Seguin's

COMPUTER
Concepts & Applications

Second Edition

Seguin's

COMPUTER
Concepts & Applications

with Microsoft® Office 2016

Second Edition

Denise Seguin
Fanshawe College, London, Ontario

PARADIGM
EDUCATION SOLUTIONS

St. Paul

Senior Vice President	Linda Hein
Editor in Chief	Christine Hurney
Senior Editor	Cheryl Drivdahl
Developmental Editor, Digital and Print	Tamborah Moore
Assistant Developmental Editors	Mamie Clark and Katie Werdick
Contributing Writer	Janet Blum
Tester	Jeff Johnson
Director of Production	Timothy W. Larson
Production Editors	Rachel Kats and Carrie Rogers
Cover and Text Designer, Senior Production Specialist	Jaana Bykonich
Copy Editor	Heidi Hogg
Indexer	Terry Casey
Vice President Sales and Marketing	Scott Burns
Director of Marketing	Lara Weber McLellan
Vice President Information Technology	Chuck Bratton
Digital Projects Manager	Tom Modl
Digital Learning Manager	Troy Weets
Digital Production Manager	Aaron Esnough
Senior Digital Production Specialist	Julie Johnston
Web Developer	Blue Earth Interactive
Video Producer	Hurix Systems

Image Credits: See page 391

ISBN 978-0-76386-880-2 (print)
ISBN 978-0-76386-886-4 (digital)

875 Montreal Way
St. Paul, MN 55102
Email: educate@emcp.com
Website: www.emcp.com

Printed in the United States of America

25 24 23 22 21 20 19 18 17 16 2 3 4 5 6 7 8 9 10

Brief Contents

Contents

Seguin's COMPUTER Applications with Microsoft® Office 2016

Preface

Course Overview

Today's students have grown up with technology all around them and are more connected to the Internet with more devices than any generation before them. They have always had the Internet as a source of information, entertainment, and communication. Students in the classroom today likely started using the Internet and a word processor before entering grade school. Some students never turn off their smartphones, even when they go to bed at night. For many, the cell phone or smartphone is integral to daily life. Being in constant touch with friends, family, and others (including classmates, teammates, colleagues, and social media followers) is a normal way of life.

So what can a textbook on introductory computer concepts and software applications provide as value to this technology driven audience? To be successful in any career, you need an understanding of computer hardware, software, and terminology. Furthermore, you need to know how to use software applications in a way that saves time and makes the best use of the available feature set. *Seguin's COMPUTER Concepts & Applications with Microsoft® Office 2016,* Second Edition, provides the tools you need to succeed immediately in your academic and personal life as well as prepare for success in your future career. In this book, you will learn computer concepts and software skills you can apply immediately to accomplishing projects and assignments for school and to organizing, scheduling, recording, planning, and budgeting for your personal needs. You will find the work you do in this course to be relevant and useful, with the content presented in a straightforward approach.

Along with well-designed textbook pedagogy, practice and problem solving will help you learn and apply computer concepts and skills. Technology provides opportunities for interactive learning as well as excellent ways to quickly and accurately assess student performance. To that end, this textbook is supported by SNAP, Paradigm Education Solution's web-based training and assessment learning management system. Details about SNAP as well as additional student and instructor resources appear on pages xxii–xxiii.

Seguin's COMPUTER Concepts & Applications with Microsoft® Office 2016, Second Edition, is divided into two parts: *Seguin's COMPUTER Concepts* and *Seguin's COMPUTER Applications*. For courses that emphasize either computer concepts or computer applications, the two parts are available as separate textbooks.

Course Goals

Seguin's COMPUTER Concepts provides instruction in achieving a basic understanding of the components that comprise computer hardware, system software, application software, Internet connectivity and resources, social media, and the security and privacy issues related to technology. No prior experience with computer concepts is required. Even those with some technological savvy can benefit from completing the course by digging deeper into topics of interest with the instructor's guidance. After completing a course that uses this part of the textbook, you will be able:

- to identify various types of computers; explain how data is converted into information; and understand technological convergence, cloud computing, green computing, and ergonomics.
- to identify hardware and software needed to connect to the Internet; explain broadband connectivity options; recognize popular web browsers, plug-ins, and players; search the web effectively; and distinguish various online services.
- to recognize and explain the components in a system unit, input devices, output devices, and network adapters; understand how data is represented on a computer; and distinguish various options for storage and storage capacity.
- to list the major functions of operating system software and recognize popular operating systems used for computing devices; explain the purpose of embedded and cloud operating systems; describe commonly used utility programs for maintaining a computer; and use troubleshooting tools in system software for solving computer issues.

- to identify productivity and multimedia applications used in workplaces and by individuals; differentiate web-based and open source applications; explain the process to acquire, install, uninstall, and upgrade software; and provide examples of mobile apps.
- to describe popular social networking, social bookmarking, media sharing, blogging, and wiki websites; and provide examples of how businesses are using social media strategies to connect and communicate with consumers.
- to explain various risks to security and privacy encountered by connected individuals, and describe strategies for protecting against security and privacy intrusions from unwanted sources.

Seguin's COMPUTER Applications offers instruction that will guide you to achieve entry-level competence with the latest versions of Microsoft Windows, web browsers, and the Microsoft Office productivity suite, including OneNote, Outlook, Word, Excel, PowerPoint, and Access. You will also be introduced to cloud computing alternatives to the traditional desktop suite. No prior experience with these software programs is required. Even those with some technological savvy can benefit from completing the course by learning new ways to perform tasks or reinforce skills. After completing a course that uses this part of the textbook, you will be able:

- to navigate the Windows operating system and manage files and folders.
- to use web browsers such as Microsoft Edge, Google Chrome, or Mozilla Firefox to navigate and search the web, as well as download content to a PC or mobile device.
- to use navigation, file management, commands, and features within the Microsoft Office suite that are standard across all applications.
- to organize and manage class notes in OneNote.
- to communicate and manage personal information in Outlook.
- to create, edit, format, and enhance documents in Word.
- to create, edit, analyze, format, and enhance workbooks in Excel.
- to create, edit, format, and enhance slides and set up a slideshow in PowerPoint.
- to create and edit tables, forms, queries, and reports in Access.
- to integrate information among the applications within the Microsoft Office suite.
- to use cloud computing technologies to create, edit, store, and share documents.

Textbook Organization and Methodology

Seguin's COMPUTER Concepts is divided into seven chapters, which can be done in any order. Some instructors will follow the chapter sequence as written; however, others may assign the chapters in a different order. For example, your instructor may prefer that you study the social media content before you learn about hardware. All the chapter content is presented in short topics with many visual aids to minimize reading time, and each topic ends with a hands-on activity that prompts you to dig deeper into the topic.

Seguin's COMPUTER Applications is divided into 15 chapters. These are best completed in sequence; however, after completing the essential skills learned in Chapters 1 through 5, instructors may opt to complete Word, Excel, PowerPoint, Access, integration, and cloud computing technologies in the order of their choice. All the chapter content is presented in short topics, with each topic focusing on related software features. Each chapter topic begins with a list of skills to be mastered and includes hands-on exercises, which consist of step-by-step instructions and illustrative screen shots.

In both parts of the textbook, each chapter opens with a brief overview, including a list of the objectives covered and a Precheck quiz that allows you to quickly discover how much you already know about the topics. The topics are presented in two or four pages, with a variety of marginal notes and other features to expand or clarify the content. At the end of each chapter, you will have a chance to review a summary of the topics, and then take a Recheck quiz to see how much you have learned and which topics require more attention.

The student ebook accompanying this textbook includes workbook pages that offer additional study tools and interactive review exercises that will reinforce and expand the knowledge and skills you've gained. Each chapter in the workbook section concludes with seven to ten assessments, some of which are to be done individually, in pairs, or within a team. Your instructor will assign assessments based on his or her goals for your level of learning.

In the workbook section of the student ebook for *Seguin's COMPUTER Concepts,* each chapter includes an assessment on green computing and an assessment on computer-related ethics so you can engage in meaningful discussions with your classmates about issues that face everyone in this digital world. In the workbook section of the student ebook for *Seguin's COMPUTER Applications,* beginning with Chapter 3, most chapters include an assessment that presents a culminating visual project in which you are to create a file similar to the examples shown. Starting in Chapter 6 and continuing to Chapter 11, some chapters include an assessment that has you listen to an audio file in the student data files for that chapter. Starting in Chapter 4, an assessment in each chapter instructs you to send output to a OneNote notebook.

What Makes This Textbook Different from Others?

Many textbooks that teach computer concepts and computer applications were designed and organized for software that was in effect one or two decades ago. As software evolves and becomes more flexible and streamlined, so too should software textbooks. With that mandate, this textbook has been designed and organized to provide a fresh look at the skills a student should know to be successful in today's world. The freedom to create a new book from scratch allowed the author to choose and place in a logical sequence the skills considered essential for today's student. Consider this book a "software survival kit for school and life." Nothing more, nothing less!

Each topic is presented in two or four pages so that reading time is minimized. Each *Seguin's COMPUTER Concepts* topic ends with a hands-on activity so that you can dig deeper into the topic. Some activities involve discussion with classmates, friends, or family members, whereas others ask you to try the technology or complete further investigative research. Many of the student data files used in the *Seguin's COMPUTER Applications* topics and assessments are based on files created by students in courses similar to those you may be enrolled in now. You will open and manipulate real work completed by someone just like you. Other files include practical examples of documents that you can readily relate to your school and personal experiences.

This Book Is Green!

Instructions to print results have been intentionally omitted for all exercises and assessments. This approach is consistent with a green computing initiative to minimize wasteful printing for nongraded topics or assessments and also provides instructors with maximum flexibility in designing their course structure.

Course Features

The following guide shows how this textbook and its digital resources use a visual approach combined with hands-on activities to help you learn and master key computer concepts and software skills.

SNAP Resources

SNAP

SNAP icons in the margins of the textbook are accompanied by blue text listing exercises and assessments that are available in SNAP. If you are a SNAP user, go to your SNAP Assignments page to complete the activities.

Interactive Resources

Arrow icons in the margins of the textbook indicate interactive resources that are available through the links menu in your student ebook and, in some cases, in SNAP.

- **Precheck quizzes** test your knowledge of the chapter content before you study the material. Use the results to help focus your study on the topics and skills you need to learn. SNAP users should go to their SNAP Assignments page to complete these quizzes.
- **Tutorials** expand on interesting tech topics and end with a brief quiz in *Seguin's COMPUTER Concepts*, and provide hands-on guided skills practice in *Seguin's COMPUTER Applications*. SNAP users should go to their SNAP Assignments page to complete these tutorials.

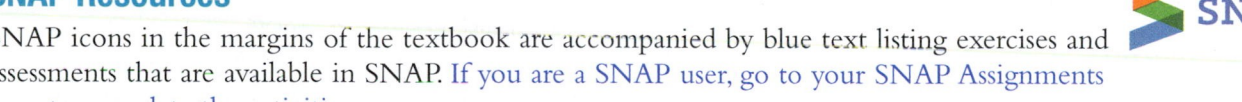

- **View Model Answer** features in *Seguin's COMPUTER Applications* link to completed model answers that you can compare with your completed work.
- The **Data Files** needed for the exercises and assessments in *Seguin's COMPUTER Applications* are downloaded as a zipped file in Chapter 1. In the workbook sections of the student ebook, you have the option of accessing individual data files as you need them to complete each assessment.
- The **Audio Files** needed for some assessments in the *Seguin's COMPUTER Applications* workbook sections of the student ebook are included in the zipped file of student data files downloaded in Chapter 1 and may also be accessed from the workbook sections of the student ebook as needed.
- A **Recheck quiz** at the end of each chapter enables you to recheck your understanding of the chapter content. You may recheck your understanding at any time and as many times as you wish. SNAP users should go to their SNAP Assignments page to complete these quizzes.
- The workbook sections of the student ebook provides study resources, review exercises, and assessments to help you reinforce and demonstrate your understanding of the topics covered in each chapter.

Textbook Elements

The following elements provide clear information and easy-to-follow instruction to help you master the key computer concepts and software skills taught in this course.

A **Skills** list presents the skills that will be learned by completing the steps in a *Seguin's COMPUTER Applications* topic.

Tutorials reinforce and supplement the concepts or skills being taught.

Simple **step-by-step instructions** accompanied by numerous **screen captures** with step numbers support mastery of the skills taught in *Seguin's COMPUTER Applications* topics. Text to be typed is presented in red font to stand out from the instructional text.

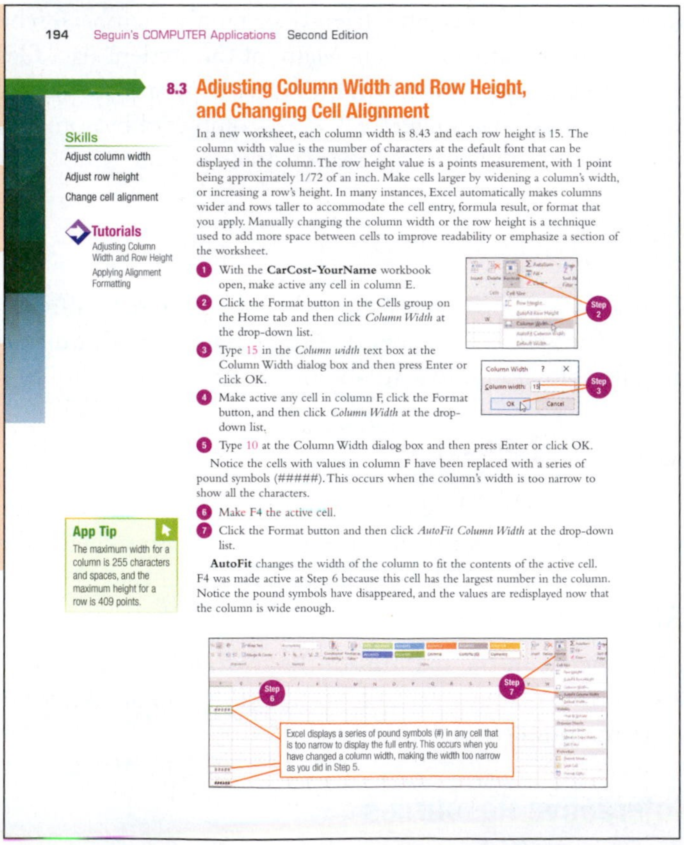

194 Seguin's COMPUTER Applications Second Edition

8.3 Adjusting Column Width and Row Height, and Changing Cell Alignment

Skills
Adjust column width
Adjust row height
Change cell alignment

Tutorials
Adjusting Column Width and Row Height
Applying Alignment Formatting

In a new worksheet, each column width is 8.43 and each row height is 15. The column width value is the number of characters at the default font that can be displayed in the column. The row height value is a points measurement, with 1 point being approximately 1/72 of an inch. Make cells larger by widening a column's width, or increasing a row's height. In many instances, Excel automatically makes columns wider and rows taller to accommodate the cell entry, formula result, or format that you apply. Manually changing the column width or the row height is a technique used to add more space between cells to improve readability or emphasize a section of the worksheet.

1. With the **CarCost-YourName** workbook open, make active any cell in column E.
2. Click the Format button in the Cells group on the Home tab and then click *Column Width* at the drop-down list.
3. Type 15 in the *Column width* text box at the Column Width dialog box and then press Enter or click OK.
4. Make active any cell in column F, click the Format button, and then click *Column Width* at the drop-down list.
5. Type 10 at the Column Width dialog box and then press Enter or click OK.

Notice the cells with values in column F have been replaced with a series of pound symbols (#####). This occurs when the column's width is too narrow to show all the characters.

6. Make F4 the active cell.
7. Click the Format button and then click *AutoFit Column Width* at the drop-down list.

AutoFit changes the width of the column to fit the contents of the active cell. F4 was made active at Step 6 because this cell has the largest number in the column. Notice the pound symbols have disappeared, and the values are redisplayed now that the column is wide enough.

App Tip
The maximum width for a column is 255 characters and spaces, and the maximum height for a row is 409 points.

Step 2
Step 3
Step 6
Step 7
Excel displays a series of pound symbols (#) in any cell that is too narrow to display the full entry. This occurs when you have changed a column width, making the width too narrow as you did in Step 5.

App Tips extend or add to your knowledge of a software feature.

App Tip

AutoCorrect operates in Excel; however, red wavy lines do *not* appear below misspelled words. Consider using the Spelling feature in the Proofing group on the

Quick Steps briefly summarize the steps to complete major tasks in software skills, for quick reference and review.

Quick Steps

Enter a Formula
1. Activate formula cell.
2. Type =.
3. Type first cell address.
4. Type operator symbol.
5. Type next cell address.
6. Continue Steps 4–5 until finished.

Check This Out features provide links to websites at which you can explore more information.

Check This Out

http://CA2.ParadigmCollege.net/Chrome

Go here to download and install Chrome on your PC or mobile device.

Oops! hints anticipate common challenges and provide solutions to help you succeed with the tasks in a software skill.

Oops!

No Cell Styles gallery? On smaller displays, the gallery is accessed by clicking the Cell Styles button in the Styles group

Good to Know features highlight interesting or fun facts or trivia about the topic.

Good to Know

Many businesses that operate globally have adopted the International Standards Organization (ISO) date format YYYY-MM-DD to avoid confusion

Blog Topic boxes offer a chance for you to write about your experience or opinions on the topic.

Blog Topic **Are You Green?**

Do you practice green computing? If yes, are there ways you can improve your green computing practices? If no, which green computing strategies can you start to use? Have you purchased a new PC or mobile device within the last year? If yes, how did you dispose of your older equipment?

Career Connection boxes give job information to spark interest and invite exploration of computer-related careers.

Career Connection **IT Jobs in Demand**

If you enjoy working with computers, consider an IT career. The 2015 Forecast survey conducted by *Computerworld* revealed that the 10 most in-demand IT jobs were as follows, ranked from most to

An **Explore Further** activity at the end of each topic invites you to dig deeper into the topic by interviewing others, trying out the technology yourself; and researching related topics.

Explore Further **Finding a Cloud Service Provider for Storing Pictu**

A popular use of cloud computing is to upload photos from your PC to a cloud storage provider so you can them on a social media website, access them from multiple devices, or have a backup if something happe mobile device.

1. Research two free cloud storage providers. Find out the amount of free storage space and look for restrictions on the file sizes that can be uploaded.
3. Save the document as **CloudFi**
4. Submit the document to your in has requested.

Alternative Method boxes present different ways to accomplish the task in a software skill.

Alternative Method **Changing Print Options Using the Page Layout Tab**

You can change some print options on the Page Layout tab, using the Margins and Orientation buttons in the Page Setup group and the Width, Height, and Scale options in the Scale to Fit group.

Beyond Basics boxes provide additional information about the feature that extends the software skills described in a topic.

Beyond Basics **Order of Operations in Formulas**

If you combine operations in a formula, Excel will automatically calculate exponentiation, multiplication, and division before addition and subtraction. You can tell Excel to perform a particular operation first by using parentheses around that part of the formula. For example, in the formula *=(A1+A2)*A3*, Excel adds the values in A1 and A2 first and then multiplies the result by the value in A3.

Security Alert boxes offer tips for security and privacy to help you learn safe computing practices.

Security Alert **Update Links with Caution**

At Step 23, you clicked the Update Links button because you knew the linked file was from a trusted source. Be aware before you click Update Links when opening a document, workbook, presentation, or database that you know where the linked object originates and that it is from a trusted source. In 2015, Sophos (an IT security company) reported a resurgence of malware circulated in Microsoft Office documents. Sophos reported the malware is targeted more towards Word and Excel files and the files are usually attached to email messages.

Tables and figures organize information in a streamlined format to minimize your reading load.

Table 8.1
Excel Features

Feature	Description
Active cell	Location in which the next typed data will be stored and that will be affected by the next command. Make a cell active by clicking it or by moving to it using the Arrow keys.
Cell pointer	Icon that displays when you are able to select cells with the mouse by clicking or dragging. On a touch device with no mouse attached, tap a cell to display selection handles (round circles) at the top left and bottom right corners.
Formula bar	Bar that displays contents stored in the active cell and is also used to create formulas.
Horizontal and vertical scroll bars	Tools used to view parts of a worksheet not shown in the current viewing area.
Name box	Box that displays the address or name of the active cell.
New Sheet button	Button on the Sheet tab bar used to insert a new worksheet.
Sheet tab	Tab that displays the name of the active worksheet. By default, new sheets are named Sheet# where # is the number of the sheet in the workbook.
	is used to navigate between worksheets.
	cating the current mode of operation; Ready / to accept new data.
	earance of the worksheet. Excel opens in Normal Page Layout and Page Break Preview. Zoom hrink the display.

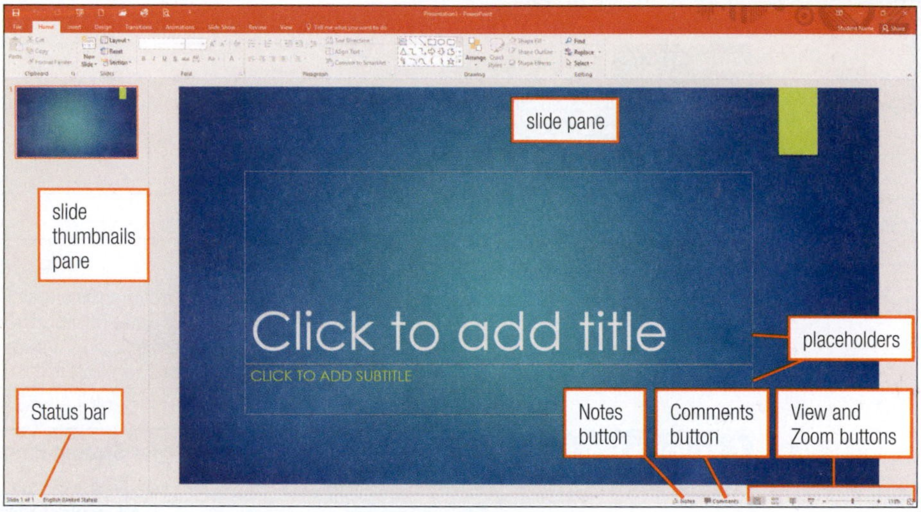

Figure 10.1
A new PowerPoint presentation with Ion theme and blue color variant in the default Normal view is shown above. See Table 10.1 for a description of screen elements.

A **Topics Review** chart at the end of each chapter summarizes the main chapter content and key words learned.

Topics Review

Topic	Key Concepts	Key Terms
8.1 Creating and Editing a New Worksheet	A spreadsheet is an application in which data is created, analyzed, and presented in a grid-like structure of columns and rows. A workbook is an Excel file that consists of a collection of individual worksheets. A new workbook opens with a blank worksheet into which you add text, insert values, and create formulas. The intersection of a column and a row is called a *cell.* The active cell is indicated with a green border, and is the location into which the next data typed will be stored, or the next command will be acted upon. Create a worksheet by making a cell active and typing text, a value, or a formula. A formula is used to perform mathematical operations on values. Formula entries begin with an equals sign and are followed by cell references with operators between the references. Edit a cell by typing new data to overwrite existing data, by double-clicking to open the cell for editing, or by inserting or deleting characters in the Formula bar.	spreadsheet application workbook worksheet cell active cell formula Clear button

Workbook Elements

The workbook sections of the student ebook provide a variety of materials you can use to review, reinforce, and demonstrate your understanding of the computer concepts and software skills covered in the textbook. For each chapter, you will find the following workbook elements.

Interactive **study tools**, including a presentation with audio support, help reinforce your understanding of the topics. These resources are accessed from the links menu.

Interactive **review exercises**, including multiple-choice, matching, and completion questions, give you an opportunity to practice and review your understanding of the skills and topics. These resources are accessed from the links menu and are also available in SNAP. SNAP users should go to their SNAP Assignments page to complete these exercises.

SNAP Exercises offer additional practice for SNAP users. SNAP Users should go to their SNAP Assignments page to complete these exercises.

Three to ten **assessments** of varying complexity provide opportunities to work individually, in pairs, or in teams to produce documents, presentations, blogs, videos, and podcasts that demonstrate your understanding of topics and how they apply to the workplace or an individual application.

Chapter 9 Working with Functions, Charts, Tables, and Page Layout Options in Excel

Study Tools

Study Tools — Study tools, including a slide presentation and Quick Steps, are available from this ebook page.

Review Exercises

Review Exercises — Multiple Choice, Matching, and Completion exercises give you an opportunity to review and reinforce your understanding of the material covered in this chapter.

SNAP — If you are a SNAP user, go to your SNAP Assignments page to complete the review exercises.

SNAP Exercises

SNAP — If you are a SNAP user, go to your SNAP Assignments page to complete additional exercises available for you.

Assessments

The following assessments offer opportunities to apply what you have learned in relevant, real-world situations. Save your solution files and URLs, and submit them for evaluation as directed by your instructor.

Data Files — **Assessment 9.1** Adding Statistical, Date, Financial, and Logical Functions to a Workbook

Type: Individual
Deliverable: Worksheet with Auction Fee Financial Analysis and Mortgage Options

1. Open **AuctionFeesandMortgagePlanner**.
2. Use Save As to change the file name to **AuctionFeesandMortgagePlanner-YourName** in a new folder named *Ch9* within the Assessments folder on your storage medium.
3. In J2 enter a formula that will insert the current date and update the date each time the workbook is opened or printed.
4. Assign the following names to the cells indicated:
   C2 AuctionFee G2 PaymentFee
5. Complete the formulas required in the worksheet using the following information:
   a. In column B, calculate the payment due dates as 5 days following the auction end date.
   b. In column D, calculate the auction fees as the sale price times the auction fee percentage. Use the range name created in Step 4 in the formula.
   c. In column E, calculate the payment processing fees as the sale price times the payment fee percentage. Use the range name created in Step 4 in the formula.
   d. In column F, calculate the net auction earnings as the sale price minus the auction fee and payment processing fee.
   e. In column G, calculate the amount to transfer to the checking account as the value that resides in net auction earnings for those instances in which

35

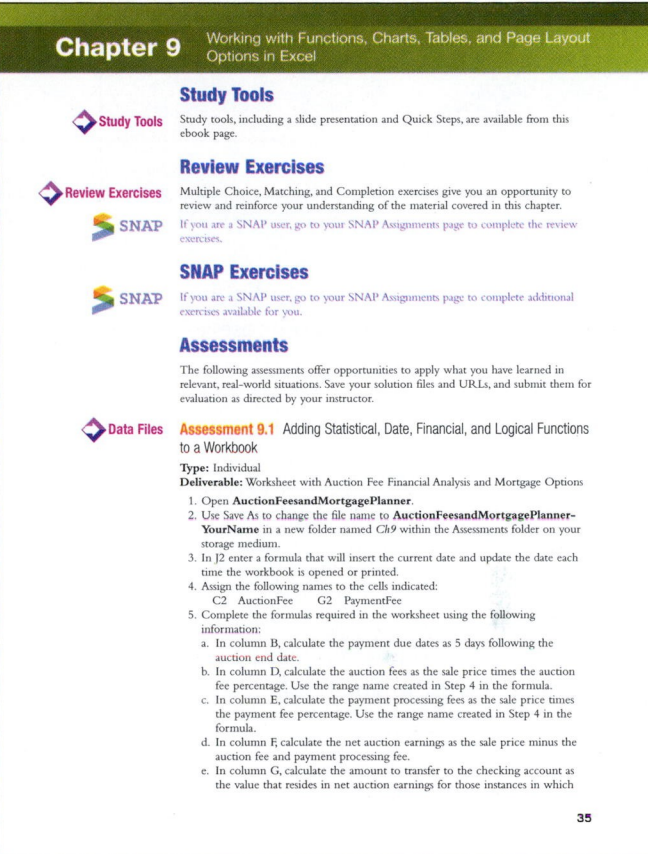

A **Green Computing assessment** prompts exploration of ways to protect the environment and make good use of its resources.

Assessment 1.6 Greener Computing—Benefits of Green Computing in a Newspaper Office

Type: Individual, Pairs, or Team
Deliverable: Blog Entry

You are involved with the school newspaper and have noticed when you are in the office that the other volunteers do not practice green computing strategies. You decide to write a blog entry that will help educate the other volunteers on the benefits to the environment of embracing green computing practices.

1. Write and post a blog entry that will educate the volunteers about green computing and encourage all of them to participate with you in adopting green computing practices at the school newspaper office.

An **Ethics Discussion assessment** engages you and your classmates in a meaningful discussion about issues that face everyone in this digital world.

Assessment 1.9 Ethics Discussion—Is It Okay to Use Work Technology for Personal Reasons?

Type: Team
Deliverable: Document, Blog Entry, or Presentation

A friend at your workplace who sits near you uses her computer for personal reasons several times throughout the day when she should be working. You have observed her updating her Facebook page, watching YouTube videos, shopping online, and looking at travel websites. One time at lunch you casually mentioned that you noticed she uses the web a lot for personal reasons, and she told you she prefers the higher speed access at work over her home setup.

1. Within your team discuss how you should handle this situation. Should you ignore the situation since you are not her manager? If you answer yes, would your answer be different if the employee was not your friend? In what instances, if any, is it OK to use employer equipment for personal use? How could you convince your friend to stop using the employer's computer for personal use? How should management deal with employees' use of company-provided technology for personal reasons?

Culminating **Visual assessments** provide opportunities to create documents similar to the example shown.

Assessment 10.5 Visual—Creating a Graduation Party Planning Presentation

Type: Individual
Deliverable: Presentation on college graduation party planning

1. Create a presentation similar to the one shown in the Assessment 10.5 Graduation Party Planning Presentation on the next page with the following additional information:
   a. The theme is *Integral* with one of the variants selected.
   b. The bullet symbols have been changed on the slide master.
   c. The font color for the slide titles has been changed on the slide master. Use your best judgment to choose a similar color.
   d. Use your best judgment to determine other formatting, placeholder size, and alignment options.
2. Save the presentation in the Ch10 folder within the Assessments folder as **GradParty-YourName**.
3. Submit the assessment to your instructor in the manner she or he has requested.
4. Close the presentation.

Audio assessments ask you to listen to instructions and then to compose a presentation as instructed.

Assessment 10.6 Audio—Internet Research and Composing a New Presentation

Type: Individual or Pairs
Deliverable: Presentation about US or Canadian historical figure

You have been asked to help the president of the school's history society with a presentation for a guest speaker at a new activity called History Conversations. Research a US or Canadian historical figure and prepare a six-slide presentation with the main facts about the person and his or her significance in US or Canadian history.

Audio File

1. Listen to the audio file named ***HistoricalFigure_Instructions***.
2. Complete the research and compose the presentation as instructed.
3. Save the presentation in the Ch10 folder within the Assessments folder as **HistoricalFigure-YourName**.
4. Submit the assessment to your instructor in the manner she or he has requested.
5. Close the presentation.

OneNote assessments instruct you to send output to a OneNote notebook.

Assessment 10.7 OneNote—Sending Assessment Work to OneNote Notebook

Type: Individual
Deliverable: New page in Shared OneNote notebook

1. Start OneNote and open the MyAssessments notebook created in Chapter 4, Assessment 4.4.
2. Make PowerPoint the active section and then add a new page titled *Chapter 10 Assessments*.
3. Switch to PowerPoint. For each assessment that you completed, open the presentation, send the slides formatted as handouts with six slides horizontal per page, and with your name in a header to OneNote 2016, selecting the *Chapter 10 Assessments* page in the *PowerPoint* section in the MyAssessments notebook, then close the presentation, saving changes if prompted to do so.
4. Close your MyAssessments notebook in OneNote and then close OneNote.
5. Close PowerPoint.
6. Submit the assessment to your instructor in the manner she or he has requested.

Course Components

The *Seguin's COMPUTER Concepts & Applications with Microsoft® Office 2016*, Second Edition, textbook contains the essential content you will need to master the key computer concepts and software skills covered. Additional resources are provided by the following digital components.

SNAP Web-Based Training and Assessment for Microsoft® Office 2016

SNAP

SNAP is a web-based training and assessment program and learning management system (LMS) for computer skills and topics and Microsoft Office 2016. SNAP offers rich content, a sophisticated grade book, and robust scheduling and analytics tools. SNAP includes a quiz and exam for each chapter, plus an item bank that can be used to create custom assessments. SNAP provides automatic scoring and detailed feedback on the program's many exercises and assessments to help identify areas where additional support is needed, evaluating student performance at both the individual level and the course level. The *Seguin's COMPUTER Concepts & Applications* SNAP course content is also available to export into any LMS system that supports LTI tools. Paradigm Education Solutions provides technical support for SNAP through 24-7 chat at ParadigmCollege.com. In addition, an online user guide and other training tools for SNAP are available.

Student eBook

The student ebook provides access to all program content from any device (desktop, tablet, and smartphone) anywhere, through a live Internet connection. The versatile ebook platform features dynamic navigation tools including a linked table of contents and the ability to jump to specific pages, search for terms, bookmark, highlight, and take notes. The student ebook offers live links to the interactive content and resources that support the textbook, including the Precheck and Recheck quizzes, tutorials, View Model Answer images, student data files, and workbook sections.

By completing all the Chapter 1 topics and assessments in *Seguin's COMPUTER Applications*, you download and extract the student data files you need for that part of the textbook and set up a folder structure for storing completed work in the course. Student data files are downloaded and extracted to a USB flash drive from a link in the ebook. As an alternative, your instructor may choose to load student data files on a network, in which case the instructor will provide alternative instructions.

Integrated into the student ebook, the workbook sections include access to study tools such as chapter-based presentations with audio support, interactive end-of-chapter review exercises, and end-of-chapter assessments. The student ebook is accessed through SNAP or online at Paradigm.bookshelf.emcp.com.

SNAP users should go to their SNAP Assignments page to complete all interactive quizzes, tutorials, and exercises in the student ebook.

Instructor eResources

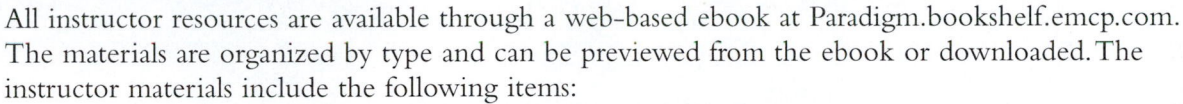

All instructor resources are available through a web-based ebook at Paradigm.bookshelf.emcp.com. The materials are organized by type and can be previewed from the ebook or downloaded. The instructor materials include the following items:

- Grading rubrics for evaluating responses to chapter assessments
- Lesson blueprints with teaching hints, lecture tips, and discussion questions
- Syllabus suggestions and course planning resources
- Chapter-based PowerPoint presentations with lecture notes
- Chapter-based quizzes and exams
- Annotated Model Answers for end-of-chapter assessments

Acknowledgments

The author and editors would like to thank the following students for their contributions to and feedback on the textbook: Karen J. Allen, Assistant Professor, Community College of Rhode Island; Lenny E. Andrews, CIT/NT Program Head, Montgomery Community College, Troy, North Carolina; Janet Blum, Professor, Fanshawe College, London, Ontario; Sharon R. Campbell, M.Ed., Pima Community College, Tucson, Arizona; Scott Cline, Southwestern Community College, Iowa; Cheryl Ann Farrell, Lecturer, Kauai Community College, Hawaii; Denise Gauthier, Lakehead University, Thunder Bay, Ontario; Keith Hare, Computer Instructor, Career/College Prep Program, St. Lawrence College, Kingston, Ontario; Lorraine Mastracchio, Professor, Senior Chairperson, Faculty/Curricula, Chair Office Technologies, The College of Westchester, White Plains, New York; Toni McBride, Fanshawe College; Nicole Oke, Fanshawe College; Patti Ann Reynolds, Fanshawe College; Michael Seguin, University of Windsor, Ontario; Barbara Shapiro, Adjunct Professor, Pima Community College; Billie Terao, Kauai Community College.

About the Author

Denise Seguin has served on the Faculty of Business at Fanshawe College of Applied Arts and Technology in London, Ontario, from 1986 until her retirement from full-time teaching in December 2012. She developed curriculum and taught a variety of office technology, software applications, and accounting courses to students in postsecondary Information Technology diploma programs and Continuing Education courses. Seguin served as Program Coordinator for Computer Systems Technician, Computer Systems Technology, Office Administration, and Law Clerk programs and was acting Chair of the School of Information Technology in 2001. Along with authoring *Seguin's COMPUTER Concepts*, First and Second Editions, and *Seguin's COMPUTER Applications with Microsoft® Office 2013*, First Edition, and *with Microsoft® Office 2016*, Second Edition, she has also authored Paradigm Education Solution's *Microsoft Outlook* 2000 to 2016 editions and co-authored *Our Digital World* First, Second, and Third Editions, *Benchmark Series Microsoft® Excel®*, 2007, 2010, and 2013, *Benchmark Series Microsoft® Access®* 2007, 2010, and 2013, *Marquee Series Microsoft® Office*, 2000 to 2013, and *Using Computers in the Medical Office*, 2003 to 2010.

In 2007, Seguin earned her Masters in Business Administration specializing in Technology Management, choosing to take her degree at an online university. She has an appreciation for those who are juggling work and life responsibilities while furthering their education, and she has taken her online student experiences into account when designing instruction and assessment activities for this textbook.

Seguin's

COMPUTER Concepts

Second Edition

Chapter 1

Living in a Digital World

Precheck
Check your understanding of the topics covered in this chapter.

Individuals and businesses interact with computers in numerous ways every day in our digital world. Some of your own interactions occur while you are at home, at work, or at school using a laptop, smartphone, or tablet. Many times you are interacting with a computing device while shopping, dining, or traveling. Consider the number of times you withdraw money from an ATM, gas up your car, swipe a debit or credit card to complete a purchase, use a self-checkout at the grocery store, or program your GPS to find a location. Many times throughout the day you are interacting with a computer without thinking about it.

To be successful in today's world, you need to use a computer independently and efficiently—which in turn requires that you have a basic understanding of computers, computer terminology, and how a computer works. These essential computer skills are often referred to as **computer literacy**. More recently the term **digital literacy** has become more widely used and is considered as important as computer literacy. To be digitally literate means that you can use various computer devices, communication technologies, and the Internet to find, assess, use, create, and share content appropriately with others.

In this chapter, you will begin your introduction to computer literacy and digital literacy by learning to distinguish the various types of computers, recognize the impact of computer innovation and convergence in our lives, explain how data is transformed into useful information, and identify trends and issues such as cloud computing, green computing, and ergonomics. This chapter is an introduction to the terminology and concepts you will explore in more detail in the chapters that follow.

SNAP If you are a SNAP user, go to your SNAP Assignments page to complete the Precheck, Tutorials, and Recheck.

Learning Objectives

1.1 Define *computer* and identify the various types of personal computers

1.2 List various mobile devices and describe wearable and embedded computers

1.3 Differentiate servers, mainframes, and supercomputers

1.4 Define *Internet of Things* and give examples of ubiquitous computing and technological convergence

1.5 Define *information technology* and explain the four operations of information processing: input, processing, output, and storage

1.6 Explain cloud computing and list its advantages and disadvantages

1.7 Describe the goals of green computing and list ways to practice this trend

1.8 Recognize ways to use computing devices that conform to good ergonomic design

1.1 Personal Computers

A **computer** is an electronic device that has been programmed to process, store, and output data that has been accepted as input. Computers come in many sizes and shapes to meet a variety of computing needs. Most people are familiar with a desktop, laptop, or tablet and recognize it as a computer. Other electronic devices that contain programmed chips—such as digital cameras, game consoles, GPSs, or even some children's toys—also have computer capabilities designed to perform limited functions.

A computer needs both **hardware** (physical components and devices) and **software** (instructions that tell the computer what to do) to be useful. You will learn about hardware in Chapter 3, operating system programs in Chapter 4, and productivity software applications in Chapter 5.

Personal Computers

A **personal computer (PC)** is a computer in which the input, processing, storage, and output are self-contained. A PC is generally used by one person at a time, although PCs can be connected to a network where other people can access PC resources, such as a file on a storage medium. A PC is sometimes referred to as a *microcomputer*.

A **desktop computer** is a PC in which the processor, memory, and main storage device are housed within a horizontal or vertical case called the **system unit**. A vertical case is sometimes referred to as a *tower*. A separate monitor, keyboard, and mouse sit alongside or near the system unit as shown in Figure 1.1. An all-in-one case integrates the system unit and monitor into one device as shown in Figure 1.2.

Figure 1.1

A desktop computer may have a vertical system unit, which is sometimes called a *tower*.

Figure 1.2

The Apple iMac sports an all-in-one case where the monitor, processor, memory, and storage media are housed in one unit.

Mobile Computers

A **mobile computer** is a PC that can be moved from place to place. Mobile computers come in a number of configurations that vary in size, shape, and weight. A **laptop computer** fits comfortably on a person's lap and is also referred to as a **notebook**. These PCs often replace desktops for today's mobile workers and for home users who want the ability to move easily from room to room with their PCs. A typical notebook (Figure 1.3) has a clamshell-style design. When the notebook is opened, the monitor swivels up to reveal a keyboard. The processor, memory, storage media, and battery are housed below the keyboard.

Figure 1.3

Laptops, also referred to as *notebooks*, have a clamshell design in which the monitor opens up to reveal the system unit.

A type of notebook that is thinner, lighter in weight, but just as powerful as a traditional notebook is called an **ultrabook**. Ultrabooks were originally named by Intel (a company that manufactures computer chips) to differentiate the new slim, lightweight notebook design that aims to achieve faster processing and storage while extending battery life. Most ultrabooks are only 0.6 to 0.7 inches thick and weigh an average of 2.5 pounds. Apple's MacBook Air, shown in Figure 1.4, is a popular ultrabook; however, all the other major hardware manufacturers also have ultrabooks.

A **netbook** is a low-cost, smaller notebook designed for people who primarily only need access to web-based applications. These notebooks contain limited software applications. Netbooks have mostly been replaced by tablets and ultrabooks.

A **tablet** (also called a *tablet PC*) is a lightweight notebook with a small screen that you interact with using touch gestures or a special pen called a *stylus*. Slate tablets have an on-screen keyboard only, while other tablets come with a keyboard that pivots or plugs in so that the tablet acts more like a traditional notebook. Figure 1.5 shows the popular Apple iPad. A laptop that can be used like a tablet by swiveling the screen and/or folding down the screen (Figure 1.6) is called a **convertible laptop** or **hybrid laptop**.

Figure 1.4

Ultrabooks such as The Apple MacBook Air are slim and lightweight, yet powerful.

Figure 1.5

The Apple iPad is a popular tablet.

Figure 1.6

A convertible (hybrid) laptop can be used as a tablet.

Security Alert: Protect, Track, and Back Up Your Mobile Device

Notebook and tablet theft is on the rise. In some areas, organized criminals use people to distract you while another person steals your device. Be aware of your surroundings and use anti-theft and tracking software and devices. Always have backups just in case!

Blog Topic: Is the PC Dead?

Smartphones and tablets are increasingly powerful, with many of the same tools offered on a notebook. Desktop sales have been steadily decreasing. Some people argue that smartphones and tablets are simply supplementing the traditional desktop and notebook and that sales data are misleading since desktops and notebooks last longer.

1. Write and post a blog entry with a paragraph that describes the number of computing devices you own and how you use them. State your response to the blog topic question *Is the PC dead?* and provide your rationale.
2. Read at least two of your classmates' blog entries and post one comment to each.
3. Submit your blog URL and the URLs of the two classmates' blogs to your instructor in the manner she or he has requested.

Explore Further: Comparing Ultrabooks with Tablets

Assume the manager at the office where you intern is interested in buying a new mobile computer. The manager is not sure whether an ultrabook or a tablet is the better choice.

1. Research the similarities and differences between ultrabooks and tablets. Choose one model of each for your comparison. Specifically, find out the physical characteristics of each (weight and screen size), connectivity options (ports, wireless, Bluetooth options), input options (keyboard, touchscreen), storage options, and processor speeds.
2. Create a document or spreadsheet to present the comparison of an ultrabook to a tablet by each criterion. Clearly identify the model of each device you are presenting and include the URLs of the websites from which you obtained the specifications.
3. Save the document or spreadsheet as **UltrabookvsTablet-YourName**.
4. Submit the document or spreadsheet to your instructor in the manner she or he has requested.

1.2 Mobile Devices, Wearable Computers, and Embedded Computers

A handheld computing device smaller than a notebook is referred to as a **mobile device**. Mobile devices have smaller screens and store programs and data within the unit or on a memory card. Some mobile devices rely entirely on touch-based input while others have a built-in or slide-out keyboard. Wearable computers are devices that can be worn on the body by attaching to an arm, a belt, a helmet, eyeglasses, or clothing. These computers are used to perform special functions such as health monitoring and to assist with other hands-free work. Embedded computers reside within electronic devices—such as household appliances and gadgets—that are designed to perform specific tasks.

Mobile Devices

Good to Know

In October 2014, CNET reported that there were more active mobile devices on planet Earth than people!

Increasingly, mobile devices are expanding computer use outside our homes and offices. Examples of these mobile devices are shown in Figure 1.7:

- A **smartphone** is a cell phone with a built-in camera that offers software applications (called *apps*), web-browsing, and messaging capabilities via cellular or other wireless networks. A smartphone that has a screen size larger than 5.25 inches but that is not as large as a typical tablet is called a **phablet** (meaning the combination of *phone* and *tablet*).
- A **portable media player** is a device used to play music, watch videos, view photos, play games, and/or read electronic books.
- An **ebook reader** (also called an *ereader*) is a device sized larger than a smartphone but smaller than a tablet and used to read electronic versions of books (called *ebooks*), newspapers, magazines, or other digital media.

Figure 1.7

A smartphone, portable media player, and ebook reader are popular mobile devices.

Wearable Computers

A computing device that can be worn on the body and functions while the individual is walking or otherwise moving around is called a **wearable computer**. These devices are usually always on, include sensors for various purposes, and provide for hands-free use with communications capability. They may allow input with voice commands, hand movements, joysticks, buttons, or touch. Wearable computers are used to assist or monitor individuals with health conditions, track items, provide real-time information, access documentation, or engage in virtual reality simulations. For example, the Department of Defense helped develop wearable computers for soldiers that monitor the battlefield environment.

Google's Project Glass eyeglasses use a heads-up virtual display that interacts with the wearer to provide information and communication technologies without the wearer having to use a smartphone. A limited number of Google Glasses were available for purchase in 2013, but in January 2015 Google announced a halt to production while it brought the project in-house for more development. Google Glass 2 was in development at the time of writing, with reports indicating the Google team is working on improvements to battery life and performance for the next generation of the wearable device.

The launch in April 2015 of Apple's smartwatch, named Apple Watch, brought digital wristwatches (Figure 1.8) to the public eye—although these products had been available for several years prior. These wearable devices connect to your smartphone and provide you with apps to manage calls, messages, appointments, alerts, and other data from your wrist.

Figure 1.8
According to a 2014 study by Acquity Group (a digital marketing company), 23 percent of participants interviewed plan to buy a smartwatch by 2019.

Embedded Computers

Numerous household appliances and consumer electronics incorporate an **embedded computer** that has a processor programmed to perform a particular task (Figure 1.9). Often, this type of device is referred to as a **smart device**. Examples can include a microwave oven that calculates defrost time depending on weight, a refrigerator that sounds an alarm when the inside temperature becomes problematic, and a washer that connects to your smartphone, allowing you to change options or start a wash cycle remotely.

Digital cameras, game consoles, electronic thermostats, electronic alarm monitoring systems, ATMs, and car navigation consoles are just a few other examples of devices with embedded systems. Digital devices are everywhere and so prevalent that many times you may not be aware you are using a computer!

Figure 1.9
Electronic devices with embedded systems—such as this handheld game console, digital camera, and electronic thermostat—are each designed to perform a specific task.

Explore Further | Favorite Computing Devices

Have you ever wondered what mobile devices the people you know most like to use? There's one way to find out....

1. Conduct a survey with at least 10 relatives, friends, neighbors, or classmates to find out each person's favorite mobile device, wearable gadget, or smart household device.
2. Compile the results of your informal survey and create a document, spreadsheet, or presentation that presents the results.
3. Save the document, spreadsheet, or presentation as **DeviceSurvey-YourName**.
4. Submit the document, spreadsheet, or presentation to your instructor in the manner she or he has requested.

1.3 Computers for Connecting Multiple Users and Specialized Processing

Larger, more powerful computers are used by organizations that need to connect many people to resources and store and process large amounts of data. Individuals use PCs to connect via a network to these larger computers for access to programs, processing, and storage resources. A high-end computer with multiple processors, large amounts of memory, and a large storage capacity can function as a server in a small network. Larger organizations purchase midrange servers and mainframes when hundreds or thousands of users need to process transactions simultaneously. Supercomputers are used when massive computing power is needed to perform advanced calculations.

Servers

A **server** is a computer with hardware and software that allows it to link together other computers to provide services such as Internet access and to share resources such as programs, data, printers, and storage. A computer that connects to a server is called a **client**. Servers are high-performance computers often stacked in racks (Figure 1.10) and stored in a **server room** that is maintained to avoid heat, humidity, and dust.

Figure 1.10

Servers mounted in racks are stored in a separate room protected from excessive heat, humidity, and dust.

Good to Know

Midrange servers used to be known as *minicomputers.*

A **midrange server** is used in small and medium-sized organizations that need to connect hundreds of client computers at the same time. Midrange servers are more powerful than a PC but not as powerful as a mainframe.

A computer connected to a network that does not store any data or software on the local PC is called a **thin client**. Some companies use thin clients to reduce costs and/or maintain tighter security on software licensing and data.

A type of thin client called a virtual desktop infrastructure (VDI) allows a computer user to access a virtual desktop from any device connected to the Internet, including a smartphone or tablet. VDI software is installed on each device, and the user's operating system, applications, and files are all stored on a central server that can be accessed from anywhere in the world.

Mainframes

A large, powerful, and expensive computer used by governments and large organizations—such as banks, insurance companies, and other corporations—to connect hundreds or thousands of users simultaneously is known as a **mainframe** (Figure 1.11). These computers have specialized hardware and software capable of processing millions of transactions and retaining massive volumes of data.

Figure 1.11

Mainframe computers connect thousands of computers simultaneously and process and store millions of transactions.

Supercomputers

The fastest, most expensive, and most powerful of all computers is a **supercomputer**. A supercomputer is capable of performing trillions of calculations per second. These massive computers are usually designed for a specific task, such as performing the complex mathematical calculations needed for weather forecasting, nuclear research, oil exploration, or scientific research analysis.

Supercomputing speed is expressed in petaflops. A **petaflop** (a measurement used in scientific calculations) represents a quadrillion floating point operations per second. Figure 1.12 shows the Stratus supercomputer installed at the National Oceanic and Atmospheric Administration agency. According to the TOP500 project, which tracks supercomputers, the United States has more of the top 500 supercomputers than any other country in the world, but China was home to the world's most powerful supercomputer in 2015.

Check This Out ✓

http://CC2.ParadigmCollege.net/Top500

Go here to read about the location of supercomputers around the world. A list of the top 500 sites for the most powerful computers is released twice per year.

Figure 1.12

Stratus, a supercomputer installed at the National Oceanic and Atmospheric Administration, performs 69.7 trillion calculations per second, allowing meteorologists to rapidly update severe weather forecasts. The microprocessors inside Stratus contain 2,000 miles of copper wiring, enough to stretch from Washington, DC, to the Grand Canyon.

Good to Know

The United States has set 2023 as the target date for the next leap in supercomputing development. The Department of Energy announced plans to develop an exascale system with IBM. One exaflop in this system equals one quintillion (1 followed by 18 zeros) calculations per second! Top researchers say the technical challenges involved in developing software for such a system may require international cooperation.

Explore Further | A History of Computing Time Line

The Computer History Museum located in Mountain View, California, offers information about the most influential people, technology, and events in computing history. Its online exhibit Timeline of Computer History offers an interactive exploration into the origins of computers.

1. Go to **http://CC2.ParadigmCollege.net/ComputerHistory** to view the online Timeline of Computer History exhibit.
2. Pick five consecutive years in the time line that are of interest to you, click the year, and read the information presented in the online exhibit. ***Note:*** *Your instructor may instead choose to assign you a time period so that a complete time line is presented to the class.*
3. Create a presentation with one slide per year and provide a brief summary in your own words that describes the significant people, technology, or event shown in the time line.
4. Save the presentation as **ComputerTimeLine-YourName**.
5. Submit the presentation to your instructor in the manner she or he has requested.

1.4 Computer Innovations and Trends

Technology is constantly evolving, meaning there will always be change in the devices and methods that we use for completing tasks at home, at work, and at school. Technologies are also converging, meaning that a device that originally was designed for one purpose, such as a cell phone designed only to make voice calls, is now capable of performing multiple functions, such as browsing the web, taking photos, sending and receiving email, and creating documents. The Internet of Things will change the way we work and play by connecting everyday objects to a network and enabling them to communicate directly with one another.

Good to Know

Intel cofounder Gordon E. Moore described a trend in 1965 in which the number of transistors that could be placed on a circuit doubled every two years. He predicted the trend would continue, and this became known as Moore's Law, which is a guiding principle for the computer industry.

Ubiquitous Computing

Dictionary.com defines *ubiquitous* as an adjective that means "existing or being everywhere, especially at the same time; omnipresent." **Ubiquitous computing** means that computing technology is everywhere within our environment and used all of the time. Effectively, the technology mostly fades into the background and users become unaware of the technology as they focus on the task at hand. Ubiquitous computing will become even more prevalent to all of us when the Internet of Things starts connecting everyday objects (such as your coffee maker) to the Internet. Consider these four examples of computer innovations in various industries:

Use your Apple Watch to view directions to your hotel, check in as you enter the lobby, and unlock your door.

Travel Starwood Hotels & Resorts is one of many companies that have developed a travel app for the Apple Watch, released in April 2015. With the SPG app on an Apple Watch, travelers can unlock the door to their rooms from their wrists. No room key is needed and the guest does not have to fumble around to point his or her smartphone at the lock. The app can also be used to view directions to the hotel and check in without having to visit the front desk.

Restaurant In 2015, McDonald's introduced self-serve kiosks at select locations. At these kiosks, customers use a tablet-style touchscreen to place an order and complete payment. They can also use the system to customize an item, including choosing from a selection of buns and toppings. At other McDonald's locations, customers are served at a table by a waiter using a tablet. Other fast-food or "fast casual" restaurants that have implemented self-serve kiosks or tablet ordering at the table include Chili's, Applebee's, and Taco Bell, to name a few.

Providing self-serve kiosks is just one way McDonald's is using new technology.

Law Enforcement Police officers are using wearable technology to provide better service and help with securing convictions. Some forces in Georgia supply officers with Google Glass eyeglasses to record everything and send information back to the station in real time. In other jurisdictions, wristwatch computers allow officers to receive information via text message or other type of alert, which can help officers in hostile situations or places where accessing a radio or smartphone will slow down or otherwise compromise their efforts and safety. Within the next decade, a Wi-Fi–enabled uniform that has a textile waveguide antenna sewn into the fabric will track a police officer's movements and remotely monitor his or her vital signs while maintaining constant communication.

Medicine In 2015, at Strong Memorial Hospital, a team of heart specialists used a 3-D printed model of a patient's heart to plan a less invasive heart valve replacement surgery for a high-risk patient. 3-D printing is also used to create custom prosthetic hands and arms for a lower cost than traditional prostheses. In March 2015, Robert Downey Jr. surprised a seven-year-old with a 3-D printed prosthetic arm that looks like the arm Downey wears as Iron Man.

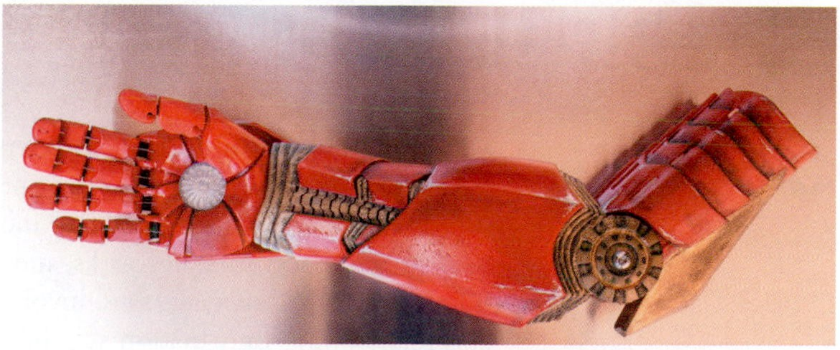

A team of volunteer engineers at Limbitless Solutions created this "Iron Man" prosthetic arm for a seven-year-old boy using 3-D printing technology.

Convergence

Technological convergence, where innovation merges several technologies into a single device, is not just about cell phones becoming multipurpose smartphones. Game consoles used to be used only to play video games, but today's multipurpose consoles are also used to play movies from Blu-ray or DVD and to stream content via the web. You can also surf the web, browse photos, and play music on newer systems.

The Internet of Things

Tutorial
What Is the Internet of Things?

An emerging trend, called the **Internet of Things (IoT)**, describes situations where everyday objects contain embedded processors and are connected to a network, allowing devices to interact with the owner and/or other connected "things." Imagine a world where every product—for example, alarm clocks, coffee makers, refrigerators, stoves, dishwashers, washing machines, clothes dryers, door locks, thermostats, and entertainment systems—can communicate via the Internet. In this connected world, imagine your day begins with the alarm clock awakening you with current weather and traffic conditions, reminding you about a meeting, adjusting the room temperature, and starting the coffee maker. This is just how your day begins! The possibilities for other interactions throughout the day are numerous. Since some of the interactions between connected devices occur without human intervention, this trend is also sometimes referred to as **machine-to-machine communications** or *M2M communications*.

Market research firm International Data Corporation (IDC) has forecasted that the global market for IoT devices and services will exceed $7 trillion by 2020.

Explore Further: What New Technology Innovation Is Occurring in Your Field of Study?

Technological innovation occurs every day, and a computer innovation will likely occur in your field of study while you are still in school.

1. Either by searching the web or by interviewing someone who works in your field of study, investigate a technology innovation that is occurring in your field or that will occur by the time you graduate.
2. Create a document with a brief description of the innovation you learned about and the impact the innovation is expected to have within the industry. At the end of the document, include the URLs of websites you used or a reference for the person you interviewed.
3. Save the document as **ComputerInnovation-YourName**.
4. Submit the document to your instructor in the manner she or he has requested.

1.5 Information Technology and the Information Processing Cycle

Tutorial
What Makes Up a Computer System?

Information technology (IT) refers to the use of computers, software, networks, and other communication systems and processes to store, retrieve, send, process, and protect information. The IT department in an organization is tasked with managing the hardware, software, networks, and other systems that form the information infrastructure. IT specialists are involved with designing, developing, implementing, and maintaining information systems.

Characters that are typed or otherwise entered into a computer are **raw data** or **data**. At the entry stage, the data is not meaningful as it is just a string of characters. Software programs provide the instructions for the computer to process and organize the data into meaningful and useful **information**. The **information processing cycle** includes the operations that transform data into information: input, processing, output, and storage, as shown in Figure 1.13 and described next. The terminology and hardware introduced in this topic will be explored in more detail in Chapter 3.

Figure 1.13
The information processing cycle includes four operations to transform raw data into useful information.

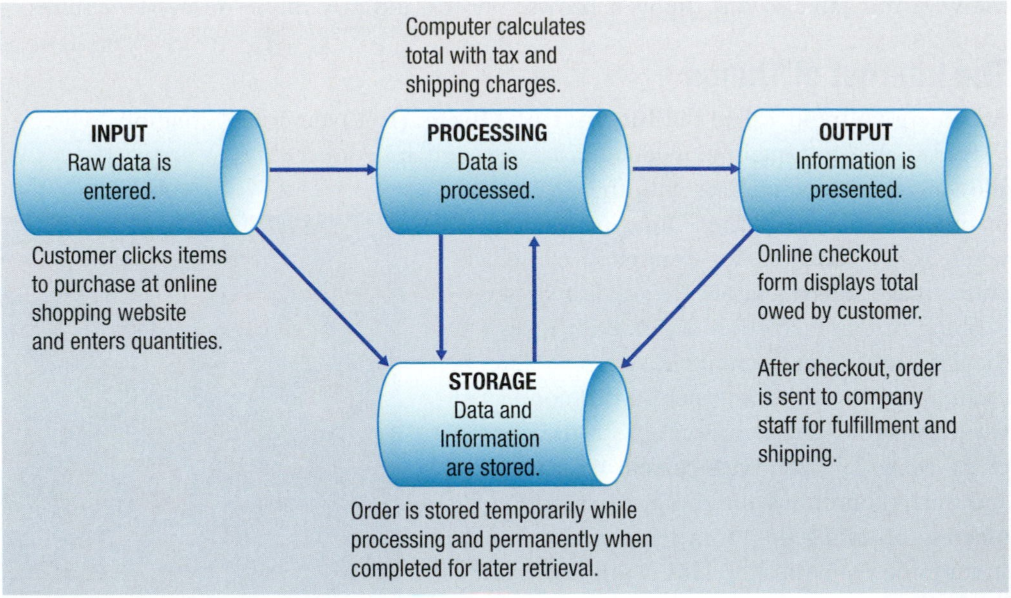

Input

Any device used to enter raw data or communicate instructions to the computer is an **input device**. Commonly used devices include a keyboard, mouse, and touchscreen similar to the ones shown in Figure 1.14. A touchpad, scanner, bar code reader, digital camera, digital pen, webcam, and microphone are just a few other examples of input devices.

Figure 1.14
A keyboard, mouse, and touchscreen are common devices used to enter input.

Processing

A computer chip called the **central processing unit (CPU)** carries out the instructions given by the software to perform the **processing** cycle. Think of the CPU as the brain of the computer. A CPU is a silicon chip referred to as the **microprocessor** and is housed on the computer motherboard (printed circuit board that contains the main computer components). Microprocessors today are typically manufactured with multiple cores, which are independent units on the same chip that can process data simultaneously. A **multicore processor** significantly increases speed and performance. Intel is a leading designer and manufacturer of microprocessors (Figure 1.15).

Figure 1.15
In September 2015, Intel announced its sixth-generation family of Core processors. These are designed to enhance performance at the lowest power levels ever and will be available for a wide range of devices, from high-end desktops to the smallest IoT gadgets.

Output

Anything used to view the information processed and organized by the computer is an **output device**. Typically, you view information on a monitor and/or print it on a printer similar to the ones shown in Figure 1.16. Other output devices include speakers and screens such as those on mobile devices and televisions.

Figure 1.16
A monitor or embedded screen, and a printer are commonly used to view information processed by the computer. The speakers and screens on mobile devices such as a smartphone or tablet can also be considered output devices.

Storage

While processing, instructions and data are temporarily stored in a holding area called **random access memory (RAM)**. RAM is also housed on the computer motherboard. RAM is temporary storage that is cleared when power to the computer is lost.

Cache memory is located either on the CPU chip or on a separate chip between the CPU and RAM and is used to store frequently used data. Speed and performance are increased with cache memory since the CPU checks cache memory first before checking RAM. The faster retrieval of frequently used data saves the processor time.

Permanent storage (Figure 1.17) is any device or location that saves data and information for later use; this type of device is referred to as a **storage medium**. Several storage media, some portable and some housed inside the system unit, are available in various capacities. An internal hard disk drive is housed inside the system unit, while USB flash drives (also called *memory sticks*), external hard drives, and optical discs such as CDs, DVDs, and Blu-ray are portable (can be easily removed from the computer). You may also connect via a network to a hard drive on another computer for storage.

Figure 1.17

Permanent storage is available in media with various capacities such as an internal hard disk drive (shown with the top metal cover removed), a USB flash drive, an external hard disk drive, and optical discs.

An increasingly popular trend is to store information using **cloud storage**, where you log in to a website and copy documents, photos, or other information to a web service. Cloud storage services such as Flickr (a website used to store photos) and Dropbox (a website where you can store any type of file) have become popular since they offer free online storage that can be shared easily or accessed anywhere you can connect to the Internet. You will learn more about cloud computing in the next topic.

Communications

In today's highly connected world, a fifth operation called *communications* is often added to the information processing cycle. Computers accept input from and send output to other computers via various wired and wireless communication channels, such as cable, telephone line, satellite, cellular, microwave, and Bluetooth transmission media. A **communications device** is any component used to facilitate the transmission of data, such as a cable modem, DSL modem, or router (Figure 1.18).

An integrated modem and wireless router are used to connect the computer devices on the home network to the Internet.
20 35

Figure 1.18
Computers connect to other computers to receive input and send output using communications devices such as the integrated modem and wireless router shown.

Career Connection

IT Jobs in Demand

If you enjoy working with computers, consider an IT career. The 2016 Forecast survey conducted by *Computerworld* revealed that the 10 most in-demand IT jobs were as follows, ranked from most to least: IT architecture, programming and application development, project management, big data, business intelligence and analytics, help desk and technical support, database administration, security and compliance administration, cloud computing, and web development. If any of these careers are of interest to you, look at courses offered in postsecondary programs in computer engineering, computer science, computer systems technician, information systems, information technology, and software engineering.

Explore Further — IT Job Profile

You have read in the Career Connection for this topic that IT jobs are in demand. You are interested in working with computers but want to learn more about specific job openings to find out what employers are looking for in new employees.

1. Using a job search website such as Monster.com, locate a current ad for an IT job that interests you within your area. ***Hint:*** *Use titles from the Career Connection.*
2. Create a document that describes the job opportunity in your own words, including the job title, the company offering the job, the duties involved in the job, and the qualifications required. Include information on compensation if the ad lists a salary range. At the end of the document, provide the URL for the job ad.
3. Save the document as **ITJobAd-YourName**.
4. Submit the document to your instructor in the manner she or he has requested.

1.6 Cloud Computing

Tutorial
How Can Cloud Computing Save Businesses Money?

Individuals and businesses are turning to providers of software and computing services that are accessed entirely on the Internet. This delivery model of software and services is called **cloud computing**. With cloud computing, all you need to get your work done is a computer with a web browser, since all the software and files are stored online.

Cloud computing got its name because the Internet has always been identified with a cloud in technology documentation. Cloud computing places the processing and storage operations of the information processing cycle at an online service provider's server and/or data center, rather than on the hardware and software of your own PC or mobile device (Figure 1.19). You can use some cloud computing services for free. For example, at Google Drive, 15 GB of cloud storage is free (with an option to pay a fee for more storage space).

Figure 1.19
Cloud computing means that your software applications and/or data are launched from a web browser and stored on the service provider's equipment. The software and data are accessible from any PC or mobile device.

The delivery of software via the Internet is referred to as **Software as a Service (SaaS)**. Advantages and disadvantages of cloud computing are listed in Table 1.1.

If you open your web browser to check email, create documents, or upload photos, music, videos, or other files to store and share with others, then you are already using SaaS services. A few popular cloud computing services

Table 1.1
Advantages and Disadvantages of Cloud Computing

Advantages	Disadvantages
Applications and data are available at any time from any place since all you need is an Internet connection.	You are totally dependent on your Internet connection; if the service goes down, you cannot access your programs or files.
Updates to software are automatic and immediately available.	You do not have control over changes made to software—upgrading is not at your discretion.
The service provider makes continual investment in hardware and software. You pay only the subscription fees after you have purchased your computer and Internet connectivity.	Over a long period, monthly subscription fees could end up costing more than the initial outlay of cash for hardware and software and ongoing Internet connectivity.
Web applications are generally easy to use and navigate.	Web applications may be too limiting to meet your needs.
Web-based applications are generally compatible with PCs, Macs, and mobile devices—you can use any device.	Some businesses may have compatibility issues with exchanging data with legacy systems or infrastructure.
Documents, photos, music, videos, and other files are stored off-site. If you experience equipment malfunction, theft, or some other disaster, all that is lost is the physical equipment, which is easily replaced.	Large cloud computing vendors have reliable and secure storage; however, there is a risk that personal and/or sensitive data could be accessed by unauthorized users. Also be mindful of who actually owns the data you are storing online—is it you or the provider?

include Google Drive, Dropbox, iCloud, and OneDrive. Many more cloud computing service providers exist to meet the growing market for web applications.

Figure 1.20 illustrates a simple three-slide presentation created in Google Slides. If you are familiar with presentation software, creating a presentation in the Google Slides web-based application will be easy since the program contains tools similar to what you would find in other presentation programs. Google Slides is just one application in the free productivity suite offered by Google. Other applications include Google Docs, Google Sheets, Google Forms, and Google Drawings.

Microsoft offers a similar suite of free web-based applications called Office Online from which you can open Word Online, Excel Online, PowerPoint Online, and OneNote Online. To start any of these applications requires that you sign up for a Microsoft account, which can be any email address you want to use as your user name. A Hotmail or Live email address is automatically a Microsoft account and means that you do not need to sign up to use the Office Online applications.

Free productivity suites in the cloud are ideal options for anyone with a need to create a simple document, presentation, or worksheet. However, web-based applications have limited features—complex work most likely requires a traditional desktop software application.

Check This Out ✓

http://CC2.ParadigmCollege.net/OfficeOnline

Go here to start a document, presentation, worksheet, or notebook using Microsoft's web-based Office Online suite. You will need to sign in with a valid Microsoft, work, or school email address to use the free software.

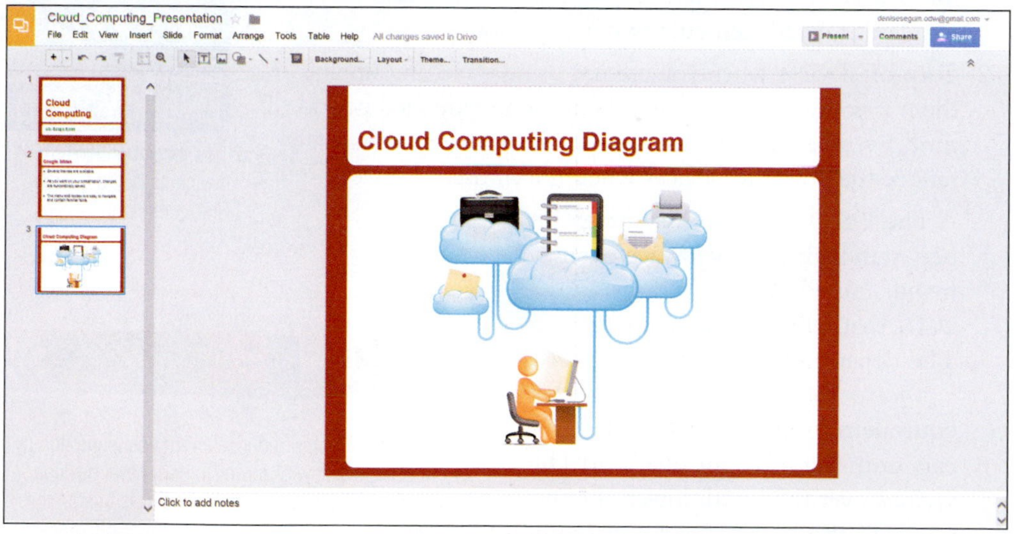

Figure 1.20

Sign in with a Gmail account at the Google home page to access Google Drive and then start Google Slides to create a presentation similar to the one shown here using free web-based software.

Security Alert: Minimize Your Risks with Cloud Storage

Data stored in the cloud is at risk of loss, theft, or breach by a hacker. One cloud security company predicts that 21 percent of data uploaded to a cloud storage provider by employees contains confidential data including a company's intellectual property. Protect against these risks by (1) never storing in the cloud a file with personal or otherwise sensitive information, (2) making sure your cloud provider encrypts data (that is, stores the file in a format unrecognizable to unauthorized users), and (3) saving a backup somewhere else just in case.

Explore Further: Finding a Cloud Service Provider for Storing Pictures

A popular use of cloud computing is to upload photos from your PC to a cloud storage provider so you can share them without posting them on a social media website, access them from multiple devices, or have a backup if something happens to the pictures on your PC or mobile device.

1. Research two free cloud storage providers. Find out the amount of free storage space and look for restrictions on the file sizes that can be uploaded.
2. Create a document that compares the two cloud providers.
3. Save the document as **CloudFileStorage-YourName**.
4. Submit the document to your instructor in the manner she or he has requested.

1.7 Green Computing

Green computing refers to the use of computers and other electronic devices in an environmentally responsible manner. Green computing can encompass new or modified computing practices, policies, and procedures. The green computing trend is growing, with more individuals and businesses adopting green strategies every year. Green strategies include reducing the energy consumption of computers and other devices; reducing the use of paper, ink, and toner; and reusing, recycling, or properly disposing of electronic waste (referred to as **e-waste** or *e-trash*).

In addition to changes in computing practices, manufacturers are working to produce electronics that are more energy efficient, reduce the amount of toxic chemicals used in computers, and incorporate more recyclable components and packaging. Finally, governments and industries are making available more recycling programs to reuse or properly dispose of electronics.

Five Ways to Go Green

Check This Out ✓

http://CC2.ParadigmCollege.net/GreenButton

Go here to read about the US Green Button standard designed to help consumers manage their energy consumption.

Good to Know

Devices that consume power when turned off or in standby mode are called energy vampires. The Department of Energy estimates the average home energy bill is 10 percent higher due to power energy vampires.

1. Make sure you use Energy Star–certified devices.

   The Energy Star label on a device means the manufacturer has reached or exceeded the minimum federal standards for reduced energy consumption.

This label identifies a device as being Energy Star compliant.

2. Turn off devices when you are not using them and unplug them if you will not be using them for an extended period of time. Even better—use smart power strips that automatically reduce the power to devices when not in use.

   The US Department of Energy set new standards for microwave ovens manufactured on or after June 17, 2016, that reduce standby energy use. The department estimates that over a 30-year period, this change will be equivalent to removing 12 million new cars from the roads for one year! The savings over time with lower energy bills will also be a bonus for consumers.

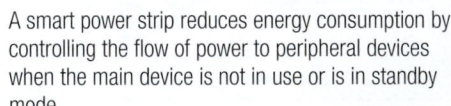

A smart power strip reduces energy consumption by controlling the flow of power to peripheral devices when the main device is not in use or is in standby mode.

3. Reduce printing to only those documents, messages, or photos that absolutely must be in paper copy and make sure what you print uses the least amount of paper.

   Make it a policy to distribute PDF copies of documents and messages and to share photos online with friends and relatives. When you must print, consider using both sides of the paper and/or using narrower margins so you can fit more on a page. The cost savings from reduced paper consumption, toner, and ink cartridges is significant. Consider also that fewer print cartridges will end up in the landfills.

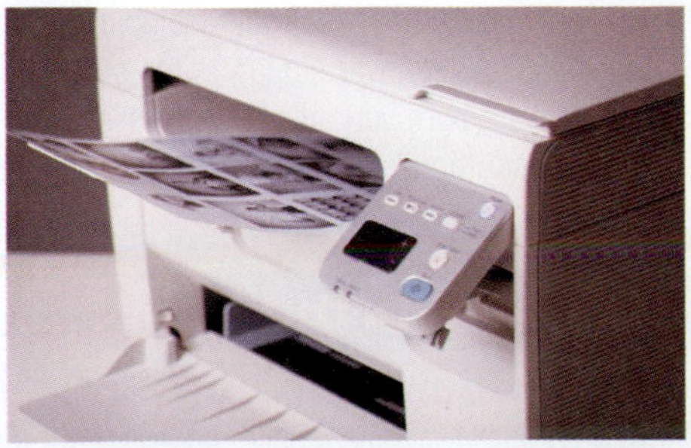
Reduce printing—only print what you absolutely must have a paper copy.

4. Modify the default power options on your computer to conserve more energy.

   Most Windows-based desktop and notebook computers default to a balanced power plan, which aims to balance performance with energy conservation. You can adjust the sleep and display settings to turn off power sooner than the default times. Choose *Power Options* in the Hardware and Sound category of the Control Panel on a Windows PC.

   On Mac computers, adjust the energy features using the Energy Saver pane in System Preferences.

Modify power options on your PC to conserve more energy.

5. Consider reselling or donating equipment you no longer need.

   Computers, cell phones, and electronics that are still in working order can be sold or donated to schools, churches, or nonprofit groups. If you must dispose of electronics, try to drop off the e-waste at an electronics recycling facility.

   In the United States, approximately 3.4 million tons of e-waste is thrown away each year. Most of this discarded electronic equipment ends up in landfills or is exported to countries such as China and India.

Whenever possible, divert e-waste from landfills.

Good to Know

According to estimates by the Environmental Protection Agency, only 27 percent of e-waste is recycled.

Blog Topic: Are You Green?

Do you practice green computing? If yes, are there ways you can improve your green computing practices? If no, which green computing strategies can you start to use? Have you purchased a new PC or mobile device within the last year? If yes, how did you dispose of your older equipment?

1. Write and post a blog entry that provides your answers to the questions.
2. Read at least two of your classmates' blogs and post one comment to each.
3. Submit your blog URL and the URLs of the two classmates' blogs to your instructor in the manner she or he has requested.

Explore Further: Locating Electronic Recycling Services in Your Area

Approximately 130 million cell phones were replaced last year in the United States. If only 27 percent of those phones were recycled, then almost 95 million cell phones ended up in landfills. This does not take into account other electronics such as game consoles, tablets, laptops, desktops, and televisions. Assume you decide to gather up some old electronics for disposal. Do you know where to take e-waste in your area?

1. Find out the nearest electronic waste drop-off location in your area. Determine the hours of operation, the items accepted for recycling, and items that are not accepted, if any.
2. Create a document that could be used as a flyer to advertise the service in your neighborhood and that contains all the information you found.
3. Save the document as **eWasteRecycling-YourName**.
4. Submit the document to your instructor in the manner she or he has requested.

1.8 Computers and Your Health

Frequent use of computing devices can adversely affect your health if you don't use proper care and preventive strategies. Physical ailments that can occur include fatigue, eyestrain, blurred vision, backaches, wrist and forearm pain, finger numbness or pain, and neck and shoulder pain. A leading job-related illness and injury in North America is **repetitive-strain injury (RSI)**. RSI is an injury or disorder of the joints, nerves, muscles, ligaments, or tendons.

Two common computer-related RSI injuries are **tendonitis** and **carpal tunnel syndrome (CTS)**. Tendonitis occurs when a tendon in your wrist becomes inflamed. CTS occurs when the nerve that connects the forearm to the palm of the hand becomes inflamed. Both conditions are caused by excessive typing, mouse scrolling, mouse clicking, and thumb typing/movements on mobile devices. Symptoms of tendonitis and CTS are listed in Table 1.2.

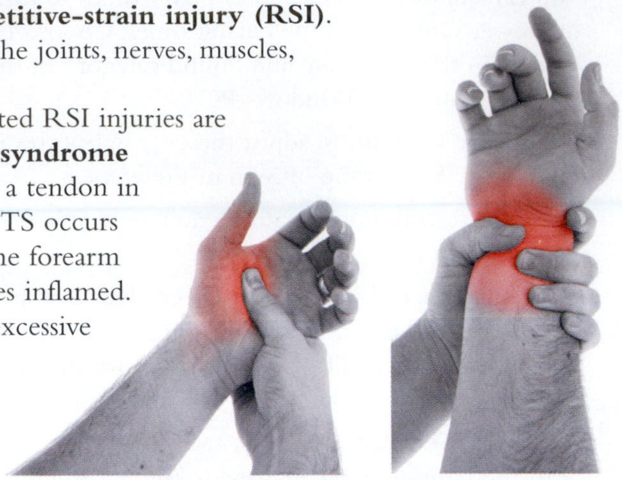

Carpal tunnel syndrome is a common RSI injury from computer use that causes pain in the hand and wrist.

Table 1.2

Symptoms Associated with RSI Injuries from Computer Use

Symptoms of Tendonitis	Symptoms of CTS
Tingling or numbness in the fingers	Numbness and tingling in the thumb and the first two fingers especially at night (can cause sleep disruptions)
Pain in the forearm and wrist	Burning sensation when the nerve is compressed
Decreased mobility of the wrist or fingers	Decreased grip strength leading the user to drop objects
Loss of strength in the hand	Loss of strength in the hand

Computer Vision Syndrome

Computer vision syndrome (CVS) is a temporary condition caused by prolonged computer use that involves eye strain; weak, itchy, burning, or dry eyes; blurred or double vision; difficulty with focus; sensitivity to light; headaches; and neck pain. According to the American Optometric Association, 50 to 90 percent of computer workers will experience some CVS symptoms.

CVS affects 50 to 90 percent of computer users.

Posture-Related Injuries

Pain in the lower back, neck, shoulders, and arms are common complaints from computer workers. Sitting for long periods of time in the same position causes fatigue and reduces circulation to muscles and tendons, which can lead to stiffness and soreness.

Neck pain is a common complaint among computer workers.

Prevention Strategies to Reduce Risk of RSI, CVS, and Muscular Pain

Knowing the three primary risk factors for developing health issues when using a computer is key to identifying strategies to reduce risk of injury: poor posture, poor technique, and excessive use. Prevention strategies are listed in Table 1.3. Many of these strategies involve the use of **ergonomics** to improve the computer workspace design. Ergonomics involves the design of equipment and a person's workspace to promote safe and comfortable operation of the equipment by the individual. In other words, good ergonomic design fits the computer equipment to the worker by adjusting components to the optimal height, distance, and angles (see Figure 1.21).

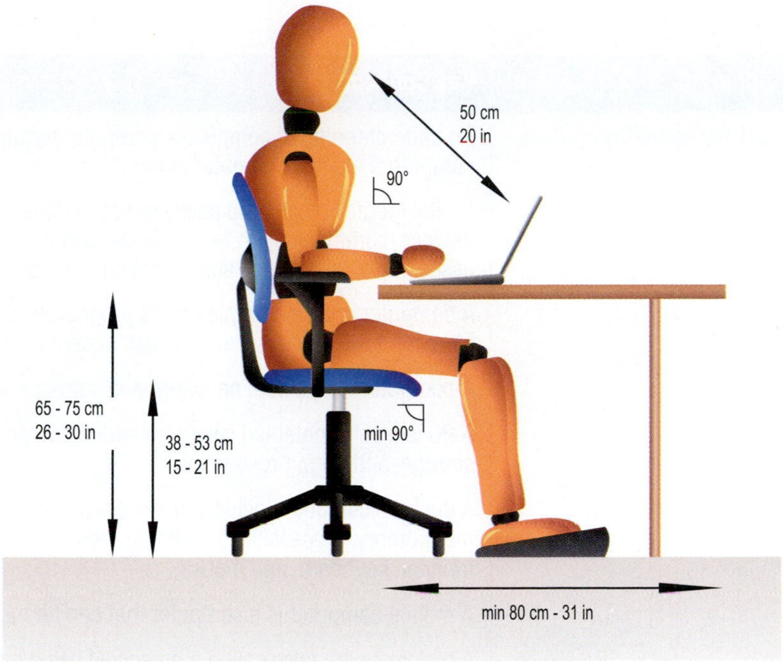

Figure 1.21
An ergonomically correct computer workspace helps prevent RSI injuries.

Table 1.3
Preventive Strategies for Avoiding Computer-Related Illness

Take frequent breaks. Get up out of the chair and walk around, stretch, and do another activity for a few moments.
Maintain good posture by sitting up straight with feet flat on the floor, shoulders relaxed, head and neck balanced and in line with torso, and your lower back supported by your chair or a rolled towel. If the desk height is not adjustable, use a foot rest.
Sit in a chair that has five legs for stability and allows adjustments to height and angle of backrest, seat, and arm rests.
When typing, the keyboard should be at elbow level with the elbows close to your body and supported by your chair. Wrists and hands should be positioned in line with forearms. If using a notebook computer, consider plugging in an external keyboard so that you can adjust the height and position.
The top of the computer screen should be at or slightly below your eye level. If using a notebook computer, consider using an external monitor that you can adjust to the correct height. Optimal viewing distance is 20 to 40 inches. Increase font size in documents and browsers if necessary to avoid eye strain.
Remember to blink—studies have shown computer users tend to blink about five times less than normal. Also minimize glare and use ambient lighting rather than overhead fluorescents if possible.
Look away from the computer screen once in a while and spend a few moments focusing on something that is off in the distance. For example, look out the window at something outside.

Check This Out ✓

http://CC2.ParadigmCollege.net/Workstation

Go here for an interactive e-tool to learn more about proper workstation setup, or view setup checklists.

Explore Further Notebook, Texting, and Smartphone Ergonomics

Good ergonomic workspace design for a notebook PC involves some factors not discussed in Table 1.3. Increased smartphone use can become a risk for some people. For example, the term BlackBerry thumb was devised to describe pain that developed from excessive texting.

1. Research ergonomics for laptops and smartphones. Specifically, find at least two articles that address the unique needs of mobile computing device users.
2. Create a document with a checklist that includes ergonomically correct usage of mobile devices. Include the URLs of the articles you used at the end of the document.
3. Save the document as **MobileErgonomics-YourName**.
4. Submit the document to your instructor in the manner she or he has requested.

Topics Review

Topic	Key Concepts	Key Terms
1.1 Personal Computers	An understanding of computers, computer terminology, and how computers work is computer literacy. Digital literacy means the ability to use various computer devices, communication technologies, and the Internet to find, assess, use, create, and share content appropriately. A computer is an electronic device programmed to process, store, and output data that has been accepted as input. A computer needs both hardware and software to work. A PC is a self-contained computer with input, processing, storage, and output resources. A desktop computer includes a system unit (a case that houses the memory, processing, and storage resources) and a separate monitor, keyboard, and mouse. A mobile computer is a computer that can be moved around. A typical laptop (also called a *notebook*) has a monitor that when swiveled up reveals a keyboard with the remaining components housed below. Ultrabooks are thinner, lighter, and more powerful notebooks. A netbook is a small notebook designed primarily for using web-based applications. A tablet is a lightweight notebook with a smaller screen that you interact with using touch or a digital pen. A laptop that can be converted into a tablet is called a *convertible laptop* or a *hybrid laptop*.	computer literacy digital literacy computer hardware software personal computer (PC) desktop computer system unit mobile computer laptop computer notebook ultrabook netbook tablet convertible laptop hybrid laptop
1.2 Mobile Devices, Wearable Computers, and Embedded Computers	A mobile device is a handheld computing device with a small screen and with programs and data stored within the unit. A smartphone is a cell phone with a built-in camera, apps, and web-browsing and messaging capabilities. A phablet is a device that is larger than a smartphone but smaller than a tablet. A portable media player is used to play games or other media, while an ebook reader is used primarily to read ebooks. A wearable computer contains sensors that are always on and provides for hands-free communications. An embedded computer is an appliance or other gadget that has a processor built-in and is designed to perform a specific task; an embedded computer is sometimes referred to as a *smart device*.	mobile device smartphone phablet portable media player ebook reader wearable computer embedded computer smart device

continued...

Topic	Key Concepts	Key Terms
1.3 Computers for Connecting Multiple Users and Specialized Processing	A server is a high-end computer that connects other computers and is stored in a specially maintained server room (a room equipped to avoid heat, humidity, and dust). A computer that connects to a server is called a *client*. Midrange servers are used to connect hundreds of clients at the same time. A computer that relies on the server for all programs and data is called a *thin client*. Mainframes are large, powerful, and expensive computers that are capable of handling hundreds or thousands of users. A supercomputer is the fastest, most expensive computer, capable of processing trillions of calculations per second. Supercomputing speed is measured in petaflops; one petaflop is a quadrillion floating point operations per second.	server client server room midrange server thin client mainframe supercomputer petaflop
1.4 Computer Innovations and Trends	Ubiquitous computing means that computing technology is everywhere within our environment and used all of the time. An Apple Watch with the Starwood Hotels & Resorts app can be used to locate a venue, check in, and unlock the door. McDonald's restaurants is one of the fast food companies that have installed self-serve kiosks and table service using tablets. Law enforcement officers use wearable technology such as Google Glass and smartwatches to improve service and help secure convictions. WiFi-enabled uniforms are expected within the next decade. 3-D printing is being used in medicine to plan difficult surgeries and make prostheses. Technological convergence involves the blending or merging of multiple technologies into a single device such as a smartphone or game console. The IoT is a trend where everyday objects are connected to a network and can interact with each other or other connected objects (referred to as *machine-to-machine communications*).	ubiquitous computing technological convergence Internet of Things (IoT) machine-to-machine communications

continued...

Topic	Key Concepts	Key Terms
1.5 Information Technology and the Information Processing Cycle	IT involves the use of technology to store, retrieve, send, process, and protect information. IT specialists are involved with designing, developing, implementing, and maintaining information systems. Raw data (or data) are characters entered into a computer that software turns into meaningful information. The Information Processing Cycle includes four operations: input, processing, output, and storage. A device used to enter raw data is an input device. The operation where instructions tell the computer what to do with the data is called *processing* and is carried out by the CPU, also called a *microprocessor*. A multicore processor has an independent unit on the same chip that allow multiple simultaneous processes. A device used to view processed and organized data or information is an output device. RAM is temporary storage used to hold data while processing. Cache memory is where frequently used data is stored. A permanent storage medium such as a hard disk drive, USB flash drive, optical disc, or cloud storage (storage at web servers) is where data is saved for later use. A communications device such as a cable modem or router transmits data to/from computers.	information technology (IT) raw data data information information processing cycle input device central processing unit (CPU) processing microprocessor multicore processor output device random access memory (RAM) cache memory storage medium cloud storage communications device
1.6 Cloud Computing	Cloud computing is a delivery model where software and computing services are accessed entirely from the web. Software over the Internet is called *SaaS*. Cloud computing places the processing and storage operations in the web. Some cloud services, such as Google Drive and OneDrive, are free. Several advantages and disadvantages of cloud computing must be considered before signing up for a cloud service. A few popular cloud computing services are Google Drive, Dropbox, iCloud, and OneDrive. Google and Microsoft both offer free web-based productivity software suites.	cloud computing Software as a Service (SaaS)

continued…

Topic	Key Concepts	Key Terms
1.7 Green Computing	Using computers and other electronic devices in an environmentally responsible manner is known as *green computing.* Green computing practices, policies, and procedures strive to reduce energy consumption; reduce use of paper and paper supplies; and reuse, recycle, or properly dispose of electronic waste (e-waste). Five ways to practice green computing are to use Energy Star rated devices, turn off or unplug devices when not in use, reduce printing of documents, modify power options on your computers, and resell or donate old equipment.	green computing e-waste
1.8 Computers and Your Health	RSI is the leading cause of job-related injury in North America and involves a disorder of the joints, nerves, muscles, ligaments, or tendons. Tendonitis occurs when a tendon in your wrist becomes inflamed. CTS occurs when the nerve that connects the forearm to the palm becomes inflamed. Both tendonitis and CTS are caused by computer overuse. Symptoms of tendonitis and CTS include pain, numbness, tingling, decreased mobility and decreased strength in the hand. CVS is temporary problems with your eyes caused by prolonged computer use. Ergonomic design involves adjusting components to optimal height, distance, and angles to prevent computer-related injury.	repetitive-strain injury (RSI) tendonitis carpal tunnel syndrome (CTS) computer vision syndrome (CVS) ergonomics

Recheck
Recheck your understanding of the topics covered in this chapter.

Workbook
Chapter review and assessment resources are available in the *Workbook* ebook.

Chapter 2

Exploring the World Using the Internet

Precheck
Check your understanding of the topics covered in this chapter.

Chances are you have used the Internet today at home, at school, or at work to search for information, access study notes, play games, watch videos or movies, update your status, upload photos, or post a comment on a social media site. For many people reading this book, the Internet has always been available to accomplish these tasks, and the ability to connect and share information online with anyone in the world is taken for granted. Society has been shaped in many ways by the proliferation of the Internet and the World Wide Web over the last 25 years. In the next few years, the emergence of Internet of Things devices into our homes and vehicles will bring even more innovation to our lives.

Today, consumers and workers need to be network and web savvy. Knowing how to find the right information quickly, connect with others, and communicate professionally are essential skills for personal and professional success. In this chapter you will learn the difference between the Internet and the World Wide Web, study the equipment options used for Internet connectivity, review the most popular web browsers, search and evaluate web content, understand how multimedia pages access plug-ins and players, and identify the various services available to you in the online world.

Following this introduction to the Internet, you will learn to communicate and connect with others using social media and web publishing options in Chapter 6.

SNAP If you are a SNAP user, go to your SNAP Assignments page to complete the Precheck, Tutorials, and Recheck.

Learning Objectives

- **2.1** Distinguish a network, the Internet, and the World Wide Web
- **2.2** Identify the hardware and various types of connectivity options for Internet service
- **2.3** Recognize the popular web browsers used to view online content
- **2.4** Describe parts of a URL and browse to web pages via web addresses and links
- **2.5** Locate content using a search engine, narrow a search using search tools, and describe content aggregators
- **2.6** Evaluate the accuracy and timeliness of web content
- **2.7** Recognize plug-ins and players used on web pages for viewing multimedia
- **2.8** Explain online services such as e-commerce, email, and VoIP

2.1 Networks, the Internet, and the World Wide Web

A **network** is two or more computers or other devices (such as a printer) that are linked together to share resources and communicate with each other. Computers are linked by a communications medium, such as a wireless signal or a cable that physically connects each device. You may have a small home network to share Internet access among a desktop, laptop, tablet, or smartphone. Often, home networks also share a printer.

Networks in business, government, and other organizations exist in a variety of sizes and types for sharing and communicating among workers. These larger networks share software, storage space, printers, copiers, and other devices in addition to Internet access. Businesses typically use the network for centralized data storage and for controlling access to computers and other equipment.

The Internet

The **Internet** or **net** is a global network that links together other networks, such as government departments, businesses, nonprofit organizations, educational and research institutions, and individuals. Think of the Internet as the physical pathway made up of thousands of other connected networks to make a worldwide network. For this network to transmit data around the world, special high-speed communications and networking equipment is needed to provide the pathway on which the data travels. For example, an email message you send to someone in another country travels through several networks, including telephone, cable, or satellite networks to reach its destination. This collection of networks is the Internet.

You connect your personal computer (PC) or mobile device to the Internet by subscribing to Internet service through an **Internet service provider (ISP)**, a company that provides access to the Internet infrastructure for a fee. You will learn about connecting to the Internet in the next topic.

Good to Know

The term *information superhighway* was made popular in the 1990s by former Vice President Al Gore, who recognized early the importance of building the Internet infrastructure and making it available to everyone. In recognition of his work, the Internet Society inducted him into the Internet Hall of Fame in April of 2012.

Check This Out

http://CC2.ParadigmCollege.net/UsageStatistics

Go here for Internet usage statistics. Check the latest Internet usage and population by country or region. For example, in June 2015, 87.9 percent of North Americans were Internet users.

The Internet is a global network connecting thousands of other networks, providing the pathway for data to travel the world.

The World Wide Web

The global collection of electronic documents circulated on the Internet in the form of web pages make up the **World Wide Web** or **web**. A **web page** is a document that contains text and multimedia content, such as images, video, sound, and animation. Web pages are usually linked to other pages so that a person can start at one page and click links to several other related pages. Web pages are stored in a format that is read and interpreted for display within a **web browser** (a software program used to view web pages). A **website** is a collection of related web pages for one organization or individual. For example, all the web pages about your school that are available for viewing on the Internet make up your school's website. All the web pages and resources such as photos, videos, sounds, and animations that make the website work are stored on a special server called a **web server**. Web servers are connected to the Internet continuously so that anyone can access them at any time from any place.

While the Internet provides the path on which a web page is transmitted, web pages are just one type of data that uses the Internet. Other services that use the same network include email messages, instant messages, Voice over Internet Protocol services (telephone services via the Internet), and file transfer services. Figure 2.1 illustrates how the Internet delivers the web content to you at your PC or mobile device, and Figure 2.2 on page 30 provides an example of web pages with multimedia.

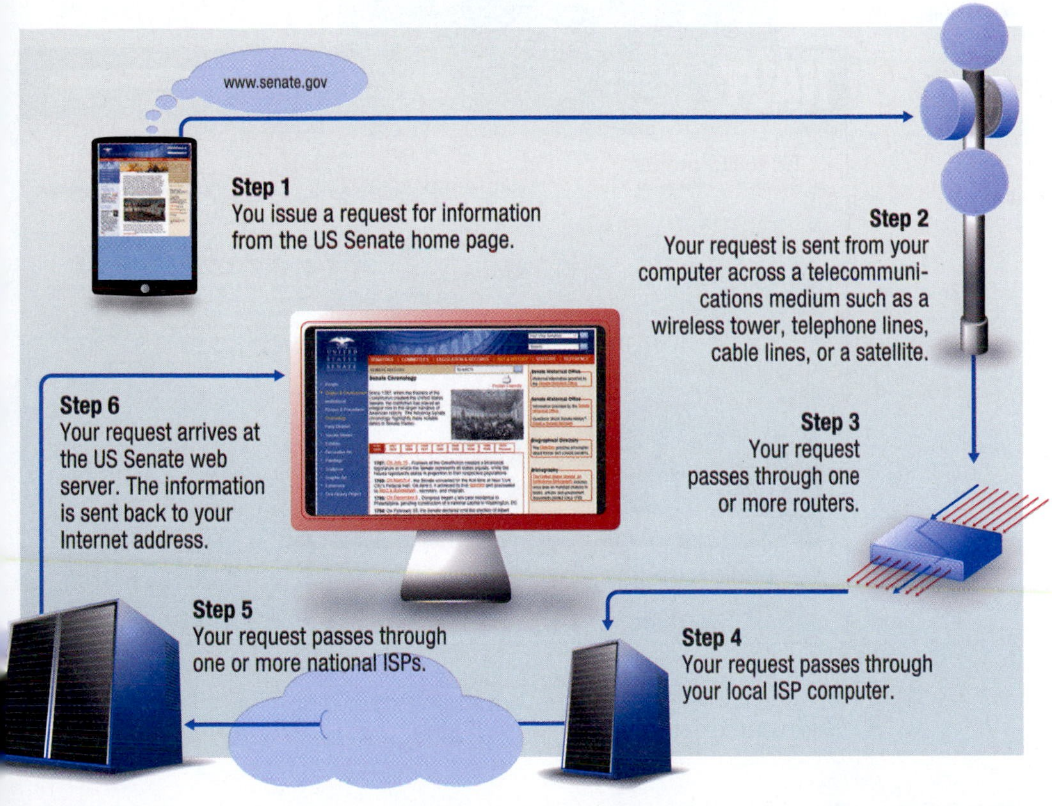

www.senate.gov
Step 1
You issue a request for information from the US Senate home page.
Step 2
Your request is sent from your computer across a telecommunications medium such as a wireless tower, telephone lines, cable lines, or a satellite.
Step 3
Your request passes through one or more routers.
Step 4
Your request passes through your local ISP computer.
Step 5
Your request passes through one or more national ISPs.
Step 6
Your request arrives at the US Senate web server. The information is sent back to your Internet address.

Figure 2.1

A web page travels along a collection of Internet networking equipment and telecommunications systems to your PC or mobile device.

Figure 2.2

Web pages can contain text, images, video, sound, and animation. A website is a collection of related web pages such as these from the US Navy.

Tutorial
How Is Web 2.0 Changing Our World?

Web 2.0 Initially, web pages mostly were a one-way communication medium where the organization or individual controlled the content and used the web simply as a means to provide information. Over time, a second generation of two-way communication web pages became available that allowed people to interact with the organization or with one another by sharing ideas, feedback, content, and multimedia. These websites that encourage and facilitate collaboration and sharing and allow users to add or edit content became known as **Web 2.0**.

Web 3.0 The next generation of the web is just starting to emerge and is known as **Web 3.0**. In this generation, meaningful connections between data and web pages will exist, allowing you to find personalized complex information more easily and quickly. Web 3.0 will use automated agents or intelligent agents, machines that will adapt and learn the type of content to show you based on previous searches and browsing you have done. Imagine starting a search with *Where is a good place to eat out tonight?* and the browser responds with a list of restaurants for the type of food you have searched for in the past within a few miles of your current location. Experts differ on the exact meaning of Web 3.0, and some even disagree with the name, preferring to call this evolution the Semantic Web. Elements of Web 3.0 already exist today. For example, the Google Now app uses predictive cards that provide you with information before you request it, such as driving directions to an upcoming appointment.

Career Connection

Careers for the Web

Web designers create the look, feel, and function of a website, while web developers program the website. Both specialists work together to create a dynamic and interactive site to support an organization's brand. Web designers and web developers that specialize in *responsive web design* are in demand. In this specialty, the website is programmed to query the device from which a request has been made to learn the screen size of the device and then adjust content for optimal viewing. For example, it will ensure that a restaurant menu is just as readable on a 5-inch smartphone screen as on a 27-inch desktop monitor. Other companies may design a separate set of web pages for smaller, mobile devices. Look up ads for web designers and web developers to see what training and experience you need if these professions are of interest to you.

Explore Further — What Is Internet2?

If the Internet is the world's largest network of networks, what is Internet2? What is the purpose of Internet2, how is it managed, and what benefits will be gained?

1. Search the web to locate answers to the above questions.
2. Create a document with a summary of your findings in your own words. Include the URLs of the web pages you used to create your summary.
3. Save the document as **Internet2-YourName**.
4. Submit the document to your instructor in the manner she or he requested.

2.2 Connecting to the Internet

At work or school, you connect to the Internet using the high-speed service installed on the organization's network. After logging in to a PC or other device by providing your user name and password, you can immediately launch a web browser and start searching the web. The networks you use in these settings are designed to handle more functions beyond sharing Internet access, such as providing access to shared software and centralized management of other resources. In this topic, you will learn about Internet connectivity options for a small home network.

Components Needed for Internet Access

Computers and mobile devices sold today are already equipped with the hardware needed to connect to a network. For example, a notebook may be sold equipped with a **network interface card (NIC)**, often referred to in computer ads as an **Ethernet port**. With this type of hardware, you plug one end of an Ethernet cable (a twisted-pair cable similar to a telephone cable but larger) into the notebook and the other end into a device that connects to the Internet. Newer PCs and all mobile devices come equipped with a built-in **wireless interface card** that allows you to connect to a network using wireless technology. Newer notebooks and mobile devices also integrate **Bluetooth** connectivity, which offers the ability to connect to another Bluetooth-enabled device, such as your smartphone.

In addition to your network-enabled PC, notebook, or mobile device, you will also need the following account service, hardware, and software to connect to the Internet and browse the web:

- an account with an ISP
- networking equipment (usually provided by your ISP), such as a cable modem, DSL modem, wireless modem, or satellite modem
- a router if you will be connecting multiple devices (however, newer modems integrate a wireless router within the same equipment)
- a web browser, such as Internet Explorer, Microsoft Edge, Firefox, Chrome, or Safari (you will learn about these software programs in the next topic)

Good to Know

A principle called *net neutrality* was in the news in February 2015 when the Federal Trade Commission passed new rules aimed to protect the flow of content. Net neutrality refers to the idea that ISPs should give consumers access to Internet content on an equal basis—without favoring one website or blocking another. The FTC's rules are meant to prevent ISPs from slowing down delivery speed for some content providers or creating a fast lane for other content providers that have paid a fee.

ISPs

ISPs are companies that sell Internet access by providing the equipment and servers that allow your PC or mobile device to connect to the Internet backbone (main data routes). Typically, you contract with a telephone or cellular provider, cable company, satellite company, or dedicated Internet access company such as EarthLink.

Fees for Internet access vary and usually are based on the connection speed that you want. High-speed access costs more than a slower connection and is usually priced at various speed levels. Also be aware of download limits (called *data caps*) in your contract. Some ISPs attach a data cap to a service, and if you exceed the cap, additional fees may be charged.

Your choice of connection speed is usually based on your anticipated usage of the Internet. If you primarily only use email and browse web pages, you can get by with a slower speed than someone who wants to play online games or stream movies, music, or radio programs.

Search at your school or library to find the best deal for ISPs in your area if you need new service. Along with Internet access, you also receive multiple email accounts and security tools to keep your PC or mobile device virus- and spam-free.

High-Speed Internet Connectivity

High-speed Internet access is called **broadband** and includes any always-on connection capable of carrying a large amount of data at a fast speed. Speed for broadband connectivity is expressed as **megabits per second (Mbps)**, meaning data transfers at the rate of 1 million bits per second. See Table 2.1 for a list of typical connection speeds by type of connection. When you evaluate ISP contracts, a higher Mbps value means a higher subscription fee. Be aware that speeds are faster for downloading content than for uploading content. Upload speeds are slower, and some ISPs restrict upload speeds. Figure 2.3 puts meaningful context to connection speed by comparing the number of photos and songs that can be downloaded at four speed levels. Typical broadband options are described next.

Good to Know

Actual connection speed will vary due to factors such as distance from ISP, time of day (congestion slows down networks), and the web activities of others sharing the connection.

Table 2.1

Average Internet Connection Speeds

Type of Internet Connectivity	Average Speed
Cable	20 to 250 Mbps
Digital subscriber line (DSL)	6 to 20 Mbps
Fiber-optic	50 to 300 Mbps, with 500 and 1,000 Mbps in some areas
Satellite	1.5 to 15 Mbps

Check This Out

http://CC2.ParadigmCollege.net/SpeedTest

Go here to perform a speed test from your PC or mobile device. Compare speed results at different times of the day until you find when speed is fastest.

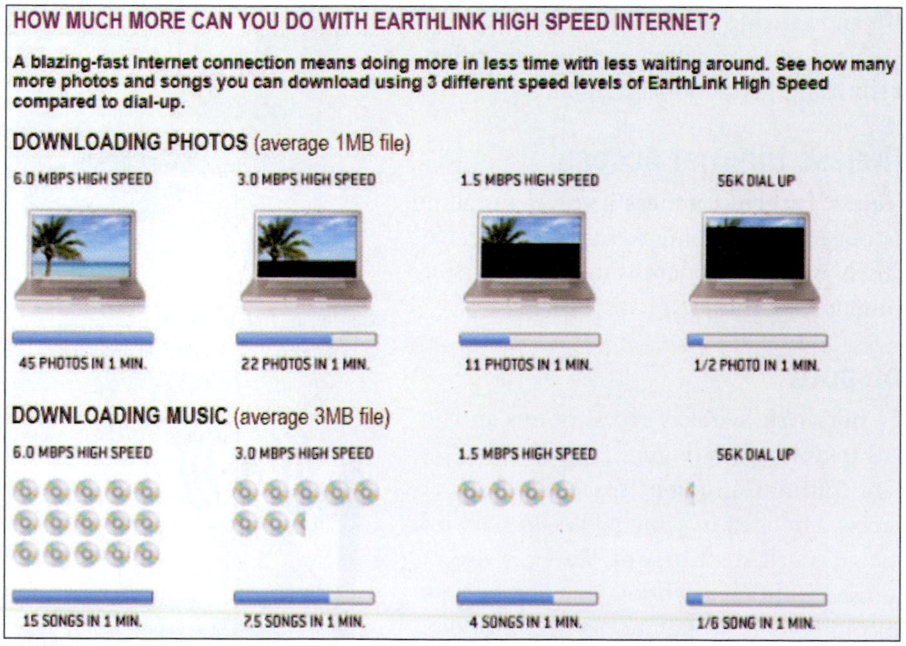

Figure 2.3

ISP EarthLink provides this chart at its website that compares the number of photos and songs that can be downloaded at various connection speeds.

Check This Out

http://CC2.ParadigmCollege.net/ProviderStats

Go here, type in your address, and click Find Broadband to view statistics about broadband providers in your area.

Cable Internet Access

Cable Internet access is provided by the same cable company with which you subscribe for television service. A cable modem connects to your cable network outlet using a coaxial cable (Figure 2.4). From the cable modem, you use a twisted-pair cable to plug into your computer or wireless router to enable Internet access. Cable connections are very fast; however, you share the connection with others in your neighborhood so performance can vary.

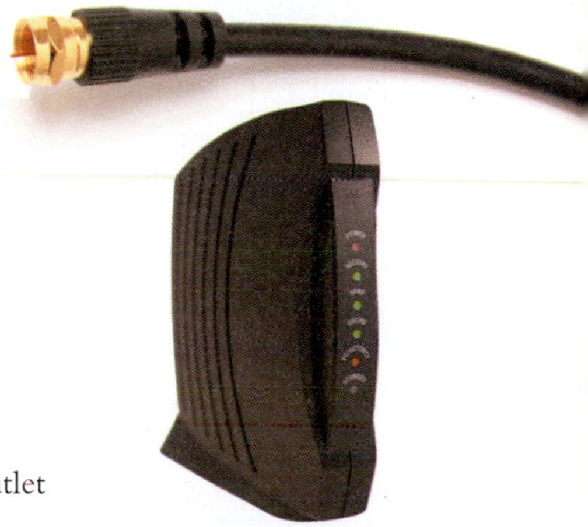

Figure 2.4

A cable modem is connected to the cable company network using coaxial cable.

Figure 2.5
A DSL modem is connected to the telephone company network using twisted-pair cable.

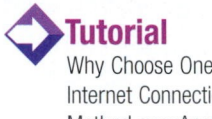

Tutorial
Why Choose One Internet Connection Method over Another?

Digital Subscriber Line Internet Access

A **digital subscriber line (DSL)** provided by your telephone company connects using telephone lines (Figure 2.5). A DSL modem uses twisted-pair cable to plug into your telephone jack and your computer or wireless router. With DSL, your telephone line is not tied up while you are using the Internet.

Fiber to the Premises Internet Access

Fiber to the premises (FTTP), also referred to as *fiber to the home (FTTH)* or *fiber-optic service (FiOS)* involves the ISP running a fiber-optic cable directly to your home or business (Figure 2.6). This is the most expensive option and not widely available. A piece of networking equipment is installed to convert optical signals transmitted over fiber-optic cable to and from the electrical signals transmitted by your computer devices.

Figure 2.6
Fiber-optic networks transmit beams of light capable of speeds measuring in the billions of bits per second.

Satellite Internet Access

Satellite Internet access is an option in rural areas where cable or DSL is not available (Figure 2.7). Satellite requires the installation of a satellite dish and satellite modem. Access is slower and more expensive although newer services offer higher speeds using geostationary satellites.

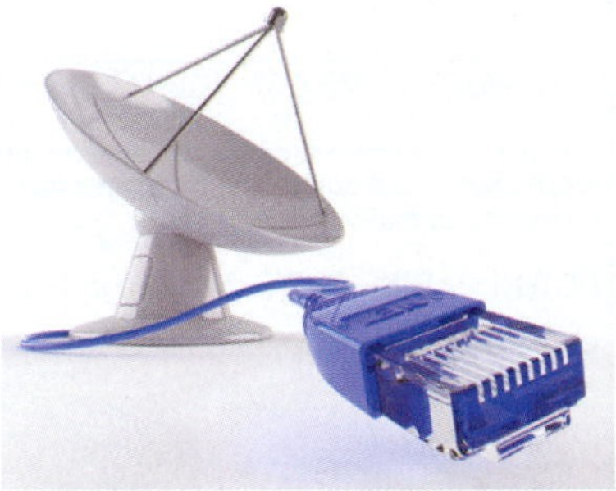

Figure 2.7
Satellite Internet is used in rural areas where cable and DSL are not available.

Fixed Wireless Internet Access

Fixed wireless Internet access involves installing an antenna outside your home to send and receive radio signals. A wireless modem is used to connect to your computer or router.

Wi-Fi Hotspots

In a **Wi-Fi network**, wireless access points and radio signals transmit data (Figure 2.8). Wi-Fi networks are common in public spaces for free Internet access. The area in which a Wi-Fi network is within range is called a **hotspot**. Wi-Fi is also commonly used in homes, schools, and workplaces to provide connectivity to notebooks and mobile devices. A Wi-Fi hotspot encompasses a short distance, making it a good option for homeowners to connect their mobile devices via a wireless router from their cable or DSL modem.

Depending on the Wi-Fi equipment being used, connection speeds fall within the range of 6 to 8 Mbps for older equipment, 25 to 30 Mbps for midrange equipment, and 150 to 1,000 Mbps for newer devices. Devices capable of transferring data at 1,000 Mbps or more express speed in **gigabits per second (Gbps)**, which is 1 billion bits per second.

Figure 2.8
A wireless access point is used in a Wi-Fi network to provide connectivity to wireless users.

Mobile Broadband Sticks

A **mobile broadband stick** (also called an *Internet dongle*) is a portable modem that plugs into a USB port on your mobile device and connects via a cellular network (Figure 2.9). The advantage to a mobile broadband stick is that you can carry your Internet connection with you.

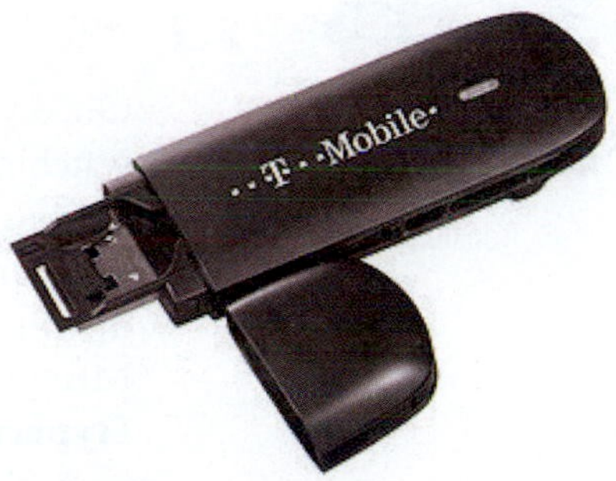

Figure 2.9

A mobile broadband stick is a portable modem that you plug into a USB port.

3G and 4G Cellular Communications

Today, smartphones are either **3G** (third generation) or **4G** (fourth generation) devices that provide Internet access through cell towers. Average speed for a 3G connection is around 1 Mbps; however, performance varies depending on location. Average speed for 4G devices is often advertised as 10 times faster than 3G, and the network connecting them is often described as a 4G **LTE** (Long-Term Evolution) **network**, which is the fastest network for mobile devices. These networks use the 4G technology standard with advanced design to improve speed. Devices have to be able to send and receive using 4G technology to take advantage of the higher speed.

In April 2015, Google announced Project Fi, a new wireless service that offers subscribers a network in which their device will automatically switch to free Wi-Fi or the fastest LTE network in the partnership as the subscriber moves around. The device intelligently moves to another network without the user's intervention. Project Fi is bound to have a positive impact for consumers, though we do not yet know how it will affect wireless service and contracts in general.

At the time of writing, a 4G LTE device on an LTE network experienced the fastest speed for a smartphone or tablet user.

In some communities, broadband Internet access may not be available, or the cost may be too high for some people. A low-cost way of connecting to the Internet is to use **dial-up**, in which you connect your PC to your telephone system via a modem built into your PC. The ISP provides you with a local telephone number that the computer dials to get on the Internet. The disadvantages to dial-up are the slow speed and the inability to use your telephone while online.

The ISP provides you with instructions to connect to the ISP network. Generally, the installation requires that you plug in the modem and run a software program. See Appendix B for help setting up a wireless network in your home.

Once you've established connectivity to your ISP service, you are ready to explore the web using a web browser.

Good to Know

5G is on its way! The wireless industry is working on 5G standards with deployments expected in 2020 and a goal to deliver 1 gigabit per second (Gbps) speed to mobile devices.

Explore Further **What Is Tethering?**

Assume you are planning a vacation in a cabin where there is no Internet access. You are bringing your smartphone and notebook with you to the cabin. Your smartphone plan includes Internet access. You decide to investigate tethering as a means to get Internet access on your notebook.

1. Search for information on tethering. Specifically, find out how a cell phone can be used as a modem for another device such as a notebook or tablet. How does it work? What do you need to do to connect the two devices? Are there any issues with tethering of which you should be aware?
2. Create a document that summarizes your answers to the questions in your own words. At the end of the document, include the URLs of the main articles you used for this topic.
3. Save the document as **Tethering-YourName**.
4. Submit the document to your instructor in the manner she or he has requested.

2.3 Popular Web Browsers

Tutorial
How Is HTML 5 Transforming the Web?

Once you are connected to the Internet, you are ready to start browsing, shopping, watching videos, playing games, or checking out what your friends and family are posting at social media websites. Web pages are viewed using browser software. A web browser is a program that locates a web page on the Internet and interprets the code in which the web page has been stored to compose the page as text and multimedia. Many web pages are created using a markup language called **HTML**, which stands for **Hypertext Markup Language**. A markup language uses tags to describe page content.

In this topic you will review the most popular web browsers for PCs: Internet Explorer, Microsoft Edge, Firefox, Chrome, and Safari. You will also be introduced to the unique needs of mobile web browsers.

Internet Explorer and Microsoft Edge

Internet Explorer (IE) is the web browser included with Microsoft Windows for editions prior to Windows 10. With the release of Windows 10 in 2015, Microsoft replaced IE with a new web browser called **Microsoft Edge**. Figure 2.10 shows the desktop version of IE version 11 (included with Windows 8.1) on the left and Microsoft Edge (included with Windows 10) on the right.

Microsoft Edge provides faster searches than IE with a cleaner and clearer reading experience. Pages can be saved to a reading list. You can highlight text, draw, or write notes on a web page, and those notations can be saved and shared. Cortana, a digital assistant, searches and helps you do things online faster. For example, while viewing a restaurant page, Cortana will pop up with the phone number, directions, and hours of operation. The Hub, a pane that you open at the right side of the screen, collects your favorites, downloads, history, and reading list in one place accessible across all devices.

Chrome

Google **Chrome** is a free web browser that runs on PCs and mobile devices, including Apple desktops, tablets, and smartphones. The browser was initially released in 2008 with features that included fast page loading and the ability to navigate and search within the Address bar. Signing in with a Google account while using Chrome allows you to sync open tabs, bookmarks, history, and saved passwords with your

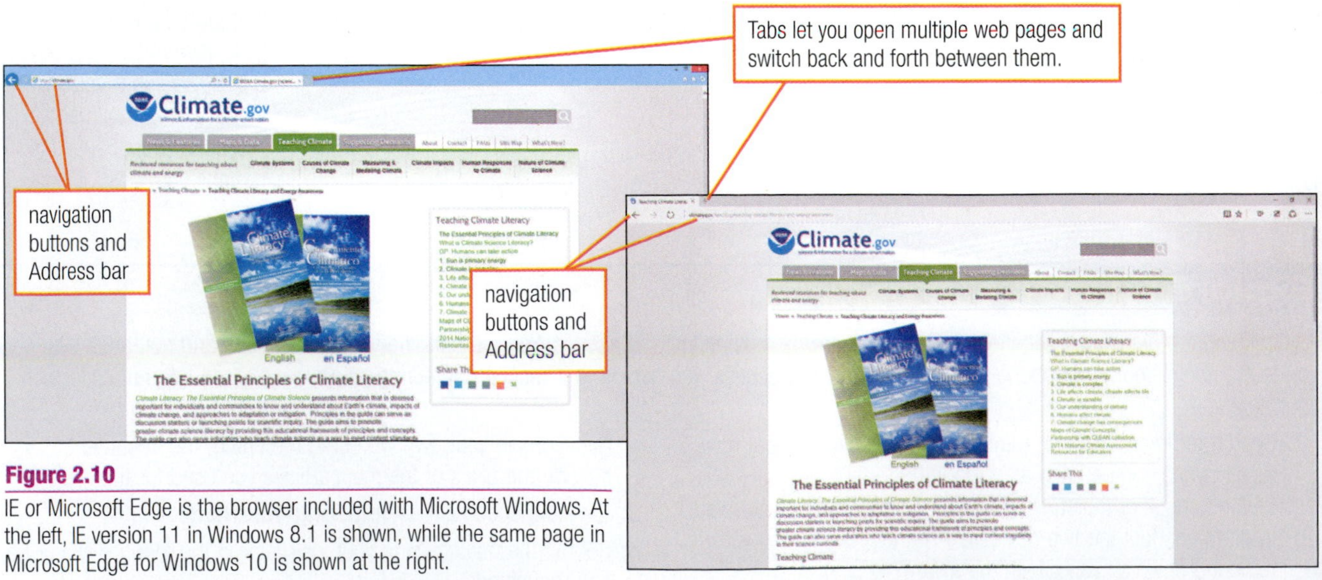

Figure 2.10
IE or Microsoft Edge is the browser included with Microsoft Windows. At the left, IE version 11 in Windows 8.1 is shown, while the same page in Microsoft Edge for Windows 10 is shown at the right.

other devices. In Figure 2.11, Chrome is shown with the web page for Grand Canyon National Park.

StatCounter, a company that measures Internet usage, reported Chrome was the browser preferred by 53 percent of web users worldwide in September 2015. Web surfers report a preference for Chrome's fast page loading, minimalist design, and synchronized searches across all devices.

> **Good to Know**
>
> The Mozilla Foundation is a nonprofit organization dedicated to promoting openness on the web. At the time of writing, over 10,000 volunteers (called Mozillians) worldwide contribute technical expertise to the development of Firefox and other open-source projects.

Firefox

Firefox is a free web browser offered by the Mozilla Foundation. The browser runs on PCs, Macs, and mobile devices. Since the initial release of Firefox version 1 in 2004, the browser has enjoyed a steadfast fan base. Figure 2.12 shows Firefox with a web page about the history of the library from the Library of Congress website.

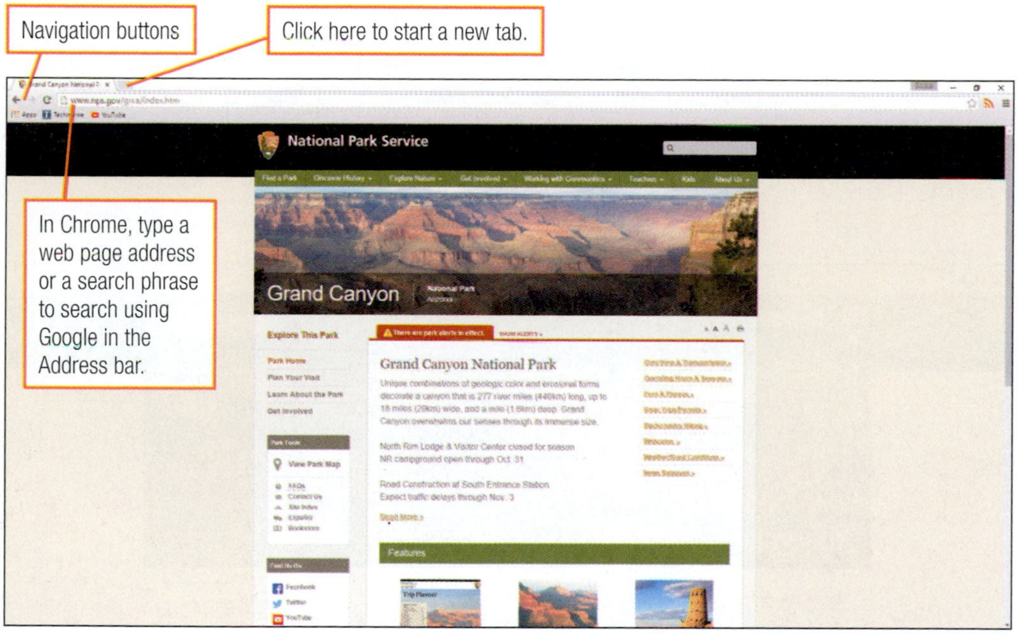

Figure 2.11

Google Chrome browser is frequently updated; version 42 is shown here. The browser is popular with people who want fast page loading within a streamlined window.

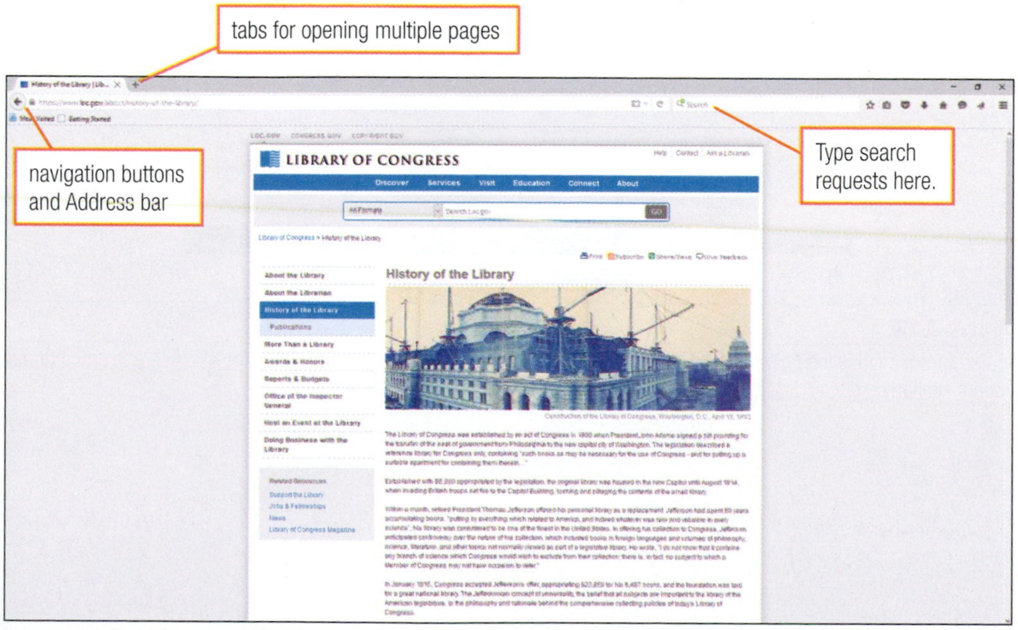

Figure 2.12

Mozilla Firefox is a free open-source browser. Version 37 is shown here.

You will notice similarities between Firefox and Chrome with the placement of the navigation buttons, Address bar, and tabs for browsing multiple pages. Firefox differs from Chrome with the search text box at the right of the Address bar. Fans of Firefox indicate they favor the browser's speed in loading web pages and believe it has better privacy and security features than IE or Chrome.

Safari

Apple **Safari** browser (Figure 2.13) is used on Mac and Apple mobile devices, such as iPads and iPhones. The browser is also available as a free download for a PC. Safari stores passwords, bookmarks, history, and the reading list in iCloud so that the information is available across all devices. Apple claims that Safari version 9 for Mac OS X El Capitan has optimized browsing to allow you to browse for up to two hours longer or watch videos for up to four hours longer than with Firefox or Chrome.

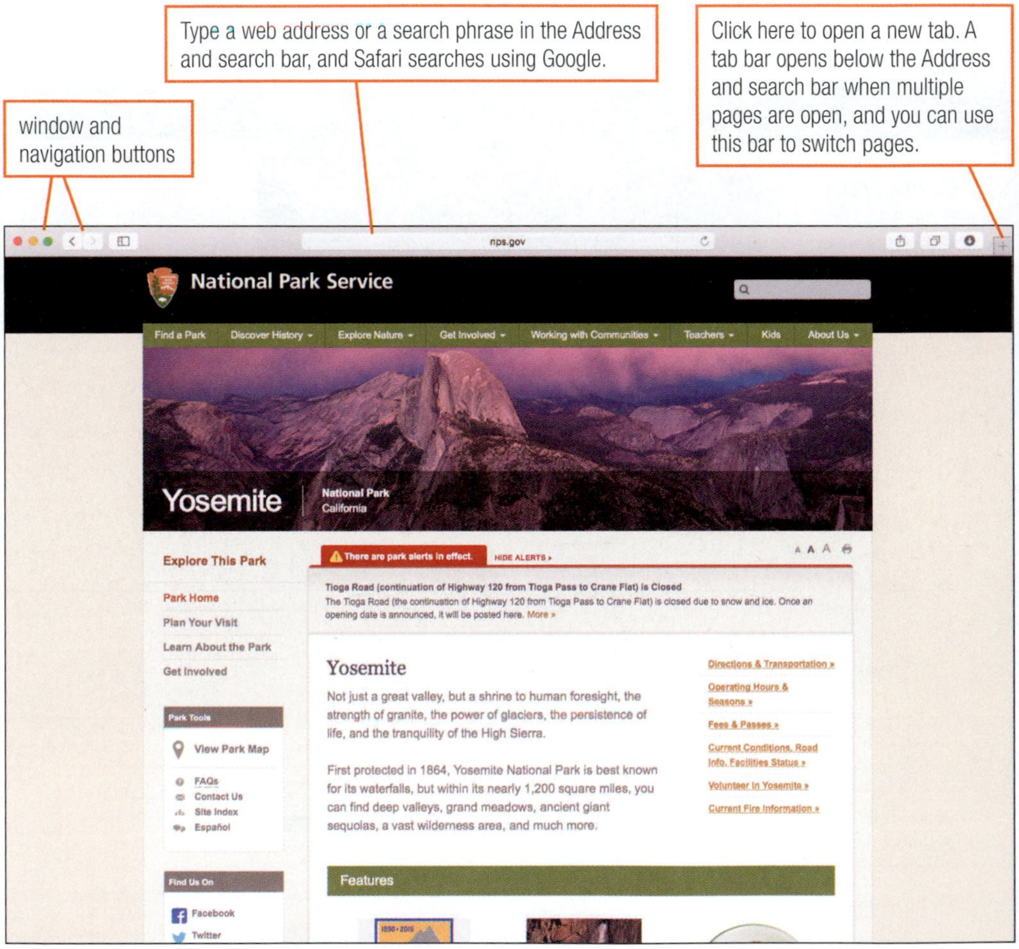

Figure 2.13

Safari for Mac OS is the browser supplied on Mac PCs and notebooks. A version of Safari for iOS on iPads and iPhones works similarly.

Mobile Browsers

A **mobile web browser** is designed to quickly display web pages optimized for the smaller screens on devices such as tablets and smartphones. The challenge for mobile browsers is that web pages designed for larger screens have to be readable in a smaller viewing area. Mobile browsers incorporate text wrapping and try to avoid the user having to scroll sideways. Mobile versions of IE, Microsoft Edge, Chrome, Firefox, and Safari are available in addition to numerous other browser apps for Android and Apple smartphones and tablets (Figure 2.14).

Figure 2.14

Google Chrome (left) and Apple Safari (right) have mobile versions for tablets and smartphones.

Blog Topic: Which Browser(s) Do You Favor?

Which browser do you use? Have you tried one of the other browsers mentioned in this topic? Do you use multiple browsers? If yes, why? If you could develop your dream browser, what would it do differently than what you use now?

1. Write and post a blog entry that answers the above questions.
2. Read at least two of your classmates' blogs and post one comment to each.
3. Submit your blog URL and the URLs of the two classmates' blogs to your instructor in the manner she or he requested.

Explore Further: What Other Web Browsers Are Available?

Other web browsers are available for PCs and Macs in addition to the ones mentioned in this topic. Each of these other web browsers is designed to be different in various ways from IE, Microsoft Edge, Chrome, Firefox, and Safari.

1. Research other web browsers for a PC or a Mac. Pick one alternative web browser and learn more about what it does and why people use it.
2. Create a document that describes the alternative web browser in your own words. At the end of the document, include the URLs of the articles you used.
3. Save the document as **AlternativeBrowser-YourName**.
4. Submit the document to your instructor in the manner she or he has requested.

2.4 Understanding Internet and Web Addresses, and Navigating Web Pages

Good to Know
ICANN allocates IP address blocks to five Regional Internet Registries (RIRs) around the world. The RIRs then allocate smaller IP address blocks to ISPs and other network operators.

Good to Know
IPv6 provides over 340 trillion trillion trillion addresses! That's enough for every person on the planet to have about 4,000 addresses.

All the popular web browsers share similar features and navigation options designed to assist with finding and viewing web pages. Regardless of the browser you use, web addressing and search techniques (discussed in the next topic) are universal.

If you are invited to visit a friend at his house, you need to know the address so you know where to go to find his home. Similarly, on the Internet, you locate a connected device (PC, smartwatch, tablet, smart appliance, and so on) by using an address. When a computing device is connected to the Internet, it is assigned a unique address called an **Internet Protocol (IP) address** so that the device can send and receive data. Two addressing systems are in use for the Internet. In Figure 2.15, the two addresses for a web server installed for the National Oceanic and Atmospheric Administration (NOAA) are shown. The **Internet Corporation for Assigned Names and Numbers (ICANN)** is a nonprofit organization that is in charge of keeping track of the Internet addresses and names all around the world.

A system of addressing that uses four groups of numbers from 0 to 255 separated by periods is referred to as *IPv4*. A new system called *IPv6* was launched in 2012 because the number of unique IPv4 addresses was running out. IPv6 uses eight groups of characters separated by colons, where a character can be a number 0 through 9 or a letter *a* through *f*. Methods are available to abbreviate the full IPv6 address. With IPv6 there will be enough IP addresses for years to come. For now, both IPv4 and IPv6 coexist since some equipment and software connected to the Internet cannot handle IPv6 addressing.

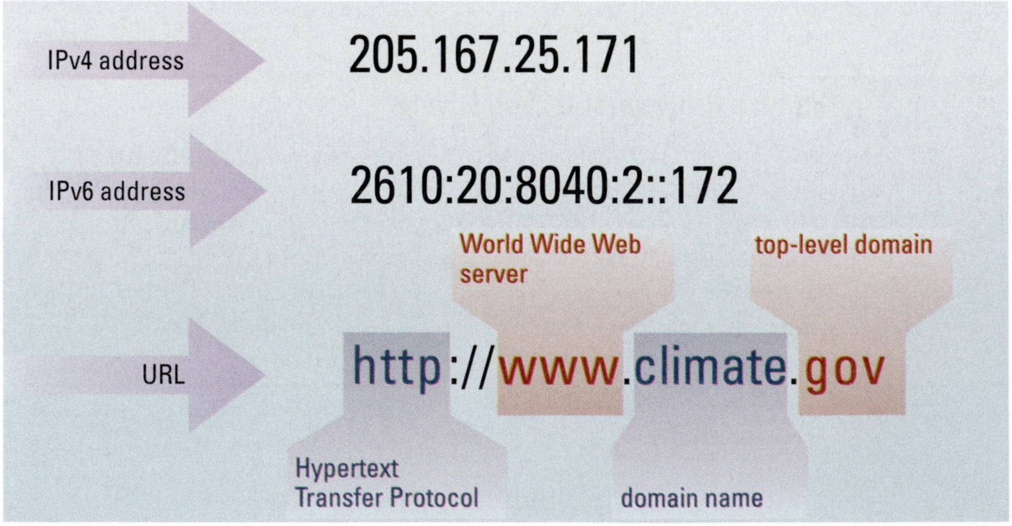

Figure 2.15
A URL contains a domain name that allows you to locate a website using a text-based name rather than the numeric IP address.

Web Addresses

Tutorial
What Are IP Addresses and Domain Names?

If you know the numeric address for a computer on the Internet, you can navigate to the site by typing it in the browser's Address bar. For example, typing 209.46.18.200 in the Address bar will bring you to the EMC Publishing, LLC, website. (EMC is a sister company to the publisher of this textbook.) However, using complicated numeric addresses to find a website is not feasible. Instead, we use a **web address**, which is a text-based address. A web address is also called a **uniform resource locator (URL)**. Figure 2.15 shows that the URL for NOAA is http://www.climate.gov. The four parts of this URL are explained in Table 2.2 (page 41). The parts of a URL are separated by punctuation consisting of a colon (:), one slash (/) or two slashes (//), and a period (.), referred to as a *dot*. When telling someone the NOAA URL, you would say "climate dot gov."

When you type a URL, a server locates the IP address for the domain name to transmit data to the correct computer. A server that holds this directory is called a **Domain Name System (DNS) server** and is owned by a business or an ISP.

Navigating Web Pages

Most people browse the web in one of two ways: by typing the web address of a company or organization to go directly to a website (Figure 2.16) or by typing a search phrase into a search engine website such as Google or Bing to search for information (Figure 2.17, page 42). In the next topic you will learn about using search engines to find information.

Table 2.2

The Parts of a URL

Part of URL	What It Represents	Examples
http	The protocol for the page. A protocol is a set of rules for transmitting data.	http Hypertext transfer protocol ftp File transfer protocol https Hypertext transfer protocol secure
www	World Wide Web server.	
climate	The organization's **domain name**, also referred to as a *second-level domain name*. Domain names are the text-based version of the IP address and are usually the name of the owner, an abbreviation of a company or organization, or an alias associated with the owner.	nytimes New York Times domain name google Google Inc. domain name navy US Navy domain name loc Library of Congress domain name
gov	The part of the domain name that identifies the **top-level domain (TLD)**. TLDs identify the type of organization associated with the domain name. Several TLDs with three or more characters are known as **generic top-level domains (gTLDs)**. ICANN is expanding the number of approved gTLDs. Watch for websites in the future with domain names such as myroadsideinn.*hotel* or mylawfirm.*legal*. A two-character TLD is a country code called a **ccTLD**.	com Commercial organizations edu Educational institution gov Government website mil Military site net Network providers such as ISPs org Nonprofit organizations biz Business ca Canada

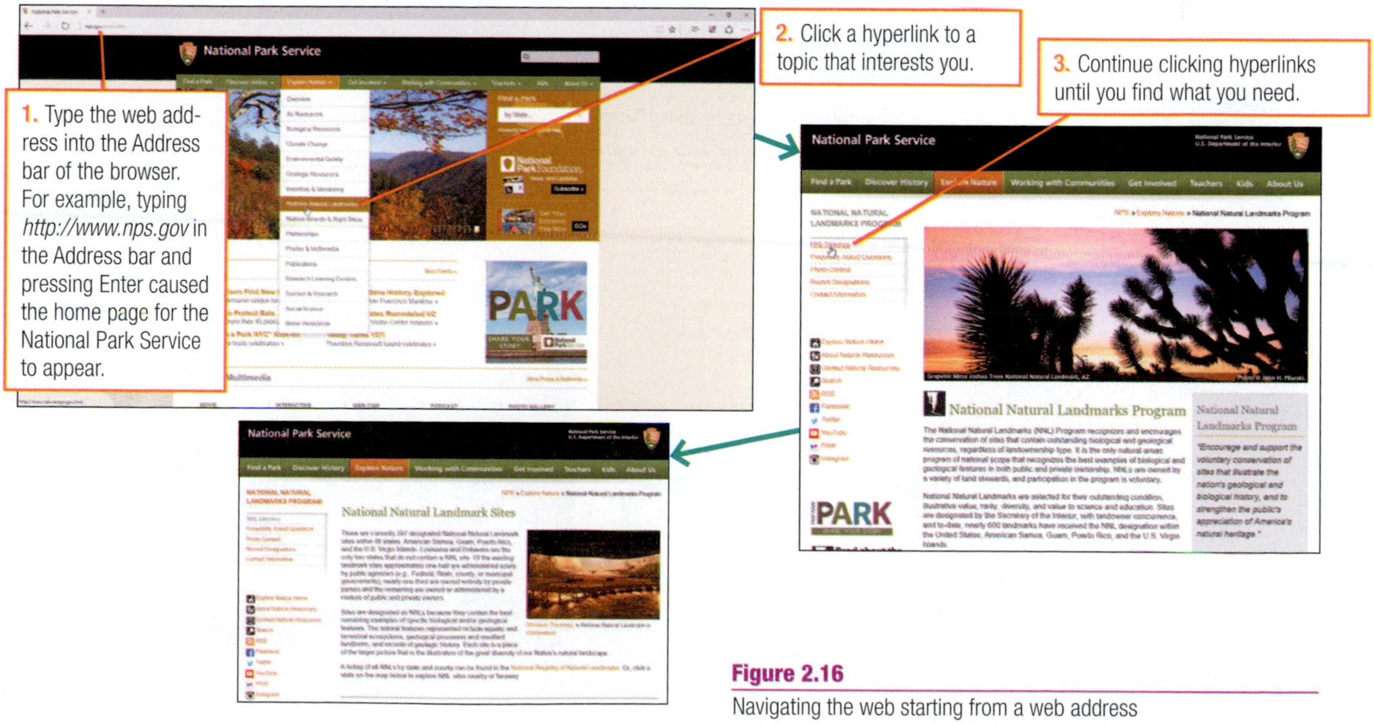
1. Type the web address into the Address bar of the browser. For example, typing http://www.nps.gov in the Address bar and pressing Enter caused the home page for the National Park Service to appear.
2. Click a hyperlink to a topic that interests you.
3. Continue clicking hyperlinks until you find what you need.
National Park Service
PARK
National Natural Landmarks Program
National Natural Landmark Sites

Figure 2.16

Navigating the web starting from a web address

Figure 2.17

You can navigate the web using a search engine website such as Bing.

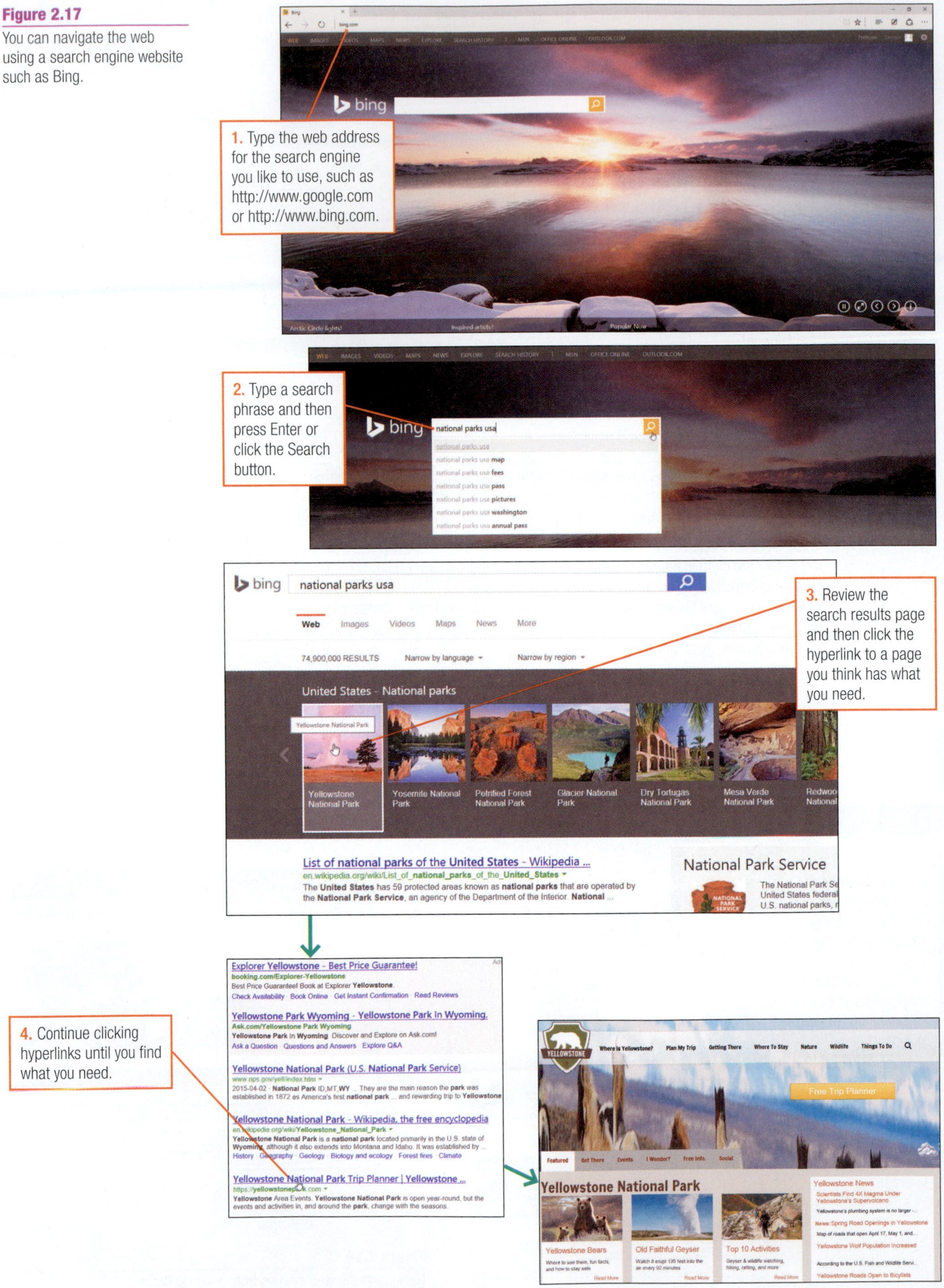

The first page of a website that displays when the web address is requested is called the **home page**. Main headings appear along the top or edges and are organized by topic to guide you to subpages within the site. Web pages contain hyperlinks (called *links* for short). A **hyperlink**, or **link** is any item on a web page that when clicked displays another page. For example, a title, word, phrase, photo, video, icon, button, or audio object may be a hyperlink. As you move a mouse pointer around a page, the white arrow pointer will change to a white hand with the index finger pointing upward when you are pointing at text or an object that is a hyperlink. Hyperlinked text is usually a different color, boldfaced, or underlined. Click when you see the icon change or click the text or object to move to the related web page.

You can also type the web address of a linked web page directly into the Address bar. For example, typing *http://www.nytimes.com/pages/todayspaper/index.html* takes you directly to "Today's Paper" at the *New York Times* website.

Blog Topic What Type of Web Activity Do You Do Most Often?

A variety of tasks are performed on the Internet, but one or two types of activities generally predominate. In what activity do you spend most of your time on the web? Is it reading news or reading or writing blogs? Is it online shopping? Is it connecting with friends and family? Is it sharing photos, videos, or music? Is it looking for information for work, school, or personal interest? How many hours per week on average do you estimate you spend on each of these activities?

1. Write and post a blog entry that answers the above questions.
2. Read at least two of your classmates' blogs and post one comment to each.
3. Submit your blog URL and the URLs of the two classmates' blogs to your instructor in the manner she or he requested.

Explore Further How Do I Register a Domain Name?

Assume you are planning to start a new business when you graduate. You know you will need to have a website but are not sure how to get a domain name for your organization.

1. Research online to find out how to check for an available domain name and how to register the name.
2. With millions of websites already in existence, the name you want to use may already be taken. Find out what alternatives you have if the domain name you want is already in use.
3. Create a document that summarizes in your own words what you learned about domain names in Steps 1 and 2. At the end of the document, include the URLs of the articles you used when researching this topic.
4. Save the document as **DomainNames-YourName**.
5. Submit the document to your instructor in the manner she or he has requested.

2.5 Searching the Web

> **Good to Know**
>
> Some browsers allow you to type a search phrase directly into the Address bar to search using a default search engine. Other browsers place an Instant Search text box near the Address bar in which you can type a search phrase.

A **search engine** is a company that searches web pages and indexes the pages by keywords or by subject. When you type a search phrase at a search engine website, a results list displays links to the web pages associated with the keywords used in the search phrase. To generate indexes, a search engine uses a program called a **spider** or **crawler** that reads web pages and other information to generate index entries. Generally, website owners submit information to search engines to make sure they are included in search results.

Some search engines display a subject directory that provides links to categories of information, such as *Music*, *News*, *Shopping*, or *Travel*. Clicking a category brings you to another page with subtopics for that category. In most cases, you can specify if you want search results to come from the entire web or from indexes associated with images, maps, news, shopping, or videos. Table 2.3 lists five popular search engines; however, be aware that many other search engines exist.

Table 2.3

Popular Search Engines

Search Engine	URL
Google	https://www.google.com/
Bing	http://www.bing.com/
Yahoo!	https://www.yahoo.com/
Ask	http://www.ask.com/
Dogpile	http://www.dogpile.com/

> **Good to Know**
>
> According to Hitwise (a company that measures Internet traffic), Google consistently ranks as the leading search engine people use for finding information (78 percent in January 2016), followed by Bing.

You will get different results from various search engines. Figure 2.18 displays the search results from the same search phrase *green computing* entered at two search engines, Bing and Ask. Differences in results can occur for a variety of reasons. For example, spider and index program parameters differ by search engine, some search engines locate and index new or updated pages at different speeds or times, and page relevance to the search phrase may be ranked differently.

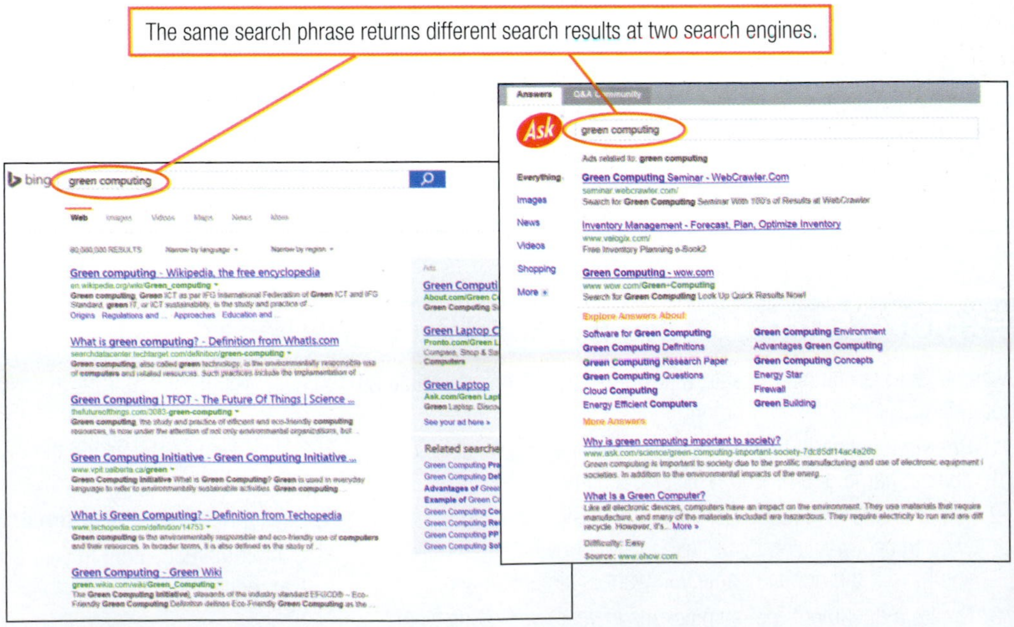
The same search phrase returns different search results at two search engines.
green computing
green computing

Figure 2.18

Search engines provide different results for the same search phrase for many reasons, including the way in which spiders and indexers find and rank pages and keywords.

Fine-Tuning a Search

Regardless of the search engine you like to use, knowing how to fine-tune a search request will make your searching quicker and easier. With practice, you will develop a search technique that works best for you. Following are some guidelines for searching:

- A search phrase in quotation marks returns pages where the keywords are in the same sequence; otherwise, the search results may have the keywords in any order. For example, "endangered animals" returns pages with the word *endangered* immediately followed by the word *animals*.
- Type a minus symbol in front of a keyword to *exclude* the keyword from the search results; for example, "endangered animals" –africa returns pages about endangered animals in continents other than Africa.
- Rather than searching the entire web, consider using search engine categories, such as News, Images, or Videos, to restrict the search results to a specific type of page or object (Figure 2.19).
- Check out advanced search tools to further refine your search terms, domain, or region (Figure 2.19).
- Most search engines allow you to restrict searches to a specific time frame; for example, in the Google search tools, you can filter results by *Past hour*, *Past 24 hours*, *Past week*, *Past month*, *Past year*, or *Custom range* (Figure 2.19).
- Look for Help at the search engine website to learn more about how the search engine indexes pages and the recommendations for searching at its site.

Tutorial
How and Why Is the Deep Web Hidden from Us?

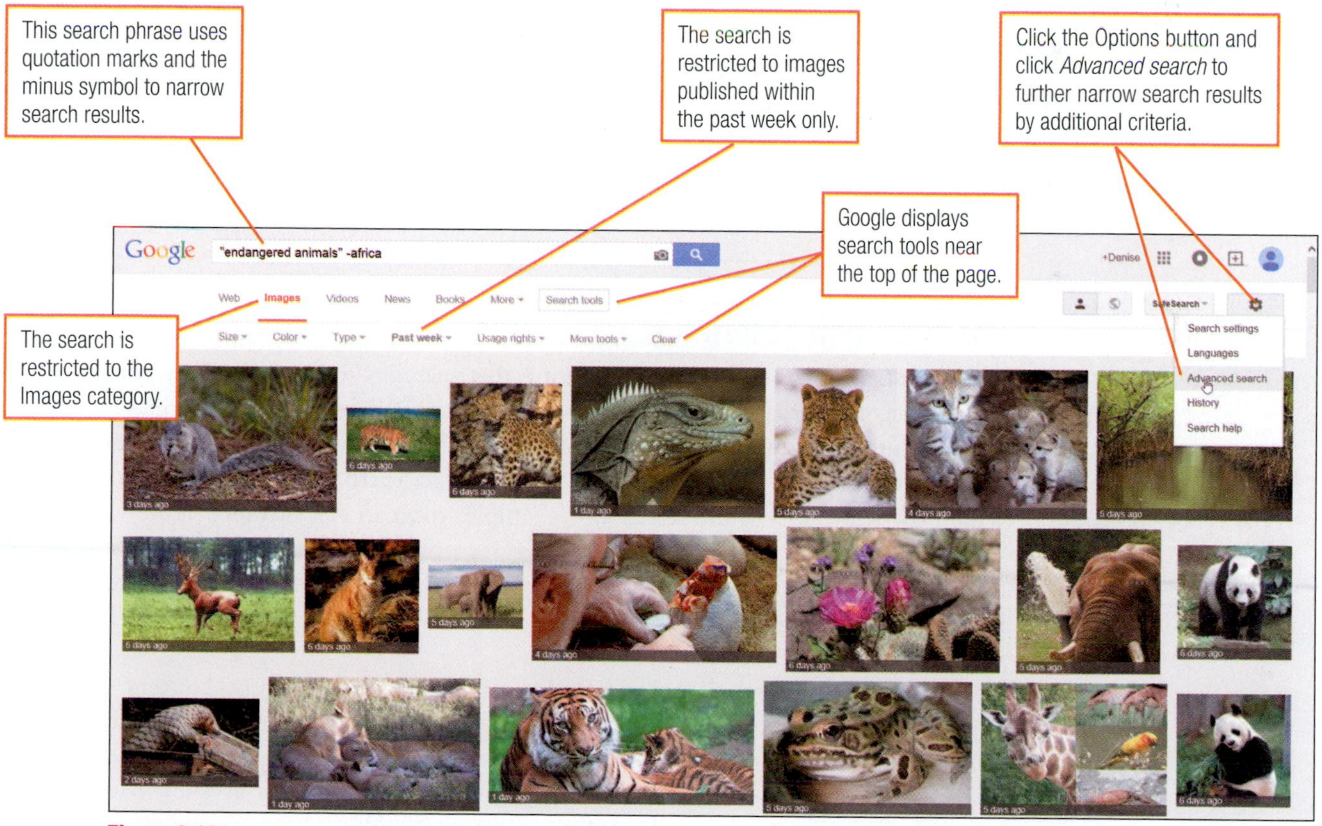
This search phrase uses quotation marks and the minus symbol to narrow search results.
The search is restricted to images published within the past week only.
Click the Options button and click *Advanced search* to further narrow search results by additional criteria.
Google displays search tools near the top of the page.
The search is restricted to the Images category.
"endangered animals" -africa
Web
Images
Videos
News
Books
More
Search tools
Size
Color
Type
Past week
Usage rights
More tools
Clear
Search settings
Languages
Advanced search
History
Search help

Figure 2.19

Using the search tools offered by a search engine can help you narrow a search.

Some search engines are metasearch search engines. A **metasearch search engine** sends your search phrase to other search engines and then compiles the results in one list. Using a metasearch search engine allows you to type your search phrase once and access results from a wider group of search engines. Dogpile is an example of a metasearch search engine that provides search results in one place from Google, Bing, and Yahoo!, among others.

Some metasearch search engines specialize in one type of search service. For example, KAYAK (http://www.kayak.com/) specializes in searching travel websites to provide you with a comparison of flights, hotels, and car rentals in one place (Figure 2.20).

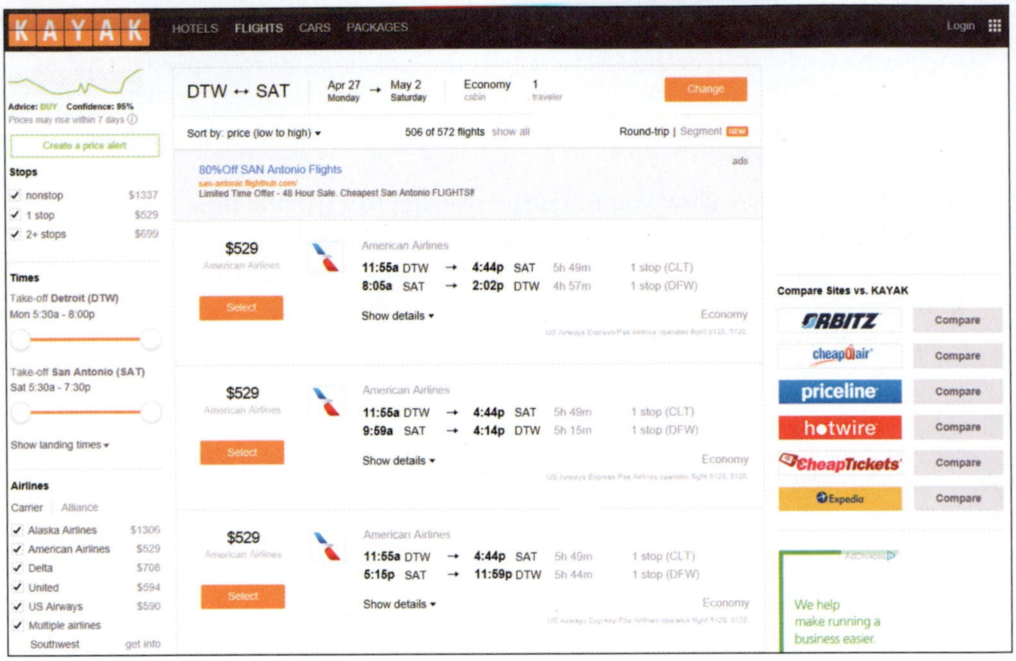

Figure 2.20
KAYAK, a metasearch search engine, specializes in searching travel websites.

Content Aggregators

A **content aggregator** is an organization that searches the web for new content, and collects and organizes the content in one place. Some content aggregators send updates automatically to subscribers. Subscribers receive an update, sometimes referred to as a **web feed** or feed based on selections made for the type of information in which the subscriber is interested. For example, you can elect to receive new items related to news or music. Some content aggregators provide this service for free, while others charge a fee to send out updates to subscribers. The advantage to subscribers is that the content aggregator does the work of searching the web and organizing related information.

Click the Feeds button at a web page to subscribe to the website's feed.

Really Simple Syndication (RSS) is a specification used by content aggregators to distribute feeds to subscribers. Feeds push content to the subscriber when something new is added to a website. An RSS reader program collects the feeds to which you subscribe and displays the headlines and/or articles. Most browsers incorporate the reader software automatically; however, several free reader apps are also available for PCs and mobile devices. **Atom** was developed as an alternative to RSS and is another specification used to distribute web feeds.

Popurls (http://popurls.com/) is a content aggregator that lists on one page all the latest headlines from the most popular sites on the Internet (Figure 2.21). Another aggregator, Techmeme (http://techmeme.com/), tracks changes to technology news and presents a summary each day.

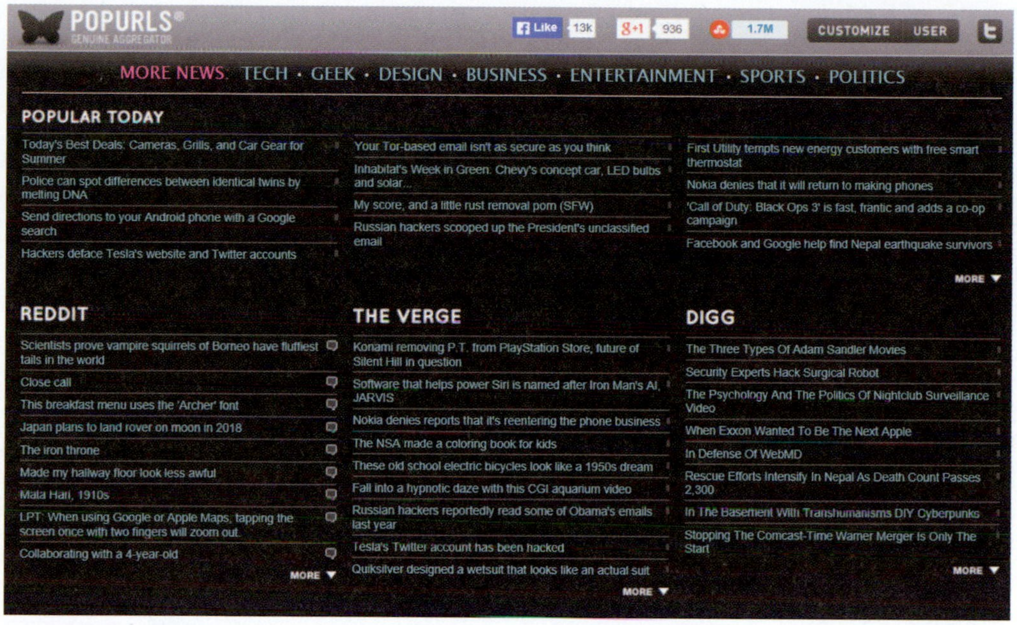

Figure 2.21

Popurls is a content aggregator that lists all the latest changes at popular websites.

Explore Further Try Out Your Search Skills

Assume you are planning a vacation to celebrate the end of the school year, and you want to use the Internet to find information for your trip.

1. Choose a destination for your vacation—anywhere in the world!
2. Use your favorite search engine to conduct a search, using only the name of the destination as the search phrase. What search phrase did you use, and how many pages were in the search results list?
3. Next explore the search engine tools for conducting advanced searches and narrow your search results by further specifying criteria and/or excluding a topic in your search. How did you refine your search, and how many pages were in the revised search results list?
4. Follow one or two links in the search results and determine if the search refinements at Step 2 were enough to find useful information. If not, further refine the search parameters and explore new links.
5. Create a presentation that summarizes your search activities. Include a slide for each of your answers in Steps 1 and 2 and for your analysis of the search results at Step 3.
6. Save the presentation as **VacationSearch-YourName**.
7. Submit the presentation to your instructor in the manner she or he has requested.

2.6 Evaluating Web Content

Increasingly, the web is becoming the only resource people turn to when looking for information, news, shopping, connecting with others, and sharing media. Anyone with an Internet connection and space allocated on a web server can publish a page on the web. Many websites rely on users to generate the content that is posted. With thousands of new websites coming online every year, how can you be sure the information presented at a site is true, accurate, and timely?

Start at the Web Address

Look at the domain name in the web address. Is the site hosted by an organization you recognize and trust? For example, an article published at http://www.nytimes.com is associated with a highly recognizable media organization, the *New York Times*. Look for the domain names of print-based publishers with which you are familiar. For example, if you are familiar with *Psychology Today* magazine, then you will be comfortable reading content at https://www.psychologytoday.com (Figure 2.22). If you do not recognize the domain name in a web address, consider doing a search for the domain name owner and then searching the owner's name to find out whether the organization is reputable.

Next look at the TLD in the web address (the three characters after the period in the domain name). A TLD with .gov, .org, or .edu is, respectively, a government department or agency, a nonprofit organization, or an educational institution—all trusted sources.

Check the domain name in the web address for a recognizable name that you trust.

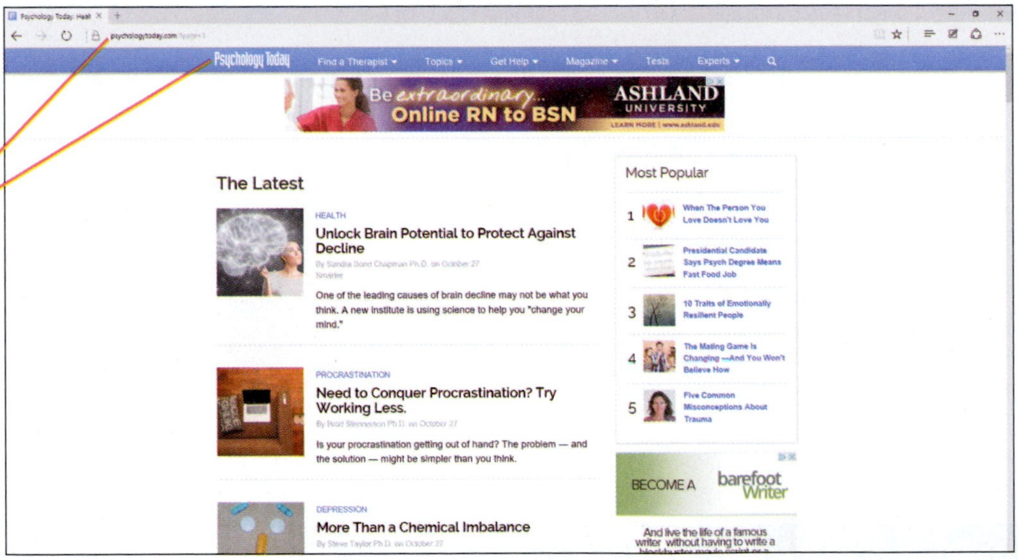

Figure 2.22

Begin evaluating web content by looking in the web address for a domain name that is an organization you recognize and trust.

Look for an Author and the Author's Affiliation

Check for an author's name at the page. Is the author affiliated with the organization in the web address? Expert authors are often identified as such in the introduction, in other biographical information, or by credentials after their names.

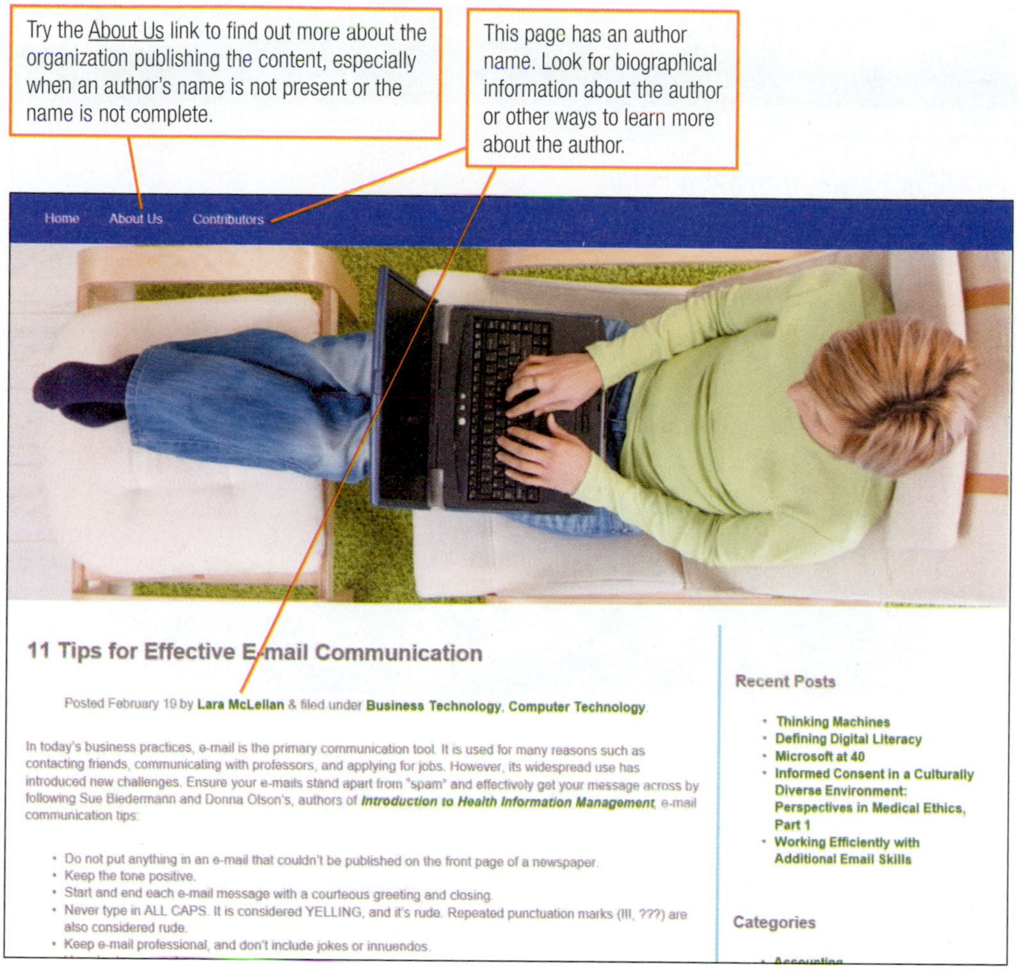

Figure 2.23

Check for an author's name on a web page; if the author has credentials or other biographical information, that helps you evaluate the validity of the content.

If no author name is shown, use other means to try to determine if the information is credible. For example, check for a link that describes the organization presenting the content. Most websites have an About Us or a Contact Us link (Figure 2.23). Check these sources to determine if a bias might exist for the information you are reading.

Check the Publication Date

In most cases, you want to find the most recent information about a topic. Look for the date of publication on the page (Figure 2.24, page 50). Use the search engine advanced search tool to filter your search results by a recent time frame and see if the page remains in the list. Sometimes the original publication date may be older, but a notation (usually near the top or bottom of the page) can provide a date the content was updated. Finally, a clue to the date of publication may appear in the web address. For example, a page may have an address similar to http://www.companyname.com/articles/2016/March/pagename.html.

If no date can be found, consider whether the content seems dated. For example, look for something in the article that may give a clue to the time frame it was published, such as a reference to an event. When in doubt, corroborate the content by finding another source that is published with a recent date.

Most pages have the publication date at the top or bottom of the page.

Figure 2.24

Always look for a publication date to evaluate if the content is current.

Purpose and Design of the Site

Finally, consider the purpose and design of the page you are reading. Is the publisher of the web page a business that markets products or services? If yes, the content may be biased toward convincing you to buy the company's goods.

Blog Topic Is *Wikipedia* a Valid Source of Information for a Research Paper?

Wikis are websites where the page content is created by the user community. Generally, anyone can add content, and additions or changes that are wrong may be visible for a while before they are caught. The openness of wikis has led some in the academic world to discredit sources such as *Wikipedia* (the most popular encyclopedia with content developed by volunteers). What do you think?

1. Go to **http://CC2.ParadigmCollege.net/Wikipedia** and read the information on the "About Wikipedia" page.
2. Create and post a blog entry with your opinion on whether *Wikipedia* content is an acceptable source for a research paper and state your rationale.
3. Read at least two of your classmates' blogs and post one comment to each.
4. Submit your blog URL and the URLs of the two classmates' blogs to your instructor in the manner she or he has requested.

A web page design, spelling, and grammar will also indicate the credibility of that page. A professionally designed, well-written page will invite trust. The page shown in Figure 2.25 may indeed present accurate information on asteroids and meteors; however, the page design uses layout, colors, and organization typically not used by professionals, and links such as ASK AN ALIEN! are cause for further inspection.

A poorly designed web page that lacks a recognizable domain name, an author's name, and a recent publication date indicates a page that you need to be careful with. The information could be accurate and credible, but you should do some additional checking to be sure.

The link ASK AN ALIEN! may be just showing the author's sense of fun. However, the wording, page design, and lack of author or date all indicate that you should verify the content on this page with another source.

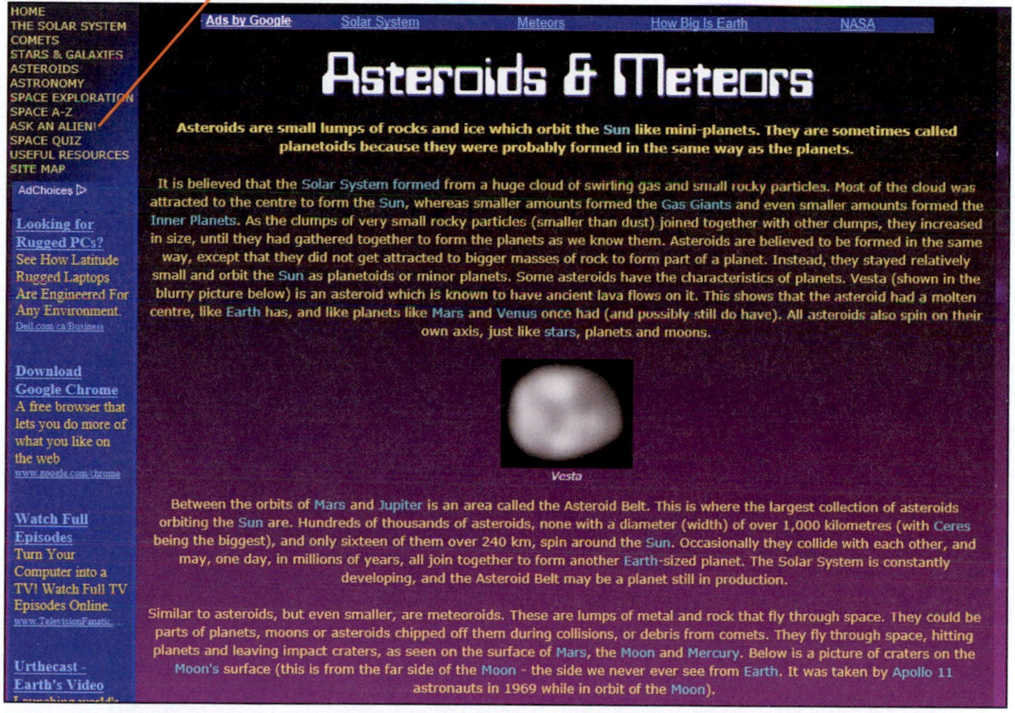

Figure 2.25

The design of a web page, including layout, organization, and choice of colors, provides clues as to whether the page was published by a professional organization.

Explore Further — Evaluate Information on Geocaching in Your Area

Geocaching is an outdoor activity where participants use a GPS or other mobile device to locate a container hidden by other participants. The container usually contains a logbook and may also have a prize of small value. When a participant finds the geocache, the participant updates the logbook and leaves a prize for the next person.

1. Find information on geocaching in your area. Pick a web page and evaluate the web page. Is the content accurate? Is the page from a credible source? Is the information current?
2. Create a document with a screen capture of the web page. Below the screen capture, list the elements that you used to evaluate the web page in Step 1. Provide the URL at the bottom of the document. ***Hint:*** *One way to make a screen capture of a web page is to display the desired web page, press the Print Screen key on your keyboard, and then use the Paste button in Word to paste the image into a document.*
3. Save the document as **Geocaching-YourName**.
4. Submit the document to your instructor in the manner she or he has requested.

2.7 Popular Web Plug-ins and Players for Multimedia Content

Most web pages have some multimedia content, such as images, animations, audio, and video. This type of rich content enhances the experience. In order for some multimedia content to work, a **plug-in** (also referred to as an **add-on**) or **player** may need to be installed. Plug-ins, add-ons, and players are all the same type of program—a software program that allows the browser to display enhanced content that it cannot display on its own.

Some plug-ins and players are included in the browser (Adobe Reader) or with your operating system (Windows Media Player). However, you might encounter a web page with a message similar to the one shown in Figure 2.26, indicating that you need to install a plug-in or player to view the content. When you encounter a message like this, a link will be provided to the source program, which you can download for free. Instead of clicking the link, you may want to open a new tab and go directly to the company's URL (see the Security Alert on page 53). At the company's site, follow the instructions to download and install the software on your PC or other device (Figure 2.27). Read each prompt carefully so that you do not install other software unintentionally. After installing the player, you may see the desired content appear immediately in the web page that gave you the message, or you may need to close

A link will be provided to the plug-in or player that is needed. You can click the link to download and install the latest version from the software program website. In this example, the link connects you to the Adobe download page. Take care when clicking such a link; see the Security Alert on the next page.

Figure 2.26

A message such as this one will appear if you display a web page that requires a plug-in or player that is not installed.

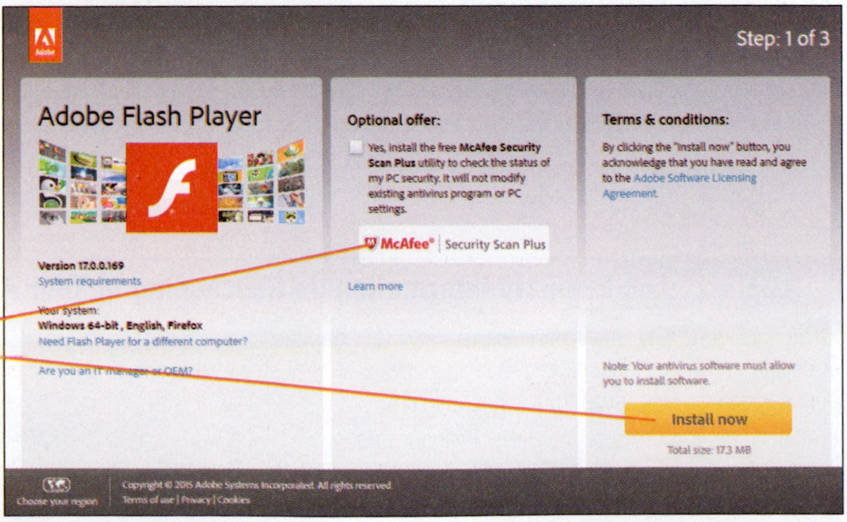

Watch for messages that will add extra software or toolbars to your browser that you may not want. If necessary, deselect these options and then click the Install now button.

Figure 2.27

Install a plug-in or player by following the steps provided at the software program website.

and reopen the browser. Some older plug-ins or players that are no longer used much are Real Player for playing music and video; Microsoft Silverlight, which Microsoft stopped developing in 2013; and the Java plug-in, which has been associated with numerous security flaws. In most cases, these programs can be uninstalled or disabled in the browser if you find them on your PC or mobile device.

Popular plug-ins and players used on the web are listed in Table 2.4. With the release of HTML 5 in October 2014, technology writers expect that plug-ins and players will become obsolete in the near future because HTML 5 supports multimedia within the browser without a plug-in. In a few years, expect that it will be unnecessary to install or update Adobe Flash or QuickTime.

Plug-in and Player Updates

From time to time, you will be prompted to install an update to a plug-in or player. Generally, when these messages occur, you should install the updates so that web pages work as expected. Adobe Flash is frequently exploited by hackers to distribute malware. If you have Adobe Flash on your device, always update it when prompted, to make sure you have the latest patches that address security issues.

Table 2.4

Common Web Plug-ins and Players

Plug-in or Player Name	Description	URL
Adobe Reader	Used to view PDF documents. PDF documents are popular for exchanging richly formatted documents on the web. PDFs are formatted as they would look when printed without requiring the source program in which the document was created to view or print.	https://get.adobe.com/reader/otherversions/
Adobe Flash Player	Used often for animations on web pages with high-quality graphics, sound, and interactivity. Many browsers include the Flash Player since it is a popular plug-in.	https://get.adobe.com/flashplayer/
Adobe Shockwave Player	Used to play interactive games, including 3-D games; complete an online course that includes interactive simulations; and navigate interactive product catalogs.	https://get.adobe.com/shockwave/
QuickTime	A player from Apple and built into Mac computers and mobile devices. PCs will also need QuickTime if the web page has video or animation provided in the QuickTime format, such as trailers found on iTunes.	https://www.apple.com/quicktime/download/

Security Alert **Be Alert for Fake Plug-Ins and Players**

Some viruses appear on web pages as spoofs of popular plug-ins and players. These viruses look like the real player, but you can find clues that they are not real. Look for typos in the name of the player or linked web page. If in doubt, do not click the link. Instead, navigate to the website of the company that publishes the player and download the software from there.

Explore Further **Add-on Toolbars for Your Browser**

Some programs, such as many antivirus applications, install add-on toolbars to your browser automatically. As shown in Figure 2.27 on page 52, you may inadvertently install an add-on when you download a plug-in or player. Some browsers refer to add-ons as *extensions*.

1. Using your favorite browser, find out how to enable and disable add-ons/extensions.
2. Create a handout that specifies the browser and version, as well as provides step-by-step instructions on how to turn on or turn off additional toolbars in the browser.
3. Save the document as **AddOnToolbars-YourName**.
4. Submit the document to your instructor in the manner she or he has requested.

2.8 E-Commerce, Messaging, and Internet Telephone and Conferencing Options

The Internet is not just for connecting with others at social media websites or looking up information you need for work, school, or your personal life. Many people turn to the Internet for e-commerce (shopping), electronic mail (email), text and instant messaging, telephone calls, and conferencing services.

E-Commerce

E-commerce is the abbreviation for electronic commerce, which involves buying or selling over the Internet (Figure 2.28). Most software is now purchased directly via the Internet, where the link to download the program becomes available once the license fee is paid. Shopping online for music, videos, books, clothing, and other merchandise may require a credit card for payment. Increasingly, however, some merchants allow customers to pay directly from their bank accounts or through third-party payment services, such as PayPal or Google Wallet. With Google Wallet, a Gmail account can be linked to a credit or debit card, which can be used for purchases at websites. E-commerce on mobile devices is a fast-growing market, as consumers love to shop for favorite apps or music to use on smartphones or tablets. Table 2.5 on page 55 describes three categories of e-commerce.

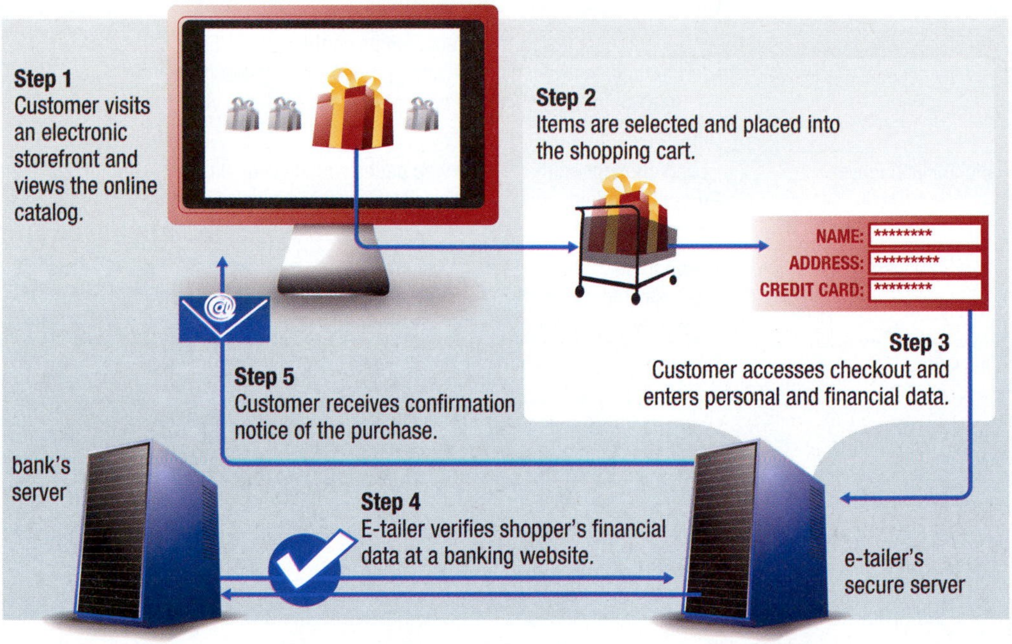

Step 1
Customer visits an electronic storefront and views the online catalog.
Step 2
Items are selected and placed into the shopping cart.
NAME: ********
ADDRESS: *********
CREDIT CARD: ********
Step 3
Customer accesses checkout and enters personal and financial data.
Step 5
Customer receives confirmation notice of the purchase.
bank's server
Step 4
E-tailer verifies shopper's financial data at a banking website.
e-tailer's secure server

Figure 2.28
The online shopping process for business-to-consumer (B2C) transactions involves the five steps illustrated here.

Table 2.5
Types of E-Commerce Transactions

E-Commerce Activity	Description
Business-to-consumer (B2C)	B2C is a familiar category of e-commerce if you have ever bought music, software, or other merchandise on the web. A business, such as Amazon, sets up a website that allows any consumer to purchase merchandise or services. A business that sells online to consumers is often referred to as an **e-tailer** (short for electronic retailer). Figure 2.28 on page 54 illustrates the typical steps in a B2C transaction.
Business-to-business (B2B)	In B2B a business sells directly to other businesses using the web. In some cases, B2B transactions occur at websites used by consumers. For example, if you are on a website that shows ads and you click the ad, a payment is charged to the business that posted the ad. B2B website ads allow website owners to provide content free of charge to consumers.
Consumer-to-consumer (C2C)	C2C activity occurs at websites such as Craigslist or eBay, where transactions occur directly between two consumers. C2C websites generally also involve B2C or B2B transactions since the website owner that provides the service charges fees to advertisers and/or sellers to post ads.

Tutorial
What Are the Differences among the Three Kinds of E-commerce?

Security Alert **Keep Your Personal Data Safe When Paying Online**

When paying online, make sure you are using a secure website before entering personal data, such as your credit card number. The web address should start with *https* (meaning the website is transferring data using encryption), and some browsers show an icon of a closed lock indicating your personal data is safe. You will learn about secure websites in Chapter 7.

Email

Electronic mail (**email**) is the sending and receiving of digital messages using the Internet, sometimes with documents or photos attached. Businesses were using the Internet for email long before consumers embraced the service when PCs became mainstream in the 1980s and 1990s. In today's workplaces, email is the standard communication medium and often is preferred over voice conversation, since email provides a written record of what has been agreed upon.

When you sign up for an account with an ISP, one or more email accounts are included with your Internet service. An **email address** is used to connect to your email account at the ISP server and is generated in the format *username@mailserver.com* or *username@mailserver.net*. Your ISP will provide the means for you to create your own user name to include before the @ symbol. The text after the @ symbol is the ISP server name. Once your email account is created, you can use a program called an **email client**, such as Microsoft Outlook or Apple Mail, to create, send, store, and receive messages.

Good to Know
In 1971 the first message was sent across a network with the @ symbol used to separate the user name from the computer name.

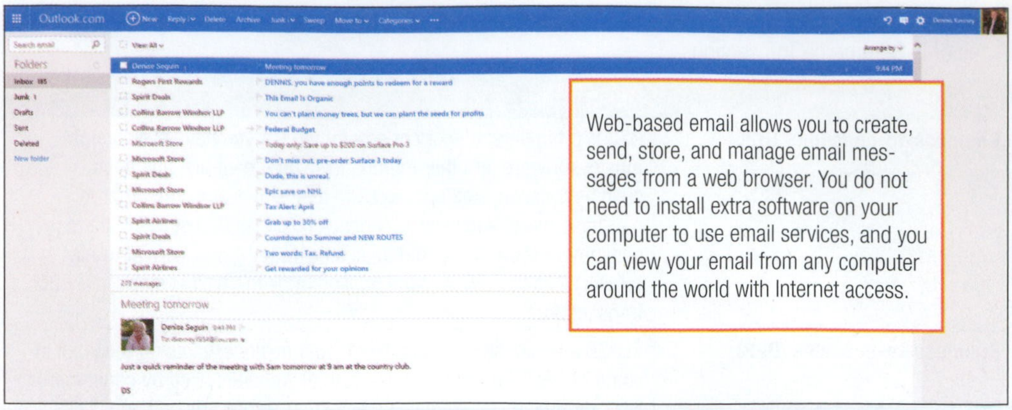

Outlook.com
Folders
Meeting tomorrow
Web-based email allows you to create, send, store, and manage email messages from a web browser. You do not need to install extra software on your computer to use email services, and you can view your email from any computer around the world with Internet access.

Figure 2.29
Microsoft Outlook.com is a popular choice for a web-based email service.

Web-based email, such as Hotmail or Gmail, are popular among email users, since you do not need a separate email client program to send and receive messages. Outlook.com or Gmail users sign in from their browsers to access email. Once logged in, all messages are created, sent, stored, and otherwise managed from the browser window as shown in Figure 2.29.

Text or instant messaging from a mobile device is a popular method of communicating with others.

Text and Instant Messaging

Messaging between mobile devices is often preferred over email since messages can be sent more quickly without a special email program. A **text message** is a short text exchange, referred to as **texting**, sent to another mobile device using a service called **short message service (SMS)**. Some mobile devices provide the ability to use **instant messaging** (exchanging text messages in real time) between other users of similar devices. Examples of instant messaging services on mobile devices are BlackBerry BBM and Apple iMessage.

Voice Conversations

The ability to engage in a voice conversation using the Internet is called **Voice over Internet Protocol (VoIP)**. Skype is a popular service example and includes the ability to make video calls using web cameras to allow each party to see one another while chatting. FaceTime is a similar service used on Apple devices. Software and hardware on your PC or mobile device convert your voice and/or picture into digital signals that travel the Internet.

Check This Out ✓
http://CC2.ParadigmCollege.net/VoIP
Go here to learn more about Internet telephone service and compare plans.

Video calls using the Internet are a popular choice for staying in touch with long distance friends or relatives.

Web Conferencing

Web conferencing programs allow individuals to connect online to engage in a meeting. Web conferencing software similar to that shown in Figure 2.30 allows each participant to talk and share ideas and information using presentations or online whiteboards. A person's desktop can be shared so that other participants can watch a demonstration. Online meetings allow businesses to save on travel expenses.

Other services use the Internet, such as newsgroups, discussion boards, chat rooms, and remote access support providers. New applications for the Internet that will make creative use of text, video, and audio are sure to be invented.

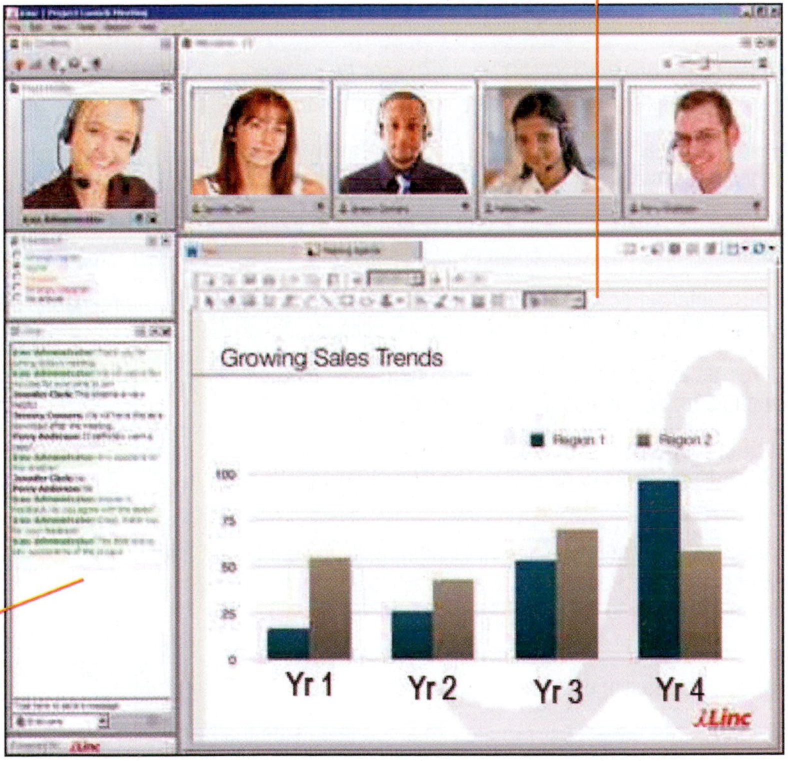
Web conferencing programs provide the ability to talk and share documents or presentations with a group of individuals. Tools are included to annotate and mark up the online whiteboard during the conference.
Participants can pose and answer questions with the group in this window.
Growing Sales Trends
Region 1
Region 2
100
75
50
25
0
Yr 1
Yr 2
Yr 3
Yr 4
iLinc

Figure 2.30
Web conferencing software allows a group of individuals to connect and collaborate using the Internet.

Explore Further Netiquette Guidelines

With so much communication taking place over the Internet, rules for acceptable social interactions have been developed called *netiquette*, which is short for *Internet etiquette*. Without the visual cues that are present in face-to-face communication, messages can often be misunderstood. What are some common netiquette guidelines?

1. Research netiquette and pick what you think are the five most important rules.
2. Create a presentation with one rule per slide, and provide an example of appropriate and inappropriate netiquette to demonstrate the rule. Include a slide at the end with the URLs of the sites from which you obtained your rules.
3. Save the presentation as **Netiquette-YourName**.
4. Submit the presentation to your instructor in the manner she or he has requested.

Topics Review

Topic	Key Concepts	Key Terms
2.1 Networks, the Internet, and the World Wide Web	Networks link computers together to share resources. The Internet is the physical structure that represents a global network linking other networks from around the world. Connection to the Internet is provided by ISPs for a fee. Web pages circulated on the Internet make up the World Wide Web, sometimes referred to simply as the *web*. Web pages stored on web servers are viewed using a web browser. Websites are a collection of related web pages. Web 2.0 refers to websites that have two-way communication, sharing, and collaboration with users. Web 3.0 incorporates automated agents that will adapt and learn the type of content you want to see on the web. This evolution is sometimes called the *Semantic Web*.	network Internet or net Internet service provider (ISP) World Wide Web or web web page web browser website web server Web 2.0 Web 3.0
2.2 Connecting to the Internet	Computers sold today have an NIC (also called an *Ethernet port*) and/or a wireless interface card to facilitate connection to the Internet. Newer notebooks and mobile devices also integrate wireless Bluetooth connectivity. ISPs provide the equipment and servers to connect to the Internet backbone with fees based on connection speed. High-speed Internet access is referred to as *broadband* and is measured in Mbps, which is 1 million bits per second. Cable Internet access requires a cable modem that connects via coaxial cable to the cable company's network. With a DSL, your telephone company supplies a DSL modem that uses twisted-pair cable to connect into a telephone jack in your home. FTTP means a fiber-optic cable is installed directly to your home, and a piece of equipment converts optical signals to electrical signals for your computer. Satellite Internet access is found in rural areas and requires the installation of a satellite dish and satellite modem. Fixed wireless Internet access requires an antenna outside the home and a wireless modem to send/receive radio signals. A Wi-Fi network uses wireless access points and radio signals to transmit data. It is often used for public spaces and homes. A hotspot is an area in range of a Wi-Fi network. New connection devices capable of transferring data at 1,000 Mbps or more express speed in Gbps instead. Mobile broadband sticks are portable modems that connect to the Internet via a cellular network. Smartphones and tablets connect using a third-generation (3G) or fourth-generation (4G) network to cellular towers, with 4G LTE networks the fastest option for mobile devices. Dial-up uses a modem to connect via a telephone line.	network interface card (NIC) Ethernet port wireless interface card Bluetooth broadband megabits per second (Mbps) cable Internet access digital subscriber line (DSL) fiber to the premises (FTTP) satellite Internet access fixed wireless Internet access Wi-Fi network hotspot gigabits per second (Gbps) mobile broadband stick 3G 4G LTE network dial-up

continued...

Topic	Key Concepts	Key Terms
2.3 Popular Web Browsers	Web pages are viewed using web browser software that interprets the code the page is stored in as text and multimedia content. HTML is a markup language used in many web pages that describes page content using tags. IE is the browser included with Microsoft Windows for Windows 8.1 and earlier editions. Windows 10 in 2015 included a new browser named Microsoft Edge with faster page loads, a streamlined design, drawing ability, Cortana, a digital assistant, and a Hub, which stores favorites, history, and a reading list. Chrome, provided free by Google, runs on PCs and mobile devices. Chrome is popular due to its fast page loading, minimalist design, and synchronized searches. Firefox is a free browser for PCs, Macs, or mobile devices available from the Mozilla Foundation. Firefox has similarities with IE. Fans prefer its speed and security. Apple Safari is used on Mac and Apple mobile devices. Safari 8 uses battery power more efficiently. Mobile web browsers are designed to quickly display web pages optimized for much smaller screens.	Hypertext Markup Language (HTML) Internet Explorer (IE) Microsoft Edge Chrome Firefox Safari mobile web browser
2.4 Understanding Internet and Web Addresses, and Navigating Web Pages	Every computing device connected to the Internet is assigned an IP address. ICANN is a nonprofit organization in charge of keeping track of IP addresses around the world. An IP address with four groups of numbers from 0 to 255 separated by periods is known as *IPv4*. IPv6, developed when the number of unique IPv4 addresses was running out, uses eight sets of characters 0 through 9 or letters *a* through *f* separated by colons. A web address, also called a *URL*, is a text-based address used to navigate to a website. A DNS server holds the directory that associates an Internet address with a web address. The *http* in a URL refers to the Hypertext Transfer Protocol used for displaying pages. A domain name is the text-based name for an organization within the URL. The three- or four-character extension in a domain name is called the *TLD* and identifies the type of organization. For example, *.gov* means government. ICANN is expanding gTLDs. A two-character extension in a domain name is a country code called a *ccTLD*. For example, *.ca* means Canada. The first page you see when you visit a website is called the *home page*. Web pages contain hyperlinks (links) that take you to a related web page when clicked.	Internet Protocol (IP) address Internet Corporation for Assigned Names and Numbers (ICANN) web address uniform resource locator (URL) Domain Name System (DNS) server domain name top-level domain (TLD) generic top-level domain (gTLD) ccTLD home page hyperlink or link

continued...

Topic	Key Concepts	Key Terms
2.5 Searching the Web	Search engines read web pages and create indexes using keywords associated with the page. Spiders and crawlers are programs used by search engines to find and index web pages. Some search engines provide categories of topics and subtopics that you can use to narrow your search. You will get different results from different search engines using the same search phrase because spider and index programs vary, pages may be updated at different times, and rankings may differ. Use the advanced tools or options to fine-tune a search. A metasearch search engine compiles results from other search engines in one place. Content aggregators are websites that collect and organize web content. Subscribers can sign up for updates (called *web feeds*) that alert the subscriber when new content is added. RSS and Atom are two specifications used for collecting, organizing, and displaying web feeds.	search engine spider crawler metasearch search engine content aggregator web feed Really Simple Syndication (RSS) Atom
2.6 Evaluating Web Content	Domain names in the web address can provide clues to the authenticity or trustworthiness of a web page. Check a web page for an author's name and affiliation; if no name is present, try reading the About Us or Contact links. Look for dates to make sure the information you are reading is the most recent; if no date exists, look for clues in the content or web address. Evaluate the purpose of a website to help decide if a bias may exist in the information presented. A poorly designed website with errors in spelling and grammar should have its content corroborated by another source.	
2.7 Popular Web Plug-ins and Players for Multimedia Content	Plug-ins, players, and add-ons are all software programs needed by a browser to display multimedia content. Adobe Reader is a program used to view PDF documents. Adobe Flash Player and Shockwave Player are programs used to view animations with high-quality graphics, sound, and interactivity. QuickTime from Apple is used for videos or animations. Proceed with caution when downloading and installing a plug-in or player since some programs will add additional unwanted software to your system or may in fact be malware designed to look like the real player. When in doubt, navigate to the company website on your own to download the software instead of using links. Once installed, plug-ins and players will periodically require updating.	plug-in add-on player

continued...

Topic	Key Concepts	Key Terms
2.8 E-Commerce, Messaging, and Internet Telephone and Conferencing Options	E-commerce involves transactions online between businesses and consumers (B2C), businesses and other businesses (B2B), and consumers and other consumers (C2C). Businesses that sell online to consumers are referred to as *e-tailers*. Shopping online generally requires a credit card or account with a third-party payment service, such as PayPal or Google Wallet. Email is the sending and receiving of messages via the Internet. An email address connects you to the ISP mail server to send, receive, and store messages. An email client is a program installed on a PC that is used to create, send, receive, and manage email messages. Text messages are short messages sent via an SMS on your smartphone or tablet (referred to as *texting*). Instant messaging is exchanging messages with someone else in real time. VoIP is technology that allows users to make telephone calls via the Internet. Web conferencing software allows a group of individuals to engage in meetings online with shared documents. Netiquette is short for *Internet etiquette* and refers to rules for acceptable social interactions on the Internet.	e-commerce e-tailer business-to-consumer (B2C) business-to-business (B2B) consumer-to-consumer (C2C) email email address email client text message texting short message service (SMS) instant messaging Voice over Internet Protocol (VoIP) web conferencing

Recheck
Recheck your understanding of the topics covered in this chapter.

Workbook
Chapter review and assessment resources are available in the *Workbook* ebook.

Chapter 3

Computer Hardware

Precheck
Check your understanding of the topics covered in this chapter.

Learning Objectives

3.1 Recognize the major components in a system unit and explain their purpose

3.2 List and recognize various types of input devices

3.3 List and recognize various types of output devices

3.4 Identify wired and wireless network adapters used for connectivity purposes

3.5 Explain how data is represented on a computer and describe typical speed and storage capacities

3.6 Describe various options for permanent storage and their corresponding storage capacities

As you learned in Chapter 1, computers come in all shapes and sizes. Whether you are working with a desktop or a notebook, ultrabook, tablet, or other mobile device, certain components are found in each one. All computers have a central processing unit (CPU), input device(s), output device(s), memory, connectivity adapters, and storage. These electronic and physical components found in a computing device are collectively known as *computer hardware*.

Some hardware is visible to you, such as the screen, keyboard, and mouse, while other hardware is housed inside the system, such as the CPU, memory, network adapter, and some storage. Hardware used for input, output, connectivity, or storage that you plug in or connect to your computer wirelessly, such as a USB storage medium or printer, is called a **peripheral**.

If you have looked at ads for computers, you know that a basic understanding of the terminology and hardware components is helpful to making a purchase decision. In Chapter 1, you were introduced to many of the hardware components found in a PC. In Chapter 2, you learned about hardware, such as cable modems and DSL modems, that provide connectivity to the Internet. In this chapter you will explore what's inside the system unit, input and output devices, network adapters, digital data representation, and storage options in more detail. Appendix A contains tips for buying a computer or mobile device.

SNAP If you are a SNAP user, go to your SNAP Assignments page to complete the Precheck, Tutorials, and Recheck.

3.1 The System Unit

As stated in Chapter 1, the system unit is the horizontal or vertical (tower) case in which the computer microprocessor, memory, and storage are located. In a mobile device, such as a laptop, tablet, or smartphone, these components are inside the unit below the integrated keyboard and/or screen. In an all-in-one system, these components are mounted in the same case in which the monitor is housed. Regardless of the configuration, the main components in the system unit are the power supply with cooling fan, motherboard, ports for plugging in peripherals, and storage devices. Figure 3.1 shows the inside view of a notebook system unit.

In this topic you will learn about the power supply, motherboard components, and ports. In Topic 3.6 you will learn about storage.

optical disc drive
In many notebooks, this drive is omitted.
cooling fan
In 2015, Apple released the first MacBook without a cooling fan. Look for more notebooks in the future to be fanless.
hard drive
motherboard
heat sink
ports for plugging in peripherals

Figure 3.1
Inside view of a notebook

Good to Know

Dead smartphone batteries could be a thing of the past for those who invest in new furniture. In 2015 IKEA released a line of home furnishings with integrated wireless chargers. Place a smartphone on the plus sign that marks the charging spot on the table, pad, or other piece of furniture equipped with the charging system, and watch the battery indicator rise!

Power Supply

All computers operate with power. In a tower or desktop the power supply is at the back of the unit where you plug in the power cord. A notebook or tablet is powered by a charged battery or the power adapter when the power adapter is plugged into a power outlet (Figure 3.2). A cooling fan is located near a power supply to draw heat away from the CPU and prevent the CPU from overheating. A heat sink is also installed near a CPU to draw heat away from the processor.

With the ubiquity of mobile devices, accessories for charging batteries are plentiful. External battery chargers that charge multiple devices at once are popular. Charging mats let you charge multiple devices without connecting the devices to the mat via a cable.

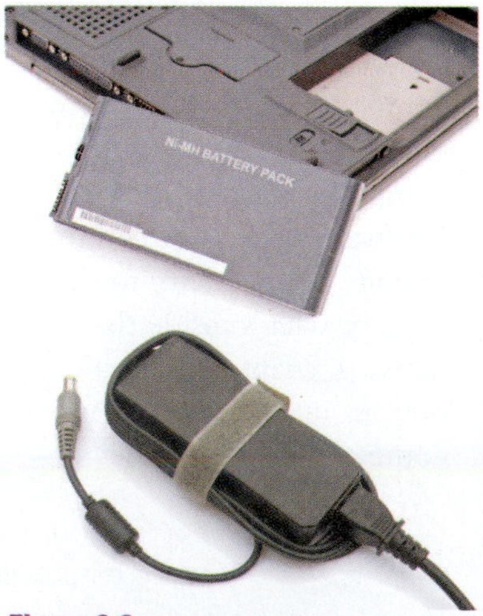
NI-MH BATTERY PACK

Figure 3.2
Notebooks are powered by a charged battery (top) or by a power adapter (bottom) plugged into a power outlet.

Motherboard

The main circuit board in the computer is called the **motherboard**. All of the other devices plug directly into or communicate wirelessly with the motherboard. Figure 3.3 shows a typical motherboard you might find inside a desktop PC.

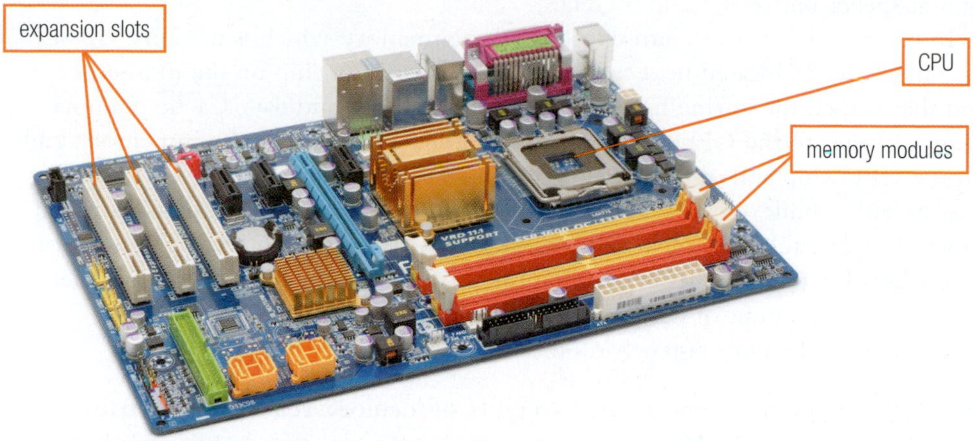

Figure 3.3

The motherboard is the hub that connects all the devices together and is designed to support a certain type of CPU.

The motherboard includes the CPU, memory, expansion slots, and circuitry attached to ports that are used to plug in external devices. Many computers integrate video and sound electronics into the main circuit board of the motherboard, while other computers may include one or more of these components as an **expansion card** that plugs into an expansion slot on the motherboard. Expansion slots are used to plug in additional circuit boards to your computer to either add or improve functionality. Another common use of an expansion card in a tower unit is to provide a network adapter into which a cable, called an Ethernet cable, is plugged for connectivity to a network. Notebook computers also have built-in card readers that allow you to insert a memory card from a digital camera or plug in a card used for wireless networking.

Data travels to the CPU and memory from the other components on the motherboard over wires called a **data bus**. Think of a data bus as a highway upon which data travels. The size and speed of a data bus affects performance since a data bus that carries more data to the CPU and memory faster performs better. Similarly, traveling by car on a four-lane highway at high speed means you arrive at a destination faster than if you traveled on a two-lane highway at a slower speed.

CPU As you learned in Chapter 1, the CPU performs the processing cycle and is often referred to as the *brain* of the computer. Today, computers do **parallel processing**, which involves having multiple microprocessor chips (more than one CPU chip on the motherboard), or a multicore processor (one CPU chip separated into independent processor cores). Parallel processing provides the ability to execute multiple instructions at the same time. Most notebooks are configured with a four-core microprocessor. Parallel processing has vastly improved system performance when combined with software written to take advantage of its capabilities.

Apple A9 Advanced RISC Machines (ARM) CPU is the processor in the 2015 edition of the popular iPhone. ARM processors use less energy than Intel processors, making them a popular choice for mobile devices.

A CPU goes through an **instruction cycle** that involves the CPU retrieving, decoding, executing, and storing an instruction. The speed at which a CPU operates is measured in the number of instruction cycles the CPU can process per second, referred to as **clock speed**. Clock speed is typically measured in **gigahertz (GHz)**, which is 1 billion cycles per second. A CPU in most notebooks and tablets sold today runs at speeds between 1 and 3 GHz.

In Chapter 1 you were introduced to cache memory, which is memory either built into the CPU or located next to the CPU on a separate chip on the motherboard and that is used for storing frequently used instructions and data. Cache memory located closest to the CPU is called **Level 1 (L1) cache**. L1 cache is memory built on the CPU chip and operates the fastest of all memory. Secondary cache memory may be either built on the CPU chip or located on the motherboard and is called **Level 2 (L2) cache**. L2 cache feeds the L1 cache. A third level of cache memory, called **Level 3 (L3) cache**, is usually located on the motherboard and feeds the L2 cache. The amount of L1, L2, and L3 cache affects performance since the CPU accesses cache memory faster than other memory.

Tutorial
What Are the Various Types of RAM?

Memory On the motherboard are two types of memory: **read-only memory (ROM)** and RAM. ROM is used for storing instructions that do not change. For example, the programming code with the instructions used when starting a computer is often stored on a ROM chip, which is called the **BIOS (basic input/output system)**, or **UEFI (Unified Extensible Firmware Interface)**. UEFI is expected to replace the older BIOS technology with a faster, more secure startup process.

Recall from Chapter 1 that RAM is temporary memory where data and instructions are stored while processing and is cleared when power is turned off. RAM is configured in modules that plug into slots on the motherboard (see Figure 3.3 on page 65). Since all software and data you are working with must reside in RAM to access the CPU, the size and type of RAM in a computer affect its performance.

A memory module like this one used in a notebook has chips on a smaller circuit board than one used in a desktop.

Desktop and notebook computers manufactured during or before 2015 have DDR3 SDRAM. DDR stands for Double Data Rate and refers to the ability to transfer data twice as often. The number after DDR represents the generation of DDR. For example, *DDR3* means third generation DDR, which is twice as fast as DDR2. SDRAM means Synchronous Dynamic Random Access Memory and refers to a type of RAM that operates at higher clock speeds than older RAM technologies. DDR4 RAM, engineered to use less power and transfer data at a faster rate, appeared in new PCs in 2015. Installing more RAM into an empty module slot can improve computer performance, extending the life of an older system.

Good to Know
A USB 3.0 device (known as a SuperSpeed USB device) can operate approximately 10 times faster than a USB 2.0 device and is easily recognizable by its blue plastic insert in the cable. In 2015, USB 3.1 Gen 2 (called SuperSpeed+) became available, and it can operate at double the USB 3.0 speed, to a maximum 10 Gbps.

Ports

A **port** is a connector located at the back, front, or side of a computer or mobile device. Ports are used to plug in external devices. The most common type of port is the **universal serial bus (USB) port**, which is used to connect an external device, such as a keyboard, mouse, printer, smartphone, or external storage medium. Most computers today provide several USB ports to accommodate multiple USB devices being used simultaneously. A USB hub can be used to increase the number of USB

ports if your computer does not provide enough to meet your needs (Figure 3.4).

A typical notebook also includes a port for plugging in an external monitor, a port for connecting to a network, and a high-definition multimedia interface (HDMI) port for connecting to a high-definition television (Figure 3.5). Ports will also be found on a notebook or other mobile device to plug in headphones, external speakers, or a microphone.

Figure 3.4
Plug in a USB hub to add more USB devices if you do not have enough USB ports.

In desktop PCs, the ports are often color coded to make it easy for someone to plug in a device with a similar end to the correct port. For example, on older desktop PCs the connectors are colored purple for the keyboard and green for the mouse so that the devices are not mixed up.

Motherboards also house other components, such as drive controllers and interfaces, to connect a hard drive or DVD drive to the motherboard via cables.

Video port
USB port. The blue connector indicates the port is USB 3.0.
Network port, also called Ethernet port. In some newer laptops, this port is no longer included as manufacturers move to wireless-only interfaces.
HDMI port

Figure 3.5
Ports at the sides, back, and sometimes front of a notebook are used to plug in external devices.

Blog Topic — Are You a Techno Enthusiast?

Manufacturers update hardware components as new developments in technology make it possible to produce faster, more energy efficient computers with expanded capabilities. How often do you update your computer hardware? Do you like to always have the latest equipment, or are you one to stick with a PC as long as possible? Do you consider yourself a technology enthusiast, or do you avoid new technology?

1. Write and post a blog entry that answers the above questions and gives your reasons.
2. Read at least two of your classmates' blogs and post one comment to each.
3. Submit your blog URL and the URLs of the two classmates' blogs to your instructor in the manner she or he requested.

Explore Further — What Is USB Type-C?

In 2015 Apple released a new MacBook with only one port—a USB Type-C port. This design created quite a stir in the technology community, which was used to multiple ports offered in notebooks. Just what is a USB Type-C port? How is USB Type-C different from the USB ports you use now? Will USB Type-C become the new standard on Windows-compatible PCs?

1. Go online and find out the answers to the questions posed.
2. Create a document that provides answers in your own words to the above questions. Include the URL(s) for the article(s) you read about the topic.
3. Save the document as **USB-TypeC-YourName**.
4. Submit the document to your instructor in the manner she or he has requested.

3.2 Input Devices

As stated in Chapter 1, any device used to enter raw data or communicate instructions to the computer is an input device. Several input devices exist, with the most common being a keyboard and mouse. Other devices used for input are also described in this topic.

Keyboards and Mice

While wired keyboards and mice were the standard for traditional desktop PCs, computer users prefer to be untethered. A wireless keyboard and/or mouse (Figure 3.6) can be used with any computer device. Wireless keyboards and mice use batteries as a source of power. A wireless receiver is plugged into a USB port and connects with the wireless keyboard and mouse. Electronic signals from the keyboard are interpreted by the keyboard device controller and sent to the computer operating system via the wireless receiver, which in turn sends the keystrokes to the active running program for display on the screen.

Figure 3.6
Wireless keyboards and mice are popular for traditional PCs and as peripherals for mobile devices.

A **keyboard** is a device used to type and input data into a computer. In addition to the alphabetic and numeric keys on a keyboard, special purpose keys (such as Esc, Insert, Delete, function keys labeled F1 through F12, the Start key on a Windows-compatible computer, and the command key on an Apple computer) allow commands to be sent to a program. Directional movement keys (such as the up, down, left, and right arrow keys, and the Home, End, Page Up, and Page Down keys) provide the ability to move around a screen. Finally, keys labeled Ctrl, Alt, and Shift allow you to use a combination of one or more of these keys with letters, numbers, and function keys to send instructions to the active program.

Notebooks include a built-in keyboard. Tablets and smartphones may or may not have integrated keyboards that are built in or slide out. Some tablets include a keyboard that you can use by plugging the tablet into a port on the top of the keyboard (called a *dock port*). Most tablets and smartphones come with touch-enabled screens that display a keyboard you use by tapping with your fingers or a stylus (Figure 3.7).

Figure 3.7
Current tablets and smartphones offer on-screen keyboards, which you tap using your fingers or a stylus (digital pen).

A **mouse** is a device used to point to, select, and manipulate objects on the screen. The mouse works by detecting its motion in relation to the surface beneath it and by the clicks of its buttons. Most mice in use today track the movement using light technology, while older mice used a trackball. As you move the mouse, the pointer on the screen moves in the same direction. Buttons on the mouse provide the ability to send a command when the pointer is resting on the target that you wish to manipulate. A wheel on the mouse facilitates scrolling.

On notebooks, a **touchpad** is located below the keyboard. This rectangular surface is used in place of a mouse to move the pointer on the screen and manipulate objects. The touchpad senses finger movement and taps much like a mouse senses movement and clicks. Depending on the touchpad device, multi-finger gestures and pinch and zoom movements can be used to scroll and zoom the display. Some notebooks and smartphones include a track pointer, which senses finger pressure for moving the pointer. Figure 3.8 shows a typical track pointer and touch pad.

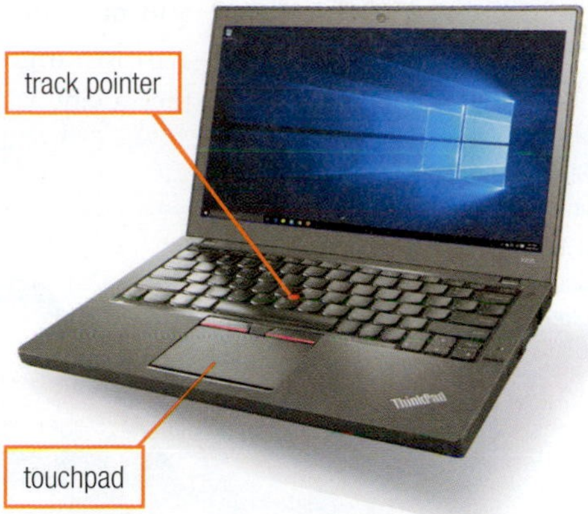

Figure 3.8

On a notebook, a touchpad and/or a track pointer (red button in middle of keyboard) moves the pointer on the screen using finger movements, while taps and buttons manipulate objects.

Touchscreens

Mobile devices, such as tablets, smartphones, and some portable media players, include a touch-enabled display, called a **touchscreen**, for accepting input. Some laptops and monitors for desktop PCs and all-in-one PCs are also touch-enabled. A touch-enabled device has a layer of capacitive material below a protective screen. When you touch the screen with your finger or with a digital pen called a **stylus**, an electrical signal is sensed by the capacitive layer, which sends data about the location you touched and any gesture you used to the computer touch processor and software that interpret the gesture.

Self-serve kiosks, such as airline check-in stations and ATMs, use touchscreens in combination with other input devices, such as keypads, buttons, and magnetic strip readers, to accept input.

Tutorial
How Do Touchscreens Work?

Good to Know

In 2015, with the release of the Apple Watch, Apple added a new feature called Force Touch. Force Touch distinguishes the level of force applied by the user and adjusts the response action. For example, a light tap performs one action, and a harder tap performs another. Force Touch is being added to other Apple devices.

Mobile devices and self-serve kiosks are touch-enabled or can be operated with a stylus.

Scanners and Readers

A **scanner** is a device that uses optical technology to analyze text and/or images and convert them into data that can be used by a computer. A scanner can be a separate input device, such as a flatbed scanner (a scanner that sits on a desk) or a handheld scanner. Many printers and photocopiers used today are multipurpose devices that also incorporate scanners.

A **bar code reader** optically scans bar codes to identify products in warehouses or at checkout counters. Even smartphones include the ability to scan a **QR (Quick Response) code**, a type of bar code that looks like a matrix of black square dots. The smartphone reads the QR code, which usually directs the device to display a website. A **magnetic strip reader** can read data from the magnetic strip on the backs of cards, such as debit cards, credit cards, or key cards used to open doors or parking gates. A **biometric device** identifies people by individual human characteristic, such as a fingerprint, iris, or voice pattern. Finally, a **radio frequency identification (RFID) reader** scans an embedded RFID tag to identify an object. RFID readers

Check This Out

http://CC2.ParadigmCollege.net/RFIDNews

Go here to read the latest news on RFID technology innovation in various industries.

and tags use tiny chips with antennas that are readable when the reader and tag are within range of each other. Typically, RFID technology is used to read tags up to 300 feet away.

Many different types of scanners and readers are used to generate input from documents, images, bar codes, biometrics, or wireless tags.

Security Alert **Keep Your Eyes on Your Cards**

Protect cards with a magnetic strip or chip that stores personal data. These cards are targets for criminals who use skimmers or readers to steal the data. If you hand over a debit or credit card to a store clerk to pay for a purchase, make sure to keep the card in your line of sight at all times and be cautious when entering a PIN.

Digital Cameras, Digital Camcorders, and Webcams

Digital cameras capture still images, while digital video cameras called *camcorders* capture live video and audio. Many of these devices are multipurpose, meaning some digital cameras could be used to capture short live-video segments, and some camcorders double as digital cameras.

A **webcam** is a video camera built into a video display screen (mounted at the top center of the screen edge) or plugged in as a peripheral and is used to provide images to the computer during live web conferencing or chatting using a program, such as Skype or FaceTime.

Smartphones and tablets have digital camera capabilities that allow you to snap pictures and record video and send them via messaging applications directly from the device.

Digital cameras, camcorders, and webcams are used to convert images and live video into a digital format.

Microphones and Voice Recognition

A **microphone** can be used in conjunction with software to create a digital audio file from voice input or other sounds captured by the device. You may also use a microphone to chat with someone online. Some games played online or with game systems accept voice commands. **Voice recognition technology** (also called *speech recognition technology*) is used to recognize voice commands as input for hands-free operation at work, with the navigation and communications system in your car, or with your mobile device. Siri on the Apple iPhone uses voice recognition to send messages, schedule meetings, or make a call. A program such as Dragon NaturallySpeaking converts input you speak into your microphone into text and commands in documents or messaging applications.

Microphones are built into notebooks and mobile devices. An external microphone or a headset with a microphone attached can also be plugged in as a peripheral (Figure 3.9).

Figure 3.9

A standalone microphone or headset microphone provides voice input during a conversation via a computer or for a voice recording.

Entertainment Controllers

Gaming systems accept input using a variety of methods, such as wired or wireless game controllers (Figure 3.10), joysticks, and motion sensors. Some games have specialized controllers, such as guitars, other musical instruments, or tennis rackets. Some exercise games use pressure sensitive mats or boards.

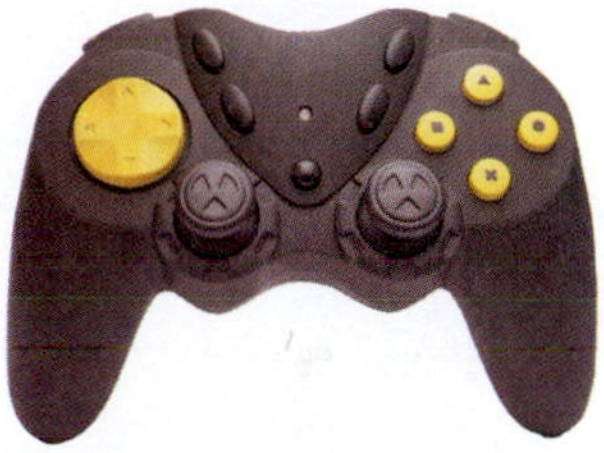

Figure 3.10

Game consoles and other entertainment systems use controllers such as the one shown here for input.

Other devices, such as keypads and magnetic ink character recognition systems, are used in specialized applications to provide input. Medical devices, such as heart rate monitors and blood glucose meters, send data to connected devices, such as smartphones, for health monitoring. Wearable keyboards and holographic inputs are no longer considered science fiction owing to new technology that works with GPS sensors to transmit location data. The Microsoft HoloLens, developed for use with Windows 10, accepts a gaze, gesture, or voice input from an untethered device for interaction with content (Figure 3.11). Imagine yourself in the future wearing your keyboard on your sleeve or responding to content via a hologram!

Figure 3.11

The Microsoft HoloLens is specialized hardware that lets you interact with holograms.

Explore Further — Virtual Reality Devices

Virtual reality devices are used with games and in commercial applications to train workers, such as simulating flights for pilots. Data input detectors may be worn on the body—for example, in headsets or gloves.

1. Research a virtual reality device for a game or training purpose.
2. Create a brief presentation that describes in your own words what you learned about the virtual reality device. Include a slide with a picture of the virtual reality device that you researched. Include the URLs of the sites from which you obtained information.
3. Save the presentation as **VirtualReality-YourName**.
4. Submit the presentation to your instructor in the manner she or he has requested.

3.3 Output Devices

In Chapter 1, you learned that devices used to view the information processed and organized by the computer are output devices. The most commonly used output device is a **monitor** or other type of screen or display in a mobile device. Computer output can also be connected to high-definition televisions, projectors, or interactive whiteboards. Other types of output devices explored in this topic include speakers, headsets, printers, and copiers.

Video Displays

An electronic device called a **video display** presents information from a computer visually. A desktop PC uses a device called a monitor to connect to the computer video port. Notebooks and other mobile devices have built-in video display screens.

Display screen size varies by device, with some smartphone screens as small as 2.5 inches and some notebooks as large as desktop monitors.

Video displays come in many different sizes, which are measured by the diagonal length of the viewing area. For a mobile device, the size of the video display is constrained by the size of the notebook, tablet, or smartphone. Small notebooks may have screens as small as 11 inches, while large notebook screens can be as big as 18.4 inches. Tablet screens typically range from 7 to 11 inches. Smartphone screens can be as small as 2.5 inches, with newer phones breaking in near 5.5 inches.

Notebooks are often connected to external video displays, such as a computer monitor or a high-definition television screen, to take advantage of larger viewing areas or to use two screens at the same time. Monitors are typically a wide-screen **liquid crystal display (LCD)** or **light-emitting diode (LED)**, both of which are flat-panel liquid crystal technology in various sizes upward from 20 inches. The difference between LCD and LED lies with the backlighting that allows light to pass through the panels. LCD screens use a type of fluorescent lamp whereas LEDs use smaller, more efficient light emitting diodes. The technology in LED screens means they consume less energy while displaying brighter, more vibrant colors than LCD screens.

Connecting two display screens to a PC or notebook is becoming commonplace, as well as streaming movies or other Internet content on a high-definition television.

Another flat-panel display screen is **plasma**. Plasma was popular with home theater enthusiasts for many years because of its truer color representation; however, LED technology has improved such that plasma is expected to eventually be obsolete.

A newer technology that is known as **organic light-emitting diode (OLED)** does not require backlighting like LCDs and LEDs, making the displays far more energy efficient for any device that runs off battery power. OLED screens without backlighting are thinner and produce the best picture quality because each organic cell behind the panel creates its own light source, meaning no light spills over into other areas of the picture.

The video display **resolution** setting affects the quality of output on the display screen. Resolution refers to the number of picture elements, called *pixels*, that make up the image shown on the screen. A **pixel** is square with red, green, and blue color values (called *RGB*) that represent each color needed to form the image. Resolution is expressed as the number of horizontal pixels by the number of vertical pixels, such as 1920 x 1080 pixels for a 17-inch notebook display. The more pixels used to render the output, the sharper the image, as shown in Figure 3.12. Displays default to recommended settings, but operating system software can be used to change the resolution.

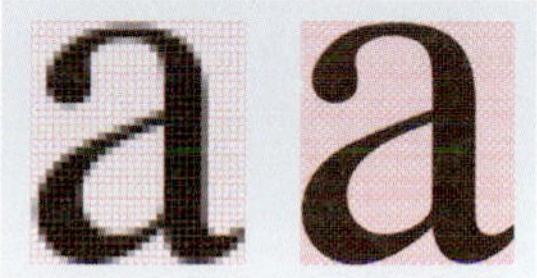

Figure 3.12
A character displayed at a low resolution using fewer pixels to form the character appears fuzzy (left) compared to the same character at a higher resolution using more pixels (right).

A newer display technology called **4K UHD** (ultra-high-definition) has found its way into display screens, such as those on monitors, televisions, and digital cameras. *4K* refers to the resolution of the display. A 4K UHD screen uses more than 4 times as many pixels as the standard high definition (HD) screen with which most of us are familiar (approximately 8 million pixels for a 4K UHD screen versus 2 million pixels for an HD screen). 5K displays are also in limited supply, and an 8K display is expected on a new iMac from Apple in 2016.

Video Display Projectors and Interactive Whiteboards

A **video display projector (VDP)** is used to project a computer output on a large screen when making presentations to groups (Figure 3.13). VDPs are often ceiling mounted in classrooms and boardrooms, while portable projectors are available for other venues. A notebook or other computer connects to the projector via a video output cable, or using wireless technology.

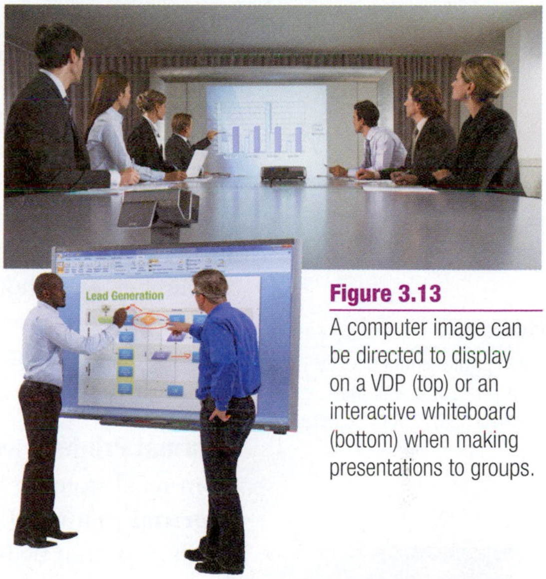

Figure 3.13
A computer image can be directed to display on a VDP (top) or an interactive whiteboard (bottom) when making presentations to groups.

An **interactive whiteboard** displays a computer output on a large white surface. Special pens are used to annotate on the whiteboard while the image is displayed for making notes or to draw attention to objects on the display. In these instances, the whiteboard is acting as both an output device and an input device. The annotations can be saved with the images as electronic files for viewing later. Tools for touch gesture interaction with the computer while the display is being viewed are also included.

Speakers and Headphones

Audio output from the computer, such as music, voice, or sound effects, is heard through internal speakers, external speakers, or headphones. PC monitors have built-in speakers. Notebooks and other mobile devices have integrated speakers. Plugging headphones or earbuds into the audio port of a computer or mobile device redirects the audio output to your headset. High-quality headphones reduce background noise improving the audio experience. External speakers can give home theater quality sound. A **Bluetooth headset** paired with a smartphone or other mobile device is used to listen to voice conversations. See Figure 3.14 for examples of these output devices.

Figure 3.14
External speakers, earbud headphones, and a Bluetooth headset are common ways to hear audio output from a computing device.

Printers and Copiers

Video displays provide output that is temporary. When the computer is turned off, the output disappears. Printed copies of computer output are called **hard copy**. Hard copy can be generated by a laser printer, inkjet printer, photo printer, thermal printer, plotter, or digital photocopier. 3-D printers manufacture objects on demand.

Figure 3.15
A laser printer is a popular choice for high volume output.

Laser Printers A **laser printer** is a popular choice for producing hard copy in offices and homes (Figure 3.15). A laser beam electrostatically charges a drum with the text and images sent for printing. A dry powder called *toner* sticks to the drum and is transferred to the paper as the paper passes through the printer. Paper feels warm when it comes out of a laser printer because heat is used to permanently adhere the toner to the paper. Color laser printers, once found only in business settings, are becoming popular with home users.

Inkjet Printers A common type of printer found in a home is an **inkjet printer** (Figure 3.16). These printers form text and images on the page by spraying drops of ink from one or more ink cartridges that move back and forth across the page. Inkjet printers allow home users to print in color relatively inexpensively.

Figure 3.16
Inkjet printers spray drops of ink on the page to form text and images.

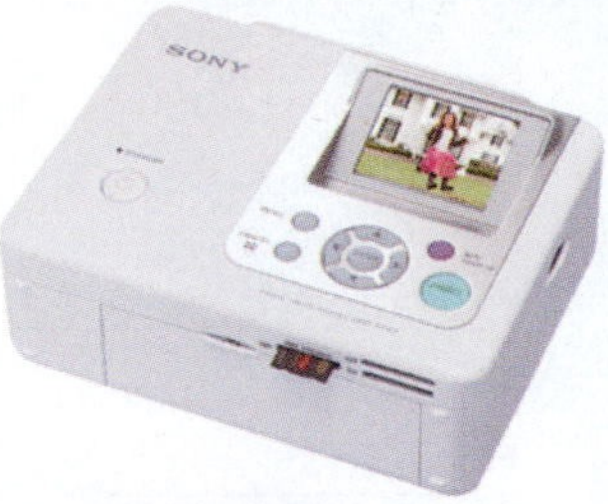

Figure 3.17
Photo printers print directly from your camera or the memory card in your camera.

Photo Printers A **photo printer** generally connects directly to a digital camera to print high-quality photos on photo paper usually using inkjet technology (Figure 3.17). Professional photo-printing service companies use higher-end photo printers that produce a high-quality image on specially treated paper for prints that last longer than those produced by inkjet printers.

Thermal Printers Most of the receipts you receive from retail stores or services are printed on a **thermal printer** (Figure 3.18). Thermal printers produce output by heating coated paper as the paper passes over the print head. These printers produce receipts quickly; however, the image fades away over time.

Figure 3.18
Thermal printers are used to print receipts and barcode labels.

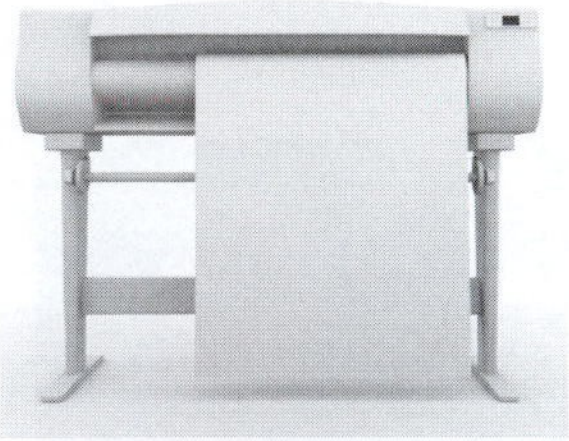

Figure 3.19
Plotters are used to print blueprints or other large technical drawings.

Plotters Blueprints, technical drawings, large drawings, and signs are often produced on a **plotter** (Figure 3.19). A plotter moves one or more pens across the surface of the paper to produce the drawing. Plotters are slow, as the movement of the pen or pens across the page takes time.

Digital Copiers A **digital copier** in an office can act as a traditional paper photocopier and, when connected to a network, accept output from computers for printing (Figure 3.20). Often these copiers are used to share color-printing capabilities in a workplace.

Figure 3.20
Digital copiers in modern offices are connected to a network to print computer output.

All-in-One Printers Many laser and inkjet printer models are multipurpose, meaning that in addition to printing, they can be used for scanning, photocopying, and sending/receiving faxes (Figure 3.21). Having a multipurpose printer saves desktop space, cuts down on multiple supply costs, and means you only have to learn to operate one device. The downside is that you cannot perform multiple functions at the same time. For example, you cannot copy a document while printing.

Figure 3.21
All-in-one printers have multifunction capability for printing, copying, scanning, and faxing.

3-D Printers A **3-D printer** can produce anything from a replacement part for a coffee maker to an entire car (Figure 3.22). At the Detroit Auto Show in 2015, the Department of Energy displayed an electric car that was produced from 3-D printed carbon fiber–reinforced plastic. 3-D objects are designed using software in which the object is created, drawn, scanned, or otherwise generated with computer assistance. The object is then printed using a technique where consecutive layers of material are placed on top of one another precisely cut to build the object. The process is sometimes referred to as *additive manufacturing*.

The 3-D printing industry is expected to generate $5.2 billion in printers and associated materials in 2015, with growth forecasted to reach $20.2 billion by 2019 according to Canalys, a global technology research and consulting firm.

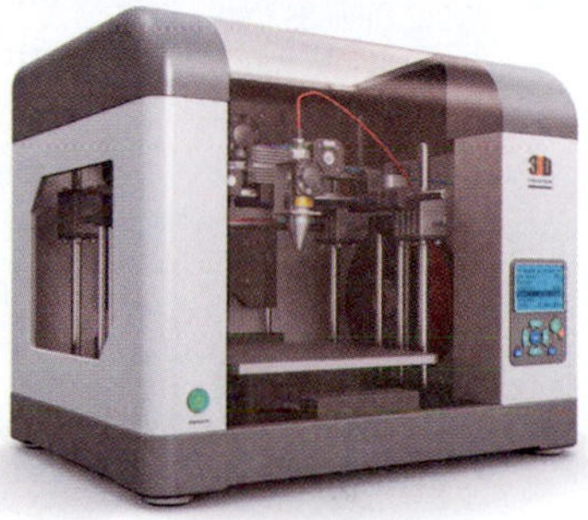

Figure 3.22
3-D printers are used to print on demand what businesses used to inventory, such as replacement parts.

Other Output Devices

Special-purpose printers, such as label printers and portable printers, are used for carrying out specific tasks. Other output devices are available, such as a document camera that displays an image from hard copy on a video display. In addition, some virtual reality devices provide output.

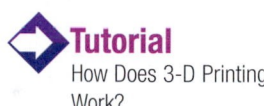

Tutorial
How Does 3-D Printing Work?

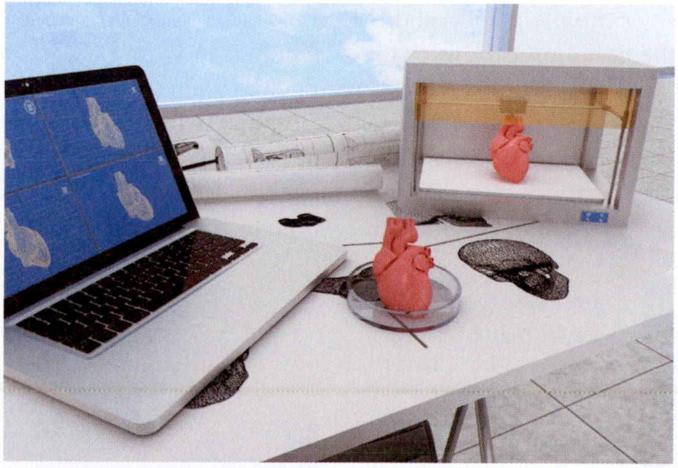

In Chapter 1, you read that a 3-D printed replica of a patient's heart was used to plan surgery on a high-risk patient. Here you can see how the heart was generated using 3-D software and a 3-D printer.

Explore Further | Laser or Inkjet—Which Printer Would You Buy?

You are looking to buy a printer and are not sure whether to buy a laser printer or an inkjet printer. You also wonder if you should buy an all-in-one printer, since you occasionally like to make copies or scan photos or documents.

1. Research the advantages, disadvantages, and costs of a laser printer and an inkjet printer. Be sure to include the costs of replacement toner or ink cartridges for comparable printers in your research.
2. Decide whether you prefer laser or inkjet and if you would buy an all-in-one printer.
3. Create a document that summarizes in your own words what you learned, your decisions, the reasons for your decisions, and the URLs of the main sources for your information.
4. Save the document as **PrinterDecision-YourName**.
5. Submit the document to your instructor in the manner she or he has requested.

3.4 Network Adapters

Recall from Chapter 1 that the term *communications device* refers to any component or device used to facilitate the transmission of data. In Chapter 2, the various types of Internet connection options were explored, and you learned about hardware used for accessing the Internet, such as cable modems, DSL modems, and mobile broadband sticks. A communications device can be thought of as both an input device and an output device since it receives data (input) from and sends data (output) to the computing device and other computers via a network. In this topic, you will examine further the hardware provided in a desktop, notebook, tablet, or mobile device that enables connectivity to a network.

Network Adapters

Tutorial
What Devices Can Be Built into Your Computer to Enable Communications?

Any device used to connect a computer to a network is called a **network adapter** (also called a *network card*). The network adapter is the interface between your computer and the other networking equipment, such as the modem or router that provides the pathway for data to travel to/from the network. All pieces of networking equipment communicate with one another using a set of standards called *protocols*. A **protocol** can be thought of as a set of rules that define how data is exchanged between two devices. A network adapter has to use the same protocols as the modem or router with which the adapter is trying to communicate for each device to understand the other. This usually becomes a factor when trying to use an older wireless network adapter with a newer router that uses a faster data transfer protocol. In that case, you can purchase a newer adapter that supports the faster protocol.

Network Adapters for Wired Connectivity

A network adapter for a wired connection is called an Ethernet port (sometimes referred to as an RJ-45 port). One end of a network cable is plugged into the network port on the computer or mobile device, and the other end is plugged into a modem or router to provide the communications channel as shown in Figure 3.23.

Ethernet refers to the type of cable used to connect two devices and the data transfer speed that the media can support. Typical ads for a computer will state Ethernet 10/100 or 10/100/1000. The numbers after Ethernet refer to the data transfer speed the adapter can support with 10 indicating 10 Mbps, 100 indicating 100 Mbps, and 1000 indicating 1,000 Mbps (or 1 Gbps, called Gigabit Ethernet).

With a wired network adapter, plug one end of a network cable into the network port of a computer and the other end into a modem or router to provide the communications pathway.

Figure 3.23
With a wired network adapter, a network cable connects two devices in a network.

Check This Out ✓
http://CC2.ParadigmCollege.net/WirelessIndustry
Go here to find articles on recent news in the wireless industry.

Network Adapters for Wireless Connectivity

Wireless connectivity is preferred by people who do not want their movements constrained by the length of a physical cable. At home, at work, or when you are on the go, a wireless network allows you the freedom to move around. Currently, computers come equipped with a wireless interface card that is integrated into the system unit as either Wi-Fi or Bluetooth.

Wi-Fi Adapters A **Wi-Fi adapter** communicates with a wireless access point or wireless router using radio frequencies to transfer data. Wi-Fi is often referred to as the **802.11 protocol**, which is the name of the standard developed to facilitate wireless communication among several hardware providers. As the protocol was improved to transmit data at faster rates, version letters were added to the 802.11 standards. At the time of writing, the latest Wi-Fi standard is 802.11ac. A computer ad may state that the integrated Wi-Fi adapter is 802.11 b/g/n/ac, which means the adapter can communicate with older Wi-Fi networks as well as the newer wireless networks.

If the integrated wireless adapter does not support a newer wireless network or you have a desktop PC that does not have a wireless interface, you can purchase an **external wireless adapter**. External wireless adapters have built-in radio transmitters and receivers to allow you to connect to a wireless modem or wireless router. The most common type of external wireless adapter is a **USB wireless adapter**, also referred to as a *USB dongle* or *USB mobile broadband stick*. A **wireless ExpressCard** adapter plugs into a narrow slot on a notebook or other mobile device. See Figure 3.24 for examples of these devices.

Figure 3.24

A USB wireless adapter or a wireless ExpressCard is often used to provide wireless connectivity or upgrade an existing Wi-Fi adapter.

Connecting with Bluetooth Bluetooth is a communications technology for short-range distances. With Bluetooth, one Bluetooth-enabled device is paired to another that is usually within a 30-foot range (though some devices can connect at distances up to 300 feet). When the Bluetooth adapter on one of the devices is activated and the other Bluetooth device is turned on, the adapter detects the wireless signal and the two devices are paired, meaning they can exchange data. Bluetooth is a popular way of connecting a smartphone to a communications system inside a car. The technology is also used to provide network access on other mobile devices, such as a notebook or tablet. Newer notebooks and mobile devices include an integrated Bluetooth adapter. You can purchase a USB Bluetooth adapter to add Bluetooth to older devices (Figure 3.25).

Figure 3.25

A USB Bluetooth adapter can be used to provide connectivity with another Bluetooth device.

Good to Know

The name Bluetooth came from 10th century King Harold Bluetooth who was instrumental in uniting warring countries in Europe. Bluetooth seemed an appropriate name, as hardware competitors had to collaborate to make devices that work with each other.

Security Alert **Use Wireless Wisely**

Wi-Fi hotspots in public areas are not secure networks. Never enter personal data at a website, in a text, or in an email message sent from a public location. Do not perform any financial transactions while using a public Wi-Fi network. At home, make sure your wireless network identification name is not obvious to your household and is secured with a strong password.

Explore Further **What Wireless Technology Is Used by Google Wallet and Apple Pay?**

Mobile payment apps, such as Google Wallet and Apple Pay, let you pay for something by placing your smartphone or smartwatch in close proximity to a reader or tapping a device that reads your information for contactless payments. The wireless data transfer is quicker than paying with cash in many cases. But just how does mobile payment technology work?

1. Research near-field communication (NFC) and how it works. Be sure to find out the range that NFC-enabled devices must be within to transfer data.
2. Create a one-page document that explains NFC and how it can be used for payments. Assume the document will be given at stores to their customers to encourage mobile payments.
3. Save the document as **MobilePaymentsNFC-YourName**.
4. Submit the document to your instructor in the manner she or he has requested.

3.5 Digital Data

Tutorial
How Does Your Computer Translate Text into Numbers?

When you type a document on a computing device, you see characters, numbers, and symbols as you type them displayed on the video display screen. However, the digital data temporarily stored in RAM, processed by the CPU, and eventually saved to permanent storage when you save the document exists as binary digits. In the **binary system**, only two possible values exist—0 and 1. Every document you save, picture on your camera, or message you send is really a series of 0s and 1s according to the computer. Understanding the way digital data is represented is helpful to put context to the speed of an Internet connection and the capacity of storage devices and memory.

Binary Bits and Bytes

Good to Know
A coding system called Unicode based on binary was developed to accommodate every letter in every language. More than 100,000 characters are represented in Unicode, with some requiring two 16-bit groups to represent a character! Unicode is the standard for programming characters in browsers and operating systems.

The smallest unit for digital data in the binary system is called a **bit**. The name *bit* is derived from *bi*nary digi*t*. A bit is either 0 or 1. By itself, a single bit of 0 or 1 is not meaningful, because only two possibilities exist. However, by adding additional bits to form a group, more possibilities to represent data are available, because different combinations of 0s and 1s can be created to represent something. By grouping 8 bits together, 256 possibilities for combinations of 0s and 1s are created. This provides enough combinations to represent each letter of the alphabet in both uppercase and lowercase, each number, and symbols (such as $, ?, and !). Each group of 8 bits is called a **byte** and represents one character. When you type the letter *A* on the keyboard and see *A* appear on the screen, one byte of RAM memory is being used to store the letter. Table 3.1 illustrates the binary equivalents for the two forms of the letter *A*, the number 4, and the $ symbol.

Table 3.1
Binary Equivalents for Letter a, Number 4, and Dollar Symbol

You type . . .	Computer stores in RAM . . .
a (lower case)	01100001
A (upper case)	01000001
4	01100100
$	00100100

Measuring Internet Speed and Data Caps

Bits are used to measure speed for transmitting data on the Internet. Recall in Chapter 2 when discussing broadband, average speeds were measured in mega*bits* per second (Mbps). One megabit was defined as 1 million bits. If it takes eight bits to represent one character, then one megabit transfers 125,000 characters. If your cable modem performs at an average speed of 20 Mbps, that means your cable modem is transmitting 2,500,000 characters per second.

Some Internet service providers (ISPs) put a limit on your monthly data transfer capacity. These limits are called *data caps* and are expressed in gigabytes. For example, a data cap of 100 GB means the ISP is limiting data transfer to 100 gigabytes in the billing period.

An average speed of 20 Mbps means 2.5 million characters per second are being transmitted!

Measuring File Size and Storage Capacity

A document, such as an essay that you create in a program like Word, is simply a collection of characters (bytes). When saved, the collection of bytes that comprises the document is called a **file**. The unique name you assign to the document when you save it is called a **file name**, and it allows you to identify that particular file among others on your storage medium. A file could potentially hold several million characters. Similarly, memory, such as RAM, and a permanent storage medium, such as a hard disk drive, can store several billion characters.

Prefixes added to the word *byte* describe progressively larger storage capacities. For example, adding *kilo* in front of *byte* creates the word **kilobyte (KB)**. One KB is 1,024 bytes, but people use the approximated value of 1,000 characters when calculating storage capacity. The next prefix is *mega*, creating the term **megabyte (MB)**. One MB is approximately 1,000,000 bytes. Table 3.2 summarizes storage units including **gigabyte (GB)** and **terabyte (TB)** with their corresponding abbreviations and capacities for the types of storage mediums you would encounter at home or at work.

Storage capacity for a USB flash drive is usually measured in GB although 1 TB flash drives are also available.

Table 3.2

Storage Units and Capacities in Bytes

Storage Unit	Abbreviation	Popular Reference	Approximate Capacity in Bytes
Kilobyte	KB	K	1,000 (one thousand)
Megabyte	MB	meg	1,000,000 (one million)
Gigabyte	GB	gig	1,000,000,000 (one billion)
Terabyte	TB	TByte	1,000,000,000,000 (one trillion)

Adding Context with Storage Capacity

Understanding that 1 MB is approximately 1,000,000 characters is more helpful to you if you can put this value into some meaningful context. According to eHow, 1 MB equals approximately 500 typed pages of text with no images. However, most documents created today have some images or other graphics added to the text to make the documents more appealing to read. The picture shown at the right of Balancing Rock uses 1.29 MB of storage space. One picture needs more digital storage space than 500 typed pages of text!

Many people like to download and store music and videos. It is not uncommon for one mp3 song to use more than 8 MB of storage and a movie file to require more than 4 GB. If you like to use your computer to store pictures, music, and movies you will need a storage medium with a large capacity.

This picture of Balancing Rock in Nova Scotia, Canada, uses 1.29 MB of storage space.

Good to Know

Big data is a term used to describe a vast amount of complex data that is analyzed for patterns or trends. The payoff to business for analyzing big data lies with better informed decisions.

Explore Further **Compressing Digital Photos**

Picture files are large because of the number of bytes needed to digitize an image. Digital image sizes are measured in pixels. For example, a typical photo taken with a digital camera may be in the range of 3000 x 2000 pixels. Such a photo would be 6 million pixels, where each pixel has its own RGB color values. RGB color information uses 24 bits for each pixel (or 3 bytes). Therefore, the file size is 18 million bytes or 18 MB (6 million pixels times 3 bytes per pixel). However, if you were to look at the file size of the picture on your digital camera memory card, the file size would be much lower than 18 MB. This occurs because of the image file format compression scheme.

1. Find out about two methods of compression: lossy and lossless and the advantages and disadvantages of each method. Which method is used by JPEG (pronounced *jay-peg*), a format for digital cameras?
2. Create a document that describes in your own words the information you learned from Step 1. Include the URLs for the articles you read.
3. Save the document as **JPEG-YourName**.
4. Submit the document to your instructor in the manner she or he has requested.

3.6 Storage Options

Saving a document, spreadsheet, or presentation makes a permanent copy of the work in a file that is available after power to the computer is turned off. When saving, a **storage device** for the file is identified. A storage device is a piece of hardware with the means to write new data to and read existing data from storage media. A storage device is often referred to as a **drive**. Each drive is identified by a unique letter and label on a Windows-compatible computer (Figure 3.26). On a Mac computer, each storage device is assigned a name, such as Macintosh HD for the hard disk drive.

Several storage options for saving a permanent copy of a file are available, such as internal and external hard disk drives, solid-state drives, network storage, USB flash memory, optical discs, and flash memory cards. Cloud storage is another option for saving files when connected to the Internet. In this topic you will learn about each of these storage devices and the cloud storage option.

Good to Know

Notice the first drive listed under Devices and drives in Figure 3.26 is the hard disk drive lettered C. Early PCs did not have HDDs and operated with one or two floppy disks (soft plastic disks that you inserted into a drive slot) assigned the letters *A* and *B*. When floppy disks became obsolete, the letters *A* and *B* were not reused.

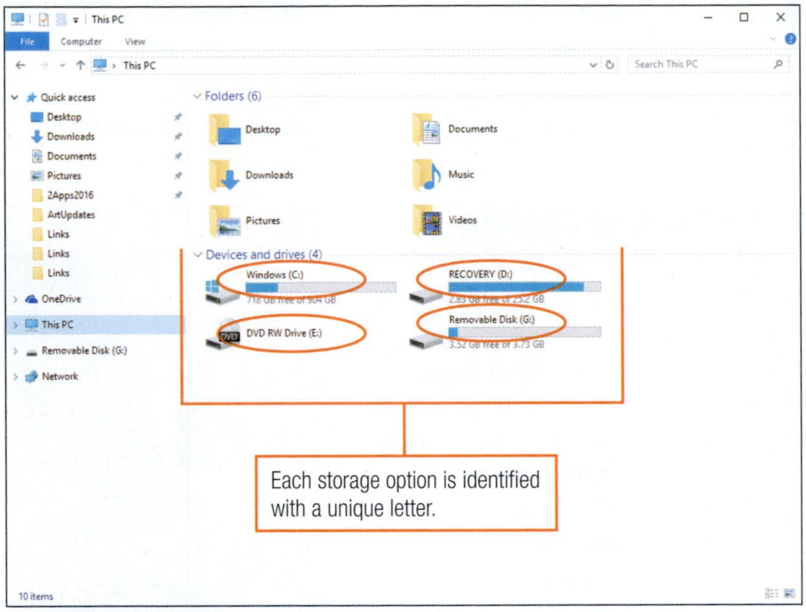

Figure 3.26

In a Windows-compatible computer, storage drives are identified with a letter.

Good to Know

A hard disk needs to be formatted before data can be stored on the drive. During formatting the disk is partitioned (assigned a logical container drive letter, such as *C*). In many cases, the HDD is split into multiple partitions for organizing programs and data files. For example, you might split a single HDD into two partitions: drive C for software programs, and drive D for data.

Hard Disk Drives

Inside the system unit of a PC is an internal **hard disk**, also called *hard drive* and *hard disk drive (HDD)* (Figure 3.27). The internal HDD is usually the largest storage device on a standalone PC and is assigned drive letter *C* on Windows-compatible computers. This is the storage medium upon which the operating system and application software programs are stored as well as data files. Hard disks are round pieces of metal called *platters* stacked inside a sealed unit with a magnetic coating on their surface. The disks spin, and a read/write head moves across the surface of the disk, magnetizing the data to the surface.

Figure 3.27

Internal hard disk with top cover plate removed to show platters and read/write head; a read/write head for each surface moves over the disks together as the platters spin.

An external HDD is a storage device that you attach to the computer using a USB port (Figure 3.28). External HDDs are a popular option for extending the storage capacity of a PC and/or for backing up documents, photos, videos, music, and other files.

Storage capacities for HDDs vary but are typically in the range of several hundred GB with newer computers having HDDs in the range of one to three TB.

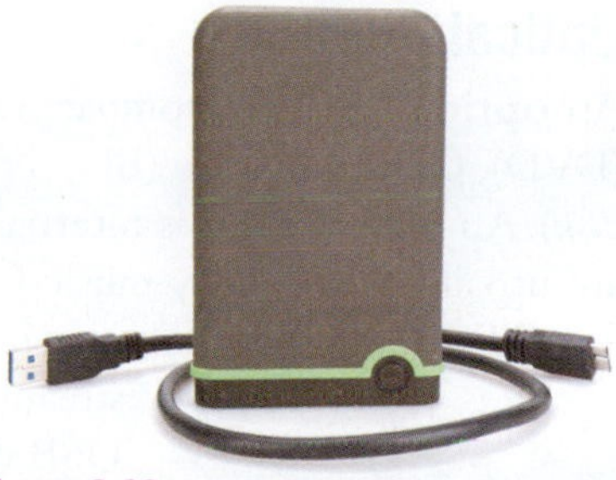

Figure 3.28

External HDDs are often used to back up an entire computer.

Good to Know

HDDs with a read/write head eventually fail. A common reason for failure involves a malfunction with the read/write head. When an HDD fails, it is often said to have crashed. You never know when an HDD will fail, so it is good to always have backup copies of important documents on another storage medium.

Solid-State Drives

Another type of drive technology called **solid-state drive (SSD)** is popular in mobile computers (Figure 3.29). SSDs use **flash memory**. Flash memory uses chips to store data electronically, instead of magnetically as on a traditional HDD. With chip-based flash memory, no mechanical parts are required inside the drive, making the device more durable. SSDs also weigh less than traditional HDDs, make no noise when operating, and require less power. Internal and external SDDs are available in storage capacities similar to those of traditional HDDs. A solid-state hybrid drive combines solid-state memory into a traditional HDD. The most frequently accessed data is stored in the solid-state area, with the rest on traditional hard disk platters.

Figure 3.29

SSDs are used in ultrabooks because they weigh less and use less power than traditional HDDs.

Network Storage

In some workplaces, data is required to be stored on a network drive for security and cost reasons. Network drives are HDDs installed in a server made available to users with access rights to the server storage via their user name and password. A network drive often has a letter assigned that is higher in the alphabet, such as drive R or drive S. Networked storage is automatically backed up daily at the server. Centralizing network storage is considered more secure than leaving data on individual HDDs scattered about a workplace.

Home users can connect various storage devices to a single wireless media hub for storing and sharing data with multiple devices and people. Wireless media hubs are also battery powered Wi-Fi routers and charging stations.

USB Flash Drives

A **USB flash drive** is a portable storage device with flash memory inside the case. USB flash drives are popular because they are easy to use, small enough to carry easily, and inexpensive. The drive is powered through the USB port of the PC. When you plug in a USB flash drive, a drive letter is assigned—usually *E*, *F*, *G*, or a higher letter, depending on the number of ports and other devices.

USB flash drives are made in all kinds of shapes, sizes, and colors. Some are disguised inside toys or cartoon characters. Others are available as plastic wristbands. Storage capacities meet all needs; some store as little as 2 to 4 GB, and some store up to 512 GB. USB flash drives with 1 TB of storage are also now available. Many other names are used to refer to a USB flash drive, such as *thumb drive*, *memory stick*, *jump drive*, *key drive*, and *pen drive*.

USB flash drives come in all shapes, sizes, colors, and capacities.

Optical Discs

An **optical disc** is a compact disc (CD), digital versatile disc / digital video disc (DVD), or Blu-ray disc (BD). Note that the spelling of this storage media is *disc* (not *disk*). An optical drive is internally mounted inside the system unit. Optical drives are usually used to play music CDs or watch movies on DVD or Blu-ray. Fewer and fewer PCs and notebooks are including optical drives because of the popularity of streaming media from the Internet and a preference to use USB drives. Netbooks and ultrabooks omit the optical drive to decrease weight and thickness and extend battery life. The optical drive is expected to become obsolete within the next few years. Optical drives are usually identified with the letter *E* or *F*, although this could vary depending on the number of other installed devices. A laser beam is used to read data from and write data to an optical disc. Recording to an optical disc is referred to as *burning a disc.*

With Blu-ray's higher storage capacity and better quality video and audio, Blu-ray media has mostly replaced DVDs.

Optical discs are sometimes used to back up important data or to make copies of music, pictures, or movies, since the removable media can be used in other devices and players and is relatively inexpensive. Optical disc types and storage capacities are listed in Table 3.3.

Table 3.3

Recordable Optical Discs and Storage Capacities

Type of Optical Disc	Media Options	Storage Capacity
CD	CD-R (write once) CD-RW (rewritable up to 1000 times)	700 MB
DVD	DVD +R or –R (write once) DVD +RW or –RW (rewriteable up to 1000 times)	4.7 GB for single-layer 8.5 GB for dual-layer
BD	BD –R (write once) BD –RE (erase and re-record multiple times)	25 GB for single-layer 50 GB for double-layer

Flash Memory Cards

Tutorial
How Can I Get More Storage on My Tablet or Smartphone?

The most common type of storage for a digital camera, smartphone, or other portable device is a **flash memory card** (Figure 3.30). A flash memory card is a small card that contains one or more flash memory chips (similar to SSDs and USB flash drives). Flash memory cards come in a variety of formats, such as Secure Digital (SD), CompactFlash (CF), and proprietary formats made by Sony and Olympus for their digital cameras. Capacities for flash memory cards can range from 1 GB to more than 60 GB. The type of flash memory card you would buy for a device depends on the formats the device can read.

Some computers and notebooks have a card reader built in for easy transfer of files stored on the flash memory card of a portable device (such as a digital camera) and the PC. Some USB hubs also contain readers.

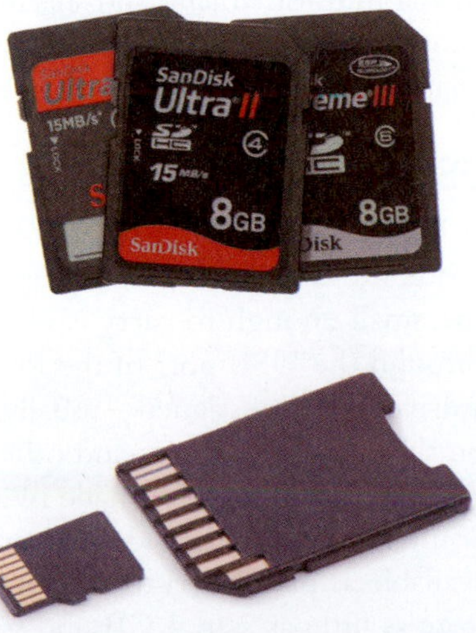

Figure 3.30

Flash memory cards are used for storage in digital cameras, smartphones, and other portable devices.

Cloud Storage

Recall from Chapter 1 that cloud computing involves accessing software and storage services from the Internet. Some cloud computing providers offer a limited amount of free storage space to account holders, with subscription plans available for those who need a higher capacity. For example, both Google Drive and Microsoft OneDrive allow 15 GB free storage at the time of writing. Other popular cloud storage providers are Dropbox and Box.

The main advantage with storing documents, pictures, video, or music using a cloud provider is the ability to access the files using a web browser from any location with Internet connectivity. You can also sync documents between multiple devices and easily share files with others. Transferring files via the Internet is fast and easy, and you no longer need to buy, organize, and store media, such as USB flash drives, CDs, DVDs, or BDs.

Storage capacities continue to grow to meet demands by consumers and businesses to store increasing amounts of data. The typical storage capacities mentioned here are likely soon to be replaced by higher capacity drives or media.

Storing files using a cloud storage provider is one way to access documents from multiple devices and easily share pictures or other files.

Good to Know

Gartner Research estimates that Amazon Web Services, a cloud service provider with about one-third of the global cloud computing market, has over 2 million servers in 11 regions around the world. In each region are located multiple data centers, and each data center can have between 50,000 and 80,000 servers!

Career Connection

Computer Technician

If you like hardware and are a good communicator, you may want to consider a career in computer hardware repair. Computer technicians troubleshoot and repair PCs and mobile devices. To succeed as a computer systems technician, you need to like working with customers as well as hardware. CompTIA's A+ certification validates entry-level knowledge and skills for computer support. Consider also enrolling in a program at a community college in PC/Desktop Support or PC Support Technician.

Explore Further — Comparing Cloud Storage Providers

Using a cloud storage provider to keep a copy of important documents or media files (such as pictures, music, and videos) has many advantages, but which provider offers the best deal?

1. Research three cloud storage providers other than Google and Microsoft. Find out how much, if any, free storage space is offered and the costs to purchase additional storage. Also learn the maximum file size that can be transferred to the provider's servers.
2. Create a presentation with one slide per provider. Describe the features, benefits, costs, and file-size limits for each provider. Include the URLs of the providers' websites where you found the information described. Conclude the presentation with a slide that states your recommendation for a cloud storage provider and give your reasons.
3. Save the presentation as **CloudStorage-YourName**.
4. Submit the presentation to your instructor in the manner she or he has requested.

Topics Review

Topic	Key Concepts	Key Terms
3.1 The System Unit	A peripheral device is hardware plugged into the system used for input, output, connectivity, or storage. The power supply is where you plug in the power cord. A cooling fan near the CPU prevents the CPU from overheating. A motherboard is the main circuit board into which all other devices connect. Expansion cards are plugged into expansion slots on the motherboard to provide or improve functionality. Data travels between components on the motherboard and the CPU via data buses. Parallel processing means the CPU can execute multiple instructions simultaneously. The instruction cycle is the process the CPU carries out to retrieve, decode, execute, and store an instruction. Clock speed is the number of instruction cycles per second the CPU processes, measured in GHz (1 billion cycles per second). L1, L2, and L3 cache affect system performance, since the CPU accesses cache memory faster than RAM. ROM stores instructions that do not change, such as the BIOS or UEFI instructions used to start up a computer. RAM is configured in modules that plug into the motherboard. The size and type of RAM affects system performance. External devices plug into a port attached to the motherboard. USB ports are the most common type of port.	peripheral motherboard expansion card data bus parallel processing instruction cycle clock speed gigahertz (GHz) Level 1 (L1) cache Level 2 (L2) cache Level 3 (L3) cache read-only memory (ROM) BIOS (basic input/output system) UEFI (Unified Extensible Firmware Interface) port universal serial bus (USB) port
3.2 Input Devices	Wireless keyboards and mice communicate with a wireless receiver plugged into a USB port. Special purpose keys on the keyboard are used to send commands to the active program running on the computer. Tablets and smartphones usually display an on-screen keyboard. A mouse detects movement using light technology and moves the pointer in the same direction you move the mouse. Buttons and a scroll wheel on a mouse are used to manipulate objects or send commands. On notebooks, a touchpad or track pointer senses finger movement and taps or finger pressure in place of a mouse. A touchscreen accepts input from finger gestures or a stylus (digital pen). A scanner uses optical technology to convert text and images into data. Other readers used for input are bar code, QR code, magnetic strip, biometric device, and RFID reader. Digital cameras, camcorders, and webcams are input devices used to provide pictures or live video to the computer or mobile device. Microphones combined with voice recognition technology are used to create data from audio sources. Various game controllers provide a means to input commands to entertainment systems.	keyboard mouse touchpad touchscreen stylus scanner bar code reader QR (Quick Response) code magnetic strip reader biometric device radio frequency identification (RFID) reader webcam microphone voice recognition technology

continued…

Topic	Key Concepts	Key Terms
3.3 Output Devices	Video display screens connect to a video port on a PC or are integrated into a notebook or mobile device. Newer monitors for PCs are wide-screen LCD or LED displays. A plasma display, often used for televisions, is expected to become obsolete due to advances in LED display technology. OLED displays are thinner and provide the best video output. Resolution is the measurement of horizontal and vertical pixels (squares with red, green, and blue color values) used to render an image. Higher resolutions produce clearer images. 4K UHD is a new display technology that uses four times the pixels as high definition. VDPs and interactive whiteboards are used to display computer output on large screens. Audio output is heard from speakers, headphones, or headsets. A Bluetooth headset is used to hear audio during voice calls. Printed copy of computer output is called *hard copy*. A laser printer uses a laser beam to charge a drum, which causes toner to stick to the paper as it passes through the printer. Inkjet printers form text and images by spraying drops of ink from ink cartridges onto a page. Photo printers are used to print high-quality pictures from digital cameras. Thermal printers heat coated paper and are often used to print receipts at retail stores. Blueprints and technical drawings are printed on plotters that move a pen across the page. Digital copiers connected to a network can be used to print output. Multipurpose printers include printing, scanning, copying, and faxing capabilities in one device. A 3-D printer produces a 3-D object by precisely cutting successive layers of material on top of one another.	video display monitor liquid crystal display (LCD) light-emitting diode (LED) plasma organic light-emitting diode (OLED) resolution pixel 4K UHD video display projector (VDP) interactive whiteboard Bluetooth headset hard copy laser printer inkjet printer photo printer thermal printer plotter digital copier 3-D printer
3.4 Network Adapters	A network adapter is any device used to connect to a network. The network adapter is the interface between a computer and a modem or router that allows data to be exchanged. Data is exchanged in a network using a system of rules called *protocols*. A network connection for a wired connection is called an Ethernet port. Ethernet refers to the type of cable used for the connection. Wi-Fi adapters are used to communicate with a wireless network. The 802.11 protocol is the name of the standard used for wireless communications in Wi-Fi networks. A USB wireless adapter and a wireless ExpressCard are external wireless adapters that can be purchased to connect to a wireless network. A Bluetooth adapter is used to provide connectivity within short ranges to other Bluetooth-enabled devices.	network adapter protocol Wi-Fi adapter 802.11 protocol external wireless adapter USB wireless adapter wireless ExpressCard

continued...

Topic	Key Concepts	Key Terms
3.5 Digital Data	Computers understand the binary system, which uses only 0s and 1s. The smallest unit in the binary system is a bit, which can have one of two values: either 0 or 1. A group of 8 bits equals a byte and represents one character, number, or symbol. Internet speed is measured in megabits per second, which is 1 million bits transferred per second. Files are permanent copies of documents, photos, or videos assigned a file name and measured in bytes. A KB is approximately 1,000 bytes. An MB is approximately 1 million bytes. A GB is approximately 1 billion bytes. A TB is approximately 1 trillion bytes. One MB can store approximately 500 pages of text. Images, music, and videos often require many MB of storage space.	binary system bit byte file file name kilobyte (KB) megabyte (MB) gigabyte (GB) terabyte (TB)
3.6 Storage Options	A storage device provides the means to read data from and write data to a permanent storage medium. Storage devices are referred to as *drives*. An internal HDD is usually the largest storage device on a standalone PC. Traditional HDDs are magnetic storage media. External HDDs are connected via a USB. SSDs use chip-based flash memory to store data; they are also more durable and use less power than HDDs. Some workplaces require data to be stored on network servers. In homes, a wireless media hub lets you store and share data among multiple devices and with other people. USB flash drives are portable, easy to use, and come in all shapes, sizes, and storage capacities. CDs, DVDs, and Blu-ray discs use optical technology to read and write data to recordable discs. Flash memory cards are used in portable devices, such as digital cameras. Some computers have a card reader built in for easy transfer of data from portable flash memory cards. Cloud storage providers allow you to store and share files that are accessible from any device with an Internet connection. Some cloud providers allow access to a limited amount of free storage space, with higher capacities available for a subscription fee.	storage device drive hard disk solid-state drive (SSD) flash memory USB flash drive optical disc flash memory card

Recheck
Recheck your understanding of the topics covered in this chapter.

Workbook
Chapter review and assessment resources are available in the *Workbook* ebook.

Chapter 4

The Operating System and Utility Programs

Precheck
Check your understanding of the topics covered in this chapter.

A computing device needs to have software installed for the device to work. *Software* is the term that describes the set of programs that contain instructions to tell the computer what to do and how to perform each task. **System software** includes the operating system that is designed to work with the hardware that is present. It also includes a set of utility programs that are used to maintain the computer and its devices. The **operating system (OS)** program provides the user interface to work with the computer, manages all the hardware resources, and provides the platform for managing files and application programs (the programs you use to perform tasks). It is the most important software on your computer, because without an operating system, the hardware and other software programs would not work.

For example, most often you go to your computing device because you have a specific task you want to do. Assume you want to log in to Facebook to check for updates from your friends. To do this, you start your computer and connect to the Facebook website. The computer first has to start the OS before you see the interface that allows you to launch the Internet browser program, such as Microsoft Edge. Without the OS, the interface would not appear, and the browser would not be able to connect to the Internet to load the Facebook page.

In this chapter, you will learn the various OSs available for computers, the typical tasks that OSs perform, and how to use a few utility programs to maintain and troubleshoot your computer.

SNAP If you are a SNAP user, go to your SNAP Assignments page to complete the Precheck, Tutorials, and Recheck.

Learning Objectives

4.1 List and describe the major functions of operating system software

4.2 Identify the operating systems in use for personal computers and describe characteristics that differentiate them from one another

4.3 Describe the functions of a mobile operating system and list the most common mobile operating systems

4.4 Explain the purpose of an embedded operating system and the purpose of a cloud operating system, and give an example of each

4.5 Describe common utility programs used to maintain a computer

4.6 Recognize and locate troubleshooting tools found in the operating system to solve computer problems

4.1 Introduction to the OS and OS Functions

The OS manages all the activities within the computer. The OS routes data between the hardware resources and the application programs as shown in Figure 4.1. The OS also starts the user interface and properly shuts down the hardware. Files that are stored on devices are managed by the OS. While you are working, the OS controls the flow of data between memory and the central processing unit (CPU). If you plug a new device into the computer, the OS looks for and installs the software that allows the device to work. Consider the OS as the conductor of a symphony; each instrument (hardware component and application program) needs the conductor (the OS) to direct when and how to play its individual piece so the song performs correctly.

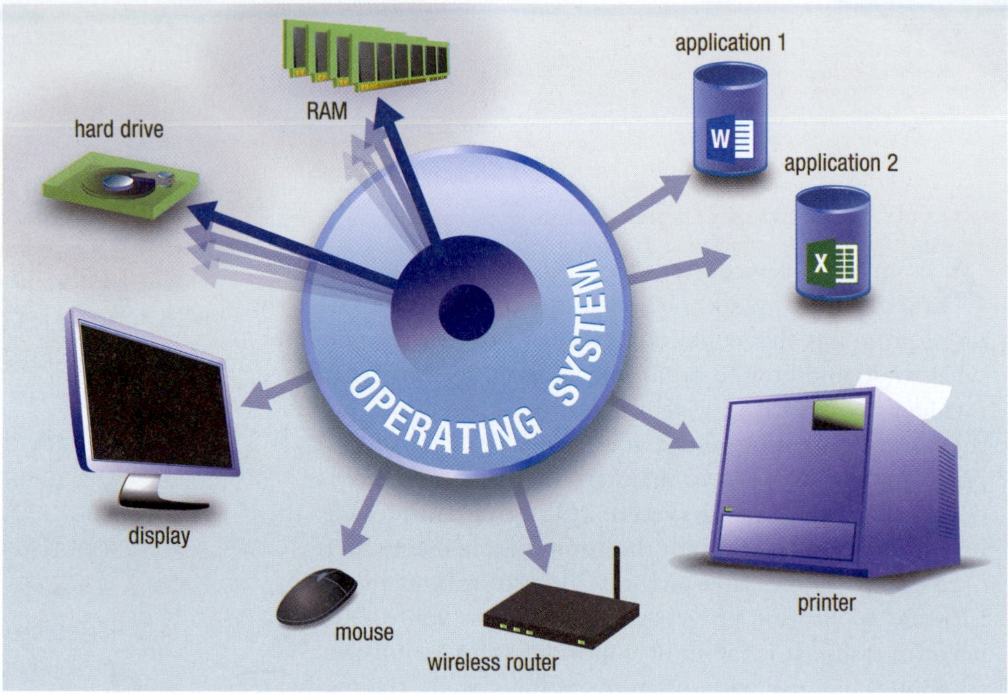

Figure 4.1
The OS controls the flow of data and manages programs and memory.

Starting and Shutting Down a Computer

Starting a computer is called **booting**. If you turn on a computer that has been shut off, you are doing a **cold boot**. If you restart a computer without turning off the power, you are doing a **warm boot**. The instructions for booting are stored on the basic input/output system (BIOS) or Unified Extensible Firmware Interface (UEFI) chip that resides on the motherboard. At startup the OS **kernel** is loaded into RAM where it remains until you power off the PC. The kernel is the core of the OS that manages memory, devices, and programs and assigns resources. Other parts of the OS are copied into RAM only when needed.

> **Good to Know**
> The term *booting* is derived from the phrase "to pull oneself up by the bootstraps." The bootstrap program contains the instruction that tells the computer where to find the OS.

As the computer is booting, a series of messages may appear on the screen depending on the OS you use. When the boot process is complete, the screen will display the user interface, the lock screen, or a sign-in screen. For example, on a computer running the Microsoft Windows 10 OS, after the lock screen is cleared, users see a sign-in screen prompting them to sign in with a Microsoft account and password. Following the sign-in process, the desktop shown in Figure 4.2 on page 89 appears.

If you decide to turn off the power to your computer, you should always perform a shutdown command so that programs and files are properly closed. Depending on the OS, choose the **Shut Down** option, which turns the computer off, or choose a

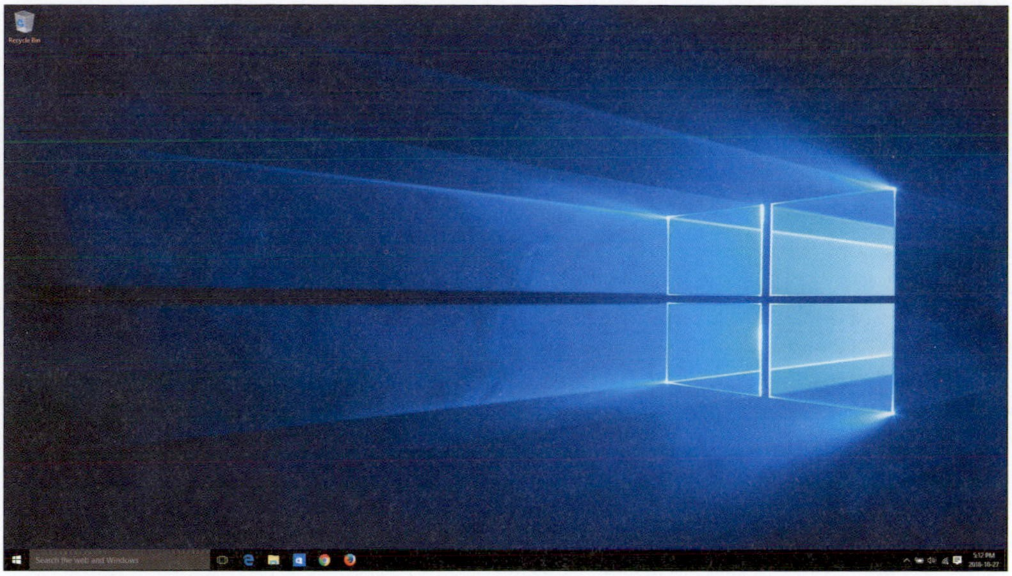

Figure 4.2
The Windows 10 desktop shown after booting and signing in to the system.

power-saving mode, such as Sleep, which saves open documents and programs while turning off unnecessary functions and devices.

Although different OSs are available for computers, most OSs perform similar functions. Most of these functions are performed automatically in the background, often without the user's awareness.

Providing a User Interface

The **user interface (UI)** is the means to interact with the computer. For example, in Windows 10, two methods can be used to launch an application program: (1) double-click a program icon on the desktop or (2) click the Start button and then click the program name or tile in the Start menu that opens. Most OSs provide the user with a **graphical user interface** (**GUI**, pronounced *gooey*) that presents visual images, such as tiles, icons, or buttons, that you click or double-click to tell the OS what you want to do.

Sometimes a **command-line interface** (see Figure 4.3) is used to interact with an OS. In a command-line interface, you type commands on the keyboard at a prompt to tell the OS what to do. Network specialists sometimes use a command-line interface to configure or troubleshoot a network device.

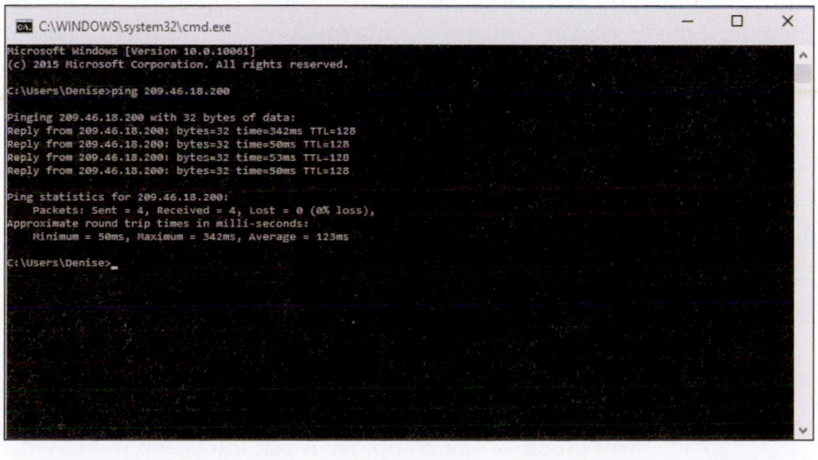

Figure 4.3
A command-line interface requires that you type commands from the keyboard at a prompt, such as C:\Users\Denise> shown in the last line of text in this window.

Managing Application Programs and Memory, and Coordinating the Flow of Data

The OS manages the installed application programs and provides you with the ability to run a program, install a new program, and uninstall a program no longer desired. When working at a computer, many people will have more than one program running at the same time. The OS manages computer resources, allocating data and software to and from the CPU and memory as needed, and determines the order in which tasks are performed. The OS also manages the flow of data between the CPU, cache memory, RAM, and the input and output devices. If you exceed the capacity of RAM, the OS uses space on the hard disk to store overflow data. The hard disk space allocated to store RAM contents is called **virtual memory**. In Windows, the Task Manager displays information about how the OS manages and coordinates computer resources (Figure 4.4).

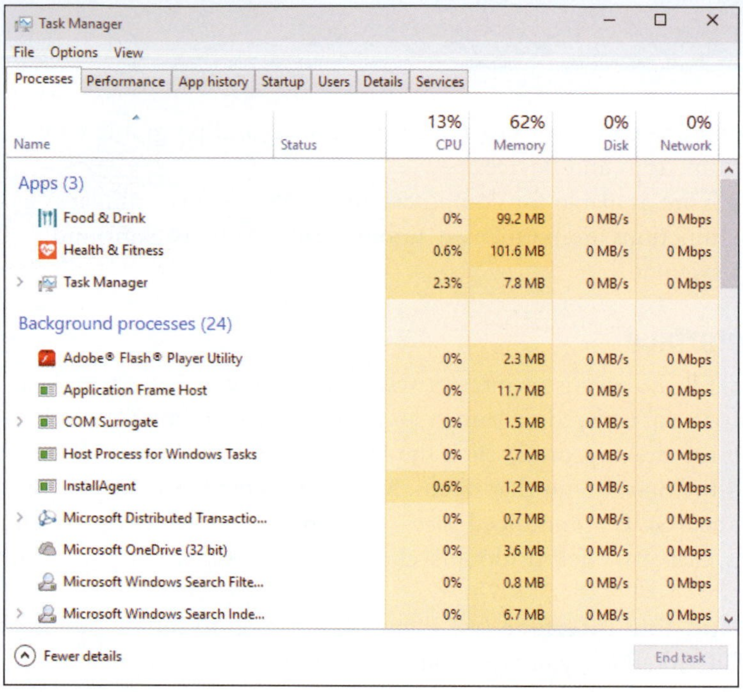

Figure 4.4
The Windows 10 Task Manager shows the many tasks the OS has to manage while you are working.

Configuring Hardware and Peripheral Devices

The OS configures all devices that are installed or connected to the computer. A small program called a **driver** contains the instructions the OS uses to communicate and route data to and from the device. When the computer is booted, the OS loads each device driver. If you plug in a new device after the computer is started, the OS searches the device for the driver, loads it automatically, and displays a message that the necessary files are being installed (Figure 4.5). This ability is called **plug and play**. If a device driver is not found, the OS will prompt you to install the driver from another source.

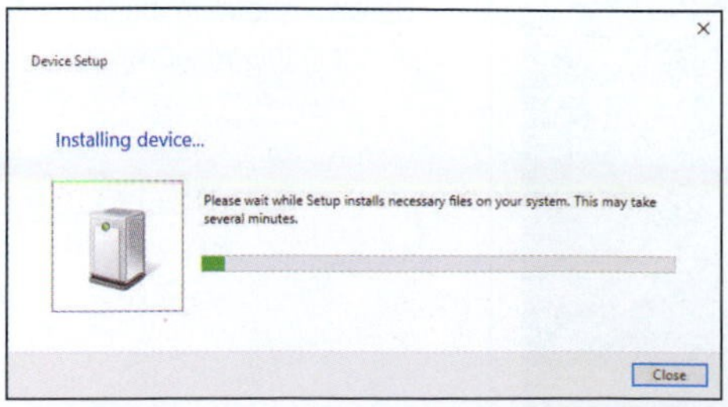

Device Setup
Installing device...
Please wait while Setup installs necessary files on your system. This may take several minutes.
Close

Figure 4.5
When new hardware has been plugged in, the OS displays a message indicating the files needed to run the device are being installed.

The OS is also used to manage other aspects of the hardware—for example, to adjust the screen's resolution, adjust the volume, and change the default settings for a device such as the window that opens when a music CD is played. The OS provides options for managing the power plan for the computer, including the time interval before the display is turned off or the computer is put into sleep mode when no activity is detected. The power plan options allow for different settings when the computer is running on battery power or plugged into a power outlet.

Providing a File System

The OS keeps track of the files stored on a computer's storage devices and provides tools you can use to find and then manage those files by moving, copying, deleting, or renaming. In addition, utility programs to search, back up, restore, clean up, and defragment storage devices are included in the OS package. Figure 4.6 shows a Windows 10 File Explorer window with a red box outlining the ribbon interface that has buttons to perform file management tasks.

Managing Software Updates and Security

Software often needs to be updated as program fixes, security enhancements, and new or modified device drivers become available. By default the OS is generally set up to download updates automatically, as shown in Figure 4.7, free of charge to registered users who have activated the software.

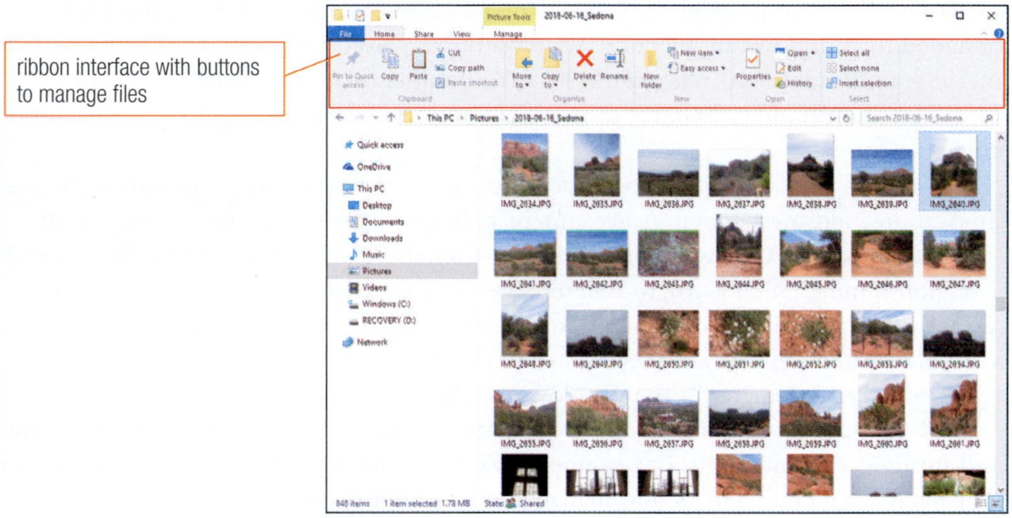

Figure 4.6

In a Windows 10 File Explorer Window, buttons on the Home tab are used to manage files and folders.

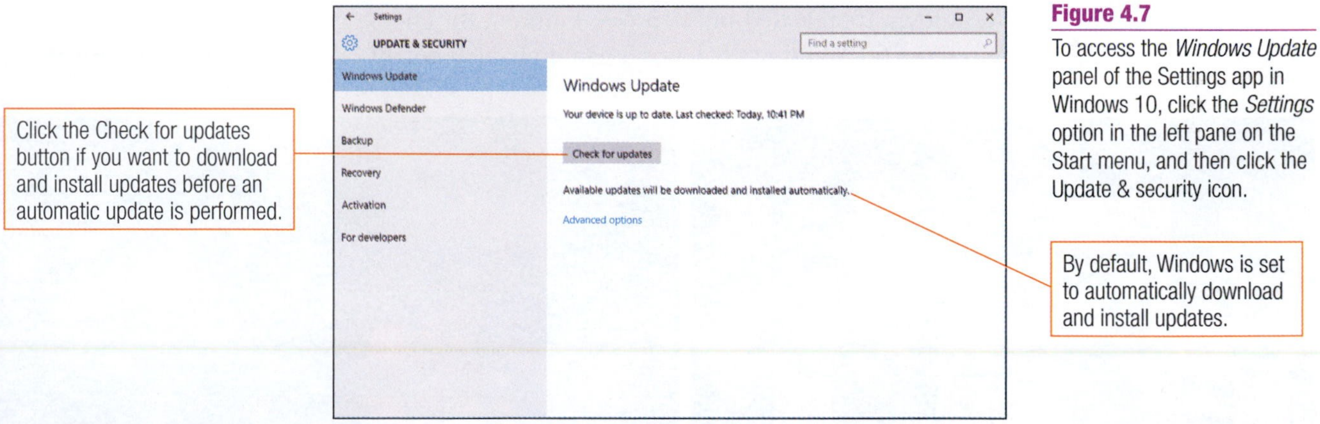

Figure 4.7

To access the *Windows Update* panel of the Settings app in Windows 10, click the *Settings* option in the left pane on the Start menu, and then click the Update & security icon.

Explore Further What Is UEFI?

UEFI was created to deal with the limitations of decades-old BIOS firmware used to boot up a computer. Many companies are replacing their old BIOS firmware with this newer interface.

1. Research to find a description of UEFI and to learn why computer companies are moving to replace BIOS with UEFI.
2. Create a document that describes, in general and in your own words, why UEFI is a more secure boot process and why BIOS is considered obsolete. Include the URLs for the websites you used to complete this activity.
3. Save the document as **UEFI-YourName** and submit it to your instructor in the manner she or he has requested.

4.2 Popular OSs for Computing Systems

Tutorial What's New in Windows 10?

When you purchase a new computing device, an OS is preinstalled so the device will work when you turn it on. The OS that is preinstalled may depend on the hardware, since some hardware is designed specifically for a particular OS. The term **computing platform** refers to the combination of hardware architecture and software design that allows applications to run. For example, buying an iMac computer means you will have the Mac OS installed because Apple computers are not designed to run Windows software. Four OSs typically installed on work, school, and home computers are Windows, Mac OS, UNIX, and Linux. You may also encounter a network OS on a PC.

Windows

Good to Know

Microsoft stopped providing support for Windows XP in April 2014. While the OS is still in use on some PCs today, home and business users are advised to upgrade to a version of Windows that is Windows 7 or higher to avoid problems that occur when updates are no longer provided. Extended support for Windows 7 is slated to end January 2020.

Windows, created by Microsoft Corporation, is the most popular OS because a wide variety of hardware is designed to run Windows and because software applications designed for Windows are plentiful. Windows has evolved from Windows 1.0, released in 1985, to Windows 10, released in 2015. You will encounter a variety of Windows OSs since the Windows brand is so prevalent and not everyone upgrades to the most current release.

Windows is updated as Microsoft develops new versions to keep up with hardware innovations, adds new functionality and/or redesigns existing functions, and overall strives to make the OS faster and more user-friendly. A new release is usually assigned a version number, such as 10, to differentiate the OS; however, with the release of Windows 10 in 2015, Microsoft adopted a new strategy: instead of releasing a new version of Windows every few years, it will use periodic updates to introduce new features and technologies in the Windows as a Service model.

Each Windows version generally comes in a variety of editions for various home and business environments. For example, Windows Server 2016 is used by businesses that need advanced security and management for networks.

The UI for Windows 8.1, released in 2013, is vastly different from the UI for Windows 10, released in 2015 (see Figure 4.8). The Start screen with live tile interface for Windows 8.1 was a game changer for PC users comfortable with the

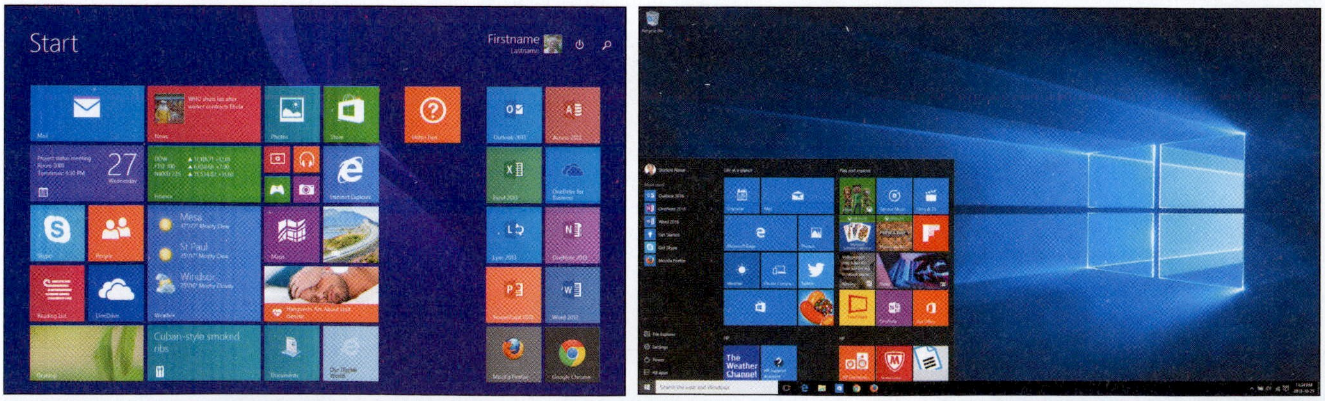

Figure 4.8
Windows 8.1 Start Screen (left) and Windows 10 Desktop with Start button menu (right)

desktop in Windows 7 and earlier releases. With Windows 10, Microsoft responded to customer feedback about Windows 8.1 and brought back the familiar desktop interface with a redesigned Start button. The redesigned Start menu offers Windows 8.1-style tiles in the right pane, along with access to all installed applications and settings in the left pane. Windows 10 also includes **Cortana**, a personal digital assistant, which can search the web, locate files on your device, and remind you of meetings or events in your calendar. Cortana responds to voice commands or keyboard input. It also keeps track of your likes and responses to alerts, and uses that information to personalize your interactive experience.

Check This Out ✓

http://CC2.ParadigmCollege.net/WindowsHistory

Go here to read the history of Windows developments from 1975 to today.

Mac OS

The **Mac OS** is the OS created by Apple, Inc., with the first release in 1984 for the Macintosh computer. The first Macintosh computer used a GUI interface and became the basis for the design of other GUI OSs down the road.

The Apple Mac OS X family is the most recent OS, with the El Capitan version, released in October 2015, shown in Figure 4.9. Apple uses a unique naming convention for Mac OS X, with a version sporting the name of an animal, such as Snow Leopard (2009) and Mountain Lion (2012), or a popular place, such as Mavericks (2013), Yosemite (2014), and El Capitan (2015). (El Capitan is also the name of a rock formation in Yosemite National Park.) Like Microsoft, Apple releases new versions to update functionality, responsiveness, and efficiencies to strive for faster, more user-friendly experiences. Server versions of Mac OS X are also available.

Historically, Macs were less prone to viruses since hackers went after Windows software because of its prevalence in the marketplace. However, with the rise in Mac sales in the past few years, virus attacks now hit the Mac world more frequently.

Mac computers have always been popular with graphic artists and those working in multimedia environments because the hardware is designed with high-end graphics processing capability. Consumer demand for mobile products from Apple, such as the iPhone and iPad, have increased brand presence of Macs in the marketplace.

Figure 4.9

Mac OS X El Capitan

UNIX

UNIX is an OS that has been around since the late 1960s and is designed for servers. Originally designed to be multi-user and multitasking, the OS is often used for web servers because of its robust ability to support many users. UNIX is available in several versions and is able to run on a variety of devices, including hardware built for Windows and Macs. In fact, the Mac OS from Apple is based on the UNIX OS. Although UNIX is a highly stable OS, the cost and higher level of skill required to install and maintain a UNIX computer make it less prevalent for typical computer users.

UNIX was designed as a server OS.

Linux

Linux was created by Linus Torvalds in 1991 and is based on UNIX. Linux can be used as a standalone OS or as a server OS. What makes Linux preferable to some users is that the OS is an **open source program**, meaning that the source code is available to the public and can be freely modified or customized. Linux, like UNIX, can run on a variety of devices and is available as a free download on the web, as well as by purchase from Linux vendors. Linux, because of its open source design, is available in many distributions (versions), such as Red Hat and Ubuntu. Figure 4.10 illustrates Linux Ubuntu. You can order some computers with Linux preinstalled upon request.

Figure 4.10

Ubuntu is one of the many distributions available for the open source Linux OS.

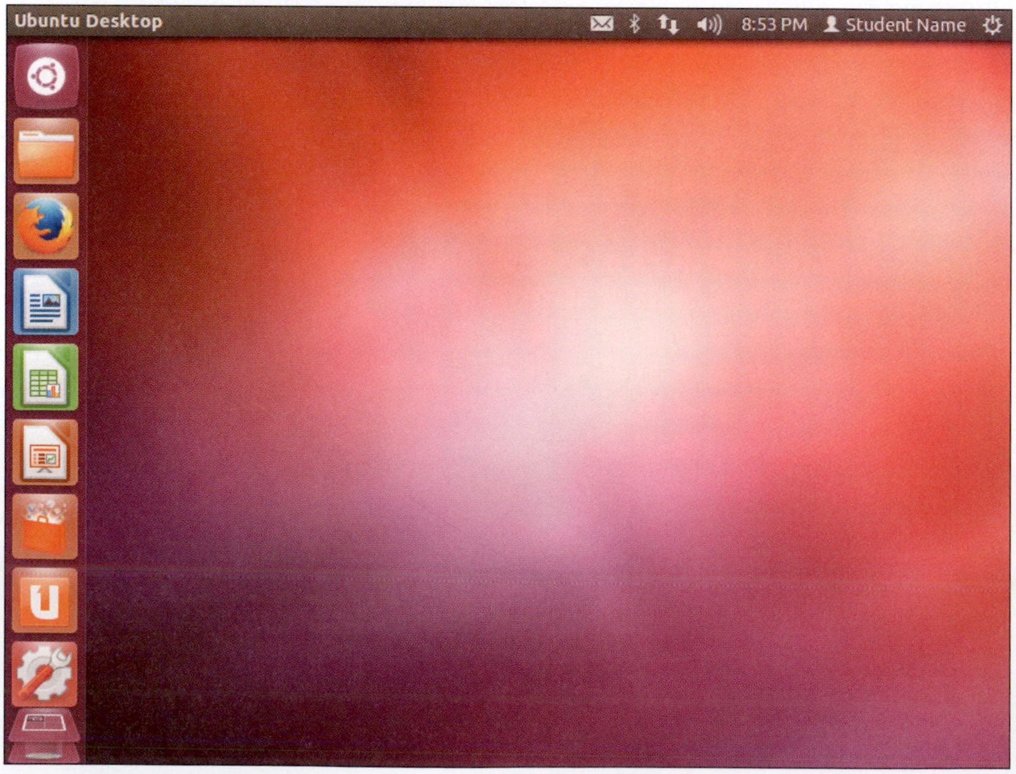

The open source software movement is increasing in large part owing to the lower costs associated with using free software. Linux can be found in use at companies such as IBM and HP, and a popular mobile OS is based on Linux.

Network OSs

A **network operating system (NOS)** incorporates enhanced functions and security features for configuring and managing computers and peripherals connected in a networked environment. Some PC OSs, such as Windows and Mac OS X, have basic networking features built in that let you connect and share files and devices within a home network. An NOS is used in the business world, where more advanced security and management features for connecting, sharing, and providing access to multiple resources are essential for maintaining large networks. Windows Server 2016 is the network OS produced by Microsoft.

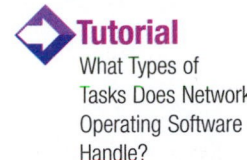

Tutorial
What Types of Tasks Does Network Operating Software Handle?

Blog Topic: To Upgrade Your OS or Not to Upgrade—What Will You Do?

When a newer version of an OS is released, some people immediately upgrade, relishing the opportunity to be on the leading edge and experience what's new. Others prefer to delay the upgrade and stick with the tried and true, assuming that it is more prudent to wait for the manufacturer to work out all the bugs.

1. Assuming that cost is not a factor in the decision to upgrade, write and post a blog entry that supports immediately upgrading or taking the wait-and-see approach. Give reasons for your position.
2. Read at least two of your classmates' blogs and post a comment to each.
3. Submit your blog URL and the URLs of the two classmates' blogs to your instructor in the manner she or he has requested.

Explore Further: Conduct a Survey and Look Up Statistics on OS Usage

Microsoft Windows and Apple Mac OS X are the most commonly used operating systems. Each of these OSs comes in several versions. Which OS and version is the most popular?

1. Survey a minimum of 10 friends, family, or classmates outside your class to find out which OS, including the version number or name, they use on their primary computing devices.
2. Next, using your favorite search engine, look up current statistics on OS market share on the web.
3. Create a document or presentation that shows the compiled results of your personal survey and the results you found on the web.
4. Add a short paragraph that describes the comparisons you found. Include the URL of the site you used for your web research.
5. Save the document or presentation as **OSStats-YourName** and submit it to your instructor in the manner she or he has requested.

4.3 Popular OSs for Mobile Devices

Tutorial
What Is 4G?

A variety of mobile devices, such as smartphones and tablets, use a **mobile operating system**, an OS designed specifically for a mobile device. The OS is stored on a ROM chip. This type of OS is designed to manage hardware and applications with less memory than a personal computer OS yet run fast and efficiently. The mobile OS often manages input from a touchscreen and/or voice commands, and routes data to and from wireless connections including cellular and Wi-Fi networks. Mobile devices also have cameras that are used for video calling and taking pictures. Mobile OSs manage small application programs, called *apps*, with support for multitasking among contacts, messages, calendars, music, video, social media updates, web browsing, and numerous other mobile tools. Several hardware manufacturers produce mobile devices, and some have developed their own OSs for use on their hardware. The most common mobile OSs include Android, iOS, and Windows 10 Mobile.

The mobile market changes rapidly as wireless technologies and software develop to take full advantage of faster speeds and capabilities. Competition in the industry is fierce, and companies that lag in new development quickly run into trouble. For example, the market share for Symbian, a mobile OS once used on most Nokia phones and popular in Europe, declined to less than 1 percent after Nokia announced a partnership with Microsoft. Consider also the struggle by BlackBerry to remain viable. A market leader in the early smartphone days, BlackBerry saw its share of the market decline to less than 2 percent in 2015 as a result of its delay in releasing a device with touch-enabled multimedia, web browsing, and apps similar to Apple and Android offerings.

Security Alert **Password Protect Your Mobile Device**

Imagine your lost smartphone or tablet resulting in someone posting embarrassing updates or photos on your Facebook account. Secure your device by locking it in case it falls into the wrong hands. Some devices provide for a touch or swipe motion to unlock; others require a typed passcode.

Android

Android is the leading mobile OS, used on many smartphones and tablets (Figure 4.11). The OS is based on Linux, making it an open source OS. In 2007, Android was released by the **Open Handset Alliance**, which is a consortium of 84 technology and mobile companies. A sampling of members includes Google, Samsung, LG, T-Mobile, and Sprint. The goal of the alliance is to develop open standards for mobile devices. Android is now maintained and developed by the **Android Open Source Project (AOSP)**, which is led by Google.

Each Android release is named after a dessert. The version in use at the time of writing is Android 6.0 Marshmallow. Android currently enjoys the highest market share for mobile devices, and Google Play, the website for Android apps, listed more than 1.7 million apps in October 2015.

Figure 4.11
Android is the OS of choice for mobile devices, including LG smartphones.

iOS

Apple developed **iOS** as the mobile OS for its iPhone, iPod, and iPad (Figure 4.12). The OS is based on Mac OS X. Users can download apps for their Apple devices only from the App store on their iPhone or iPad, or from iTunes on a Mac. Development of new apps for Apple devices is tightly controlled by Apple, meaning that new apps are generally virus-free, stable, and reliable. In the summer of 2015, over 1.5 million apps and games were available in the App Store and iTunes for Apple devices.

Figure 4.12
The Apple iPad Air tablet uses the iOS interface.

Windows 10 Mobile

Microsoft Windows 10 Mobile (Figure 4.13) is the edition that replaced the earlier mobile OS from Microsoft, Windows Phone. Windows Phone introduced the tile interface, which became the basis for Windows 8.1 for standalone (desktop) computers. In all three versions of Windows (Phone, 8.1, and 10), live tiles stream updates to the user's mail, calendar, and web apps.

Windows 10 Mobile for smartphones is considered to be just like the desktop edition of Windows 10 but optimized for the smaller screen—apps and settings operate similarly in both versions of Windows 10. The consistent design of Windows 10 across devices means that if you clear an alert on your smartphone, the alert also disappears on your laptop or tablet.

BlackBerry OS

BlackBerry (formerly Research in Motion) developed **BlackBerry OS** for BlackBerry devices (Figure 4.14). Although known for its superior messaging security and its BlackBerry Messenger tool, BlackBerry suffered a huge decline in market share before releasing four new smartphones in 2015 as part of a turnaround campaign. One of the new smartphones, called the Priv, incorporates the renowned BlackBerry security with the Android OS, which allows users to download apps from the Google Play store. Although no longer common as a consumer device, BlackBerry smartphones are still found in corporate and government offices.

Figure 4.13
Windows 10 Lumia 950 smartphone.

Figure 4.14
The BlackBerry Priv smartphone was released by BlackBerry in 2015 as part of a turnaround campaign to gain back customers.

Explore Further — Which Smartphone Would You Choose?

Assume you have just won a contest in which the prize is a free talk, text, and data plan for one year that more than meets your needs. All you need to do to claim your prize is to buy any smartphone you want.

1. Visit your preferred smartphone provider store or use the Internet to conduct your survey of smartphone providers and find your dream smartphone.
2. Once you have made your selection, create a document that explains your smartphone choice, the features of the smartphone, and your rationale. Include in your rationale a discussion of the mobile OS that resides on the smartphone and whether the mobile OS influenced your choice.
3. Include the URLs of any websites you used and/or the name and location of the store you visited.
4. Save the document as **Smartphone-YourName** and submit it to your instructor in the manner she or he has requested.

4.4 Embedded OSs and Cloud OSs

Computing consoles such as automated tellers, GPS navigation systems, video game controllers, medical equipment devices, point-of-sale cash registers, digital cameras, and a multitude of other consumer and commercial electronics need a specialized OS designed for the device's limited use. In these computing devices, an **embedded operating system** is installed. Embedded OSs are smaller and interact with fewer resources to perform specific tasks fast and reliably. Smart TVs use an embedded OS referred to as a *TV OS* to present a UI and manage the content options.

Cloud OSs, while not yet widely used, are a viable option for people with multiple devices who want seamless integration of software and documents.

Windows Embedded

Windows Embedded is a family of OSs in various releases, based on the familiar Windows OS, designed for use in task-specific devices that need to present a UI and manage input, output, and limited resources. For example, Windows Embedded and Windows Embedded Compact are variations recommended by Microsoft for an ATM or a digital picture frame.

Embedded Linux

Embedded Linux applications can be found running smart appliances, in-flight entertainment systems, personal navigation systems, and a variety of other consumer and commercial electronics. Similar to the standalone Linux OS, Embedded Linux has several distributions because it is an open source program.

TV OSs Embedded in Smart TVs

Televisions have evolved into entertainment hubs with a variety of choices for viewing content—traditional cable and satellite signal programming, streamed music, videos, movies, news, and more. Inside newer smart TVs an OS is embedded that is a **TV operating system**. The TV OS is the program that runs the set-top box, runs other connected devices, presents the interface for accessing content, and allows the viewer to navigate channels or streamed media. A TV OS uses apps to connect to resources, such as Netflix and YouTube, and accepts input from the remote control device or via wireless keyboard, smartphone, or tablet. A variety of TV OSs are in use, such as the LG webOS, Samsung Tizen, and Panasonic Firefox OS.

ATMs are just one of many kinds of electronic devices that require an embedded OS.

Car console and navigation systems use embedded OSs.

A TV OS presents a UI with access to apps that enable users to access content from a variety of resources in today's smart TVs.

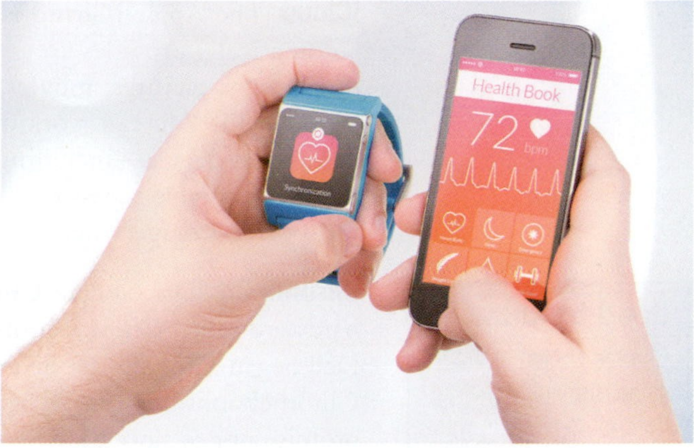

Android Wear is the OS embedded in some smartwatches.

Android Embedded in Devices

Android, the Linux-based OS, is not just for smartphones and tablets. Some home automation systems that control lighting, heating, air conditioning, and interactions with a smart appliance, such as a washer or dryer, are using an embedded version of the Android OS. Android Auto may be the OS running the console and navigation system in your car, Android TV may be the OS on your game console, and you might be checking time on a smartwatch controlled by Android Wear.

Cloud OSs

Some companies, such as Google, are developing OSs that operate like a virtual desktop. The interface may look and feel like a traditional desktop, but your settings, documents, pictures, contacts, and other files are stored in the cloud. This means you can access the objects from any device anywhere you have an Internet connection. A **web-based operating system** is not a true OS like Windows, and you still need a standalone OS on the computer to start your computer and access the web browser. The appeal of these systems is that extra software for applications does not have to be installed, and the ability to synchronize documents among multiple devices seamlessly is worthwhile as more people use multiple computers.

Cloud OSs are like a virtual desktop, with all settings, applications, and documents stored on cloud servers.

Check This Out ✓

http://CC2.ParadigmCollege.net/CloudOS

Go here to learn about eyeOS, a free cloud-based OS for those who register and create a user account.

Security Alert Protect Your Documents in the Cloud

Storing all your files in the cloud is not without risk of hackers or others making unwanted intrusions into your personal data. Make sure the service provider encrypts data, and choose a password that is difficult to hack. See Chapter 7 for information on encryption and creating strong passwords.

iCloud The Apple **iCloud** is built into every new iOS device. Once set up, iCloud automatically provides access to your email, contacts, calendar, notes, reminders, documents, pictures, movies, and more, on multiple Apple devices, as shown in Figure 4.15. You can work on documents in the cloud and access them from any connected device—including a Windows-based PC. If you download an app on one device, you have access to it on your other devices too. Apple typically includes 5 GB of free storage when you sign up for iCloud.

Good to Know

Chrome OS led to the establishment of the Chromium projects with the goal to develop a fast, simple, and secure open source OS for people who spend most of their time on the web.

Chrome OS The Google **Chrome OS** is a Linux-based OS available on specific hardware called Chromebooks, manufactured by Acer, Asus, Toshiba, and HP. In 2014 Dell began shipping the first Chromeboxes, desktop PCs with the Chrome OS. Chromebooks boast fast startup with built-in virus protection, automatic updates that promise not to slow down your device over time, and cloud-based applications, such as Google Docs, Gmail, Google Drive, and Cloud Print. You can also sync your favorite websites, documents, and settings with other devices that use the Chrome browser.

Google is constantly updating Chrome OS as it receives feedback from users and reviewers. Figure 4.16 shows the desktop edition with version 19.

Figure 4.15

After signing in with your Apple ID, the iCloud service connects you to Mail, Contacts, Calendar, and Find iPhone, and synchronizes documents, pictures, and movies from any other connected Apple device or PC

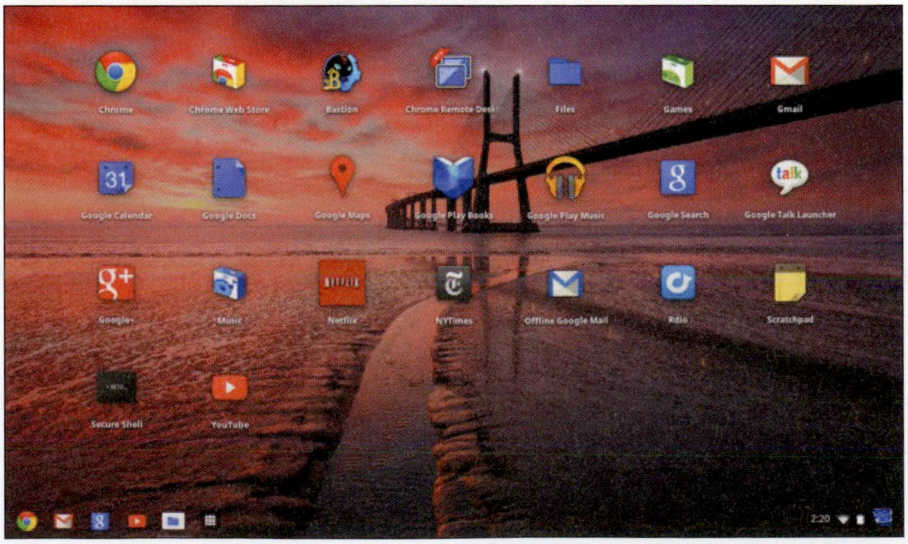

Figure 4.16

The desktop in Google Chrome OS version 19.

Career Connection

Careers in the Cloud

Cloud computing is growing, and businesses that use and supply cloud services are looking for IT professionals with the right cloud technology skill sets. According to Forbes.com, in 2015 there were 3.9 million jobs in the United States affiliated with cloud computing. The following skills were the top five most in demand: Structured Query Language (SQL), Java, overall software development expertise, Linux, and JavaScript. If you are interested in a career in cloud computing, look for certificate, diploma, or degree programs in that field. Cloud certification exams from companies such as Amazon, VMware, Cloud U, CompTIA, and Google are also available, although these exams are better suited to individuals with some work experience in an IT environment.

Blog Topic Is the Future Bright for Web-Based OSs?

Within a team, discuss the following question: *Will cloud-based OSs eventually take over from traditional computing environments in which all the software and files are stored on a local hard drive?* Consider the advantages and disadvantages of using a system in which all settings and files are stored in the cloud. What, if any, barriers will prevent these working environments from becoming commonplace?

1. Write and post a blog entry for your team with a summary of your team's position.
2. Read at least two of your classmates' team blogs and post one comment from your team to each.
3. Submit your team's blog URL and the URLs of the two classmates' team blogs to your instructor in the manner she or he has requested.

Explore Further Favorite Electronic Gadgets

Of all the many electronic gadgets available, which are the most popular? You can get some idea by working with a classmate to survey family and friends and analyzing your results.

1. Ask at least 10 family members or friends to name their favorite electronic gadget other than a smartphone or tablet. Examples can include MP3 player, GPS, gaming system, and digital camera.
2. Compare the results of your informal survey with a classmate's results and discuss the following questions: Which devices are named most often in both lists? Are there any devices that appear on only one list? Was there a response that surprised you?
3. Create a document that summarizes the two survey results and your discussion.
4. Save the document as **FavoriteDevices-YourName** and submit it to your instructor in the manner she or he has requested.

4.5 OS Utilities for Maintaining System Performance

Just as a car needs regular tune-ups to keep it running smoothly and efficiently, so does a computer. Files on the computer should be regularly maintained by removing unwanted files, and regularly backing up important files to prevent loss of data. Most OSs provide a utility to schedule regular maintenance. File maintenance utilities often include a file manager, a utility to clean up unwanted files, a disk defragmenter, and a backup and restore program.

Utilities that protect your computer from malware, such as viruses and spyware, are discussed in Chapter 7, Computer Security and Privacy.

File Manager

You open a **File Explorer** window to perform file management tasks, such as moving, copying, deleting, and renaming files. You can also set up your filing system by creating a new **folder**, which is where you store related files. A folder on a computer is similar to a paper file folder you would use in an office for paper documents you want to keep together. Open File Explorer in Windows 10 by clicking the File Explorer icon on the Windows taskbar.

In Mac OS X, the **Finder** utility is used to perform file management routines. Open a Finder window by clicking the Finder icon on the dock. See Figure 4.17 for a comparison of the Windows File Explorer and Mac Finder.

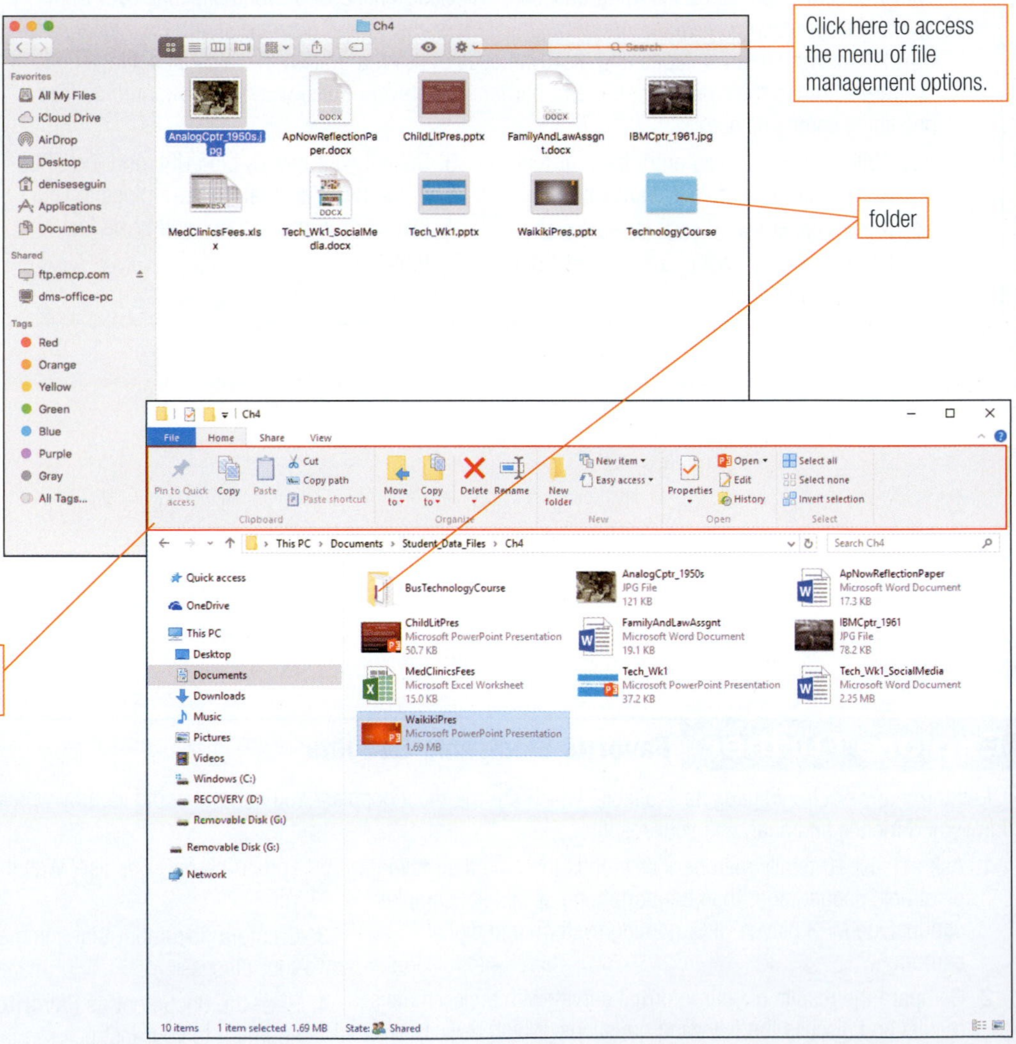
Click here to access the menu of file management options.
folder
Use buttons on the Home tab to perform file management tasks.

Figure 4.17
Perform file management tasks in a Finder window on a Mac (left), or in a File Explorer window (right) on a Windows PC.

Disk Cleanup Utility

The Windows **Disk Cleanup** utility (Figure 4.18) allows you to scan a particular storage device or drive to select various types of files to be deleted. Files the utility will flag for deletion include temporary Internet files, temporary application files, downloaded files, files moved to the Recycle Bin, and offline web pages. To open Disk Cleanup in Windows 10, click in the search box on the Windows taskbar, type *Disk Cleanup*, and then press Enter.

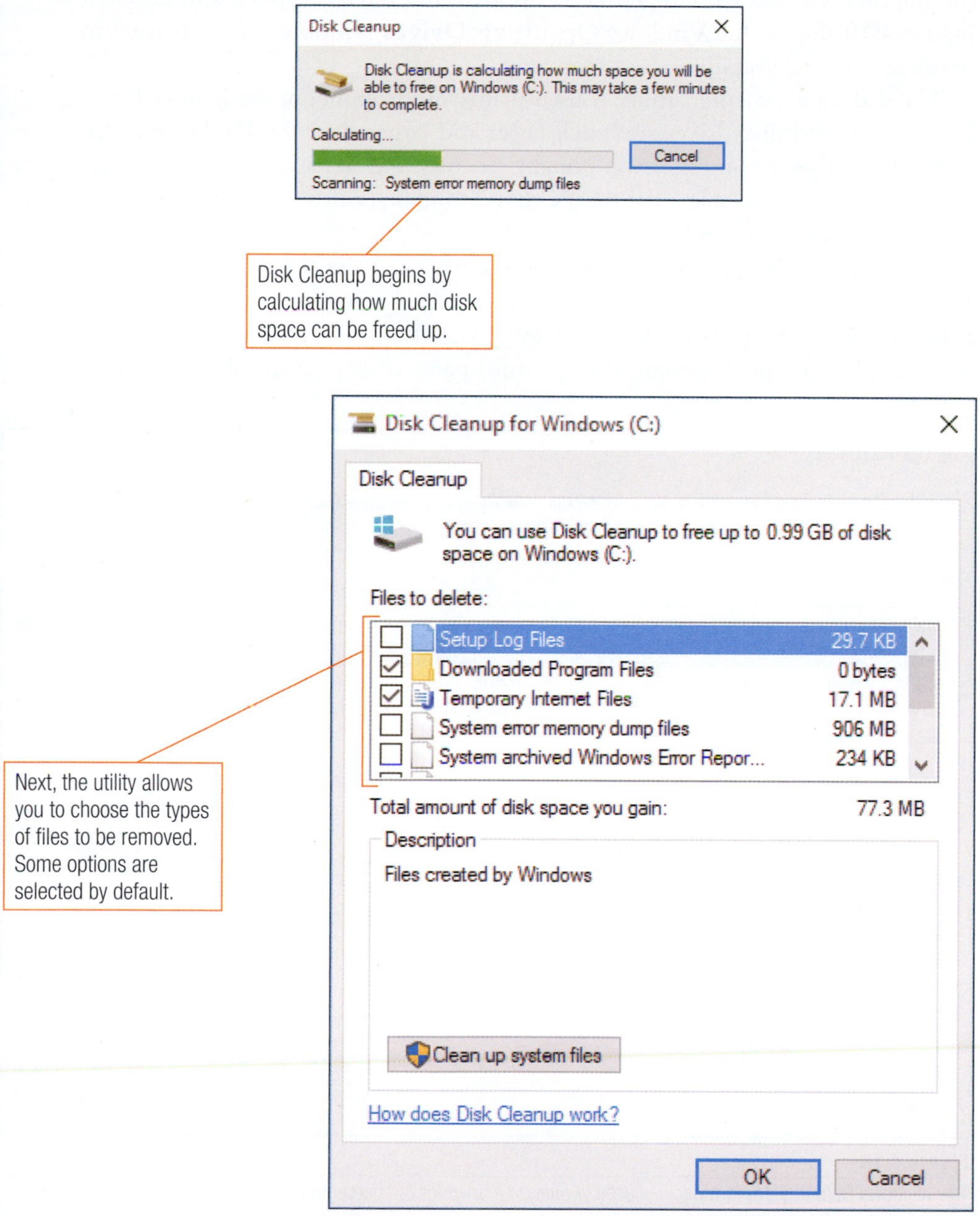

Figure 4.18

In Windows, the Disk Cleanup utility is used to help remove unnecessary files that clutter a hard disk drive.

Disk Defragmenter

As time passes, a disk can become fragmented as a result of files being moved or deleted. Files are stored on a disk in groups called *clusters*, and several clusters are sometimes needed to store one document. Sometimes the clusters needed for a document are not stored adjacent to one another. This is called a **fragmentation**. When you reopen a document that has been fragmented, the OS has to gather back together all the fragmented clusters and arrange them in the correct order. As more fragmentation occurs, disk efficiency decreases. A **disk defragmenter** rearranges the fragmented files back together to improve file retrieval speed and efficiency. Figure 4.19 shows the Windows **Optimize Drives** window, which is used to perform a disk defragmentation manually.

The disk defragmenter utility is used primarily by someone with an older PC. Today's hard disk drives are much faster and larger than the HDDs in older computers. If your computer was bought recently and has a large hard disk drive with lots of free space available, or if the PC has a solid-state drive, you do not need to run the disk defragmenter utility.

The Mac OS X file system works differently than the file system used on a Windows PC. Mac users do not generally need to defragment a disk because a Mac automatically defragments files on its own. For those rare instances when Mac users need to defragment their hard disks, a third party utility program is needed.

Good to Know

Solid-state drives (SSDs) that use flash memory are treated differently than traditional hard disk drives (HDDs) by the Optimize Drives utility. While a traditional HDD is scheduled to be defragmented weekly by default, an SSD is defragmented monthly. This is because SSDs do not become as fragmented as an HDD and have a finite number of times that data can be written before the drive is at risk of failure.

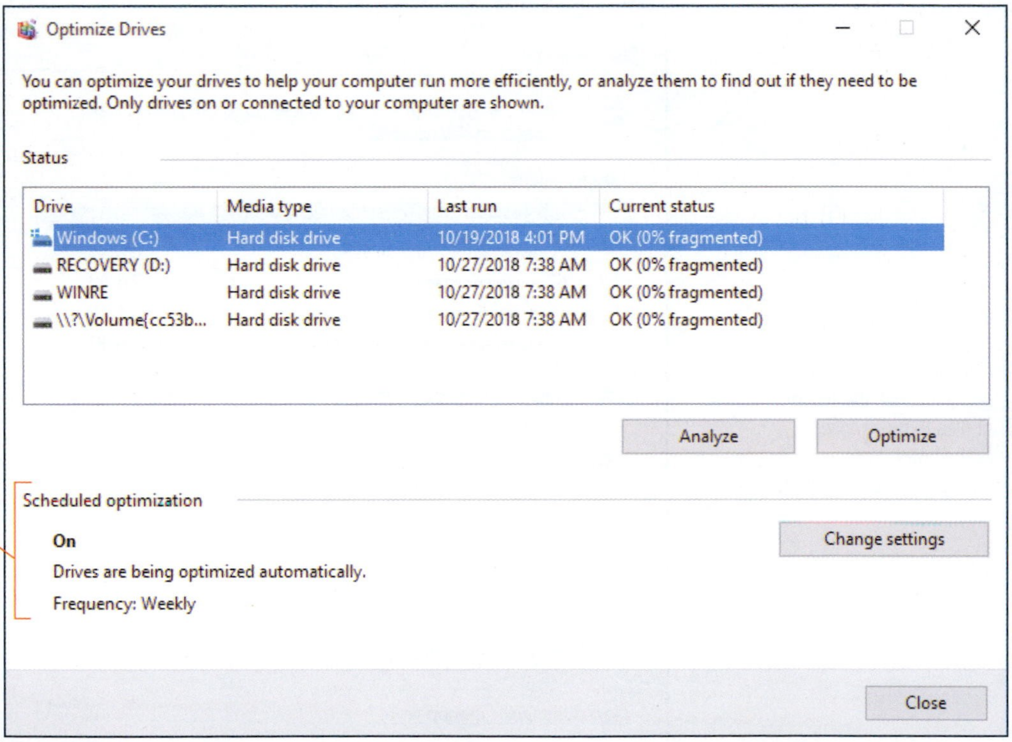

An HDD is scheduled to be optimized weekly by default.

Figure 4.19

The Windows Optimize Drives window is used to analyze a drive for the percentage of fragmentation, optimize the drive, and change optimization settings.

Back Up and Restore Utility

All computer users should back up important files regularly to prevent loss of data from disk corruption, accidental deletion, or other damage that keeps the files from being usable. A **backup utility** is a program that allows you to back up selected files or an entire disk to another storage medium. To begin a backup in Windows, go to the System and Security category in the Control Panel and then click the link to **File History**.

Files backed up using a backup utility are not stored in a readable format because they are compressed to save space. To copy files back to a disk drive in their original state, the files need to be restored. During a restore, a file or group of files is decompressed. Open the File History window to restore a file or group of files from a backup in Windows.

In Mac OS X, the **Time Machine** is used to back up and restore files. Click the Time Machine icon on the dock to start a backup operation. Figure 4.20 shows the Mac Time Machine utility and the Windows File History utility.

Good to Know

In the IT community, the Backup 3-2-1 rule is considered a best practice. Simply stated the rule is this: Have at least 3 copies of your data (original plus two backups); keep the backups on two different media (e.g., one on an external hard drive, one on a USB); and keep one copy of a backup offsite.

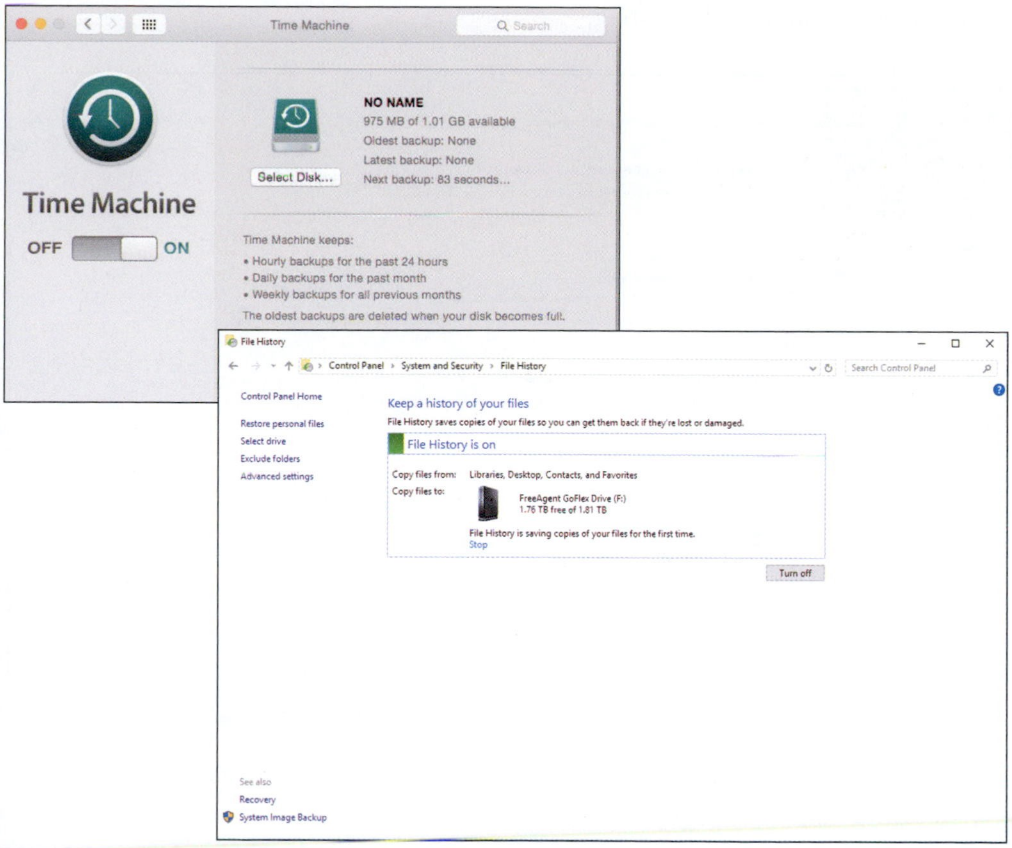

Figure 4.20

Go to Time Machine (left) on a Mac or File History (right) on a Windows PC to back up or restore files.

Explore Further — A Computer Maintenance Checklist

This topic introduced a sampling of common utility programs that are provided with the OS and used to perform computer maintenance. A comprehensive computer maintenance plan includes other tasks, such as wiping clean the screen and other peripherals.

1. Search the web for articles on computer maintenance to learn about other tasks recommended by computer experts.
2. Individually or working with a classmate, develop a computer maintenance checklist that you could use at home or at work to maintain your computer. Group the tasks by frequency, such as daily, weekly, monthly, and yearly.
3. Create the checklist in a document and arrange it in a format that is easy to follow.
4. Save the document as **MaintenanceChecklist-YourName** and submit it to your instructor in the manner she or he has requested.

4.6 OS Troubleshooting Tools

In a perfect world, the printer would always print, the connection to the Internet would always work, and your computer would always operate at blazing fast speed! Causes of computer problems can be complex and not easily resolved. However, knowing how to use a few of the tools provided in the OS package can help you fix some problems and get back to work.

Windows Security and Maintenance Window

The Windows Security and Maintenance window opened from the Control Panel shown in Figure 4.21 is a good place to begin when something is not working. The window displays messages when the OS has detected potential issues that need your attention. If the problem you are experiencing is not listed in one of the messages, click the Troubleshooting link to open the Troubleshooting window, and then click the link that most closely describes the problem you are having to open tools to help you resolve the problem. The prompts that display in those tools will vary depending on the issue you are troubleshooting.

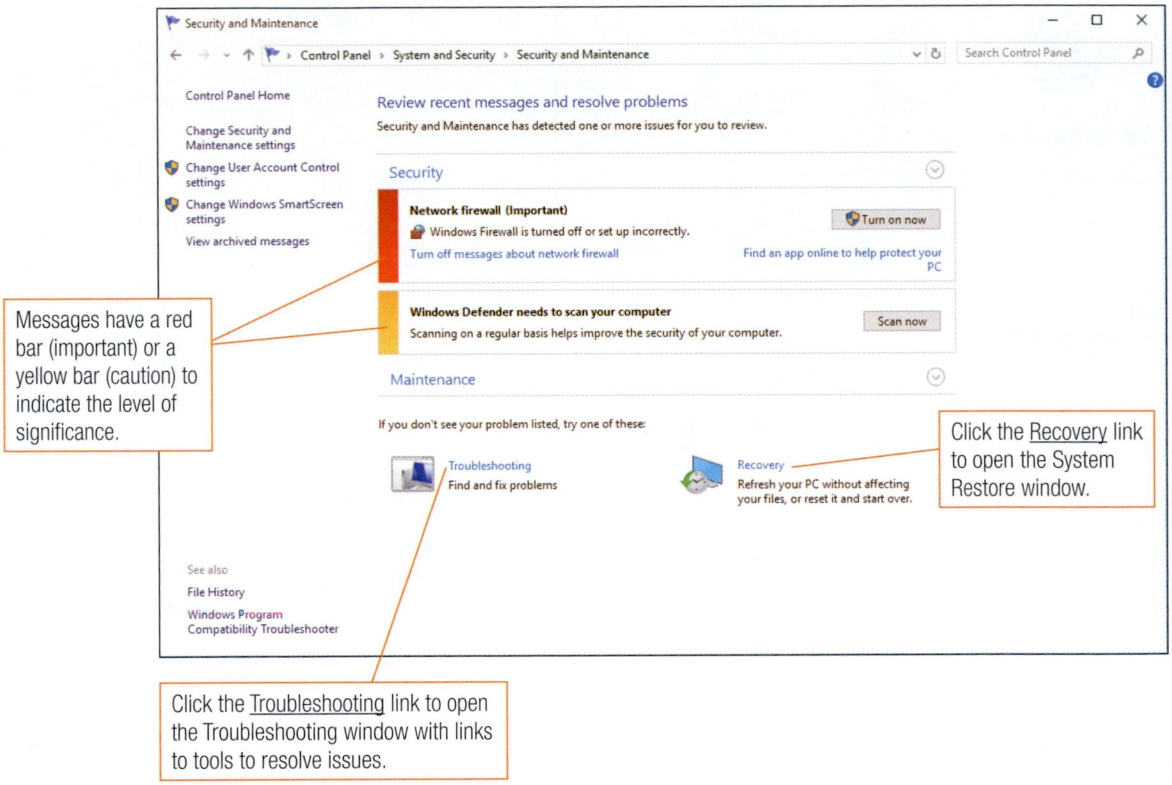

Figure 4.21

The Windows Security and Maintenance window displays messages about issues encountered on your computer and provides buttons and links to tools that can be used to resolve the issues.

Windows System Restore Feature

Sometimes a problem occurs after installing something new like a device driver, an application, or an update that inadvertently cause a problem with something else. Or you may accidentally delete or write over a system file and as a result cause a program or device to become unusable. In these cases, **System Restore** is a way for you to turn back the clock to when the computer was functioning normally. System Restore will undo a recent change while leaving all documents intact. You can access System Restore from the Security and Maintenance window. Click the Recovery link located at the bottom right of the window (see Figure 4.21 on page 106), and then click the Open System Restore link. At the first System Restore window (shown in Figure 4.22), click Next to begin a restore operation. At the next window, select an event from a list of changes that have been made to your system (Figure 4.23) and then follow the prompts that appear.

> **Good to Know**
>
> You can use a Windows utility named *Refresh* located in the *Update & security* panel of the Settings app to restore the OS without losing your personal files, personalization settings, or Windows Store apps. All software you installed from CDs, DVDs, or websites, is removed. Refresh is like reinstalling Windows but without losing your data files.

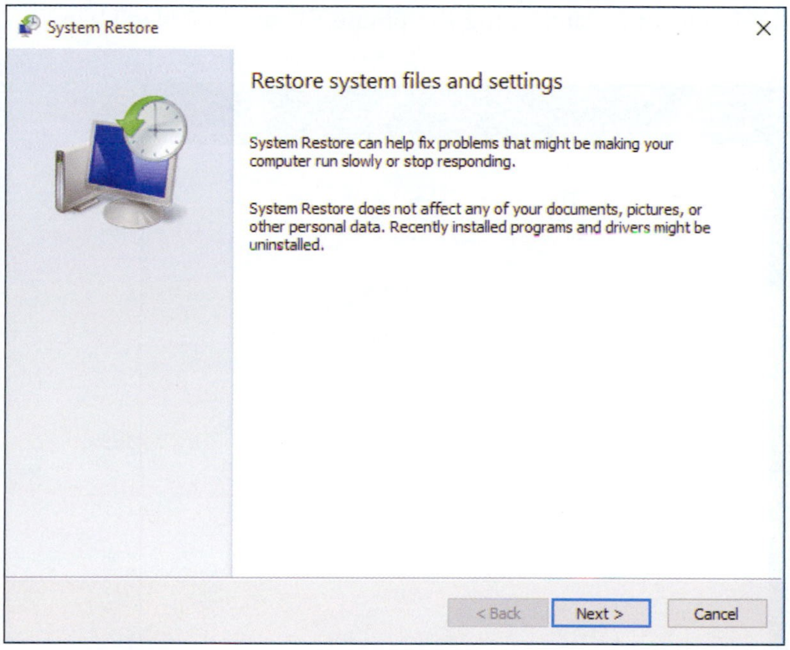

Figure 4.22
Click the Next button in the first System Restore window to start the process of undoing changes made to your Windows computer.

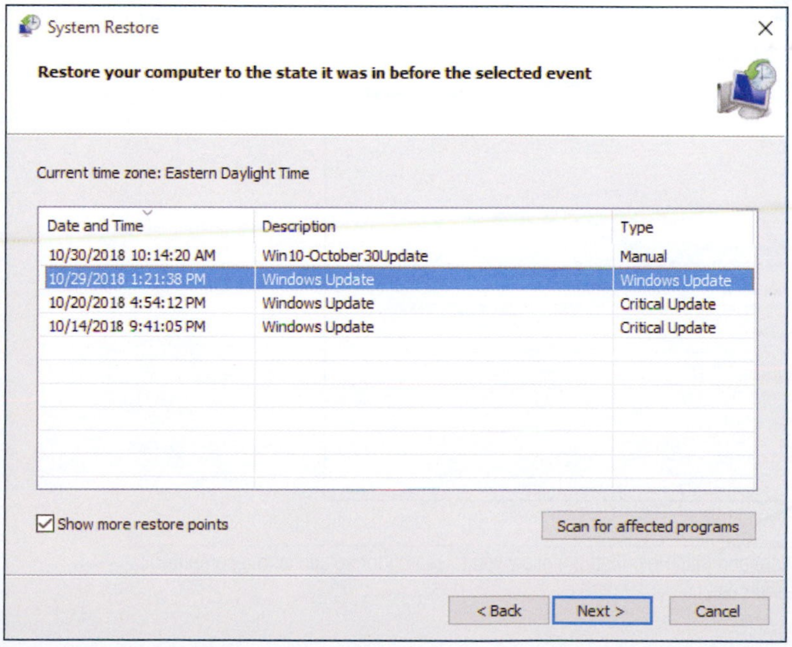

Figure 4.23
At the second System Restore window, select the restore point from the event list and then click Next to begin the restore process.

Help and Support

Check This Out ✓

http://CC2.ParadigmCollege.net/MicrosoftSupport

http://CC2.ParadigmCollege.net/AppleSupport

Go to the support website for Microsoft or Apple to find help by searching for articles, fixes, downloads, or other resources. Each company also hosts a community forum at its support website, where users share tips and solutions.

OSs offer extensive help and support that you can search to find answers to most questions and issues. In Windows you can access the Get Started app by typing *Help* in the search box on the Windows taskbar, and then clicking *Get Started* at the top of the search results list. In the Get Started app, click a category in the left panel to view available help topics displayed as icons in the right panel. Click an icon to read help information. Figure 4.24 shows the help topic icons for the Get connected category in the Get Started app.

In most cases, you can locate help more quickly by typing a short phrase that describes the feature or other issue in the search box on the Windows taskbar and then clicking a link in the search results list.

On a Mac device, access the Help utility from the menu bar along the top of the screen, type a search phrase in the search text box, and then select a topic in the results list that appears, or choose *Show All Help Topics* to browse help in a window. Figure 4.24 shows the results of a search using the phrase *fix sound* in Mac Help.

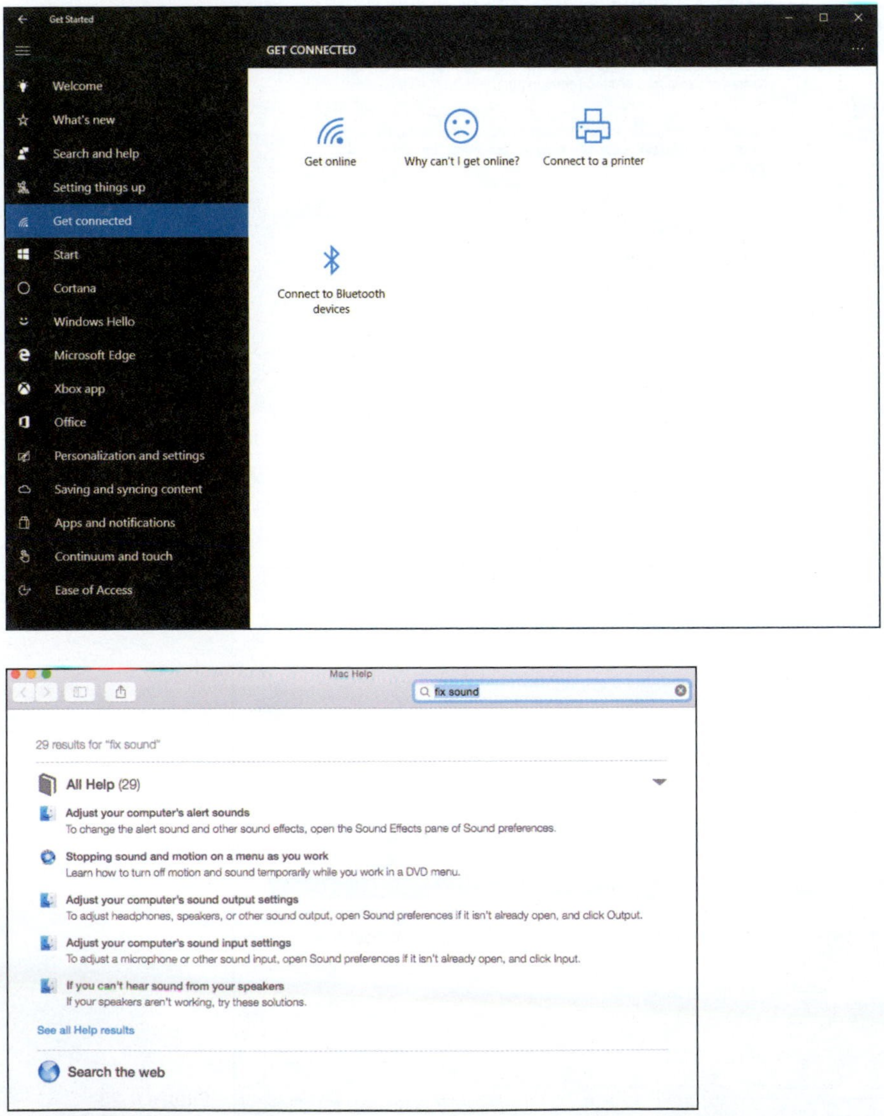

Figure 4.24

Windows Get Started app (top) and Mac Help (bottom) allow you to search for solutions to a computer issue in extensive online resources.

Career Connection

Careers in Technical Support

Help desk and technical support ranked sixth among the 10 most in-demand IT skills forecast for 2016 by *Computerworld*. IT executives reported a growing need for help desk and support technicians because of a growth in projects and bring-your-own-device programs that have added complexity and volume of work to the IT department. Certifications to demonstrate your ability to work well in this field include CompTIA A+ certification geared toward workers in desktop support, and MTA (Microsoft Technology Associate), MCSA (Microsoft Certified Solutions Associate), and MCSE (Microsoft Certified Solutions Expert), which validate your skills in troubleshooting Microsoft technology. Go to **http://CC2.ParadigmCollege.net/Certifications** to learn more about Microsoft certifications.

Blog Topic How I Fixed My Computer

Almost everyone has had to troubleshoot a computer issue at some point. Think about the last time you had a problem with your computer and how you resolved the problem. If you do not have an experience that you can recall, ask a family member or friend to describe his or her experience to you.

1. Write and post a blog entry that relates the computer issue and the way it was resolved. Include tips or techniques learned from the experience to prevent the problem from reoccurring.
2. Read at least two of your classmates' blogs and post one comment to each.
3. Submit your blog URL and the URLs of the two classmates' blogs to your instructor in the manner she or he has requested.

Explore Further Common Computer Problems

Everyone who uses a computer will eventually experience a problem. Some computer problems seem to crop up more commonly than others. Knowing about these common computer problems and their solutions will save you time when you encounter them.

1. Find articles that describe five common computer problems and how to fix them.
2. Create a presentation with one issue per slide and include recommendations for how to fix each problem.
3. At the end of your presentation, add a slide listing the URL(s) of websites that you used for research.
4. Save the presentation as **ComputerProblems-YourName** and submit it to your instructor in the manner she or he has requested.

Topics Review

Topic	Key Concepts	Key Terms
4.1 Introduction to the OS and OS Functions	System software consists of the OS plus a set of utility programs used to maintain a computer. OS software provides a UI, manages the computer's hardware and software, and provides a system for managing files. Starting a computer is called *booting*; starting from a no-power state is a cold boot and restarting a powered-on computer is a warm boot. At startup, the OS core called the kernel, which manages memory, devices, and programs, is loaded into RAM. Use the Shut Down command to turn off the power to a computer so that programs and files are properly closed. The UI is the method with which you interact with the computer. A GUI uses visual images, such as icons, that the user clicks. With a command-line interface, commands are typed at a prompt. The OS coordinates the flow of data and activities between hardware resources and application programs. For example, when RAM has reached capacity, the OS uses hard disk space, called *virtual memory*, to store RAM contents. The OS configures hardware and peripheral devices by using a driver. A driver is a small program with instructions that tell the OS how to communicate with a device. With plug and play capability, a driver is automatically installed by the OS when a new device is plugged in. The OS keeps track of all files stored on a system and provides the tools with which to manage those files. The OS performs automatic updates for program fixes, security enhancements, and new or modified drivers.	system software operating system (OS) booting cold boot warm boot kernel Shut Down user interface (UI) graphical user interface (GUI) command-line interface virtual memory driver plug and play
4.2 Popular OSs for Computing Systems	A computing platform is a combination of hardware architecture and software design for a specific OS. Windows is the most popular OS. A variety of hardware is designed to run Windows OS and Windows applications. Windows 10 restored the familiar desktop interface and introduced a redesigned Start button that combines the live tile interface from Windows 8.1 with a menu system. Cortana, in Windows 10, is a personal digital assistant that responds to voice commands or keyboard input to help you work. Mac OS X is the OS used for Apple Mac computers. Mac OS was the originator of the GUI. UNIX was developed in the 1960s for servers and is a popular choice for web servers. Linux, created in 1991, is an open source OS (meaning that it can be freely modified or customized) that runs on a variety of devices. A NOS, such as Windows Server 2016, has enhanced functions and security features for managing networked environments.	computing platform Windows Cortana Mac OS UNIX Linux open source program network operating system (NOS)

continued…

Topic	Key Concepts	Key Terms
4.3 Popular OSs for Mobile Devices	Mobile OSs, stored on a ROM chip, handle smaller hardware and apps with less memory. Mobile OSs include support for cameras, touchscreen and/or voice commands for input, and video calling. Android was released by the Open Handset Alliance, a collaboration of 84 technology and mobile companies that develops open standards for mobile devices. The AOSP is now tasked with maintaining and developing Android. iOS is the mobile OS developed by Apple for the iPhone, iPod, and iPad. Windows 10 Mobile is the mobile OS developed by Microsoft for Windows smartphones. BlackBerry developed the BlackBerry OS to support its family of BlackBerry devices.	mobile operating system Android Open Handset Alliance Android Open Source Project (AOSP) iOS BlackBerry OS
4.4 Embedded OSs and Cloud OSs	Consumer and commercial electronic devices use an embedded OS designed for their limited use. Windows Embedded is a family of embedded OSs used on a variety of task-specific devices. Embedded Linux is similar to standalone Linux and is used in a variety of consumer and commercial electronics. Smart TVs use an embedded OS called a TV OS to present a UI, manage content, and manage input from a remote control, wireless keyboard, smartphone, or tablet. Android is used as the embedded OS for many electronic devices and includes releases such as Android Auto and Android Wear. A web-based OS is a virtual desktop for accessing files and apps anywhere via the Internet. iCloud is built into every iOS device and syncs documents in the cloud to all devices, including PCs. Chrome OS is available on Chromebooks and supports cloud-based Google apps.	embedded operating system Windows Embedded Embedded Linux TV operating system web-based operating system iCloud Chrome OS
4.5 OS Utilities for Maintaining System Performance	File Explorer for Windows and Finder for Mac are utilities for file maintenance, such as moving or deleting files. A folder is a place for storing associated files. Disk Cleanup is a utility used to remove unwanted files. Fragmentation occurs when file clusters for the same file are not stored next to each other. A disk defragmenter utility, such as Windows Optimize Drives, increases disk speed and efficiency by putting file clusters back together. Newer computers with faster and very large hard disks or solid-state drives do not need to be defragmented. A backup utility, such as the Windows File History or Mac Time Machine, is used to back up files and restore backed-up files to their original state.	File Explorer folder Finder Disk Cleanup fragmentation disk defragmenter Optimize Drives backup utility File History Time Machine

continued...

Topic	Key Concepts	Key Terms
4.6 OS Troubleshooting Tools	The Windows Security and Maintenance window displays messages about issues and has tools to resolve problems. System Restore reverses a recent system change. The Windows Get Started app or Mac Help is used to find answers to questions or issues.	System Restore

Recheck

Recheck your understanding of the topics covered in this chapter.

Workbook

Chapter review and assessment resources are available in the *Workbook* ebook.

Chapter 5

Application Software

Precheck

Check your understanding of the topics covered in this chapter.

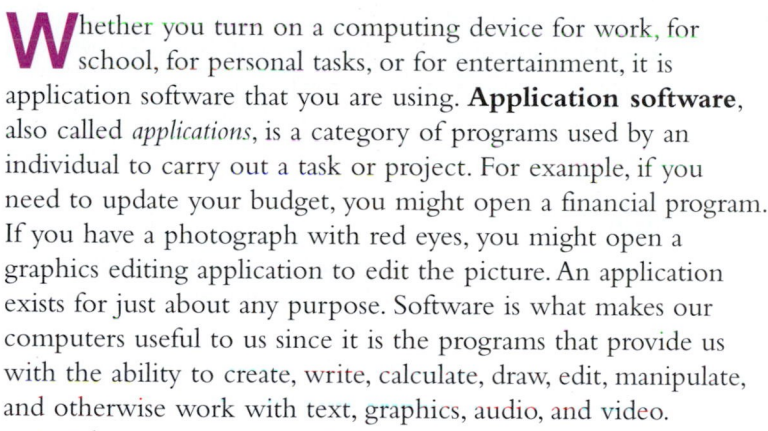

Whether you turn on a computing device for work, for school, for personal tasks, or for entertainment, it is application software that you are using. **Application software**, also called *applications*, is a category of programs used by an individual to carry out a task or project. For example, if you need to update your budget, you might open a financial program. If you have a photograph with red eyes, you might open a graphics editing application to edit the picture. An application exists for just about any purpose. Software is what makes our computers useful to us since it is the programs that provide us with the ability to create, write, calculate, draw, edit, manipulate, and otherwise work with text, graphics, audio, and video.

In Chapter 4, you learned about system software and the role of the operating system (OS) to route and manage data between the hardware and the other programs that are running. Once a computer is started and the OS is loaded, you are ready to start the application in which you want to work. In this chapter, you will learn about software applications commonly used in the workplace and by individuals. You will also learn how to manage the software on your computing device, and you will survey mobile apps for a smartphone, tablet, or wearable device.

Learning Objectives

5.1 Describe typical uses for a word processor, spreadsheet, presentation, and database management software application

5.2 Identify personal information management, accounting, project management, and document management software applications

5.3 Distinguish applications used for graphics, publications, multimedia, and web projects

5.4 List and explain types of applications intended for personal use

5.5 Describe the uses and benefits of web-based and open source applications

5.6 Explain how to acquire, install, uninstall, and upgrade software programs

5.7 Describe the functionality of a mobile application and give examples of mobile apps

SNAP If you are a SNAP user, go to your SNAP Assignments page to complete the Precheck, Tutorials, and Recheck.

5.1 Productivity Applications for the Workplace

> **Check This Out ✓**
> **http://CC2.ParadigmCollege.net/MicrosoftOfficeOnline**
> Go here to access the free web-based versions of Microsoft Office software: Word Online, Excel Online, and PowerPoint Online. You will learn more about these web-based applications in Topic 5.5.

Software for the workplace generally includes programs for producing word processing documents (working with text), spreadsheets (calculating and managing numbers), presentations (slide shows), and database management systems (keeping track of data). These software programs are called **productivity software** because they are used in the workplace to perform a wide variety of business-related tasks.

A group of productivity software applications will typically be bundled together in what is called a **software suite** or **productivity suite**. While many variations of a software suite exist, a minimum bundle includes word processing, spreadsheet, presentation, and email applications. For example, the Microsoft Office Standard Suite includes Microsoft Word for word processing documents, Microsoft Excel for spreadsheets, Microsoft PowerPoint for presentations, and Microsoft Outlook for email. Microsoft offers its popular Office suite in several different bundles (called *editions*) to provide groups of programs to suit a variety of office environments.

Microsoft also publishes a version of Office designed for Mac computers. Alternatives to Microsoft Office and Apple productivity applications include OpenOffice, a free productivity suite made available by the open source community, and web-based productivity software offered by cloud providers, such as Google and Zoho. These applications are introduced in Topic 5.5.

Regardless of the suite you use, the productivity applications will have similar features. In this topic, you will learn the features and uses for four productivity applications: word processing, spreadsheet, presentation, and database management software.

Word Processing Applications

A **word processing application** is software used to create documents containing mostly text. Images and other multimedia are often included with text in a document to add visual appeal and assist with understanding content. Figure 5.1 presents a trip planner document for the Grand Canyon in Microsoft Word. Apple's word processor is called Pages. With a word processing program, individuals create a variety of documents, such as essays, reports, letters, memos, contracts, brochures, catalogs, menus, newsletters, mailings, labels, articles, blogs, and journals. Word processing programs generally include the following features:

- text formatting options to change the typestyle, color, size, and style of text, called *fonts* and *font attributes*
- bold, underline, italic, and other text effects, such as shadow and strikethrough
- spelling and grammar checking, as well as a thesaurus

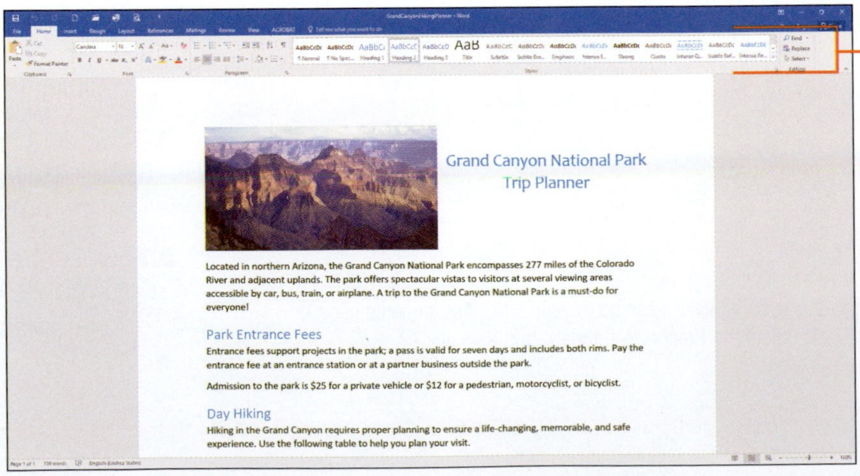

Figure 5.1
A word processor is used to create any kind of document that is mostly text, such as this trip planner for the Grand Canyon created in Microsoft Word.

- paragraph alignment options, spacing, tabs, indents, borders, and shading
- page numbering, margins, columns, and page breaks for formatting pages
- bulleted or numbered lists, tables, images, charts, and other graphics
- footnotes, endnotes, captions, and citations
- preformatted templates for cover pages, reports, letters, and other documents
- personalization of a standard document and labels for a mailing
- collaboration tools such as track changes, comments, share, and compare

> **Good to Know**
> You will encounter different versions of Microsoft Office in the workplace, because some business offices do not upgrade to the most recent version. You are most likely to see Microsoft Office 2010, Microsoft Office 2013, or Microsoft Office 2016 on Windows computers. Microsoft will stop providing support for Microsoft Office 2010 in October 2020.

Spreadsheet Programs

A software program in which you work primarily with numbers that you organize, calculate, and chart is called a **spreadsheet application**. Data is entered in a cell within a worksheet. A worksheet is a grid of columns and rows, with each column and row intersecting at a placeholder for data called a *cell*. You perform calculations on values stored in cells, and those calculations can be simple mathematical operations or complex formula statements.

Formulas in spreadsheets automatically recalculate whenever you change a number in a cell that is included in a formula. People like to perform "what-if" analysis with spreadsheets, which involves changing a value or formula to see what will happen to another value. For example, in a budget spreadsheet, you could increase your income in one cell and watch how that change affects the amount of money you have left after paying expenses in another cell. Spreadsheet programs also have charting capabilities so you can graph the values in a pie, column, or other type of chart. Figure 5.2 illustrates a school budget worksheet in Microsoft Excel. The Apple spreadsheet program is called Numbers.

Spreadsheets are used for any work that primarily tracks numbers such as budgets, revenue, expenses, asset tracking, inventory control, production control, gradebooks, research data, payroll, billing, costing, estimating, attendance recording, and scheduling. Spreadsheet programs generally include these features:

- preprogrammed formulas used in statistics, finance, math, date, and logic analysis
- formatting options to change typestyle, color, size, alignment, and numeric display
- sorting and filtering options to organize large blocks of data
- various chart styles and options to graph data and add other visual elements
- multiple worksheet tabs for grouping, consolidating, and managing data

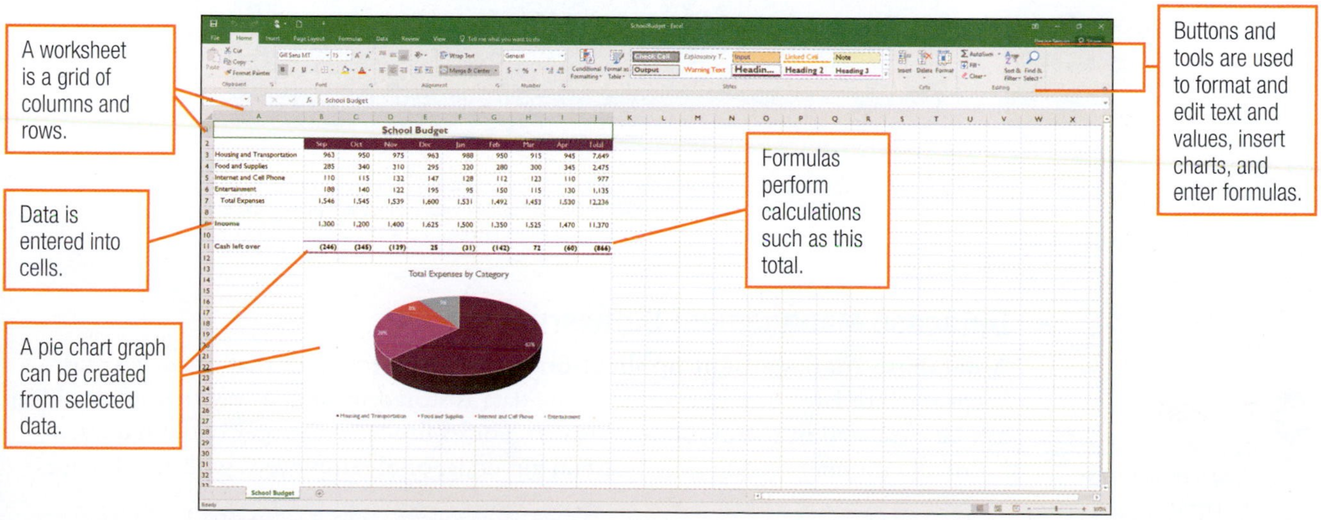
A worksheet is a grid of columns and rows.
Data is entered into cells.
A pie chart graph can be created from selected data.
Formulas perform calculations such as this total.
Buttons and tools are used to format and edit text and values, insert charts, and enter formulas.
School Budget
Total Expenses by Category

Figure 5.2

Spreadsheet software is used to track, analyze, and graph numerical data such as this school budget worksheet in Microsoft Excel.

- page layout and format options for printing large worksheets
- tools to perform what-if analysis
- collaboration tools such as track changes, comments, and share

Presentation Software

Slides for an electronic slide show that may be projected on a screen during an oral presentation or on a video display at a self-running kiosk are created in a **presentation application**, such as Microsoft PowerPoint or Apple Keynote. Presentation software helps you organize, describe, and explain key points, facts, figures, messages, or ideas. Slides allow you to use text, images, audio, and video plus animation and transition effects to provide a dynamic presentation experience. Figure 5.3 shows a group of slides in a presentation created with Microsoft PowerPoint. Presentation programs generally include the following features:

- several slide layouts for arrangement of titles and content
- predesigned presentation designs and themes for backgrounds, colors, fonts, and effects
- formatting options to change typestyle, color, size, and alignment of content
- tools for inserting pictures, clipart, photos, shapes, charts, tables, and other graphics
- sound and video media options
- slide transition and animation schemes to make dynamic slide shows
- options for customizing a slide show
- collaboration tools such as track changes, comments, and share

The slide pane shows miniatures of all the slides in the presentation. Icons let you know if animation and/or transition effects have been applied.

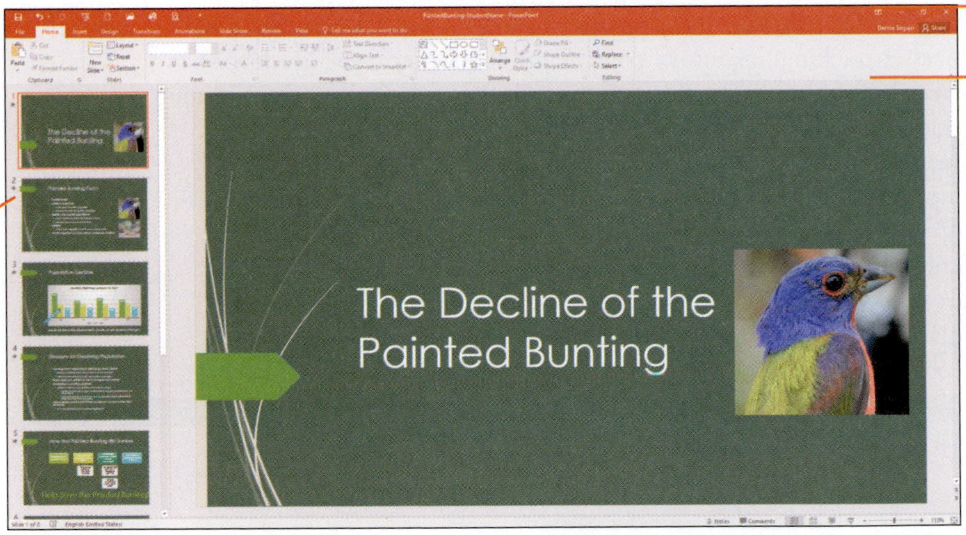

Buttons and tools are used to insert slides, format text, apply transition and animation schemes, and insert graphics, audio, and video.

Figure 5.3

Presentation software, such as Microsoft PowerPoint, is used to create a series of slides that are presented in a slide show.

Database Management Software

Tutorial
How Can Databases Make a Difference in Our Lives?

A **database management application** is a software program that organizes and keeps track of large amounts of data. The data is stored in such a way that information can be extracted in useful lists and reports. For example, a manager could request a list of all customers residing in a certain zip code, or all employees with no absences.

With database software, you set up the structure for storing data, input and maintain the data, and produce lists and reports to serve a variety of purposes. Businesses use databases to keep track of customers, patients, clients, vendors, employees, products, inventory, assets, contacts, claims, equipment, service records, and more. Any data that needs to be organized and stored can be set up in a database. Figure 5.4 illustrates a database created in Microsoft Access to keep track of used textbooks for sale. Database applications generally include these features:

- tables for designing the structure of data in columns (called *fields*) and rows (called *records*)
- forms for entering and maintaining data in a user-friendly interface
- queries for extracting and displaying data by criteria
- reports for printing or displaying data with rich text formatting options
- the ability to join related tables for queries and reports that extract data from two or more tables

Good to Know

As of May 2015, more than 1.2 billion people were using Microsoft Office—that's one in seven people on the planet!

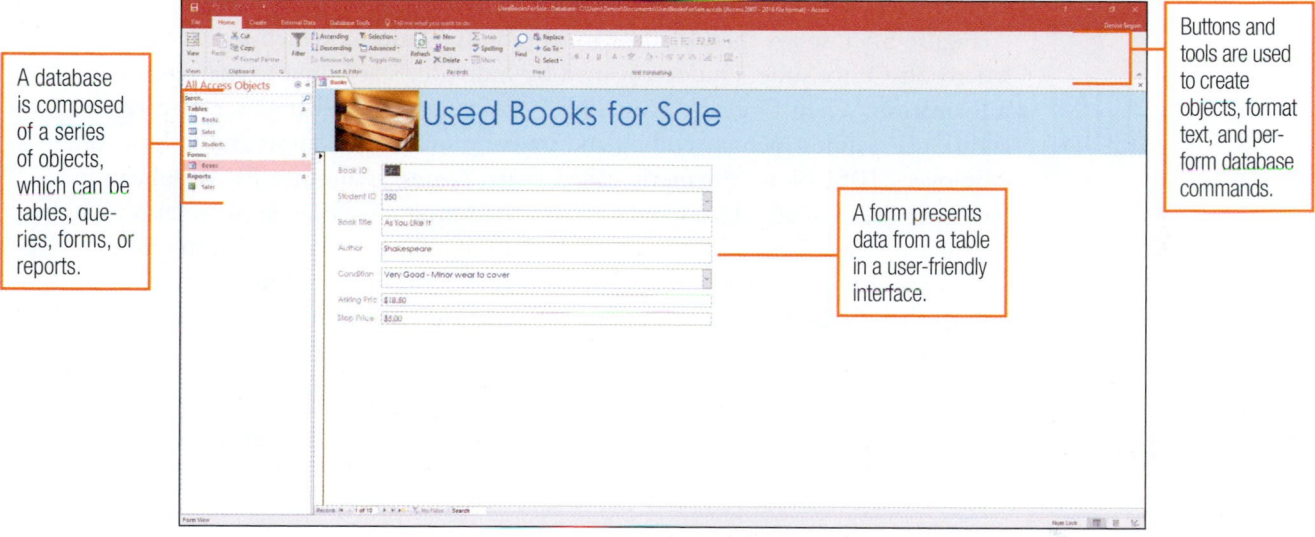

A database is composed of a series of objects, which can be tables, queries, forms, or reports.

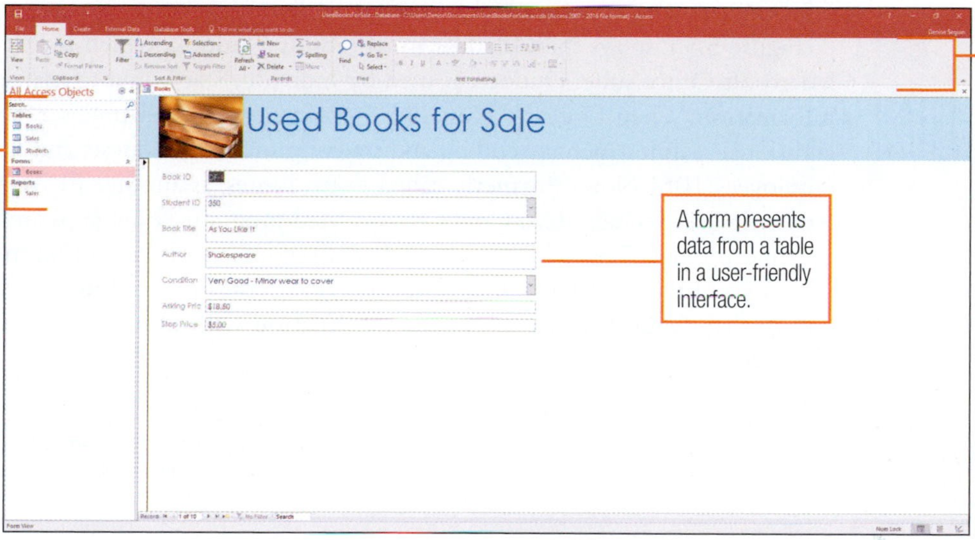

Buttons and tools are used to create objects, format text, and perform database commands.

A form presents data from a table in a user-friendly interface.

Figure 5.4

Database management software helps a business track and organize data such as this used textbook database shown in Microsoft Access.

Explore Further Tips for Using Microsoft Word, Excel, or PowerPoint

Many people are self-taught Microsoft Office users who have learned how to get their work done by trial and error, by looking up a feature, or by being shown how to use a feature by someone else. Learning tips and tricks for one of the applications might save you some time or effort the next time you need to create a document, spreadsheet, or presentation.

1. Pick Microsoft Word, Microsoft Excel, or Microsoft PowerPoint—the application for which you most want to learn a few tips—and find and read one online article with tips for using the software.
2. From the article, choose the five tips you found most helpful and create a one-page handout that explains the tips in your own words. Include the URL for the article.
3. Save the document as **MSOfficeTips-Your Name**.
4. Submit the document to your instructor in the manner she or he has requested.

5.2 Other Workplace Productivity Applications

Tutorial
How Do You Identify the Format That a File Is Saved In?

Businesses use software to do more than deliver information through documents, spreadsheets, presentations, and databases. They also use applications to manage communications, calendars, contacts, financial information, projects, and documents. In some industries, specialized software is designed to complete tasks unique to the industry, and large companies use enterprise-wide software programs to manage large-scale operations. In this topic, you will be introduced to some of these other types of applications found in a workplace.

Personal Information Management Software

Managing messages, schedule, contacts, and tasks can be onerous with the volume of emails, appointments, contacts, and to-do lists a typical worker encounters. A **personal information management (PIM) application** helps you organize this type of information. Reminders and flags help you remember and follow up on important emails, appointments, events, or tasks.

Figure 5.5 displays the Calendar in Microsoft Outlook, which is part of the Microsoft Office suite. Outlook is used by individuals at home to manage personal information. When Outlook is used in a workplace, an Exchange server gives users additional features such as sending and tracking meeting requests and tasks to other employees. IBM Notes (formerly called Lotus Notes) is another PIM application. Apple devices include iCal, Contacts, and Mail programs. PIM apps are also included on smartphones. The ability to sync calendars, contacts, and email on multiple devices means you have the latest information wherever you may be. PIM software also allows you to share your calendar or contact information with other people inside or outside your workplace.

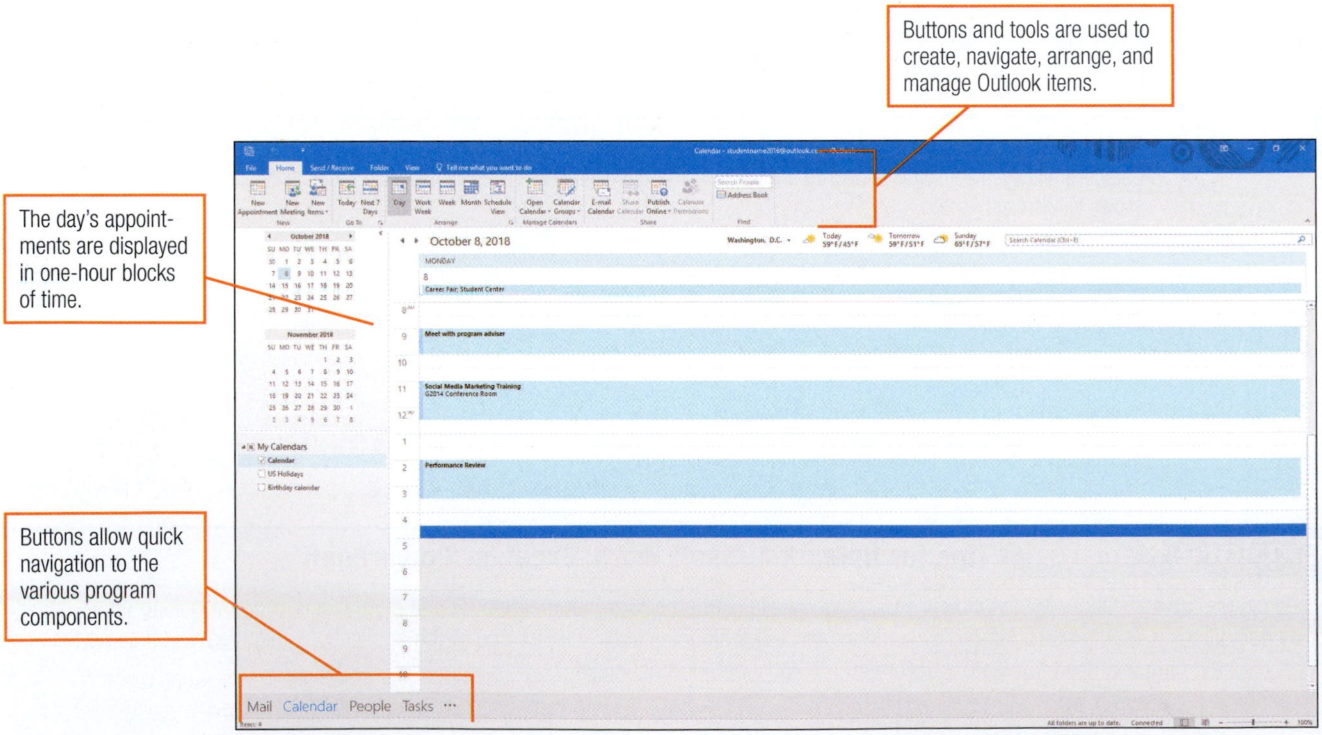

Figure 5.5
Microsoft Outlook is an application you can use to manage messages, schedules, contacts, and tasks.

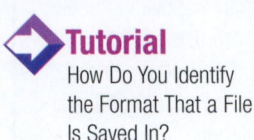

Accounting Software

All businesses need an **accounting application** to record and report financial information related to assets, liabilities, equity, revenue, and expenses. These programs provide the basis for financial reporting and tax calculations. Accounting software is generally organized by accounting activity, such as invoicing, purchasing, inventory, payroll, banking, bill paying, payment receiving, and memo processing. Accounting programs also support costing and estimating features for customer- and vendor-related functions. Several accounting software programs are designed for small, medium, and large businesses. Figure 5.6 shows the payroll summary screen for QuickBooks, an accounting program used by many small businesses.

Good to Know

Sage software is another popular accounting program. Formerly called Simply Accounting, Sage is used by over 6 million small- and medium-sized businesses to keep track of transactions around the globe.

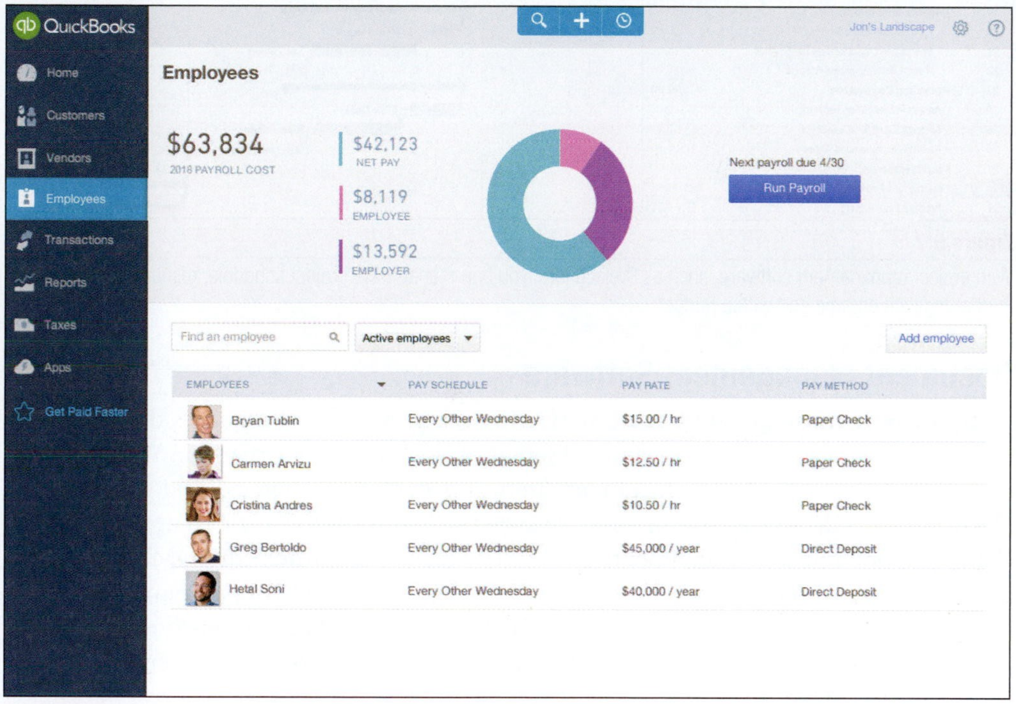

Figure 5.6

QuickBooks is a popular accounting software application for recording and reporting the financial activities for a small business. The payroll module shows a summary of payroll costs and employees.

Project Management Software

Large projects that need several resources and are to be completed on a schedule and within a budget are often managed using a **project management application**. Project management software is used to enter all the tasks needed to get a project done, establish time frames, assign resources, and allocate budget money to each task. Once the project is created, the program develops a project schedule and shows interdependencies between tasks for any tasks that cannot start until a previous task is completed. A typical way to display a schedule is in a Gantt chart, which plots tasks in time lines as shown in Figure 5.7 on page 120. Maintaining the data also allows you to view the impact on the schedule or budget if changes are made to tasks, resources, or time lines. Several project management software programs are available, including Microsoft Project, Clarizen, Wrike, Mavenlink, Basecamp, and ProjectLibre.

One advantage to using project management software is the collaborative tools included with the program. Each team member can be given access to the project file to update his or her task information and view other tasks or documents related to the project. This allows everyone to stay up-to-date and deal with issues that arise in a timely manner.

Check This Out

http://CC2.ParadigmCollege.net/PMI

Go here to learn about the Project Management Institute, the leading nonprofit professional association for project managers. The PMI develops globally recognized project management standards, certifications, professional development tools, and other resources for individuals and businesses.

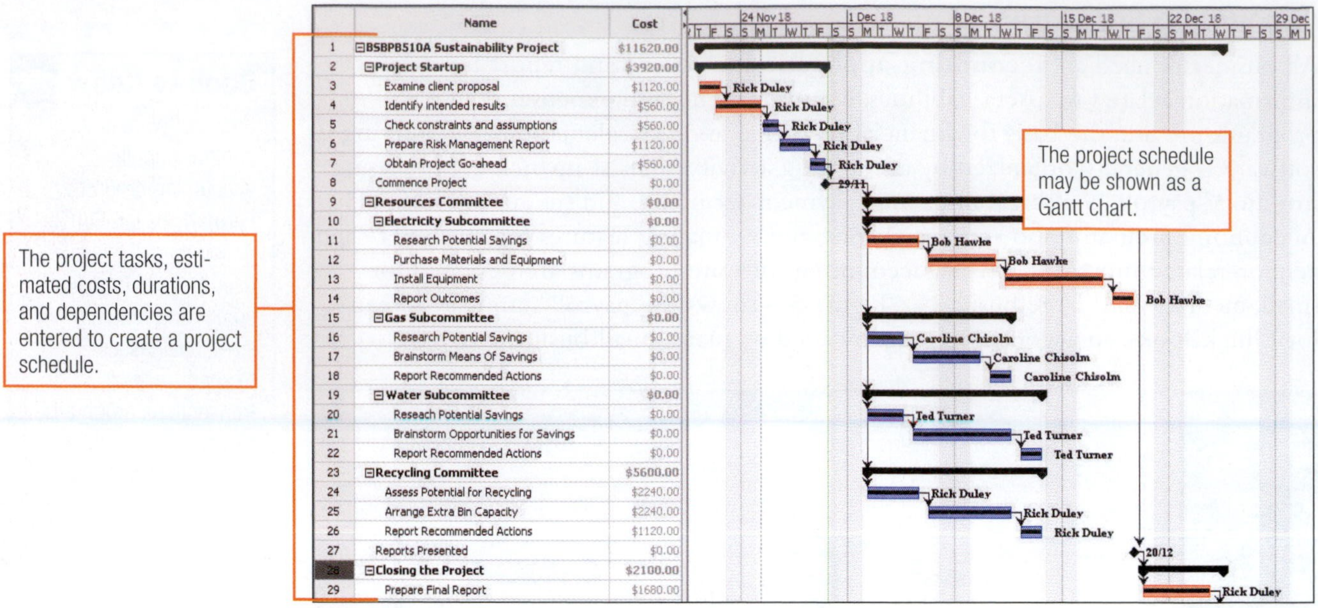

Figure 5.7

With project management software, such as ProjectLibre, you can manage the project schedule, resources, and budget to finish on time and within budget.

Document Management Software

A **document management system (DMS)** is a program that manages the creation, storage, retrieval, history, and eventual disposal of documents or other files stored in a central repository. Paper documents are scanned, coded or tagged, and stored electronically. DMS programs provide advanced search tools for retrieval as well as sharing of documents. A document's life cycle is managed through the DMS, and all documents are stored in a common file format, such as PDF. DMS programs use secure servers and controlled access to ensure privacy and security. Some industries, such as the legal industry, use DMS programs to manage the thousands of documents that are

Career Connection

Project Manager—Among the Top 25 Jobs Posted Online

Any organization that launches a large project involving many resources and multiple teams needs to have a skilled project manager to keep the project on time and on budget. According to PayScale, a company that compiles salaries from over 40 million individuals, the average salary for a project manager in information technology was $86,378 in May 2015. WANTED Analytics, a company that collects and analyzes hiring trend data from over 150 countries, reported in May 2015 that project manager was among the top 25 most common jobs posted online. If you are well organized, like to lead groups of diverse teams, and have excellent communication skills, consider investigating what it takes to be a project manager.

exchanged between lawyers in litigation cases. A DMS is the cornerstone of a paperless office. The DMS program called LogicalDOC is shown in Figure 5.8.

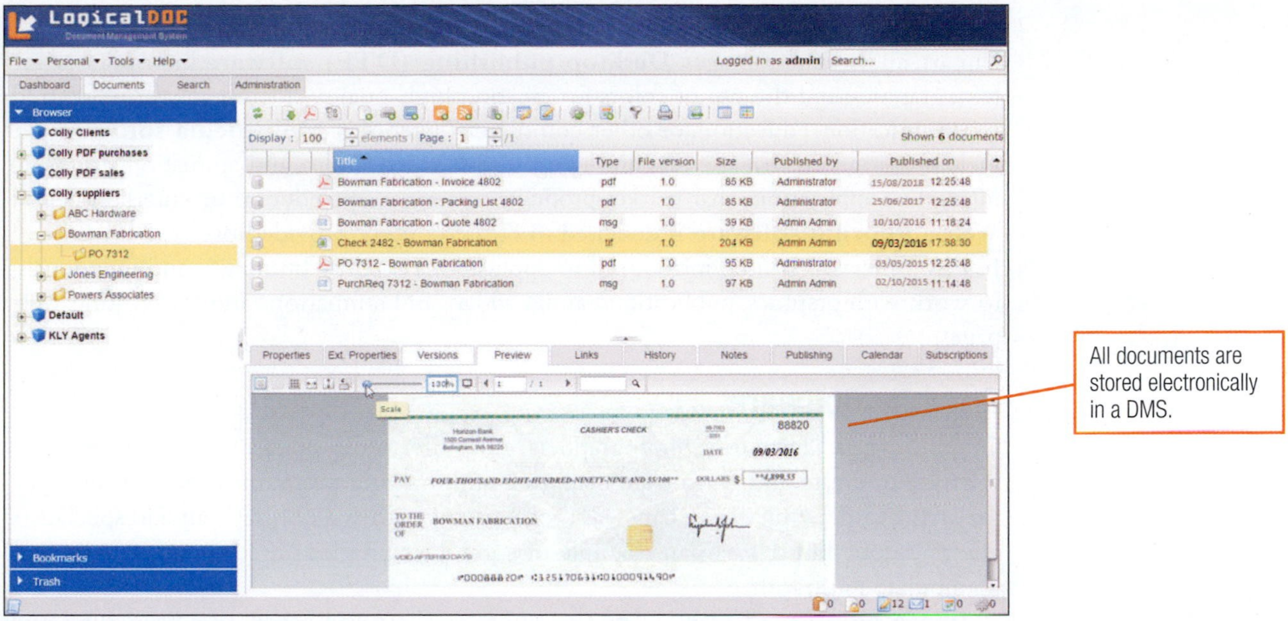

Figure 5.8

Companies use a DMS program such as LogicalDOC to electronically manage all documents, including paper documents that are scanned, coded, and stored on central servers.

Other Specialized Software

Industries such as automotive, construction, manufacturing, and engineering use industry-specific software—for example, computer-aided design (CAD) or computer-aided manufacturing (CAM) programs—to create complex designs and drawings. Medical establishments use medical software programs to track patient records, billings, and insurance claims. Hotels and travel agencies use programs to manage bookings, guests, and resources. These are just a few examples of industry-specific software applications.

Large companies, referred to as *enterprises*, have higher-level needs to manage the multitude of activities and processes involved in transactions with customers, vendors, inventories, and human resources. These companies often use an **enterprise resource planning (ERP) application**, which is a software solution designed for large-scale organizations. Companies such as SAP and Oracle provide ERP software for these environments, often along with extensive customization, training, and support.

Explore Further — Which Industry-Specific Software Will You Use?

Chances are, industry-specific software is used in your field of study. For example, contractors use materials- and labor-estimating software, restaurants use meal service software, and airlines use reservation systems. What industry-specific software will you be required to use in your future career?

1. Research industry-specific software applications used in your field of study. If possible, interview someone who works in your field and ask that person to describe specialized software he or she uses in the workplace.
2. Create a document that describes the software applications used in your field and how the software is used to track, manage, and report information.
3. Save the document as **MyIndustrySoftware-YourName**.
4. Submit the document to your instructor in the manner she or he has requested.

5.3 Applications for Working with Graphics, Publications, Multimedia, and the Web

Graphics software is used for creating, editing, and manipulating drawings, photos, clip art, and scanned images. **Desktop publishing (DTP) software** incorporates text, graphics, and the use of colors for creating high-quality documents for marketing, communication, education, or other commercial purposes. **Multimedia software** includes programs that use text and images with video, audio, and animations to create interactive applications that market products or services, or educate or entertain people. **Web authoring software** is designed to create content provided over the Internet. In this topic, you will be introduced to applications used by businesses and individuals to work with graphics, publications, audio, video, and animations and for creating web pages.

Graphics Software

Graphic artists, illustrators, photographers, and other professionals use specialized software to create and edit images. Painting and drawing programs provide tools for artists to draw pictures, shapes, and other images to which they can add special effects. Adobe Illustrator is an example of a graphics program used to create, edit, and manipulate illustrations.

Photo editing software is used by photographers and others to edit pictures and add special effects and text to pictures taken with a digital camera. Adobe Photoshop is a popular choice of both professionals and individuals. Tools are available in Photoshop to crop out unwanted portions of a picture, remove red eye, retouch areas, correct color brightness and contrast, add text, add special effects, and even add in a person or object copied from another photo. Figure 5.9 shows a photo edited using Adobe Photoshop to add a blue sky background and butterfly to baby's feet.

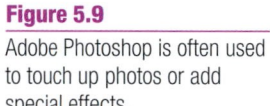

Figure 5.9
Adobe Photoshop is often used to touch up photos or add special effects.

Desktop Publishing Software

Word processing software provides tools to arrange text and graphics in a document; however, a word processor does not let you precisely position objects and control text flow around objects. For professional publications, desktop publishing software is used to produce a print-based document, such as a corporate newsletter, annual report, price list, restaurant menu, catalog, brochure, or book. Programs such as Adobe InDesign, Microsoft Publisher, and QuarkXPress are popular choices for desktop publishing. DTP programs use rulers, grids, and guides as well as other tools and features that allow DTP professionals to precisely place text and graphics on a page. In addition, the software provides more control over word spacing, space between and around objects and text, and a wider range of fonts, sizes, and colors for text formatting. Figure 5.10 illustrates an advertising circular in QuarkXPress for Mac.

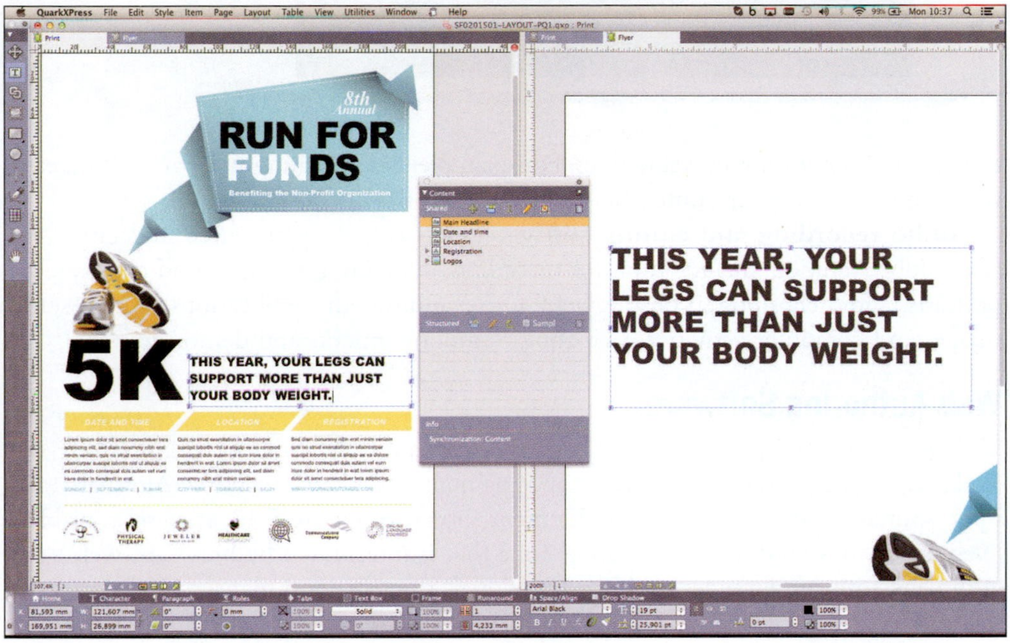

Figure 5.10
QuarkXPress is a desktop publishing application used to do page layout for professional publications.

Multimedia Software

For content delivered via the web or distributed on CD, DVD, or Blu-ray disc, professionals use multimedia programs to create animations, add audio and video, and author interactive multimedia applications. **Animation software** is used to create images or objects that have movement or otherwise interact with users. Adobe Flash is an application often used to create interactive applications delivered over the web on Windows-based PCs and for desktop applications. In Flash, the designer works with a time line and a stage in which text, graphics, and other objects are placed in the sequence the movement or interaction is supposed to occur.

In 2015, YouTube changed its standard for delivery of video from Flash to HTML5, which is supported across all devices (Apple devices do not support Flash content). HTML5 also delivers video content over the Internet more efficiently than Flash. This change at YouTube is widely believed to signal the obsolescence of Flash within the technology community, although Adobe is still supporting Flash for the desktop environment. Web browsing via a smartphone or tablet is expected to grow, leading to the expectation that HTML5 will replace Flash as the new standard for developing multimedia content.

Video editing software, such as Final Cut Pro from Apple (Figure 5.11 on page 124) and Adobe Premiere Elements, provide tools to create videos referred to as *clips*. Video shot with a digital camera can be manipulated by cutting, adding, or moving scenes; creating split screens; or adding music, audio effects, or text for titles or credits. Some audio editing capability is also included, as well as tools to organize the

Figure 5.11
Final Cut Pro video editing software from Apple is a package used by many professional multimedia producers.

display of content on removable discs. For example, video editing programs also create the menus and burn the content to a DVD or Blu-ray disc.

Audio recording and editing software, such as free, open source Audacity and Adobe Audition, include tools for recording and editing music, sound clips, and podcasts (audio clips posted on the web). Other multimedia applications capture screen images and computer activity for creating training segments and demonstrations.

Web Authoring Software

Web authoring programs, such as Adobe Dreamweaver and Microsoft Expression Web, are used by businesses to create and maintain interactive websites. Alternative open source programs, such as openElement shown in Figure 5.12, are also available. Web pages are stored in programming code that is interpreted by browsers. Web authoring software provides tools for individuals to create and manage all the pages and external resources for a website by working in either design view or code view. Nonprogrammers can create a web page in design view and let the software automatically generate the programming code needed for browsers. Experienced web developers often work in code view and switch between views as pages are fine-tuned. Figure 5.12 is a web page shown in code view, with the software prompting the user that an unnecessary semicolon is present.

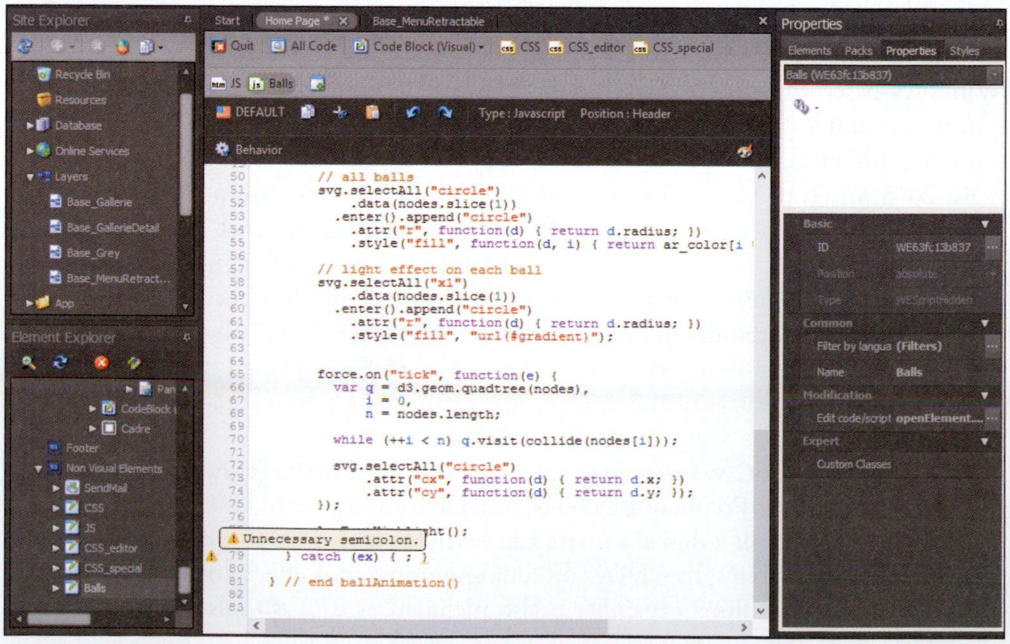

Figure 5.12
The web page source code in Javascript is shown here using the web authoring software program called openElement, an open source program. Web browsers interpret this code to display the text and multimedia that you see when you view the page.

Multimedia for the Nonprofessional

A variety of graphics and multimedia programs are available to meet the needs of both professional and nonprofessional users. Most of the programs showcased in this topic are more expensive software programs geared toward professionals or hobby enthusiasts. Less expensive or free programs are used by nonprofessionals or individuals who want to work with multimedia at home. For example, Windows Live Essentials is a free suite offered to Windows users that includes a program to work with video (Movie Maker) and photos (Photo Gallery). The Windows OS also includes programs for drawing (Paint) and recording sound (Voice Recorder). Figure 5.13 shows how the exposure of a photograph can be adjusted using Photo Gallery. Apple devices are packaged with the iLife suite which includes iPhoto, iMovie, and GarageBand for working with photos, video, and audio.

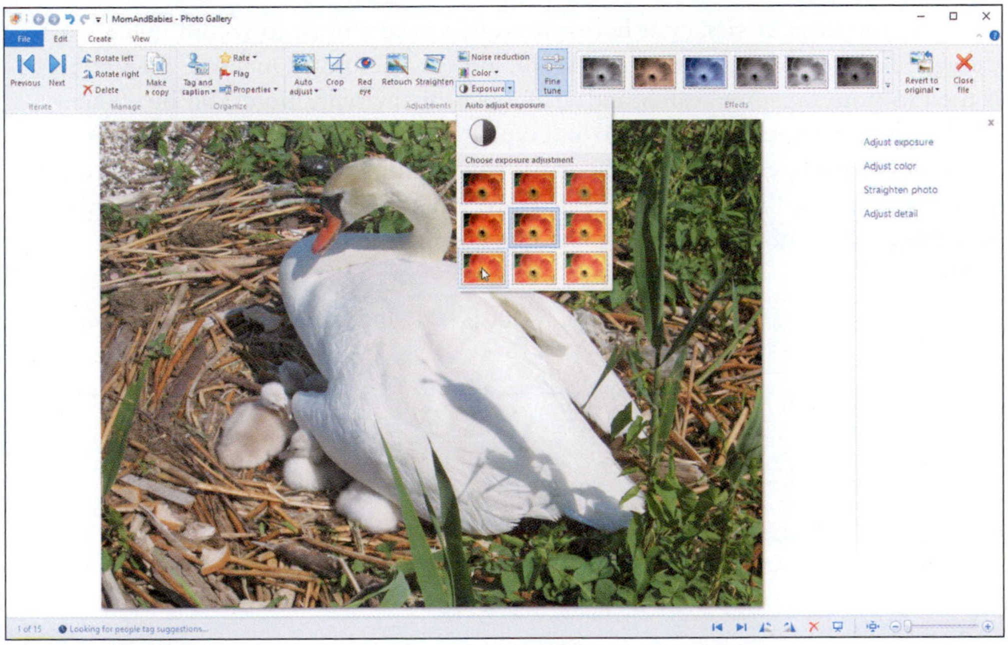

Figure 5.13

Photo exposure can be adjusted using Windows Live Photo Gallery, part of the free Windows Live Essentials suite from Microsoft.

Check This Out ✓

http://CC2.ParadigmCollege.net/WindowsLiveEssentials

Go here to download Windows Live Essentials for free.

Check This Out ✓

http://CC2.ParadigmCollege.net/Picasa

Go here to download Picasa—a free image editing and organizing program from Google. Pictures are stored in web albums, which can be shared with others.

Explore Further — Are You a Skilled Photo Editor?

Web-based photo editing software programs allow you to edit photos without downloading and installing software on your computer. Each program offers a basic set of tools for nonprofessionals.

1. Find a free online image editing program for which you want to experiment editing a photo.
2. Using a digital camera, take a photo of something related to your field of study. For example, take a picture of a park if you are going to be a landscape designer, a house if you are going to work in construction, or a hospital if you plan to work in the medical field. Upload the photo to the image editing website and experiment with the software's editing tools to edit the image. For example, crop out a part of the picture, change the color, retouch the photo, add shapes, add special effects, add text, and so on.
3. Save the revised image as **PhotoEditing-YourName**.
4. Submit the original photo and the edited photo to your instructor in the manner she or he has requested.

5.4 Software Applications for Personal Use

Software programs for personal use include a wide range of applications that cover almost every hobby, interest, and need. For example, you can install software to help you manage personal notes, ideas, and thoughts at work, at school, or at home, manage your personal finances, prepare tax returns, play games, design a garden, and create a genealogy map. Programs help you organize recipes and plan trips, as well as educate and provide reference information. In this topic, you will survey a variety of applications for personal use.

If you have an interest or a hobby that is not mentioned in this topic, chances are that a related software program has already been created. Search the web for an application if you have not already found one.

Note Taking Software

While in meetings, classes, or at home, you often need a place to record notes, thoughts, or ideas. **Note taking software**, such as Microsoft OneNote (Figure 5.14), is used to store, organize, search, and share notes of any type. Notes can be entered by clicking anywhere on the screen and typing or writing by hand using a stylus. Documents, audio, video, images, emails, appointments, contacts, and web links can be attached or inserted into a note to collect everything related to a topic in one place. You can organize notes into notebooks and tabs and use search and share tools.

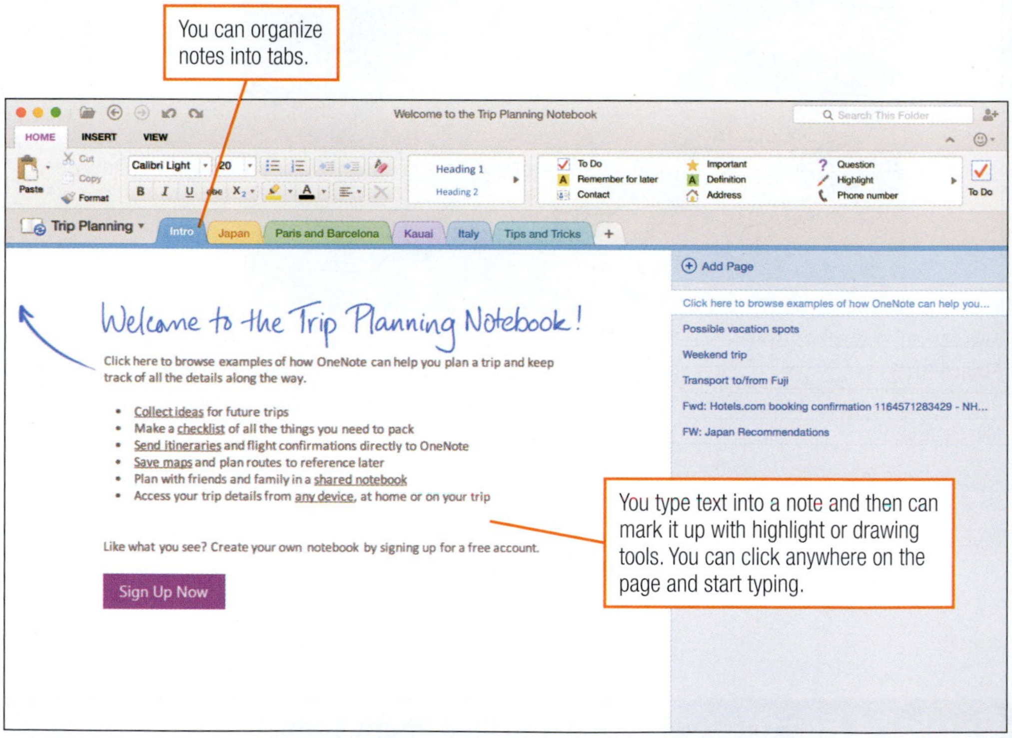

Figure 5.14
Microsoft OneNote, shown here in the Mac edition, is a useful tool to organize notes on any topic related to school, work, or home.

Software to Manage Personal Finances and Taxes

Keeping track of a checking or savings account and personal investments is accomplished with **personal finance software**. Most personal finance software programs allow you to download activity from your banking account directly into the personal finance program. You can balance your checking account, analyze home expenses, and track investments. Quicken (Figure 5.15) is a popular program used for managing finances.

Tax preparation software guides you through the completion of the complex forms required to file your income taxes with the government. These programs generally estimate your tax bill using an interview-style series of questions and input boxes. Programs generally alert you to missing information and/or deductions that can help minimize taxes. Tax forms can be printed and can also be filed with the government electronically.

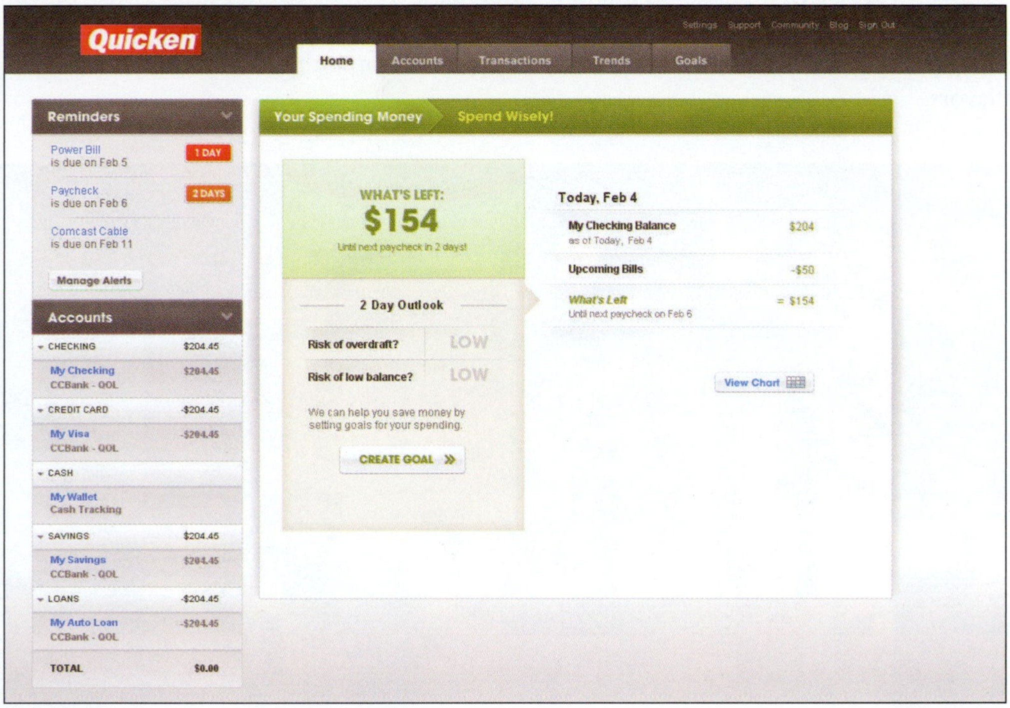

Figure 5.15
Quicken is a software program for managing personal finances such as cash and personal expenses.

Legal Software

Legal software, such as Quicken WillMaker, MyAttorney, and Family Lawyer, help you prepare legal documents such as wills, contracts, leases, loan agreements, and living trusts. These programs provide standard legal documents that you customize for your purposes by responding to a series of questions, forms, or dialog boxes that prompt you for input.

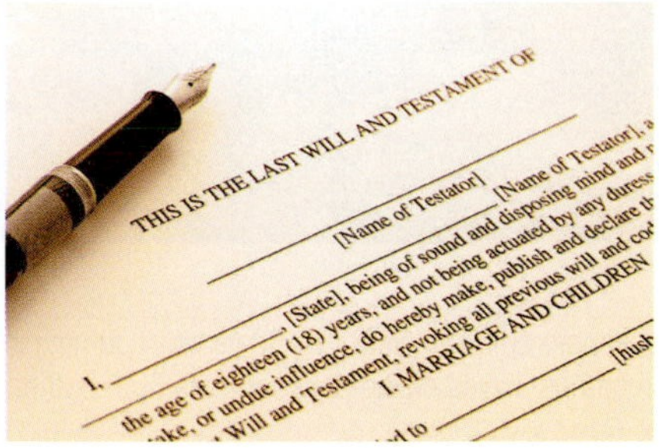

Legal software helps individuals create legal documents such as a last will and testament.

Hobby Software

Software applications for creating a family tree; scrapbooking; planning trips; managing recipes and planning meals; designing homes, decks, and gardens; and creating and printing custom greeting cards are just a few examples of **hobby software** you can use to pursue your favorite leisure activities.

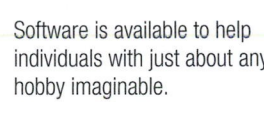

Software is available to help individuals with just about any hobby imaginable.

Entertainment Software

> **Good to Know**
>
> According to Newzoo (a games market research company), worldwide spending on games is expected to reach $107 billion in 2017, with China and the United States vying for first place as the biggest game market.

Entertainment software includes programs for playing interactive games and videos. Some games are designed to be played individually. Others involve subscribing to online services where you can join hundreds of thousands of other game enthusiasts and play against others online. For example, with more than 7 million subscribers, World of Warcraft (WoW) is a highly successful online game involving role-playing and multiple players that boasts a 2014 Guinness World Record for the longest video game marathon at 29 hours and 31 minutes.

Games are often available in multiple versions such as an edition for a PC, a version that can be played online through a browser, and a smaller app for downloading to a smartphone. Tetris (Figure 5.16) is one example of a game that is available in all these flavors.

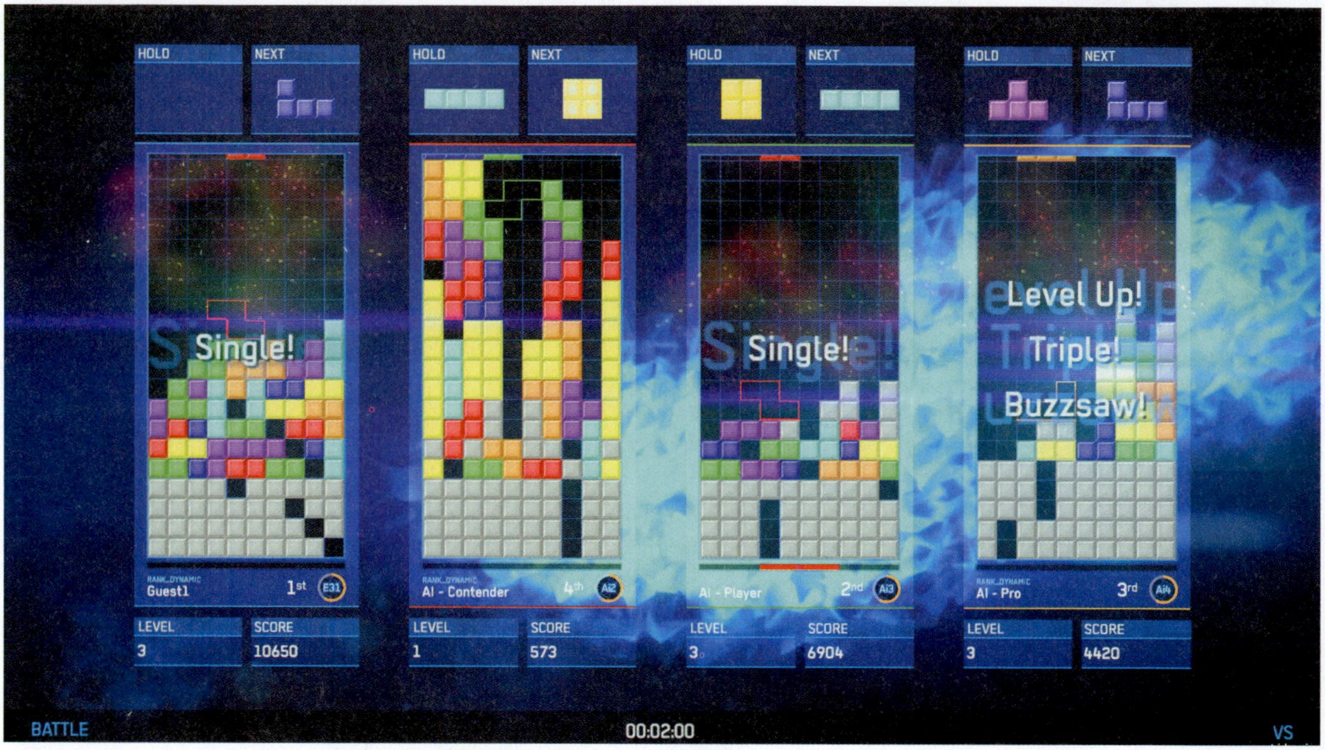

Figure 5.16

Tetris, shown here in the four-player ultimate edition, celebrated 30 years of gaming in 2014. The fan favorite puzzle game had over 425 million paid downloads, and more than one billion games played online per year at its 30th birthday!

> **Blog Topic** **What Is Your Favorite Game?**
>
> Do you play video games? If yes, which game is your favorite? Which game do you find most challenging, or the most relaxing? How much time per week do you spend playing games?
>
> 1. Write and post a blog entry with your answers to the questions. If you do not play computer games, ask someone you know who does to describe a favorite game for you.
> 2. Read at least two of your classmates' blog entries and post one comment to each.
> 3. Submit the URLs of your blog and the two classmates' blogs to your instructor in the manner she or he has requested.

Education and Reference Software

Educational software is designed to teach children and adults about subjects such as math, spelling, grammar, geography, science, and history through an interactive reference or game format. Figure 5.17 shows the ScienceFlix program created by Scholastic for teaching children in grades four through nine about science. You can also find software to help you learn a foreign language and to teach you how to type. **Reference software** uses multimedia tools to provide rich content information in encyclopedias, dictionaries, translation guides, atlases, and other reference resources.

Tutorial
How Can Software Help You Learn?

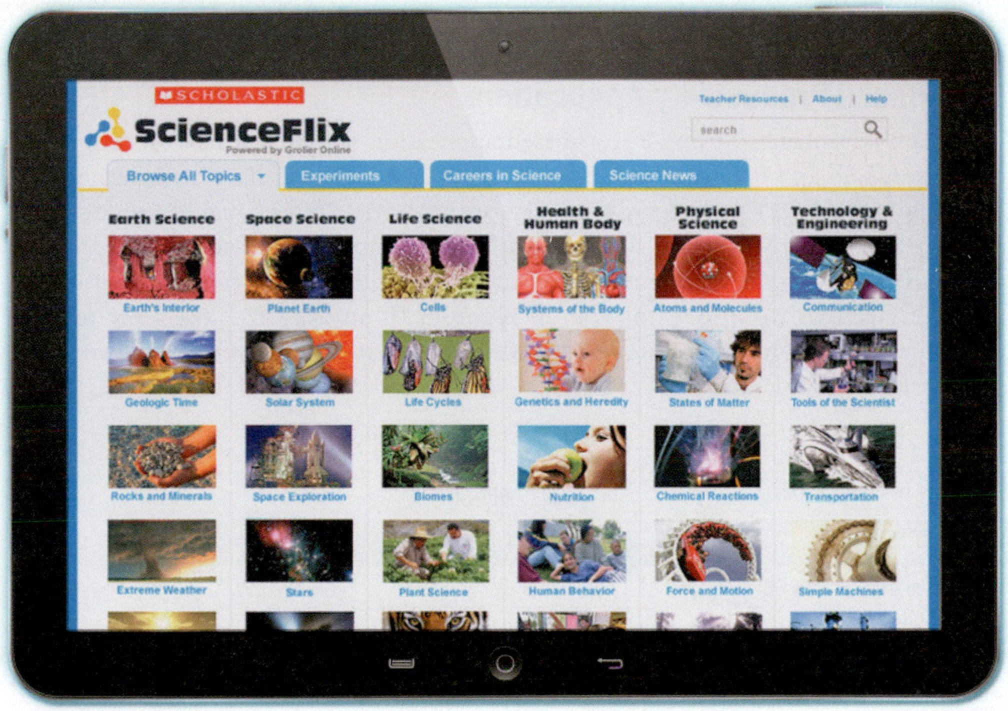

Figure 5.17
Scholastic educational materials are found in schools all over the world. The interactive ScienceFlix program contains over 4,000 objects for students to explore about science topics.

Security Alert Be Cautious with Free Software

The lure of free software can be enticing. Be cautious with web ads that offer free software of any type, but especially those that offer to manage personal finances. Read the details, including the fine print, before downloading the software or submitting your email address or any other personal information. Often these programs are used to collect personal information for resale, or they may contain malicious code such as a virus.

Explore Further Survey Note Taking Software

The ability to organize, store, sort, and search notes electronically can save you time finding information, and help you study for tests and exams. Several free note taking applications are available for PC, Mac, Android, iOS, and Linux. Which note taking software would you like to use?

1. Search for online reviews on free note taking software and read at least two articles.
2. Decide on one program that you think would work best for you, given the program's features and ease of use.
3. Create a document that describes the note taking application you selected and give your reasons for choosing it. Include the URLs of the articles you read for this topic.
4. Save the document as **NoteTakingSoftware-YourName**.
5. Submit the document to your instructor in the manner she or he has requested.

5.5 Cloud and Open Source Applications

Good to Know

Market intelligence provider IDG (International Data Group) predicts that SaaS delivery will grow five times faster than the software market as a whole, and by 2018, one of every five dollars spent on software will be for a cloud product.

Check This Out

http://CC2.ParadigmCollege.net/Prezi

Go here to learn about Prezi—a cloud-based presentation program that uses a virtual canvas for presenting ideas. By signing up for a free account, you agree that your prezis will be searchable, accessible, and reusable by anyone.

In Chapter 1, you were introduced to Cloud Computing and the SaaS delivery model for software applications. Recall that SaaS stands for *software as a service* and means that the software you are using is not installed on your computing device. SaaS applications are hosted by a third party and made available to you from a web browser. Open source programs are often provided for free, meaning that you can download and install the software on a computer without paying a license fee. In this topic, you will survey three web-based and two open source software alternatives for productivity applications. If you need new software, consider using one of the programs described in this topic, or search for another cloud or open source alternative application.

Web-Based Productivity Applications

The main advantage to using a web-based application is that you have access to the software and your files from any location at which you have an Internet connection. Table 5.1 provides a summary of three popular web-based productivity application alternatives. If you decide to use a cloud application, consider spending time working with a few different suites until you find the one with the features and interface that works best for you. In Figure 5.18 on page 131, the same text is shown in the word processing application from each of the three providers summarized in Table 5.1.

Table 5.1

Summary of Three Popular Web-Based Productivity Applications

Criterion	Google Drive	Office Online	Zoho
Amount of free storage offered at time of writing	15 GB	15 GB	5 GB
Applications	Documents Spreadsheets Presentations Forms Drawings	Word Online Excel Online PowerPoint Online OneNote Online	Sheet (Spreadsheet) Show (Presentation) Writer (Word Processor) Plus several apps for collaboration and business processes
URL	https://www.google.com	https://office.live.com	http://www.zoho.com
Sign-in process	Sign in with a Gmail account and then click Google Apps, Drive, New, and the desired application.	Sign in with a Microsoft account and then click the desired application.	Sign in with a Zoho account and then click the desired application.

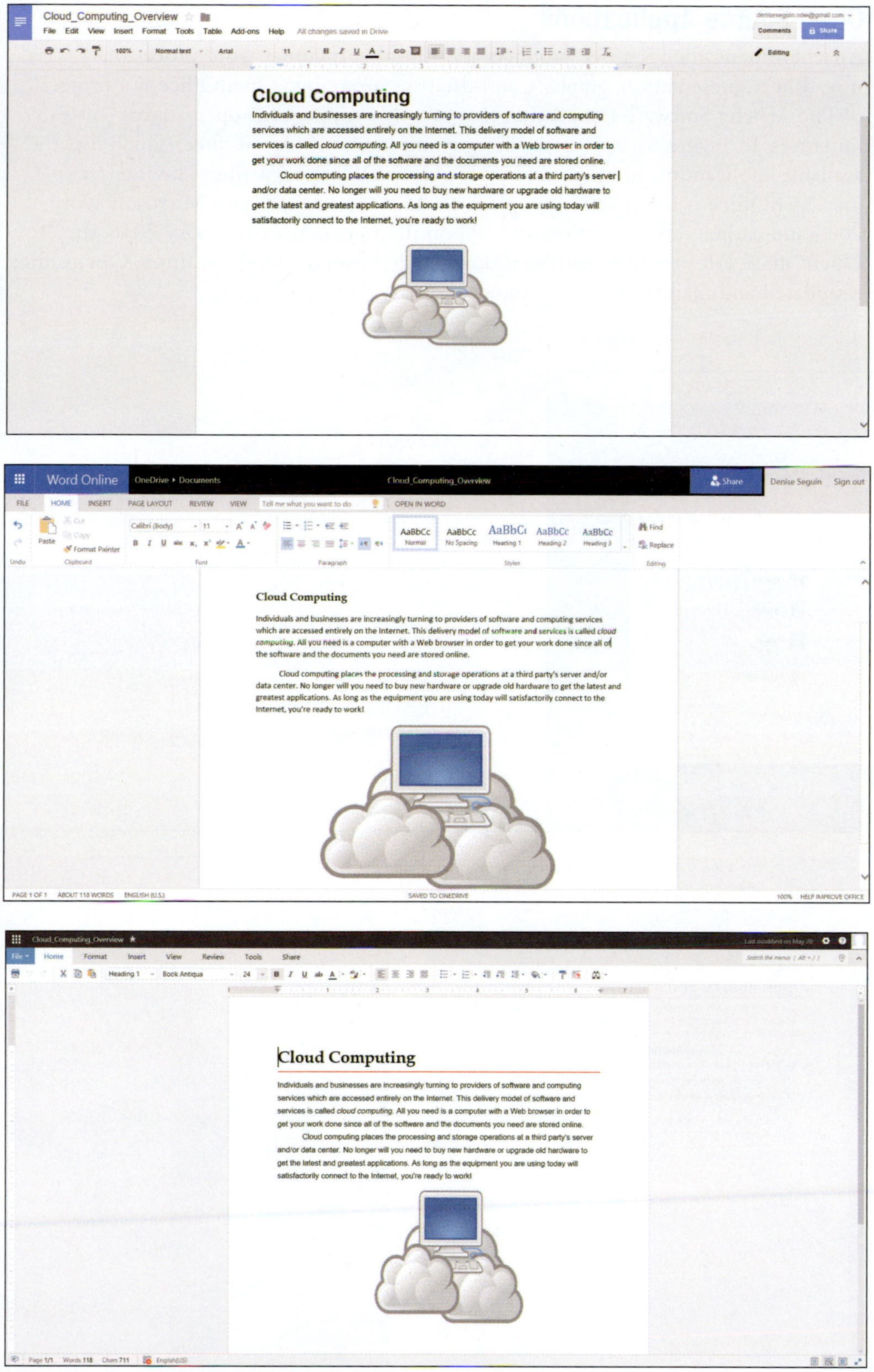

Figure 5.18

Web-based programs from different developers vary slightly. For example, compare the text formatting options in the Google, Microsoft, and Zoho online word processing applications.

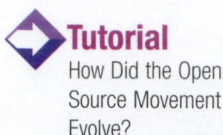

Tutorial
How Did the Open Source Movement Evolve?

Check This Out
http://CC2.ParadigmCollege.net/OpenOffice
Go here to learn more about OpenOffice.

Open Source Applications

Apache OpenOffice is a free productivity suite that includes word processor, spreadsheet, presentation, graphics, and database programs. OpenOffice is a project of The Apache Software Foundation that provides support for open source software initiatives. In Figure 5.19, you see the opening menu of OpenOffice, which lists the available applications, and the window for OpenOffice.org Writer. The interface for OpenOffice is intuitive for people who have experience with Microsoft Word 2003 and earlier versions (before the ribbon interface). As of February 2016, the OpenOffice software suite had been downloaded over 160 million times. OpenOffice is updated and maintained by volunteers.

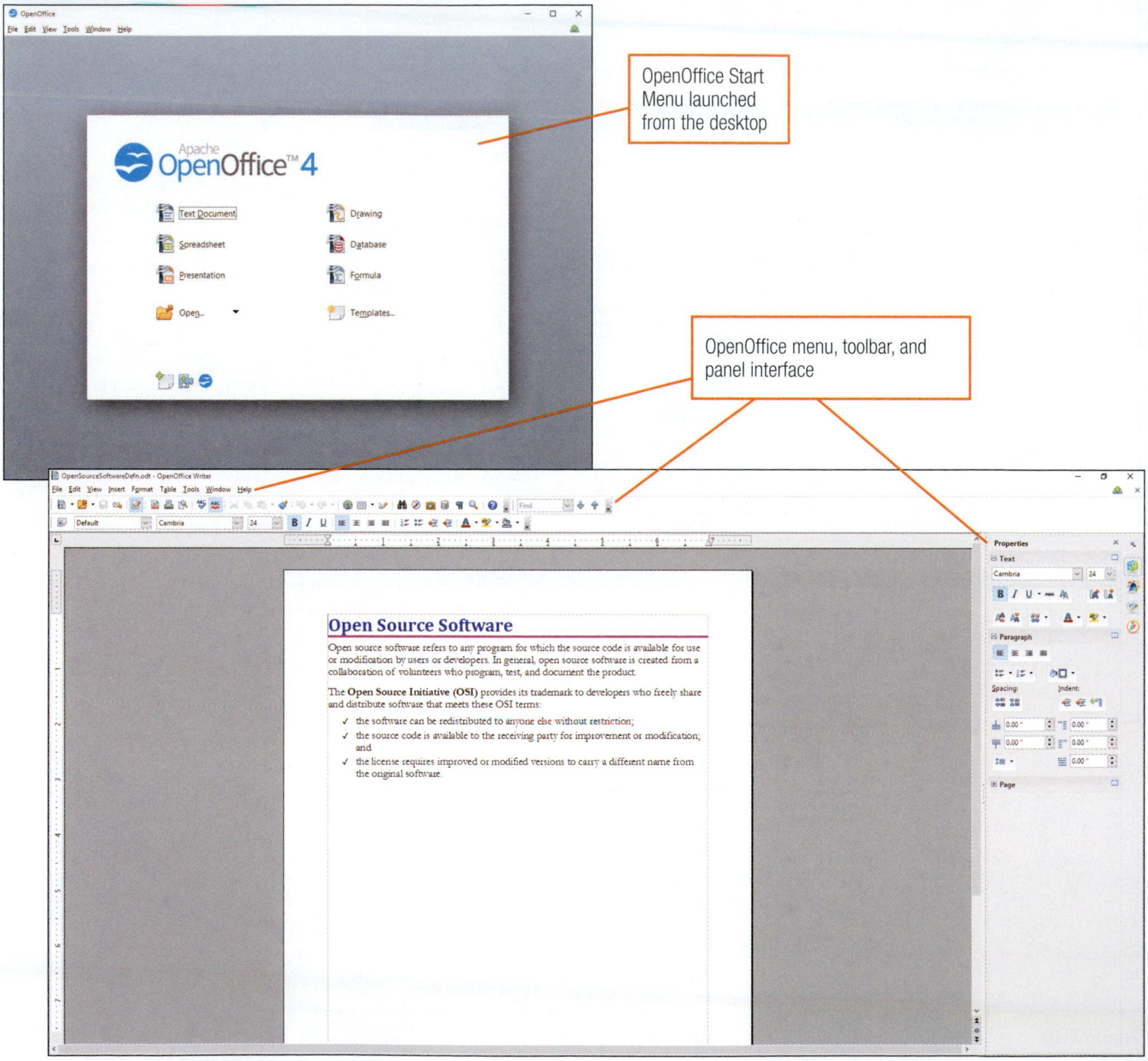

Figure 5.19
OpenOffice is a free, open source productivity suite that includes a word processor (shown here) as well as spreadsheet, presentation, drawing, database, and formulas applications.

Another free open source productivity suite is LibreOffice (Figure 5.20). LibreOffice runs on Windows, Macintosh, and Linux computers and includes the applications Writer, Calc, Impress, Draw, Base, and Math. LibreOffice is a project of the not-for-profit organization The Document Foundation. Similar to OpenOffice, LibreOffice is created and maintained by volunteers, and was actually born when a team of OpenOffice developers decided to create LibreOffice as a separate suite.

A few writers in the technical community have speculated that LibreOffice will overtake OpenOffice as the preferred open source productivity suite, and some are predicting that the two projects will merge, creating one open source desktop suite. Given the similarities in the two programs, a merge of the two programs into one would be a likely scenario.

Check This Out ✓

http://CC2.ParadigmCollege.net/LibreOffice

Go here to learn more about LibreOffice.

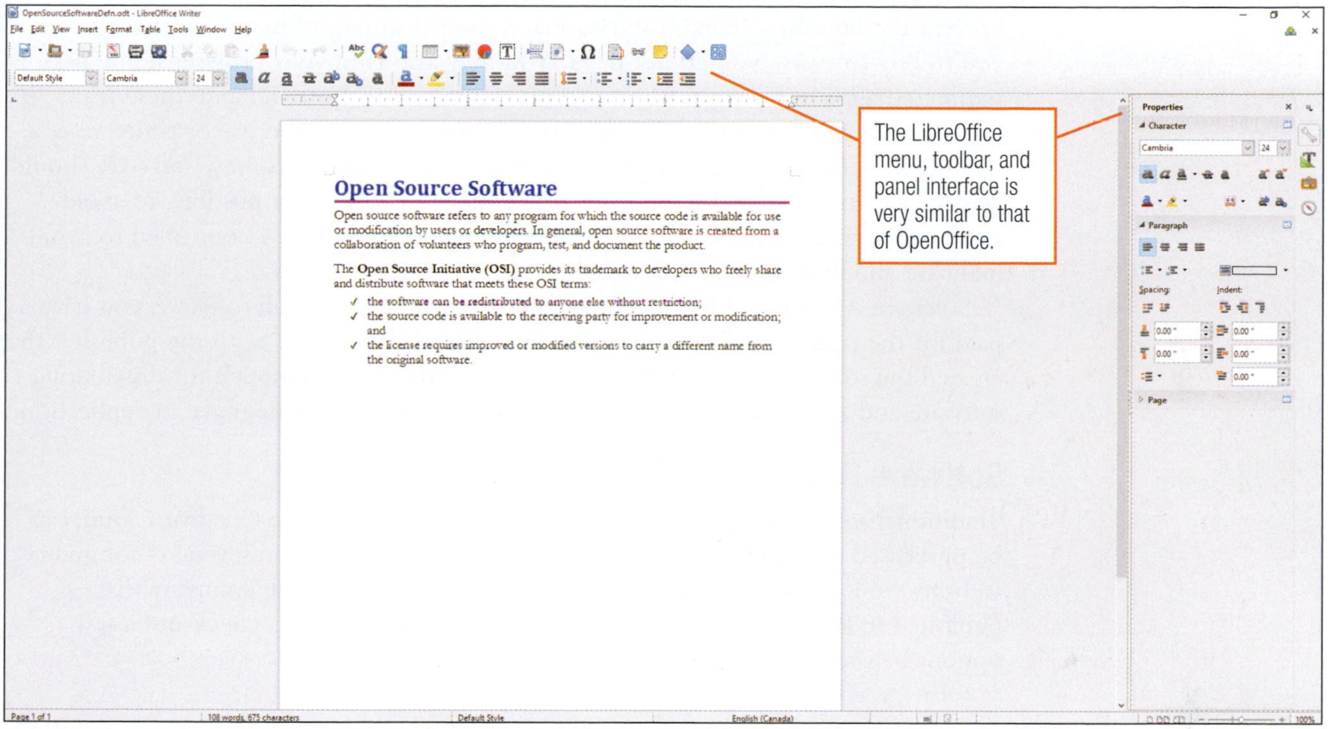

Figure 5.20

LibreOffice is another free open source productivity suite with the same applications as OpenOffice. The word processor shown here is very similar to the one in OpenOffice—a result of LibreOffice being created by OpenOffice developers.

Explore Further Discover Zoho

Zoho is a web-based applications provider with 15 million users in 2015. Try out Zoho and compare it with what you are using now for productivity applications. ***Note:*** *If you are already a Zoho user, complete this activity using another web-based productivity application.*

1. Go to **http://CC2.ParadigmCollege.net/Zoho**, sign up, and activate a free account.
2. Launch Writer, Sheet, or Show—the application you want to use for your comparison—and experiment with the program to learn the available features. For example, enter some sample text and try formatting options and spell check features.
3. Create a document that compares the Zoho application with the same type of application you normally use. Consider doing the comparison in a table or chart to compare the two programs feature by feature.
4. Save the document or spreadsheet as **ZohoComparison-YourName**.
5. Submit the document or spreadsheet to your instructor in the manner she or he has requested.

5.6 Acquiring, Installing, Uninstalling, and Upgrading Software

Tutorial
How Does a Software as a Service (SaaS) License Differ from a Traditional Software License?

Software applications can be acquired in various ways such as purchasing from a retailer either in the store or online, buying directly from the software publisher, or downloading from a website such as Tucows downloads (http://www.tucows.com/downloads). At software download websites, people often look for software that is low cost or free. You should exercise caution when using software download websites. Many times, free software is bundled with other programs you do not want, and the installation screens can be confusing to navigate as you try to avoid getting the extra unwanted software. Many download websites advertise that all software has been tested to be virus and spyware free; however, this does not prevent the bundling of extra software and the placement of many ads that entice you to buy software you do not need. You may also find your browser home page is redirected after installing software from a download website. Despite these issues, if you are careful, and you need a software program for a limited use or timeframe, a download website can be a good resource. On Mac computers, new software should be acquired and installed within the Mac App Store whenever possible, to avoid these issues. The Apple software distribution platform is strictly controlled to avoid malware and unwanted additional software.

Software is a licensed product, meaning that when you install software, you have paid for the right to use the product, while ownership remains with the publisher that created the software. In this topic, you will learn the various models for distributing software and the general steps you take to install, uninstall, or upgrade an application.

Software Distribution Models

Traditional software suites, such as Microsoft Office and Adobe Creative Cloud, can be purchased as **packaged software** at a retailer's store or from several e-commerce websites. You can also buy the software online directly from the company that published it. Pricing for software suites can vary, so it is wise to check out a few options before making a purchase.

Other ways to acquire software include the following:

- **Shareware** is available to download for a free trial period. Once the trial period expires, you need to pay a fee to the software publisher to unlock the application. Other forms of shareware continue to work beyond the trial period but generally have features made inaccessible until the fee is paid.
- **Freeware** can be downloaded and installed at no cost and without restrictions. An example of a popular freeware program is Apple iTunes.
- Open source software is generally available for free and downloaded from a website.
- **Subscription software** is purchased from providers that generally charge a monthly or annual fee for access to the software and storage services. Fees vary based on the number of users and the amount of storage space.

Good to Know

Software packages that have been opened are generally not returnable. Check the system requirements before paying for packaged software to make sure the software will work with your PC hardware and with your OS.

Installing Software

When you buy packaged software at a retail store, you usually receive a DVD inside the package. Insert the DVD into the appropriate drive on your computing device, and the software will automatically begin the installation process. Follow the prompts to complete the installation routine.

In some cases, you may purchase a license card, which has instructions to go to a website, download the software, and install the software with the license key printed on the card. If you have downloaded software from a website, you generally have two methods for installing the software on a Windows-based computer:

Packaged software purchased at a retailer generally includes a DVD that you use to install the software.

- You can opt to run the installation program directly from the website. After clicking the download link, you will have the option to run or save the installation file. Choose run to install the program directly from the source website and then follow the prompts that appear. In the Windows OS, you will be prompted with a security warning message and will have to allow the installation to proceed.
- Alternatively, you can save the downloaded file to your hard drive and run the installation later. After clicking the download link, select the save option to download the file to the default downloads folder, or choose Save as to either navigate to another drive and folder or create a new folder in which to store the file. When the download is complete, open the window to view the file and then double-click the file name to start the installation routine. Follow the prompts that appear in the installer window (Figure 5.21). In the Windows OS, you need to click the option to allow the installation to proceed at the security warning message. Choose the method that saves the downloaded file if you want to have a copy of the software program installation file in case you need to reinstall it again at a later date.
- On a Mac computer, downloaded software is saved automatically to the Downloads folder located next to the Trash icon on the dock. Open the folder and double-click the installer program to start the installation. Some installer programs open a pop-up window instructing you to drag the installer program to the Applications folder, while other installer programs automatically copy the file to the Applications folder and begin the software installation. Follow the prompts that appear once the installer program is running.

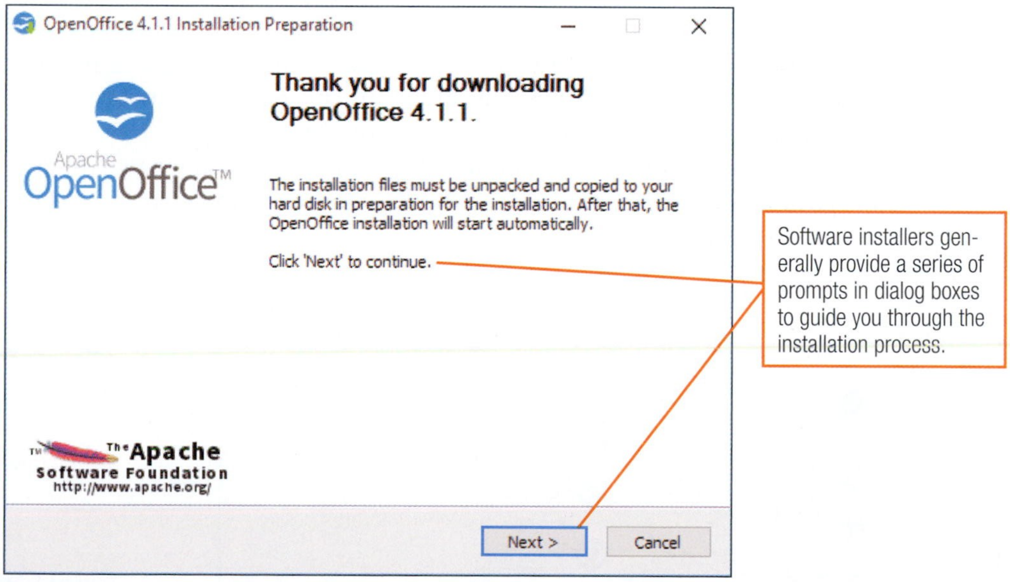

Figure 5.21

Installing software you have downloaded generally involves proceeding through an installer wizard that prompts you along the way.

When you install software, you are required to accept a license agreement (unless the software product is open source) similar to the one shown in Figure 5.22. The license agreement, called a **software license agreement (SLA)** or **end-user license agreement (EULA)**, varies by software publisher. Although the terms and conditions are generally long and filled with legal terminology, you should read the agreement and not just blindly click I Accept or I Agree or Yes to move on. The SLA or EULA specifies the number of computers you can legally install the software on. For example, some publishers will allow installation on up to three computers, while others may restrict it to one.

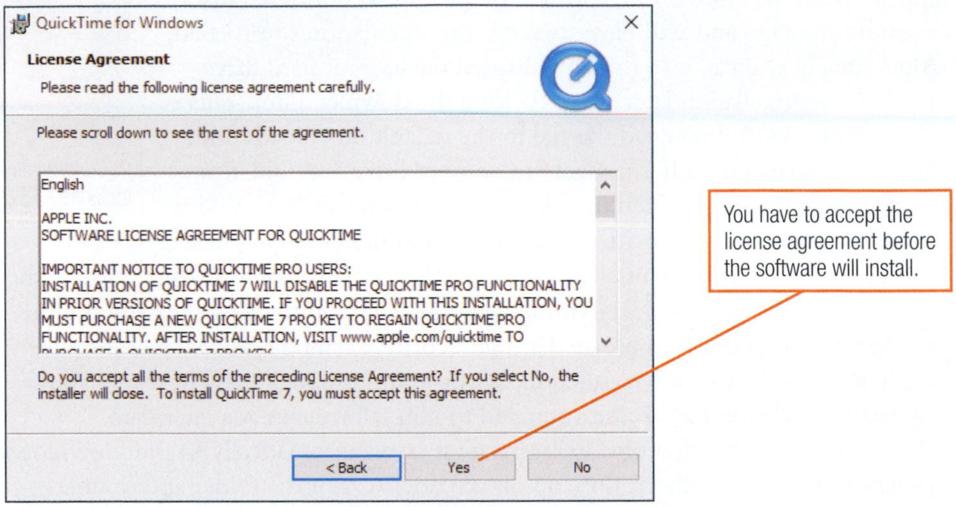

Figure 5.22

Software such as Apple QuickTime requires that you agree to a license agreement for the software installation to proceed.

Uninstalling Software

If you have installed a software application that you no longer use, uninstall the program from the hard drive to free up resources. To do this on a Windows-compatible computer, open the Control Panel and click the link Uninstall a program in the *Programs* category (Figure 5.23). At the Programs and Features window, click to select the program you want to remove in the list of software applications and then click the Uninstall button. An uninstall routine will automatically run. Close the Control Panel when finished. In some cases, programs are not completely removed until you restart your computer.

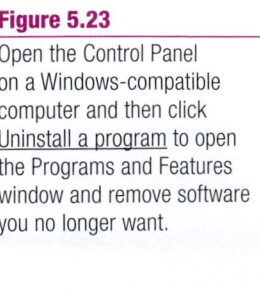

Figure 5.23

Open the Control Panel on a Windows-compatible computer and then click Uninstall a program to open the Programs and Features window and remove software you no longer want.

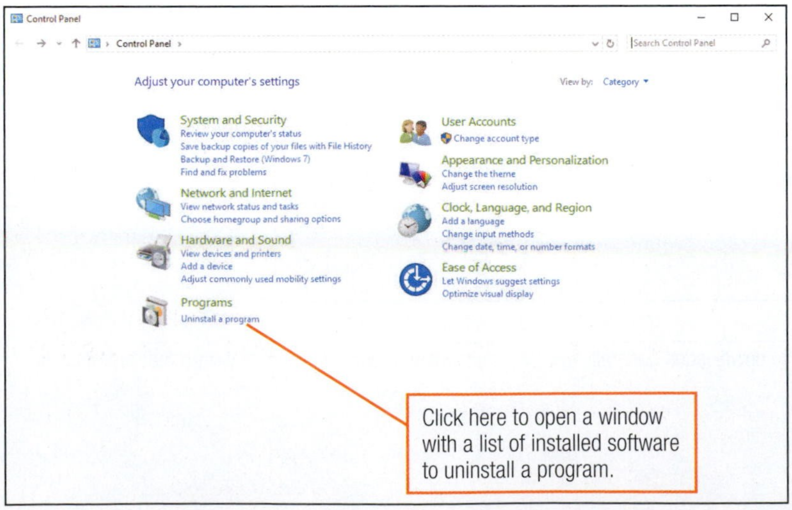

On a Mac computer, you uninstall an application by finding the application icon (in the Finder window) and dragging the icon to the Trash. The icon is a shortcut to the program's installation bundle, which includes all related program files. To remove a program's shortcut icon from the dock, simply drag the icon off the dock.

Upgrading Software

Upgrading software means installing a newer version of a program you are already licensed to use (not to be confused with updating, which installs fixes or patches to the existing version). Usually, when you install an upgrade, the older version is replaced; however, in some applications, you can opt to keep the older version and the newer version on the same computer. Some software applications prompt you when an upgrade is available, and clicking the prompt will take you to the website where you can download the newer version. Some upgrades are free, while others require payment for the upgrade at a price lower than the original purchase. Registering software when you buy it is a good idea because it helps ensure you are notified of upgrades and qualify for reduced pricing.

Blog Topic: Why Pay for Software?

As you have learned in this chapter, there are several alternatives to paying for a software license for a traditional packaged suite such as Microsoft Office. Despite these free alternatives, software suites like Microsoft Office have loyal supporters who consistently buy upgrades. Why do you think people pay for software? What benefits do paying customers receive that users of freeware do not?

1. Write and post a blog entry with your thoughts on why people prefer to pay for software such as Microsoft Office, instead of using OpenOffice, LibreOffice, or other free, web-based applications.
2. Read at least two of your classmates' blog entries and post one comment to each.
3. Submit the URLs for your blog and your two classmates' blogs to your instructor in the manner she or he has requested.

Security Alert: Downloader Beware

Exercise caution at software review websites that provide links to download free software. Many of these sites have ads with links that look deceptively similar to the actual download links you are supposed to click. These links lead to software the advertiser wants you to download, not the software you are looking for. Clicking one of these links by mistake often means you end up with unwanted software on your PC that can be difficult to remove completely. To be safe, download a program from the actual company's website, and be careful to click the download link in the main body of the web page (not around the outside edge where ads are typically run). These precautions can help ensure you get the software you want.

Explore Further: SLA Terms for Microsoft Office

Do you know the usage rights in the Microsoft Office SLA? For example, can you legally install the software on more than one computer?

1. Find and read the software license agreement for Microsoft Office desktop application software at **http://CC2.ParadigmCollege.net/MicrosoftSLA**. Specifically, find out how Internet activation works, whether the software can be transferred to another user, and the number of computers the software can be installed on.
2. Create a document with the answers to the questions in your own words.
3. Save the document as **MSOffice-SLA-YourName**.
4. Submit the document to your instructor in the manner she or he has requested.

5.7 Mobile Apps

Mobile devices, such as smartphones, tablets, and smartwatches, have a different software edition designed specifically for mobile use. A program for a smartphone or tablet is called a **mobile application** or *app*. An app is designed usually for one purpose, to work on a smaller screen, and to accept touch input from finger gestures. Functionality for on-screen keyboards, handwriting recognition, and speech recognition capabilities are also part of app design. Other important features include compatibility and synchronization with PC software and information sharing with other programs or users. In this topic, you will survey apps for mobile devices.

Good to Know

As of January 2016, Microsoft revealed that the free Microsoft Office Mobile apps for Android and Apple devices had been downloaded more than 340 million times, surpassing the downloads tally for Windows 10.

Downloading Apps for a Smartphone or Tablet

Apps by the thousands are available for Android, Apple, Windows, and BlackBerry devices to accomplish just about any type of task you can imagine. For example, apps are available for working with emails, schedules, contacts, maps, GPS data, weather information, news, travel details, games, banking, calculating, currency conversion, messaging, and social media such as Facebook, Twitter, and Instagram. These are just a few of the categories of apps you will find at the Android, Apple, Windows, and BlackBerry stores. Smartphones and tablets have an icon or tile that you tap to launch the store where you find and download apps. Figure 5.24 displays the Google Play store website, where Android apps are bought and downloaded.

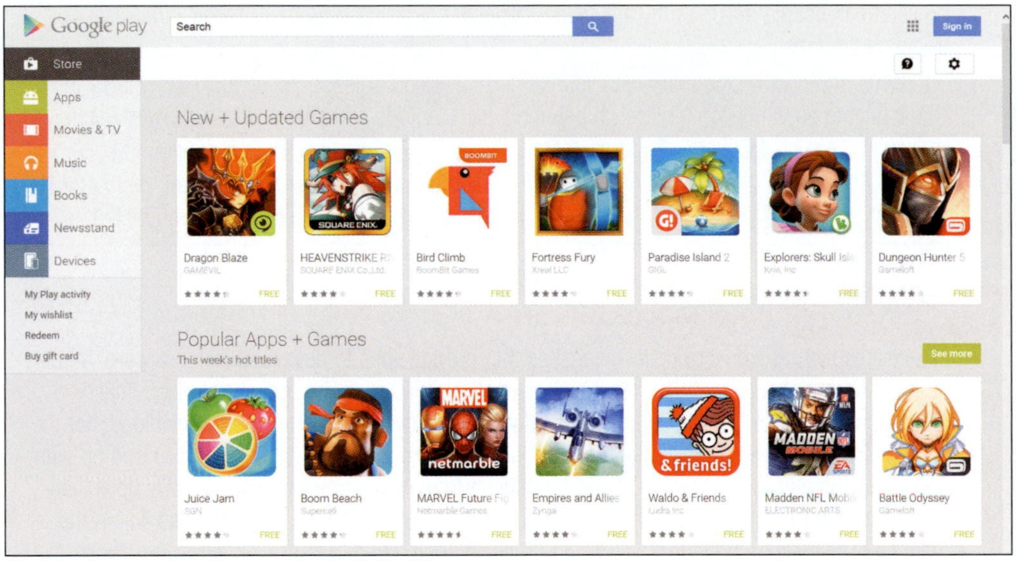

Figure 5.24

Android apps are found at Google Play. New apps are added frequently, with many offered for free or at a low cost.

Blog Topic What Is Your Favorite Mobile App?

What is your favorite smartphone or tablet app? Why? How often do you use the app in a typical day?

1. Write and post a blog entry that describes your favorite app, why it is your favorite, and how often you use it in a typical day.
2. Read at least two of your classmates' blog entries and post one comment to each.
3. Submit your blog URL and the URLs of the two classmates' blogs to your instructor in the manner she or he has requested.

Built-in Apps

Android, Apple, Windows, and BlackBerry smartphones and tablets come equipped with several built-in apps, such as the ones shown on the iPhone in Figure 5.25. Typically, PIM apps for keeping track of appointments, contacts, to-do lists, reminders, and notes are standard, as are apps for email, messaging, maps, music, games, and social networks.

Figure 5.25

Smartphones and tablets come equipped with built-in apps, such as the ones shown on this iPhone. Apple includes a mobile edition of productivity applications such as Numbers, Pages, and Keynote.

Mobile Productivity Apps

Microsoft has Word, Excel, PowerPoint, and OneNote editions designed for a smartphone or tablet. You can review, edit, and sync documents to and from email, OneDrive, Sharepoint, or other web-based services. Microsoft has released Office Mobile apps for Android in the Google Play store and for iPhone and iPad in the iTunes store as free downloads. Apple has mobile editions of Pages, Keynote, and Numbers for the iOS devices iPhone and iPad (Figure 5.25). Google Mobile is a suite of productivity apps for Android devices. Figure 5.26 shows the Office mobile app screen for Microsoft Excel and Microsoft Word.

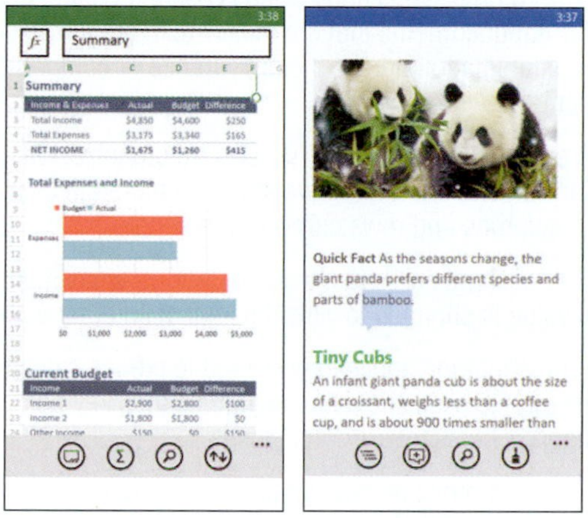

Figure 5.26

Microsoft Excel Mobile (left) and Microsoft Word Mobile (right) are used to view, edit, and create spreadsheets and documents on your smartphone or tablet.

Wearable Technology Apps

The growth of wearable technology devices is also driving growth in the development of wearable technology apps. The challenges for wearable app developers are the constraints of battery life, small screen, and less computing power. These are the same challenges encountered for smartphone app developers, but they are magnified for developers of wearable devices. Developers also have to consider the usage for a wearable app. In most cases, the wearer will want a quick interaction with a display that provides information at a glance, while withstanding constant movement. Fitness apps are abundant for bands and smartwatches—everything from apps that measure heart rate to apps that monitor glucose levels and issue fatigue alerts. Alarms, billable hours trackers, maps, weather forecasts, schedule and note reminders, email alerts, shopping lists, recipe card displays, boarding passes, and conversion tools are just a few of the other wearable tech apps now available.

Productivity apps for wearable devices will see growth as the devices become prevalent in the workplace. To coincide with the release of the Apple Watch in 2015, Microsoft released a smartwatch PowerPoint app that lets the wearer navigate slides in a presentation, view the time elapsed, and see the number of slides in the deck. Watch for innovative wearable apps to come soon!

Mobile apps for wearable technology are a growing trend, with IDG predicting that 111.9 million wearable devices will be sold in 2018.

Explore Further **Popular Apps for Android, Apple, and Windows Mobile Devices**

With thousands of apps available for mobile devices, finding the most useful apps for a smartphone or tablet might not be easy.

1. Find and read at least two online articles that rate the top free apps for an Apple, Android, or Windows mobile device. Pick five apps that you think are noteworthy.
2. Create a presentation that contains five slides describing the five apps—one app on each slide. Include a sixth slide with the URLs of the articles you used.
3. Save the presentation as **MyTop5Apps-YourName**.
4. Submit the presentation to your instructor in the manner she or he has requested.

Topics Review

Topic	Key Concepts	Key Terms
5.1 Productivity Applications for the Workplace	Application software, or apps, are programs used by individuals to carry out tasks, or otherwise get things done. A productivity suite, also known as a *software suite*, is a group of bundled programs that includes a word processing, spreadsheet, presentation, and database management program. The Microsoft Office suite is offered in several editions, some of which include Microsoft Word, Microsoft Excel, Microsoft PowerPoint, Microsoft Outlook, and Microsoft Access. A word processing application is used to create, edit, and format documents that are mostly text, but may also include multimedia to improve the appearance or comprehension of content. A spreadsheet application is used to organize, calculate, edit, format, and chart numbers that are entered in cells within a grid of columns and rows called a worksheet. Spreadsheets are often used to perform what-if analysis, where a value is changed to view the impact on other values. A presentation application is used to create slides for an electronic slide show that communicates key points, facts, figures, messages, or other ideas. Large amounts of data are organized, stored, and maintained in a program called a database management application. In database management software, you set up the structure to store data, input data, maintain data, and then produce lists and reports for various purposes.	application software productivity software software suite productivity suite word processing application spreadsheet application presentation application database management application
5.2 Other Workplace Productivity Applications	Personal information management (PIM) software is used to organize emails, appointments, contacts, and to-do lists. Accounting software applications are used to record and report the financial activities of a business related to assets, liabilities, equity, revenue, and expenses. A business will use project management software to create and maintain a project schedule and project budget. Document management software is used for managing the storage, retrieval, history, and eventual disposal of documents stored in a central repository. Industry-specific software applications are programs used to perform tasks unique to a specific business environment, such as computer-aided design or travel bookings. Enterprise resource planning (ERP) software is designed to support large-scale operations with higher level needs.	personal information management (PIM) software accounting application project management application document management system (DMS) enterprise resource planning (ERP) application

continued...

Topic	Key Concepts	Key Terms
5.3 Applications for Working with Graphics, Multimedia, and the Web	Graphics software refers to painting and drawing programs with tools to create, edit, and apply special effects to pictures, shapes, or other images. Desktop publishing software is used to place text and graphics on a page with more control over spacing and a wider range of fonts, sizes, and colors for professional, print-based publications. A multimedia software program uses text with images, video, audio, and animations to create interactive applications. A website and its associated web pages are created and maintained using a web authoring program. Photo editing software is used to edit pictures and add special effects and text. Animation software applications are used by a multimedia professional to create images with movement or otherwise interact with viewers. Video editing software is used to manipulate video recorded with a camcorder and add music, audio effects, and text to create videos called clips. Recording and editing music clips, sound clips, or podcasts is done using an audio recording and editing software program. Low-cost or free multimedia programs are available for nonprofessionals to work with graphics, pictures, video, and sound.	graphics software desktop publishing (DTP) software multimedia software web authoring software photo editing software animation software video editing software audio recording and editing software
5.4 Software Applications for Personal Use	Note taking software provides a way to store, organize into notebooks and tabs, search, and share notes of any type. Personal finance software allows you to balance your bank accounts and manage personal investments. Prepare and file your tax return using a tax preparation software program. Legal documents, such as wills and contracts, can be prepared using legal software, which contains forms for completing legal documents. Hobby software applications are available to help you with just about any type of leisure activity, such as scrapbooking, meal planning, or genealogy. A program for playing a game or video is referred to as *entertainment software*. Learning about subjects such as math and geography is made easier using an educational software program that uses multimedia to add interactivity and games to improve comprehension and retention of content. A reference software program uses multimedia tools to provide rich content in an encyclopedia, translation guide, and other references.	note taking software personal finance software tax preparation software legal software hobby software entertainment software educational software reference software

continued...

Topic	Key Concepts	Key Terms
5.5 Cloud and Open Source Applications	The main advantage to using a web-based application is that you have access to the software and your documents from any location with an Internet connection. Google Drive, Office Online, and Zoho are all cloud providers that offer free storage space and a suite of productivity applications for free. Apache OpenOffice, a free, open source productivity suite updated and maintained by volunteers, includes a word processor, spreadsheet, presentation, graphics, and database program. LibreOffice, a project of The Document Foundation, is another open source productivity suite with applications called Writer, Calc, Impress, Draw, Base, and Math.	
5.6 Acquiring, Installing, Uninstalling, and Upgrading Software	Software is a licensed product, meaning that you pay for the right to use the software but you do not own the program code. Packaged software is a program or suite that can be purchased in a retail store, at e-commerce websites, or directly from the software publisher. Shareware is a downloadable software program for which you pay a small fee if you decide to keep the program after a trial period. Freeware is a software program provided for your use without purchase, such as Apple iTunes. Subscription software is a program generally purchased from cloud computing providers where you pay a monthly or annual charge. Packaged software contains a DVD or license card inside the package with which you install the application. Download and install software directly from a website by running the install program at the source website or by saving the install program on your hard disk drive to install at a later time. All software programs except open source applications require that you agree to or accept a software license agreement (SLA) or end-user license agreement (EULA) which contains the terms and conditions for using the program. For example, the agreement specifies the number of computers you can legally install the software on. Uninstall software from the computer when you are no longer using it to free up computer resources by opening the Control Panel on a Windows PC or by dragging the program icon and dock shortcut to the trash on a Mac. Installing a newer version of a software program is called *upgrading*; upgrades are generally made available for free or at a price lower than purchasing the software new.	packaged software shareware freeware subscription software software license agreement (SLA) end-user license agreement (EULA)

continued…

Topic	Key Concepts	Key Terms
5.7 Mobile Apps	A mobile application, or app, is a program designed for use on a mobile device such as a smartphone, tablet, or smartwatch that is designed to work on a smaller screen. The app accepts input from touch, handwriting, and voice, and includes compatibility with PC software. All smartphones and tablets come equipped with several built-in apps that typically include personal information management, communication, messaging, maps, music, and game apps. Microsoft, Google, and Apple all have separate mobile productivity apps that run on their smartphones and tablets. Wearable technology apps are designed for use on devices, such as fitness bands and smartwatches. These apps accommodate smaller hardware resources that provide for a quick interaction, display information at a glance, and withstand constant movement.	mobile application

Recheck

Recheck your understanding of the topics covered in this chapter.

Workbook

Chapter review and assessment resources are available in the *Workbook* ebook.

Chapter 6

Using Social Media to Connect and Communicate

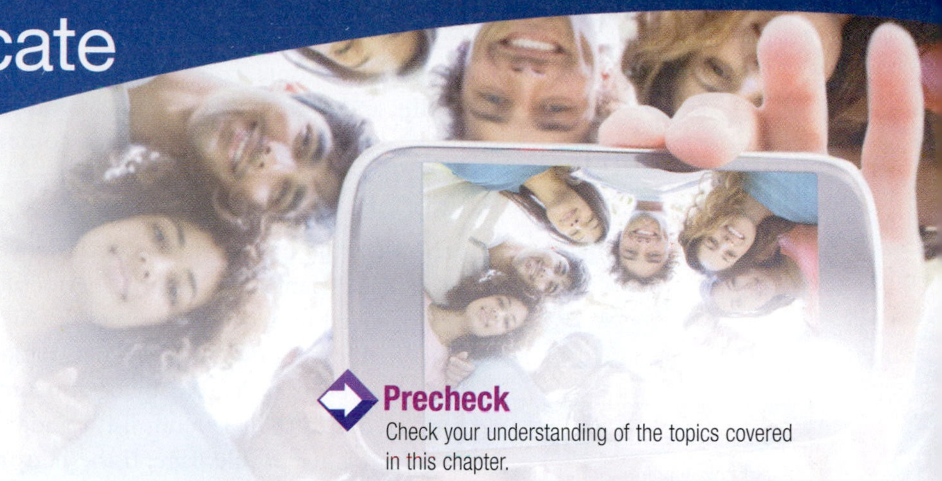

Precheck

Check your understanding of the topics covered in this chapter.

Learning Objectives

6.1 Describe social networking and list popular social networking websites

6.2 Explain how social bookmarking is used to track and share information, and give examples of social bookmarking websites

6.3 List key features of popular websites used for sharing music, videos, photos, and presentations

6.4 Identify websites used for blogging and explain how to create a blog and a blog post

6.5 Describe how wikis generate content from users and describe two well-known wiki websites

6.6 Relate examples of social media strategies used by businesses to connect and communicate with customers

In Chapter 2, you learned that Web 2.0 refers to second-generation websites that provide for two-way communication, where individuals interact with organizations and with one another by sharing ideas, feedback, content, and multimedia. A large component of Web 2.0 involves social networking sites, such as Facebook, Twitter, and Instagram, that are used daily by millions of people of all ages around the world. Businesses and other organizations also use social media technologies to connect and interact with customers or clients. Media sharing services, blogs, and wikis are other components of Web 2.0 that focus on user-generated content.

In this chapter, you will learn about social networking, social bookmarking, media sharing, blogging, and wikis. You will also be introduced to ways organizations have incorporated social media technologies into their strategies to increase brand loyalty or attract new business.

NOTE: *The nature of social media websites is such that they constantly evolve in response to innovation or new trends. The screens shown and instructions provided in this chapter are subject to change. Often, updates or changes to software mean that changes occur to the layout, design, or procedures. You can use the Help function at a website if the figures or steps provided in this chapter do not match what you are seeing on your screen.*

SNAP If you are a SNAP user, go to your SNAP Assignments page to complete the Precheck, Tutorials, and Recheck.

6.1 Social Networking

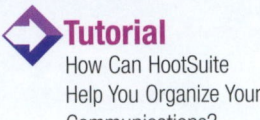

Tutorial
How Can HootSuite Help You Organize Your Communications?

Social media is a term used to describe any online tool in which users generate content and interact with others. A website that provides a platform for people to connect with groups of people and interact is called a **social networking website**. Generally, social networking sites provide a means to build a list of friends, with whom you share information, and publish a profile that contains information about yourself. In this topic, you will be introduced to the social networking sites Facebook, LinkedIn, and Google+ (which help you connect with friends, family, and business contacts) and reddit (an open source community for sharing stories).

Facebook

Facebook is the most popular social networking site used by people who want to connect with friends and family. The social network ranked first in a 2015 worldwide survey of social networking websites by Statista (an Internet statistical portal) and by GlobalWebIndex (a digital consumer market research company).

New Facebook users start by creating an account, setting up their profile, and adding friends to their Friends list. To add friends, you search by a person's name and look at his or her profile page. If the person is someone you want to add to your Friends list, click the Add Friend button. A friend request is sent to the individual, who can then accept or ignore it. Once an individual accepts your friend request, the two of you can see each other's Facebook activity.

People post updates to Facebook about what they're doing and share links, photos, videos, music, games, news items, quotes, and just about anything else that appears to be of interest. People comment on a person's Facebook posts, generally with brief notes. Users can chat with friends who are online or use the Facebook Messenger tool to send private messages.

Users can create or join Facebook groups to gather with people who share a similar interest or goal. Businesses and other organizations create Facebook pages to share information and interact with customers, clients, or other interested visitors. For example, Figure 6.1 shows the Facebook page for the US Department of Education.

Good to Know
Facebook was founded in February 2004 as a network for college students only. In 2006, Facebook opened up to everyone, and quickly exploded to become the most used social network worldwide. In December 2015, Facebook reported more than 1.59 billion active monthly users, with mobile users representing 1.44 billion.

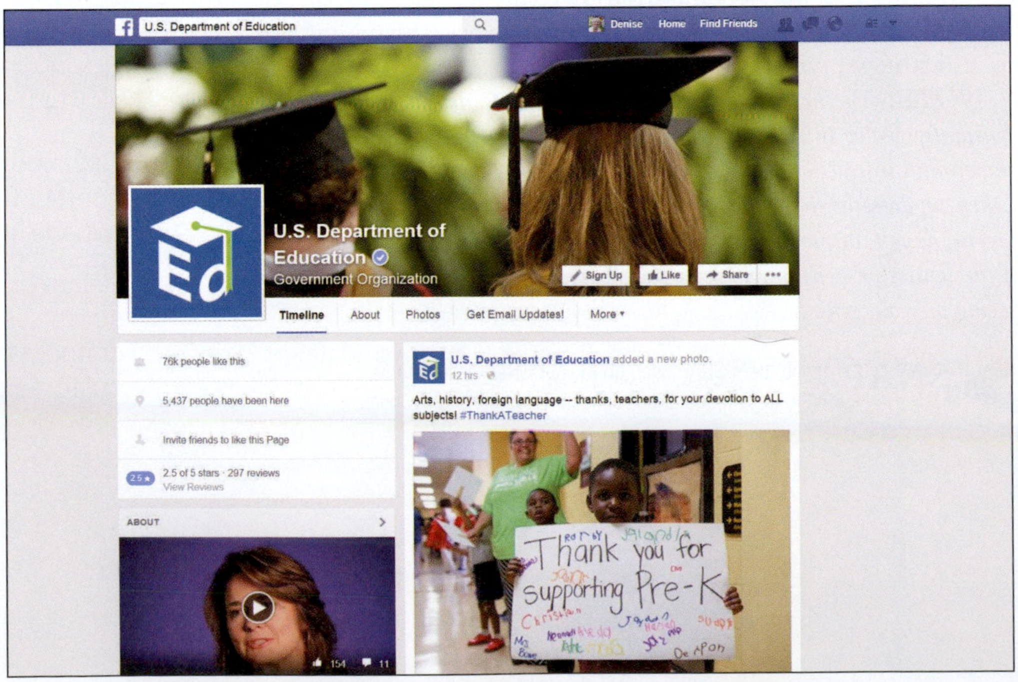

Figure 6.1
Education news is shared and discussed in comments with the general public on the Facebook page for the US Department of Education.

Check This Out
http://CC2.ParadigmCollege.net/FBSeguinConcepts
Go here to see the Facebook page for this textbook.

LinkedIn

LinkedIn, the most visited business-related social networking site, launched in May 2003 and reports that new members join the network at a rate of more than two per second. The social network ranked seventh in the March 2015 worldwide survey by Statista. LinkedIn reports over 414 million members, with students and recent college graduates the fastest growing demographic. It is a professional network where users connect with business contacts.

Creating an account with LinkedIn allows you to create a professional profile with your current and past employment positions, education credentials, and links to websites (such as your current company's website). Your profile can be expanded to represent in resume-like fashion a summary of your qualifications and prior work experiences. Once your profile is established, you begin connecting through LinkedIn with people in your workplace and with other professionals in your field and related fields. The Search tool in LinkedIn can be used to find people by name, job title, company name, or location. You can also join professional association groups to keep up with news in your field.

A Jobs board shows current job listings and includes a search tool to find job listings by job title, keywords, or company name. Figure 6.2 shows the LinkedIn Careers page for Adobe.

Tutorial
How Can Social Media Help You Land a Job?

Good to Know
LinkedIn mobile users viewed 1.45 million jobs per day in 2014.

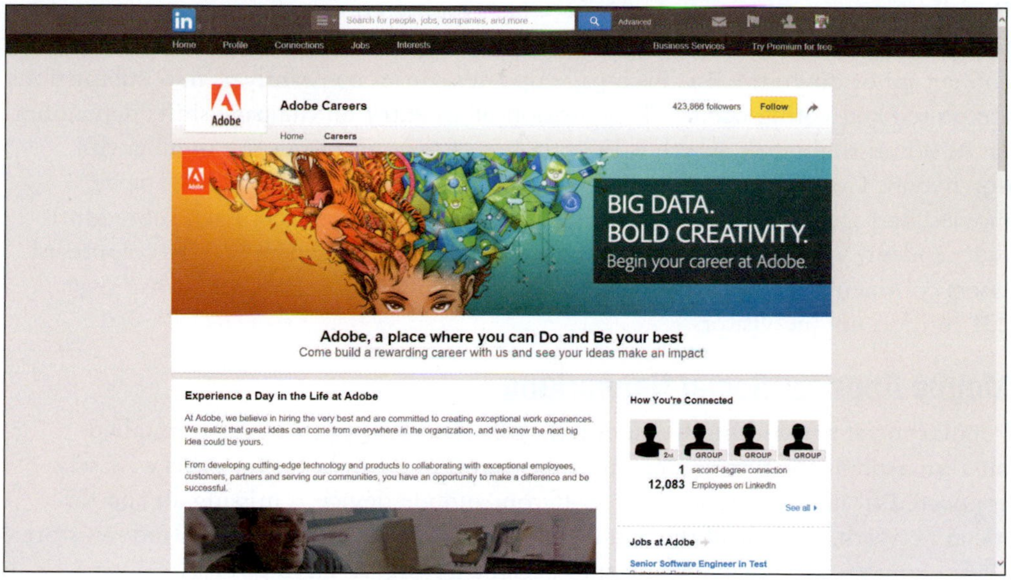

Figure 6.2
The LinkedIn Careers page for Adobe has information about working at Adobe and current job postings.

Google+

In 2011, Google launched a social networking site called **Google+**. The social network ranked ninth in a March 2015 survey by Statista, with 300 million active monthly users. Sign in at Google+ with your Gmail account or create a new account, add content to your profile, and then start adding people to your network.

In Google+, people or websites that you connect with are organized into categories called *circles*. The default circles are Family, Friends, Acquaintances, and Following. By maintaining your social network in separate circles, you can share activity with only the people for whom the content is of interest. For example, you can post information about a family reunion and share it only with your Family circle. Add websites with which you want to keep up-to-date to your Following circle. Type a note, upload a photo or video, or enter a link at the *Share what's new* box at the top of your page, and then share the item by adding names, names of circles, or email addresses.

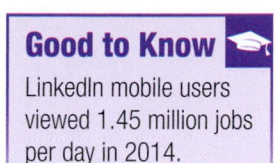

Businesses and other organizations have Google+ pages. Figure 6.3 shows a page of photos posted by the US Navy on its Google+ page.

Figure 6.3

At the US Navy Google+ page, you can scroll through photos that show live action of navy activities.

Reddit

The Reddit mascot is named *Snoo.*

Reddit is a social networking website where registered users submit content with text, links, or photos. Other registered users, called *redditors,* vote to move the content up or down the list. Each page updates stories constantly as new submissions are posted and voting occurs. The position of an entry on the page shifts depending on its submission score, which is the number of upvotes minus the number of downvotes. Content is organized by categories, such as gaming, videos, news, movies, and sports, called *subreddits,* to which you can subscribe. Each subreddit is independent, with a set of guidelines and rules to follow, moderated by volunteers. Users comment on stories and can add friends. In January 2016, reddit had over 231 million unique visitors.

Mobile Apps for Social Networking

Popular social networking websites have free mobile apps that are preinstalled on a smartphone so that you can post messages, upload photos, or otherwise stay connected from your mobile device. If your mobile device is missing an app for a social network, download the app from Google Play, iTunes, or the Windows store.

Anonymous social networking apps became a rising trend in 2014. An **anonymous social network** allows users to post content viewable by everyone on the network without using their real names. One popular anonymous social network is Yik Yak, a free mobile app for Android or iOS devices. Yik Yak uses GPS technology to pinpoint the location of mobile devices and then allows users to create and view posts, called *yaks,* within a small radius—anyone within 1.5 miles of a message can read and respond to yaks. Yik Yak began as a popular app among college and university students to communicate about class cancellations and campus life. The app soon spread to high school and middle school students. The app's developers had to build geofencing technology into their system to block the app from being used on high school or middle school grounds after complaints that the app became a vehicle for misuse and cyberbullying by the younger student population.

Another anonymous social network, Secret, shut down its network in April 2015 after just 16 months of operation. Although the future of anonymous social networking is unclear, many of these apps have a large number of active users.

Table 6.1 lists three mobile social networking apps that ranked in the top 15 worldwide for active accounts in March 2015, according to Statista.

Social networking apps are free for a mobile device.

Table 6.1

Three Top 15 Ranked Social Networking Apps

Social Network	Number of Active Users in March 2015	Rank in Top 15
WhatsApp	700 million	Third
WeChat	468 million	Sixth
Skype	300 million	Eighth

Security Alert Know Your Privacy Settings

Make sure you check the privacy settings at the social networks you use when you set up your account. Recheck the settings periodically to be sure you are not sharing more personal information than you intended. Always recheck your settings when a network updates or changes its privacy options or policies. Ask your friends not to tag you in photos they post if you don't want friends of friends to see what you've been up to.

Blog Topic Is It Fair That Social Media Posts Can Be Used Against You?

You have probably seen news stories about athletes who lost scholarships, college applicants whose admission offers were rescinded, and employees who were fired—all because they posted on a social network something considered inappropriate or offensive. Do you think your social network posts should affect your ability to attend school or to work? Should a social network post be treated the same as a notice on a public bulletin board? Is it fair that an employer or potential employer can judge you based on your social media activity?

1. Write and post a blog entry that answers the above questions and gives your reasons.
2. Read at least two of your classmates' blogs and post one comment to each.
3. Submit your blog URL and the URLs of the two classmates' blogs to your instructor in the manner she or he has requested.

Explore Further Find a New Social Network

This topic surveyed only four social networks; many more exist. The popularity of mobile social networking is leading to the development of new social networks every year. What new social network would you like to explore?

1. Find a social networking app or website that you have not used before. Learn the purpose of the social network and read reviews and user ratings. Think about whether you would use the network or stick with your existing social networks.
2. Create a document or presentation that describes the app, whether you would use it, and give your reasons. Include the URLs for the websites you used.
3. Save the document or presentation as **NewSocialNetwork-YourName**.
4. Submit the document or presentation to your instructor in the manner she or he has requested.

6.2 Social Bookmarking

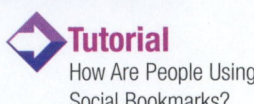

Tutorial
How Are People Using Social Bookmarks?

A category of social networking that provides tools to organize, store, and share content with others is known as **social bookmarking**. You have probably saved or bookmarked a link that you visit frequently within your browser. Bookmarked links are stored in folders on your local hard drive. Social bookmarking is similar to browser bookmarking except that a saved link, called a **bookmark**, is saved in a social network that is accessible from any device with Internet connectivity. At social bookmarking sites, you can search bookmarks that others have created.

Bookmarks can be organized by tagging a website. A **tag** is a keyword you assign to describe or categorize a selected photo, article, or item on a web page. Tags help users at the social bookmarking site find content. For example, if you find a recipe for Greek souvlaki you want to share, you can tag the recipe at the source website, while creating the bookmark with keywords such as *recipe*, *greek souvlaki*, *greek*, and *entrée*.

Each social bookmarking website has a **bookmarklet**. A bookmarklet is an icon that allows you to perform an action on the current web page with one click. For a social bookmarking website, the bookmarklet captures the current web page's URL and saves the page reference for you in your bookmarks account. The bookmarklet performs actions in the social bookmarking website similar to what happens when you add a web page to the Favorites list or bookmarks bar in your browser. When you create an account at a social bookmarking website, look for instructions on copying the bookmarklet to your browser's toolbar.

Many web pages display bookmarklets for popular websites near content you might want to bookmark. Depending on the bookmarklet, you may need to select the desired content and sign in to your account before the bookmark is created. Web pages also display bookmarklets you can use to share content via a social media account. For example, a Facebook or Twitter bookmarklet may be used to post content on your Facebook page or Twitter account. Figure 6.4 shows three bookmarklets that can be clicked to bookmark or share the content shown.

In this topic, you will explore three social bookmarking sites: Pinterest, StumbleUpon, and Delicious.

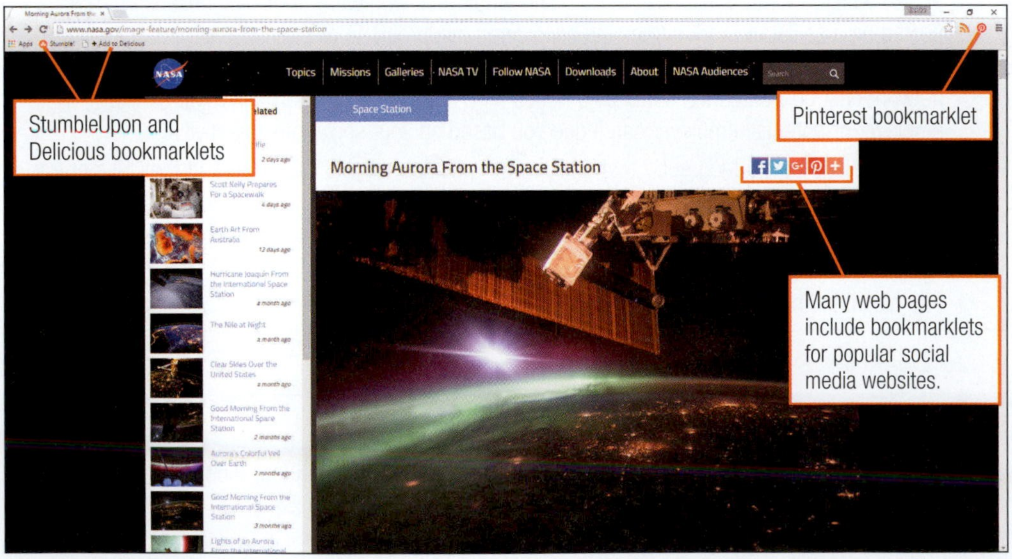

Figure 6.4
Bookmarklets on the Chrome toolbar and NASA web page can be used to bookmark or share content.

Pinterest

Pinterest is a virtual pinboard, or visual bookmarking tool to find and save ideas or other content of personal interest. The website launched in March 2010 and quickly joined the ranks of Facebook and Twitter in the top 10 social networking websites. Users click the Pin It button (bookmarklet) to pin pictures of things they have seen on the Internet that they like and want to share. Pinterest users can add a Pin It button to their browser's toolbar, or many websites include the Pin It button next to an image or other content that can be copied to Pinterest. Click the Pin It button, select the image to pin, and then choose the board to pin it to. You can also upload your own pictures to share on a board.

A board is a collection of related pictures and users can assign boards unique names. For example, you can create a board for technology and collect pictures of cool gadgets. You can browse and follow boards created by other Pinterest users to get ideas for yourself. If you like something you find on someone else's board, you can repin the item to your own. In August 2014, Pinterest launched a messaging feature that allows users to discuss a shared pin without leaving the social bookmarking website.

Figure 6.5 displays items in the Travel category that could be pinned to an individual board or shared via the messaging feature.

Good to Know

According to Pinterest, 75 percent of its daily traffic initiates from a smartphone or tablet. Pinterest also says one-third of all new Pinterest accounts come from men, despite the widely held belief that Pinterest is a female-dominated social network.

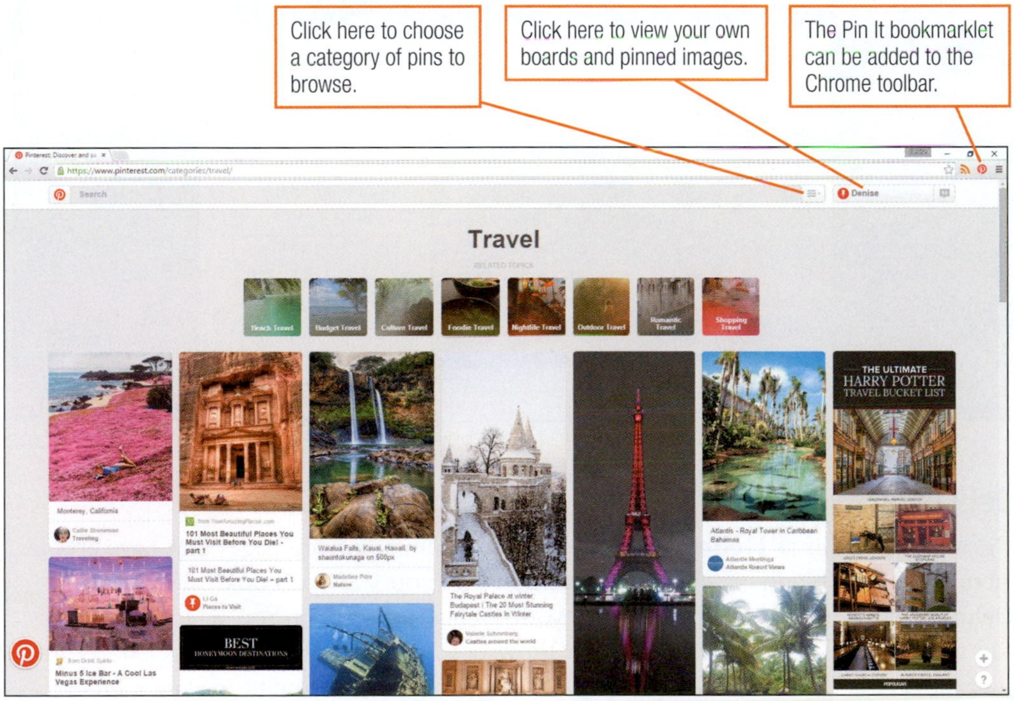

Click here to choose a category of pins to browse.
Click here to view your own boards and pinned images.
The Pin It bookmarklet can be added to the Chrome toolbar.
Travel

Figure 6.5

Pinterest is a visual social bookmarking site where users pin pictures to boards that link to items of interest.

StumbleUpon

StumbleUpon allows you to browse recommended web pages and save the pages you like to a personal profile. When you join StumbleUpon, you choose which content categories you want to see. Once your interests are established, you navigate through various web pages StumbleUpon finds for you by clicking the Stumble button in the black StumbleBar at the top of the screen (Figure 6.6). Use the Like (thumbs-up) button and the Dislike (thumbs-down) button on the StumbleBar as you view pages so that StumbleUpon can tailor the recommendations to your preferences. Each time you click the Stumble button, another web page appears. You can share a page you find with others, and you can follow another StumbleUpon user (called a Stumbler) if you like the same web pages.

View web pages you have liked, add more categories to your interests, and browse lists, channels, or other Stumbler pages once you have created a profile and used StumbleUpon to like pages. Click your avatar and explore pages using the options that appear.

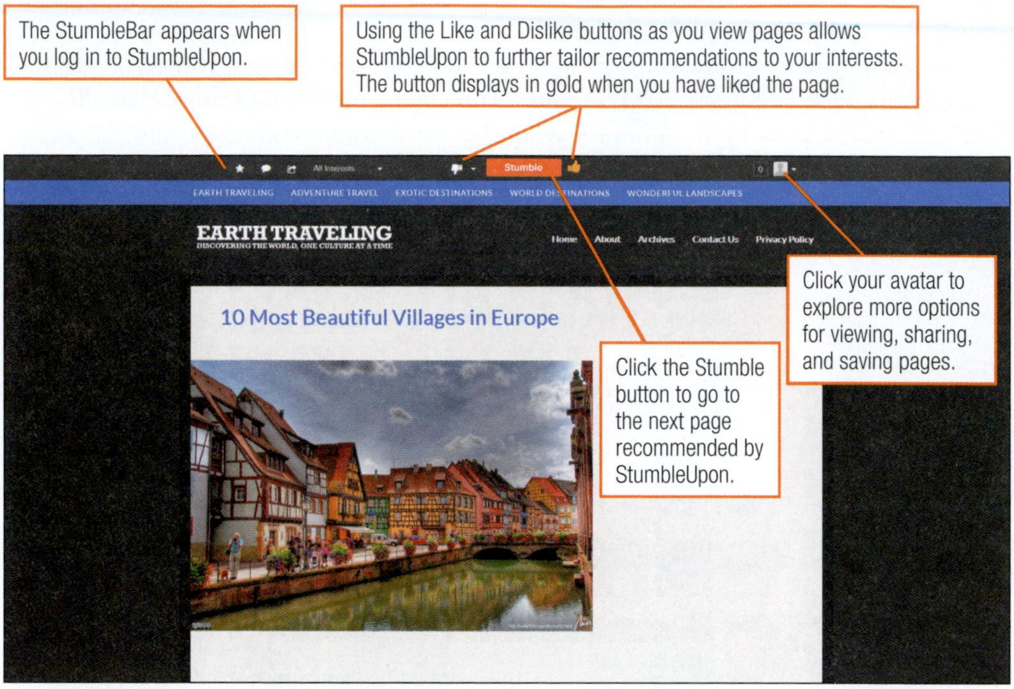
The StumbleBar appears when you log in to StumbleUpon.
Using the Like and Dislike buttons as you view pages allows StumbleUpon to further tailor recommendations to your interests. The button displays in gold when you have liked the page.
Stumble
EARTH TRAVELING
ADVENTURE TRAVEL
EXOTIC DESTINATIONS
WORLD DESTINATIONS
WONDERFUL LANDSCAPES
EARTH TRAVELING
DISCOVERING THE WORLD, ONE CULTURE AT A TIME
Home
About
Archives
Contact Us
Privacy Policy
10 Most Beautiful Villages in Europe
Click your avatar to explore more options for viewing, sharing, and saving pages.
Click the Stumble button to go to the next page recommended by StumbleUpon.

Figure 6.6
StumbleUpon shows recommended web pages for you based on your likes and dislikes.

+ Add to Delicious

Click the Delicious bookmarklet to save a link to your account.

Delicious

Create an account at **Delicious** to save and share links to web pages that have articles, pictures, videos, blogs, or some other content that you want to bookmark. Use the Delicious bookmarklet to save links in your Delicious account. You will have to add the Delicious bookmarklet to your browser's Favorites or Bookmarks bar. As an alternative, use the *Add Link* option in the Delicious sidebar menu to type a link that you want to save. Delicious has an import utility found on the Manage tab of its Settings page that will import bookmarks you have saved in a browser.

When viewing a web page that you decide to save, click the Delicious bookmarklet, sign in to your account if you are not already logged in, enter tags or accept the default tags, type a comment if desired, and then click the Save link button. You can mark links as private or public, and you can follow other Delicious users.

Once you have a collection of links, you can sort and search your personal collection or the collections of people you are following. Figure 6.7 on page 153 displays a Delicious page with saved bookmarks.

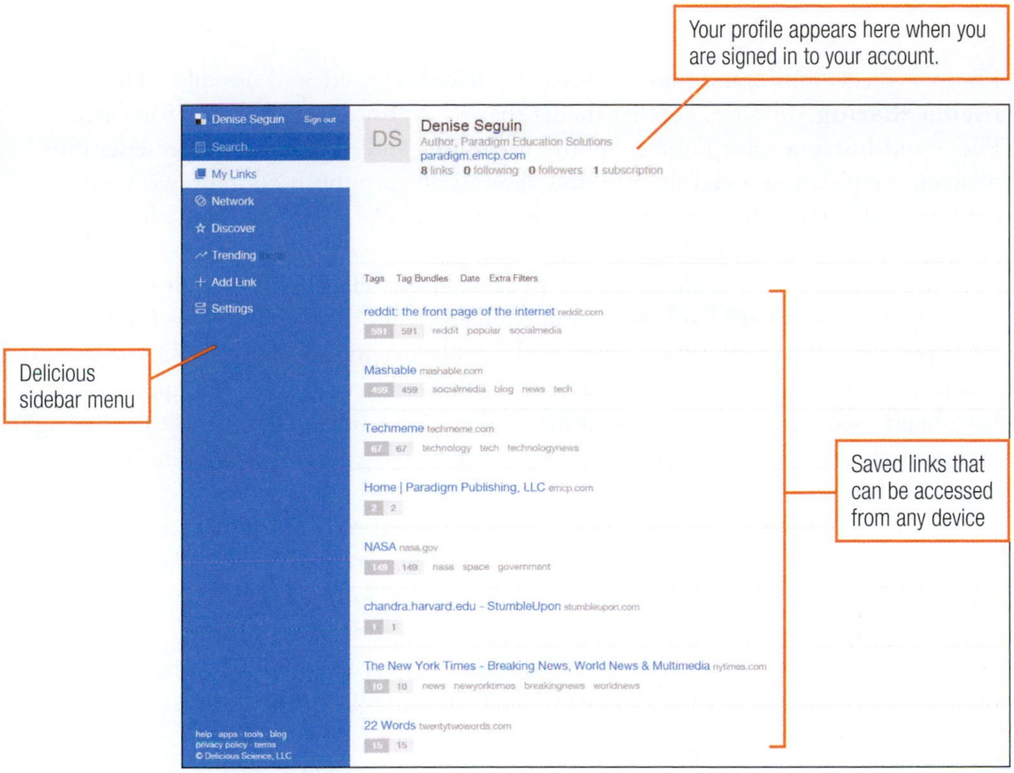

Figure 6.7

Use Delicious to collect links to websites, pictures, videos, blog entries, articles, or any other web content you want to save and/or share.

Some social bookmarking websites have connectors to Facebook and Twitter, allowing users to register using an existing Facebook or Twitter account instead of an email address.

Table 6.2 provides names and URLs to six social bookmarking sites, including the three discussed in this topic.

Table 6.2

Social Bookmarking Websites

Social Bookmark	URL
Delicious	https://delicious.com/
Digg	http://digg.com/
Diigo	https://www.diigo.com/
Newsvine	http://www.newsvine.com/
Pinterest	https://www.pinterest.com/
StumbleUpon	http://www.stumbleupon.com/

Explore Further Start Social Bookmarking

Explore a social bookmarking website to learn what it offers.

1. From the list in Table 6.2, choose a social bookmarking website you have not used before and create an account at the website.
2. Experiment with the tools available at the site by adding at least 10 bookmarks to content that you like on the web. Bookmark different types of content, such as a blog, news article, picture, and video. Consider also customizing your profile and sharing some links with others.
3. Capture an image of your page at the social bookmarking website, showing your saved links. Use a screen capture program, such as Windows Snipping Tool or PrintScreen. Depending on the method used, save the image as a JPEG file or paste the image into a document. Save the image or document as **SocialBookmarks-YourName**.
4. Submit the image or document to your instructor in the manner she or he has requested.

6.3 Media Sharing

Tutorial
How Can You Safely Share Videos?

Good to Know

A video sharing app named Vine, owned by Twitter and released in 2013, quickly gained popularity. The app lets users record and edit a video clip up to six seconds long, called a *vine*. The video is published on the Vine social network or shared on Facebook or Twitter as a looping video. According to Twitter, five vines are tweeted every second.

Photos, videos, music, and presentations are shared, viewed, and downloaded using **media sharing** websites. Popular media sharing websites are YouTube for videos, Flickr and Instagram for photos, Spotify for music, and Slideshare for presentations. Sharing media using social sharing sites allows you to publish content, work with content collaboratively, and distribute content to several people more easily than sending files or links as message attachments.

Some websites have applications for **peer-to-peer (P2P) file sharing**, in which users access each other's hard drives and exchange files directly over the Internet. BitTorrent is a P2P application often used for file sharing. People use P2P applications to share software, games, movies, music, and other content. Some P2P applications have been used to share copyrighted material without permission from the copyright owner, such as exchanging movies or music tracks between users, and are often the target for litigation from copyright holders.

Digital audio and video files are sometimes shared on the Internet as podcasts. A **podcast** is an audio or video post that is usually part of a series to which people subscribe. A software program called a **podcatcher** automatically downloads new podcast episodes to your computer or mobile device for you to listen to or watch whenever you like. Other podcasts are streamed from a website. In this topic, you will survey the media sharing services YouTube, Flickr, Spotify, and Instagram.

YouTube

YouTube, which is owned by Google, is the most popular video sharing website in the world. A YouTube video becomes a **viral video** when it spreads quickly via forwarded or shared links or word-of-mouth. With a YouTube account, you can search, browse, and watch videos; upload a video you have created; subscribe to someone's YouTube channel; and share videos with friends. Figure 6.8 shows a page from YouTube EDU, which hosts educational videos, some of which are lessons from teachers or full courses from leading universities. According to YouTube, over 1 billion users watch YouTube videos, with more than 50 percent watching from a mobile device. New content is uploaded at the rate of 300 hours of video every minute! Many people also go to YouTube to stream music or watch music videos.

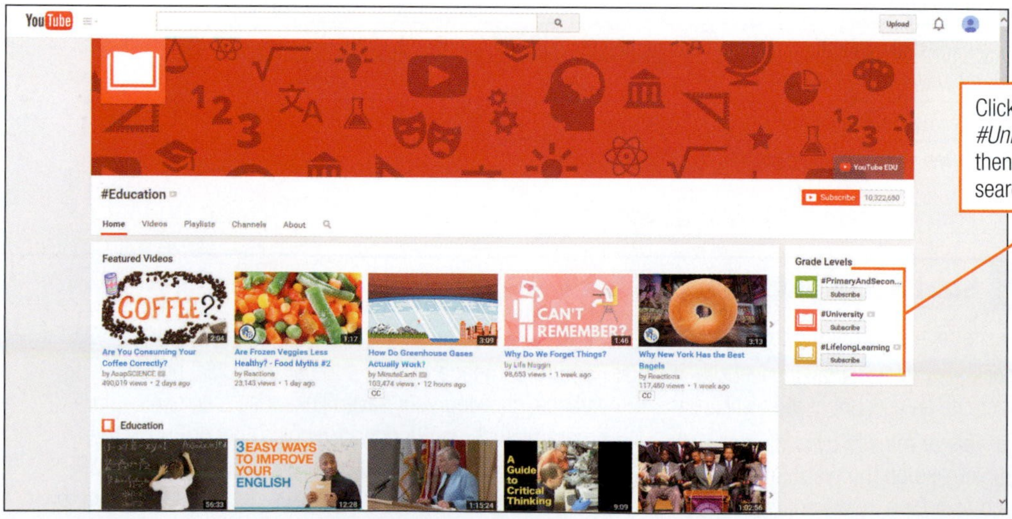

Click *#PrimaryAndSecondaryEducation*, *#University*, or *#LifelongLearning* and then pick a subcategory to browse or search educational videos by subject.

Figure 6.8
Go to YouTube EDU (**http://CC2.ParadigmCollege.net/YouTubeEDU**) to watch free lectures, courses, or other educational videos.

Flickr

Sharing photos is a popular media sharing activity because most people have digital photos they want family and friends to see. Uploading photos to a sharing site lets you easily send a link to share your photo album with other people. Although social networking sites such as Facebook and Twitter let you upload and share photos, these sites generally have lower photo storage limits than do dedicated photo sharing websites.

Many dedicated photo sharing websites are available. **Flickr** was among the original services, started in Vancouver, Canada, in 2004. In 2005, Flickr was bought by Yahoo. See Table 6.3 to review other photo sharing websites.

Generally, photo sharing websites let you upload pictures organized into albums, sets, or folders; tag and comment on pictures; and share the photos with others. You can share with other users of the site, or you can link to the photos through Facebook, Twitter, or blog posts, or through emails and other messaging tools. You can search for pictures uploaded by others, and some sites include a feature (such as the Commons at Flickr) that lets you search public photography archives. Figure 6.9 shows the Explore page for photos uploaded to Flickr.

Some photo sharing websites, such as Google Photos, include photo editing tools. In May 2015, Google announced the launch of Google Photos. Previously part of Google+, the Photos app was converted to a new standalone product that allows for free, unlimited storage of photos and videos from Apple or Android devices, or via the web. The free, unlimited storage applies for pictures with a maximum resolution of 16 megapixels and video with a maximum resolution of 1080p (also called *Full HD*).

Good to Know

A mobile app for photo and video sharing called Snapchat had over 200 million monthly users in 2016. The app, for Apple and Android devices, lets users take photos, record videos, add text and drawings, and then send the media, called *snaps*, to a list of recipients. Users set a time limit for which a recipient can see the snap, which ranges from 1 to 10 seconds. When the time period expires, the snap is deleted from Snapchat servers.

Table 6.3

Sampling of Photo Sharing Websites

Photo Sharing Website	Restrictions for Free Accounts	URL
Flickr	1 TB for photos and videos up to 3 minutes each	https://www.flickr.com/
Google Photos	Unlimited photos and videos for images up to 16 megapixels and video up to 1080p	https://photos.google.com/
Photobucket	2 GB for photos and videos up to 10 minutes each	http://photobucket.com/
Shutterfly	Unlimited photos	https://www.shutterfly.com/
Snapfish	Unlimited photos	http://www.snapfish.com/photo-gift/welcome

flickr
Explore
By default, Flickr searches everyone's uploads. Click Explore to browse recently uploaded photos or videos, or type a keyword or phrase to find photos using the search text box.

Figure 6.9

The recent photos on the Explore page at Flickr change constantly as new photos are added. As of May 2015, Flickr had approximately 11 billion photos stored on its servers.

Spotify

Good to Know

In 2014, Taylor Swift made headlines by pulling all of her songs from Spotify. Swift said she felt that Spotify did not offer enough value for artists. Spotify pays artists based on a royalty per play. According to Spotify, on average, a record label earns less than a penny per play from its site—a payment that is split between the record label company and the recording artist.

Spotify is a music and video streaming service launched from Sweden in 2008 that quickly became popular by allowing users to listen to music on most devices connected to the Internet. Spotify was one of the first to offer streaming of music via the web instead of requiring individuals to download tracks to a device. Spotify is also popular because of its vast collection of music, which includes over 30 million tracks and 2 billion playlists. The service was available in 58 countries and reported over 75 million active users in 2016. Spotify offers both a free account and a paid subscription account. A free account has ads between tracks and delivers music at a lower quality. The paid account, called Spotify Premium, is ad free and streams high-definition music. In addition, Premium users can listen to music offline.

Spotify users can share playlists and tracks that are currently playing with friends on the service. A feature called Discover Weekly delivers a personalized playlist of two hours of tracks every Monday to your phone or other device. The weekly playlist is compiled based on the previous tracks you have played and similar tracks listened to by other users. In 2015, Spotify announced it was adding video to its streaming service.

To use Spotify, sign up for an account at the Spotify website (see Table 6.4), and then download the app to your PC or mobile device and install it. Figure 6.10 displays the Spotify app for a PC. You can browse for tracks by genre or use the search text box to find a song by artist, title, playlist, or record label. You can easily save favorite tracks to your music library using the Save icon next to a track.

Table 6.4

Music Streaming Services

Music Service	URL
Apple Music	http://www.apple.com/music
Deezer	https://www.deezer.com
Google Music	https://play.google.com/music/listen#/sww
Rdio	http://www.rdio.com/home/en-us/
Spotify	https://www.spotify.com/us/
YouTube	https://www.youtube.com/

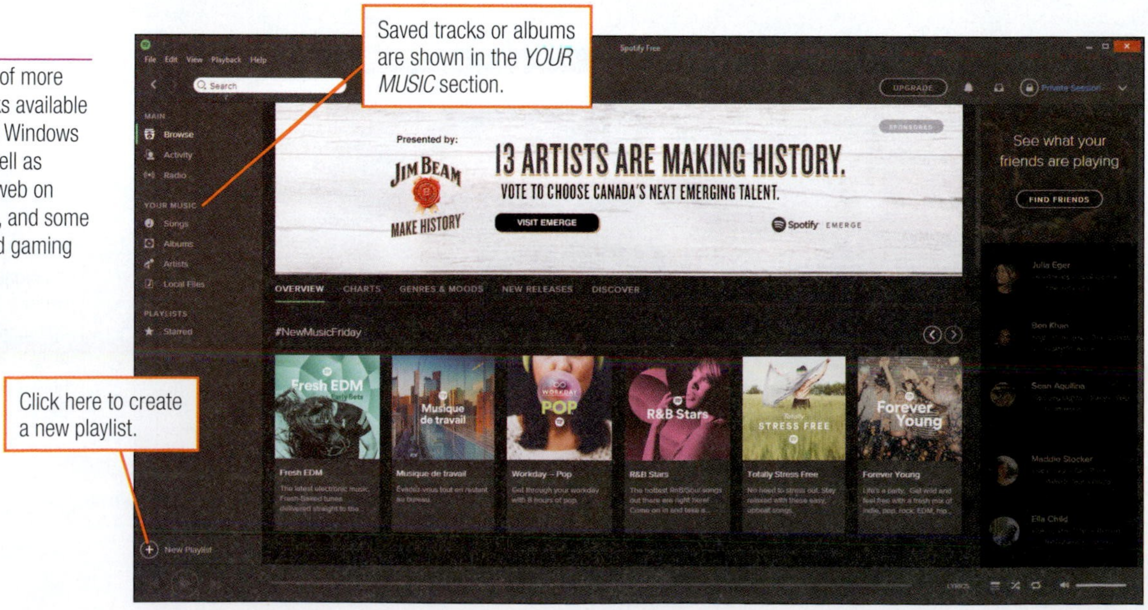

Figure 6.10

Spotify has a library of more than 30 million tracks available on iOS, Android, and Windows Phone devices, as well as streaming from the web on your desktop, laptop, and some smart televisions and gaming consoles.

Music sharing sites are often the target of litigation by major music recording labels for copyright violations. For example, Grooveshark, a music sharing website started in 2007, became embroiled in lawsuits in 2010 for copyright infringements from four major music labels: EMI Music Publishing, Universal Music Group, Sony Music, and Warner Music Group. In April 2015, the company ceased operations as part of a settlement with the record labels. At the time Grooveshark shut down, the site streamed over 1 billion songs per month, stored over 15 million songs on servers, and had 20 million active users.

Check This Out ✓

http://CC2.ParadigmCollege.net/MusicResource

Go here to find a music resource authorized by the Recording Industry Association of America and the Music Business Association.

Instagram

Instagram is a free app used by over 400 million users for sharing photos from an Apple or Android phone or tablet. After taking a photo with a mobile device, you can use Instagram to add a special effects filter to the picture, and then share the photo to your Instagram page or your favorite social networking site. In March 2015, Instagram added a new feature called Layout that lets you combine multiple pictures into one, and then flip and rotate images to create interesting visuals. Figure 6.11 shows the Layout feature being used to flip an image. You can download the Instagram app from the App Store or Google Play.

Instagram was started in October 2010 and grew to one million users in just over two months. In April 2012, Facebook purchased Instagram. According to Instagram, on average, approximately 80 million photos are posted each day.

Check This Out ✓

http://CC2.ParadigmCollege.net/Mashable

Go here for up-to-date news on digital culture, social media, and technology.

Figure 6.11

The Layout feature in Instagram (left) is used to flip an image, creating the result shown at the right.

Explore Further — Share a Presentation

Slideshare is a website at which you upload and share presentations created in PowerPoint, PDFs, Keynote, or OpenOffice. The slide hosting website also allows you to upload and share documents and videos. In this activity, you will experiment with sharing a presentation.

1. Create a presentation with at least three slides that describes the methods or websites that you use to share media, such as photos, videos, or music. If you do not share media, create one slide for each of the websites mentioned in this topic that summarizes what you learned.
2. Save the presentation as **MediaSharing-YourName**.
3. Go to **http://CC2.ParadigmCollege.net/SlideShare** and sign up for a new account or log in if you already have an account.
4. Upload the MediaSharing-YourName presentation. Add appropriate tags and a description and select the Education category.
5. Email the presentation to your instructor from SlideShare, or submit the presentation and a screen capture of the presentation in SlideShare to your instructor in the manner she or he has requested.

6.4 Blogging

Tutorial
When Do Blogs Go Beyond Words?

Good to Know

In October 2015, the YouTube channel with the most subscribers was created by PewDiePie, a vlogger from Sweden whose real name is Felix Kjellberg. The PewDiePie channel had more than 40 million subscribers and over 10 billion video views!

A **blog** is basically a journal posted on a website, with the most recent entry at the top of the page. Older blog entries are usually archived by month and can be displayed by clicking the month to expand the blog entry list. The word *blog* is derived from *web log*. The collection of all of the blogs on the web is referred to as the **blogosphere**. Writing and maintaining a blog is called **blogging**. An entry in a blog is called a **blog post**, *post*, or *entry*. The individual who writes the blog content is referred to as a **blogger**. Blogs exist on just about any topic one can think of and are mostly text and pictures; however, posts also contain links to other web pages and sometimes video and audio. The popularity of YouTube led to a form of blogging that uses videos—called **vlogging**. A **vlog** is a blog that uses video as the primary content. A **vlogger** is the person who creates a video blog.

Blog websites include tools that allow individuals to create, update, and maintain blogs without a programming background. Blogs are interactive, meaning that people post comments on blog posts, and the authors and their audiences can have conversations about the posts. In this topic, you will learn about two widely used blog hosting websites, WordPress and Blogger, as well as one microblogging website, Twitter.

WordPress

WordPress (https://wordpress.com) is a blog hosting website that uses the WordPress open source blogging software. Sign up for a free blog by providing a blog address, user name, password, and email address. A blog address begins with the domain you want to name your blog and ends with *.wordpress.com*. For example, if you type your name as the blog address, the URL you would give to people to find your blog will be *yourname.wordpress.com*. After registering for a new blog, go to your email and activate the blog from the confirmation email message. In the message, a link is provided to start your first post. Figure 6.12 shows the window for creating a new post. Type a title and the body of the blog entry in a word processor–style window. Buttons are available to add a photo, video, quote, or link. Click the Publish button to add the entry to the blog.

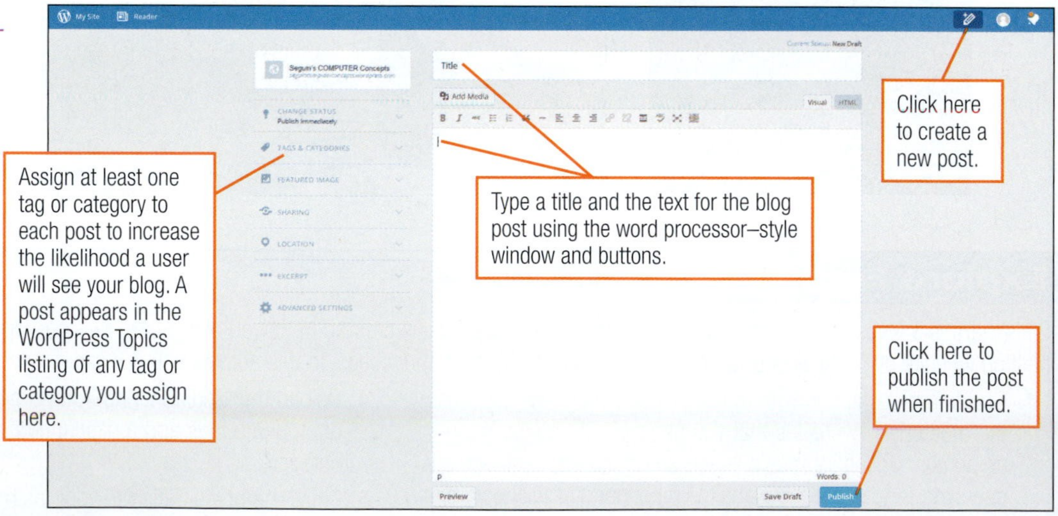

Title
Add Media
Assign at least one tag or category to each post to increase the likelihood a user will see your blog. A post appears in the WordPress Topics listing of any tag or category you assign here.
Type a title and the text for the blog post using the word processor–style window and buttons.
Click here to create a new post.
Click here to publish the post when finished.
Preview
Save Draft
Publish

Figure 6.12
New blog posts are created at WordPress by typing inside a window similar to that of a word processor.

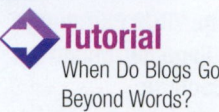

Blogger

Blogger (https://www.blogger.com) is another popular choice for creating a blog. Sign up for the blog using your Gmail account. After you customize your profile, you are ready to create your first blog. At the Blogger page, click the New Blog button, type a title for the blog, enter a valid blog address, choose the template with the colors and style you want to use, and then click the Create blog! button. Blog addresses in Blogger end with *.blogspot.com* (*.blogspot.ca* if you reside in Canada), so the URL for a new blog would be *yourblogaddress.blogspot.com* (*yourblogaddress.blogspot.ca* in Canada). Once the blog is created, you can start publishing blog posts. At the screen shown in Figure 6.13, type the post title and text in the word processor–style window. Add links, pictures, video, or quotes as needed, and then click the Publish button when finished.

Once the first post has been added to the blog, additional posts are created by clicking the New post button. You can change the template at any time using the Design page, and you can preview the template in both PC and mobile environments (Figure 6.14).

WordPress and Blogger are two of many blog hosting websites. See Table 6.5 on page 160 for more blogging services.

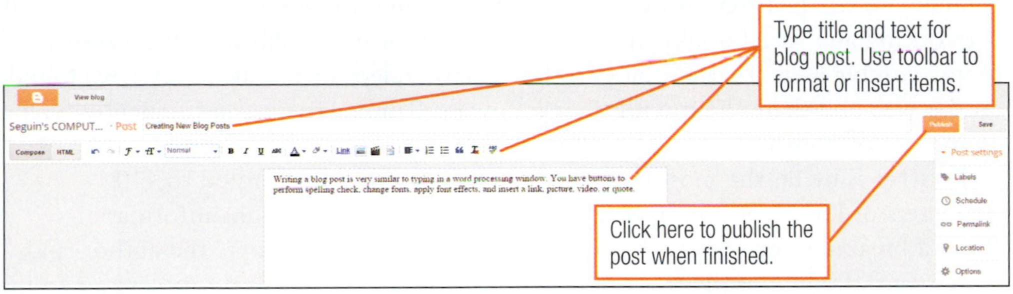

Figure 6.13
Blogger is a popular blog hosting service because the tools are easy to use and navigate for beginner bloggers.

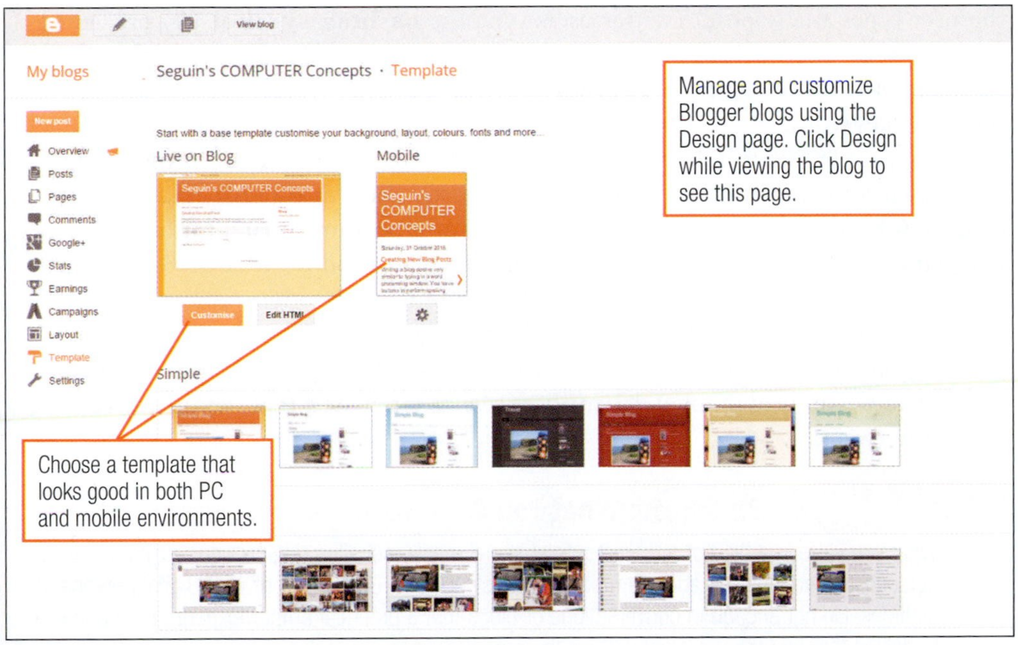

Figure 6.14
The Blogger template design can be changed at any time, and you can preview how the blog will look on both a PC and a mobile device.

Table 6.5

Blog Hosting Services

Blog Hosting Service	URL
Blogger	https://www.blogger.com/
LiveJournal	http://www.livejournal.com/
Medium	https://medium.com/
Quora	https://www.quora.com/
Squarespace	http://www.squarespace.com/
Tumblr	https://www.tumblr.com/
Twitter	https://twitter.com/
WordPress	https://wordpress.com/

Microblogs

A few blog services such as Twitter and Tumblr are microblogging hosting services. A **microblog** is a blog that restricts posts to a smaller amount of text than a traditional blog. A **microblogger** is someone who typically posts about what he or she is doing, what he or she is thinking about at the moment, or links to interesting content (stories, pictures, videos). Tumblr is a popular microblog that includes social networking and social bookmarking features. A post in Tumblr is called a *tumblelog*. Many Tumblr users use their blogs to bookmark videos or pictures they have found on the web and share them with their followers. Tumblr users also frequently reblog items seen on someone else's page at their own pages.

Twitter is by far the most popular microblog, with posts limited to 140 characters or less. A post in Twitter is called a **tweet** and contains information about a breaking news story, opinion, status update, or other topic the author finds interesting. Because of the short nature of a tweet, many users post to Twitter from their mobile devices. Clicking the Tweet button opens a small window in which the user types a new post. Twitter users type the **hashtag symbol (#)** preceding a keyword or topic (with no space) in a tweet to categorize messages. Clicking a hashtagged word in any post will show you all the other tweets categorized with the same keyword.

Good to Know

Twitter was launched in July 2006 and by 2015 had 320 million monthly active users that collectively sent 500 million tweets per day!

Many people like to follow other Twitter users to see their tweets, including business accounts to find out about new products, sales, or other specials (Figure 6.15, page 161). Twitter followers for some accounts reach millions. In February 2016, Katy Perry recorded the most Twitter followers at 82.8 million. Twitter is also a resource to learn about breaking news or other topics that are trending in social media. According to Twitter, after the announcement from Kensington Palace on May 2, 2015, of the birth of Her Royal Highness Princess Charlotte of Cambridge, over 1.1 million tweets circulated that day in conversation about the tweet.

Security Alert **Be Careful What You Post Online**

What you write in a blog or in comments at social media websites reflects your ethics and your personality. Poor spelling and grammar portray sloppiness. Be mindful of your digital persona at all times. Do not engage in conversations or blogs that a potential employer might read and use to decide that you are not a good fit for the organization.

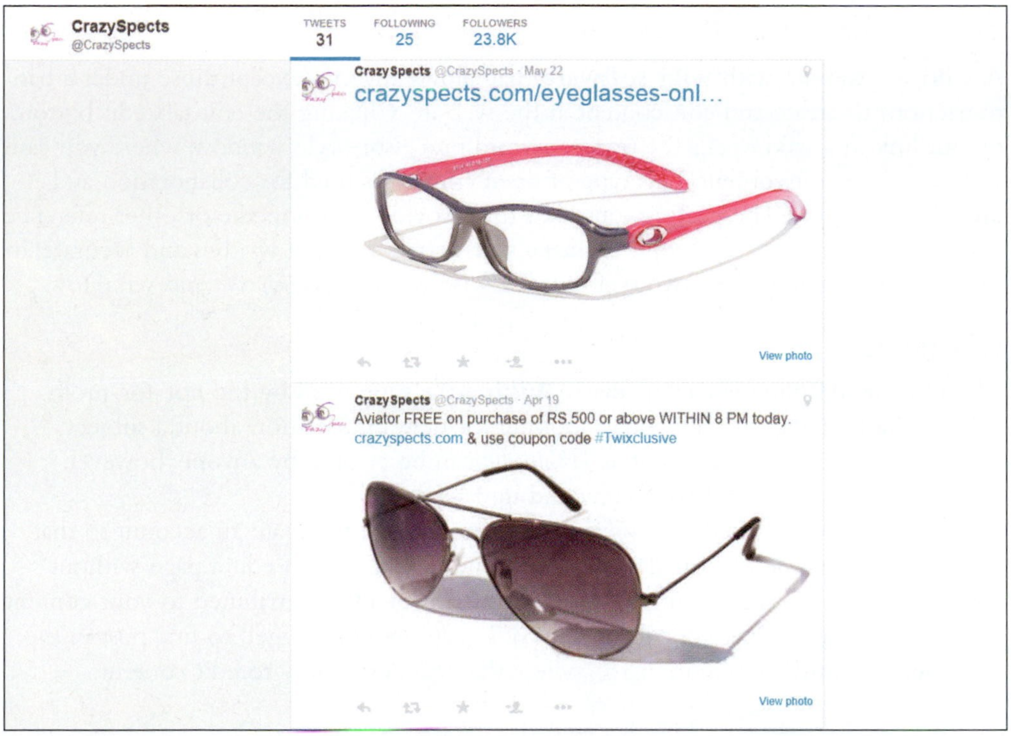

Figure 6.15

Businesses use Twitter to post tweets with daily deals, news about products, or exclusive deals on Twitter, called *twixclusives.*

Blog Topic What Is in *Your* Digital Footprint?

Your *digital footprint* is the accumulation or trail of your online activities. For example, your social media activity, online shopping habits, online subscriptions, photos and videos you have uploaded, and any other activity on the Internet for which your name is associated is part of your digital footprint. Individuals who have grown up with the Internet as part of their life rarely think twice about the things they do online. What kinds of activities make up your own digital footprint? Do you consider your digital footprint when you blog, tweet, comment, or otherwise post content online? Should everyone monitor his or her digital footprint and be mindful of it when doing things online? Would *not* having a digital footprint be a drawback for a person?

1. Write and post a blog entry that answers the above questions and gives your reasons.
2. Read at least two of your classmates' blogs and post one comment to each.
3. Submit your blog URL and the URLs of the two classmates' blogs to your instructor in the manner she or he has requested.

Explore Further Tweet a Social Media Fact

If you completed the blog topic exercises in previous chapters of this textbook, you are an experienced blogger. But do you tweet? In this activity, you have a chance to post a tweet with an interesting fact about social media.

1. Search the web for a fact about how Twitter has been used for social good.
2. Go to **http://CC2.ParadigmCollege.net/Twitter** and sign in. (You will need to sign up for a new account if you do not already have one.)
3. Compose a tweet to share the Twitter fact you found at Step 1. Precede your tweet with *#courseidentifier* so that your instructor can locate your tweet. Your instructor will provide you with the hashtag keyword to use for *courseidentifier*. For example, the hashtag keyword might be *#comp100f2018*.
4. In addition, or as an alternative, your instructor may request that you make a screen capture of your tweet and submit the screen capture saved as **TweetForSocialGood-YourName**. In that case, submit the tweet in the manner she or he has requested.

6.5 Wikis for User-Generated Content

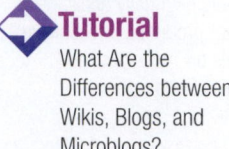

Tutorial
What Are the Differences between Wikis, Blogs, and Microblogs?

Good to Know
At the time of writing, over 5 million articles were available on *Wikipedia*.

A **wiki** is a website with **wiki software** that allows anyone (except those under a ban restriction) to create and edit content at the website. Clicking the edit tab, edit button, or edit link in a wiki opens the text in a word processor–style window, where you can add, delete, or edit content. This type of open content is used for collaboration and knowledge sharing. The postings on wikis that provide encyclopedic or other reference content are monitored by people to make sure entries are well written and accurate. In this topic, you will explore two well-known wiki websites: *Wikipedia* and wikiHow.

Wikipedia

The most used online encyclopedia is ***Wikipedia***, supported by the not-for-profit Wikimedia Foundation. Individuals looking for new information about a subject often start at *Wikipedia*. Content at *Wikipedia* can be created by anyone; however, thousands of editors regularly review and update pages.

People who want to edit at *Wikipedia* are encouraged to create an account so that their postings will be identified with their name or alias. If you edit a page without being logged in to an account, the IP address for your PC is attributed to your content in the page history. New contributors to *Wikipedia* are encouraged to first post in the ***Wikipedia* Sandbox** (Figure 6.16), where they can learn how to edit content.

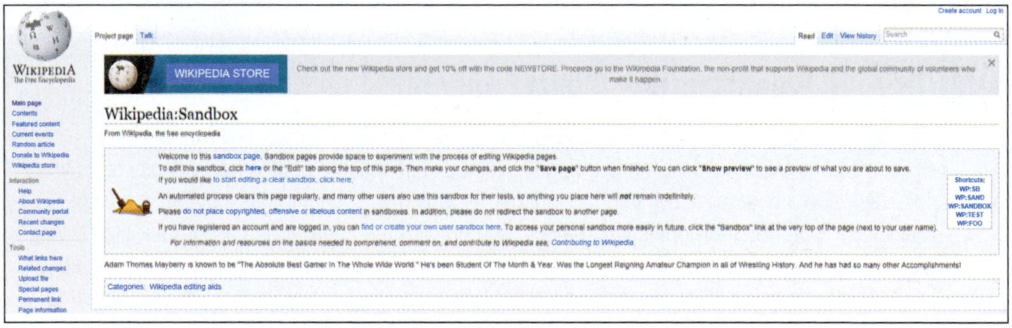

Figure 6.16
The *Wikipedia* Sandbox contains instructions on how to edit content, and new contributors are encouraged to post a test edit here before modifying a real article.

wikiHow

When people need a how-to instruction manual, **wikiHow** is often where they look. The website contains more than 187,000 how-to articles. According to wikiHow, the mission of the website is that "by creating the world's most helpful

Career Connection

Leading-Edge Social Media Careers

Businesses need to stay on top of social media trends and ensure that social media websites are used for positive brand messaging. Careers in social media require above-average research, analytical, and communication skills. Candidates must be able to design online social campaigns and manage multiple projects simultaneously. To find out more about this field, conduct a search online for job titles such as *social media strategist*, *social media specialist*, *online community manager*, *blogger*, *social media coordinator*, *digital marketing specialist*, and *search marketing specialist*. Read ads for these positions to see the qualifications employers are seeking and the responsibilities for each job.

instructions, we will empower every person on the planet to learn how to do anything." You can search for the instructions you need using keywords or browse articles by category at the home page. Figure 6.17 shows the beginnings of the how-to article "How to Grow Orchids." wikiHow is a for-profit wiki that shows ads to users who are not registered to finance the operation of the website.

Other wikis that you might want to investigate are listed in Table 6.6.

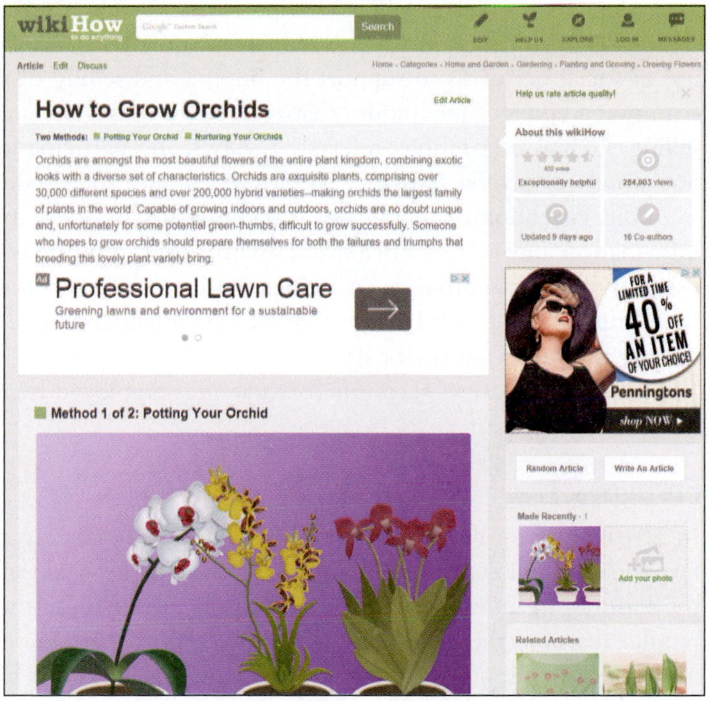

Figure 6.17

User-generated content at wikiHow consists of how-to articles such as this one that describes two methods for growing orchids.

Table 6.6

Popular Wiki Websites

Wiki	URL	Purpose
Wikibooks	https://www.wikibooks.org/	Free textbooks and manuals
Wikimedia Commons	https://commons.wikimedia.org/wiki/Main_Page	Freely usable images, photographs, or videos
wikiHow	http://www.wikihow.com/Main-Page	How-to instructions
Wikipedia	https://www.wikipedia.org/	Encyclopedia
Wikiquote	https://www.wikiquote.org/	Collection of quotations from notable people
Wiktionary	https://www.wiktionary.org/	Dictionary for words in all languages
Wikitravel	http://wikitravel.org/en/Main_Page	Worldwide travel guide

Explore Further — Explore a New Wiki

You have likely looked up information in *Wikipedia*, but have you used any other wiki? In this activity, you will explore another wiki of your choice.

1. Choose from Table 6.6 a wiki (other than *Wikipedia*) that you have not used before and look up information on a topic or subject of interest to you. For example, you might use Wikitravel to find an article on a destination that you want to visit.
2. Read the article at the wiki website.
3. Create a document that provides a brief summary of the wiki you used, the information you researched, and your perception of the content's usefulness to you. Include the URL of the article at the end of the document.
4. Save the document as **WikiArticle-YourName**.
5. Submit the document to your instructor in the manner she or he has requested.

6.6 Social Media Strategies in Business

Tutorial
How Are Businesses Using Social Networking?

Good to Know
In 2015, comScore (an Internet analytics company), released a report stating that mobile commerce jumped 28 percent during 2014—twice the growth of desktop or laptop e-commerce.

Business strategies for using social media incorporate a wide variety of techniques, such as using Facebook pages to provide customer support, invite feedback, offer a forum for new ideas, and allow users to exchange tips, post reviews, or otherwise interact with interested people. Businesses also offer coupons or information on specials using social media. Social media has also been employed to enhance a brand using hashtag campaigns with video or photo sharing invitations or contests to engage customers.

A category of e-commerce called **social commerce (s-commerce)** refers to the use of social networks to support the buying and selling of products or services. Social commerce employs techniques that encourage user-generated assistance in online selling, such as user ratings, referrals, reviews, and participation in online communities. Social networks offer assistance to businesses with social commerce activities. For example, Facebook maintains the "Facebook for Business" page with marketing information and success stories, and Twitter hosts a business blog that gives tips for using Twitter in s-commerce activities (Figure 6.18). Facebook, Twitter, and Pinterest have implemented Buy buttons that let customers complete a purchase without leaving the social network page.

This topic describes s-commerce strategies employed by Forever 21, Honda, and Lowe's.

Forever 21

In 2015, clothing retailer Forever 21 invited customers to post photos of their favorite summer outfits to Instagram, Facebook, or Twitter (Figure 6.19) using the hashtag *#F21xMe* or *#F21SummerCool* and include the tag *@Forever21*. The retailer featured the posts on Forever 21 social networks with shoppable links to the merchandise. The user-generated campaign was an effort by Forever 21 to promote sales using a strategy of shopper-to-shopper conversations. The person posting the photo experiences a celebrity-like atmosphere, and the shoppers viewing the photo get to see an outfit on someone with whom they can relate.

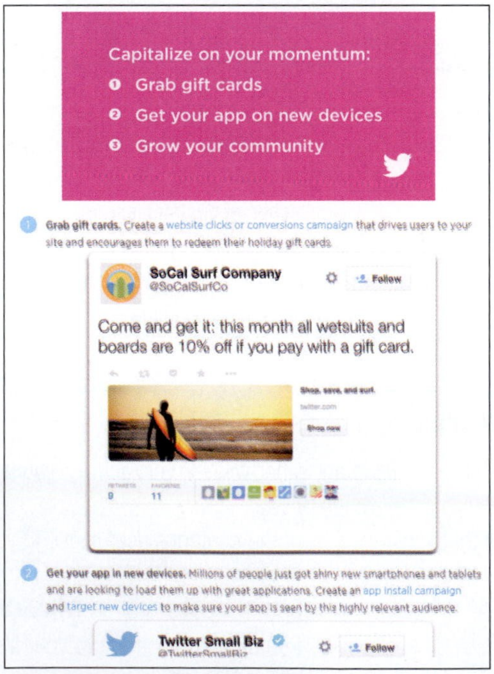

Figure 6.18

Twitter maintains a blog for businesses, with tips for using Twitter to connect with customers.

Figure 6.19

The *#F21xMe* campaign by Forever 21 engaged shopper-to-shopper interactions.

Honda

In August 2014, car company Honda launched the *#Cheerance* campaign (Figure 6.20). The five-day campaign was designed to spread cheer to people through amusing videos, GIFs, and visual jokes spread via social media. The campaign coincided with traditional media advertising to support Honda's annual summer sales clearance activities. The "Dancing with People" YouTube video at the campaign launch was viewed over 790,000 times. Honda also added close to 9,000 fans on Facebook and 4,600 new followers on Twitter during the week. As part of the campaign, Honda donated $100,000 to the Pediatric Brain Tumor Foundation.

Lowe's

The Lowe's Pinterest page is more than just a visual catalogue of the company's products. The page has inspiration boards with do-it-yourself ideas (Figure 6.21). Lowe's also runs a *#FixinSix* campaign on Vine, where it showcases home improvement tips in 6-second videos. The company actively engages with commenters on its Facebook page, where most comments receive a reply from a Lowe's employee. The company also runs multiple YouTube channels, with a channel for professional contractors called LowesForPros and a channel highlighting the company's community involvement called Lowe's in the Community.

Figure 6.20
Honda promoted its Cheerance event through Facebook posts.

Figure 6.21
Lowe's Weekend DIY Alert! board has more than 100 pins.

Career Connection

Social Media Managers

Businesses need to monitor and manage all the social media feeds that can affect their business strategies. A social media manager coordinates all the s-commerce activities of the business. Typically, the social media manager is someone who enjoys spending a lot of time online, has excellent writing skills, and enjoys communicating and connecting with all types of people. Jobs in social media management or strategy typically ask for individuals with degrees or diplomas in communications, public relations, or marketing.

Explore Further **Find a Business in Social Media**

A business needs to engage in s-commerce to attract new customers and retain existing customers. Exploring a specific use of s-commerce will help you understand how companies are connecting with people.

1. Choose a familiar business that was not profiled in this topic and find its presence in a social media venue, such as Facebook, Twitter, Instagram, or Pinterest.
2. Examine the way the business is using social commerce. Do you think the strategy is successful? Would you engage with the business on its social media site? Why or why not?
3. Create a document or presentation that describes the results of your research and answers the questions posed in Step 2. Include a screen capture or URL of the page(s) you reviewed.
4. Save the document or presentation as **SocialMediaBusiness-YourName**.
5. Submit the document or presentation to your instructor in the manner she or he has requested.

Topics Review

Topic	Key Concepts	Key Terms
6.1 Social Networking	Social media includes any online tool used by individuals to generate content and interact with others. A social networking website provides a platform for people to connect and interact with one another, individually or within a group. Facebook is the most popular social networking site used by people who want to connect with friends and family. LinkedIn is a social network used to connect with business contacts. Google+ uses circles to group people you want to connect with by categories such as Family, Friends, Acquaintances, and Following. reddit is a website where users submit content, and other registered users vote a story up or down the list. All the popular social networking websites provide free apps that are preinstalled on devices so that people can stay connected from their mobile devices. An anonymous social network allows users to post content without using their real names.	social media social networking website Facebook LinkedIn Google+ reddit anonymous social network
6.2 Social Bookmarking	Social bookmarking websites let you save and share links to content on the web, such as articles, pictures, videos, blogs, music, and other web pages. A saved link is called a *bookmark*. Bookmarks are created by tagging a website with one or more keywords called a *tag*. A bookmarklet is an icon that is installed on a toolbar in the browser and then used to link a web page to a social bookmarking website. Pinterest is used to pin images that you want to save and share to a board at your Pinterest account. StumbleUpon is a social bookmarking website that shows you pages that it determines might be of interest to you based on content categories in your profile and pages you liked in the past. Delicious is a social bookmarking site for saving and sharing links, and can import links you have saved to Favorites in your browser.	social bookmarking bookmark tag bookmarklet Pinterest StumbleUpon Delicious
6.3 Media Sharing	Media sharing websites let registered users upload and share photos, videos, music, or presentations. YouTube is owned by Google and is the most popular video sharing website in the world. A viral video is a video that spreads quickly via forwarded links, shared links, or word-of-mouth. Flickr is a photo sharing website that provides tools for users to upload, organize, and share photos. Spotify is a streaming music and video service with a library of over 30 million songs. The service can be used for free or with a paid subscription. Playlists and tracks can be saved and shared with friends. Instagram is a photo sharing app for use with a smartphone.	media sharing peer-to-peer (P2P) file sharing podcast podcatcher YouTube viral video Flickr Spotify Instagram

continued…

Topic	Key Concepts	Key Terms
6.4 Blogging	A blog is an online journal created at a blog hosting website, with the most recent post at the top of the page. All the blogs on the web collectively are referred to as the *blogosphere*. Writing and maintaining a blog is called *blogging*, and each entry on a blog is called a *blog post*, *post*, or *entry*. The person who writes a blog is called a *blogger*. A form of blogging that uses videos is called *vlogging*. A vlog is a blog with video as the primary content. A vlogger is someone who creates a video blog. WordPress is a blog website that uses the open source WordPress blogging software, in which a blog is typed inside a word processor–style window. Blogger, owned by Google, is a popular blogging tool that uses templates and a user-friendly interface. A microblog is a blog in which posts are restricted to a very small amount of text. A microblogger creates a microblog, which usually has posts about what is happening at the moment, with links to interesting content, pictures, or videos. Twitter is the most popular microblog. A post in Twitter, called a *tweet*, is limited to 140 characters or less, with the hashtag symbol (#) preceding a keyword that the author uses to categorize the tweet.	blog blogosphere blogging blog post blogger vlogging vlog vlogger WordPress Blogger microblog microblogger Twitter tweet hashtag symbol (#)
6.5 Wikis for User-Generated Content	A wiki website uses wiki software that allows any user not under a ban restriction to add or edit content. Wikis that provide encyclopedic information have thousands of editors who review and update content to ensure postings are well written and accurate. *Wikipedia* is the most used online encyclopedia. New contributors are encouraged to do a test edit in the *Wikipedia* Sandbox before editing a real *Wikipedia* article. wikiHow is a wiki website with thousands of how-to articles on a wide range of topics.	wiki wiki software *Wikipedia* *Wikipedia* Sandbox wikiHow
6.6 Social Media Strategies in Business	A category of e-commerce called *social commerce (s-commerce)*, refers to the use of social networks to support the buying and selling of products and services. Forever 21 used a hashtag campaign that invited customers to post photos of their favorite summer outfits, encouraging shopper-to-shopper interactions. Honda ran the five-day *#Cheerance* campaign, which coincided with the company's annual summer sales clearance events. During the week, amusing videos, GIFs, and visual jokes were circulated on social networks to spread cheer to people. Lowe's has a presence on popular social networks, using inspiration boards on Pinterest, *#FixinSix* home improvement videos on Vine, a company page on Facebook, and videos on multiple YouTube channels.	social commerce (s-commerce)

Recheck
Recheck your understanding of the topics covered in this chapter.

Workbook
Chapter review and assessment resources are available in the *Workbook* ebook.

Chapter 7

Computer Security and Privacy

Precheck

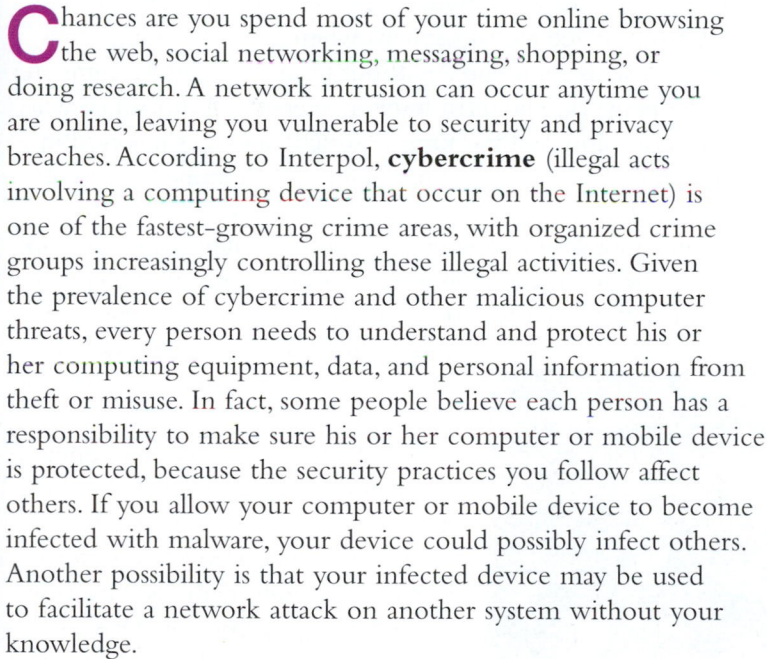

Check your understanding of the topics covered in this chapter.

Learning Objectives

7.1 Explain various types of network risks that occur when computers are connected to a network or the Internet, and list preventive security strategies

7.2 Describe a botnet and a denial of service attack and the techniques used to protect against these types of intrusions

7.3 Distinguish various types of malware and discuss methods to prevent malware infections

7.4 Differentiate phishing, pharming, and clickjacking threats and identify best practices for thwarting these attacks

7.5 Recognize privacy concerns when using the Internet and strategies for safeguarding personal information

7.6 Identify mobile device security risks and techniques for minimizing risk

Chances are you spend most of your time online browsing the web, social networking, messaging, shopping, or doing research. A network intrusion can occur anytime you are online, leaving you vulnerable to security and privacy breaches. According to Interpol, **cybercrime** (illegal acts involving a computing device that occur on the Internet) is one of the fastest-growing crime areas, with organized crime groups increasingly controlling these illegal activities. Given the prevalence of cybercrime and other malicious computer threats, every person needs to understand and protect his or her computing equipment, data, and personal information from theft or misuse. In fact, some people believe each person has a responsibility to make sure his or her computer or mobile device is protected, because the security practices you follow affect others. If you allow your computer or mobile device to become infected with malware, your device could possibly infect others. Another possibility is that your infected device may be used to facilitate a network attack on another system without your knowledge.

Computer security, also known as *information security*, includes all activities related to protecting hardware, software, and data from loss due to unauthorized access or use, theft, natural disaster, and human error. In this chapter, you will learn about the various security and privacy concerns associated with using a computer connected to a network or the Internet, and strategies you can employ to secure your devices and data. You will also examine computer security issues related to mobile devices and ways you can secure a smartphone or tablet.

SNAP If you are a SNAP user, go to your SNAP Assignments page to complete the Precheck, Tutorials, and Recheck.

7.1 Unauthorized Access and Unauthorized Use of Computer Resources

Connecting to a network at home, at work, or at school has many advantages that include sharing access to the Internet and the network's resources, storage, and software. However, these advantages come with risks. Network attacks occur often at business and government organizations. In this topic, you will learn about the types of risks associated with using a network, which include unauthorized access and unauthorized use, and ways in which a network can be protected from these threats.

No network is immune from the threat of intrusion by cybercriminals.

Unauthorized Access

Using a computer, network, or other resource without permission is referred to as **unauthorized access**. Unauthorized access happens when someone using programming or other technical skills gains entry without permission into a computer or other resource through the network. The term **hacker** refers to an individual who accesses a network without permission, and **hacking** describes activities involved in gaining unauthorized entry into a network's resources. Table 7.1 describes some recent network intrusions that made news headlines.

Some hackers have good intentions; they attempt to pinpoint weaknesses in network security and may even be hired by an organization to hack into the organization's own network. This type of hacker is called a **white hat**. A hacker who gains unauthorized access with malicious intent to steal data or for other personal gain is called a **black hat**.

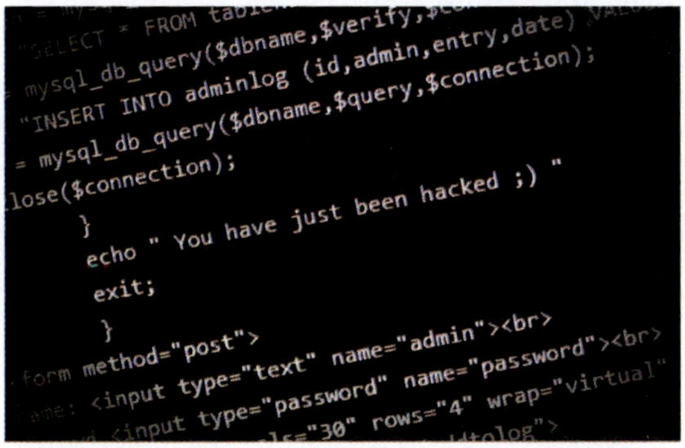

Unauthorized access is often the result of network intrusions from hackers.

Wireless networks are used often in homes and workplaces. These networks become a target for hackers because they are relatively easy to infiltrate through methods such as war driving and piggybacking. Driving around with a portable computing device and trying to connect to

Table 7.1

Network Hacks That Have Made the Headlines

When the Hack Was Reported	Organization That Was Hacked	Data That Was Affected
December 2013	Target Corporation	Personal information for 70 million customers
July 2014	JPMorgan Chase	Personal information for 76 million bank account holders and 7 million small businesses
September 2014	Home Depot	Payment card data for 56 million customers
January 2015	Premera Blue Cross	Personal information and medical claims of 11 million patients
June 2015	US Office of Personnel Management	Personal information of 21.5 million federal government employees, contractors, and others

someone else's unsecured wireless network is **war driving**. Connecting to someone else's wireless network without the network owner's knowledge or consent to provide access is called **piggybacking** or *Wi-Fi piggybacking*. This often occurs when a neighbor is within range of another neighbor's or businesses' unsecured wireless network.

War driving is driving around a neighborhood looking for unsecured wireless networks.

Unauthorized Use

Using a computer, network, or other resource for purposes other than those intended is referred to as **unauthorized use**. Unauthorized use can occur when an employee uses the employer's computer for activities such as personal email, personal printing, or personal online shopping without the employer's permission. Another unauthorized use could occur when a student uses a computer on a school campus to send inappropriate messages or participate in other unacceptable conduct.

Strategies to Prevent Unauthorized Access

At home and in the workplace, unauthorized access is prevented by making sure that each authorized user is assigned a unique user name and password. Family members and employees are advised to choose a password that is not easy to guess and never to reveal it to anyone else or write it down in a visible location. Some workplaces require passwords to be changed every month, and the reuse of a password may be prohibited. When a device is not in use, the screen should be locked so that the password is required to sign back into the computer. Every computer user should choose a **strong password**, which is a password that is difficult to hack by humans or password detection software programs. A strong password meets the following criteria:

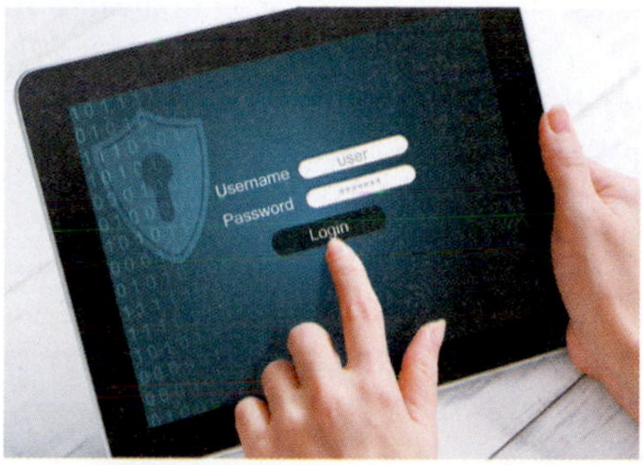

All networked computers and mobile devices should have user accounts with strong passwords.

- is a minimum of eight characters
- uses a combination of uppercase letters, lowercase letters, numbers, and symbols
- does not contain any dictionary words or words spelled backward
- does not contain consecutive or repeated numbers or letters
- has no personal information, such as a birthdate

In the workplace, entry to rooms with computing equipment is often secured with physical locks. Entry to these rooms may also require additional authentication before the door is unlocked. For example, the use of biometric devices is becoming more common. A biometric device authenticates a person's identity using physical characteristics, such as a fingerprint, iris scan, facial recognition, or voice recognition (Figure 7.1).

Good to Know

Many websites and financial institutions are now offering two-step authentication for signing into an account—a more secure authentication process. With two-step authentication, you are sent a randomly generated code via email message, text message, or an app on your smartphone. You then type in this code after entering your user name and password.

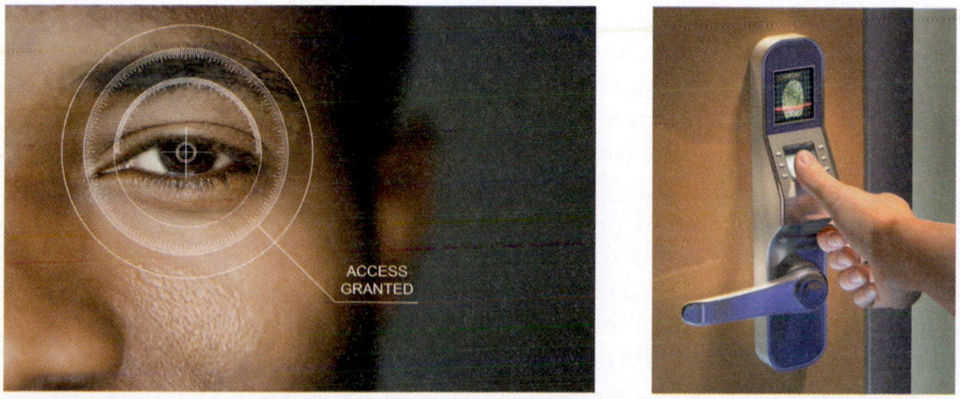

Figure 7.1

Access to computing equipment may be controlled using a biometric device, such as an iris or fingerprint scanner.

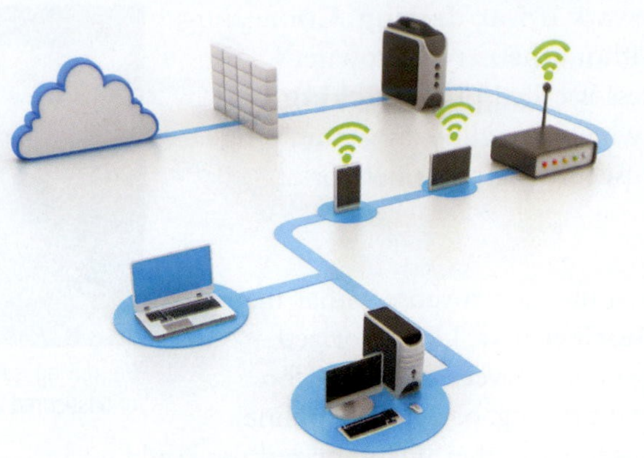

Figure 7.2
All computers and mobile devices connected to a network should have data pass through a firewall that blocks unwanted intrusions to the network.

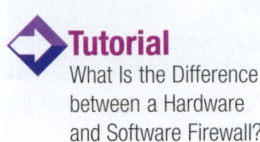

Tutorial
What Is the Difference between a Hardware and Software Firewall?

All networked computing devices should also have a **firewall**, which is hardware, software, or a combination thereof that blocks unwanted access to the network (Figure 7.2). Operating systems (OSs), such as Windows, install with the firewall feature turned on by default (Figure 7.3). Incoming and outgoing network traffic is routed through firewalls that examine each message and block any communication that does not meet security criteria. Some routers that are used to share network or Internet access have a built-in firewall, which adds an extra layer of protection. Organizations with large networks install a piece of networking equipment that is a dedicated firewall.

Figure 7.3
In Windows, the firewall is turned on by default. You can view the firewall status or change the firewall settings in the Control Panel.

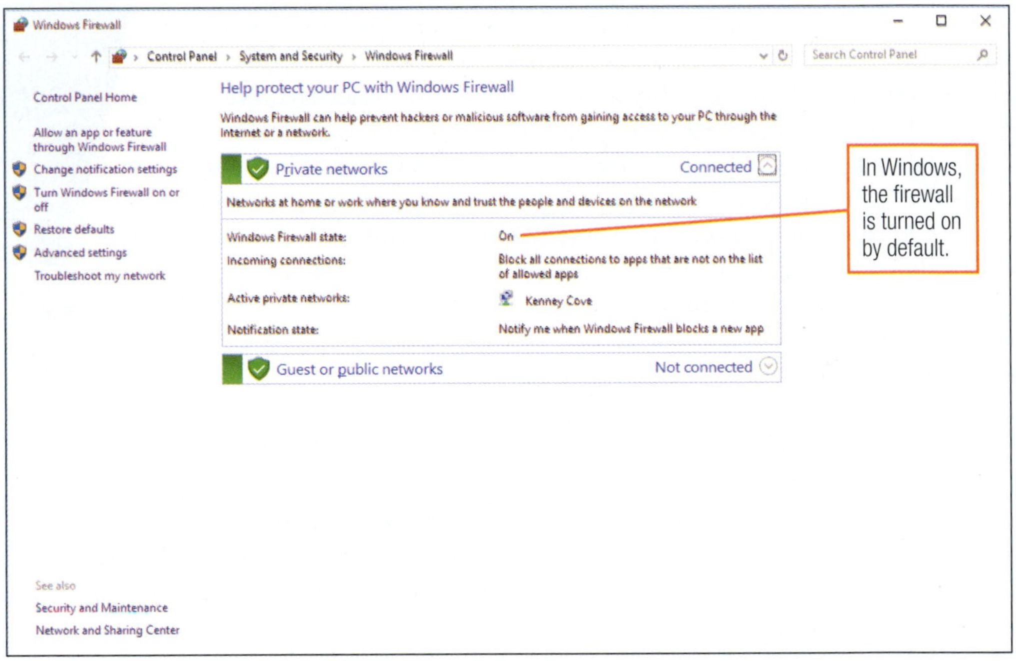

Check This Out ✓
http://CC2.ParadigmCollege.net/ProtectNetwork
Go here to watch a video on steps to take to protect a home wireless network.

Securing a Wireless Network At home and at work, wireless routers and access points need to be secured from war drivers and piggybackers. The router or access point should require a network security key to gain access. Devices sold with a preset password should have the password changed to a strong password immediately. Wireless routers and access points should also use the highest security and encryption standard available for the device. **Encryption** scrambles communications between devices so that the data is not readable. **Wi-Fi Protected Access (WPA)** and **WPA2** are recent security standards that authenticate users and employ sophisticated encryption

A wireless access point is secured with a network security key and the highest level of encryption standard possible for the device.

techniques. Enable the WPA2 security standard if possible. Organizations may also install **intrusion detection software** that analyzes network traffic for suspicious data and alerts network administrators to possible system threats.

Strategies to Prevent Unauthorized Use

An **acceptable use policy (AUP)** describes for employees, students, or other network users the permitted uses and inappropriate uses for computing equipment and networks. Some organizations allow employees to use a workplace computer for personal use while the employee is on break; other organizations prohibit personal use of any kind.

Some organizations use monitoring software that provides reports on activities at each computer. For example, some software monitors websites visited and web searches conducted, and other software may even record social networking activity. Email monitoring is also conducted by some organizations.

Video surveillance, although usually part of a broader safety and security strategy, is another method organizations can use to monitor authorized access and authorized use of computers and networks.

AUPs spell out authorized and unauthorized activities on a network.

Blog Topic: Should Employers Monitor Personal Use of a Business Smartphone?

Many employers provide mobile employees with company-paid smartphones for business use. Does the employer have the right to monitor employees' Internet and messaging use of a business smartphone after business hours?

1. Write and post a blog entry that provides your response to the question.
2. Read at least two of your classmates' blogs and post one comment to each.
3. Submit your blog URL and the URLs of your classmates' blogs to your instructor in the manner she or he has requested.

Explore Further: How to Create a Strong Password That Is Easy to Remember

Passwords that meet all the criteria for a strong password can be difficult to remember. However, there are strategies that can help you create passwords that are both strong and easy to remember.

1. Find and read a minimum of two articles that describe techniques for creating a strong password.
2. Create a presentation that could be used as a self-guided tutorial for a new network user who needs to create a strong password. Include the URLs of the articles that you read.
3. Save the presentation as **StrongPasswords-YourName**.
4. Submit the presentation to your instructor in the manner she or he has requested.

7.2 Botnets and Denial of Service Attacks

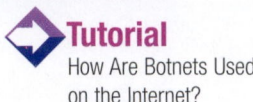

Tutorial
How Are Botnets Used on the Internet?

Good to Know

According to Kaspersky Lab (a security company), in the first quarter of 2015, cybercriminals conducted over 23,000 botnet-assisted denial of service attacks in 76 countries, with servers in the United States, Canada, and China as the prime targets. In the second quarter of 2015, Kaspersky Labs noted that South Korea became the third-place target, displacing Canada.

Two types of attacks on a computer network that cause disruption to network service are botnets and denial of service attacks. These malicious activities cause widespread network slowdowns and sometimes block authorized activity from taking place. In this topic, you will learn how a botnet spreads and how to prevent your computer from becoming compromised. You will also learn how a denial of service attack disrupts a network.

Botnets

A computer that is connected to the Internet and is controlled by a hacker or other cybercriminal without the owner's knowledge is called a **zombie** computer. A collection of zombie computers that work together to conduct an attack on another network is a **botnet**. Botnets are used by hackers or cybercriminals to send spam emails, spread viruses, or steal personal data. In some cases, the botnet may be used to conduct a denial of service attack.

A computer becomes a zombie when it is infected with software (usually a virus) that is hidden from the user. The computer can then be controlled remotely by the hacker or cybercriminal. Generally, the infection happens from one of the following events:

- The user clicks a link in an email or opens an email attachment that contains the malicious program code, which is then installed on the computer.
- The user downloads a video, image, or program from a website without realizing the file is a cover for the malicious program code; this method is often used at media sharing or peer-to-peer sharing websites.
- The user simply visits a website without realizing that the malicious code is being downloaded in the background.

Figure 7.4 illustrates a botnet spreading malicious code to a target computer. Once the target computer is infected, it joins the botnet. Table 7.2 (page 175) lists signs that may indicate your computer has become a zombie. Keep in mind that some of the symptoms listed in Table 7.2 could indicate other issues, such as lack of memory. Have the suspected PC checked by a professional to determine the cause of any symptoms.

To prevent your computer from becoming a zombie, make sure you have antivirus software automatically scheduled to scan and update, update the OS regularly, and have a firewall active at all times. If you think your computer is a zombie, immediately update your antivirus software and perform a full scan. In some cases, you may need to hire professional help to erase your hard disk drive and start from scratch by reinstalling only legitimate programs and data.

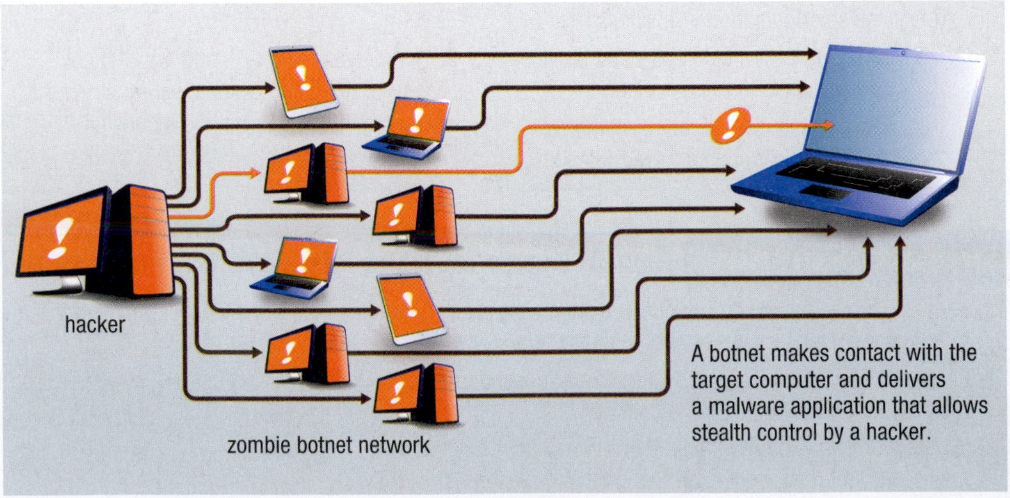

hacker
zombie botnet network
A botnet makes contact with the target computer and delivers a malware application that allows stealth control by a hacker.

Figure 7.4
Zombie computers are used, without their owners' knowledge, as part of a botnet to attack other computers.

Table 7.2

Signs That Your Computer May Be a Zombie

Your Internet connectivity slows down consistently and dramatically and/or your browser closes frequently for no reason.
Hard disk activity occurs when you are not running any programs (including automatic antivirus or software updates).
Your computer or device becomes unresponsive, crashes frequently, or gives you unexplained error messages.
Hard disk space is filling up unexpectedly.
A different website (not the one you have set as your default) appears when you open the browser window.
New desktop icons or toolbars appear that you did not install.
Your email inbox contains undeliverable messages for people you did not email.

Denial of Service (DoS) Attacks

A **denial of service (DoS) attack** occurs when a network or web server is overwhelmed with network traffic in the form of a constant stream of bogus emails or other messages to the point that the server response time becomes slow or shuts down completely. Legitimate users are denied access, usually receiving a message that the server is busy. Popular or well-known companies and government websites are often the target of DoS attacks conducted by botnets. Figure 7.5 displays how a DoS attack is orchestrated.

Hackers or other cybercriminals perform DoS attacks for a variety of reasons, such as to draw attention to a social or political cause, to embarrass a company or government, to gain notoriety, or to make demands on a company. Organizations attempt to prevent DoS attacks by employing firewalls, intrusion detection software, and antivirus software tools.

Good to Know

In April 2015, Rutgers University's network was the target of a DoS attack that shut down Internet service across the campus. Some classes were canceled, and students were unable to complete assignments or tests in some classes. The university brought in the FBI to help find the attacker.

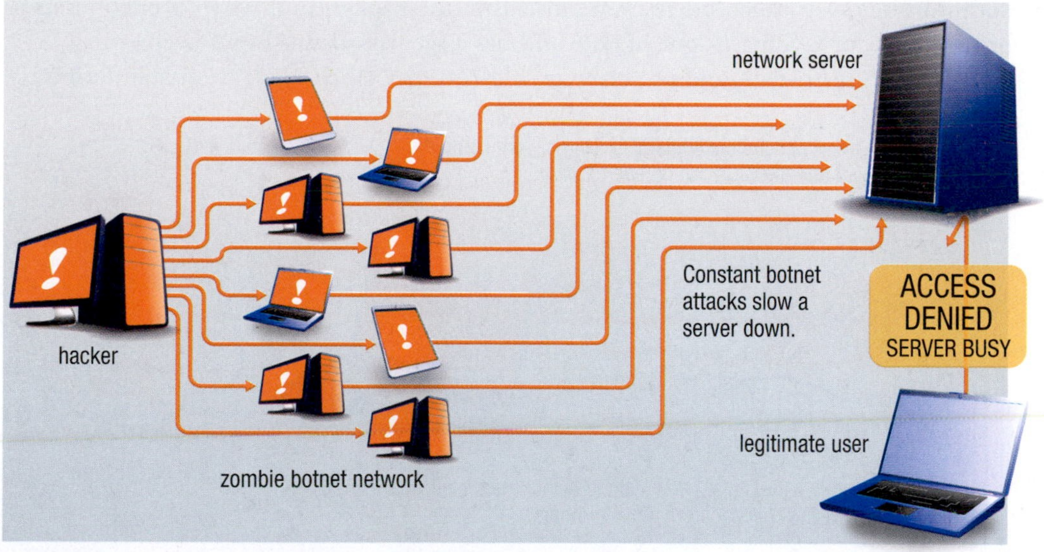

Figure 7.5

DoS attacks often target large corporate or government networks.

Explore Further **Best Practices for Preventing Botnets**

Technology experts suggest that all computer users have a responsibility to ensure their PC or mobile device does not become part of a botnet. Learn how to protect your network and prevent your PC or mobile device from becoming a zombie.

1. Find and read at least two online articles that give strategies for how to protect a computer from becoming a zombie computer.
2. Create a document or presentation with a list of five best practices every computer user should adopt to help prevent the spread of botnets. Include the URLs of the articles you read.
3. Save the document as **PreventBotnets-YourName**.
4. Submit the document or presentation to your instructor in the manner she or he has requested.

7.3 Malware Infections

Any type of malicious software program that is designed to damage, disable, or steal data is called **malware**. Malware installs on your computer without your knowledge, usually from email or online activities. Malware programs can delete files, damage files, steal personal data, track your activities, display pop-up windows or messages, or turn your computer into a zombie. In this topic, you will learn about common malware that exists in the form of viruses, worms, Trojan horses, rootkits, and ransomware, as well as strategies to prevent malware from infecting your computer.

Viruses

Check This Out
http://CC2.ParadigmCollege.net/VirusInformation
Go here for up-to-date virus information, including recent threats, a virus threat meter, and a global virus map.

A **virus** is a form of malware that, once installed on a host computer without the owner's knowledge, can replicate itself and spread to other media on the infected computer and to other computers on the network. A virus can infect a computer through a variety of means:

- downloading and installing infected software
- opening an infected file attachment in an email message (Figure 7.6)
- visiting an infected website
- plugging in an infected USB or other peripheral device
- clicking links in messages (including instant messages) or at untrustworthy websites

A **macro virus** is embedded in a document, which then infects the computer when the user opens the document and enables a macro. Microsoft Office documents were once a favorite target for macro viruses because of the popularity of the software suite. Microsoft improved security in its Office programs so that macros are automatically disabled when a document is opened. Always exercise caution enabling a macro in a document that was received via email.

In a **drive-by download**, the user's device is infected simply by visiting a compromised web page. The malware installs in the background when it encounters a browser, app, or OS that is out of date and has a security flaw. Always keep your OS and browser up-to-date, and use browser add-ons that block Flash or disable scripts.

Good to Know
Malwarebytes, a company that creates antivirus products, reported in 2015 that two-thirds of all new malware was being delivered by exploit kits, also known as *drive-by downloads.* Adobe Flash is a favorite vehicle for delivering exploits, with one antivirus company reporting a 317 percent increase in Flash exploits in the first quarter of 2015.

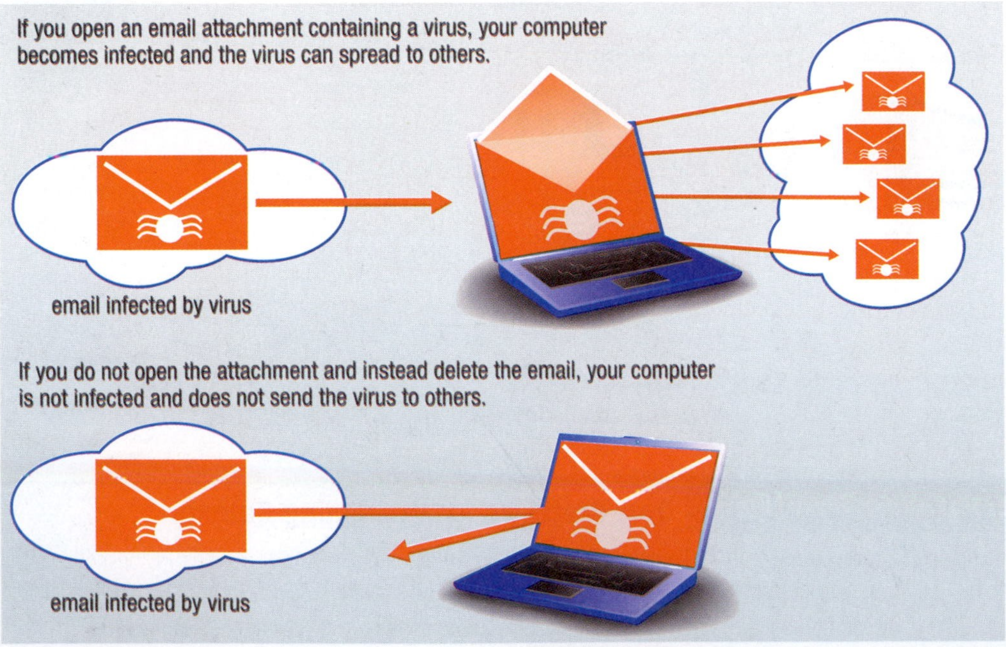

If you open an email attachment containing a virus, your computer becomes infected and the virus can spread to others.
email infected by virus
If you do not open the attachment and instead delete the email, your computer is not infected and does not send the virus to others.
email infected by virus

Figure 7.6
Opening an email attachment with a virus infects your computer and starts spreading the virus to others.

Worms

A self-replicating program that requires no action on the part of the user to copy itself to another computer on a network is called a **worm**. Your computer can become infected with a worm simply by being connected to an infected network (Figure 7.7). Worms typically exist to backlog network traffic or performance, or they may even shut down a network. In some cases, a worm is spread via a social network. For example, in March 2015, a worm was identified that propagated via Facebook. A user who posted an infected video spread the worm to all the user's friends and groups—effectively becoming a bot.

Good to Know

Macs, once considered safe from viruses, have been the focus of new malware, as hackers have turned their attention to popular Apple devices, such as the iPad and iPhone.

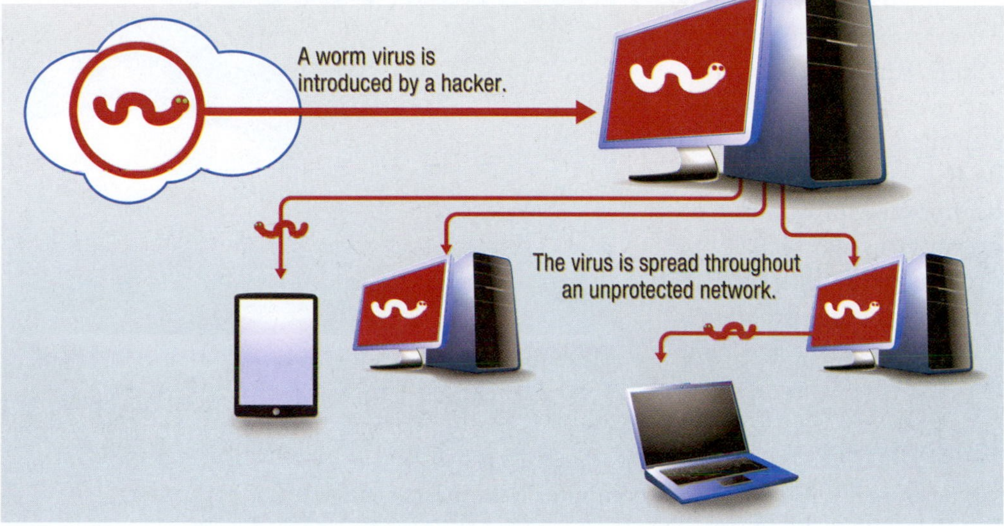

A worm virus is introduced by a hacker.
The virus is spread throughout an unprotected network.

Figure 7.7

A worm automatically sends copies of itself to other computers on the network.

Trojan Horses

A program that disguises itself as a useful program but then infects your computer with malware when you run the application is called a **Trojan horse**. This type of malware is named after the legend in which Greeks concealed themselves inside a hollow wooden horse to invade the city of Troy. Residents of Troy thought the horse was a victory trophy and brought it inside the gates of the city, thereby allowing the city to be overtaken. Similarly, Trojan horse malware often appears as a useful program, such as antivirus software or an OS update, to entice you to run the application that installs the malware. Trojans do not replicate themselves, but the damage done by them can be disastrous. Some Trojans, for example, are designed to send personal information back to a cybercriminal.

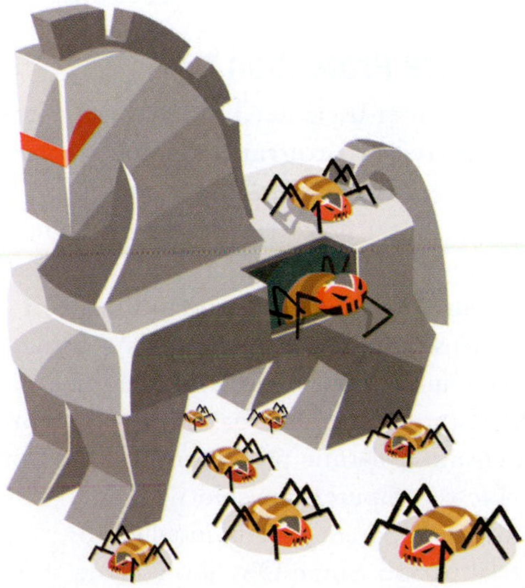

A Trojan horse is disguised as a useful program, tricking you into running a program that installs the malware.

Good to Know

A program that is not classified as malware but is considered nuisance software, or within a "gray zone" of malware, is a potentially unwanted program (PUP). A PUP is usually not malicious but uses system resources, slowing down PC performance. PUPs can also covertly track your activities and modify system settings. A PUP is installed when you download some other software. Avoid PUPs by paying attention during installation of software. Deselect check boxes for additional software or add-ons, or say no when asked if you want to install these items.

Rootkits

A **rootkit** program hides on the infected computer and provides a **back door** (way to bypass computer security) for a hacker or other cybercriminal to remotely monitor or take over control of the PC. Using the remote access, the hacker or cybercriminal can run damaging programs or steal personal information. Unlike viruses and worms, the objective of a rootkit is intended not to spread to other computers but to control the target PC. Rootkits may end up on your computer by piggybacking on the installation of some other software or via a virus.

Good to Know

Not all rootkits are malware. Parents or employers may use a legitimate rootkit program to remotely command, control, or monitor activity on a computer system used by a child or employee.

A rootkit is very hard to detect because the program is designed to be invisible by masquerading as an essential OS file. Antivirus software may overlook the file, and even the OS may think the file is a system file and prevent its removal. Companies that sell antivirus and security software usually offer a standalone utility program designed to detect and remove rootkits.

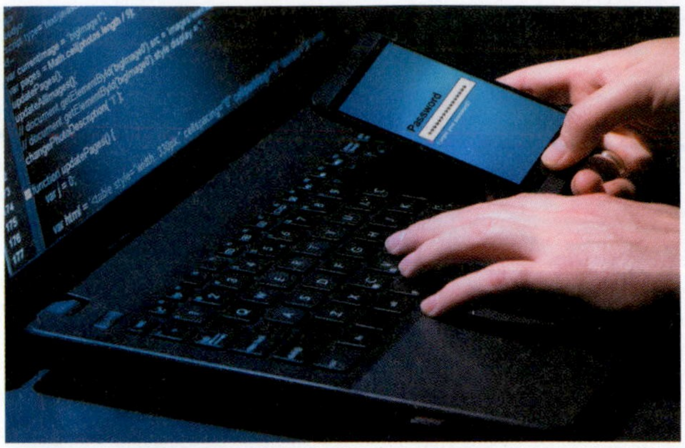

A hidden program called a *rootkit* can allow a hacker to monitor your activity or steal personal data.

Ransomware

A type of malware that locks a computer or restricts access to the computer, demanding that the user pay the malware creator to unlock the device or provide an unlock code, is called **ransomware**. In some cases, the contents of the hard drive are encrypted by the malware. Initially, ransomware installed when a user opened an email attachment that contained the malware. However, early in 2015, the FBI warned the public that it was seeing more incidents of users infecting their computers simply by clicking on a compromised website, often after being lured to the website via an email message or pop-up ad. In the first quarter of 2015, McAfee Labs (an Internet security company) reported a 165 percent increase in ransomware over 2014.

Malware Protection

Check This Out ✓

http://CC2.ParadigmCollege.net/Bitdefender

Go here for a free antivirus program run from a browser that can scan your system whenever you like.

All computer users need to have an up-to-date **antivirus program** running on their computers at all times. This type of program is set up to run automatic scans on a regular basis during a time when the computer is not likely to be in use. Most antivirus programs also scan all incoming emails automatically. You will need to check the settings in a particular program to ensure real-time protection is turned on.

New computers are sold with an antivirus program already installed for a trial period. Some OSs also include malware protection. However, you may want to use a different program or upgrade to a comprehensive suite of online threat

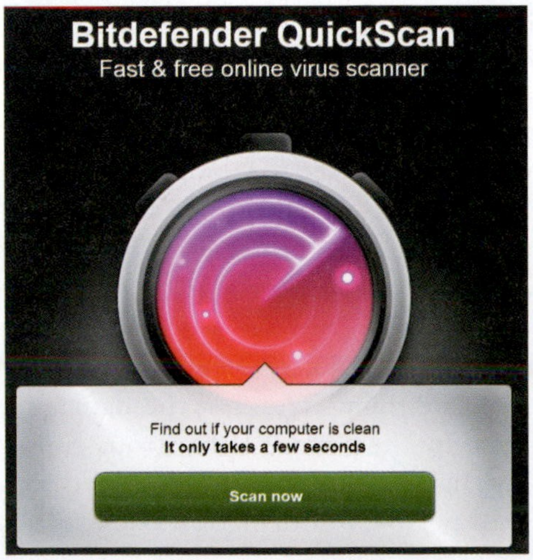

Some antivirus companies, such as Bitdefender, offer a free online scanning tool.

protection. Check reviews and look for information from trusted sources about the antivirus program that detects and removes malware the best. For example, you can buy a program or subscription for Bitdefender, Kaspersky, Webroot, or McAfee—these are just four of several companies that offer antivirus programs. Most antivirus software companies offer programs packaged in a suite of Internet security utilities or separate, standalone security programs. If you have one or more mobile devices, look for a suite that includes protection for smartphones and tablets. You will also find free antivirus software available from companies such as Microsoft or AVG. Microsoft provides Windows Security Essentials free for computers using Windows 7, and Windows Defender free for computers using Windows 8.1 and later (Figure 7.8).

Be wary of downloading free antivirus software from an ad or pop-up window that appears when you are on a website. Go directly to the website of a company that you know is trusted, and download free software from there. Regardless of the malware protection program you choose, make sure it runs automatically and scans regularly, and that a firewall is always active.

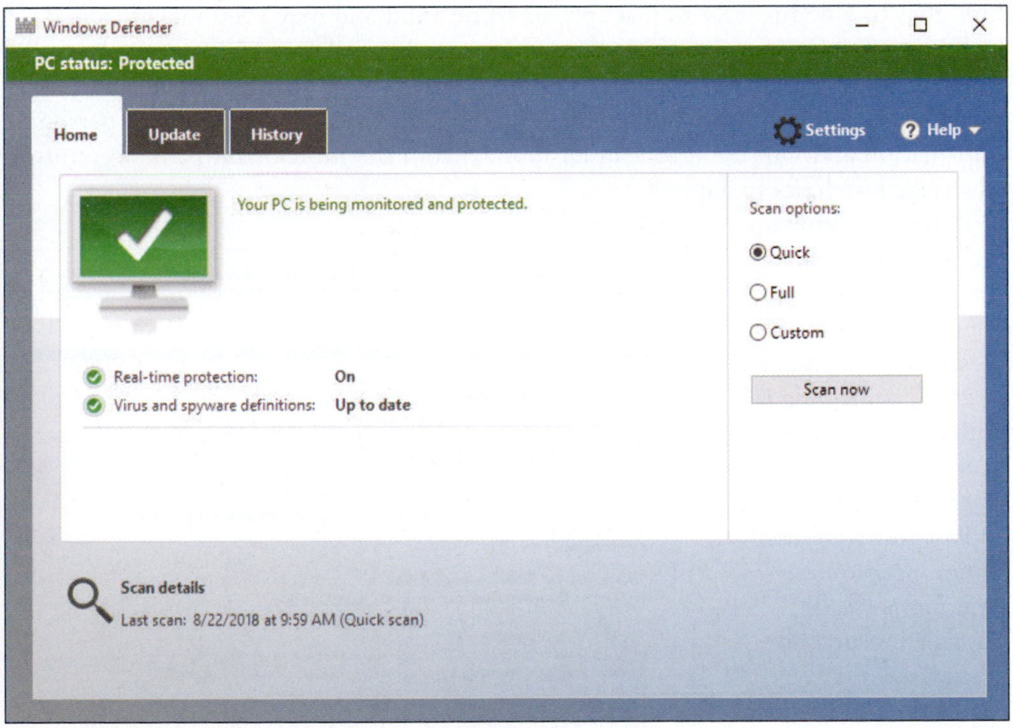

Figure 7.8
Windows Defender is included with Windows 10 and runs automatically to provide protection against malware and other unwanted software.

Security Alert **Do Regular Backups**

Making regular backups of your data will provide the best protection of all. Create a routine to back up data regularly. Should malware strike your system, you will have another copy of important information safely stored somewhere else.

Explore Further **What Is a Logic Bomb?**

Another type of malware that can cause damage to your computer is a logic bomb virus. What are the characteristics of this type of malware? What is the most common type of activity that activates the virus? Are there uses for a logic bomb that are not malicious?

1. Search online for information on logic bombs and read at least two articles to find answers to the above questions.
2. Create a document or presentation that summarizes in your own words what you learned about logic bombs. Include the URLs of the websites you used.
3. Save the document or presentation as **LogicBombs-YourName**.
4. Submit the document or presentation to your instructor in the manner she or he has requested.

7.4 Phishing, Pharming, and Clickjacking Threats

A growing area of cybercrime involves online fraud or scams designed to trick unsuspecting users into revealing personal information so the criminal can steal money from the individual or engage in identity theft. **Identity theft** occurs when an individual's personal information is obtained by a criminal, who then uses the information to buy products or services under the victim's name or to pose as the victim for financial gain. In this topic, you will learn about three scams used to obtain personal information: phishing, pharming, and clickjacking.

Phishing

Tutorial
What Are Current Trends in Phishing Attacks?

Good to Know
According to the 2015 *Anti-Phishing Working Group* report, over 1 million unique phishing email reports were filed by consumers from January to September, which was double the number of reports received in 2014.

Check This Out
http://CC2.ParadigmCollege.net/ReportPhishing
Go here to submit a report about a phishing message you have received.

Phishing (pronounced *fishing*) is the term that describes activities that appear to be initiated by a legitimate organization (such as a bank) in an attempt to obtain personal information that can be used in fraud, theft, or identity theft. A popular email phishing technique involves receiving a message that appears to be from a bank or credit card company and directs the user to click a link (Figure 7.9). The link goes to a bogus website that appears to be valid and may even include a real bank's logo and color scheme. At the phishing website, the user is prompted to enter personal information, such as a user name, password, bank account number, or credit card number. If the individual complies, a criminal now has critical personal information and will use it to transfer money from the individual's bank accounts or to charge purchases to a credit card.

Phishing is growing on social networking sites, owing to the high volume of activity on these sites. For instance, in 2015, coinciding with the excitement of the launch of the Apple Watch, Facebook and Twitter were used to lure people into entering personal information in a fake giveaway. Those who succumbed to the scam entered their full names and Facebook handle and were then asked to invite 100 friends to do the same—with 100 invites earning the user an Apple Watch. Twitter users who mentioned the smartwatch in a tweet were also directed to the scam at fake accounts named Apple Giveaways.

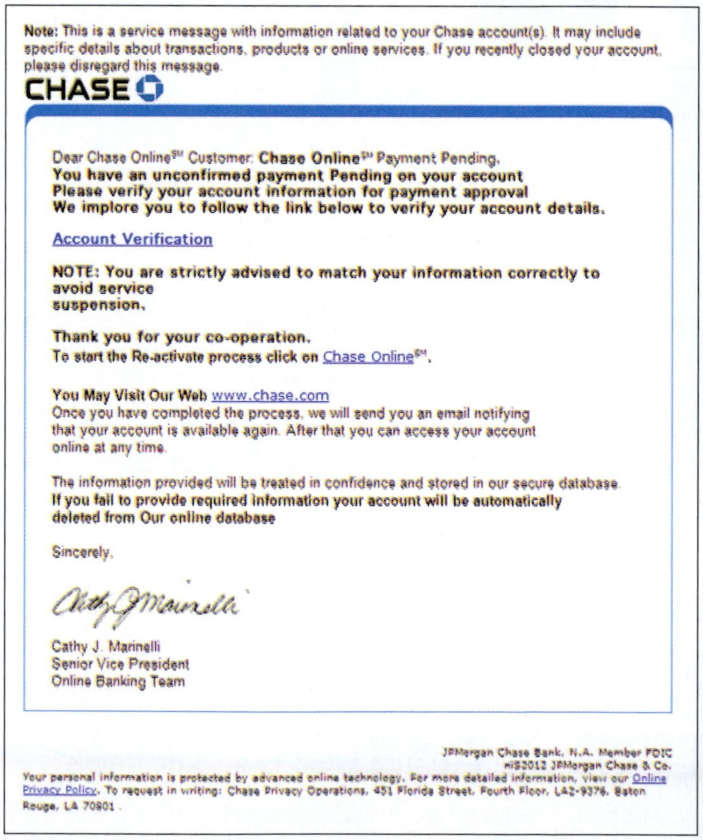
Note: This is a service message with information related to your Chase account(s). It may include specific details about transactions, products or online services. If you recently closed your account, please disregard this message.

CHASE

Dear Chase Online℠ Customer: **Chase Online℠ Payment Pending.**
You have an unconfirmed payment Pending on your account
Please verify your account information for payment approval
We implore you to follow the link below to verify your account details.

Account Verification

NOTE: You are strictly advised to match your information correctly to avoid service suspension.

Thank you for your co-operation.
To start the Re-activate process click on Chase Online℠.

You May Visit Our Web www.chase.com
Once you have completed the process, we will send you an email notifying that your account is available again. After that you can access your account online at any time.

The information provided will be treated in confidence and stored in our secure database.
If you fail to provide required information your account will be automatically deleted from Our online database

Sincerely,

Cathy J. Marinelli
Senior Vice President
Online Banking Team

JPMorgan Chase Bank, N.A. Member FDIC
©2012 JPMorgan Chase & Co.
Your personal information is protected by advanced online technology. For more detailed information, view our Online Privacy Policy. To request in writing: Chase Privacy Operations, 451 Florida Street, Fourth Floor, LA2-9376, Baton Rouge, LA 70801.

Figure 7.9
This message received by Chase customers was a phishing attempt to trick users into clicking the links and revealing account information.

Pharming

Pharming is similar to phishing except that the individual is tricked into typing in personal information at a phony website that appears to be the real website. One type of pharming attack generates an email that installs code on the user's computer without the user's knowledge, and the code then modifies files on the computer. In other pharming cases, the attack compromises the IP address for a Domain Name System (DNS) server. When an individual enters the correct web address for a website, such as his or her bank, the malicious code redirects the URL, sending the victim to a fake web page. The web page at the pharming website looks legitimate, so the individual proceeds to enter personal information.

Phishing and pharming scams employ **spoofing** techniques, in which a sender's email address is altered to a phony address that appears legitimate to the email recipient, or an IP address is altered to appear to be a trusted source.

Pharming scams redirect you to a phony website where you are prompted to enter personal information.

Clickjacking

Clickjacking occurs when a button, graphic, or link on a web page appears to be real but, when clicked, causes malicious software to run. The malicious software code is hidden so that users have no idea that they are not clicking a real link. The bogus button, graphic, or link directs users to another website, where personal information is requested or malware is installed.

In some Facebook clickjacking schemes, a bogus Like button redirects users to advertising pages where the scammers receive money for each wayward clicker. Techniques used in clickjacking scams often involve a breaking news story, exclusive content or contest lure, or a trending news item. Be cautious of clicking links or buttons for something that appears too good to be true or seems unlikely, such as a celebrity death hoax.

Identity theft scams often initiate in email. Delete messages you receive that ask you to click a link to update information. Never click links in unsolicited email messages. Before typing personal information on any web page, examine the URL and other text on the page. Phony websites usually have spelling or grammar errors, or the URL for a false website will have a slightly different domain name or character substitution in the name, such as the number *1* instead of the letter *i*.

Clickjacking scams use buttons, graphics, or links to redirect users from legitimate websites or run malicious software.

Explore Further — What Is Social Engineering?

Security experts know that the weakest link in computer security is human. Unfortunately, cybercriminals also know this and employ social engineering tactics to gain unauthorized access to a network or trick individuals into revealing personal information. How will you know a social engineer is trying to trick you?

1. Search online for articles on social engineering. Find and read at least two articles that describe social engineering tactics, including tactics used at social networking websites.
2. Create a document or presentation that summarizes in your own words what you learned about social engineering. Include the URLs of the websites you used.
3. Save the document or presentation as **SocialEngineering-YourName**.
4. Submit the document or presentation to your instructor in the manner she or he has requested.

7.5 Information Privacy

With so much information collected and stored online, individuals and companies are increasingly concerned with information privacy. **Information privacy** is the right of individuals or organizations to control the information collected about them. Consider all the websites at which you have set up accounts and the personal information you provided at each site. Consider also that some websites track the pages you visit and store information about you. Software may be installed on your computer that is tracking everything you do. In this topic, you will learn about privacy concerns related to online activities.

Cookies

A web server may send a small text file to be stored on your computer hard disk that contains data about you, such as your user name and the pages you visited. This text file is called a **cookie** and is used to identify you when you return to the website. In many cases, the use of cookies is welcomed; they are helpful when used to prefill a login screen or customize your viewing preferences at an e-commerce site. However, cookies might also be used for unwanted purposes, such as tracking your activities or gathering information about you without your permission.

All Internet browsers provide the ability for you to control how cookies are handled. Figure 7.10 shows the Cookies section in the Advanced settings panel for Microsoft Edge, where you can choose how to manage cookies. The default setting is *Don't block cookies*. This setting can be changed to *Block all cookies* or *Block only third-party cookies*. Blocking all cookies is not recommended because signing in to websites that you use frequently becomes difficult without the website cookie installed on your hard drive. A third-party cookie is a cookie placed on your hard drive by a domain that is different from the domain of the web page you are visiting. For example, if you are viewing a web page from the domain shoppingsite.com and a cookie is placed on your system from adtracker.com while viewing that page, the adtracker.com cookie is considered a third-party cookie. Third-party cookies are often designed to track your surfing habits. Many people choose to block third-party cookies as a precaution against behind-the-scenes tracking by websites.

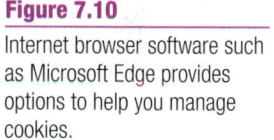

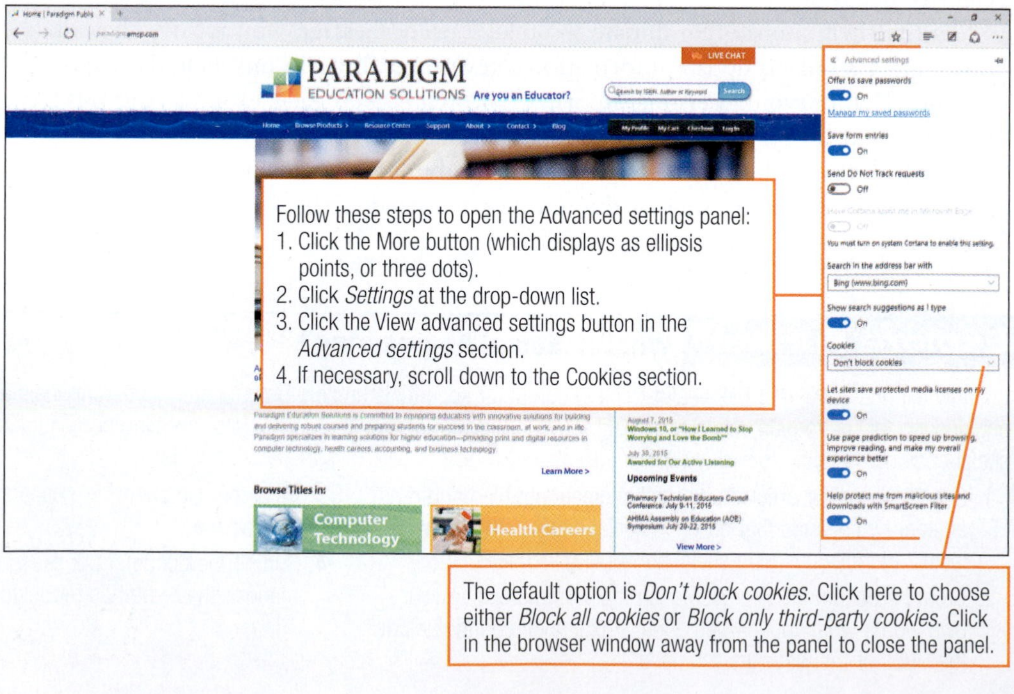
PARADIGM
EDUCATION SOLUTIONS
Are you an Educator?
LIVE CHAT
Follow these steps to open the Advanced settings panel:
1. Click the More button (which displays as ellipsis points, or three dots).
2. Click *Settings* at the drop-down list.
3. Click the View advanced settings button in the *Advanced settings* section.
4. If necessary, scroll down to the Cookies section.
Cookies
Don't block cookies
Browse Titles in:
Computer Technology
Health Careers
Upcoming Events
View More >
The default option is *Don't block cookies*. Click here to choose either *Block all cookies* or *Block only third-party cookies*. Click in the browser window away from the panel to close the panel.

Figure 7.10

Internet browser software such as Microsoft Edge provides options to help you manage cookies.

Spyware

Software programs that exist on your computer without your knowledge and track your activities are referred to as **spyware**. Some spyware may be on your workplace computer so that your employer can monitor your online activities. Other spyware may be used by websites to target ads to your preferences. Antivirus programs typically include spyware detection and removal.

A version of spyware called **keystroke logger**, or *keylogger*, may be activated as part of a rootkit or Trojan horse that records every keystroke you type and sends it back to a cybercriminal. Keystroke loggers may be used to obtain your bank account number and password or other personal information that leads to identity theft. Some keystroke logger software is promoted on the Internet to businesses as a computer security tool and to parents who want to monitor their children's online activity.

Spyware tracks your online activities.

Programs responsible for pop-up ads that appear on your desktop or while viewing web pages are the result of software referred to as **adware**. These unwelcome ads often piggyback spyware onto your computer. Early in 2015, technology company Lenovo made headlines when an adware program called Superfish, preinstalled on new Lenovo PCs, was found to have a flawed design that left users vulnerable to a **man-in-the-middle (MITM) attack**. An MITM attack occurs when a hacker intercepts communications between a user and a website, usually for purposes of capturing personal information. In the Lenovo case, Superfish adware left a hole in the security on the user's PC that meant a hacker could install malware on the device. In May 2015, Lenovo was served with a class action lawsuit over the adware debacle.

Good to Know

The United States Secret Service issued an advisory in July 2014 about keystroke logger malware used on computers in business centers at major hotels in the Dallas/Fort Worth area to obtain large amounts of sensitive personal information from guests.

Spam

Spam is electronic junk mail—unsolicited email sent to a large group of people at the same time. Spam messages entice readers to buy something, are phishing messages, or are vehicles used to distribute Trojan viruses in attachments or via a link the user clicks in the message, or are vehicles used to distribute Trojan viruses in attachments or via a link the user clicks in the message. Spam messaging has infiltrated social networks and text messages. According to Kaspersky Lab (an Internet security company), on average, between 53 and 62 percent of email was spam in the first half of 2015. A Kaspersky Lab analyst wrote that an increase in the use of real-life tragic events in spam was noticed in 2015. For example, the April 2015 Nepalese earthquake was used by spammers in emails asking the recipient to make a donation to help earthquake victims. Never click a link in an unsolicited email to make a donation. A **Twitter bot** is software programmed to follow people based on popular keywords. When a user clicks a link in the comment that appears as a response to a tweet, they receive spam or malware. Beware of followers with strange handles.

Spyware called a *keystroke logger* records every keystroke you type.

Obtaining a store loyalty card or registering for free accounts often requires you to provide your email address. These databases of names and email addresses are sold for marketing purposes, which is how you end up with spam. Many people use a free web-based email account at hosts such as Outlook.com or Gmail for online activities only. This helps to reduce the amount of spam invading the email inbox you use for personal or work messaging. Sign up for a new account when spam at the free account becomes onerous.

Spam is estimated to account for more than 53 percent of all email traffic!

Tutorial
How Does Encryption Work?

Check This Out ✓
http://CC2.ParadigmCollege.net/ElectronicPrivacy
Go here for up-to-date information on privacy issues from the Electronic Privacy Information Center.

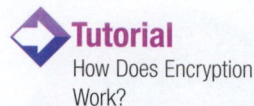

Ways to Protect Personal Information

When shopping online or conducting other business that requires a financial transaction, make sure the URL at the website begins with *https* and that you see a small closed padlock next to the Address bar or in the Status bar of the browser window. These signs indicate a secure website using a protocol that protects data sent to the site with **Transport Layer Security (TLS)**, which encrypts transmitted data so that the data is unreadable if intercepted.

Table 7.3 provides strategies you can use to protect personal information while pursuing online activities. Ultimately, you are responsible for keeping sensitive information private and being diligent at websites where you provide personal data. Check privacy policies and do not reveal information that you do not feel is necessary for the purpose of the visit.

Table 7.3
Ways to Minimize Tracking of Your Personal Information

Fill in only the fields marked with asterisks at websites that ask you for personal information when registering for an account; these are the minimum fields required to obtain an account.
Consider changing the privacy option in the browser that you use to block third-party cookies.
At websites that require a birthdate, such as Facebook, make sure you hide the date in your profile.
Have different user names and use strong passwords for online shopping, social networks, and banking. Make sure the answers to security questions you have set up to recover your password from websites are not easily gleaned from other information about you that is online.
Do not allow apps or websites to tag your location. Geo-location apps on your smartphone may sound cool, but consider that a third party could be tracking your every movement.
Use a free web-based email account for online shopping and social networks and keep your regular email address for other purposes.
If your ISP does not use a spam filter on your email account, find and install anti-spam software on your own.
Delete spam messages right away without opening them.
Unsubscribe to mailing lists that you think are selling your email address for marketing purposes.
Regularly clear the history in your browser.
Make sure the antivirus program you use includes antispyware and that the program is set to automatically update and scan your computer regularly.
Make sure a firewall is active at all times you are online.
Do not reveal personal details in status updates or other posts that may allow someone to determine where you live.
Shred documents with personal information before discarding them.

Data Privacy in the Cloud

When storing pictures, documents, or other data at a cloud provider website, such as Flickr or Dropbox, find out the privacy and security policies that affect your data. Typically, you control the data privacy by restricting who can see a file. However, unanticipated issues could arise, such as an employee of the cloud provider being able to view the contents of your files. To be safe, never post at a cloud provider files containing sensitive information, such as your birthdate and social security number, that could make you vulnerable to identity theft.

At social networks, such as Facebook and Twitter, make sure you review and change privacy settings so that only the information you want public is viewable by anyone. In Facebook, check the information about you that is public. To do this, go to your Profile page in your Facebook account, click the button next to View Activity Log with the ellipsis (three dots), and then click *View As*. The next page shows you what your profile looks like to anyone who searches for your name in Facebook.

Change your profile if you see personal information that should not be shared with the general public. When posting information at social networks, also consider that friends who see the information could inadvertently share something personal about you with someone else.

Cybercriminals are trolling social networks for personal data they can mine for financial gain. Three popular methods cybercriminals use on social networks is to place offers for free gifts (such as a smartphone), post scandalous news or a death hoax about a celebrity, or post news about a tragic world event. Generally, once you click one of these items in your news feed, you are asked to fill out a survey, invited to download software that is really malware, or redirected to a website with a drive-by download. Often, you are encouraged to share the post on your timeline to entice your friends to do the same activity. Don't answer surveys in social networks, and do practice the advice *Think before you click!*

Change privacy settings at social networks, such as Facebook, and at cloud provider websites to control information about you that is available for others to view.

Good to Know

In Facebook, run the Privacy Checkup tool to go through a three-step process to review your current privacy settings. To start Privacy Checkup, click the Privacy Shortcuts button (to the right of the Notifications button) at the top of the your account window, then click *Privacy Checkup*. The utility shows you the audience for your posts, the apps you have logged in to using Facebook, and information in your profile that is visible to others.

Blog Topic: Is Employer Monitoring an Invasion of Privacy?

Video cameras, email monitoring, website monitoring, and keystroke loggers are some of the ways employers can keep tabs on what their employees are up to at the workplace. Generally, employees should not have an expectation of privacy when using employer-owned computing equipment. Still, is all this monitoring of activities an invasion of privacy? What about using the employer's computer during lunch hours and breaks? Shouldn't that be considered the employee's personal time?

1. Write and post a blog entry that provides your opinion about the questions.
2. Read at least two of your classmates' blogs and post one comment to each.
3. Submit your blog URL and the URLs of your classmates' blogs to your instructor in the manner she or he has requested.

Explore Further: Learning about Privacy Notices

Websites that collect personal information also have a privacy notice that spells out how the organization will use the personal data you provide. Have you ever read a privacy notice? What should a typical privacy notice include?

1. Go to the website of an e-tailer that you have used in the past, and find and read the privacy policy or privacy notice link. If you have not made an online purchase, visit the website of a well-known e-tailer, such as Amazon.
2. Create a document or presentation with a summary in your own words of how personal information will be used, stored, and safeguarded by the e-tailer. Include the URL to the policy you used.
3. Save the document or presentation as **PrivacyPolicy-YourName**.
4. Submit the document or presentation to your instructor in the manner she or he has requested.

7.6 Mobile Device Security

Mobile devices such as notebooks, ultrabooks, tablets, and smartphones have untethered people from their homes and offices; however, the portable nature of these devices makes them vulnerable to security risks. In this topic, you will examine the various security risks for mobile users and methods used to protect hardware and data from loss due to cybercrime, theft, or other circumstances.

Mobile Malware

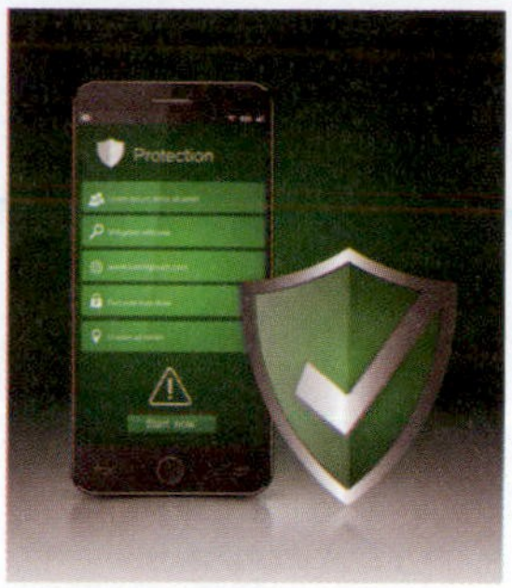

Mobile malware is increasing each year. Each smartphone and tablet should be protected with mobile security software.

According to Internet security company McAfee Labs, **mobile malware** (viruses designed for mobile devices) increased 49 percent from the last quarter of 2014 to the first quarter in 2015. Android devices are a popular target for malware because of the open source nature of their OS; however, no mobile OS is without risk. A smartphone or tablet may get a virus via an infected app downloaded from an app store or the web, an infected computer connected to the device, an attachment sent via email or text message, or a Bluetooth connection in close proximity.

Make sure your smartphones and tablets have mobile security software to shield the devices from malware. All app stores offer free mobile security apps.

Good to Know

In May 2015, smartphone owners were urged to be cautious when a wave of ransomware viruses spread to mobile devices. The viruses locked devices and demanded payment to an offshore bank account for an unlock code.

Lost or Stolen Mobile Devices

Securing a mobile device with locks, biometrics, and/or remote tools is necessary to protect against the loss of a device due to theft or absentmindedness. While the hardware may be easily replaced, the personal information and data stored on the device usually has the higher value for individuals and employers. The following tools assist with securing mobile devices and data (see also Figure 7.11):

- Many devices are equipped with fingerprint readers that restrict access to the authenticated user only.
- A strong password or passcode for access to the device should be enabled; should the device be stolen or lost, the password/passcode may provide enough time to employ remote wiping utilities.
- Physical locks with cables that attach a notebook to a table or desk in a public place are a deterrent to thieves looking for an easy target.
- Technology for remote wiping, locking, and tracking of a lost or stolen mobile device lets the owner wipe the device clean of data and track its location.
- Regular backups of data stored on mobile devices should be mandatory.

Figure 7.11

Mobile devices can be secured with fingerprint readers, passcodes or passwords, and physical cable locks to restrict access.

Bluetooth Risks

Tutorial
What Risks Are Involved in Using Bluetooth?

Bluetooth technology, which wirelessly connects and exchanges data between two devices in close proximity, is subject to risk from intrusion by others within range. Bluetooth range can be from 3 to 300 feet, depending on the power class of the device. When using Bluetooth in a public space with many people nearby, a risk exists that someone else can connect to your device and send you a virus or access personal data. Turn Bluetooth on only when needed and turn it off as soon as you are finished with it. Consider installing a Bluetooth firewall app that will secure your device from unwanted intrusions.

Mobile devices carry risks unique to their portable nature. Employers may require employees with mobile devices to abide by a mobile computing policy. A mobile computing policy usually requires employees to take responsible measures to secure notebooks, tablets, or smartphones while away from the office, make frequent backups to a secure site, and password protect all sensitive company documents stored on the device.

To reduce security risks, turn off Bluetooth when using a mobile device in a crowded place.

Security Alert Be Aware of Shoulder Surfers

If you are viewing sensitive or confidential information on a mobile device, protect your screen from shoulder surfers. Privacy screens for notebooks, tablets, and smartphones prevent shoulder surfers from seeing what is on your screen. Be aware of your surroundings!

Career Connection

Computer Security Experts

Computer security is a top priority for many organizations as they strive to protect against network attacks and cybercrime activities. A 2016 report from Cisco Systems (a network hardware manufacturer) estimates that one million job openings exist for cybersecurity professionals. Security professionals are among the highest paid IT workers. A bachelor's degree in computer science or computer security is generally required for a computer security career. Certifications attract higher salaries, and a wide variety of security certifications are available. For someone starting out in the field, the CompTIA Security+ and the GIAC Security Essentials certification from the Global Information Assurance Certification organization are a good foundation.

Explore Further Using Public Wi-Fi Wisely

Public Wi-Fi networks are unsecured to make them as convenient to use as possible. What precautions should you take when using a public Wi-Fi network to connect your notebook, tablet, or smartphone?

1. Find and read at least two online articles with tips for using public Wi-Fi networks safely. Choose the five tips you think are the most important.
2. Create a presentation with one slide for each tip that describes what you learned. Include a sixth slide with the URLs of the articles you used.
3. Save the presentation as **PublicWi-Fi-YourName**.
4. Submit the presentation to your instructor in the manner she or he has requested.

Topics Review

Topic	Key Concepts	Key Terms
7.1 Unauthorized Access and Unauthorized Use of Computer Resources	Illegal acts involving a computing device on the Internet is cybercrime. Computer security activities are related to protecting hardware, software, and data from loss due to unauthorized access, unauthorized use, theft, natural disaster, or human error. Unauthorized access occurs when someone gains entry without permission to a computer through a network. A hacker is an individual who accesses a network without permission, while hacking describes activities used to gain unauthorized access to a network. A white hat is a hacker who gains entry into a network to pinpoint weaknesses in the network security. A black hat is a hacker who gains entry into a network with malicious intent. War driving occurs when someone drives around with a portable device trying to connect to someone else's unsecured wireless network. Piggybacking refers to connecting to a wireless network without the network owner's permission. Unauthorized use is performing activities on a computer other than the intended uses. A strong password is difficult to hack by humans or password detection software programs. Physical entry to rooms with computing equipment at workplaces is secured by locks and biometric devices. A biometric device uses physical characteristics of an individual to authenticate identity. A firewall is hardware, software, or a combination thereof that blocks unauthorized access. Encryption scrambles communications between devices so that the data is unreadable to anyone except the originator and intended recipient of a transmission. Wi-Fi Protected Access (WPA) and WPA2 are the most recent encryption standards used in wireless routers and access points. Organizations may use intrusion detection software that analyzes network traffic for suspicious data to thwart network attacks. An acceptable use policy (AUP) spells out appropriate and inappropriate use of computing equipment in the workplace.	cybercrime computer security unauthorized access hacker hacking white hat black hat war driving piggybacking unauthorized use strong password biometric device firewall encryption Wi-Fi Protected Access (WPA) WPA2 intrusion detection software acceptable use policy (AUP)

continued…

Topic	Key Concepts	Key Terms
7.2 Botnets and Denial of Service Attacks	A zombie is a computer controlled by a hacker or cybercriminal without the owner's knowledge. A collection of zombie computers that attack a network is called a *botnet*. A computer becomes a zombie by being infected with software, usually from a virus, that is hidden from the user. To prevent a computer from becoming a zombie, scan regularly with up-to-date antivirus software, update the OS regularly, and make sure a firewall is always active. A denial of service (DoS) attack occurs when a botnet attacks a network by sending a constant stream of messages that slow down or completely shut down a server. Organizations use firewalls, intrusion detection software, and antivirus tools to prevent DoS attacks.	zombie botnet denial of service (DoS) attack
7.3 Malware Infections	Malware refers to any type of malicious software. A virus is a form of malware that replicates itself, spreading to other media on the infected computer and to other computers. A macro virus is a virus embedded in a document macro; when the user enables the macro, the virus infects the computer. A drive-by download occurs when the user's computer is infected simply by visiting a compromised website using an out-of-date browser, app, or OS that has a security flaw. A worm is a self-replicating program that infects other computers on a network without user action. A Trojan horse is a program that appears to the user to be a useful program but which in fact is malware. Rootkit programs provide a back door (a way to bypass security) for a hacker or cybercriminal to control a computer remotely. Ransomware is a form of malware where the target device is locked or encrypted and a demand for payment is made by the malware creator to provide the owner with an unlock code. Antivirus programs detect and remove malware.	malware virus macro virus drive-by download worm Trojan horse rootkit back door ransomware antivirus program
7.4 Phishing, Pharming, and Clickjacking Threats	Identity theft occurs when personal information is obtained by a criminal who uses the information for financial gain. Phishing activities usually occur in messages that appear to be legitimate but are intended to steal personal information by convincing the user to click a link to a phishing website where the user enters personal information. Pharming is where malicious code redirects a URL to a fake web page after a person types a web address at which the unsuspecting user enters personal information. Spoofing techniques alter a sender's email address or a web address so that they appear legitimate. Clickjacking occurs when a user clicks a phony button, image, or link and is redirected to another website or a virus downloads to the device.	identity theft phishing pharming spoofing clickjacking

continued…

Topic	Key Concepts	Key Terms
7.5 Information Privacy	Information privacy refers to the rights of individuals to control information that is collected about them. A cookie is a small text file placed on your hard drive by a web server with information about your user name and the pages you visited. Spyware is software that tracks your activities without your knowledge. Keystroke loggers, or keyloggers, record every keystroke you type and send the data to a cybercriminal. Adware displays pop-up ads on your desktop or at web pages and will sometimes piggyback spyware onto your computer. A man-in-the-middle (MITM) attack occurs when a hacker intercepts communications between a user and a website for purposes of capturing personal information. Spam is unsolicited email sent to large groups of people. A Twitter bot is software programmed to follow people based on popular keywords and usually results in spam or malware when a user clicks a link in a tweet posted by a bot. A closed padlock next to the Address bar and *https* at the beginning of a website address are signs indicating that the website is a secure website using Transport Layer Security (TLS), which encrypts transmitted data. Find out the privacy and security policies in effect at cloud-providing websites where you store pictures and documents. Review and change privacy settings at social networks, such as Facebook and Twitter.	information privacy cookie spyware keystroke logger adware man-in-the-middle (MITM) attack spam Twitter bot Transport Layer Security (TLS)
7.6 Mobile Device Security	Mobile malware are viruses designed for mobile devices. Android devices are attacked more frequently due to their open source mobile operating system. A smartphone or tablet gets a virus by downloading an infected app, by being connected to an infected computer, from a message attachment, or via a Bluetooth connection. All mobile devices including tablets and smartphones should have mobile security software installed. Mobile devices should be secured with locks, biometrics, or remote wiping and tracking tools in case of loss or theft. Using Bluetooth in a public space leaves you vulnerable; someone else with a Bluetooth device can access your smartphone, tablet, or notebook and send you a virus or steal personal data. Employers may require mobile workers to abide by a mobile computing policy that requires them to take responsible measures to secure their devices.	mobile malware

Recheck
Recheck your understanding of the topics covered in this chapter.

Workbook
Chapter review and assessment resources are available in the *Workbook* ebook.

Appendix A

Buying a New Computing Device

Buying a new notebook, tablet, or smartphone requires an understanding of the technical jargon that often appears in computer ads. An experienced electronics sales associate will help you choose the right device; however, some people like to shop online or find out in advance the features that are important to consider. In this appendix, you will learn to shop for a device that meets your needs using a step-by-step buying process model.

Buying a New PC or Tablet

Are you in the market for a new computer or are you looking to add a second device to supplement a computer you already own? Many people own more than one computing device. Perhaps you have a desktop PC and want a notebook or tablet to use for school. The following pages will guide you through a decision-making process that will help you make an informed purchase. Spending a little time planning your requirements will save time and money and help you avoid making an impulse purchase you may regret.

A section with tips for making a smartphone purchase is included at the end of the appendix. The following steps are geared toward deciding how to buy a personal computer or tablet.

Step 1: Determine Your Maximum Budget

Before you start browsing computer ads, know how much money you can afford to spend. Computers are sold in a wide range of prices, from a few hundred dollars to a few thousand dollars, to suit a variety of budgets. Setting your maximum price will help narrow the search when you are ready to shop.

Start by setting the maximum budget.

Step 2: Decide on a Desktop, Notebook, Ultrabook, or Tablet

Desktop PCs are declining in usage, but nevertheless, some people prefer the stationary system unit that sits on or under a desk with an attached monitor, keyboard, and mouse. If you normally work in one place and have the physical space to accommodate the larger PC, a desktop is a good value. The desktop PCs of today last longer than earlier desktops and are easier to upgrade than most mobile devices. All-in-one PCs pack all the system unit components behind the monitor, which requires less desktop space. Desktop PCs also include a larger screen for easier viewing of content.

You will need to decide between a desktop PC, notebook, ultrabook, convertible laptop, or tablet.

If you are looking for a portable computer for school or work that you can move around the house, that has a full-size keyboard with all the power and capability of a traditional desktop, and that has a medium-size screen, then a notebook or ultrabook is what you need. Which option you choose will depend on how you plan to use it. A notebook computer provides everything a traditional desktop PC provides, in a portable case that you can carry around. Notebooks are available in a wide variety of configurations and screen sizes. The weight of a notebook varies: some smaller units weigh in at 2.5 pounds, but those with a larger screen can top the scales at over 7 pounds. An ultrabook is lighter and slimmer than a notebook, with most models weighing less than 3 pounds. The battery on an ultrabook lasts longer than that in a traditional notebook. If your computing needs are primarily just surfing the web, and sending and receiving email, a low-cost notebook with a small screen, sometimes called a *netbook*, may be for you.

Tablets are smaller and lighter than notebooks. Typically, people buy a tablet as a secondary device, with a desktop or notebook PC serving as their primary device. However, the available options include convertible tablet PCs (with screens that rotate 180 degrees to fold over a keyboard) and tablets supplied with a docking station that includes a full-size keyboard. If you want to use a touchscreen, or a stylus to handwrite notes, a tablet is the way to go.

Step 3: Decide on the Software Applications and Operating System

Computers come with an operating system and some software applications preinstalled, so you may be tempted to skip this step. However, this step is important because it can help you keep within your budget. Watch for systems that preinstall limited trial editions of software applications. These applications usually expire within a short time frame, such as 90 days, or at some point within the first year after purchase. Following expiration, you have to pay a license fee to continue using the software. You need to find out in advance if you will have to set aside money to pay for software applications separately.

Check your school's computer store to see if you can buy software applications at academic pricing, or even get software for free. For example, Microsoft provides free software, such as Microsoft Office, to eligible students at some qualifying schools (see Figure A.1). Some academic licenses have to be purchased through your school to qualify for student discounts; however, increasingly, retailers are able to offer the same pricing upon proof of student registration.

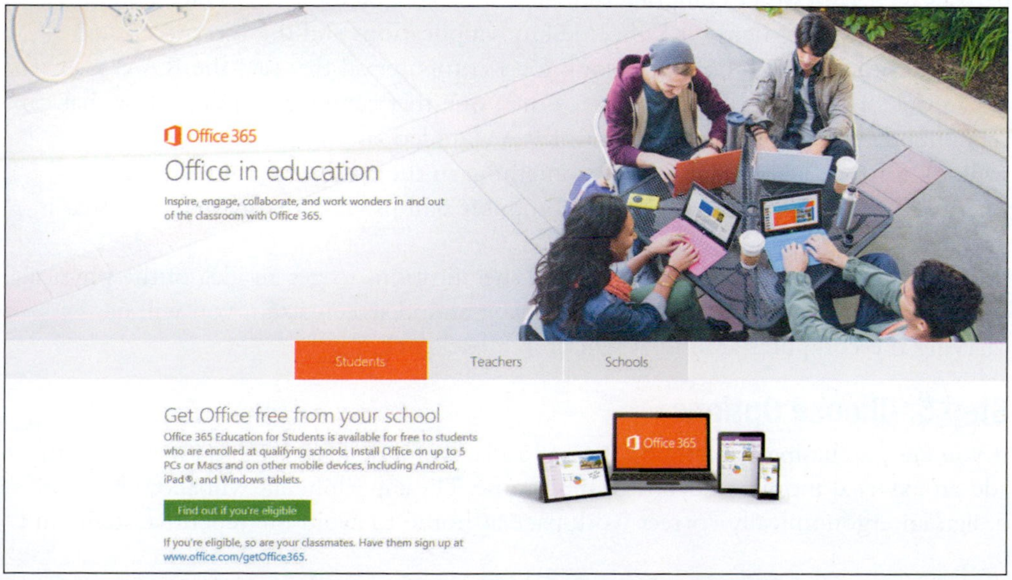

Figure A.1
The Microsoft Education program provides Microsoft software for free to some qualifying schools.

It pays to shop around for the best price on the software application you want to install. Some software publishers offer coupons for web-based purchases, and some retailers can offer attractive pricing when you package the software with your hardware. Look for a software suite that will bundle together multiple applications in one product. These are always a better value than buying individual applications.

Deciding on the software applications you want to use will help you choose the appropriate hardware and OS. All software applications will specify the system requirements for running the software. You will notice that software companies specify minimum and recommended system requirements. Go for the recommended requirements in a new purchase because performance is usually slower at the minimum requirements. Pay particular attention to the specified operating system that is needed to run the application, the amount of RAM, the processor speed, and the disk storage used by the application(s).

Apple PCs and mobile devices are generally more expensive than Windows-compatible computers, but fans argue the money is well spent.

Software applications are typically available in a Mac or a Windows-compatible edition. With the popularity of cloud-based software that functions on either platform, deciding between Mac and PC is becoming less dependent on software and more a personal choice and budget issue. Apple PCs are more expensive than Windows-compatible PCs. The Apple iPad and iPhone are also more expensive than Windows-compatible or Android tablets and smartphones.

Apple fans are fiercely loyal to the brand and will argue that the extra money for Apple is well worth the investment. Ultimately, if you are not partial to either platform or OS family of products, you should try both environments at your school or at a store to determine whether you become a Mac or a PC owner.

Step 4: Compare Hardware Components to Match Software Needs

Table A.1 (page 195) provides an overview of specifications you should check in a typical ad for a Windows-compatible notebook computer. If necessary, review Chapter 3 for more information on any of the hardware components that are listed.

If you can afford to spend more, buy more than you need to meet the recommended requirements. This will ensure you have a computer that will meet your needs into the future. In a nutshell, go for the computer with the fastest processor, most RAM, and largest internal hard disk drive. These systems will typically be packaged with other components that will be adequate for an average computer user working with Microsoft Office desktop applications and the Internet. If you cannot afford to spend more now, look for a computer ad that says the RAM is expandable. This will be a better choice than one that cannot be upgraded or that can accommodate only a limited amount of RAM added later.

Look for this logo, which tells you the device is energy efficient.

Look for the Energy Star logo or something in the ad that says the device is Energy Star qualified. This means the computer will use less energy than one that is not rated.

Examine the width, height, and weight specifications to get an idea of the physical characteristics. Pay particular attention to weight and screen size if you will be carrying the computer around at school in a backpack.

Step 5: Choose Options

If you are purchasing a notebook to use in place of a desktop PC, you may want to add an external monitor, keyboard, and mouse. These peripherals will allow you to design an ergonomically correct workspace at home to avoid the repetitive strain and

Table A.1

Hardware Components Typically Advertised for a Notebook PC

Processor	Intel Core, Atom, AMD, or ARM processors are commonly found in notebooks and tablets. Notebooks and tablets are sold with multiple-core CPUs, usually dual- or quad-core. Look for the amount and type of cache memory (L1, L2, or L3) with the CPU and the highest processor speed (1.5 GHz and higher).
RAM	RAM works with the CPU to give you high-speed performance. The more RAM you have, the better your system will perform. Look for a minimum of 4 GB of RAM on a notebook and 2 GB on a tablet. Check if RAM is expandable in modules that can be added to the device at a later time. A system with a higher level of expandable RAM will last longer.
Screen	A desktop PC will have a larger screen than a notebook or tablet, typically 19 inches or more. A notebook or ultrabook will have a screen size in the range of 15 inches or higher. Tablet screens are smaller, ranging from 9 to 12 inches. Screen size is measured diagonally from corner to corner.
Video Card	In most cases, the video card supplied with a notebook is adequate. If you are going to use your computer for gaming or high-end graphics design, pay attention to the graphics card, video memory, and GPU. Look for higher specifications for these items to achieve faster graphics processing capabilities.
Hard Disk Space	The larger the amount of hard disk storage space you can get, the better. However, keep in mind that you can always buy external hard disk drives to store digital photos, videos, and music files. Many notebooks are now supplied with a 1 TB HDD, but capacity varies. Look for a minimum of 500 GB.
Optical Disc Drives	Some notebooks include a DVD or Blu-ray Disc drive. Ultrabooks do not have optical drives (although you can purchase one as a peripheral). Optical drives are expected to become obsolete in the next few years as more people opt to stream movies and music.
Digital Media Reader	Transferring data from a digital camera or smartphone is easier if the notebook has a digital media card reader. Most notebooks are equipped with a reader or include a slot for one.
Networking Capabilities	Notebooks are equipped with integrated Wi-Fi networking capabilities. Some also come with integrated Bluetooth connectivity. An Ethernet port provides the added capability of plugging in to a wired network using a twisted-pair cable (sometimes called an *RJ-45 connector*). At school, some classrooms, lounges, or libraries may be equipped with network plug-ins that will give you faster Internet access than the wireless network.
Battery Life	Check the battery life to see how long the computer will operate before requiring power from an outlet. Battery life is important if you will be using the notebook away from power outlets for long periods of time.
Ports	Check the number and type of ports that are available on the notebook. The more USB ports the better, although you can buy an inexpensive USB hub if you need to expand the port availability. An HDMI port will allow you to plug in the notebook to a high-definition television screen for watching movies. A video port is also typically included to allow you to plug in an external monitor.
Integrated Web Cam	Most notebooks are equipped with a web cam. If you plan to do video calling, this feature will be important to you.

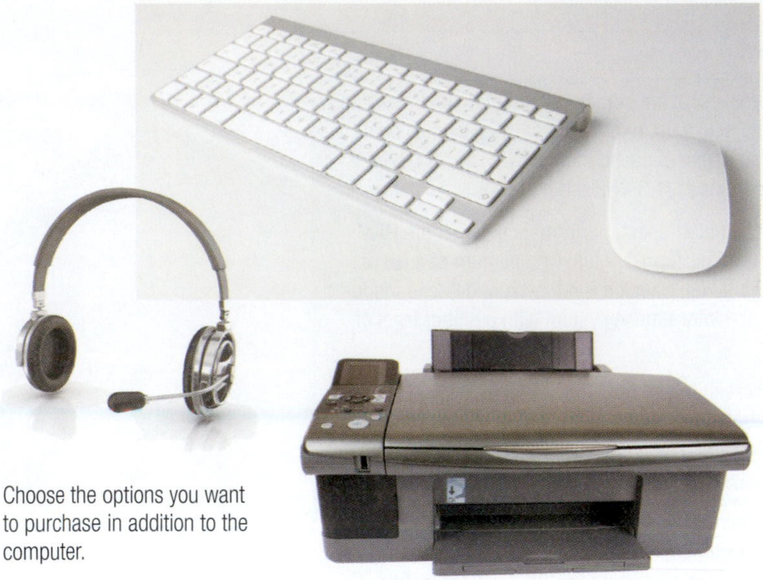

Choose the options you want to purchase in addition to the computer.

eye strain that occur from prolonged use of notebooks. Wireless keyboards and mice allow you to adjust your workspace to more comfortable positions.

If you like listening to music or watching movies, you may want to invest in external speakers or high-quality, noise-canceling headphones. A headset with a microphone is desirable if you plan to use voice technology in many applications.

If you need to print at home, consider whether you want a laser or inkjet printer. Compare the cost of toner versus ink and the number of pages you can print before replacing supplies to help you decide on the type of printer. Some computers are bundled with a printer. Make sure the printer included in such a package is one you want; if you would prefer a better quality printer, try to negotiate a discount on it rather than accepting the packaged device. Consider an all-in-one printer that includes scanning and copying capabilities. All-in-one printers are a good value and will use less desk space than multiple devices.

If you are purchasing a computing portable device, think about how you will carry it and buy a well-padded case or backpack. Consider buying a case with wheels if you will be carrying a notebook along with your textbooks at school. For tablets, consider buying a sleeve or case that you can use to protect the screen surface.

Many mobile devices are subject to theft or loss. Consider biometric options such as a fingerprint reader, or tracking software and hardware that will allow you to remotely monitor or wipe the device should it be stolen or lost.

Step 6: Decide Whether to Buy an Extended Warranty

Most computer equipment carries a one-year parts and labor warranty.

Computers come with a limited parts and labor warranty that is typically good for one year. Consider if you want to buy the extended warranty plans that are offered when you buy a new computer. These warranties are priced depending on the value of the device, and some retailers' warranties will fix mishaps not covered by the manufacturer. Decide if you want to spend the money on these plans. Some people believe extended warranties are a waste of money, while others prefer the peace of mind that comes with knowing they are covered for anything that might happen.

If you have a credit card that includes a buyer protection plan, find out if you must make the purchase using the card and check the policy to see if the credit card insurance will cover you for any accidental damage or loss. If you have coverage, you may not need the extra protection from a retailer's extended warranty.

Step 7: Shop Around, Ask About Service, and Check Reviews

Spend some time on the web before deciding what to purchase, comparing two or three devices in the same price range that you can afford. Also compare the pricing at in-store electronics retailers and online e-tailers. Be mindful of shipping costs that you may incur if you buy from a web-based store. Consider creating a spreadsheet to compare a few options side by side.

Make sure to visit your school's computer store. Schools often offer attractive deals from hardware manufacturers that have discounts negotiated for the large school audience. School staff will also be able to help you choose a computer for programs with specialized hardware or software requirements.

If you are comfortable negotiating at an electronics store, you may be able to convince the retailer to upgrade some options for you in a package price. For example, it would not hurt to ask the sales associate to throw in a wireless keyboard or mouse, or a set of speakers, with a new notebook PC.

Make sure to inquire about service options. Ask where warranty work and other repairs are performed. Some stores will do warranty repairs or out-of-warranty repairs onsite, while others have to ship the PC back to the manufacturer. If the retailer ships the computer elsewhere, ask how long a typical repair will take. In some cases, you could be without your PC for more than week if the store ships the repair offsite. Ask who pays for the shipping to and from the repair center. Finally, some stores do not offer any assistance with repairs—avoid these locations if you are not technically savvy or are adverse to risk.

Some people prefer to pay a little more for a computer that they can have serviced at the store of purchase in case of malfunction. You will have to decide how important the repair facility is to you before making a purchase. Be sure to ask all these questions to help you make the choice with which you are most comfortable.

Search the web for reviews of the product you are considering and the retailer from which you want to purchase it. While reviews are not always helpful (many are negative and the positive ones may not be authentic), they do provide insight into the questions you should ask and the issues for which you want to be on the alert.

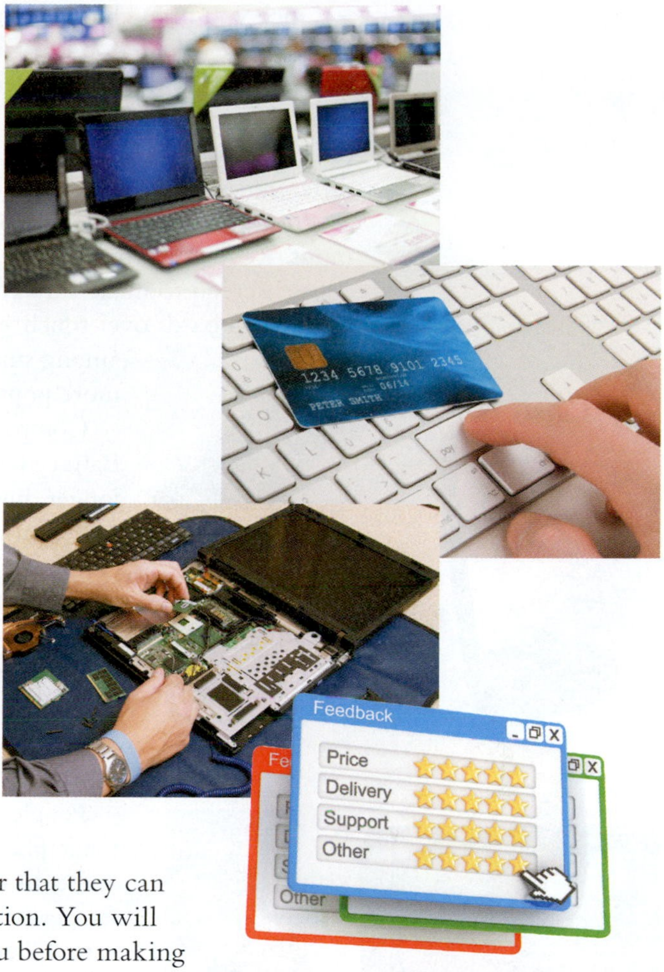

Compare prices at in-store and online retailers, investigate service options, and read reviews on the web.

Considerations for Buying a Smartphone

Before buying a smartphone, choose the provider with which you want to subscribe, the data plan that will meet your needs, and the features you want in a smartphone. Consider whether the provider you have chosen includes the cost of the smartphone in the contract. Some wireless providers will provide a base model smartphone free of charge or at a discounted price, or an upgraded model at a low price, if you sign up for a specified contract period. Watch for limits, caps, and time-of-use charges that may apply. For example, a plan may advertise unlimited use, but the unlimited use may apply in certain hours only. Note that some tablets may also include 3G or 4G wireless access and will need a data plan from a wireless carrier to take advantage of a cellular network when you are not in range of a Wi-Fi hotspot.

Good to Know

Some people prefer to buy an unlocked smartphone. An unlocked smartphone is not tied to a specific wireless carrier. This means you can buy a month-to-month voice and data plan without being locked into a long-term contract. To activate the phone, you will need to purchase a SIM card (a card you insert into the phone with your phone number, contacts, and call history) from the wireless carrier you choose.

Once you have chosen a data plan, compare the smartphones the carrier offers. Visit a store where you can try out a few smartphone models in advance. You will want to try models with different screen sizes. Larger screens might be nice, but consider how you will carry the smartphone and whether it will fit in your hand, pocket, or purse conveniently. You will want to try out messaging and browsing on different size screens to find the one with which you are comfortable. Input can be touch-based with an onscreen keyboard or you can use a keyboard with trackpad input. Keyboards may slide out or be built in below the screen. Try a few tasks with a touchscreen to make sure you are comfortable with touch input. Some people prefer keyboards over touch-enabled screens; however, you will find more selection among smartphones with touch-enabled screens because they are more popular.

When acquiring a smartphone, start with a data plan and then try out various smartphones to choose the one that suits you. Consider the screen size, input method, battery life, and memory card options.

Compare the battery life of various smartphone models. Battery technology is improving and newer batteries last longer, but often battery life does not live up to the advertised specifications. Talk time is the standard by which to base comparisons. Look on the web for reviews that have tested models and provide actual talk time statistics. You may want to inquire about purchasing a second battery if you will often be away from charging stations and think you will use the phone more than the advertised specifications. Another option is to purchase an external battery pack, which can be used with other devices as well as your smartphone.

People use their smartphones to do much more than just make phone calls—to take pictures or record video, play music, and communicate using messaging applications. The apps for performing these tasks need storage space on a memory card. Check the size of the memory card that comes with the smartphone and consider if you will need to buy a larger memory card. Check the compatibility of the memory card with your notebook or other computing devices so that you can easily exchange media files among them.

Ask if a car charger adapter comes with the smartphone or if you have to buy the car charger separately. This could be a negotiating item if you think you will use a car charger often.

Replacing an Older Device?

When you buy a new device, try to sell your older device, donate it to charity, or trade it in if the seller accepts trade-ins. If you cannot sell, give away, or trade in older electronics, remember to look into disposal options for e-waste that will properly recycle the device. Go to http://CC2.ParadigmCollege.net/EWaste for more information on recycling electronics.

Appendix **B**

Wireless Networking

A wireless network is the standard for most homes. People prefer a wireless network so that a network cable does not have to be installed from room to room through floors or ceilings in their home. With a wireless network, you can move freely around the house and outside to your yard, with your computing device, and not lose a network connection. You can connect PCs, tablets, smartphones, wearable devices, gaming consoles, smart appliances, and smart TVs. Family members browse the Internet, watch YouTube, and stream movies from any room in the house. In this appendix, you will learn the basic steps for setting up a wireless network and connecting devices to the network in a home. You will also learn how to set up a wireless network on Apple equipment, and how to connect to a public wireless network.

Setting Up a Wireless Network at Home

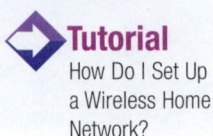

Tutorial
How Do I Set Up a Wireless Home Network?

Good to Know

The term *802.11* refers to a set of specifications developed by the Institute of Electrical and Electronics Engineers (IEEE) that tells wireless devices how to connect with each other using a series of access points and radio frequencies to transmit data. The letter or letters after 802.11 (for example, *ac*) reference the version of the standard being used.

Wi-Fi uses a combination wireless router / wireless access point and radio signals to transmit data within a limited range. The speed you will experience in a wireless network will vary depending on the equipment, the ISP service, the number of people sharing the connection, and the type of bandwidth being used by each connected user. Most wireless routers in use are either wireless ac (802.11ac) routers, or wireless n (802.11n) routers. A wireless ac router can operate approximately three times faster than a wireless n router, with ac routers tested in real world environments maintaining a speed of just under 1 Gbps. While this speed sounds lightning fast, bear in mind that the equipment can only deliver the Internet speed for which you have subscribed (see Step 1). You also need to have devices that are compatible with the wireless router to take advantage of newer technology.

Even with a wireless network, some homes will have a desktop PC that is connected by plugging in a network cable to the wireless router. The following steps describe the general process for setting up a wireless network. Different routers provide slightly different software interfaces; however, the general steps will be the same.

A modem provides Internet access. A wireless router allows you to share that access among multiple devices. Newer devices combine a modem and router into one unit.

Step 1: Subscribe to High-Speed Internet Service with an ISP

As you learned in Topic 2.2 in Chapter 2, to connect to the Internet, you need an account with an Internet service provider (ISP). Contact a telephone company, cable company, or dedicated Internet service company for high-speed Internet access. Each provider will offer different pricing levels that vary according to the speed, with faster speeds costing more per month than slower speeds.

A telephone company will provide you with a DSL modem, and a cable company will provide you with a cable modem. Newer modems provided by ISPs are a combination wireless router and modem in one piece of equipment called a *modem router*. Some installations may require two pieces of equipment: a DSL or cable modem, plus an additional wireless router. To proceed to Step 2, you need the ISP service activated, as well as a DSL or cable modem router, or a modem plus wireless router. If your ISP does not provide a wireless router, you can buy one at an electronics store. Brand names for commonly used wireless routers are Linksys, D-Link, and Cisco.

Your ISP may also provide instruction documentation when you subscribe for service

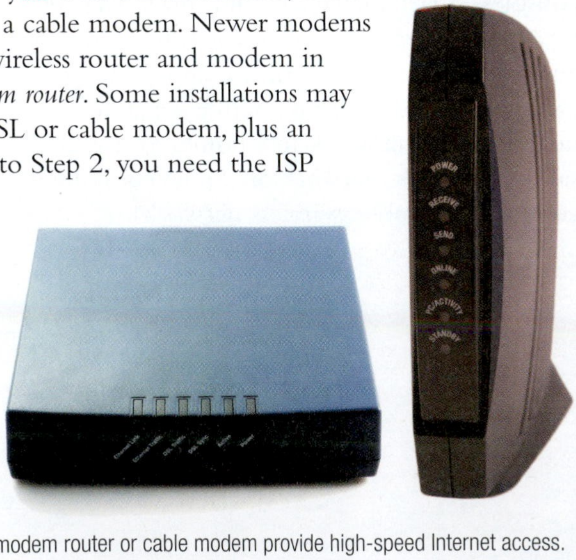

A modem router or cable modem provide high-speed Internet access.

and may give you a USB flash drive or DVD that automates the setup process if the company's technician does not go to your residence to do an on-site installation. New subscribers generally have a technician visit their home to set up the service and install and configure the equipment. Subscribers with existing service who are upgrading a router or modem will generally do the installation themselves, possibly with telephone assistance from the ISP. If the documentation from your ISP contains instructions that vary from the steps below, complete the steps according to the instructions from the ISP.

Step 2: Connect the Networking Hardware Equipment

Connect one end of a coaxial cable (cable modem) or twisted-pair cable (DSL modem) to the modem and the other end to the cable or telephone line coming into your house. Plug the power adapter into the modem and into a power outlet. You should see lights illuminate on the front of the modem, indicating power and connectivity are live.

Next, connect the modem to the wireless router if you need a standalone router (if your ISP did not provide you with a combination modem router). To do this, plug one end of a network cable into the back of the modem and the other end into the back of the wireless router. Plug the power adapter into the wireless router and into a power outlet. You should also see lights illuminate on the front of the standalone router.

If you have a desktop PC in the same room as your networking equipment, you can connect the PC to the integrated modem router or standalone router by plugging one end of a network cable into the PC network port and the other end into the back of the modem router or standalone router. This allows the PC to use a wired connection to the router, while the remaining devices in your home will use a wireless connection.

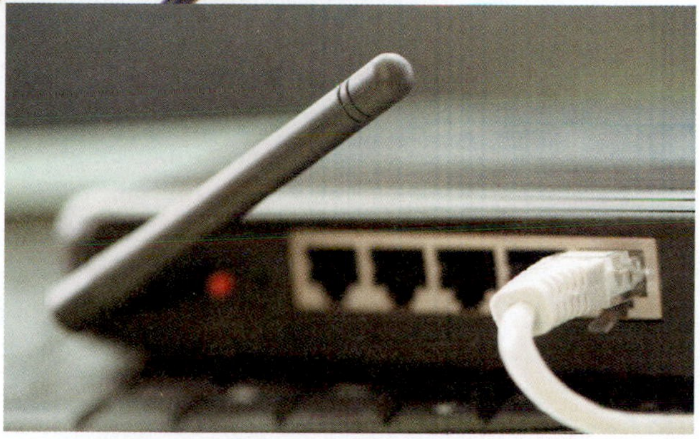

Connect a cable or DSL modem to a wireless router using a network cable.

Once the networking equipment is connected and has power, you can move on to Step 3.

Step 3: Configure the Wireless Router

Integrated modem routers or standalone routers may come with an installation CD, DVD, or USB flash drive that walks you through the steps to set up the router, or you may be instructed to go to a website to configure the router. One computer will need to be plugged into the wireless router while you configure it. After this step, you can unplug the PC from the router and connect wirelessly afterward.

Start with the computer connected to the router through the Ethernet port and the configuration medium installed or website open in your browser (Figure B.1, page 202). Proceed by following the instructions that appear in the setup program. The software interface is user-friendly, and prompts assist you at each step. Generally, you need to do three tasks: assign the router a name (called the *service set identifier [SSID]*) and security key, change the administrative password for the router, and choose the security standard you want to use.

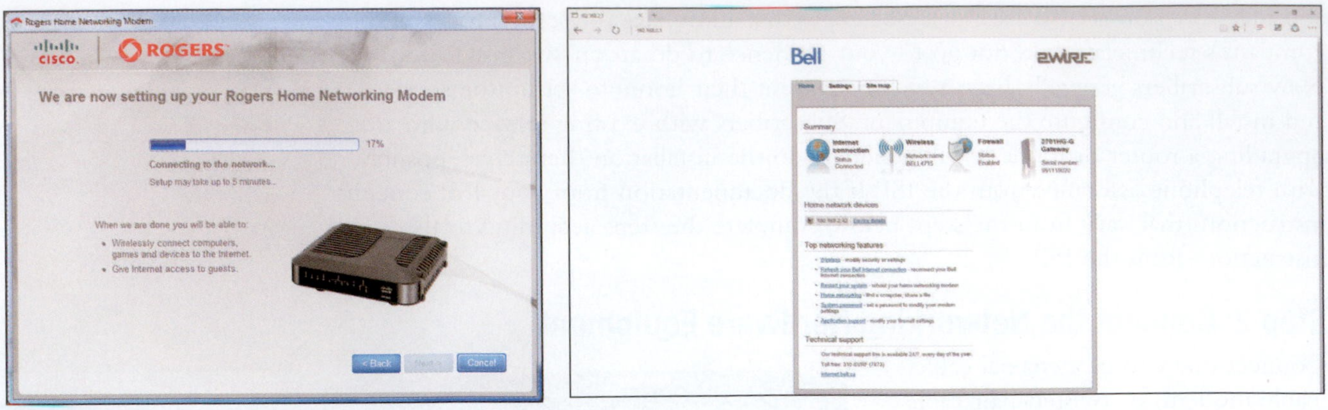

Figure B.1

Insert the CD, DVD, or USB flash drive into a PC to start the router setup program (left), or open a browser window and type in the URL given to you by the ISP (right).

If you did not receive an installation medium with a preprogrammed setup process, look for instructions that came with the equipment that provide a URL or IP address to configure the router. Open a browser window and type the URL or IP address to start the software interface as shown in the image in Figure B.1. Note that the software interface for each router will vary. If in doubt about how to proceed, call the technical support assistance telephone number given to you.

Wireless routers come with a default user name and password—usually *admin* for both user name and password, or *admin* and *password*. Log on to the router device and proceed to change the settings as needed.

When giving the router a new name, try not to use an obvious name that will identify you with the router. For example, do not use your name or your address. If you use an obscure name, then when someone is within range of your router, they will not associate the network name with you and try to break into your Internet access (this can help you avoid situations such as a neighbor trying to piggyback your connection). A good idea is to prevent the router from broadcasting the router SSID. Although free public Wi-Fi networks, such as those at airports, coffee shops, and libraries, use a recognizable name to provide unsecured network access to everyone who is within range, home users should choose a name that is not easily associated with the location. Also assign a security key that your neighbors or anyone who knows you would not be able to guess.

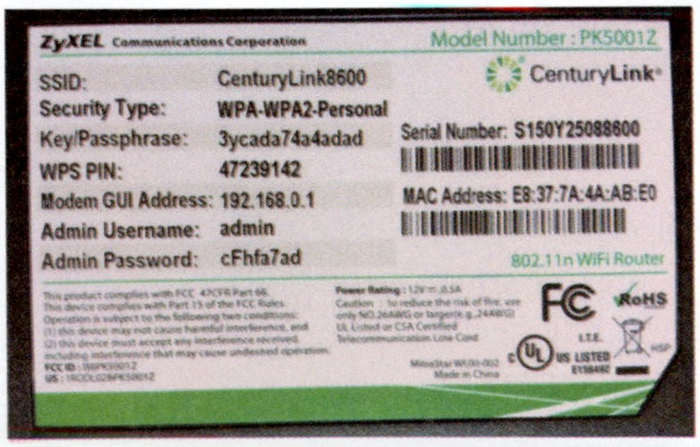

Wireless routers may include a CD, DVD, or USB that automates the setup process. If none of these are provided, look on the bottom of the router for the address to type into a browser window.

Change the default administrator password to a strong password known only to you. The administrative password will be needed if you ever want to change the router settings in the future. If necessary, write down the user name and password for administering the router and store it in a secure location.

Activate the security standard for the router, preferably using Wi-Fi Protected Access WPA2. Some older devices may not support WPA2; in that case, use WPA. Avoid using the less secure WEP standard. WPA2 secures your wireless network with encryption. People will not be able to connect to the wireless router unless they know the security key, and data transmitted across the wireless network will be encrypted.

If you used a notebook PC to configure the wireless router, you can unplug it when finished and proceed to connect each wireless device to the router as described in Step 4. You can leave a desktop PC plugged into the router if the desktop PC does not have a wireless network adapter or you do not want to use it wirelessly.

Step 4: Connect Individual Devices to the Wireless Router

Notebooks, tablets, wearable devices, and smartphones come equipped with a built-in wireless interface card, called a *network adapter*. Generally, the wireless network adapter turns on by default when the device is powered on. For smartphones and some tablets, you may need to turn on Wi-Fi connectivity.

If a PC or other computing device does not have a built-in wireless interface card, you can purchase a network adapter for wireless networking. For a desktop PC, buy a USB wireless network adapter; for a notebook PC, buy a wireless network card adapter. A tip for ensuring a smooth setup process is to buy a wireless network adapter made by the same manufacturer as your wireless router.

For each device you want to connect to the wireless router, follow the steps similar to those illustrated in Figure B.2.

Connect a television, gaming console, or other smart device by following instructions provided by the device manufacturer. In most cases, you have two options. One is to use a push button on the router to instruct the device to automatically detect the router. The other option is to use a remote control to enter the device name and security key in an on-screen menu on the appliance.

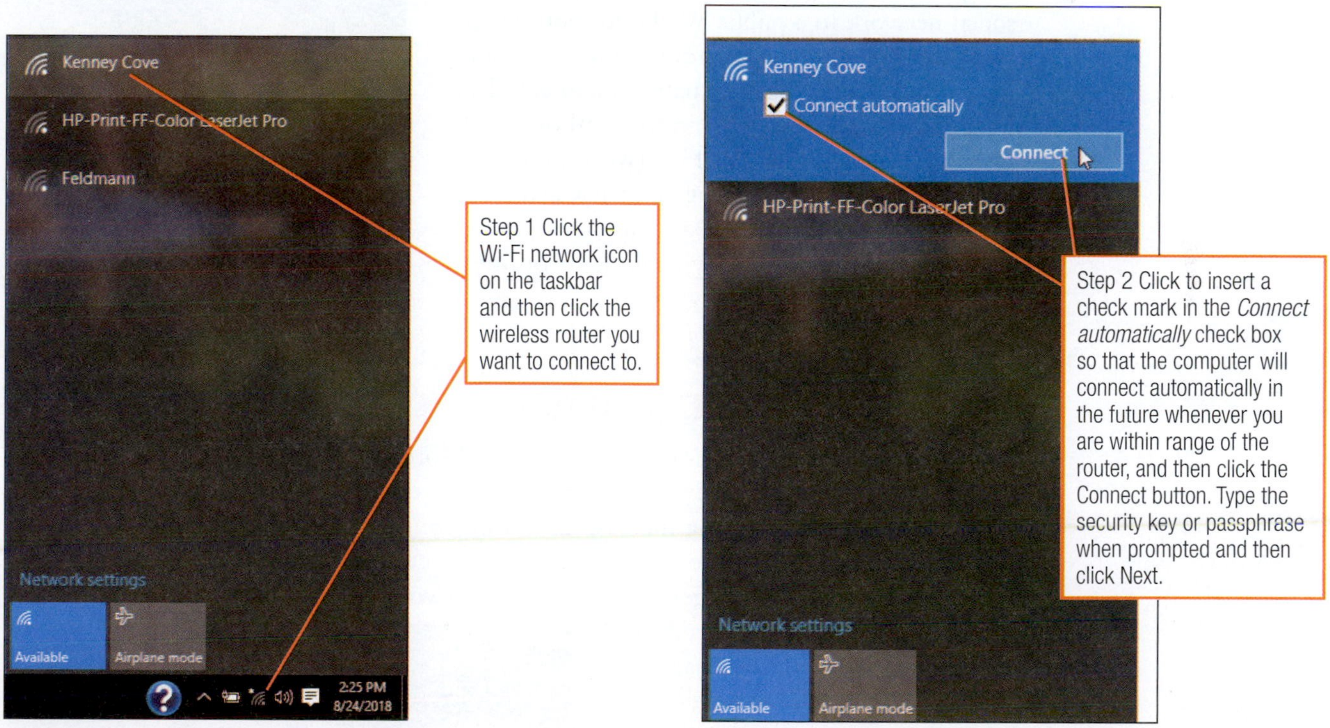

Figure B.2

There are two steps to connecting to a wireless router manually in Windows 10.

Setting Up a Wireless Network on Apple Equipment

To set up a wireless network with Apple computers, you will need a Wi-Fi router, which Apple calls an AirPort. AirPort Express is the name of Apple's 802.11n router, and Airport Extreme is the name of Apple's 802.11ac router. Another device, called AirPort Time Capsule, combines an 802.11ac router with up to 3 TB of storage for backing up data in one device. Plug the Airport Express, Airport Extreme, or Time Capsule device into the high-speed cable or DSL modem from your ISP and then follow the instructions that appear in the AirPort Utility program that appears on your computer or iOS device.

Connecting to a Public Wireless Hotspot

Follow the steps to manually connect to a public wireless hotspot shown in Figure B.2 on page 203. The network name should be obvious in the list of available networks; however, if necessary you can ask a staff person (such as a store clerk, hotel clerk, or airport worker) for the network name and password. Exercise caution when using a public Wi-Fi hotspot, and do not transmit personal or confidential data, as public networks are not secured with encryption and are at risk of interception by hackers. Never perform financial transactions using a public Wi-Fi hotspot. If you must check email or sign in to a social network in a public Wi-Fi hotspot, do so with awareness of your surroundings and avoid entering confidential information in an email or post. If you frequently sign in to email or social networks using public Wi-Fi networks, consider having a different user name and password for these services than the ones you use for other online activities—especially banking or online shopping accounts.

The Future of Wireless Networking

Wireless networking is becoming ubiquitous. More home devices are becoming Internet-enabled—even beyond smart appliances and televisions. The Internet of Things is expected to bring increasingly more connected objects into our day-to-day activities. As you move into this more connected future, it will become even more important to be diligent with wireless network security to ensure that your personal data is not subjected to unwanted access. If you change to a new modem or router, remember to use an SSID that is not easily associated with you or your home or disable the broadcast of the SSID. Also be sure to always use a strong password for both the network and the router administration.

Glossary/Index

integrated web cam, 195
Intel, 4, 10
manufacturer of microprocessors, 13
interactive whiteboard a device that displays a computer output on a large white surface, on which special pens can be used to annotate and draw, 73
Internet (net) a global network that links together other networks, such as government departments, businesses, nonprofit organizations, educational and research institutions, and individuals, 28
components needed for access, 32
connecting to, 32–35
connection speed, 32–34
evaluating web content, 48–51
fees for access to, 32
measuring speed of, and data caps, 78
navigating web pages, 41–43
path of web content delivery, 29
web addresses, 40–41
Internet Corporation for Assigned Names and Numbers (ICANN) a nonprofit organization that keeps track of the Internet addresses and names all around the world, 40
Internet dongle, 35
Internet Explorer (IE) the web browser included with Microsoft Windows editions prior to Windows 10, 36
Internet of Things (IoT) an emerging trend where everyday objects contain embedded processors and are connected to a network from which human-to-machine interactions and machine-to-machine interactions occur. See also *machine-to-machine communications,* 11
Internet Protocol (IP) address a unique address assigned to a computing device when it is connected to the Internet so that the device can communicate with other computers, 40
Internet service provider (ISP) a company that provides access to the Internet infrastructure for a fee, 28
connection speed, 32–34
email address and, 55
fees for, 32
high-speed service for wireless network, 200–201
measuring Internet speed and data caps, 78
intrusion detection software programs that analyze network traffic for suspicious data and alert network administrators to possible system threats, 173
iOS proprietary mobile OS from Apple used for its iPhone and and iPad, 97
IPv4, 40
IPv6, 40

J

Java
plug-in, 53
jump drive, 81

K

Kaspersky Lab, 174, 179, 183
KAYAK, 46
kernel the core of the OS that manages memory, devices, and programs and assigns resources, 88
keyboard a device used to type and input data into a computer, 68
wireless, 68, 196
key drive, 81
keylogger, 183
keystroke logger spyware that is activated as part of a rootkit or Trojan horse that records every keystroke you type. Also known as a *keylogger,* 183
kilobyte (KB) 1,024 bytes or more commonly associated with the approximate value of 1,000 bytes, 79
Kjellberg, Felix, 158

L

laptop computer a PC that has a monitor that when swiveled up reveals a keyboard with the remaining components housed below. Also called *notebook,* 4
laser printer an output device in which a laser beam electrostatically charges a drum with the text and images sent for printing. A dry powder called toner sticks to the drum and is transferred to the paper, 74
legal software programs that help you prepare legal documents, such as wills, contracts, leases, loan agreements, and living trusts, 127
Lenova, 183
Level 1 (L1) cache cache memory that is built on the CPU chip and operates the fastest of all memory, 66
Level 2 (L2) cache cache memory stored on the CPU chip or built on the motherboard that feeds the L1 cache, 66
Level 3 (L3) cache cache memory that is usually built on the motherboard and feeds the L2 cache, 66
LG, 96
webOS, 98
LibreOffice, 133
light-emitting diode (LED) a wide-screen flat-panel technology that uses small, more efficient light-emitting diodes to allow light to pass through panels to display text and images. LEDs consume less energy and show more vibrant colors than LCDs, 72
link any text or other object on a web page that, when clicked, displays a related web page. Also called *hyperlink,* 43
LinkedIn a professional social network through which you connect with your business contacts, 147
Linux an open source, free OS created by Linus Torvalds and based on UNIX. It can be used as a standalone OS or as a server OS. Linux is available in many distributions, such as Red Hat and Ubuntu, 94
embedded, 97
liquid crystal display (LCD) a flat-panel, wide-screen technology widely used for desktop PC monitors in which fluorescent lighting allows light to pass through panels to create the display text and images, 72
Live email, 17
LiveJournal, 160
Lowe's, s-commerce strategy, 165
LTE (Long-Term Evolution) network a Long-Term Evolution network, which is the fastest network for mobile devices that is based upon the 4G standard using cellular towers. See also 4G, 35

M

M2M communications, 11
Mac. *See also* Apple Inc.
backup, 105
buying new computer considerations, 194
disk defragmentation-OS, 104
Finder utility-OS, 102
Help utility, 108
installing software, 134, 135
malware and, 177
operating system for, 93
Time Machine, 105
uninstalling software, 137
wireless network setup for, 204
machine-to-machine communications an environment in which everyday objects with embedded processors and connectivity interact with other objects without human intervention. See also *Internet of Things (IoT),* 11
Mac OS a proprietary operating system created by Apple, 93
macro virus a type of virus that is embedded in a document and infects the computer when the user opens the document and enables a macro, 176
magnetic ink character recognition systems, 71
magnetic strip reader a device that reads the magnetic strip on the back of cards, such as debit cards, credit cards, or key cards used to open doors or parking gates, 69
mainframe a large, powerful, and expensive computer used by the government and large organizations, such as banks, insurance companies, and other corporations, to connect hundreds or thousands of users simultaneously, 8
malware any type of malicious software program that is designed to damage, disable, or steal data, 176
antivirus program, 178–179
ransomware, 178
rootkit, 178
Trojan horse, 177
viruses, 176
worms, 177
Malwarebytes, 176
man-in-the-middle (MITM) attack occurs when a hacker intercepts communications between a user and a website for purposes of capturing personal information, 183
Mavenlink, 119
Mavericks, 93
McAfee Labs, 178, 179, 186
McDonald's, 10
media sharing websites that allow you to share, view, and download photos, videos, music, and presentations, 154
most popular websites for, 154–157
Medium, 160
megabits per second (Mbps) the speed for broadband connectivity in which data transfers at the rate of 1 million bits per second, 33
measuring Internet speed, 78
megabyte (MB) approximately 1 million bytes, 79
memory
cache memory, 14, 66
flash memory, 81
operating system managing, 90
random access memory, 14, 66
read-only, 66
virtual, 90
memory stick, 14, 81

P

packaged software traditional desktop software that can be purchased at a retail store, from an e-commerce website, or directly from the software publisher, 134
Panasonic Firefox OS, 98
parallel processing a computer configuration that involves having multiple microprocessor chips or a multicore processor to execute multiple instructions simultaneously, 65
passwords
  criteria for strong, 171
  protection for mobile devices, 96
PayPal, 54
peer-to-peer (P2P) file sharing a form of file sharing facilitated by a website at which users exchange files directly with one another over the Internet, 154
pen drive, 81
peripheral hardware used for input, output, connectivity, or storage that you plug in or connect to your computer wirelessly, 63
  operating system configuring, 90
  options and buying new computer, 194, 196
personal computer (PC) a computer in which the input, processing, storage, and output are self-contained, 4
  buying a new, 192–197
personal finance software programs used to keep track of a checking or savings account, investments, or other personal financial information, 126
personal information management (PIM) application a software program that helps you organize messages, schedules, contacts, and tasks, 118
petaflop a measurement used in scientific calculations that represents a quadrillion floating point operations per second, 9
PewDiePie, 158
phablet means the combination of a *phone* and *tablet* and describes a smartphone with a screen larger than 5.25 inches but not as large as a typical tablet, 6
pharming a scam in which an individual is tricked into typing in personal information at a phony website that appears to be the real website requested by the individual, 181
phishing activities that appear to be initiated by a legitimate organization in an attempt to obtain personal information that can be used in fraud, theft, or identity theft, 180
Photobucket, 155
photo editing software programs used to edit pictures and add special effects and text to photos taken with a digital camera, 122
photo printer an output device that connects directly to a digital camera to print high-quality photos on photo paper using inkjet technology, 74
photos
  mobile apps for sharing, 155, 157
  websites for sharing, 155
Picasa, 155
piggybacking connecting to someone else's wireless network without the network owner's knowledge or consent, 171
Pinterest a website with virtual pinboards on which people pin pictures of things they have seen on the Internet that they like and want to share using the Pin It button, 151
pixel a square with red, green, and blue color values that represent each color needed to form an image. Millions of pixels make up the image shown on a screen, 73
plasma a flat-panel technology that provides truer color representation but is expected to become obsolete by the improved technology in LEDs, 72
platter, 80
player a software program that allows the browser to display enhanced content that it cannot display on its own. Also called add-on or plug-in, 52
  installing tips, 52–53
  popular, 53
  updates, 53
plotter an output device that moves one or more pens across the surface of the paper to produce a drawing, 74
plug and play OS technology in which the OS searches a newly plugged-in device for the driver, loads it automatically, and displays a message when the device is ready to use. See also *driver,* 90
plug-in a software program that allows the browser to display enhanced content that it cannot display on its own. Also called *add-on* or *player,* 52
  installing tips, 52–53
  popular, 53
  updates, 53
podcast an audio or video file that is usually a part of a series and is streamed or downloaded to your computer or mobile device, 154
podcatcher a software program that automatically downloads new podcasts for which the user has subscribed to a computer or mobile device, 154
Popurls, 47
portable media player a device on which to play music, watch videos, view photos, play games, and/or read electronic books, 6
port a connector located at the back, side, or front of a computer or mobile device that is used to plug in external devices, 66–67
  dock port, 68
  specification when buying computer, 195
posture-related injuries, 20
potentially unwanted program (PUP), 177
presentation application software used to create slides for an electronic slideshow that may be projected on a screen or displayed at a self-running kiosk, 116
printers
  options and buying new computer, 196
  types of, 74–75
Priv, 97
privacy issues
  awareness of shoulder surfers, 187
  cookies, 182
  data privacy in cloud, 184–185
  social network privacy setting, 149
  spam, 183
  spyware, 183
  ways to protect personal information, 184
processing one of the four progressions in the information processing cycle in which data is manipulated or otherwise acted upon by the central processing unit, 13
  in information processing cycle, 13
processor, 195
productivity software, 114
  mobile apps for, 139
  for workplace, 114–121
productivity suite programs used in the workplace that includes word processing, spreadsheets, presentations, and database management. Also known as *software suite,* 114
ProjectLibre, 119, 120
project management application a software program used to enter all the tasks needed to get a project done, establish time frames, assign resources, and allocate budget money to each task, 119–120
protocol a set of rules that defines how data is exchanged between two devices, 76

Q

QR (Quick Response) code a type of bar code that looks like a matrix of black square dots and directs the device (usually a smartphone) to display a website, 69
QuarkXPress, 123
QuickBooks, 119
Quicken, 127
QuickTime, 53
Quora, 160

R

radio frequency identification (RFID) reader a device that scans an embedded RFID tag (a chip with an antenna) to identify an object, 69–70
random access memory (RAM) temporary storage for instructions and data that is cleared when power to the computer is lost, 14
  on motherboard, 66
  specification when buying computer, 195
ransomware a type of malware that locks or restricts access to a device, and the malware creator demands a ransom payment in exchange for unlocking the device or providing the unlock code, 178
raw data characters that are typed or otherwise entered into a computer, 12
Rdio, 156
read-only memory (ROM) memory built on the motherboard that is used for storing computer instructions that do not change, 66
Really Simple Syndication (RSS) a specification used by content aggregators to distribute updates to subscribers. See also *Atom,* 46
Real Player, 53
reddit a social networking website where registered members post content, which other members vote up or down to create a submission score. The score determines the position of the entry on the page, 148
redditors, 148
Red Hat, 94
reference software programs that use multimedia tools to provide rich content information in encyclopedias, dictionaries, translation guides, atlases, and other reference resources, 129
repetitive-strain injury (RSI) an injury or disorder of the joints, nerves, muscles, ligaments, or tendons, 20
  prevention strategies for, 21
  symptoms of, 20

spoofing techniques in which a sender's email address is altered to a phony address that appears legitimate to the email recipient, or an IP address is altered to appear to be a trusted source, 181
Spotify a music and video streaming service that lets you listen to music or watch video from devices connected to the Internet via the Spotify app, 156–157
spreadsheet application software in which you work primarily with numbers that you organize, calculate, and chart, 115–116

spyware software programs that exist on your computer without your knowledge and track your activities, 183

storage device the piece of hardware with the means to write new data to and read existing data from storage media, 80

storage medium any device where data and information are saved for later use, 14

strong password a password that is difficult to hack by humans or password detection software programs, 171
StumbleUpon a social bookmarking website on which you can browse recommended web pages and save the pages you like to your profile, 151–152
stylus a digital pen, 5, 69

subscription software programs purchased from a software provider that generally charges a monthly or annual fee per user for access to the software and storage services, 134
supercomputer the fastest, most expensive, most powerful computer, capable of performing trillions of calculations per second and usually designed for a specific task that involves complex calculations, 9

System Restore a Windows utility program that will undo a recent system change while leaving all documents intact, 106
system software the OS designed to work with the present hardware, as well as a set of utility programs that are used to maintain the computer and its devices, 87
system unit a horizontal or vertical case in which the processor, memory, and main storage device of a desktop computer are housed, 4

T

tablet a lightweight notebook with a smaller screen that you interact with using a touch screen or stylus. Also called a *tablet PC,* 5

tag a keyword you assign to content you add to a social bookmarking site that describes or categorizes a photo, article, or item from a web page, 150
tax preparation software programs that guide you through the completion of the complex forms required to file your income taxes, 127

technological convergence the place where innovation merges several technologies into a single device, 11
tendonitis a common computer-related repetitive-strain injury that occurs when a tendon in the wrist becomes inflamed. It is caused by excessive typing, mouse scrolling, mouse clicking, and thumb typing/movements on mobile devices, 20
terabyte (TB) approximately 1 trillion bytes, 79

texting sending text messages to another mobile device, 56
text message a short text exchange using mobile devices, 56
thermal printer an output device that heats coated paper as the paper passes over the print head and is usually used for receipts, 74
thin client a computer connected to a network that does not store any data or software on the local PC, 8
3-D printer an output device that prints a 3-D digital object using a technique where consecutive layers are placed on top of one another precisely cut to build the object, 74

3G (third generation) third generation network for mobile devices that provides Internet access through cell towers. Average speed for a 3G connection is around 1 Mbps, 35

Time Machine backup utility program on Mac computers for backing up and restoring files, 105

top-level domain (TLD) the part of the URL that identifies the type of organization associated with the domain name. See also *generic top-level domains (gTLDs),* 41

touchpad a rectangular surface with buttons, located below the keyboard on a notebook, that is used in place of a mouse to move the pointer on the screen and manipulate objects. The touchpad senses finger movement and taps similar to a mouse, 69
touchscreen a display that accepts input from finger gestures on mobile devices or other PCs. Also known as *touch-enabled display,* 69

Transport Layer Security (TLS) a protocol used on the Internet that encrypts transmitted data so the data is unreadable if intercepted, 184
Trojan horse a program that disguises itself as a useful program that infects your computer with malware when you run the application, 177

TV operating system the operating system installed on a smart TV that displays apps, manages connected devices, and accepts input from a remote control, wireless keyboard, tablet, or smartphone, 98
tweet a post on Twitter, limited to 140 characters or less, 160
Twitter bot software programmed to follow people based on popular keywords, 183
Twitter the most popular microblog, with posts limited to 140 characters or less, 160

U

ubiquitous computing an idea that computing technology is everywhere within our environment and used all of the time, 10–11

UEFI (Unified Extensible Firmware Interface) programming code stored on a ROM chip that includes instructions used when starting a computer. See also *BIOS,* 66
ultrabook a type of notebook that is thinner and lighter, but just as powerful as a traditional notebook, 4–5

unauthorized access using a computer, network, or other resource without permission, 170

unauthorized use using a computer, network, or other resource for purposes other than the intended use, 171

uniform resource locator (URL) a text-based address to navigate to a website. Also called *web address,* 40

universal serial bus (USB) port the most common type of port that is used to connect an external device, such as a keyboard, mouse, printer, smartphone, or external storage media, to a computer, 66–67

UNIX an OS created in the 1960s designed for servers and popular for web servers because of its robust ability to support many users, 94

Photo Credits

Microsoft images used with permission from Microsoft.

Chapter 1 *Page 3*: Shutterstock ID 222048700/Syda Productions. *4*: ©Shutterstock/Oleksly Mark; ©2015 with express permission from Apple; ©Shutterstock/Galatia Romania; ©iStock.com/CostinT. *5*: ©Shutterstock/Kiev, Ukraine; ©2015 with express permission from Apple; ©iStock.com/Abalcazar. *6*: ©Shutterstock/Asif Islam; ©Shutterstock/Ijansempoi; ©Shutterstock/iQoncept. *7*: ©Shutterstock/Denys Prykhodov; ©iStock.com/scanrall; ©iStock.com/adventtr; ©Shutterstock/lucadp. *8*: ©iStock.com/CostinT; ©iStock.com/xenotar. *9*: ©National Oceanic and Atmospheric Administration (United States Department of Commerce). *11*: ©a-image/Shutterstock.com; ©Paradigm. *12*: ©iStock.com/kevinjeon00; ©iStock.com/Lee Rogers; ©iStock.com/Anatolii Babii. *13*: ©Intel; ©iStock.com/Emir Memedovski; ©iStock.com/ambrits; ©iStock.com/scanrall; ©Shutterstock/Audrey Popov. *14*: ©iStock.com/jpa1999; ©iStock.com/krzyscin; ©iStock.com/wolv; ©iStock.com/AudreyTTL. *15*: ©iStock.com/pictafolio; ©iStock.com/Chris Schmidt. *16*: ©Monicaodo/Dreastime.com. *17*: Google and the Google logo are registered trademarks of Google Inc., used with permission. *18*: Photo courtesy Bits Limited; ©Shutterstock/Marco Prati. *19*: ©Shutterstock/S. Dashkevych. *20*: ©iStock.com/hidesy; ©iStock.com/hidesy; ©iStock.com/deliormanli; ©iStock.com/Yuri.

Chapter 2 *27*: ©iStock.com/RapidEye. *28*: ©Shutterstock/Anton Balazh. *31*: ©iStockphoto.com/nullplus. *33*: ©iStockphoto.com/sambrogio; ©iStockphoto.com/Kameleon007. *34*: ©iStockphoto.com/4x6; ©iStockphoto.com/happymoron; ©iStockphoto.com/Asian; ©iStockphoto.com/Talaj; Image by Krish Dulal, distributed under a CC-By 2.0 license; ©iStockphoto.com/naikon. *35*: ©Shutterstock/autsawin uttisin. *37*: Google and the Google logo are registered trademarks of Google Inc., used with permission. *38*: ©2015 with express permission from Apple. *39*: ©Shutterstock/Your Design; ©iStockphoto.com/Stephen Krow. *45*: Google and the Google logo are registered trademarks of Google Inc., used with permission. *47*: ©popurls.com. *52*: ©2015 with express permission from Apple.

Chapter 3 *63*: ©iStockphoto.com/sturti. *64*: ©Shutterstock/Romash Denis; © iStockphoto.com/Freer Law; ©Shutterstock/jcjgphotography. *65*: ©Shutterstock/Norman Chan. *66*: ©iStockphoto.com/stocksnapper. *67*: ©Kelvin Wong/Shutterstock.com; ©Shutterstock/JIPEN. *68*: ©iStockphoto.com/Andy445; ©iStockphoto.com/pictafolio. *69*: ©Shutterstock/Sergey Nivens; ©Shutterstock/Sorbis. *70*: ©iStockphoto.com/erikthame; ©iStockphoto.com/nicolas_; ©iStockphoto.com/OJO_Images; © Dreamstime.com/Pressureua; ©iStockphoto.com/JacobH; ©iStockphoto.com/infografick; ©iStockphoto.com/scanrail; ©Shutterstock/Bloomua. *71*: ©Shutterstock/no author; ©iStockphoto.com/alehdats. *72*: ©iStockphoto.com/vovan13; ©Shutterstock/Zeynep Demir; ©iStockphoto.com/alexeys; ©Shutterstock/Mark Oleksly. *73*: ©Shutterstock/bikeriderlondon; ©SMART Technologies, Inc.; ©iStockphoto.com/jian wang; ©iStockphoto.com/LifesizeImages; ©Shutterstock/flydragon. *74*: ©Shutterstock/Maksym Dykha; ©Shutterstock/tankist276; ©Shutterstock/vetkit; ©Shutterstock/Alfonso de Tomas; ©Shutterstock/Sylvie Bouchard. *75*: ©wabeno/Dreamstime.com; ©Shutterstock/Mark Oleksly; ©iStockphoto.com/belekekin. *76*: ©iStockphoto.com/Visualfield; ©iStockphoto.com/zokara. *77*: ©iStockphoto.com/scanrail; ©iStockphoto.com/yozks. *78*: ©iStockphoto.com/loops7. *79*: ©iStockphoto.com/c-photo; ©Trevor Allen/Dreamstime.com. *80*: ©iStockphoto.com/sqback. *81*: ©Yevgen Romanenko; ©iStockphoto.com/scanrail; ©Shutterstock/nikolamaster; ©Shutterstock/ekler. *82*: ©Shutterstock/PixDeluxe; ©iStockphoto.com/nkbimages; ©Shutterstock/Kovalchuk Oleksandr. *83*: ©Shutterstock/cifotart; ©Shutterstock/Image Team.

Chapter 4 *87*: ©iStockohoto.com/zhang bo. *94*: ©iStockphoto.com/z80. *96*: ©Shutterstock/Zeynep Demir. *97*: ©Shutterstock/Bloomua. *98*: ©Shutterstock/Denys Prykhodov; ©Shutterstock/Chesky. *99*: ©Shutterstock/Gts; ©Shutterstock/Alexey Boldin; Google and the Google logo are registered trademarks of Google Inc., used with permission. *100*: ©2015 with express permission from Apple; Google and the Google logo are registered trademarks of Google Inc., used with permission. *101*: ©iStockphoto.com/kjekol. *108*: ©2015 with express permission from Apple. *109*: ©iStockphoto.com/darrenwise.

Chapter 5 *113*: ©Shutterstock/Rawpixel.com. *119*: Reprinted with permission © Intuit Inc. All rights reserved. *120*: ©Shutterstock/Yuri Arcurs. *122*: ©Shutterstock/Svetlana Larina. *123*: ©Quark Software Inc. *124*: ©2015 with express permission from Apple. *127*: ©Shutterstock/atm2003; ©iStockphoto.com/malerapaso; ©Michele Pacclone. *131*: ©2015 with express permission from Apple; ©2015 with express permission from Apple. *135*: © iStockphoto.com/Kamaga. *136*: ©2015 with express permission from Apple. *138*: Google and the Google logo are registered trademarks of Google Inc., used with permission. *139*: ©Shutterstock/Andrey_Popov; ©Shutterstock/Brues.

Chapter 6 *145*: ©Shutterstock/wavebreakmedia. *146*: ©Facebook.com. *147*: Image courtesy of Linkedin; Google and the Google logo are registered trademarks of Google Inc., used with permission. *148*: Google and the Google logo are registered trademarks of Google Inc., used with permission; Image courtesy of reddit. *149*: ©iStockphoto.com/winhorse. *150*: Image courtesy of Bookmarklet. *151*: Image courtesy of Pinterest; Image courtesy of StumbleUpon. *152*: Image courtesy of StumbleUpon; Image courtesy of Delicious. *153*: Image courtesy of Delicious. *154*: Image courtesy of Delicious. *155*: Image courtesy of Flickr. *157*: Image courtesy of Beats Music; Image courtesy of Instagram; Image courtesy of WordPress. *158*: Image courtesy of WordPress. *159*: Images courtesy of Blogger. *160*: Image courtesy of Twitter. *161*: Image courtesy of Twitter. *162*:Image courtesy of Wikipedia; ©Shutterstock/Dustin. *164*: Image courtesy of Twitter. *165*: Image courtesy of Facebook; ©iStockphoto.com/ferlistockphoto.

Chapter 7 *169*: ©Shutterstock/Rawpixel.com. *170*: ©iStockphoto.com/RapidEye; ©iStockphoto.com/Kirbyphoto. *171*: ©iStockphoto.com/RonBailey; ©Shutterstock/mama_mia; ©Shutterstock/BlueSkyImage; ©Shutterstock/Andrea Danti. *172*: ©Shutterstock/hywards; ©Shutterstock/Slawomir Fajer. *173*: ©Shutterstock/alexskopje. *177*: ©iStockphoto.com/sukmaraga. *178*: ©Shutterstock/scyther5; Image courtesy of Bitdefender. *181*: iStockphoto.com/Carlos_bcn; ©Facebook.com. *183*: ©Shutterstock/alexskopje; ©Shutterstock/Syda Productions; ©iStockphoto.com/PaulPaladin. *185*: ©iStockphoto.com/Stratol. *186*: ©Shutterstock/Es sarawuth; ©Shutterstock/ptnphoto; ©Shutterstock/ymgerman; ©iStockphoto.com/Khosrownia. *187*: ©Shutterstock/Monkey Business Images; ©Shutterstock/improvise.

Appendix A *191*: ©Shutterstock/Oleksiy Mark; ©Shutterstock/Oleksiy Mark. *192*: ©iStockphoto.com/sqback; ©iStockphoto.com/alexsl; ©iStockphoto.com/CostinT; ©iStockphoto.com/Stephen Krow; ©iStockphoto.com/LL28; ©Shutterstock/Kathy Burns-Millyard. *194*: ©Shutterstock/mama_mia. *196*: ©iStockphoto.com/Rüstem GÜRLER; ©iStockphoto.com/ewg3D; ©Shutterstock/Murat Baysan; ©Shutterstock/GalaStudio. *197*: ©iStockphoto.com/97; ©iStockphoto.com/Jirsak; ©iStockphoto.com/Andrew_Howe; ©iStockphoto.com/JuSun. *198*: ©iStockphoto.com/pictafolio; ©iStockphoto.com/Balster; ©iStockphoto.com/luxxtek; ©Shutterstock/Zeynep Demir; ©iStockphoto.com/scanrail; ©iStockphoto.com/adventtr. *199*: © Shutterstock/Monkey Business Images; ©iStockphoto.com/vladru. *200*: ©iStockphoto.com/appleuzr; ©iStockphoto.com/sambrogio; ©iStockphoto.com/pflorendo. *201*: ©iStockphoto.com/infomages; ©iStockphoto.com/deepblue4you.

Appendix B *204*: ©iStockphoto.com/adamdodd; ©Shutterstock/Rigelp.

Seguin's

COMPUTER Applications

with Microsoft® Office 2016

Second Edition

Chapter 1

Using Windows 10 and Managing Files

Precheck

Check your understanding of the topics covered in this chapter.

Windows 10 is the operating system (OS) software published by Microsoft Corporation. An OS provides the user interface that allows you to work with a computer or mobile device. The OS also manages all the hardware resources, routes data between devices and applications, and provides the tools for managing files and application programs. Every computing device requires an OS; without one your computer would not function. Think of the OS as the data and device manager that ensures data flows to and from each device and application. When you touch the screen, click the mouse, or type words on a keyboard, the OS recognizes the input and sends the data to the application or device that needs it. If a piece of hardware is not working, the OS senses the problem and displays a message to you. For example, if a printer is not turned on, the OS communicates that the printer is offline. When you power on a computer or mobile device, the OS loads automatically into memory and displays the user interface when the computer is ready.

Computers and mobile devices have an OS preloaded and ready to use. Some tasks require you to interact with the OS directly, such as when you launch an app, program, or system setting window, switch windows, and manage your files and folders. In this chapter, you will learn to navigate in Windows 10 and manage files on a storage medium.

Note: *You will need a removable storage medium (USB flash drive) with enough space to download a copy of the student data files for this textbook.*

SNAP If you are a SNAP user, go to your SNAP Assignments page to complete the Precheck, Tutorials, and Recheck.

Learning Objectives

- **1.1** Navigate Windows 10 using touch, a mouse, or a keyboard
- **1.2** Sign in to Windows 10, launch an app, and switch between apps
- **1.3** Use the search text box and minimize, maximize, close, and snap windows
- **1.4** Use icons in the notification area to view the status of a setting and view customization options for the notification area
- **1.5** Lock the screen, sign out, and shut down Windows 10
- **1.6** Use and customize the Start menu
- **1.7** Personalize the Lock screen, desktop background, and color scheme
- **1.8** Describe file, folder, download, and extract student data files
- **1.9** Browse files with File Explorer
- **1.10** Create new folders and copy files and folders
- **1.11** Move, rename, and delete files and folders and safely eject a USB flash drive

1.1 Using Touch, Mouse, and Keyboard Input to Navigate Windows 10

Skills

Describe Windows 10 touch gestures

Describe basic mouse actions

List common keyboard commands for Windows 10

Windows 10, released in July 2015, is the latest edition of the Microsoft OS for personal computers (PCs) and mobile devices. The Windows 10 **user interface (UI)** incorporates the familiar desktop and Start menu from Windows 7, with the tiles and enhanced touchscreen functionality from Windows 8.1. The UI uses icons, a Start menu, and other means to interact with users. The **Start menu** is a pop-up menu that displays when you click the **Start button** located at the bottom left corner. In the left pane of the Start menu are links to your most-used applications; options to launch File Explorer, Settings, the All apps menu; and a Power button. The right pane contains tiles. A **tile** is a square or rectangle that, when clicked, starts an app, application, or other Windows feature. An **app** is a smaller program used on a smartphone, tablet, or PC that is designed usually for one purpose, to work on a touchscreen, to use less power than an application, and to use fewer network resources. An **application**, which is more powerful than an app, is a program used to get a task done with a wide range of functions and features. Applications make use of a full-size keyboard and a mouse, and they are designed for a larger screen and more powerful computing resources.

Windows 10 works with touchscreen input, mouse input, and keyboard input devices. Becoming familiar with input actions using touch, the mouse, and the keyboard will help you navigate the UI.

Using Touch to Navigate Windows 10

App Tip

You can adjust settings for some touch actions in the Pen and Touch dialog box accessed from the Control Panel.

On a touchscreen, you perform actions using gestures. A **gesture** is an action or motion you perform with one or two fingers, a thumb, or a stylus. Table 1.1 (page 5) explains the gestures used with the Windows interface.

In Windows, touch actions are called *gestures.*

On a touchscreen, when a task requires typed characters, such as an email address, message text, or web address, the **touch keyboard** shown in Figure 1.1 is used. Tapping the area that requires typed input generally causes the touch keyboard to appear. The touch keyboard is also available in thumb keyboard mode (Figure 1.2, page 5) and in handwriting mode (Figure 1.3, page 6). The touch keyboard changes some buttons depending on the application in use. For example, in the Mail app the @ symbol is located to the right of the spacebar, while in Microsoft Edge the slash (/) displays in that keyboard location.

Figure 1.1

The full touch keyboard in Windows appears when typed characters are expected.

Table 1.1

Windows Touch Gestures

Gesture	Description and Mouse Equivalent	What It Does	What It Looks Like
Tap or Double-tap	One finger touches the screen and immediately lifts off the screen once or twice in succession. **Mouse:** Click or double-click left mouse button.	• Launches an app or application • Follows a link • Performs a command or selection from a button or icon	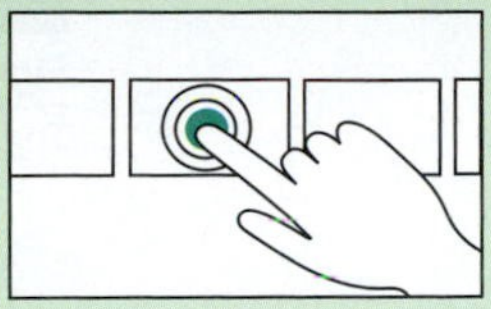
Press and hold	One finger touches the screen and stays in place for a few seconds. **Mouse:** Point or right-click.	• Shows a context menu • Shows pop-up information or details	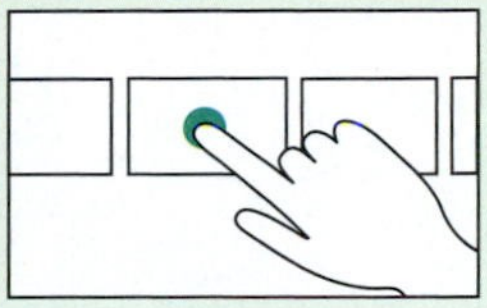
Slide	Move one or two fingers in the same direction. **Mouse:** Drag (may need to drag or scroll using scroll bars).	• Used to drag, pan, or scroll through lists or pages	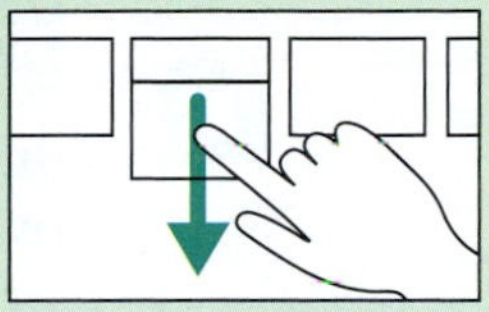
Swipe	Move one finger in from the left or right a short distance. **Mouse:** Click the Notification icon on the taskbar.	• In from the right reveals the Action Center panel with Notifications and quick action tiles at the bottom	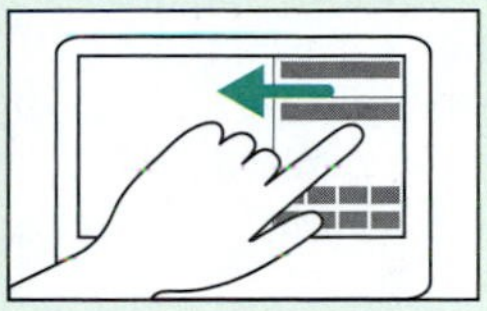
	Mouse: Click the Task View button on the taskbar.	• In from the left shows thumbnails of open windows so you can switch to another window	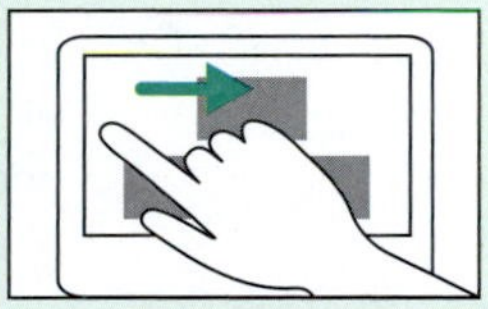
Zoom Out	Two fingers touch the screen apart from each other and move closer together. **Mouse:** Ctrl + scroll mouse wheel toward you.	• Shrinks the size of text, an item, or tiles on the screen	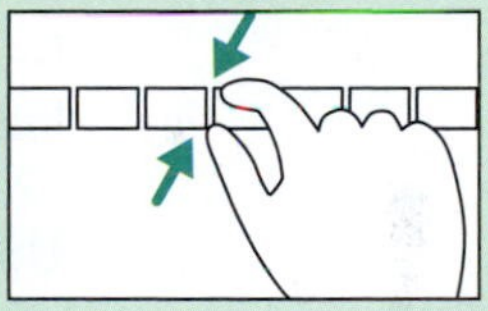
Zoom In	Two fingers touch the screen together and move farther apart. **Mouse:** Ctrl + mouse scroll wheel away from you.	• Expands the size of text, an item, or tiles on the screen	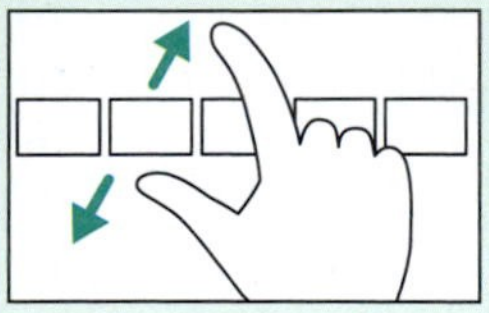

Figure 1.2

The Windows touch keyboard in thumb mode has the keys split on either side of the screen.

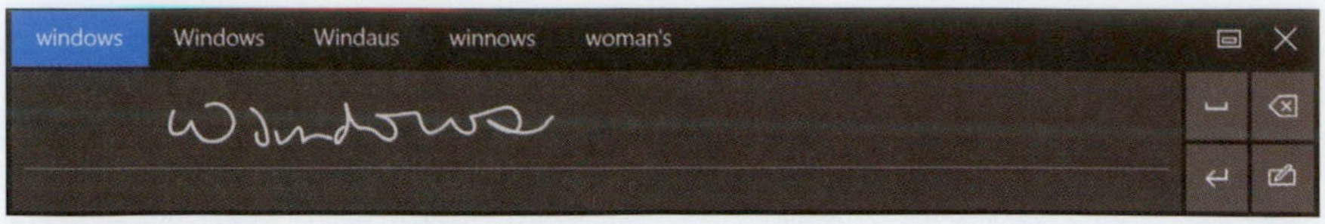

Figure 1.3
The Windows touch keyboard in handwriting mode is shown.

For some purposes, you still use a mouse and traditional keyboard with a touch-enabled device. For example, typing an essay for a school project is easier using a traditional keyboard, and doing precise graphics editing is easier with a mouse. Connect a universal serial bus (USB) or wireless mouse and/or keyboard for intensive work like this.

Using a Mouse to Navigate Windows 10

App Tip

If you run out of desk surface, lift the mouse up off the desk, place it back down, and then continue moving in the same direction to extend the mouse movement further.

For traditional desktops, laptops, or notebook PCs, navigating the Windows user interface requires the use of a **mouse**, **trackball**, **touchpad**, or other pointing device. These devices are used to move and manipulate a **pointer** (displayed as) on the screen; however, the white arrow pointer can change appearance depending on the action being performed.

To operate the mouse, move the device up, down, right, or left on the desk surface to move the pointer on the screen in the corresponding direction. A scroll wheel on the top of the mouse can be used to scroll up or down. Newer mice include the ability to push on the left or right side of the scroll wheel to scroll right or left. Left and right buttons on the top of the mouse are used to perform actions when the pointer is resting on an item. Table 1.2 (page 7) provides a list and description of mouse actions.

To use a touchpad, move your finger across the surface of the touchpad in the direction required. Tap the touchpad or a button below it to perform an action.

A mouse, trackball, or touchpad can be used as a pointing device to navigate Windows.

Using a Keyboard to Navigate Windows 10

Most actions in Windows are performed using touch gestures or a mouse; however, some people like to use a **keyboard command** (also called a *keyboard shortcut*) because it is fast and easy to use. The Windows logo key is positioned at the bottom left of a keyboard between the Ctrl or Function key (labeled Fn) and the Alt key. Many keyboard shortcuts use the Windows logo key. For example, press the Windows logo key at any time to bring up the Start menu. Useful keyboard commands are described in Table 1.3 (page 7).

If you prefer using keyboard commands, search the web for articles that give other Windows 10 keyboard navigational commands.

Press the Windows logo key with a letter to perform an action.

Note: *Instructions in this textbook are written with mouse actions. If necessary, check with your instructor for the equivalent touchpad or other pointing device action. If you prefer to use touch gestures, refer to the gestures with mouse equivalent actions provided in Table 1.1 on page 5.*

Table 1.2

Mouse Movements and Actions

Term or Action	Description
Point	Move the mouse in the direction required to rest the white arrow pointer on a button, icon, option, tab, link, or other screen item.
Click	Quickly tap the left mouse button once while the pointer is resting on a button, icon, option, tab, link, or other screen item.
Double-click	Quickly tap the left mouse button twice. On the desktop, a program is launched by double-clicking the program's icon.
Right-click	Quickly tap the right mouse button. Within a software application such as Word or Excel, a right-click causes a shortcut menu to appear. Shortcut menus in software applications are context-sensitive, meaning that the menu that appears varies depending on the item the pointer is resting upon when the right-click occurs.
Drag	Hold down the left mouse button, move the mouse up, down, left, or right, and then release the mouse button. Dragging is an action often used to move or resize an object.
Scroll	Use the scroll wheel on the mouse to scroll in a window. If the pointing device you are using does not include a scroll wheel, click the scroll arrows on a horizontal or vertical scroll bar at the right or bottom of a window, or drag the scroll box in the middle of the scroll bar up, down, left, or right.

Table 1.3

Keyboard Commands or Shortcuts

Keyboard Shortcut	What It Does
Windows logo key	Displays Start menu
Windows logo key + a	Opens the Action Center panel at the right side of the screen
Windows logo key + d	Returns to the desktop from an app or application window
Windows logo key + e	Opens a File Explorer window
Windows logo key + l	Locks the screen
Windows logo key + q	Starts a search for apps, files, settings, and web links
Windows logo key + Tab	Displays Task View to switch to another window
Alt + F4	Closes app, application, or other active window
Alt + Tab	Switches between open apps
Up, Down, Left, or Right Arrow keys	Moves selection on Start menu to an app or application name, setting, folder name, or tile; pressing the Enter key launches the selection

App Tip

To use a keyboard command, hold down the Windows logo key or Alt, press and release the letter or function key, and then release the Windows logo key or Alt.

Beyond Basics Windows 10 is Software as a Service

With the release of Windows 10, Microsoft adopted a new model called *Windows as a service*. This means that new features and technologies will be released periodically as updates rather than Microsoft accumulating new features and issuing a new version every few years. The default setting is for automatic updates to download and install as they become available. Expect that the Windows 10 you see in this textbook may vary slightly as quarterly or semiannual updates will become routine.

1.2 Starting Windows 10 and Exploring Apps

Skills

Start and sign in to Windows 10

Launch an app

Switch apps

Tutorials

Sign In to and Out of Windows 10

Explore the Windows 10 Desktop, Taskbar, and Start Menu

Open and Close Applications from the Start Menu

Move between Open Windows

If you are turning on your PC from a no power state, the **Lock screen** shown in Figure 1.4 appears. The Lock screen also appears if you resume computer use after the system has gone into sleep mode. Depending on your PC or mobile device, turning on or resuming system use from sleep mode involves pressing the Power button or moving a mouse.

Each person who uses a PC or mobile device will have his or her own **user account**. A user account includes a user name and a password or personal identification number (PIN). Windows stores program and settings information for each user's account so that each person can customize options without conflicting with the settings for other people who use the computer. In Windows, Microsoft offers two types of user accounts at sign-in: a Microsoft account or a local account.

App Tip

Signing in with a Microsoft account is considered connecting to the cloud. Your apps, games, music, photos, files, and settings are stored online and can be used or viewed from any other Windows device.

Signing In with a Microsoft Account

A user account set up as a **Microsoft account** means you sign in to Windows using an email address from hotmail.com, live.com, or outlook.com (referred to as a Windows Live ID). A Microsoft account means you can download new apps from the Windows store, see live updates from messaging and social media services in tiles on the Start menu, and sync your Windows and browser settings online so that they are the same across all devices.

Signing In with a Local Account

A user account set up as a **local account** means Windows and browser settings on a PC or mobile device cannot be shared with other devices. Automatic connections to messaging and social media services also do not work with a local account.

Note: *The screens shown throughout this textbook show Windows signed in with a Microsoft account.*

App Tip

Touch user? Swipe up from the bottom edge of the screen to reveal the sign-in screen.

1. Turn on the computer or mobile device, or resume system use from sleep mode.
2. At the Lock screen shown in Figure 1.4, click anywhere on the screen, or press any key on the keyboard to reveal the sign-in screen.

You can customize the image that appears on the Lock screen. Your lock screen may show a different picture.

Icons that show power and network connectivity status and notifications for Mail and Calendar (if any are available) appear on the lock screen.

10:29
Friday, July 10
Your date and time will vary.

Figure 1.4

The Windows 10 lock screen.

3 Depending on the system, the next step will vary. Complete the sign in by following the steps in 3a, 3b, or 3c that match the configuration of your device:

a. Type your password in the *Password* text box below your Microsoft account name and email address and press Enter or click the Submit button (right-pointing arrow).

b. Type your PIN in the text box below your Microsoft account name and email address, or perform the touch gestures over your account's picture password.

A picture password uses a picture from your Pictures library that you perform three touch gestures over. A PIN code lets you sign in faster using a numeric code.

App Tip

To set up a picture password or PIN, click Start, Settings, *Accounts*, and *Sign-in options*, and then follow the on-screen prompts. Note that not all systems support these sign-in options. You have to enroll in Windows Hello to use a PIN. Windows Hello uses biometric authentication that lets you unlock a device using facial recognition, an iris scan, or a fingerprint scan.

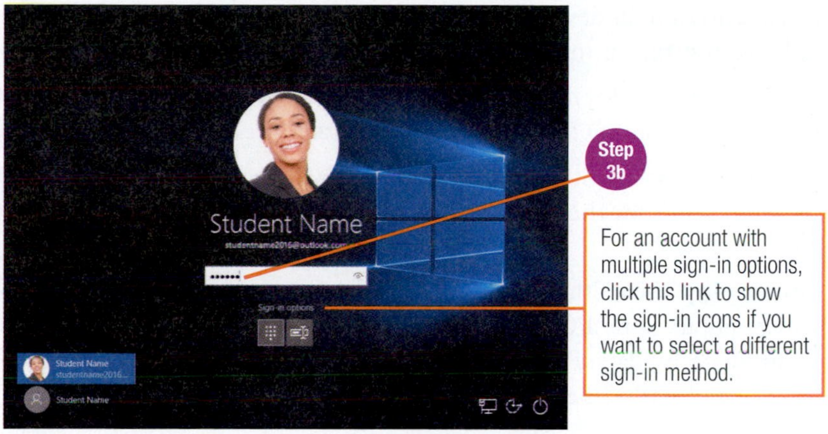

c. If the active account is not your account, click the account name, picture, or silhouette icon at the bottom left of the sign-in screen, type your password in the *Password* text box, and then press Enter or click the Submit button (right-pointing arrow).

The Desktop

Once signed in, the desktop, similar to the one shown in Figure 1.5, appears. The **desktop** displays icons that are used to launch programs or open other windows and

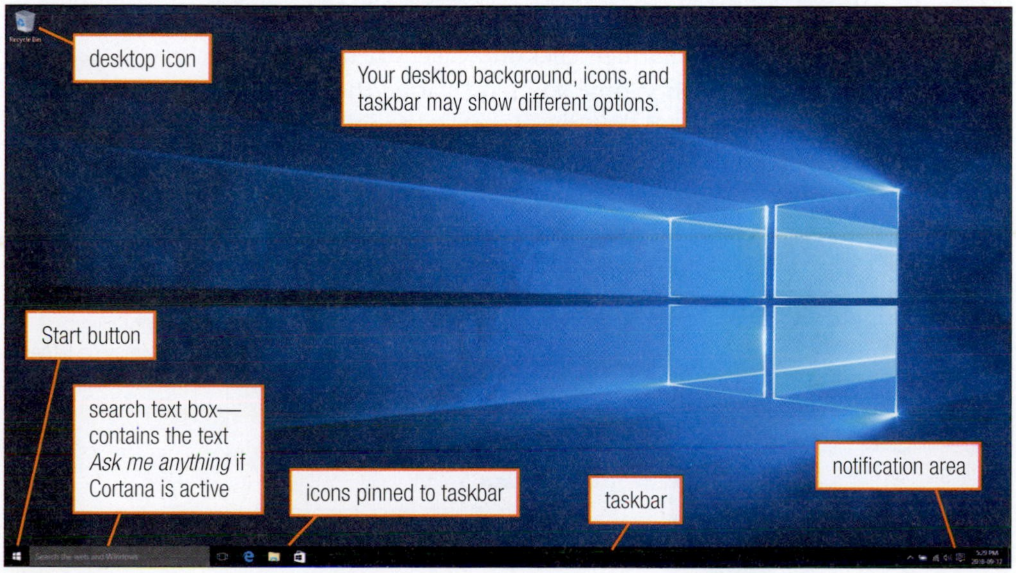

Figure 1.5

The Windows 10 desktop displays icons and a taskbar at the bottom.

App Tip

Signing in to Windows 10 on a tablet or other touchscreen device converts the display to *tablet mode*, in which the Start screen displays tiles for common apps, a menu button, a power button, and a back button to navigate the UI.

> **App Tip**
> If your setup includes multiple monitors, the search text box appears on the main display only—a search icon (magnifying glass) appears in place of the search text box on the secondary monitor.

a taskbar along the bottom of the screen. The **taskbar** has the Start button, the search text box, icons to start programs, and the notification area. The **search text box** is used to locate apps, programs, settings, files on your PC, or find information on the web. The **notification area** at the right end of the taskbar shows the current date and time, and icons to view or change the status of system settings. When you sign in, Windows opens the Start menu on the desktop for you.

Launching an App

Built-in apps for Windows 10 include Photos, Maps, Mail, Calendar, Groove, and Movies & TV, to name a few. The Windows 10 family of apps is designed to look and operate consistently on all devices. To launch an app, click the Start button and then click the tile for the app in the right pane.

> **Oops!**
> No Photos tile? Type Photos in the search text box and then press Enter or click *Photos* in the search results list. You will learn how to add a tile to the Start menu in a later topic.

Note: *If you are using a tablet, turn off tablet mode by swiping in from the right edge and then tapping the Tablet mode quick action tile.*

4. If necessary, click the Start button. Click the Photos tile in the right pane on the Start menu to launch the Photos app.

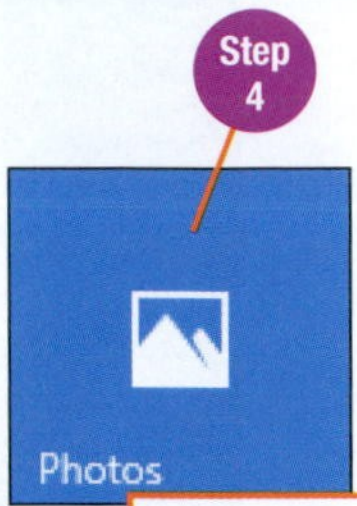

Your Photos tile may be larger and will vary if the tile is live.

The **Photos app** shows thumbnails of the photos stored in the Pictures library on a PC, tablet, smartphone, and in OneDrive, grouped by date. Photos are set to auto-enhance and can be easily shared with others from the app.

Photos on your screen will be grouped by date and will vary from this example.

> **App Tip**
> Pressing the Windows logo key on the keyboard also brings up the Start menu.

5. Click the Start button, and then click the Calendar tile in the right pane. If this is the first time you have started the app, click the Get started button, and then the Ready to go button to set up the app with your Microsoft account.

Your Calendar tile may be larger and will vary if the tile is live.

The **Calendar app** shows appointments and reminders for events stored in your Microsoft account. The calendar for the current month loads. Birthday reminders for those accounts connected to Facebook are shown in the calendar.

> **Oops!**
> Are you also asked if the app can use your location? Click Yes or No depending on your preference. Locations services are optional.

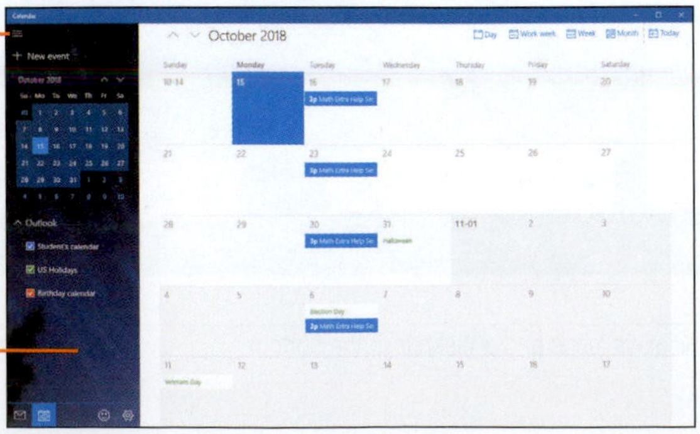

In Windows 10 apps, the Menu button shows the app commands, settings, and views.

Your month and calendar entries will vary.

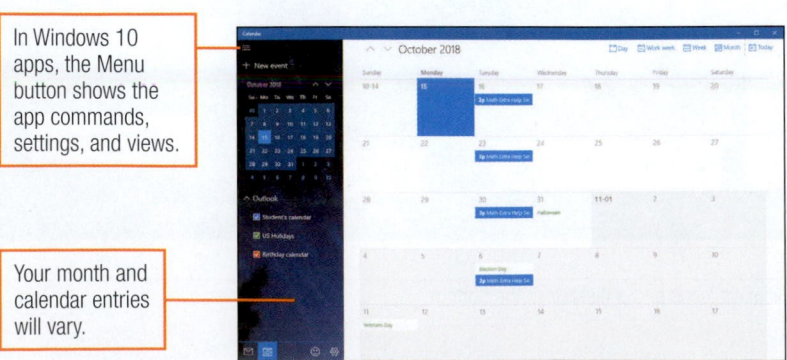

6 Click the Store icon on the taskbar.

In the **Store app**, you can search for and download new apps for your PC or mobile device.

Switching between Apps

You can switch between apps by clicking the button on the taskbar for the app, by viewing open apps in Task View, or by using the keyboard shortcut Alt + Tab. Each app, program, or other window that is opened has a button on the taskbar. Pointing to a button on the taskbar causes a thumbnail to appear above the button with a preview of the window and its active contents. The preview is helpful when you have multiple documents open in the same program to select the correct window.

7 Click the Photos button on the taskbar.

The Photos app moves to the foreground.

8 Click the Task View icon on the taskbar.

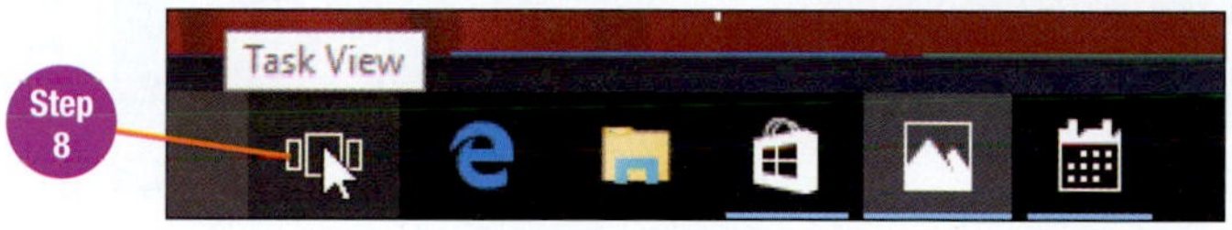

9 Click the Calendar thumbnail.

Task View is a new view in Windows 10 that shows all open apps in the middle of the screen with larger thumbnails to easily see the active contents in each window. Click the thumbnail for the desired app to switch to another window.

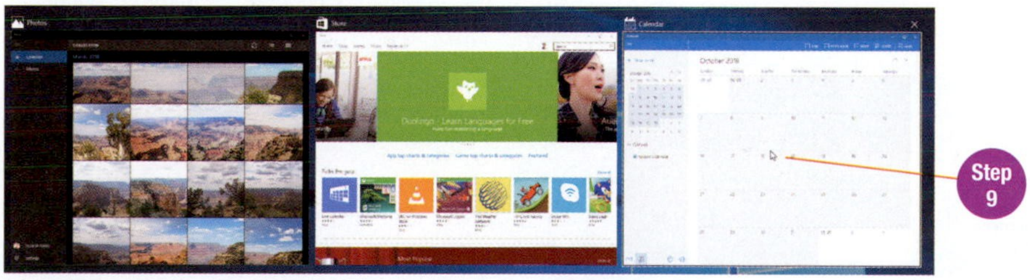

Alternative Method — Switching Apps Using the Keyboard

You can switch to another app by holding down the Alt key and pressing the Tab key. This brings up thumbnails for open apps in the middle of the screen. Continue to hold down the Alt key while pressing and releasing Tab until the desired app is selected (outlined with a white box). Release Alt to switch to the highlighted window.

Quick Steps

Start Windows 10 and Sign In
1. Turn on power or resume system from sleep mode.
2. Click or press any key to remove Lock screen.
3. Type password and press Enter or click Submit button, type PIN, or perform touch gestures on picture.

Launch an App
Click Start button and then click desired tile in right pane on Start menu.

Switch between Apps
Click desired button on taskbar; *or*
1. Click Task View on taskbar.
2. Click desired thumbnail.

App Tip

On a touchscreen, swipe in from the left edge of the screen to show Task View.

Beyond Basics — Other Windows 10 Apps to Explore

In this topic, you briefly viewed the Photos app, Calendar app, and Windows Store. These are just three of several universal apps installed with Windows 10. Other useful apps worth exploring include Alarms & Clock, Calculator, Groove Music (requires an XBox profile to run), Maps, Money, Movies & TV, News, People, Sports, Voice Recorder, and Weather. Click All apps in the left pane of the Start menu to view the full list.

1.3 Using the Search Text Box and Working with Windows

Skills

Use the search text box to start an app

Minimize, maximize, restore down, close, and snap windows

Tutorials

Open and Close Applications Using the Search Box

Search with Cortana

Manipulate Windows

Oops!

No Search text box on taskbar? Right-click the taskbar, point to *Search*, and then click *Show search box*. If the *Show search box* option does not appear, then the taskbar is set to show small buttons only. In that case, right-click the taskbar, click *Properties*, then click the *Use small taskbar buttons* check box to remove the check mark. Click OK.

Oops!

Don't have four windows open? If you closed one or all three of the windows that were opened in the previous topic, return to Topic 1.2 and reopen them.

The search text box is a quick way to start an app, launch an application, locate a file or setting, find information from the web, or find information on how to use a Windows feature. Click in the search text box and then start typing the first few letters of the app or program name, file name, or other topic. The search text box is the fastest way to locate help on anything in Windows 10. The search text box contains the dimmed text *Ask me anything* or *Search the web and Windows* depending on whether Cortana is active. Cortana is the new personal assistant included with Windows 10.

1. Click in the search text box and then type al.

Watch the entries appear in the results list above the search text box as you type. Each character you add in the search text box further refines the list. Notice that options appear in the *Settings* section and web links appear in the *Web* section of the results list.

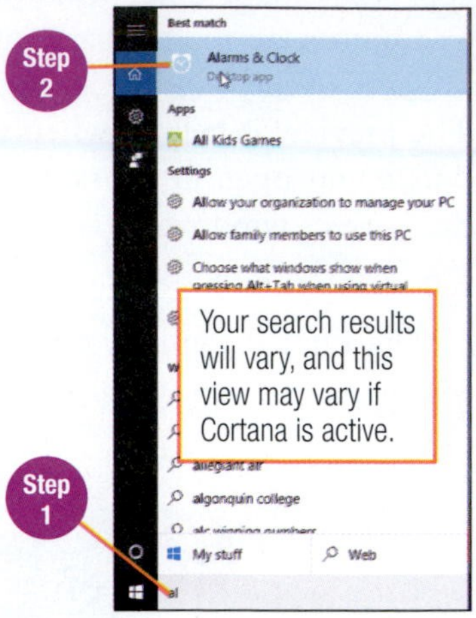

2. Click *Alarms & Clock* in the *Best match* section of the results list.

You should now have four windows overlapping each other on your desktop.

Each app, application, setting, or other feature opens in a window, which allows you to view and work on multiple tasks at the same time. Each window contains standard features for moving, resizing, and closing a window so you can arrange items on your desktop to suit your work preferences. Figure 1.6 identifies the standard window features.

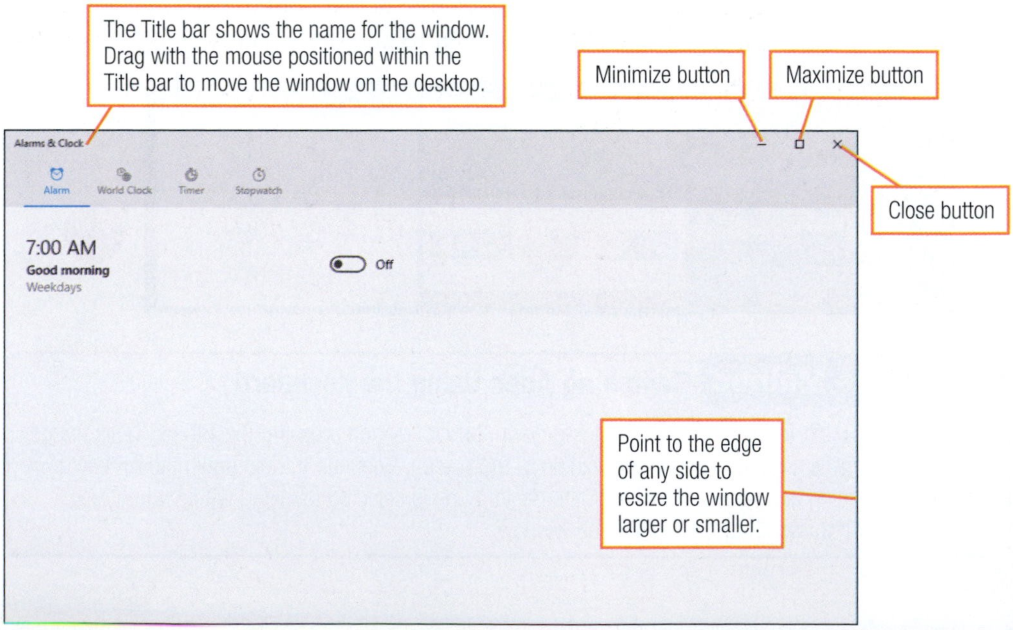

Figure 1.6

Shown above, is the Alarms & Clock window displaying standard features.

3. Click the Minimize button located at the top right of the Alarms & Clock window.

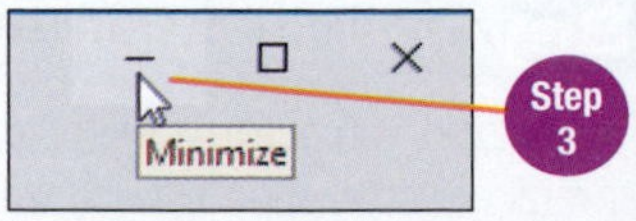

The **Minimize** button is used to reduce the window to a button on the taskbar.

4 With the Calendar window now active, click the Close button to close the Calendar app.

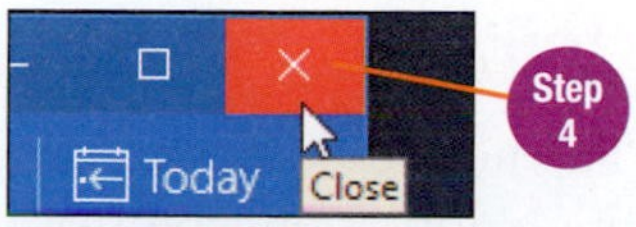

The **Close** button is used to close the window. In a window that contains an open document, the document is also closed, and you are prompted to save changes before closing if changes have been made since the last save operation.

5 With the Photos window now active, click the Maximize button.

Clicking the **Maximize** button expands the window size to fill the entire desktop, and the Maximize button changes to the Restore Down button. **Restore Down** returns the window to its previous size after a window has been maximized.

6 Click the Restore Down button on the Photos window title bar.

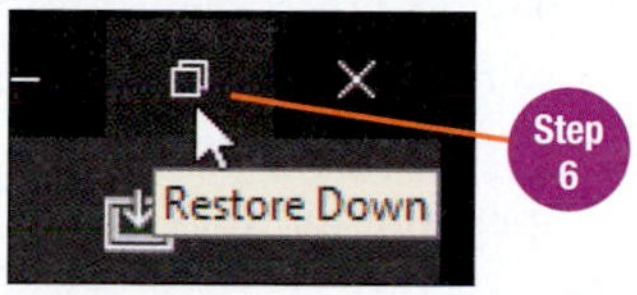

7 Position the mouse pointer on the Photos window Title bar and then drag the window up, down, left, or right a few inches to practice moving the window on the desktop.

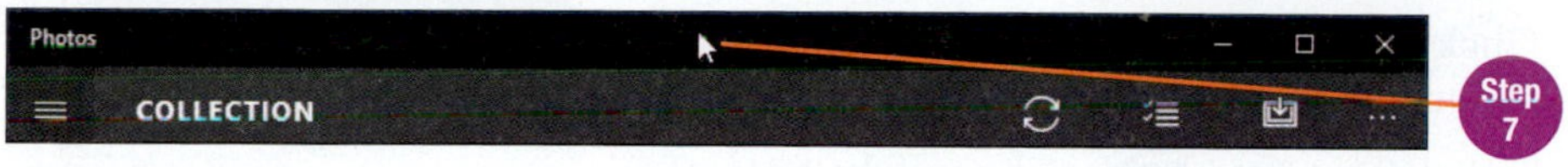

8 Click the Alarms & Clock button on the taskbar to restore the window to the desktop.

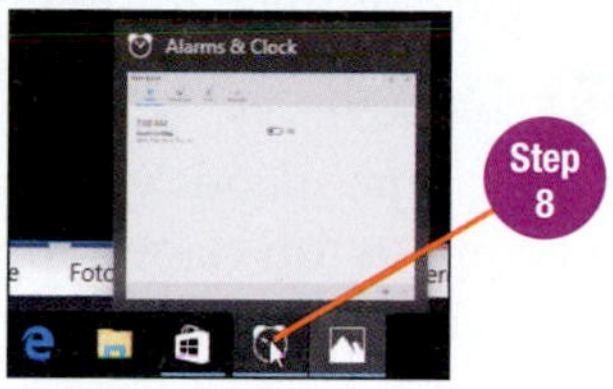

The **Snap** feature in Windows lets you dock a window to one side of the screen without moving and then resizing the window manually. To snap a window to the left or right side of the screen, drag the title bar to the desired edge, then release the mouse when you see the window outline fill the right or left half. In Windows 10, you can snap a window to one of four quadrants by dragging it to a corner. The **Snap Assist** feature pops up when a window is snapped, leaving part of the screen empty and other windows open. In the empty portion of the screen, Snap Assist shows thumbnails of the remaining windows. Click the thumbnail for the window you want to fill the remainder of the screen.

9 Drag the Alarms & Clock Title bar to the left edge of the screen until the outline of a window in the left half of the screen appears, and then release the mouse.

The Alarms & Clock window now fills the left half of the desktop, and Snap Assist shows you thumbnails for the Photos and Store windows in the empty space on the right.

10 Click the Photos window thumbnail.

The screen is now split in half, with the Alarms & Clock window in the left half and the Photos window in the right half.

11 Close the Photos, Alarms & Clock, and Store windows.

Quick Steps

Search for an App, Application, Setting, File, or Web Link

1. Click in the search text box.
2. Type first few letters of app, application, setting, or topic.
3. Click desired item in results list.

App Tip

You can also maximize a window by double-clicking the Title bar or by dragging the window's title bar to the top edge of the screen until the window maximizes.

App Tip

Cortana is the personal assistant included in Windows 10 that operates from the search text box on the taskbar. Cortana responds to text typed in the search text box or to voice commands if you use the microphone icon. Cortana personalizes content the more you use the feature. Some things Cortana will do include helping you find a file on your PC, find a restaurant on the web, track your flight status, and give you a reminder from your calendar.

1.4 Using the Notification Area

Skills

View system information in the notification area on the taskbar

View the Notifications and actions panel in the Settings app

Tutorials

Adjust the Sound Volume

Connect to and Disconnect from a Wireless Network

Modify Screen Brightness and Resolution

The notification area at the right end of the taskbar shows the current date and time, the Notification icon that opens the Action Center panel, the Speaker icon used to adjust the volume, and the Network icon, which shows network connectivity. A Power icon appears next to the network icon if the device uses a battery. Additional icons may appear depending on the applications installed on your PC or mobile device. You use the notification area to view or manage the status of a setting, or other feature.

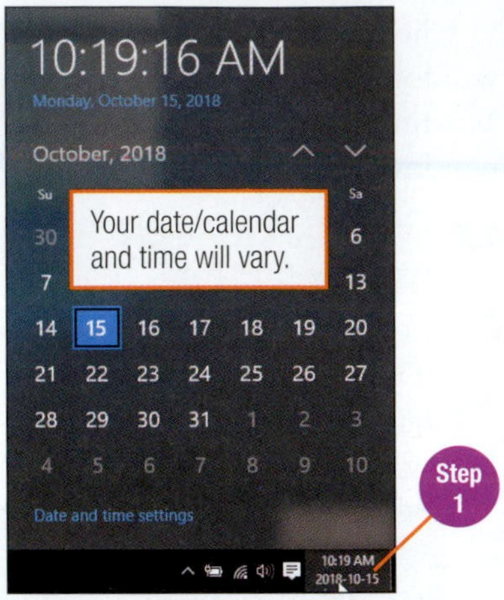

1. Click the current date and time in the notification area at the right end of the taskbar.

   A calendar appears above the date and time displaying the current month. Change the month using the up and down pointing arrows, or change the system date by clicking Date and time settings to open the Settings app.

2. Click in an unused area on the desktop to remove the pop-up calendar.

3. Click the Speaker icon in the notification area on the taskbar.

   The volume control slider opens. Take note of the current value for the volume level.

4. Drag the slider right to adjust the volume higher.

   A chime sounds when you release the mouse at the new volume level. If you are in a computer lab classroom without speakers and do not have headphones plugged in, you will not hear the chime.

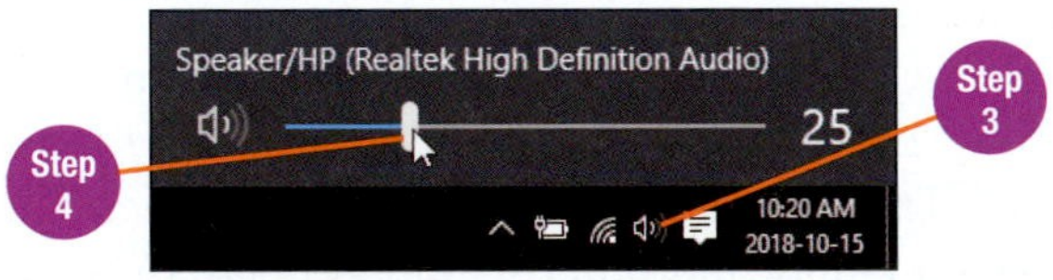

5. Drag the slider left to restore the volume control to the original level.

6. Click in an unused area on the desktop to remove the volume control slider.

7. Click the Network icon in the notification area on the taskbar.

   A list of Wi-Fi networks within range are shown with the active network shown as *Connected*. At the bottom of the panel in the *Network settings* section are quick action tiles. A **quick action tile** is a link to a setting. Clicking the quick action tile for a wireless network you are connected to turns the Wi-Fi connection off. Click the Airplane mode quick action tile to turn on the airplane mode setting, which turns off all wireless communications for your device. You use the Network panel to manage your network connectivity by disconnecting from your current Wi-Fi network or by connecting to another one. To connect to another Wi-Fi network, click the network name and then follow the prompts that appear.

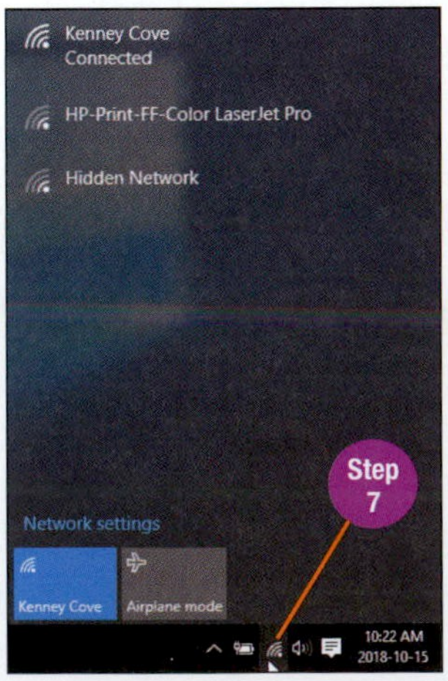

Oops!

Your network panel differs from the one shown here? If you are plugged in to a network via a network cable, the icon shows as a screen with a network plug, and the quick action tiles at the bottom of the panel shown here are not visible because no Wi-Fi connection is active.

8 Click in an unused area on the desktop to remove the Network panel.

9 Click the Power icon in the notification area. Skip to Step 11 if you do not see a Power icon similar to the one shown because you are using a PC that does not use a battery.

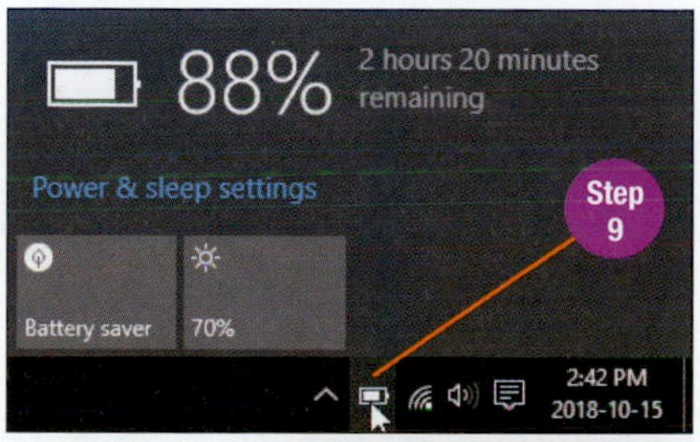

The Power & sleep settings link opens the Settings app with the Power & sleep panel active, where you can adjust the time periods when the screen turns off or sleep mode is activated. The Battery saver quick action tile turns on the feature, which limits background activity to conserve the battery. Cycle through various screen brightness settings using the Brightness quick action tile. The brightness setting affects the battery life.

10 Click in an unused area on the desktop to remove the pop-up Power panel.

11 Click the Notifications icon to open the Action Center panel.

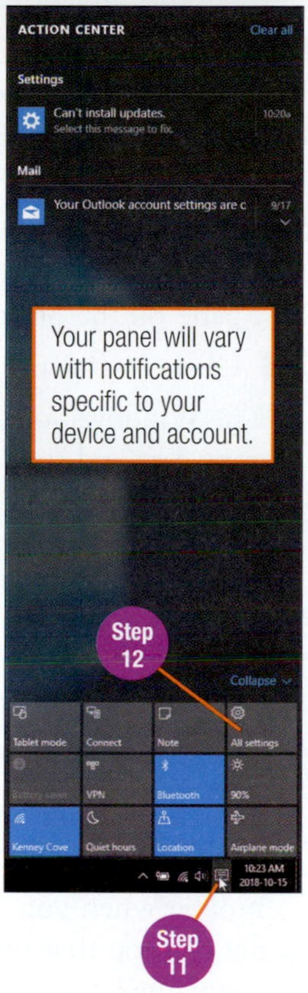

In the top section of the **Action Center** panel, notifications appear from settings, apps, applications, and your connected accounts. For example, you will see messages regarding installed updates, new mail, or a birthday reminder from the Calendar app. At the bottom of the panel are rows of quick action tiles. The tiles shown vary depending on the type of device in use.

12 Click the All settings quick action tile in the Action Center panel to start the Settings app.

13 Click System (first option) in the Settings app window.

14 Click Notifications & actions in the left pane of System Settings.

15 Scroll down and review the options for customizing Notifications.

Drag to slide a switch from On to Off or vice versa to change any of the Notifications options.

16 Click the Select which icons appear on the taskbar link and then review the options.

17 Click the Back button and then click the Turn system icons on or off link.

18 Review the system icon options that can be turned on or off and then close the Settings app window.

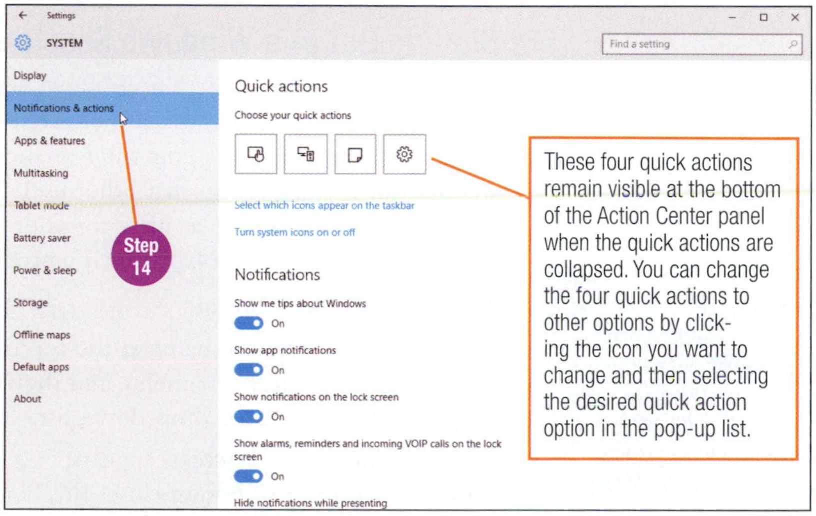

Quick Steps

View the Status of or Change a System Setting Using the Notification Area

Point at or click the icon in the notification area at the right end of the taskbar.

App Tip

On a touchscreen, swipe in from the right edge of the screen to display the Action Center panel.

App Tip

The Notifications icon is white when new notifications are available.

1.5 Locking the Screen, Signing Out, and Shutting Down Windows 10

Skills

Lock the Screen

Sign out of Windows 10

Shut down Windows 10

If you need to leave your PC or mobile device for a short period of time and do not want to close all your apps and documents, you can lock the device. Locking the system causes the lock screen image to appear full screen so someone else cannot see your work. All your apps, applications, and documents are left open in the background, and you can resume work right away once you unlock the device with your password, PIN, or picture password.

1. Click the Start button, type photos in the search text box and press Enter, or click the Photos tile to launch the Photos app.
2. Click the Start button.
3. Click your account name at the top of the left pane on the Start menu.
4. Click *Lock* at the drop-down list.

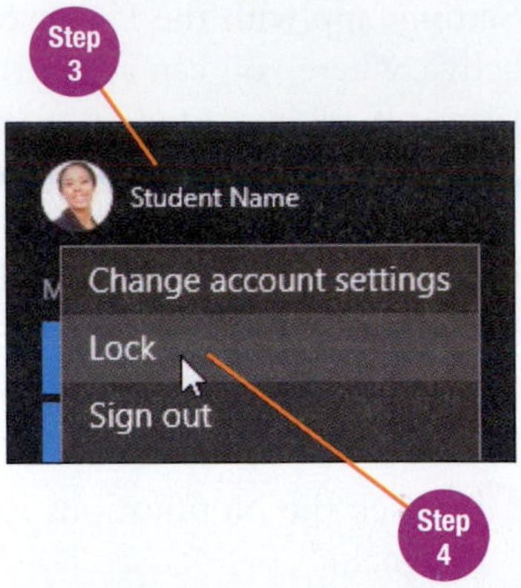

The Windows lock screen appears with the current date and time and notifications, if any are available.

5. Click anywhere on the lock screen or press any key on the keyboard to display the sign-in screen.
6. Type your password in the *Password* text box and press Enter, type your PIN, or perform the touch gestures on your picture password.

Notice when you are back at the desktop that the Photos app remained open while the device was locked.

Signing Out of a Windows Session

When you are finished with a Windows session, you should **sign out** of the PC or mobile device. Signing out is also referred to as *logging off*. Signing out closes all apps, applications, and files. If a computer or mobile device is shared with other people, signing out is expected so that other users can sign in to their accounts. Signing out and locking also provide security for your device because someone would need to know your password, PIN, or touch gestures to access programs or files.

7. Click the Start button.
8. Click your account name at the top of the left pane on the Start menu, and then click *Sign out* at the drop-down list.

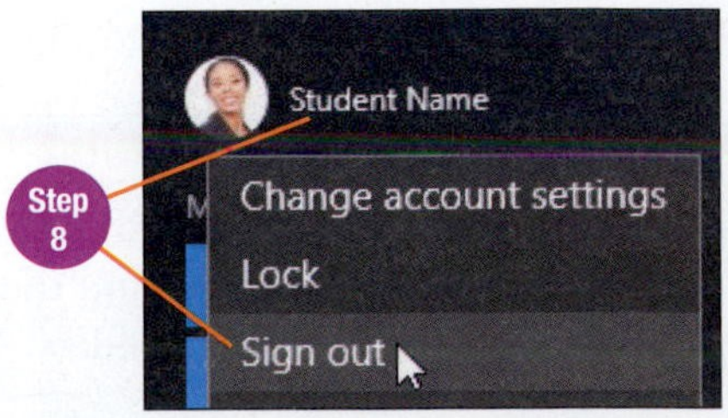

The Windows lock screen appears; however, this time Windows closes the Photos app automatically.

> **App Tip**
> If you have documents open with unsaved changes, Windows prompts you to save the documents before proceeding with the sign-out process.

9 Display the sign-in screen, type your password and press Enter, type your PIN, or perform the touch gestures on your picture password.

Notice the Photos app is not on the desktop because it was closed when you signed out of the previous Windows session.

Shutting Down the PC or Mobile Device

If you want to turn off the power to your computer or mobile device, perform a **shut down**. Shutting down the system ensures that all Windows files are properly closed. The power will turn off automatically when shut down is complete.

10 If necessary, click the Start button.

11 Click Power near the bottom of the left pane on the Start menu.

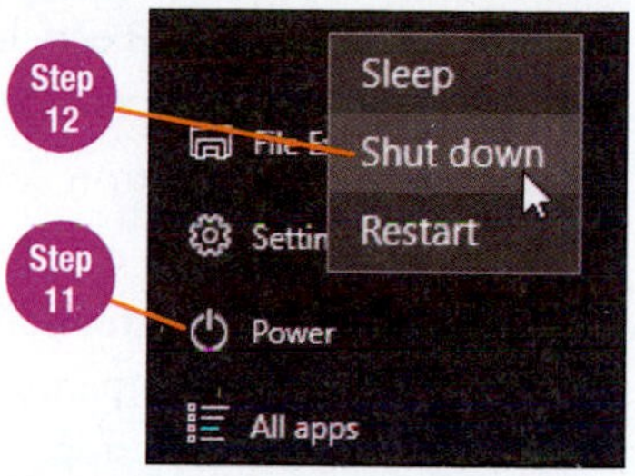

Note: *Check with your instructor before proceeding to Step 12 because some schools do not allow students to shut down computers. If necessary, click in an unused area on the desktop to remove the Start menu and proceed to the next topic.*

12 Click *Shut down* at the pop-up list.

If someone else is signed in on the device you are shutting down, a message will display informing you the other user could lose unsaved work if you proceed. Click *Shut down anyway* to proceed with turning off the device, or click in an unused area on the desktop to remove the message and cancel the shutdown operation.

The system will perform the shutdown operation, and in a few seconds the power will turn off. In some instances, system updates will be installed during a shutdown operation.

13 Wait a moment or two and then press the Power button to turn the PC or mobile device back on.

14 When the lock screen appears, display the sign-in screen and then sign back in to Windows.

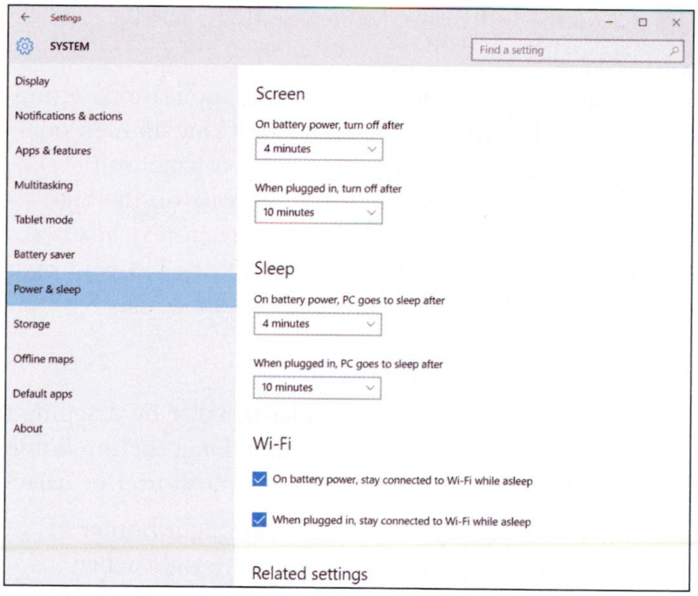

Figure 1.7

The Power & sleep panel is shown in the Settings app.

Quick Steps

Lock PC or Mobile Device

1. Click Start button.
2. Click account name at top of left pane on Start menu.
3. Click *Lock*.

Sign Out of Windows

1. Click Start button.
2. Click account name at top of left pane on Start menu.
3. Click *Sign out*.

Shut Down PC or Mobile Device

1. Click Start button.
2. Click Power.
3. Click *Shut down*.

Beyond Basics — Other Power Options

The *Sleep* option from the Power pop-up list is used when you are away from the computer and want to leave all programs and documents open but use less power. A system goes into sleep mode after a period of time elapses with no activity. See Figure 1.7 to view the Power & sleep panel in the Settings app where you can change the options. Choose *Restart* to shut down Windows and immediately start it up again without turning off the power. A restart is used when a system is not performing correctly or is otherwise not responding.

1.6 Using and Customizing the Start Menu

Skills

Navigate the Start menu

Resize the Start menu

Pin/unpin a tile to/from the Start menu

Move a tile

Resize a tile

Turn on and off live updates

The Start menu is divided into two panes. The left pane contains links to the apps or applications most used or recently added at the top of the pane, and File Explorer, Settings, Power, and All apps are at the bottom of the pane. The right pane, as you learned in Topic 1.2, contains tiles to apps, applications, or other features. The Start menu can be customized to suit your preferences by adding or removing tiles, rearranging tiles, resizing a tile, and by turning a live tile on or off to enable or stop notifications or other content from appearing on the tile.

Note: *In some school computer labs, the ability to change Windows settings is disabled. If necessary, complete this topic and the next topic on your PC or mobile device at home.*

1. Double-click the Recycle Bin icon on the desktop to open the Recycle Bin window.

2. Click the Start button, and then click Settings to open the Settings app.
3. Click the Start button, click All apps, scroll down the apps list in the left pane, and then click Money to launch the Money app.

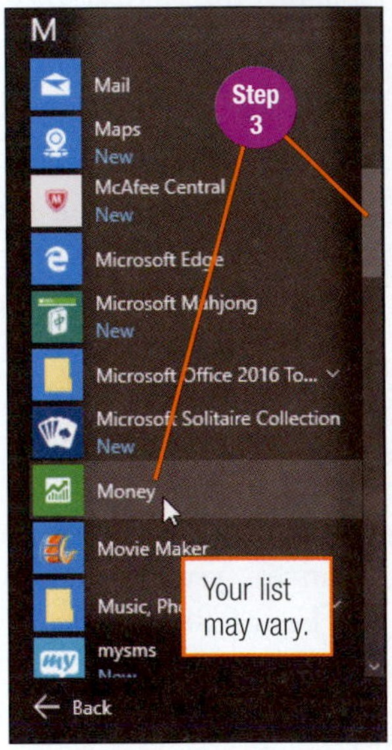

4. Click the Start button, click All apps, then click Back to return the left pane to the previous list.
5. Click in the search text box, type calc, and then press Enter to launch the Calculator app.
6. Close the Calculator, Money, Settings, and Recycle Bin windows.

Whether you choose to start an app, application, setting, or open another window by double-clicking an icon on the desktop, clicking an option in the left pane on the Start menu, clicking a tile in the right pane on the Start menu, or by typing a name using the search text box is a personal preference. Over time, you will develop your own style for using the Start menu and desktop.

App Tip

Right-click the Start button to open the Quick Access menu, which provides access to advanced system tools, such as Device Manager, Computer Management, Task Manager, and Control Panel to name a few.

Resizing the Start Menu

You can make the Start menu wider or taller by dragging the top or right border of the Start menu upward or to the right. Drag the top border downward or the right border to the left to make the Start menu shorter or narrower.

7. Click the Start button, point at the right border of the Start menu, and then drag to the right when the pointer changes to a left- and right-pointing arrow to make the menu wider.

8. With the Start menu still open, point at the top border and then drag upward when the pointer changes to an up- and down-pointing arrow to make the menu taller.

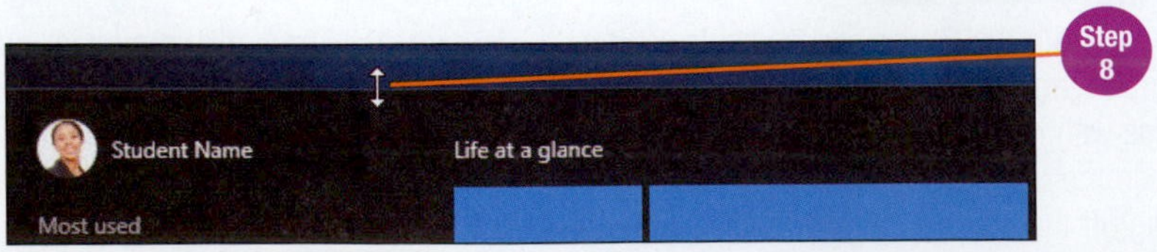

Pinning and Unpinning Tiles to and from the Start Menu

Right-click a tile to reveal the shortcut menu with the options Unpin from Start, Resize, or More, which is used to access the options Turn live tile on or Turn live tile off (depending on its current state), and Pin to taskbar. Click **Unpin from Start** to remove the tile from the Start menu. A tile can be added to the Start menu by right-clicking the app or application name in the All apps list on the Start menu, and then clicking **Pin to Start**. The shortcut menu offers more or fewer choices depending on the app or application name that you right-click on the Start menu.

9. With the Start menu open, right-click the Photos tile and then click *Unpin from Start* at the shortcut menu.

The tile is removed, and the Start menu remains open.

10. Click All apps in the left pane on the Start menu, scroll down the All apps menu, and then right-click Photos.
11. Click *Pin to Start* at the shortcut menu.

The Photos tile is added back to the Start menu, and the Start menu remains open. Notice that the tile is not added back to the same location from which it originated.

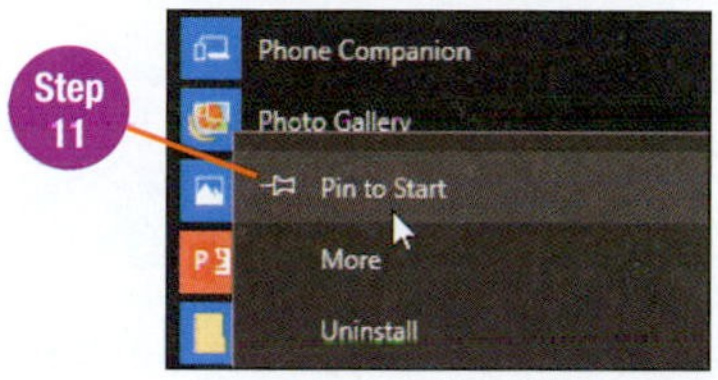

> ### Quick Steps
> **Remove a Tile from the Start Menu**
> 1. Right-click tile.
> 2. Click *Unpin from Start*.
>
> **Add a Tile to the Start Menu**
> 1. Click Start button and then click All apps.
> 2. Scroll down All apps list to locate desired app or application name.
> 3. Right-click app or application name.
> 4. Click *Pin to Start*.
>
> **Rearrange Tiles**
> Drag tile to desired location.
>
> **Resize a Tile**
> 1. Right-click tile.
> 2. Point to *Resize*.
> 3. Click desired size.
>
> **Turn Off/On Live Updates**
> 1. Right-click tile, then point to *More*.
> 2. Click *Turn live tile off* or *Turn live tile on*.

Rearranging Tiles

Tiles can be moved to a new location on the Start menu by dragging the tile to the desired location.

12. Drag the Photos tile back to its original location in the right pane on the Start menu.

As you drag a tile around on the Start menu, the tiles are dimmed, and you will notice other tiles shifting around to make room for the tile.

Resizing a Tile and Turning Live Updates Off or On

Tiles are either square or rectangular in shape and can be sized Small, Medium, Wide, or Large using the Resize option on the shortcut menu. Some tiles do not offer all size options. Some tiles display live updates, with notifications, headlines, or pictures displayed on the tile. Change the live update status using the **Turn live tile off** or **Turn live tile on** option at the shortcut menu.

13. With the Start menu open, right-click the Calendar tile, point to *Resize*, and then click *Large*.
14. Right-click the Calendar tile, point to *Resize*, and then click *Medium*. If necessary, drag the Mail or other tile back upward to fill in the space next to the Calendar tile.
15. Right-click the Mail tile, point to *More*, and then click *Turn live tile off*.

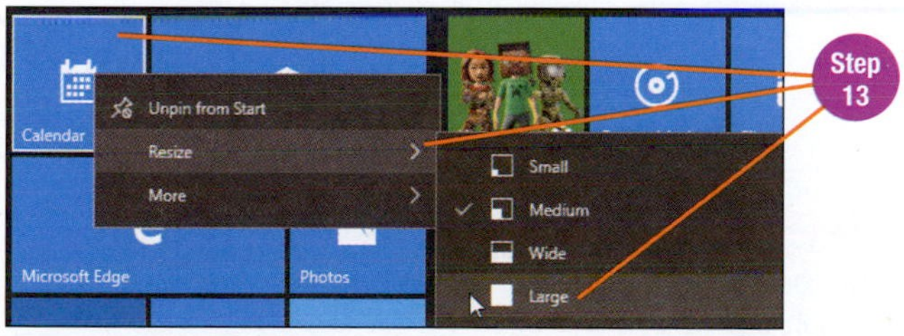

16. Right-click the Mail tile, point to *More*, and then click *Turn live tile on*.
17. Resize the Start menu back to its original height and width if desired.
18. If necessary, rearrange tiles or make other changes as needed to restore the Start menu to its original settings and then click in an unused area of the desktop to close the Start menu.

1.7 Personalizing the Lock Screen and the Desktop

Skills

Change the Lock screen background image

Add an app to the Lock screen notifications

Change the desktop background image

Change the color scheme

Tutorial
Personalize the Desktop

Most people like to put a personal stamp on their PC or mobile device. In Windows 10, you can personalize the Lock screen by changing the picture that displays and the apps that provide notifications when the screen locks. The desktop background can be personalized to a different image and color scheme. A theme changes the background image, color, and sound scheme in one step. The Start menu by default shows the most used and recently added apps or applications in the left pane. You can turn one or both of these categories off.

Open the Settings app and choose *Personalization* to make changes to the lock screen, desktop background, colors, themes, and Start menu.

1. Click the Start button and then click Settings.
2. Click *Personalization* in the Settings app window.

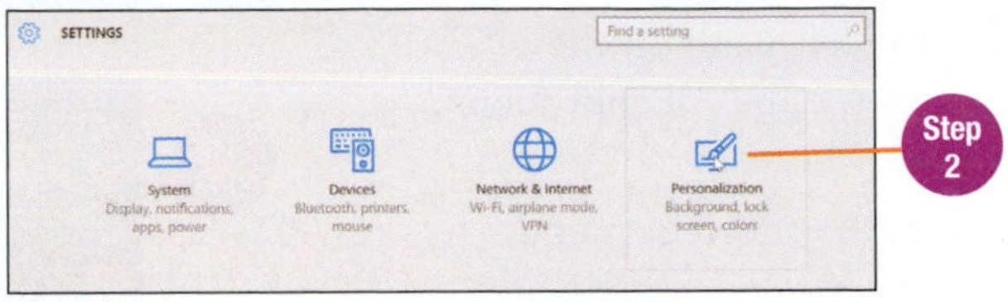

3. Click Lock screen in the left pane of the Settings app window.

The current Lock screen image is shown above five thumbnails for other background pictures in the right pane, as shown in Figure 1.8. Click a different picture to preview the image or click the Browse button to choose a picture on your PC or mobile device to use as the Lock screen image. You can also opt to show a slideshow for the lock screen by changing the Background option from Picture to Slideshow.

Figure 1.8
The Lock screen pane is shown in the Settings app.

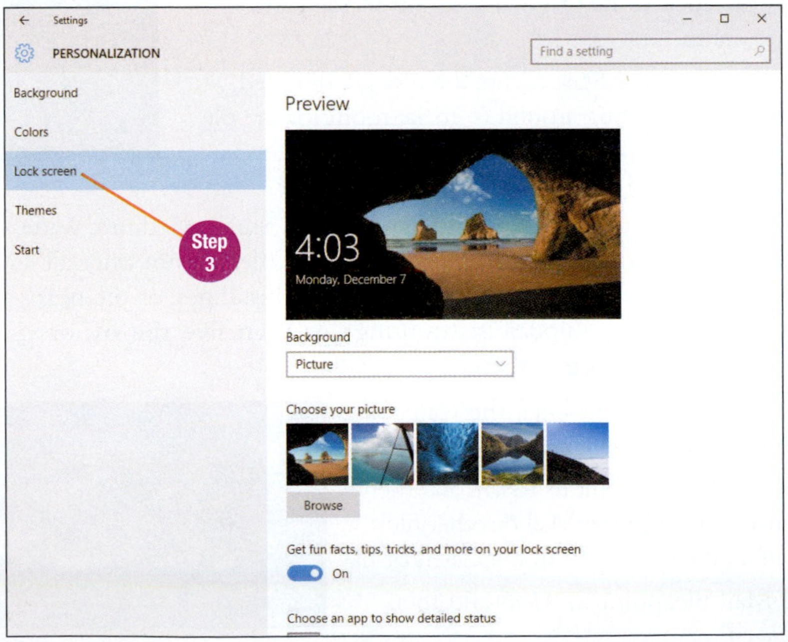

Oops!
No background thumbnails? The Background option below the Preview is at a different setting (such as *Windows spotlight*). Click the *Background* option box arrow and then click *Picture.*

4. Click one of the five background thumbnails below the current Lock screen image. You determine the background image you want to view.

The app buttons below the background thumbnails control which apps give notifications on the lock screen image.

5 If necessary, scroll down to view the Lock screen app buttons. Click the first button with a plus symbol in the *Choose apps to show quick status* section and then click *Weather* at the pop-up list.

The Weather app will now provide notifications when the screen is locked.

6 Click Background in the left pane of the Settings app window.

7 Click one of the five background thumbnails in the *Choose your picture* section. You determine which picture you want for your background. If the *Choose your picture* thumbnails are not visible, click the Background option box arrow and then click *Picture*.

8 Click Colors in the left pane.

9 Click a color square in the *Choose your accent color* section and then close the Settings app window. You determine the accent color you want to use for tiles and window accents.

The new background image is shown on the desktop.

10 Click the Start button and look at the new accent color used on tiles.

11 Lock the screen and notice the new picture on your lock screen.

12 Sign back in to unlock the system.

13 If necessary, click the Start button. Click Settings, then repeat Step 2 to Step 9 restoring the lock screen, background, and color scheme to their original settings. At Step 5, click *None* in the Weather button pop-up list to remove the app on the lock screen.

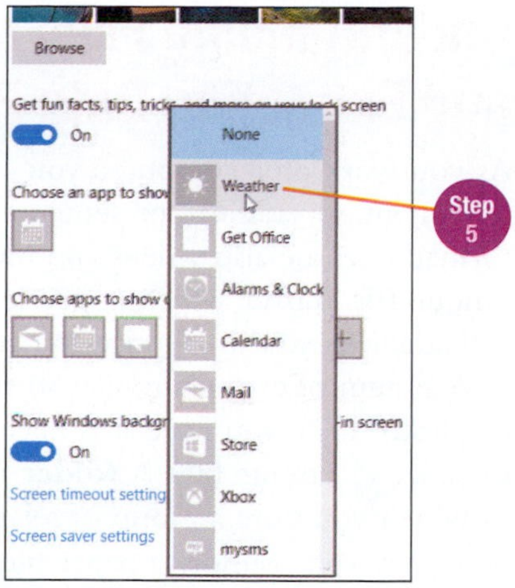

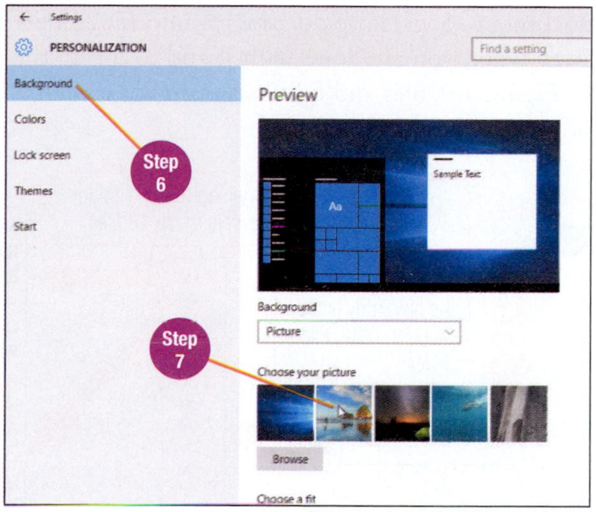

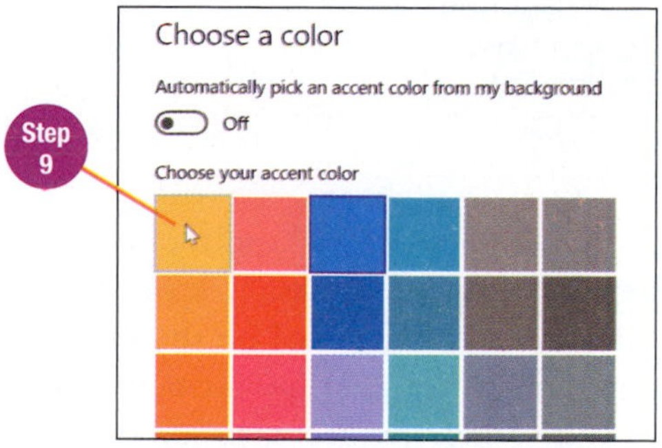

Quick Steps

Change the Lock Screen Options

1. Click Start button.
2. Click Settings.
3. Click *Personalization*.
4. Click Lock screen in left pane.
5. Change desired lock screen options.

Change Background

1. Click Start button.
2. Click Settings.
3. Click *Personalization*.
4. Click Background in left pane.
5. Click desired thumbnail image.

Change Color Scheme

1. Click Start button.
2. Click Settings.
3. Click *Personalization*.
4. Click Colors in left pane.
5. Click desired color square.

App Tip

When you are signed in with a Microsoft account, your personalization settings are saved online. Sign in from another PC or mobile device and your new lock screen, background, and color scheme will appear on the other device.

Beyond Basics: Adding a Picture for Your Account

To add a picture of yourself to your Microsoft account so that your picture shows in place of the silhouette icon, begin by clicking the Start button, clicking your account name at the top of the left pane, and then clicking *Change account settings*. In the Settings app window with *Your account* active in the left pane, click the Browse button below the silhouette, navigate to the image you want to use, and then double-click the file. You can also use the Camera button to take a new picture of yourself using your PC or mobile device webcam.

1.8 Understanding Files and Folders and Downloading and Extracting Data Files

Skills

Define file, file name, and folder

Download and extract student data files to a USB flash drive

Tutorials

Create a Compressed Archive (ZIP) File

Download and Extract Student Data Files

As you work on a computer, you are creating and modifying files. A **file** is a document, spreadsheet, presentation, picture, or any other data that you save in digital format. Files are also videos and music that you play on a device. Each file has a unique **file name**, which is a series of characters you assign to the file when you save it that allows you to identify and retrieve the file later.

A system of organizing files so that you can find and retrieve a specific document or photo when you need it is necessary. Folders are created on a storage device to organize electronic files. A **folder** is a name assigned to a placeholder or container in which you store a group of related files. Think of a folder on the computer in the same way you consider a paper file folder in a desk drawer at your home. You might have one file folder for your household bills and another file folder for your school documents. Separating documents into file folders makes it easy to put a document away when you are done with it and to locate the document when you need it again. In Figure 1.9, files and folders are shown to help you understand how digital data is organized on a storage device.

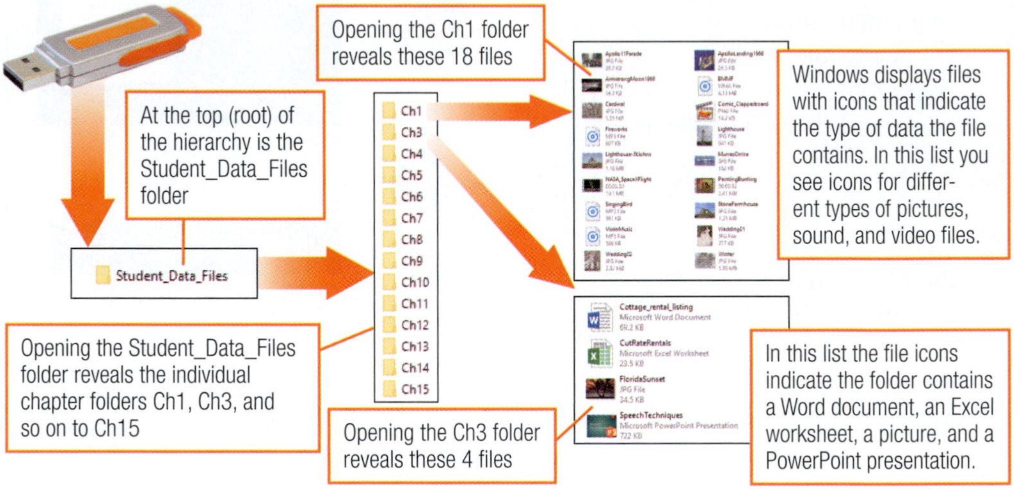
Opening the Ch1 folder reveals these 18 files
At the top (root) of the hierarchy is the Student_Data_Files folder
Student_Data_Files
Ch1
Ch3
Ch4
Ch5
Ch6
Ch7
Ch8
Ch9
Ch10
Ch11
Ch12
Ch13
Ch14
Ch15
Windows displays files with icons that indicate the type of data the file contains. In this list you see icons for different types of pictures, sound, and video files.
Opening the Student_Data_Files folder reveals the individual chapter folders Ch1, Ch3, and so on to Ch15
Cottage_rental_listing
Microsoft Word Document
CutRateRentals
Microsoft Excel Worksheet
FloridaSunset
SpeechTechniques
Microsoft PowerPoint Presentation
Opening the Ch3 folder reveals these 4 files
In this list the file icons indicate the folder contains a Word document, an Excel worksheet, a picture, and a PowerPoint presentation.

Figure 1.9

Digital data is stored in files, which are organized into folders.

To complete the tasks in the rest of this textbook, a set of student data files must be copied to a USB flash drive or other storage medium. Check with your instructor for his or her preference on the storage medium to use for completing the work in your course. You may be instructed to save files to a network folder at your school or in your OneDrive account. Substitute another storage medium if necessary when the USB flash drive is used in the remaining topics.

The student data files are copied from the accompanying ebook. The files are packaged so that you need to download only one file, called an *archive file*, or a ZIP file. A **ZIP file** assembles and compresses a group of files under one name that looks like a folder name with a .zip file extension. The files are compressed so that the ZIP file size is as small as possible, meaning the file will copy faster over a network. A ZIP file should be uncompressed before the files stored within it are used so that each file is restored to its original size and put back in the folder from which the file originated. To restore the files within a ZIP file to their original size and folder structure, you perform a process called *extracting*.

App Tip

You can recognize a ZIP file in a file list because Windows displays the icon as a file folder with a zipper.

Note: *You will need a USB flash drive to complete the steps in this topic and the next three topics. Check with your instructor for alternative instructions if he or she prefers that you save files somewhere else, such as in a network folder on a school server.*

1. Insert a USB flash drive into an available USB port on your PC. Skip this step if you are saving files to another storage medium.
2. Go to your ebook for this textbook and navigate to this page in the ebook.
3. Click the Ancillary Links button as shown in the image at the right. The button may appear at the top or along the side of the window depending on the window size.

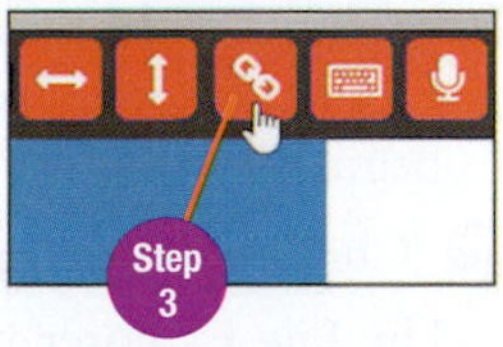

4. Click the Student_Data_Files hyperlink that appears in the Ancillary Links dialog box as shown in the image at the right.
5. Click the Download hyperlink at the top of the OneDrive window.

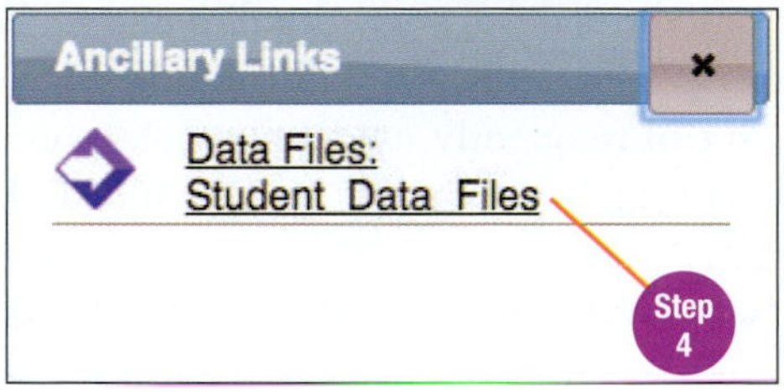

The ZIP archive file will start copying to the Downloads folder. The download will take a few moments depending on the speed of your network connection. Watch the progress of the download at the bottom of the browser window.

6. Click the Open button that appears when the message displays that Student_Data_Files.zip finished downloading.

A File Explorer window opens. The Compressed Folder Tools Extract tab appears because the file opened is a ZIP archive file. **File Explorer** is the utility used to browse files and folders on storage devices and perform file management routines. You will learn more about File Explorer in the next three topics.

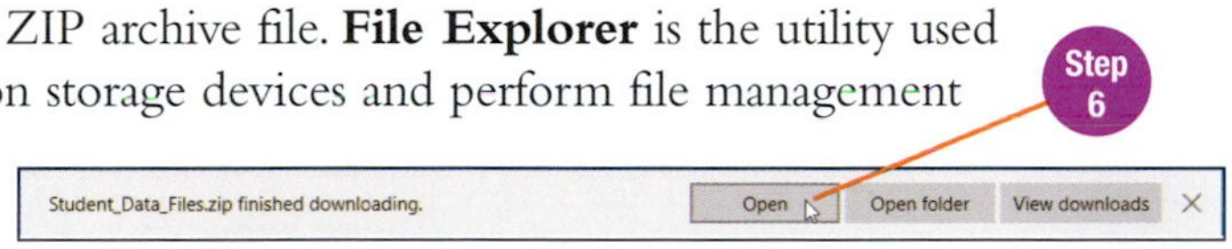

7. If necessary, click the Compressed Folder Tools Extract tab.
8. Click the Extract all button.
9. Click the Browse button in the Extract Compressed (Zipped) Folders dialog box.

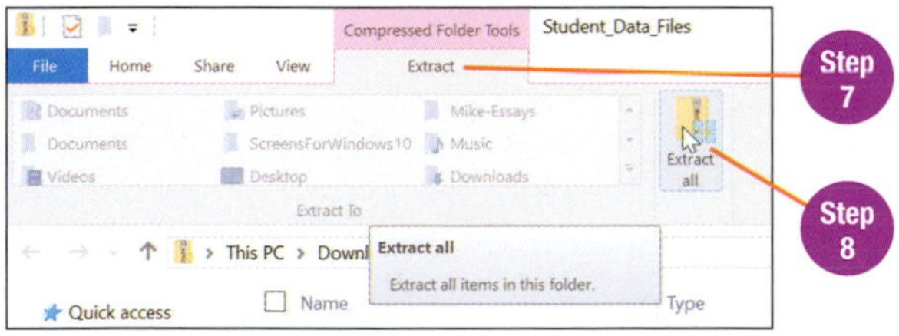

10. Click your USB flash drive in the left pane of the Select a destination dialog box, and then click the Select Folder button.

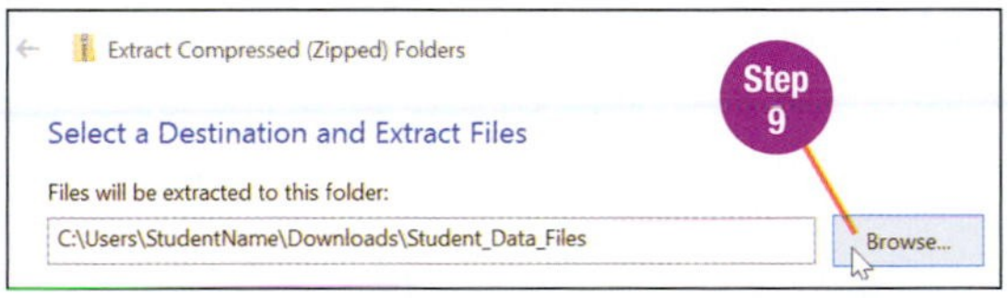

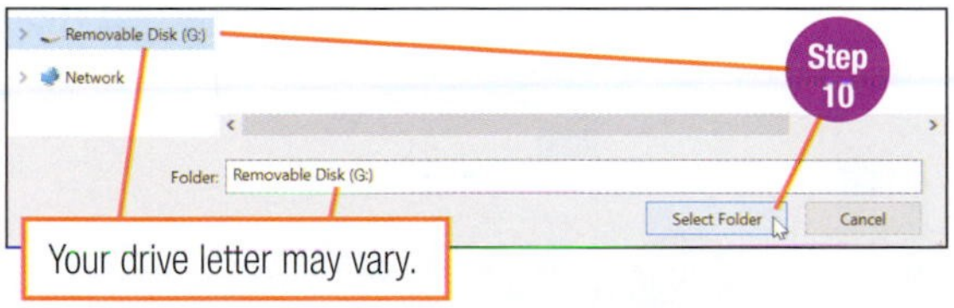

11. Click Extract in the Extract Compressed (Zipped) Folders dialog box.

A progress message displays the status of the operation. When finished a new File Explorer window opens with the Student_Data_Files folder shown.

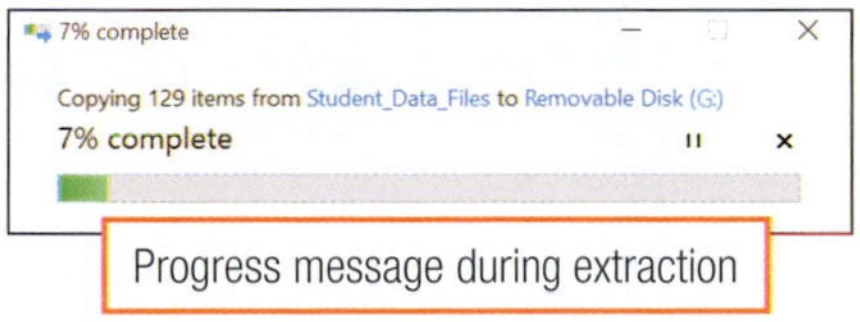

12. Close all the open windows including the OneDrive browser window.

Data Files
Student_Data_Files

Quick Steps
Download and Extract Student Data Files
1. Navigate to this page in ebook.
2. Click Ancillary links button, then Student_Data_Files hyperlink.
3. Click Download hyperlink in OneDrive.
4. Click Open.
5. If necessary, click Compressed Folder Tools Extract tab.
6. Click Extract all button.
7. Click Browse button.
8. Click USB flash drive in left pane, then Select Folder.
9. Click Extract.

Oops!
A window other than File Explorer opens at Step 6? If there is another ZIP archive program installed on your device (such as 7-Zip), your file may open in the archive program window. In that case, close the window that opened. Click the File Explorer icon on the taskbar. Click Downloads in the left pane. Right-click the file Student_Data_Files.zip in the right pane, point to *Open with*, click *Windows Explorer*, and then proceed to Step 7.

1.9 Browsing Files with File Explorer

Skills

Identify features in a File Explorer window

Browse files on a device using File Explorer

Tutorial

Navigate between Local Volumes and Folders in File Explorer

To view or manage the files on a storage device, open a File Explorer window by clicking the File Explorer icon on the taskbar or near the bottom of the left pane on the Start menu. In File Explorer, you perform file maintenance tasks, such as creating new folders to organize files, renaming files, copying files, moving files, and deleting files. To begin, you will learn how to navigate the File Explorer window (see Figure 1.10).

1 Click the File Explorer icon on the taskbar.

The File Explorer window is divided into two panes. The Navigation pane at the left displays the list of places associated with the device. The right pane, called the Content pane, displays the files and folders stored on the selected item. The window opens by default in Windows 10 in a new view called **Quick access**, which shows a list of frequently used and recently used files. Each frequent folders list contains at least four folders: Desktop, Downloads, Documents, and Pictures.

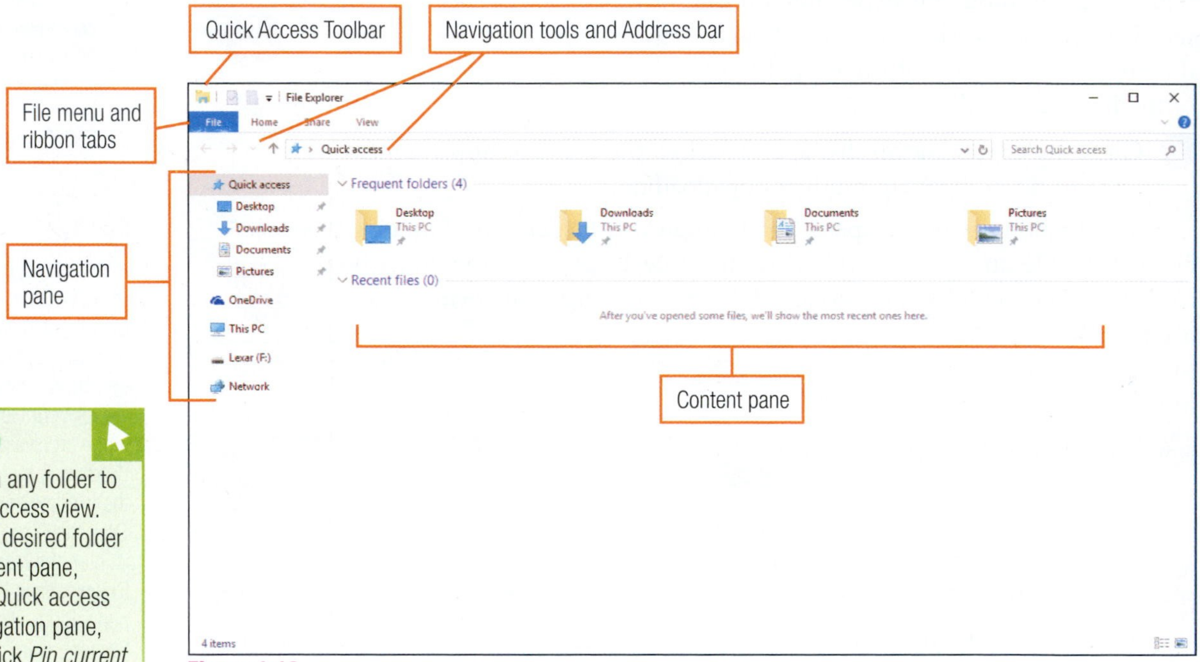

Figure 1.10

The File Explorer window

App Tip

You can pin any folder to the Quick access view. Display the desired folder in the Content pane, right-click Quick access in the Navigation pane, and then click *Pin current folder to Quick access*.

2 Click This PC in the Navigation pane.

A This PC window displays all the available storage options on the computer.

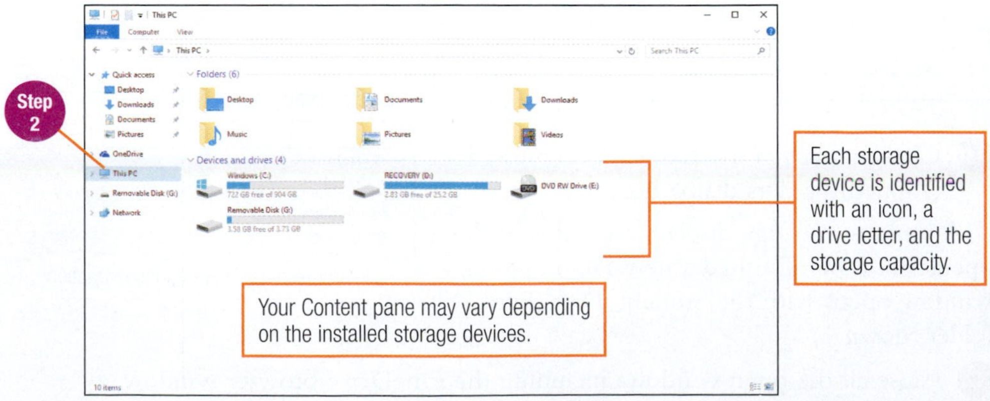

App Tip

You can set File Explorer to always open with This PC active instead of the new Quick access view. To do this, right-click Quick access in the Navigation pane, click *Options*, change the *Open File Explorer* option to *This PC*, and then click OK.

3 If necessary, insert your USB flash drive into an available USB port. If a new window opens when you insert the USB flash drive, close the window.

4 Double-click the icon for the Removable Disk representing your USB flash drive in the *Devices and drives* section to view the contents in the Content pane.

The Content pane shows the name of the folder you extracted from the ZIP file in the previous topic. Your content pane may show additional files if you did not use a blank USB flash drive.

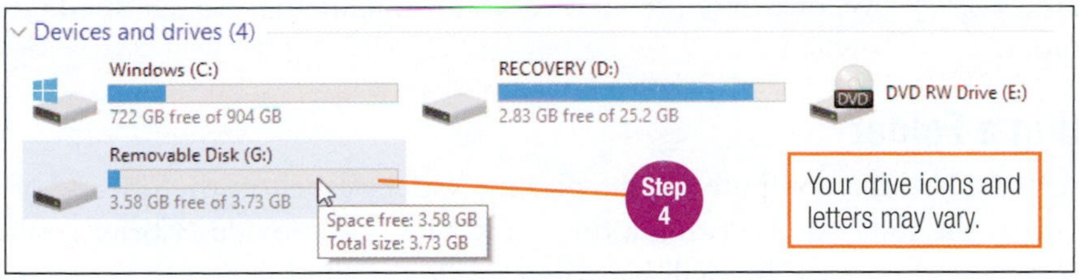

5 Double-click the folder *Student_Data_Files*.

A list of folders stored within the Student_Data_Files folder appears. A folder within another folder is sometimes referred to as a **subfolder**.

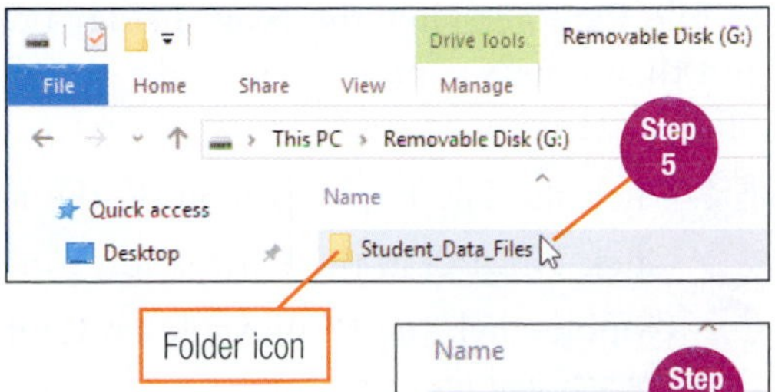

6 Double-click the folder *Ch1*.

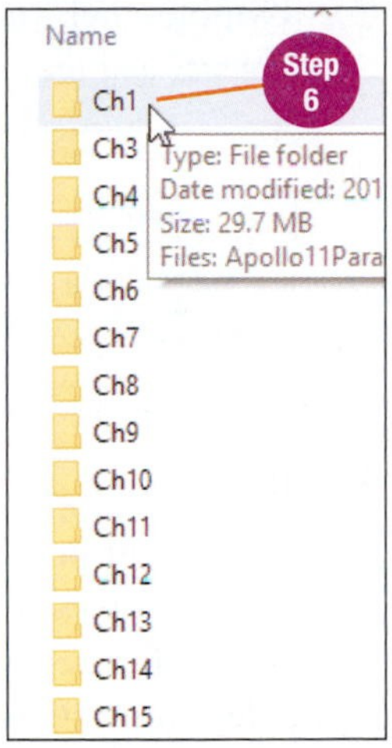

A list of files stored in the Ch1 subfolder appears in the Content pane.

7 Click the View tab.

8 Click the *Tiles* option in the Layout group.

Use the Layout options to view files in the Content pane as small, medium, large, and extra large icons; in a list format with or without file details, such as the date and time the file was created or last updated and the file size; in a list with the file type and file properties such as author (Content); or as tiles (shown below).

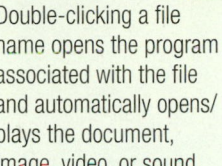

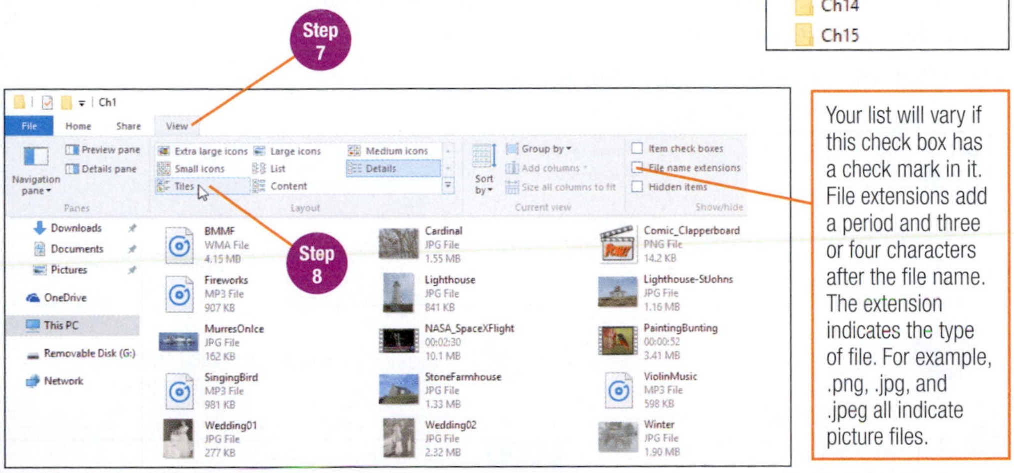

9 Click Desktop in the Navigation pane.

Browse content in File Explorer by clicking names in the Navigation pane, or by double-clicking device or folder names in the Content pane.

10 Close the File Explorer window.

Note: *Leave the USB flash drive in the device for the next topics.*

Quick Steps

Browse Files in File Explorer

1. Click File Explorer icon on taskbar.
2. If necessary, insert a removable storage medium such as a USB flash drive.
3. Click desired location or device in Navigation pane, *or* double-click a folder or device name in Content pane.

App Tip

Double-clicking a file name opens the program associated with the file and automatically opens/plays the document, image, video, or sound.

App Tip

Changing the view to tiles or icons lets you easily locate a file you are looking for when browsing pictures or videos.

1.10 Creating Folders and Copying Files and Folders

Skills

Create a folder and subfolder

Copy files and folders

Tutorials

Create and Rename a File or Folder

Move and Copy Using Copy and Paste

Move and Copy Using Drag-and-Drop

As you work with software applications, such as Word or Excel, you will create many files that are documents or spreadsheets. You may also download files from a digital camera or a website and receive other files from email or text messages. Storing the files in an organized manner with recognizable names will mean you can easily locate the document or picture later. Creating folders in advance of creating files means having an organizational structure already in place. From time to time, you also need to rename, copy, move, or delete files and folders to maintain a storage medium in good order.

Creating a Folder

Creating a folder on a computer is like placing a sticky label on the outside of an empty paper file folder and writing a title on it. The title provides a brief description of the type of documents that will be stored inside the file folder. On the computer, in File Explorer, click the **New folder** button in the New group on the Home tab, and then type a name for the folder to set up the electronic equivalent of a paper filing system.

1. Click the File Explorer icon on the taskbar.
2. Click This PC in the Navigation pane of the File Explorer window.
3. Double-click the Removable Disk representing your USB flash drive in the *Devices and drives* section.

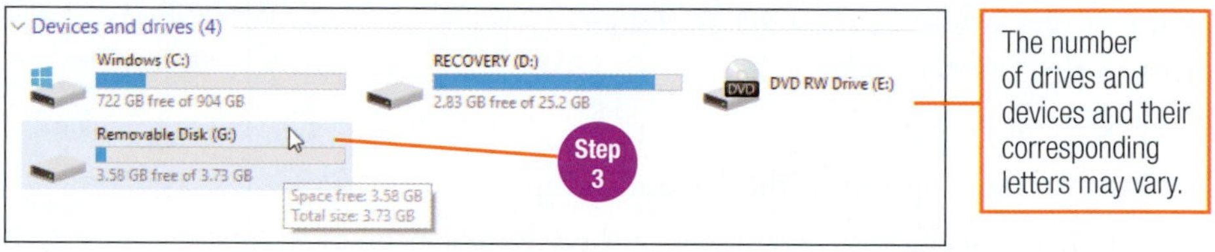

App Tip

Tabs and/or buttons on the ribbon change and become available or unavailable depending on what is selected in the window.

4. If necessary, click the Home tab to display the ribbon interface.

The **ribbon** provides the buttons you need to perform file management tasks. Buttons are organized into the tabs Home, Share, View, and Manage. Within each tab, buttons are further organized into groups, such as Clipboard, Organize, New, Open, and Select (on the Home tab).

5. Click the New folder button in the New group on the Home tab.

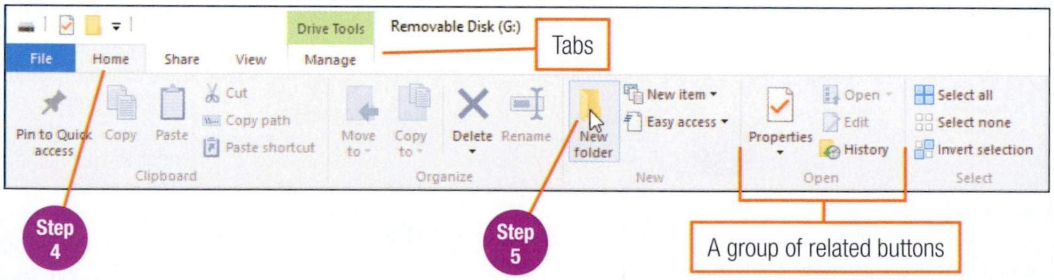

App Tip

In the folder structure you are creating, no spaces between words are used. Windows allows the use of spaces; however, a good practice is to avoid spaces in folder names.

6. Type ComputerCourse and then press Enter.

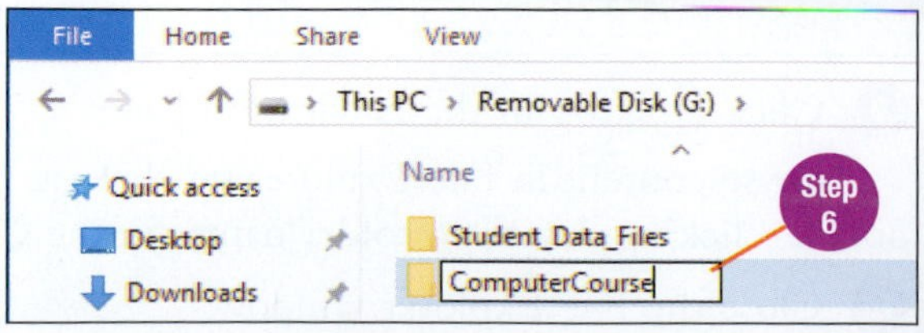

7 Click the View tab and then click the *List* option in the Layout group.

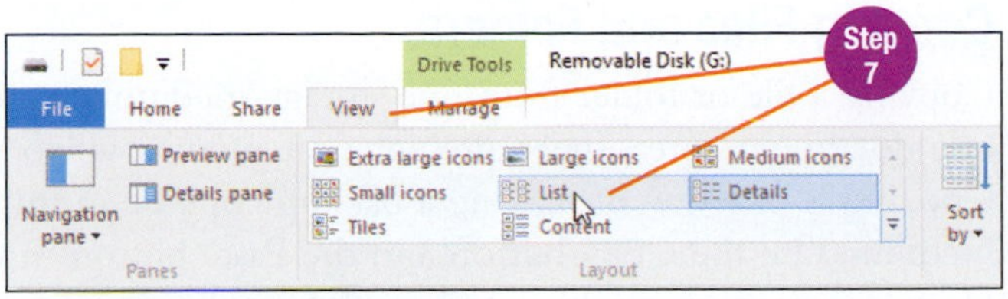

List view displays names with small icons representing each file or folder and without details such as the date or time the file or folder was created or modified, the file type, and the file size. Each folder can have a different view.

8 Click the Home tab. If the ribbon is not currently expanded, a pushpin icon displays below the Close button near the top right of the window. Click the pushpin to expand the ribbon; otherwise, proceed to Step 9.

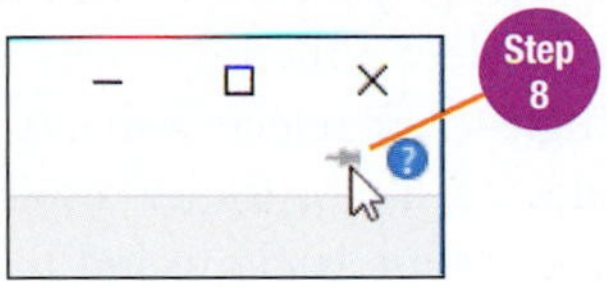

The pushpin expands the ribbon permanently in the window. The pushpin icon changes to an up-pointing arrow (like a caret ^ symbol), which is the Minimize the Ribbon icon.

9 Double-click the *ComputerCourse* folder name in the Content pane.

You have now opened the ComputerCourse folder. File management tasks performed next will occur inside this folder.

10 With the Home tab active, click the New folder button, type ChapterTopicsWork, and then press Enter.

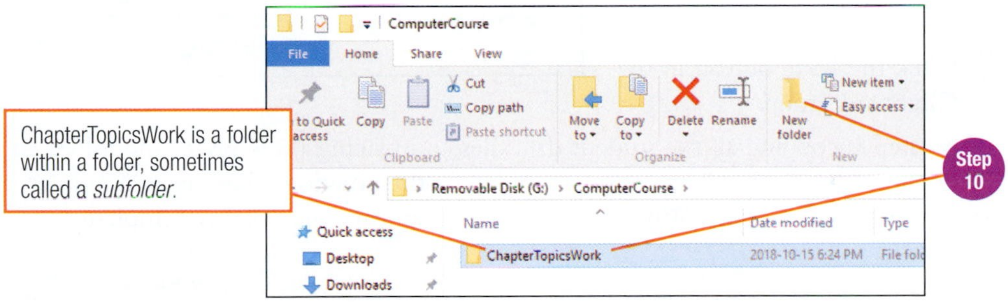

11 Click the New folder button, type Assessments, and then press Enter.

You now have two folders (or subfolders) within the ComputerCourse folder.

12 Click the Up arrow button at the left of the Address bar.

Notice you now see only the ComputerCourse folder and the Student_Data_Files folder. The two folders created in Steps 10 and 11 are no longer visible because they are *inside* the ComputerCourse folder.

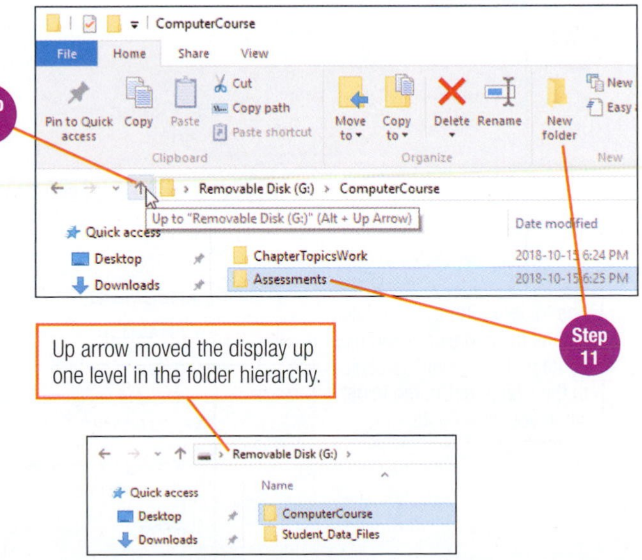

Quick Steps

Create a Folder

1. Click File Explorer icon on taskbar.
2. Navigate to desired storage medium and/or folder.
3. If necessary, click Home tab.
4. Click New folder button.
5. Type folder name.
6. Press Enter.

Oops!

No pushpin icon below the Close button? Then your ribbon is already pinned in the window. Skip Step 8.

App Tip

The terms *folder* and *subfolder* are used interchangeably when a subfolder exists. Windows does not distinguish a subfolder from a folder; however, some people prefer to use *subfolder* to differentiate a folder within the hierarchy on a disk.

App Tip

The Back button (left-pointing arrow) returns the display to the previous folder list.

Copying Files and Folders

Copying a file or folder from one storage medium to another makes an exact copy of a document, spreadsheet, presentation, picture, video, music file, or other object. Copying is one way of making a backup copy of an important file on another storage medium. Use the Copy button and the Paste button in the Clipboard group on the Home tab to copy a selected file or folder.

13 Click to select the folder *Student_Data_Files*.

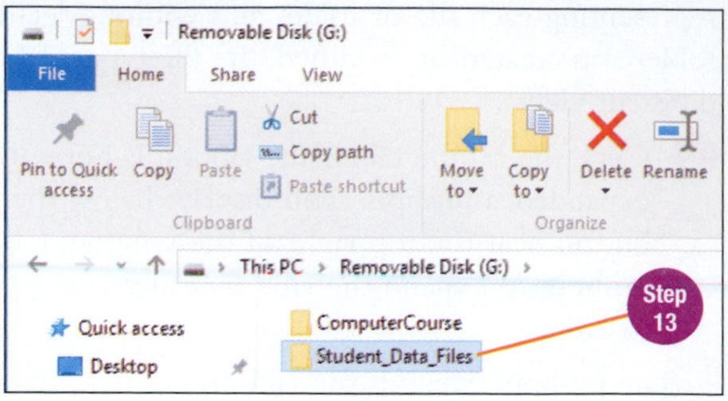

Before you can copy, you must first select a file or folder—a single-click selects a file. A selected file or folder displays with a blue background in the Content pane. On touchscreen devices, a check box also displays next to folder and file names; a check mark in the check box indicates the file is selected.

App Tip

Ctrl + C is the universal keyboard shortcut to Copy.

14 Click the Copy button in the Clipboard group on the Home tab.

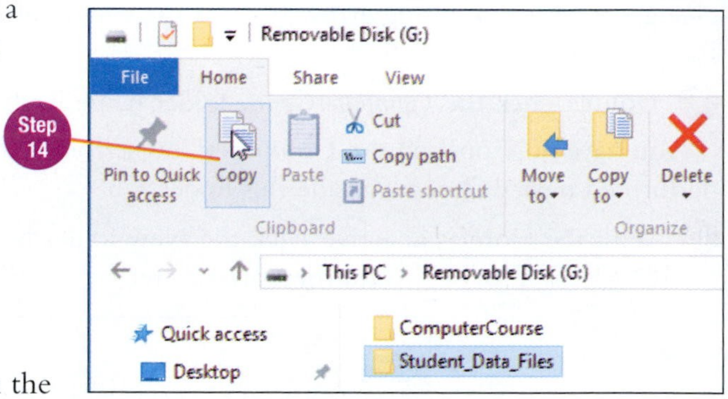

App Tip

Ctrl + V is the universal keyboard shortcut to Paste.

15 Double-click the folder *ComputerCourse* in the Content pane.

16 Click the Paste button in the Clipboard group.

This step is copying all the student data files and placing the copy of the folder and all its contents in the ComputerCourse folder. As the copying takes place, Windows displays a progress message. When the message disappears, the copy is complete.

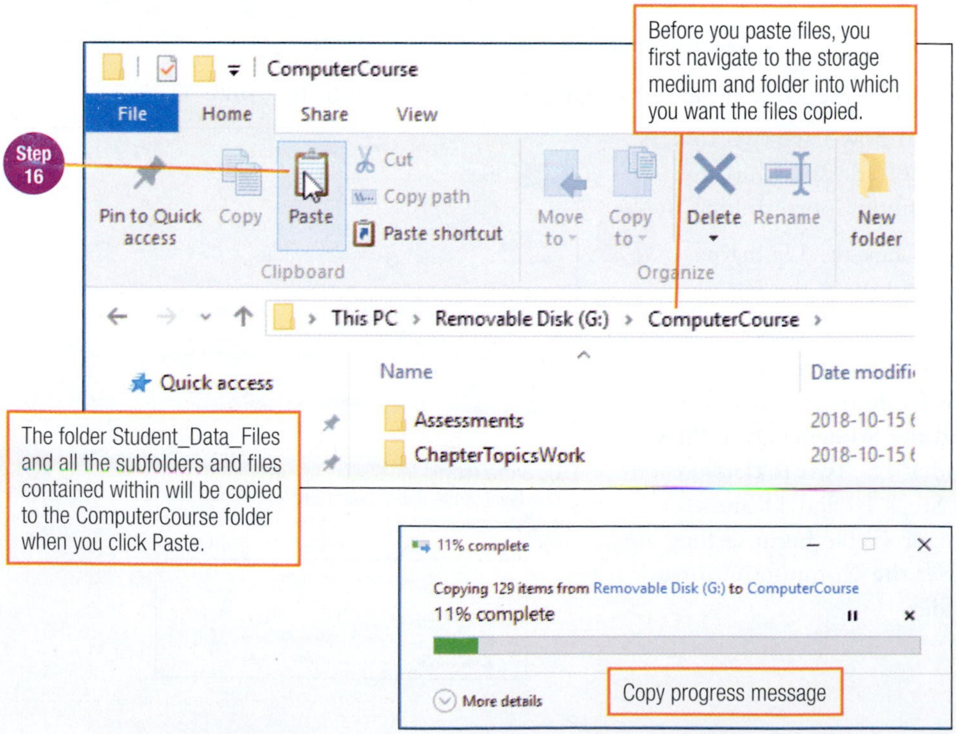

17 Double-click the *Student_Data_Files* folder name.

18 Double-click the *Ch1* folder name.

In the next steps, you will copy individual files to another folder.

19 If necessary, click the View tab and then click List in the Layout group to show only the file names in the Ch1 folder. Skip this step if List view is already active.

20 Click to select ***Lighthouse***, hold down the Shift key, and then click to select ***Winter***.

This action selects all the files, starting with **Lighthouse** and ending with **Winter**. Holding down the Shift key while clicking a file name instructs Windows to select all files from the file name selected first to the file name selected second.

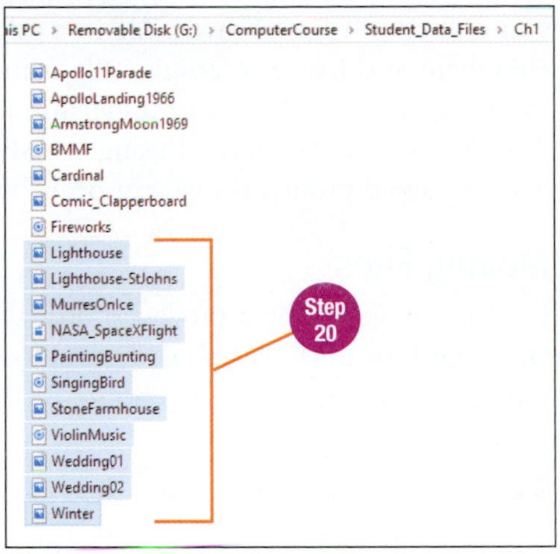

Another way to select multiple files is to hold down the Ctrl key while clicking a file name. Use the Ctrl key if you do not want all the files in between to be selected. In other words, Ctrl + click is used to select multiple files that are not next to each other.

21 If necessary, click the Home tab.

22 Click the Copy button.

23 Click *ComputerCourse* in the Address bar.

Clicking a device or folder name in the Address bar is another way to navigate to devices or folders.

24 Double-click *ChapterTopicsWork* in the Content pane.

25 Click the Paste button.

The selected files are copied into the ChapterTopicsWork folder.

26 Click the Close button to close the File Explorer window.

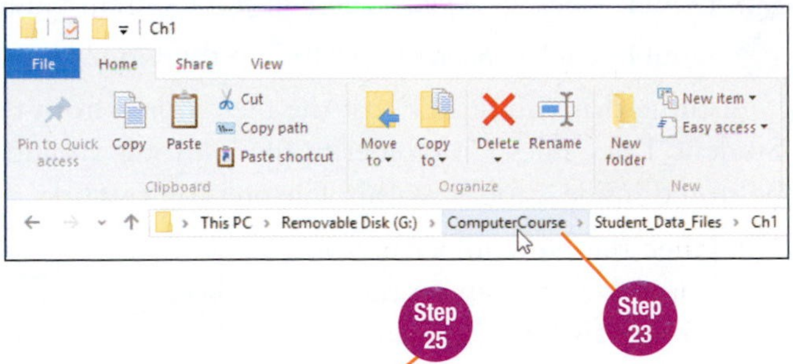

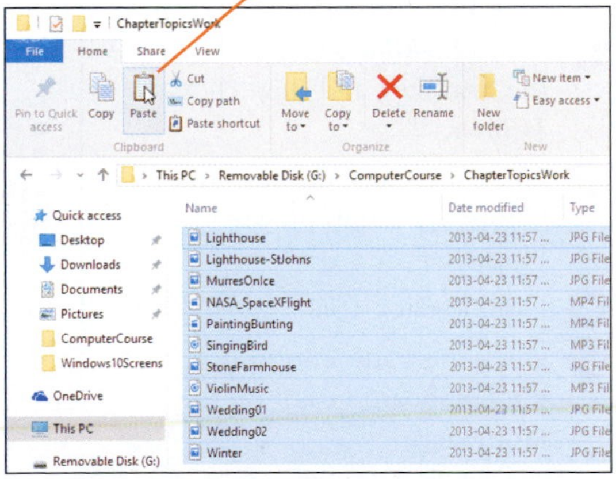

Quick Steps

Copy Files or Folders

1. Open File Explorer.
2. Navigate to source data storage medium and/or folder.
3. Select file(s) or folder(s) to be copied.
4. If necessary, click Home tab.
5. Click Copy button.
6. Navigate to destination storage medium and/or folder.
7. Click Paste button.

Alternative Method: Copying Files or Folders in File Explorer Using Other Methods

- Select files, choose the Copy to button in the Organize group on the Home tab, and then choose the destination folder.
- Select files, right-click inside selection, click Copy, navigate to the destination folder, right-click in Content pane, and then click Paste.
- Drag and drop folders/files from the source location to the destination location.

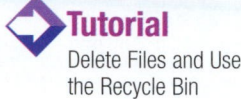

1.11 Moving, Renaming, and Deleting Files and Folders and Ejecting a USB Flash Drive

Skills

Move a file or folder

Rename a file or folder

Delete a file or folder

Empty the Recycle Bin

Eject a USB flash drive

Tutorial
Delete Files and Use the Recycle Bin

File Explorer is also used to move, rename, and delete files and folders. Sometimes you will copy a file or save a file in a folder and later decide you want to move it elsewhere. You may also assign a file name to a file or folder and later decide you want to change the name. Files or folders no longer needed can be deleted to clean up the disk. When you are finished using a USB flash drive, you should properly eject the drive to avoid problems that can occur when files are not properly closed.

Moving Files

Files are moved using a process similar to copying. Begin by selecting files and choosing **Cut** in the Clipboard group on the Home tab in File Explorer. Navigate to the destination location and choose Paste. When files are cut they are removed from the source location.

1. Click the Start button and then click File Explorer in the left pane on the Start menu.
2. Click This PC in the Navigation pane and then double-click the Removable Disk for your USB flash drive in the *Devices and drives* section.
3. Double-click *ComputerCourse* in the Content pane.
4. Double-click *ChapterTopicsWork* in the Content pane.

Assume that you decide that the files copied from the Student_Data_Files Ch1 folder in the last topic should be stored inside a folder within ChapterTopicsWork.

5. Click the New folder button in the New group on the Home tab, type Ch1, and then press Enter.
6. Click ***Lighthouse***, hold down the Shift key, and then click ***Winter***.
7. Click the Cut button in the Clipboard group on the Home tab.
8. Double-click *Ch1*.
9. Click the Paste button in the Clipboard group on the Home tab.

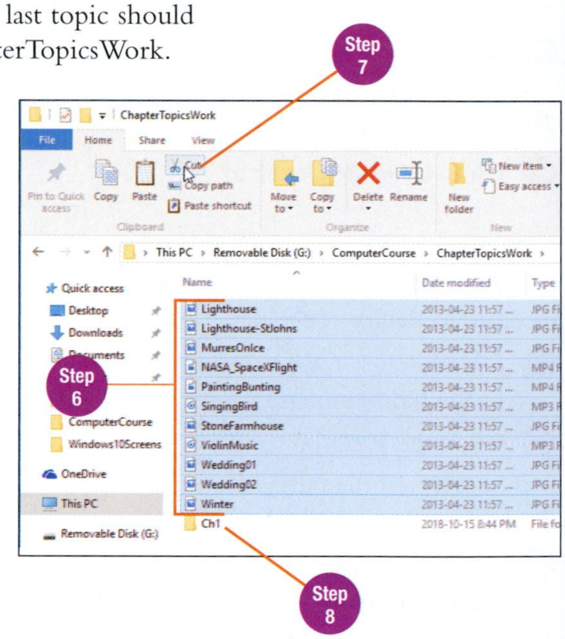

App Tip
Ctrl + X is the universal keyboard shortcut to Cut.

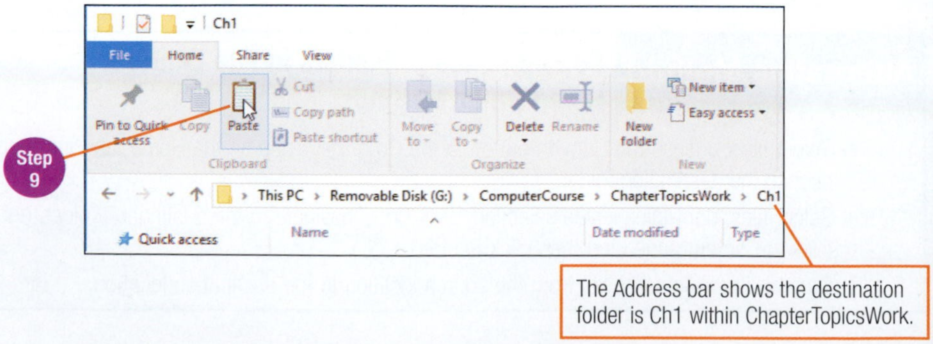

Step 9
The Address bar shows the destination folder is Ch1 within ChapterTopicsWork.

The files are removed from the ChapterTopicsWork folder and placed within the Ch1 folder.

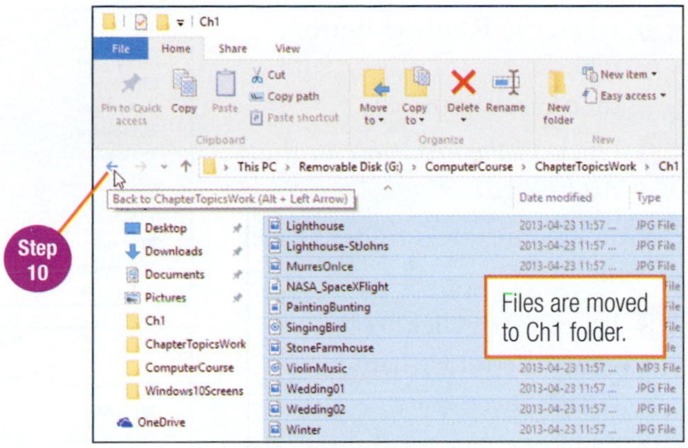

10. Click the Back button to return to the previous list.

Notice the files are no longer in the ChapterTopicsWork folder.

11. Click the Forward button (right-pointing arrow next to Back button) to return to the Ch1 folder.

Quick Steps

Move Files or Folders

1. Open File Explorer.
2. Navigate to source data storage medium and/or folder.
3. Select files or folder to be moved.
4. If necessary, click Home tab.
5. Click Cut button.
6. Navigate to destination storage medium and/or folder.
7. Click Paste button.

Rename Files or Folders

1. Open File Explorer.
2. Navigate to data storage medium and/or folder.
3. Select file to be renamed.
4. If necessary, click Home tab.
5. Click Rename button.
6. Type new name and press Enter.

Renaming Files and Folders

At times you will receive a file from someone else and decide you want to rename the file to something more meaningful to you, or you may decide upon a new name for a file or folder after the file or folder was created. Change the name of a file or folder with the **Rename** button in the Organize group on the Home tab.

12. Double-click ***Winter*** in the Content pane. The photograph opens in the Photos app unless your system is set up to display images in another application. If a message window appears asking *How do you want to open this file?*, double-click Photos to open the picture in the Photos app window.

Assume a friend sent you this picture of a weeping birch tree laden with snow in a winter scene. You decide to rename the picture.

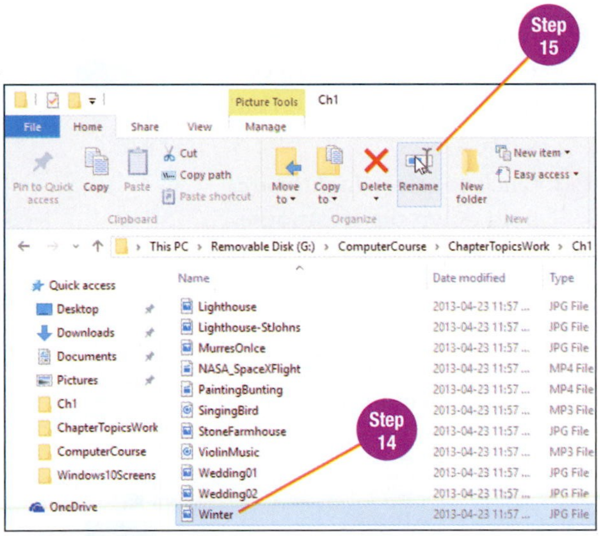

13. Close the Photos app window (or other picture viewing application) to return to the File Explorer window.

14. If necessary, click to select ***Winter*** in the Content pane.

15. Click the Rename button in the Organize group on the Home tab.

16. Type BirchTreeInWinter and then press Enter.

17. Click to select the file named ***ViolinMusic***.

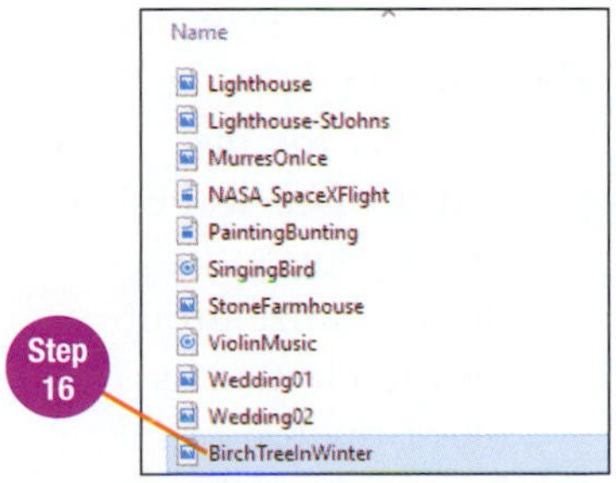

Assume this file is the song Danny Boy played on a violin and recorded by you as you heard the song at an outdoor event.

18. Click the Rename button, type DannyBoyViolin, and then press Enter.

19. Click *ComputerCourse* in the Address bar.

You can rename a folder as well as a file.

20. If necessary, click to select the folder named *ChapterTopicsWork*.

21. Click the Rename button, type CompletedTopicsByChapter, and then press Enter.

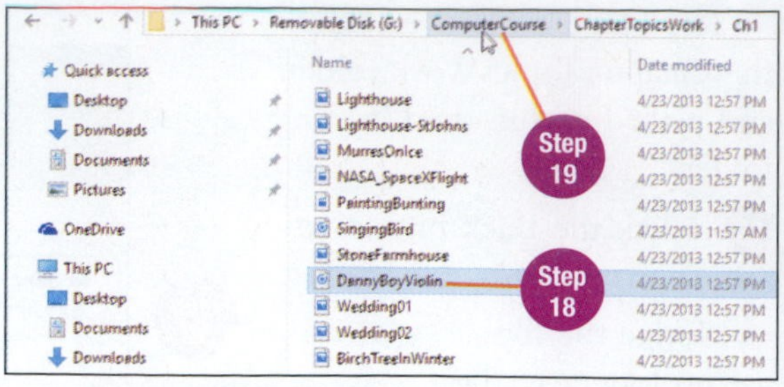

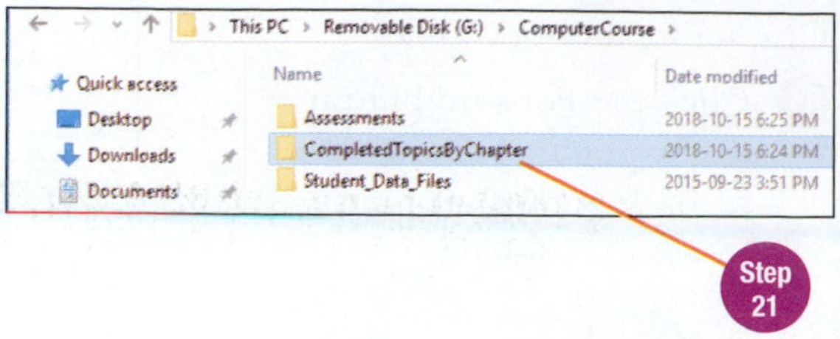

Deleting Files and Folders

> **App Tip**
>
> On each PC, the Recycle Bin is set to hold a maximum number of megabytes (MB). Be aware that when the maximum is reached, some files will be permanently deleted to make room for new deleted files. To check the maximum size, click the Recycle Bin properties button on the Recycle Bin Tools Manage tab.

Delete files or folders when you no longer need to keep them. You should also delete files or folders if you have copied them to a removable storage medium for archive purposes and want to free up space on the local disk. In File Explorer, select the files or folders to be deleted and then click the **Delete** button in the Organize group on the Home tab. Files and folders deleted from the local hard disk are moved to the Recycle Bin. While it is in the Recycle Bin, you can restore the file to its original location if you deleted the file in error. Files deleted from a USB flash drive are not sent to the Recycle Bin; therefore, exercise caution when deleting a file from a USB flash drive.

22. Double-click the folder *CompletedTopicsByChapter* and then double-click the folder *Ch1*.

23. Click to select ***Lighthouse***, hold down the left mouse button and then drag the file to Desktop in the Navigation pane.

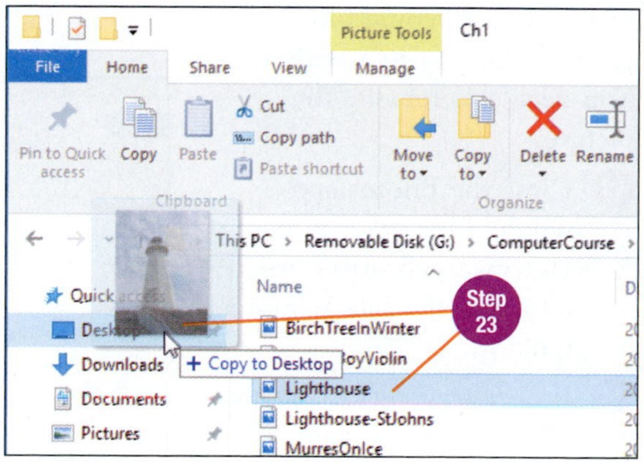

Dragging a file from a folder on one storage medium to a location on another storage medium copies the file.

> **App Tip**
>
> Dragging a file or folder on the same storage medium moves the file. To be sure of the operation you want to perform, drag a file or folder to another location using the right-mouse button. When you release the mouse, a shortcut menu appears at which you can choose to Copy or Move.

24. Click Desktop in the Navigation pane.

25. Click ***Lighthouse*** to select the file and then click the Delete button in the Organize group on the Home tab (click the top of the button—not the down-pointing arrow).

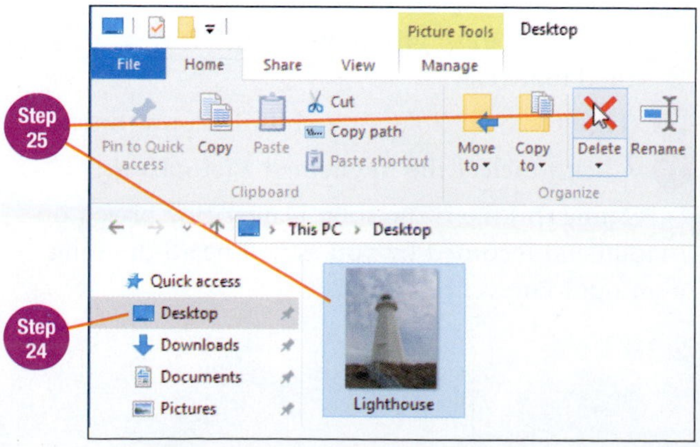

26 Click This PC in the Navigation pane and then double-click the Removable Disk for your USB flash drive in the *Devices and drives* section.

27 Double-click *ComputerCourse*, *CompletedTopicsByChapter*, and then *Ch1*.

28 Click to select ***SingingBird*** and then click the Delete button in the Organize group on the Home tab.

29 Click Yes at the Delete File message box that appears.

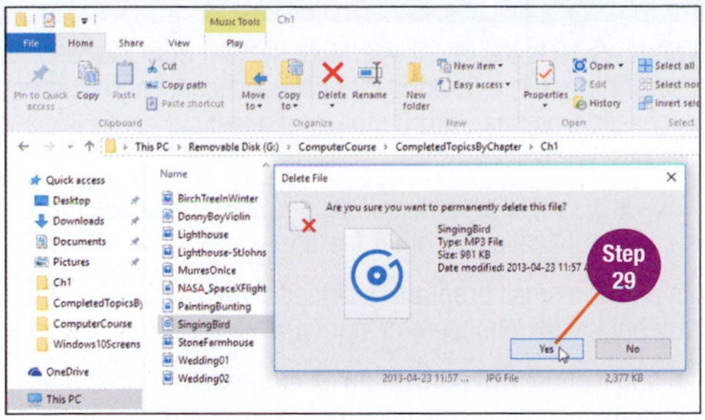

The confirmation message appears when you delete a file from a USB flash drive because the files are permanently deleted, not sent to the Recycle Bin from which the file could be restored.

30 Close the File Explorer window.

31 Double-click the Recycle Bin icon on the desktop.

32 Click the Empty Recycle Bin button in the Manage group on the Recycle Bin Tools Manage tab.

33 Click Yes to permanently delete the file at the Delete File message box.

34 Close the Recycle Bin window.

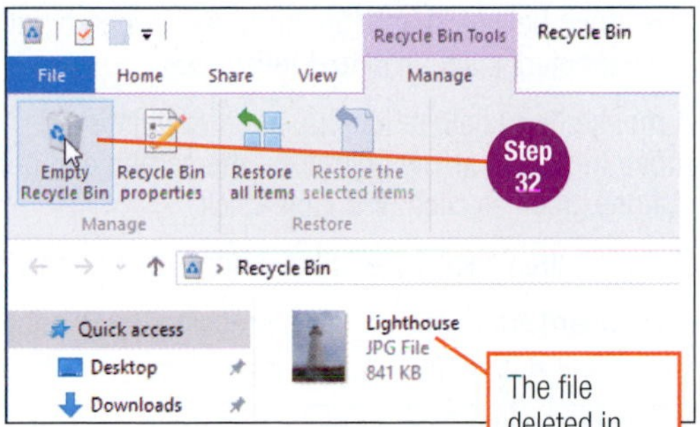

The file deleted in Step 25 was moved here.

When you are finished with a USB flash drive, you should always use the **Safely Remove Hardware and Eject Media** feature before pulling the drive out of the USB port to make sure all files are properly closed to avoid data corruption.

35 Click Show hidden icons (up-pointing arrow) in the notification area on the taskbar and then click the Safely Remove Hardware and Eject Media icon.

36 Click *Eject Storage Media* at the pop-up menu. Your menu may show *Eject Disk* or *Eject USB Flash Drive* depending on the device.

37 Remove your USB flash drive from the computer when the message appears that it is safe to do so.

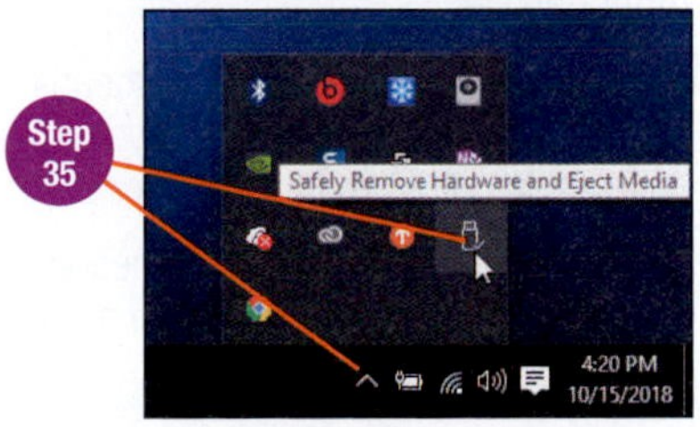

If multiple USBs are plugged in, click the correct drive in the list.

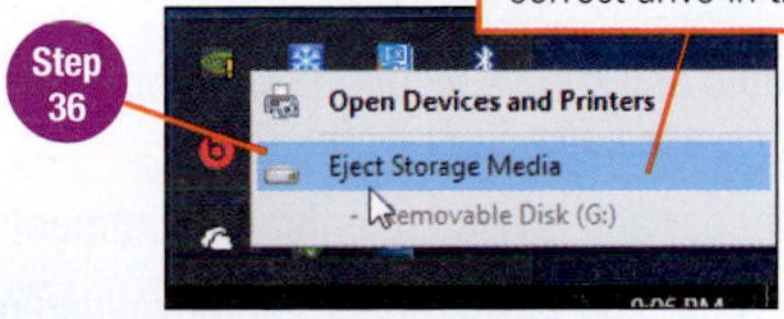

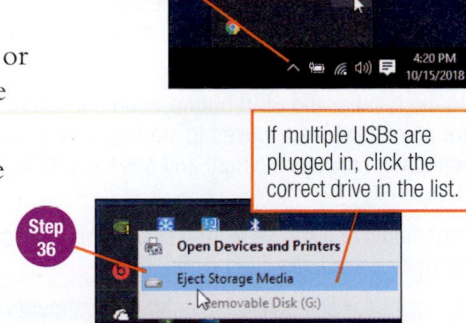

A message appears when the USB can be safely removed.

Safe To Remove Hardware
The 'USB Mass Storage Device' device can now be safely removed from the computer.

Quick Steps

Delete Files or Folders

1. Open File Explorer.
2. Navigate to data storage medium and/or folder.
3. Select file(s) or folder(s) to be deleted.
4. If necessary, click Home tab.
5. Click Delete button.
6. If prompted, click Yes.

Empty the Recycle Bin

1. Double-click Recycle Bin icon on desktop.
2. Click Empty Recycle Bin.
3. Click Yes.

Oops!

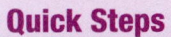

Other files in your Recycle Bin? Other files may appear in your Recycle Bin from previous work. To be safe, select and delete only the ***Lighthouse*** file in this activity.

Oops!

The Safely Remove Hardware and Eject Media icon is not always hidden; you may not have to reveal it with the Show hidden icons up-pointing arrow.

Topics Review

Topic	Key Concepts	Key Terms
1.1 Using Touch, Mouse, and Keyboard Input to Navigate Windows 10	Windows 10 is the latest operating system from Microsoft. The user interface is a desktop that includes icons, a Start menu accessed from the Start button, and a taskbar along the bottom of the screen. A tile is a square or rectangle on the Start menu used to launch an app, application, or other feature. An app is a small program designed for a smartphone, tablet, or notebook with touchscreen input and is mainly for one task. An application is a more complex program that does more tasks than an app, uses full-size keyboards, uses a mouse, and requires more extensive hardware resources. A gesture is an action or motion you perform with your finger or stylus on a touch-enabled device, such as a tap or swipe motion. The touch keyboard appears on-screen when typed characters are expected, such as in text messages. A mouse, trackball, touchpad, or other pointing device is used to move the white arrow pointer on the screen and perform mouse actions, such as click or double-click. Pressing the Windows logo key brings up the Start menu. A keyboard command involves pressing the Windows logo key, Ctrl, Alt, or a function key with a letter.	Windows 10 user interface (UI) Start menu Start button tile app application gesture touch keyboard mouse trackball touchpad pointer keyboard command
1.2 Starting Windows 10 and Exploring Apps	The Lock screen appears when you start Windows or resume use from sleep mode. A user account is a user name and password used to sign in to Windows. Signing in to Windows using a hotmail.com, live.com, or outlook.com email address is considered a Microsoft account and means that your settings are stored online and synced with other devices. Signing in with a local account means that your settings are not shared with other devices, and you do not see live updates on some of the tiles on the Start menu. Once signed in, the desktop appears and the Start menu opens. The desktop has icons to launch programs and a taskbar along the bottom of the screen. On the taskbar, the Start button, search text box, and icons are pinned, which are used to start apps or applications. A notification area at the right end has icons to show system status. The Photos app shows pictures stored on the local PC and from connected accounts such as OneDrive. The Calendar app is used to enter appointments or events. Use the Store app to search for and download new apps. Switch between apps using the app button on the taskbar or by displaying Task View using the Task View icon on the taskbar to click the desired thumbnail.	Lock screen user account Microsoft account local account desktop taskbar search text box notification area Photos app Calendar app Store app Task View

continued…

Topic	Key Concepts	Key Terms
1.3 Using the Search Text Box and Working with Windows	Click in the search text box, type the first few letters of what you are looking for, and then click the item in the search results. The Minimize button reduces a window to a button on the taskbar. Click the Close button to close a window and any content within the window. The Maximize button expands a window size to fill the entire desktop. The Maximize button changes to the Restore Down button when a window is maximized. Use Restore Down to return the window to its previous size. The Snap feature lets you dock a window to the left or right half of the window, or to one of four quadrants by dragging the window left, right, or to a corner. Snap Assist shows thumbnails of open windows when you snap a window and leave part of the screen empty.	Minimize Close Maximize Restore Down Snap Snap Assist
1.4 Using the Notification Area	Click the current date and time at the right end of the taskbar to view a pop-up calendar. Click the Speaker icon to adjust the volume. Click the Network icon to manage network connectivity. A quick action tile displays in Notification panels and is used to turn on or turn off a setting or open a setting window. The Power icon displays the battery status and provides quick actions and links to manage power options. Click the Notifications icon to open the Action Center panel where you can view system messages or access several quick action tiles for managing settings.	quick action tile Action Center
1.5 Locking the Screen, Signing Out, and Shutting Down Windows 10	Lock the screen if you need to leave your PC or mobile device for a short period of time by clicking Start, your account name, and then Lock. Locking leaves all documents and apps open but unavailable to anyone but yourself. Click Start, your account name, and then Sign out to close all apps and documents (also referred to as *logging off*). Perform a shutdown command if you want to turn off the power to the PC or mobile device. Shut down is accessed from the Power option on the Start menu.	sign out shut down

continued…

Topic	Key Concepts	Key Terms
1.6 Using and Customizing the Start Menu	Apps or applications can be started by double-clicking an icon on the desktop, by clicking a tile on the Start menu, by scrolling the options in the left pane on the Start menu, or by typing the first few letters of the name in the search text box. Resize the Start menu by dragging the right border or the top border left, right, up, or down as desired. Right-click a tile and click *Unpin from Start* to remove the tile from the Start menu; locate an app or application in the All apps menu, right-click the name, and click *Pin to Start* to add a tile for the program to the Start menu. Move tiles to a new location on the Start menu by dragging the tile. App tiles are either square or rectangular in shape and can be resized larger or smaller. The Turn live tile off command stops a tile from displaying notifications or status updates; use Turn live tile on to restore the tile's notifications.	Unpin from Start Pin to Start Turn live tile off Turn live tile on
1.7 Personalizing the Lock Screen and the Desktop	Click the Start button, click Settings, then click *Personalization* in the Settings app to personalize the lock screen and desktop options. You can choose from five other pictures for the Lock screen or browse to a picture on your PC or mobile device. You can also change the apps that display notifications on the lock screen. Change the desktop background image and/or the color scheme in the Settings app using the Background and Colors panels.	
1.8 Understanding Files and Folders and Downloading and Extracting Data Files	A file is any document, spreadsheet, picture, or other text or image saved as digital data. When you create a file, you assign a unique file name that allows you to identify and retrieve the file. A folder is a name assigned to a placeholder where a group of related files are stored. A group of files and folders can be compressed and saved as a ZIP file, which bundles everything together in one file with a .zip file extension. When you open a ZIP file, a window opens with the Extract all button used to restore the files and folders from the zipped package, allowing you to use them in their original state and folder structure. File Explorer is the Windows utility used to browse files and perform file management tasks.	file file name folder ZIP file File Explorer

continued…

Topic	Key Concepts	Key Terms
1.9 Browsing Files with File Explorer	In Windows 10, File Explorer opens in the new Quick access view, which shows frequently used and recently used files. The left pane in File Explorer is the Navigation pane, and the right pane is the Content pane. Click This PC in the Navigation pane to view all the available storage devices. You browse content by clicking names in the Navigation pane or double-clicking names in the Content pane. Use options in the Layout group on the View tab to change how the files and folders display in the Content pane. A folder created within another folder is sometimes called a *subfolder*.	Quick access subfolder
1.10 Creating Folders and Copying Files and Folders	Click the New folder button in the New group on the Home tab in File Explorer to create a new folder. A ribbon in File Explorer provides buttons organized into tabs and groups used to carry out file management tasks. Copying a file or folder makes an exact duplicate of a document, spreadsheet, presentation, picture, video, music file, or other object in another folder and/or storage medium. Begin a copy task by first selecting the file or folder to be copied and then use the Copy and Paste buttons in the Clipboard group on the Home tab.	New folder ribbon Copy Paste
1.11 Moving, Renaming, and Deleting Files and Folders and Ejecting a USB Flash Drive	Files are moved by selecting the files or folders, choosing Cut, navigating to the new destination drive and/or folder, and choosing Paste. Click the Rename button in the Organize group on the Home tab, type a new name, and then press Enter to change the name of the selected file or folder. Files deleted from a hard disk drive are sent to the Recycle Bin and remain there until the Recycle Bin is emptied. Files deleted from a USB flash drive are not sent to the Recycle Bin. Select files or folders to be deleted and then click the Delete button in the Organize group on the Home tab. Open the Recycle Bin from the desktop to view files deleted from the hard disk drive. Emptying the Recycle Bin permanently deletes the files or folders. Eject a USB flash drive using the Safely Remove Hardware and Eject Media icon in the notification area on the taskbar.	Cut Rename Delete Safely Remove Hardware and Eject Media

Recheck

Recheck your understanding of the topics covered in this chapter.

Workbook

Chapter review and assessment resources are available in the *Workbook* ebook.

Chapter 2

Navigating and Searching the Web

Precheck

Check your understanding of the topics covered in this chapter.

For many people reading this textbook, the Internet is part of daily life, used to search for information, connect with friends and relatives, watch videos, listen to music, play games, or shop. Mobile devices, such as tablets and smartphones, allow people to browse the web anywhere at any time. Being able to effectively navigate and search the web is a requirement for all workers and consumers.

In this chapter, you will learn definitions for Internet terminology and how to navigate the web using three different web browsers. You will also learn to use search tools to find and print information, view multiple websites in a browsing session, bookmark web pages you visit often, and copy an object from a website to your computer.

***Note:** While the emphasis in this chapter is on using Microsoft Edge, which is included with Windows 10, feel free to work through the topic activities and projects using Google Chrome or Mozilla Firefox. In that case, be aware that for some topics, the steps provided may need to be altered to suit the Chrome or Firefox browser.*

If you are using a computer with Windows 7, Internet Explorer is the web browser from Microsoft included with the operating system. The steps you complete and screens you see will vary from the ones shown in this chapter. If necessary, check with your instructor for alternate instructions.

No student data files are required to complete this chapter.

SNAP If you are a SNAP user, go to your SNAP Assignments page to complete the Precheck, Tutorials, and Recheck.

Learning Objectives

2.1 Describe the Internet, World Wide Web, web browser, web page, hyperlink, and web address

2.2 Navigate the web using Microsoft Edge, use tabs to view multiple websites, and add a page to the Favorites list

2.3 Navigate the web using Chrome, use tabs to view multiple websites, bookmark a page, and use the Find bar

2.4 Navigate the web using Firefox, use tabs to view multiple websites, bookmark a page, use the Find bar, and locate information using the Search bar

2.5 Use a search engine website to find information, refine a search using advanced search tools, and print a web page

2.6 Download a picture from a web page

2.1 Introduction to the Internet and the World Wide Web

Skills

Define Internet

Define World Wide Web

Explain web browser, web page, and hyperlink

Describe web address

The **Internet** or **net** is a global network that links other networks such as individuals, businesses, schools, government departments, nonprofit organizations, and research institutions. The worldwide system of interconnected networks using standardized communication protocols to transmit data is known as the Internet. High-speed communications and networking equipment are used on the Internet to transmit data from one computer to another. For example, a request sent from your computer to display a web page showing flight times from an airline schedule, would travel through several other networks, such as telephone, cable, or satellite company networks, to reach the airline web server.

The World Wide Web

The collection of electronic documents circulated on the Internet in the form of web pages make up the **World Wide Web** or **web**. A **web page** is a document that contains text and multimedia content, such as images, video, sound, and animation (Figure 2.1, page 41). Web pages also contain hyperlinks. A **hyperlink**, also called a **link**, is text, a picture, an icon, or another object on a web page that moves you to another related page when clicked. Web pages are stored in a format that is read and interpreted for display within a **web browser**, which is a software program used to view web pages. A website is a collection of related web pages for one organization or individual. For example, the collection of web pages linked to the main page for your school make up your school website. All the web pages and resources such as photos, videos, sounds, and animations that make the website work are stored on a computer called a *web server*. Web servers are connected to the Internet continuously.

You connect your PC or mobile device to the Internet by subscribing to Internet service through an **Internet service provider (ISP)**, a company that provides access to Internet infrastructure for a fee. The ISP will provide you with the equipment needed to connect to its network, as well as instructions for installing and setting up the equipment to work with your computer and other mobile devices. Once your account and equipment are set up, you can start browsing the web using a browser, such as Microsoft Edge, Chrome, or Firefox.

Many people connect wirelessly to the Internet from multiple devices.

Web Addresses

Each web page has a unique text-based **web address** that allows you to navigate to the page. A web address is also called a **uniform resource locator (URL)**. One way to navigate the web is to type a web address into the Address bar of a web browser. For example, to view the main web page for the publisher of this textbook, you would use the web address *http://paradigm.emcp.com*. If *http* is left out when typing a web address in a browser, it is assumed. For this reason, many people often go to a page by typing only the portion of the address after *http://*. The parts of the web address (URL) https://www.nasa.gov/topics/journeytomars/index.html shown in Figure 2.1 are explained in Table 2.1.

Many times when you go to the web to look for information, you do not know the web addresses for the pages you need. In this case, search tools help you find web pages. You will learn to find web pages using search tools in Topic 2.5.

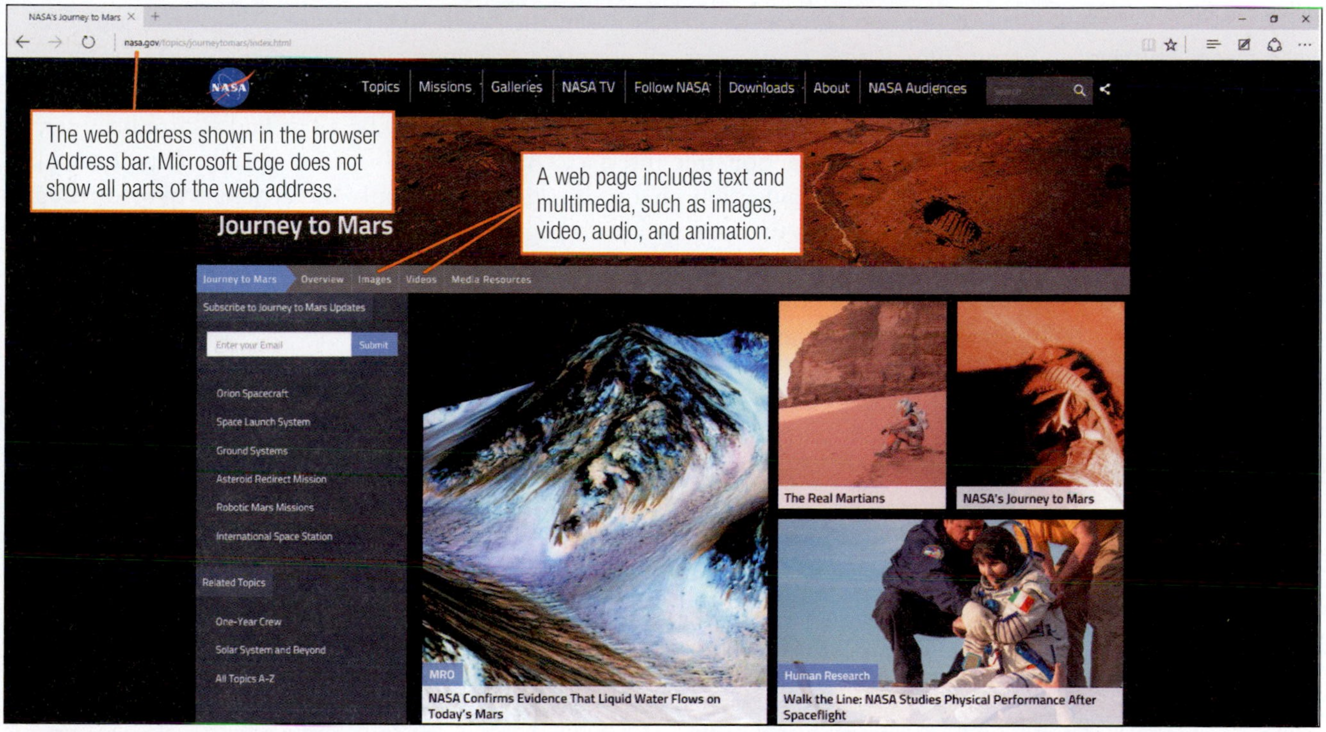

Figure 2.1

A web page from NASA that includes multimedia content is shown in a Microsoft Edge browser window.

Table 2.1

The Parts of the Web Address (URL) https://www.nasa.gov/topics/journeytomars/index.html

Part of URL	What It Means	Examples
https://	Hypertext Transfer Protocol Secure. A set of rules for transmitting data in encrypted format over the Internet. Https is used for exchanging data in online transactions. Other websites are starting to use the protocol to provide authentication of the website and to protect data. Other protocols used are http to transfer data without encryption and ftp to transfer a file.	http ftp https
www.nasa.gov	Domain name. A text-based address for the web server on the Internet that stores the web page. The last three letters (gov) are the extension and tell you the type of organization. Some domain names end with a two-character country code, such as eBay.ca for the Canadian auction site eBay. Using *www* in a domain name is becoming less common. In the *Examples* column are four domain names to show a sampling of a variety of extensions. More extensions are used, such as .net, .biz, .legal, and .realtor.	google.com (Google) harvard.edu (Harvard University) navy.mil (US Navy) wikipedia.org (Wikipedia online encyclopedia)
/topics/journeytomars/	Folder path to the web page. The forward slash (/) and text after the slash are the folder names on the web server where the page is stored.	path folder names will vary
index.html	Web page file name. The file name extension indicates the language used to create the web page. Html stands for *Hypertext Markup Language*, which uses tags to describe content and is widely used.	file names will vary

2.2 Navigating the Web Using Microsoft Edge

Skills

Navigate the web using Microsoft Edge

View multiple websites within the same window

Add a page to Favorites

Tutorials

Get Started with the Microsoft Edge Browser

Use Tabbed Browsing

Save and Reopen Favorites

Microsoft Edge is the web browser included with Windows 10. The new browser replaces the Internet Explorer web browser included with earlier Windows versions. Similar to the Windows apps you learned about in Chapter 1, where an app looks and feels the same on all devices, Microsoft Edge is the browser for all Windows 10 devices, including smartphones and tablets.

When you launch the web browser, the Start page (Figure 2.2) loads with news and information feeds unless the browser has been customized to display another page. For example, many schools will customize browsers to show the student portal when started. Microsoft Edge was designed to be a fast and secure browser, with a clean, distraction-free interface. A new Reading view option strips away all the sidebars and navigation on a web page to show only the article. Microsoft Edge also provides tools to annotate a web page with markup, highlights, handwriting, or typed notes, saving the page as a web note for reading in the Reading list, a OneNote notebook, or shared via email. See Beyond Basics for information on creating a web note.

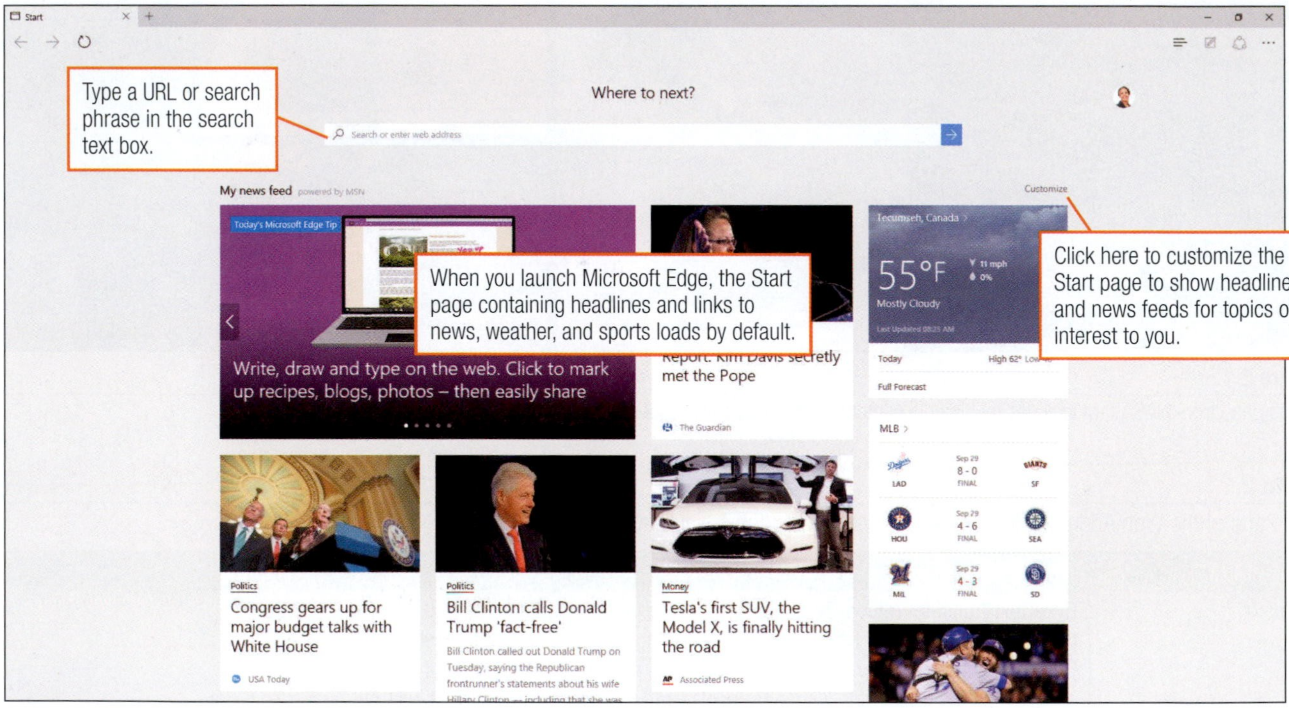

Figure 2.2

The Microsoft Edge Start page is shown.

Starting Microsoft Edge and Displaying a Web Page

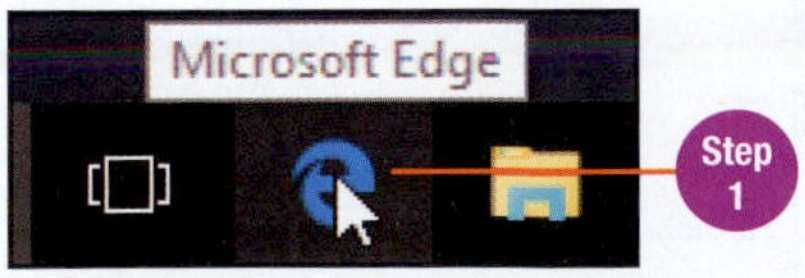

1. Click the Microsoft Edge icon on the taskbar.

   The Microsoft Edge browser window opens to the Start page shown in Figure 2.2 unless the browser has been customized to display another page.

2. With the insertion point positioned in the search text box (contains the dimmed text *Search or enter web address*), type nps.gov/grca and then press Enter. If a message box appears asking you to sign up for national park news, close the message using the × at the top right corner. Review the layout and tools in the Microsoft Edge window shown in Figure 2.3 (page 43).

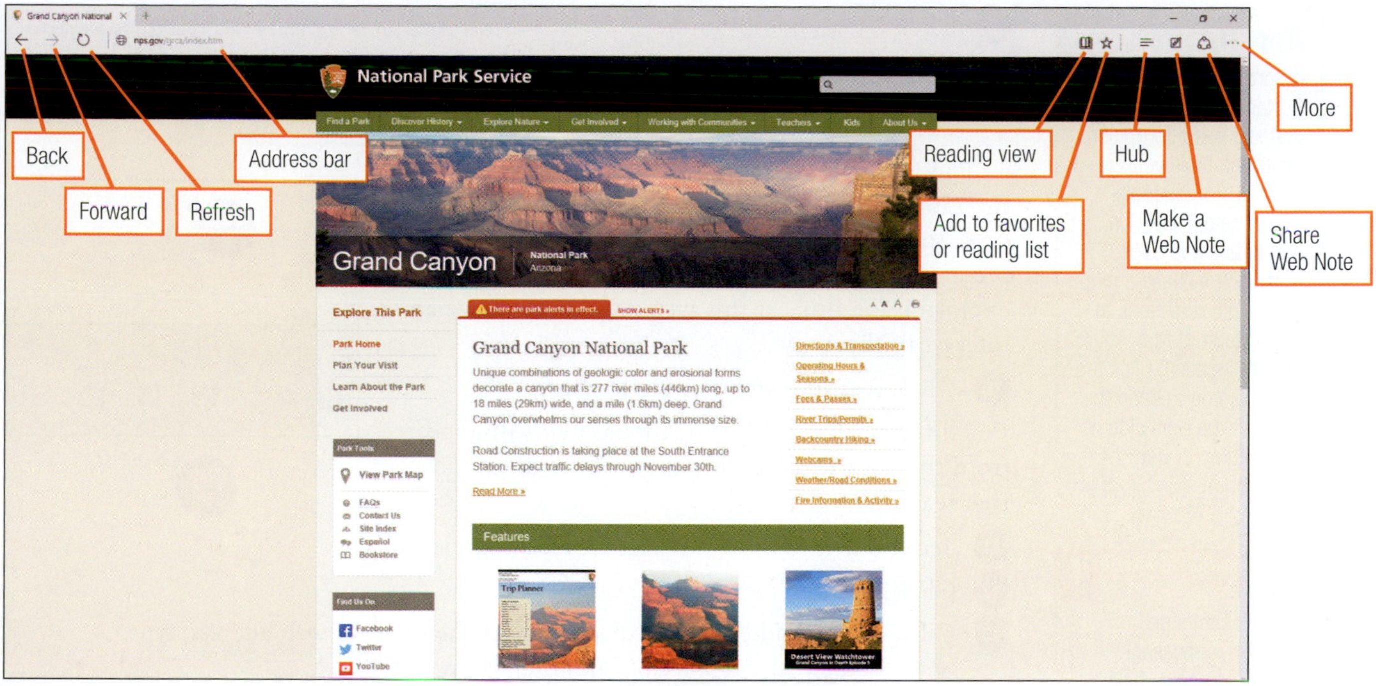

Figure 2.3
The National Park Service Grand Canyon web page is shown in a Microsoft Edge browser window.

3 Click About Us near the top right of the web page.

4 Click Overview.

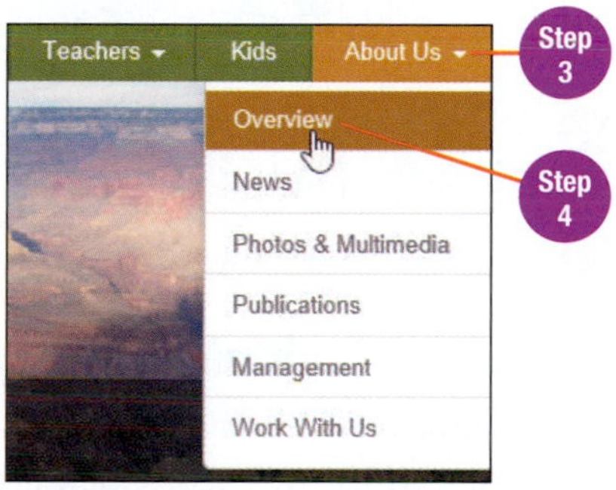

Navigating web pages involves clicking hyperlinks to move from one page to another at a website or to a web page stored at another website. Click **Back** to return to the previous page viewed or click **Forward** to move forward one web page viewed. To display a different web page, click in the **Address bar** to select the current entry, or drag to select the current text in the Address bar, type the web address, and then press Enter.

App Tip

As you begin typing a URL, Microsoft Edge displays matches below the Address bar that begin with similar text. Click the page if it appears in the list before you finish typing.

5 Click in the Address bar or drag to select the existing web address, type loc.gov, and then press Enter.

The Library of Congress home page appears. The starting page for a website is called the **home page**.

6 Click Digital Preservation in the *Resources & Programs* section at the right side of the Library of Congress page.

7 Click Back to return to the Library of Congress home page (move back one web page).

8 Click Forward to return to the Digital Preservation page (move forward one web page).

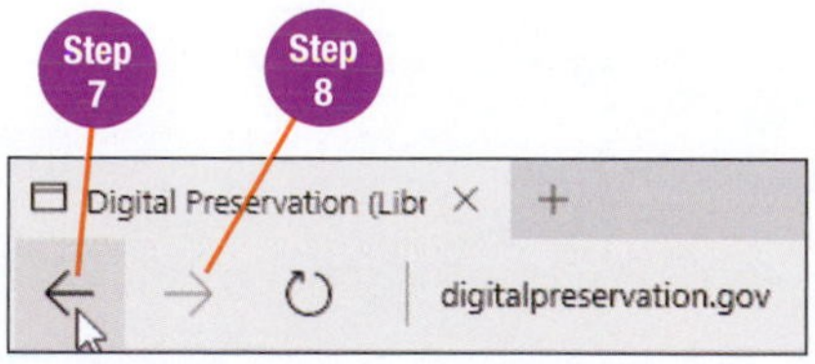

App Tip

If Cortana is active, Cortana may alert you that she has information about the topic you are viewing. For example, if you are displaying a restaurant web page, Cortana may have a map ready with directions to the restaurant from your current location. Click the Cortana icon to open the panel at the right side of the window to view the information.

Oops!

Can't reach page error? This message occurs when you have made a typing mistake when entering the web address. Click in the Address bar and try again.

9. Click View the tips in the *Personal Digital Archiving: Preserving Your Digital Memories* section.

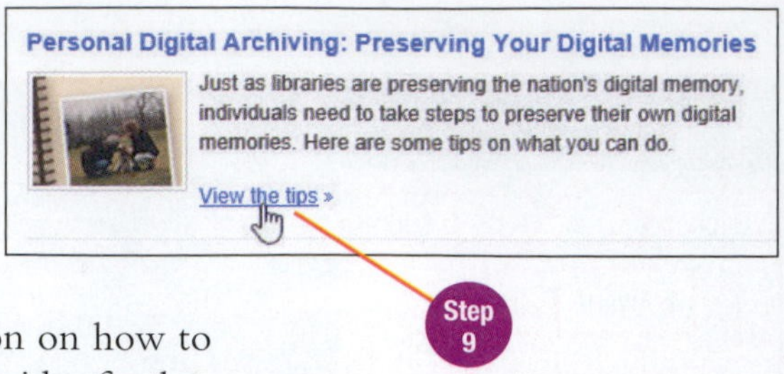

The Personal Archiving page at the Library of Congress contains links to articles with useful information on how to preserve your personal memories. Consider further exploring the links at this web page if you have an interest in this topic.

10. Click Reading view on the toolbar.

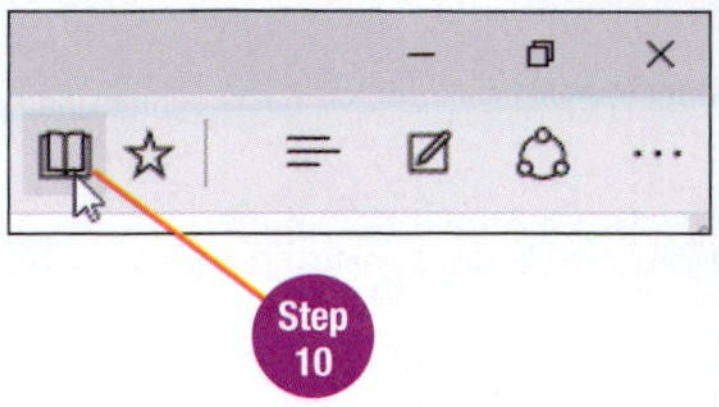

All the sidebars and navigational items disappear from the page leaving only the text for distraction-free reading.

11. Scroll down to view the page in Reading view.
12. Click Reading view to turn off the view.
13. Click in the Address bar or drag to select the existing web address, type www.nasa.gov/topics/history, and then press Enter.

14. Scroll down and click a link to a story that interests you. Read the story using Reading view.
15. Turn off Reading view and then click Back to return to the NASA History page.

Displaying Multiple Web Pages and Adding a Page to Favorites

Open multiple web pages within the same Microsoft Edge window by displaying each page in its own tab. Click **New tab** (displays as a plus symbol) to open a new page in the window. Switch between web pages by clicking the tab for the page you want to view. This is called **tabbed browsing**. The web address for a page you visit frequently can be saved to the **Favorites** list by displaying the page and then using the star on the toolbar to add the page to Favorites.

App Tip

Click Refresh (next to Forward) to update a web page. Sometimes you need to do this if the page stops loading properly or otherwise hangs, or you want to reload the page because the page you are viewing is not the current version.

16. Click New tab (plus symbol) next to the tab for the NASA History page at the top of the window.

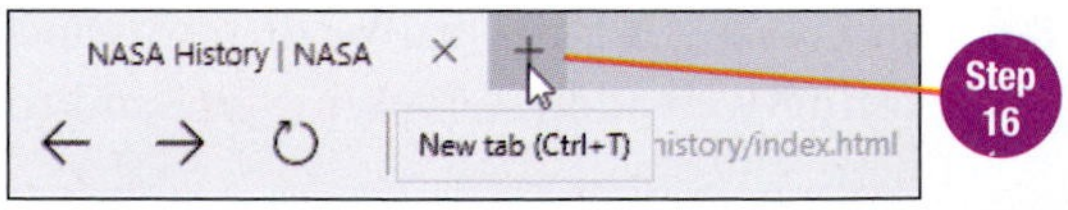

17. Type www.flickr.com/commons in the search text box and then press Enter.

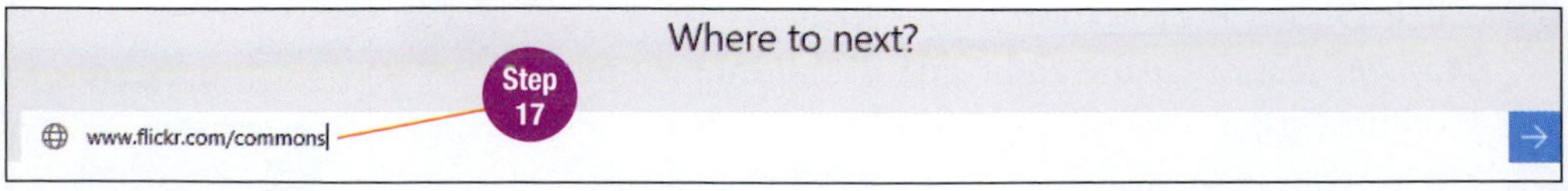

The Commons at flickr.com contains public photography archives from around the world. Images in the commons have no known copyright restrictions. The next time you need a picture or photo for a project, consider sourcing an image from this website.

18 Click the NASA History page tab to change the web page displayed in the window.

19 Click Close tab (displays × on tab) on the NASA History tab.

20 With The Commons page at flickr.com displayed in the window, click the star at the right end of the Address bar on the toolbar.

21 Click the Add button to accept the default option to save the page in Favorites. The page will display in the Favorites list with the name Flickr: The Commons.

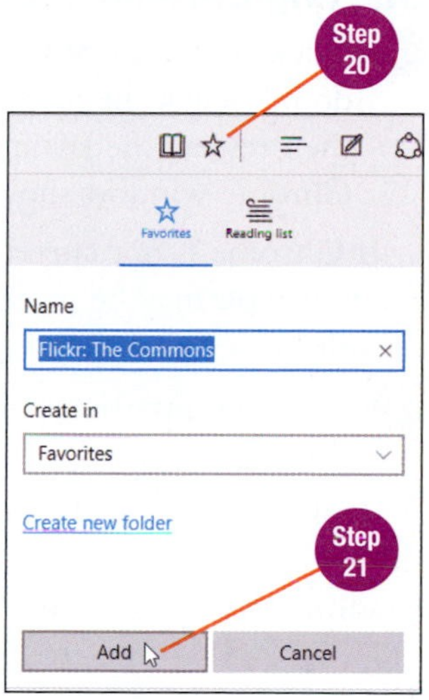

The star turns gold for a page that is added to the Favorites list.

22 Click Hub to open the Hub panel at the right side of the window.

Open the **Hub** to view the Favorites list, Reading list, History list, or Downloads list.

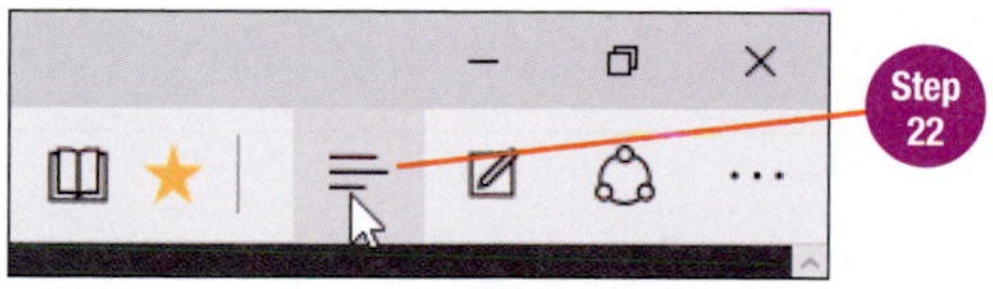

23 If necessary, click the star in the Hub panel to view the Favorites list if another list is currently active.

24 Click Hub to close the Hub panel.

25 Close the Microsoft Edge window.

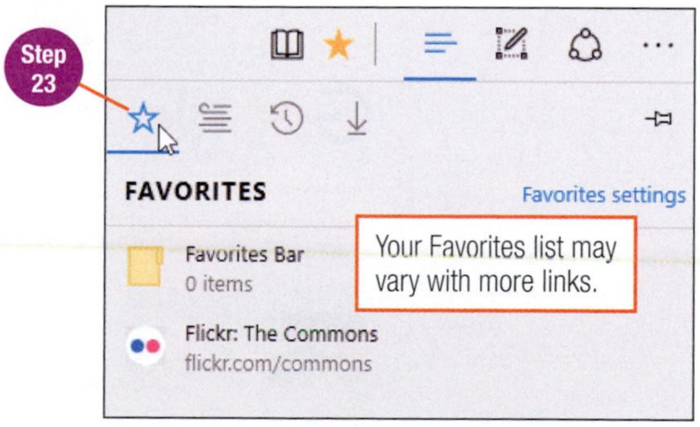

Quick Steps

Start Microsoft Edge
Click Microsoft Edge icon on taskbar.

Display a Web Page
Type web address in the search text box on Start page or in Address bar of existing page.

Display Multiple Web Pages
1. Click New tab.
2. Type URL for new page.
3. Press Enter.

Add link to web page to Favorites
1. Display page in window.
2. Click star on toolbar.
3. Click Add button.

App Tip

Use the Reading list in the Hub to save links to articles or other pages that you want to read at a later time. With the web page displayed, click the star, click Reading list, and then click the Add button.

App Tip

Open the Hub to view your browsing history by clicking the History icon (clock) at the top of the panel.

Beyond Basics Annotating a Web Page in Microsoft Edge

Add a note, highlight text on a page, or draw markings using the tools from Make a Web Note. Click Make a Web Note to display the Web Note toolbar on the current page. The tab control and Web Note toolbar display purple. Use the Pen, Highlighter, Eraser, Typed note, and Clip tools to annotate the web page. When finished, save the annotated page to a OneNote notebook using the Save Web Note button or click the Share Web Note button to send the Web Note in an email message or via OneNote. Click Exit to remove the Web Note tools when finished.

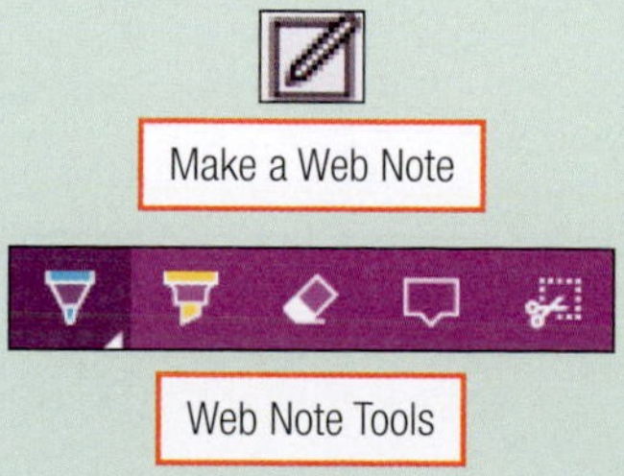

2.3 Navigating the Web Using Chrome

Skills

Navigate the web using Chrome

View multiple websites within the same window

Bookmark a page

Use the Find bar

Oops!

Insertion point not positioned in the blank Address bar? On some tablets and PCs, Chrome starts with the insertion point in the search text box. Click to select the current entry in the web address first, before typing the address at Step 2.

Google **Chrome** is a free web browser for Windows-compatible PCs, Macs, or Linux PCs. Chrome was reported in 2015 by StatCounter (a company that measures web traffic) to be the browser of choice for approximately 50 percent of desktop and tablet users, and 30 percent of smartphone users worldwide. The browser has gained a significant following since its release in 2008 due to its fast page loading and searching directly from the Address bar using the Google search engine. Complete the steps in this topic if you have the Chrome web browser installed on your device; otherwise, skip to the next topic.

Starting Chrome and Displaying a Web Page

1. Click the Chrome icon on the taskbar or double-click the icon on the desktop, and then review the layout and tools in the Chrome window shown in Figure 2.4.

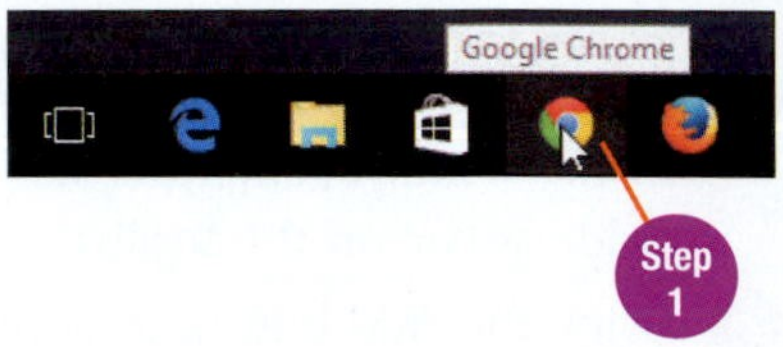

If Chrome is not currently set as the default browser, you may be prompted to set it as the default browser in a message bar below the Address bar.

2. With the insertion point positioned in the Address bar, type techmeme.com and then press Enter.

Techmeme is a technology news site that posts each day the top news headlines from the industry.

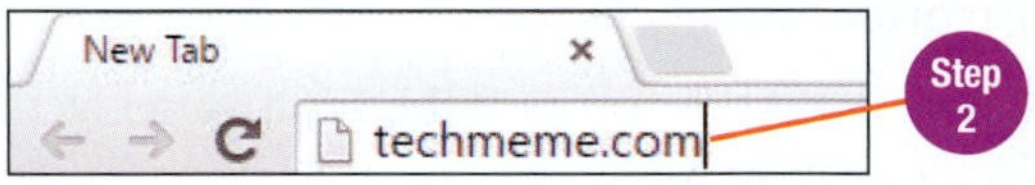

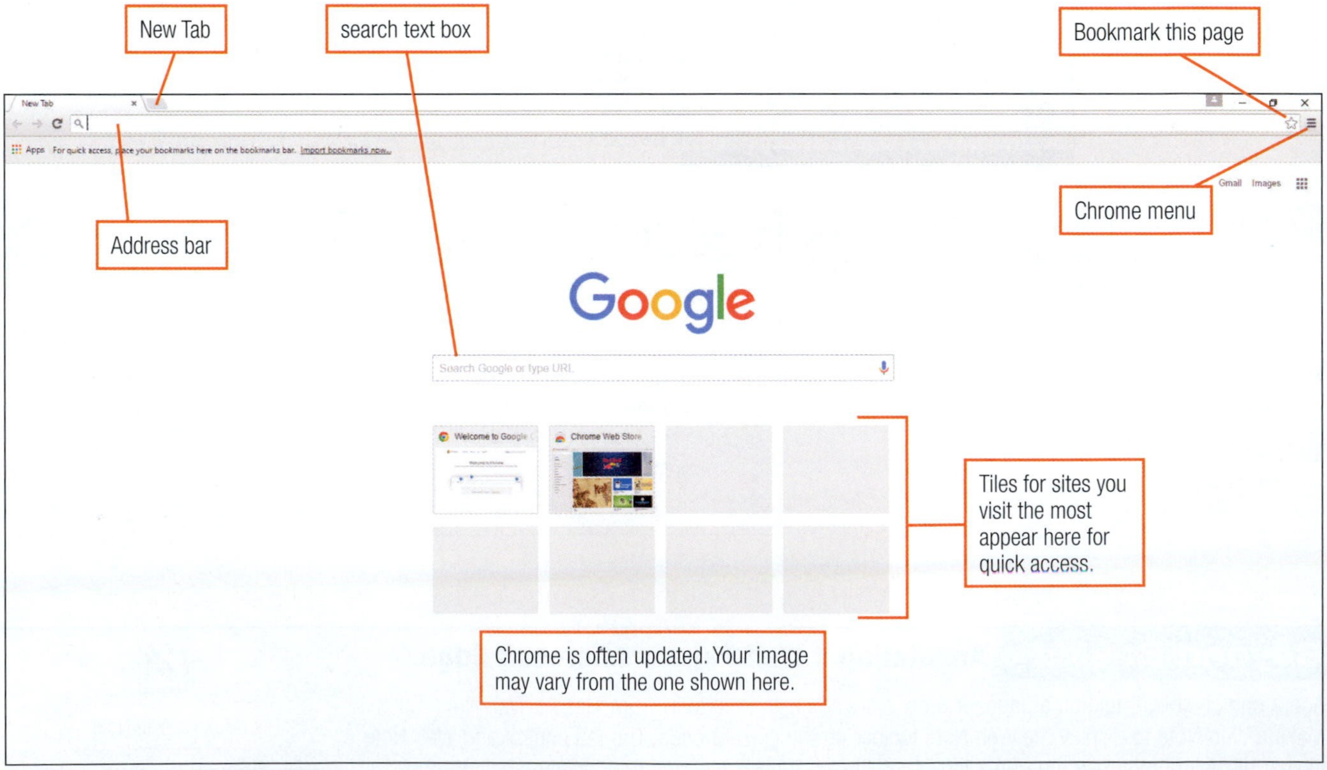

Figure 2.4

The Google search engine is shown displayed in the Chrome browser.

3. Click a link to a technology story that interests you on the Techmeme page.

Techmeme is a content aggregator—a company that searches, collects, and organizes content in one place. Clicking a link to a story on the Techmeme page takes you to another website.

4. Click Back to return to the Techmeme page.

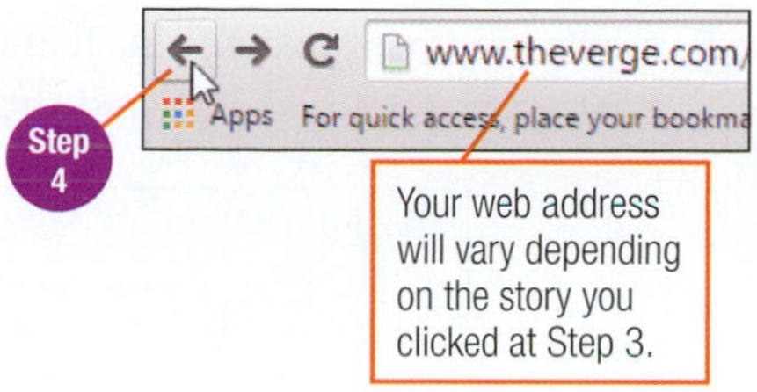

Check This Out

http://CA2.ParadigmCollege.net/Chrome

Go here to download and install Chrome on your PC or mobile device.

Displaying Multiple Web Pages and Bookmarking Pages

Similar to Microsoft Edge, Chrome uses tabbed browsing to display more than one web page within the same browser window. Open a new tab and navigate to a web address to browse a new site without closing the existing web page. Chrome displays a page name at the top of the tab along with a close control. Web pages you visit frequently can be bookmarked by clicking the white star at the end of the Address bar (displays the ScreenTip *Bookmark this page*).

Good to Know

If you sign in to Chrome using your Google account, your bookmarks and other browser preferences are saved and can be accessed on other PCs or mobile devices.

5. With techmeme.com the active web page, click the white star at the end of the Address bar.

The white star changes to gold, and the Bookmark dialog box appears.

6. Click Done to close the Bookmark dialog box.

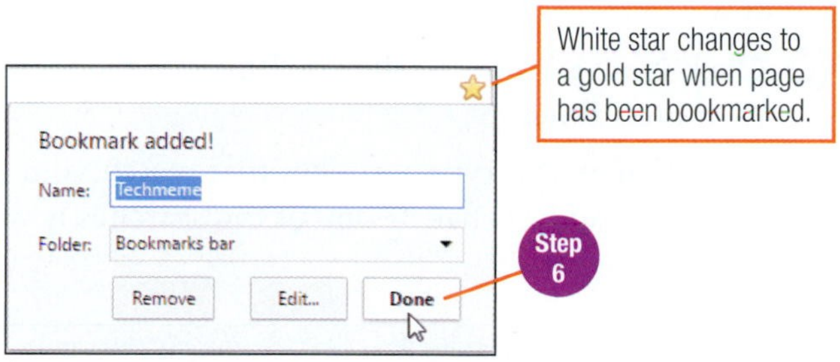

The **Bookmarks bar** displays below the Address bar and is turned on by default when Chrome is installed. To turn the Bookmarks bar off or on, display the menu system by clicking the **Chrome menu** (displays three bars, often called a *hamburger button*) near the top right of the window.

Good to Know

A button or icon with three bars is called a *hamburger button* because it resembles a hamburger patty between a top and bottom bun. The button is commonly used in apps to indicate a menu.

7. Click the Chrome menu (displays as three bars with the ScreenTip *Customize and control Google Chrome*) and then point to *Bookmarks*. A check mark next to *Show bookmarks bar* (shown below) means that the bar is turned on. In that case, click in a blank area away from the menu to close the menu; otherwise, click *Show bookmarks bar* to turn the bar on.

App Tip

By default, bookmarks are added to the bookmarks bar, which is docked below the Address bar.

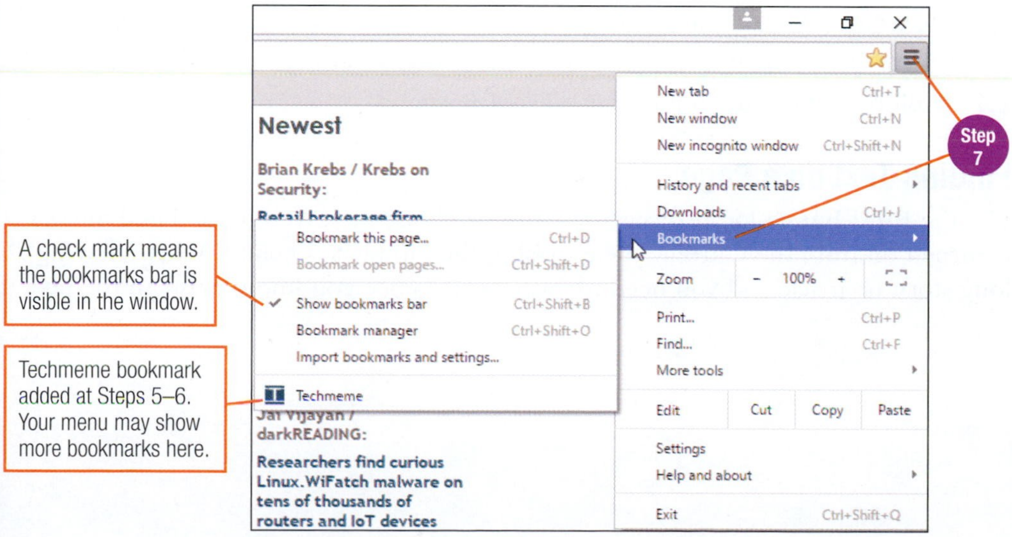

8. Click New tab next to the Techmeme tab to open a new page in the window, type www.youtube.com, and then press Enter.

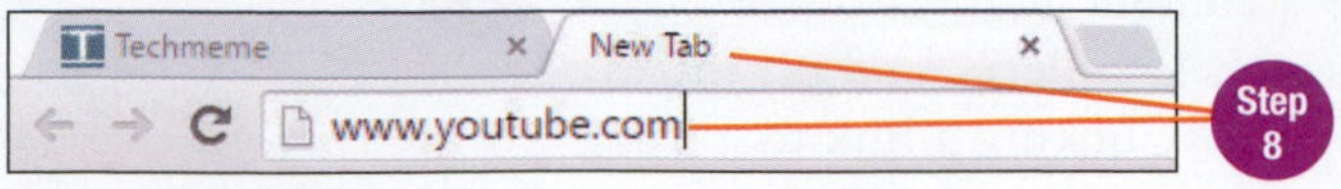

9. Click the white star and then click Done to add youtube.com to the Bookmarks bar.

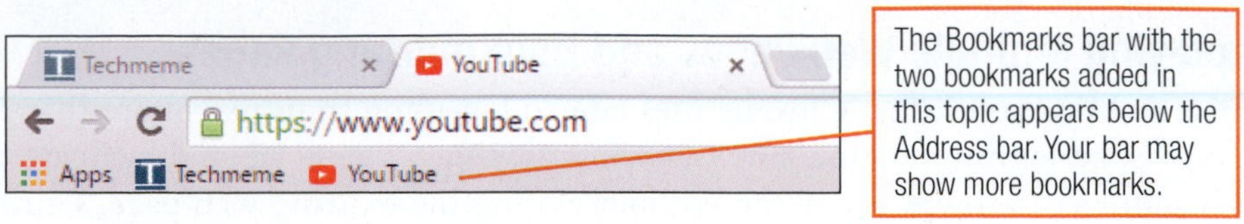

Searching the Web from the Address Bar

> **App Tip**
> Go to *Settings* on the Chrome menu to change the default search engine in the *Search* section on the Settings page.

Like Microsoft Edge, Chrome allows you to type a search phrase in the Address bar. Search results from Google (or other default search engine) appear in the window.

10. Click New tab next to the YouTube tab, type seven wonders of the world, and then press Enter.

Notice that as you type, searches that match your entry appear in a drop-down list below the Address bar. If one of the searches is what you are looking for, click the entry in the list.

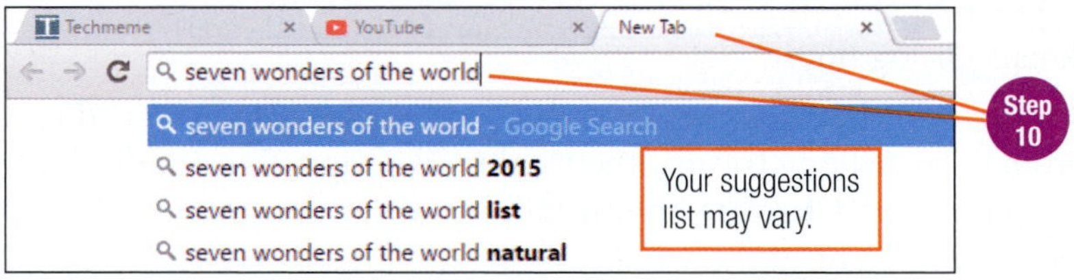

11. Click Images for seven wonders of the world in the Google search results and then scroll down to view the pictures.
12. Click in the Address bar to select the current web address, type great wall of china, and then press Enter.
13. Click Great Wall of China - Wikipedia, the free encyclopedia, then scroll down to review the *Wikipedia* page about the Great Wall of China.
14. Scroll back up to the top of the *Wikipedia* page.

Finding Text on a Page

> **App Tip**
> In Microsoft Edge the Find bar is accessed by clicking More, then *Find on page.*

Use the **Find bar** to locate a specific word or phrase on a web page. The Find bar is turned on from the Chrome menu. Using the Find bar is helpful when viewing a long story or article and you need to locate a reference you know exists in the text.

15 Click the Chrome menu and then click *Find*.

The Find bar opens at the right side of the window below the bookmarks bar with the insertion point positioned in the Find bar text box.

16 Type first emperor in the Find bar text box.

The currently selected match is shaded with an orange background on the page, and the number of matches found on the web page displays in the Find bar next to the find text. Additional matches below the current selection are shaded yellow.

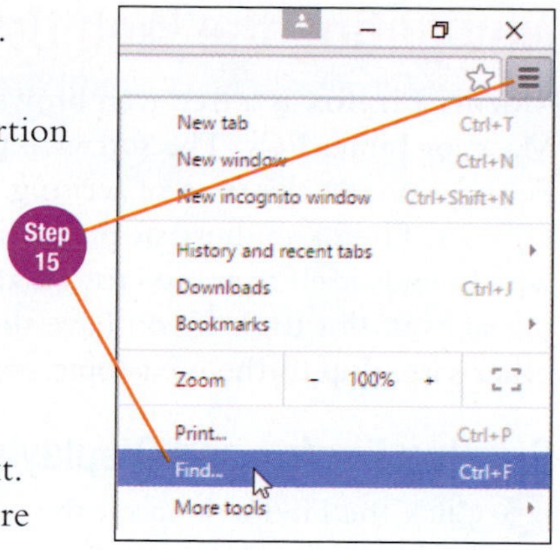

17 Click Next (down-pointing arrow) on the Find bar to scroll the page to the next occurrence of *first emperor*.

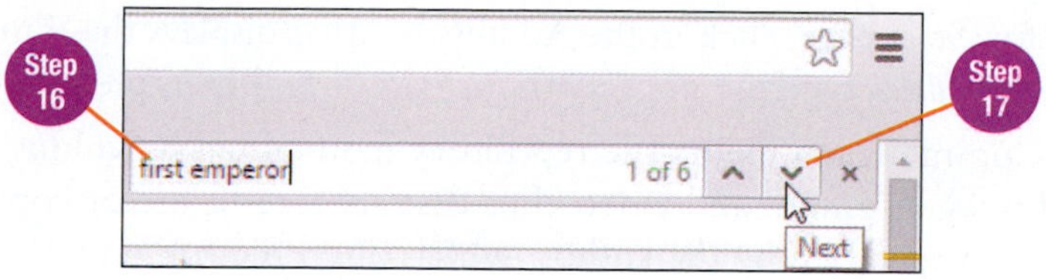

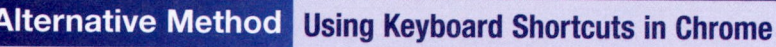

18 Continue clicking Next until you have seen all occurrences.

19 Close the Chrome window.

Quick Steps

Start Chrome
Click Chrome icon on the taskbar or double-click the icon on the desktop.

Display a Web Page
Click in Address bar, type URL, and then press Enter.

Display Multiple Web Pages
1. Click New tab.
2. Type URL for new web page.
3. Press Enter.

Bookmark a Web Page
1. Display desired web page.
2. Click white star.
3. Click Done.

Find Text on a Web Page
1. Click Chrome menu.
2. Click *Find*.
3. Type text to find.
4. Click Next for each occurrence.

Alternative Method Using Keyboard Shortcuts in Chrome

Use these shortcut keys to perform routine actions faster in Chrome:

Open a new tab	Ctrl + T
Show or hide Bookmarks bar	Ctrl + Shift + B
Turn Find bar on	Ctrl + F

Beyond Basics Incognito Browsing in Chrome

Click the Chrome menu and then click *New incognito window* to open a new tab for private browsing. Web pages you visit while using an incognito tab will not appear in the browser history or search history, and any cookies that are created are automatically deleted after all incognito windows are closed. Be aware that browsing using incognito tabs does not prevent an employer or ISP from tracking the websites you visit because they use special software to monitor usage.

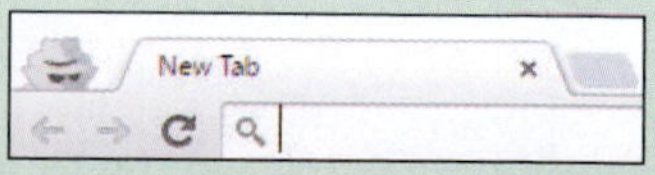

Incognito tab

2.4 Navigating the Web Using Mozilla Firefox

Skills

Navigate the web using Firefox

View multiple websites within the same window

Bookmark a page

Use the Find bar

Use the Search bar

Mozilla **Firefox** is a free web browser that runs on Windows-compatible PCs, Macs, or Linux PCs. The software program is published by the nonprofit Mozilla Foundation. At the time of writing, Firefox was the third most popular web browser. Firefox enthusiasts prefer the nonprofit open source software environment, which lends itself to more customization options in the Firefox browser. Complete the steps in this topic if you have the Firefox web browser installed on your device; otherwise, skip to the next topic.

Starting Firefox and Displaying a Web Page

1. Click the Firefox icon on the taskbar or double-click the icon on the desktop. Click Not now if prompted to set Firefox as the default browser. Review the layout and tools in the Firefox window shown in Figure 2.5.

2. At the Firefox Start page, click in the Address bar that displays the dimmed text *Search or enter address*, type commons.wikimedia.org, and then press Enter.

Wikimedia Commons is a media file repository maintained by volunteers. Go to this site to find images, sound, and video clips that are free to use or copy by following the terms specified by the author, which often require only that you credit the source.

Check This Out ✓

http://CA2.ParadigmCollege.net/Firefox

Go here to download and install the Firefox web browser on your PC or mobile device.

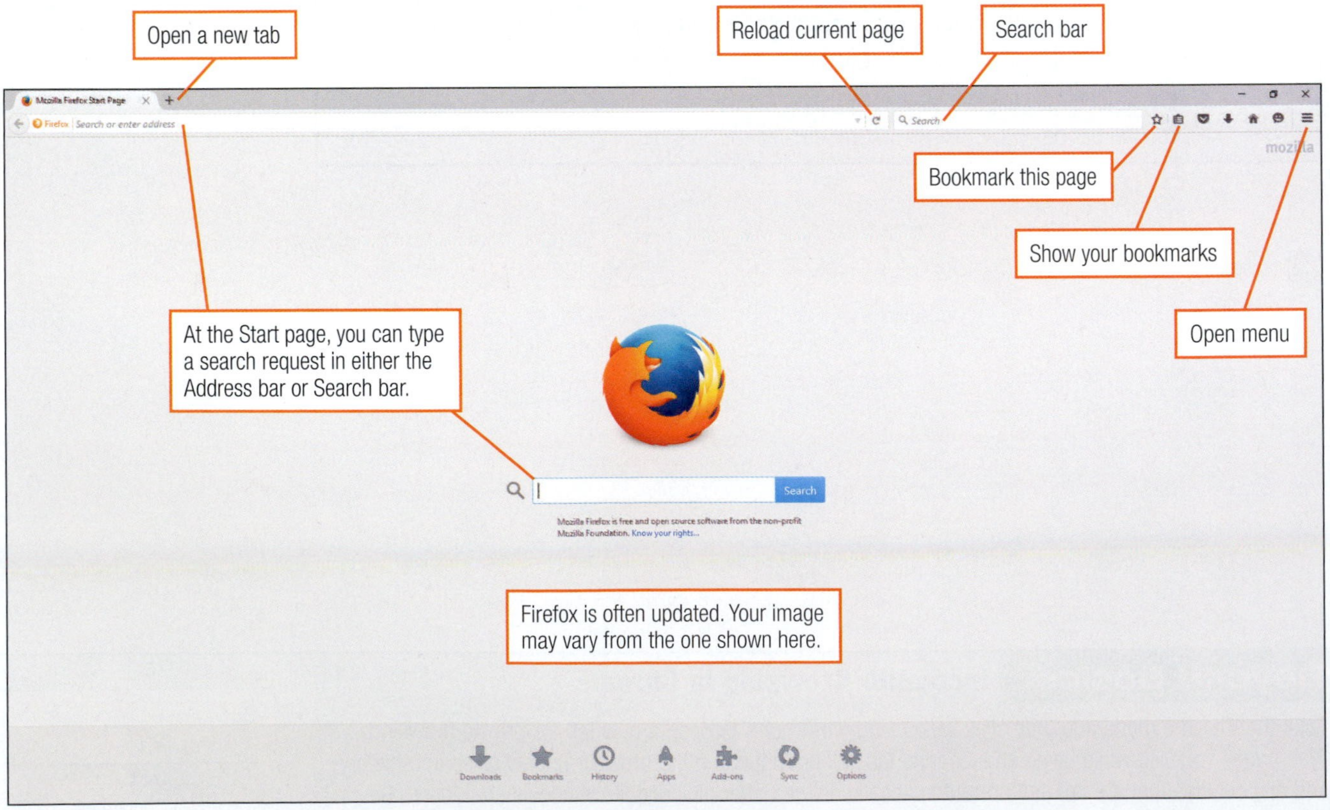

Figure 2.5

The Firefox window is shown.

3. Click in the *Search Wikimedia Commons* text box near the top right of the Wikimedia Commons page that displays the dimmed word *Search*, type clownfish, and then press Enter or click Go (magnifying glass).

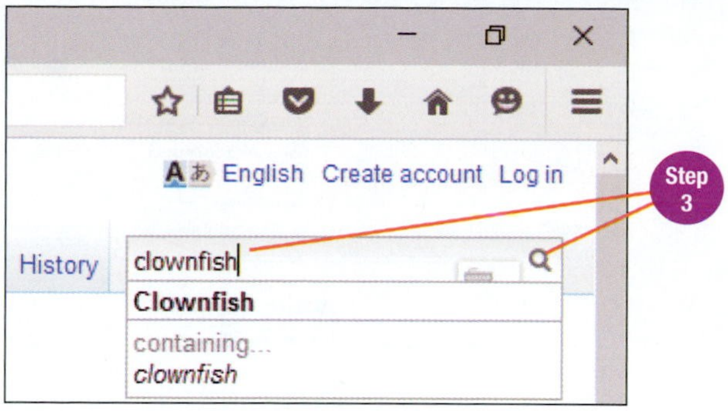

4. Scroll down and view the pictures of clownfish.

Good to Know

At the time of writing, more than 28 million free-use images, sound clips, and other media files were available at Wikimedia Commons.

Displaying Multiple Web Pages and Bookmarking Pages

Similar to Microsoft Edge and Chrome, Firefox provides for tabbed browsing. Click **Open a new tab** (displays as a plus symbol), type a web address in the Address bar, and then press Enter to display a new page in its own tab. Web pages you visit frequently can be saved by clicking the star on the toolbar next to the Search bar (displays the ScreenTip *Bookmark this page*). Click **Show your bookmarks** located on the toolbar next to the star to display the bookmarks menu, which is used to navigate to a bookmarked page or turn on the Bookmarks toolbar.

5. Click the star on the toolbar (displays the ScreenTip *Bookmark this page*).

The star turns blue for a bookmarked page.

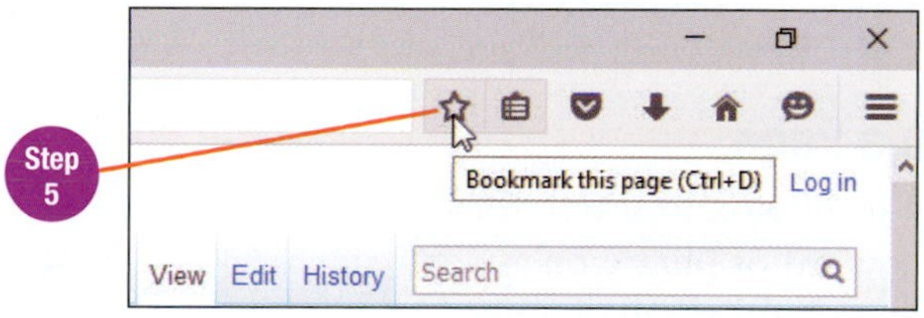

6. Click Open a new tab (displays as a plus symbol) next to the Wikimedia tab. If a message box opens on the new page with information about updates made to New Tab, click the Got it! button.
7. If necessary, click in the address bar on the new page. Type wikitravel.org and then press Enter.

Wikitravel is a worldwide travel guide written and updated by travelers.

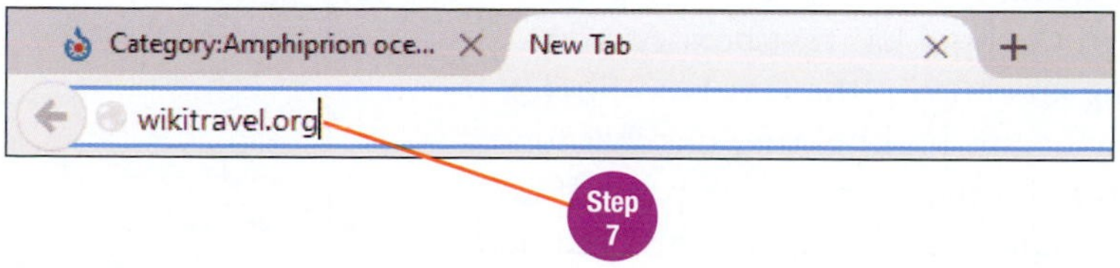

8. Click the star to bookmark the page.

App Tip

Firefox includes a Bookmarks toolbar that displays below the Address bar. Turn on the Bookmarks toolbar from the Show your bookmarks menu. Add a web page to the Bookmarks toolbar by displaying the page and then dragging the page tab onto the Bookmarks toolbar.

9. Click Show your bookmarks next to the star on the toolbar, click *Recently Bookmarked*, and then click *Category:Amphiprion ocellaris - Wikimedia Commons* at the side menu.

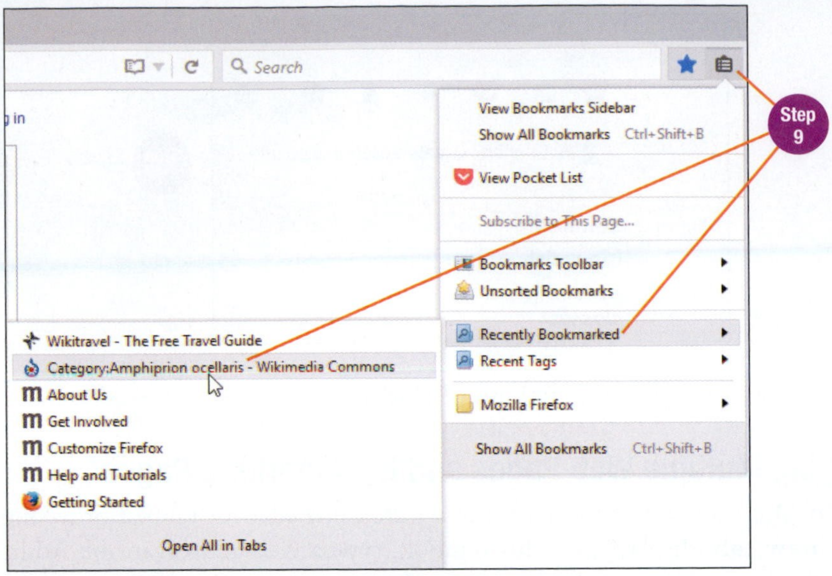

10. Click Close Tab (displays as × on the tab) in the second tab titled Category:Amphiprion ocellaris - Wikimedia Commons to close the page.

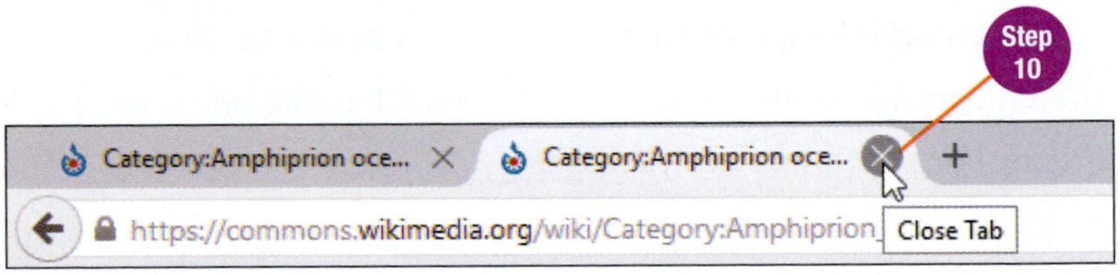

Finding Text on a Page

Open the Find bar in Firefox to search for all occurrences of a word or phrase on a web page. The Find bar is useful when you need to quickly locate a specific reference or other text on a page.

11. Click Open menu (displays three bars) at the end of the toolbar and then click *Find*.

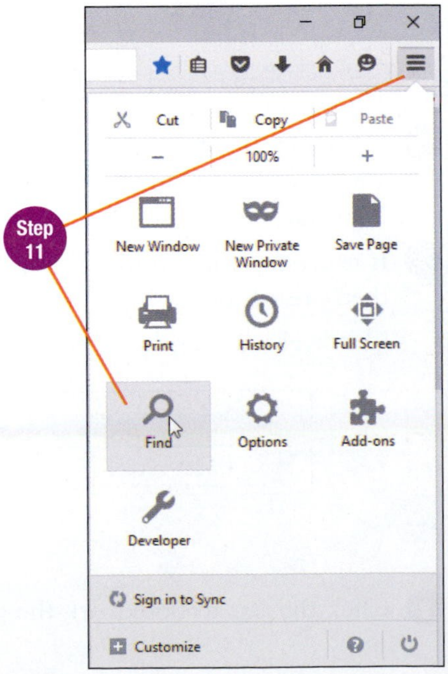

The Find bar opens at the bottom left of the Firefox window with an insertion point positioned in the Find bar text box. As you begin typing an entry in the text box, Firefox immediately begins highlighting matches for the search text on the current web page. If no matches are found, Firefox shades the Find box pink. Use the next and previous navigation buttons to move to each occurrence of the search word or phrase.

12 With the insertion point positioned in the Find bar text box (contains dimmed text *Find in page*), type aquarium.

The first matched occurrence of the search text is shaded green on the page.

13 Click Next to move to the next occurrence of *aquarium* on the page.

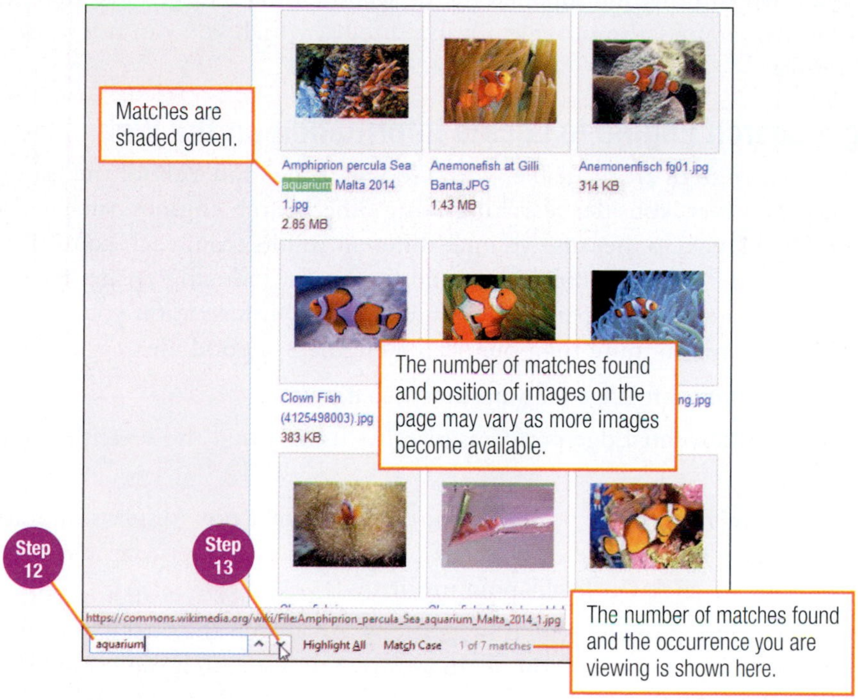

14 Continue clicking Next until you return to the first occurrence on the page.

15 Press Esc or click Close find bar (displays with an ×) at the right end of the Find bar.

Searching the Web Using the Search Bar

Search for information using a search engine, such as Google, Yahoo, or Bing, by typing a search word or phrase in the **Search bar** next to the Address bar in the Firefox window.

16 Click in the Search bar, type tropical fish, and then press Enter or click Search (right-pointing arrow).

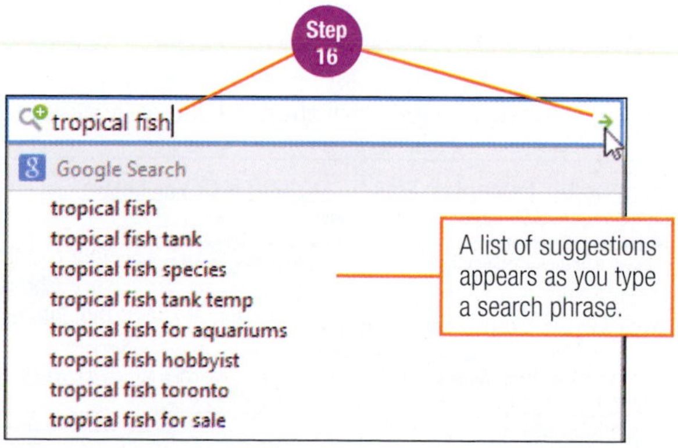

17 Click a link to a web page that interests you from the search results list.

18 Close the Firefox window.

Quick Steps

Start Firefox
Click Firefox icon on taskbar or double-click icon on desktop.

Display a Web Page
Click in Address bar, type URL, and then press Enter.

Display Multiple Web Pages
1. Click Open a new tab.
2. Type URL for new web page.
3. Press Enter.

Bookmark a Web Page
1. Display desired web page.
2. Click star.

Display a Recently Bookmarked Page
1. Click Show your bookmarks.
2. Click *Recently Bookmarked*.
3. Click desired bookmark.

Open the Find Bar
1. Click Open menu.
2. Click *Find*.

Search Using the Search Bar
Type search phrase in Search bar and then press Enter.

App Tip

Choose a different search engine for a search by clicking the magnifying glass in the Search bar and then clicking the desired search engine at the drop-down list. Click *Change Search Settings* at the drop-down list to change the default search engine that is used when searching.

2.5 Searching for Information and Printing Web Pages

Skills

Use search tools to find information on the web

Narrow search results by applying advanced search options

Print a web page, including selected pages only

Tutorials

Use Search Engines to Find Content

Print a Web Page

A **search engine** is a company that indexes web pages by keywords and provides a search tool with which you can search their indexes to find web pages. To create indexes, search engines use a program called a **spider** or **crawler** that reads web pages and other information supplied by the website owner to generate index entries. Search engines also provide advanced tools, which you can use to narrow search results.

Using a Search Engine to Locate Information on the Web

Several search engines are available, with Google, Bing, and Yahoo! the leading companies; however, consider searching using other search engines, such as Dogpile, Ask, and DuckDuckGo, because you get different results from each company. Spider and crawler program capabilities and timing for indexing create differences in search results among companies. Depending on the information you are seeking, performing a search in more than one search engine is a good idea.

1 Click the Microsoft Edge icon on the taskbar.

By default, Microsoft Edge performs searches using Bing, the search engine from Microsoft.

2 With the insertion point positioned in the search text box (displays dimmed text *Search or enter web address*) on the Start page, type cover letter examples and then press Enter or click Go (right-pointing arrow).

Notice that Bing provides search suggestions that match the characters you type in a drop-down list as soon as you begin typing. Click a search suggestion in the list if you see a close match.

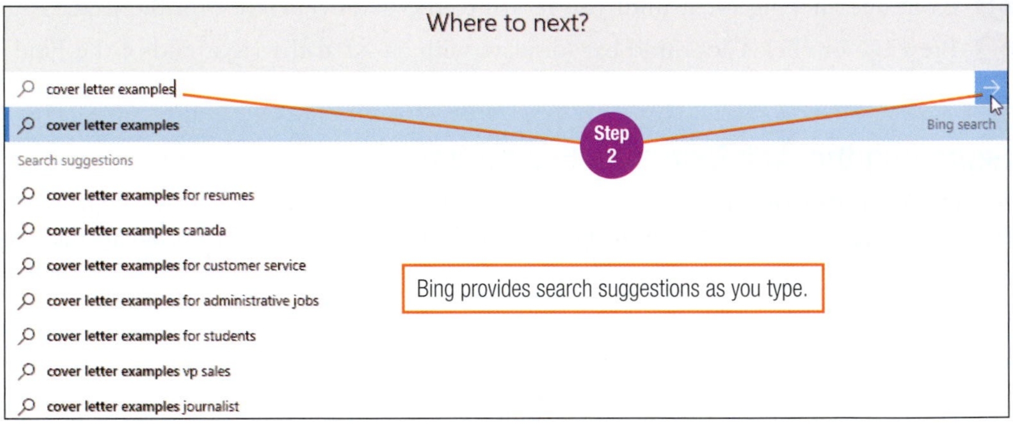

3 Scroll down the search results page and click a link to a page that interests you.

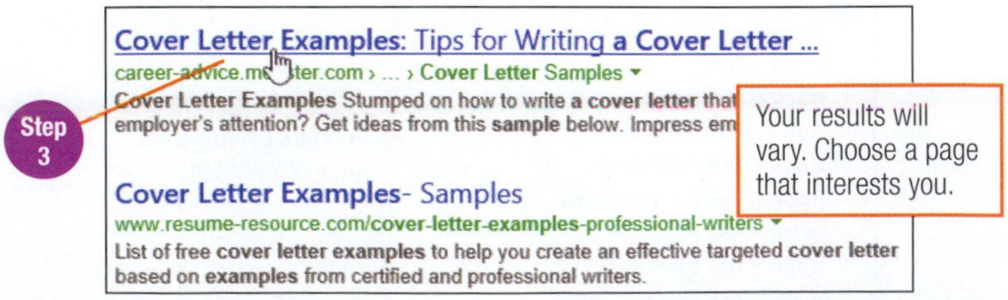

Check This Out

http://CA2.ParadigmCollege.net/Dogpile

Go here to perform a search using a metasearch search engine. Metasearch search engines send your search phrase to other search engines and show you one list of search results from the wider group.

4. Read a few paragraphs about cover letters at the page you selected.
5. Click Back to return to the search results list.
6. Click in the Address bar or drag to select the current web address in the Address bar, type yahoo.com, and then press Enter.
7. With the insertion point positioned in the search text box, type cover letter examples and then press Enter, or click the Search Web button.

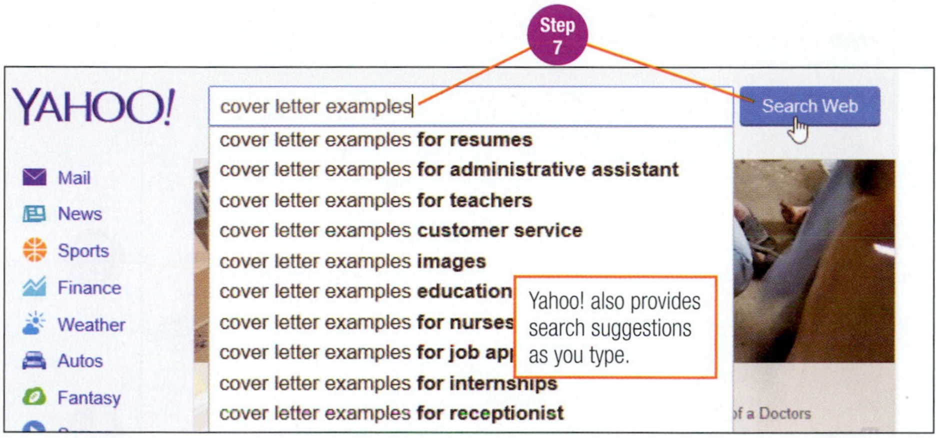

> **App Tip**
> Click a category above a search box or along the top of a search engine web page to restrict search results to a specific type of content such as Images, Videos, Maps, or News.

8. Scroll down the search results page. Notice that some links are to the same web pages that you saw in the Bing search results; however, the same page may be in a different order in the list or you may notice new links not shown by Bing.

Using Advanced Search Options

In both Bing and Yahoo!, the search results for the cover letter examples resulted in millions of links in the results pages. Search engines provide tools to help you narrow the search results. Each search engine provides different tools. Explore the options at the search engine you prefer or look for a help link that provides information on how to use advanced search tools.

9. Click in the Address bar or drag to select the current web address, type google.com, and then press Enter.
10. With the insertion point positioned in the search text box, type cover letter examples, and then press Enter.
11. Click the Options button (displays as gear icon near top right of the page), and then click Advanced search at the drop-down list.

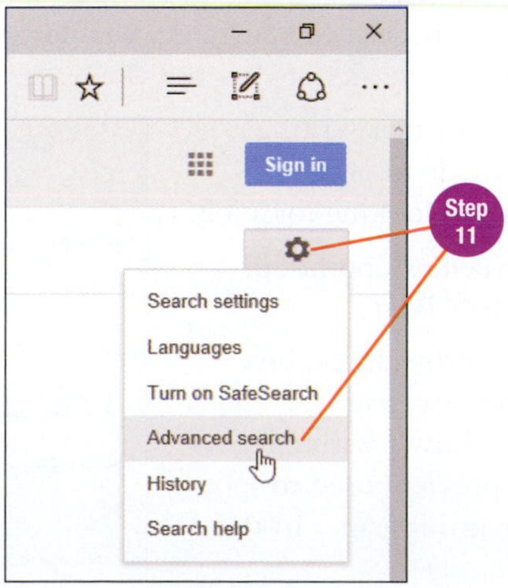

App Tip

The Google advanced search tools include specifying words in an exact order, key words to include or exclude, and restricting searches to a specific file format, country, or language.

12 Click in the *site* or *domain* text box, and then type edu. You may need to scroll down the screen to locate the option.

An edu domain is restricted to US accredited postsecondary institutions.

13 Click the Advanced Search button near the bottom of the Advanced Search page.

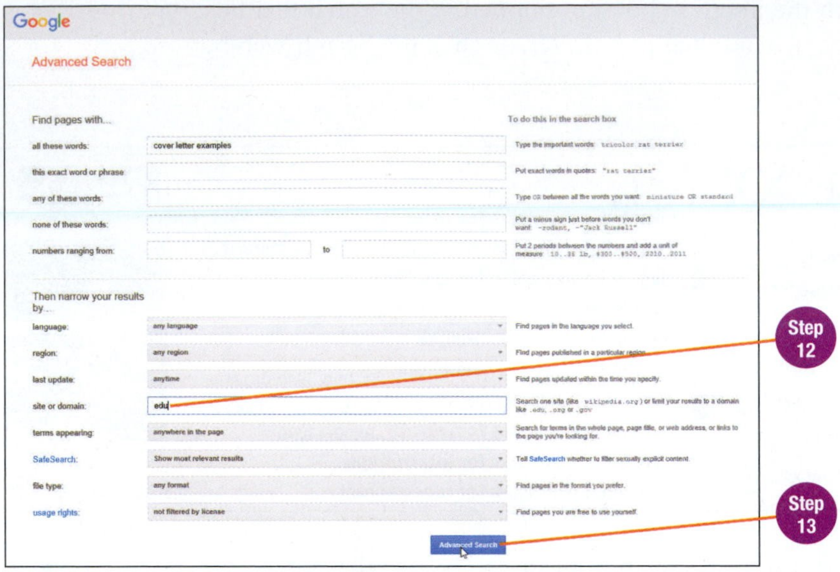

App Tip

Narrowing a searh to edu domains limits pages in the search results to those from accredited US postsecondary institutions.

14 Click Search tools above the search results, click Any time, and then click Past month.

The search results list is now significantly reduced from the millions in the prior results list.

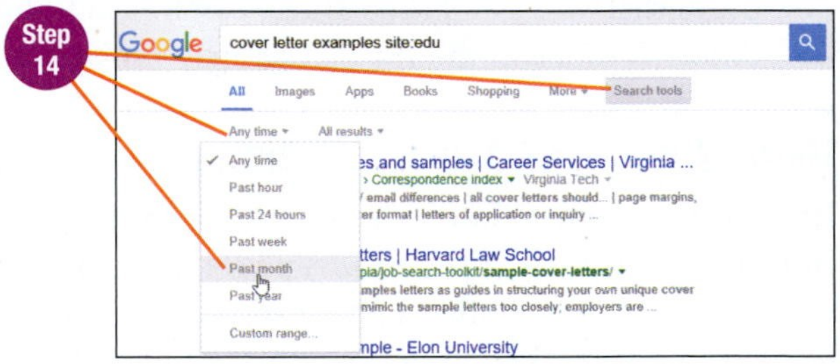

15 Scroll down the search results page and then click a link to a page that interests you. Notice that all URLs are .edu domains and all dates are within the past month.

Printing a Web Page

Printing a web page can sometimes be frustrating, because web pages are designed for optimal screen viewing (not printing). Many times you may print a web page only to discard a second or third page that you did not need, or the content printed did not fit the width of the paper and the printout was unusable.

App Tip

Ctrl + P is the universal keyboard command to open the Print dialog box in any browser or program.

16 Click in the Address bar or select the current web address, type www.usf.edu/career-services/students/cover-letter-dos-and-donts.aspx, and then press Enter.

This page contains several tips for writing cover letters. Assume you decide to print the page for later use when you are looking for a job.

17 Click More (displays as ellipsis points, or three dots) and then click *Print*.

The page displays in the Print dialog box shown in Figure 2.6 on the next page. A preview of the first page is shown with a right-pointing arrow above the preview used to navigate and view the remaining pages in the printout.

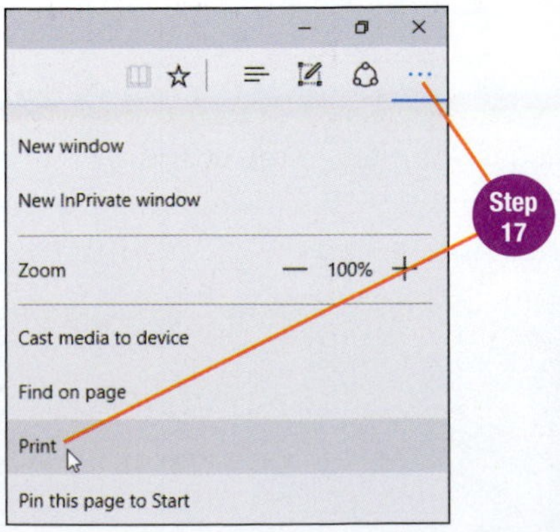

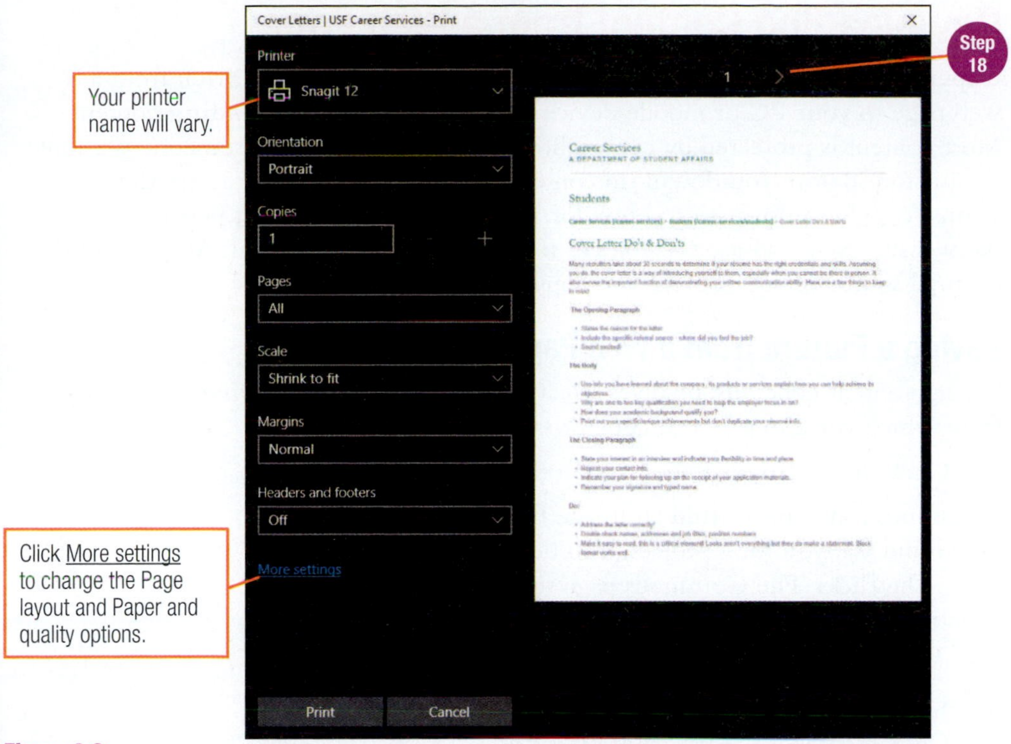

Figure 2.6

The Print dialog box in Microsoft Edge.

Option boxes are available to change the destination printer, page orientation, number of copies, pages to print, scaling, margins, and to add a header and/or footer.

18 Click the Next page arrow (right-pointing arrow) above the preview page to view the second page that will be printed.

19 Click the Next page arrow again to view the third page that will be printed.

The web page needs three pages to print, with the last page being unnecessary as it contains links only.

20 Click the *Pages* option box and then click *Page range* at the drop-down list.

21 Click in the *Range* text box and then type 1-2.

22 Click the Print button or click the Cancel button if you are not connected to a printer to close the Print dialog box.

Only pages 1 and 2 of the web page print. Avoid wasting paper whenever possible when printing web pages by taking the time to preview, ensuring you use only the pages that you need.

23 Close the Microsoft Edge window. Click Close all if prompted to close all tabs.

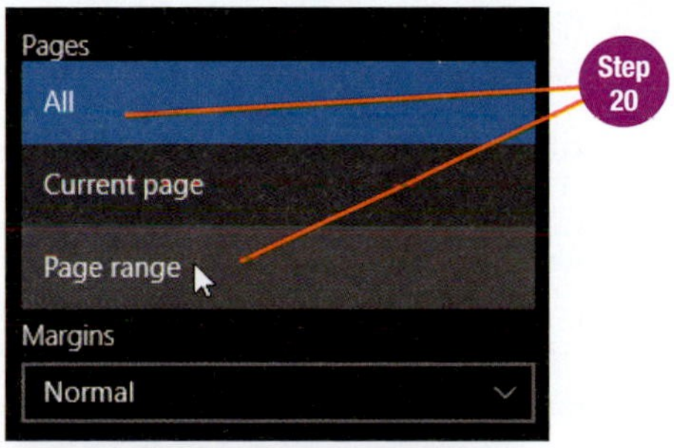

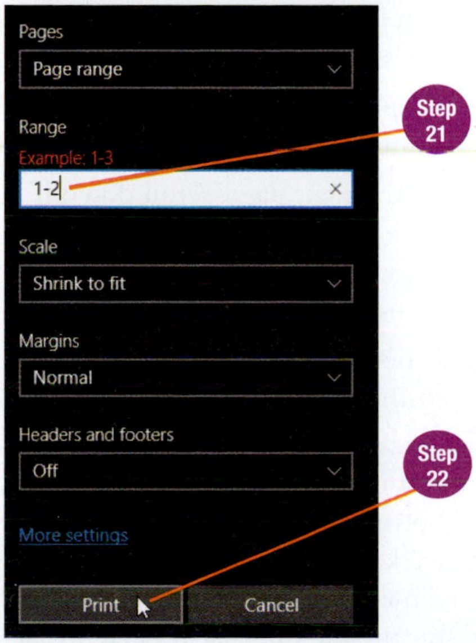

Quick Steps

Use a Search Engine to Find Information

1. Start a web browser.
2. Type URL for desired search engine in Address bar and then press Enter.
3. Type search phrase in search text box and then press Enter.

Use the Google Advanced Search Options

1. Start a web browser.
2. Type google.com in Address bar and then press Enter.
3. Type search phrase in search text box and then press Enter.
4. Click Options button (gear icon).
5. Click Advanced search.
6. Select desired advanced search options.
7. Click Advanced Search button.

Print a Web Page

1. Display desired web page.
2. Display Print dialog box. (In Microsoft Edge, click More, then *Print*.)
3. Preview pages to be printed.
4. Set print options as desired.
5. Click Print button.

Good to Know

Some web pages provide a link to view the page in a printable format. Look for a View Printable hyperlink, which reformats the content for a letter-size page that prints only the article or story.

2.6 Downloading Content from a Web Page

Skills

Download a picture from a web page

Tutorial

Download a File from a Website

Copying an image, audio clip, video clip, or music file (such as MP3) from a web page to your PC or mobile device is referred to as **downloading** content. Most content is protected by copyright law from being used by someone without permission. Before you download content, check the website for restrictions against copying information. Look for a contact link and request permission from the website owner to use the content if no restrictions are shown. Always cite the original source of any content you copy from a web page.

Saving a Picture from a Web Page

Saving content generally involves selecting an object and displaying a context menu from which you can select to copy or save the object.

1. Click the Microsoft Edge icon on the taskbar.

   Assume you want to find an image from the Grand Canyon for a project. You decide to use the flickr The Commons page to find a picture in the public domain that can be used without copyright restrictions.

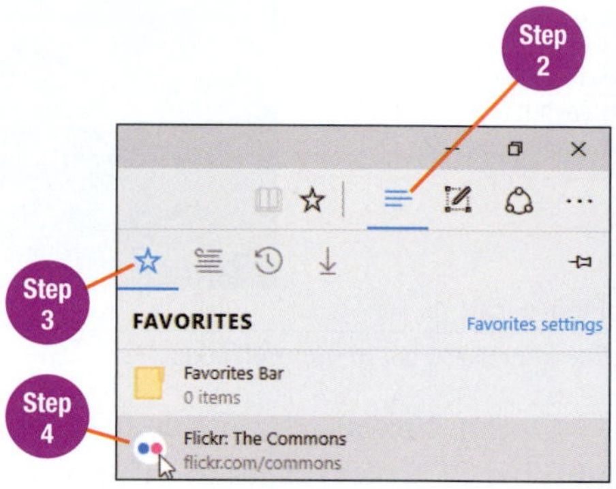

2. Click Hub.
3. Click the star if the Favorites list is not currently displayed in the Hub.
4. Click Flickr: The Commons in the Favorites list (you added this link to the Favorites list in Topic 2.2).
5. If necessary, scroll down to the section titled *A Commons Sampler*.
6. Click in the *Search The Commons* text box, type grand canyon, and then press Enter, or click the SEARCH button.

Oops!

Don't have Flickr: The Commons in your Favorites list? If necessary, type flickr.com/commons in the Address bar and then press Enter.

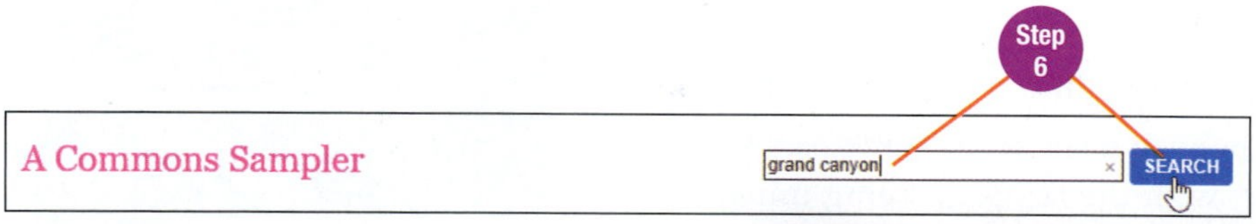

Good to Know

The Commons at flickr.com was started in 2008 as a joint project between flickr and the Library of Congress. The goal is to increase access to publicly held photographs. In 2015, the project had expanded to over 100 library, museum, and other public collections worldwide.

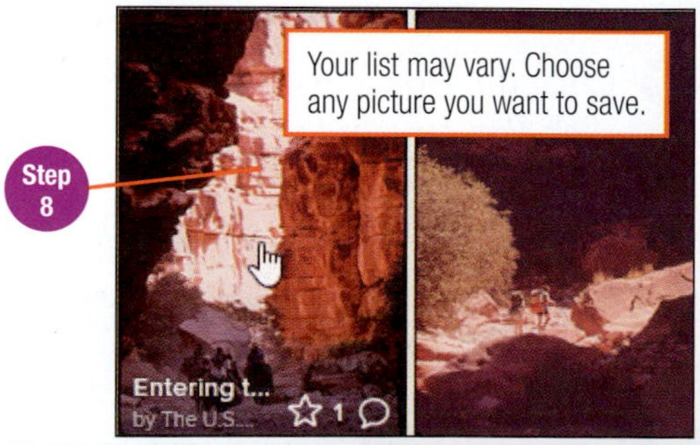

7. Scroll down and view the images in the search results page.
8. Click a picture that you like and want to save.
9. At the next page, scroll down if necessary and read the description below the photograph. Note the access and use restrictions, if any.
10. If necessary, scroll back up the page to the picture preview.
11. Click the Download this photo icon (displays as a down-pointing arrow above a bar) at the bottom right of the picture preview area and then click Medium at the pop-up list. Note that the dimensions for each size option will vary depending on the picture that is currently selected.

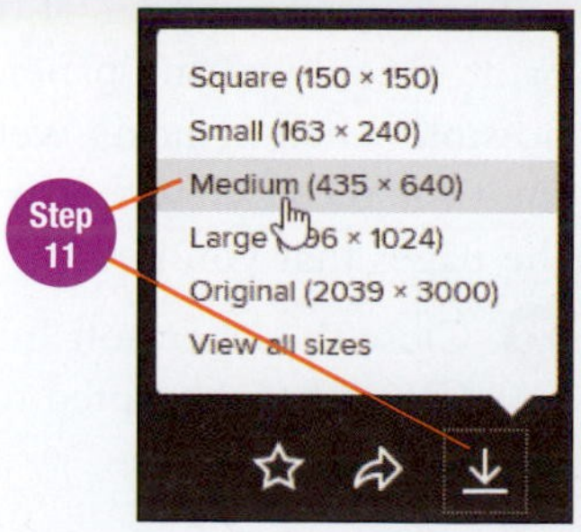

12 Close the message bar that displays when the picture has finished downloading. A message box appears if you do not have a Yahoo account connected with your Microsoft account. Click the close button at the top right of the message box and proceed to Step 13 if you do not wish to create a new Yahoo account by clicking the Sign up with Yahoo button.

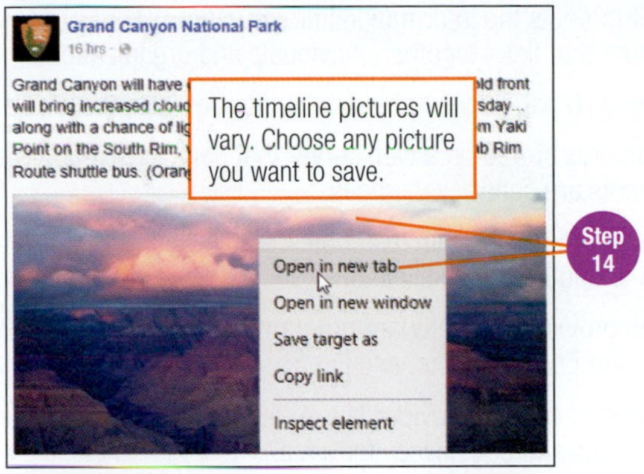

13 Click in the Address bar to select the current web address, type facebook.com/GrandCanyonNationalPark, and then press Enter. You may be prompted to sign in to Facebook to view the page. If necessary, skip to Step 18 if you cannot view the Facebook page.

14 Scroll down the timeline to a picture that you would like to save, right-click the picture, and then click *Open in new tab*.

15 If necessary, click the new tab to view the photo on its own page.

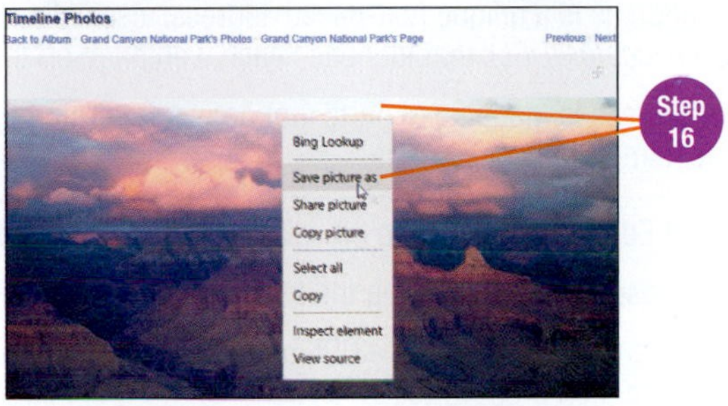

16 Right-click the photo and then click *Save picture as*.

17 At the Save As dialog box, click Downloads in the Navigation pane, select the current text in the *File name* text box, type GrandCanyon, and then click Save.

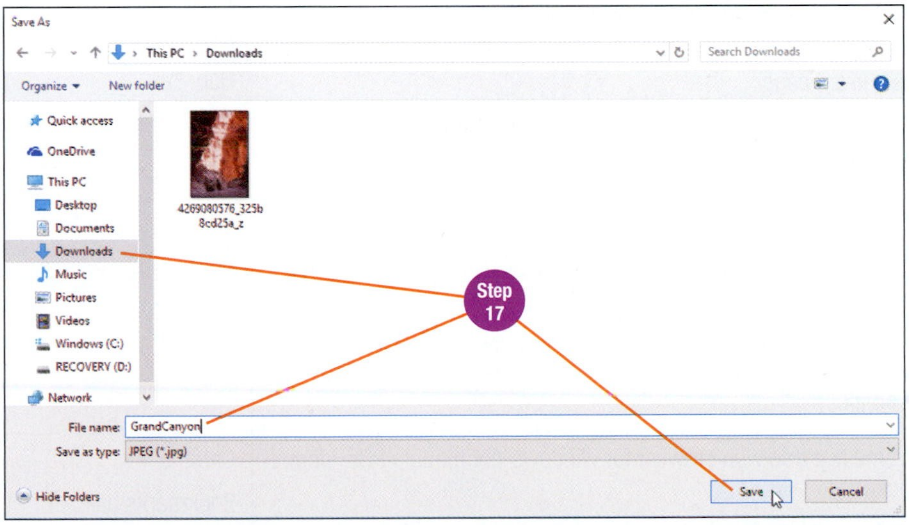

18 Close the Microsoft Edge window. Click Close all when prompted to close all tabs.

19 Click the File Explorer icon on the taskbar.

20 Click Downloads in the Navigation pane.

You will see the two downloaded pictures in the Content pane.

21 Double-click each picture you downloaded to view the picture in the Photos app or other picture viewing window and then close the window.

22 Close File Explorer.

Quick Steps

Save a Picture from a Web Page

1. Display desired web page.
2. Right-click image.
3. Click *Save picture as*.
4. Navigate to desired storage medium, type file name if necessary, then click Save.

Oops!

Different context menu? In Chrome and Firefox, select *Open link in new tab* and *Save image as* at the shortcut menus in Steps 14 and 16.

App Tip

A picture downloaded from a web page can be inserted into a document or presentation by opening an Insert Picture dialog box and specifying the drive, folder, and file name for the image.

Topics Review

Topic	Key Concepts	Key Terms
2.1 Introduction to the Internet and the World Wide Web	The Internet is the information infrastructure that represents the global network that links together individuals and organizations. All the web pages circulated on the Internet form the World Wide Web. Documents stored on a web server that contain text and multimedia elements are called *web pages*. A web page can contain hyperlinks, also called *links*, that move from one page to another when clicked. A web browser is a software program used to view web pages, such as Microsoft Edge, Chrome, and Firefox. An Internet service provider is a company that provides Internet service to individuals and businesses for a fee. A web address is a unique text-based address, also called a *uniform resource locator (URL)*, that identifies each web page on the Internet. A web address is made up of parts that define the protocol, domain, folder, and file name for the web page.	Internet (net) World Wide Web (Web) web page hyperlink (link) web browser Internet service provider (ISP) web address uniform resource locator (URL)
2.2 Navigating the Web Using Microsoft Edge	Microsoft Edge is the new web browser included with Windows 10. Start Microsoft Edge by clicking the Microsoft Edge icon on the taskbar. To display a web page, type the URL or enter a search phrase in the search text box and then press Enter. Click Back to move back one page; click Forward to move forward one page. Click in the Address bar and type a new URL or search phrase to display a different web page in the window. The first page that displays for a website is called the *home page*. Click New tab to open a new page in the window and click Close tab to remove the current page. Tabbed browsing means you have multiple web pages open in a window, with each web page on a separate tab. Display a web page, click the star on the toolbar, and then click the Add button to save a page to the Favorites list. Open the Hub to show Favorites, Reading list, History, and Downloads in a panel at the right side of the window. Click Make a Web Note on the current page to display the Web Note tools for annotating a web page that can be saved to a OneNote notebook or shared via email.	Microsoft Edge Back Forward Address bar home page New tab tabbed browsing Favorites Hub
2.3 Navigating the Web Using Chrome	Google Chrome is a free web browser for Windows-compatible PCs, Linux PCs, or Macs. Start Chrome by clicking the Chrome icon on the taskbar or by double-clicking the icon on the desktop. Display a web page by typing a URL or search phrase in the Address bar. Click the white star to bookmark the current web page. Use the Chrome menu to access the Bookmarks menu and turn on or turn off the display of the Bookmarks bar that docks below the Address bar. Open the Find bar from the Chrome menu to locate all occurrences of a word or phrase on the current web page.	Chrome Bookmarks bar Chrome menu Find bar

continued...

Topic	Key Concepts	Key Terms
2.4 Navigating the Web Using Firefox	Mozilla Firefox is a free web browser for Windows-compatible PCs, Linux PCs, or Macs. Start Firefox by clicking the Firefox icon on the taskbar or by double-clicking the icon on the desktop. Display a web page by typing a URL or search phrase in the Address bar and then pressing Enter. Bookmark the current web page by clicking the star. A bookmarked page displays a blue star. Click Show your bookmarks to show the bookmarks menu system. Click Open menu, then click *Find* to open the Find bar and locate all occurrences of a word or phrase on the current web page. Type a search word or phrase in the Search bar to search for information using the default search engine.	Firefox Open a new tab Show your bookmarks Search bar
2.5 Searching for Information and Printing Web Pages	A company that indexes web pages by keywords using programs called *spiders* or *crawlers* and provides a search tool to find the pages is called a *search engine*. Use more than one search engine because you will get different results from each due to differences in spider and crawling programs and timing differentials. To find information using a search engine, launch a web browser, type the URL for the desired search engine, type a search word or phrase in the search text box, and then press Enter. Each search engine provides tools for advanced searching, which narrows the search results list. For example, at Google, the Advanced Search page provides options to include or exclude words in the search and restrict search results to types of domains, file formats, country, or language. Preview and print a web page by accessing the Print option from a menu in the browser (in Microsoft Edge, go to the More menu, then click *Print*).	search engine spider crawler
2.6 Downloading Content from a Web Page	Copying an image, audio clip, video clip, or music file from a web page to your PC or mobile device is called *downloading*. Some websites, such as flickr.com, provide a download tool that facilitates downloading an image on their website to the Downloads folder. If no download tool is on the web page, saving content generally involves right-clicking the object and selecting a save option at the shortcut menu.	downloading

Recheck

Recheck your understanding of the topics covered in this chapter.

Workbook

Chapter review and assessment resources are available in the *Workbook* ebook.

Chapter **3**

Exploring Microsoft Office 2016 Essentials

Precheck
Check your understanding of the topics covered in this chapter.

Microsoft Office 2016 is a suite of software programs that includes applications such as Word, Excel, PowerPoint, Access, Outlook, and OneNote. The suite is available in various editions that package the programs in collections geared toward a home, business, or student customer using the programs under a one-time purchase for a PC installation or a subscription installation called Office 365. The Office Professional 2016 edition for PC installation and the Office 365 Home subscription include all the programs used in this textbook.

One reason the Microsoft Office suite is popular is because several features or elements are common to all the programs. Once you learn your way around one of the applications in the suite, another application looks and operates similarly, making the learning process faster and easier.

In this chapter, you will navigate the Microsoft Office 2016 interface and perform file-related tasks or routines common to all the applications. You will customize the Quick Access Toolbar and choose options using multiple methods. You will also save and open files to and from OneDrive, an online file storage option.

SNAP If you are a SNAP user, go to your SNAP Assignments page to complete the Precheck, Tutorials, and Recheck.

Data Files
Before beginning this chapter, be sure you have copied the student data files for this course to your storage medium. Steps on downloading and extracting the data files are provided in Chapter 1, Topic 1.8, on pages 22–23.

Learning Objectives

3.1 Start an Office program, identify common features, and explore the ribbon interface

3.2 Open, save, print, export, close, and start new documents in the backstage area

3.3 Customize and use the Quick Access Toolbar

3.4 Select text and objects, perform commands using the ribbon and Mini toolbar, and select options in a dialog box

3.5 Copy and paste using buttons in the clipboard and format an object using a task pane

3.6 Use the Tell Me feature to find options and help resources

3.7 Save files to and open files from OneDrive, navigate longer documents, and use Undo

3.8 Change the Zoom setting and screen resolution

3.1 Starting and Switching Programs, Starting a New Presentation, and Exploring the Ribbon Interface

Skills

Start an Office program

Switch between programs

Start a new presentation

Explore the ribbon interface

Tutorials

Opening a Blank Document

Opening a Document from the Recent Options List

All the programs in the Microsoft Office suite begin at a Start screen and share some common features and elements. An application can be started using an icon on the desktop, from a tile or program name on the Start menu, or by using the search text box on the taskbar.

Microsoft Office 2016 Editions

The Microsoft Office 2016 suite is packaged in various collections of programs as one-time purchased software. Table 3.1 lists three of these editions. The suite is also available through a monthly or annual subscription as Office 365. **Office 365** includes Word, Excel, PowerPoint, OneNote, Outlook, Publisher, and Access, along with Skype calling minutes, additional OneDrive storage, and technical support from Microsoft. Other advantages to an Office 365 subscription is the suite is accessible on up to five devices, which can include Apple and Android devices, and updates to the software are automatically pushed to each installation.

Microsoft also offers a special edition of Office 365 for students called Office 365 University, which is available only to verified students and faculty of postsecondary institutions. Other editions for installation on a Mac computer and collections of software and services geared toward business environments are available.

Table 3.1

Microsoft Office 2016 One-Time Purchase Editions

Edition	What It Includes
Office Home and Student 2016	Word, Excel, PowerPoint, and OneNote
Office Home and Business 2016	Word, Excel, PowerPoint, OneNote, and Outlook
Office Professional 2016	Word, Excel, PowerPoint, Access, Publisher, OneNote, and Outlook

Microsoft Office 2016 System Requirements

Table 3.2 on the next page provides the standard system requirements for installing Microsoft Office 2016. Generally, if the PC can successfully run Windows 7, Windows 8.1, or Windows 10, then Office 2016 will also work on the same hardware, provided there is enough free disk space for the program files.

Starting a Program in the Microsoft Office 2016 Suite

To start a program in the Microsoft Office 2016 suite, double-click the program icon on the desktop or click the program tile in the right pane on the Start menu. If a tile for the application is not in the right pane on the Start menu, click *All apps* in the left pane, scroll down, and then click the program name in the left pane.

A quick way to find and start an application is to type the first few letters of the program name in the search text box on the taskbar and then click the name in the search results list or press Enter if you have typed the entire program name. For example, type Word 2016 in the search text box and then press Enter to start Microsoft Word 2016.

Table 3.2

Microsoft Office 2016 System Requirements

Hardware Component	Requirement
Processor	1 gigahertz (GHz) or faster processor
Memory	2 gigabytes (GB) of RAM Mac computer requires 4 GB RAM
Disk space	3.0 GB available free space Mac computer requires 6.0 GB available disk space
Operating system	Windows 7, Windows 8.1, or Windows 10 Mac computer requires Mac OS X 10.10 or newer
Display setting	1280 x 800 screen resolution or higher
Browser	Current versions of Microsoft Edge, Chrome, Firefox, Safari, Internet Explorer

1. Click in the search text box on the taskbar, type word 2016, and then press Enter.

Word 2016 is the application within the Microsoft Office suite used to create, edit, and format text-based documents. When you start Word, the Start screen appears. The **Start screen** for Microsoft Office applications shows the *Recent* option list used to open a document worked on recently.

2. Click the Maximize button ☐ near the top right of the window if Word does not fill the screen. Skip this step if you see the Restore button ❐ since the window is already maximized.
3. Compare your screen with the Word Start screen shown in Figure 3.1.

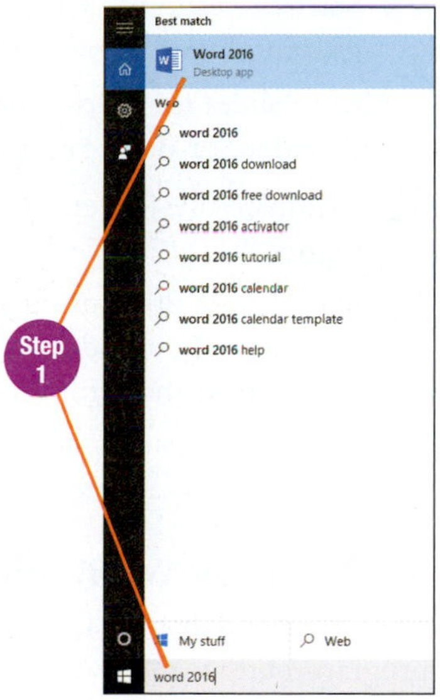

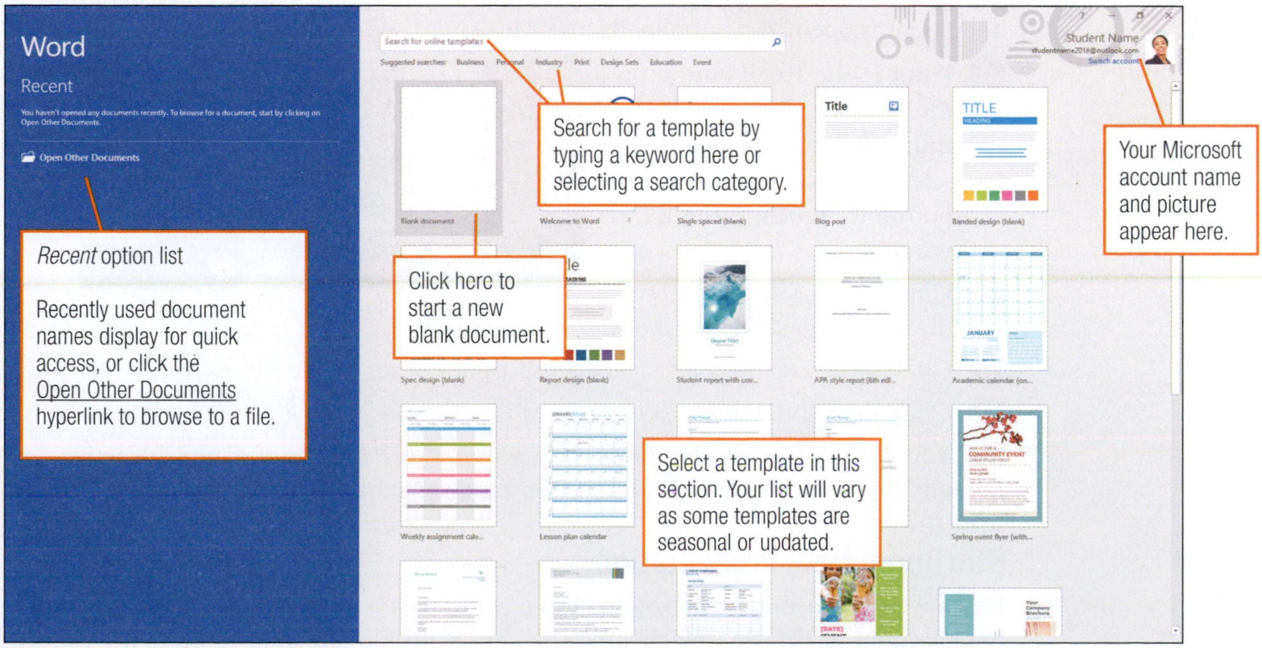

Figure 3.1

Word 2016 opens with the Word Start screen shown above.

4. Click the Start button and then click the Excel 2016 tile in the right pane on the Start menu. If an Excel 2016 tile is not available, click *All apps* in the left pane, scroll down the program list, and then click *Excel 2016*. Click the Maximize button if the Excel window does not fill the screen.

Use **Excel 2016** when your focus is on entering, calculating, formatting, and analyzing numerical data.

5. Compare the Excel Start screen with the Word Start screen shown in Figure 3.1 on the previous page.

Each Office application offers templates in the template gallery on the Start screen. A template is a preformatted document, worksheet, presentation, or database. Click a thumbnail to preview a larger picture of the template. The first thumbnail is used to start a new blank document, workbook, presentation, or database.

App Tip

Each Office program has its own color scheme. Word is blue, Excel is green, PowerPoint is orange, and Access is maroon.

6. Start PowerPoint 2016 by typing PowerPoint 2016 in the search text box and pressing Enter or by using the Start menu. If necessary, maximize the window.

Create slides for an oral or kiosk-style presentation that includes text, images, sound, video, or other multimedia in **PowerPoint 2016**.

7. Compare the PowerPoint Start screen with the Word Start screen shown in Figure 3.1.

8. Start Access 2016 using any method described in Step 1 or Step 4. If necessary, maximize the window and then compare the Access Start screen with the Word Start screen shown in Figure 3.1.

Access 2016 is a database program in which you organize, store, and manage related data, such as information about customers or products.

Switching between Office Programs

As learned in Chapter 1, you switch to another open program by clicking the program button on the taskbar. Point to a button on the taskbar to see a thumbnail appear above the button with a preview of the open document. If more than one document is open, the thumbnails make it easy to switch to the correct window.

9. Point to the Excel button on the taskbar to preview the thumbnail of the Excel Start screen and then click the button to switch to the Excel window.

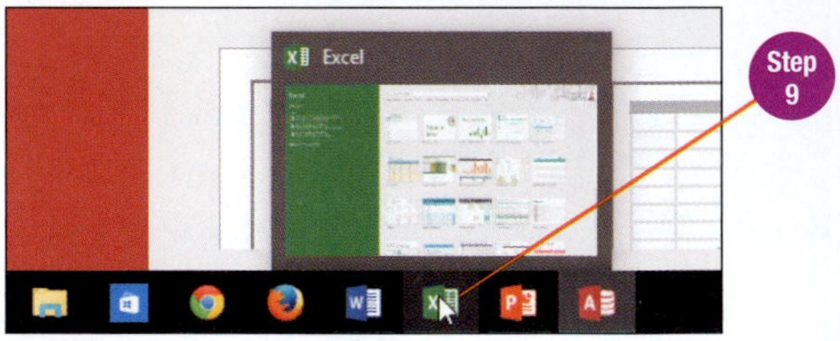

10. Click the Access button on the taskbar to switch to the Access window.

11. Click the Close button (×) at the top right corner of the Access window.

12. Click the Close button to close Excel.

13. You should now see the PowerPoint window. If PowerPoint is not the active window, click the PowerPoint button on the taskbar.

Starting a New Presentation

For any program in the Microsoft Office suite, start a new document, workbook, presentation, or database by clicking the new blank document, workbook, presentation, or database thumbnail in the Templates gallery on the Start screen.

14 Click *Blank Presentation* in the Templates and themes gallery on the PowerPoint Start screen.

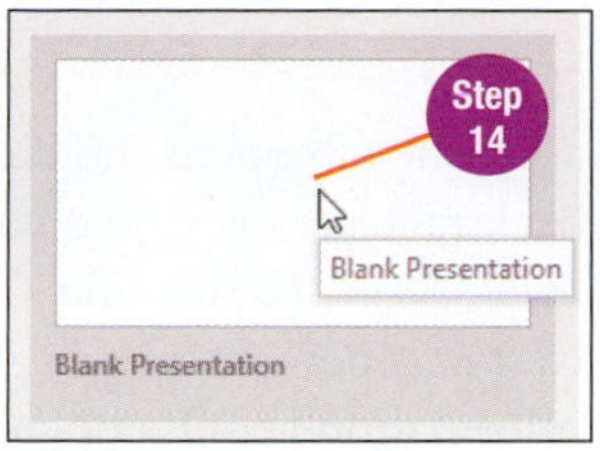

Exploring the Ribbon Interface

The ribbon interface appears along the top of each Office application. Buttons within the ribbon are used to access commands and features within the program. The ribbon is split into individual tabs, with each tab divided into groups of related buttons, as shown in Figure 3.2. Word, Excel, PowerPoint, and Access all have the File and Home tabs as the first two tabs in the ribbon. The File tab is used to perform document-level routines, such as saving, printing, and exporting. This tab is explored in the next topic. The Home tab always contains the most frequently used features in each application, such as formatting and editing buttons.

Quick Steps

Start a New Office Document, Workbook, Presentation, or Database

Click thumbnail for new blank document, blank workbook, blank presentation, or blank desktop database in the Templates gallery or the Templates and Theme gallery on the Start screen.

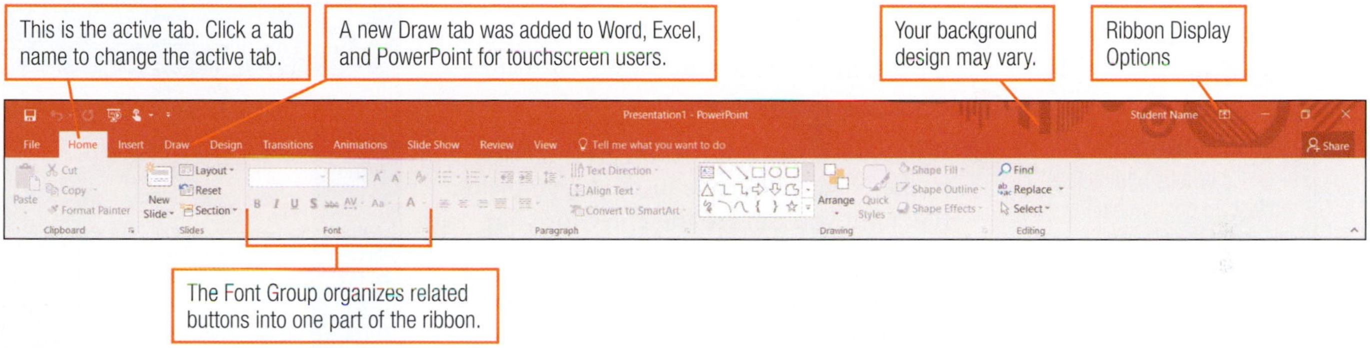

Figure 3.2

The PowerPoint ribbon appears along the top of the application window, as it does for all Office applications. Shown here is the PowerPoint ribbon for a touchscreen device.

The **Ribbon Display Options** button near the top right of the window is used to change the ribbon display from *Show Tabs and Commands* to *Show Tabs*, which hides the command buttons until you click a tab, or *Auto-hide Ribbon*, which displays the ribbon only when you click along the top of the window.

15 Click the Insert tab to view the groups and buttons on the Insert tab ribbon for PowerPoint.

16 Click the Word button on the taskbar and then click *Blank document* on the Start screen to start a new Word document.

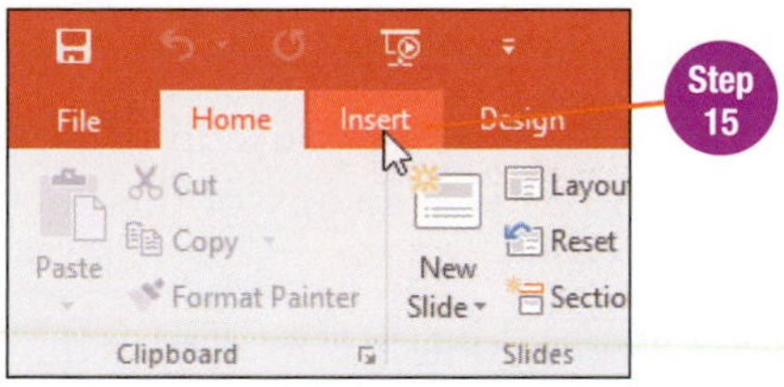

17 Click the Insert tab to view the groups and buttons on the Word Insert tab ribbon.

18 Click the Design tab in Word and then review the buttons on the Word Design tab ribbon.

19 Switch to PowerPoint and then click the Design tab.

20 Spend a few moments exploring other tabs and then close PowerPoint.

21 Spend a few moments exploring other tabs in Word and then close Word.

Oops!

Ribbon is showing more or fewer buttons, or the buttons look different than shown in Figure 3.2? The screen resolution for your PC or mobile device affects the ribbon display. In Topic 3.8, you will learn how to change the display. For now, the instructions will not ask you to click anything you cannot see or identify by the button label or icon.

3.2 Using the Backstage Area to Manage Documents

Skills

Open, Save As, Print, and Close a document

Export a document as a PDF file

Tutorials

Printing a Document

Previewing and Printing

Managing Folders

Managing Documents

Closing a Document and Closing Word

App Tip

The *Recent* option list at the Open backstage area displays by default the last 25 documents opened. If the file you want is in the *Recent* option list, click the file name to open the document.

The File tab opens the **backstage area** in the Microsoft Office applications. The backstage area is where you find file management options, such as *Open*, *Save*, *Save As*, *Print*, *Share*, *Export*, and *Close*. You also go to the backstage area within an application to start a new document. Other tasks performed in the backstage area include displaying information about a document, protecting a document, and managing the document properties and versions.

Each application in the Microsoft Office suite provides options that can be personalized at the backstage view in the Options dialog box. Your Microsoft account and/or connected services and the background or theme for all the Office applications are managed in the Account backstage area.

Note: *If necessary, insert your USB flash drive into an empty USB port before starting this topic. Close the File Explorer window if it opens after you insert the USB flash drive.*

1. Start Word 2016.
2. At the Word Start screen, click Open Other Documents in the left pane.
3. Click the *Browse* option.
4. If necessary, scroll down the list of places in the Navigation pane in the Open dialog box until you can see the entry for your USB flash drive.
5. Click the entry in the Navigation pane for your USB flash drive.
6. Double-click *Student_Data_Files* in the Content pane.
7. Double-click *Ch3*.

The Word document **Cottage_rental_listing** is displayed in the Content pane. Within an Office application, the Open dialog box by default shows only files created in the active application.

8. Double-click ***Cottage_rental_listing***.

In the next steps, you will use the Save As command to save a copy of the document in another folder.

9. Click the File tab to display the backstage area.

When a document is open, the backstage area displays the *Info* option with document properties for the active file and buttons to protect, inspect, and manage versions of the document.

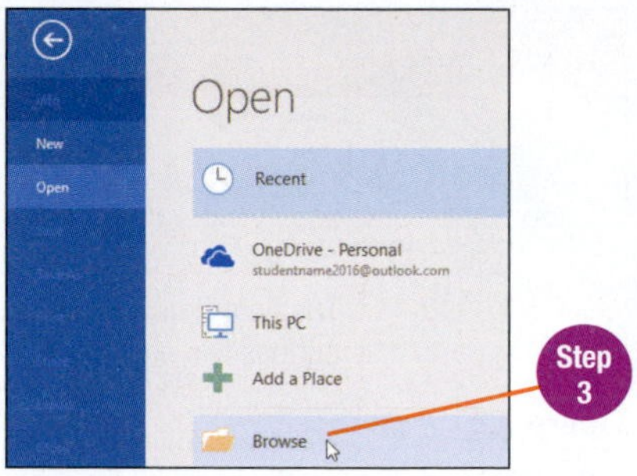

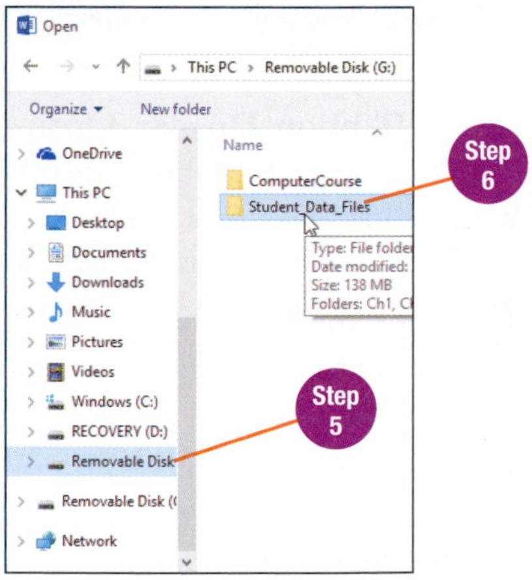

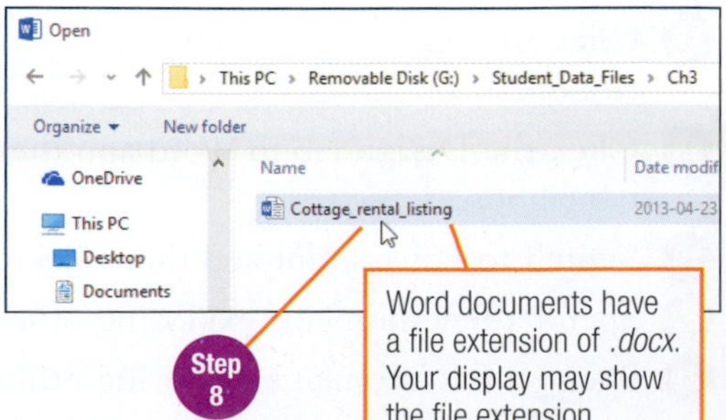

Word documents have a file extension of *.docx*. Your display may show the file extension.

10 Click *Save As*.

The Save As command is used to save a copy of a document in another location or to save a copy of the document in the same location but with a different file name.

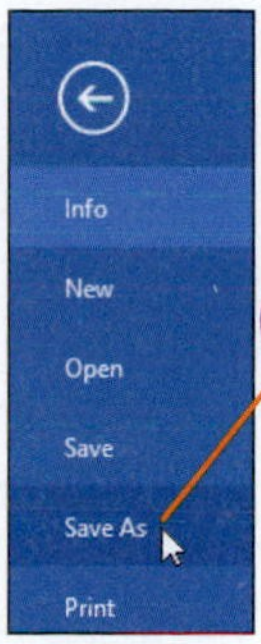

11 With *This PC* already selected in the Save As backstage area, click the More options hyperlink below the location, file name text box, and file type option box that displays at the top of the right panel.

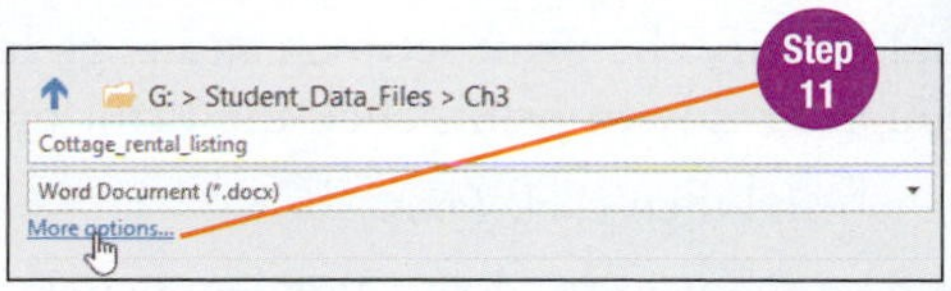

12 Click the Up arrow button at the left of the Address bar.

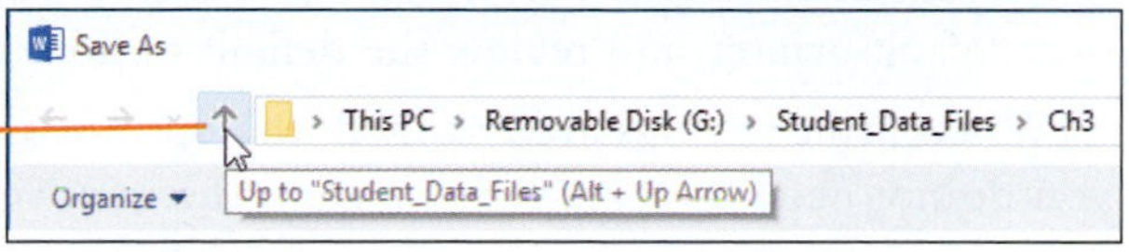

13 Click the Up arrow button a second time.

14 Double-click *ComputerCourse* and then double-click *CompletedTopicsByChapter* in the Content pane.

15 Click the New folder button on the Command bar, type Ch3, and then press Enter.

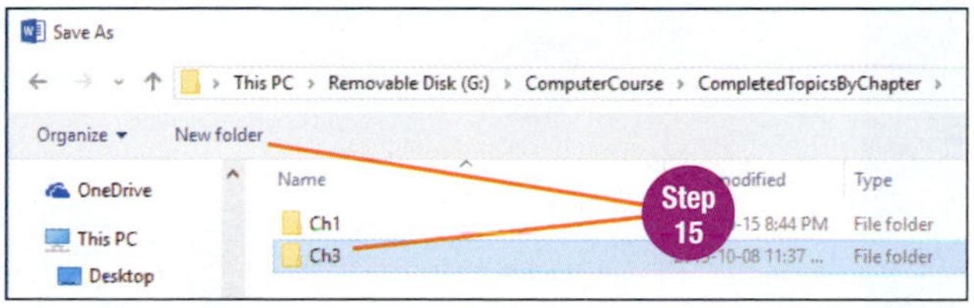

16 Double-click *Ch3*.

17 Click in the *File name* text box or drag to select the current file name, type CottageListing-YourName, and then press Enter or click the Save button.

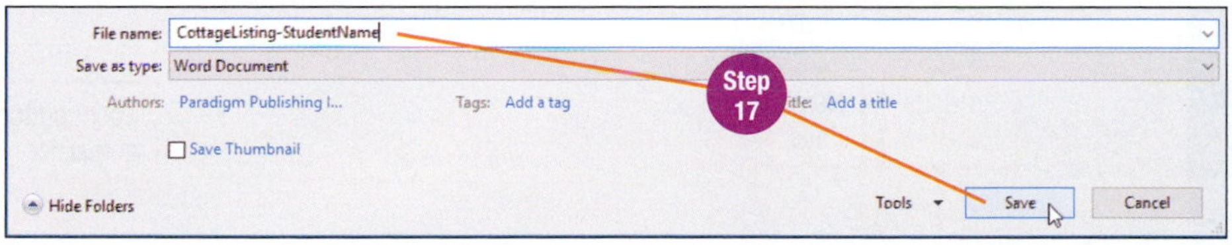

18 Click in the document next to *List Date:* below the address *3587 Bluewater Road* (in the second column of the table) and then type the current date.

19 Click next to *Assigned Agent:* below the date (in the second column of the table) and then type your name.

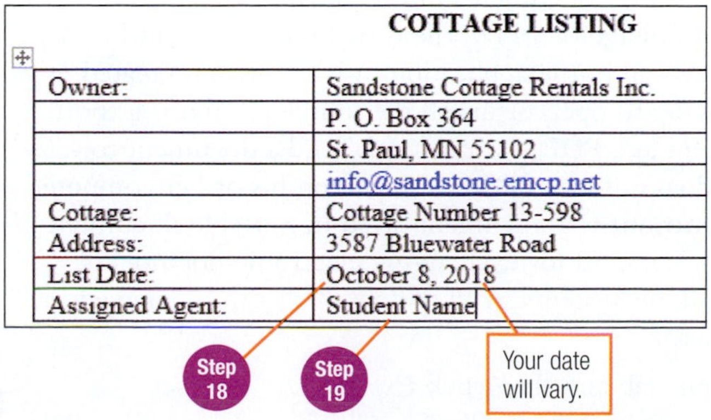

COTTAGE LISTING

Owner:	Sandstone Cottage Rentals Inc.
	P. O. Box 364
	St. Paul, MN 55102
	info@sandstone.emcp.net
Cottage:	Cottage Number 13-598
Address:	3587 Bluewater Road
List Date:	October 8, 2018
Assigned Agent:	Student Name

Quick Steps

Open a Document
1. At Word Start screen, click the hyperlink Open Other Documents.
2. Click *Browse*.
3. Navigate to drive and/or folder and then double-click file name.

Use Save As to Save a Copy of a Document
1. Click File tab.
2. Click *Save As*.
3. Click More options hyperlink in right panel
4. Navigate to desired drive and/or folder.
5. If necessary, change file name.
6. Click Save.

App Tip

You do not need to open the Save As dialog box if you want to save a copy of the document in another folder on the same drive or change the file name. Use the Up arrow button and/or the file name text box at the top of the right panel at the Save As backstage area to make the desired changes.

Oops!

Typing mistake? Press Backspace to delete what you have typed if you make an error and then retype the text. You can also drag across text and press Delete.

Printing a Document

> **App Tip**
> Change *Print All Pages* in the *Settings* section to print a selection of text only, the current page only, or specific pages or a range of pages. To print specific pages, change Print All Pages to *Custom Print* and then type the pages separated by commas in the *Pages* text box.

Display the Print backstage area when you want to preview and print a document. Before printing, review the document in the **Print Preview** panel of the backstage area shown in Figure 3.3. The bottom of the Print Preview panel shows the number of pages needed to print the document, and navigation buttons are included to move to the next page and previous page in a multipage document.

In the Print panel, choose the printer on which to print the document in the *Printer* section, and modify the print settings and page layout options in the *Settings* section. When you are ready to print, click the Print button.

20. Click the File tab and then click *Print.*
21. Examine the document in the Print Preview panel, check the name of the default printer, and review the default options in the *Settings* section.

When print settings are changed, the options are stored with the document, so you do not need to change them again the next time you want to print.

22. Click the Print button to print the document.

The document is sent to the printer, and the backstage area closes.

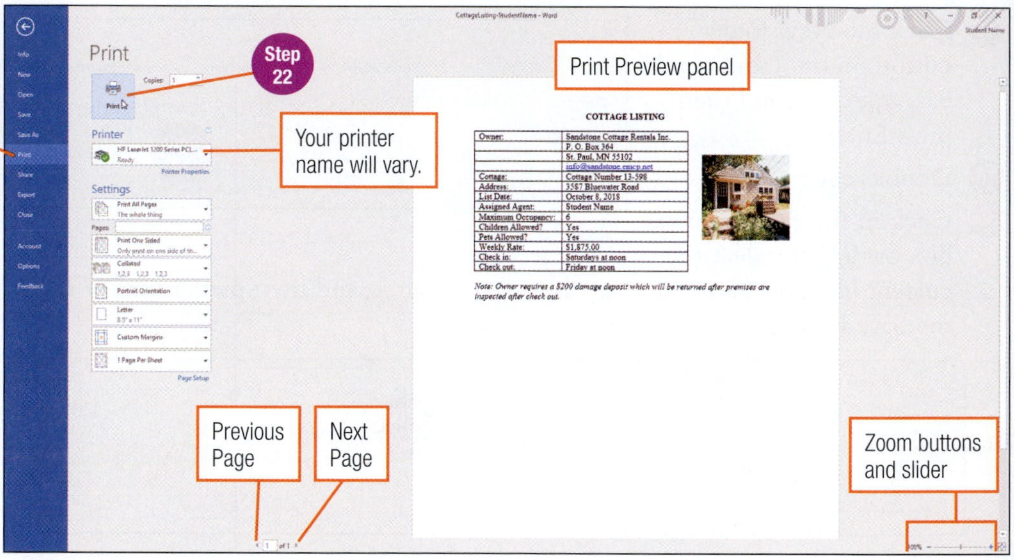

Figure 3.3

Print backstage area

Exporting a Document as a PDF File

> **App Tip**
> In Word you can open a PDF document, and Word converts the PDF into an editable document.

Many people exchange documents in PDF format via email or websites. The advantage of a PDF file is that the document looks and prints as it would in the application in which it was created but without having to open or install the source program. Export a Word document as a PDF if you need to send a document to someone who does not have Word installed on his or her computer.

A **PDF document** is a document saved in portable document format, an open standard for exchanging electronic documents developed by Adobe Systems. A PDF document can be viewed in any web browser.

23. Click the File tab and then click *Export.*

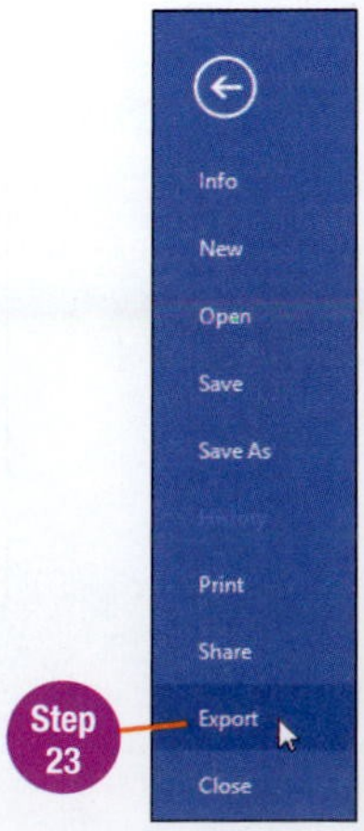

24 With *Create PDF/XPS Document* selected in the Export backstage area, click the Create PDF/XPS button.

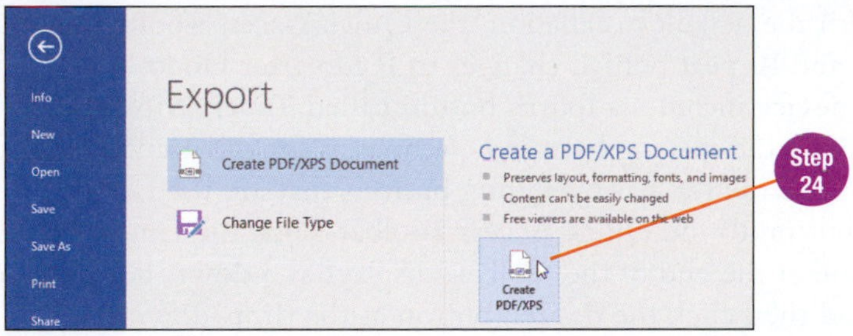

Quick Steps

Print a Document

1. Click File tab.
2. Click *Print*.
3. Preview and/or change options as necessary.
4. Click Print.

Export as PDF

1. Click File tab.
2. Click *Export*.
3. Click Create PDF/XPS.
4. Click Publish.

25 Click the Publish button at the Publish as PDF or XPS dialog box.

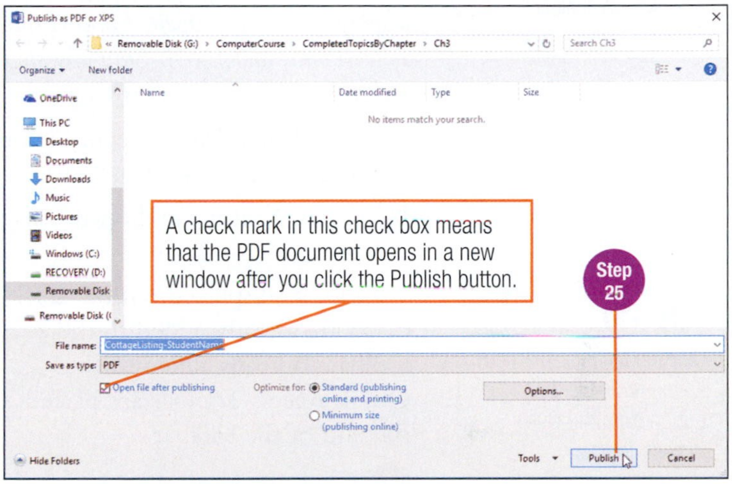

By default, the PDF is created in the same drive and folder in which the Word document resides and with the same file name but with the file extension *.pdf*. Because PDF files have a different file extension, the same name can be used for both the Word document and the PDF document.

26 The published PDF document opens in a reader app, such as Windows Reader or Adobe Reader, or in a browser window. If no program is associated with PDF documents, a message box similar to the one shown at the right opens with the prompt *How do you want to open this file?* In that case, click OK to open the PDF document in the selected option *Microsoft Edge*.

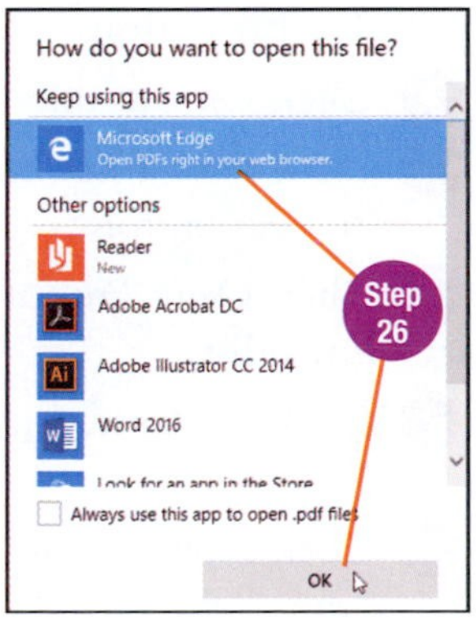

Oops!

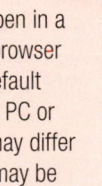

PDF does not open in a Reader app or browser window? The default settings on your PC or mobile device may differ and the option may be turned off. In that case, skip Steps 26 and 27.

27 Close the window in which the PDF document opened to return to Word.

28 Click the File tab and then click *Close*.

29 Click the Save button when prompted at the message box asking if you want to save your changes. Leave Word open for the next topic.

Close a document when you are finished editing, saving, printing, and publishing. A blank window displays when no documents are open.

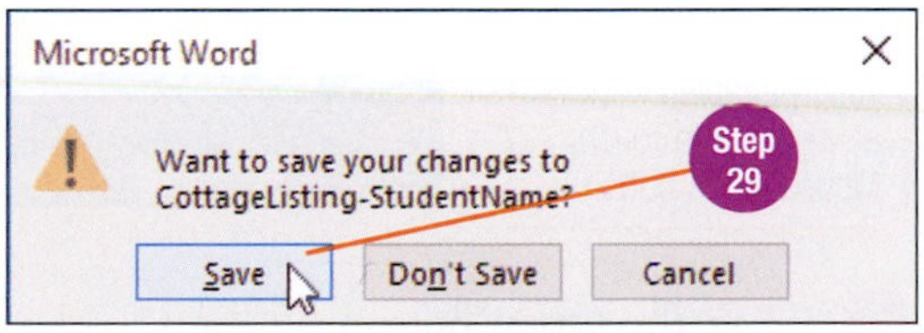

View

Model Answer

Compare your completed file with the model answer.

Beyond Basics — Pinning Documents and Folders to *Recent* option lists

At the Open backstage area, you can pin a frequently used file to the *Recent* option list so that the file name always appears in the *Recent* option list. Point to the file name in the *Recent* option list and then click the pushpin icon that displays at the right to pin the item to the list.

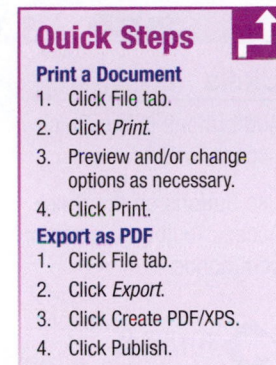

3.3 Customizing and Using the Quick Access Toolbar

Skills

Add buttons to the Quick Access Toolbar

Use buttons on the Quick Access Toolbar to perform commands

Tutorial
Customizing the Quick Access Toolbar

The **Quick Access Toolbar** is at the top left corner of each Office application window. With the default installation, the Quick Access Toolbar has buttons to Save, Undo, and Repeat (which changes to Redo after Undo has been used). A touchscreen device includes a fourth button called Touch/Mouse Mode that is used to optimize the spacing between commands for the mouse or for touch. Most people customize the toolbar by adding buttons that are used often.

To add a button to the Quick Access Toolbar, click the Customize Quick Access Toolbar button at the end of the toolbar (displays as a down-pointing arrow with a bar above) and then click the desired button at the drop-down list.

***Note:** Skip this topic if the Quick Access Toolbar on the computer you are using already displays the New, Open, Quick Print, and Print Preview and Print buttons in Word, PowerPoint, and Excel. Skip any steps in which a drop-down list option already displays with a check mark, which means the button is already on the toolbar.*

1. At a blank Word screen, click the Customize Quick Access Toolbar button.

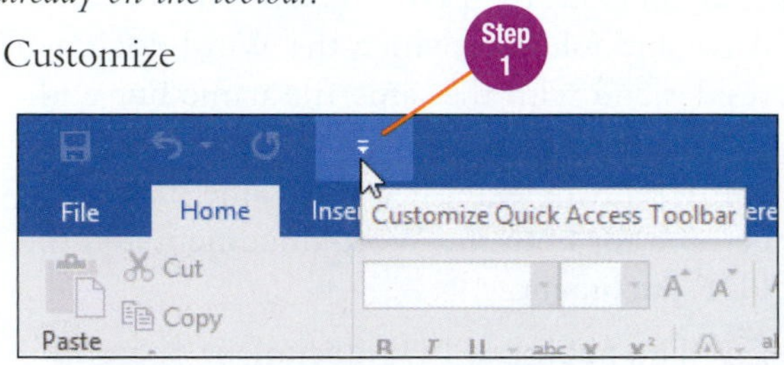

2. Click *New* at the drop-down list.

Options displayed with a check mark are already added to the toolbar. Buttons added to the Quick Access Toolbar are placed at the end of the toolbar.

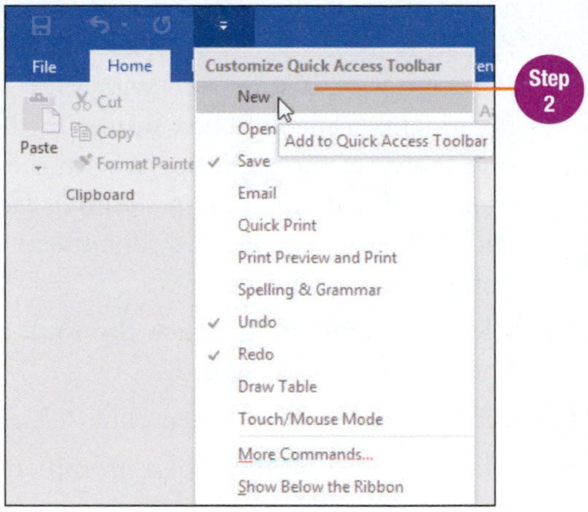

3. Click the Customize Quick Access Toolbar button.
4. Click *Open* at the drop-down list.
5. Click the Customize Quick Access Toolbar button.
6. Click *Quick Print* at the drop-down list.
7. Click the Customize Quick Access Toolbar button.
8. Click *Print Preview and Print* at the drop-down list.

App Tip
Clicking a check-marked option removes the button from the Quick Access Toolbar.

App Tip
Right-click any button on the ribbon and then click *Add to Quick Access Toolbar* to add the button.

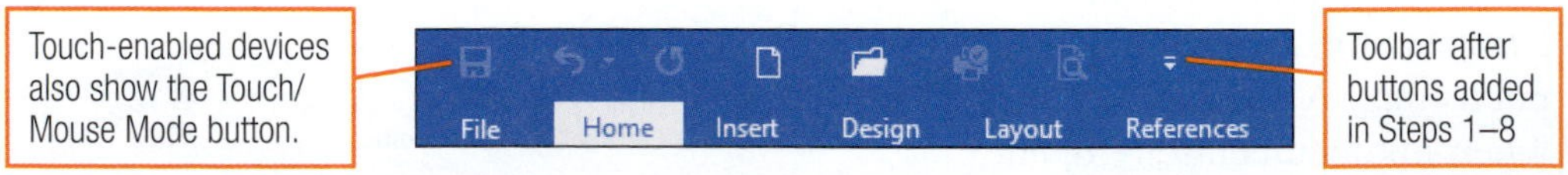

9. Click the Open button on the Quick Access Toolbar.

The Open backstage area opens with the *Recent* option list.

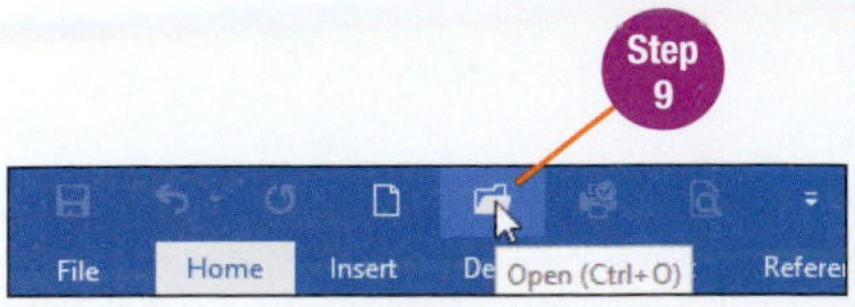

10 Click the file named ***CottageListing-StudentName*** in the *Recent* options list.

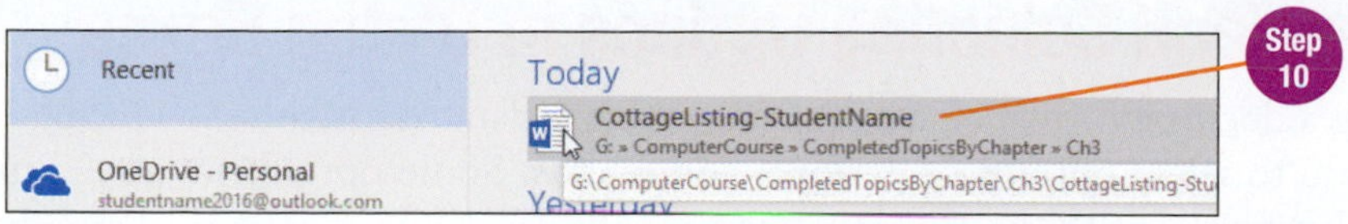

11 Click the Print Preview and Print button on the Quick Access Toolbar.

The Print backstage area opens.

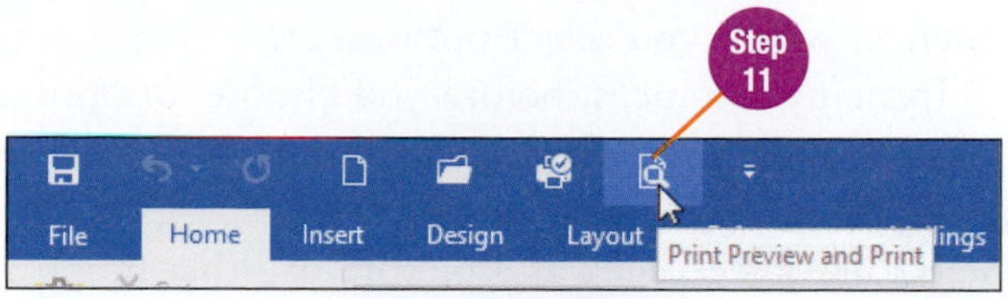

12 Click the Back button (left-pointing arrow inside circle) to return to the document without printing.

13 Start PowerPoint 2016.

14 Click Blank Presentation at the PowerPoint Start screen.

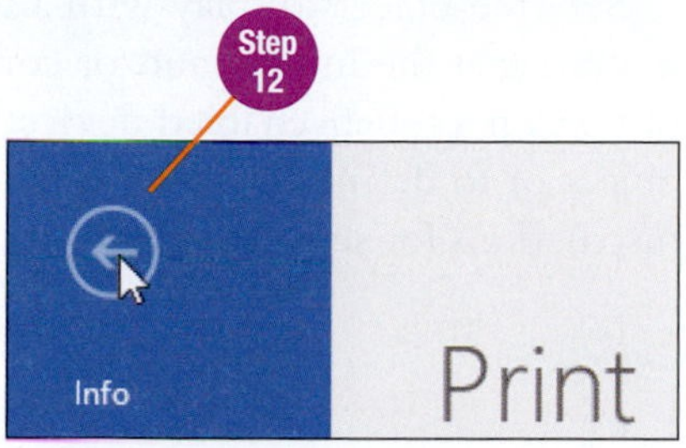

Notice the customized Word Quick Access Toolbar does not carry over to other Microsoft applications.

15 Customize the Quick Access Toolbar in PowerPoint by adding the New, Open, Quick Print, and Print Preview and Print buttons.

16 Close PowerPoint.

17 Start Excel 2016 and then click Blank Workbook at the Excel Start screen.

18 Customize the Excel Quick Access Toolbar to add the New, Open, Quick Print, and Print Preview and Print buttons.

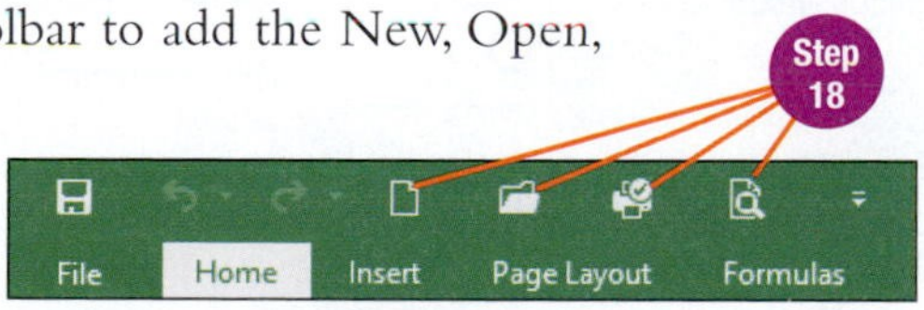

19 Close Excel.

20 At the Word document, click the File tab and then click *Close*.

21 Click the New button on the Quick Access Toolbar.

A new blank document window opens. Leave this document open for the next topic.

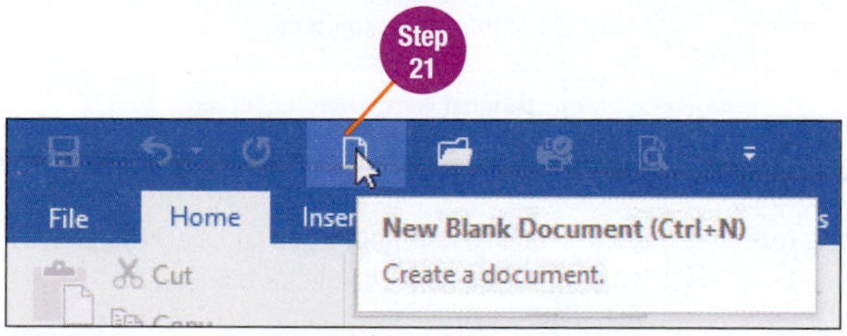

Quick Steps

Add a Button to the Quick Access Toolbar

1. Click Customize Quick Access Toolbar button.
2. Click desired button at drop-down list.

App Tip

The Quick Print button added to the Quick Access Toolbar automatically sends the current document to the printer using the active printer and print settings.

App Tip

For Office applications, the keyboard command Ctrl + F4 closes the current document and Alt + F4 closes the program.

Beyond Basics: Moving the Quick Access Toolbar below the Ribbon

You may prefer to have the Quick Access Toolbar display below the ribbon so that the buttons are closer to the area in which you are working. To do this, click the Customize Quick Access Toolbar button and then click *Show Below the Ribbon* at the drop-down list.

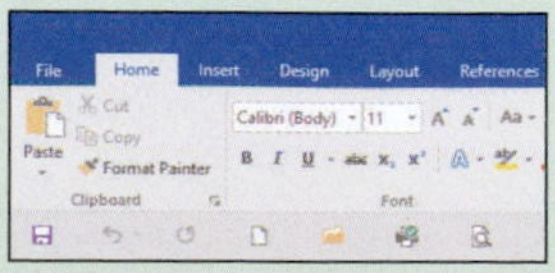

Quick Access Toolbar below the ribbon

3.4 Selecting Text or Objects, Using the Ribbon and Mini Toolbar, and Selecting Options in Dialog Boxes

Skills

- Select text and objects
- Perform commands using the ribbon and Mini toolbar
- Display a task pane and dialog box
- Choose options in a dialog box

Tutorials

- Selecting, Replacing, and Deleting Text
- Applying Font Formatting Using the Mini Toolbar
- Applying Font Formatting Using the Font Dialog Box

Creating a document, worksheet, presentation, or database involves working with the ribbon to select options or perform commands. Some options involve using a button, list box, or gallery, and some commands cause a task pane or dialog box to open in which you select options.

In many instances, before you choose an option from the ribbon, you first select text or an object as the target for the action. Select text by clicking within a word, paragraph, cell, or placeholder or by dragging across the text you want to select. Select an object, such as a picture or other graphic, by clicking the object.

Selected objects display with a series of selection handles. A **selection handle** is a circle at the middle and/or corners of an object, or at the beginning and end of text on a touch-enabled device. Selection handles are used to manipulate the object or to define the selection area on a touch-enabled device. Table 3.3 provides instructions for selecting text using a mouse or touch and for selecting an object.

Table 3.3

Selecting Text and Objects Using the Mouse and Touch

Selecting Text Using a Mouse	Selecting Text Using Touch	Selecting Objects
Point at the beginning of the text or cell to be selected. The pointer displays as I, called an *I-beam* in Word and PowerPoint, or as ✜, called a *cell pointer* in Excel. Hold down the left mouse button and drag to the end of the text or cells to be selected. Release the mouse button. 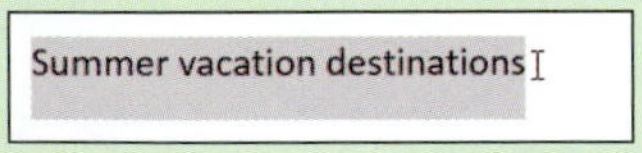 In some cases, a Mini toolbar displays when you release the mouse after selecting text. 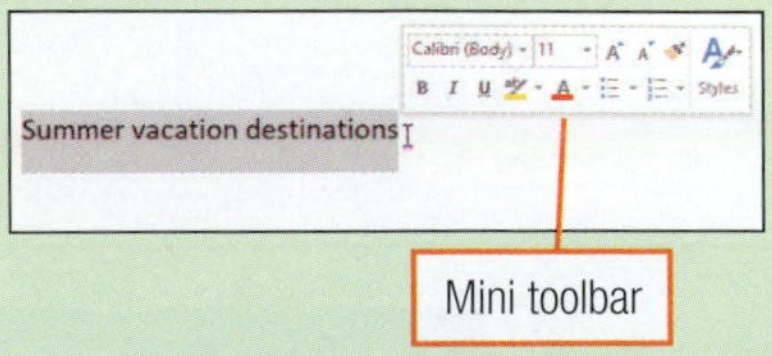 	Tap at the beginning of the text to be selected. A selection handle appears below the text (displays as an empty circle). 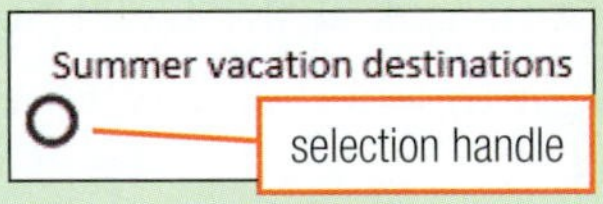 Slide the selection handle right to move the insertion point to edit text. Alternatively, double-tap at the beginning of the text to select the first word and show a second selection handle, then slide the right selection handle to extend the selection. 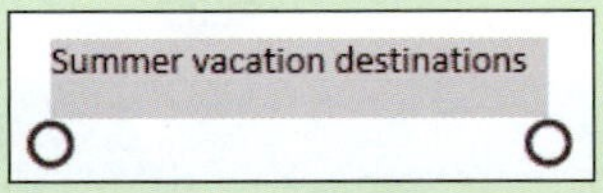 After releasing your finger, you can slide the left or right selection handle to redefine the area if necessary. To display the Mini toolbar, press and hold inside the selected text area. The toolbar appears when you release your finger and displays already optimized for touch. 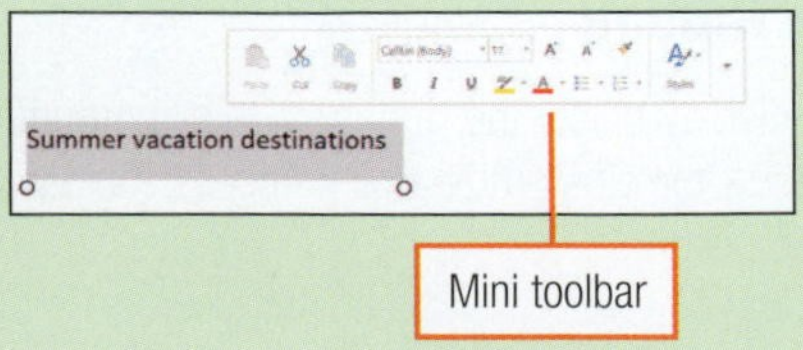 	Click anywhere over the object. Selection handles appear at the ends, corners, and middle (depending on width and height) of each side of the object. A Layout Options button also appears next to a selected object with options for aligning and moving the object with surrounding text. 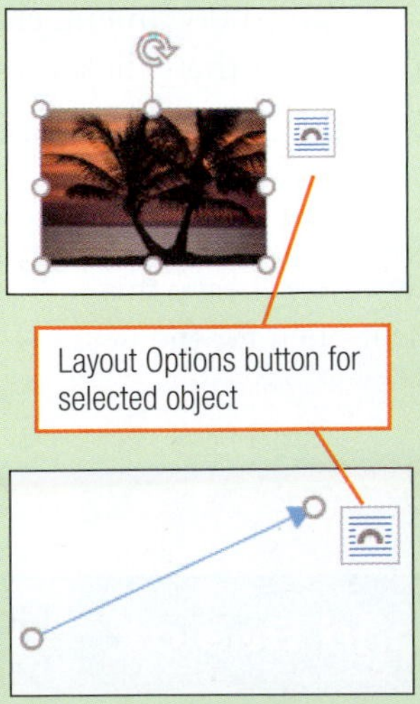

1 At a blank Word screen, type Summer vacation destinations and then press Enter.

2 Type Explore the beaches of Florida and experience the Florida sunset with friends or family. and then press Enter.

3 Select the title *Summer vacation destinations* to display the Mini toolbar.

The **Mini toolbar** appears near text after text is selected or with the shortcut menu when you right-click a selection. The toolbar contains frequently used formatting commands for quicker access within the work area than using the ribbon.

If necessary, refer to the instructions in Table 3.3 (page 74) for selecting text using the mouse or touch.

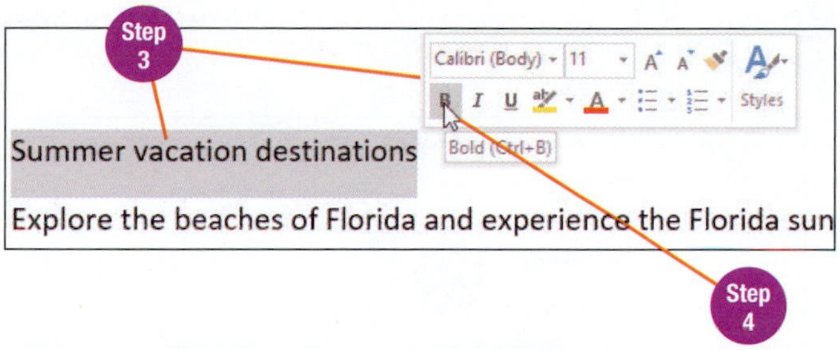

4 Click the Bold button on the Mini toolbar.

5 Click in the blank line below the sentence that begins with *Explore* to deselect the title.

6 Click the Insert tab on the ribbon.

7 Click the Pictures button in the Illustrations group.

This opens the Insert Picture dialog box.

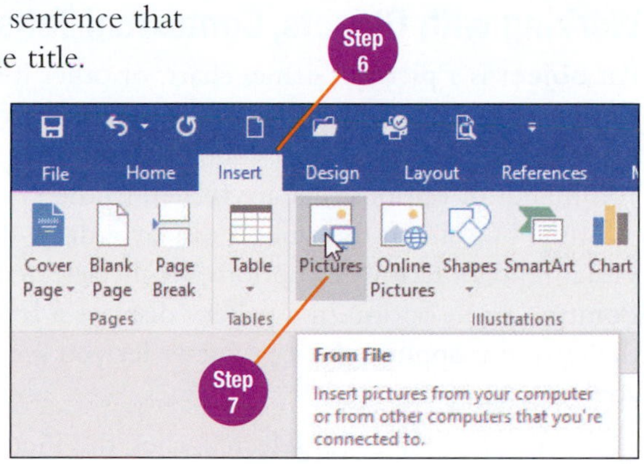

8 If necessary, scroll down the list of places in the Navigation pane. Click the entry in the Navigation pane for your USB flash drive.

9 Double-click *Student_Data_Files*, double-click *Ch3*, and then double-click ***FloridaSunset***.

The FloridaSunset picture is inserted in the document and is automatically selected.

10 Drag the selection handle at the bottom right corner of the image until the picture is resized to the approximate height and width shown at the right.

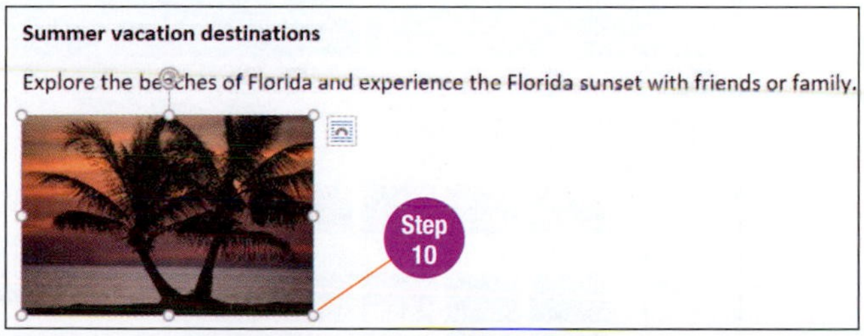

The mouse pointer changes shape to a double-headed diagonal arrow (⤡) when you point at the bottom right corner of the image. Drag downward and to the right when you see this icon. The pointer changes shape to a crosshairs—a large, thin, black cross (+)—while you drag the mouse. When you release the mouse, the selection handles reappear.

Quick Steps

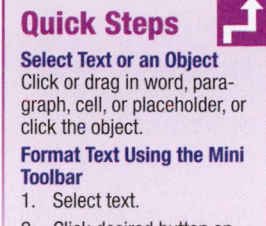

Select Text or an Object
Click or drag in word, paragraph, cell, or placeholder, or click the object.

Format Text Using the Mini Toolbar
1. Select text.
2. Click desired button on Mini toolbar.

App Tip

All the buttons available on the Mini toolbar are also available on the ribbon.

Oops!

No selection handles? If you click away from the object, the selection handles disappear. Click the picture to redisplay the selection handles.

> **App Tip**
>
> The first time a document is saved, the Save As backstage area appears so the document can be assigned a file name. Once the document is named, clicking Save on the Quick Access Toolbar saves changes using the existing name and storage location.

11. Click the Save button on the Quick Access Toolbar.

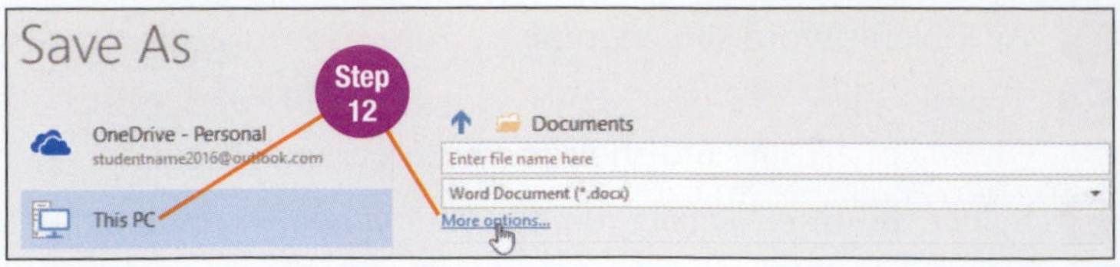

12. Click *This PC* and then click the More options hyperlink in the right panel. At the Save As dialog box, navigate to the Ch3 folder within CompletedTopicsByChapter and ComputerCourse on your USB flash drive.
13. Type VacationDestinations-YourName and then press Enter or click the Save button.

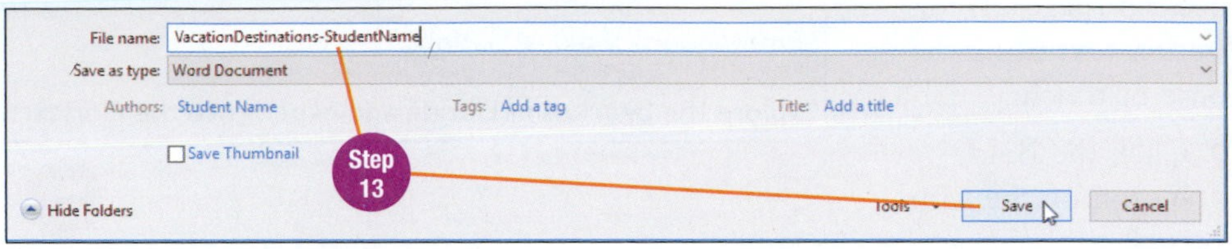

Working with Objects, Contextual Tabs, and Dialog Boxes

An **object** is a picture, shape, chart, or other item that can be manipulated separately from text or other objects around it. When an object is selected, a contextual ribbon tab appears. More than one contextual tab may appear. A **contextual tab** contains commands or options that are related to the type of object that is currently selected.

Some buttons in the ribbon display a drop-down gallery. A **gallery** displays visual representations of options for the selected item in a drop-down list or grid. Pointing to an option in a gallery displays a **live preview** of the text or object if the option is applied. Live previews let you see how formatting will look before applying an option.

> **App Tip**
>
> Live preview lets you see the effect of a change without applying the option. Watch the text or object change as you move the mouse over each option.

> **Oops!**
>
> Picture Tools Format tab not visible? This tab appears only when a picture is selected. Click the picture to display the contextual tab.

14. With the image still selected, click the Picture Tools Format tab if the tab is not the active tab, and then click the Corrections button in the Adjust group.
15. Point to the last option in the Corrections gallery. Notice the picture brightens significantly when you point to the option.
16. Click the last option in the Corrections gallery to apply the *Brightness: +40% Contrast: +40%* correction.

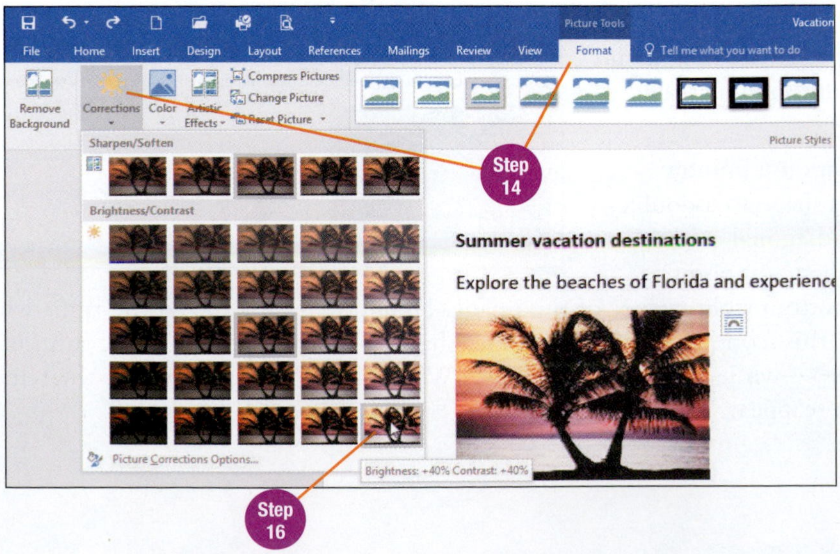

Some ribbon groups have a small button at the bottom right corner of the group that is a diagonal downward-pointing arrow (⧉). This button is called a **dialog box launcher**. Clicking the button causes a task pane or a dialog box to appear. A **task pane** appears at the left or right side of the window, whereas a **dialog box** opens in a separate window above (or, from the viewer's perspective, in front of) the document. Task panes and dialog boxes contain more options as buttons, lists, sliders, check boxes, text boxes, and option buttons.

Quick Steps

Display the Contextual Tab
Click to select object.

Display a Task Pane or Dialog Box
Click dialog box launcher at bottom right of group on ribbon.

Oops!

Measurement displays with cm? In Canada, Office installs with the metric measurement system. At Step 20, type 3 in or change to inches at the Options dialog box from the File tab. Click *Advanced* in the left pane, scroll down to the *Display* section, and then change the *Show measurements in units of* option.

17 Click the dialog box launcher at the bottom right corner of the Picture Styles group.

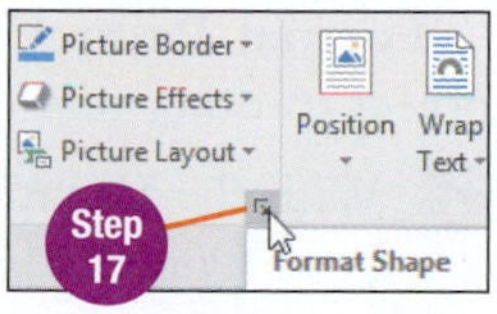

The Format Picture task pane opens at the right. You will work in a task pane in the next topic.

18 Click the Close button (×) at the top right corner of the Format Picture task pane to close the pane.

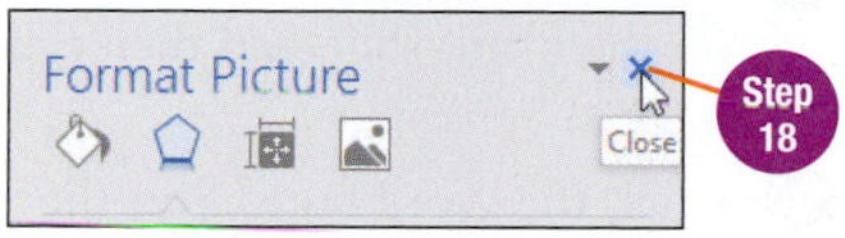

19 Click the dialog box launcher at the bottom right corner of the Size group.

The Layout dialog box opens with the Size tab active.

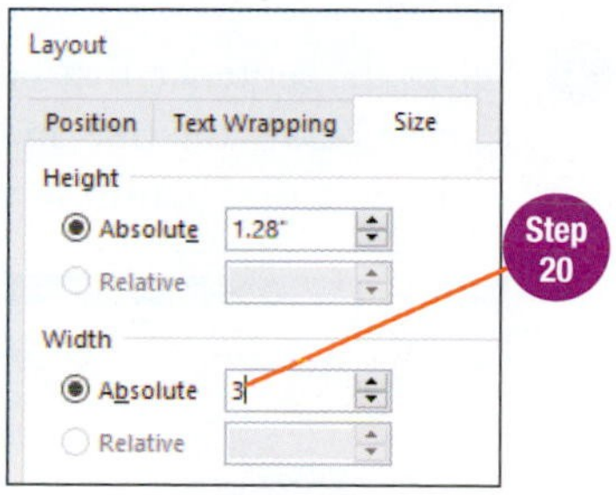

20 Select the current value in the *Absolute* text box in the *Width* section and then type 3.

21 Click the Text Wrapping tab and then click the *Square* option in the *Wrapping style* section.

22 Click OK.

23 With the picture still selected, position the pointer on top of the picture and then drag the picture up to the top of the document, releasing it when the green horizontal and vertical alignment guides show the picture aligned at the top and left margins.

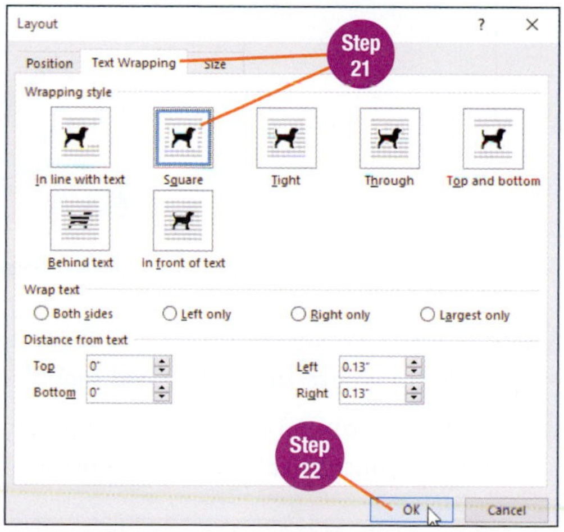

An **alignment guide** is a colored horizontal or vertical line that appears when you are moving an object to help you align and place the object within the document boundaries or in relation to surrounding text or other nearby objects.

24 Click the Save button on the Quick Access Toolbar. Leave the document open for the next topic.

Because the document has already been saved once, the Save button saves the changes using the existing file name and location.

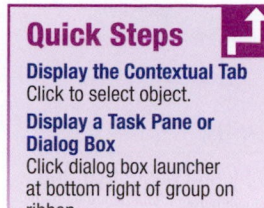

3.5 Using the Office Clipboard and Formatting Using a Task Pane

Skills

Copy and paste text and an object

Copy and paste formatting options using Format Painter

Use a task pane to format a selected object

Tutorials

Cutting, Copying, and Pasting Text

Using the Paste Options Button

Using the Clipboard Task Pane

Formatting with Format Painter

Applying Font Formatting Using the Font Group

The Clipboard group is standardized across Microsoft Office programs. The buttons in the Clipboard group are Cut, Copy, Paste, and Format Painter. You used Cut, Copy, and Paste in Chapter 1 when you learned how to move and copy files and folders. Cut, Copy, and Paste are also used to move or copy text or objects.

Format Painter is used to copy formatting options from selected text or an object to other text or another object.

1. With the **VacationDestinations-YourName** document still open, start PowerPoint 2016, and then click *Blank Presentation.*
2. Click anywhere in *Click to add title* on the blank slide and then type Florida Sunset.

3. Click the Word button on the taskbar.
4. Select the sentence that begins with *Explore* below the title and then click the Copy button in the Clipboard group on the Home tab.

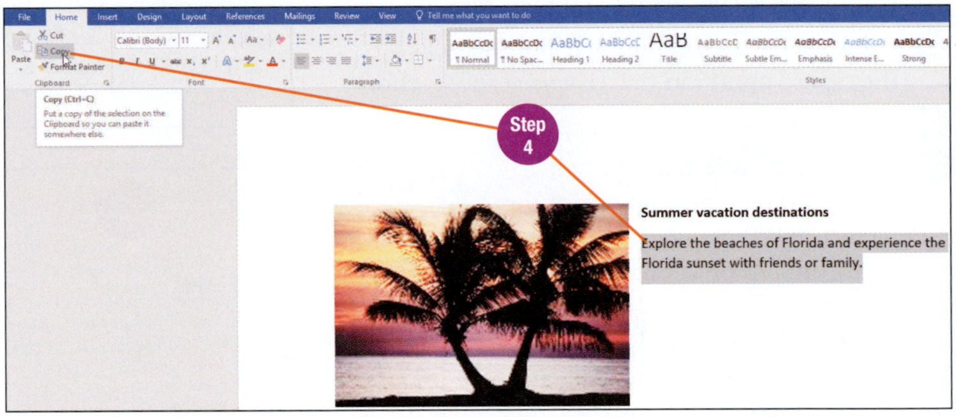

5. Click the PowerPoint button on the taskbar to switch to PowerPoint and then click anywhere in *Click to add subtitle* on the slide.
6. Click the top part of the Paste button in the Clipboard group. (Do *not* click the down-pointing arrow on the button.)

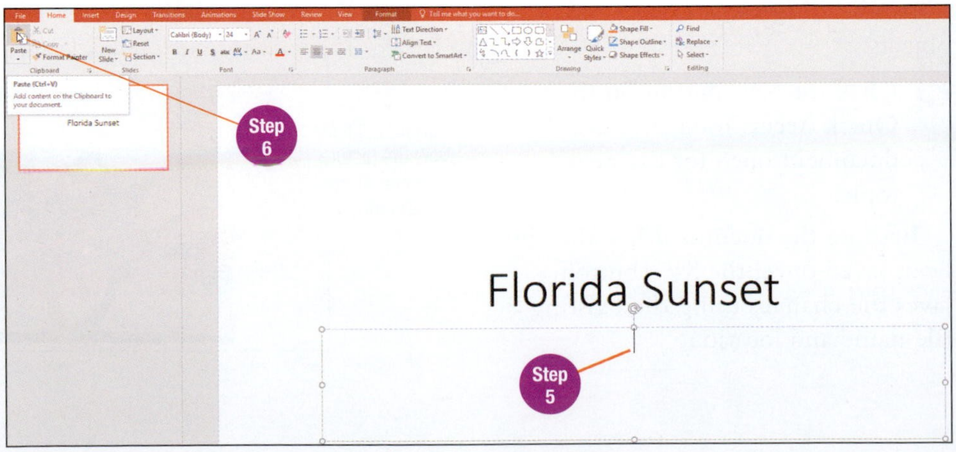

App Tip

Some buttons in the ribbon have two parts. Clicking the top or left of the button causes the default action to occur. Clicking the bottom or right of the button (arrow) displays a list of options to modify the action that occurs.

The selected text that was copied from Word is pasted on the slide in PowerPoint. Notice also the Paste Options button that appears below the pasted text.

7 Click the Paste Options button to display the Paste Options gallery.

Paste Options vary depending on the pasted text or object. Buttons in the gallery allow you to change the appearance or behavior of the pasted text or object in the destination location.

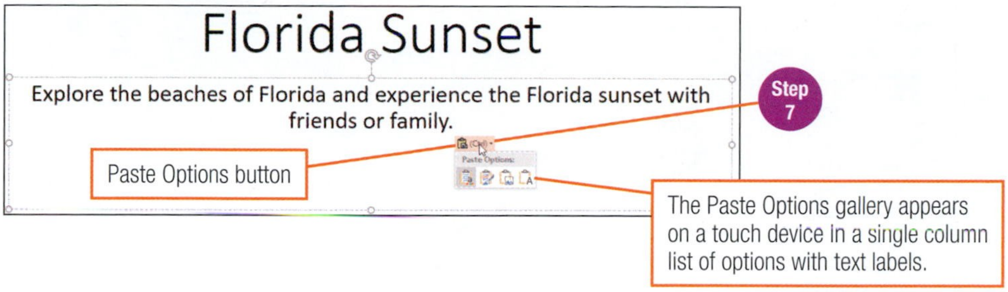
Florida Sunset
Explore the beaches of Florida and experience the Florida sunset with friends or family.
Step 7
Paste Options button
The Paste Options gallery appears on a touch device in a single column list of options with text labels.

8 Click the Word button on the taskbar to switch to Word.

9 Click to select the picture, click the Copy button, click the PowerPoint button on the taskbar, and then click the Paste button. (Remember not to click the down-pointing arrow on the Paste button.)

The pasted picture is dropped onto the slide overlapping the text.

10 Click the Paste Options button. Notice that the Paste Options for a picture are different than the Paste Options for text.

Step 10
Explore the beaches of
the Florida sunset with

11 Click in white space away from the picture to remove the Paste Options gallery.

12 If necessary, click to select the picture object.

13 Drag the selected picture below the text. Release the picture when the orange guide shows the picture is aligned with the middle of the text placeholders.

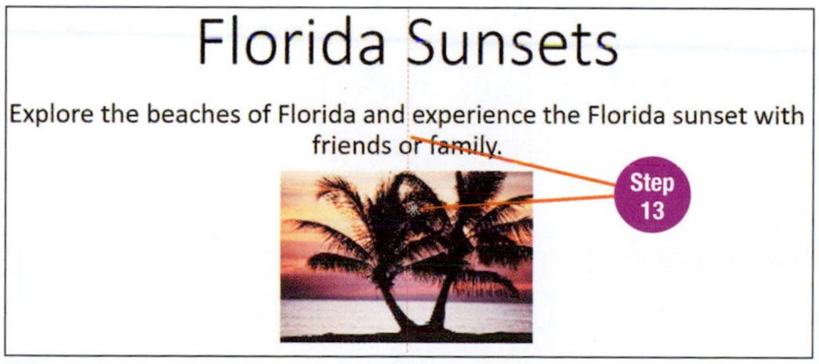
Florida Sunsets
Explore the beaches of Florida and experience the Florida sunset with friends or family.
Step 13

14 Click the Save button on the Quick Access Toolbar.

Quick Steps

Copy and Paste Text or an Object

1. Select text or object.
2. Click Copy button.
3. Navigate to destination document or location within current document.
4. Click Paste button.

Oops!

A Design Ideas task pane opened after you pasted the picture on the slide? Click No Thanks at the bottom of the task pane to close it. PowerPoint Designer is a new service that opens when you add a photo to a title slide.

App Tip

Paste Options are helpful if different formatting exists between the source or destination documents, and you want to control which formatting is applied to the pasted text or object.

15 At the Save As backstage area, click *This PC* and then click *Browse.*

16 Navigate to the Ch3 subfolder in the CompletedTopicsByChapter folder on your USB flash drive.

17 Select the current text in the *File name* text box, type FloridaSunset-YourName, and then press Enter or click Save.

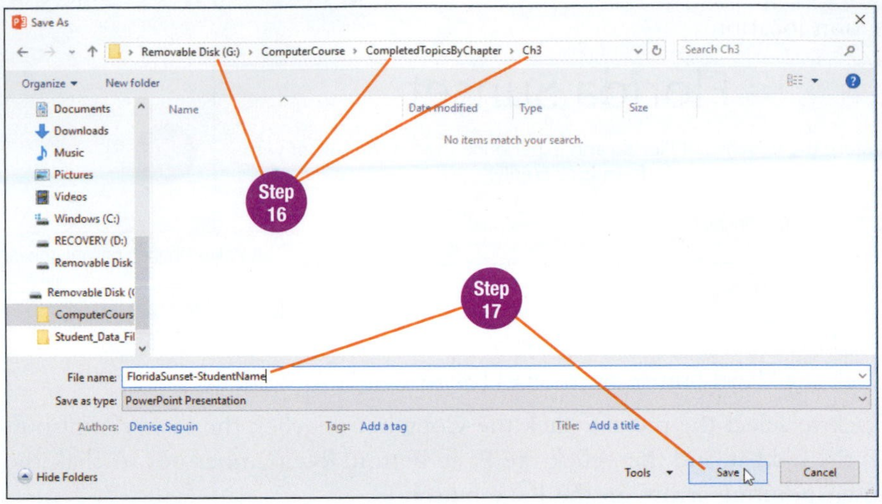

Using Format Painter to Copy Formatting Options

Sometimes instead of copying text or an object, you want to copy formatting options. Format Painter copies to the clipboard the formatting attributes for selected text or an object.

Click the Format Painter button to do a one-time copy of formatting options or double-click the button if you want to paste the formatting options multiple times. Double-clicking the Format Painter button turns the feature on until you click the button again to turn the feature off. A button that operates as on or off is called a **toggle button**.

18 Select the first occurrence of the word *Florida* in the subtitle on the slide.

19 Click the Font Color button arrow (down-pointing arrow at the right of the Font Color button) in the Font group on the Home tab.

20 Click the *Purple* square (the last square in the *Standard Colors* section).

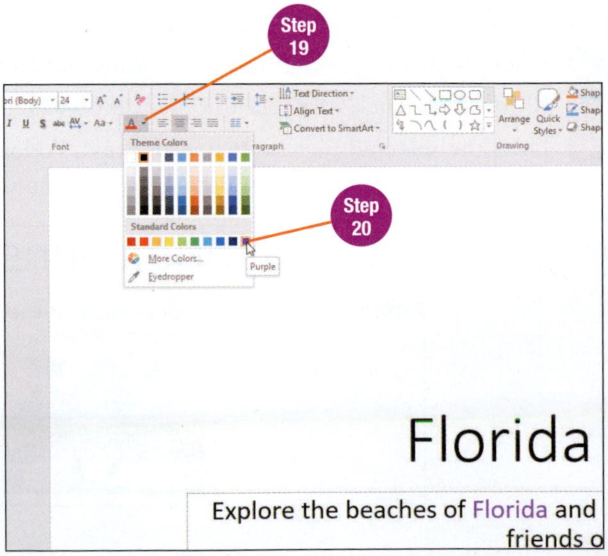

21 With the text still selected, click the Italic button in the Font group on the Home tab.

22 With the text still selected, click the Format Painter button (displays as a paint brush) in the Clipboard group.

23 Drag the mouse pointer with the paintbrush icon across the second occurrence of the word *Florida* in the subtitle.

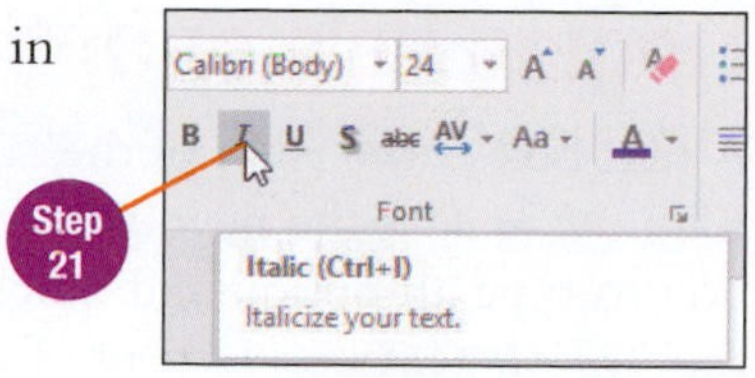

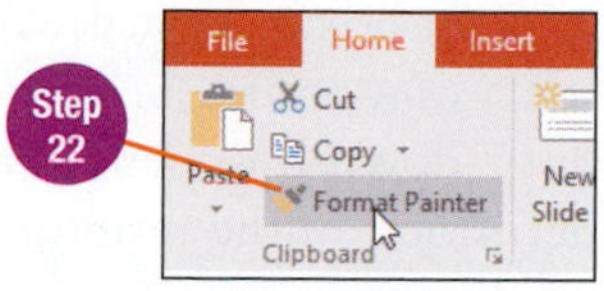

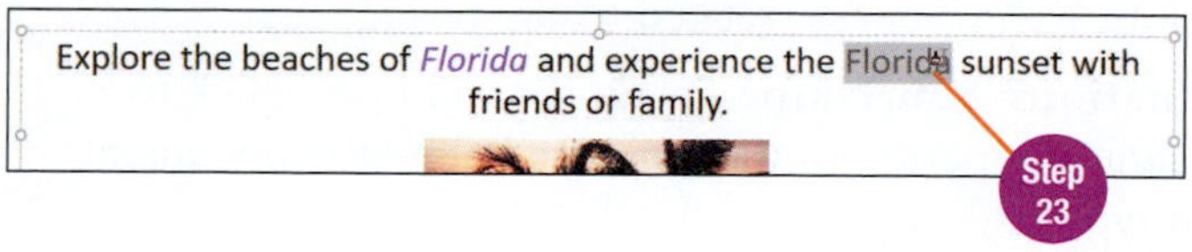

Quick Steps

Copy and Paste Formatting Options

1. Select text or object with desired formatting applied.
2. Click Format Painter button.
3. Click object or drag to select desired text to which formatting is to be copied.

24 Click in white space away from the selected text to deselect the text.

25 Click the Save button on the Quick Access Toolbar.

26 Click to select the picture and display the contextual tab.

27 Click the Picture Tools Format tab.

28 Click the *Drop Shadow Rectangle* option in the Picture Styles gallery (fourth picture style option).

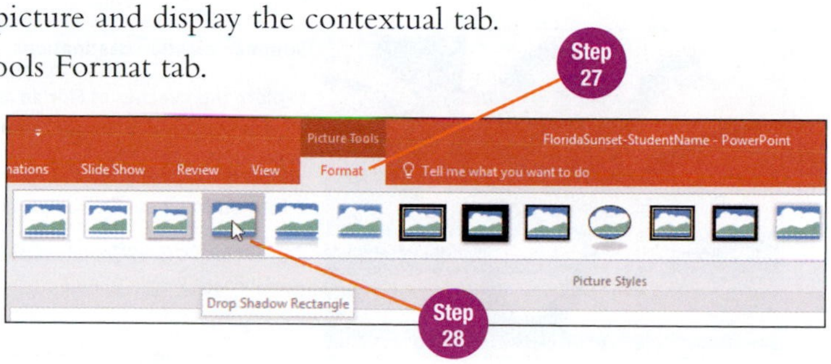

29 With the picture still selected, click the Home tab, click the Format Painter button, and then click the title text *Florida Sunset* at the top of the slide.

30 With the Florida Sunset placeholder selected, click the dialog box launcher in the Drawing group on the Home tab to open the Format Shape task pane at the right side of the window.

31 Click the Size & Properties tab (last option) in the Format Shape task pane.

32 Click Text Box to reveal the options below Text Box in the task pane.

33 Click the *Vertical alignment* option box arrow (down-pointing arrow at the right of *Bottom*) and then click *Middle*.

34 Close the Format Shape task pane.

35 Save and then close PowerPoint. Leave the Word document open for the next topic.

App Tip

You can also align text in a PowerPoint placeholder using the Align Text button in the Paragraph group on the Home tab.

View

Model Answer

Compare your completed file with the model answer.

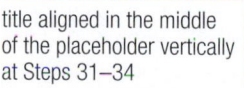

title aligned in the middle of the placeholder vertically at Steps 31–34

3.6 Finding Help or Options Using the Tell Me Feature

Skills

Use Tell Me to locate an option

Use Tell Me to look up a definition

Use Tell Me to find help information

Tutorials

Using the Tell Me Feature

Using the Help Feature

A text box at the right of the last tab on the ribbon containing the text *Tell me what you want to do* is the new **Tell Me** feature in Microsoft Office 2016. Use the text box to type an option and quickly access the command or feature directly from the *Tell Me* text box instead of navigating the ribbon tabs. You can also use the *Tell Me* text box to type a word or phrase and search resources in a Help window to learn how to use an option or feature. The **Smart Lookup** option on the Tell Me drop-down list opens a task pane at the right side of the window that lets you see a definition of the term or explore web resources related to the term.

1. With the **VacationDestinations-YourName** document still open, click to place the insertion point after the period in the sentence below the document title, press Enter, and then type Visit http://ParadigmCollege.net/FloridaTours for information on our Florida vacation packages..
2. Press Enter and then type Our exclusive Got2GoSunset package is our most popular booking..

3. Click to place the insertion point after the last "t" in Got2GoSunset.

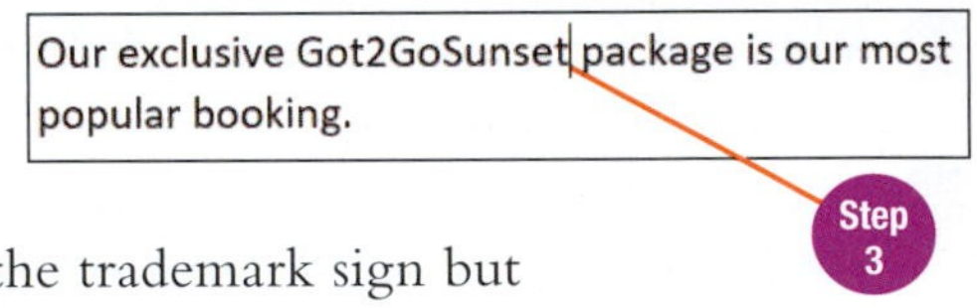

Assume that Got2GoSunset is a trademarked name and you want to insert the trademark sign but do not know where the symbol feature is located.

4. Click in the *Tell Me* text box that contains the text *Tell me what you want to do* at the right of the View tab on the ribbon and then type insert trademark symbol.
5. Click *Insert a Symbol* in the drop-down list and then click the trademark symbol ™ in the Symbol palette that appears.

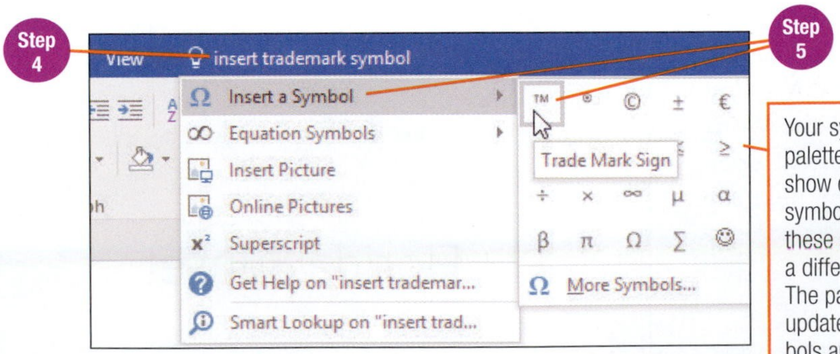

Your symbol palette may show different symbols and/or these symbols in a different order. The palette updates as symbols are used.

trademark sign inserted at Step 5

Check This Out

http://CA2.ParadigmCollege.net/OfficeSupport

Go here to find help at the Office website. Use the search text box to type a word or feature you need help with, or navigate the support website using the links below the search text box. Microsoft provides tutorials and video training by product at the Office Training Center accessed at this page.

6. Click in the *Tell Me* text box and then type watermark.
7. Click *Smart Lookup on "watermark"*.

The Smart Lookup task pane opens at the right side of the window. In the Explore tab of the task pane are web links to resources related to watermark. In the Define tab, you can view a definition of watermark.

8. Click the Got it button in the Smart Lookup task pane if a message displays about data sent to Bing regarding the highlighted term and surrounding content. Skip this step if no message about privacy displays in the task pane.
9. Click the Define tab in the Smart Lookup task pane and then read the definition for watermark in the pane.
10. Close the Smart Lookup task pane.
11. Click in the *Tell Me* text box, type watermark, and then click *Get Help on "watermark"*.

A Word 2016 Help window opens with links to help articles about watermarks.

12. Scroll down if necessary and then click Insert a Watermark in Word 2016 for Windows in the Help window. Read the next page that provides information and the steps to add a watermark.
13. Click Back to return to the previous page.
14. Close the Help window.

Inside the Help window, you can continue searching for other help information by typing a keyword or phrase in the search text box just below the toolbar and pressing Enter.

15. Click in the *Tell Me* text box, type watermark, click *Watermark* at the drop-down list, and then click *SAMPLE 1* in the watermark gallery.
16. Scroll down to view the SAMPLE watermark added to the document background.
17. Click the Save button on the Quick Access Toolbar and then close the Word window. Click No if prompted to save the copied item.

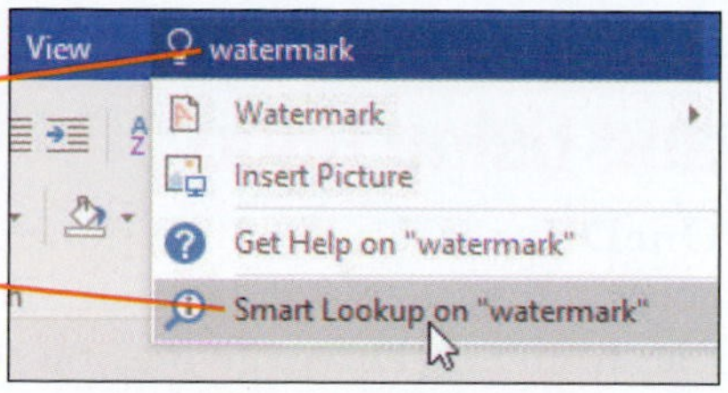

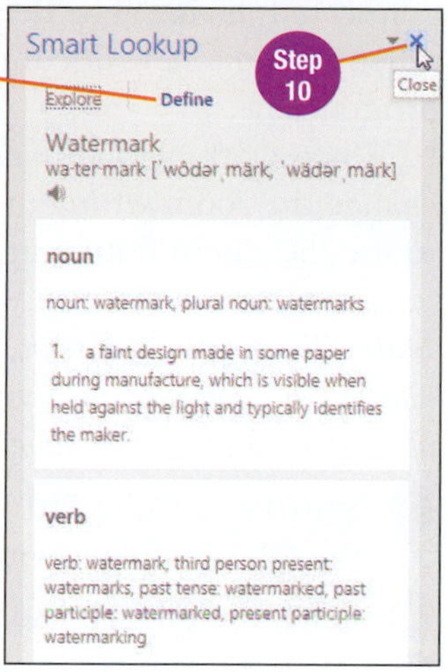

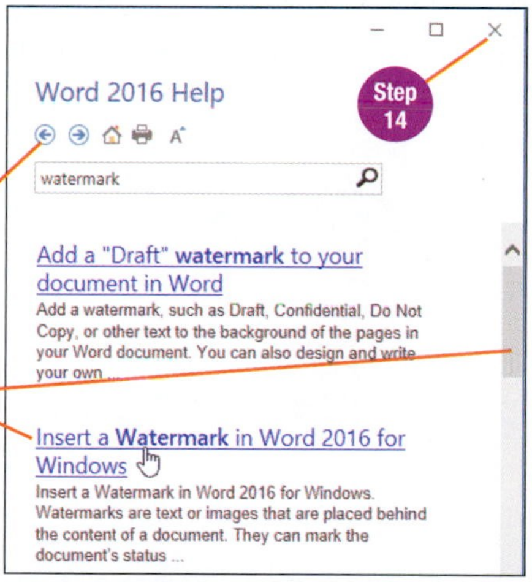

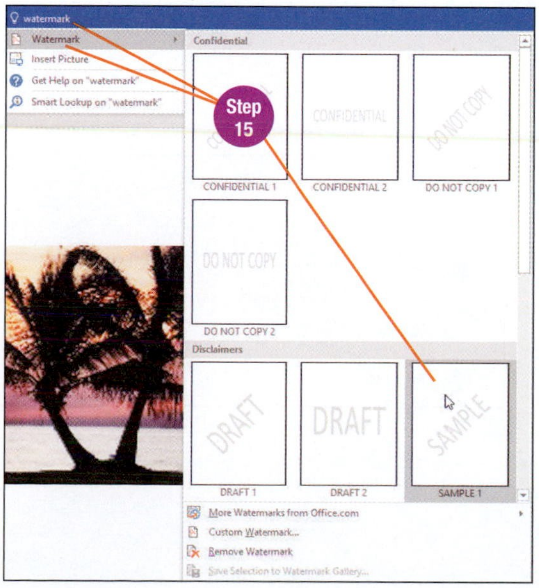

Quick Steps

Use Tell Me Feature

1. Click in *Tell Me* text box.
2. Type option, feature, or a short description of the task you want to complete.
3. Click option in drop-down list to access the feature, open the Help window with links to help information, or perform a Smart Lookup.

Oops!

Word Help window looks different than the screen shown here? Help is updated often and may not appear exactly as shown. Another possibility is that you are seeing offline help results if you are not connected to the Internet. Click a link to watermark help that appears in your window.

Check This Out

http://CA2.ParadigmCollege.net/MicrosoftCommunity

Go here to look for information in Microsoft Community, a free discussion forum where you can post questions about Microsoft products and receive answers from other community members. You need to sign in to ask a question or start a discussion, but if you just want to search for and read other questions and answers, navigate by category or use the search text box at the top of the page.

View

Model Answer

Compare your completed file with the model answer.

3.7 Using OneDrive for Storage, Scrolling in Documents, and Using Undo

Skills

Save and open files to and from OneDrive

Navigate in longer documents

Use Undo

Tutorials

Scrolling

Using Undo and Redo

OneDrive is secure online storage available to individuals signed in with a Microsoft account (often referred to as *cloud storage*). You can save files to and open files from OneDrive, giving you the ability to access the files from any Internet-connected device. The default storage location at the Save As backstage area when saving a new document, workbook, or presentation is OneDrive for Office programs.

When working with longer documents, you will need to scroll the display or change the zoom setting to see more or less text in the window. You will learn how to use the Zoom feature in the next topic. Undo reverses an action and is used often to restore a document when you make a mistake.

***Note:** To complete this topic, you need to be signed in with a Microsoft account. If you do not have a Microsoft account, skip the OneDrive section in Steps 2 to 19 and proceed to Step 20 after opening the presentation.*

1. Start PowerPoint 2016 and then open the presentation **SpeechTechniques** from the Ch3 subfolder within the Student_Data_Files folder on your USB flash drive.
2. Click the File tab and then click *Save As*.
3. Click the *OneDrive - Personal* option at the Save As backstage area.
4. Click the *Documents* folder in the right panel.

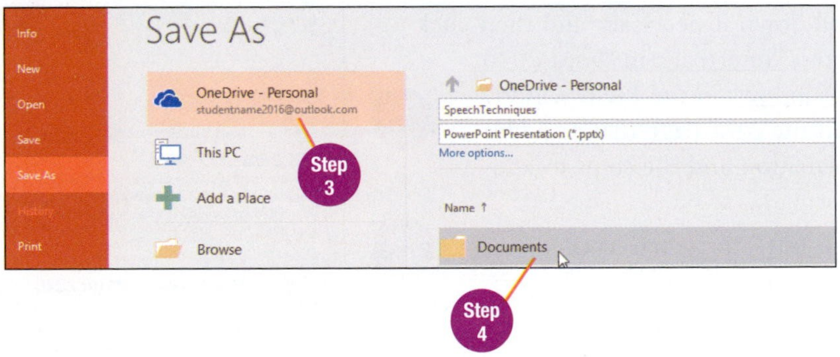

App Tip

You can access the file you will save to OneDrive from any device, even if the device does not have a local copy of PowerPoint. You will learn about the Office Online applications in Chapter 15.

5. Select the text in the *File name* text box at the top of the right panel, type SpeechTechniques-YourName and then click the Save button.

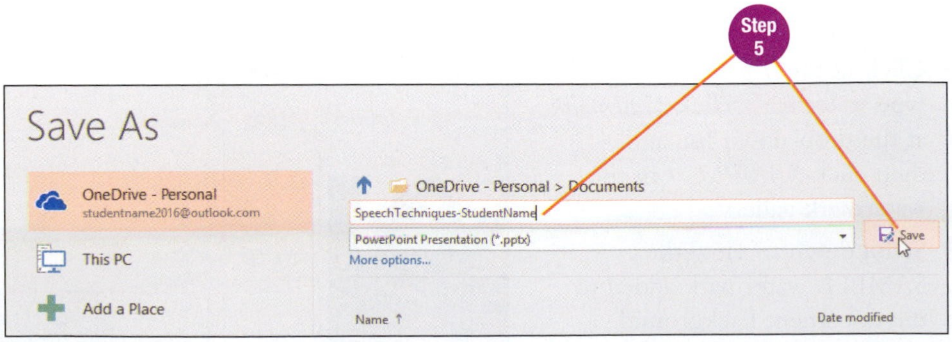

App Tip

The Save button on the Quick Access Toolbar displays with two rounded arrows in a circle when you are working with a document saved to OneDrive.

A progress message displays in the Status bar as the file is uploaded.

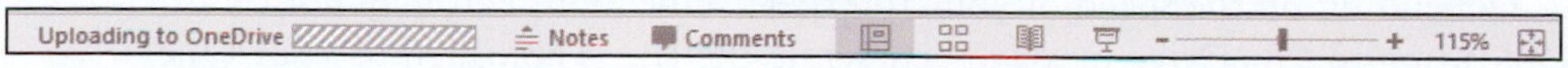

If you decide to use OneDrive for saving work, you should use folders to organize files. In the next steps, you will save the presentation to OneDrive a second time by creating a folder as you save the file.

6 Click the File tab and then click the *Save As* option.

7 With your OneDrive account already selected at the Save As backstage area, click the *Browse* option.

8 At the Save As dialog box, click the New folder button on the Command bar.

Notice that the file saved at Step 5 appears in the Content pane.

9 Type CompletedTopicsByChapter and then press Enter.

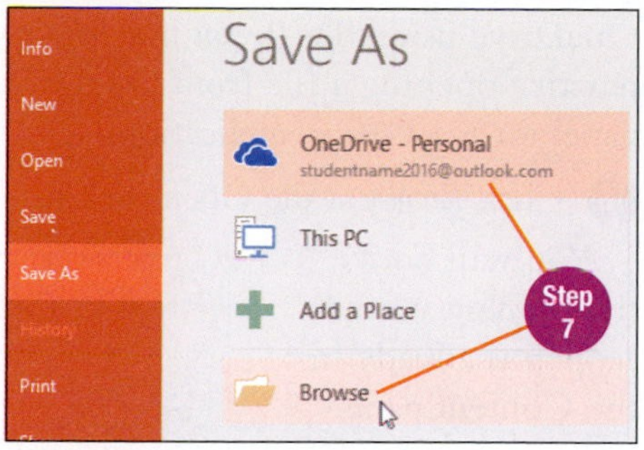

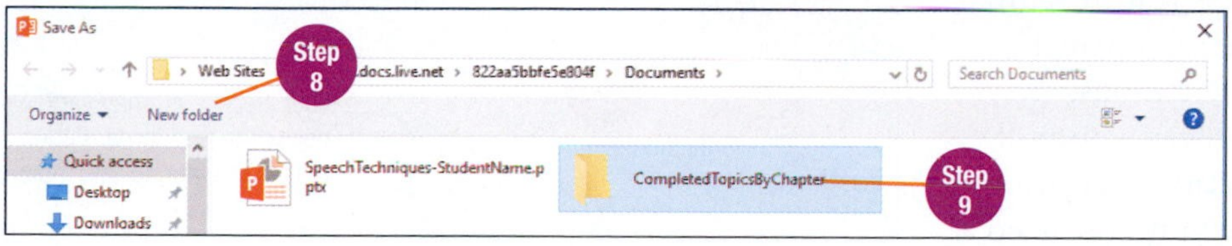

10 Double-click *CompletedTopicsByChapter*.

11 Click the New folder button on the Command bar, type Ch3, and then press Enter.

12 Double-click *Ch3*.

13 Click the Save button to save the presentation using the same name as before.

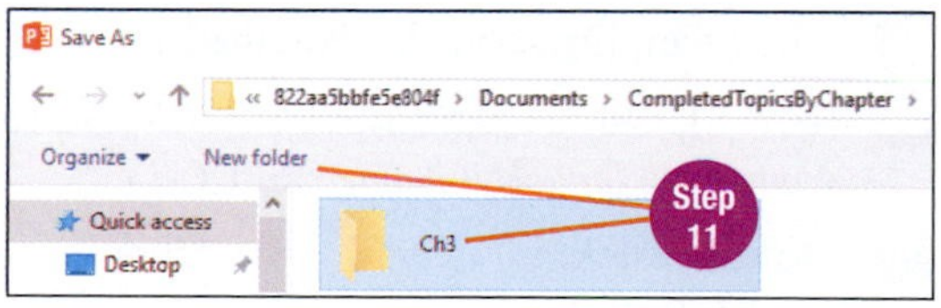

You now have two copies of the presentation saved on OneDrive.

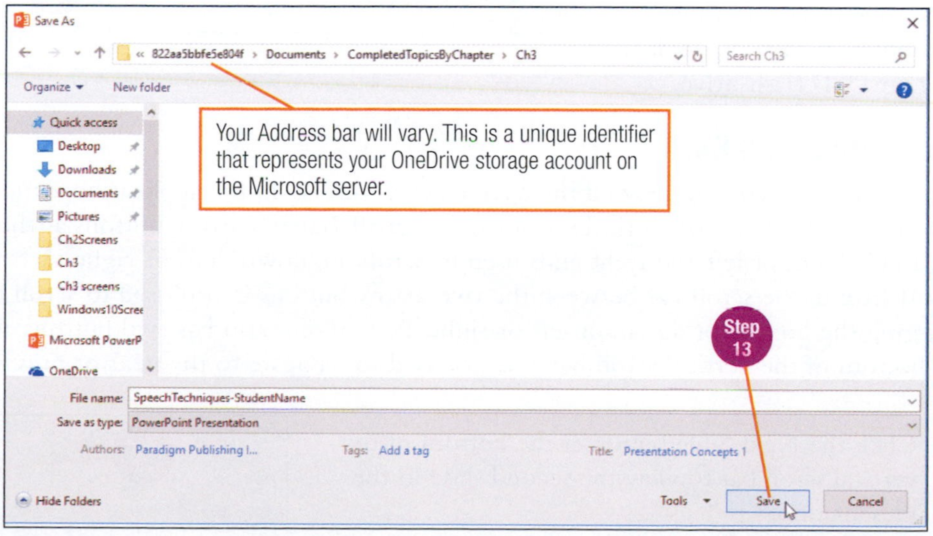

Quick Steps

Save a File to OneDrive

1. Click File tab.
2. Click *Save As*.
3. If necessary, click OneDrive account name.
4. Click folder in right panel or click *Browse*.
5. If necessary, navigate to desired folder at Save As dialog box.
6. Type name for file in *File name* text box.
7. Click Save.

App Tip

You may notice a one- or two-second delay when navigating folders in the Open or Save As dialog box when working on OneDrive. When that happens, wait a few seconds for the screen to update—do not click options or commands a second time.

14 Click the File tab and then click *Close.*

Depending on the speed of your Internet connection, you may notice an Uploading to OneDrive message box while the file is uploaded to your OneDrive account.

15 Click the Open button on the Quick Access Toolbar.

Because you just closed the presentation, you will notice the presentation appears twice in the *Recent* list in the right panel. Notice that your OneDrive account is associated with each of these entries. You could reopen the presentation from OneDrive using the *Recent* list; however, in the next steps, you will use Browse to practice opening a file from OneDrive in case a file you need is not in the *Recent* panel for the Office application.

16 Click *Browse* at the Open backstage area.

You will notice the file you want to reopen is already in the Content pane because the Quick access feature shows recently opened presentations; however, you will practice navigating in case you ever need a file that has not been recently opened.

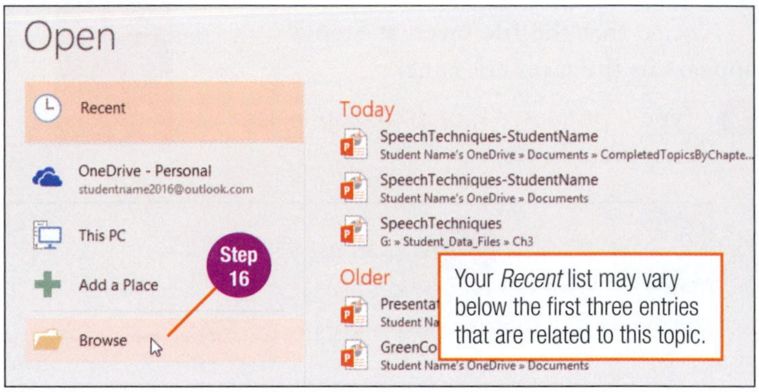

App Tip

When you work with files on OneDrive, the file you are updating is a copy of the file saved on your local device. A green check mark on folder and file names in the Content pane means that the local copy matches the copy on OneDrive; a red x means the file or folder is not synchronized. Synchronization occurs automatically in the background whenever Internet connectivity is available.

17 Click OneDrive in the Navigation pane.

18 In the Content pane, double-click the folders *Documents*, *CompletedTopicsByChapter*, and *Ch3*.

19 Double-click ***SpeechTechniques-YourName*** in the Content pane.

Navigate folders on OneDrive using the same methods as navigating folders on your USB flash drive.

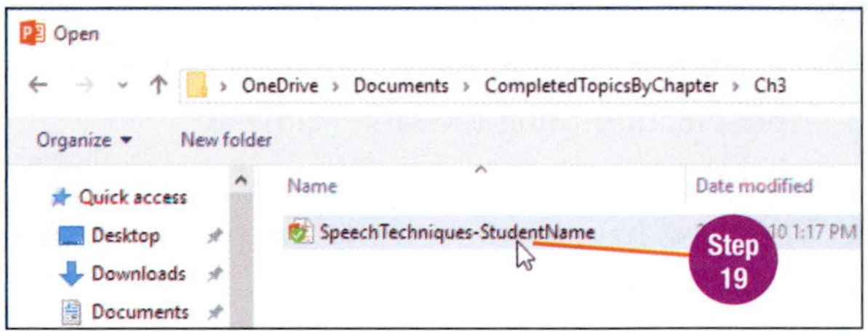

Using the Scroll Bars

App Tip

Horizontal and vertical scroll bars appear only when the file exceeds the viewing area.

Larger files with content beyond the current view display in the application window with a horizontal and/or vertical scroll bar. A **scroll bar** has arrow buttons at the top and bottom or left and right ends used to scroll up, down, left, or right. A **scroll box** in the scroll bar between the two arrow buttons is also used to scroll by dragging the box up or down, or left or right. PowerPoint also has two buttons at the bottom of the vertical scroll bar that are used to navigate to the next or previous slide.

20 Click the Next Slide button at the bottom of the vertical scroll bar to view the second slide in the presentation.

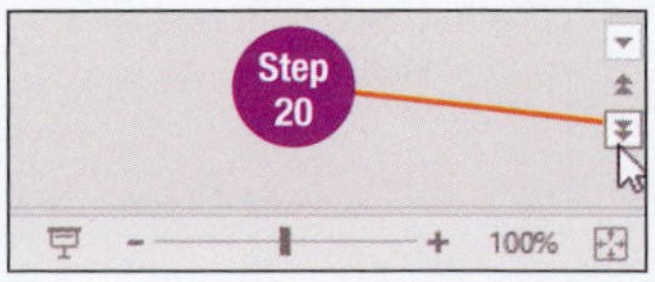

21 Click the Next Slide button two more times to move to Slide 4.

22 Click the up arrow button at the top of the vertical scroll bar repeatedly until you are returned to the first slide.

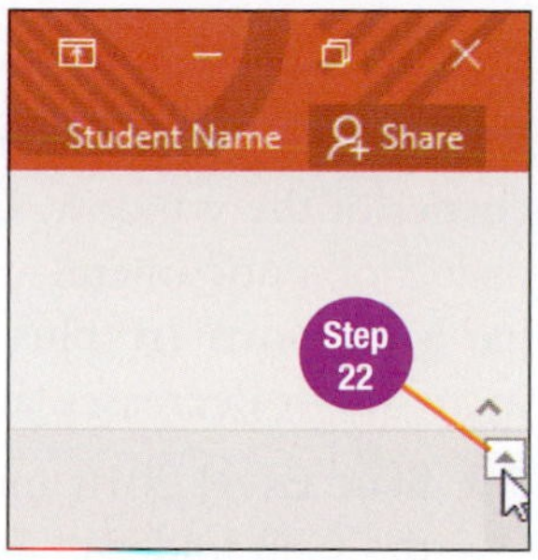

23 Drag the scroll box at the top of the vertical scroll bar downward until you reach the end of the slides.

As you drag the scroll box downward, a ScreenTip displays the slide numbers and titles for the slides so you know when to release the mouse.

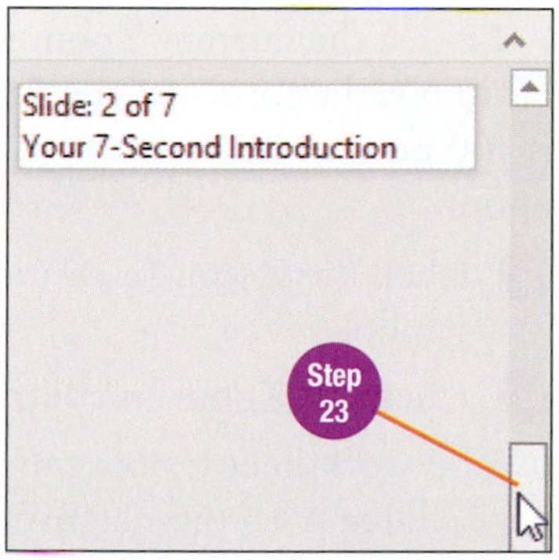

24 Press Ctrl + Home.

Ctrl + Home is the universal keyboard shortcut for returning to the beginning of a file.

25 Press Ctrl + End.

Ctrl + End is the universal keyboard shortcut for navigating to the end of a file.

Quick Steps

Scroll within a File
Click arrow button for desired direction to scroll in horizontal or vertical scroll bar, or drag scroll box in horizontal or vertical scroll bar.

Use Undo
Click Undo button on the Quick Access Toolbar.

Oops!

Using Touch Keyboard? Skip Steps 24 and 25 because the Touch Keyboard does not have Home and End keys.

Using Undo

The **Undo** command in all Office applications can be used to restore a document, presentation, worksheet, or Access object to its state before the last action that was performed. If you make a change to a file and do not like the results, immediately click the Undo button on the Quick Access Toolbar. Some actions, such as Save, cannot be reversed with Undo.

26 Navigate to the first slide in the presentation.

27 Select the title text *Speech Techniques*.

28 Click the Bold button on the Mini toolbar or in the Font group on the Home tab.

29 With the text still selected, click the Underline button on the Mini toolbar or in the Font group on the Home tab.

30 Click on any part of the slide away from the selected text to deselect the title text.

31 Click the Undo button on the Quick Access Toolbar. Do *not* click the down-pointing arrow on the button.

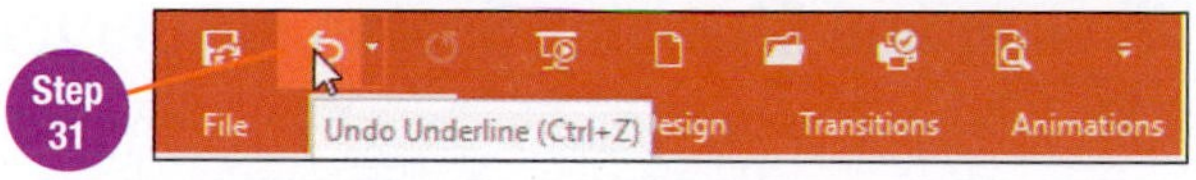

The underline is removed from the title text and the text is selected.

32 Click the Undo button a second time to remove the bold formatting.

33 Click on the slide away from the selected text to deselect the text and then click the Save button on the Quick Access Toolbar.

34 Close the presentation and then close PowerPoint.

App Tip

Undo stores multiple actions. To undo an action that was not the last action performed, click the Undo button arrow and then click the desired action in the drop-down list.

App Tip

Use the Redo button on the Quick Access Toolbar if you change your mind after using Undo and want the action reapplied to the document.

View

Model Answer
Compare your completed file with the model answer.

3.8 Changing the Zoom Option and Screen Resolution

Skills

Change the Zoom setting

View the screen resolution and change the setting if possible to match textbook illustrations

Tutorial
Changing the Zoom

Word, Excel, and PowerPoint display a **Zoom slider** bar near the bottom right corner of the window. Using the slider, you can zoom out or zoom in to view more or less of a document, worksheet, slide, or presentation. At each end of the slider bar is a **Zoom In** (plus symbol) and a **Zoom Out** (minus symbol) control that increases or decreases the magnification by 10 percent at each click.

1. Start Excel 2016 and then open the workbook named **CutRateRentals** from the Ch3 folder in Student_Data_Files.

Notice the current Zoom setting near the bottom right corner of the Excel window, which is 100 percent if the setting is at the default option.

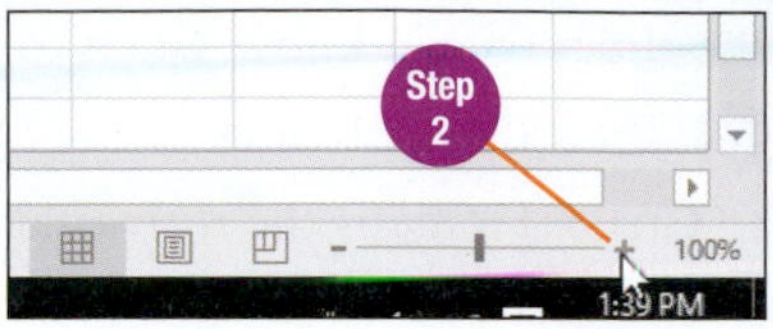

2. Click the Zoom In control (displays as a plus symbol).
3. Click the Zoom In control two more times.

The worksheet is now much larger in the display area with the magnification increased 30 percent.

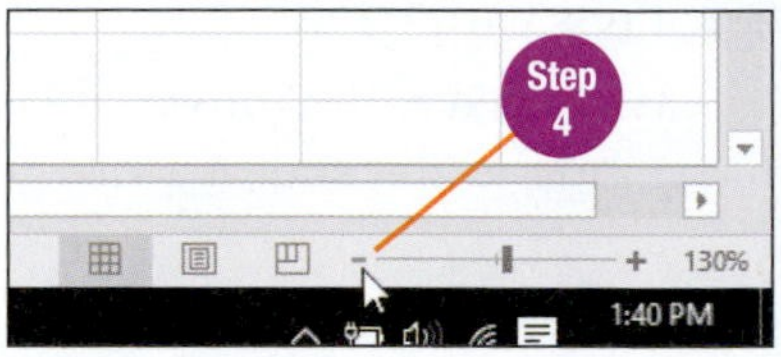

4. Click the Zoom Out control (displays as a minus symbol).
5. Drag the Zoom slider left or right and watch magnification of the worksheet decrease or increase as you move the slider.

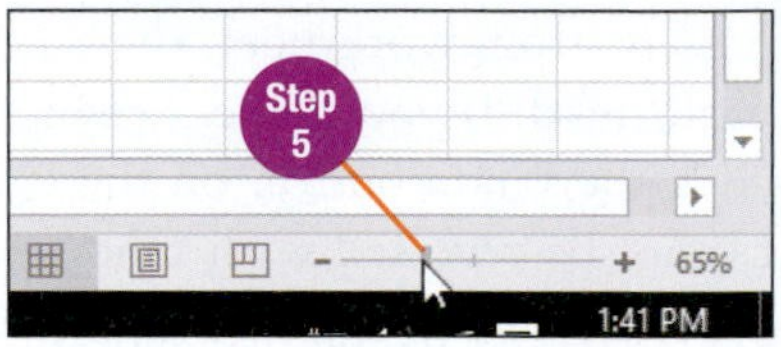

6. Drag the Zoom slider to the middle of the slider bar to change the zoom to 100 percent.
7. Click *100%* at the right of the Zoom In control.

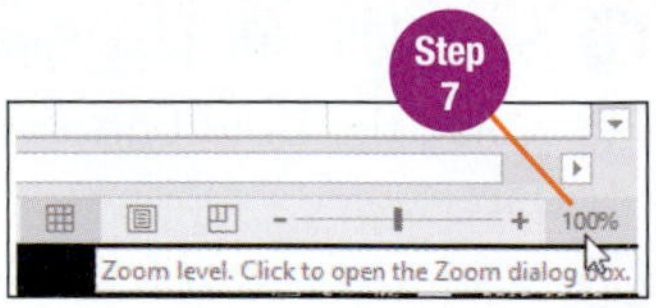

This opens the Zoom dialog box, where you can choose a predefined magnification, type a custom percentage value, or choose the *Fit selection* option to fit a group of selected cells to the window.

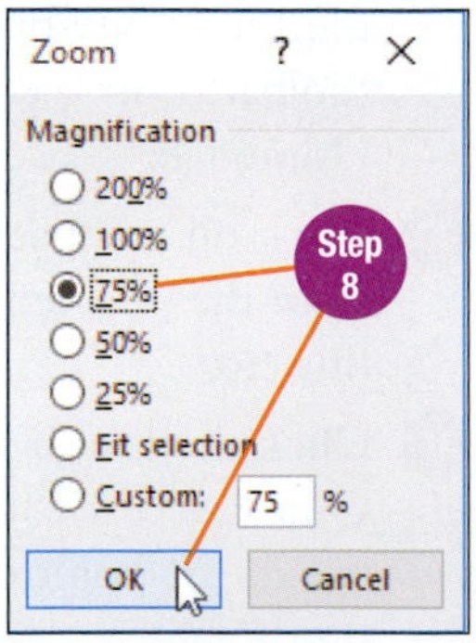

8. Click *75%* and then press Enter or click OK.
9. Return the zoom magnification to 100 percent by dragging the Zoom slider to the middle of the slider bar.

Zoom In, Zoom Out, the Zoom slider, and the Zoom dialog box function the same in Word and PowerPoint.

Oops!

Having trouble using the Zoom slider on a touch device? Tap the controls or the percentage number to open the Zoom dialog box (Steps 7–8), or use the Zoom buttons on the View tab on the ribbon.

App Tip

The View tab in Word, PowerPoint, and Excel contain a Zoom group with buttons to change zoom magnification. Access does not include the Zoom feature.

Viewing and Changing Screen Resolution

The ribbon on your computer may show fewer or more buttons than the illustrations in this textbook, or some buttons may show icons only (no labels). The appearance of the ribbon is affected by the screen resolution (Figure 3.4 on page 89).

Screen resolution refers to the number of picture elements, called *pixels*, that form the image on the display. A pixel is a square with color values. Millions of pixels are used to render display images. Resolution is expressed as the number of horizontal pixels by the number of vertical pixels.

Note: *Check with your instructor before proceeding onward. Some schools do not allow the display properties to be changed. If necessary, perform Steps 10–18 on your home PC.*

10. Minimize the Excel window to display the desktop.

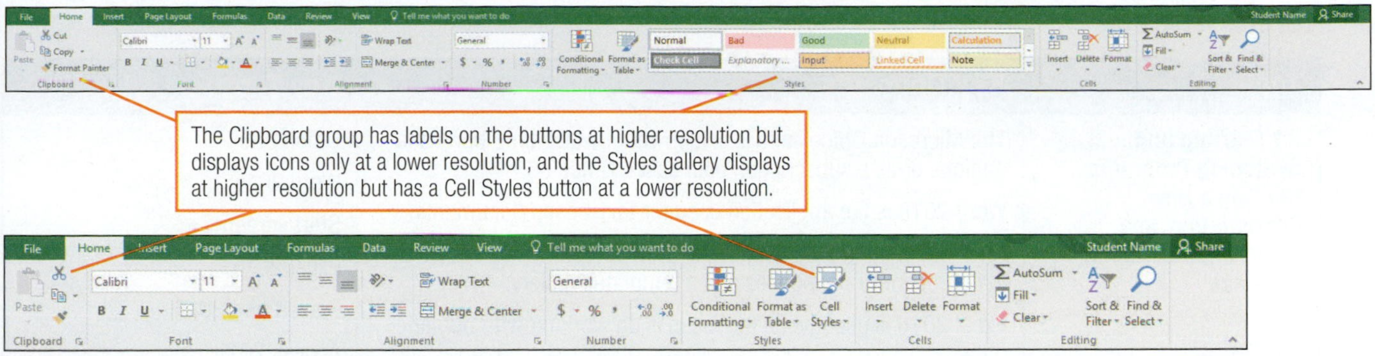

The Clipboard group has labels on the buttons at higher resolution but displays icons only at a lower resolution, and the Styles gallery displays at higher resolution but has a Cell Styles button at a lower resolution.

Figure 3.4

Shown is the Excel Home tab at 1920 x 1080 (top) and at 1280 x 1024 (bottom).

11 Right-click a blank area on the desktop and then click *Display settings*.

12 Click *Advanced display settings* at the bottom of the Customize your display panel in the Settings app with *Display* selected in the left pane. You may need to scroll down to the bottom of the right panel to find the option.

13 If the current setting for *Resolution* is *1920 x 1080*, skip to Step 16; otherwise, click the *Resolution* option box and then click *1920 x 1080* if the option is available; otherwise, use the resolution option that displays with *(Recommended)*.

14 Click the Apply button.

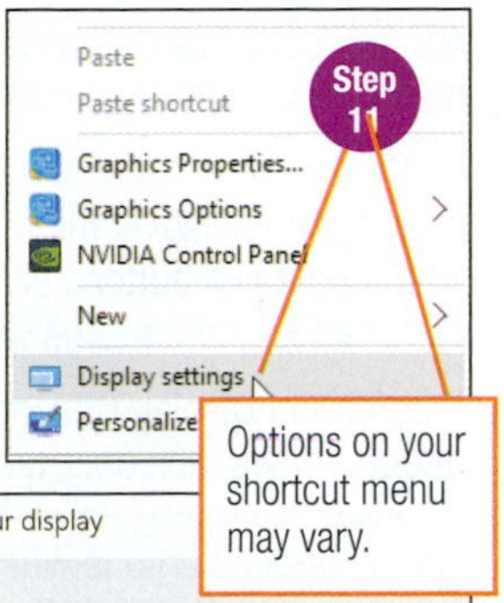

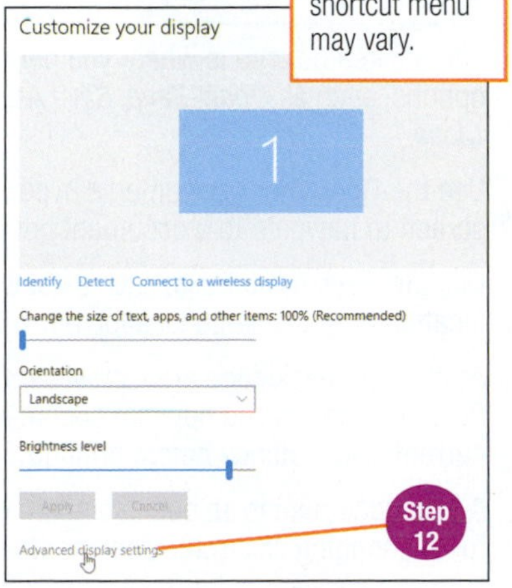

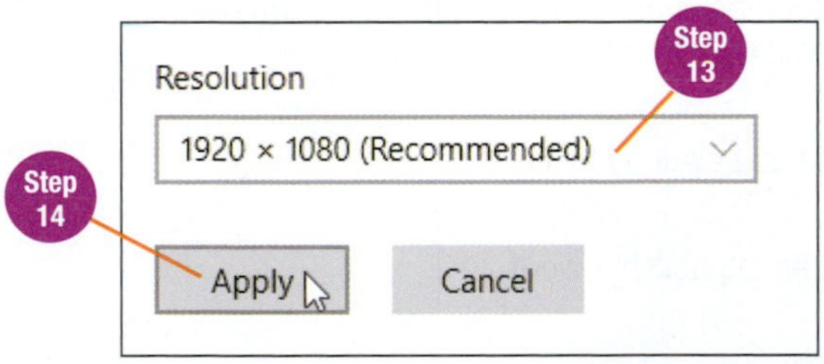

Quick Steps

Change Zoom Magnification

Click Zoom In or Zoom Out button or drag Zoom slider to desired setting

OR

1. Click zoom percentage.
2. Select desired zoom option at Zoom dialog box.
3. Click OK.

App Tip

Screen resolution is an operating system setting. A higher resolution uses more pixels and means the image quality is sharper or clearer. It also means more content can be displayed in the viewing area.

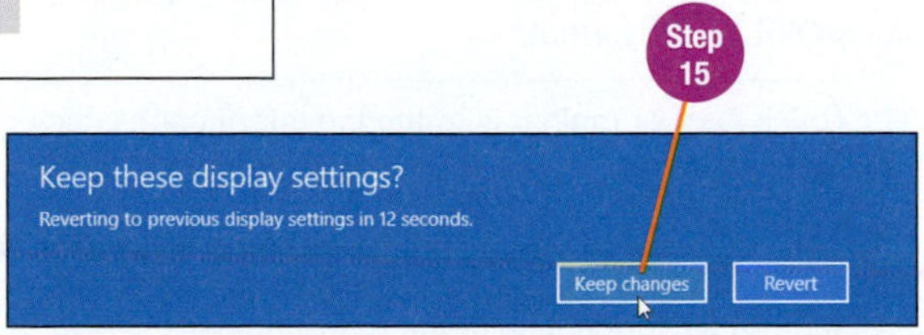

15 Click the Keep changes button.

16 Close the Settings app window.

17 Click the Excel button on the taskbar to view the Excel window at the new screen resolution.

18 If you changed your screen resolution, examine the screen to see if you like the new setting. If the interface is not of good quality, repeat Steps 10 to 16 to restore the resolution option to its original setting. The setting that displays with *(Recommended)* is usually the best choice for your device.

You do not need to change the screen resolution to the same setting used for the images in this textbook. Just be aware that some illustrations may not match exactly what is on your display if your resolution is at a different setting.

19 Close the **CutRateRentals** worksheet and then close Excel.

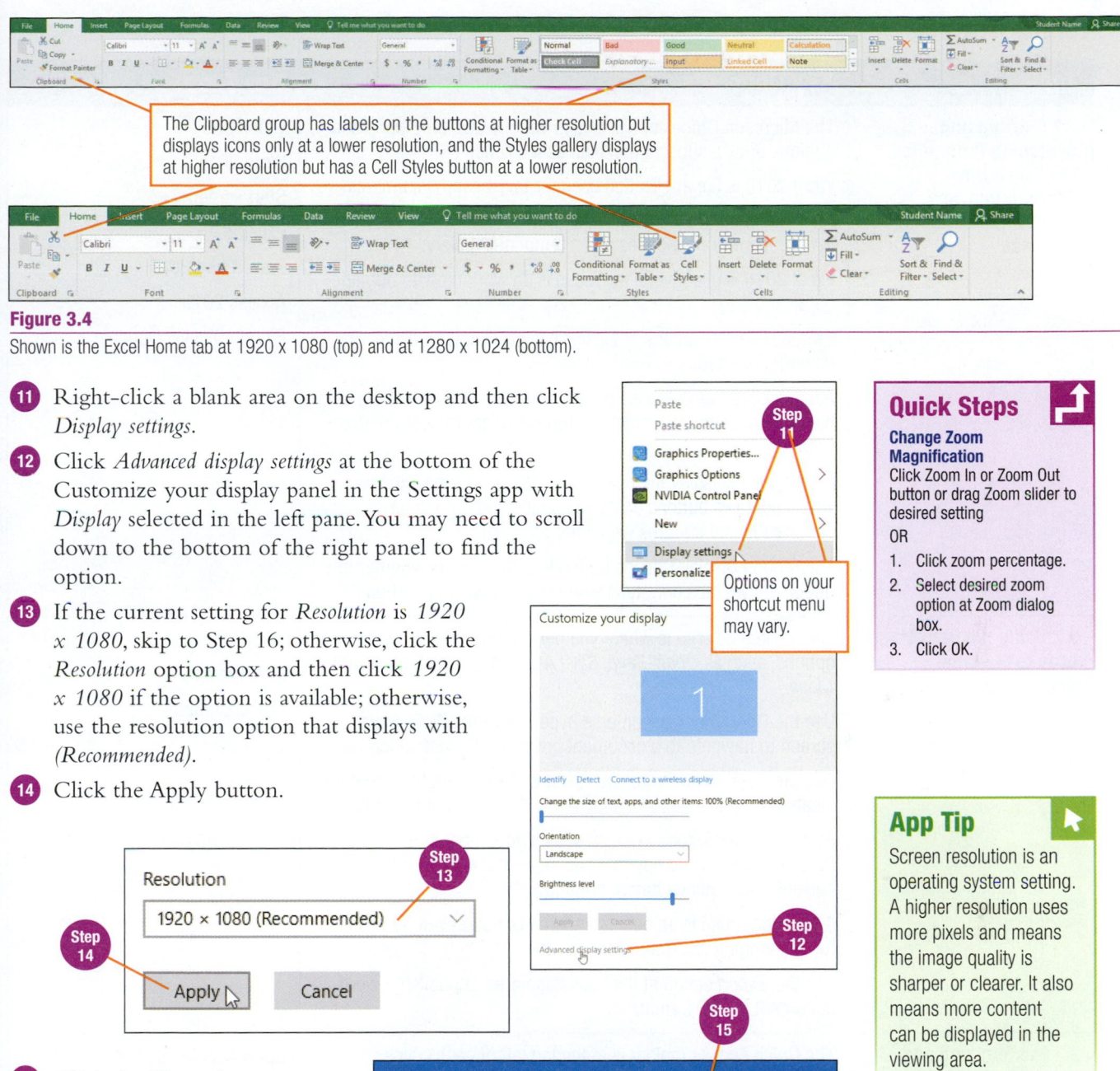

Topics Review

Topic	Key Concepts	Key Terms
3.1 Starting and Switching Programs, Starting a New Presentation, and Exploring the Ribbon Interface	The Microsoft Office suite is sold in various one-time purchase editions or as a subscription plan called Office 365. Word 2016 is the application used for text-based documents. An Office program starts with the Start screen, which shows a list of recently opened files and a templates gallery. Excel 2016 is used when the focus is on working with numeric data. Create slides for an oral or kiosk-style presentation using PowerPoint 2016. Access 2016 is a database program used to organize, store, and maintain related data, such as information about customers or products. All programs display the ribbon along the top of the window, which contains buttons divided into tabs and groups for commands and features within the program. The Ribbon Display Options button lets you control whether the ribbon shows tabs only, tabs with commands, or no ribbon.	Office 365 Word 2016 Start screen Excel 2016 PowerPoint 2016 Access 2016 Ribbon Display Options
3.2 Using the Backstage Area to Manage Documents	The backstage area is where you perform document-level options, such as *Open*, *Save*, *Save As*, *Print*, *Share*, *Export*, and *Close*. Use the Open Other Documents hyperlink at the Word Start screen to navigate to a document not in the *Recent* option list. Use the *Save As* option to save a copy of a document in another location or in the same location but with a different file name. At the Print backstage area, preview a document in the Print Preview panel to see how the document will look with the current print settings before printing. A PDF document is an open standard created by Adobe Systems for exchanging electronic documents. Use the *Export* option at the backstage area to publish a Word document in PDF format.	backstage area Print Preview PDF document
3.3 Customizing and Using the Quick Access Toolbar	The Quick Access Toolbar is at the top left of each Office application window. Add to or remove buttons from the Quick Access Toolbar by clicking the Customize Quick Access Toolbar button and then clicking the desired option at the drop-down list. The Quick Access Toolbar can be customized individually for each Office application.	Quick Access Toolbar

continued...

Topic	Key Concepts	Key Terms
3.4 Selecting Text or Objects, Using the Ribbon and Mini Toolbar, and Selecting Objects in Dialog Boxes	A selected object displays with circles around the perimeter called *selection handles*, which are used to resize or otherwise manipulate the object. The Mini toolbar contains the same buttons as the ribbon and appears near selected text or with the shortcut menu. Dragging a selection handle resizes a picture, shape, chart, or other item referred to as an *object*. A contextual tab appears when an object is selected with buttons related to the object. A gallery is a drop-down list or grid with visual representations of options. A live preview shows the text or object as it will look if the option on which the mouse is resting is applied. The dialog box launcher is located at the bottom right of a group on the ribbon and displays a task pane or dialog box when clicked. Task panes and dialog boxes provide additional options for the related ribbon group as buttons, lists, sliders, check boxes, text boxes, and option buttons. Colored horizontal and vertical alignment guides appear when moving an object to help you place and align the object with text, margins, or other nearby objects.	selection handle Mini toolbar object contextual tab gallery live preview dialog box launcher task pane dialog box alignment guide
3.5 Using the Office Clipboard and Formatting Using a Task Pane	The Clipboard group on the ribbon is standardized across all Office applications. Use Cut, Copy, and Paste buttons to move or copy text or objects. A Paste Options button appears when you paste text or an object with options for modifying the paste action. Use the Format Painter button to copy formatting options. A button, such as the Format Painter button, that operates in an on or off state is called a *toggle button*.	Format Painter toggle button
3.6 Finding Help or Options Using the Tell Me Feature	Click in the *Tell Me* text box that displays *Tell me what you want to do* and then type a term or option to locate the option directly from the Tell Me list or to look up help resources about the feature in a Word 2016 Help window. Click the *Smart Lookup* option from the Tell Me drop-down list to open a task pane with web links and definitions for the term.	Tell Me Smart Lookup
3.7 Using OneDrive for Storage, Scrolling in Documents, and Using Undo	OneDrive is cloud storage where you can save files that can be accessed from any other Internet-connected device by selecting your OneDrive account at the Open and Save As backstage areas. Horizontal and vertical scroll bars with arrow buttons and a scroll box are used to navigate larger documents. The Undo feature is used to reverse an action performed restoring a document to its previous state.	OneDrive scroll bar scroll box Undo

continued...

Topic	Key Concepts	Key Terms
3.8 Changing the Zoom Option and Screen Resolution	Use the Zoom In, Zoom Out, Zoom slider, and Zoom dialog box in Word, Excel, and PowerPoint to increase or decrease the magnification setting. Screen resolution refers to the number of horizontal and vertical pixels used to render an image on the display. The screen resolution setting for your PC or mobile device affects the display of the ribbon.	Zoom slider Zoom In Zoom Out screen resolution

Recheck

Recheck your understanding of the topics covered in this chapter.

Workbook

Chapter review and assessment resources are available in the *Workbook* ebook.

Chapter 4

Organizing and Managing Class Notes Using OneNote

Precheck

Check your understanding of the topics covered in this chapter.

OneNote is a note-taking software application referred to as a *digital notebook*. Think of OneNote as the electronic equivalent of a binder with notes written on loose leaf paper organized by dividers. Note-taking software can store, organize, search, and share notes of any type, including typed notes, handwritten notes on a tablet, web pages, pictures, documents, presentations, worksheets, email messages, appointments, contacts, and more. A OneNote notebook can collect everything you want to keep track of for a subject or topic in one place.

OneNote notebooks can be stored on OneDrive so that you can access the notes from any Internet-connected device. Another advantage to storing a notebook on OneDrive is that you can share it with others so that more than one person can edit a page. For group projects, OneNote is a useful tool for collaborating and sharing ideas, research, and content.

In this chapter, you will learn how to open an existing notebook; create a new OneNote notebook; add sections, pages, and content; tag and search notes; and share a notebook with others.

Learning Objectives

4.1 Open an existing notebook, add a note, apply color to note text, add a section, and add a page

4.2 Insert web content into a notebook

4.3 Insert a picture and document, and embed a copy of a presentation into a notebook

4.4 Tag a note, view tags, and jump to a tagged note

4.5 Search notes and close a notebook

4.6 Create a new notebook and share a notebook

SNAP If you are a SNAP user, go to your SNAP Assignments page to complete the Precheck, Tutorials, and Recheck.

Data Files

Before beginning this chapter, be sure you have copied the student data files for this course to your storage medium. Steps on downloading and extracting the data files are provided in Chapter 1, Topic 1.8, on pages 22–23.

4.1 Opening a Notebook and Adding Notes, Sections, and Pages

Skills

- Open an existing notebook
- Create and move a note
- Apply color to note text
- Add a section and page

OneNote 2016 is the note-taking application within the Microsoft Office suite. A **OneNote notebook** is organized into sections, which are accessed by tabs across the top of the notebook. Think of sections as the dividers you would use in a binder to organize notes by subject, topic, or category. Within each section you add pages. Notes or other content are added to a page. You can add as many sections and pages as you like to organize a notebook. Notes or other content can be added anywhere on a page.

1. Click in the search text box on the taskbar, type OneNote 2016, and then press Enter. Windows 7 users may be prompted to sign in with their Microsoft account before OneNote starts for the first time.

The OneNote Start screen (Figure 4.1) appears with tips for using OneNote and links to how-to videos. By default a personal notebook for your Microsoft account is created and opened. The notebook is stored in OneDrive. You can put everything in one notebook or create separate notebooks for keeping notes organized. For example, you may want to create one notebook for school-related content and another for personal content.

Note: *The Start screen shown in Figure 4.1 may not appear depending on the configuration for the computer you are using.*

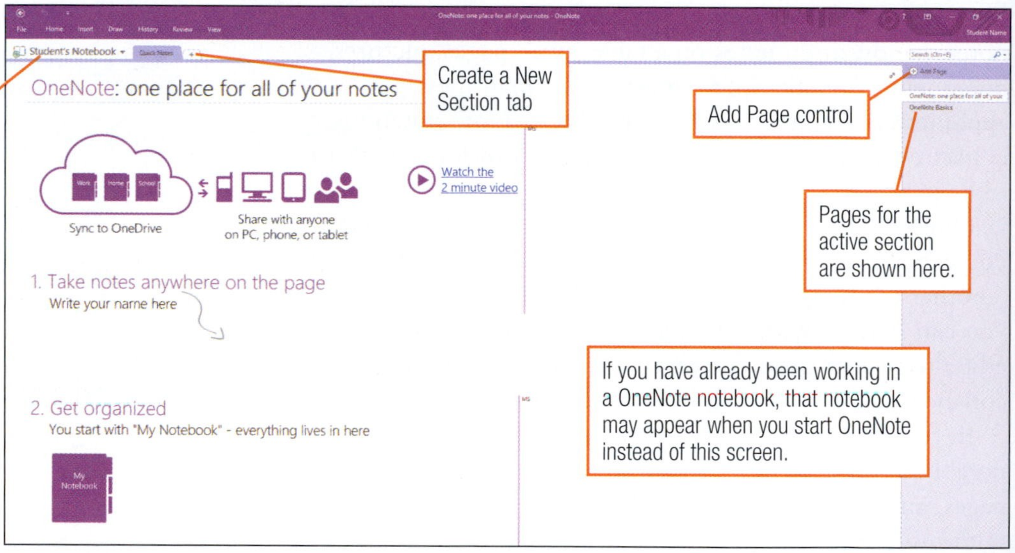

Figure 4.1

The OneNote Start screen is shown with your personal notebook open and the Quick Notes tab active.

> **Oops!**
>
> Does a message display telling you Microsoft OneNote is not the default program for OneNote hyperlinks and asking if you want to change the associations? Click Yes, then click OK at the next message telling you to change the associations in the Settings app. The Start screen will load next.

2. Click Student's Notebook (where *Student's* is your first name), or other notebook name, and then click *Open Other Notebooks.*

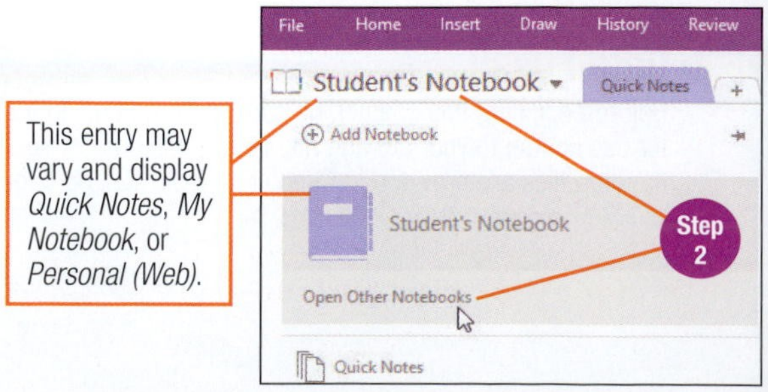

3 At the Open Notebook backstage area, click *Browse* in the *Open from other locations* section.

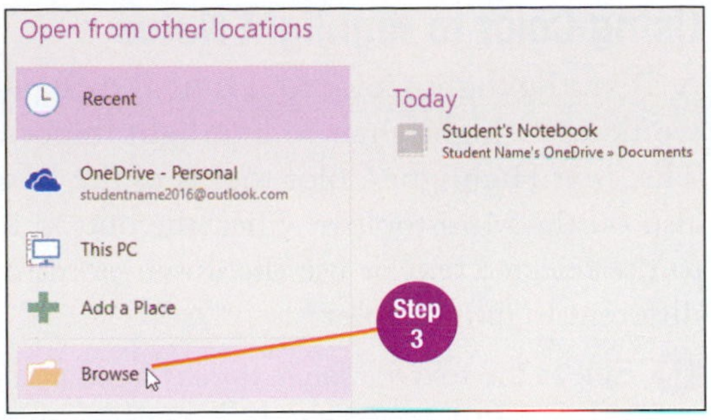

4 Navigate to the entry for your storage medium in the Navigation pane and then double-click the *Student_Data_Files* and *Ch4* folder names in the Content pane at the Open Notebook dialog box.

5 Double-click the *TechnologyCourse* folder name.

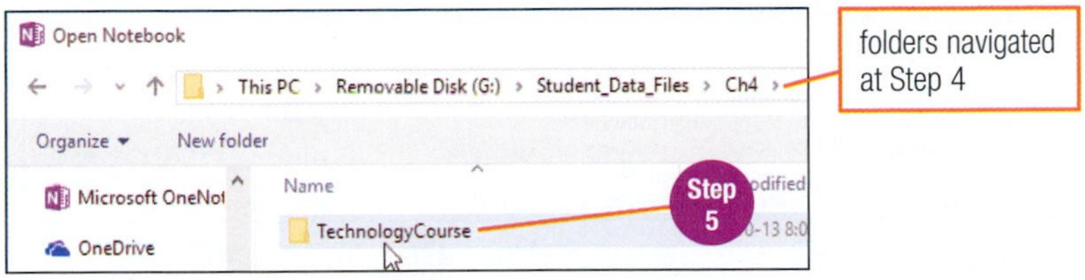

6 Double-click ***Open Notebook***.

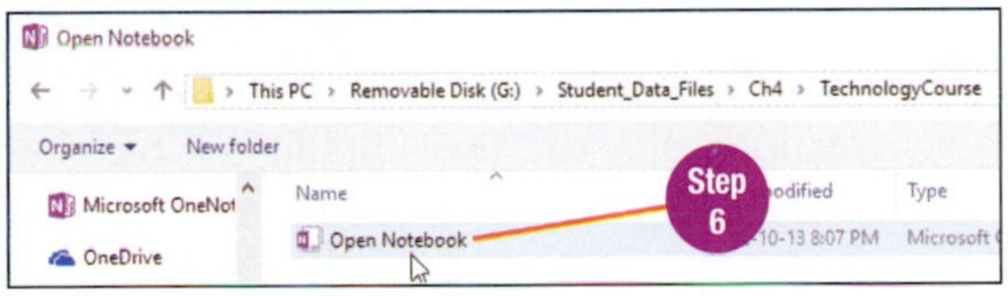

By default, OneNote creates a table of contents file named Open Notebook saved within a folder that is named the notebook name. The Open Notebook file is similar to a table of contents for a book in that it stores the name of each section added to the notebook. OneNote saves each section as a separate file within the notebook folder.

7 Review the information on the Business Technology page in the *Course Information* section. If necessary, scroll down to view all information.

8 Click anywhere in the text *Prof. J. Wickham*.

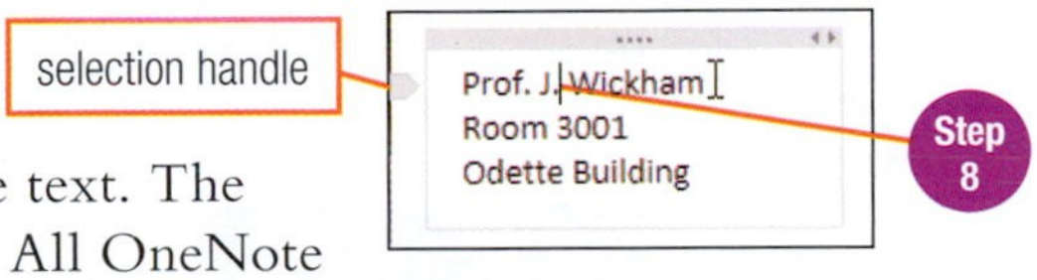

Notice that a box surrounds the note text. The box is referred to as a **note container**. All OneNote content is placed inside a note container. Notice also that a selection handle appears at the left side of the note container when the pointer is resting on note text.

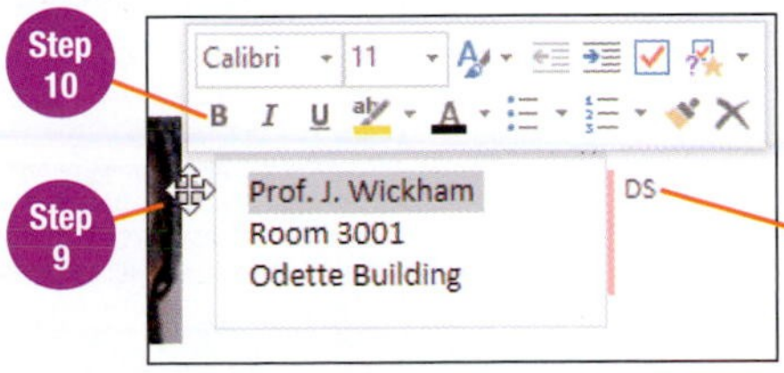

9 Click the selection handle at the left of the note container to select the text *Prof. J. Wickham*.

10 Click the Bold button on the Mini toolbar.

11 Click in any blank space at the right of the Prof. J. Wickham note container and then type Office hours every Tuesday from 12:00 to 1:00.

12 Drag the gray bar at the top of the note container to move the note below the *Prof. J. Wickham* note container in the approximate location shown at the right.

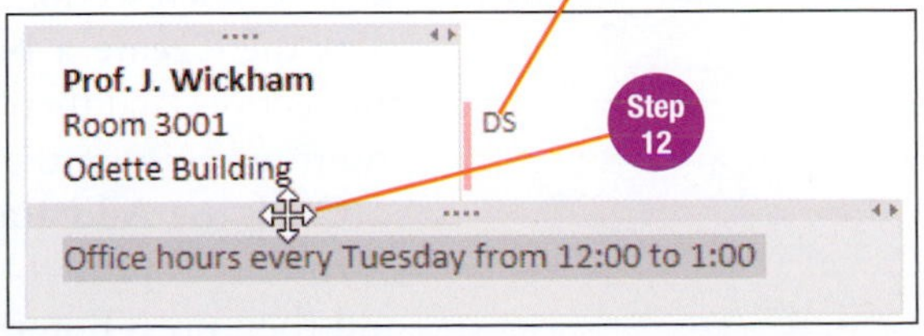

A four-headed white arrow pointer appears when you point to the top gray bar on the note container. Drag when you see this pointer.

App Tip

You can also open a notebook at the Open backstage area by clicking the File tab and then clicking *Open*.

App Tip

OneNote differs from other Office programs in that the name that appears as the notebook name is the name of a *folder* (not an individual file). Each OneNote section is a *separate file saved within the notebook folder.*

App Tip

To delete a note, select the note text using the selection handle or the gray bar at the top of the note container and then press the Delete key on the keyboard or choose Cut in the Clipboard group on the Home tab.

OneNote keeps track of the author name for new notes. To show or hide author initials, click the History tab and then click Hide Authors. The Hide Authors button is a toggle that turns on or turns off the author initials.

Using Color to Highlight Notes

A Text Highlight Color tool is used to apply color highlighting to notes just as you would use a highlighter to highlight important points while reading a textbook. The Text Highlight Color tool is in the Basic Text group on the Home tab and also on the Mini toolbar. Click the button to apply the default yellow highlighting to the selected text or use the down-pointing arrow on the button to choose a different highlight color.

13 Select the text *Examine various social media and communications applications* in the Learning Objectives note container and then click the Text Highlight Color button on the Mini toolbar to highlight the text using the default yellow color.

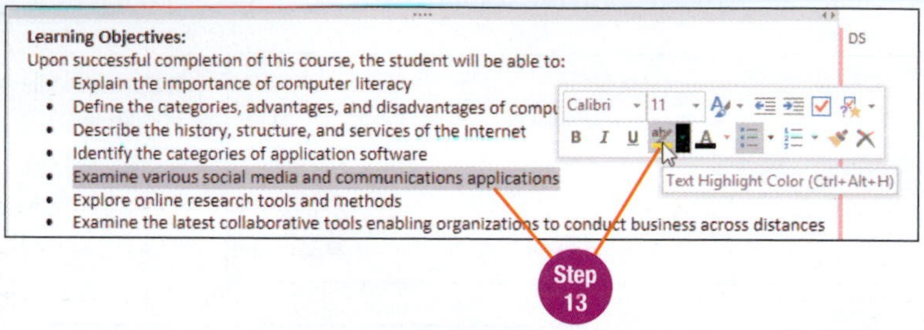

Oops!

Only ribbon tabs visible? Click the Home tab and then click the pushpin icon at the bottom right corner of the ribbon to keep the ribbon visible while you work.

14 Select the text *blogging, podcasting, VoIP, and Twitter* in the Course Description note container, click the Text Highlight Color button arrow on the Mini toolbar or in the Basic Text group on the Home tab, and then click the *Green* option (second color option in the first row).

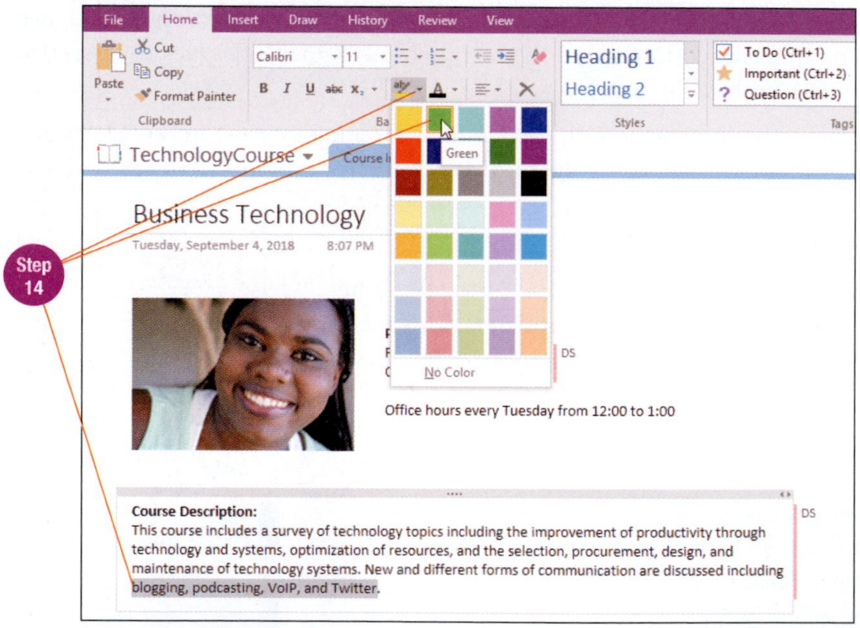

Adding Sections and Pages

A section is like a divider in a binder. Sections organize content by category, topic, or subject. Each section can have multiple pages. To create a new section in a notebook, click the **Create a New Section** tab (displays as a plus symbol), type a name for the section, and then press Enter. A new blank page opens for the section with an insertion point in the page title area. Type a title for the page and then press Enter.

Click the **Add Page** control (displays as a plus symbol inside a circle) at the top of the Pages pane to add a new page within the section. Type a title for the page and then press Enter.

15 Click the Create a New Section tab (displays as a plus symbol) next to the Course Information tab.

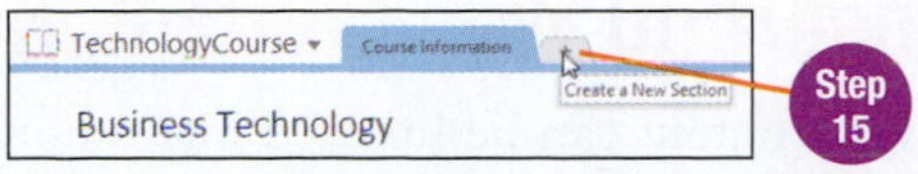

16 Type Web Pages and then press Enter.

17 With the insertion point positioned in the page title area, type Technology Web Pages and then press Enter.

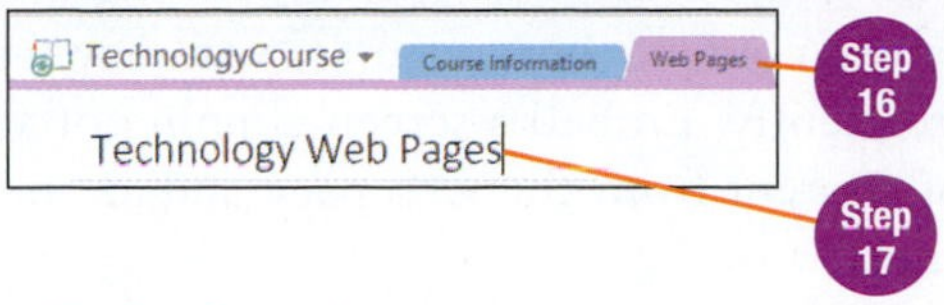

18 Click the Create a New Section tab, type Technology Images, and then press Enter.

19 Type Pictures for Technology Topics as the page title and then press Enter.

20 Click the Web Pages tab to display the section.

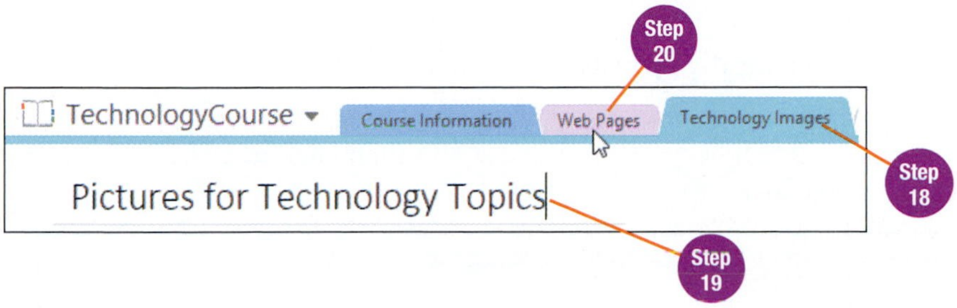

21 Click the Add Page control (displays as a plus symbol inside a circle) in the Pages pane.

22 Type Technology Web Links as the page title and then press Enter. Leave OneNote open for the next topic.

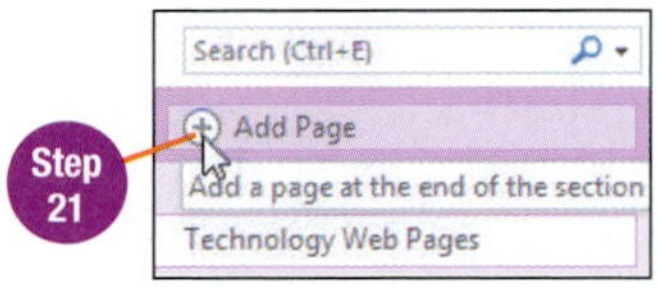

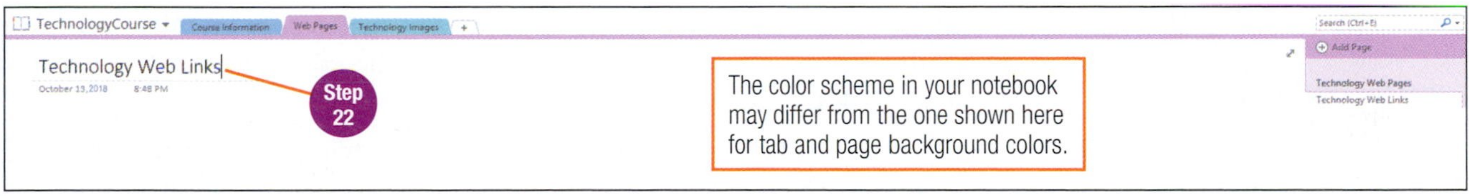

Quick Steps

Open a Notebook
1. Click notebook name left of section tabs.
2. Click *Open Other Notebooks*.
3. Navigate to drive and/or notebook folder name.
4. Double-click *Open Notebook*.

Add a Note to a Page
1. Click at desired location on page.
2. Type note text.
3. Click in blank space outside note container.

Add a Section and Page to a Notebook
1. Click Create a New Section tab.
2. Type section title and press Enter.
3. Type page title and press Enter.

Add a Page to a Section
1. Make the desired section tab active.
2. Click Add Page control.
3. Type page title and press Enter.

App Tip

A Save button is not provided in OneNote; changes are saved automatically.

Beyond Basics: Creating a Table in a Note and Calculating Expressions

OneNote automatically formats text into a table when you type some text and then press the Tab key. Each time you press Tab, a new column is inserted into the table. Press Enter to add a new row. You can also perform a calculation in OneNote by typing an expression. When you press the spacebar after an equals sign, OneNote calculates the expression. For example, typing *15*12=* and then pressing the spacebar causes OneNote to calculate the result and show *15*12=180* in the note container.

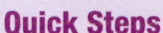

4.2 Inserting Web Content into a Notebook

Skills

Insert a link to a web page

Insert a screen clipping from a web page

Web content can be inserted into a notebook as a link or as a screen clipping. The method you use will vary depending on the content and the frequency of updates to the content. For example, you may want to use a link if a web page updates frequently. Embed a screen clipping of a web page if you want to copy a portion of content from the web page and are not concerned with updates to the captured content.

You can also use the standard copy and paste tools to select and copy text from a web page and paste it into a notebook. When you paste text copied from a web page, OneNote automatically includes the source URL below the pasted text.

1. With the TechnologyCourse notebook open and an insertion point active on the Technology Web Links page, type https://twitter.com/Techmeme and then press Enter twice.

OneNote automatically formats web addresses as hyperlinks.

2. Type Techmeme provides daily summaries of leading technology stories and tweets headlines with links throughout the day. and then click in a blank area away from the note container.

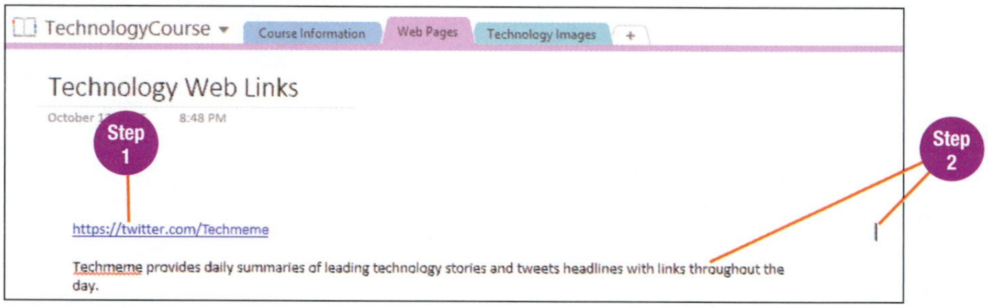

Oops!

Web page not found? Check that you typed the web address as shown. As an alternative, find an article on Tim Berners-Lee you can embed into OneNote.

3. Click https://twitter.com/Techmeme to view the Twitter page in Microsoft Edge or other browser window. If a window opens with the message *How do you want to open this?*, click OK to accept Microsoft Edge.
4. Click in the Address bar to select the web address or drag to select the web address, type https://en.wikipedia.org/wiki/Tim_Berners-Lee, and press Enter.

To embed a copy of content from a web page into a notebook, use the *Take screen clipping* option from the **New quick note** button (OneNote button with scissors on the taskbar, or revealed by clicking Show hidden icons in the Notification area on the taskbar).

App Tip

From Microsoft Edge or any Office application, you can also send a copy of the current document to OneNote by printing the document using the Send to OneNote 2016 printer.

5. If necessary, click the Show hidden icons button in the Notification area on the taskbar to reveal the New quick note button.
6. Right-click the New quick note button.
7. Click *Take screen clipping* at the shortcut menu.

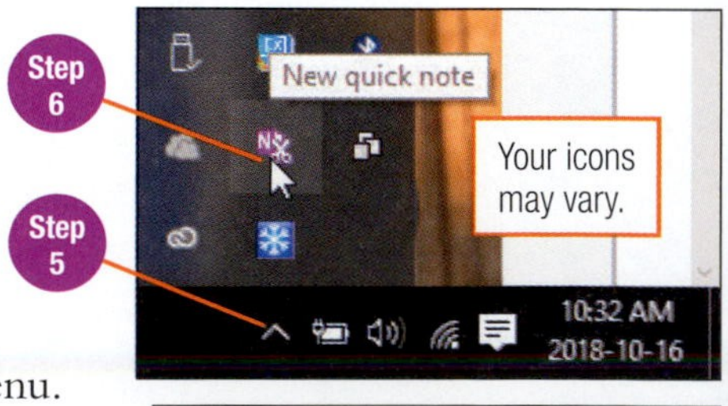

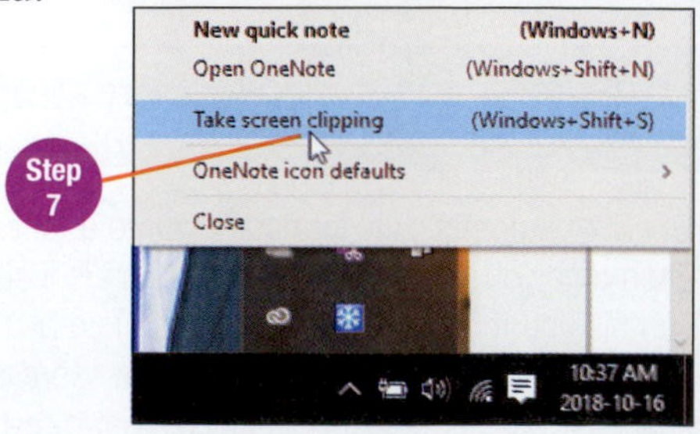

The screen dims and a crosshairs (+) displays. A screen clipping is used to capture a portion of a web page that you want to save in a notebook by dragging the crosshairs across the content that you want to copy.

8 Drag the crosshairs from just above the *Wikipedia* page title to the bottom of the Sir Tim Berners-Lee box at the right side of the page as shown below.

9 At the Select Location in OneNote dialog box, click the expand button (displays as a plus symbol) next to TechnologyCourse in the *All Notebooks* section.

10 Click the expand button next to Web Pages.

11 Click *Technology Web Pages* and then click the Send to Selected Location button.

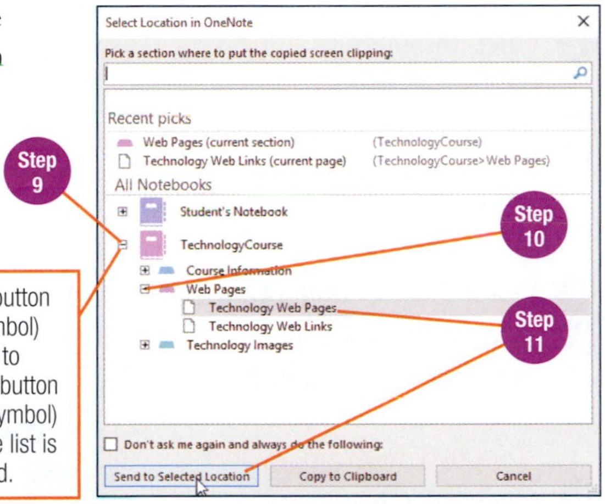

Expand button (plus symbol) changes to collapse button (minus symbol) when the list is expanded.

12 Click in the Address bar or select the web address, type wikipedia.org/wiki/3D_printing, and then press Enter.

Assume you want to save the picture of the 3-D printer shown on the *Wikipedia* page about 3-D printing.

13 Repeat Step 5 to Step 7 to start the OneNote screen clipping tool.

14 Drag the crosshairs from the top left to the bottom right of the 3-D printer image at the right side of the *Wikipedia* page as shown at the right. Note that the image shown at the right may have been replaced with another picture.

15 At the Select Location in OneNote dialog box, click the expand button next to TechnologyCourse, click the expand button next to Technology Images, click *Pictures for Technology Topics*, and then click the Send to Selected Location button.

16 Close the browser window to return to the OneNote window and view the 3-D printer image embedded in a note container on the notebook page. Notice the date and time you took the screen clipping appears below the image. Leave OneNote open for the next topic.

Quick Steps

Add a Link to a Web Page

Click anywhere on the page and type web address.

Capture a Portion of a Web Page as a Screen Clipping

1. Open notebook.
2. Open browser and go to desired web page.
3. If necessary, click Show hidden icons on taskbar.
4. Right-click New quick note button.
5. Click *Take screen clipping*.
6. Drag to select area to capture.
7. Select section and page in notebook.
8. Click Send to Selected Location.

Oops!

Picture shown not on the web page? Capture an image of another picture from the page if the one shown is no longer available.

App Tip

A quick note is a short reminder for things you might write on a sticky note. To create a quick note, click Show hidden icons in the Notification area on the taskbar, and then click the New quick note button. Type the quick note text in the note window that opens and then close the window. Each quick note is a separate page in the *Quick Notes* section, which can be viewed by selecting *Quick Notes* at the Notebooks drop-down list.

4.3 Inserting Files into a Notebook

Skills

Insert a picture

Insert a link to a document

Embed a copy of a presentation

Pictures, documents, presentations, workbooks, contacts, email messages, appointment details, and more can be added to a notebook as a link to the source content or as a copy of the content. Consider using a OneNote notebook as a repository to collect all the data related to a course, subject, or other topic. The advantage to assembling all the content in one place is that you no longer need to keep track of web links or web pages separately from documents and other notes for a subject.

Items are inserted into a OneNote page using buttons on the Insert tab. A document can be inserted as an icon that links to the source file, or the text and other content from the document can be embedded into the notebook. Once inserted, you can add annotations with your own notes.

1. With the TechnologyCourse notebook open and the Pictures for Technology Topics page active in the *Technology Images* section, click the Insert tab.
2. Click the Pictures button in the Images group.
3. At the Insert Picture dialog box, navigate to the Ch4 folder in Student_Data_Files on your storage medium.
4. Double-click ***AnalogCptr_1950s***.
5. With an insertion point positioned in the note container below the image, type Analog computer from the 1950s.
6. Click the Create a New Section tab, type Documents as the section title, and then press Enter.
7. Type Course Documents as the page title and then press Enter.

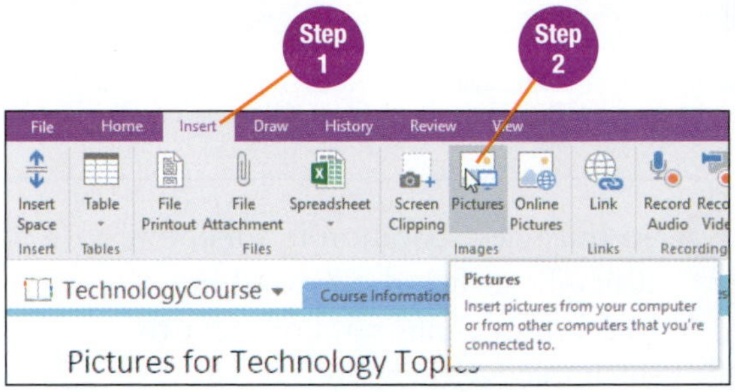

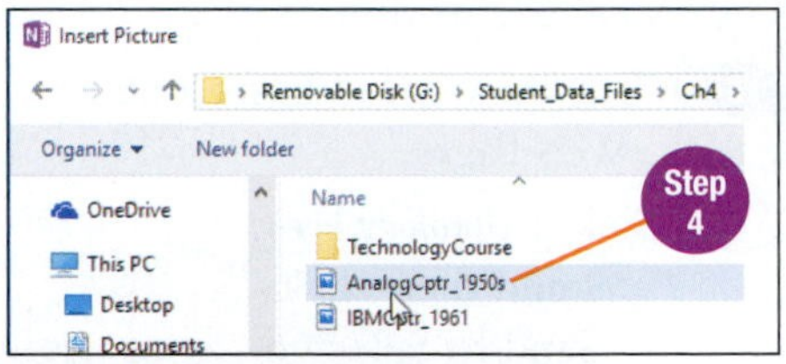

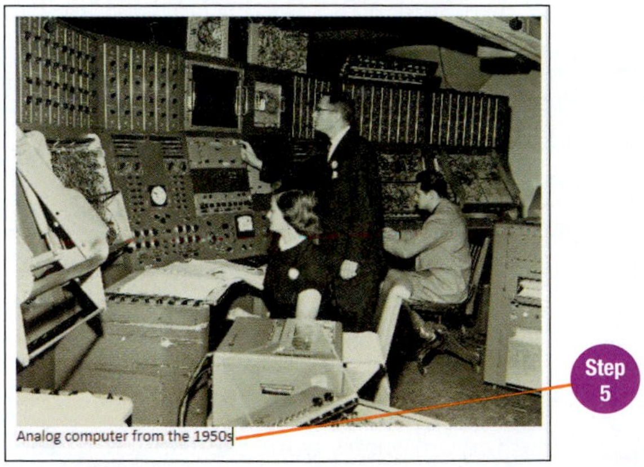

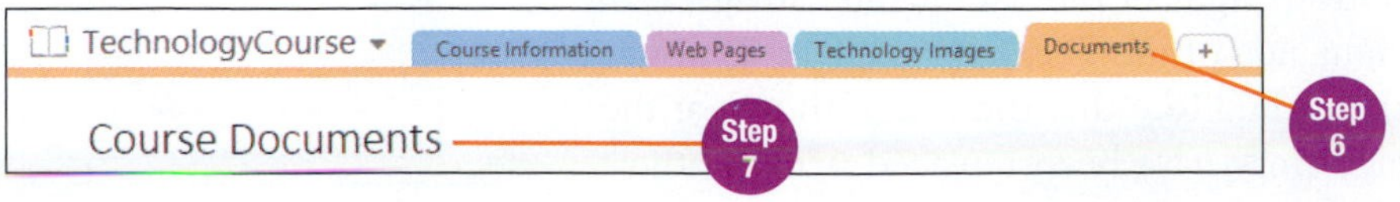

App Tip

You can also drag and drop a picture onto a OneNote page from a File Explorer window.

8. Click the File Attachment button in the Files group on the Insert tab.

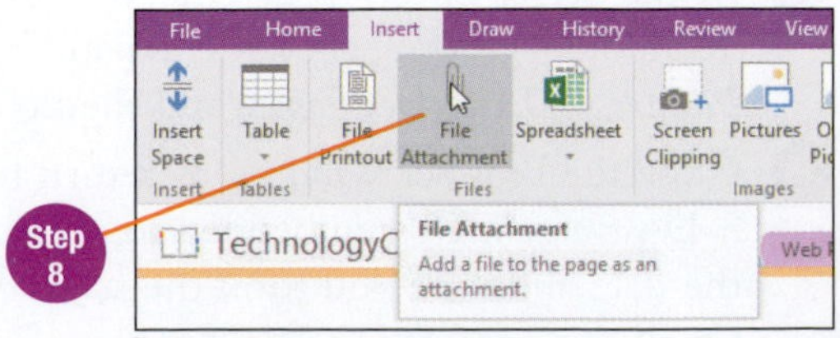

9 With the Ch4 folder in Student_Data_Files active, double-click the Word document ***Tech_Wk1_SocialMedia*** at the Choose a file or a set of files to insert dialog box.

10 Click Attach File at the Insert File dialog box.

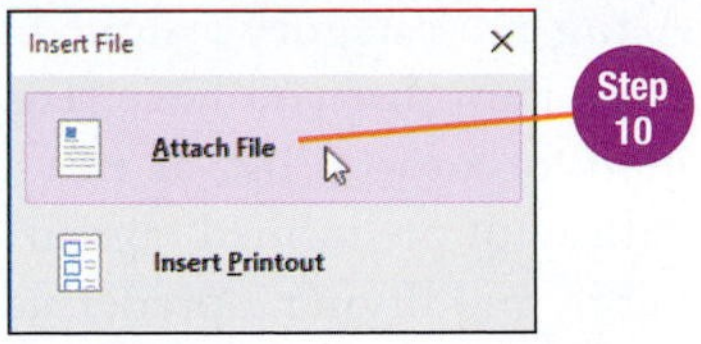

11 With an insertion point positioned in the note container below the Word document icon and file name, type Week 1 Assignment.

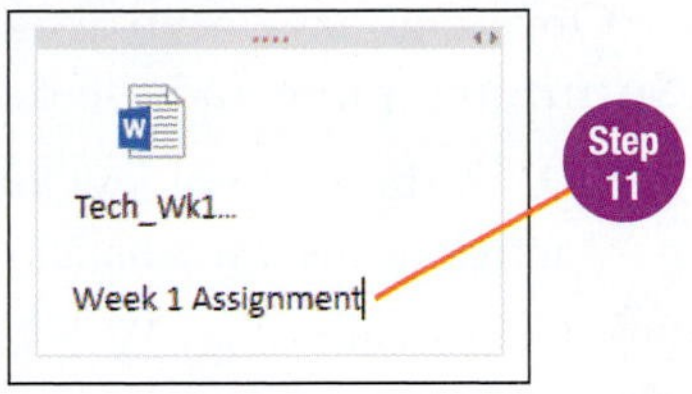

The file is linked to the source document and can be opened from OneNote.

12 Double-click the document icon. If you are using a touchscreen, tap Open. Click OK at the Warning message that opening attachments could harm your computer or data.

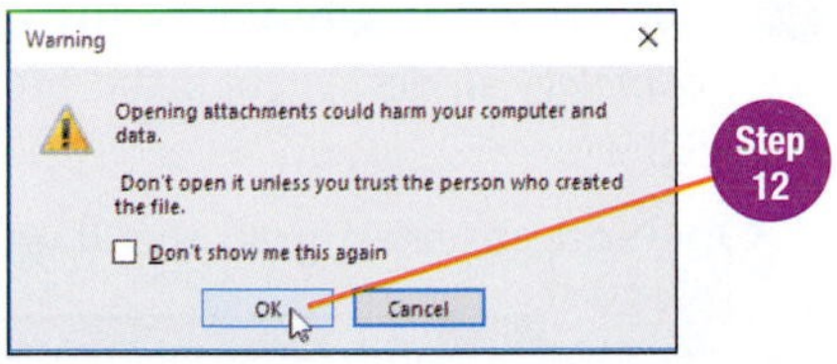

13 Scroll down to review the Word document and then close Word.

14 Create a new section *Presentations* with a page title *Course Presentations*.

15 With the Course Presentations page active, click the File Printout button in the Files group on the Insert tab.

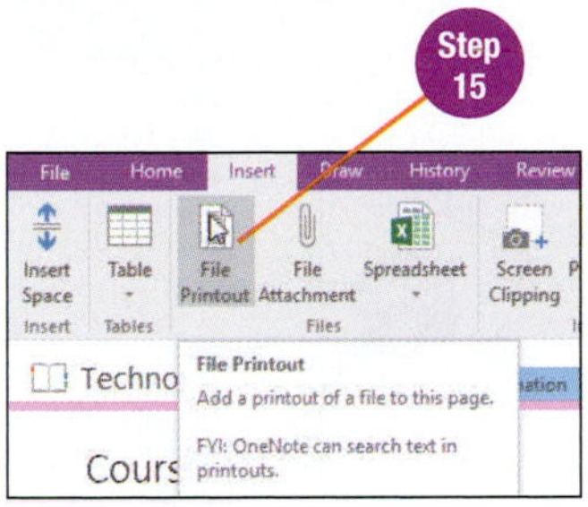

16 Double-click the PowerPoint presentation ***Tech_Wk1***.

Use File Printout to embed a copy of the content of the file onto the current page. This option allows you to add your own notes within the content. For example, embed a presentation in advance of a lecture so that you can type your own notes directly on or next to a slide as the teacher is teaching the class.

17 Scroll down and review the PowerPoint slides inserted on the OneNote page. Leave OneNote open for the next topic.

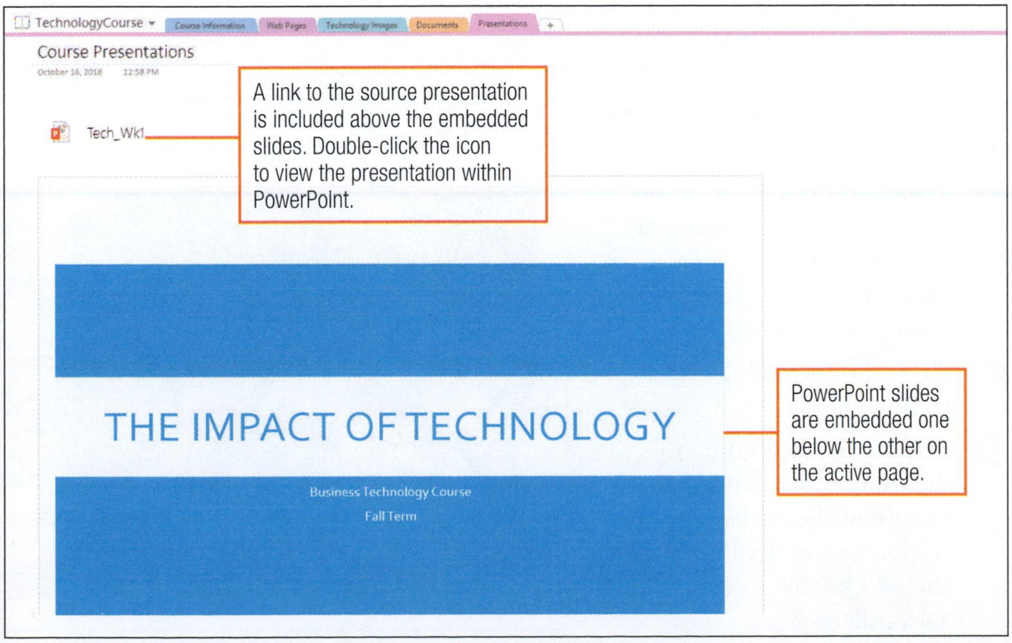

Quick Steps

Insert a Picture

1. Make desired page active.
2. Click Insert tab.
3. Click Pictures button.
4. Navigate to drive and/or folder.
5. Double-click image file name.
6. If necessary, type descriptive note.

Insert a File as a Linked Icon

1. Make desired page active.
2. Click Insert tab.
3. Click File Attachment button.
4. Navigate to drive and/or folder.
5. Double-click file name.
6. Click Attach File.
7. If necessary, type descriptive note.

Embed a Copy of File Contents

1. Make desired page active.
2. Click Insert tab.
3. Click File Printout button.
4. Navigate to drive and/or folder.
5. Double-click file name.
6. If necessary, type descriptive note.

App Tip

Changes that occur in the file after it has been inserted into OneNote as a printout are not updated. Be aware that the note container may not contain the most up-to-date content.

4.4 Tagging Notes, Viewing Tags, and Jumping to a Tagged Note

Skills

Tag a note

View and jump to tagged notes

A **tag** is a category assigned to a note. The tag allows you to identify the note later as an item that you have flagged as important, as a question, as a definition, as an item for a to-do list, as an idea, or for some other purpose. OneNote includes a gallery of predefined tags in the Tags group on the Home tab. You can customize a tag by modifying a predefined OneNote tag or by creating a new tag of your own.

Once tags have been assigned to items in the notebook, you can display the **Tags Summary pane** and use the pane to navigate to a tagged item.

1. With the TechnologyCourse notebook open and the Course Presentations page active in the *Presentations* section, click the Web Pages section tab.
2. Click Technology Web Links in the Pages pane.
3. Click at the beginning of the note text *Techmeme provides daily summaries of leading technology stories…*, click the Home tab, and then click *Important* in the Tags gallery.

OneNote inserts a gold star (tag icon) for the Important tag next to the note text.

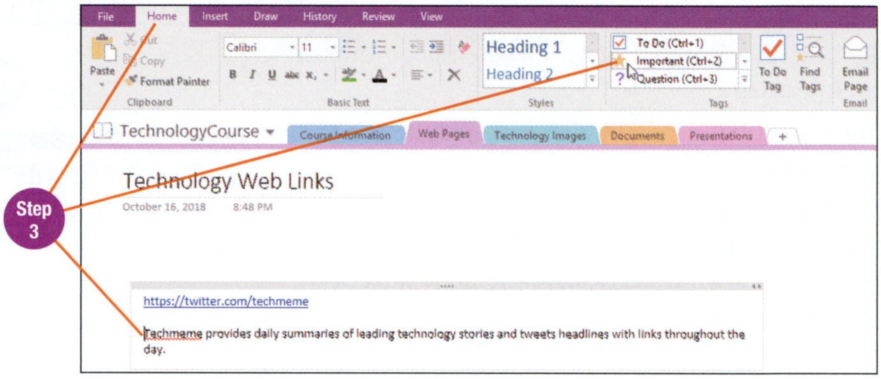

4. Click Technology Web Pages in the Pages pane.
5. Double-click after the bolded title *Tim Berners-Lee* to place an insertion point and then click *Important* in the Tags gallery.

The tag is inserted inside a new note container on the page.

6. Type Use this information in Assignment 1. If necessary, drag the top gray bar to move the note container if it overlaps other text.
7. Click the Technology Images section tab.
8. Click at the beginning of the caption text below the picture of the analog computer and then click *? Question* in the Tags gallery.

A purple question mark appears next to the caption text.

9 Click the Presentations section tab.

10 Scroll down the page of embedded PowerPoint slides to the slide with the title *REFLECTION BLOG* and then double-click to place the insertion point at the right of the slide title.

11 Click the More button (displays as a down-pointing arrow below a bar) at the bottom of the Tags gallery to display more predefined tag options.

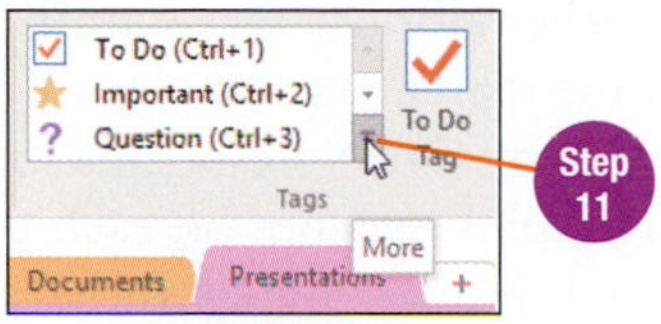

12 Click *Remember for blog* in the drop-down gallery.

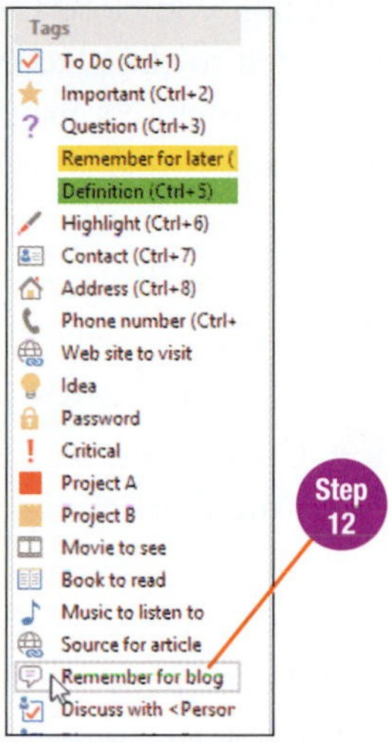

13 Type Blog entry homework in the note container next to the tag icon. If necessary, move the note container if it overlaps existing text.

Once tags have been applied to notes, you can view all the tagged notes and jump to a specific item that you need to review. Click the **Find Tags** button in the Tags group on the Home tab to display in a Tags Summary pane at the right side of the OneNote window a list of tagged items grouped by tag category.

14 Click the Find Tags button in the Tags group.

The Tags Summary pane opens at the right side of the OneNote window.

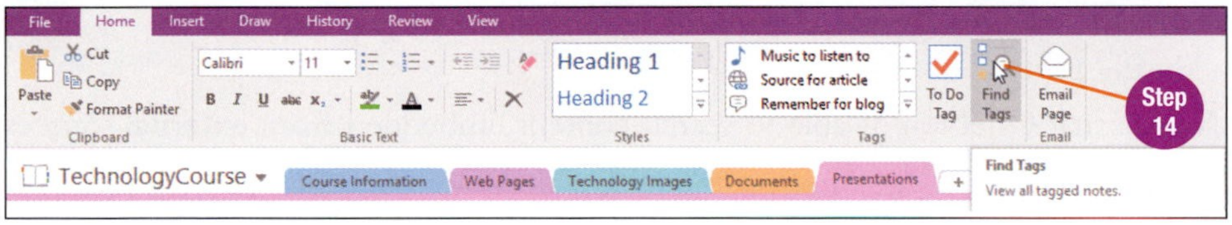

15 Click Techmeme provides daily summa... in the Tags Summary pane. The hyperlinks may show more or less text in the Tags Summary pane on the computer you are using depending on the screen size and screen resolution.

OneNote jumps to the Technology Web Links page in the *Web Pages* section of the notebook and selects the entry in the note container.

16 Click each of the other tags in the Tags Summary pane to jump to each tagged item in the notebook.

17 Click the Close button at the top right of the Tags Summary pane. Leave OneNote open for the next topic.

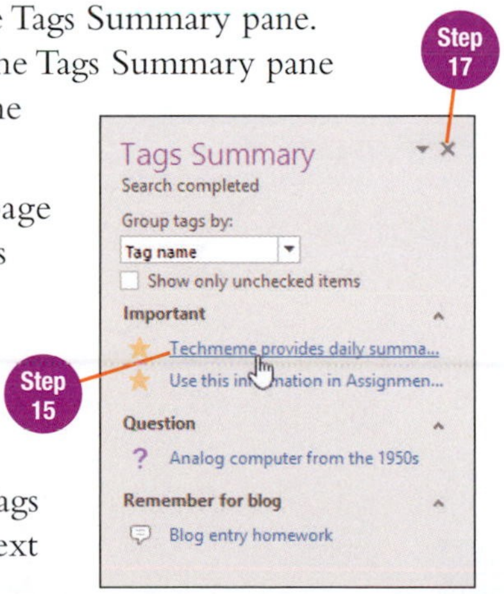

Quick Steps

Tag a Note

1. Position insertion point at beginning of note or item.
2. Click Home tab.
3. Click desired tag in Tags gallery.

View All Tags

1. Click Home tab.
2. Click Find Tags button.

Jump to a Tagged Item

Click desired tagged note in Tags Summary pane.

App Tip

Use the search list box at the bottom of the Tags Summary pane to specify locations that should be searched for tags. For example, you can view tags from all open notebooks or from the active section only.

Beyond Basics Using the To-Do Tag

You can use the Tags feature to create a to-do list by tagging items in your notebook with the To Do tag. OneNote inserts a blank check box at the left of note text tagged with *To Do*. Click the check box when a task has been completed to mark the item finished.

4.5 Searching Notes and Closing a Notebook

Skills

Search notes

Close a notebook

An advantage to using an electronic notebook instead of a paper-based notebook is the ability to search all the pages in the notebook for a keyword or phrase and instantly locate each occurrence of the note text. The search feature in OneNote searches all the pages within all open notebooks. Type a search keyword or phrase in the search text box located above the Pages pane at the right side of the OneNote window. OneNote begins listing pages with matches in a drop-down list and highlights matches on each page as soon as you begin typing. Click a page in the search results to view the matches.

When you close OneNote, the active notebook is left open so that you are returned to the place you left off when you start OneNote again. You may instead choose to close a notebook when you are finished working. One reason to close a notebook is that when you want to search for a keyword in a specific notebook but it also exists in the current notebook, closing the current notebook will avoid pages showing up in search results that you are not interested in reviewing.

1 With the TechnologyCourse notebook open, click the Course Information section tab.

2 Click in the search text box above the Pages pane that contains the text *Search* and then type Tim Berners-Lee.

OneNote begins displaying matches as soon as you start typing.

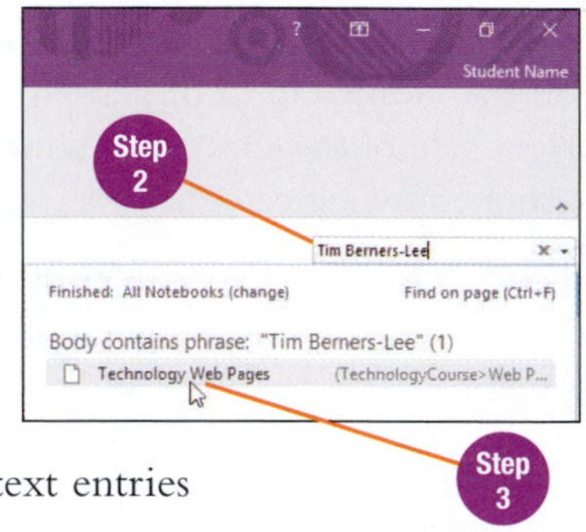

3 Click the entry in the search results list to navigate to the page and review the highlighted text entries on the page.

Notice that OneNote is able to search content embedded from external sources.

4 Click *Tim Berners-Lee* or select the text in the search text box and then type analog.

5 Click *Pictures for Technology Topics* in the search results list to navigate to the page with the picture of the analog computer.

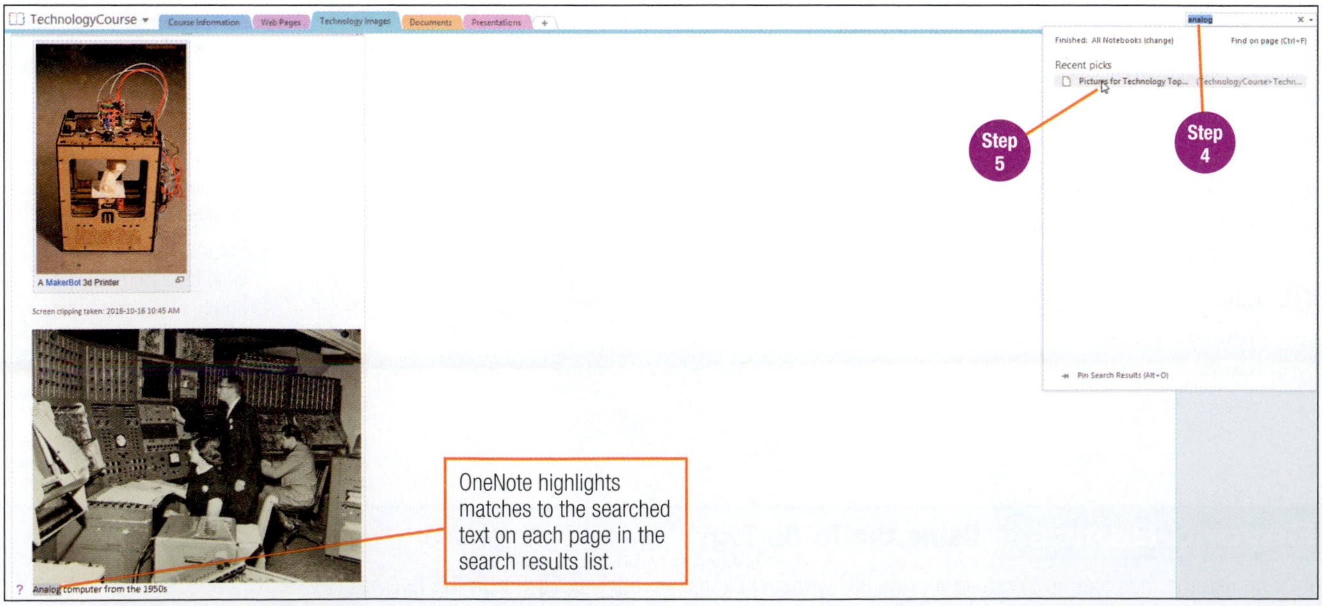

6 Click *analog* or select the text in the search text box and then type blog.
7 Click each entry in the search results list to review each item.
8 Click the Close button at the right of the search text box to close the search results list.

Your search results may vary.

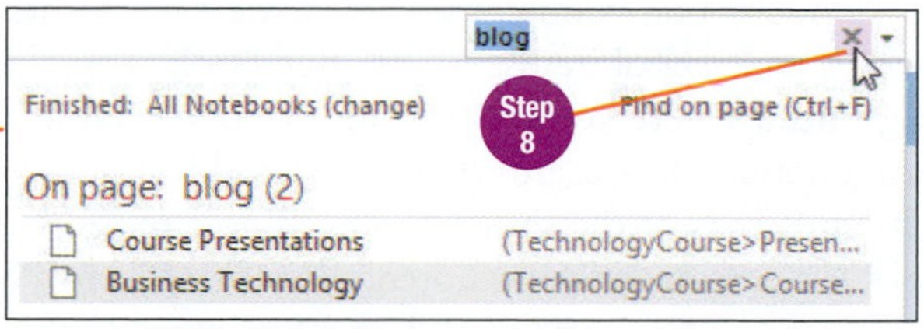

Because OneNote automatically saves changes to notebooks as you work, you can leave all your notebooks open and be assured that changes are being saved. However, if you want to close a notebook, click the *Close* option in the Settings button drop-down list at the **Notebook Information backstage area**.

9 Click the File tab.
10 Click the Settings button next to TechnologyCourse at the Notebook Information backstage area.
11 Click *Close* at the Settings button drop-down list to close the notebook.

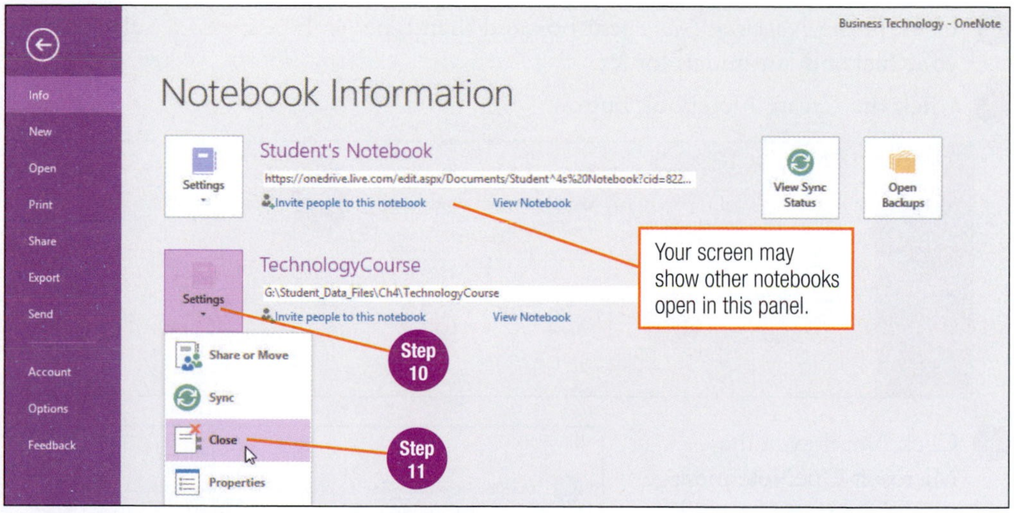

Your screen may show other notebooks open in this panel.

Quick Steps

Search Notes

1. Click in the search text box.
2. Type search keyword or phrase.
3. Click pages in search results list.

Close a Notebook

1. Click File tab.
2. Click Settings button.
3. Click *Close*.

Alternative Method: Searching Content on the Active Page Only

To search for a keyword or phrase on the active page only, press Ctrl + F. OneNote displays *Find on page* in a yellow box next to the search text box. Type the search keyword or phrase in the search text box. OneNote displays an up and down arrow in the yellow box with the number of matches found. Click the arrows to navigate to the matches on the current page.

Beyond Basics: Printing and Exporting Notebook Sections

Print a notebook section by making the desired section active, clicking the File tab, and then clicking *Print*. Use Print Preview at the Print backstage area to view and modify print settings, such as the print range, paper size, and page orientation. Consider exporting a page, section, or notebook as a PDF file instead of printing. Display the Export backstage area, choose to export a page, a section, or the entire notebook, choose the export file format, and then click the Export button. OneNote displays the Save As dialog box in which you choose the drive, folder, and file name for the exported file.

4.6 Creating a New Notebook and Sharing a Notebook

Skills

Create a new notebook

Share a notebook using OneDrive

Some people may choose to organize all their notes for all purposes within one notebook (the default notebook file), using sections and pages to create an organizational structure. Others may choose to create separate notebooks in which to organize notes. For example, you may want to maintain separate notebooks for home, work, and school items. A new notebook is created at the **New Notebook backstage area** where you specify the notebook name and storage location.

A shared notebook is useful if you are working on a group project. With a shared notebook, members of the group can each post research, links, ideas, or other notes in one place. Share an existing notebook at the **Share Notebook backstage area**. A shared notebook has to be stored on OneDrive. One person creates the notebook and is referred to as the notebook *owner.* He or she shares the notebook by entering each person's email address at the Share Notebook backstage area. Each group member receives an invitation to view the notebook by email message.

Note: *Check with your instructor for the name of the classmate with whom you will share the notebook created in this topic. At Step 13 you will need the Microsoft account email address for the classmate. If necessary, you can practice sharing the notebook with a friend or relative.*

1. Click the File tab and then click *New.*
2. Click your OneDrive account name at the New Notebook backstage area if OneDrive is not automatically selected.
3. Click in the *Notebook Name* text box and then type MyElectives-xx. Substitute your first and last initials for *xx*.
4. Click the Create Notebook button.

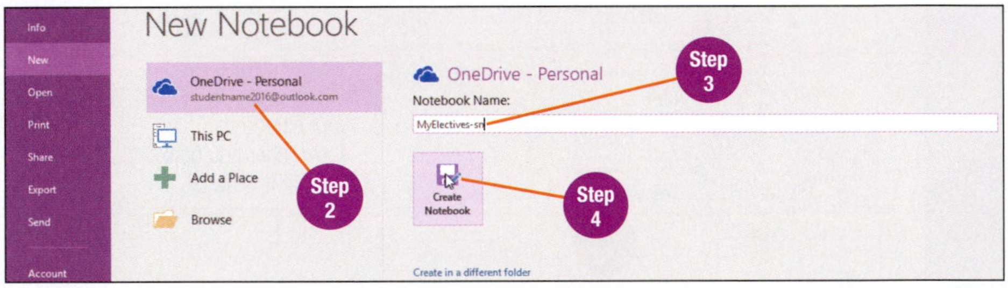

App Tip

By default, each person with whom you share a notebook can make changes to the notebook. To share a notebook and only allow the other person to view the content, click the permissions option box arrow (displays *Can edit*) at the right of the email addresses text box and then click *Can view.*

5. Click Not now at the Microsoft OneNote message box asking if you would like to share the notebook with other people.

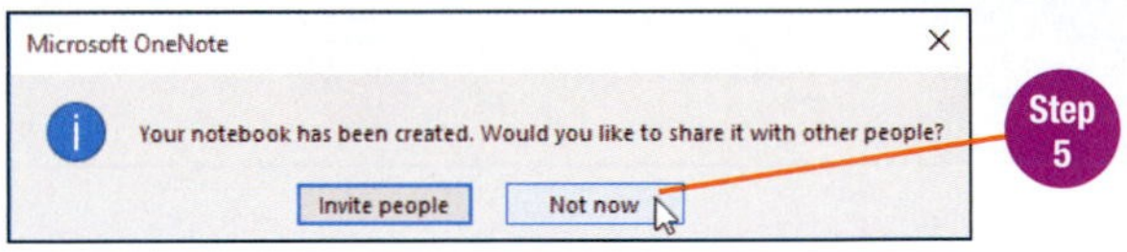

You will set up the sharing feature later in this topic. OneNote opens a new notebook with one section created titled *New Section 1.*

6. Right-click the New Section 1 section tab and then click *Rename.*
7. Type Child Lit and then press Enter.
8. Type Children's Literature as the page title and then press Enter.

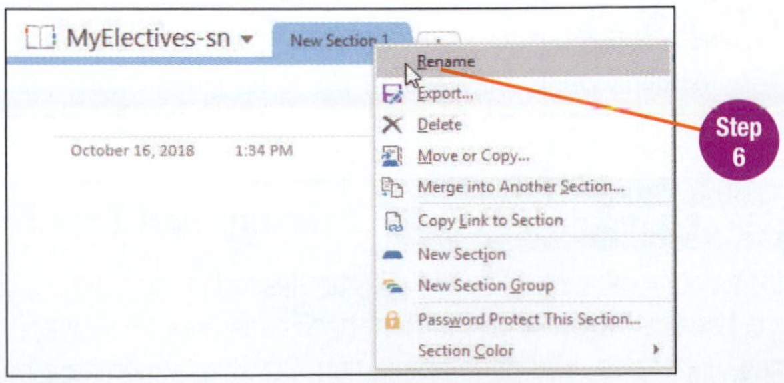

Oops!

Don't remember how to embed files? Refer to Topic 4.3, Step 15.

9. Embed a copy of the PowerPoint presentation ***ChildLitPres*** on the page.

10 Add a second section tab named *Film* with the page title *Film Genres* and then embed a copy of the Word document ***ApNowReflectionPaper***.

You decide to share the notebook with a classmate taking the same electives as you, so you can each add notes to the notebook.

A notebook stored online displays this icon indicating the content is synced with OneDrive.

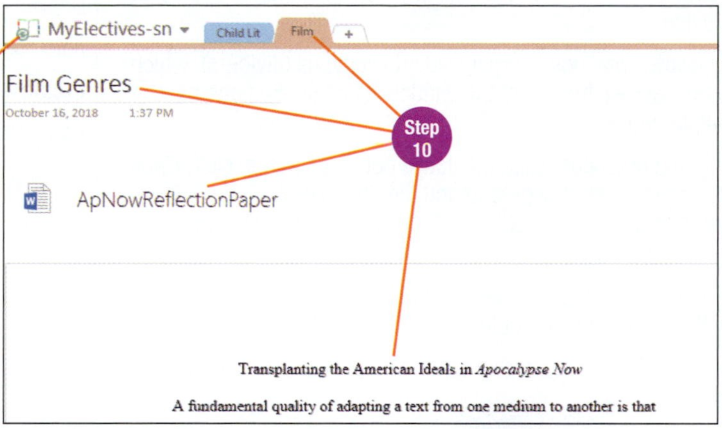

11 Click the File tab.

12 Click the Settings button next to MyElectives-xx and then click *Share or Move*.

13 At the Share Notebook backstage area, click in the *Type names or e-mail addresses* text box and then type the classmate's Microsoft account email address.

14 Click in the message box and then type Here is a notebook I created that we can use to share notes for our electives.

15 Click the Share button.

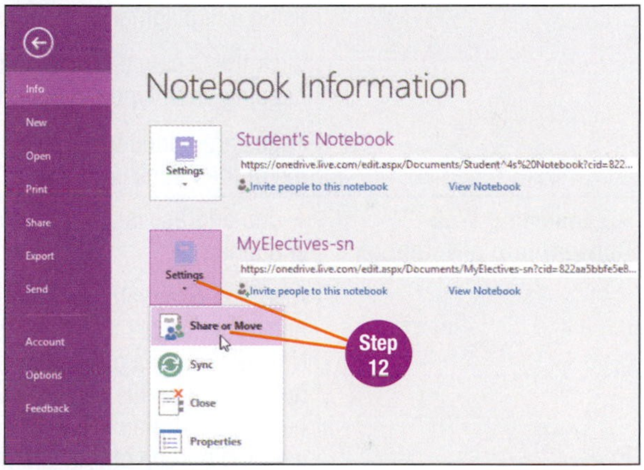

When sharing is completed, the student's name is shown in the *Shared with* section of the backstage area.

16 Click the Back button.

17 Close the MyElectives-xx notebook and then close OneNote.

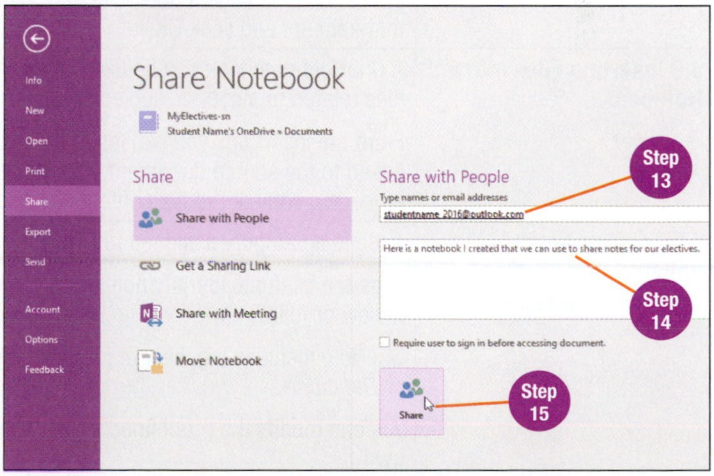

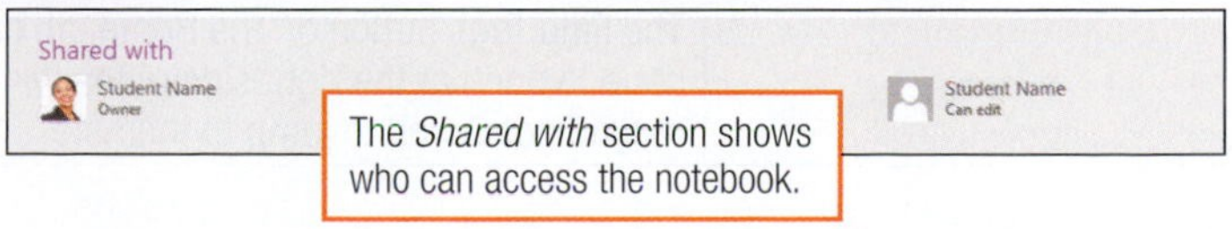

Optional

18 Open a browser window, navigate to https://outlook.com, and sign in if you are not automatically signed in.

19 At the Inbox, click the message received from a classmate with subject text similar to *MyElectives-xx has been shared with you* to open the message.

20 Click the View in OneDrive button in the message to open the notebook in OneNote Online. Click Unblock if a message pops up informing you parts of the message have been blocked.

21 Add a note to one of the pages. (You determine the note text.)

22 Close the browser window.

Quick Steps

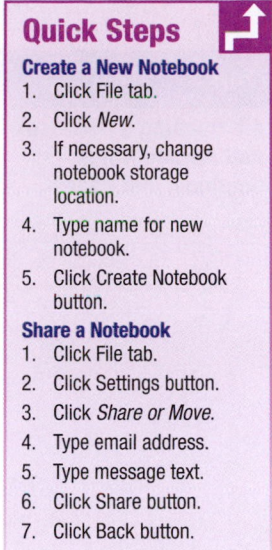

Create a New Notebook
1. Click File tab.
2. Click *New.*
3. If necessary, change notebook storage location.
4. Type name for new notebook.
5. Click Create Notebook button.

Share a Notebook
1. Click File tab.
2. Click Settings button.
3. Click *Share or Move.*
4. Type email address.
5. Type message text.
6. Click Share button.
7. Click Back button.

Topics Review

Topic	Key Concepts	Key Terms
4.1 Opening a Notebook and Adding Notes, Sections, and Pages	OneNote 2016 is a note-taking software application that is the electronic equivalent of a binder with loose leaf notes separated by dividers. A OneNote notebook is organized into sections (dividers), which are tabs across the top of the window. Each section can have multiple pages. To open a notebook, click the active notebook name, click *Open Other Notebooks*, navigate to and then double-click the file *Open Notebook* stored within a folder named the same as the notebook name. Each note on a page is stored within a note container, which is a box that surrounds the note text. Drag the gray bar along the top of the note container to move a note. Use the Text Highlight Color tool to add color to notes similarly to using a highlighter to emphasize text in a textbook. Click the Create a New Section tab to type a new section heading, then type a page title to start a new section. Pages are added to a section using the Add Page control at the top of the Pages pane.	OneNote 2016 OneNote notebook note container Create a New Section Add Page
4.2 Inserting Web Content into a Notebook	A web address is automatically converted to a hyperlink in a note container. A portion of a web page can be captured and inserted into a notebook. To do this, click the Show hidden icons button in the Notification area on the taskbar if the New quick note button is not already visible on the taskbar, right-click the New quick note button, and then click *Take screen clipping*. Drag the crosshairs over the portion of the web page you want to embed. Next, select the destination page in the Select Location in OneNote dialog box that appears and click OK.	New quick note
4.3 Inserting Files into a Notebook	A OneNote notebook can be used as a repository to collect all the files related to a course, subject, or other topic. From the Insert tab, you can insert a picture, a file as an icon linked to the source document, or a file as a printout, which embeds a copy of the file contents into the notebook.	
4.4 Tagging Notes, Viewing Tags, and Jumping to a Tagged Note	A tag is a category assigned to a note. Tags are useful to identify notes that you want to flag for later review or follow up. OneNote includes a gallery of predefined tags, such as *Important* or *Definition*. You can modify the predefined tags or create a new tag of your own. The Find Tags button on the Home tab causes the Tags Summary pane to open at the right side of the window with links to each tagged note used to jump to the note.	tag Tags Summary pane Find Tags

continued...

Topic	Key Concepts	Key Terms
4.5 Searching Notes and Closing a Notebook	OneNote can search all pages in all open notebooks for a keyword or phrase typed in the search text box. OneNote begins highlighting matches to the search keyword or phrase and displays pages in the search results list as soon as you begin typing. Close a notebook using the Settings button at the Notebook Information backstage area.	Notebook Information backstage area
4.6 Creating a New Notebook and Sharing a Notebook	Create a new notebook at the New Notebook backstage area. A notebook saved to OneDrive can be shared with other people. More than one person can edit a page at the same time when a notebook is shared. Use the Settings button at the Notebook Information backstage area to access the Share Notebook backstage area. You can then share a notebook by typing the email address and a short message for each invitee.	New Notebook backstage area Share Notebook backstage area

Recheck

Recheck your understanding of the topics covered in this chapter.

Workbook

Chapter review and assessment resources are available in the *Workbook* ebook.

Chapter 5

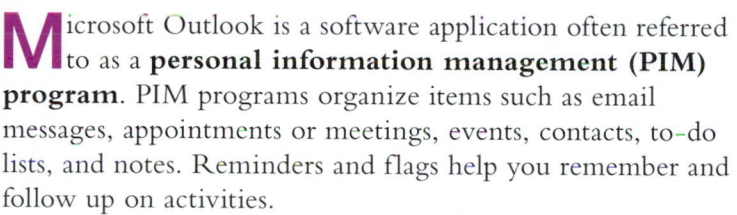

Communicating and Scheduling Using Outlook

Precheck

Check your understanding of the topics covered in this chapter.

Learning Objectives

5.1 Create, send, read, reply to, and forward email messages

5.2 Attach a file to a message, delete a message, and empty the Deleted Items folder

5.3 Preview, open, and save a file attachment

5.4 Schedule an appointment and an event

5.5 Schedule a recurring appointment and edit an appointment

5.6 Schedule and accept a meeting request

5.7 Add and edit contact information

5.8 Add, update, and delete a task

5.9 Search Outlook messages, appointments, contacts, or tasks

Microsoft Outlook is a software application often referred to as a **personal information management (PIM) program**. PIM programs organize items such as email messages, appointments or meetings, events, contacts, to-do lists, and notes. Reminders and flags help you remember and follow up on activities.

In the workplace, Outlook is often used with an Exchange server, which allows employees within the organization to easily share calendars, schedule meetings, and assign tasks with one another. Consider using Outlook on your home PC or mobile device to connect to the mail server supplied by your ISP and manage your messages. Outlook can also help you organize your time, activities, address book, and to-do list.

In this chapter, you will learn how to use the desktop application PIM program Microsoft Outlook 2016 for creating and sending email messages; scheduling appointments, events, and meetings; creating contacts; and maintaining a to-do list.

If you do not have access to the desktop software application, you can use Outlook.com to practice the skills taught in this chapter. However, be aware that the screens shown and the step-by-step instructions are for the desktop Outlook application. The web-based program Outlook.com uses a different interface. Where possible, instructions or marginal notes direct you to the method used in Outlook.com. In some cases, a feature available in the desktop application is not available in Outlook.com, and you will not be able to complete all the tasks in the topic.

SNAP If you are a SNAP user, go to your SNAP Assignments page to complete the Precheck, Tutorials, and Recheck.

Data Files

Before beginning this chapter, be sure you have copied the student data files for this course to your storage medium. Steps on downloading and extracting the data files are provided in Chapter 1, Topic 1.8, on pages 22–23.

5.1 Using Outlook to Send Email

Skills

Create and send an email message

Reply to a message

Forward a message

Electronic mail (email) is communication between individuals by means of sending and receiving messages electronically. Email is the business standard for communication in the workplace. Individuals also use email to communicate with relatives and friends around the world. While text messaging is popular for brief messages between individuals, email is still used to send longer messages.

Setting Up Outlook

The screen that you see when you start Outlook for the first time depends on whether a prior version of Outlook existed on the computer you are using. **Outlook 2016** can transfer information from an older version of Outlook to a new data file or, if no prior data file exists, will present a Welcome to Outlook 2016 screen at start-up. Click Next at the welcome screen and then click Next at the second screen to accept the option to connect an email account. At the Add Account dialog box shown in Figure 5.1, enter your name, email address, and your password twice and then click Next. Outlook automatically configures the mail server settings displaying progress messages as each part is completed. Click Finish when completed to start Outlook.

In instances where Outlook cannot automatically set up your email account, additional information will be required such as the incoming and outgoing mail server address. Contact your ISP if necessary for this information.

Note: *The instructions in this chapter assume Outlook has already been set up and that you are connected to the Internet with an always-on connection (high-speed Internet service) at school or at home. If necessary, connect to the Internet and sign in to your email account before starting the topic activities. Check with your instructor for assistance if you are not sure how to proceed.*

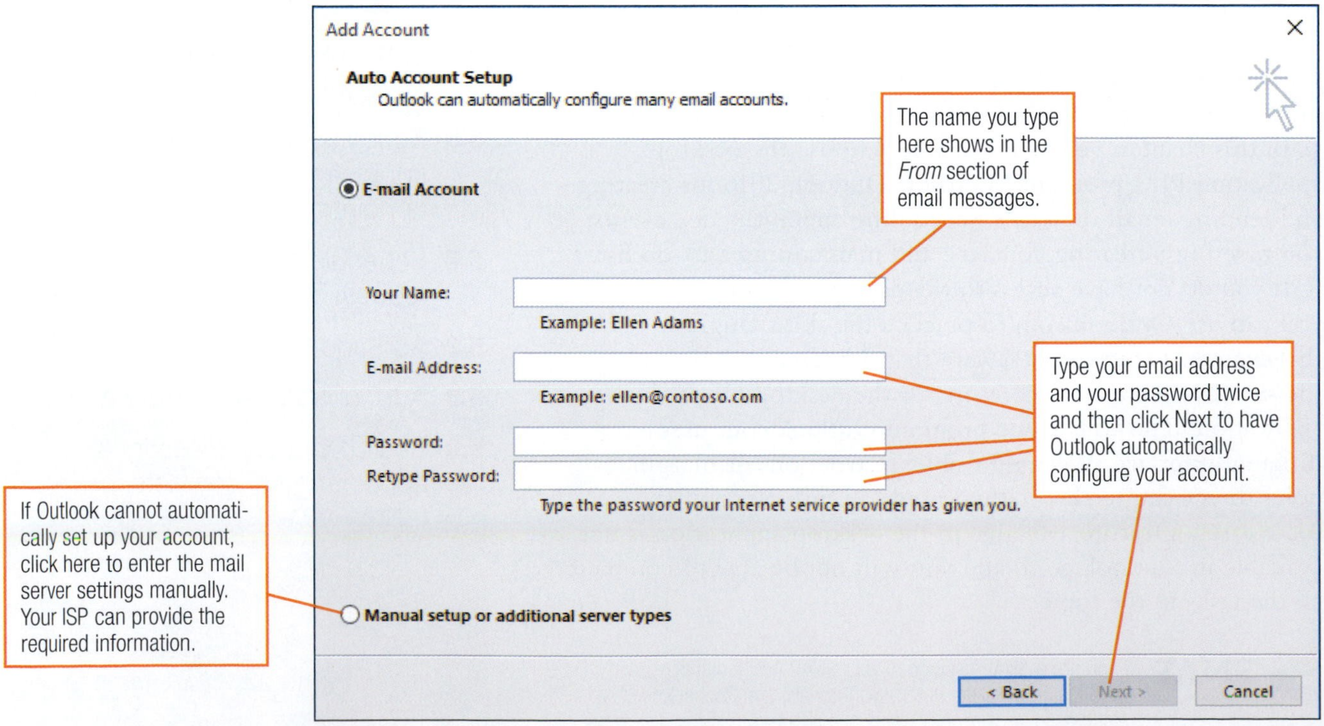

Figure 5.1

Outlook automatically sets up most email accounts once you enter your name, email address, and email password.

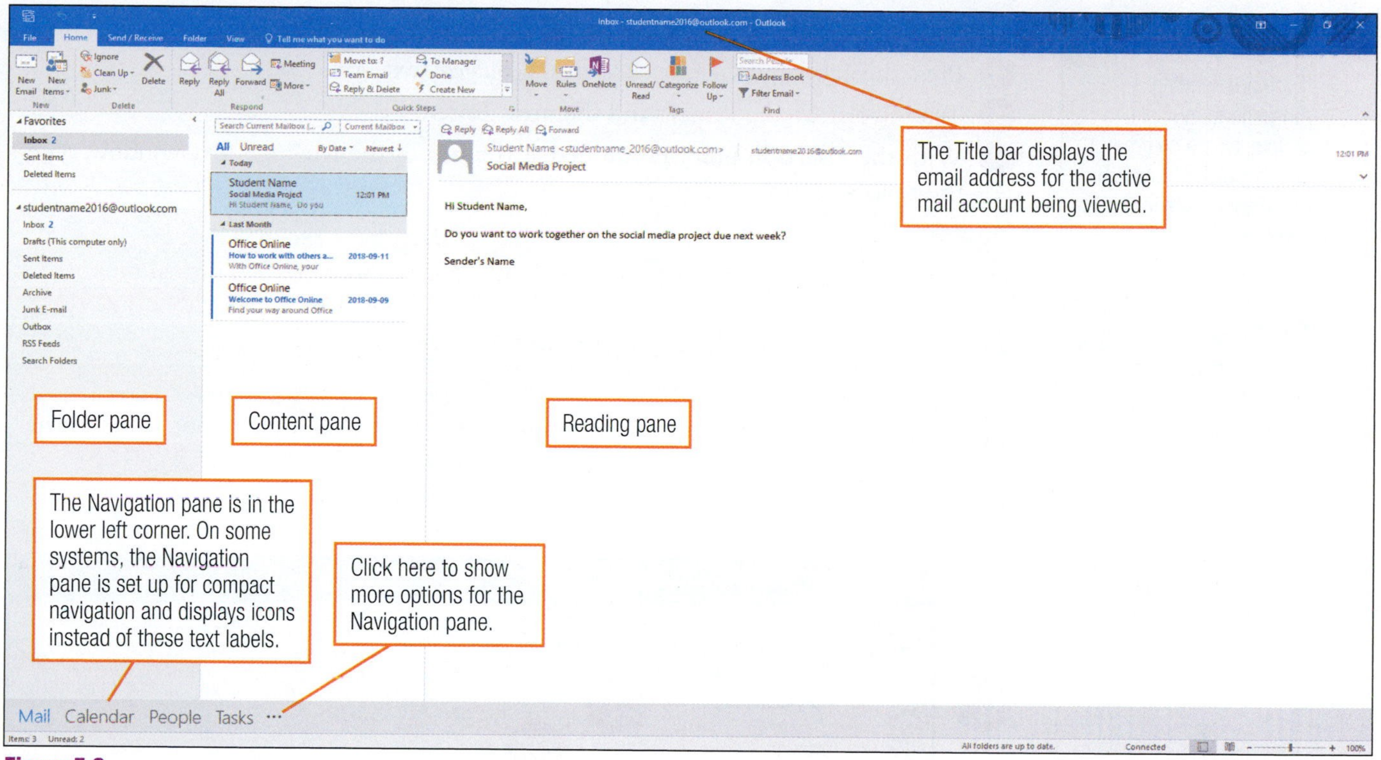
The Title bar displays the email address for the active mail account being viewed.
Folder pane
Content pane
Reading pane
The Navigation pane is in the lower left corner. On some systems, the Navigation pane is set up for compact navigation and displays icons instead of these text labels.
Click here to show more options for the Navigation pane.
Mail Calendar People Tasks ···
Hi Student Name,
Do you want to work together on the social media project due next week?
Sender's Name

Figure 5.2

The Outlook window. Outlook checks for new messages automatically when the program is started.

Once Outlook has been set up with an email account, the Outlook window appears, similar to the one shown in Figure 5.2. By default, **Mail** is the active component, with **Inbox** the mail folder shown when Outlook starts. Messages in the Content pane are shown with the newest message received at the top of the message list. The left pane, called the Folder pane, is used to switch the display to another mail folder. At the bottom of the Folder pane is the Navigation pane, used to navigate to another Outlook component, such as Calendar. The right pane, called the Reading pane, displays the contents of the selected message.

App Tip

Click the View tab, click the Folder Pane button in the Layout group, and choose *Normal*, *Minimized*, or *Off* to change the Folder pane. The Reading Pane button in the same group is used to display the Reading pane at the right or bottom of the screen or to turn off the Reading pane.

Creating and Sending a Message

Click the **New Email** button in the New group on the Home tab to start a new email message. Type the recipient's email address in the *To* text box, type a brief description in the *Subject* text box, and then type your message text in the white message text box. Click the Send button when finished.

Note: *Check with your instructor for instructions on whom you should exchange messages and meeting requests with for this chapter. Your instructor may designate an email partner for each person or allow you to choose your email partner. If necessary, send messages to yourself.*

Oops!

A Welcome to Outlook 2016 message box appears? This screen appears the first time Outlook is started with no email account set up. Refer to the instructions on the previous page to configure your email account first before you can proceed to Step 2.

1. Click in the search text box on the taskbar, type Outlook 2016, and then press Enter to start Outlook 2016. If you are using Outlook.com, open a browser window, navigate to https://outlook.com, and sign in to your Microsoft account if you are not automatically signed in.

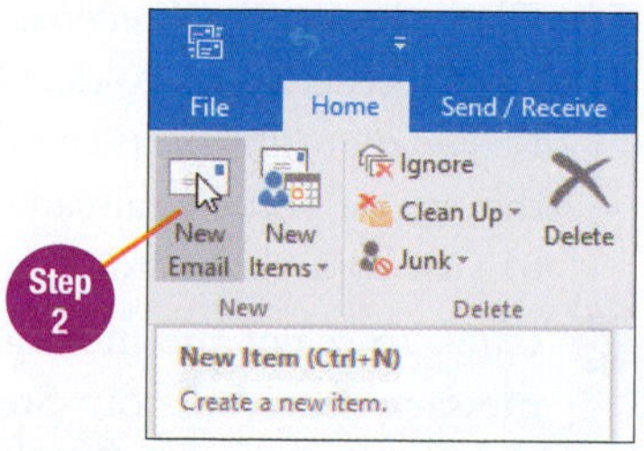
Step 2
File
Home
Send / Receive
New Email
New Items
Ignore
Clean Up
Junk
Delete
New
Delete
New Item (Ctrl+N)
Create a new item.

2. Click the New Email button in the New group on the Home tab or click the New button next to Outlook.com.

App Tip

If you are sending a message to multiple people, type a comma (,) or semicolon (;) between email addresses in the *To* text box.

App Tip

As a courtesy to the recipient, always include a *Subject* line that accurately describes the purpose of the message. People who receive many email messages in a day use the subjects to prioritize their Inboxes.

3. Type the email address for the recipient in the *To* text box.
4. Press the Tab key twice or click in the *Subject* text box.
5. Type Social Media Project and the press Enter.
6. With the insertion point positioned at the top of the Message text window, type the following text:

   Hi (type recipient's name), [press Enter twice]

   I think we should do our project on Pinterest.com. Pinterest is a virtual pinboard where people pin pictures of things they have seen on the Internet that they want to share with others. [press Enter twice]

   What do you think?
7. Press Enter twice at the end of the message text and then type your name as the sender.
8. Click the Send button.

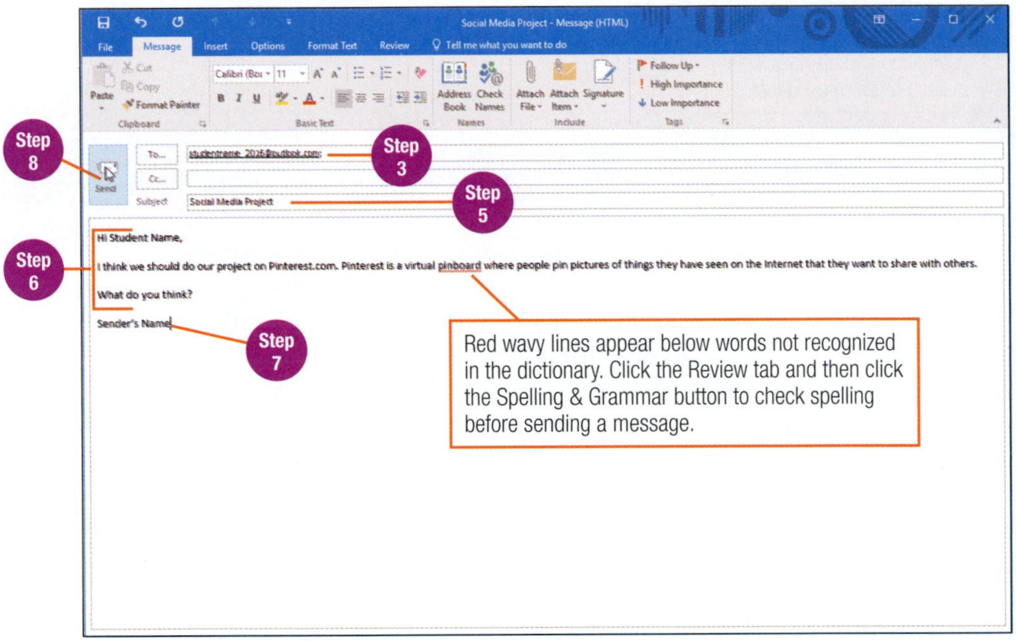

Quick Steps

Create and Send an Email Message

1. Click New Email button.
2. Type address in *To* text box.
3. Type brief description in *Subject* text box.
4. Type message text in message window.
5. Click Send.

Reply to a Message

1. Click Reply button in Reading pane.
2. Type reply message.
3. Click Send.

Replying to a Message

New messages appear at the top of the message list in the Content pane with message headers that show the sender, subject, time, and first line of message. Click to select a message header and reply directly from the Reading pane using the **Reply** button. Replying from the Reading pane is called an **inline reply**. You can also double-click the message header in the Content pane to open the message in a Message window from which you can choose to Reply or Forward the message.

9. Click the Send / Receive tab and then click the Send/Receive All Folders button in the Send & Receive group to update the Content pane. Skip this step if you can already see the message sent to you by a classmate or yourself from Step 8.
10. Click to select the message header for the message received from Step 8 and then read the message text in the Reading pane.

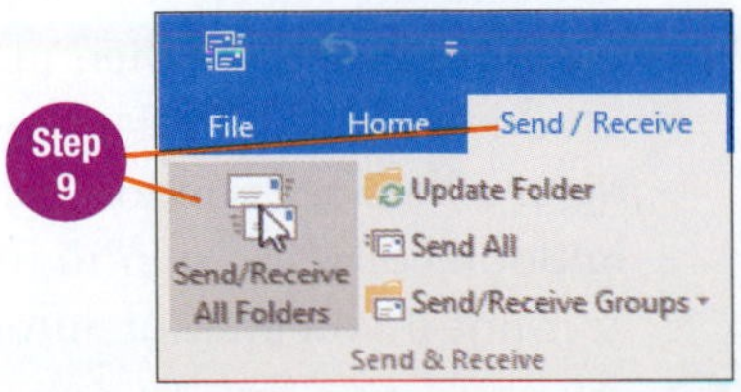

App Tip

If you are online when a new message is received, a chime sounds and a preview of the message appears in a desktop alert near the bottom right corner of your screen.

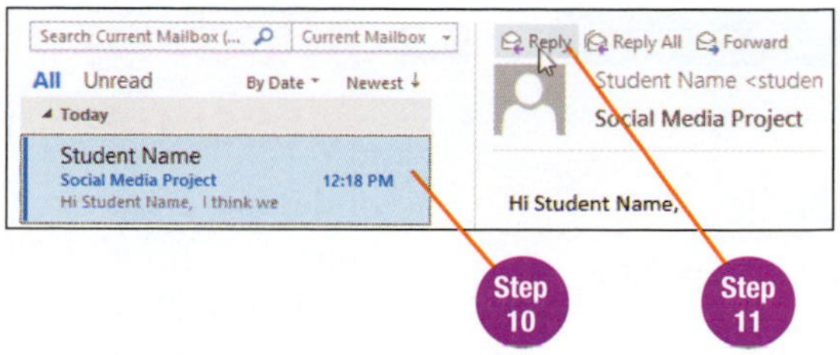

11. Click the Reply button at the top of the message in the Reading pane.
12. Type the following reply message text and then click the Send button.

(Type the name of the person from whom you received the message), [press Enter twice]

I agree. I have a few pictures we can use to practice with if you want to set up a sample account at Pinterest.com. [press Enter twice]

(Type your name)

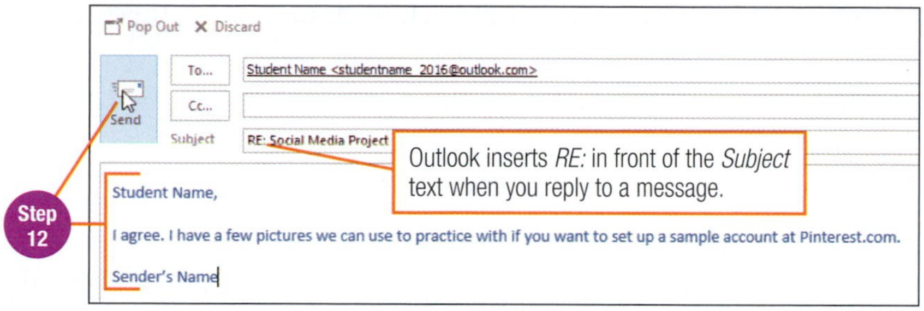

Forwarding a Message

Forward a message if you want someone else to receive a copy of a message you have received. Choose the **Forward** button, type the email address for the person to whom you want to forward the message, and type a brief explanation if desired before sending the message.

Think carefully before forwarding a message to be certain that the original sender would not object to another person reading the message without his or her permission. If in doubt, do not forward the message.

13. With the message header for the message selected at Step 10 still active, click the Forward button in the Reading pane. In Outlook.com, click the arrow next to Reply and then click Forward.

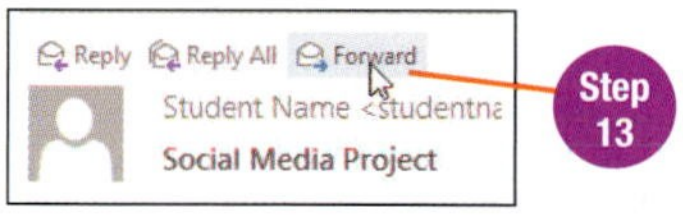

14. Type the email address for another classmate in the *To* text box.
15. Click in the message window above the original message text and then type the following text:

Hi (type recipient's name), [press Enter twice]

Do you want to join our group for the social media project? See message below discussing Pinterest.com. [press Enter twice]

(Type your name)

16. Click the Send button.

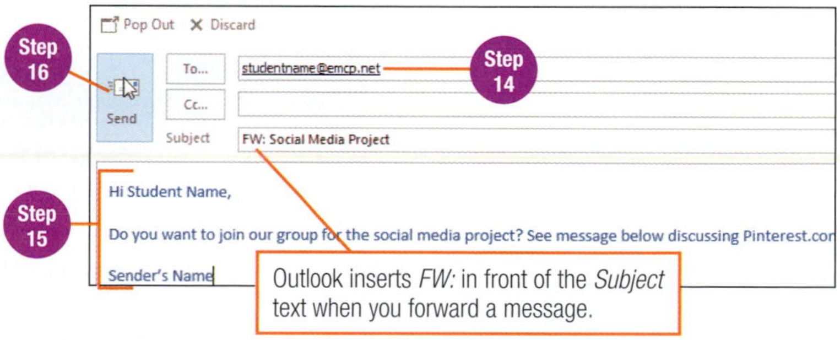

Oops!

Reading pane off? Turn on the Reading pane by clicking the View tab, Reading Pane button, then *Right*.

App Tip

Use Reply All to send a reply in which more than one person was included in the initial message. Use good judgment with Reply All and be sure that all the other recipients really need to see your response.

Quick Steps

Forward a Message

1. Click Forward button in Reading pane.
2. Type address in *To* text box.
3. Type message.
4. Click Send.

Beyond Basics Email Signatures

A signature is a closing automatically inserted at the bottom of each sent message. Signatures usually include contact information for the sender, such as name, title, department, company name, and contact telephone numbers. To create a signature, open a message window, click the Signature button on the Message tab in the Include group, and then click *Signatures*.

5.2 Attaching a File to a Message and Deleting a Message

Skills

Attach a picture to a message

Delete a message

Empty Deleted Items folder

Files are often exchanged between individuals via email. To attach a file to an email message, use the **Attach File** button in the Include group on the Message tab. The recipient of an email message with a file attachment can choose to open the file from the mail server or save it to a storage medium to open later.

Messages that are no longer needed should be deleted to keep your mail folders to a manageable size. You can delete a message in the Inbox folder if you replied to the message because you can view the original text with your reply from Sent Items. Consider setting aside a time each week to clean up your Inbox by deleting messages.

1 With Outlook open and Inbox the active folder, click the Home tab if Home is not the active tab.

2 Click the New Email button in the New group.

3 Type the email address for the recipient in the *To* text box.

Notice that as you begin typing an email address, Outlook provides email addresses that match what you are typing in a drop-down list. This feature is referred to as **AutoComplete**. Rather than type the entire email address, you can click the correct recipient in the AutoComplete list. People in the workplace who use Outlook connected to a special server called an Exchange server can send a message to someone within the organization by typing just the name of the recipient.

4 Press the Tab key twice or click in the *Subject* text box.

5 Type Picture for Pinterest and then press Enter.

6 With the insertion point positioned in the Message text window, type the following text:

Hi (type recipient's name), [press Enter twice]

Attached is a picture we can put on Pinterest.

7 Press Enter twice at the end of the message text and then type your name as the sender.

8 Click the Attach File button in the Include group on the Message tab in the message window.

Oops!

Using Outlook.com? Click the Insert button and then click *Files as attachments* at the drop-down list.

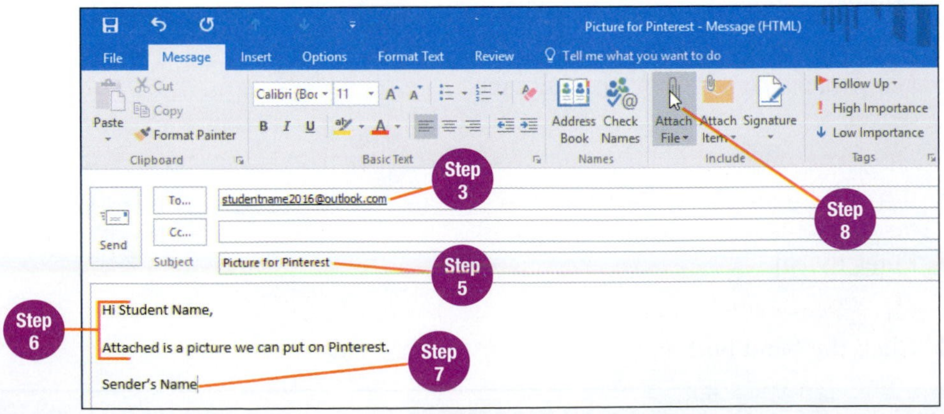

App Tip

New in Outlook 2016 is the Recent Items list on the Attach File button drop-down list. Files you have worked with recently show in this list, so you can attach one to a message with just one click.

9 Click *Browse This PC* at the drop-down list.

10 At the Insert File dialog box, navigate to the Student_Data_Files folder on your storage medium and then double-click *Ch5*.

11 Double-click the image file ***MurresOnIce***.

Outlook adds the file to an *Attached* area below the *Subject* text box.

12 Click the Send button.

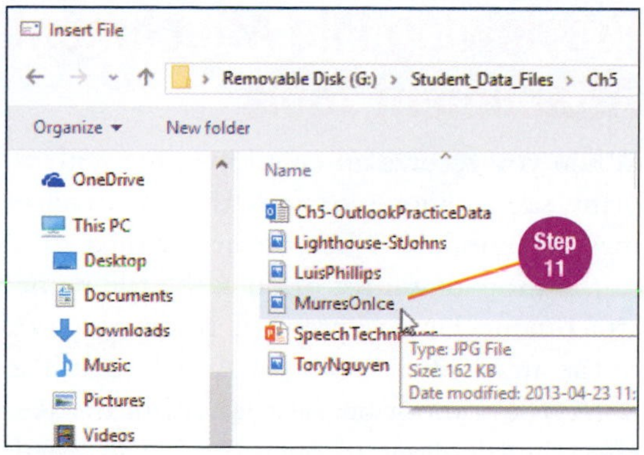

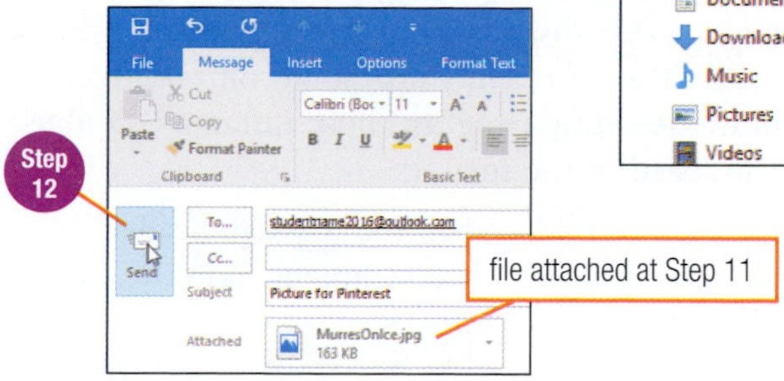

Over time your mail folders (Inbox and Sent Items) become filled with messages that are no longer needed. To delete a message, select the message header in the Content pane and then click the Delete button in the Delete group on the Home tab. Deleted messages are moved to the **Deleted Items** folder where the message can be restored if needed. Periodically, empty the Deleted Items folder to permanently delete the messages.

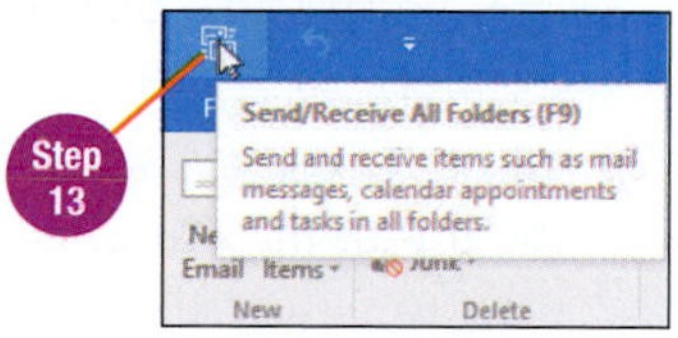

13 Click the Send/Receive All Folders button on the Quick Access Toolbar (first button) to update the Inbox. Skip this step if you can already see the message sent to you by a classmate or yourself in Step 12.

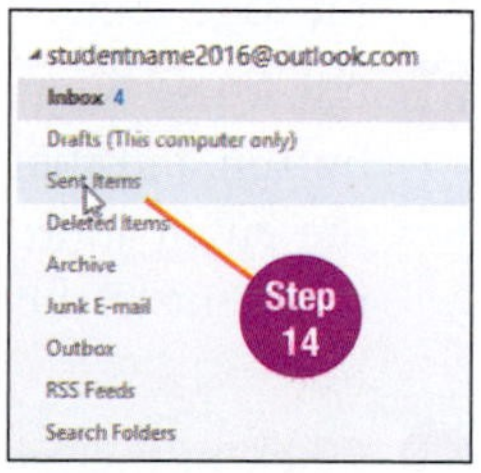

14 Click *Sent Items* in the Folder pane.

15 If necessary, click to select the message header for the message with the picture attached that you sent to a classmate or yourself in this topic.

16 Click the Delete button in the Delete group on the Home tab.

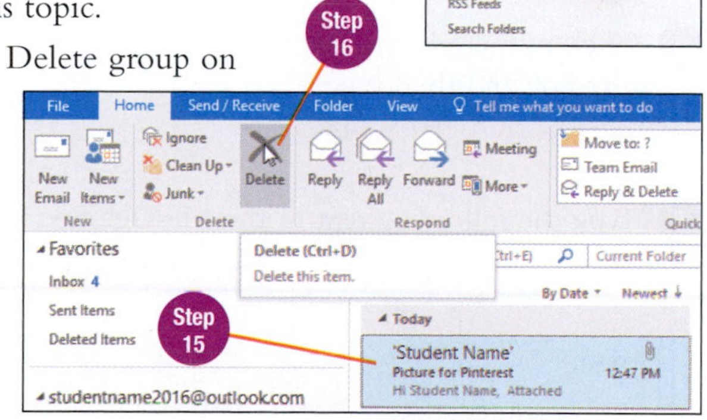

17 Click *Deleted Items* in the Folder pane.

Notice the message you deleted appears in the Content pane.

18 Right-click *Deleted Items* in the Folder pane and then click *Empty Folder*.

19 Click *Yes* at the Microsoft Outlook message box asking if you want to continue to permanently delete everything in the Deleted Items folder.

20 Click *Inbox* in the Folder pane.

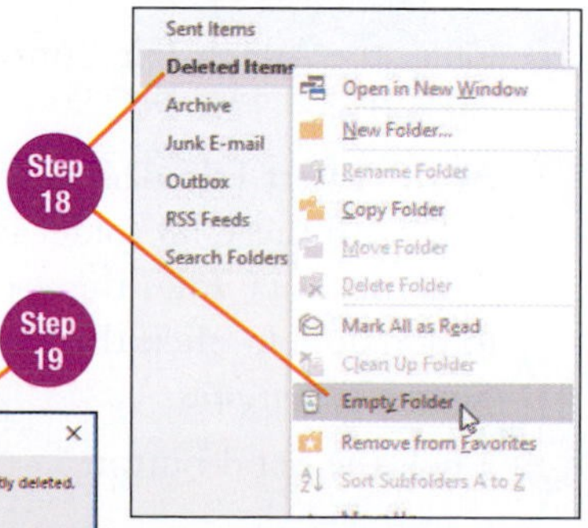

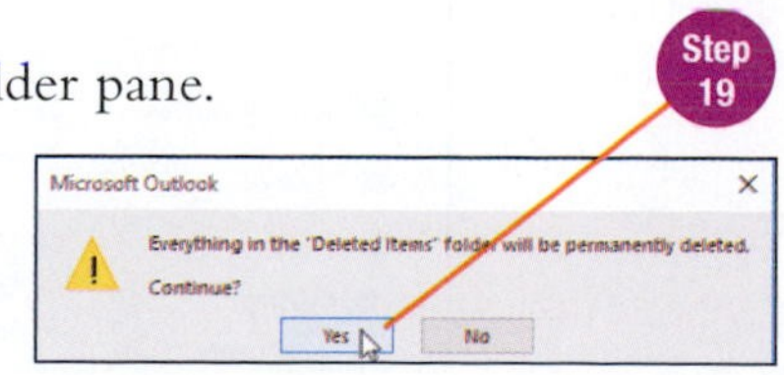

Quick Steps

Attach a File to a Message

1. Open new message window.
2. Type address in *To* text box.
3. Type brief description in *Subject* text box.
4. Type message text in message window.
5. Click Attach File button.
6. Click desired file in Recent Items list or click *Browse This PC*.
7. At Insert File dialog box, navigate to desired drive and/or folder.
8. Double-click file name.
9. Click Send.

Delete a Message

1. Select message in Content pane.
2. Click Delete button.

Empty Deleted Items Folder

1. Right-click *Deleted Items* in Folder pane.
2. Click *Empty Folder*.
3. Click Yes.

Oops!

Folder pane off or minimized? Click View tab, Folder Pane button, and then *Normal*.

App Tip

Select multiple messages for deletion using the Windows standards: Shift + click to select adjacent message headers, or Ctrl + click to select message headers that are not next to each other.

Oops!

Lots of messages in *Deleted Items*? As a precaution, click No at Step 19. At a later time, review all the messages in Deleted Items to ensure it is safe to permanently delete them.

5.3 Previewing File Attachments and Using File Attachment Tools

Skills

Preview a file attachment

Open a file attachment

Save a file attachment

When you receive an email message with a file attached, you can preview, open, print, save, remove, or copy the file attachment from the Reading pane or from a message window. Click the arrow next to the file name to select the desired action in the drop-down list or click the file name in the Reading pane to preview the attachment. During preview, the message text disappears, replaced with the contents of the attached file, and the Attachment Tools Attachments tab becomes active. Some files cannot be viewed within the Reading pane. In those instances, double-click the file name to open the file attached to the message.

1. With Outlook open and Inbox the active folder, click the message header for the message received in the previous topic with the file attachment. Skip this step if the message header is already selected.

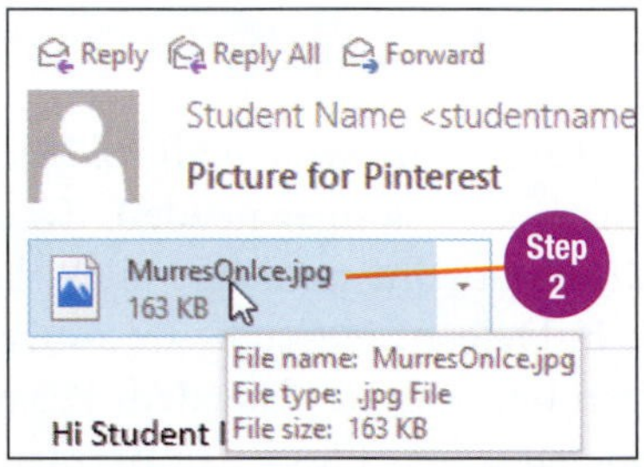

2. Click the file name ***MurresOnIce.jpg*** in the Reading pane. Do *not* click the arrow at the right of the file name.

Outlook removes the message text and displays in the Reading pane the picture attached to the message. Notice also that the Attachment Tools Attachments tab is active on the ribbon.

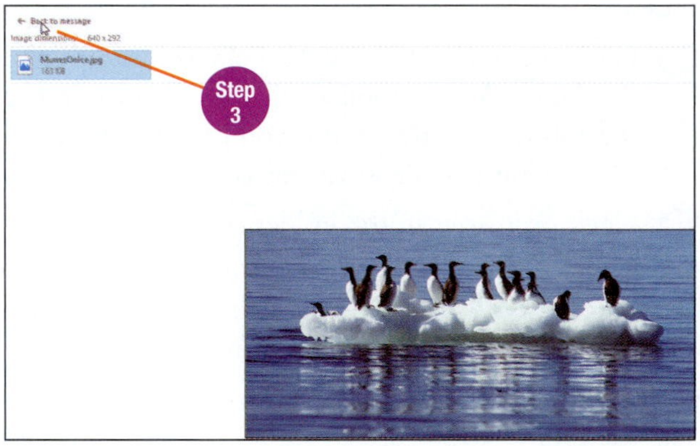

3. Click *Back to message* at the top of the Reading pane to restore the message text.
4. Click the New Email button and then type the email address for the recipient in the *To* text box.
5. Click in the *Subject* text box and then type Presentation for Business Class.
6. Type the following text in the Message text window:

   Hi (type recipient's name), [press Enter twice]

   Attached is the PowerPoint presentation for our group project. [press Enter twice]

   (Type your name)
7. Click the Attach File button in the Include group on the Message tab and then click *Browse This PC*.

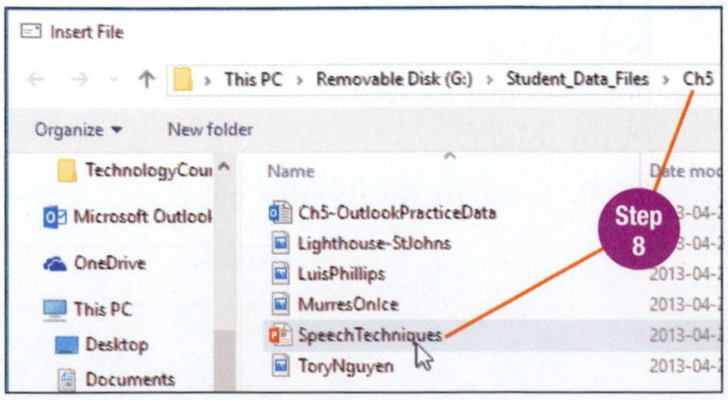

8. At the Insert File dialog box, with the Ch5 folder in Student_Data_Files the active folder, double-click the file ***SpeechTechniques***.
9. Click the Send button.

App Tip

If you are using Outlook .com, clicking the file name in the message pane offers three options: View online, Save to OneDrive, and Download. When a picture is attached to an email the picture is automatically previewed when the message header is clicked and two options appear below the image: Download as zip and Save to OneDrive.

App Tip

If you are using Outlook .com, the file is uploaded to the server and may take a few seconds to complete the upload.

10 Click the Send/Receive All Folders button on the Quick Access Toolbar to update your Inbox folder. Skip this step if you can already see the message sent to you by a classmate or yourself in Step 9.

11 Click the message header for the message received with the subject *Presentation for Business Class*.

12 Click the arrow at the right of the file name ***SpeechTechniques.pptx*** in the Reading pane and then click *Preview*.

13 Scroll down the Reading pane to the last slide in the presentation.

14 Click the file name button in the Reading Pane, and then click the Open button in the Actions group on the Attachment Tools Attachments tab.

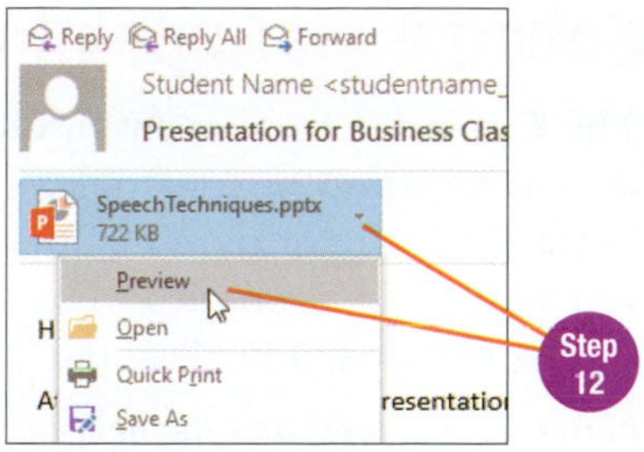

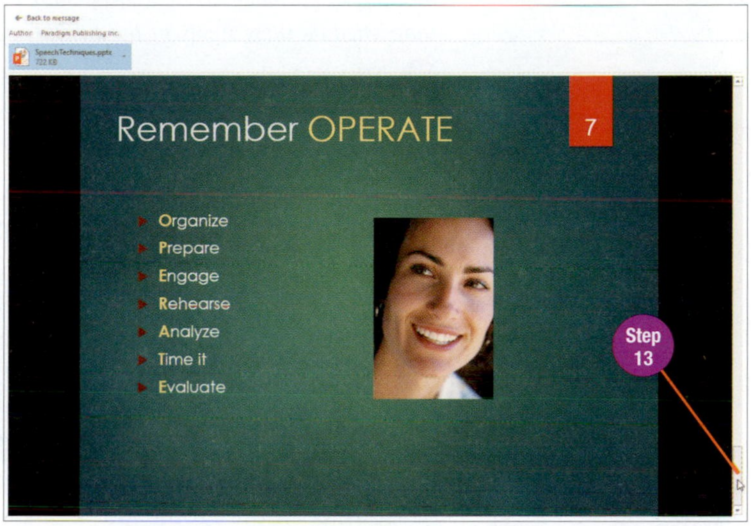

PowerPoint starts with the **SpeechTechniques** file open. Notice the Title bar and Message bar displayed below the ribbon tabs indicate the presentation is open in **Protected View**. Protected View allows you to read the file content in the source application; however, editing the file is not permitted until you click the Enable Editing button on the Message bar. The presentation remains in Read-Only mode with editing enabled until you save the file to another location because the file was opened from an email message.

15 Close PowerPoint to return to Outlook.

16 Click the file name button in the Reading Pane, and then click the Save As button in the Actions group on the Attachment Tools Attachments tab.

17 At the Save Attachment dialog box, navigate to the CompletedTopicsByChapter folder on your storage medium and then create a new folder *Ch5*.

18 Double-click the *Ch5* folder and then click the Save button.

19 Click the file name button in the Reading Pane, and then click the Show Message button in the Message group on the Attachment Tools Attachments tab to close the presentation preview in the Reading pane.

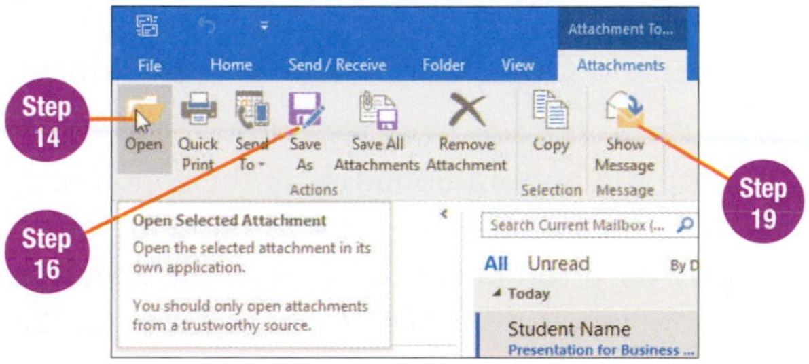

App Tip

Clicking the file name button in the Reading pane automatically previews the file. Click the arrow at the right of the file name button to access other attachment options.

Quick Steps

Preview a File Attached to a Message

Click file name button in Reading pane.

Open a File Attached to a Message

1. Click file name button in Reading pane.
2. Click Open button in Actions group on Attachment Tools Attachment tab.

Save a File Attached to a Message

1. Click file name button in Reading pane.
2. Click Save As button in Actions group on Attachment Tools Attachment tab.
3. Navigate to drive and/or folder.
4. Click Save.

Security Alert — Be Cautious Opening File Attachments!

Outlook blocks certain file types attached to messages that are known to be the target for viruses and are considered unsafe. However, even with the protection Outlook provides, you should exercise caution when opening a file received in an email message. Open files only from people you know and trust and always make sure you have real-time, up-to-date virus protection turned on. When in doubt, delete without opening any emailed files you were not expecting.

5.4 Scheduling Appointments and Events in Calendar

Skills

Schedule an appointment

Schedule an event

The **Calendar** component in Outlook is used to schedule appointments and events, such as meetings or conferences. An **appointment** is any activity where you want to track the day or time that the activity begins and ends in your schedule or when you want to be reminded to be somewhere. An appointment in Calendar can be a class, a meeting, a medical test, or a lunch date.

Note: *In this topic and the next two topics, you will schedule appointments, an event, and a meeting in October 2018. Check with your instructor, if necessary, for alternate instructions that schedule these items in the current month or in October of the current year.*

1. With Outlook open and Inbox the active folder, click Calendar in the Navigation pane.

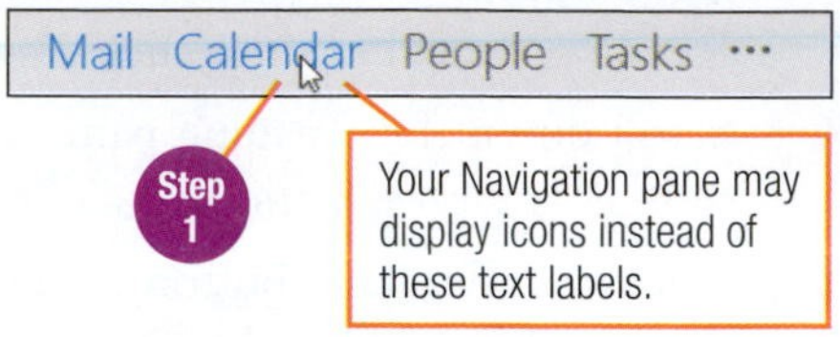

Outlook displays the current date, week, or month in the Content pane in Day, Week, or Month view. A **Date Navigator** displays at the top of the Folder pane with the current month and next month, along with directional arrow buttons to browse forward or back to upcoming or previous months. Open the **Go To Date** dialog box to navigate to a specific date that is not easily seen using the Date Navigator or the buttons in the Go To group on the Home tab.

2. If necessary, click the Day button in the Arrange group on the Home tab and then click the Go to Date launcher button (downward-pointing diagonal arrow) at the bottom right of the Go To group.

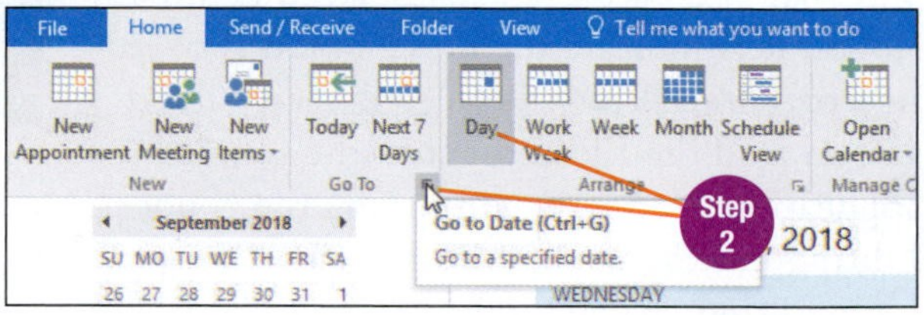

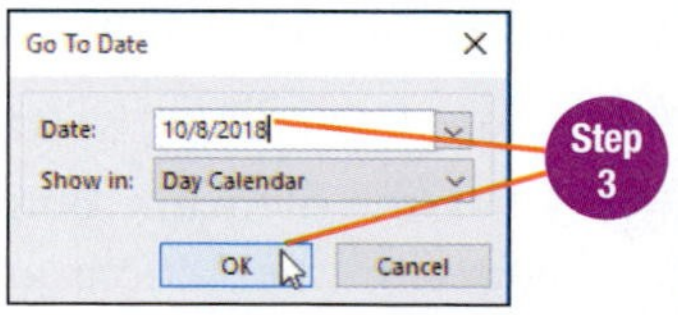

3. At the Go To Date dialog box, type 10/8/2018 and then press Enter or click OK.

4. Click next to 9:00 a.m. in the Appointment area, type Meet with program adviser, and then press Enter or click in another time slot outside the appointment box.

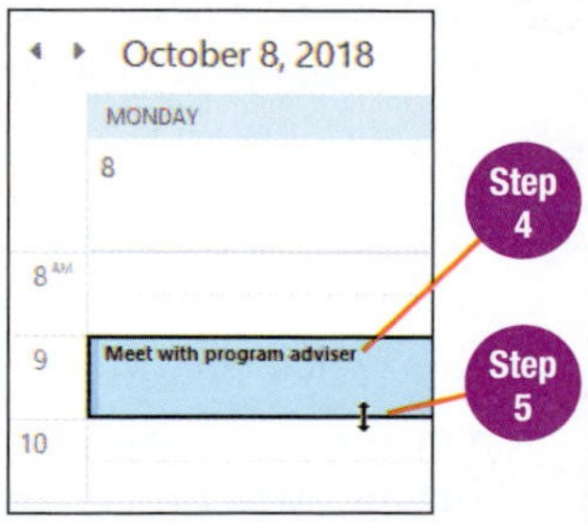

By default, Outlook schedules an appointment for a half hour.

5. Drag the bottom boundary of the appointment box to 10:00 a.m. If you are using a touchscreen, you may need to double-tap to open the appointment, tap the *End time* option box arrow, tap *10:00 AM (1 hour)*, and then tap Save & Close. Skip this step if you are using Outlook.com.

6. Click next to 11:00 a.m. in the Appointment area.

7. Click the New Appointment button in the New group on the Home tab.

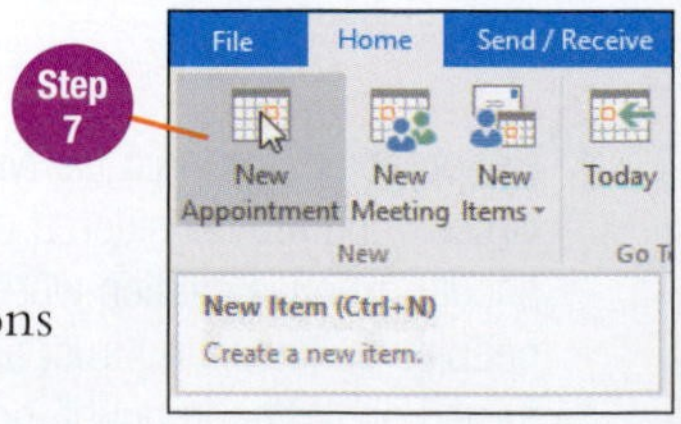

Click the **New Appointment** button to open an Appointment window in which you can provide more details about the appointment or select more options to apply to the appointment.

Oops!

Using Outlook.com? Click the Microsoft Apps button (it displays as a waffle icon) at the top left of the window and then click the Calendar tile in the drop-down list. Click View near the top right of the window and then click Day if the view is not currently Day.

Oops!

August 10 displayed instead of October 8? The Region Format in the Control Panel is not set to English (United States). Try Step 3 again, typing the date as October 8, 2018 instead of 10/8/2018.

App Tip

A feature called *peek* displays a pop-up with current information when you point to an item. For example, point to an appointment in your calendar to view a pop-up with information about the appointment. You can also peek at the appointments for the day without leaving Mail by simply pointing to Calendar in the Navigation pane.

8 Type Intern Interview in the *Subject* text box.

9 Press Tab or click in the *Location* text box and then type Room 3001. If you are using Outlook.com, click View details to open the Details panel in which you enter the location.

10 Click the *End time* option box arrow and then click *12:00 PM (1 hour)* at the drop-down list. Skip this step if you are using Outlook.com.

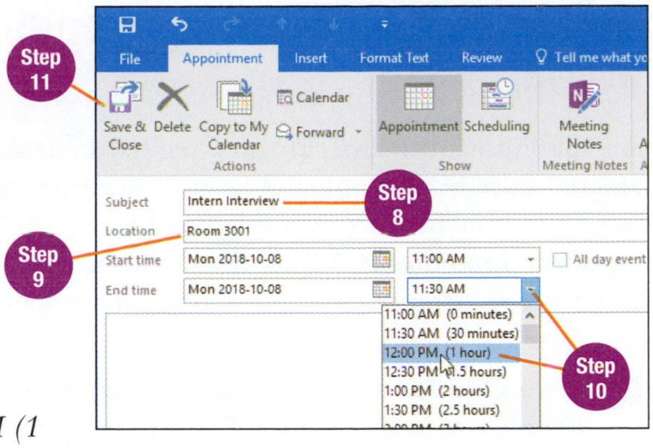

11 Click the Save & Close button in the Actions group on the Appointment tab in the Appointment window.

An **event** differs from an appointment in that it is an activity that lasts an entire day or longer. Examples of events include conferences, trade shows, or vacations. An event does not occupy a time slot in the Calendar. Event information appears in a banner along the top of the day in the Appointment area.

12 Click the New Items button in the New group on the Home tab and then click *All Day Event* at the drop-down list to open an Event window.

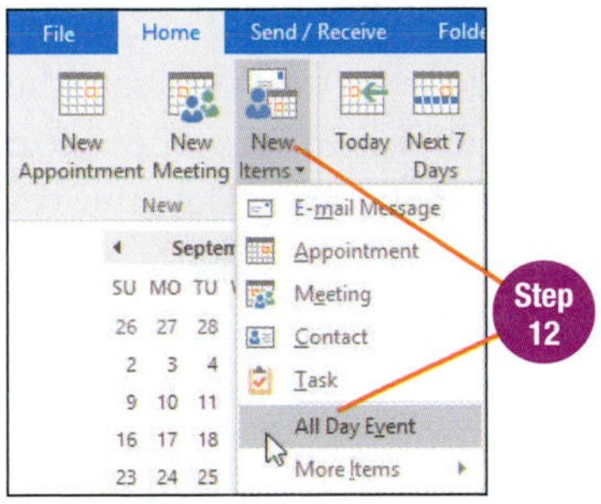

13 Type Career Fair in the *Subject* text box.

14 Press Tab or click in the *Location* text box and then type Student Center.

15 Click the Save & Close button in the Actions group on the Event tab in the Event window. Notice the event appears at the top of the Appointment area before the 8 a.m. time slot.

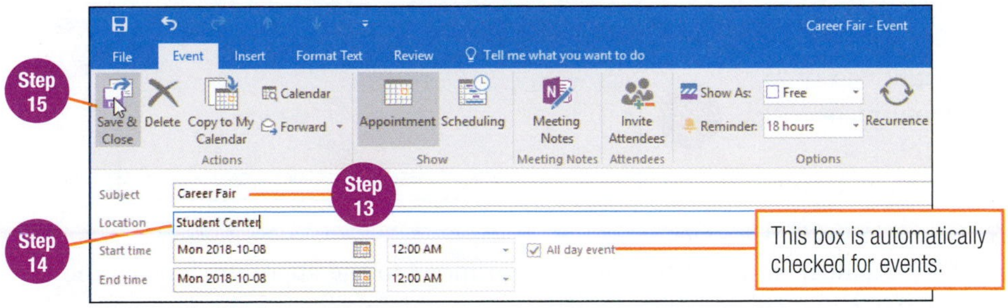

Quick Steps

Schedule an Appointment

1. Display the Calendar.
2. Navigate to appointment date.
3. Click next to appointment time.
4. Type appointment description.
5. Press Enter.

OR

1. Display the Calendar.
2. Navigate to appointment date.
3. Click next to appointment time.
4. Click New Appointment button.
5. Enter appointment details in Appointment window.
6. Click Save & Close.

Schedule an Event

1. Display the Calendar.
2. Navigate to event date.
3. Click New Items button and then click *All Day Event.*
4. Enter event description.
5. Enter event location.
6. Click Save & Close.

Oops!

Using Outlook.com? Click the down-pointing arrow on the New button and then click *Event* at the drop-down list.

App Tip

Change the End time date if the event lasts more than one day.

Beyond Basics — Appointment Reminders and Tags

By default, new appointments have a reminder set at 15 minutes. Turn off the reminder or change the reminder time by clicking to select an appointment in the Appointment area and then using the *Reminder* option box in the Options group on the Calendar Tools Appointment tab.

Assign one or more tags to a selected appointment with buttons in the Tags group on the Calendar Tools Appointment tab. Click the Private button for a personal appointment so that other people with access to your calendar cannot see the appointment details. Click the High Importance button to remind you of an important appointment.

5.5 Scheduling a Recurring Appointment and Editing an Appointment

Skills

Schedule a recurring appointment

Edit an appointment

An appointment that occurs on a regular basis at fixed intervals need only be entered once in Outlook and set up as a recurring appointment. To do this, open the Appointment Recurrence dialog box by clicking the **Recurrence** button in the Options group on the Appointment tab or the Calendar Tools Appointment tab. Enter the recurrence pattern for a repeating appointment, click OK, and then save and close the appointment.

1. With Outlook open and Calendar active for October 8, 2018, click the Forward button to display October 9, 2018 in the Appointment area.

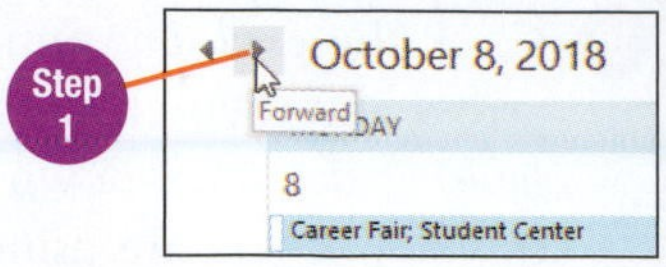

2. Click next to 3:00 p.m. in the Appointment area, type Math Extra Help Sessions, and then press Enter.

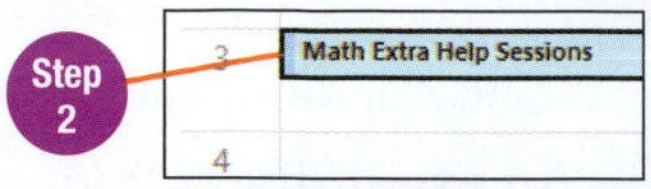

3. With the Math Extra Help Sessions appointment box selected in the Appointment area, click the Recurrence button in the Options group on the Calendar Tools Appointment tab.

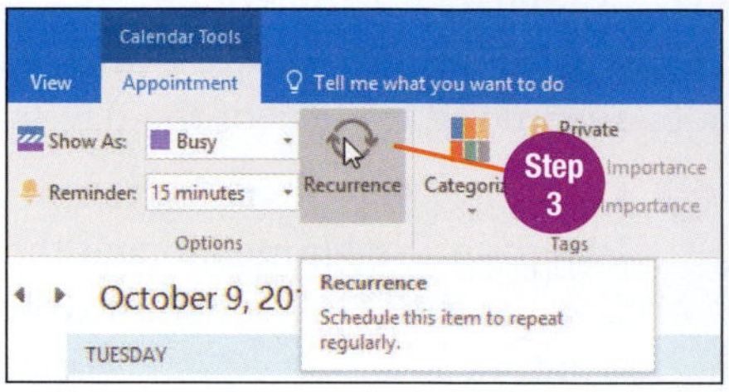

By default, Outlook sets the *Recurrence pattern* details for the appointment to recur *Weekly* at the same day and time as the appointment.

4. At the Appointment Recurrence dialog box, select *10* in the *End after* text box in the *Range of recurrence* section and then type 5.
5. Click OK.

A recurring icon displays at the right end of the appointment box in the Appointment area.

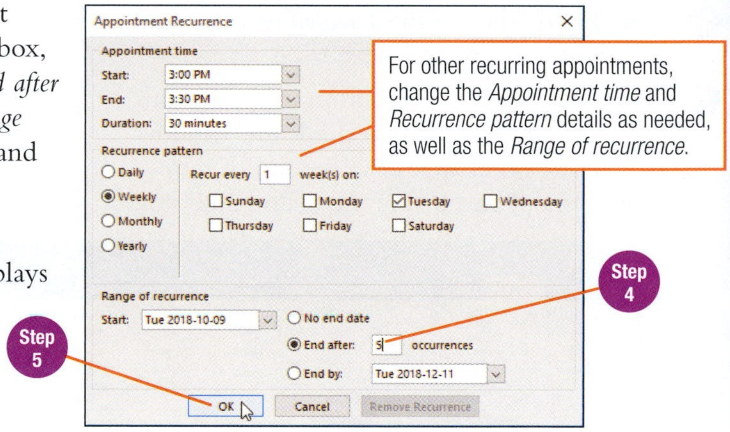

6. Click *16* in the October 2018 calendar in the Date Navigator to move to the appointments for the following Tuesday and view the Math Extra Help Sessions appointment.
7. Click *23* in the October 2018 calendar in the Date Navigator to view the Math Extra Help Sessions appointment in the Appointment area.
8. Click the Go to Date launcher button in the Go To group, type 11/13/2018 in the Go To Date dialog box, and then press Enter or click OK.

Notice the Math Extra Help Sessions appointment does not appear in the Appointment area because the range of recurrence has ended.

Oops!

Calendar Tools Appointment tab not visible? Click the appointment box to select the appointment and display the contextual tab.

Oops!

Using Outlook.com? Set the recurrence option by displaying the appointment Details panel and then changing *How often* to *Weekly*.

App Tip

Consider entering your class schedule in the Outlook calendar for the current semester as recurring appointments.

Quick Steps

Schedule a Recurring Appointment

1. Display Calendar.
2. Navigate to appointment date.
3. Click next to appointment time.
4. Type appointment description.
5. Press Enter.
6. Click Recurrence button.
7. Enter recurrence pattern and/or range details.
8. Click OK.

Edit an Appointment

1. Select appointment.
2. Click Open button.
3. Change appointment details as needed.
4. Click Save & Close.

Assign options or tags to an existing appointment by selecting the appointment and using the buttons in the Calendar Tools Appointment tab. Change the subject, location, day, or time of an appointment by double-clicking appointment to open the Appointment window.

9 Display October 8, 2018 in the Calendar.

10 Click to select the appointment scheduled at 11:00 a.m.

A selected appointment box displays with a black outline. A pop-out opens at the left with the appointment details when you point at an appointment.

11 Click the Open button in the Actions group on the Calendar Tools Appointment tab. Click the View details hyperlink if you are using Outlook.com.

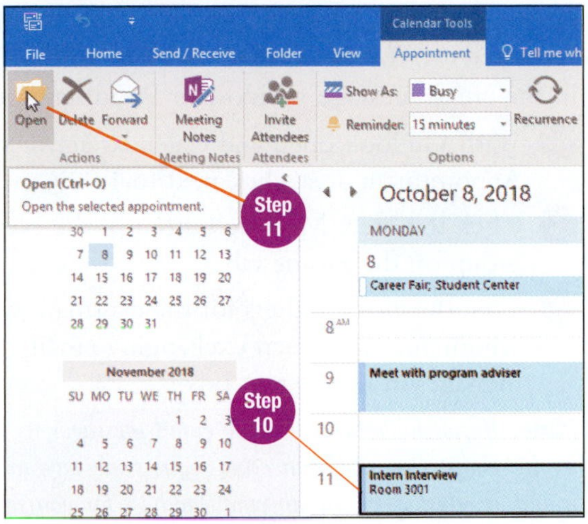

Assume the intern interview has been rescheduled to Tuesday.

12 Click the calendar icon at the right end of the *Start time* text box.

13 Click *9* in the drop-down calendar.

14 Click Save & Close in the Actions group on the Appointment tab.

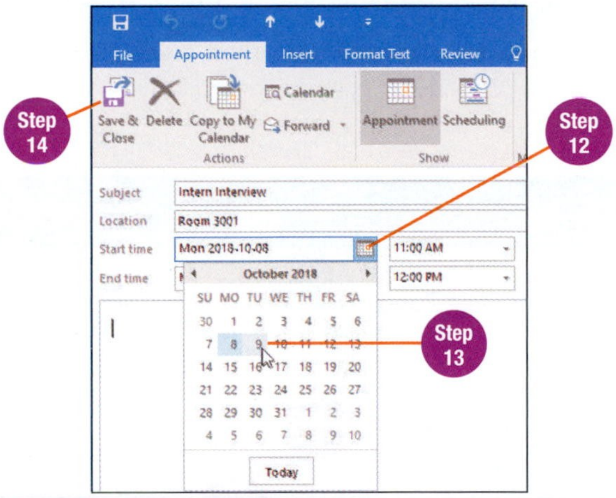

15 Display October 9, 2018 in the Appointment area.

Notice the Intern Interview appointment appears next to 11:00 a.m.

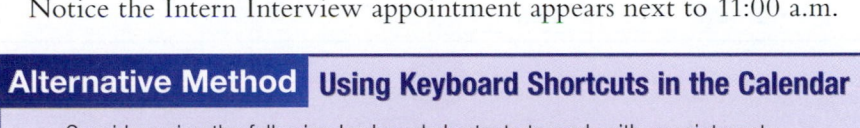

Alternative Method **Using Keyboard Shortcuts in the Calendar**

Consider using the following keyboard shortcuts to work with appointments:

Ctrl + N to open a new Appointment window

Ctrl + O to open the Appointment window for the selected appointment

Ctrl + G to open the Go To Date dialog box

Ctrl + P to print the appointments for the current day

5.6 Scheduling a Meeting

Skills

Schedule a meeting

Respond to a meeting request

Schedule a **meeting** by selecting the day and time and then clicking the **New Meeting** button in the New group on the Home tab. At the Meeting window, enter the email addresses for the individuals to invite to the meeting in the *To* text box. Type the meeting subject, location, and other details as needed and then click the Send button. Meeting attendees receive a **meeting request** email message. Responses to the meeting request are sent back to the meeting organizer via buttons in the email message window or Reading pane.

1. With Outlook open and Calendar active with October 9, 2018 displayed in the Appointment area, click next to 1:00 p.m.
2. Click the New Meeting button in the New group on the Home tab.
3. Type the email address for the classmate with whom you have been exchanging email messages in the *To* text box.

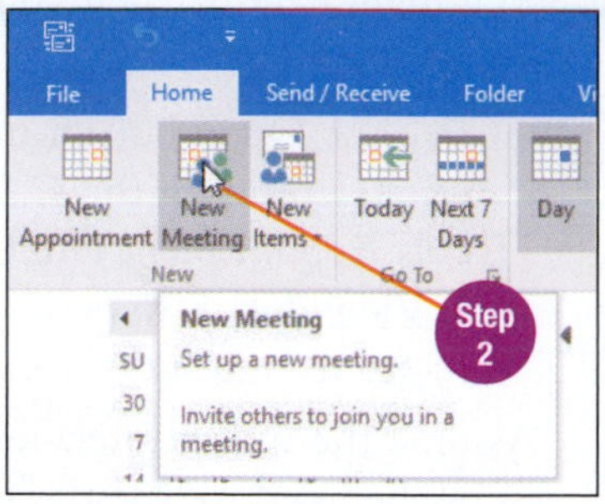

Note: *If you have been sending email messages to yourself in this chapter, send the meeting request message to a friend or relative, or use an email address for yourself that is different from your Microsoft account address because you cannot send a meeting request to yourself. You will not be able to complete Step 8 to Step 16 if you do not receive a meeting request message from someone else.*

Oops!

Using Outlook.com? Create an appointment, display the Details panel, and click the Attendees tab (next to Details). Enter the email address for the meeting participant in the *Invite people* text box. Click Send invite to send the meeting request messages.

4. Press Tab or click in the *Subject* text box and then type Fundraising Planning Meeting.
5. Press Tab or click in the *Location* text box and then type Room 1010.
6. Click the *End time* option box arrow and then click *2:30 PM (1.5 hours)* at the drop-down list.
7. Click the Send button.

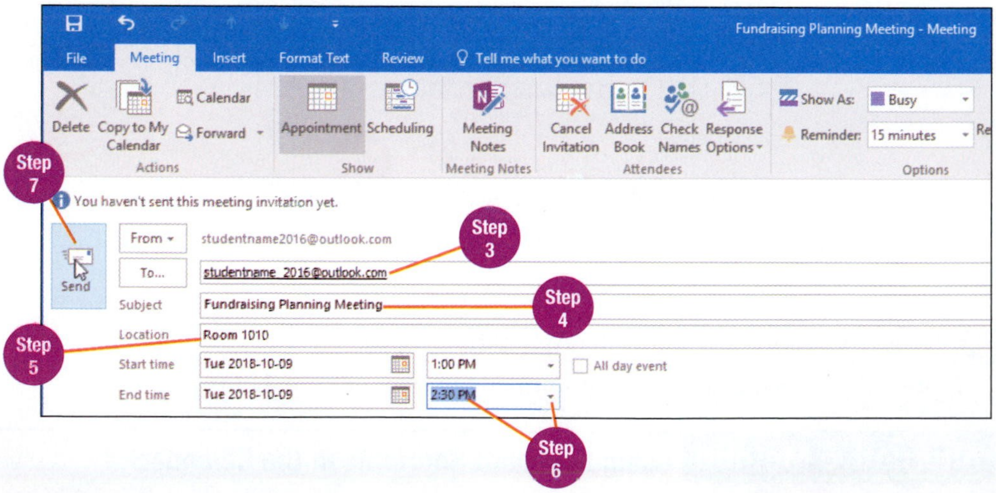

App Tip

Consider using the space in the message window below *End time* to type a meeting agenda or other explanatory text to inform attendees about the purpose of the meeting.

8. Click Mail in the Navigation pane.
9. Click the Send/Receive All Folders button on the Quick Access Toolbar to update your Inbox folder. Skip this step if you can already see the meeting request message sent to you by a classmate at Step 7.

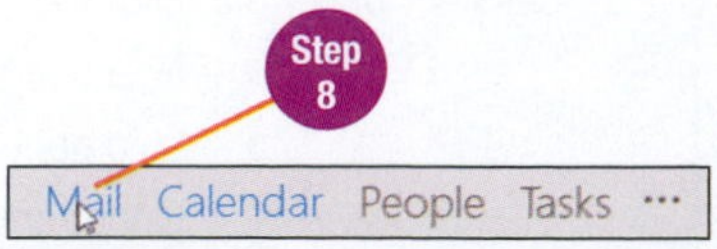

10 Click to select the message header for the meeting request to view the message details in the Reading pane.

Buttons along the top of the Reading pane or in the Respond group on the Meeting tab in a Message window for a meeting request are used to respond to the meeting organizer. Click the **Accept** button to send a reply that you will attend the meeting. Use the Tentative, Decline, or Propose New Time buttons if you are not required, or unable to attend a scheduled meeting. Outlook also provides a Calendar button at the top of the Reading pane, which is used to view your appointments for the meeting day and time to see if you are available before you send a response to the meeting organizer.

11 Double-click the message header to open the meeting request message with the Meeting tab active.

12 Click the Accept button in the Respond group on the Meeting tab.

13 Click *Send the Response Now* at the drop-down list.

Notice that the meeting request email message is deleted from your Inbox after you responded to the meeting invitation.

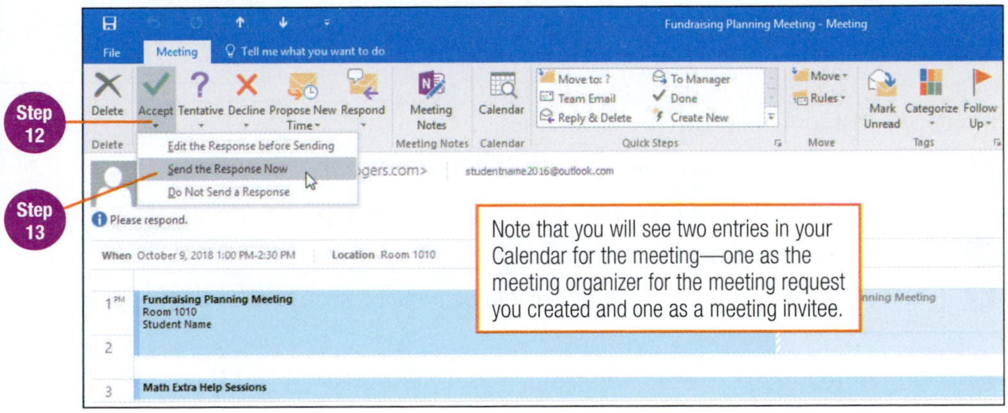

14 Click *Sent Items* in the Folder pane.

15 Click the message header for the message sent to the meeting organizer with your Accepted reply and then read the message you sent to the meeting organizer in the Reading pane.

16 Click *Inbox* in the Folder pane.

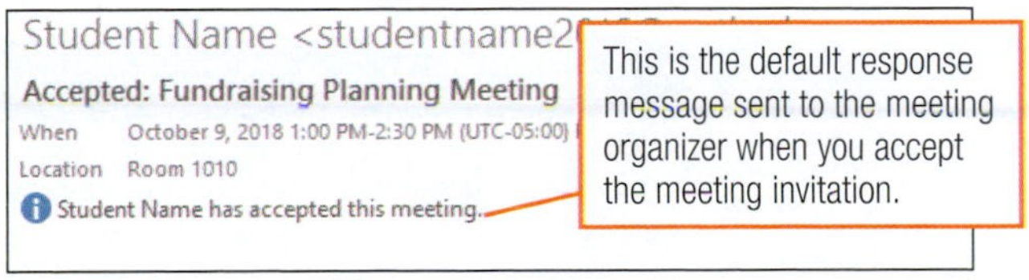

Quick Steps

Schedule a Meeting

1. Display Calendar.
2. Navigate to meeting date.
3. Click next to meeting time.
4. Click New Meeting button.
5. Enter meeting details.
6. Click Send.

Accept a Meeting Request

1. Display Inbox.
2. Select meeting request message header OR open Meeting window.
3. Click Accept button.
4. Click *Send the Response Now*.

Beyond Basics Updating and Canceling a Meeting

If you need to reschedule a meeting, open the Meeting window; make the required changes to the day, time, or location; and then click the Send Update button. Outlook will send an email message to each attendee with the updated information. To delete a meeting, open the Meeting window and then click the Cancel Meeting button in the Actions group on the Meeting tab. Outlook sends an email message to each attendee informing them that the meeting is canceled and removes the meeting from each person's calendar.

5.7 Adding and Editing Contacts in People

Skills

Add a Contact

Edit a Contact

The **People** component in Outlook is used to store and organize contact information, such as email addresses, mailing addresses, telephone numbers, and other information about the people with whom you communicate. Think of People as an electronic address book. To add information about a person, click the **New Contact** button in the New group on the Home tab. Contacts display alphabetically in the People list in the Content pane. Click a contact name to display the information about the person in a **People card** in the Reading pane.

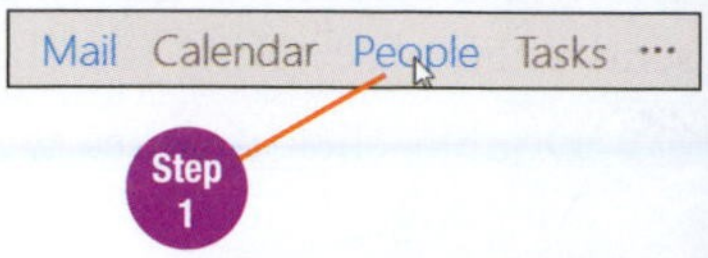

1. With Outlook open and Inbox the active folder, click People in the Navigation pane.
2. Click the New Contact button in the New group.
3. Type Tory Nguyen in the *Full Name* text box in the Contact window.
4. Press Tab or click in the *Company* text box.

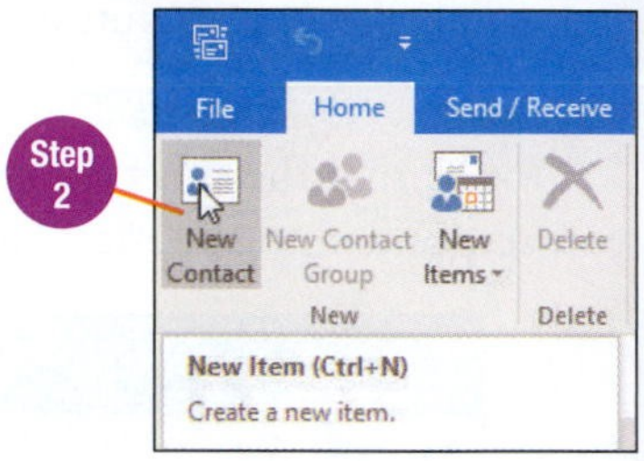

Notice the *File as* text box automatically updates when you move past the *Full Name* entry with the last name of the person followed by the first name. The *File as* entry is used to organize the People list alphabetically by last names.

5. Type NuWave Personnel in the *Company* text box.
6. Press Tab or click in the *Job title* text box and then type Recruitment Specialist.
7. Click in the *E-mail* text box and then type tory@emcp.net.
8. Click in the *Business* text box in the *Phone numbers* section and then type 8885559840.
9. Click in the *Mobile* text box in the *Phone numbers* section and then type 8885553256.

Notice that the phone numbers automatically format to show brackets around the area code, a space, and a hyphen in the number when you move past the field. In Outlook.com, the formatting of telephone numbers does not occur. Type the brackets and hyphens if desired.

10. Click the Add Contact Picture control that displays as a silhouette in a box between the name and business card sections of the Contact window.

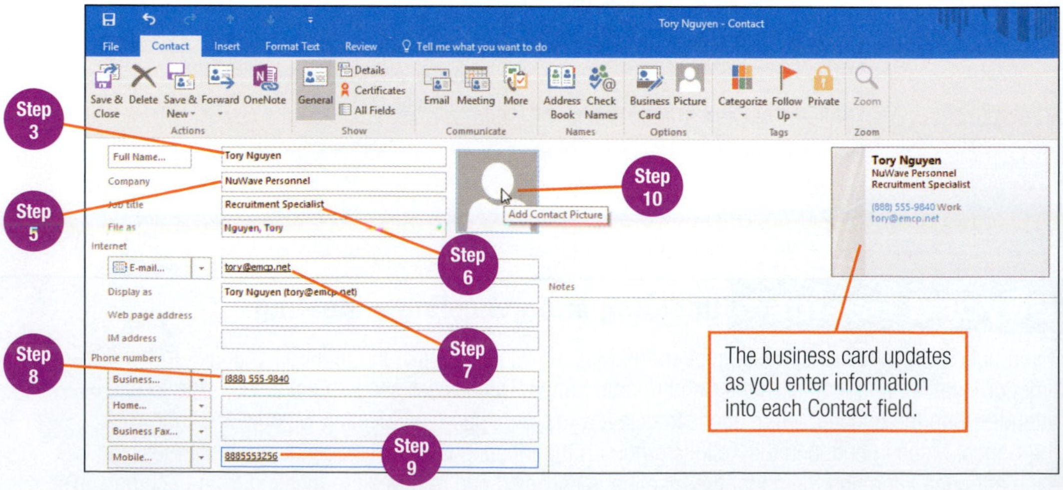

Oops!

Using Outlook.com? Click the Microsoft Apps button (it displays as a waffle icon) at the top left of the window and then click the People tile in the drop-down list. Click the New button to add a new contact. Click the expand buttons (plus symbol inside circle) to locate more options for entering data in the Add new contact panel.

App Tip

You can also add a picture using the Picture button in the Options group on the Contact tab.

11 At the Add Contact Picture dialog box, navigate to the Ch5 folder in the Student_Data_Files folder and then double-click the image file ***ToryNguyen***.

12 Click the Save & Close button in the Actions group on the Contact tab.

A selected person's information displays in the Reading pane in a People card with links to schedule a meeting or send an email to that person. Click *Edit* to open the People card fields for editing in the Reading pane, or double-click the name in the People list to add or modify information in a People card window.

13 Click Edit near the top right of the Reading pane with Tory Nguyen's information displayed.

14 Click at the end of the *Work* telephone number *(888) 555-9840,* press the spacebar, and then type extension 3115.

15 Click the Save button at the bottom right of the Reading pane.

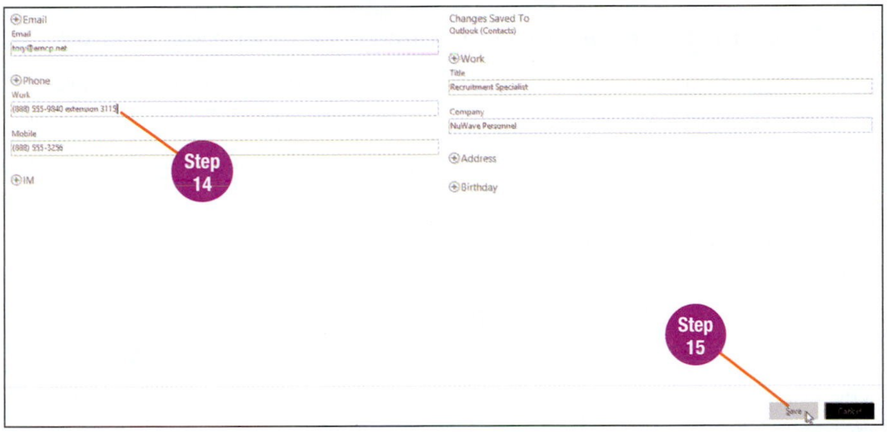

16 Double-click in the white space below the last entry in the People list.

Double-clicking in blank space in the People list opens a new Contact window.

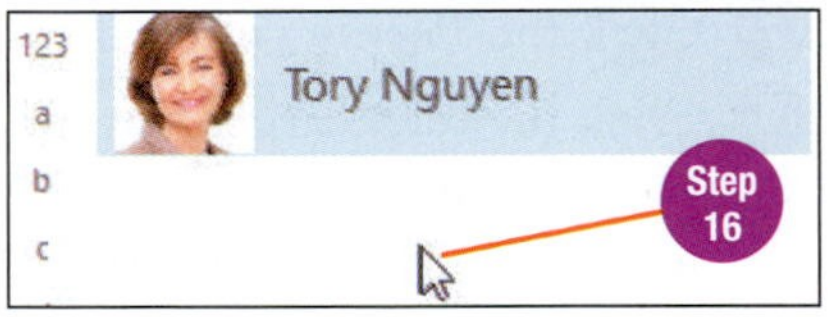

17 Enter the name of your instructor, the name of your school, and the email address of your instructor in the Contact window and then click Save & Close.

Alternative Method **Editing Contact Information Using the Contact Window**

You can also edit a contact by opening the full Contact window and clicking the Outlook (Contacts) hyperlink below *View Source* in the Reading pane for the selected person. This causes the same Contact window to open that you used to add the person. Use this method if you need to change the picture of a contact or access the complete set of data or ribbon options.

Quick Steps

Add a Contact

1. Display People.
2. Click New Contact button.
3. Enter contact information as required.
4. Click Save & Close.

Edit a Contact

1. Click to select contact in People list.
2. Click Edit in Reading pane.
3. Edit information as required.
4. Click Save.

Oops!

No Reading pane? Your Contact view may be set to Business Card or Card. Click People in the Current View group on the Home tab. If necessary, click the View tab, Reading Pane button, then *Right*.

Oops!

A Check Full Name dialog box may appear after you enter a name. This happens when Outlook cannot determine the first and last name. Typing errors or hyphenated names can cause the dialog box to open. Enter or edit the text as needed and click OK when the dialog box appears.

5.8 Adding and Editing Tasks

Skills

Add a task

Edit a task

Delete a task

Mark a task complete

Oops!

Using Outlook.com? Add a task by displaying the Calendar. Click the arrow on the New button and then click Task. Tasks display in a pane below the Calendar.

The **Tasks** component in Outlook maintains a to-do list. You can track information about each task, such as how much of the task is completed, how much time has been spent on the task, and the priority of the task. In **To-Do List** view, uncompleted tasks are shown grouped in descending order by the due date.

1. With Outlook open and People active, click *Tasks* in the Navigation pane and then click the *To-Do List* option in the Current View group on the Home tab if To-Do List is not the active view.

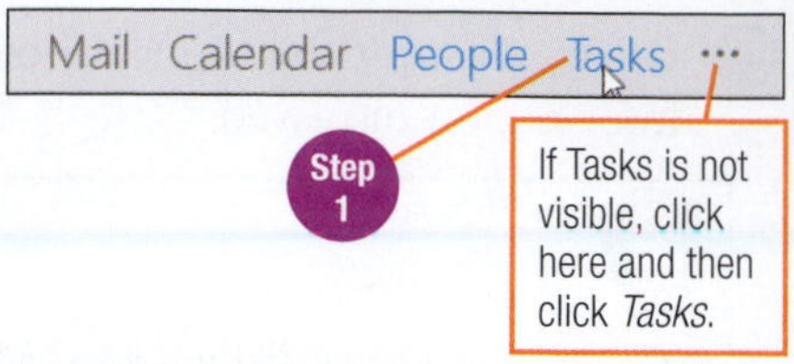

2. Click in the text box at the top of the To-Do List that displays the dimmed text *Type a new task* or *Click here to add a new Task*, type Do research on Pinterest, and then press Enter.

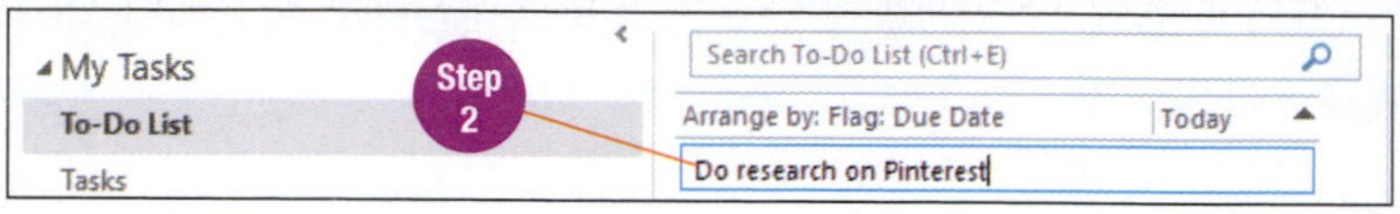

Outlook adds the task to the To-Do List under a flag with the heading *Today*.

3. Type Gather pictures to create Pinterest pinboard and then press Enter.
4. Type Create resume for Career Fair and then press Enter.

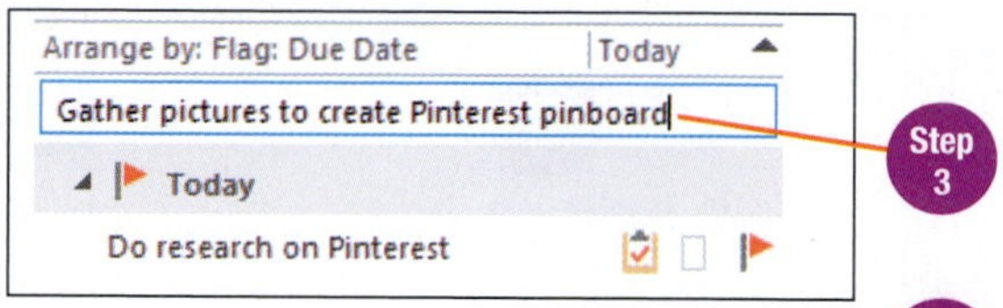

To add a task with more details and options, open a Task window by clicking the **New Task** button.

5. Click the New Task button in the New group on the Home tab.

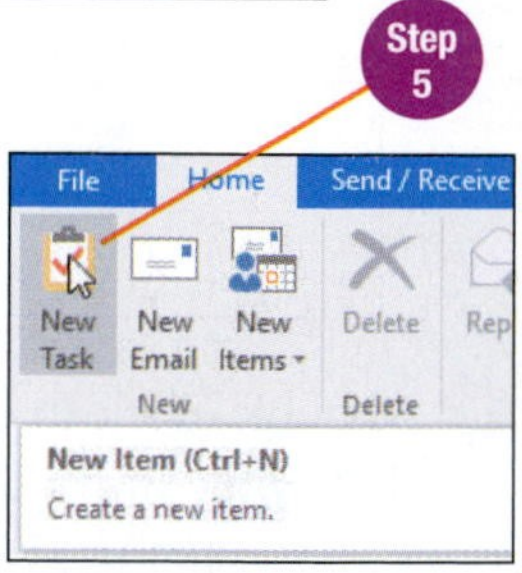

6. Type Prepare study notes for exams in the *Subject* text box.
7. Click the *Priority* option box arrow and then click *High*.
8. Click the calendar icon at the right end of the *Due date* text box, navigate to the last month of the current semester, and then click the Monday that is one week before the last week of your semester.
9. Click the Save & Close button in the Actions group on the Task tab.

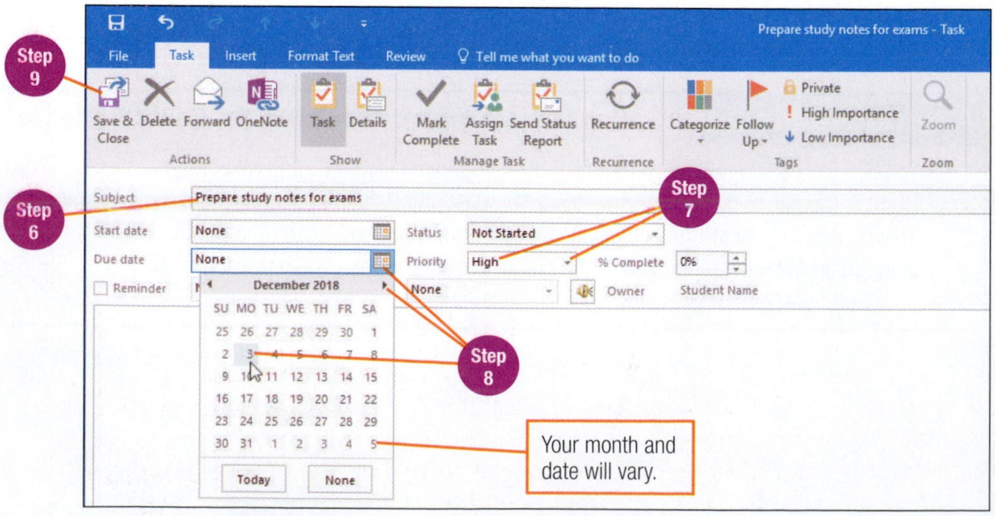

Editing or updating a task can include activities such as assigning or changing a due date, assigning a priority, entering the percentage of completion, or changing the status of a task. When a task is completed, use the Remove from List button in the Manage Task group on the Home tab or mark the task as complete in the Task window.

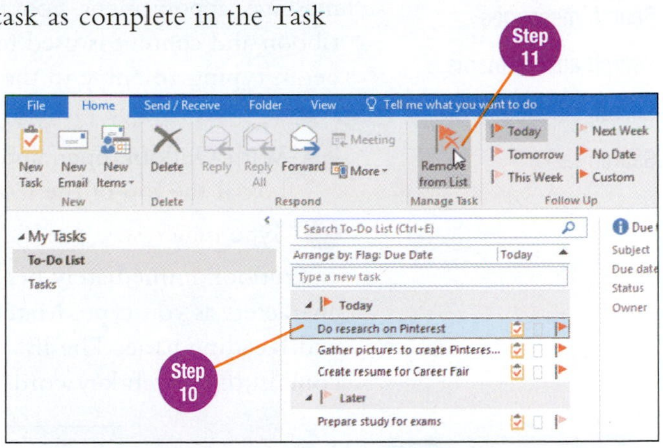

10 Click to select the task *Do research on Pinterest.*

11 Click the Remove from List button in the Manage Task group on the Home tab.

Notice the task is removed from the To-Do List. You can also use the Delete button in the Delete group on the Home tab to remove a task.

12 Double-click the task *Create resume for Career Fair* to open the Task window.

13 Click the Mark Complete button in the Manage Task group on the Task tab.

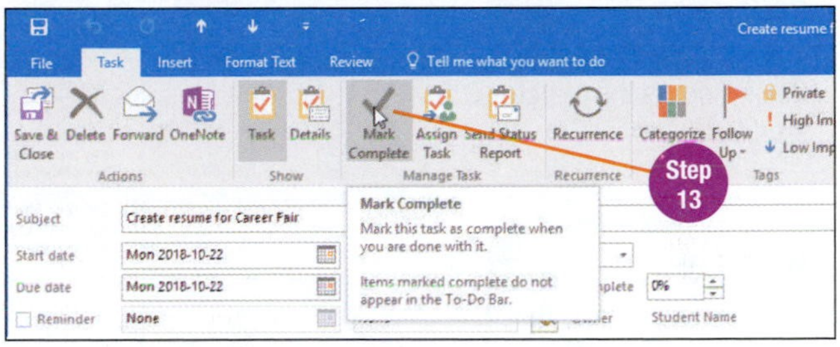

14 Double-click the task entry *Gather pictures to create Pinterest pinboard.*

15 Click the *Status* option box arrow and then click *Waiting on someone else.*

16 Click in the text box with white space below the *Reminder* options and then type Waiting for Leslie to send me pictures from her renovation clients..

17 Click the Save & Close button. Notice the updated task details appear in the Reading pane for the selected task.

18 Click the Simple List option in the Current View group on the Home tab.

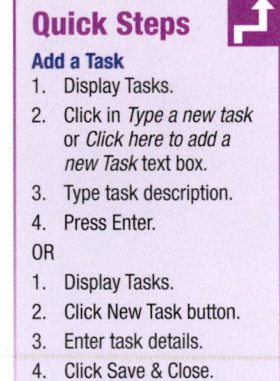

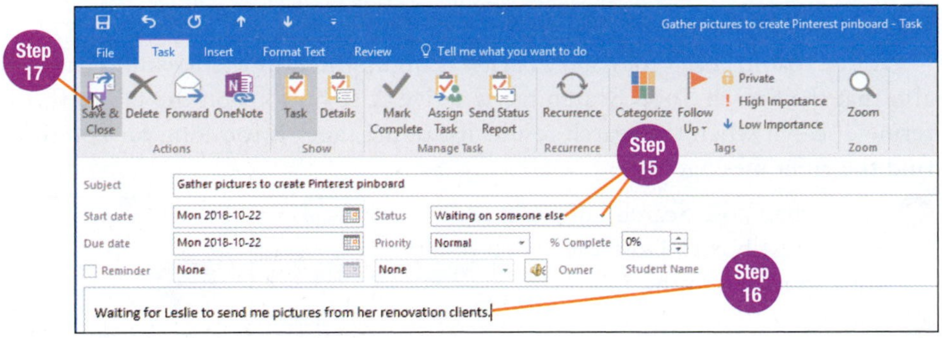

Quick Steps

Add a Task

1. Display Tasks.
2. Click in *Type a new task* or *Click here to add a new Task* text box.
3. Type task description.
4. Press Enter.

OR

1. Display Tasks.
2. Click New Task button.
3. Enter task details.
4. Click Save & Close.

The list changes to include tasks marked completed. See Beyond Basics to read about the difference between Remove from List and Mark Complete options.

19 Display the Inbox folder in Mail.

Beyond Basics — Remove from List versus Mark Complete

Remove from List deletes the task, while Mark Complete retains the task in the task list with a line drawn through the task and a gray check mark showing the task is finished. Mark Complete should be used if you need to retain task information for timekeeping or billing purposes. Display the complete Tasks list by clicking *Tasks* in the Folder pane.

5.9 Searching Outlook Items

Skills

- Search messages
- Search appointments
- Search contacts
- Search tasks

The search feature in Outlook, referred to as Instant Search, is used to locate a message, appointment, contact, or task. A search text box located between the ribbon and content is used to find items. Outlook begins a search as soon as you begin typing an entry in the search text box. Matched items are highlighted in the search results. Once located, you can open an item to view or edit the information.

1. With Outlook open and Inbox the active folder in Mail, click in the search text box at the top of the Content pane (contains the text *Search Current Mailbox*).
2. Type pinterest.

Outlook immediately begins matching messages in the Content pane with the characters as you type. Matched words are highlighted in both the Content pane and Reading pane. The list that remains is filtered to display all messages that contain the search keyword.

App Tip

The keyboard shortcut Ctrl + E opens the search text box.

App Tip

Instant Search shows the first 30 matches. Click the More hyperlink at the bottom of the search results list to view up to 250 matches.

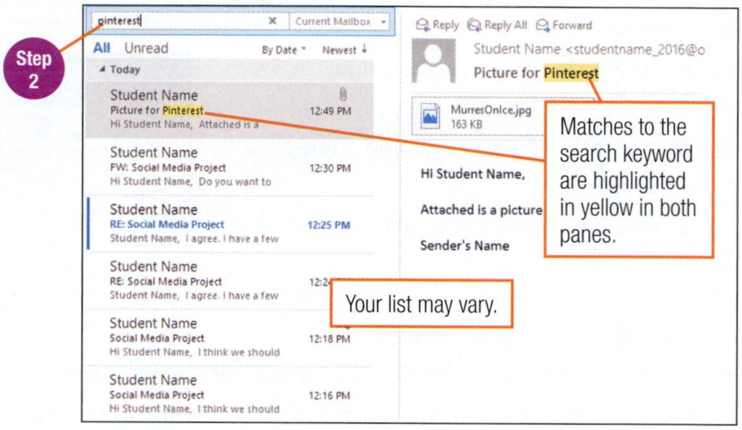

3. Click to view each message in the search results list.

Notice that for each message *Pinterest* is highlighted in the Reading pane. Notice also that the Search Tools Search tab is active. Use buttons on the tab to further refine a search when the search results list of messages is too long for you to easily find the right message.

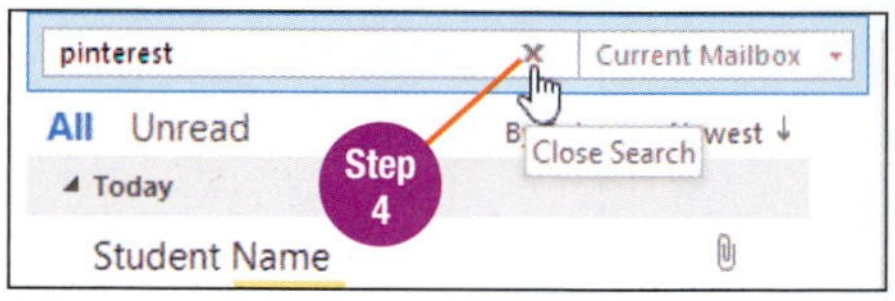

4. Click the Close Search button in the search text box to close the search results list and return to the Inbox.
5. Display the Calendar.
6. Click in the search text box at the top right of the Appointment area (contains the text *Search Calendar*) and then type career fair.

Outlook displays the appointment found with the search keywords in a filtered list.

7. Double-click the entry in the filtered list to view the details in the Event window and then close the window.
8. Click the Close Search button to restore the Calendar to the appointments for the current day.

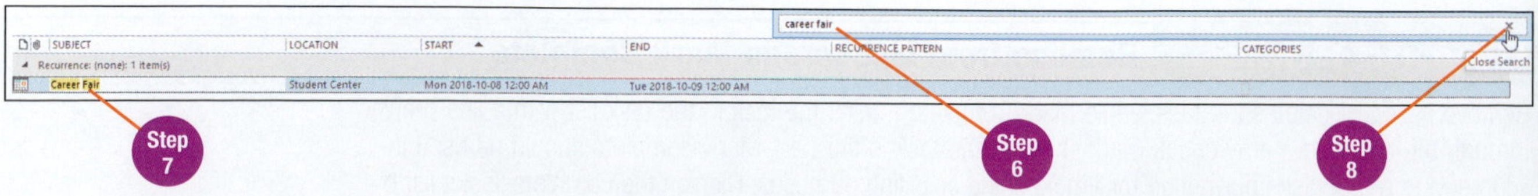

9 Display People.

10 Click in the search text box at the top of the People list (contains the text *Search Contacts*) and then type nuwave.

Outlook displays the contact for Tory Nguyen who works at NuWave Personnel. You can use the search feature to find any Outlook item by any entry saved for the message, appointment, contact, or task. For example, you could find a contact by name, job title, company name, or even telephone number.

> **Quick Steps**
>
> **Search for an Outlook Item**
> 1. Display Mail, Calendar, People, or Tasks.
> 2. Click in search text box.
> 3. Type search keyword.

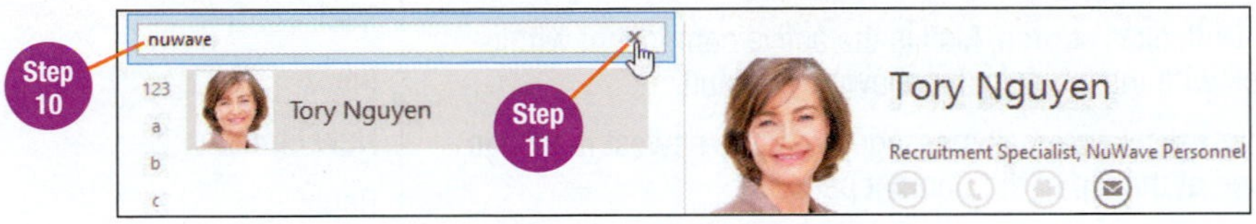

11 Click the Close Search button to restore the People list.

12 Display Tasks.

13 Click in the search text box at the top of the task list (contains the text *Search To-Do List* or *Search Tasks* depending on the active selection in the Folder pane.) and then type ex.

Outlook displays the task entry *Prepare study notes for exams*. Outlook can match items with only a partial entry for a word.

14 Click the Close Search button in the Close group on the Search Tools Search tab.

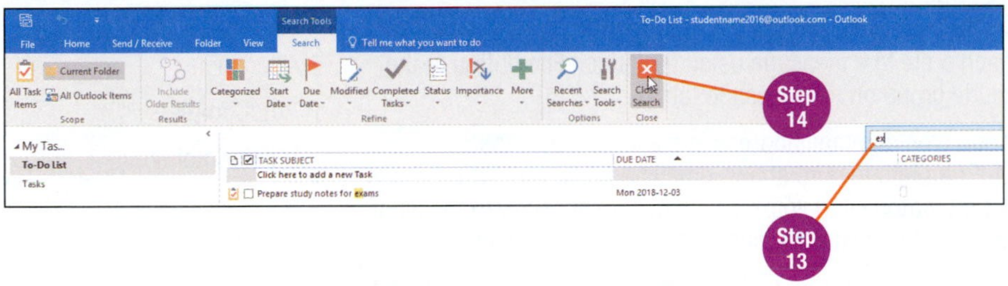

15 Display Mail with the Inbox folder.

16 Close Outlook.

Beyond Basics Other Search and Filter Techniques

The Home tab for Mail, Calendar, People, and Tasks contains a search text box (contains the text Search People) in the Find group. Use this text box to find a contact from any Outlook area. You can click a person in the search results list to view the contact information in a People card.

In Mail, the Find group also contains a Filter Email button. Use this button to filter the message list by categories such as *Unread*, *Has Attachments*, *This Week*, *Flagged*, or *Important*.

Topics Review

Topic	Key Concepts	Key Terms
5.1 Using Outlook to Send Email	Microsoft Outlook 2016 is an application for organizing messages, appointments, contacts, and tasks referred to as a *personal information management (PIM) program*. Electronic mail (email) is the exchange of messages between individuals electronically. When Outlook is started, Mail is the active component within Outlook with the Inbox folder shown by default. The Inbox displays email messages with the newest message received at the top of the Content pane. Create and send a new email message using the New Email button in the New group on the Home tab. Click the message header for a new message received to read the message contents in the Reading pane. Reply directly to a message by clicking the Reply button in the Reading pane (referred to as an *inline reply*). Send a copy of a message you have received to someone else using the Forward button. A signature is a closing containing your name and other contact information that is inserted automatically at the end of each message.	personal information management (PIM) program electronic mail (email) Outlook 2016 Mail Inbox New Email Reply inline reply Forward
5.2 Attaching a File to a Message and Deleting a Message	Attach a file to a message using the Attach File button in the Include group on the Message tab. As you type an email address in the *To* text box, the AutoComplete feature shows email addresses in a drop-down list that match what you are typing. Click an entry in the list if the correct recipient appears before you finish typing. Delete messages from mail folders that are no longer needed to keep folders to a manageable size. Deleted messages are moved to the Deleted Items folder. Empty the Deleted Items folder to permanently delete messages.	Attach File AutoComplete Deleted Items
5.3 Previewing File Attachments and Using File Attachment Tools	Preview a file attached to a message by clicking the file name in the Reading pane. While a file is being previewed, message text is temporarily removed from the Reading pane. Some files cannot be viewed in the Reading pane and must be viewed by double-clicking the file name to open the file. Open or Save a file using buttons in the Actions group on the Attachment Tools Attachments tab or with options from the drop-down list accessed by clicking the arrow at the right of the file name in the Reading pane. A file opened from a message is opened in Protected View in the source application, which allows you to read the contents. You cannot edit the file until you click the Enable Editing button on the Message bar. Certain types of files known to contain viruses are automatically blocked by Outlook.	Protected View

continued...

Topic	Key Concepts	Key Terms
5.4 Scheduling Appointments and Events in Calendar	The Calendar component is used to schedule appointments and events. An appointment is any activity for which you want to record the occurrence by day and time. A Date Navigator at the top of the Folder pane displays the current month and next month with directional arrows to browse to the previous or next month. Use the Go To Date dialog box to navigate directly to a specific date you want to display in the Appointment area. Click next to the time in the Appointment area and then type a description to enter a new appointment. Click the New Appointment button in the New group on the Home tab to enter details for a new appointment in an Appointment window. An event is an appointment that lasts an entire day or longer. Click the New Items button in the New group on the Home tab and then click *All day event* to create an event in an Event window.	Calendar appointment Date Navigator Go To Date New Appointment event
5.5 Scheduling a Recurring Appointment and Editing an Appointment	An appointment that occurs at fixed intervals on a regular basis can be entered once, and Outlook schedules the remaining appointments automatically. Click the Recurrence button to set the recurrence pattern and range of recurrence details for a recurring appointment. Click to select an appointment in the Appointment area to assign options or tags to the appointment using buttons on the Calendar Tools Appointment tab. Open the Appointment window to make changes to the subject, location, day, or time of a scheduled appointment.	Recurrence
5.6 Scheduling a Meeting	A meeting is an appointment to which you invite people. Information about a meeting is sent to people via a meeting request, which is an email message sent to meeting participants. Click the New Meeting button in the New group on the Home tab to create a new meeting request by entering the email addresses for meeting attendees and the meeting particulars. A meeting attendee responds to a meeting request from the Reading pane or the message window by clicking a respond button, such as Accept. Meetings can be updated or canceled, and Outlook automatically informs all attendees via email messages.	meeting New Meeting meeting request Accept

continued...

Topic	Key Concepts	Key Terms
5.7 Adding and Editing Contacts in People	Use the People component to store and organize contact information for people with whom you communicate in a People card. Click the New Contact button or double-click in a blank area of the People list to open a Contact window and add information to a People card. Click the picture image control for a contact to select a picture of a contact in the Add Contact Picture dialog box. A contact's picture displays in the People card. The People card for a selected individual in the People list displays in the Reading pane. Click *Edit* in the Reading pane or double-click a person's name to edit the contact information in the People card.	People New Contact People card
5.8 Adding and Editing Tasks	Use Tasks in Outlook to maintain a To-Do List. Click in the *Type a new task* text box to add a task to the To-Do List or click the New Task button to enter a new task in a Task window. Open a Task window to add a due date or to add other task information, such as a priority or status. Select a task and use the Remove from List button when a task is completed. Open a task and use the Mark Complete button to indicate a task is completed; completed tasks are retained in the Task list but removed from the To-Do List.	Tasks To-Do List New Task
5.9 Searching Outlook Items	A search text box appears at the top of Mail, Calendar, People, and Tasks in which you can quickly search for an item by typing a keyword or phrase. Outlook begins to match items as soon as you begin typing a search keyword. Matches to the search keyword are highlighted in the filtered lists and in content in the Reading pane. A search text box also appears in the Find group on the Home tab in Mail, Calendar, People, and Tasks with which you can search for people and view the People card for an individual from any Outlook component.	

Recheck

Recheck your understanding of the topics covered in this chapter.

Workbook

Chapter review and assessment resources are available in the *Workbook* ebook.

Chapter 6

Creating, Editing, and Formatting Word Documents

Precheck
Check your understanding of the topics covered in this chapter.

Microsoft Word (referred to as *Word*) is a **word processing application** used to create documents that are mostly text for personal, business, or school purposes. Word documents can also include pictures, charts, tables, or other visual elements to make the document more interesting and easier to understand. Letters, essays, reports, invitations, recipes, agendas, contracts, and resumes are examples of documents that can be created using Word. Any text-based document you need to create can be generated using Word.

Word automatically corrects some errors as you type and indicates other potential spelling and grammar errors for you to consider. Other features provide tools to format and enhance a document. In this chapter, you will learn how to create, edit, and format documents. You will create new documents starting from a blank page and other documents by selecting from the template gallery in Word.

Note: *If you are using a tablet, consider connecting it to a USB or wireless keyboard because parts of this chapter involve a fair amount of typing.*

Learning Objectives

- **6.1** Create a new document and insert, delete, and edit text
- **6.2** Insert symbols and check spelling and grammar
- **6.3** Find and replace text
- **6.4** Move text and create bulleted and numbered lists
- **6.5** Format text using font options and change paragraph alignment
- **6.6** Indent paragraphs, change line spacing, and change spacing before and after paragraphs
- **6.7** Apply a style to text and change the style set
- **6.8** Create a new document from a template

SNAP If you are a SNAP user, go to your SNAP Assignments page to complete the Precheck, Tutorials, and Recheck.

Data Files
Before beginning this chapter, be sure you have copied the student data files for this course to your storage medium. Steps on downloading and extracting the data files are provided in Chapter 1, Topic 1.8, on pages 22–23.

6.1 Creating and Editing a New Document

Skills

Enter text

Describe AutoCorrect actions

Describe AutoFormat actions

Edit, insert, and delete text

Tutorials

Exploring the Word Screen

Entering Text

Undoing an AutoCorrect Correction

Adding and Deleting an AutoCorrect Entry

Saving with the Same Name

Saving with a New Name

Moving the Insertion Point and Inserting and Deleting Text

Recall from Chapter 3 that when Word starts, the Word Start screen appears, and you can choose to open an existing document, create a new blank document, or search for and select a template to create a new document. Creating a new document includes typing the document text, editing the text, and correcting errors. As you type, the AutoCorrect and AutoFormat features in Word help you fix common typing errors and apply formatting to characters or paragraphs.

1. Start Word 2016.
2. At the Word Start screen, click *Blank document* in the Templates gallery and compare your screen with the one shown in Figure 6.1.

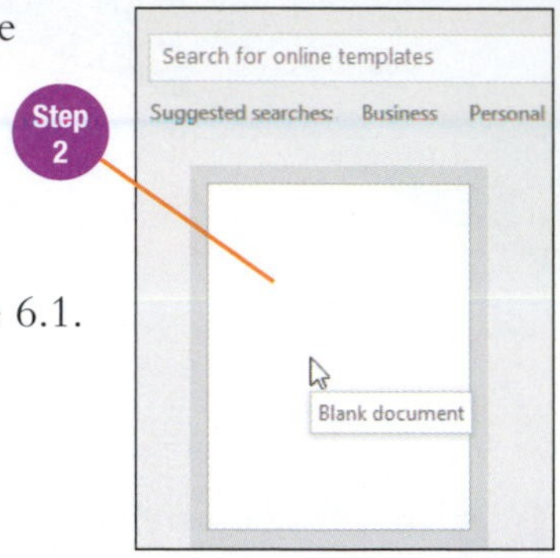

If necessary, review the ribbon interface and Quick Access Toolbar described in Chapter 3. Table 6.1, p. 137, describes the elements shown in Figure 6.1.

3. Type Social Bookmarking and press Enter.

Notice that extra space is automatically added below the text before the next line.

4. Type the text on the next page allowing the lines to end automatically; press Enter only where indicated.

Word will move text to a new line automatically when you reach the end of the current line. This feature is called **wordwrap**. Word will also put a red wavy line below the word *bookmarklet*. Red wavy lines appear below words that are not found in the dictionary Word uses, indicating a possible spelling error. Correct typing mistakes as you go using the Backspace key to delete the character just typed and then retyping the correct character. You will learn other editing methods later in this topic.

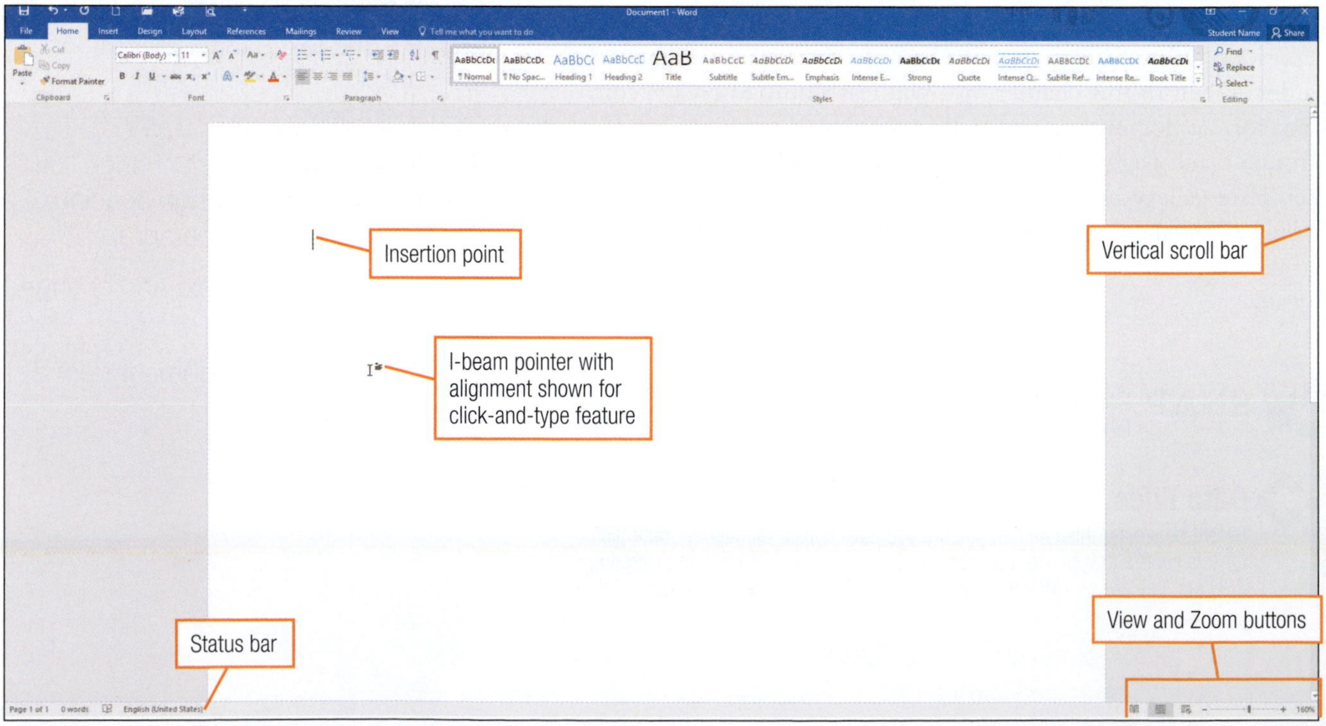

Figure 6.1

A new blank document screen is shown. The default settings in Word show a new document in Print Layout view and with rulers turned off; your display may vary if settings have been changed on the computer you are using. See Table 6.1, p. 137, for a description of screen elements.

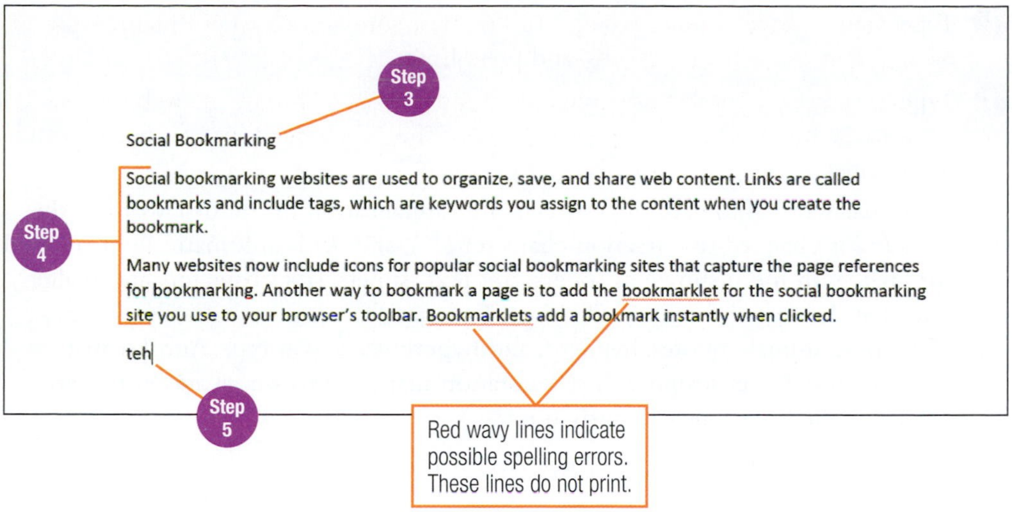
Step 3
Social Bookmarking
Step 4
Social bookmarking websites are used to organize, save, and share web content. Links are called bookmarks and include tags, which are keywords you assign to the content when you create the bookmark.
Many websites now include icons for popular social bookmarking sites that capture the page references for bookmarking. Another way to bookmark a page is to add the bookmarklet for the social bookmarking site you use to your browser's toolbar. Bookmarklets add a bookmark instantly when clicked.
teh
Step 5
Red wavy lines indicate possible spelling errors. These lines do not print.

Social bookmarking websites are used to organize, save, and share web content. Links are called bookmarks and include tags, which are keywords you assign to the content when you create the bookmark. [press Enter]

Many websites now include icons for popular social bookmarking sites that capture the page references for bookmarking. Another way to bookmark a page is to add the bookmarklet for the social bookmarking site you use to your browser's toolbar. Bookmarklets add a bookmark instantly when clicked. [press Enter]

5 Type teh and press the spacebar. Notice that Word changes the text to *The.*

A feature called **AutoCorrect** changes commonly misspelled words as soon as you press the spacebar.

Table 6.1

Word Features

Feature	Description
Insertion point	Blinking vertical bar indicates where the next character typed will appear.
I-beam pointer	Pointer appearance for text entry or selection when you move the pointer using a mouse or trackpad. The I-beam pointer displays with a paragraph alignment option (left, center, or right) depending on the location of the I-beam within the current line. You can double-click and type text anywhere on a page, and the alignment option will be left-aligned, center-aligned, or right-aligned. This feature is called **click and type**.
Status bar	Displays page number with total number of pages and number of words in the current document. The right end of the Status bar has view and zoom options. The default view is Print Layout view, which shows how a page will look when printed with current print options.
Vertical scroll bar	Use the scroll bar to view parts of a document not shown in the current window.
View and Zoom buttons	By default, Word opens in Print Layout view. Other view buttons include Read Mode and Web Layout view. Read Mode maximizes reading space and removes editing tools, providing a more natural environment for reading. Zoom buttons, as you learned in Chapter 3, are used to enlarge or shrink the display.

App Tip

AutoCorrect also fixes common capitalization errors, such as two initial capitals, no capital at the beginning of a sentence, and no capital in the name of a day. AutoCorrect also turns off the Caps Lock key and corrects text when a new sentence is started with the key left on. Use Undo if AutoCorrect changes text that you don't want changed.

6. Type popular social bookmarking site Pinterest.com is used to pin pictures found on the Web to virtual pinboards. and press Enter.
7. Type a study by a marketing company found that 1/2 of frequent web surfers use a social bookmarking site, with Pinterest the 1st choice for most females. and press Enter.

App Tip
AutoFormat does not recognize all fractions. For example, typing *1/3* will not format to the one-third fraction character. You will learn about inserting symbols for these characters in the next topic.

Notice that Word automatically corrects the capitalization of the first word in the sentence, *1/2* is changed to a fraction character (½), and *1st* is automatically formatted as an ordinal, with the *st* shown as superscript text (superscript characters are smaller text placed at the top of the line). The **AutoFormat** feature automatically changes some fractions, ordinals, quotes, hyphens, and hyperlinks as you type. AutoFormat also converts straight apostrophes (') or quotation marks (") to smart quotes ('smart quotes'), also called *curly quotes* ("curly quotes").

8. Click the Save button on the Quick Access Toolbar.

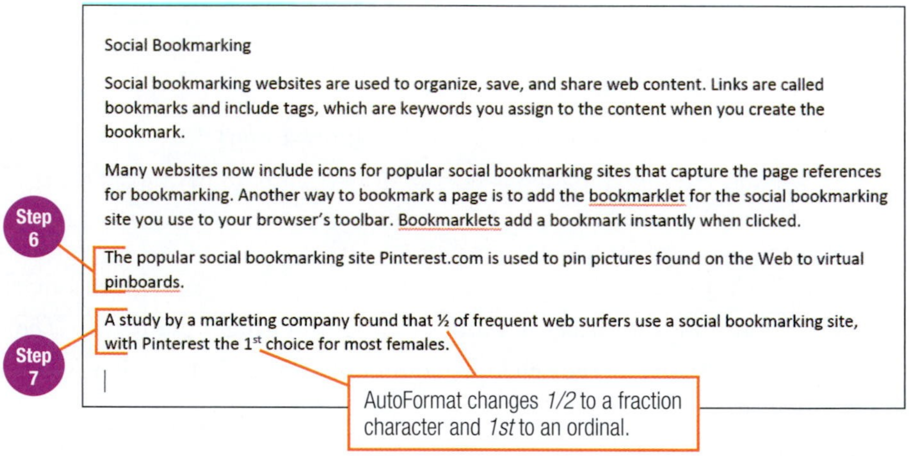
Social Bookmarking
Social bookmarking websites are used to organize, save, and share web content. Links are called bookmarks and include tags, which are keywords you assign to the content when you create the bookmark.
Many websites now include icons for popular social bookmarking sites that capture the page references for bookmarking. Another way to bookmark a page is to add the bookmarklet for the social bookmarking site you use to your browser's toolbar. Bookmarklets add a bookmark instantly when clicked.
Step 6
The popular social bookmarking site Pinterest.com is used to pin pictures found on the Web to virtual pinboards.
Step 7
A study by a marketing company found that ½ of frequent web surfers use a social bookmarking site, with Pinterest the 1st choice for most females.
AutoFormat changes 1/2 to a fraction character and 1st to an ordinal.

Because this is the first time the document has been saved, the Save As backstage area appears.

9. Click the option at the Save As backstage area that represents the location for your storage medium and then click the Browse button. For example, click *This PC* if you are saving files to a USB flash drive and then click *Browse*.
10. At the Save As dialog box, navigate to the CompletedTopicsByChapter folder on your storage medium and then create a new folder, *Ch6*.
11. Double-click the *Ch6* folder name.
12. Select the current text in the *File name* text box, type SocialMediaProject-YourName, and then press Enter or click the Save button.

App Tip
You can move the insertion point by pressing the Up, Down, Left, or Right arrow keys to move within a document. Hold down an arrow key to rapidly move the insertion point.

When creating a new document, changes often need to be made to the text after the text has been typed. You may need to correct typing errors, change a word or phrase to some other text, add new text, or remove text. Making changes to a document after the document has been typed is called **editing**. The first step to edit text is to move the insertion point to the location of a change.

13. Click to position the insertion point at the beginning of the last paragraph that begins with the text *A study by a marketing company* (insertion point will be blinking just left of *A*), type Experian Hitwise, and then press the spacebar.

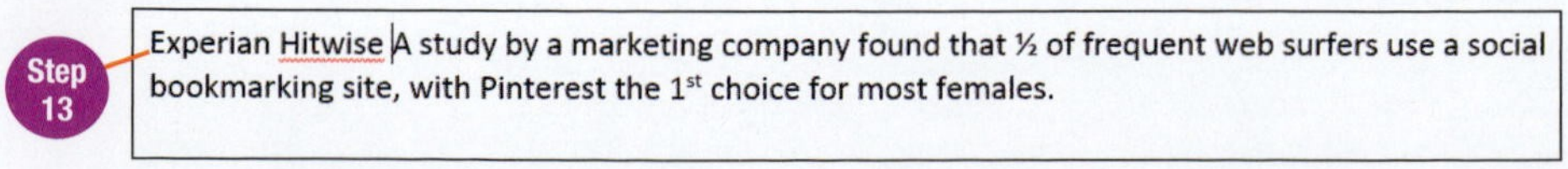
Step 13
Experian Hitwise A study by a marketing company found that ½ of frequent web surfers use a social bookmarking site, with Pinterest the 1st choice for most females.

Word automatically inserts the new text and moves existing text to the right.

14. With the insertion point still positioned at the left of *A* in *A study*, press the Delete key until you have removed *A study by*, type (, click to position the insertion point just after the *y* in *company*, and then type) conducted a survey of frequent web surfers and.

15. Position the insertion point just left of ½, press the Delete key until you have removed ½ *of frequent web surfers*, and then type one-half.

16. Position the insertion point at the left of *1st*, delete *1st*, and then type first.

17. Position the insertion point below the last paragraph and then type your first and last name.

18. Check your text with the document shown in Figure 6.2. If necessary, make further corrections by moving the insertion point and inserting and deleting characters as needed.

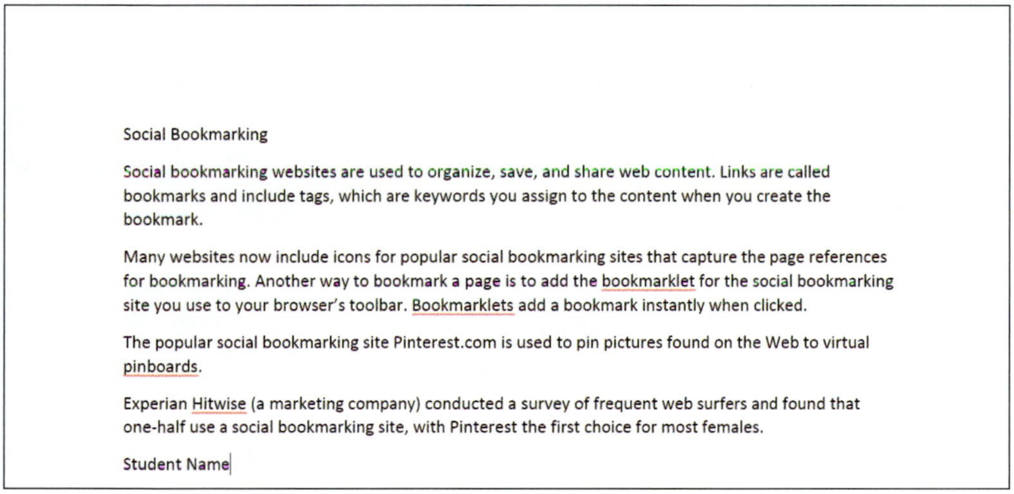
Social Bookmarking

Social bookmarking websites are used to organize, save, and share web content. Links are called bookmarks and include tags, which are keywords you assign to the content when you create the bookmark.

Many websites now include icons for popular social bookmarking sites that capture the page references for bookmarking. Another way to bookmark a page is to add the bookmarklet for the social bookmarking site you use to your browser's toolbar. Bookmarklets add a bookmark instantly when clicked.

The popular social bookmarking site Pinterest.com is used to pin pictures found on the Web to virtual pinboards.

Experian Hitwise (a marketing company) conducted a survey of frequent web surfers and found that one-half use a social bookmarking site, with Pinterest the first choice for most females.

Student Name

Figure 6.2

The document text for SocialMediaProject-StudentName is shown.

19. Click the Save button on the Quick Access Toolbar. Leave the document open for the next topic.

Because the document has already been assigned a file name at Step 12, the Save button saves the document changes using the same name.

Oops!

Insertion point will not go below last paragraph? Click to place the insertion point at the end of the last sentence and then press Enter to move down to a blank line.

Quick Steps

Create a New Document
1. Start Word 2016.
2. Click *Blank document*.
3. Type text.

Save a New Document
1. Click Save button on the Quick Access Toolbar.
2. Navigate to drive and/or folder.
3. Enter file name.
4. Click Save.

Save a Document Using the Existing Name
Click Save button on the Quick Access Toolbar.

Edit a Document
1. Position insertion point at location of change.
2. Type new text or delete text as needed.
3. Save changes.

Beyond Basics — Line Breaks versus New Paragraphs

You press Enter only at the end of a short line of text (such as the title) or at the end of a paragraph. Pressing Enter creates a hard return, and in Word creates a new paragraph. By default, line spacing in Word 2016 is set to 1.08, and 8 points of space is added after each paragraph. A point is a measurement system in which 1 point is approximately equal to the height of 1/72 inch. Think of 8 points as approximately .11 of an inch of space added after each hard return.

To end a short line of text and not add an extra 8-point space after the line, use the Line Break command Shift + Enter (hold down the Shift key while pressing Enter). A line break moves to the next line without creating a new paragraph. For example, use Shift + Enter when typing an address in a letter after the street number and street name to move to the next line.

6.2 Inserting Symbols and Completing a Spelling and Grammar Check

Skills

Insert a symbol and special character

Check spelling and grammar

Tutorials

Inserting Symbols

Inserting Special Characters

Checking Spelling and Grammar

In some documents, you need to insert a symbol or special character, such as a copyright symbol (©), registered trademark (™), or a fraction character for a fraction that AutoCorrect does not recognize, such as one-third (⅓). Symbols and special characters are inserted using the **Symbol gallery** or the Symbol dialog box.

The **Spelling & Grammar** button on the Review tab starts the Spelling and Grammar feature used to correct errors. The Spelling feature matches words in the document with words in a dictionary and flags a word not found as a possible error. The Spelling task pane opens at the right side of the window with suggestions for a word not found and with buttons to ignore, to change, or to add the word to the dictionary. The feature also checks for duplicate words and prompts you to remove the repeated word. Spelling and Grammar helps you correct many errors; however, you still need to proofread your documents. For example, the errors in the following sentence escaped detection: The plain fair was expensive!

1. With the **SocialMediaProject-YourName** document open, position the insertion point after *n* in *Experian* in the last paragraph.

Experian is a registered trademark, so you will add the registered trademark symbol after the name.

2. Click the Insert tab.
3. Click the Symbol button in the Symbols group.
4. Click *Trade Mark Sign*. Note that the symbol may appear in a different position than shown in the image at the right.

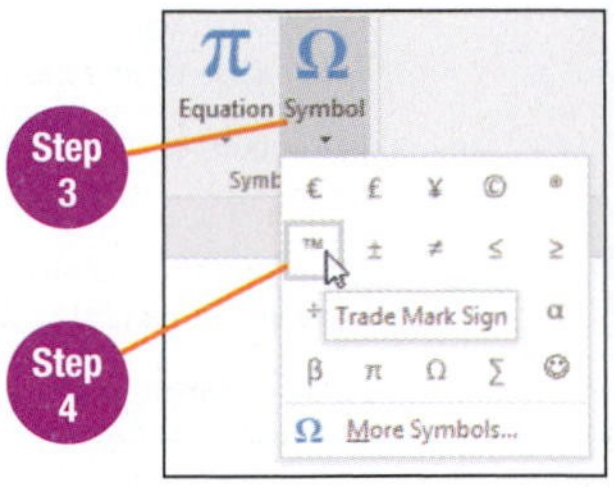

5. Position the insertion point after the period at the end of the paragraph that begins *Experian* and press the spacebar to insert a space.
6. Type The survey sample size of 1,000 interviews provides a standard error at 95% confidence of and then press the spacebar.
7. Click the Symbol button and then click *More Symbols*.

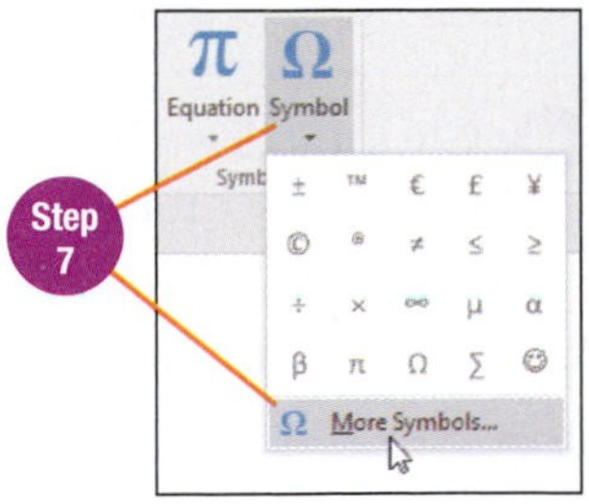

8. At the Symbol dialog box, with *Font* set to *(normal text)* and *Subset* set to *Letterlike Symbols*, scroll up the symbol list until the *Subset* changes to *Latin-1 Supplement*, click ±, and then click the Insert button.

Oops!

Different font and/or subset? Use the *Font* or *Subset* list arrow to change the option to *(normal text)* and *Letterlike Symbols* if the Symbol dialog box has different settings.

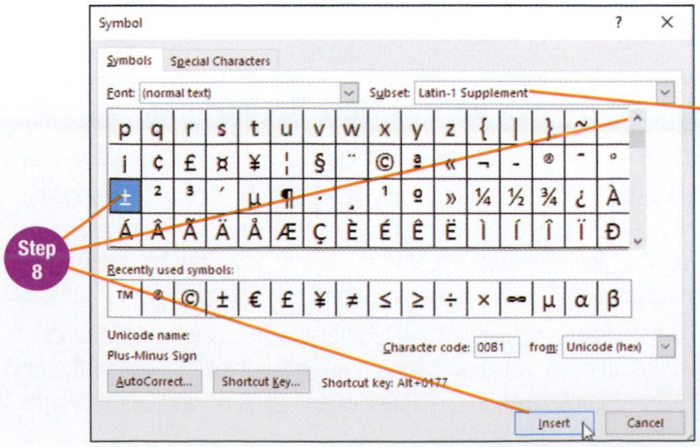

Scroll up the dialog box at Step 8 until the *Subset* changes to *Latin-1 Supplement* and you can see the plus-minus symbol.

9 Click the Close button to return to the document and then type 3%..

You may have noticed the Plus-Minus Sign symbol in the Symbol gallery. In Steps 7 to 9, you practiced using the Symbol dialog box so that you will know how to find a symbol that is not shown in the Symbol gallery.

10 Click the Review tab and then click the Spelling & Grammar button in the Proofing group.

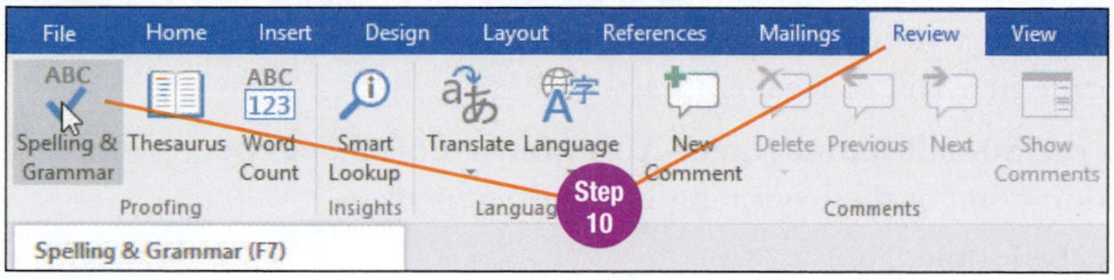

11 When the word *bookmarklet* is selected, click the Ignore All button in the Spelling task pane.

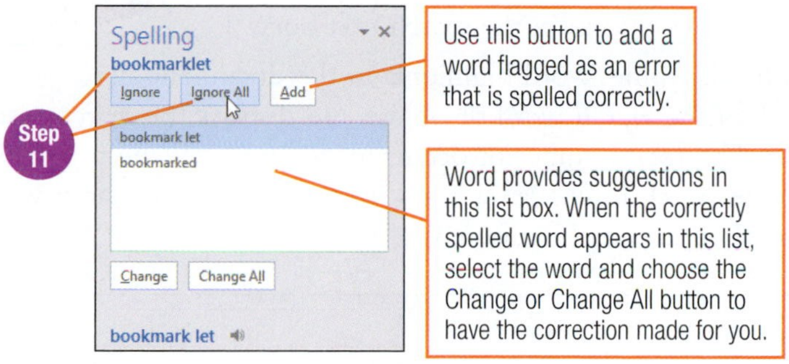

12 When the word *bookmarklets* is selected, click the Ignore All button in the Spelling task pane.

13 Choose Ignore when *pinboards* is selected.

14 Choose Ignore when *Hitwise* is selected.

15 Click OK at the message that the spelling and grammar check is complete.

16 Save the document using the same name. Leave the document open for the next topic.

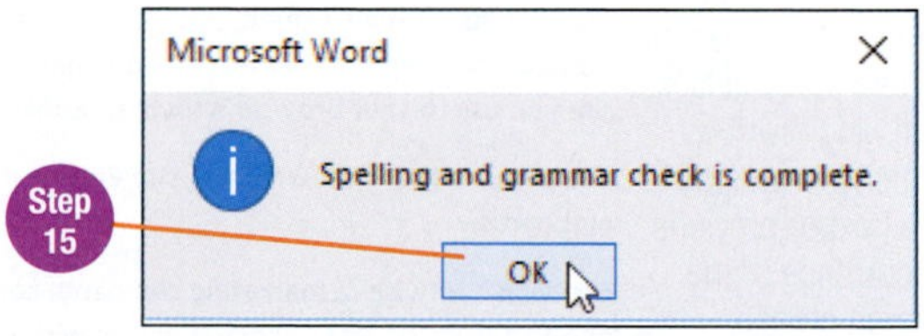

Alternative Method Inserting a Symbol Using a Keyboard Shortcut

Type (c) to have AutoCorrect insert the copyright symbol ©.

Type (r) to have AutoCorrect insert the registered symbol ®.

Type (tm) to have AutoCorrect insert the registered trademark symbol ™.

To view the complete list of AutoCorrect entries, click the File tab, then click *Options* at the backstage area. At the Word Options dialog box, click *Proofing* in the left pane and then click the AutoCorrect Options button.

App Tip

Right-click a word with a red wavy line to view suggested replacements in a shortcut menu. You can also instruct Word to *Ignore All* or *Add to Dictionary* at the shortcut menu.

Oops!

Spell check stopped at a different word? Respond to other errors as needed to correct variations that have occurred when you typed the document text in the previous topic.

Quick Steps

Insert Symbol from Symbol Dialog Box

1. Position insertion point.
2. Click Insert tab.
3. Click Symbol button.
4. Click *More Symbols.*
5. If necessary, change font or subset.
6. Scroll to locate symbol.
7. Click to select desired symbol.
8. Click Insert button.
9. Click Close button.

Perform a Spelling and Grammar Check

1. Click Review tab.
2. Click Spelling & Grammar button.
3. Choose Ignore, Ignore All, Add, Change, or Change All as needed at each error.
4. Click OK.

6.3 Finding and Replacing Text

Skills

Use Find Command

Use Replace Command

Tutorials

Finding Text

Finding and Replacing Text

Navigating Using the Navigation Pane

Using the Thesaurus

The **Find** feature moves the insertion point to each occurrence of a word or phrase. Find is helpful if you think you have overused a particular term and want to review how many times it appears in a document, or if you want to move the insertion point to a specific location in the document very quickly and a unique word or phrase exists near the location. **Replace** looks for each occurrence of a word or phrase and automatically changes the text to another word or phrase that you specify. Use Replace to make a global change throughout the document, such as changing a person's name in a will or legal contract.

1. With the **SocialMediaProject-YourName** document open, position the insertion point at the beginning of the document.
2. Click the Home tab.
3. Click the Find button in the Editing group.

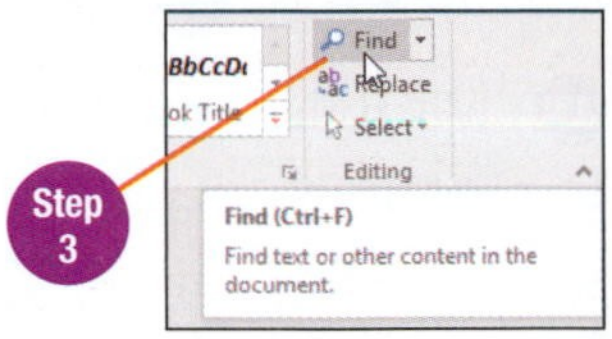

Find
Replace
Select
Editing
Step 3
Find (Ctrl+F)
Find text or other content in the document.

This opens the Navigation pane at the left side of the Word document window.

4. Type social bookmarking in the search text box.

When you finish typing, Word highlights in the document all the occurrences of the search word or phrase and displays the search results below the search text box. The total number of occurrences appears at the top of the Results list. Each entry in the search results list is a link that moves to the search word location in the document when clicked (Figure 6.3).

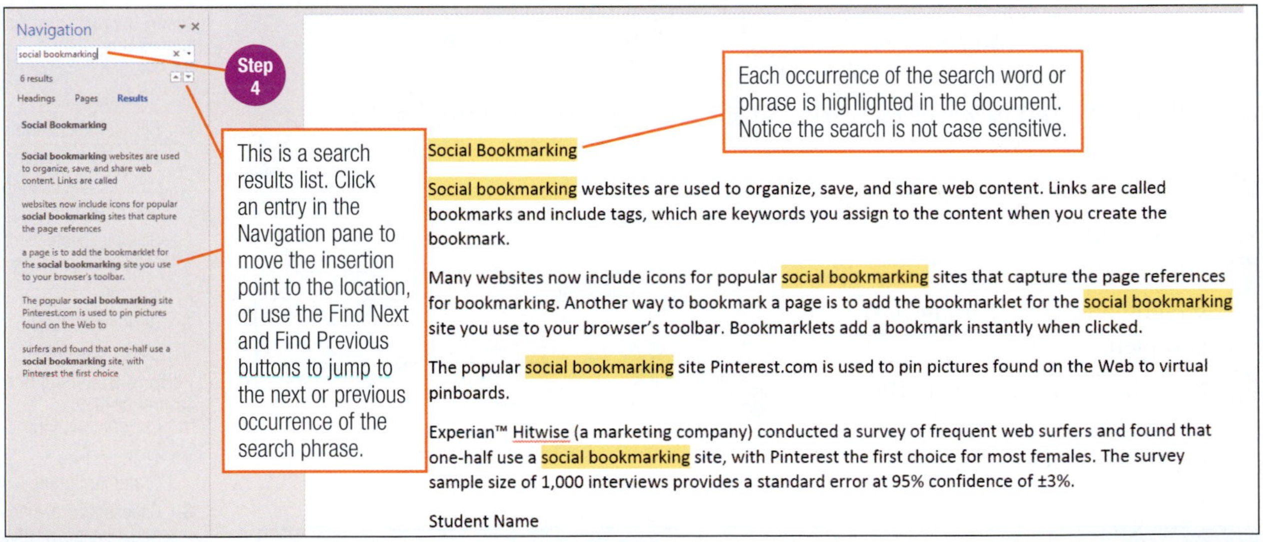

Navigation
social bookmarking
6 results
Headings Pages Results
Step 4
This is a search results list. Click an entry in the Navigation pane to move the insertion point to the location, or use the Find Next and Find Previous buttons to jump to the next or previous occurrence of the search phrase.
Each occurrence of the search word or phrase is highlighted in the document. Notice the search is not case sensitive.
Social Bookmarking
Social bookmarking websites are used to organize, save, and share web content. Links are called bookmarks and include tags, which are keywords you assign to the content when you create the bookmark.
Many websites now include icons for popular social bookmarking sites that capture the page references for bookmarking. Another way to bookmark a page is to add the bookmarklet for the social bookmarking site you use to your browser's toolbar. Bookmarklets add a bookmark instantly when clicked.
The popular social bookmarking site Pinterest.com is used to pin pictures found on the Web to virtual pinboards.
Experian™ Hitwise (a marketing company) conducted a survey of frequent web surfers and found that one-half use a social bookmarking site, with Pinterest the first choice for most females. The survey sample size of 1,000 interviews provides a standard error at 95% confidence of ±3%.
Student Name

Figure 6.3

Search results for *social bookmarking* are highlighted in the SocialMediaProject-YourName document.

App Tip

You can find text using a partial word search. For example, entering *exp* would find *Experian*, *expert*, and *experience*. Use partial word searches if you are not sure of correct spelling.

5. Click each entry one at a time in the Results list in the Navigation pane.

Notice that each occurrence of the search word is selected as you move to the phrase location.

6. Click the Close button at the top right of the Navigation pane to close the pane.

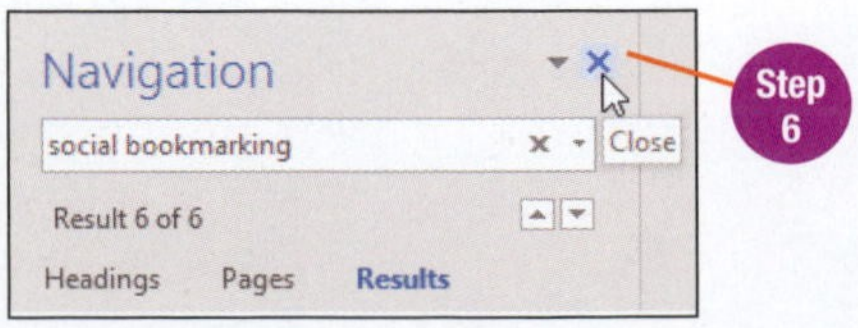

Navigation
social bookmarking
Close
Result 6 of 6
Headings Pages Results
Step 6

7 Position the insertion point at the beginning of the document.

Find and Replace searches begin from the location of the insertion point in the document.

8 Click the Replace button in the Editing group on the Home tab.

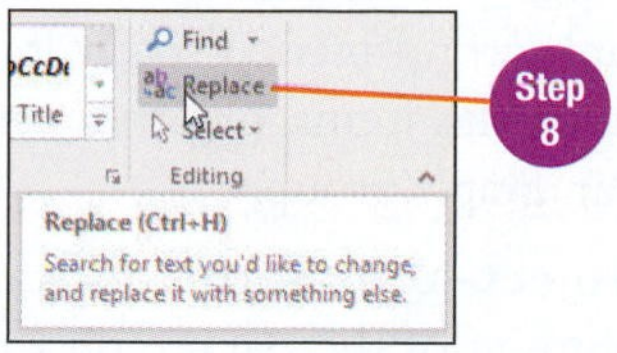

9 At the Find and Replace dialog box, with *social bookmarking* selected in the *Find what* text box, type bookmarklet.

10 Press Tab or click in the *Replace with* text box and then type bookmark button.

11 Click the Replace All button.

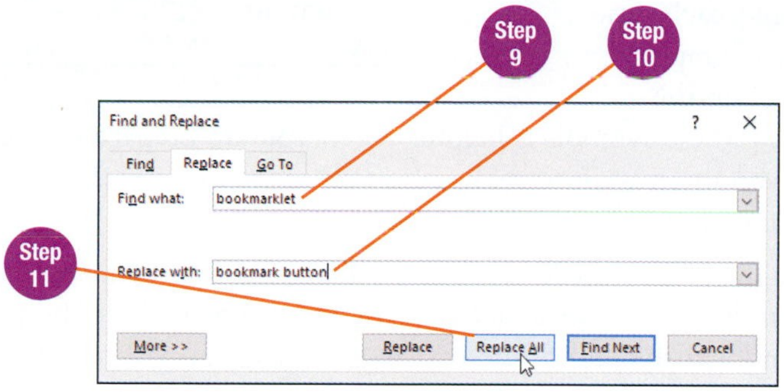

12 Click OK at the message that 2 replacements were made.

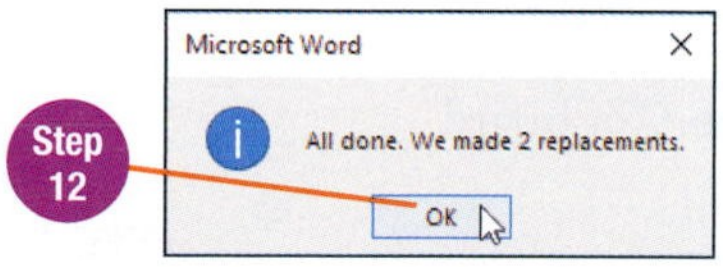

13 Click the Close button to close the Find and Replace dialog box.

Notice that Word matches the correct case of a word when the word is replaced at the beginning of a sentence, as seen in the last sentence of the paragraph that begins with *Many websites now include.*

14 Save the document using the same name. Leave the document open for the next topic.

App Tip

Ctrl + Home moves the insertion point to the beginning of a document.

App Tip

Click Find Next to replace text as you go through the document stopping at each occurrence if you do not want to globally replace the text.

Oops!

No replacements made? Click OK and check your spelling in the *Find what* text box. Correct the text and try Replace All again. Still have 0 replacements? Cancel the Replace command and check the spelling of *bookmarklet* within your document. Correct the text in the document and repeat Steps 8 to 12.

Quick Steps

Find Text

1. Position insertion point at beginning of document.
2. Click Find button.
3. Type search text.
4. Review Results list.

Replace Text

1. Position insertion point at beginning of document.
2. Click Replace button.
3. Type *Find what* text.
4. Press Tab or click in *Replace with* text box.
5. Type replacement text.
6. Click Replace All.
7. Click OK.
8. Click Close button.

Beyond Basics — Using the Thesaurus to Replace a Word

Sometimes when you find yourself overusing a word, you are stuck for an alternative word to use in its place in one or two occurrences. Consider using the Thesaurus to help you find a word with a similar meaning. Thesaurus is located in the Proofing group on the Review tab. Position the insertion point anywhere within a word you want to change, click the Thesaurus button, point to a word you want to change the occurrence to in the results list in the Thesaurus task pane, click the down-pointing arrow that appears, and then click *Insert*.

6.4 Moving Text and Inserting Bullets and Numbering

Skills

Move text

Create a bulleted list

Create a numbered list

Tutorials

Cutting, Copying, and Pasting Text

Creating Bulleted Lists

Creating Numbered Lists

The Cut button in the Clipboard group is used to move a selection of text from one location in the document to another location. Bulleted and numbered lists set apart information that is structured in short phrases or sentences. A bulleted list is text set apart from a paragraph with a list of items that are in no particular sequence. The **Bullets button** in the Paragraph group is used to create this type of list. A numbered list is used for a sequential list of tasks, items, or other text and is created using the **Numbering button** in the Paragraph group.

1. With the **SocialMediaProject-YourName** document open, position the insertion point at the beginning of the paragraph that begins with *The popular social bookmarking site.*

2. Click the Show/Hide button in the Paragraph group on the Home tab.

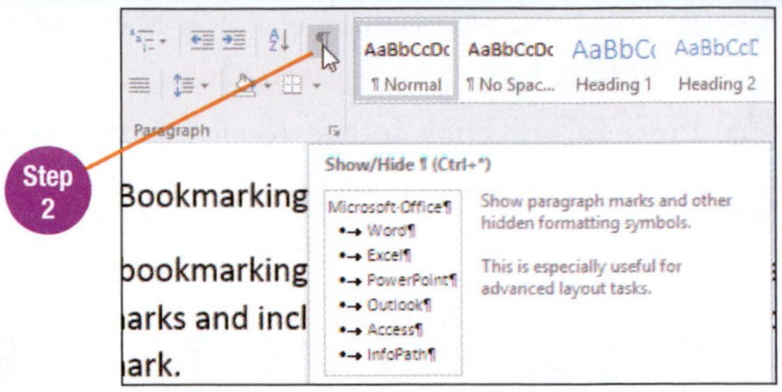

Show/Hide turns on the display of hidden formatting symbols. For example, each time you press Enter, a paragraph symbol (¶) is inserted in the document. Revealing these symbols is helpful when you are preparing to move or copy text because you often want to make sure you move or copy the paragraph symbol with the paragraph.

App Tip

The dot that appears between words when hidden formatting symbols are displayed indicates you pressed the spacebar.

3. Select the paragraph *The popular social bookmarking site Pinterest.com is used to pin pictures found on the Web to virtual pinboards.* Make sure to include the paragraph formatting symbol at the end of the text in the selection as shown below.

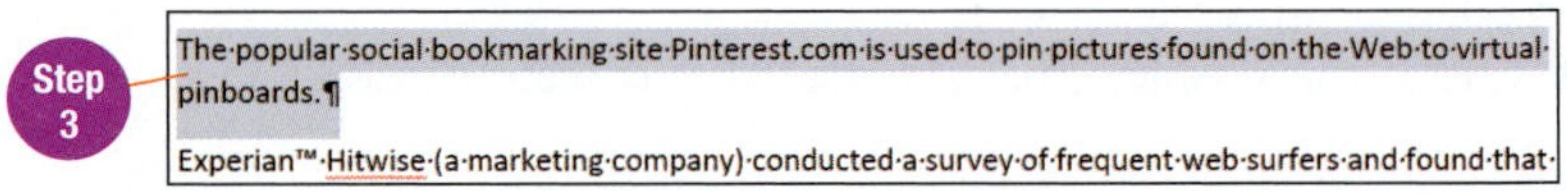

Step 3
text pasted at Step 6
The·popular·social·bookmarking·site·Pinterest.com·is·used·to·pin·pictures·found·on·the·Web·to·virtual·pinboards.¶
A Paste Options button appears whenever you paste text with buttons in a gallery that can change how the text is pasted. The button disappears when you start a new task or press the Esc key.
Experian™·Hitwise·(a·marketing·company)·conducted·a·survey·of·frequent·web·surfers·and·found·that·

Oops!

Forgot how to select text? Refer to Topic 3.4 in Chapter 3 for help with selecting text and objects.

4. Click the Cut button in the Clipboard group on the Home tab.

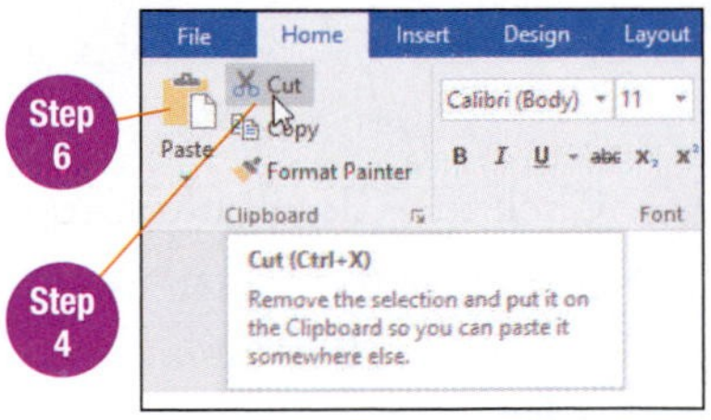

The text is removed from the current location and placed in the Clipboard.

5. Position the insertion point at the beginning of the paragraph that begins with *Many websites now include.*

6. Click the top of the Paste button in the Clipboard group (do *not* click the down-pointing arrow on the button).

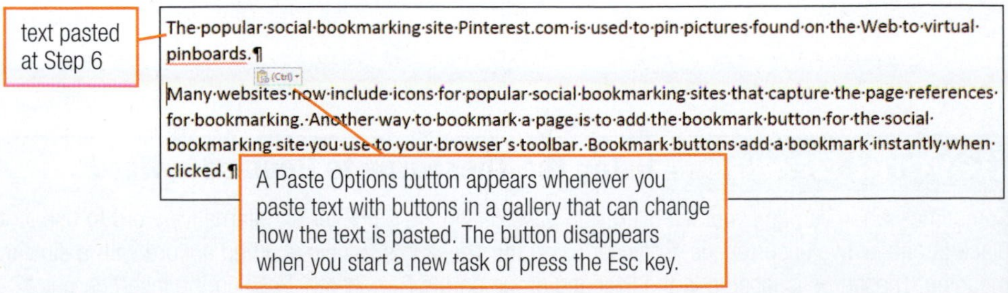

7. Click the Show/Hide button to turn off the display of hidden formatting symbols.

8 Position the insertion point after the period that ends the sentence *The popular social networking site Pinterest.com is used to pin pictures found on the Web to virtual pinboards*, press the spacebar, type Other social bookmarking sites include:, and then press Enter.

9 Click the left part of the Bullets button in the Paragraph group on the Home tab (do *not* click the down-pointing arrow on the button).

Step 9

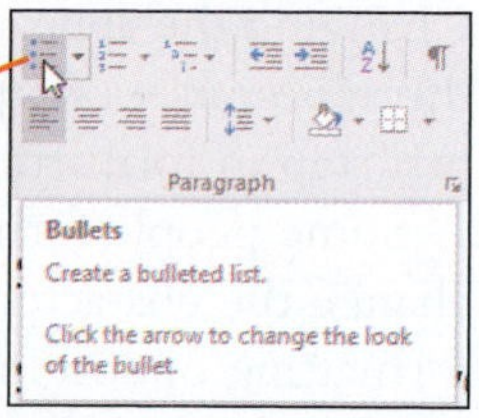
Paragraph
Bullets
Create a bulleted list.
Click the arrow to change the look of the bullet.

This action indents and then inserts the default bullet character, which is a solid round bullet.

10 Type StumbleUpon.com and press Enter.

11 Type Delicious.com and press Enter.

12 Type Digg.com and press Enter.

13 Type Newsvine.com.

Steps 10-13

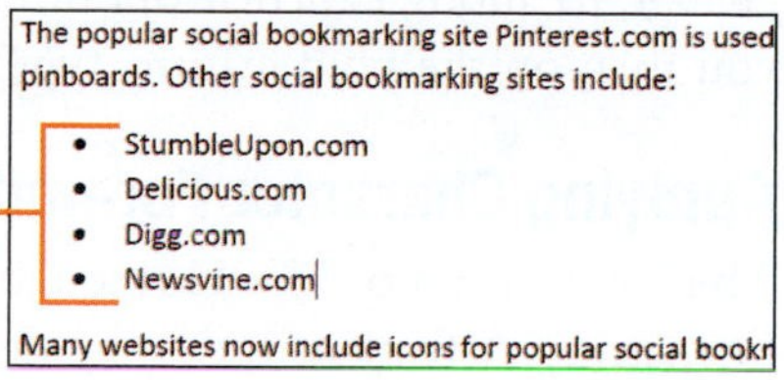
The popular social bookmarking site Pinterest.com is used
pinboards. Other social bookmarking sites include:

- StumbleUpon.com
- Delicious.com
- Digg.com
- Newsvine.com

Many websites now include icons for popular social bookm

14 Position the insertion point after the period that ends the sentence *Bookmark buttons add a bookmark instantly when clicked*, press the spacebar, type To add a bookmark button:, and then press Enter.

15 Click the left part of the Numbering button in the Paragraph group on the Home tab (do *not* click the down-pointing arrow on the button).

This indents and inserts 1.

16 Type Display the browser's Favorites toolbar or Bookmarks bar. and then press Enter.

17 Type Right-click the bookmark button and then choose Add to favorites. and then press Enter.

18 Type Choose Add button at dialog box that appears..

Steps 16-18

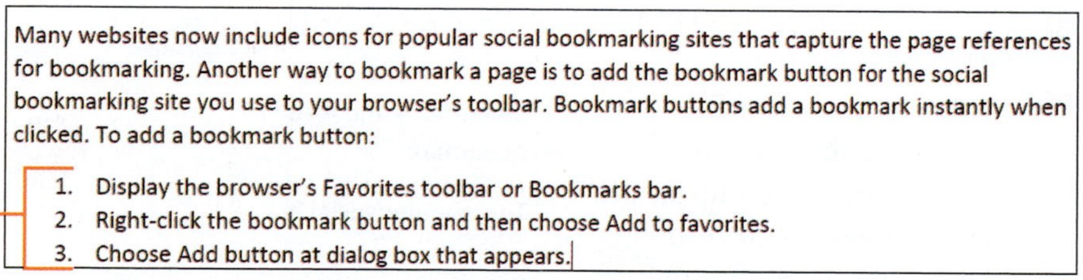
Many websites now include icons for popular social bookmarking sites that capture the page references for bookmarking. Another way to bookmark a page is to add the bookmark button for the social bookmarking site you use to your browser's toolbar. Bookmark buttons add a bookmark instantly when clicked. To add a bookmark button:

1. Display the browser's Favorites toolbar or Bookmarks bar.
2. Right-click the bookmark button and then choose Add to favorites.
3. Choose Add button at dialog box that appears.

19 Save the document using the same name. Leave the document open for the next topic.

Alternative Method Automatically Creating a Bulleted or Numbered List

The AutoFormat as You Type feature creates automatic bulleted and numbered lists when you do the following:

Type *, >, or –, press the spacebar, type text, and then press Enter (bulleted list).

Type 1., press the spacebar, type text, and press Enter (numbered list).

Immediately use Undo if an automatic list appears and you do not want to create a list.

App Tip

The Bullets button arrow is used to choose a different bullet character from the Bullet library.

App Tip

The Numbering button arrow is used to choose a different number format from the Numbering library.

Quick Steps

Move Text

1. Select text.
2. Click Cut button.
3. Position insertion point.
4. Click Paste button.

Create a Bulleted List

1. Click Bullets button.
2. Type first list item.
3. Press Enter.
4. Type second list item.
5. Press Enter.
6. Continue typing until finished.

Create a Numbered List

1. Click Numbering button.
2. Type first numbered item.
3. Press Enter.
4. Type second numbered item.
5. Press Enter.
6. Continue typing until finished.

6.5 Formatting Text with Font and Paragraph Alignment Options

Skills

Change font and font options

Change paragraph alignment

Tutorials

Applying Font Formatting Using the Font Group

Changing Paragraph Alignment

The process of altering the appearance of the text is referred to as **formatting**. Changing the appearance of characters is called **character formatting**. Changing the appearance of a paragraph is called **paragraph formatting**. In some cases, the first step in formatting is to select the characters or paragraphs to be changed.

Some people format text as they type the document. In that case, you can change the character or paragraph option before typing the text. Depending on the formatting option in use, you may have to turn off the option after typing text or change to another format option. For example, if you apply bold to text as you type, you turn on the bold feature, type the text, then turn off the bold feature.

Applying Character Formatting

The Font group on the Home tab contains the buttons used to change character formatting. A **font** includes the design and shape of the letters, numbers, and special characters of a particular *typeface*. A large collection of fonts is available from simple to artistic character design. The font size is set in points, with one point equal to approximately 1/72 of an inch in height. The default font in a new document is 11-point Calibri.

The Font group includes buttons to increase or decrease the font size; change the case; change the font style (bold, italic, or underline) or font color; highlight text; add the effects strikethrough, subscript, or superscript; or add an artistic look using the Text Effects and Typography button (outline, shadow, glow, and reflection accents).

App Tip

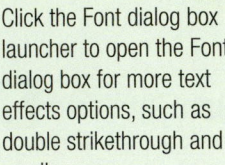

Click the Font dialog box launcher to open the Font dialog box for more text effects options, such as double strikethrough and small caps.

Oops!

Mini toolbar disappeared? This happens when you move the mouse away from the toolbar after selecting text. Use the *Font* option box arrow in the Font group on the Home tab instead.

1. With the **SocialMediaProject-YourName** document open, select the title text at the top of the document *Social Bookmarking*.
2. Click the *Font* option box arrow on the Mini toolbar.
3. Scroll down and then click *Century Gothic*.
4. With the title text still selected, click twice the Increase Font Size button on the Mini toolbar or in the Font group on the Home tab.

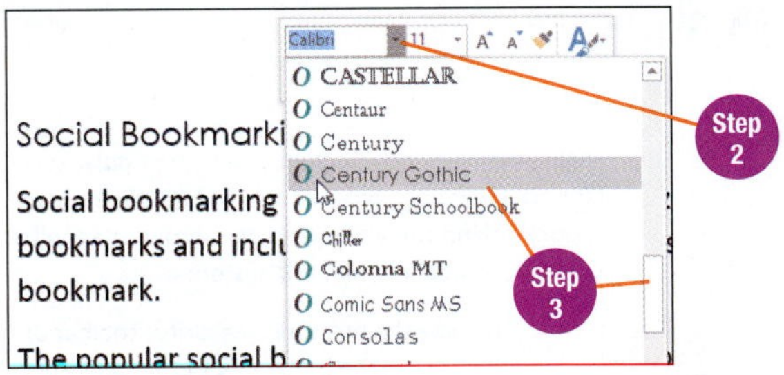

The first time you increase the font size, the size changes to 12 points. The second time, the size changes to 14 points and continues to increase 2 point sizes each time until you reach 28. After 28 points, the size changes to 36, 48, and then 72.

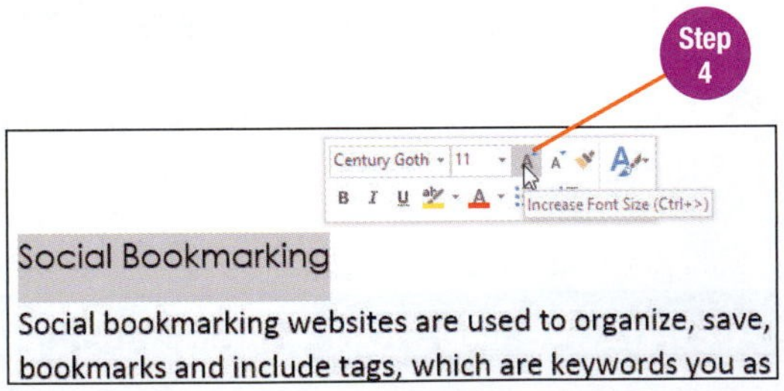

App Tip

Use the Font Color button arrow to choose a color other than red. Once the color is changed, the new color can be applied to the next selection without using the button arrow. The color on the button resets to red after Word is closed.

5. With the title text still selected, click the Bold button on the Mini toolbar or in the Font group on the Home tab.
6. With the title text still selected, click the Font Color button (do *not* click the Font Color button arrow) on the Mini toolbar or in the Font group on the Home tab.

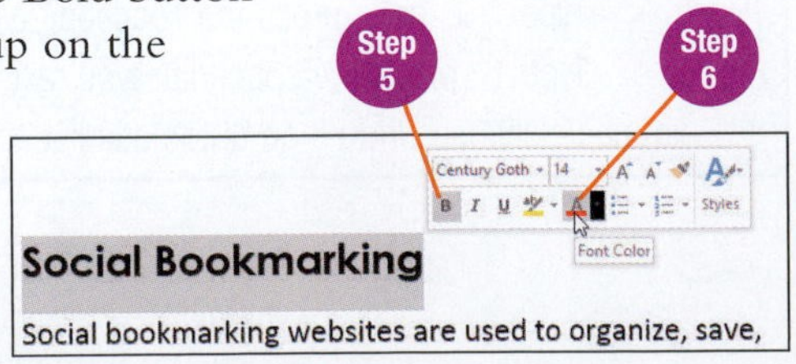

The default Font Color is Red.

7. Click in the document away from the selected title to deselect the text.

Applying Paragraph Formatting

The Paragraph group on the Home tab contains the buttons used to change paragraph formatting. The bottom row of buttons in the group contains the buttons for changing the alignment of paragraphs from the default **Align Left** to **Center**, **Align Right**, or **Justify**. Justified text adds space within a line so that the text is distributed evenly between the left and right margins. You will explore other buttons in the Paragraph group in the next topic.

8. Click to place the insertion point anywhere within the title text *Social Bookmarking*.

To format a single paragraph, you do not need to select the paragraph text because paragraph formatting applies to all text within the paragraph to the point where a hard return was inserted.

9. Click the Center button in the Paragraph group on the Home tab.

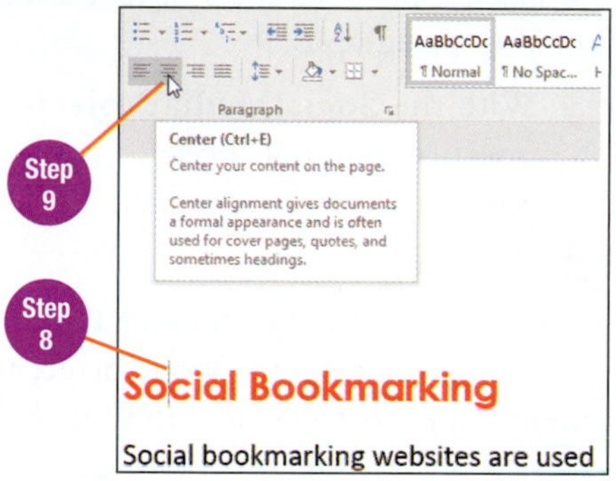

10. Click to place the insertion point anywhere within the first paragraph of text and then click the Justify button in the Paragraph group on the Home tab.

Justified text spreads the lines out so that the text ends evenly at the right margin.

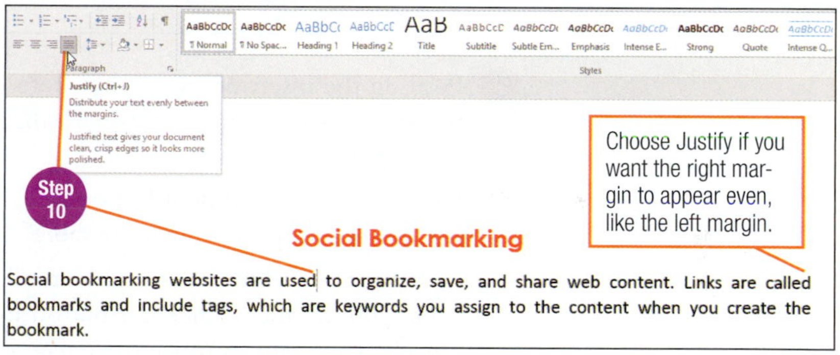

11. With the insertion point still positioned in the first paragraph, click the Align Left button in the Paragraph group on the Home tab.

12. Save the document using the same name. Leave the document open for the next topic.

Select more than one paragraph first if you want to apply the same alignment option to multiple paragraphs.

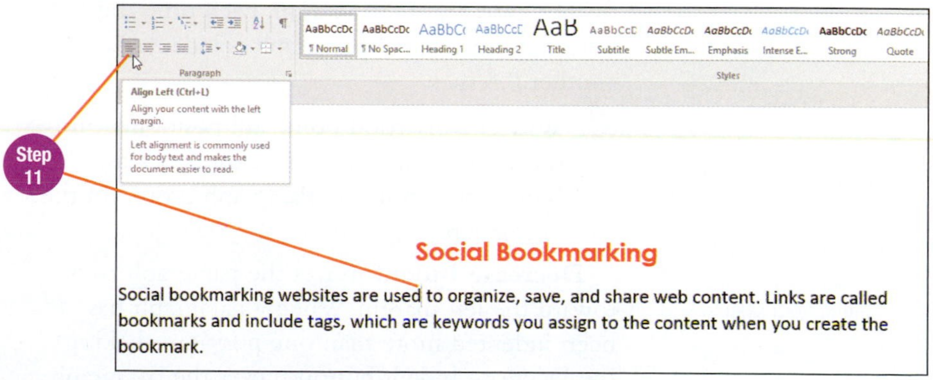

Quick Steps

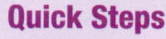

Change Font
1. Select text.
2. Click *Font* option box arrow.
3. Scroll down to desired font.
4. Click font.

Increase Font Size
1. Select text.
2. Click Increase Font Size button.

Change Font Color to Red
1. Select text.
2. Click Font Color button.

Change Paragraph Alignment
1. Click in paragraph.
2. Click Align Left, Center, Align Right, or Justify button.

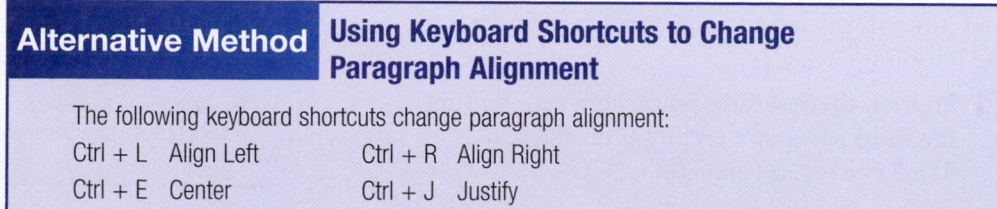

Alternative Method: Using Keyboard Shortcuts to Change Paragraph Alignment

The following keyboard shortcuts change paragraph alignment:

Ctrl + L	Align Left	Ctrl + R	Align Right
Ctrl + E	Center	Ctrl + J	Justify

6.6 Indenting Text and Changing Line and Paragraph Spacing

Skills

Indent text

Change line spacing

Change spacing after paragraphs

Tutorials

Indenting Text

Changing Line Spacing

Changing Spacing Before and After Paragraphs

Paragraphs are indented to set the paragraph apart from the rest of the document. In reports, essays, or research papers, long quotes are indented. A paragraph can be indented for the first line only, or for all lines in the paragraph. Paragraphs can also be indented from the right margin. A paragraph where the first line remains at the left margin but subsequent lines are indented is called a **hanging indent**. Hanging indents are used in bulleted lists, numbered lists, bibliographies, and lists of cited works.

Use the **Line and Paragraph Spacing** button in the Paragraph group to change the spacing between lines of text within a paragraph and to change the spacing before and after paragraphs.

1. With the **SocialMediaProject-YourName** document open, position the insertion point at the left margin of the first paragraph (begins with the text *Social bookmarking websites*).
2. Press the Tab key.

Pressing the Tab key indents the first line of a paragraph 0.5 inch and is referred to as a *first line indent*. The AutoCorrect Options button may also appear. Use the button when it appears to change the first line indent back to a Tab, to stop setting indents when you press Tab, or to change other AutoFormat options.

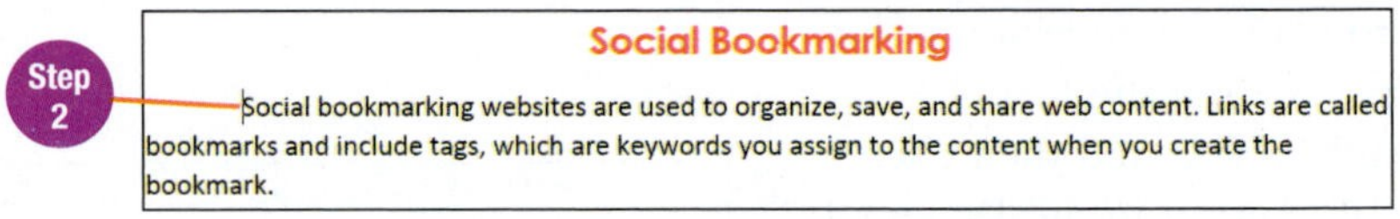

Step 2
Social Bookmarking
Social bookmarking websites are used to organize, save, and share web content. Links are called bookmarks and include tags, which are keywords you assign to the content when you create the bookmark.

3. Position the insertion point anywhere within the second paragraph (begins with the text *The popular*).
4. Click the Increase Indent button in the Paragraph group on the Home tab.

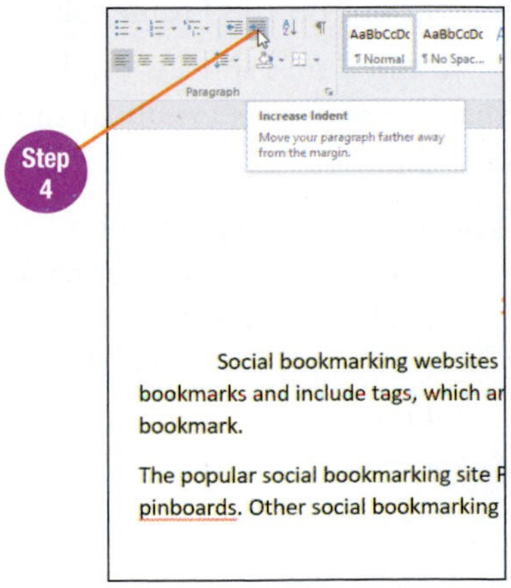

Step 4
Paragraph
Increase Indent
Move your paragraph farther away from the margin.
Social bookmarking websites
bookmarks and include tags, which ar
bookmark.
The popular social bookmarking site
pinboards. Other social bookmarking

The **Increase Indent** button indents all lines of a paragraph 0.5 inch. Click the button more than once if you want to move the paragraph further away from the margin. Each time the button is clicked, the paragraph is indented another 0.5 inch.

5. With the insertion point still positioned in the second paragraph, click the Decrease Indent button in the Paragraph group on the Home tab.

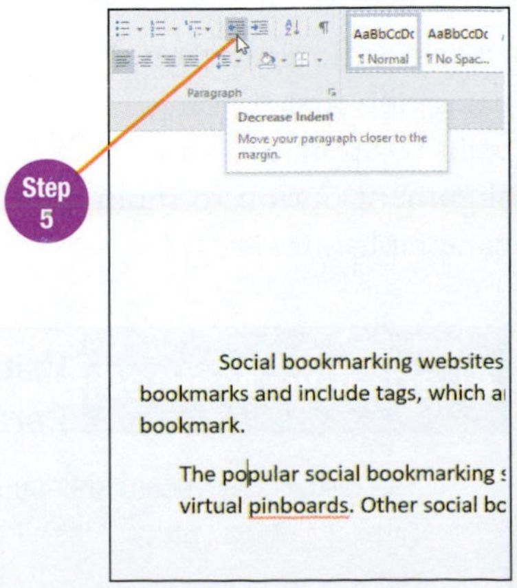

Step 5
Paragraph
Decrease Indent
Move your paragraph closer to the margin.
Social bookmarking websites
bookmarks and include tags, which a
bookmark.
The popular social bookmarking
virtual pinboards. Other social bc

Decrease Indent moves the paragraph back toward the left margin. When a paragraph has been indented more than one position, clicking the Decrease Indent button moves the paragraph back towards the left margin 0.5 inch each time the button is clicked.

6. Position the insertion point anywhere within the third paragraph (begins with the text *Many websites now include*).

App Tip

Use the Clear All Formatting button in the Font group to remove all formatting from selected text.

7 Click the Line and Paragraph Spacing button in the Paragraph group on the Home tab, and then click *Line Spacing Options* at the drop-down list.

8 At the Paragraph dialog box, select the current entry in the *Left* text box and then type 0.5.

9 Select the current entry in the *Right* text box and then type 0.5.

10 Click OK.

The paragraph is indented from both margins by 0.5 inch.

11 With the insertion point still positioned in the paragraph that begins with the text *Many websites*, click the Line and Paragraph Spacing button and then click *Line Spacing Options*.

12 Change the entry in the *Left* and the *Right* text boxes to *0*.

13 Click the *Special* list box arrow and then click *First line*.

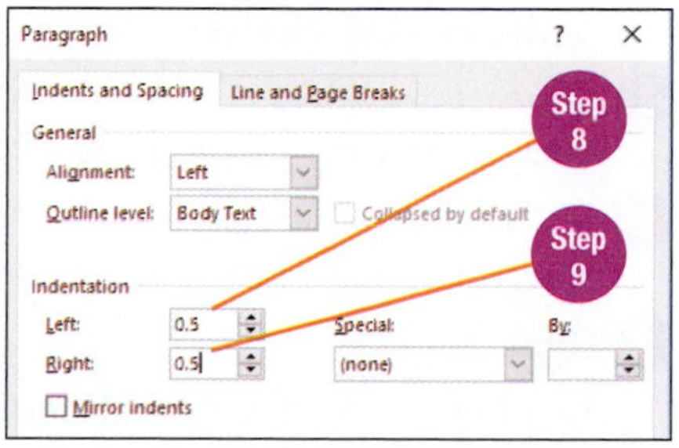

14 Click OK.

15 Format the second paragraph that begins with the text *The popular* and the last paragraph that begins with the text *Experian* with a first line indent by opening the Paragraph dialog box and then changing the *Special* list box option to *First line*.

16 Click the Select button in the Editing group on the Home tab and then click *Select All* at the drop-down list.

17 Click the Line and Paragraph Spacing button and then click *1.5* at the drop-down gallery.

The line spacing is changed to 1.5 lines for the entire document. Notice the other line spacing options are *1.0*, *1.15*, *2.0*, *2.5*, and *3.0*.

18 With the entire document still selected, click the Line and Paragraph Spacing button and then click *Remove Space After Paragraph* at the drop-down gallery.

19 Click in any section of the document to deselect the text.

20 Save the document using the same name. Leave the document open for the next topic.

Alternative Method **Changing Indents and Paragraph Spacing Using the Layout and Design tabs**

In the Paragraph group on the Layout tab, use the *Left* and *Right* text boxes to indent paragraphs and the *Before* and *After* text boxes to change the spacing before and after paragraphs.

On the Design tab, use the Paragraph Spacing button in the Document Formatting group to set line and paragraph spacing options for the entire document, including new paragraphs.

Quick Steps

Indent a Paragraph from Both Margins

1. Position insertion point in paragraph.
2. Click Line and Paragraph Spacing button.
3. Click *Line Spacing Options*.
4. Change *Left* value.
5. Change *Right* value.
6. Click OK.

Add Space Before Paragraphs or Remove Space After Paragraphs

1. Position insertion point or select paragraphs.
2. Click Line and Paragraph Spacing button.
3. Click *Add Space Before Paragraph* or *Remove Space After Paragraph*.

App Tip

Ctrl + A is the keyboard shortcut to Select All.

App Tip

Open the Paragraph dialog box to specify the amount of space to insert before and after a paragraph, measured in points, in the *Before* and *After* text boxes.

View Model Answer

Compare your completed file with the model answer.

6.7 Formatting Using Styles

Skills

Apply styles

Change style set

Tutorials

Applying Styles and Style Sets

Applying and Modifying a Theme

A **style** is a set of predefined formatting options that can be applied to selected text or paragraphs with one step. The Styles group on the Home tab shows the styles available in Word. You can also create your own styles. Use the More button at the bottom of the scroll bar at the right of the styles gallery to show more style options and the *Create a Style*, *Clear Formatting*, and *Apply Styles* options.

Once styles have been applied to text in the document, buttons in the Document Formatting group on the Design tab change the **style set**, which changes the look of a document by applying a group of formatting options to styles. Each style set has different formatting options associated with it.

1. With the **SocialMediaProject-YourName** document open, click the File tab and then click *Save As*.
2. If necessary, select the storage location option where you are saving your work such as *This PC* or *OneDrive - Personal* at the Save As backstage area.
3. Click in the *File name* text box, and then click a second time to place the insertion point at the end of the word *Project* and before -*YourName*.
4. Type WithStyles.

   The file name is now **SocialMediaProjectWithStyles-YourName**.
5. Click the Save button.

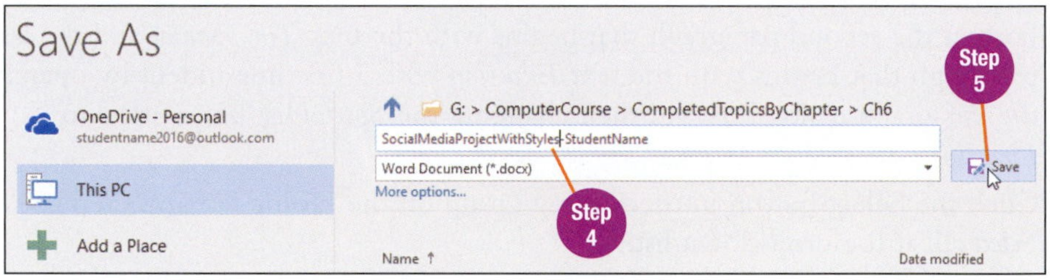

6. Position the insertion point anywhere within the title text *Social Bookmarking*.
7. Click the *Title* style in the styles gallery on the Home tab.

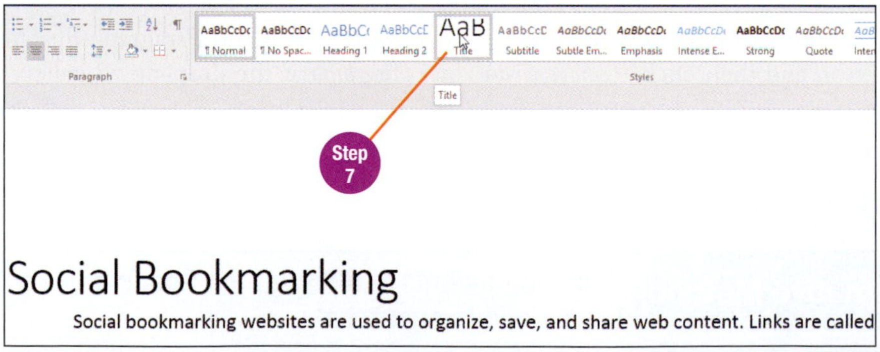

8. Position the insertion point anywhere within the first paragraph of text below the title.
9. Click the *Quote* style option in the styles gallery. If the *Quote* style option is not visible, click the More button ( ) at the bottom of the scroll bar located at the right of the styles gallery to display more style options, and then click the *Quote* style option.

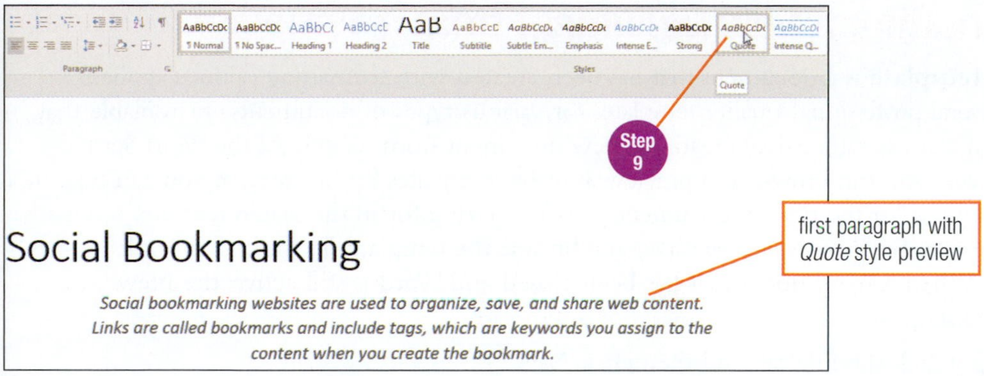

Step 9
Quote
Social Bookmarking
Social bookmarking websites are used to organize, save, and share web content. Links are called bookmarks and include tags, which are keywords you assign to the content when you create the bookmark.
first paragraph with *Quote* style preview

Quick Steps

Format Using Styles
1. Select text or position insertion point.
2. Click desired style option.

Change Style Set
1. Click Design tab.
2. Click desired style set.

10 Select *Pinterest.com* in the second paragraph and then click the *Intense Reference* style.

11 Deselect *Pinterest.com*.

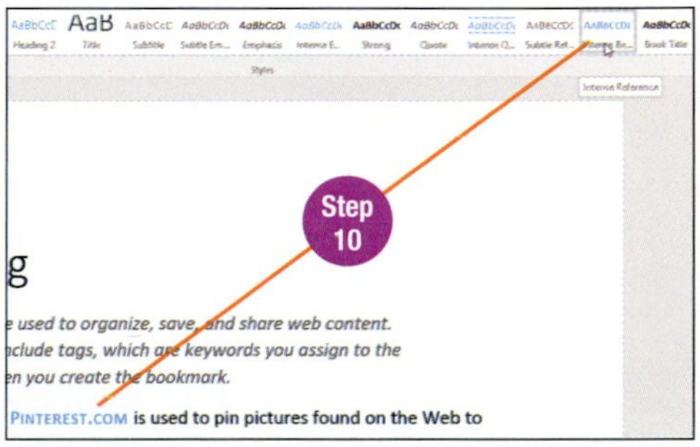

Once styles have been applied to text, you can experiment with various style sets in the Document Formatting group on the Design tab. Changing the style set changes font and paragraph formatting options.

12 Click the Design tab.

13 Click the *Basic (Stylish)* style set in the Document Formatting gallery (fourth option from left).

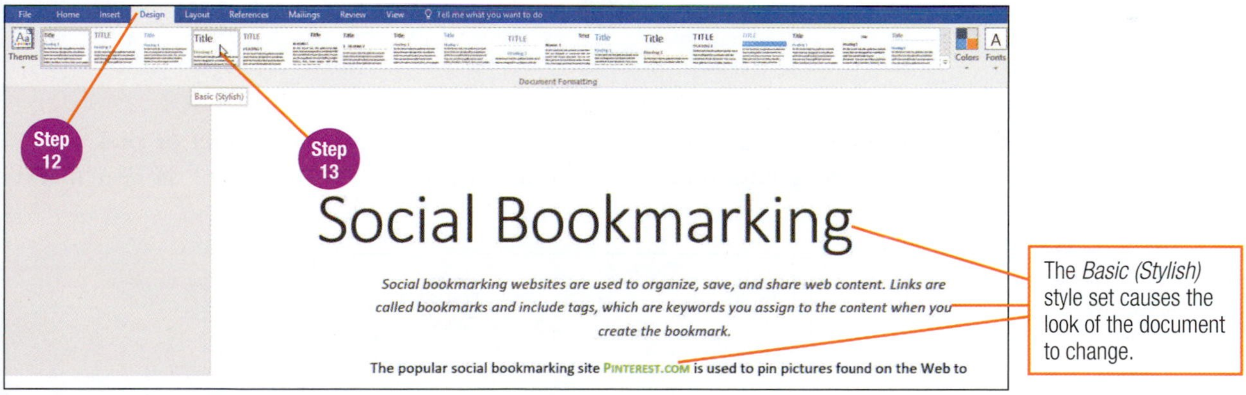

14 Position the insertion point anywhere within the title text *Social Bookmarking*, click the Home tab, and then click the *Heading 1* style.

The title text formats with the options for the Heading 1 style in the new style set. The formatting applied by a style is determined by the **Theme**. Each theme has a color scheme and a font scheme that affects style options.

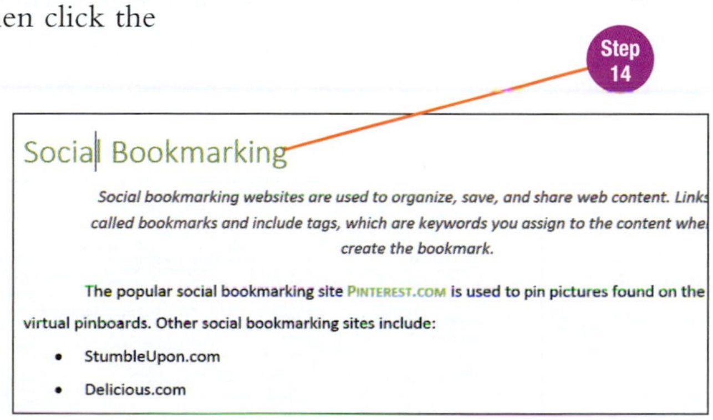

App Tip

Change the theme from the Themes button on the Design tab.

15 Save the document using the same name (**SocialMediaProjectWithStyles-YourName**).

16 Click the File tab and then click *Close* to close the document, leaving Word open for the next topic.

View Model Answer

Compare your completed file with the model answer.

6.8 Creating a New Document from a Template

Skills

Create a new document from a template

Tutorial

Creating a Document Using a Template

A **template** is a document that has been created with formatting options applied. Several professional-quality templates for various types of documents are available that you can use rather than creating a new document from scratch. At the Word Start screen, you can browse and preview available templates by category, or you can type in a keyword for the type of document you are looking for in the search text box (contains the text *Search for online templates*) and browse the templates in the search results.

When a Word document has been closed and Word is still active, the New backstage area is used to browse for a template.

1. Click the File tab and then click *New*.
2. At the New backstage area, click Business in the *Suggested searches* section.

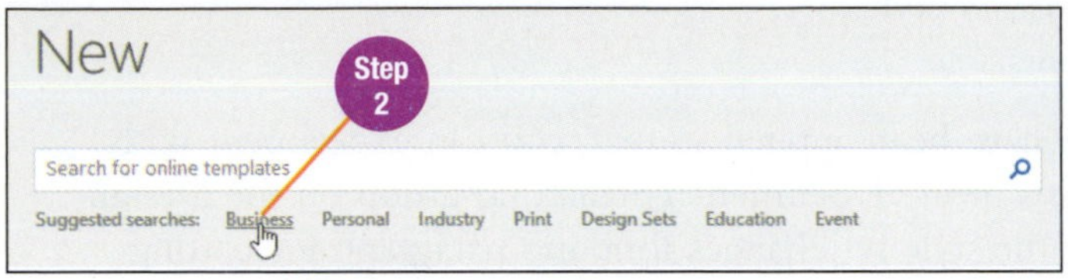

3. Scroll down and review the various types of business templates available, then click Home at the top of the New backstage area.

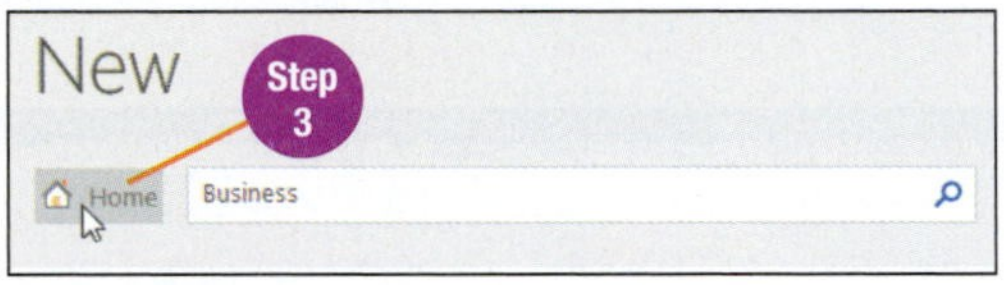

4. Click in the search text box, type time sheet, and then press Enter or click the Start searching button (displays as a magnifying glass at the end of the search text box).

Oops!

Your *Time sheet* template looks different? Available templates are changed often. If the first template looks different, close the preview and look for one that is closest to the one shown. If necessary, adjust the remaining instructions to suit the available templates.

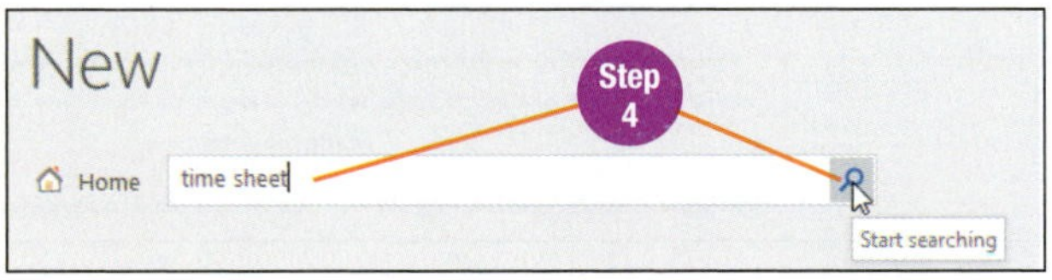

5. Click the first *Time sheet* template in the Templates gallery.

A preview of the template opens with a description that provides information on the template design.

6. Click the Create button.

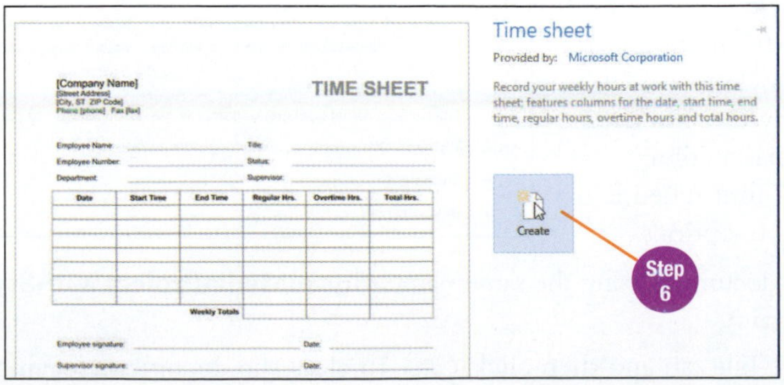

7 Click *[Company Name]* and then type A+ Tutoring Advantage.

8 Click *[Street Address]* and then type 1015 Montreal Way.

9 Click *[City, ST ZIP Code]* and then type St. Paul, MN 55102.

10 Click *[phone]* and then type 888-555-3125.

11 Click *[fax]* and type 888-555-3445.

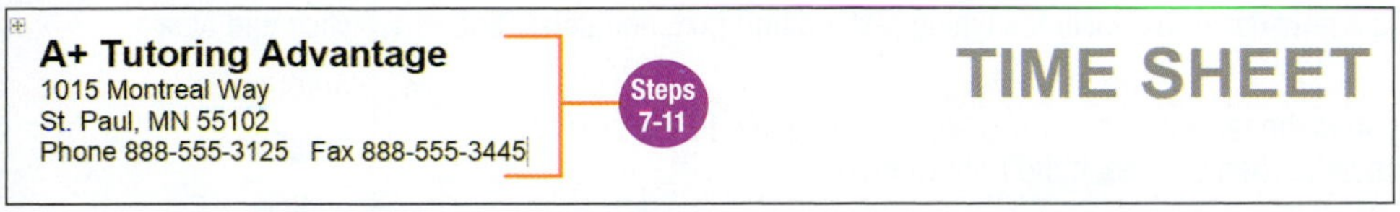

A+ Tutoring Advantage
1015 Montreal Way
St. Paul, MN 55102
Phone 888-555-3125 Fax 888-555-3445

TIME SHEET

12 Click next to *Employee Name* and then type your name.

13 Complete the remainder of the time sheet document using the text shown in Figure 6.4 by completing a step similar to Step 12.

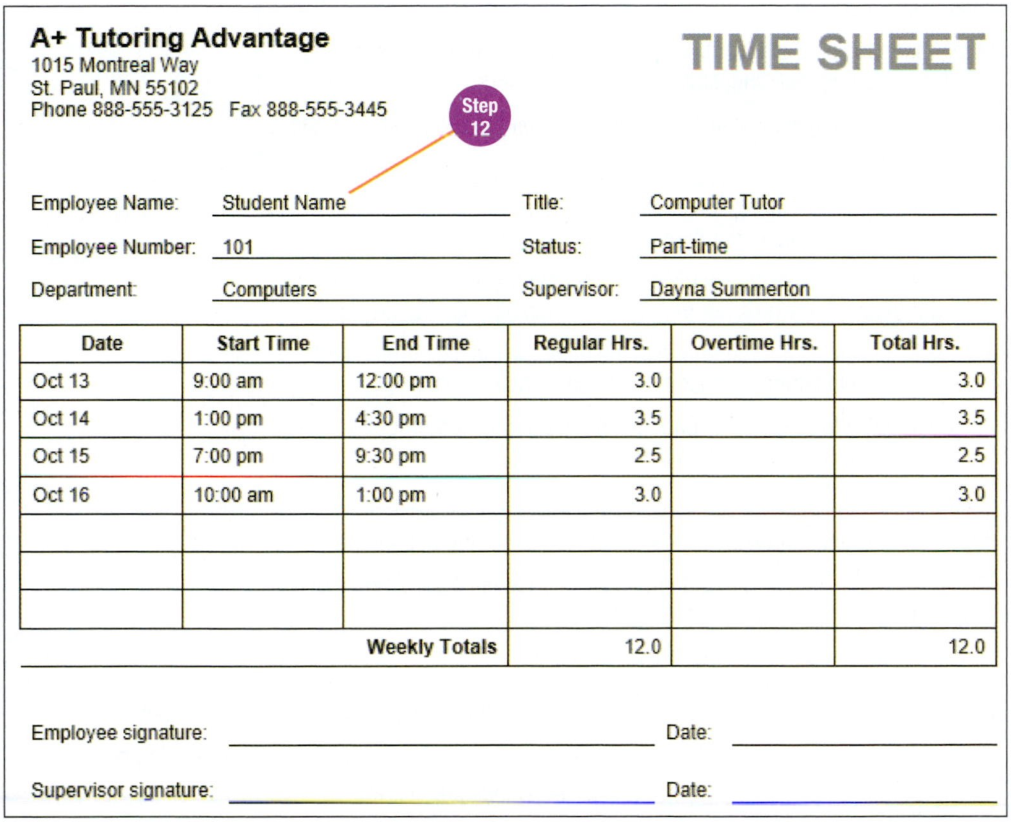

A+ Tutoring Advantage
1015 Montreal Way
St. Paul, MN 55102
Phone 888-555-3125 Fax 888-555-3445

TIME SHEET

Employee Name: Student Name Title: Computer Tutor
Employee Number: 101 Status: Part-time
Department: Computers Supervisor: Dayna Summerton

Date	Start Time	End Time	Regular Hrs.	Overtime Hrs.	Total Hrs.
Oct 13	9:00 am	12:00 pm	3.0		3.0
Oct 14	1:00 pm	4:30 pm	3.5		3.5
Oct 15	7:00 pm	9:30 pm	2.5		2.5
Oct 16	10:00 am	1:00 pm	3.0		3.0
		Weekly Totals	12.0		12.0

Employee signature: Date:

Supervisor signature: Date:

Figure 6.4

Shown is a completed Oct13to16Timesheet-YourName document.

14 Save the completed time sheet in the Ch6 folder in the CompletedTopicsByChapter folder on your storage medium as **Oct13to16TimeSheet-YourName**. Choose OK when a message displays that the document will be upgraded to the newest file format.

15 Close the document.

App Tip

[Company Name] is referred to as a *text placeholder*. Look for these placeholders in a template to indicate where to personalize the document. Other templates include descriptive text within the template that describes how to use the template.

Quick Steps

Create New Document from a Template

1. Click File tab.
2. Click *New*.
3. Browse or search for template design.
4. Click desired template.
5. Click Create button.
6. Complete document as required.

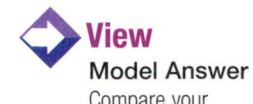

View

Model Answer

Compare your completed file with the model answer.

Beyond Basics Template Designs

Templates are available for any type of document. The next time you need to type a letter, memo, report, invitation, announcement, flyer, or labels, look for a template design.

Topics Review

Topic	Key Concepts	Key Terms
6.1 Creating and Editing a New Document	A word processing application is software used to create documents that are composed mostly of text. Start a new blank document from the Word Start screen. Creating a new document includes typing text, editing text, and correcting errors. Wordwrap is the term that describes Word moving text to the next line automatically when you reach the right margin. Double-clicking on the page in blank space and typing is referred to as *click and type*. Text is automatically aligned left, center, or right depending on the location in the line at which click and type occurs. As you type new text, AutoCorrect fixes common misspellings, and AutoFormat automatically converts some text to fractions, ordinals, quotes, hyphens, and hyperlinks. A change made to text that has already been typed is referred to as *editing* and involves inserting, deleting, and replacing characters. The first step in editing is to position the insertion point at the location of the change.	word processing application wordwrap click and type AutoCorrect AutoFormat editing
6.2 Inserting Symbols and Completing a Spelling and Grammar Check	Symbols or special characters, such as a copyright symbol or registered trademark, are entered using the Symbol gallery or Symbol dialog box. The Spelling & Grammar button is used to match words in the document with words in the dictionary; words not found are flagged as potential errors. During a spell check, a word not found in the dictionary is highlighted and suggestions for replacement appear in the Spelling task pane. Ignore, Ignore All, Add, Change, or Change All are buttons in the Spelling task pane used to respond to each potential error.	Symbol gallery Spelling & Grammar
6.3 Finding and Replacing Text	The Find feature highlights all occurrences of a keyword or phrase and provides in the Navigation pane a link to each location in the document. Use Replace if you want Word to automatically change each occurrence of a keyword or phrase with another word or phrase. Find a word with a similar meaning in the Thesaurus.	Find Replace
6.4 Moving Text and Inserting Bullets and Numbering	Turn on the display of hidden formatting symbols using the Show/Hide button in the Paragraph group on the Home tab. Hidden formatting symbols, such as the paragraph symbol, are inserted in a document whenever the Enter key is pressed. Displaying formatting symbols is helpful when moving text to make sure the paragraph symbol is selected before cutting the text. Bullets are items in a list that is set apart from the paragraph and are entered in no particular sequence. A numbered list is a sequential series of tasks or other items that are each preceded by a number.	Bullets button Numbering button

continued…

Topic	Key Concepts	Key Terms
6.5 Formatting Text with Font and Paragraph Alignment Options	Changing the appearance of text is called *formatting*. Character formatting involves applying changes to the appearance of characters, whereas paragraph formatting changes the appearance of an entire paragraph. A font is also called a *typeface* and refers to the design and shape of letters, numbers, and special characters. Change a font, font size, case, font style, font color; highlight text; and add font effects to change character formats. Change a paragraph's alignment from the default Align Left to Center, Align Right, or Justify using the buttons in the Paragraph group on the Home tab. Justified text has extra space within a line so that the left and right margins are even.	formatting character formatting paragraph formatting font Align Left Center Align Right Justify
6.6 Indenting Text and Changing Line and Paragraph Spacing	Press Tab at the beginning of a paragraph to indent only the first line or change *Special* to *First line* at the Paragraph dialog box. A paragraph in which all lines are indented except the first line is called a *hanging indent*. Indent all lines of a paragraph using the Increase Indent button or change the *Left* text box entry at the Paragraph dialog box. A paragraph indents 0.5 inch each time the Increase Indent button is clicked. Use the Decrease Indent button to move a paragraph closer to the left margin; the paragraph moves left 0.5 inch each time the button is clicked. Indent a paragraph from both margins using the *Left* and *Right* text boxes in the Paragraph dialog box. Change line spacing by selecting the desired spacing option from the Line and Paragraph Spacing button. Extra space can be added or removed before or after paragraphs using options from the Line and Paragraph Spacing button or the Paragraph dialog box.	hanging indent Line and Paragraph Spacing Increase Indent Decrease Indent
6.7 Formatting Using Styles	Format text by applying a style, which is a set of predefined formatting options. Change the style set using buttons in the Document Formatting group on the Design tab. Each style set applies a different set of formatting options for the styles on the Home tab, meaning you can change the appearance of a document by changing the style set. A Theme is a set of colors, fonts, and font effects that alter the appearance of a document.	style style set Theme
6.8 Creating a New Document from a Template	A template is a document that is already set up with text and/or formatting options. Browse available templates in the template gallery at the Word Start screen or at the New backstage area. Find a template by browsing the gallery by a category or by typing a keyword in the search text box. Click a template design to preview the template and create a new document based upon the template. Within a template, text placeholders or instructional text is included to help you personalize the document.	template

Recheck

Recheck your understanding of the topics covered in this chapter.

Workbook

Chapter review and assessment resources are available in the *Workbook* ebook.

Chapter 7

Enhancing a Word Document with Special Features

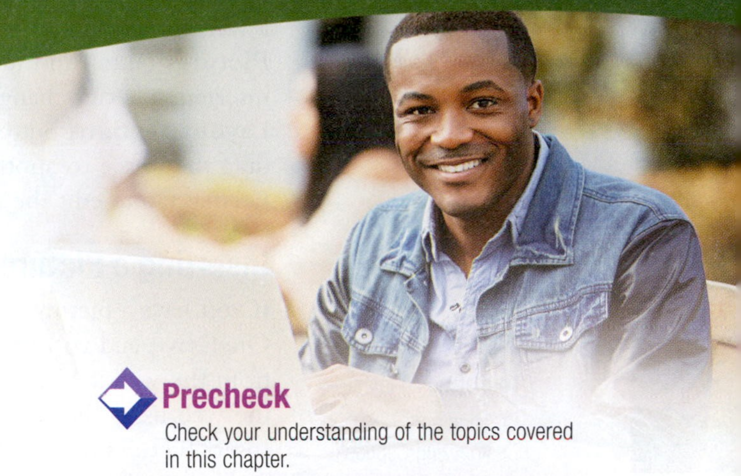

Precheck

Check your understanding of the topics covered in this chapter.

Several features in Word allow you to add visual appeal, organize information, or format a document for a special purpose, such as a research paper. Word provides different views to work in and navigate a document and includes collaborative tools, such as comments, for working on a document with other people. Several resume and cover letter templates are available in Word to help you build job search documents.

In this chapter, you will enhance documents already typed and finalize an academic research paper by adding formatting, citations, and a Works Cited page. Lastly, you will create a resume and cover letter using templates.

Learning Objectives

7.1 Insert, edit, and label pictures in a document

7.2 Add borders and shading to text and insert a text box in a document

7.3 Insert a table in a document

7.4 Format and modify a table

7.5 Change layout options

7.6 Add text and page numbers in a header for a research paper

7.7 Insert and edit citations in a research paper

7.8 Create a Works Cited page for a research paper and display a document in different views

7.9 Insert and reply to comments in a document

7.10 Create a resume and cover letter from templates

SNAP If you are a SNAP user, go to your SNAP Assignments page to complete the Precheck, Tutorials, and Recheck.

Data Files

Before beginning this chapter, be sure you have copied the student data files for this course to your storage medium. Steps on downloading and extracting the data files are provided in Chapter 1, Topic 1.8, on pages 22–23.

7.1 Inserting, Editing, and Labeling Pictures in a Document

Skills

Insert a picture from a web resource

Insert a picture from a file on your computer

Edit a picture

Insert a caption

Tutorials

Inserting, Sizing, and Positioning an Image

Formatting an Image

Creating and Customizing Captions

Good to Know

According to Microsoft, Bing Image Search applies a copyright filter so that the results displayed are only those tagged with a Creative Commons license. A Creative Commons license means that you have to provide attribution (credit the source). A link to the source of each image is included so that you can properly credit the picture creator.

App Tip

The Online Video button in the Media group on the Insert tab is used to add and play videos within a Word document.

Adding a graphic element, such as a picture, not only adds visual appeal to a document but can also help a reader understand content. You can insert a picture from a web resource or from an image file stored on your computer using the **Online Pictures** button in the Illustrations group on the Insert tab. Once an image has been inserted, you can change the way text wraps around the sides of the image using the **Layout Options** button that appears. Resize the image with the selection handles or drag the image to another position in the document. Use buttons on the Picture Tools Format tab to edit the image.

Inserting a Picture from an Online Source

If you have a picture stored at an online service, such as Flickr, Facebook, or OneDrive, and you have those services connected to Word, you can insert the image from the website within the Word document. You can also search for an image on the web using the search text box to the right of the *Bing Image Search* option at the Insert Pictures dialog box and insert the image into the Word document.

1. Start Word 2016 and open the document **InsulaSummary** from the Ch7 folder in Student_Data_Files.
2. Click the File tab and then click *Save As*. At the Save As backstage area, click *Browse*. At the Save As dialog box, navigate to the CompletedTopicsByChapter folder on your storage medium, create a new folder *Ch7*, and then save a copy of the document within the Ch7 folder as **InsulaSummary-YourName**.
3. Position the insertion point at the beginning of the first paragraph of text.
4. Click the Insert tab and then click the Online Pictures button in the Illustrations group.
5. At the Insert Pictures dialog box, with the insertion point positioned in the search text box to the right of the *Bing Image Search* option, type brain and then press Enter or click the Search button (displays as a magnifying glass).

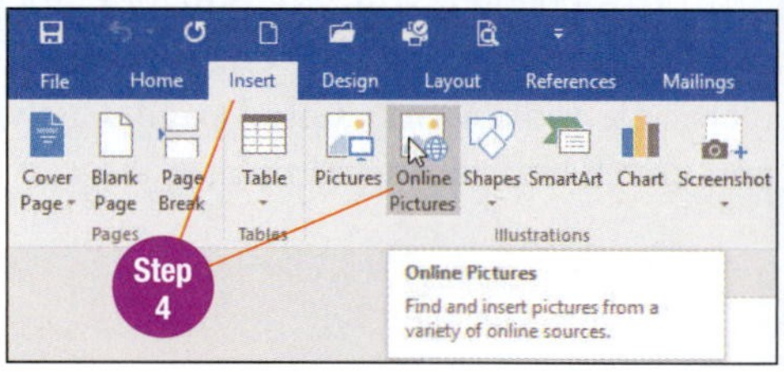

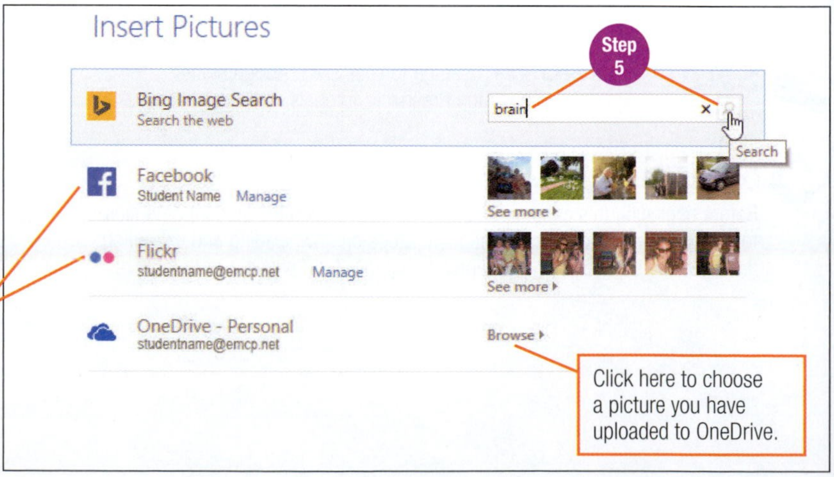

Pictures you have stored at Flickr and Facebook show here if you have connected your Flickr and Facebook accounts to your Microsoft account.

6. Scroll down the search results list to the image shown at the right, click to select the image, and then click the Insert button. If you cannot locate the image shown, close the Insert Pictures dialog box and then insert the image using the Pictures button in the Illustrations group (see Steps 13 to 14) using the image file ***Brain*** in the Ch7 folder in Student_Data_Files.

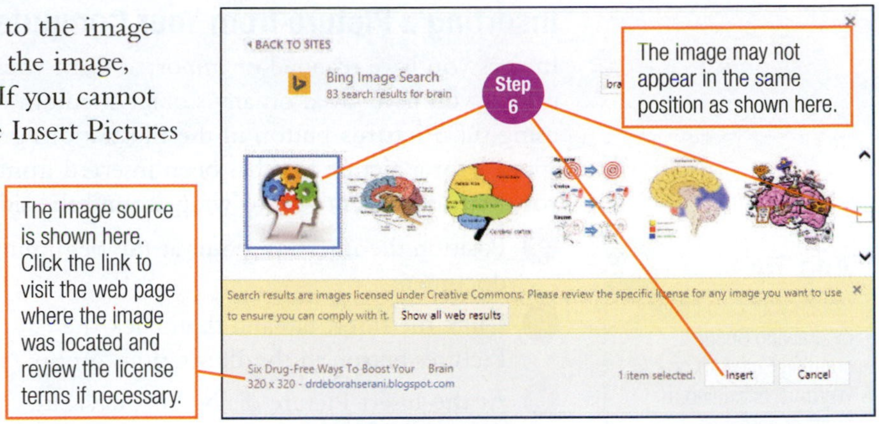

7. Click the Layout Options button that appears at the top right of the inserted image.

8. Click *Square*, the first option in the *With Text Wrapping* section of the LAYOUT OPTIONS gallery, and then click the Close button.

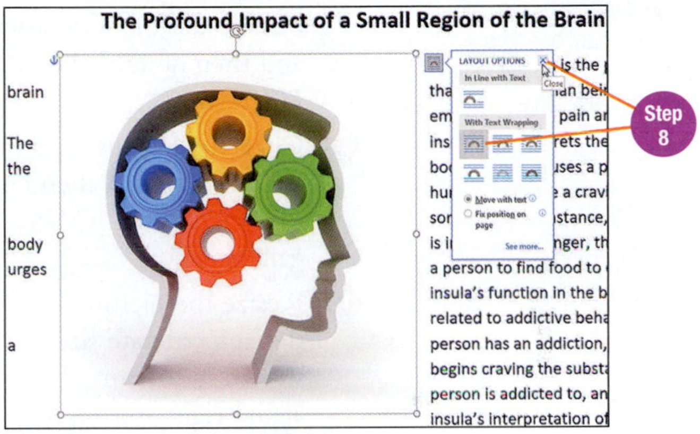

The LAYOUT OPTIONS gallery provides choices to control how text wraps around the picture object and to control whether the picture should remain fixed at its current position or move with the text. Notice also that the Picture Tools Format tab becomes active when a picture is selected. You will work with buttons in this tab later in this topic.

9. Drag the picture to the right until the right edge of the picture is aligned at the right margin.

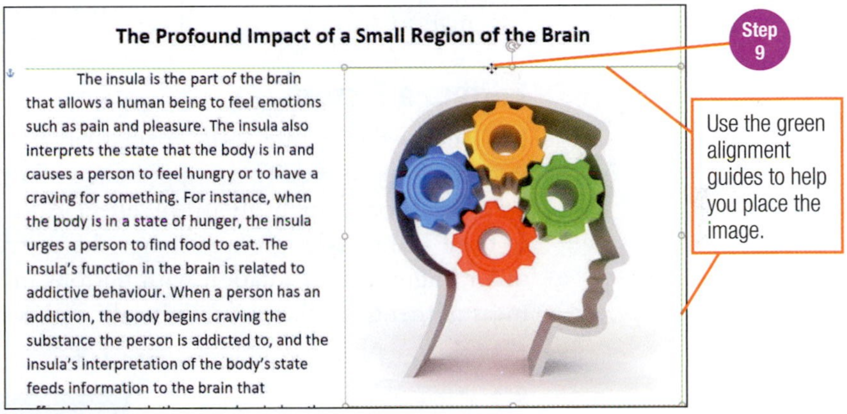

As you move the picture, green alignment guides help you position the image at the top of the paragraph and at the right margin.

10. Drag the bottom left corner selection handle on the image up and toward the right until the picture is resized to the approximate size shown in the Step 10 illustration.

11. Save the revised document using the same name (**InsulaSummary-Your Name**).

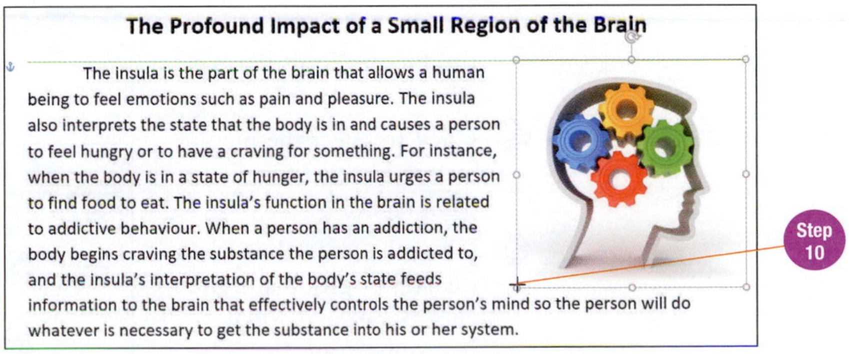

Inserting a Picture from Your Computer

Images you have scanned or imported from your digital camera to your PC or other images you have saved on any storage medium can be inserted into a document using the **Pictures** button in the Illustrations group. The Layout Options button also appears for a picture that has been inserted from your PC for you to specify the way you want document text to wrap around the sides of the picture.

> **App Tip**
> Create your own images by drawing Shapes, creating SmartArt or WordArt, or adding a chart or screenshot. Explore these features if you want to add a graphic but do not have a picture available.

12. Position the insertion point at the beginning of the second paragraph in the document.
13. Click the Insert tab and then click the Pictures button in the Illustrations group.

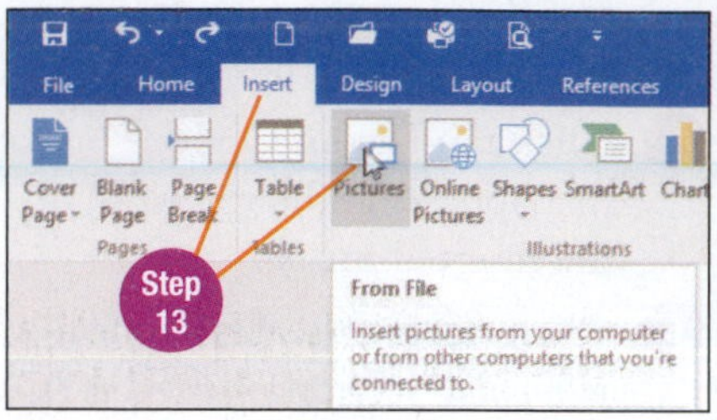

14. At the Insert Picture dialog box, navigate to the Ch7 folder in the Student_Data_Files folder on your storage medium, and then double-click the image named ***USCPhoto***.
15. Click the Layout Options button, click *Square*, and then close the LAYOUT OPTIONS gallery.
16. Resize the picture to the approximate size shown in the image at the right and align the photo at the left margin.

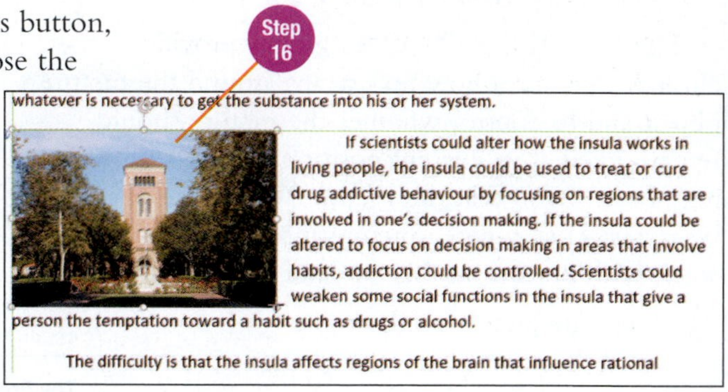

Step 16
whatever is necessary to get the substance into his or her system.
If scientists could alter how the insula works in living people, the insula could be used to treat or cure drug addictive behaviour by focusing on regions that are involved in one's decision making. If the insula could be altered to focus on decision making in areas that involve habits, addiction could be controlled. Scientists could weaken some social functions in the insula that give a person the temptation toward a habit such as drugs or alcohol.
The difficulty is that the insula affects regions of the brain that influence rational

Editing a Picture

Buttons on the Picture Tools Format tab are used to edit an image. Use buttons in the Adjust group to modify the appearance of a picture, such as the sharpness, contrast, or color tone, or to apply an artistic effect. Add a border or picture effect with options in the Picture Styles group. Change the picture's position, text wrapping option, order, alignment, or rotation with buttons in the Arrange group. Crop or specify exact measurements for the picture's height and width with buttons in the Size group.

17. Click to select the picture inserted in the first paragraph.
18. Click *Soft Edge Rectangle* (sixth option) in the Picture Styles group on the Picture Tools Format tab.

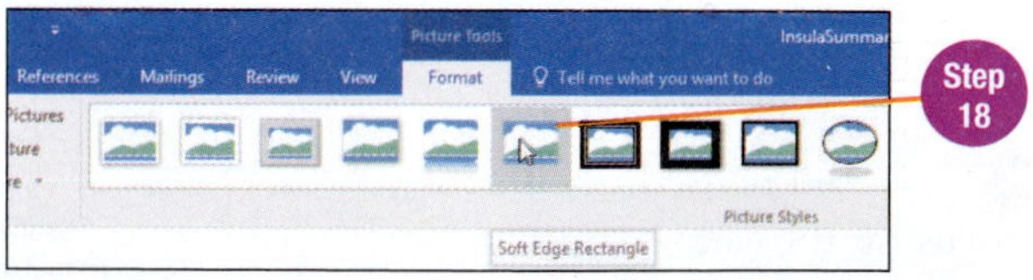

19. Click to select the picture inserted in the second paragraph.
20. Click the Color button in the Adjust group and then click *Saturation: 400%* (last option) in the *Color Saturation* section of the drop-down gallery.

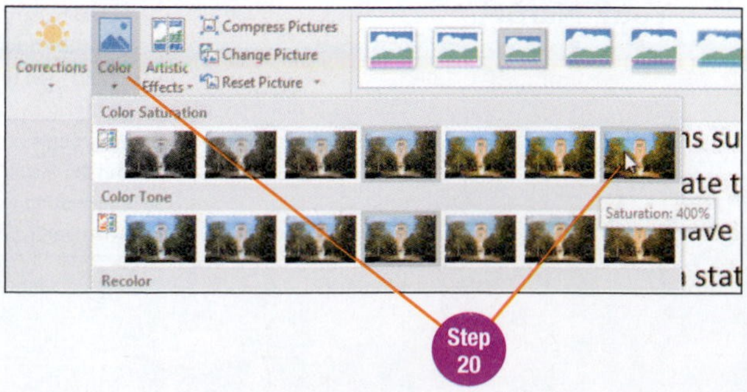

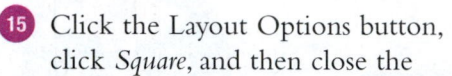

Notice the picture appears brighter than it did before. Saturation refers to the purity of colors in a photo. Some digital cameras use a low saturation level, making the colors seem dull; increasing the saturation level brightens a picture.

Inserting a Caption with a Picture

Adding a caption below a photograph can help a reader understand the context of a picture, or you can use captions to number figures in a report. With the **Insert Caption** feature, Word automatically numbers pictures, inserting the number after the label *Figure*.

21 With the picture in the second paragraph still selected, click the References tab.

22 Click the Insert Caption button in the Captions group.

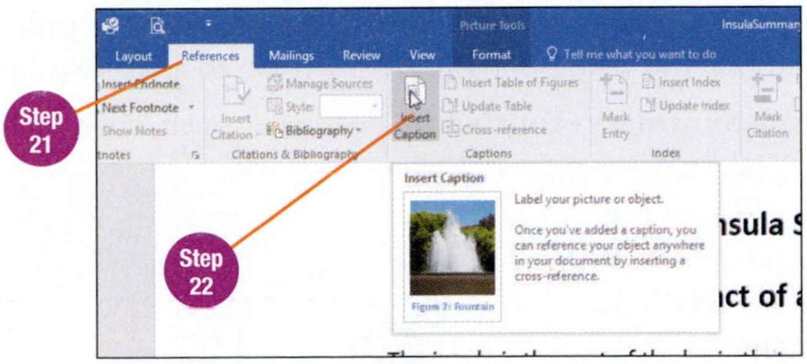

23 At the Caption dialog box, with the insertion point positioned in the *Caption* text box, press the spacebar and then type Insula research is being done at the University of Southern California.

24 Press Enter or click OK.

25 Click in the document outside the caption box to deselect the caption.

26 Save the revised document using the same name (**InsulaSummary-YourName**). Leave the document open for the next topic.

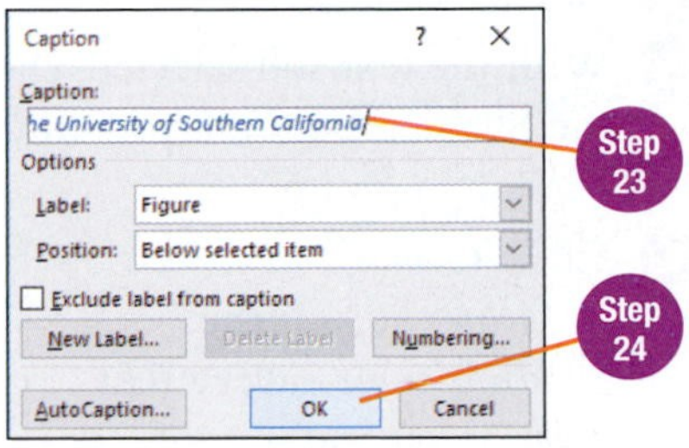

App Tip

For advanced documents, such as a research report, Word can automatically generate a Table of Figures from captions.

Quick Steps

Insert Online Photo
1. Position insertion point.
2. Click Insert tab.
3. Click Online Pictures button.
4. Type search word or phrase.
5. Select desired image.
6. Click Insert.

Insert Image from a Computer
1. Position insertion point.
2. Click Insert tab.
3. Click Pictures button.
4. Navigate to drive and/or folder.
5. Double-click desired image.

Edit a Picture
1. Select image.
2. Change layout options, resize, move, or otherwise edit picture as needed.

Insert a Caption
1. Select image.
2. Click References tab.
3. Click Insert Caption button.
4. Type caption text.
5. Click OK.

Beyond Basics: Cropping and Removing the Background of a Picture

You can remove unwanted portions of a picture with the Crop tool in the Size group on the Picture Tools Format tab. Click the Crop button and then use the crop handles to modify the picture. The portion of the image that will remain appears normal, while the cropped area becomes dark gray. Click outside the image to complete the crop action.

The Remove Background button in the Adjust group on the Picture Tools Format tab is another tool you can use to remove portions of a photo. With this button, you can focus on an object in the foreground of a picture and remove the background. For example, with a photo of an airplane in the sky, you can select the airplane and have Word remove the sky in the background.

7.2 Adding Borders and Shading, and Inserting a Text Box

Skills

Add a paragraph border

Add shading within a paragraph

Add a border to a page

Insert a text box

Tutorials

Applying Borders

Inserting a Page Border

Applying Shading

Inserting a Text Box

Formatting a Text Box

Add a border and/or add color behind text (called **shading**) to make text stand out from the rest of a document. You can add borders and shading to a single paragraph or to a group of selected paragraphs. With the **Page Borders** button, you can add a border around the edges of the entire page. Add a line that spans the entire page width above the insertion point location by clicking *Horizontal Line* at the **Borders gallery**.

A text box is used to set a short passage of text apart from the rest of a document. Word includes several built-in text box styles that can be used for this purpose. Inserting text inside a box is a way to draw the reader's attention to an important quote or point in a document. A quote inside a text box is called a **pull quote**. Click the **Text Box** button in the Text group on the Insert tab to add a text box.

1. With the **InsulaSummary-YourName** document open, click the Home tab.
2. Select the first two lines of the document that are the title and subtitle text and then click the Borders button arrow in the Paragraph group.

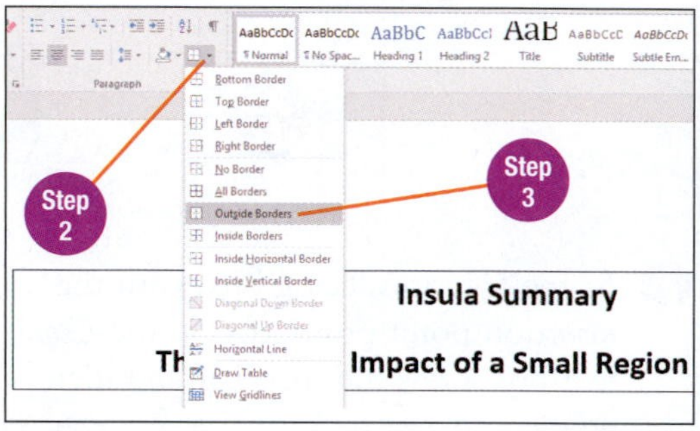

3. Click *Outside Borders*.
4. With the text still selected, click the Shading button arrow in the Paragraph group.
5. Click *Orange, Accent 6, Lighter 80%* at the Shading color gallery (last color in second row of *Theme Colors* section).

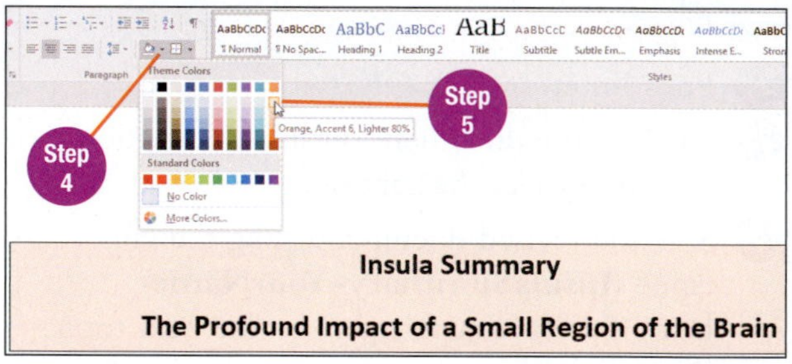

6. Click in any paragraph to deselect the text.
7. Click the Design tab.
8. Click the Page Borders button in the Page Background group.

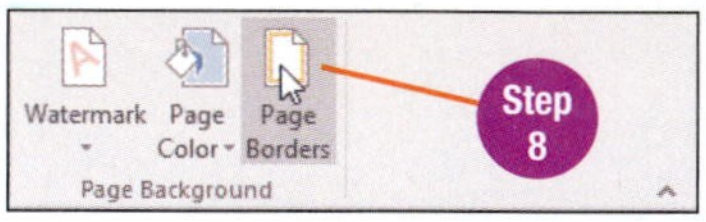

9. At the Borders and Shading dialog box, with the Page Border tab selected, click the page graphic next to *Shadow* in the *Setting* section.
10. Click the *Width* list box arrow and then click *1 ½ pt* at the drop-down list.
11. Click OK.

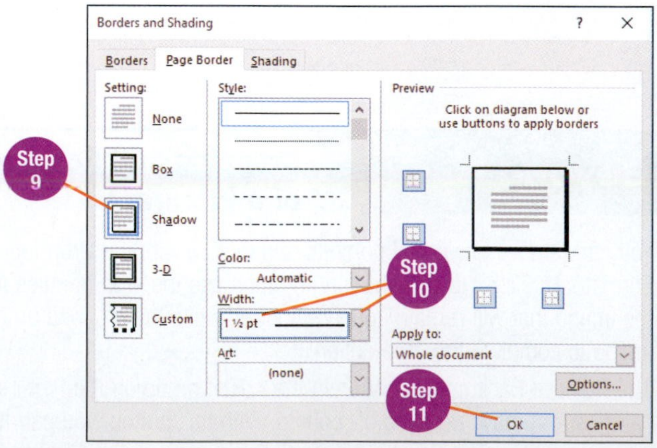

App Tip

Use *Borders and Shading* from the Borders gallery to create a custom border in the Borders and Shading dialog box by changing the border style, color, and width options.

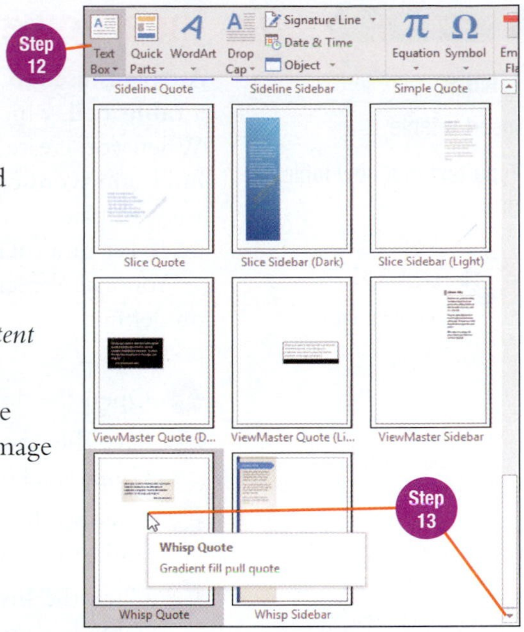

12 Click the Insert tab and then click the Text Box button in the Text group.

13 Scroll down and then click *Whisp Quote* at the drop-down list.

Word adds a text box overlapping other text in the document and with default text already selected inside the text box.

14 Type Some people with damage to the insula were able to quit smoking instantly!.

15 Right-click *[Cite your source here.]* and then choose *Remove Content Control* at the shortcut menu.

16 Point to the border of the box and then drag the text box to the bottom of the page to the approximate location shown in the image below.

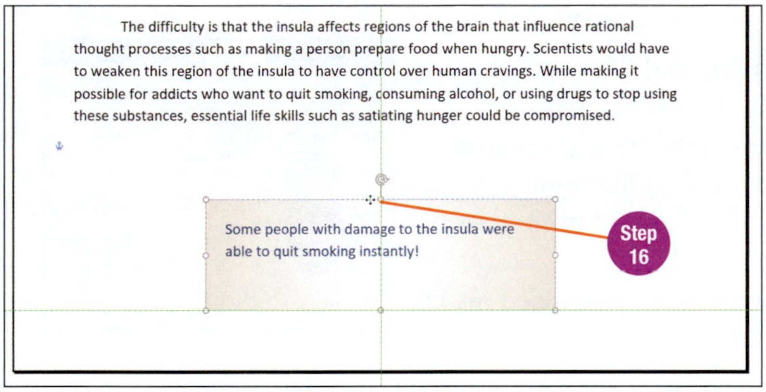

17 Drag the bottom middle selection handle up to reduce the height of the text box as shown in the image below.

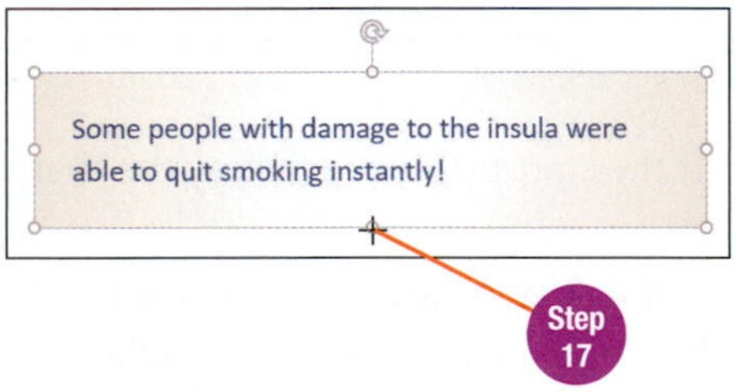

18 Click in any paragraph to deselect the text box and then save the revised document using the same name (**InsulaSummary-YourName**).

19 Close the document.

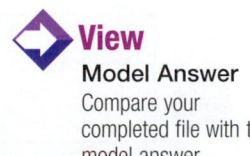

View Model Answer
Compare your completed file with the model answer.

Quick Steps

Add a Paragraph Border
1. Select paragraph(s).
2. Click Borders button arrow.
3. Click desired border style.

Add Shading to a Paragraph
1. Select paragraph(s).
2. Click Shading button arrow.
3. Click desired color.

Add a Page Border
1. Click Design tab.
2. Click Page Borders button.
3. Select desired *Setting* and *Style*, *Color*, *Width*, or *Art* options.
4. Click OK.

Insert a Text Box
1. Click Insert tab.
2. Click Text Box button.
3. Click desired text box style.
4. Type text.
5. Move and/or resize box as needed.

Beyond Basics — Formatting Tools to Edit a Text Box

When a shape, line, drawing, or other graphic object is selected, the Drawing Tools Format tab becomes available. Use buttons on the tab to edit the object. For example, with a selected text box, you can change the text box shape style, fill, or outline and add shape effects. Edit the appearance of the text inside the box by applying a WordArt style, changing the text fill or outline, adding text effects, or changing the alignment or direction of the text.

7.3 Inserting a Table

Skills

Insert a table

Type text in a new table grid

Tutorial

Creating a Table

A table is used to organize and present data in columns and rows. Text is typed within a **table cell**, which is a rectangular box that is the intersection of a column with a row. When you create a table, you specify the number of columns and rows the table will hold, and Word creates a blank grid in which you type the table text. Text that you want to place side by side in columns, or in rows, is ideal for a table. For example, a price list or a catalog with items and descriptions is ideal for a table.

You can also create a table using the Quick Tables feature. A **Quick Table** is a predefined and formatted table with sample data that you can replace with your own text.

1. Open the document **RezMealPlans**.
2. Save the document as **RezMealPlans-YourName** in the Ch7 folder in CompletedTopicsByChapter.
3. Position the insertion point at the left margin in the blank line below the subheading *Meal Plans with Descriptions*.
4. Click the Insert tab and then click the Table button in the Tables group.
5. Click the square in the drop-down grid that is three columns to the right and two rows down (*3x2 Table* displays above grid).

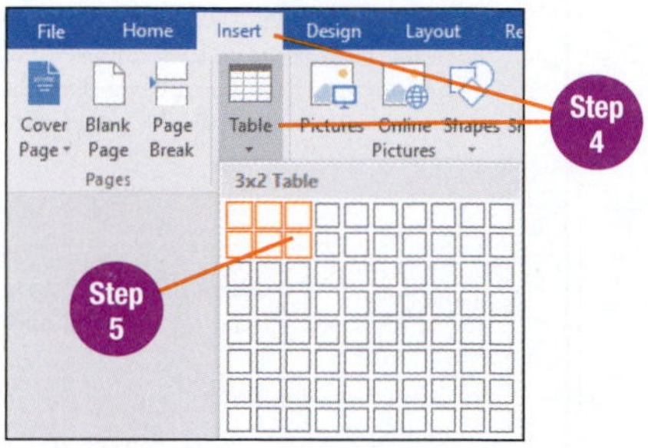

6. With the insertion point positioned in the first table cell, type Meal Plan Name and then press Tab or click in the next table cell.
7. Type Cost and then press Tab or click in the next table cell.

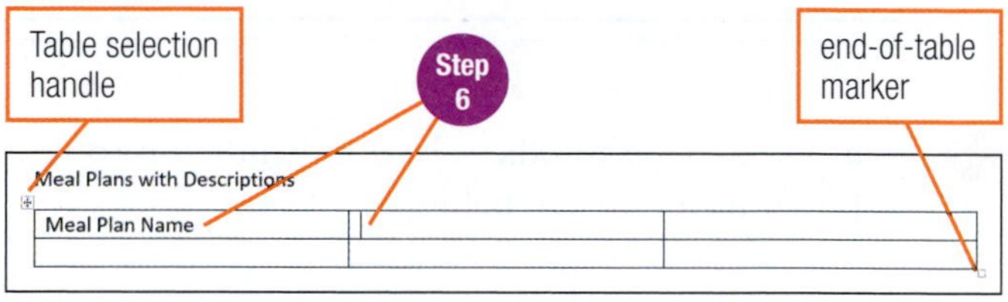

8. Type Description and then press Tab or click in the first table cell in the second row.
9. Type the second row of data as follows. When you finish typing the text in the last column, press Tab to add a new row to the table automatically.

Minimum	$2,000	Suitable for students with small appetites who plan to be away from residence most weekends.

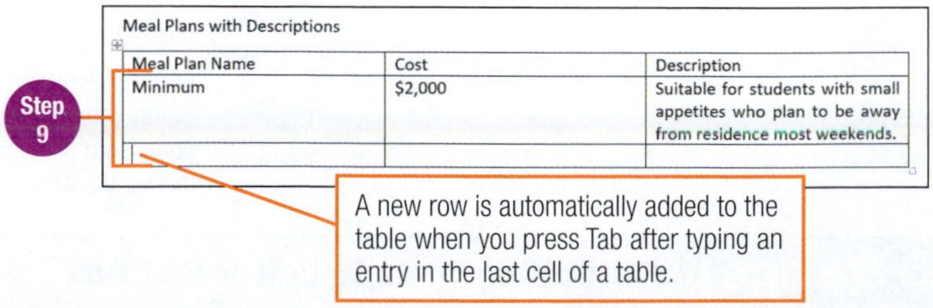

10. Type the remainder of the table as shown in Figure 7.1 on page 165 by completing steps similar to those in Steps 6 to 9, except do not press Tab after typing the last table cell entry.

App Tip

The advantage to using a table versus typing information in tabbed columns is that information can wrap around within a table cell.

Oops!

Added a new row by mistake? Click the Undo button to remove the extra row.

Meal Plans with Descriptions

Meal Plan Name	Cost	Description
Minimum	$2,000	Suitable for students with small appetites who plan to be away from residence most weekends.
Light	$2,200	Best plan for students with a lighter appetite who spend occasional weekends on campus.
Full	$2,400	Full is the most popular plan. This plan is for students with an average appetite who will stay on campus most weekends.
Plus	$2,600	Students with a hearty appetite who will stay on campus most weekends choose the Plus plan.

The column alignment is Justified because of the style set in the document. Generally, cells are aligned left in new tables.

Figure 7.1

Text for first table with the design and layout options for the current document style is shown.

11 Position the insertion point at the left margin in the blank line below the subheading *Meal Plan Fund Allocations*.

12 Click the Insert tab, click the Table button, and then click *Insert Table*.

You can also insert a new table using a dialog box in which you specify the number of columns and rows.

13 At the Insert Table dialog box, with the value in the *Number of columns* text box already set to *5*, press Tab or select the value in the *Number of rows* text box, type 5, and then press Enter or click OK.

14 Type the data in the new table as shown in Figure 7.2. Click in the paragraph below the table after typing the text in the last table cell.

15 Save the document using the same name (**RezMealPlans-YourName**). Leave the document open for the next topic.

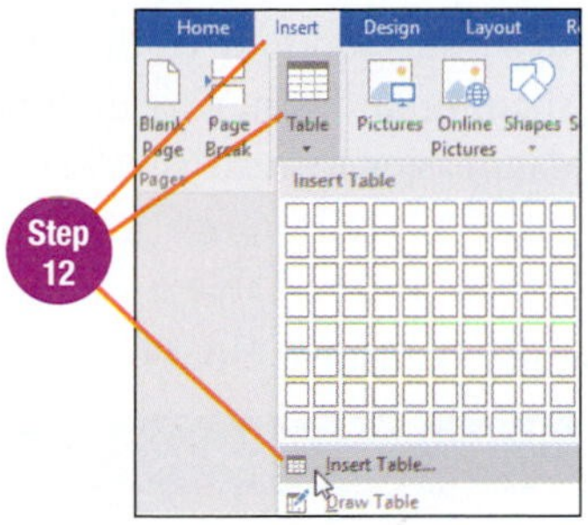

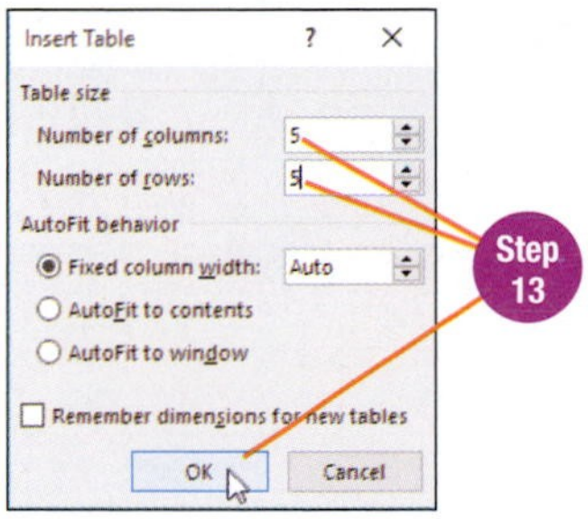

Quick Steps

Insert a Table

1. Click Insert tab.
2. Click Table button.
3. Click square in drop-down grid that represents the desired number of columns and rows.
4. Type table text.

OR

1. Click Insert tab.
2. Click Table button.
3. Click *Insert Table.*
4. Type number of columns.
5. Type number of rows.
6. Click OK.
7. Type table text.

Meal Plan Fund Allocations

Meal Plan Name	Total Cost	Operating Fund	Basic Fund	Flex Fund
Minimum	$2,000	$200	$1,575	$225
Light	$2,200	$200	$1,725	$275
Full	$2,400	$200	$1,775	$425
Plus	$2,600	$200	$1,850	$550

Note that the Basic fund is tax exempt and is designed for use at all on-campus restaurants. Flex fund purchases are taxable.

Click outside the table grid after typing the last table cell entry to avoid adding a new row to the table.

Figure 7.2

Text for second table is shown above.

7.4 Formatting and Modifying a Table

Skills

Apply and customize a table style

Insert and delete rows and columns

Change column width

Change cell alignment

Merge cells

Tutorials

Changing the Table Layout

Changing the Table Design

Customizing Cells in a Table

Once a table has been inserted into the document, use buttons in the Table Tools Design and Layout tabs to format the table and to add or delete rows and columns. Choose from a predesigned collection of formatting options to add borders, shading, and color to a table from the **Table Styles** gallery.

1. With the **RezMealPlans-YourName** document open, position the insertion point in any table cell within the first table.
2. Click the Table Tools Design tab.
3. Click the More button located at the bottom of the scroll bar at the right of the Table Styles gallery.
4. Click *Grid Table 4 – Accent 2* (tenth option in second row in *Grid Tables* section; the location may vary on your screen depending on your screen size and resolution setting).

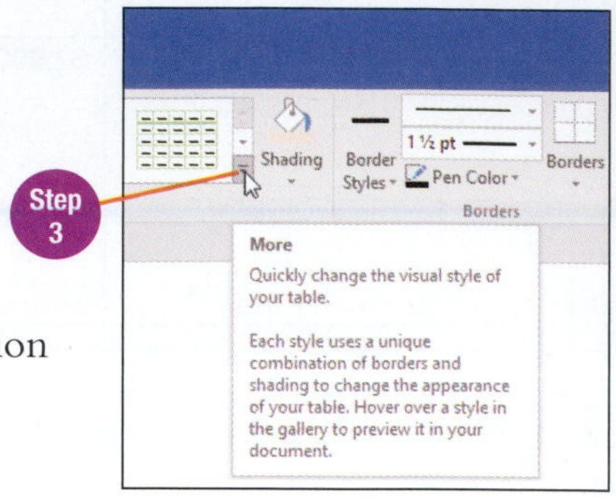

Notice the formatting applied to the column headings and text in the first column. A row with shading and other formatting applied uniformly to every other row to make the data easier to read is referred to as a **banded row**. The border around each cell is now colored orange. The check boxes in the Table Style Options group, the Shading button in the Table Styles group, and the buttons in the Borders group are used to further modify the table formatting.

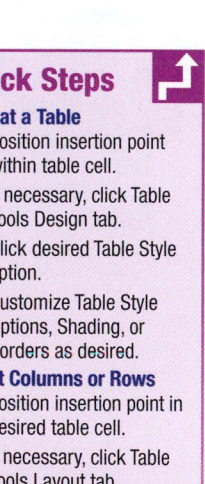

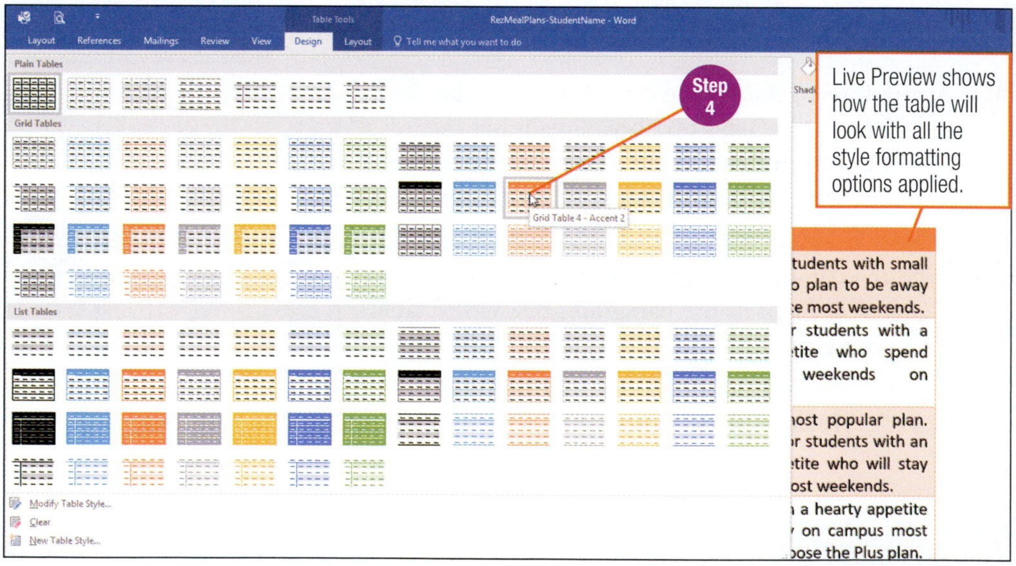

5. Click the *First Column* check box in the Table Style Options group to clear the check mark.

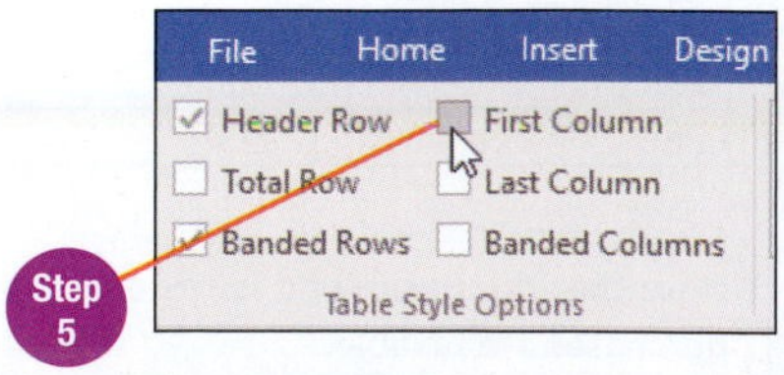

Notice the bold formatting is removed from the text in the first column.

Quick Steps

Format a Table

1. Position insertion point within table cell.
2. If necessary, click Table Tools Design tab.
3. Click desired Table Style option.
4. Customize Table Style Options, Shading, or Borders as desired.

Insert Columns or Rows

1. Position insertion point in desired table cell.
2. If necessary, click Table Tools Layout tab.
3. Click Insert Above, Insert Below, Insert Left, or Insert Right button.

Delete Columns or Rows

1. Position insertion point in desired table cell.
2. If necessary, click Table Tools Layout tab.
3. Click Delete button.
4. Click desired option at drop-down list.

6. Select the column headings in the first row of the table, click the Shading button arrow on the Mini toolbar or in the Table Styles group on the Table Tools Design tab, and then click *Orange, Accent 2, Darker 50%* (sixth option in last row of *Theme Colors* section).

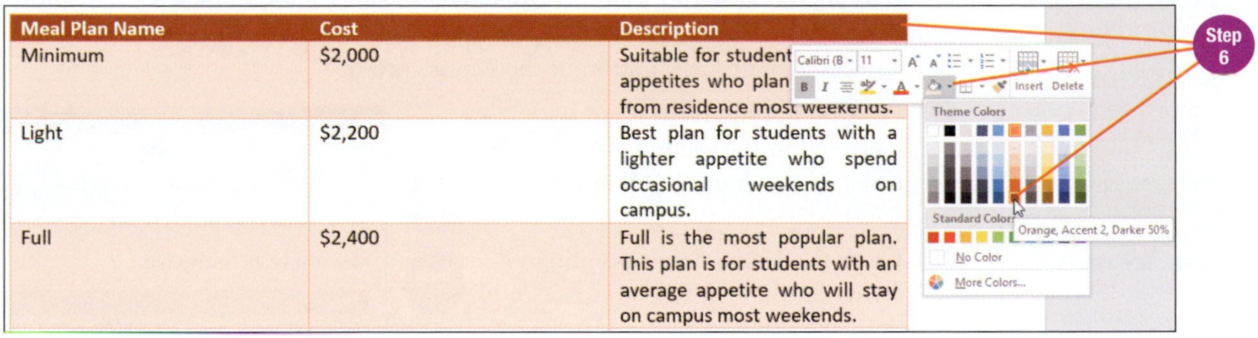

Meal Plan Name
Cost
Description
Minimum
$2,000
Suitable for student appetites who plan from residence most weekends.
Light
$2,200
Best plan for students with a lighter appetite who spend occasional weekends on campus.
Full
$2,400
Full is the most popular plan. This plan is for students with an average appetite who will stay on campus most weekends.
Theme Colors
Standard Colors
Orange, Accent 2, Darker 50%
No Color
More Colors...
Insert
Delete
Step 6

Inserting and Deleting Columns and Rows

Buttons in the Rows & Columns group on the Table Tools Layout tab are used to insert or delete columns or rows. Position the insertion point within a table row and click the Insert Above or Insert Below button to add a new row to the table. The Insert Left and Insert Right buttons are used to add a new column to the table.

Position the insertion point within a table cell, select multiple rows or columns or select the entire table, and then click the Delete button to delete cells, a column, a row, or the table.

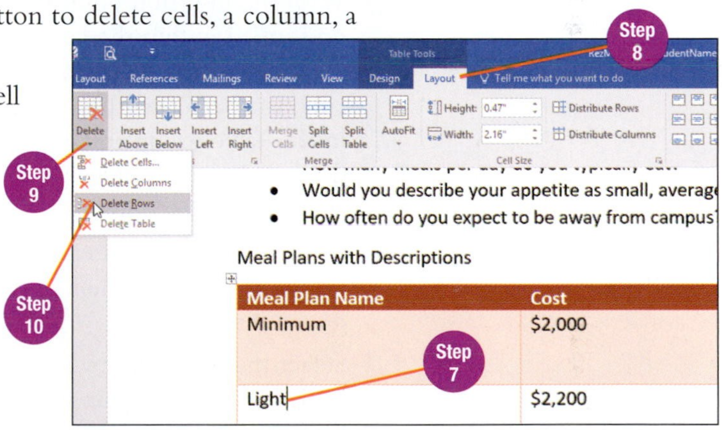

7. Position the insertion point within any table cell in the third row of the first table (begins with *Light*).
8. Click the Table Tools Layout tab.
9. Click the Delete button in the Rows & Columns group.
10. Click *Delete Rows*.
11. Position the insertion point within any table cell in the third row of the second table (begins with *Light*), click the Delete button, and then click *Delete Rows*.
12. Position the insertion point within any table cell in the last column of the first table.
13. Click the Insert Left button in the Rows & Columns group.

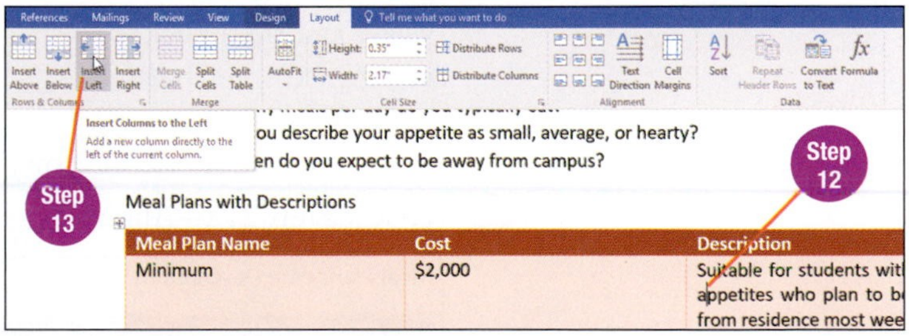

A new column is created between the *Cost* and *Description* columns. Notice that Word adjusts each column to be the same width. New rows are inserted by following a similar process.

14. Position the insertion point within the table cell in the first row of the new column (between *Cost* and *Description*) and then type Daily Spending.
15. Type the values below the column heading in rows 2, 3, and 4 as follows:

    $18.35

    $22.00

    $23.85

Modifying Column Width and Alignment and Merging Cells

Adjust the width of a column by dragging the border line between columns left or right. You can also enter precise width measurements in the *Width* text box in the Cell Size group on the Table Tools Layout tab. Use the buttons in the Alignment group to align text within cells horizontally and vertically. Combine two or more cells into one cell using the Merge Cells button or divide a cell into two or more cells using the Split Cells button in the Merge group.

Quick Steps

Modify Column Width
1. Position insertion point within table cell in desired column.
2. If necessary, click Table Tools Layout tab.
3. Change *Width* measurement value to desired width.

Modify Cell Alignment
1. Select column, row, or table cells.
2. If necessary, click Table Tools Layout tab.
3. Click desired button in Alignment group.

Merge or Split Cells
1. Select column, row, or table cells.
2. If necessary, click Table Tools Layout tab.
3. Click Merge Cells or Split Cells button.

16 Position the insertion point within any table cell in the second column of the first table (column heading is *Cost*).

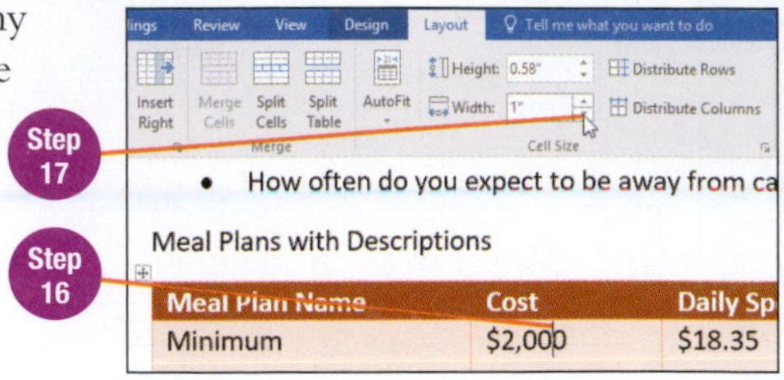

17 Click the *Width* down-pointing arrow in the Cell Size group until the value is *1"*.

18 Position the insertion point within any table cell in the last column of the first table (column heading is *Description*) and then click the *Width* up-pointing arrow until the value is *2.3"*.

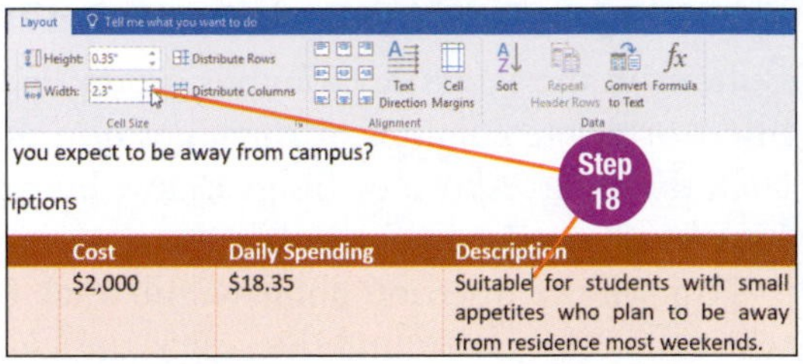

19 With the insertion point still positioned within the last column of the first table, click the Select button in the Table group and then click *Select Column* at the drop-down list.

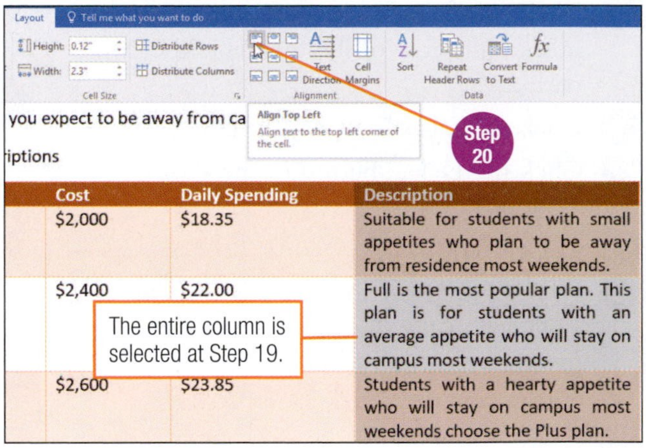

20 Click the Align Top Left button in the Alignment group (first button).

21 Select the first column in the first table (column heading is *Meal Plan Name*) and then click the Align Center button in the Alignment group (second button in second row).

22 Repeat Step 21 to Align Center the second and third columns in the first table.

Meal Plans with Descriptions

Meal Plan Name	Cost	Daily Spending	Description
Minimum	$2,000	$18.35	Suitable for students with small appetites who plan to be away from residence most weekends.
Full	$2,400	$22.00	Full is the most popular plan. This plan is for students with an average appetite who will stay on campus most weekends.
Plus	$2,600	$23.85	Students with a hearty appetite who will stay on campus most weekends choose the Plus plan.

Steps 21-22

23 Position the insertion point within any table cell in the first row of the second table, click the Table Tools Layout tab if necessary, and then click the Insert Above button in the Rows & Columns group.

24 With the new row already selected, click the Merge Cells button in the Merge group.

25 With the new row still selected, type Breakdown of Meal Plan Cost by Fund and then click the Align Top Center button in the Alignment group (second button in first row).

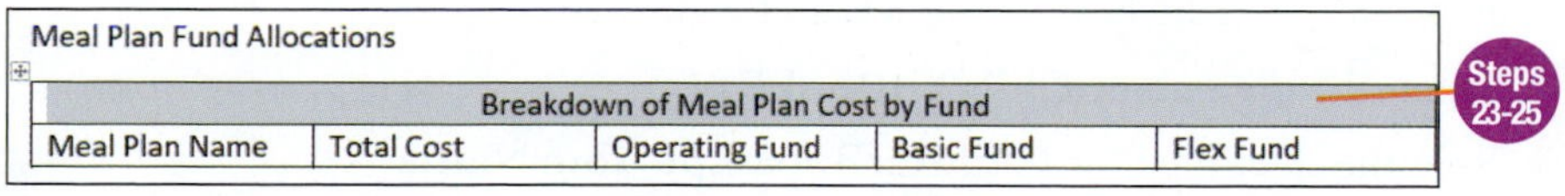
Meal Plan Fund Allocations
Breakdown of Meal Plan Cost by Fund
Meal Plan Name
Total Cost
Operating Fund
Basic Fund
Flex Fund
Steps 23-25

26 Select the column headings and all the values in columns 2, 3, 4, and 5 in the second table and then click the Align Center button.

27 With the insertion point positioned within any table cell in the second table, click the Select button and then click *Select Table.*

28 Click the Table Tools Design tab.

29 Click the Borders button arrow in the Borders group and then click *No Border.*

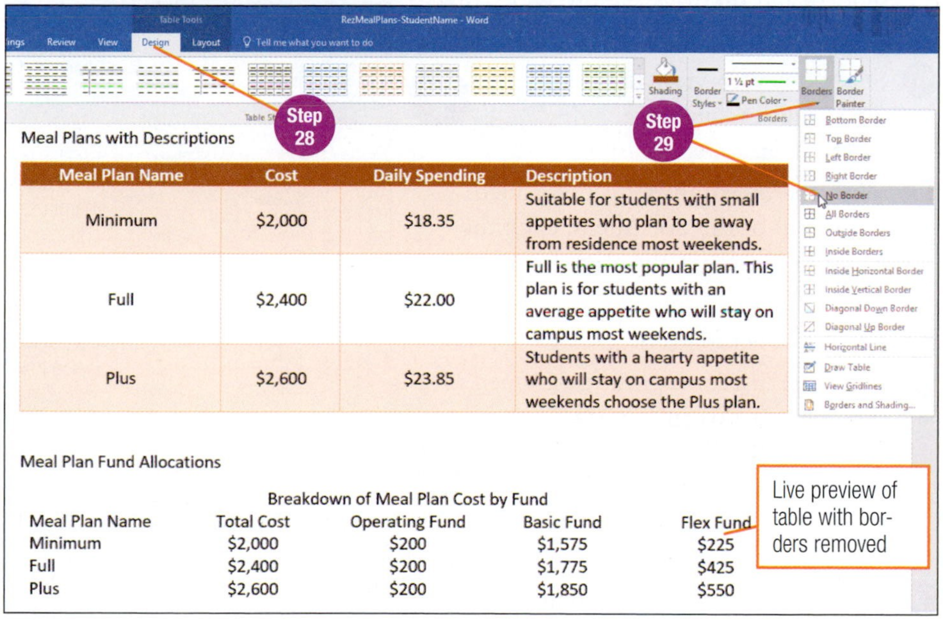

30 Click in the paragraph below the table to deselect the table.

31 Apply the Heading 2 style to the text *Meal Plans with Descriptions* and *Meal Plan Fund Allocations* above the first and second tables.

32 Save the document using the same name (**RezMealPlans-YourName**) and then close the document.

Oops!

Merged row selected too? Select the cells by dragging the mouse—do not use the Select button because *Select Column* will include the merged cell.

App Tip

You can also select the table with a mouse by clicking the Table selection handle at the top left corner of the table.

App Tip

Create a table for any type of columnar text instead of setting tabs—tables are simpler to create and have more formatting options.

Alternative Method: Modifying a Table Using the Shortcut Menu or Mini Toolbar

Right-click within a table cell or with table cells selected to display a context-sensitive shortcut menu and Mini toolbar. Use options from the shortcut menu or Mini toolbar to insert or delete cells, columns, or rows; merge or split cells; change a border style; or modify table properties.

View

Model Answer

Compare your completed file with the model answer.

7.5 Changing Layout Options

Skills

Change page orientation

Change margins

Insert a page break

Tutorials

Changing Page Orientation

Changing Paper Size

Changing Margins

Inserting and Removing a Page Break

Inserting and Deleting a Section Break

By default, new documents in Word are set up for a letter-sized page (8.5 x 11 inches) in portrait orientation with 1-inch margins at the left, right, top, and bottom. **Portrait** orientation means the page is vertically oriented (taller than it is wide). In portrait mode, a page has a standard 6.5-inch line length (8.5 inches minus 2 inches for the left and right margins). This is the orientation commonly used for documents and books. You can change to **landscape** orientation (the page is rotated to make it wider than it is tall). In landscape orientation, the text has a 9-inch line length (11 inches minus 2 inches for the left and right margins).

1. Open the document **ChildLitBookRpt**.
2. Save the document as **ChildLitBookRpt-YourName** in the Ch7 folder in CompletedTopicsByChapter.
3. Click the Layout tab.
4. Click the Orientation button in the Page Setup group and then click *Landscape*.

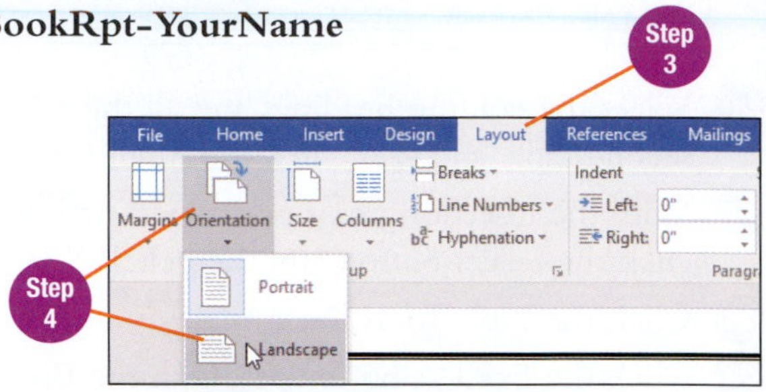

Notice the width of the page is extended, and the page is now wider than it is tall.

5. Scroll down to view the document in landscape orientation.
6. With the insertion point positioned at the top of the document, click the Margins button in the Page Setup group.
7. Click *Custom Margins*.
8. With the insertion point positioned in the *Top* text box in the *Margins* section of the Page Setup dialog box, press Tab twice or select the current value in the *Left* text box and then type 1.2.
9. Press Tab or select the current value in the *Right* text box, type 1.2, and then press Enter or click OK.
10. Scroll down to view the document with the new left and right margin settings.

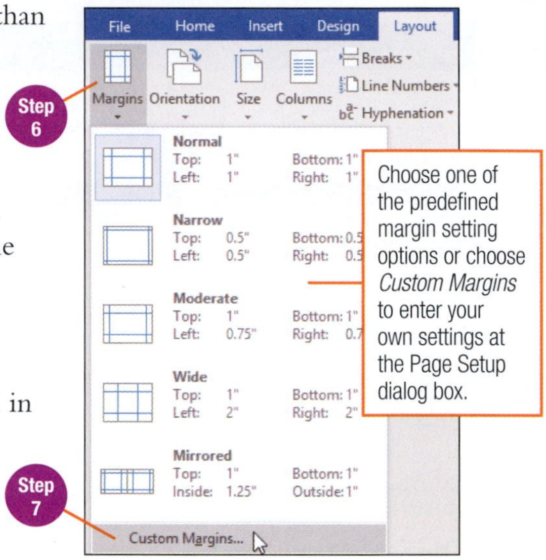

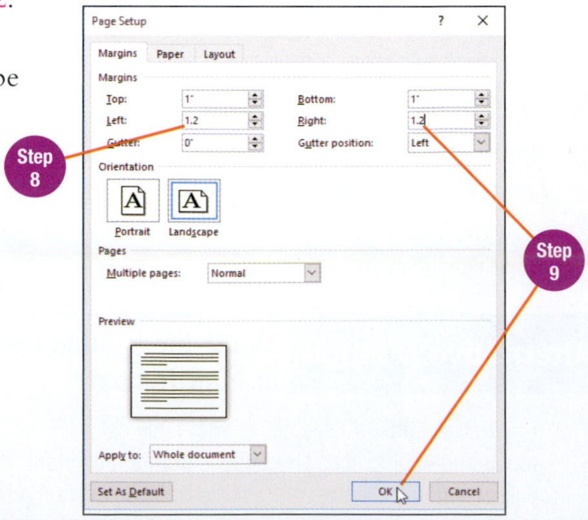

App Tip

Use the Size button in the Page Setup group to change the paper size to legal (8.5 x 14), envelope, or several other predefined photo or index card sizes.

App Tip

The Columns button in the Page Setup group formats a document into two or more newspaper-style columns of text.

Sometimes you want to end a page before the point at which Word ends a page automatically and starts a new page (referred to as a **soft page break**). Soft page breaks occur when the maximum number of lines that can fit within the current page size and margins has been reached. A page break that you insert at a different location is called a **hard page break**.

11 Position the insertion point at the left margin next to the subtitle *The Allegories* near the bottom of page 1.

12 Click the Insert tab.

13 Click the Page Break button in the Pages group.

Notice that all the text from the insertion point onward is moved to page 2.

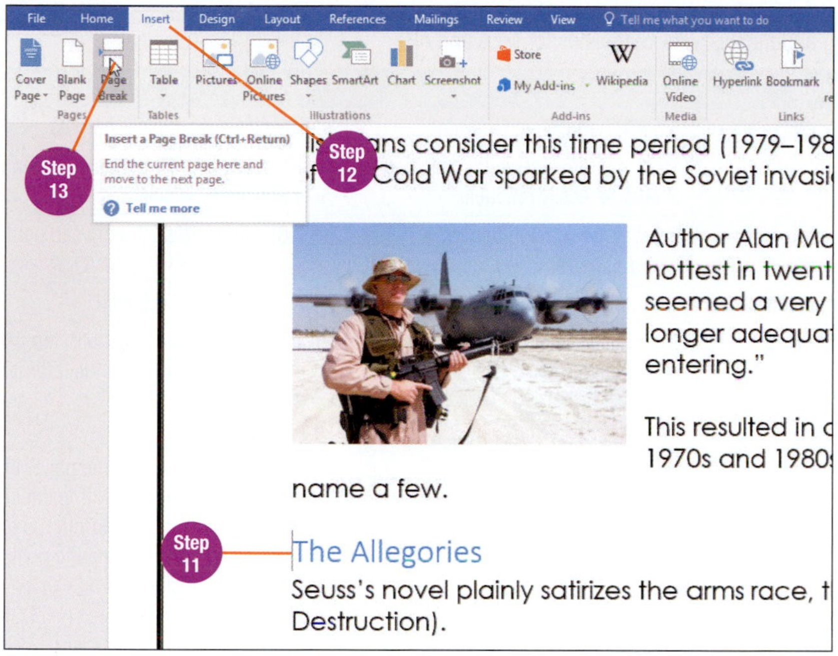

14 Scroll up and down to view the book report with the new page break.

15 Save the document using the same name (**ChildLitBookRpt-YourName**) and then close the document.

Alternative Method: Creating a Page Break Using the Layout Tab or with a Keyboard Shortcut

You can also insert a page break using the Breaks button in the Page Setup group on the Layout tab or by using the keyboard command Ctrl + Enter.

App Tip

Insert hard page breaks as your last step in preparing a document, because hard page breaks do not adjust if you add or delete text.

Oops!

Page break at wrong location? Press Backspace until the page break is deleted or use Undo to remove the page break. Position the insertion point at the correct location and try Step 13 again.

Quick Steps

Change to Landscape Orientation
1. Click Layout tab.
2. Click Orientation button.
3. Click *Landscape*.

Change Margins
1. Click Layout tab.
2. Click Margins button.
3. Click predefined margin option.

OR

1. Click Layout tab.
2. Click Margins button.
3. Click *Custom Margins*.
4. Enter custom measurements.
5. Click OK.

Insert a Hard Page Break
1. Position insertion point.
2. Click Insert tab.
3. Click Page Break button.

View
Model Answer
Compare your completed file with the model answer.

Beyond Basics: Changing Page Layout for a Section of a Document

By default, changes such as margins or orientation affect the entire document. A section break is inserted to change page layout options for a portion of a document. The Breaks button in the Page Setup group on the Layout tab is used to insert a section break. Choose *Next Page* to insert a section break that also starts a new page or choose *Continuous* to have the section break start at the insertion point position without starting a new page. For example, use section breaks if you want one page in a document to be landscape while the other pages are portrait. To do this, insert a section break where you want a landscape page, change the orientation to landscape, then insert another section break after the landscape page and return the orientation to portrait.

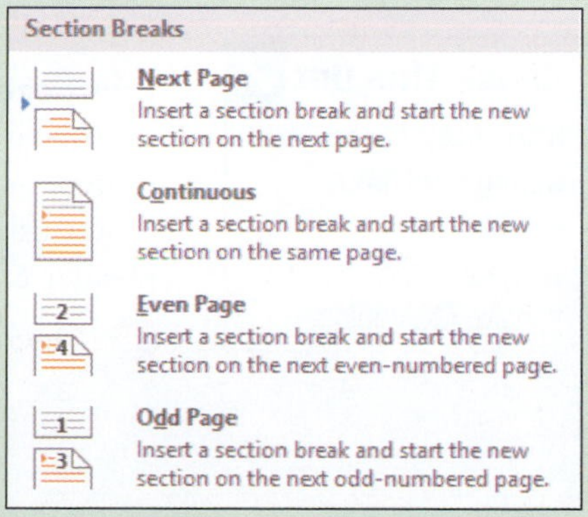

7.6 Adding Text and Page Numbers in a Header for a Research Paper

Skills

Add text in a header

Insert page numbers in a header in MLA style

Tutorials

Inserting and Removing Page Numbers

Inserting and Removing a Predesigned Header and Footer

Editing a Header and Footer

Formatting a Report in MLA Style

Creating a Different First Page Header and Footer

Creating Odd and Even Page Headers and Footers

Formatting a Report in APA Style

During the course of your education, chances are you will have to submit a research paper or essay that is formatted for a specific **style guide** (a set of rules for paper formatting and referencing). Style guides are used in academic and professional writing; MLA (Modern Language Association) and APA (American Psychological Association) are two guides used often. See Table 7.1 for general MLA and APA guidelines. Always check an instructor's assignment instructions in case he or she has requirements that may be in addition to the formatting guidelines in Table 7.1.

Table 7.1

Formatting and Page Layout Guidelines for MLA and APA

Layout Item	MLA	APA
Paper size and margins	8.5 x 11 with 1-inch margins	8.5 x 11 with 1-inch margins
Font size	12-point; typeface is not specified but should be easily readable	12-point, with Times New Roman the preferred typeface
Line and paragraph spacing	2.0 with no spacing between paragraphs	2.0 with no spacing between paragraphs
Paragraph indent	Indent first line 0.5 inch	Indent first line 0.5 inch
Page numbering	Top right of each page one space after your last name	Top right of each page with the title of the paper all uppercase at the left margin on the same line
Title page	No (unless specifically requested by your instructor)	Yes Running Head: title of the paper at the left margin all uppercase with page number at the right margin 1 inch from the top. In the upper half of the page centered horizontally include: Title of the paper Your name School name
First page	Top left corner (double-spaced): Your name Instructor's name Course title Date A double-space below the above headings center the title (title case) and then begin the paper.	Center the word *Abstract* at the top of the page. Type a brief summary of the paper in a single paragraph in block format (no indents). Limit yourself to approximately 150 words. Start paper on a new page after the Abstract with the title of the paper centered (title case) at the top of the page.
Bibliography	Create separate Works Cited page at the end of the document organized alphabetically by author.	Create separate References page at the end of the document organized alphabetically by author.

Check This Out ✓

http://CA2.ParadigmCollege.net/MLAGuide

Go here for a comprehensive MLA guide.

A **header** is text that appears at the top of each page, and a **footer** is text that appears at the bottom of each page. Word provides several predefined headers and footers or you can create your own. Page numbering is added within a header or footer using the **Page Number** button in the Header & Footer group on the Header & Footer Tools Design tab.

1 Open the document **China&TibetEssay**.

2 Save the document as **China&TibetEssay-YourName** in the Ch7 folder in CompletedTopicsByChapter.

3 Scroll down and review the formatting in the essay. Notice the paper size, font, margins, line and paragraph spacing, and first line indents are already formatted.

4 Position the insertion point at the beginning of the document and replace the text *Michael Seguin* with your first and last name.

The first four lines of this report are set up in MLA format for a first page; however, you need to add the page numbering for an MLA report.

5 Click the Insert tab and then click the Header button in the Header & Footer group.

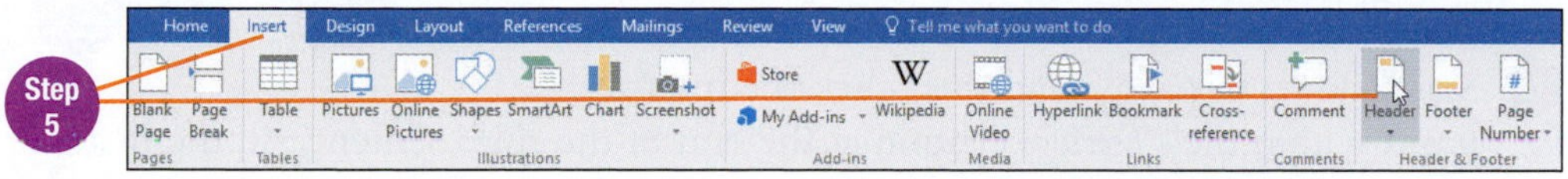

6 Click *Edit Header* at the drop-down list.

7 Press Tab twice to move the insertion point to the right margin, type your last name, and then press the spacebar.

8 Click the Page Number button in the Header & Footer group.

9 Point to *Current Position* and then click *Plain Number*.

10 Select your last name and the page number in the Header pane.

11 Click the *Font* option box arrow on the Mini toolbar, scroll down the font list, and then click *Times New Roman*.

12 Click the *Font Size* option box arrow on the Mini toolbar and then click *12*.

13 Click within the Header pane to deselect the text.

14 Click the Close Header and Footer button in the Close group on the Header & Footer Tools Design tab.

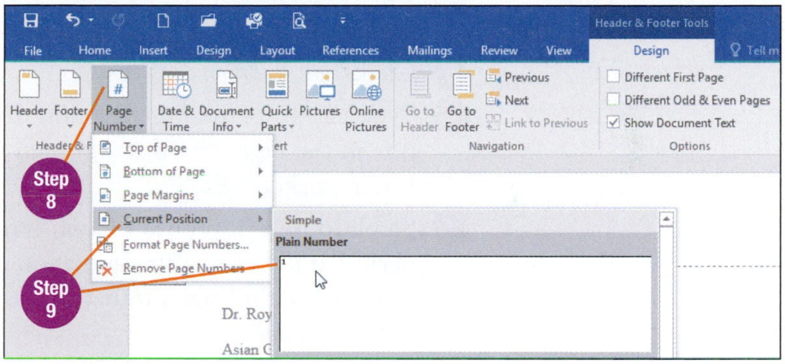

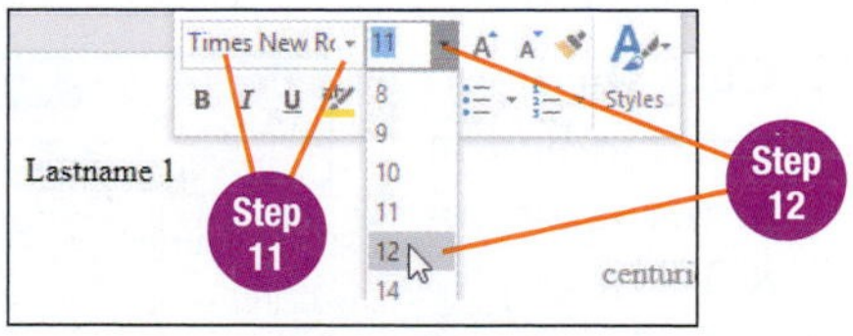

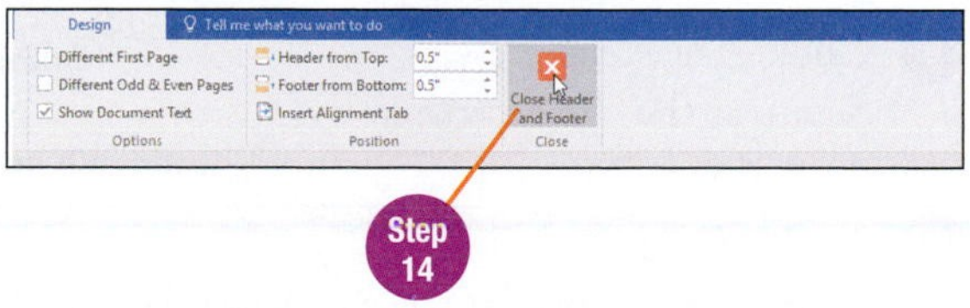

15 Scroll down through the document to view your last name and the page number at the top of each page.

16 Save the document using the same name (**China&TibetEssay-YourName**). Leave the document open for the next topic.

Quick Steps

Insert a Header or Footer

1. Click Insert tab.
2. Click Header or Footer button.
3. Click built-in option or choose *Edit Header* or *Edit Footer*.
4. Type text and/or add options as needed.
5. Click Close Header and Footer button.

Insert Page Numbering

1. Within Header or Footer pane, click Page Number button.
2. Point to *Current Position*.
3. Click desired page number option.
4. Click Close Header and Footer button.

Oops!

Mini toolbar not visible? Click the Home tab and change the font and font size using the buttons in the Font group. Click the Header & Footer Tools Design tab at Step 13.

Check This Out

http://CA2.ParadigmCollege.net/APAGuide

Go here for a comprehensive APA guide.

Beyond Basics — Removing Page Number from First Page

In many reports or books, a header and/or page number is not shown on the first page. Click the *Different First Page* check box on the Header & Footer Tools Design tab to create a First Page header that you can leave blank.

7.7 Inserting and Editing Citations

Skills

Edit a citation

Insert a citation

Tutorials

Inserting Sources and Citations

Editing a Citation and a Source

Direct quotations copied from sources or material you have paraphrased from another source needs to be referenced in a **citation** (source of the information used). Word provides tools to manage sources, insert citations, and edit citations.

1. With the **China&TibetEssay-YourName** document open, click the References tab.

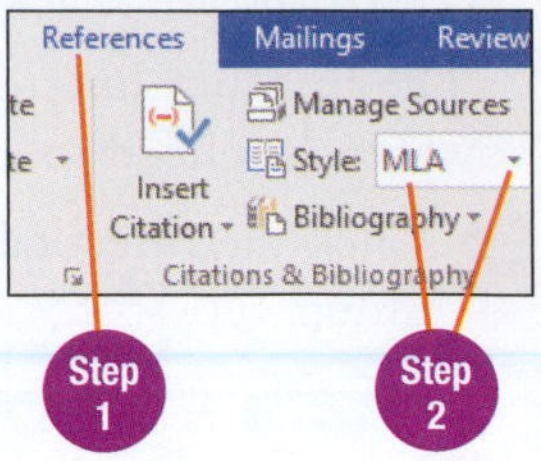

2. Look at the *Style* option in the Citations & Bibliography group. If the *Style* is not *MLA*, click the *Style* option box arrow and then click *MLA*. (You may need to slide or scroll down the list.)

You will begin by editing an existing citation.

3. Scroll down to page 3 and then click the insertion point within the *(Tsering)* citation at the end of the third sentence in the first paragraph (sentence begins with *When delegates disagreed . . .*) to display the citation placeholder.
4. Click the Citation Options arrow that appears.

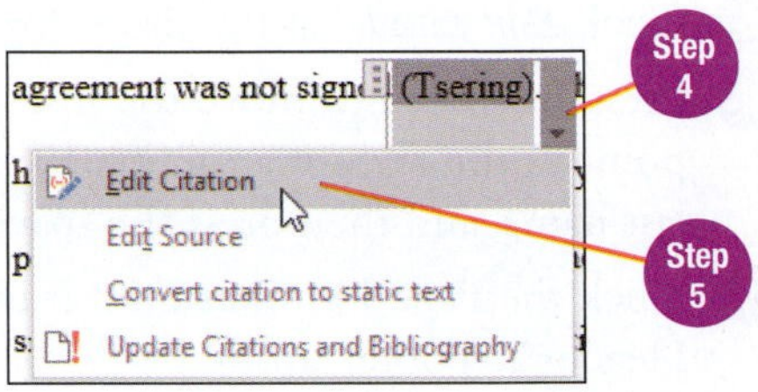

5. Click *Edit Citation*.
6. Type par. 12 at the Edit Citation dialog box in the *Pages* text box and then press Enter or click OK.

7. Scroll to page 1, position the insertion point left of the period at the end of the quotation in the first sentence in the second paragraph that begins *China currently claims . . .* and then press the spacebar.
8. Click the Insert Citation button in the Citations & Bibliography group.
9. Click *Add New Source* at the drop-down list.

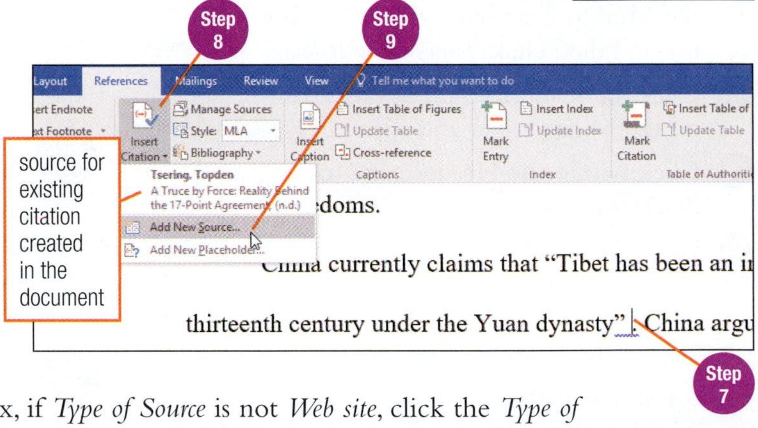

10. At the Create Source dialog box, if *Type of Source* is not *Web site*, click the *Type of Source* list box arrow and then click *Web site*. (You may need to slide or scroll down the list.)
11. Click in the *Author* text box and then type Bajoria, Jayshree.
12. Click in the *Name of Web Page* text box and then type The Question of Tibet.
13. Press Tab or click in the *Year* text box and then type 2008.
14. Continue to press Tab or click in the designated text boxes and then type the information as shown below:

Month	December	*Month Accessed*	November
Day	5	*Day Accessed*	15
Year Accessed	2018	*Medium*	Web

Good to Know

In the seventh edition of the MLA handbook, URLs are no longer required. MLA advises writers to include URLs only if a reader is unlikely to find the source without the web address.

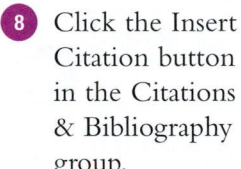

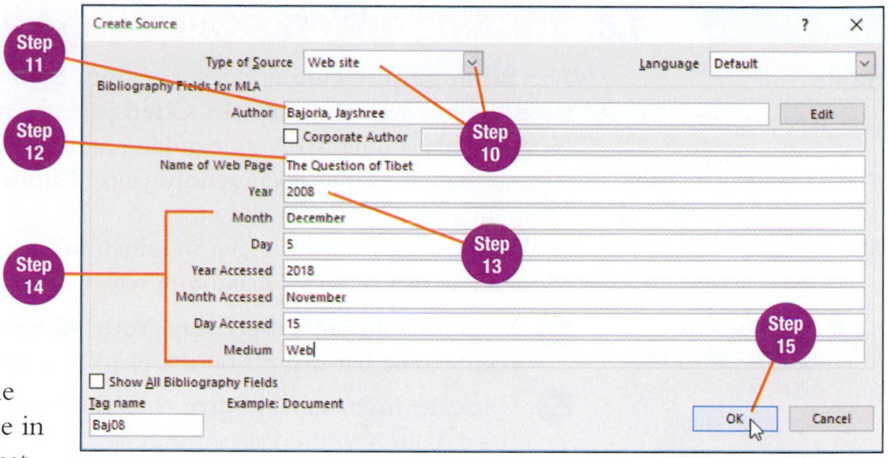

15. Click OK.
16. Click in the *(Bajoria)* citation, click the Citation Options arrow, and then click *Edit Citation*.
17. Type par. 2 in the *Pages* text box at the Edit Citation dialog box and then click OK.
18. Position the insertion point left of the period at the end of the quoted text in the fourth sentence in the second paragraph (sentence that begins *Praag points out. . .*), press the spacebar, click the Insert Citation button, and then click *Add New Source*.
19. Enter the information in the designated text boxes in the Create Source dialog box with the *Type of Source* set to *Web site* as follows.

Author	Praag, Michael C.
Name of Web Page	The Historical Status of Tibet: A Summary
Year	1996
Month	June
Day	26
Year Accessed	2018
Month Accessed	November
Day Accessed	14
Medium	Web

20. Edit the Praag citation to add *par. 18* in the citation by completing steps similar to Steps 16 to 17.
21. Position the insertion point left of the period at the end of the fourth sentence in the second paragraph on page 2 that begins *While independence was* . . . and then press the spacebar.

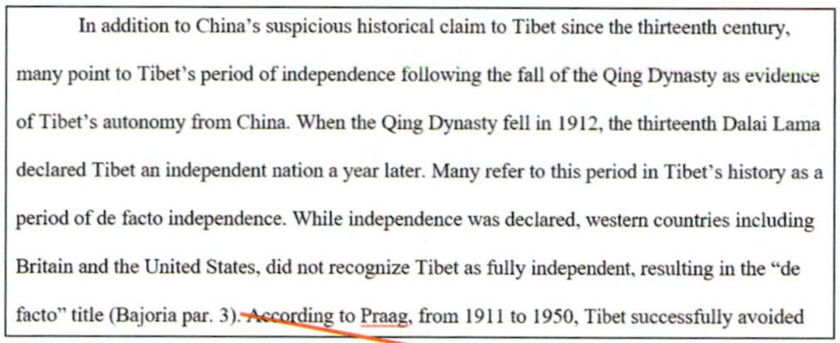
In addition to China's suspicious historical claim to Tibet since the thirteenth century, many point to Tibet's period of independence following the fall of the Qing Dynasty as evidence of Tibet's autonomy from China. When the Qing Dynasty fell in 1912, the thirteenth Dalai Lama declared Tibet an independent nation a year later. Many refer to this period in Tibet's history as a period of de facto independence. While independence was declared, western countries including Britain and the United States, did not recognize Tibet as fully independent, resulting in the "de facto" title (Bajoria par. 3). According to Praag, from 1911 to 1950, Tibet successfully avoided

22. Click the Insert Citation button and then click *Bajoria, Jayshree*.
23. Edit the citation to add *par. 3* in the citation.
24. Save the document using the same name (**China&TibetEssay-YourName**). Leave the document open for the next topic.

Quick Steps

Insert a Citation with a New Source
1. Position insertion point.
2. Click References tab.
3. Click Insert Citation button.
4. Click *Add New Source*.
5. If necessary, change *Type of Source*.
6. Enter required information.
7. Click OK.

Insert a Citation with an Existing Source
1. Position insertion point.
2. Click References tab.
3. Click Insert Citation button.
4. Click required source.

Edit a Citation
1. Position insertion point in citation.
2. Click Citation Options button.
3. Click *Edit Citation*.
4. Type page or other reference.
5. Click OK.

Good to Know

MLA recommends the abbreviations *n. pag.* for a source without page numbers, *n.d.* for a source without a date, and *n.p.* for a source without a publisher.

Beyond Basics — Editing a Source

To change the source information for a citation, position the insertion point within the citation, click the Citation Options arrow, and then click *Edit Source*. This action opens the Edit Source dialog box in which you can make changes to the bibliography fields for the reference.

7.8 Creating a Works Cited Page and Using Word Views

Skills

Insert a page break

Create a Works Cited page

Browse a document in different views

Tutorials

Inserting a Works Cited Page

Managing Sources

Inserting Footnotes and Endnotes

Changing Document Views

The **Bibliography** button in the Citations & Bibliography group on the References tab is used to generate a **Works Cited** page for MLA papers or a References page for APA papers. The MLA style guide requires a Works Cited page to be on a separate page at the end of the document organized alphabetically by author's name or by title when an author's name is absent.

Word provides various views in which to review a document, including Read Mode view that provides maximum screen space for reading longer documents.

1. With the **China&TibetEssay-YourName** document open, move the insertion point to the left margin on the blank line below the last paragraph.
2. Click the Insert tab and then click the Page Break button in the Pages group to start a new page.

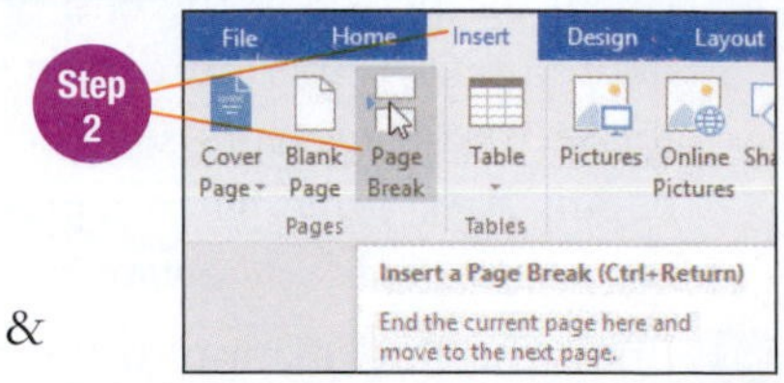

3. Click the References tab.
4. Click the Bibliography button in the Citations & Bibliography group.
5. Click *Works Cited* in the drop-down list.

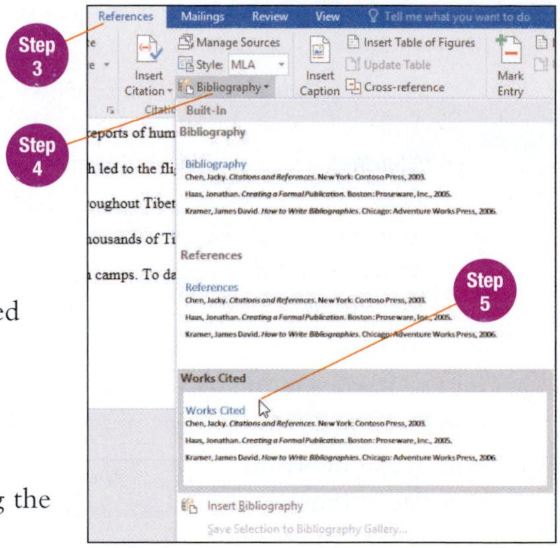

Word automatically generates the Works Cited page. In the next steps, you will format the text to match the font, size, and spacing of the rest of the document.

6. Select all the text in the Works Cited page.

Word surrounds the entire text on the page with a border and displays a Bibliographies button and an Update Citations and Bibliography button along the top of the placeholder.

7. Click the Home tab and then make the following changes to the selected text:
   a. Change the font to 12-point Times New Roman.
   b. Change the line spacing to 2.0.
   c. Open the Paragraph dialog box and change *Before* and *After* in the *Spacing* section to *0 pt*.
8. Select the title text *Works Cited*, change the font color to Automatic (black), and center the title.

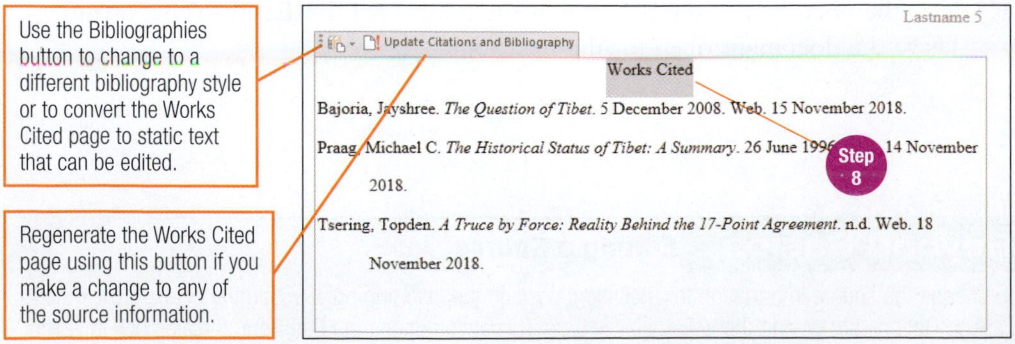

App Tip

Do not change formatting until you are sure your Works Cited page is complete, because the page will revert to predefined formats if you make changes to sources and then update the Works Cited page.

Good to Know

The seventh edition of the MLA guide now requires all entries in a reference list to include the medium in which the reference has been published, such as film, print, or web.

The default view for new documents is **Print Layout view**, which displays the document as it will appear when printed. **Read Mode view** displays a document full screen in columns, allowing you to read longer documents more easily without screen elements such as the Quick Access Toolbar and ribbon. **Draft view** hides print elements, such as headers and footers. **Web Layout view** displays a document as it would appear as a web page, and **Outline view** displays content as bulleted points.

9 Position the insertion point at the beginning of the document.

10 Click the View tab and then click the Read Mode button in the Views group.

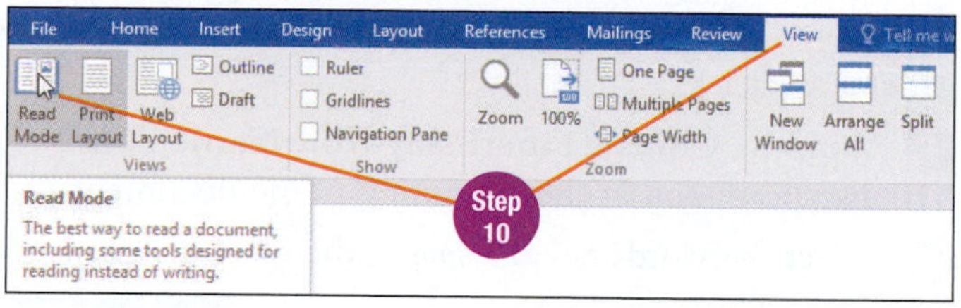

Use Read Mode to view a document without editing.

11 Click the View tab, point to *Layout*, and then click *Paper Layout* to display the document as single pages. Skip this step if your screen is already displaying the document as single pages.

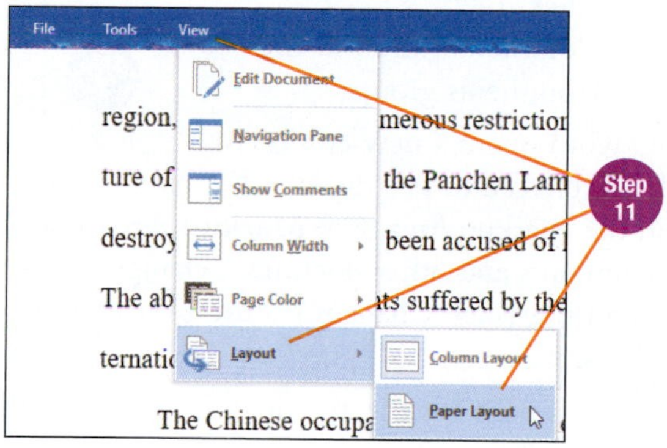

12 Scroll down to the end of the document to view the document in Read Mode, then click the View tab, point to *Layout*, and then click *Column Layout*.

13 Click the Previous Screen button (left-pointing arrow inside circle at the middle right of the screen) to move back to the previous screen until you have returned to the beginning of the document.

14 Click the View tab and then click *Edit Document* to return to Print Layout view.

15 Click the Draft button in the Views group on the View tab to view just the text in the document and then browse the document.

16 Click the Print Layout view button near the right end of the Status bar.

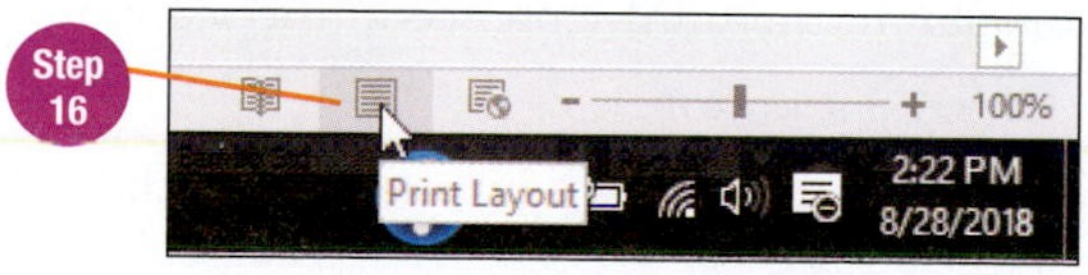

17 Save the document using the same name (**China&TibetEssay-YourName**). Leave the document open for the next topic.

App Tip

The *Welcome back!* balloon appears at the right side of the screen when you reopen a document. Click the balloon to scroll to where you left the document when you closed it.

App Tip

In Print Layout view, turn on the Navigation pane (View tab, Navigation Pane check box in the Show group) and click *Pages* at the top of the pane to move through a document by clicking miniature page thumbnails.

Quick Steps

Generate a Works Cited Page

1. Position insertion point at end of document.
2. Insert page break.
3. Click References tab.
4. Click Bibliography button.
5. Click *Works Cited*.
6. Format as required.

Change Document View

1. Click View tab.
2. Click desired view button.

Beyond Basics — Footnotes and Endnotes

In some academic papers, you need to insert footnotes or endnotes. Footnotes are explanatory comments or source information placed at the bottom of a page. Endnotes are explanatory comments or source information that appear at the end of a section or document. Position the insertion point and use the Insert Footnote or Insert Endnote button on the References tab to add these elements.

7.9 Inserting and Replying to Comments

Skills

Insert comments

Change the markup view

Reply to a comment

Mark a comment done

Tutorials

Inserting Comments

Managing Comments

Tracking Changes in a Document

App Tip

New to Word 2016 is the Real Time Presence feature that lets you see who else is editing a shared document you have open and the changes each person is making in real time.

Comments is a collaborative tool in Word that is useful when working on a document with another person or team. A **comment** is a short note associated with text that provides explanatory information to a reader. A comment can also be used to pose a question to document reviewers. You can reply to a comment made by someone else and mark a comment as done.

When working in teams or on group projects, consider using comments in documents to explain portions of your text, ask questions of your teammates, or add general feedback.

1. With the **China&TibetEssay-YourName** document open, position the insertion point at the beginning of the document.
2. Select the words *Sakya Lama* in the second sentence in the first paragraph.
3. Click the Review tab.
4. Click the New Comment button in the Comments group.

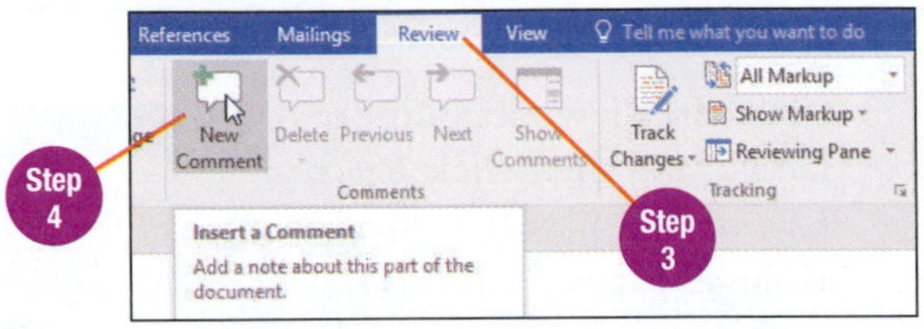

Word opens a new comment box (referred to as a *comment balloon*) in the Markup Area. The **Markup Area** is at the right side of the screen, where comments and other document changes, such as insertions and deletions, are shown when the Track Changes feature is turned on.

5. Type Consider adding more explanation about Sakya Lama and the Yuan dynasty and then click in the document outside the comment box.

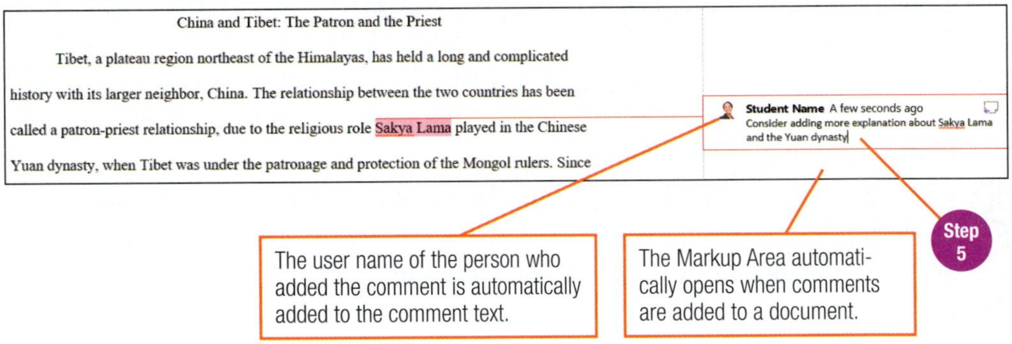

6. Select *modern historians* in the third sentence in the second paragraph.
7. Click the New Comment button.
8. Type Provide a few names of modern historians? and then click in the document.

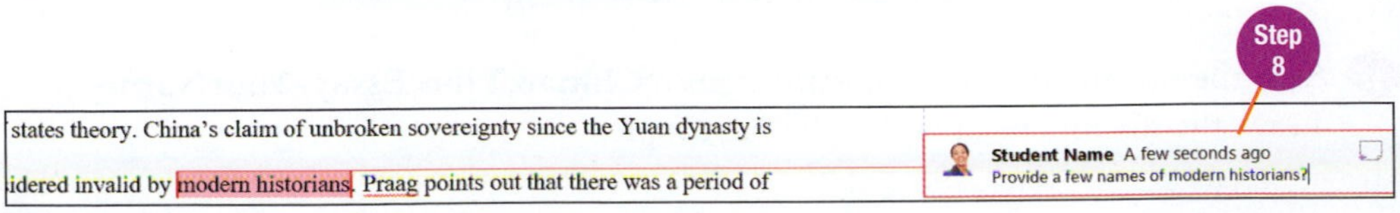

9. Position the insertion point at the beginning of the document.
10. If necessary, click the Review tab.
11. Click the Display for Review button arrow in the Tracking group (currently displays *All Markup* or *Simple Markup*) and then click *No Markup* at the drop-down list.

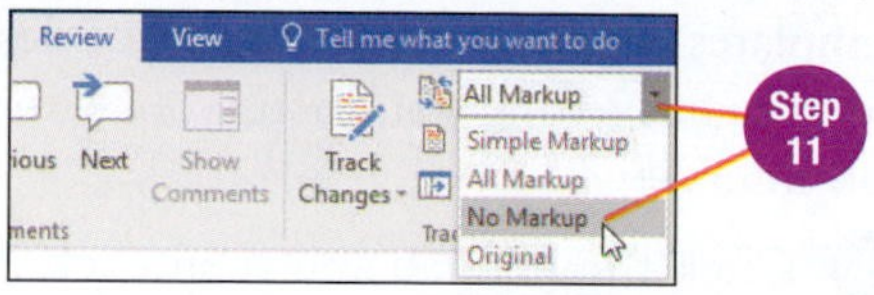

Notice the two comments on page 1 are removed from the document display.

12. Click the Display for Review button arrow and then click *Simple Markup* at the drop-down list.
13. If the Show Comments button in the Comments group is not active, click Show Comments to turn on the display of comment text, then point to the first comment balloon on page 1.

Notice Word shows a callout line pointing to the text with which the comment is associated. The comment box also displays a Reply button.

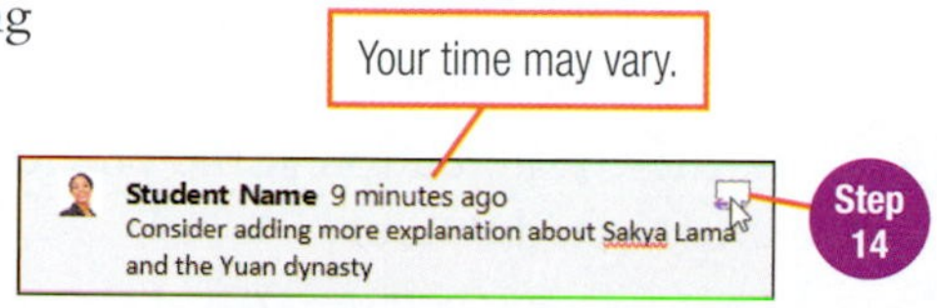

14. Click the Reply button (displays as a small white page with a left-pointing arrow) in the first comment box.
15. Type Asked Dr. Smith and he said this is not necessary and then click in the document.

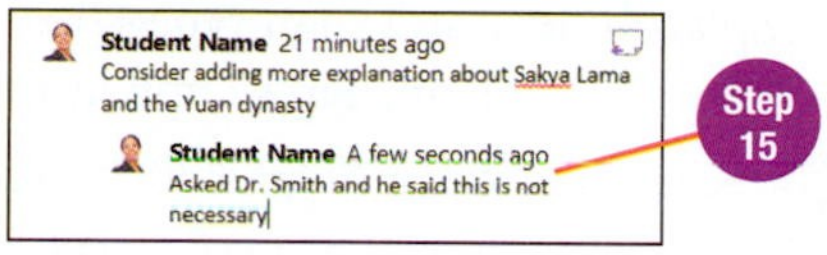

Notice the reply comment text is indented below the original comment in a conversation-style dialogue.

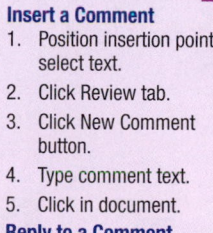

16. Point to the second comment balloon on page 1 and then click the Reply button.
17. Type I'll check with Jose to see if he wants to include a few names.
18. Right-click the first comment balloon on page 1 and then click *Mark Comment Done* at the shortcut menu.
19. Click in the document outside the comment box.

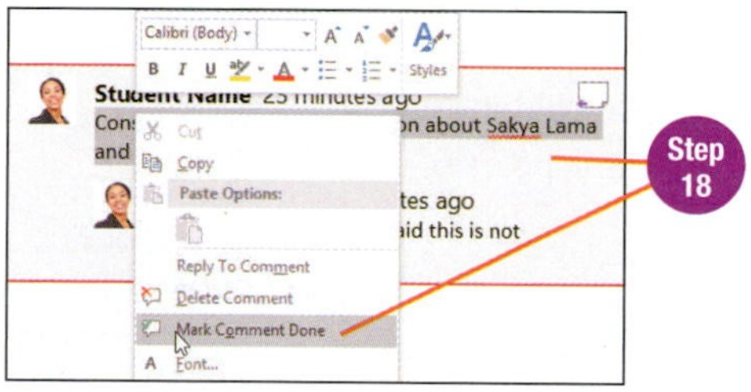

Notice the comment text is dimmed for the comment marked as done. You can also delete a comment instead of marking the comment done.

20. Save the document using the same name (**China&TibetEssay-YourName**) and then close the document.

App Tip

Simple Markup revision view sports a less cluttered look at the changes and comments in a document.

Quick Steps

Insert a Comment
1. Position insertion point or select text.
2. Click Review tab.
3. Click New Comment button.
4. Type comment text.
5. Click in document.

Reply to a Comment
1. Point to comment balloon.
2. Click Reply button.
3. Type reply text.
4. Click in document.

Mark a Comment Done
1. Right-click comment.
2. Click *Mark Comment Done.*

Change Display for Review
1. Click Review tab.
2. Click Display for Review button arrow.
3. Click desired markup view.

View

Model Answer

Compare your completed file with the model answer.

Beyond Basics — Tracking Changes Made to a Document

In situations when a document will be circulated to multiple readers for revisions, turning on track changes is a good idea. Track changes (Review tab) logs each person's insertions, deletions, and formatting changes. Changes can be reviewed, accepted, and rejected in the Revisions pane.

7.10 Creating a Resume and Cover Letter from Templates

Skills

Create a resume

Create a cover letter

> **Check This Out**
>
> **http://CA2.ParadigmCollege.net/CareerAdvice**
>
> Go here for articles and examples on how to write effective resumes and cover letters.

> **Good to Know**
>
> Most recruiters advise job seekers to begin a job search with a reverse chronological resume style which lists your work experience from most to least recent.

> **App Tip**
>
> Print multiple copies of a resume by changing the *Copies* value at the Print backstage area.

> **Oops!**
>
> Having trouble removing spaces in the resume? The resume is formatted as a table. Use the skills you learned in Topic 7.4 to delete table rows to remove space between sections where you deleted template content.

Word provides several professionally designed and formatted resume and cover letter templates that take the work out of designing and formatting these two crucial documents, letting you focus your efforts on writing documents that will win you a job interview!

1. Click the File tab and then click *New*.
2. At the New backstage area, click in the search text box, type entry level resume, and then press Enter or click the Start searching button (displays as a magnifying glass).

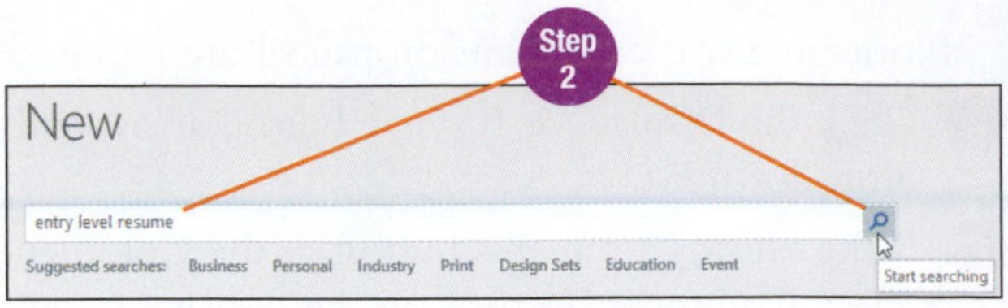

3. Click the thumbnail for *Resume for recent college graduate* in the Templates gallery.

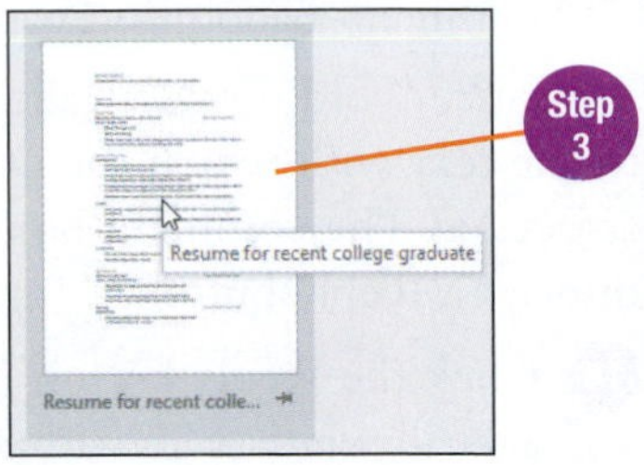

4. Click the Create button at the preview window for the selected resume.
5. Select the text *STUDENT NAME* in the *Author* placeholder and then type Dana Jelic. Note that the text will appear all uppercase.
6. Right-click the *Street Address* placeholder and then click *Remove Content Control* at the shortcut menu.

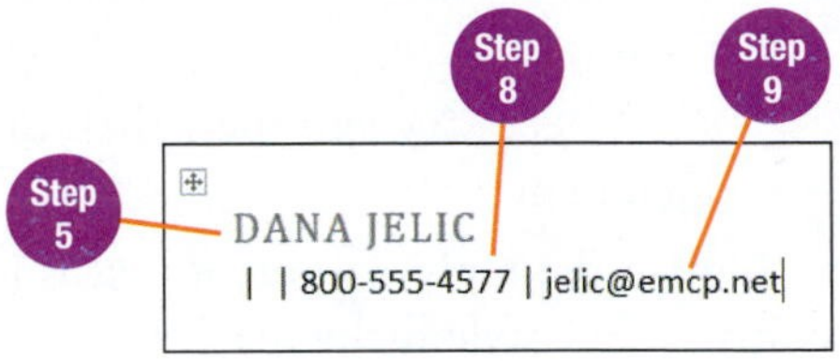

7. Delete the *City, ST ZIP Code* placeholder by completing a step similar to Step 6.
8. Click to select the *Phone Number* placeholder and then type 800-555-4577.
9. Click to select the *E-mail Address* placeholder and then type jelic@emcp.net.
10. Type the remainder of the resume as shown in Figure 7.3 by selecting and editing text in placeholders or by deleting placeholders or text.

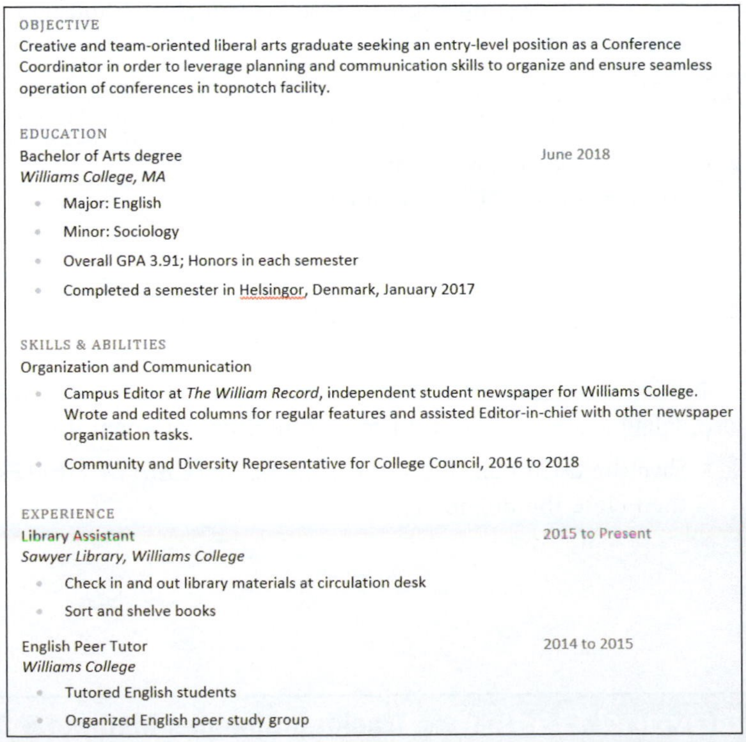

OBJECTIVE

Creative and team-oriented liberal arts graduate seeking an entry-level position as a Conference Coordinator in order to leverage planning and communication skills to organize and ensure seamless operation of conferences in topnotch facility.

EDUCATION

Bachelor of Arts degree — June 2018

Williams College, MA

- Major: English
- Minor: Sociology
- Overall GPA 3.91; Honors in each semester
- Completed a semester in Helsingor, Denmark, January 2017

SKILLS & ABILITIES

Organization and Communication

- Campus Editor at *The William Record*, independent student newspaper for Williams College. Wrote and edited columns for regular features and assisted Editor-in-chief with other newspaper organization tasks.
- Community and Diversity Representative for College Council, 2016 to 2018

EXPERIENCE

Library Assistant — 2015 to Present

Sawyer Library, Williams College

- Check in and out library materials at circulation desk
- Sort and shelve books

English Peer Tutor — 2014 to 2015

Williams College

- Tutored English students
- Organized English peer study group

Figure 7.3

Shown is the resume text for Topic 7.10.

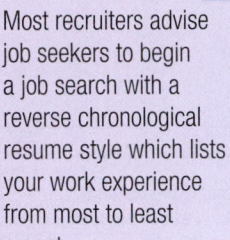

11 Save the document as **JelicResume-YourName** in the Ch7 folder in CompletedTopicsByChapter. Click OK if a message appears about upgrading to the newest file format.

12 Close the resume document and then display the New backstage area.

13 Type cover letter in response to technical position in the search text box and then press Enter or click the Start searching button.

14 Select and create a document using the template *Sample cover letter in response to a technical position advertisement.*

15 Create the letter as shown in Figure 7.4 by selecting and editing text in placeholders, adding more space between text, or by deleting placeholders or text. (Note that the letter closing in the template is not shown in Figure 7.4. Use the default text in this section.)

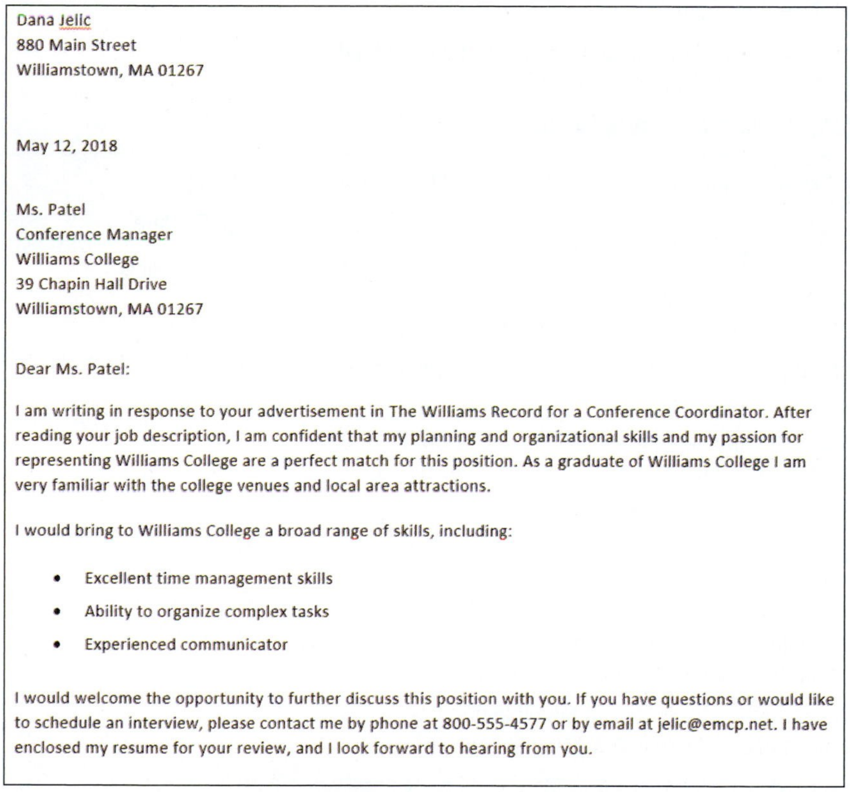
Dana Jelic
880 Main Street
Williamstown, MA 01267

May 12, 2018

Ms. Patel
Conference Manager
Williams College
39 Chapin Hall Drive
Williamstown, MA 01267

Dear Ms. Patel:

I am writing in response to your advertisement in The Williams Record for a Conference Coordinator. After reading your job description, I am confident that my planning and organizational skills and my passion for representing Williams College are a perfect match for this position. As a graduate of Williams College I am very familiar with the college venues and local area attractions.

I would bring to Williams College a broad range of skills, including:

- Excellent time management skills
- Ability to organize complex tasks
- Experienced communicator

I would welcome the opportunity to further discuss this position with you. If you have questions or would like to schedule an interview, please contact me by phone at 800-555-4577 or by email at jelic@emcp.net. I have enclosed my resume for your review, and I look forward to hearing from you.

Figure 7.4

Use this cover letter text for Topic 7.10.

16 Click the Layout tab and then click the Page Setup dialog box launcher.

17 If necessary, click the Layout tab in the Page Setup dialog box.

18 Click the *Vertical alignment* list box arrow, click *Center* at the drop-down list, and then click OK.

19 Save the document as **JelicCoverLetter-YourName** in the Ch7 folder in CompletedTopicsByChapter and then close the document.

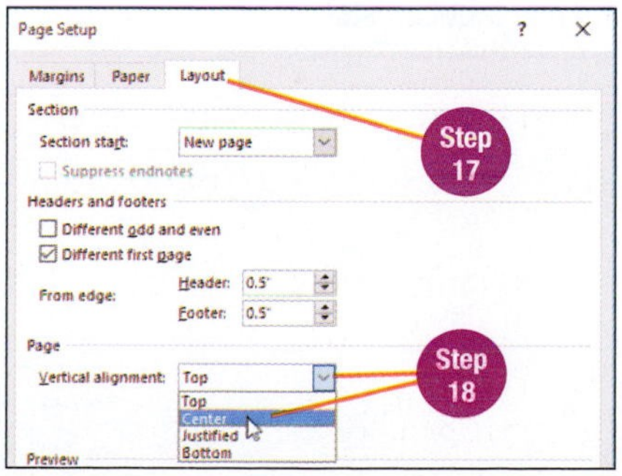

App Tip

Use the Envelopes or Labels button in the Create group on the Mailings tab to generate an envelope or label for a letter.

Quick Steps

Create a Resume

1. Click File tab.
2. Click *New.*
3. Type entry in the search text box and press Enter.
4. Click desired template.
5. Click Create button.
6. Edit as required.

Create a Cover Letter

1. Click File tab.
2. Click *New.*
3. Type entry in the search text box and press Enter.
4. Click desired template.
5. Click Create button.
6. Edit as required.

App Tip

Vertically center a letter to make sure the letter has a professional appearance. For short letters, add extra space between letter elements to balance the content on the page.

View

Model Answer

Compare your completed file with the model answer.

Topics Review

Topic	Key Concepts	Key Terms
7.1 Inserting, Editing, and Labeling Pictures in a Document	Graphic elements assist with comprehension and/or add visual appeal to documents. Insert a picture from a web resource or an online service, such as Flickr, Facebook, or OneDrive, using the Online Pictures button in the Illustrations group on the Insert tab. Buttons in the Layout Options gallery are used to control how text wraps around the picture and the position of the picture on the page. The Pictures button on the Insert tab is used to insert pictures from image files stored on your computer. Edit the appearance of an image and/or add special effects using buttons on the Picture Tools Format tab. A caption is explanatory text above or below a picture that is added using the Insert Caption button on the References tab. Word automatically numbers pictures as Figures.	Online Pictures Layout Options Pictures Insert Caption
7.2 Adding Borders and Shading, and Inserting a Text Box	Add a border or shading to paragraphs to make text stand out on a page. Shading is color applied to the page behind the text. Apply a border to selected text using the Borders gallery from the Borders button arrow in the Paragraph group on the Home tab. Add shading using the Shading button arrow in the Paragraph group on the Home tab. A page border surrounds the entire page and is added from the Page Borders button in the Page Background group on the Design tab. A pull quote is a quote placed inside a text box. Insert text inside a box using the Text Box button in the Text group on the Insert tab.	shading Page Borders Borders gallery pull quote Text Box
7.3 Inserting a Table	A table is a grid of columns and rows in which you type text and is used when you want to arrange text side by side or in rows. A table cell is a rectangular-shaped box in the table grid that is the intersection of a column and a row into which you type text. Create a table by clicking a square in a drop-down grid or by entering the number of columns and rows in the Insert Table dialog box. Pressing Tab in the last table cell automatically adds a new row to the table. A Quick Table is a predesigned table with sample data, such as calendars and tabular lists.	table cell Quick Table

continued…

Topic	Key Concepts	Key Terms
7.4 Formatting and Modifying a Table	Apply a predesigned collection of borders, shading, and color to a table using an option from the Table Styles gallery. Shading or other formatting applied to every other row to make the table data easier to read is called a *banded row*. Check boxes in the Table Style Options group are used to customize the formatting applied from a Table Styles option. Apply shading or borders using buttons in the Table Styles and Borders group on the Table Tools Design tab. New rows and columns are inserted above, below, left, or right of the active table cell using buttons in the Rows & Columns group on the Table Tools Layout tab. Remove selected table cells, rows, or columns or the entire table using options from the Delete button in the Rows & Columns group. Adjust the width of a column by changing the *Width* text box value in the Cell Size group on the Table Tools Layout tab or by dragging the column border. Buttons to change alignment options for selected table cells are found in the Alignment group on the Table Tools Layout tab. Cells in a table can be merged or split using buttons in the Merge group on the Table Tools Layout tab.	Table Styles banded row
7.5 Changing Layout Options	Portrait orientation means the text on the page is oriented to the taller side (8.5-inch width), while landscape orientation rotates the text to the wider side of the page (11-inch measurement becomes the page width). Change the margins by choosing one of the predefined margin options or by entering measurements for the top, bottom, left, and right margins at the Page Setup dialog box. A soft page break is a page break that Word inserts automatically when the maximum number of lines that can fit on a page has been reached. A hard page break is a page break inserted by you in a different location than where the soft page break occurred. A section break is inserted from the Breaks button in the Page Setup group on the Layout tab and is used to format a portion of a document with different page layout options.	portrait landscape soft page break hard page break
7.6 Adding Text and Page Numbers in a Header for a Research Paper	A style guide is a set of rules for formatting and referencing academic papers. A header is text that appears at the top of each page, while a footer is text that appears at the bottom of each page. Click the Insert tab and choose the Header or Footer button to create a header or footer in the Header or Footer pane. Page numbers are added to a document at the top or bottom of a page within a Header or Footer pane using the Page Number button on the Header & Footer Tools Design tab.	style guide header footer Page Number

continued...

Topic	Key Concepts	Key Terms
7.7 Inserting and Editing Citations	A citation provides a reader with the reference for information quoted or paraphrased within an academic paper. Position the insertion point where a citation is needed and use the Insert Citation button on the References tab to create a reference. Click *Add New Source* at the Insert Citation drop-down list to enter information for a new reference for a citation. Edit a citation to add a page number or paragraph number to the reference.	citation
7.8 Creating a Works Cited Page and Using Word Views	A Works Cited page is a separate page at the end of the document with the references used for the paper. Use the Bibliography button in the Citations & Bibliography group on the References tab to generate a Works Cited page formatted for the MLA style guide. Print Layout view displays the document as it will appear when printed. Read Mode view displays a document full screen in columns or pages without editing tools. Draft view hides print elements, such as headers, footers, and page numbering. Web Layout view displays the document as a web page. Outline view displays content as bullet points. Footnotes are sources or explanatory comments placed at the bottom of a page, while endnotes are sources or explanatory comments placed at the end of a section or document in an academic paper.	Bibliography Works Cited Print Layout view Read Mode view Draft view Web Layout view Outline view
7.9 Inserting and Replying to Comments	A comment is a short note associated with text that provides explanatory information or poses a question to a reader. Select text that you want to associate with a comment and type the comment text inside a comment balloon by clicking the New Comment button on the Review tab. Comment balloons display in the Markup Area, which is a pane that opens at the right side of the document when comments are added. A document with comments can be shown with *No Markup*, *Simple Markup*, or *All Markup*, which refers to the way comment boxes are displayed. Point at a comment balloon and use the Reply button to enter reply text that responds to a comment. Mark a comment as done to retain the comment text but display the comment dimmed in the Markup Area.	comment Markup Area
7.10 Creating a Resume and Cover Letter from Templates	At the New backstage area, search for a resume template and a cover letter template in various styles, themes, and purposes. Personalize a resume and cover letter by adding content and deleting content controls not needed using the placeholders in a resume or cover letter template.	

Recheck

Recheck your understanding of the topics covered in this chapter.

Workbook

Chapter review and assessment resources are available in the *Workbook* ebook.

Chapter 8

Creating, Editing, and Formatting Excel Worksheets

Precheck
Check your understanding of the topics covered in this chapter.

Microsoft Excel (referred to as *Excel*) is a **spreadsheet application** used to create, process, and present information that is organized in a grid of columns and rows. In Excel, data can be calculated, analyzed, and graphed in a chart. The ability to do "what-if" analysis is a popular feature of the application; in this type of analysis, one or more values are changed to view the effect on other values. Excel is used for budget, income, expense, investment, loan, schedule, grading, attendance, inventory, and research data. Any information that can be set up in a grid-like structure is suited to Excel.

A file that you save in Excel is called a **workbook**. A workbook contains a collection of worksheets; a **worksheet** is the structure into which you enter, edit, and manipulate data. Think of a workbook as a binder and a worksheet as a page within the binder. Initially, a workbook has only one worksheet (page), but you can add more as needed.

Many of the features that you learned about in Word operate the same or similarly in Excel, which will make learning Excel faster and easier. You will begin by creating new worksheets in a blank workbook and then open other worksheets to practice navigating, editing, sorting, and formatting tasks.

Note: *If you are using a tablet, consider connecting it to a USB or wireless keyboard because parts of this chapter involve a fair amount of typing.*

SNAP If you are a SNAP user, go to your SNAP Assignments page to complete the Precheck, Tutorials, and Recheck.

Data Files
Before beginning this chapter, be sure you have copied the student data files for this course to your storage medium. Steps on downloading and extracting the data files are provided in Chapter 1, Topic 1.8, on pages 22–23.

Learning Objectives

8.1 Create and edit a new worksheet

8.2 Format cells with font, number, border, and merge and center options

8.3 Adjust column width and row height, and change cell alignment

8.4 Use the Fill feature to enter and copy data, and use AutoSum to add a column or row of values

8.5 Insert and delete rows and columns

8.6 Sort data and apply cell styles

8.7 Change page orientation, scale a worksheet, and display formulas in cells

8.8 Insert and rename a worksheet, copy cells, and indent data within a cell

8.9 Use Go To to move to a cell, freeze panes, apply shading options, and wrap text and rotate cell entries

8.1 Creating and Editing a New Worksheet

Skills

Open a new blank workbook

Enter text and values

Create formulas

Edit cells

Tutorials

Opening a Blank Workbook

Entering Data

Changing the Zoom

Entering Formulas Using the Keyboard

Entering Formulas Using the Mouse

Editing Data

Clearing Cell Contents and Formatting

Checking Spelling

Determining the Order of Operations

When you start a new blank workbook, you begin at a worksheet, which is divided into columns and rows. The intersection of a column and a row is called a **cell**, and in each cell you can type text, a value, or a formula. The cell with the green border is called the **active cell**. The active cell is the location in which the next entry you type is stored. The active cell is also the cell affected by the next command (action) you perform. Each cell is identified with the letter of the column and the number of the row that intersect to form the cell. For example, A1 refers to the cell in column A, row 1. A new workbook starts with one worksheet labeled *Sheet1* that has columns labeled A to Z, AA to AZ, BA to BZ, and so on to the last column, which is labeled XFD. Rows are numbered 1, 2, 3, up to 1,048,576.

Creating a New Worksheet

Begin a new worksheet by entering titles, column headings, and row headings to give the worksheet an organizational layout and provide context for the reader. Next, enter values in the columns and rows. Complete the worksheet by inserting formulas that perform calculations or otherwise summarize data.

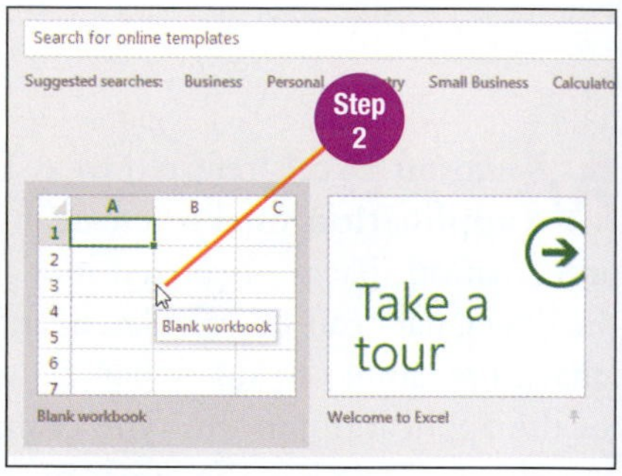

1. Start Excel 2016.
2. At the Excel Start screen, click *Blank workbook* in the Templates gallery. Compare your screen with the one shown in Figure 8.1, and read the descriptions of screen elements in Table 8.1 on page 187.

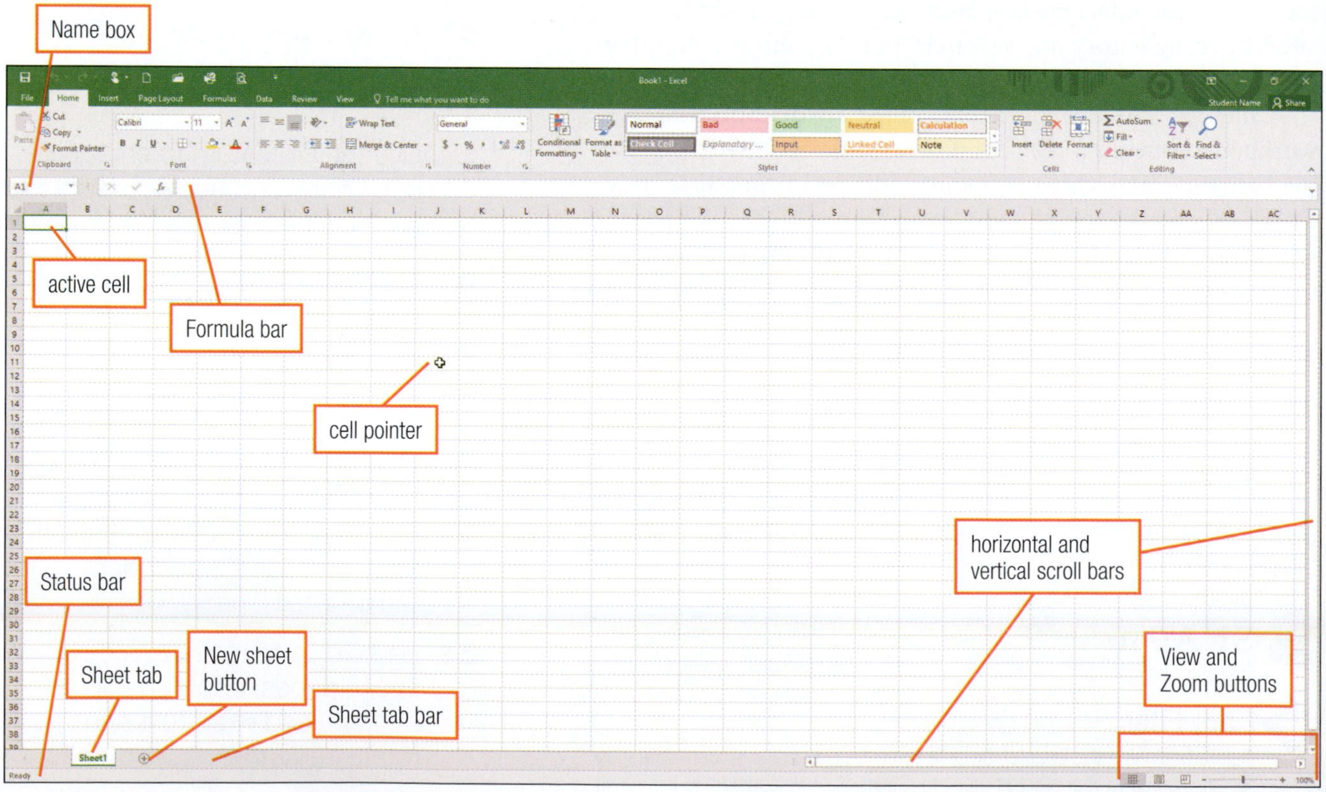

Figure 8.1

A new blank worksheet in Excel is shown here. The worksheet area below the ribbon is divided into columns and rows, creating cells into which data and formulas are typed and stored.

Table 8.1

Excel Features

Feature	Description
Active cell	Location in which the next typed data will be stored and that will be affected by the next command. Make a cell active by clicking it or by moving to it using the Arrow keys.
Cell pointer	Icon that displays when you are able to select cells with the mouse by clicking or dragging. On a touch device with no mouse attached, tap a cell to display selection handles (round circles) at the top left and bottom right corners.
Formula bar	Bar that displays contents stored in the active cell and is also used to create formulas.
Horizontal and vertical scroll bars	Tools used to view parts of a worksheet not shown in the current viewing area.
Name box	Box that displays the address or name of the active cell.
New Sheet button	Button on the Sheet tab bar used to insert a new worksheet.
Sheet tab	Tab that displays the name of the active worksheet. By default, new sheets are named Sheet# where # is the number of the sheet in the workbook.
Sheet tab bar	Bar that displays sheet tabs and is used to navigate between worksheets.
Status bar	Bar that displays messages indicating the current mode of operation; Ready indicates the worksheet is ready to accept new data.
View and Zoom buttons	Buttons used to change the appearance of the worksheet. Excel opens in Normal view. Other view buttons include Page Layout and Page Break Preview. Zoom buttons are used to enlarge or shrink the display.

Entering Text and Values

When you start a new worksheet, the active cell is A1 at the top left corner of the worksheet. Entries are created by activating a cell and typing text, a value, or a formula.

3 With A1 the active cell, type Car Purchase Cost and then press Enter or click A2 to make A2 the active cell.

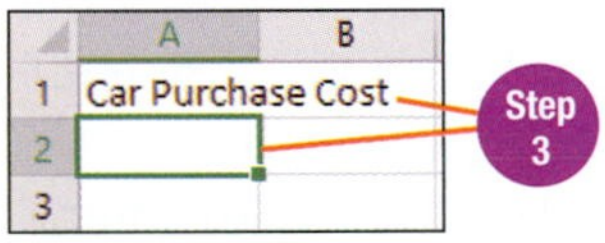

4 Type Preowned Ford Focus Sedan and then press Enter twice or click A4.

5 Type Total Purchase Price and then click A6.

6 Type Loan Details: and then click B7.

7 Type the remaining row headings by moving the active cell and typing the text shown in the image at right.

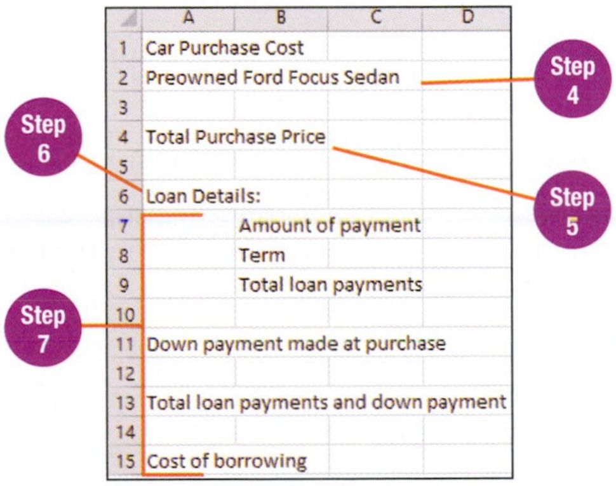

8 Click F4, type 16700.00, and then click E7.

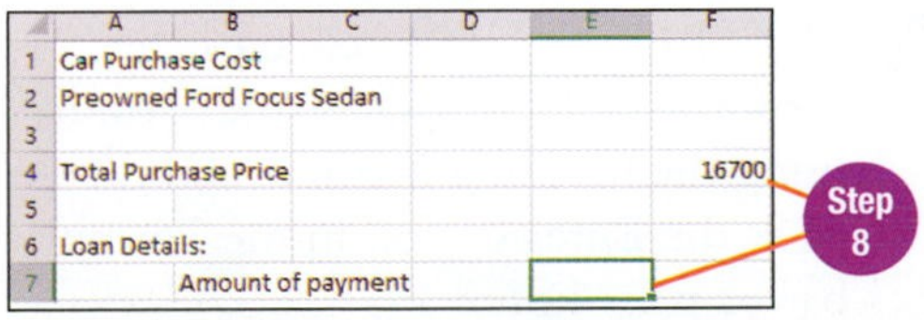

Zeros to the right of a decimal are not stored or shown. You will learn how to format a cell to show the decimal place values in Topic 8.2.

App Tip

You can use Arrow keys to move up, down, left, or right from cell to cell.

App Tip

Excel's AutoComplete matches an entry in the same column with the first few characters that you type. Accept an AutoComplete entry by pressing Tab, Enter, or an Arrow key, or continue typing to ignore the suggestion.

App Tip

By default, text entries align at the left edge of a cell and numeric entries are right aligned.

9 Type the remaining values by activating the cell and typing the numbers shown below.

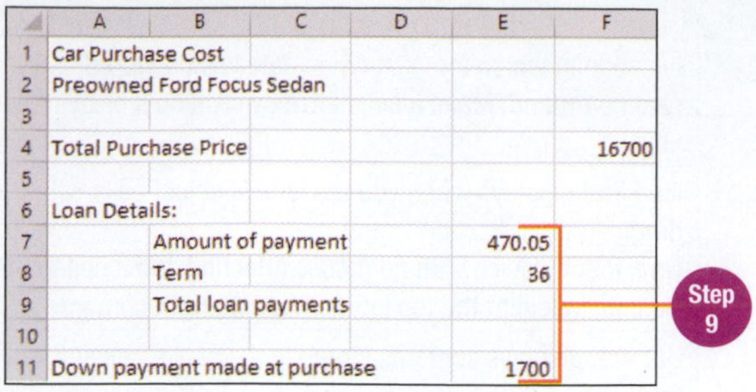

Car Purchase Cost
Preowned Ford Focus Sedan
Total Purchase Price 16700
Loan Details:
Amount of payment 470.05
Term 36
Total loan payments
Down payment made at purchase 1700
Step 9

Creating Formulas to Perform Calculations

A **formula** is used to perform mathematical operations on values. A formula entry begins with the equals sign (=) to indicate to Excel the entry that follows is a calculation. Following the equals sign, type the first cell address that contains a value you want to use, type a mathematical operator, and then type the second cell address. Continue typing mathematical operators and cell addresses until finished. The mathematical operators are + (addition), - (subtraction), * (multiplication), / (division), and ^ (exponentiation).

10 Click E9 to make it the active cell and then type =e7*e8.

11 Click the Enter button in the Formula bar.

Excel calculates the result and displays the value in E9. Notice that the cell in the worksheet area displays the formula result, while the Formula bar displays the formula used to calculate the result. Notice also that Excel capitalizes column letters in cell addresses within formulas.

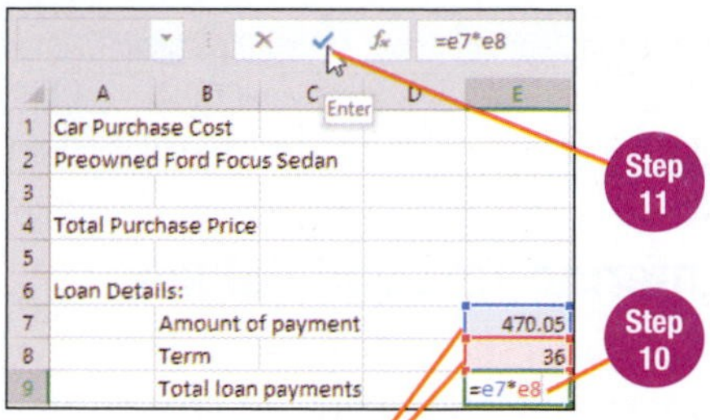

Color references make it easy to check which values are part of the formula or to help find errors.

Another way to enter a formula is to use the pointing method, in which you click the desired cells instead of typing their cell addresses.

12 Make F13 the active cell and then type =.

13 Click E9.

A moving dashed border surrounds E9, the cell is color coded, and the address *E9* is inserted in both cell F13 and the Formula bar.

14 Type +.

15 Click E11 and then click the Enter button in the Formula bar or press Enter.

16 Make F15 the active cell, type the formula =f13-f4 or enter the formula using the pointing method, and then click the Enter button in the Formula bar or press Enter.

The result, *1921.8*, displays in the cell.

Oops!

Clicked the wrong cell? Just click the correct cell—the cell reference is not fixed in the formula until you type an operator. You can also press the Esc key to start over.

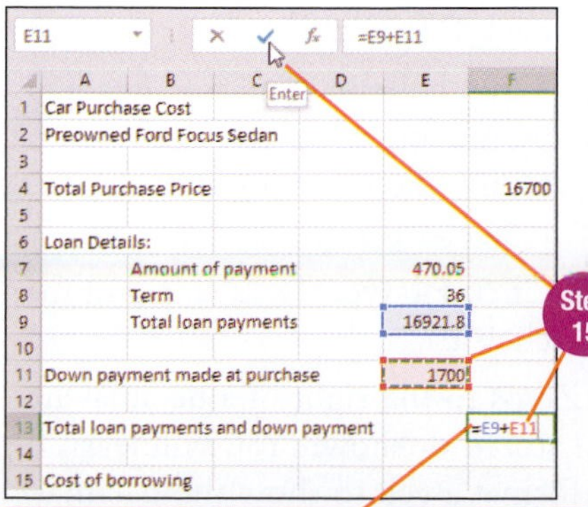

The formula created in Steps 12 to 15 by typing the equals sign (Step 12), clicking cells (Steps 13 and 15), and typing the operator (Step 14).

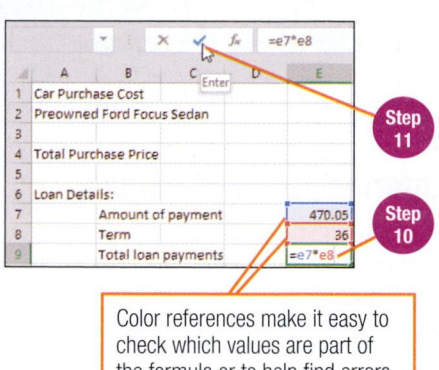

Editing Cells

An entire cell entry can be changed by making the cell active and typing a new entry to replace the existing contents. Double-click a cell to open it for editing in the worksheet area; this will allow you to change the entry rather than replace it. You can also edit a cell's contents by making the cell active and then inserting or deleting characters or spaces in the Formula bar.

To delete the contents of an active cell, press the Delete key or click the **Clear button** in the Editing group on the Home tab and then click *Clear All* at the drop-down list.

17 Make E7 the active cell, type 480.95, and then press Enter.

Notice that the new payment amount causes the values in E9, F13, and F15 to update.

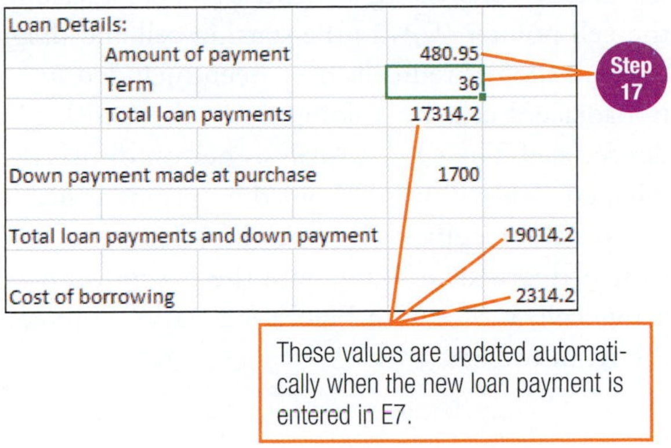

18 Double-click F4, position the insertion point between *6* and *7*, press Backspace to remove *6*, type 5, and then click any other cell.

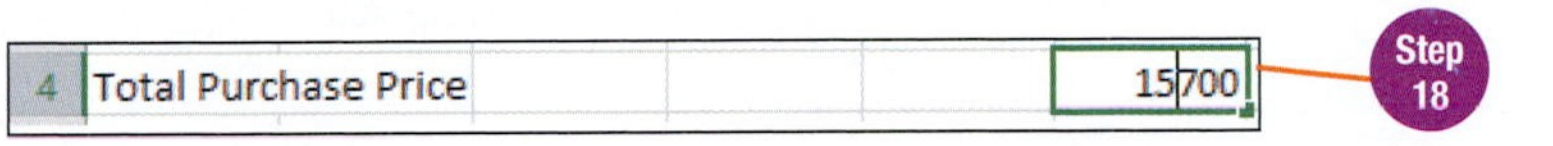

19 Make E11 the active cell, click in the Formula bar, position the insertion point between *1* and *7*, press Backspace to remove *1*, and then click any other cell.

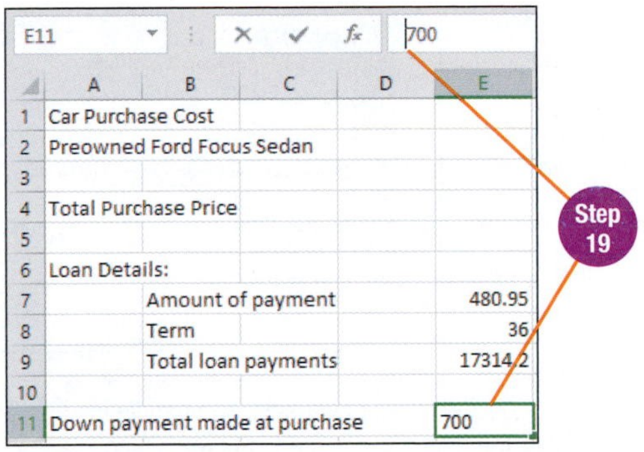

20 Save the new workbook as **CarCost-YourName** in a new folder named *Ch8* in the CompletedTopicsByChapter folder on your storage medium. Leave the workbook open for the next topic.

Quick Steps

Enter a Formula

1. Activate formula cell.
2. Type =.
3. Type first cell address.
4. Type operator symbol.
5. Type next cell address.
6. Continue Steps 4–5 until finished.
7. Press Enter.

Edit a Cell

1. Double-click cell.
2. Position insertion point.
3. Insert or delete characters or spaces as needed.
4. Press Enter.

App Tip

F2 is the keyboard command to edit a cell.

App Tip

AutoCorrect operates in Excel; however, red wavy lines do *not* appear below misspelled words. Consider using the Spelling feature in the Proofing group on the Review tab to spell check all worksheets.

Beyond Basics — Order of Operations in Formulas

If you combine operations in a formula, Excel will automatically calculate exponentiation, multiplication, and division before addition and subtraction. You can tell Excel to perform a particular operation first by using parentheses around that part of the formula. For example, in the formula *=(A1+A2)*A3*, Excel adds the values in A1 and A2 first and then multiplies the result by the value in A3.

8.2 Formatting Cells

Skills

- Select cells
- Change the font
- Apply bold formatting
- Format values
- Add borders
- Merge cells

Tutorials

- Selecting Cells
- Merging and Centering Cells
- Applying Font Formatting
- Adding Borders to Cells
- Applying Number Formatting
- Applying Formatting Using the Format Cells Dialog Box

Much like the Home tab in Word, the Home tab in Excel contains the formatting options for changing the appearance of text, values, or formula results. The Font group contains buttons to change the font, font size, and font color, and to apply bold, italic, underline, borders, and shading. The Alignment group contains buttons to align text or values within the cell edges.

Selecting Cells and Applying Font Formatting

To select cells using a mouse: Select adjacent cells with a mouse by positioning the cell pointer (✚) in the starting cell and dragging in the required direction until all the desired cells have been included in a shaded selection rectangle. Select nonadjacent cells by holding down the Ctrl key while you click the mouse in each desired cell. The Quick Analysis button displays when a group of cells has been selected. You will learn about the options available from this button in Chapter 9.

To select cells using touch: Selecting cells on a touch device in Excel is similar to selecting text in Word, with the exception that two selection handles display in the active cell, as shown in Figure 8.2. As in Word, tap inside the selection area to display the Mini toolbar.

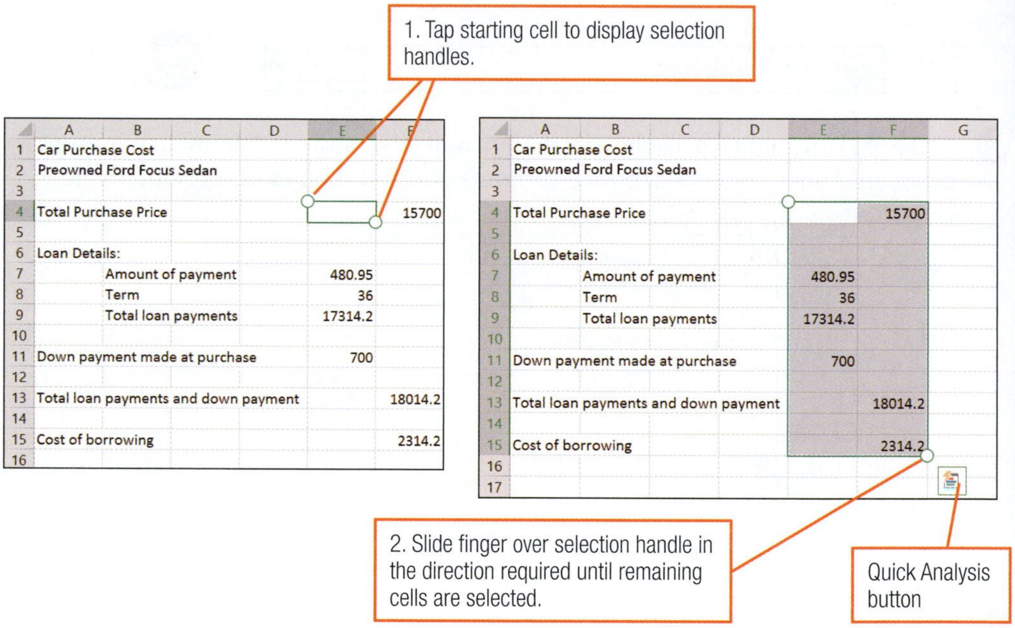

Figure 8.2

Selecting cells on a touch device is not much different from selecting cells using a mouse.

App Tip

Select cells using the keyboard by holding down the Shift key while you press an Arrow key (Up, Down, Left, or Right).

1 With the **CarCost-YourName** workbook open, starting at cell A1, select all the cells down and right to F15.

A rectangular-shaped group of cells is referred to as a **range**. A range is referenced with the address of the cell at the top left corner, a colon (:), and the address of the cell at the bottom right corner. For example, the reference for the range selected in Step 1 is *A1:F15*.

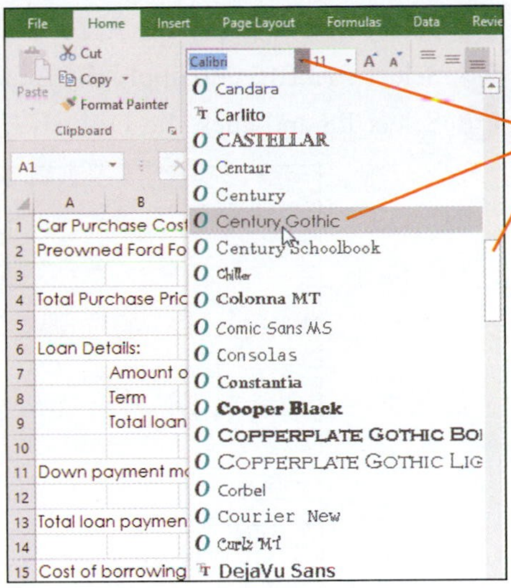

2 Click the Font list box arrow in the Font group on the Home tab, scroll down the gallery, and then click *Century Gothic*.

3 Click any cell to deselect the range.

4 Select A1:A2 and then click the Bold button in the Font group.

Notice the entire text in A1 and A2 is bold, including the characters that spill over the edge of column A into columns B, C, and D. This is because the entire text entry is stored in the cell that was active when the text was typed. Overflow text that displays in adjacent columns is not problematic when the adjacent columns are empty. You will learn how to widen a column to fit overflow text in the next topic.

5 Select cell F15 and then click the Bold button.

Formatting Numbers

By default, cells in a new worksheet are all in the General format, which has no specific appearance options. Buttons in the Number group on the Home tab are used to format the appearance of numeric entries in a worksheet. Add a dollar symbol, insert commas to indicate thousands, and/or adjust the number of decimal places to improve the appearance of values. Use the Percent Style format to convert decimal values to percentages and include the percent symbol.

Use the *Number Format* option box arrow (next to *General*) to choose other formats for dates, times, fractions, or scientific values, or to open the Format Cells dialog box from the *More Number Formats* option.

6 Select E4:F15.

7 Click the Comma Style button in the Number group.

Comma Style formats values with a comma in thousands and two decimal places.

8 Select F4 and then click the Accounting Number Format button in the Number group. (Do not click the down-pointing arrow on the button.)

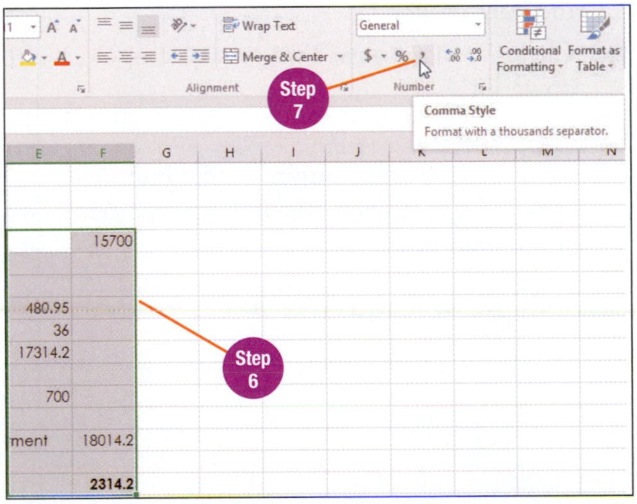

Accounting Number Format adds a currency symbol ($ for the United States and Canada), commas to indicate thousands, and two decimal places. Use the Accounting Number Format button arrow to choose a format that uses a currency symbol other than the dollar symbol (such as €, which stands for Euro).

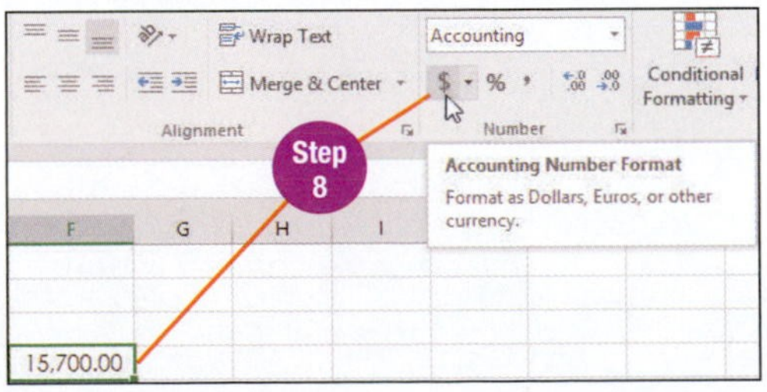

App Tip

Excel automatically widens columns as needed when you apply a format that adds more characters to a column, such as Comma Style.

App Tip

Accounting Number Format aligns the currency symbol at the left edge of the cell. The *Currency* option (in the Number Format drop-down list) places the currency symbol immediately to the left of the value. Use Accounting Number Format if you want all dollar symbols to align at the same position.

9 Select E7 and apply the Accounting Number Format.

10 Select F13:F15 and apply the Accounting Number Format.

11 Select E8 and click the Decrease Decimal button twice.

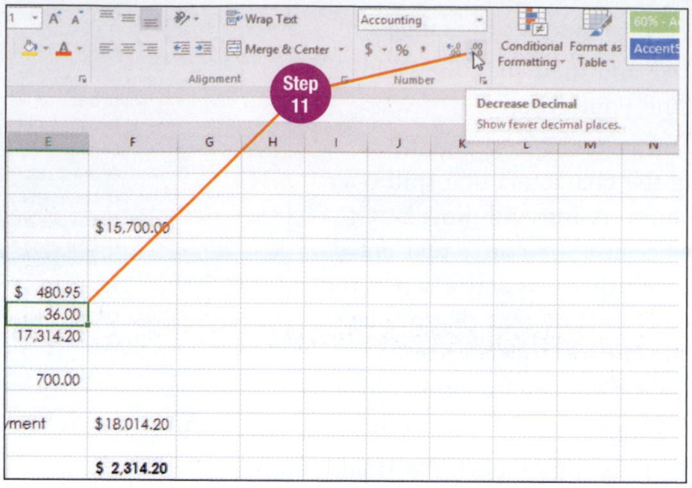

Oops!

Apply the wrong format to a cell or range? Use the Undo command, or simply apply the correct format to the cell or range.

One decimal place is removed from the active cell or range each time you click the **Decrease Decimal button**. Click the **Increase Decimal button** to add one decimal place.

Adding Borders

Borders in various styles and colors can be added to the top, left, bottom, or right edge of a cell. Borders are used to underscore column headings or totals, or to otherwise emphasize cells.

12 Select F13.

13 Click the Bottom Border button arrow in the Font group.

14 Click *Top and Bottom Border* at the drop-down list.

15 Select F15.

16 Click the Top and Bottom Border button arrow and then click *Bottom Double Border* at the drop-down list.

17 Click any other cell to view the border style applied to F15.

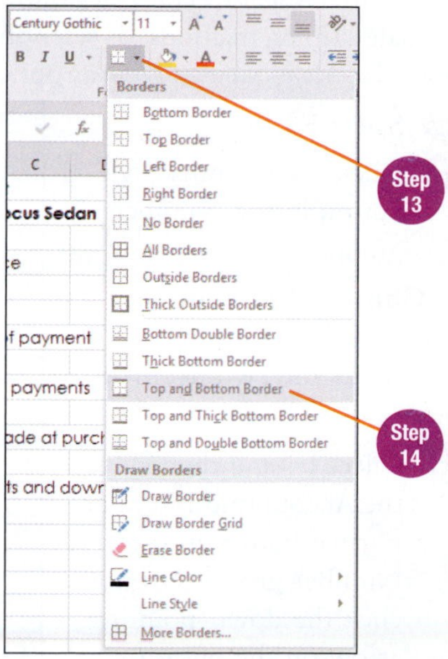

App Tip

The Borders button updates to the most recently selected border style so that you can apply the same border to another cell or range by simply clicking the button (not the arrow).

Merging and Centering Cells

A worksheet title is often centered across the columns used in the worksheet. The **Merge & Center button** in the Alignment group is used to combine a group of cells into one large cell and center its contents. Use the Merge & Center button arrow to merge without centering, or to unmerge a merged cell.

18 Select A1:F1.

19 Click the Merge & Center button in the Alignment group.

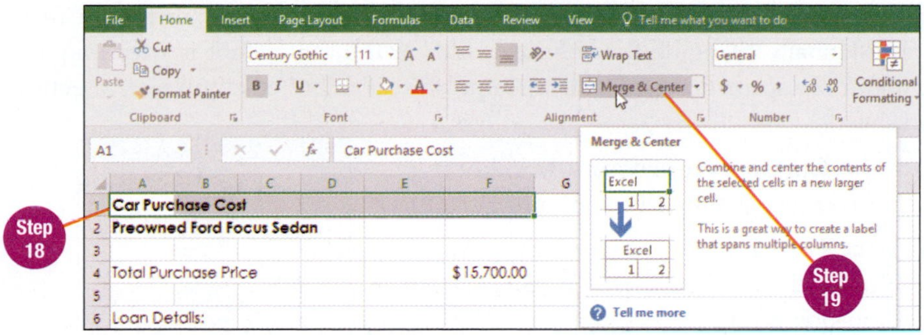

20 Select A2:F2 and then click the Merge & Center button.

21 Save the workbook using the same name (**CarCost-YourName**). Leave the workbook open for the next topic.

Quick Steps

Change a Font
1. Select cell(s).
2. Click Font list box arrow.
3. Click desired font.

Change Number Format
1. Select cell(s).
2. Click *Number Format* option box arrow, Accounting Number Format button, Percent Style button, or Comma Style button.
3. Click format option if needed.

Adjust Decimal Places
1. Select cell(s).
2. Click Increase Decimal or Decrease Decimal button.

Add Borders
1. Select cell(s).
2. Click Borders button arrow.
3. Click border style.

Merge Cells
1. Select cells.
2. Click Merge & Center button.

Alternative Method — Formatting with the Mini Toolbar or Keyboard Shortcuts

Consider applying formatting with the Mini toolbar, which you display by right-clicking inside selection area. Alternatively, you can use these keyboard shortcuts:

Ctrl + B	Apply bold formatting
Ctrl + I	Apply italic formatting
Ctrl + 1 (one)	Open the Format Cells dialog box
Ctrl + Shift + $	Apply US currency formatting
Ctrl + Shift + %	Apply percent style formatting

Beyond Basics — Format Cells Dialog Box

Click the dialog box launcher located at the bottom right of the Font, Alignment, or Number group to open the Format Cells dialog box. Use the dialog box to apply multiple formats in one operation, to further customize format options, or to apply font effect options *Strikethrough*, *Superscript*, and *Subscript*.

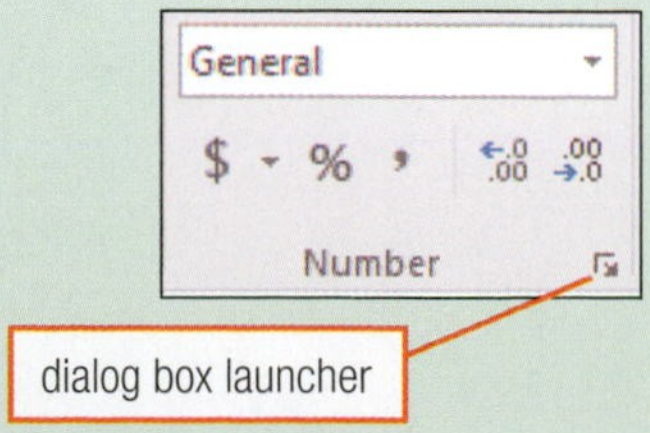

8.3 Adjusting Column Width and Row Height, and Changing Cell Alignment

Skills

Adjust column width

Adjust row height

Change cell alignment

Tutorials

Adjusting Column Width and Row Height

Applying Alignment Formatting

In a new worksheet, each column width is 8.43 and each row height is 15. The column width value is the number of characters at the default font that can be displayed in the column. The row height value is a points measurement, with 1 point being approximately 1/72 of an inch. Make cells larger by widening a column's width, or increasing a row's height. In many instances, Excel automatically makes columns wider and rows taller to accommodate the cell entry, formula result, or format that you apply. Manually changing the column width or the row height is a technique used to add more space between cells to improve readability or emphasize a section of the worksheet.

1. With the **CarCost-YourName** workbook open, make active any cell in column E.
2. Click the Format button in the Cells group on the Home tab and then click *Column Width* at the drop-down list.

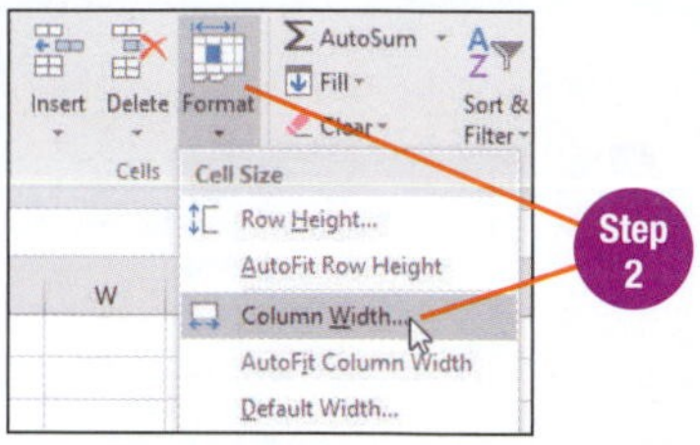

3. Type 15 in the *Column width* text box at the Column Width dialog box and then press Enter or click OK.

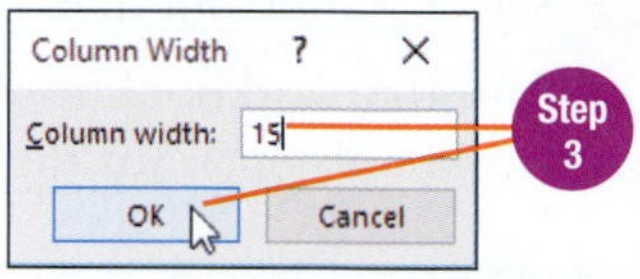

4. Make active any cell in column F, click the Format button, and then click *Column Width* at the drop-down list.
5. Type 10 at the Column Width dialog box and then press Enter or click OK.

Notice the cells with values in column F have been replaced with a series of pound symbols (#####). This occurs when the column's width is too narrow to show all the characters.

6. Make F4 the active cell.
7. Click the Format button and then click *AutoFit Column Width* at the drop-down list.

App Tip

The maximum width for a column is 255 characters and spaces, and the maximum height for a row is 409 points.

AutoFit changes the width of the column to fit the contents of the active cell. F4 was made active at Step 6 because this cell has the largest number in the column. Notice the pound symbols have disappeared, and the values are redisplayed now that the column is wide enough.

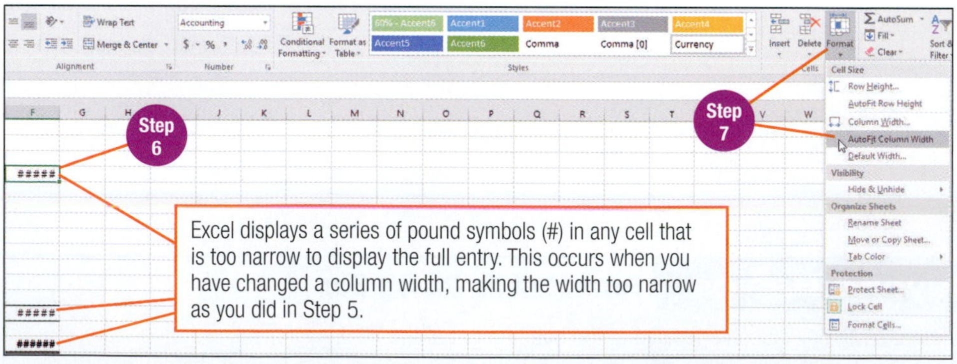

8 Select A1:A2.

Select cells in multiple rows or columns to change the height or width of more than one row or column at the same time.

9 Click the Format button and then click *Row Height* at the drop-down list.

10 Type 26 in the *Row height* text box at the Row Height dialog box, and then press Enter or click OK.

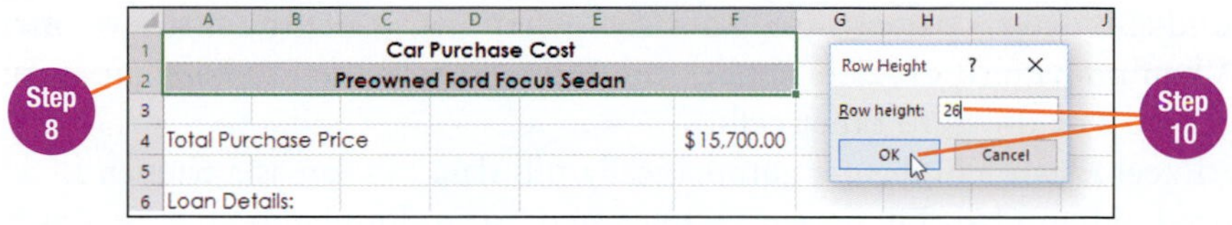

The Alignment group on the Home tab contains buttons to align the entry of a cell horizontally and/or vertically. You can align at the left, center, or right horizontally, or at the top, middle, or bottom vertically.

11 With A1:A2 still selected, click the Middle Align button in the Alignment group.

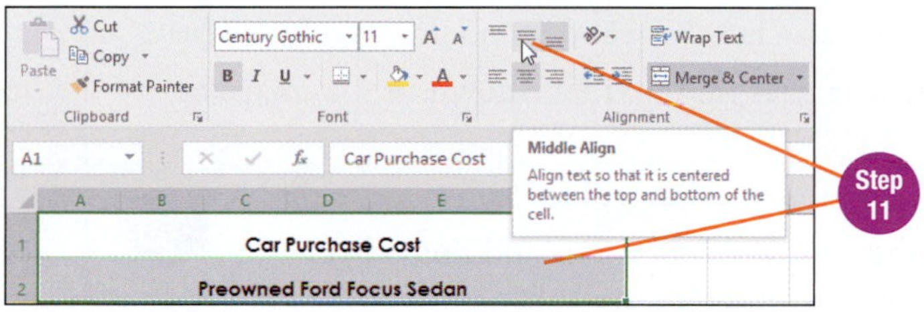

Middle Align centers text vertically between the top and bottom edges within a cell.

12 Make active any cell in row 15.

13 Click the Format button, click *Row Height*, type 26, and then press Enter or click OK.

14 Select A15:F15 and then click the Middle Align button.

15 Click any cell to deselect the range.

16 Save the workbook using the same name (**CarCost-YourName**).

17 Click the File tab and then click *Close* to close the workbook.

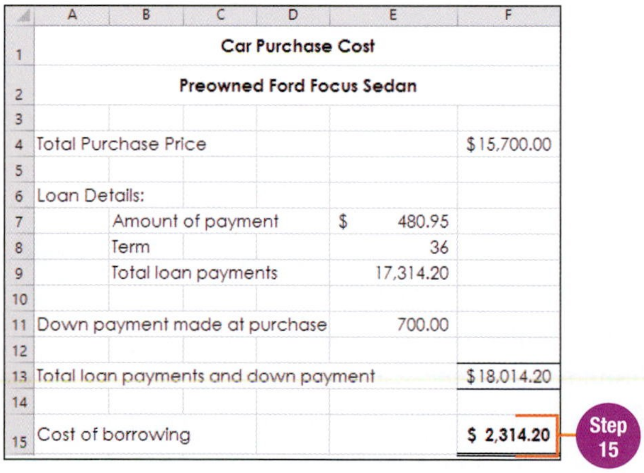
Car Purchase Cost
Preowned Ford Focus Sedan
Total Purchase Price
$15,700.00
Loan Details:
Amount of payment
$ 480.95
Term
36
Total loan payments
17,314.20
Down payment made at purchase
700.00
Total loan payments and down payment
$18,014.20
Cost of borrowing
$ 2,314.20
Step 15

Quick Steps

Change Column Width
1. Activate any cell within column.
2. Click Format button.
3. Click *Column Width*.
4. Type width.
5. Click OK.

Change Row Height
1. Activate any cell within row.
2. Click Format button.
3. Click *Row Height*.
4. Type height.
5. Click OK.

AutoFit Column Width or Row Height
1. Activate cell with contents that are longest in the column or tallest in the row.
2. Click Format button.
3. Click *AutoFit Row Height* or *AutoFit Column Width*.

View
Model Answer
Compare your completed file with the model answer.

Alternative Method Changing Column Width or Row Height Using a Mouse

Change column widths using a mouse by dragging the column boundary at the right of the column letter to the right to increase the width or to the left to decrease the width. Change row height using a mouse by dragging the row boundary below the row number up to decrease the height or down to increase the height. Double-click the right column boundary or the bottom row boundary to AutoFit the column width or row height.

8.4 Entering or Copying Data with the Fill Command and Using AutoSum

Skills

Use Auto Fill to enter a series

Use Fill Right to copy a value

Use the fill handle to enter data

Add a column with AutoSum

Tutorials

Populating Data Using Flash Fill

Entering Formulas Using the AutoSum Button

Entering Data Using the Fill Handle

Copying Formulas

Using Undo and Redo

The **Auto Fill** feature in Excel is used to enter data automatically based on a pattern or series that exists in an adjacent cell or range. For example, if *Monday* is entered in cell A1, Auto Fill can enter *Tuesday*, *Wednesday*, and so on automatically in the cells immediately to the right of or below A1. Excel fills many common text or number series, and also detects patterns for other data when you select the first few entries in a list. When no pattern or series applies, the **Fill** feature is used to copy an entry or formula across or down to other cells.

The Excel **Flash Fill** feature automatically fills data as soon as a pattern is recognized. When Flash Fill presents a suggested list in dimmed text, press Enter to accept the suggestions, or ignore the suggestions and continue typing. A Flash Fill Options button appears when a list is presented with options to undo Flash Fill, accept the suggestions, or select changed cells.

Using Auto Fill and Fill Right

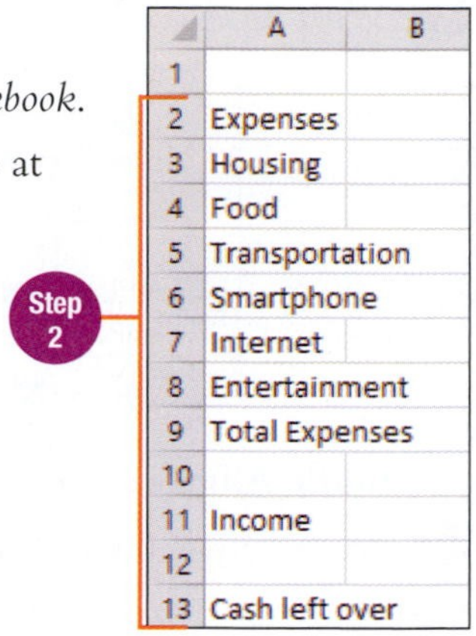

1. Click the File tab, click *New*, and then click *Blank workbook*.
2. Type the text entries in A2:A13 as shown in the image at right.
3. Change the width of column A to 18.
4. Make B1 the active cell, type Sep, and then click the Enter button on the Formula bar.
5. Select B1:I1.
6. Click the Fill button in the Editing group, and then click *Series* at the drop-down list.

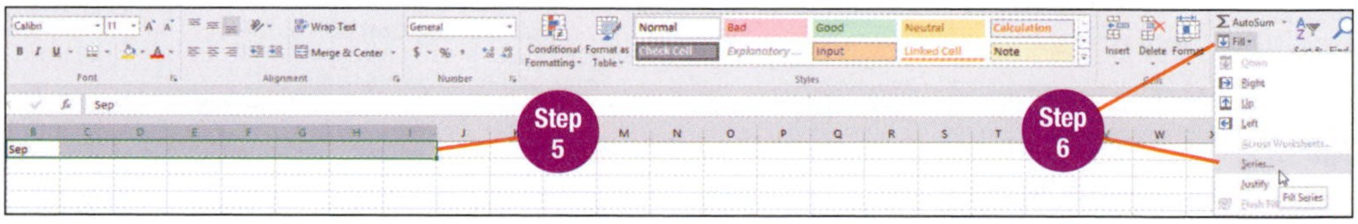

7. Click *AutoFill* in the *Type* section of the Series dialog box and then click OK.

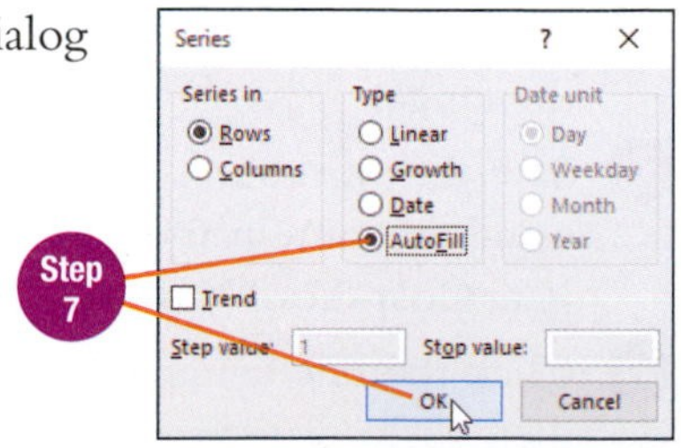

Auto Fill enters the column headings *Oct* through *Apr* in the selected range.

8. Make B3 the active cell, type 875, and then click the Enter button.
9. Select B3:I3, click the Fill button, and then click *Right* at the drop-down list.

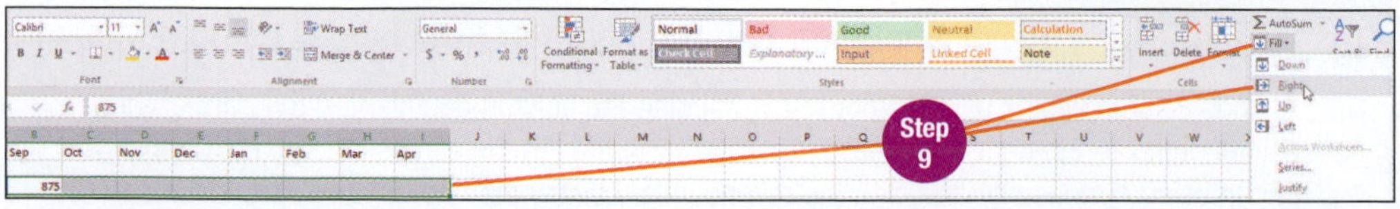

Fill Right copies the entry in the first cell to the other cells within the selected range.

10 Enter the remaining values as shown in the image at right. In rows 5, 6, and 7, use Fill Right to enter the data by completing tasks similar to those in Steps 8 and 9.

	A	B	C	D	E	F	G	H	I
1		Sep	Oct	Nov	Dec	Jan	Feb	Mar	Apr
2	Expenses								
3	Housing	875	875	875	875	875	875	875	875
4	Food	260	340	310	295	320	280	300	345
5	Transportation	88	88	88	88	88	88	88	88
6	Smartphone	48	48	48	48	48	48	48	48
7	Internet	42	42	42	42	42	42	42	42
8	Entertainment	150	110	95	175	100	85	95	120
9	Total Expenses								

Step 10

Using the Fill Handle to Copy Cells

The **fill handle** is a small, green square at the bottom right corner of the active cell or range. The fill handle can be used to copy data from a cell or range to adjacent cells.

To use the fill handle with a mouse: When you point at the square with a mouse, the cell pointer changes appearance from the large white cross to the fill handle (**+**). Drag right or down when you see the fill handle icon to copy data or a formula, or to extend a series from the active cell or range to adjacent cells.

To use the fill handle on a touch device: Tapping a cell on a touch device displays the active cell with two selection handles instead of the fill handle. See Figure 8.3 for instructions on how to use the fill handle on a touch device.

App Tip

The Auto Fill Options button appears when you release the mouse after dragging the fill handle to copy a cell. Use the button to instruct Excel to fill the cells with the formatting options only from the copied cell (no data is copied), or to copy the data with no formatting options (only data is copied).

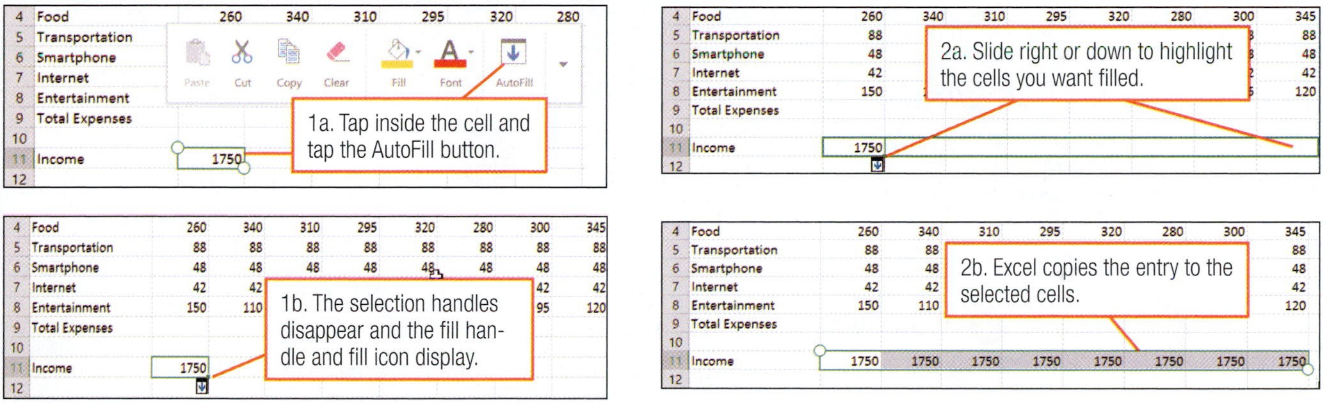

Figure 8.3

How to use the fill handle on a touch device.

11 Make B11 the active cell, type 1750, and then click the Enter button.

12 Drag the fill handle right to I11.

The value *1750* is copied to the cells in the selected range. See Beyond Basics at the end of this topic for more information about using the versatile fill handle.

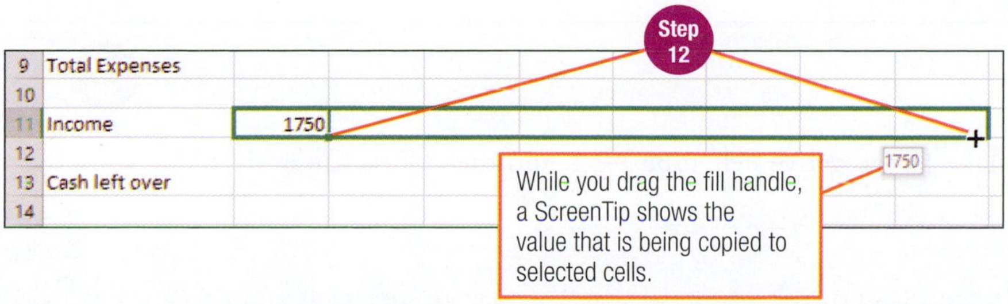

Oops!

Don't see the fill handle? The feature may have been turned off. Open the Advanced panel at the Excel Options dialog box (click File, *Options*, *Advanced*), and then click *Enable fill handle and cell drag-and-drop* to insert a check mark.

> **App Tip**
>
> In most cases, the range that is selected by AutoSum is correct; however, always check to make sure the included cells have the correct values to be added. If necessary, drag to select a different range before completing the formula.

Using the SUM function and AutoSum

To add the expenses in B9, you could type the formula *=B3+B4+B5+B6+B7+B8*; however, Excel includes a built-in preprogrammed function called SUM that can be used to add a column or row of numbers. The SUM function is faster and easier to use. To add the expenses in B9 using SUM, you would type the formula *=SUM(B3:B8)*. Notice after *=SUM* you need to provide only the range of cells to add enclosed in parentheses, rather than all the individual cell references and addition symbols. Because the SUM function is used frequently, an **AutoSum button** is included in the Editing group on the Home tab and the AutoSum feature automatically detects the range to be added.

13 Make B9 the active cell.

14 Click the AutoSum button in the Editing group on the Home tab. (Do not click the down-pointing arrow at the right of the AutoSum button.)

Excel inserts the formula *=SUM(B3:B8)* in B9 with the suggested range *B3:B8* selected.

15 Click the Enter button or press Ctrl + Enter to complete the formula. (Ctrl + Enter completes the entry and keeps B9 as the active cell.)

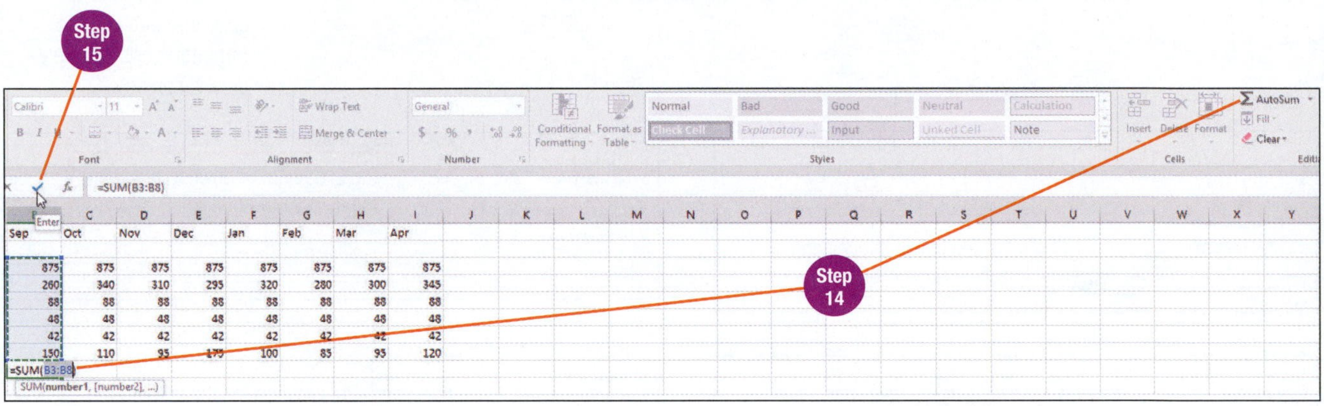

16 With B9 the active cell, drag the fill handle right to I9.

In this instance, using the fill handle copies the formula in B9 to the selected cells.

17 Make B13 the active cell, type =b11-b9, and then click the Enter button or press Ctrl + Enter.

18 With B13 the active cell, drag the fill handle right to I13.

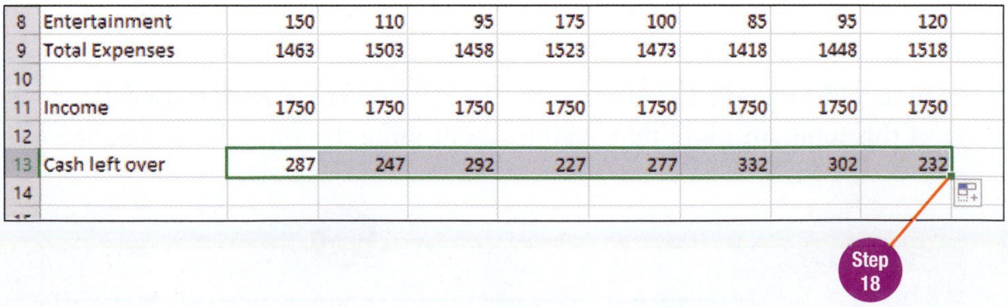

19 Make J1 the active cell, type Total, and then press Enter.

20 Make J3 the active cell and then click the AutoSum button.

In this instance, Excel suggests the range B3:I3 in the SUM function. Excel looks for values immediately above or to the left of the active cell. Because no value exists above J3, Excel correctly suggests adding the values to the left in the same row.

21 Click the Enter button to accept the formula.

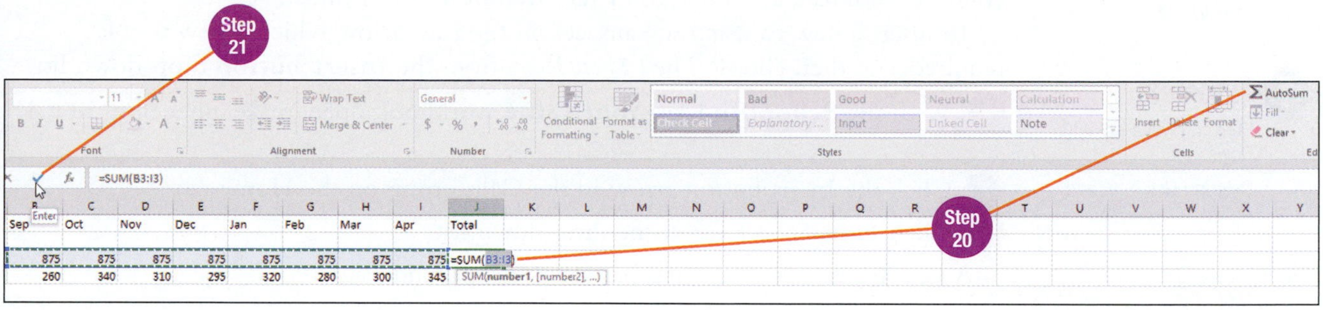

22 With J3 the active cell, drag the fill handle down to J13.

23 Make J10 the active cell, and then either press the Delete key or click the Clear button in the Editing group and then click *Clear All* at the drop-down list.

24 Make J12 the active cell and repeat the instruction in Step 23.

	A	B	C	D	E	F	G	H	I	J
1		Sep	Oct	Nov	Dec	Jan	Feb	Mar	Apr	Total
2	Expenses									
3	Housing	875	875	875	875	875	875	875	875	7000
4	Food	260	340	310	295	320	280	300	345	2450
5	Transportation	88	88	88	88	88	88	88	88	704
6	Smartphone	48	48	48	48	48	48	48	48	384
7	Internet	42	42	42	42	42	42	42	42	336
8	Entertainment	150	110	95	175	100	85	95	120	930
9	Total Expenses	1463	1503	1458	1523	1473	1418	1448	1518	11804
10										
11	Income	1750	1750	1750	1750	1750	1750	1750	1750	14000
12										
13	Cash left over	287	247	292	227	277	332	302	232	2196

Step 24

25 Save the new workbook as **SchoolBudget-YourName** in the Ch8 folder in CompletedTopicsByChapter on your storage medium. Leave the workbook open for the next topic.

Quick Steps

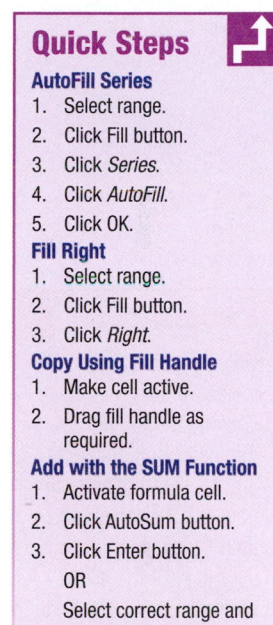

AutoFill Series
1. Select range.
2. Click Fill button.
3. Click *Series*.
4. Click *AutoFill*.
5. Click OK.

Fill Right
1. Select range.
2. Click Fill button.
3. Click *Right*.

Copy Using Fill Handle
1. Make cell active.
2. Drag fill handle as required.

Add with the SUM Function
1. Activate formula cell.
2. Click AutoSum button.
3. Click Enter button.

OR

Select correct range and then click Enter button.

Beyond Basics More Examples of Using the Fill Command

The Excel Fill command can detect patterns in values, dates, times, months, days, years, or other data. A pattern is detected based on the cells selected before dragging the fill handle. Following are some examples of series the fill handle can extend. In each example, you would select the range of cells in column A and column B, and then drag the fill handle to the right to extend the data.

Column A	Column B	Columns C, D, E, and so on
10	20	30, 40, 50, and so on
9:00	10:00	11:00, 12:00, 1:00, and so on
2018	2019	2020, 2021, 2022, and so on
Year 1	Year 2	Year 3, Year 4, Year 5, and so on

8.5 Inserting and Deleting Rows and Columns

Skills

Insert a new row

Insert a new column

Delete a row

Tutorials

Inserting Columns and Rows

Deleting Columns and Rows

New rows or columns are inserted or deleted using the Insert or Delete buttons in the Cells group on the Home tab. New rows are inserted above the row in which the active cell is positioned, and new columns are inserted to the left. Cell references within formulas and formula results are automatically updated when new rows or columns with data are added to or removed from a worksheet.

To insert a new row, activate any cell in the row below which a new row is required, and then choose *Insert Sheet Rows* from the **Insert button** drop-down list.

1. With the **SchoolBudget-YourName** workbook open, make any cell in row 4 active.
2. Click the Insert button arrow in the Cells group on the Home tab.
3. Click *Insert Sheet Rows* at the drop-down list.

   A new blank row is inserted between *Housing* and *Food*.

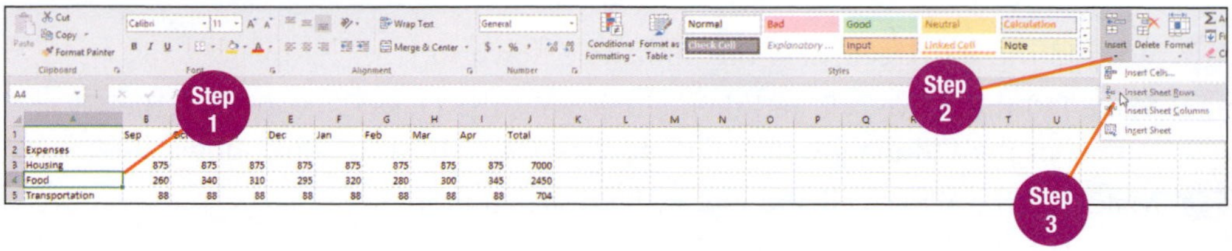

4. Type the following entries in the cells indicated:

A4	Utilities	F4	128
B4	110	G4	106
C4	115	H4	118
D4	132	I4	112
E4	147		

5. Make J3 the active cell and then drag the fill handle down to J4 to copy the SUM formula to the new row.

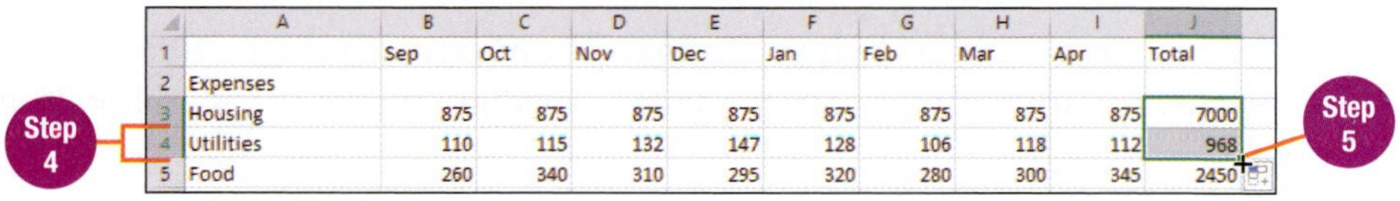

6. Select A1:A2, click the Insert button arrow, and then click *Insert Sheet Rows*.

   Two rows are inserted above A1.
7. Make the new cell A1 the active cell and then type Proposed School Budget.
8. Make the new cell A2 the active cell and then type First Year of Program.
9. Use Merge & Center to format the range A1:J1.
10. Use Merge & Center to format the range A2:J2.

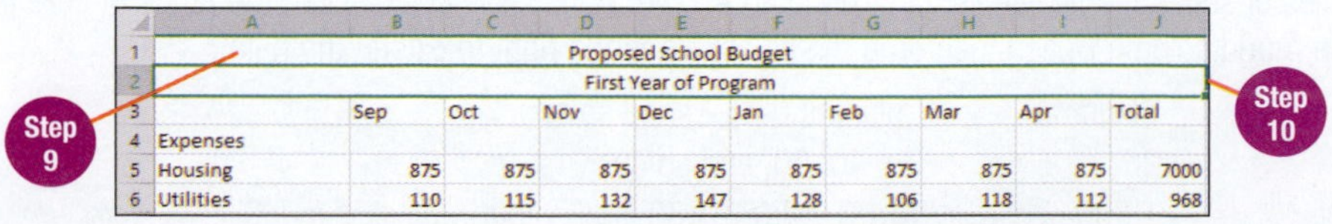

Oops!

Only one cell is inserted instead of an entire row? Clicking the top part of the Insert button inserts a cell instead of an entire new row. Use Undo and then try again, making sure to click the arrow on the bottom part of the Insert button to access the drop-down list.

App Tip

To insert multiple rows, select row numbers along the left edge of the worksheet area, right-click, and then click *Insert*. Excel will insert the same number of blank rows as you selected and it will insert the blank rows above the first row you selected.

11 Make any cell in column J active.

12 Click the Insert button arrow and then click *Insert Sheet Columns* at the drop-down list.

A new column is inserted between *Apr* and *Total*. Notice also an **Insert Options button** ( ) appears below and right of the active cell. Options from this button are used to format the new column the same as the column at its left or right, or to clear formatting in the new column.

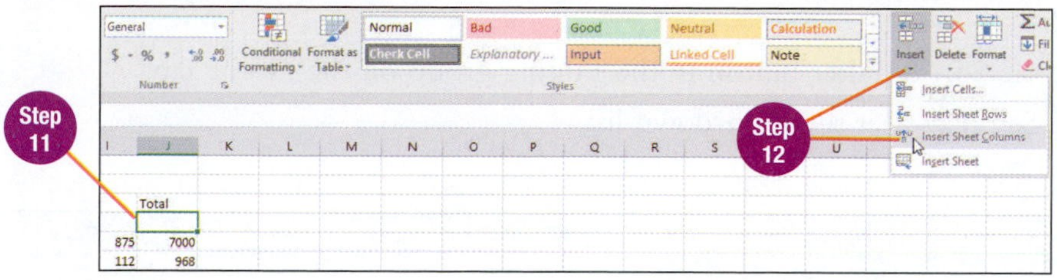

Quick Steps

Insert Rows or Columns
1. Activate cell or select range.
2. Click Insert button arrow.
3. Click *Insert Sheet Rows* or *Insert Sheet Columns*.

Delete Rows or Columns
1. Activate cell or select range.
2. Click Delete button arrow.
3. Click *Delete Sheet Rows* or *Delete Sheet Columns*.

To delete a single row or column, position the active cell within that row or column, and then choose *Delete Sheet Rows* or *Delete Sheet Columns* from the **Delete button** drop-down list. Remove multiple rows or columns from the worksheet by first selecting the range of rows or columns to be deleted.

13 Make any cell in row 10 active.

14 Click the Delete button arrow and then click *Delete Sheet Rows* at the drop-down list.

Row 10 is removed from the worksheet, and existing rows below are shifted up to fill in the space.

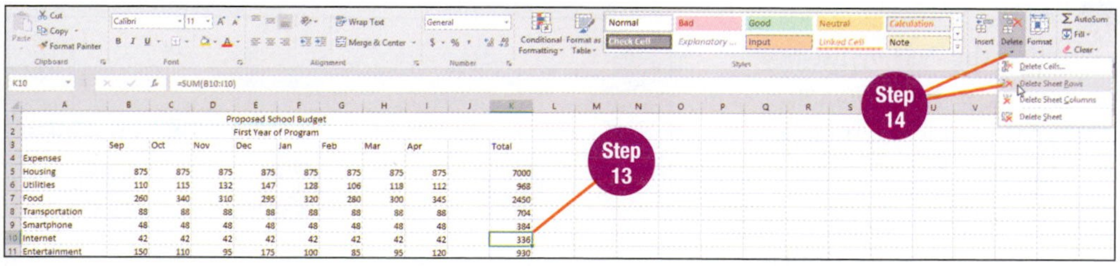

App Tip

Delete a column by performing actions similar to those in Steps 13–14 except click *Delete Sheet Columns* at the Delete button drop-down list.

15 Save the workbook using the same name (**SchoolBudget-YourName**). Leave the workbook open for the next topic.

Beyond Basics Inserting and Deleting Cells

The Insert and Delete buttons are also used to insert and delete cells within a worksheet. Select the range of cells you need to add and then choose *Insert Cells* at the Insert button drop-down list. At the Insert dialog box, choose whether to shift existing cells right or down.

Select the range of cells to delete, choose *Delete Cells* at the Delete button drop-down list, and then select whether to shift existing cells left or up to fill the space.

8.6 Sorting Data and Applying Cell Styles

Skills

Sort rows of data

Apply cell styles

Tutorials

Sorting Data

Applying Cell Styles

Applying and Modifying Themes

A range in Excel can be rearranged by sorting in either ascending or descending order on one or more columns. For example, you can sort a list of names and cities first by the city and then by the last name. To sort by more than one column, select the range and open the Sort dialog box from the **Sort & Filter button** drop-down list.

1 With the **SchoolBudget-YourName** workbook open, select A5:K10.

Notice you do not include the heading (in A4) or the totals (in A11:K11) in the sort range.

2 Click the Sort & Filter button in the Editing group on the Home tab.

3 Click *Sort A to Z* at the drop-down list.

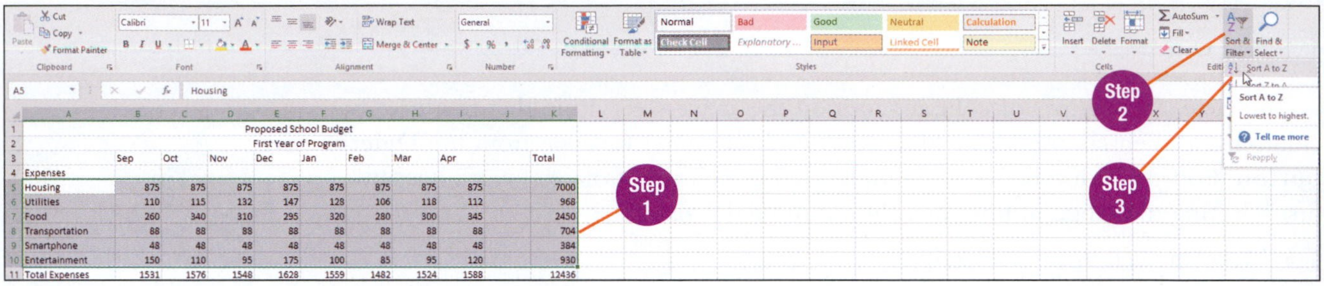

4 Click any cell to deselect the range, and review the new order of the expenses.

5 Select A5:K10.

6 Click the Sort & Filter button and then click *Custom Sort* at the drop-down list.

7 At the Sort dialog box, click the *Sort by* list box arrow in the *Column* section, and then click *Column K*.

8 Click the *Order* list box arrow (currently displays *Smallest to Largest*) and then click *Largest to Smallest*.

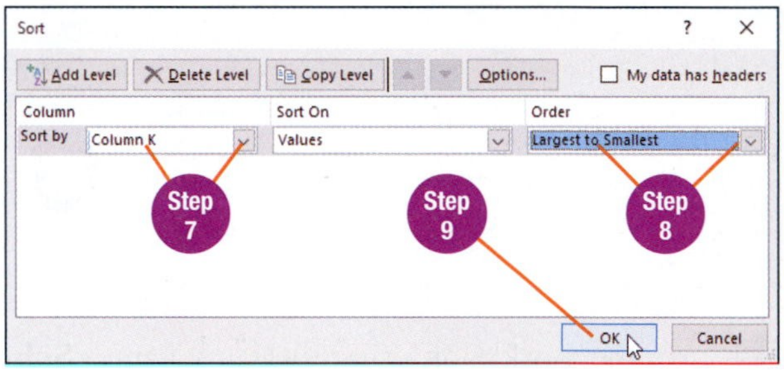

9 Click OK.

The range is rearranged in descending order from highest expense total to lowest.

10 Click any cell to deselect the range, and review the new order of expenses.

Similar to Word Styles feature, **Cell Styles** in Excel offers a set of predefined formatting options that can be applied to a single cell or a range. Using Cell Styles to format a worksheet is fast and promotes consistency. The Cell Styles gallery groups styles by the sections *Good, Bad and Neutral*; *Data and Model*; *Titles and Headings*; *Themed Cell Styles*; and *Number Format*.

11 Make A1 the active cell and then click the More button located at the bottom right of the Cell Styles gallery in the Styles group on the Home tab.

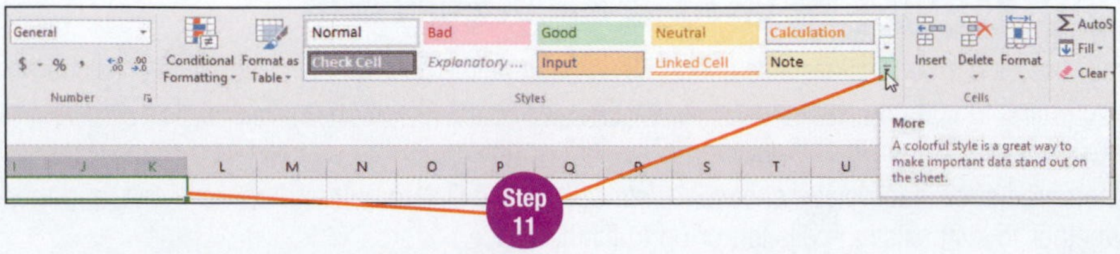

12 Click *Heading 1* in the *Titles and Headings* section of the Cell Styles gallery.

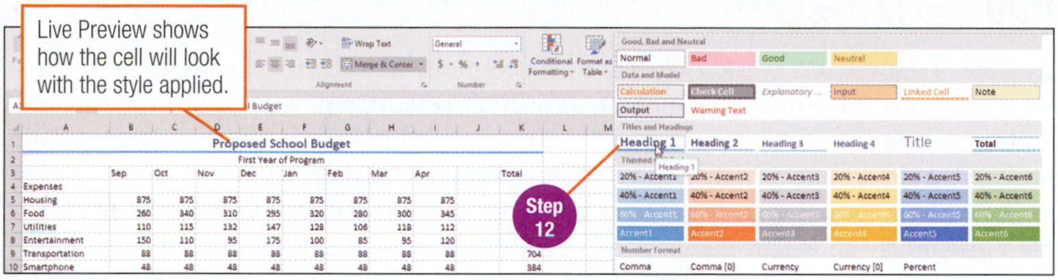

Live Preview shows how the cell will look with the style applied.
Step 12

13 Make A2 the active cell, click the More button in the Cell Styles gallery, and then click *Heading 4* in the *Titles and Headings* section.

14 Apply the Heading 4 cell style to A4, A13, and A15.

15 Select B3:K3, apply the Accent1 style in the *Themed Cell Styles* section of the Cell Styles gallery, and then center the content of those cells.

16 Select B5:K15 and apply the Comma [0] style in the *Number Format* section of the Cell Styles gallery.

17 Select B15:K15 and apply the Total style in the *Titles and Headings* section of the Cell Styles gallery.

18 Click any cell to deselect the range and compare your worksheet with the one shown in Figure 8.4.

19 Save the workbook using the same name (**SchoolBudget-YourName**). Leave the workbook open for the next topic.

	A	B	C	D	E	F	G	H	I	J	K
1	Proposed School Budget										
2	First Year of Program										
3		Sep	Oct	Nov	Dec	Jan	Feb	Mar	Apr		Total
4	Expenses										
5	Housing	875	875	875	875	875	875	875	875		7,000
6	Food	260	340	310	295	320	280	300	345		2,450
7	Utilities	110	115	132	147	128	106	118	112		968
8	Entertainment	150	110	95	175	100	85	95	120		930
9	Transportation	88	88	88	88	88	88	88	88		704
10	Smartphone	48	48	48	48	48	48	48	48		384
11	Total Expenses	1,531	1,576	1,548	1,628	1,559	1,482	1,524	1,588		12,436
12											
13	Income	1,750	1,750	1,750	1,750	1,750	1,750	1,750	1,750		14,000
14											
15	Cash left over	219	174	202	122	191	268	226	162		1,564

Figure 8.4

This is the sorted worksheet with cell styles applied.

Oops!

No Cell Styles gallery? On smaller displays, the gallery is accessed by clicking the Cell Styles button in the Styles group on the Home tab.

App Tip

You can hold down the Ctrl key and click A4, A13, and A15 to format all three cells in one operation.

Quick Steps

Sort a Range by the First Column

1. Select range.
2. Click Sort & Filter button.
3. Click *Sort A to Z* or *Sort Z to A*.

Custom Sort

1. Select range.
2. Click Sort & Filter button.
3. Click *Custom Sort*.
4. Change options and/or add levels as needed.
5. Click OK.

Apply Cell Styles

1. Select cell or range.
2. Click desired cell style in Styles gallery.

Beyond Basics Workbook Themes

Options in the *Titles and Headings* and *Themed Cell Styles* sections in the Cell Styles gallery change depending on the active theme (set of colors, fonts, and effects). Change the theme for a workbook using the Themes gallery, accessed by clicking the Themes button arrow in the Themes group on the Page Layout tab.

8.7 Changing Orientation and Scaling, and Displaying Cell Formulas

Skills

Preview a worksheet

Change orientation

Display cell formulas

Change scaling

Tutorials

Printing a Worksheet

Displaying Formulas

By default, new Excel workbooks have print options set to print the active worksheet on a letter-size page (8.5 x 11 inches), in portrait orientation, with 0.75-inch top and bottom margins, and 0.7-inch left and right margins. Preview a new worksheet before printing to determine whether these print options are appropriate.

Workbooks are often distributed as PDF files and circulated electronically. A PDF file is essentially an electronic view of a printed worksheet and has the same default settings. Always preview a worksheet and change print options as needed before exporting as a PDF.

1. With the **SchoolBudget-YourName** workbook open, click the File tab, click *Print*, and then compare your screen with the one shown in Figure 8.5.
2. Click the Next Page button at the bottom of the preview panel to view the second page of the worksheet.
3. Click the *Orientation* list box arrow in the *Settings* category and then click *Landscape Orientation* at the drop-down list.

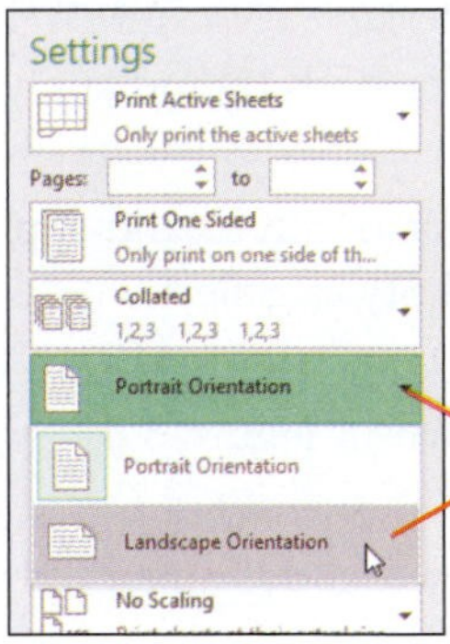

Notice the worksheet now fits on one page. Landscape is a common layout used for wide worksheets.

4. Click the Back button to return to the worksheet and then save the revised workbook using the same name (**SchoolBudget-YourName**).

Quick Steps

Change the Orientation

1. Display Print backstage area.
2. Click *Orientation* list box arrow.
3. Click *Landscape Orientation.*

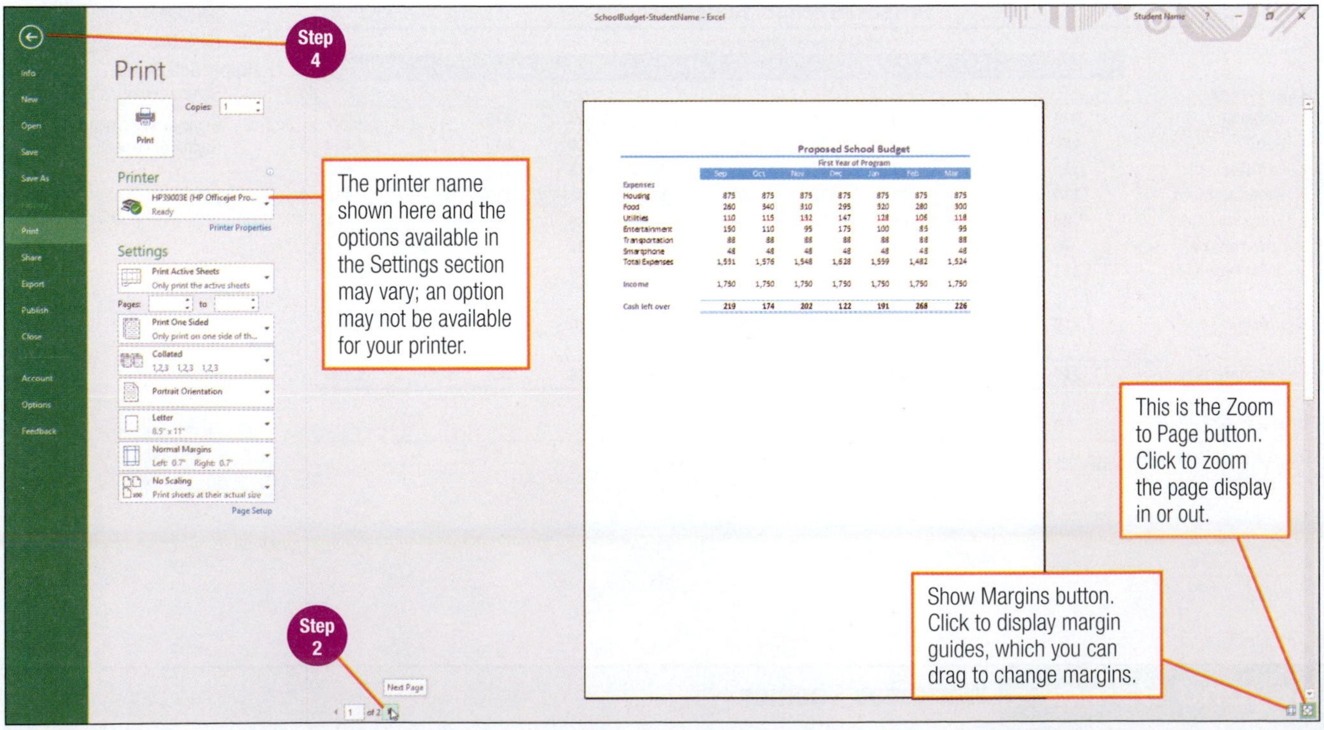

Figure 8.5

Print backstage area is shown with first page displayed for the **SchoolBudget-StudentName** worksheet.

On a printed copy of the worksheet, only the formula result is printed. You may want to print a second copy of the worksheet with the formulas displayed in the cell as a backup or documentation strategy for a complex or otherwise important worksheet.

5 Click the Formulas tab.

6 Click the Show Formulas button in the Formula Auditing group.

The **Show Formulas button** is a toggle button that switches the display between showing the formula in each cell, and showing the result in each cell.

7 Scroll right if necessary to review the worksheet with formulas displayed.

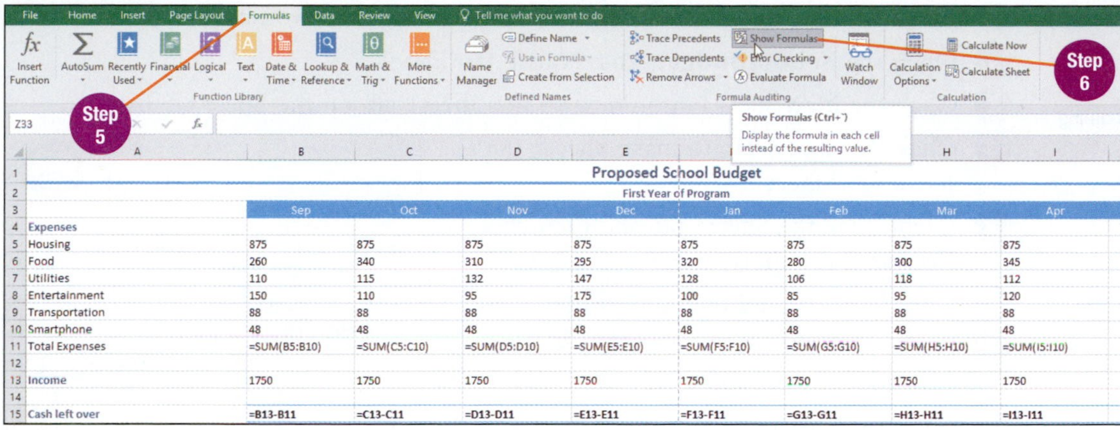

8 Display the Print backstage area.

9 Click the *Scaling* list box arrow in the *Settings* category and then click *Fit Sheet on One Page*.

Fit Sheet on One Page shrinks the size of text on the printout to fit all columns and rows on one page.

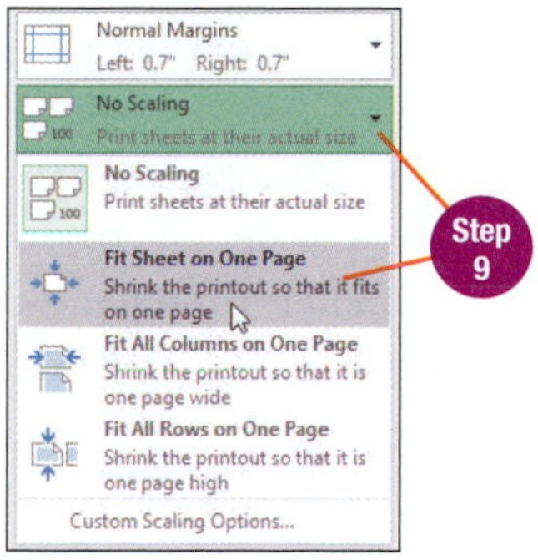

10 Click the Back button to return to the worksheet.

11 Use Save As to save a copy of the worksheet with the formulas displayed, named **SchoolBudget-Formulas-YourName** in the Ch8 folder in CompletedTopicsByChapter.

12 Close the workbook.

Alternative Method — Changing Print Options Using the Page Layout Tab

You can change some print options on the Page Layout tab, using the Margins and Orientation buttons in the Page Setup group and the Width, Height, and Scale options in the Scale to Fit group.

App Tip

Ctrl + ` (grave accent, usually located above the Tab key) is the keyboard command to turn on or off the display of formulas.

App Tip

Other methods used to print wide worksheets are decreasing the margins, and changing the scaling percentage.

View

Model Answer

Compare your completed file with the model answer.

Quick Steps

Display Cell Formulas

1. Click Formulas tab.
2. Click Show Formulas button.

Scale a Worksheet

1. Display Print backstage area.
2. Click *Scaling* list box arrow.
3. Click required scaling option.

Beyond Basics — More Scaling Options

In the Print backstage area, the scaling option *Fit All Columns on One Page* shrinks the size of text until all the columns fit the page width; more than one page may print if there are many rows. *Fit All Rows on One Page* shrinks the size of text until all the rows fit the page height; more than one page may print if there are many columns.

8.8 Inserting and Renaming a Worksheet, Copying Cells, and Indenting Cell Contents

Skills

Insert a new worksheet

Rename worksheets

Copy cells

Indent cells

Tutorials

Inserting and Renaming Worksheets

Copying and Pasting Cells between Worksheets

Moving Cells

Using Format Painter and the Repeat Command

Navigating and Scrolling

A workbook can contain more than one worksheet. Use multiple worksheets as a method to organize or group data into manageable units. For example, a homeowner might have one household finance workbook and keep track of bills and loans in one worksheet, savings and investments in a second worksheet, and a household budget in a third worksheet. Insert, rename, and navigate between worksheets using the sheet tabs in the **Sheet tab bar** near the bottom of the window. Use the **New sheet button** in the Sheet tab bar to add a new worksheet to the workbook.

1. Open the **SchoolBudget-YourName** workbook.
2. Click the New sheet button next to the Sheet1 tab on the Sheet tab bar.
3. Click the Sheet1 tab to make Sheet1 the active worksheet.
4. Right-click the Sheet1 tab and then click *Rename* at the shortcut menu.
5. Type First Year and then press Enter.
6. Right-click the Sheet2 tab, click *Rename*, type Second Year, and then press Enter.
7. Click the First Year tab to make First Year the active worksheet.
8. Select A4:A15 and then click the Copy button in the Clipboard group on the Home tab.
9. Make Second Year the active worksheet, make A4 the active cell, and then click the top portion of the Paste button (not the down-pointing arrow) in the Clipboard group.
10. Click the Paste Options button and then click *Keep Source Column Widths*.
11. Make First Year the active worksheet, select A1:K3, and then click the Copy button.
12. Make Second Year the active worksheet, make A1 the active cell, and then click the Paste button.
13. Edit A2 in the Second Year worksheet to change *First* to *Second* so that the title now reads Second Year of Program.

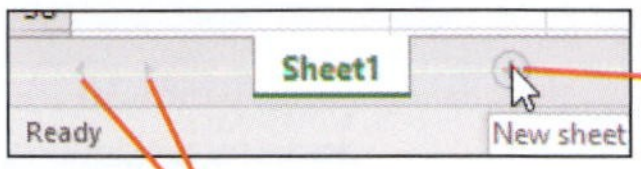

Step 2

The left- and right-pointing arrows are used to scroll sheet tabs.

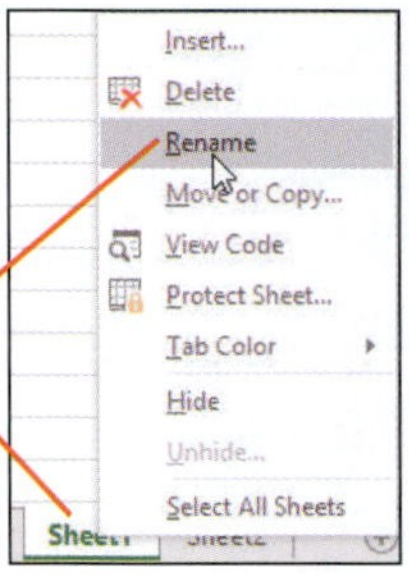

Step 4

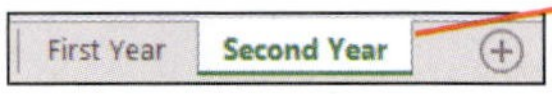

Step 6

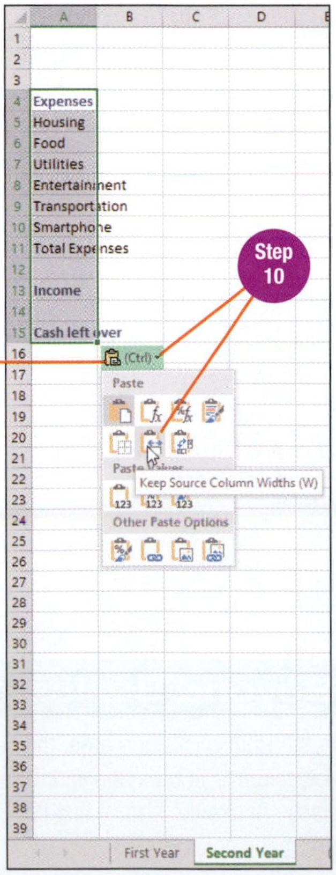

Step 10

On a touch device, the Paste Options button does not appear here after text is pasted into the worksheet; instead, the options must be accessed by tapping the Paste button on the ribbon.

App Tip

Other options on the sheet tab shortcut menu are used to delete, move, copy, hide, or protect entire sheets, and to change the color of the background in the sheet tab.

Oops!

Pasted to the wrong starting cell? Drag the border of the selected range to the correct starting point, or use Cut and Paste to move cells.

14 Enter the data, complete the formulas for the cells in row 15 and column K, and format the cells in the Second Year worksheet, as shown in Figure 8.6.

	A	B	C	D	E	F	G	H	I	J	K
1	Proposed School Budget										
2	Second Year of Program										
3		Sep	Oct	Nov	Dec	Jan	Feb	Mar	Apr		Total
4	Expenses										
5	Housing	910	910	910	910	910	910	910	910		7,280
6	Food	245	330	298	285	308	275	295	355		2,391
7	Utilities	112	118	140	151	131	118	122	124		1,016
8	Entertainment	160	95	100	185	110	95	90	125		960
9	Transportation	90	90	90	90	90	90	90	90		720
10	Smartphone	50	50	50	50	50	50	50	50		400
11	Total Expenses	1,567	1,593	1,588	1,671	1,599	1,538	1,557	1,654		12,767
12											
13	Income	1,800	1,800	1,800	1,800	1,800	1,800	1,800	1,800		14,400
14											
15	Cash left over	233	207	212	129	201	262	243	146		1,633

Figure 8.6

The completed Second Year worksheet is shown here.

> **App Tip**
>
> Use the fill handle, copy formulas from the First Year sheet to the Second Year sheet, and/or use the Format Painter feature whenever possible.

> **Quick Steps**
>
> **Insert a Worksheet**
> Click New sheet button.
>
> **Rename a Worksheet**
> 1. Right-click sheet tab.
> 2. Click *Rename*.
> 3. Type new name.
> 4. Press Enter.
>
> **Indent Cells**
> 1. Activate cell or select range.
> 2. Click Increase Indent button.

The Increase Indent button in the Alignment group on the Home tab moves an entry approximately one character width inward from the left edge of a cell each time the button is clicked. Use this feature to indent entries in a list below a subheading. The Decrease Indent button moves an entry approximately one character width closer to the left edge of the cell each time the button is clicked.

15 With Second Year still the active worksheet, select A5:A10 and then click the Increase Indent button in the Alignment group on the Home tab.

16 Make A11 the active cell and then click the Increase Indent button twice.

17 Change the orientation to landscape for the Second Year worksheet.

18 Make First Year the active worksheet, indent A5:A10 once, and indent A11 twice.

19 Save the workbook using the same name (**SchoolBudget-Your Name**) and then close the workbook.

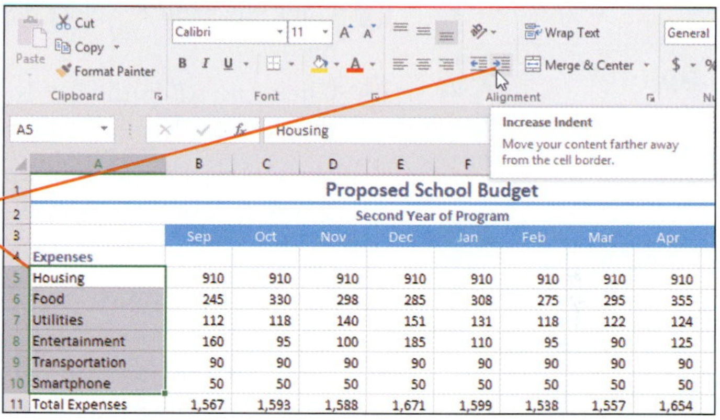

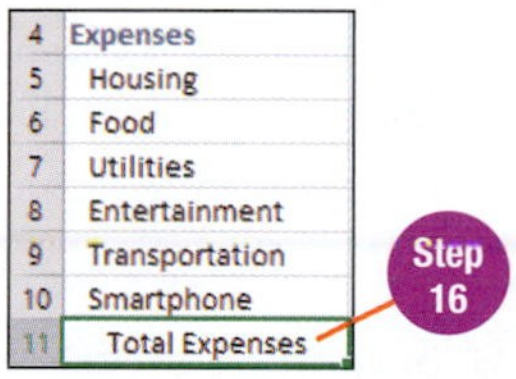

> **View**
> **Model Answer**
> Compare your completed file with the model answer.

> **Alternative Method** **Renaming a Worksheet**
>
> Another way to rename a worksheet is to double-click the sheet tab, type a new name, and then press Enter.

> **App Tip**
>
> Each worksheet has its own page layout and print options.

> **Beyond Basics** **Scrolling Sheet Tabs in the Sheet Tab Bar**
>
> Use the left- and right-pointing arrows to the left of the first sheet tab to scroll to sheet tabs not currently visible, or right-click an arrow to open the Activate dialog box, click the sheet to make active, and then click OK.

8.9 Using Go To; Freezing Panes; and Shading, Wrapping, and Rotating Cell Entries

Skills

Use Go To

Freeze panes

Add fill color

Wrap text

Rotate text

Tutorials

Freezing and Unfreezing Panes

Adding Fill Color to Cells

In large worksheets where you cannot see all cells at once, the **Go To** and **Go To Special** commands accessed from the **Find & Select button** in the Editing group on the Home tab are used to move the active cell to a specific location in a worksheet. Column or row headings not visible when you scroll right or down beyond the viewing area can be fixed in place using the **Freeze Panes** option when working with large worksheets.

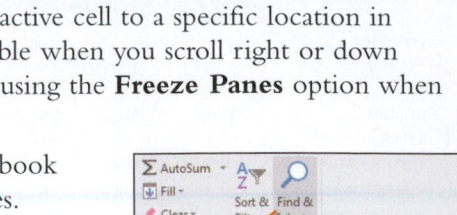

1. Open the **NSCSuppliesInventory** workbook from the Ch8 folder in Student_Data_Files.
2. Save the workbook as **NSCSuppliesInventory-YourName** in the Ch8 folder in CompletedTopicsByChapter.
3. Scroll down the worksheet area until the titles and column headings are no longer visible.
4. Click the Find & Select button in the Editing group on the Home tab and then click *Go To* at the drop-down list.

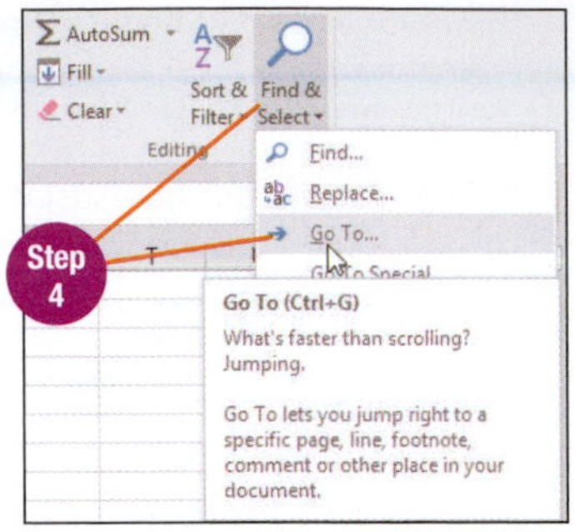

5. At the Go To dialog box, type a4 in the *Reference* text box and then press Enter or click OK.

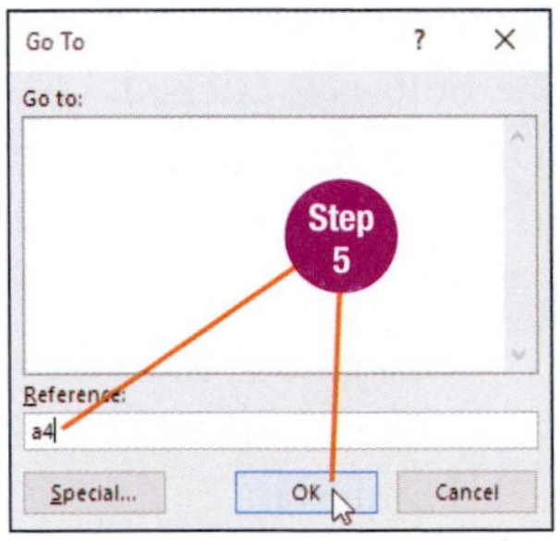

6. Click the Find & Select button and then click *Go To Special*.
7. Click *Last cell* in the Go To Special dialog box and then click OK.

Use the *Last cell* option in the Go To Special dialog box in a large worksheet to move the active cell to the bottom right of the worksheet.

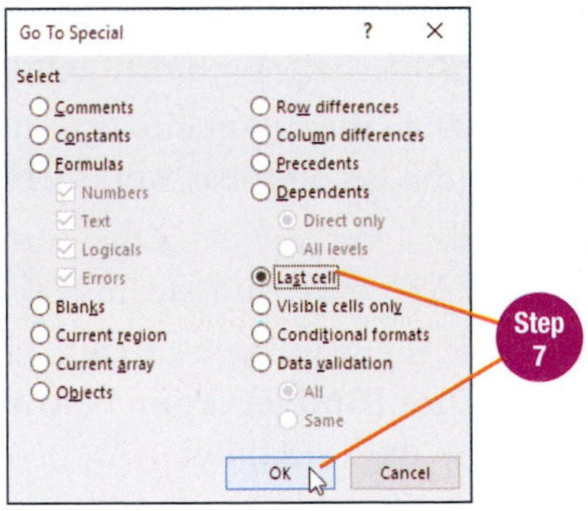

8. Use Go To to move the active cell back to A4.
9. Scroll up until you can see the first three rows, containing titles and column headings.
10. With A4 still the active cell, click the View tab and then click the Freeze Panes button in the Window group.
11. Click *Freeze Panes* at the drop-down list.
12. Scroll down past all data. Notice that rows 1 to 3 do not scroll out of the viewing area.

App Tip

Ctrl + G is the keyboard command for Go To.

App Tip

The active cell position determines which rows and columns are fixed—all rows above and all columns left of the active cell are frozen.

App Tip

Once cells have been frozen, *Freeze Panes* at the Freeze Panes button drop-down list changes to *Unfreeze Panes*.

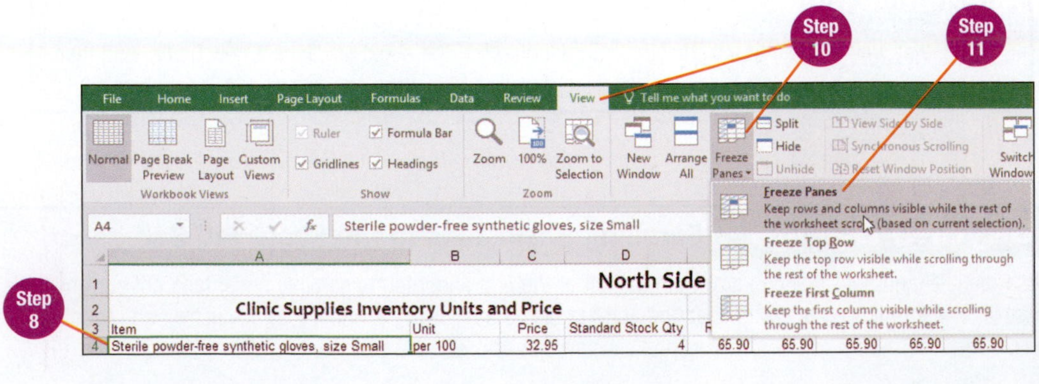

Column headings can be formatted to stand out from the rest of the worksheet by shading the background of the cell using the **Fill Color button** in the Font group on the Home tab or by rotating the cell entries. Cells with long entries can be housed in narrower columns by formatting the text to automatically wrap within the width of the cell using the **Wrap Text button** in the Alignment group on the Home tab. In Steps 13–20 you will format the worksheet headings to match the appearance shown in Figure 8.7.

App Tip

Consider rotating column headings diagonally or vertically in narrow columns.

13. Scroll to the top of the worksheet and then select A1.
14. Click the Home tab, click the Fill Color button arrow in the Font group, and then click *Orange, Accent 6* (last color in first row of *Theme Colors* section) at the drop-down gallery.

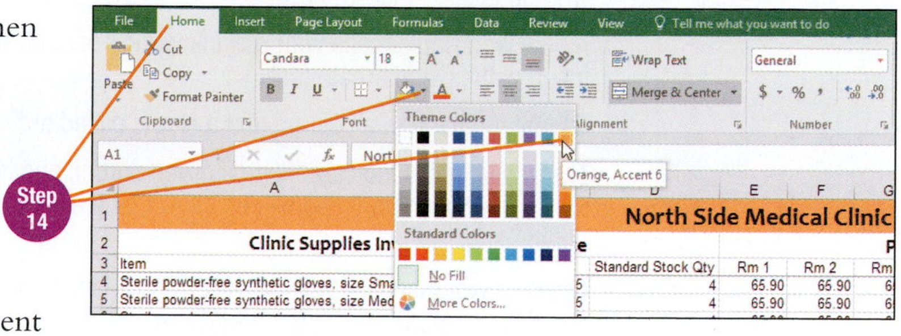

15. Select A2:M2 and apply the Orange, Accent 6, Lighter 60% fill color (last option in third row of *Theme Colors* section).
16. Select A3:M3 and apply the Orange, Accent 6, Lighter 80% fill color (last option in second row of *Theme Colors* section).
17. Make M3 the active cell, change the row height to 30, and then change the column width to 10.
18. With M3 still the active cell, click the Wrap Text button in the Alignment group.

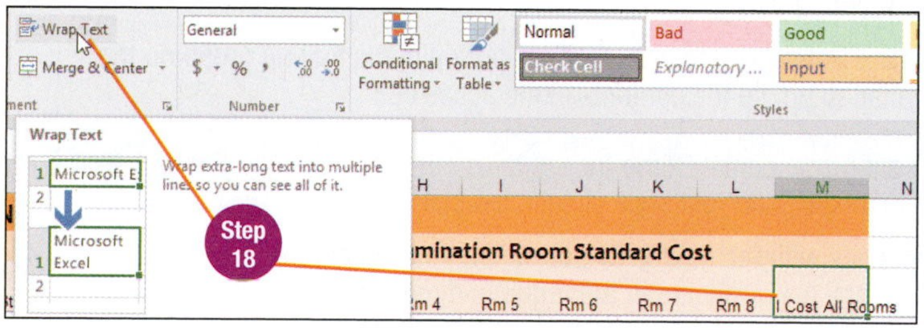

The entire column heading is visible again, with the text wrapping within the cell.

19. Make D3 the active cell, change the column width to 9, and then click the Wrap Text button.
20. Select E3:L3, click the Orientation button in the Alignment group, and then click *Angle Counterclockwise* at the drop-down list.

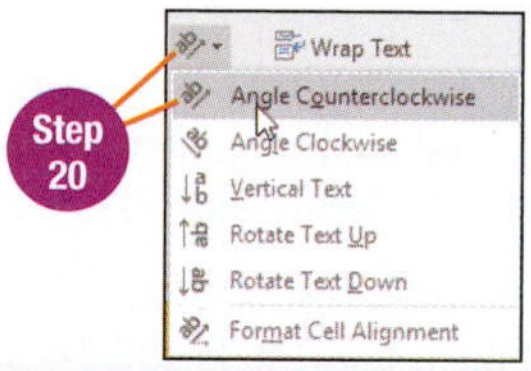

Angle Counterclockwise rotates the text within the cell boundaries 45 degrees.

21. Click any cell to deselect the range and then display the Print backstage area.
22. Change settings to *Landscape Orientation* and *Fit All Columns on One Page* and then go back to the worksheet display.
23. Save the workbook using the same name (**NSCSuppliesInventory-YourName**) and then close the workbook.

Quick Steps

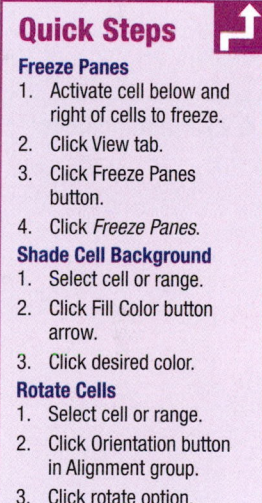

Freeze Panes
1. Activate cell below and right of cells to freeze.
2. Click View tab.
3. Click Freeze Panes button.
4. Click *Freeze Panes.*

Shade Cell Background
1. Select cell or range.
2. Click Fill Color button arrow.
3. Click desired color.

Rotate Cells
1. Select cell or range.
2. Click Orientation button in Alignment group.
3. Click rotate option.

View
Model Answer
Compare your completed file with the model answer.

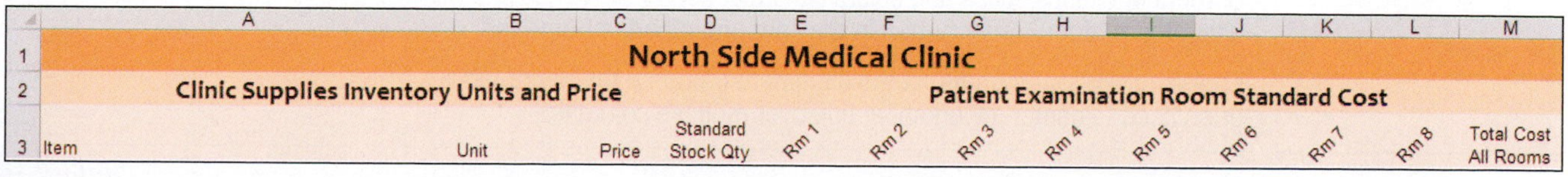

Figure 8.7
This worksheet shows the formatted headings.

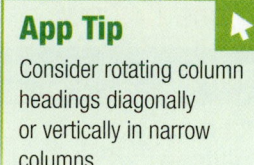

Topics Review

Topic	Key Concepts	Key Terms
8.1 Creating and Editing a New Worksheet	A spreadsheet is an application in which data is created, analyzed, and presented in a grid-like structure of columns and rows. A workbook is an Excel file that consists of a collection of individual worksheets. A new workbook opens with a blank worksheet into which you add text, insert values, and create formulas. The intersection of a column and a row is called a *cell*. The active cell is indicated with a green border, and is the location into which the next data typed will be stored, or the next command will be acted upon. Create a worksheet by making a cell active and typing text, a value, or a formula. A formula is used to perform mathematical operations on values. Formula entries begin with an equals sign and are followed by cell references with operators between the references. Edit a cell by typing new data to overwrite existing data, by double-clicking to open the cell for editing, or by inserting or deleting characters in the Formula bar. Press the Delete key, or use the Clear button in the Editing group on the Home tab to delete the contents in the active cell.	spreadsheet application workbook worksheet cell active cell formula Clear button
8.2 Formatting Cells	The Font group on the Home tab contains buttons to change the font, font size, font color, and font style of selected cells. Select cells with the mouse by positioning the cell pointer over the starting cell and dragging in the required direction. Select cells using touch by tapping the starting cell, and then sliding your finger over a selection handle until the remaining cells are inside the selection rectangle. A rectangular-shaped group of cells is called a *range*, and is referenced with the starting cell address, a colon, and the ending cell address (e.g., A1:F15). By default, cells in a new worksheet have the General format, which has no specific formatting options. The Comma Style button in the Number group on the Home tab adds a comma in thousands and two decimal places. The Accounting Number Format button in the Number group on the Home tab adds a dollar symbol, a comma in the thousands place, and displays two digits after the decimal point. The Decrease Decimal button and Increase Decimal button in the Number group on the Home tab remove or add one decimal place each time the button is clicked. Borders in various styles and colors can be added to the edges of a cell using the Bottom Border button in the Font group on the Home tab. The Merge & Center button in the Alignment group on the Home tab is often used to center a worksheet title over multiple columns.	range Comma Style button Accounting Number Format button Decrease Decimal button Increase Decimal button Merge & Center button

continued…

Topic	Key Concepts	Key Terms
8.3 Adjusting Column Width and Row Height, and Changing Cell Alignment	A technique to add more space between cells to improve readability or emphasize a section is to widen a column or increase the height of a row. Open the Column Width dialog box from the Format button in the Cells group on the Home tab to enter a new value for the width of the column in which the active cell is positioned. Excel displays a series of pound symbols when a column width is too narrow to display all the cell contents. AutoFit changes the width of a column to fit the contents of the active cell. Open the Row Height dialog box from the Format button in the Cells group on the Home tab to enter a new value for the height of the row in which the active cell is positioned. Align a cell at the left, center, or right horizontally, or top, middle, or bottom vertically using buttons in the Alignment group. The Middle Align button in the Alignment group on the Home tab centers cell contents vertically.	AutoFit Middle Align
8.4 Entering or Copying Data with the Fill Command and Using AutoSum	Auto Fill can be used to automatically enter data in a series or pattern based upon an entry in an adjacent cell. When no pattern is detected the Fill feature copies an entry or formula to other cells. The Flash Fill feature automatically suggests entries when a pattern is detected. Select a range and use the Fill button to open the Series dialog box or choose Down, Right, Up, or Left to copy an entry. The small, green square at the bottom right of an active cell is the fill handle and can be used to copy data and formulas or to enter a series. Excel includes the AutoSum button in the Editing group on the Home tab that is used to enter a SUM function to add a column or row of numbers.	Auto Fill Fill Flash Fill Fill Right fill handle AutoSum button
8.5 Inserting and Deleting Rows and Columns	A new row is inserted above the active cell or selected range. A new column is inserted left of the active cell or selected range. Use the Insert button in the Cells group on the Home tab to insert new rows or columns. Options for formatting new rows or columns are available from the Insert Options button that appears when rows or columns are inserted. Delete rows or columns using the Delete button in the Cells group on the Home tab. The Insert and Delete buttons can also be used to insert or delete cells within the worksheet.	Insert button Insert Options button Delete button
8.6 Sorting Data and Applying Cell Styles	Select a range and choose the sort order option from the Sort & Filter button in the Editing group on the Home tab to arrange the rows by the entries in the first column. Open the Sort dialog box to sort by more than one column or to choose a different column in the range by which to sort. Cell Styles are a set of predefined formatting options applied to selected cells using options in the Cell Styles gallery in the Styles group on the Home tab. Use Cell Styles to format faster and/or promote consistency among worksheets.	Sort & Filter button Cell Styles

continued...

Topic	Key Concepts	Key Terms
8.7 Changing Orientation and Scaling, and Displaying Cell Formulas	New workbooks print on a letter-size page, in portrait orientation, with top and bottom margins of 0.75 inch, and left and right margins of 0.7 inch. Change print options even if you are only exporting the workbook as a PDF because PDFs are generated using the print settings. Change to landscape orientation using the Orientation list box at the Print backstage area. Landscape is a common layout used for wide worksheets. Turn on or turn off the display of formulas in cells instead of the results of formulas by clicking the Formulas tab, and then clicking the Show Formulas button in the Formula Auditing group. Fit Sheet on One Page scales text on a printout so that all columns and rows print on one page. Fit All Columns on One Page is a scaling option that shrinks text to fit all columns in one page width. Fit All Rows on One Page is a scaling option that shrinks text to fit all rows in one page height.	Show Formulas button Fit Sheet on One Page
8.8 Inserting and Renaming a Worksheet, Copying Cells, and Indenting Cell Contents	The Sheet tab bar near the bottom left of the window is used to insert, rename, and navigate among sheets in a workbook. Click the New sheet button on the Sheet tab bar to insert a new worksheet. Right-click a sheet tab and choose Rename to type a new name for a worksheet. Copy and paste cells between worksheets using the Copy and Paste buttons in the Clipboard group. *Keep Source Column Widths* from the Paste Options button lets you paste new cells with the same column width as the source cell.	Sheet tab bar New sheet button
8.9 Using Go To; Freezing Panes; and Shading, Wrapping, and Rotating Cell Entries	The Go To dialog box and Go To Special dialog box from the Find & Select button in the Editing group on the Home tab are used to move to a specific cell in a large worksheet. Freeze Panes fixes rows and/or columns in place for scrolling in large worksheets so that column and row headings do not scroll out of the viewing area. All rows above and all columns left of the active cell are frozen when Freeze Panes is turned on. Cells are shaded with color using the Fill Color button in the Font group on the Home tab. Long text entries in cells can be displayed in narrow columns by wrapping text within the cell column width using the Wrap Text button in the Alignment group on the Home tab. *Angle Counterclockwise* is an option from the Orientation button in the Alignment group on the Home tab that rotates text within a cell 45 degrees.	Go To Go To Special Find & Select button Freeze Panes Fill Color button Wrap Text button *Angle Counterclockwise*

Recheck

Recheck your understanding of the topics covered in this chapter.

Workbook

Chapter review and assessment resources are available in the *Workbook* ebook.

Chapter 9

Working with Functions, Charts, Tables, and Page Layout Options in Excel

Precheck

Check your understanding of the topics covered in this chapter.

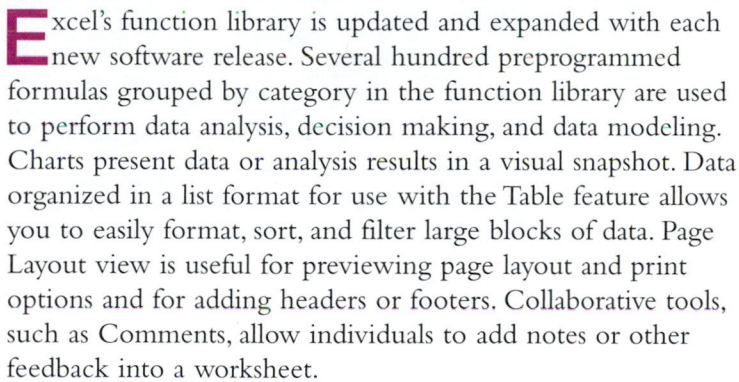

Excel's function library is updated and expanded with each new software release. Several hundred preprogrammed formulas grouped by category in the function library are used to perform data analysis, decision making, and data modeling. Charts present data or analysis results in a visual snapshot. Data organized in a list format for use with the Table feature allows you to easily format, sort, and filter large blocks of data. Page Layout view is useful for previewing page layout and print options and for adding headers or footers. Collaborative tools, such as Comments, allow individuals to add notes or other feedback into a worksheet.

In this chapter, you continue working with formulas by learning the types of references used in formulas and how to use functions to perform statistical, date, financial, and logical analysis. Next, you explore strategies for presenting data using charts, comments, and tables, as well as formatting a worksheet using page layout options and print options.

Learning Objectives

9.1 Create formulas with absolute addresses and range names

9.2 Create formulas with AVERAGE, MAX, and MIN statistical functions

9.3 Enter and format dates and use the TODAY date function

9.4 Perform decision making using the logical IF function

9.5 Use the PMT function to calculate a loan payment

9.6 Create and edit a pie chart

9.7 Create and edit a column chart

9.8 Create and edit a line chart

9.9 Use Page Layout view, insert a header, change margins, and center a worksheet

9.10 Create and edit sparklines and insert comments into a worksheet

9.11 Sort and filter a range defined as a *table*

SNAP If you are a SNAP user, go to your SNAP Assignments page to complete the Precheck, Tutorials, and Recheck.

Data Files

Before beginning this chapter, be sure you have copied the student data files for this course to your storage medium. Steps on downloading and extracting the data files are provided in Chapter 1, Topic 1.8, on pages 22–23.

9.1 Using Absolute Addresses and Range Names in Formulas

Skills

Create a formula with an absolute address

Create a range name

Create a formula with a range name

Tutorials

Absolute Addressing

Naming and Using a Range

Managing Range Names

The formulas in the previous chapter used cell references that are considered a **relative address**, where a column letter and row number change relative to the destination when a formula is copied. For example, the formula *=SUM(A4:A10)* becomes *=SUM(B4:B10)* when copied from a cell in column A to a cell in column B. Relative addressing is the most common addressing method.

Sometimes you need a formula in which one or more addresses should not change when the formula is copied. In these formulas, use cell references that are an **absolute address**. A dollar symbol precedes a column letter and/or row number in an absolute address, for example, *=$A$10*. Some formulas have both a relative and an absolute reference; these are referred to as a **mixed address**. See Table 9.1 for formula addressing examples.

Table 9.1

Cell Addressing and Copying Examples

Formula	Type of Reference	Action If Formula Is Copied
=B4*B2	relative	Both addresses will update.
=$B$4*$B$2	absolute	Neither address will update.
=B4*$B$2	mixed	The address B4 will update; the address $B$2 will not update.
=B4*$B2	mixed	The address B4 will update; the row number in the second address will update, but the column letter will not.
=B4*B$2	mixed	The address B4 will update; the column letter in the second address will update, but the row number will not.

1. Start Excel 2016 and open the workbook named ***FinancialPlanner*** from the Ch9 folder in Student_Data_Files.
2. Use Save As to save a copy of the workbook as **FinancialPlanner-YourName** in a new folder, Ch9, in the CompletedTopicsByChapter folder.
3. Review the worksheet noticing the three rates in row 2; these rates will be used to calculate gross pay, payroll deductions, and savings.
4. Make C4 the active cell, type =b4*b2, and then click the Enter button on the Formula bar, or press Ctrl + Enter.

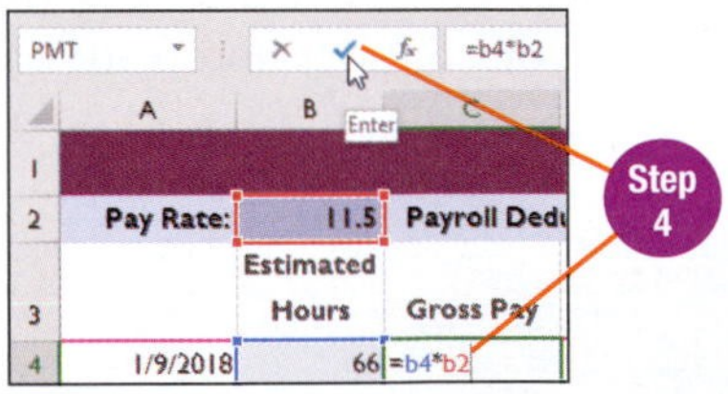

5. Use the fill handle in C4 to copy the formula to C5:C30.
6. Make C5 the active cell and look at the formula in the Formula bar.

The #VALUE! error occurs because B3 is a label and has no mathematical value.

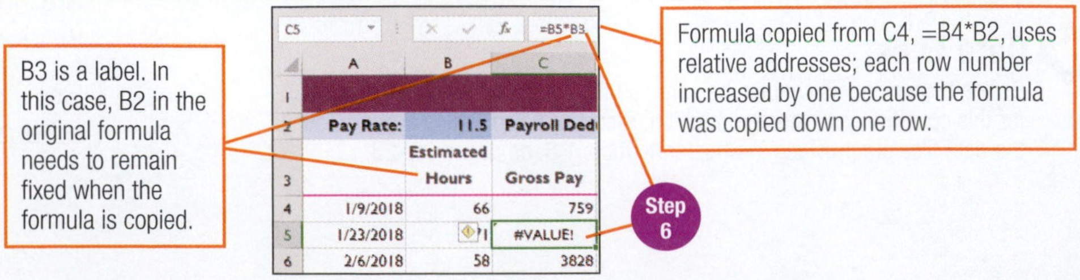

7 Select C5:C30 and press the Delete key or click the Clear button in the Editing group on the Home tab and then click *Clear All*.

8 Make C4 the active cell and edit the formula so that it reads *=B4*$B$2*.

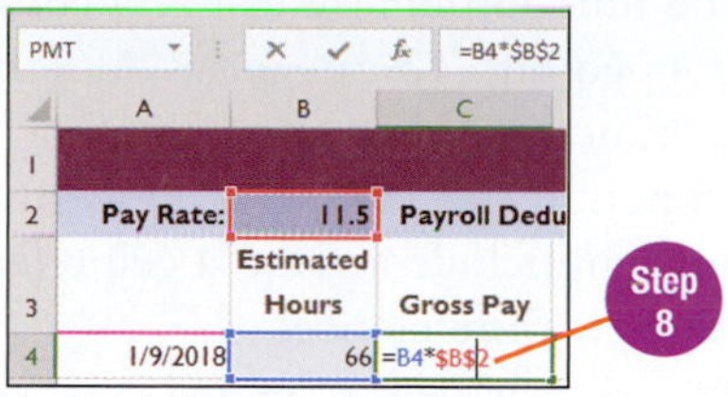

9 Use the fill handle in C4 to copy the formula to C5:C30.

10 Make D4 the active cell and enter the formula =c4*e2.

11 Make E4 the active cell and enter the formula =c4-d4.

12 Select D4:E4 and use the fill handle to copy the formulas to D5:E30.

A cell or a range can be referenced by a descriptive label, which makes a formula easier to understand. For example, the formula *=Hours*PayRate* is readily understood. Names are also used when a formula needs an absolute reference because a cell or range name is automatically absolute. Cell or range names are assigned using the Name box at the left end of the Formula bar. Use the Name Manager button in the Formulas tab to manage cell names after they are created.

13 Make G2 the active cell, click in the Name box at the left end of the Formula bar, type SaveRate, and then press Enter.

A range name can use letters, numbers, and some symbols. Spaces are not valid in a range name, and the first character in a name must be a letter, an underscore, or a backward slash (\).

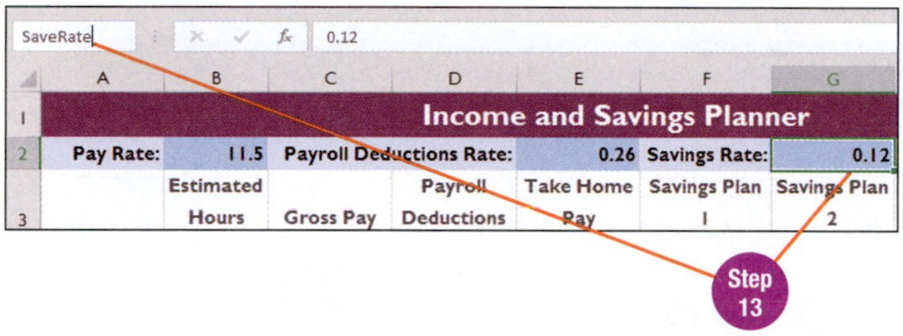

14 Make F4 the active cell, type =e4*SaveRate, and then press Ctrl + Enter or click the Enter button.

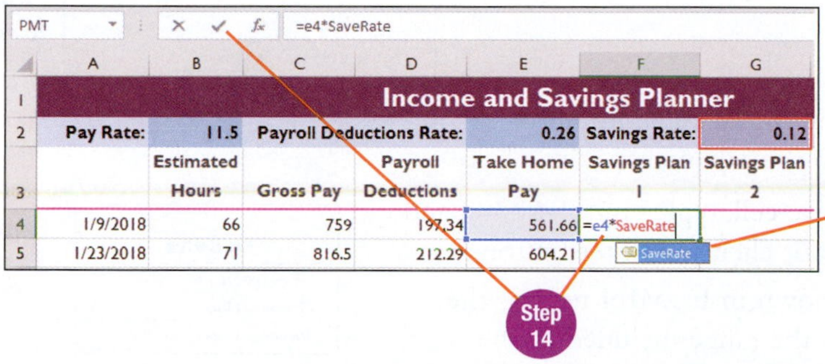

AutoComplete displays range names in the current workbook. Press Tab to accept the name in the list, or select the name (when necessary), and then press Tab.

15 Use the fill handle in F4 to copy the formula to F5:F30.

16 Save the revised workbook using the same name (**FinancialPlanner-YourName**). Leave the workbook open for the next topic.

App Tip

Press Function key F4 to make an address absolute. F4 cycles through variations of absolute and mixed addresses for the reference in which the insertion point is positioned.

Quick Steps

Make Cell Reference Absolute
Type dollar symbol before column letter and/or row number, or press F4 to cycle through variations of addressing.

Name a Cell or Range
1. Select cell or range.
2. Type name in Name box.
3. Press Enter.

App Tip

A range name can also be used in the Go To dialog box to move the active cell.

App Tip

Upper and lowercase letters separate words in a range name; however, range names are not case sensitive—*SaveRate* and *saverate* are considered the same name.

9.2 Entering Formulas Using Statistical Functions

Skills

Enter AVERAGE formula

Enter MAX formula

Enter MIN formula

Tutorial

Using Statistical Functions

The function library in Excel contains more than 400 preprogrammed formulas grouped into 13 categories. All formulas based on functions begin with the name of the function followed by the function's parameters in parentheses. The parameters for a function (referred to as an **argument**) will vary depending on the formula chosen and can include a value, a cell reference, a range, multiple ranges, or a combination of values with references.

1. With the **FinancialPlanner-YourName** workbook open, make I4 the active cell.

2. Click the AutoSum button arrow in the Editing group on the Home tab and then click *Average* at the drop-down list.

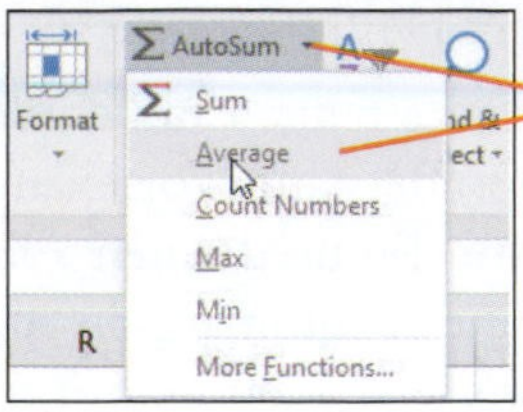

Excel enters *=AVERAGE(B4:H4)* in the cell with the range *B4:H4* selected. In this instance, Excel suggests the wrong range.

3. With the range B4:H4 highlighted in the formula cell, select B4:B30, and then press Enter or click the Enter button.

Excel returns the result *68.96296296* in the formula cell, which is the arithmetic mean of the hours in column B. If empty cells or cells containing text are included in the formula's argument, they are ignored.

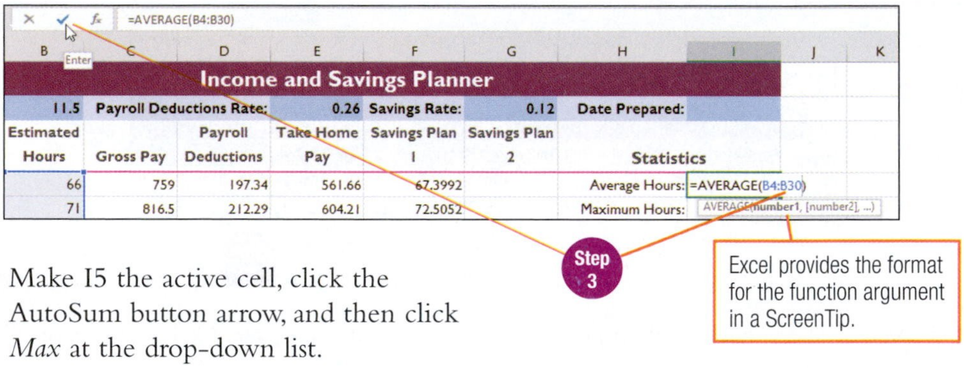

4. Make I5 the active cell, click the AutoSum button arrow, and then click *Max* at the drop-down list.

5. Type b4:b30 and then press Enter or click the Enter button.

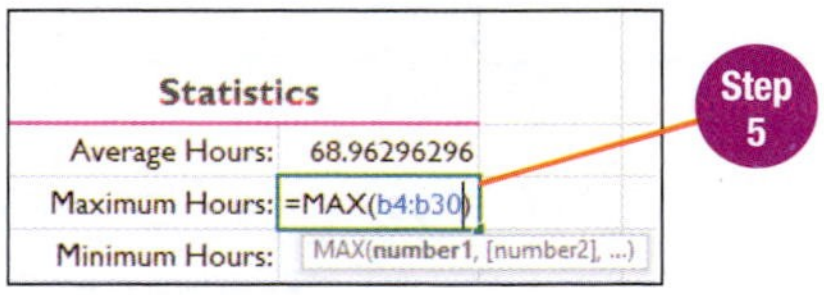

Excel returns the value *80* in the formula cell. MAX returns the largest value found in the range included in the argument.

6. Make I6 the active cell, type =min(b4:b30), and then press Enter or click the Enter button.

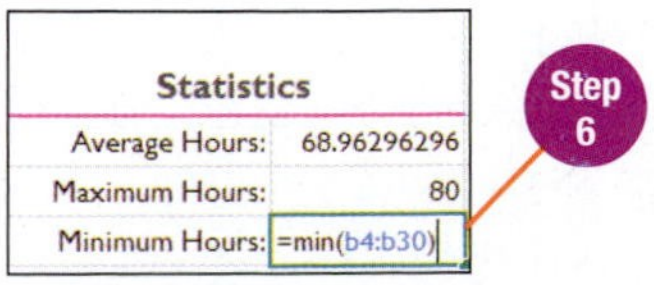

The result *48* is shown in I6. MIN returns the smallest value within the range included in the argument.

Excel's Insert Function dialog box assists with finding and entering functions and their arguments into a formula cell. A variety of methods can be used to open the Insert Function dialog box, including clicking the Insert Function button on the Formula bar or clicking the Formulas tab and then clicking the Insert Function button in the Function Library group.

App Tip

Shift + F3 is the keyboard shortcut to open the Insert Function dialog box.

7 Make I8 the active cell and then click the Insert Function button on the Formula bar (button right of Enter button).

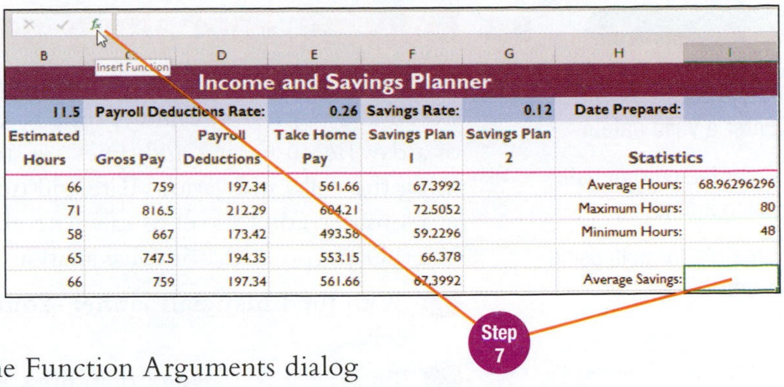

8 Click the *Or select a category* list arrow and then click *Statistical* at the drop-down list.

9 Click *AVERAGE* in the *Select a function* list box and then click OK.

10 Type f4:f30 in the *Number1* text box at the Function Arguments dialog box and then press Enter or click OK.

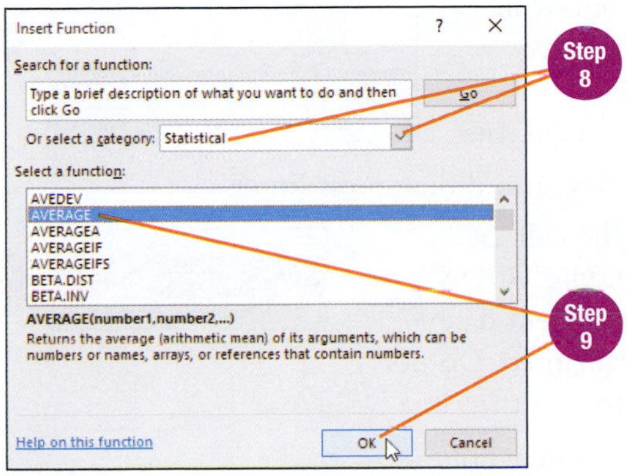

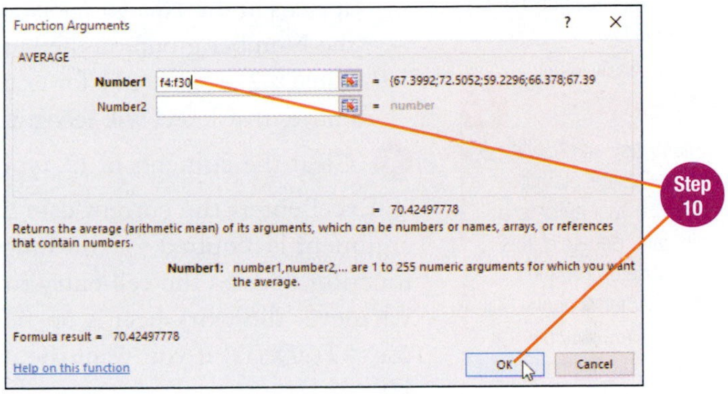

11 Make I9 the active cell, click the AutoSum button arrow, and then click *More Functions* at the drop-down list.

12 With the text already selected in the *Search for a function* text box, type max and then press Enter or click the Go button.

13 With MAX selected in the *Select a function* list box, click OK.

14 Type f4:f30 in the *Number1* text box at the Function Arguments dialog box, and then press Enter or click OK.

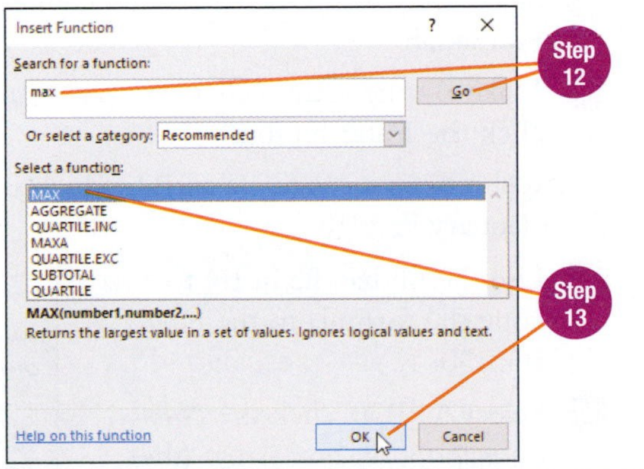

15 Make I10 the active cell, click the AutoSum button arrow, and then click *Min* at the drop-down list.

16 Type f4:f30 and then press Enter, or click the Enter button.

17 Save the revised workbook using the same name (**FinancialPlanner-YourName**). Leave the workbook open for the next topic.

Quick Steps

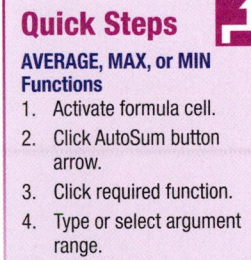

AVERAGE, MAX, or MIN Functions

1. Activate formula cell.
2. Click AutoSum button arrow.
3. Click required function.
4. Type or select argument range.
5. Press Enter.

Beyond Basics COUNT Function

Count Numbers from the AutoSum button arrow inserts a COUNT function, which returns the number of cells in the argument range that have values. Use the function COUNTA if you want to count all the cells within the argument range including cells that contain text. Empty cells are ignored in both cases.

9.3 Entering, Formatting, and Calculating Dates

Skills

Enter a valid date

Enter the current date using a function

Create a formula using a date

Format dates

Tutorial
Using Date and Time Functions

Oops!

General instead of *Date* appears? Excel did not recognize your entry as a valid date. Generally, this is because of a typing error. Try Step 2 again. Still *General*? You may need to check the Region in the Control Panel.

App Tip

The function *=NOW()* returns the current date and time in the active cell.

A date typed into a cell in normal date format, such as *May 1, 2018* or *5/1/2018,* is stored as a numerical value. A time is stored as a decimal value representing a fraction of a day. Because dates and times are stored as values, calculations can be performed using the cells, and various date and time formats can be applied to the results.

Consider using Excel to calculate elapsed time for scheduling, payroll, membership, or other purposes that involve analysis of date or time.

1. With the **FinancialPlanner-YourName** workbook open, make I2 the active cell.
2. Type 12/20/2018 and then press Enter.
3. Make I2 the active cell and notice that *Date* appears in the *Number Format* option box in the Number group on the Home tab. See Table 9.2 on page 219 for examples of cell entries that Excel will recognize as a valid date.

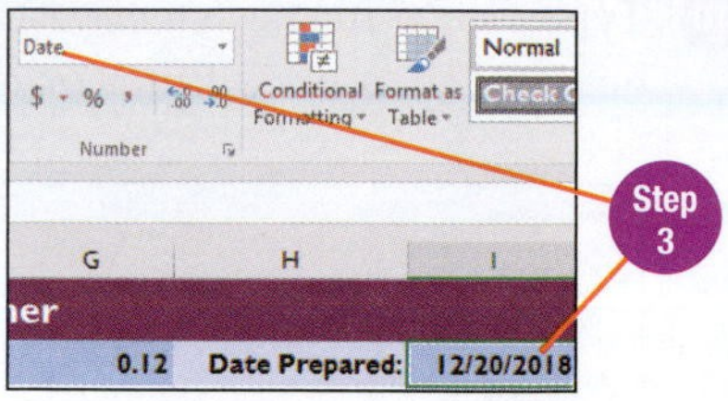

4. Clear the contents of I2, type =today(), and then press Enter.

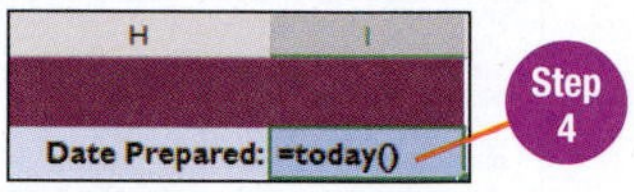

Excel enters the current date into the cell. No argument is required for this function. The TODAY function updates the cell entry to the current date whenever the worksheet is opened or printed. Do not use *=TODAY()* if you want the date to stay the same.

5. Make B3 the active cell and insert a new column.
6. Type Pay Date in B3 and then click A3.
7. Type End Date in A3 and then click the Enter button.
8. Select A3:B3 and then click the Center button in the Alignment group on the Home tab.
9. Make B4 the active cell, type =a4+7, and then click the Enter button.

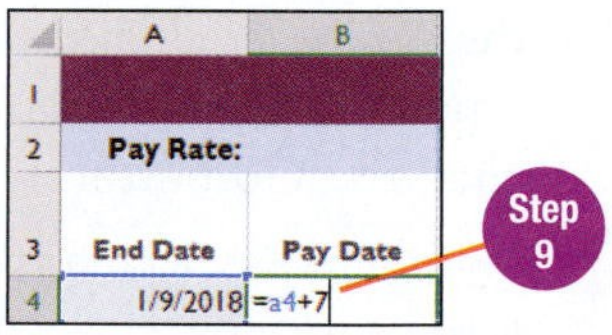

Excel returns *1/16/2018* in B4, which is seven days from January 9, 2018.

10. Use the fill handle in B4 to copy the formula to the range B5:B30.
11. Select A4:B30, click the *Number Format* option box arrow (the arrow next to *Date*), and then click the *More Number Formats* option at the bottom of the drop-down list.
12. At the Format Cells dialog box with *Date* selected in the *Category* list box, click *14-Mar-12* in the *Type* list box and then click OK.

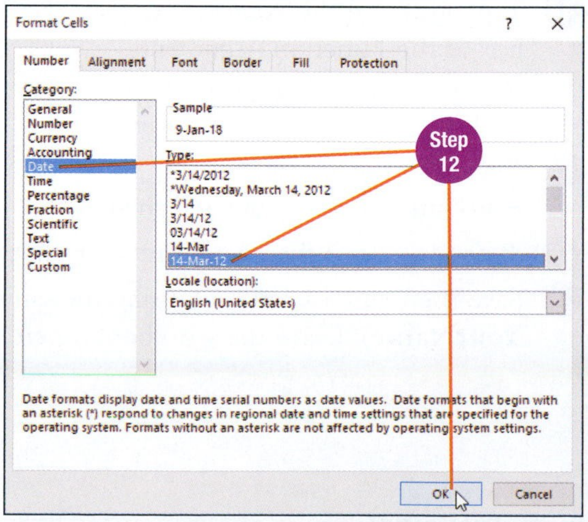

13 Click any cell to deselect the range.

14 Save the revised workbook using the same name (**FinancialPlanner-YourName**). Leave the workbook open for the next topic.

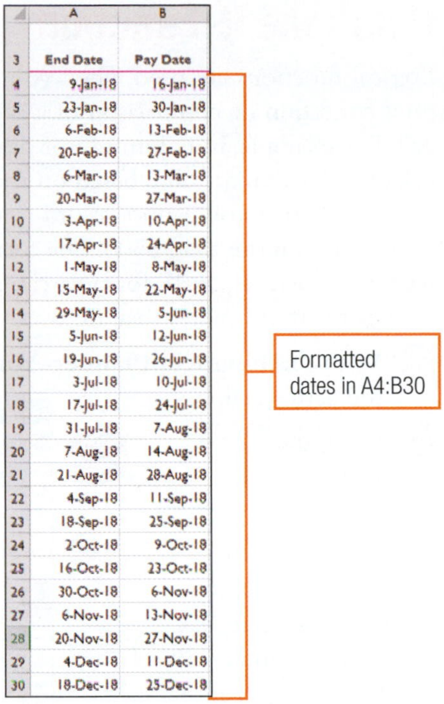

	A	B
3	End Date	Pay Date
4	9-Jan-18	16-Jan-18
5	23-Jan-18	30-Jan-18
6	6-Feb-18	13-Feb-18
7	20-Feb-18	27-Feb-18
8	6-Mar-18	13-Mar-18
9	20-Mar-18	27-Mar-18
10	3-Apr-18	10-Apr-18
11	17-Apr-18	24-Apr-18
12	1-May-18	8-May-18
13	15-May-18	22-May-18
14	29-May-18	5-Jun-18
15	5-Jun-18	12-Jun-18
16	19-Jun-18	26-Jun-18
17	3-Jul-18	10-Jul-18
18	17-Jul-18	24-Jul-18
19	31-Jul-18	7-Aug-18
20	7-Aug-18	14-Aug-18
21	21-Aug-18	28-Aug-18
22	4-Sep-18	11-Sep-18
23	18-Sep-18	25-Sep-18
24	2-Oct-18	9-Oct-18
25	16-Oct-18	23-Oct-18
26	30-Oct-18	6-Nov-18
27	6-Nov-18	13-Nov-18
28	20-Nov-18	27-Nov-18
29	4-Dec-18	11-Dec-18
30	18-Dec-18	25-Dec-18

Quick Steps

TODAY Function

1. Activate formula cell.
2. Type =today().
3. Press Enter.

Good to Know

Many businesses that operate globally have adopted the International Standards Organization (ISO) date format YYYY-MM-DD to avoid confusion with a date written as 02/04/03, which could mean February 4, 2003 (US), or April 2, 2003 (UK). Another strategy is to format a date with the month spelled out like the format used at Step 12.

Table 9.2

Entries Excel Recognizes as Valid Dates or Times

Dates	Times
12/20/18; 12-20-18	4:45 (stored as 4:45:00 AM)
Dec 20, 2018	4:45 PM (stored as 4:45:00 PM)
20-Dec-18 or 20 Dec 18 or 20/Dec/18	16:45 (stored as 4:45:00 PM)

Note: *The year can be entered as two digits or four digits and the month as three characters or spelled in full. Times are generally entered as hh:mm, but in situations that require a higher level of accuracy, they are entered as hh:mm:ss.*

Alternative Method **Entering a Date Using a Date Function Formula**

You can also enter dates into cells as DATE functions. A DATE function is typed as *=DATE(Year,Month,Day)*. For example *=DATE(2018,12,20)*. Use the Date & Time button in the Function Library group on the Formulas tab to browse other Date or Time functions.

Beyond Basics **Region Setting and Dates**

The Region setting in the Control Panel affects the format that Excel 2016 will recognize as a valid date. Following are examples of date format by region:

English (United States)	*m/d/yy*
English (Canada)	*yy/m/d* (Windows 10) or *d/m/yy* (Windows 7)
English (United Kingdom)	*d/m/yy*

To change the Region, open the Control Panel from the desktop and select the Region icon or the Clock, Language, and Region category.

9.4 Using the IF Function

Skills

Enter IF function

Tutorial

Using Logical IF Functions

Logical functions are used when you need a formula to perform a calculation based on a condition or comparison of a cell, with a value or the contents of another cell. For example, in column G of the Income and Savings Planner worksheet, you calculated a savings value based on the take-home pay amounts in column F. Suppose you decide that you cannot afford to contribute to your savings plan unless your take-home pay is more than $500. The formula in column G does not accommodate this scenario; however, an IF formula can analyze the take-home pay and calculate the savings for those values that are over your minimum.

1. With the **FinancialPlanner-YourName** workbook open, make H4 the active cell.

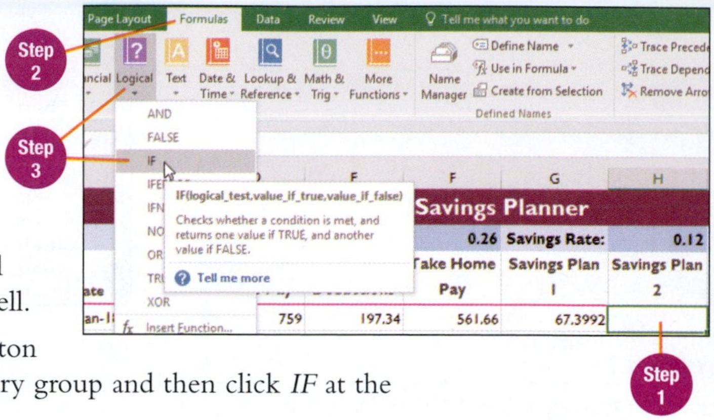

2. Click the Formulas tab.

   The category drop-down lists in the Function Library group are another way that you can find an Excel function to insert into a cell.

3. Click the Logical button in the Function Library group and then click *IF* at the drop-down list.

4. With the insertion point positioned in the *Logical_test* text box at the Function Arguments dialog box, type f4>500 and then press Tab or click in the *Value_if_true* text box.

   A logical test is a statement to evaluate a comparison so that one of two actions can be performed. In this case, the statement *f4>500* tells Excel to determine if the value that resides in F4 is greater than 500. All logical tests result in either a true or a false response—either the value is greater than 500 (true) or the value is not greater than 500 (false). See Table 9.3 on page 221 for more examples of logical tests.

5. Type f4*SaveRate and then press Tab or click in the *Value_if_false* text box.

   The statement in the *Value_if_true* text box is the formula you want Excel to calculate when the logical test proves true. In other words, if the value in F4 is greater than 500, you want Excel to multiply the value in F4 times the value in the cell named SaveRate (.12).

6. Type 0 and then click OK.

App Tip

Formulas, values, or text are all valid entries for the *Value_if_true* and *Value_if_false* text boxes.

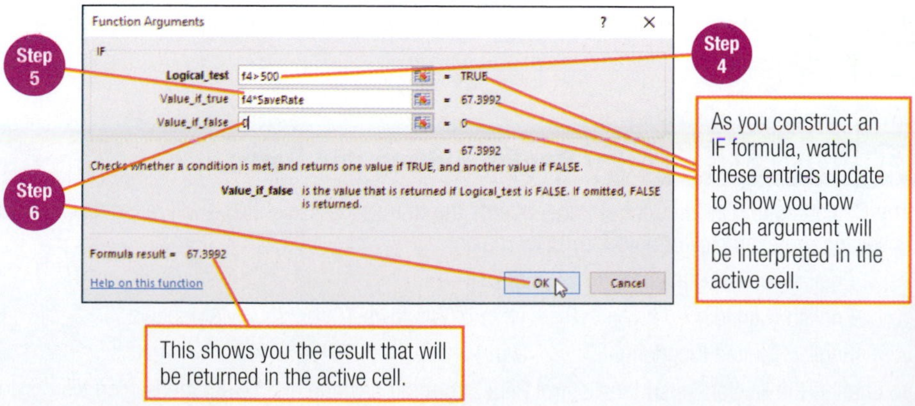

The *Value_if_false* statement is the formula you want Excel to calculate when the logical test proves false. In other words, if the value in F4 is 500 or less, you want zero placed in the cell because you have decided that you cannot afford to contribute to your savings plan.

7 Look in the Formula bar at the IF statement entered into the active cell *=IF(F4>500,F4*SaveRate,0)*.

Using the Function Arguments dialog box to build an IF statement is a good idea because the commas and parentheses are inserted automatically in the correct positions within the formula.

8 Use the fill handle in H4 to copy the formula to the range H5:H30.

9 Review the results in H5:H30. Notice the cells that have 0 appear in a row where the take-home pay value in column F is 500 or less.

10 Select C4:H30, and then click the Quick Analysis button that appears below the selection.

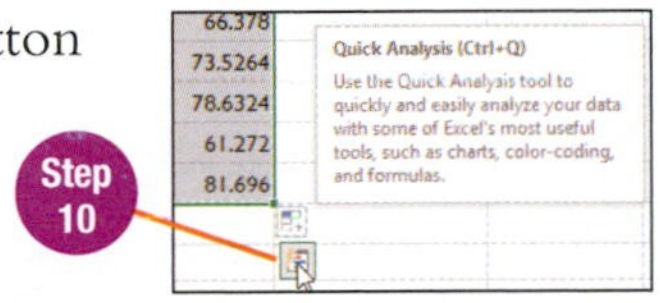

11 Click the Totals tab, and then click the Sum button in the *Totals* gallery (first button).

Excel creates SUM functions for each column in the selected range and enters them in row 31.

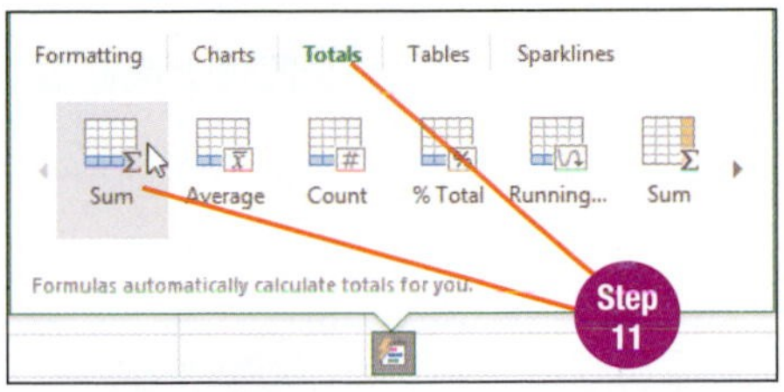

12 Select D4:H31, click the Home tab, and then click the Comma Style button.

13 Apply the Comma Style format to C2 and J4:J10.

14 Apply the Percent Style format to F2 and H2.

15 Select C31:H31 and then add a Top and Double Bottom Border.

16 Save the revised workbook using the same name (**FinancialPlanner-YourName**). Leave the workbook open for the next topic.

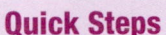

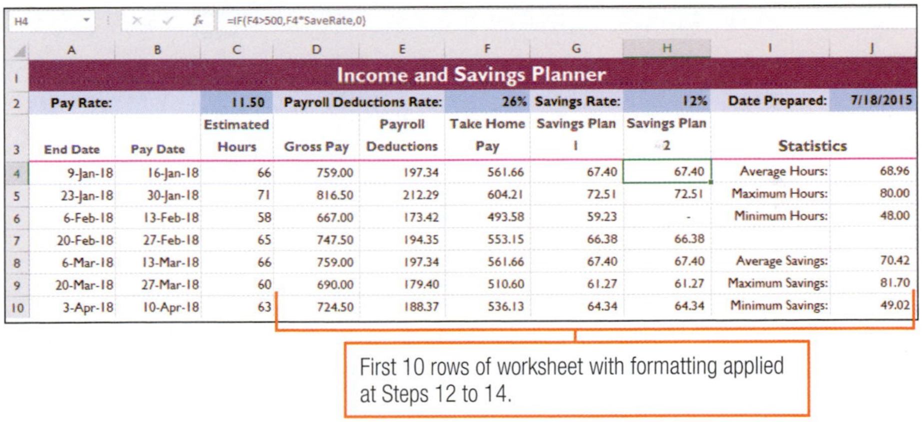

H4 =IF(F4>500,F4*SaveRate,0)

	A	B	C	D	E	F	G	H	I	J
1	Income and Savings Planner									
2	Pay Rate:		11.50	Payroll Deductions Rate:		26%	Savings Rate:	12%	Date Prepared:	7/18/2015
3	End Date	Pay Date	Estimated Hours	Gross Pay	Payroll Deductions	Take Home Pay	Savings Plan 1	Savings Plan 2	Statistics	
4	9-Jan-18	16-Jan-18	66	759.00	197.34	561.66	67.40	67.40	Average Hours:	68.96
5	23-Jan-18	30-Jan-18	71	816.50	212.29	604.21	72.51	72.51	Maximum Hours:	80.00
6	6-Feb-18	13-Feb-18	58	667.00	173.42	493.58	59.23	-	Minimum Hours:	48.00
7	20-Feb-18	27-Feb-18	65	747.50	194.35	553.15	66.38	66.38		
8	6-Mar-18	13-Mar-18	66	759.00	197.34	561.66	67.40	67.40	Average Savings:	70.42
9	20-Mar-18	27-Mar-18	60	690.00	179.40	510.60	61.27	61.27	Maximum Savings:	81.70
10	3-Apr-18	10-Apr-18	63	724.50	188.37	536.13	64.34	64.34	Minimum Savings:	49.02

First 10 rows of worksheet with formatting applied at Steps 12 to 14.

Quick Steps

IF Function

1. Activate formula cell.
2. Click Formulas tab.
3. Click Logical button.
4. Click *IF*.
5. Type *Logical_test* statement.
6. Type value or formula in *Value_if_true* text box.
7. Type value or formula in *Value_if_false* text box.
8. Click OK.

App Tip

Percent Style multiplies the value in the cell by 100 and adds a percent symbol (%) to the cell.

Table 9.3

IF Statement Logical Test Examples

Logical Test	Condition Evaluated	IF Statement Example
F4>=500	Is the value in F4 greater than or equal to 500?	=IF(F4>=500,F4*SaveRate,0)
F4<500	Is the value in F4 less than 500?	=IF(F4<500,0,F4*SaveRate)
F4<=500	Is the value in F4 less than or equal to 500?	=IF(F4<=500,0,F4*SaveRate)
F4=$K$2	Is the value in F4 equal to the value in K2? Assume value in K2 is the take-home pay value for which you will set aside savings.	=IF(F4=$K$2,F4*SaveRate,0)
Hours<>0	Is the value in the cell named Hours not equal to 0?	=IF(Hours<>0,Hours*PayRate,0) Calculates Gross Pay when hours have been logged

9.5 Using the PMT Function

Skills

Enter PMT function

Tutorial
Using Financial Functions

Financial functions in Excel can be used for a variety of tasks that involve saving or borrowing money, such as calculating the future value of an investment, calculating the present value of an investment, or calculating borrowing criteria, such as interest rates, terms, or payments. If you are considering a loan or mortgage, use Excel's PMT function to determine an estimated loan payment. The PMT function uses a specified interest rate, number of payments, and loan amount to calculate a regular payment. Once a payment is shown, you can manipulate the interest rate, term, or loan amount to find a payment with which you are comfortable.

1. With the **FinancialPlanner-YourName** workbook open, click the LoanPlanner sheet tab.

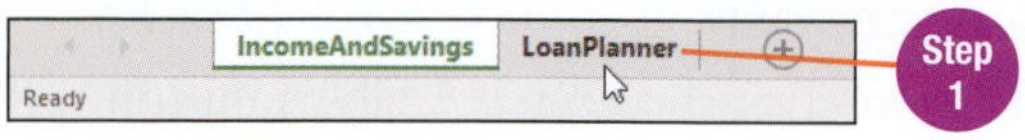

2. Make B7 the active cell.
3. Click the Formulas tab, click the Financial button in the Function Library group, scroll down the drop-down list, and then click *PMT*.

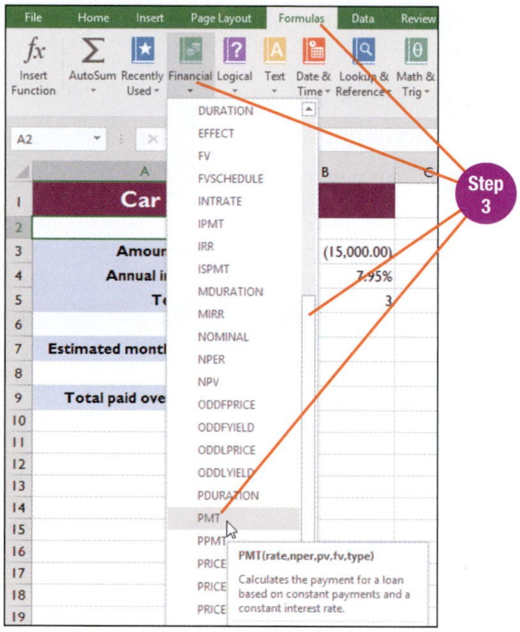

Oops!

Can't see B4? Drag the Function Arguments title bar right until the dialog box is no longer obscuring your view of columns A and B.

4. With the insertion point positioned in the *Rate* text box at the Function Arguments dialog box, click B4 and then type /12.

The interest rate in B4 is expressed as the interest rate per year. Typing /12 after B4 causes Excel to divide the interest rate in B4 by 12 to calculate the monthly interest rate. To use the PMT function correctly, you need to ensure that the time periods are all the same. In other words, if you want to find a monthly payment, you need to make sure the rate and terms are also in monthly units. Most lending institutions express interest with the annual rate (not monthly) but compound the interest monthly.

5. Click in the *Nper* text box, click B5, and then type *12.

The value in B5 is the number of years you will take to pay back the loan. Multiplying the value times 12 will convert the value to the number of months to repay the loan. Most lending institutions express the repayment term in years (not months).

6 Click in the *Pv* text box and then click B3.

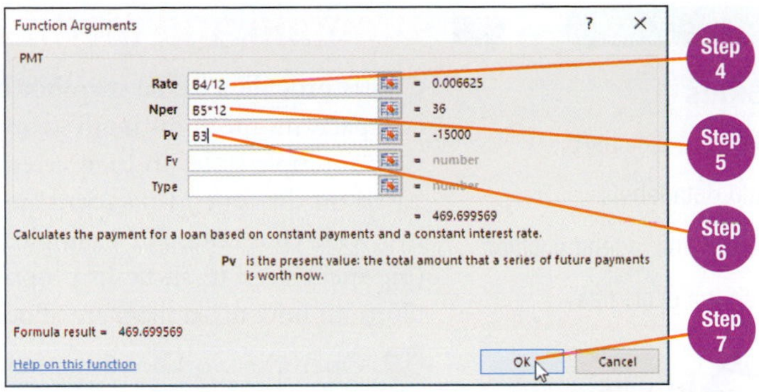

Pv stands for *present value* and represents the amount you want to borrow (referred to as the *principal*). Notice the amount borrowed is entered as a negative value in this worksheet. By default, Excel considers payments as negative values because money is subtracted from your bank balance when you make a loan payment. By entering a negative number for the amount borrowed, the PMT formula will return a positive value for the calculated loan payment. Whether you prefer to show a negative value for the amount borrowed or for the estimated monthly loan payment is a matter of personal preference; both options are acceptable.

7 Click OK.

Excel returns the payment *$469.70* in B7.

8 Look in the Formula bar at the PMT statement entered into the active cell *=PMT(B4/12,B5*12,B3)*.

9 Make B9 the active cell and enter the formula =b7*b5*12.

Excel calculates the total cost for the loan to be $16,909.18.

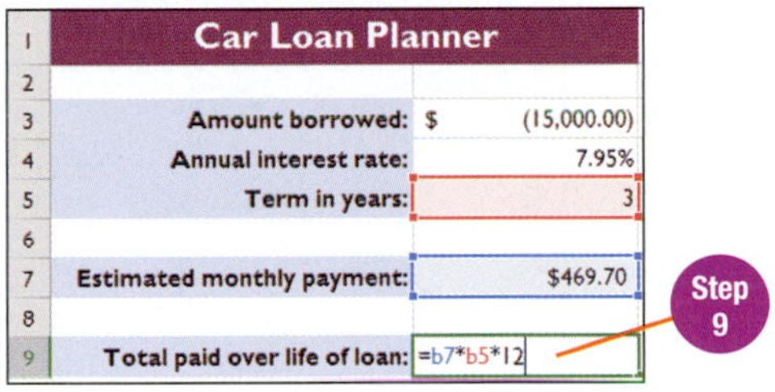

10 Change the value in B5 from *3* to *4*.

Notice that increasing the term one more year reduces your monthly payment; however, the total cost of the loan increases because you are making more payments.

11 Save the revised workbook using the same name (**FinancialPlanner-YourName**) and then close the workbook.

Quick Steps

PMT Function

1. Activate formula cell.
2. Click Formulas tab.
3. Click Financial button.
4. Scroll down list.
5. Click *PMT*.
6. Enter *Rate* particulars.
7. Enter *Nper* particulars.
8. Enter *Pv* value or reference.
9. Click OK.

App Tip

PMT assumes a constant payment and a constant interest rate; this function cannot be used to estimate loan payments where the payment or interest rate is variable.

View

Model Answer

Compare your completed file with the model answer.

App Tip

Type a negative symbol in front of PMT if the amount borrowed is a positive value and you want the payment to be a positive value. For example, *=-PMT(B4/12,B5*12,B3)*.

Beyond Basics

Using FV to Calculate the Future Value of an Investment

Another useful financial function is FV, which is used to calculate the future value of a series of regular payments that earn a constant interest rate. For example, if you deposit $100 each month for 10 years into an investment account that earns 9.75% per year (compounded monthly), the FV function *=FV(9.75%/12,10*12,100)* calculates the value of the account after the 10-year period to be $20,193.76.

9.6 Creating and Modifying a Pie Chart

Skills

Create a pie chart

Add data labels

Modify the legend position

Edit the chart title

Tutorials

Creating Charts

Formatting with Chart Buttons

Inserting a Shape

Formatting a Shape

Changing Chart Design

Changing Chart Formatting

Charts provide a visual snapshot of data. Charts can illustrate trends, proportions, and comparisons more distinctly than numbers alone. Excel provides 15 categories of charts with multiple styles in each category. The Quick Analysis button recommends charts based on the type of data you are analyzing and allows you to preview the chart style live with your data. For example, a **pie chart** is a circular graph with each data point (pie slice) sized to show its proportion to a total. Governments often use a pie chart to illustrate how tax dollars are allocated across various programs and services.

1. Open the workbook named ***SocialMediaStats***.
2. Use Save As to save a copy of the workbook as **SocialMediaStats-YourName** in the Ch9 folder in CompletedTopicsByChapter.
3. Select A5:B10.

Before you can insert a chart you first need to select the data that you want Excel to represent in a chart.

4. Click the Quick Analysis button that appears below the selection area and then click the Charts tab.
5. Click *Pie* at the *Charts* gallery.

Excel graphs the data in a pie chart and places the chart overlapping the cells within a chart object window. Notice also that the chart object is selected with selection handles, three chart editing buttons, and the Chart Tools Design and Format tabs in the ribbon.

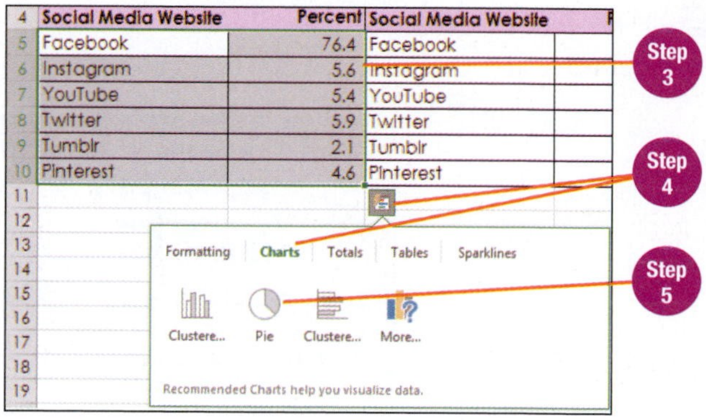

App Tip

Roll the mouse over the chart options to see a live preview of the data graphed in the chart above the gallery.

6. With the chart selected, drag the chart with the mouse positioned over any white unused area inside the chart borders, to the approximate location shown below.

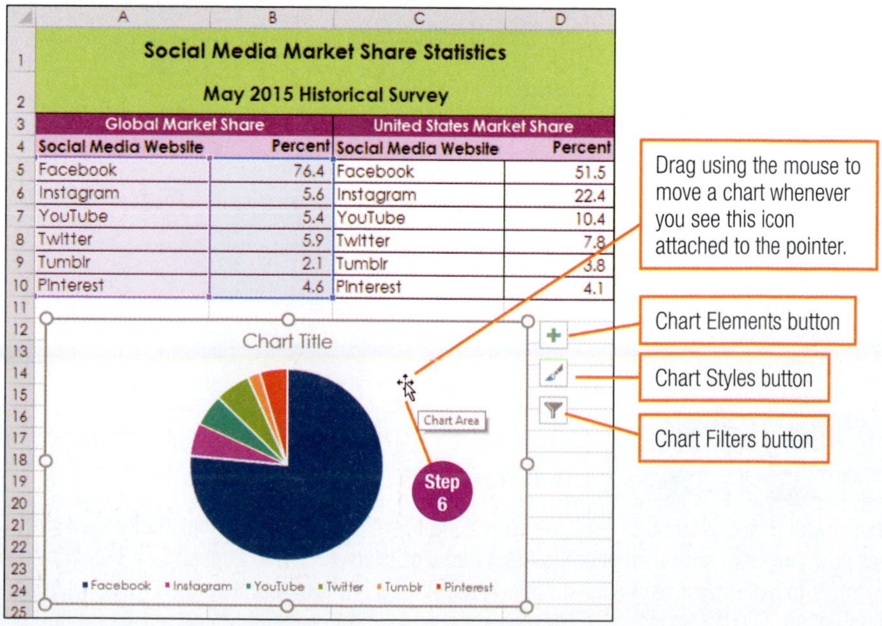

7 Click the Chart Elements button (displays as a plus symbol next to the chart).

8 Click the *Data Labels* check box to insert a check mark, click the right-pointing arrow that appears at the right end of the *Data Labels* option, and then click *Outside End*.

Although pie charts show proportions well, adding data labels allows a reader to include context with the size of each pie slice.

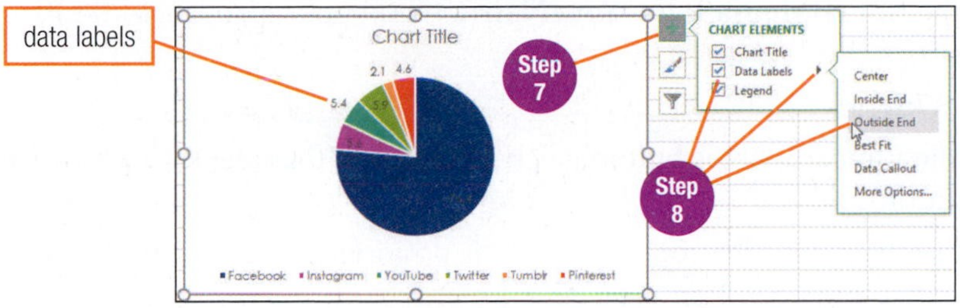

9 With Chart Elements still displayed, click at the right end of *Legend* when the right-pointing arrow appears and then click *Right*.

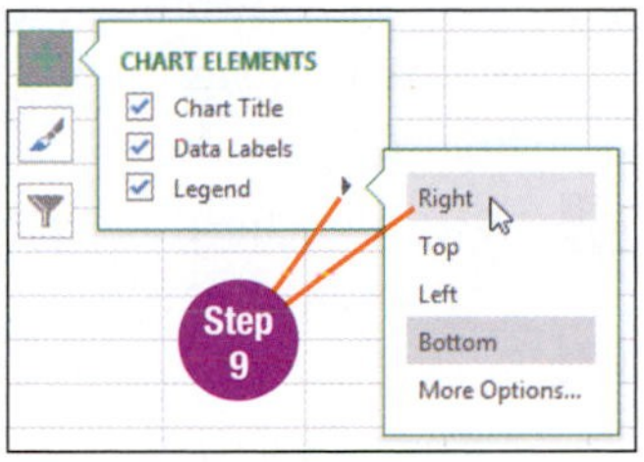

10 Click to select the *Chart Title* object inside the chart window, drag to select *Chart Title*, type Global Market Share, and then click in any white, unused area within the chart to deselect the title.

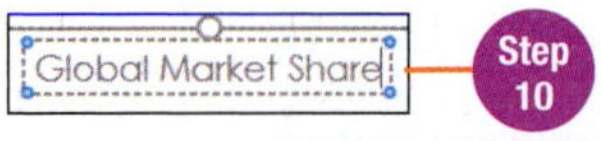

11 Select C5:D10 and insert a second pie chart, as shown in Figure 9.1, by completing steps similar to those in Steps 4 to 10.

12 Save the revised workbook using the same name (**SocialMediaStats-YourName**). Leave the workbook open for the next topic.

Quick Steps

Create a Pie Chart

1. Select range.
2. Click Quick Analysis button.
3. Click Charts.
4. Click *Pie*.
5. Move and/or modify chart elements as required.

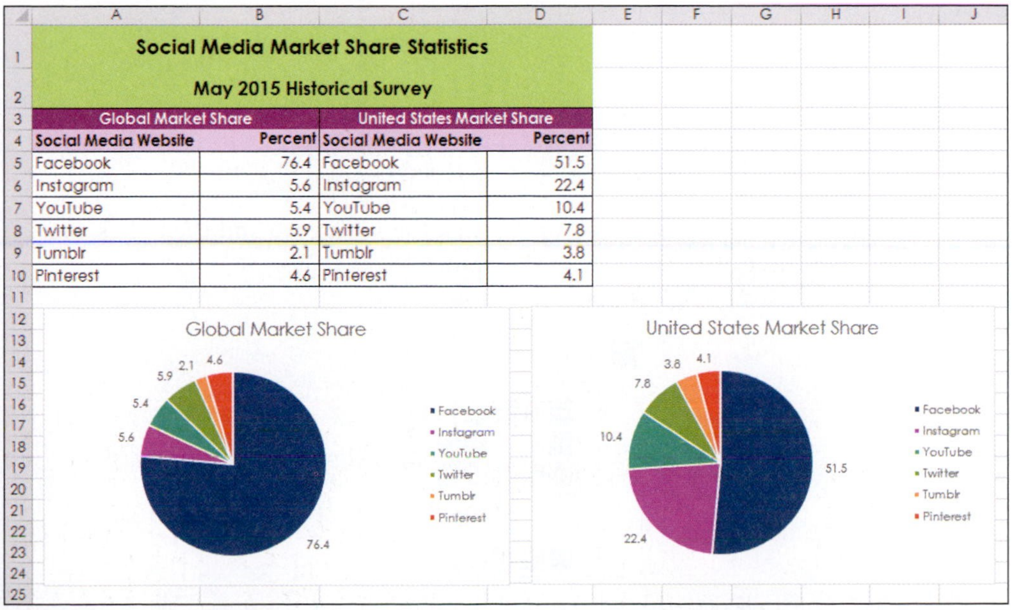

Figure 9.1

The revised workbook shows side-by-side pie charts for Social Media Market Share Statistics.

App Tip

A popular technique to emphasize a pie slice is to move the slice away from the rest of the pie (called a *point explosion*). To do this, click to select the pie slices, then click to isolate the individual slice and drag the slice away from the pie.

9.7 Creating and Modifying a Column Chart

Skills

Create a column chart

Change the chart style

Change the chart color scheme

Add axis titles

In a **column chart**, each data point is a colored bar that extends up from the **category axis** (horizontal axis, also called *x-axis*) with the bar height representing the value of the data points on the **value axis** (vertical axis, also called *y-* or *z-axis*). Use a column chart to compare one or more series of data side by side. Column charts are often used to identify trends or illustrate comparisons over time or categories.

1. With the **SocialMediaStats-YourName** workbook open, click the Facebook sheet tab.
2. Select A7:B14.
3. Click the Quick Analysis button, click Charts, and then click *Clustered Column* (first button).
4. Drag the chart until the top left corner is positioned in row 1 under column letter C (see Figure 9.2 on page 227).
5. Drag the bottom right selection handle down and right to resize the chart until the bottom right corner is at approximately the bottom right border of J16 (see Figure 9.2).
6. With the chart selected, click the Chart Styles button (displays as a paintbrush next to the chart).
7. Scroll down to the bottom of the Style list and then click the last option in the gallery (*Style 16*).

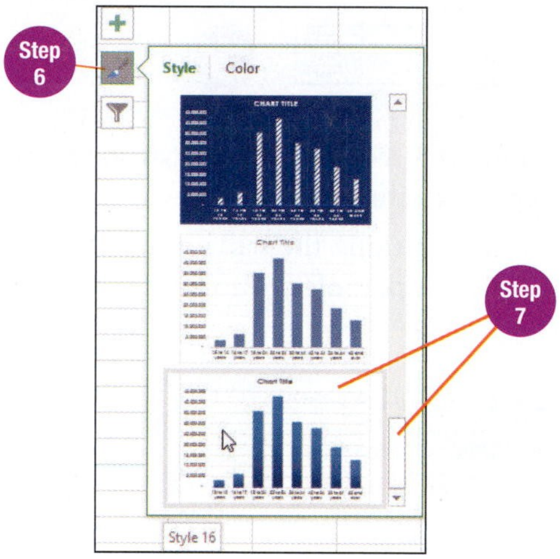

8. With the *Chart Styles* gallery still open, click the Color tab and then click the third row in the *Colorful* section of the color gallery (*Color 3*).

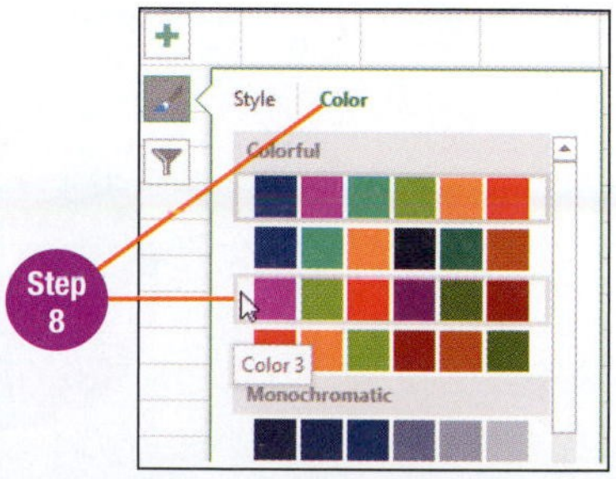

9. Click the Chart Elements button.

Additional chart elements options are available for column charts that are not possible with a pie chart.

10 Click the *Axis Titles* check box to insert a check mark.

Excel adds an Axis Title object to the vertical axis and to the horizontal axis.

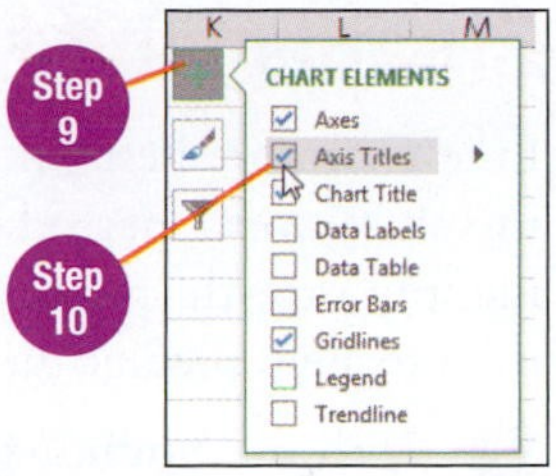

11 With the Axis Title object along the vertical axis already selected, select the title text and type North American Users.

12 Click to select the *Axis Title* object along the horizontal axis and press Delete to remove the object.

13 Edit the *Chart Title* to Facebook Audience by Age Group.

14 Compare your chart to the one shown in Figure 9.2. If necessary, redo an action in Steps 4 to 13.

15 Save the revised workbook using the same name (**SocialMediaStats-YourName**). Leave the workbook open for the next topic.

Quick Steps

Create a Column Chart

1. Select range.
2. Click the Quick Analysis button.
3. Click Charts.
4. Click *Clustered Column*.
5. Move and/or modify chart elements as required.

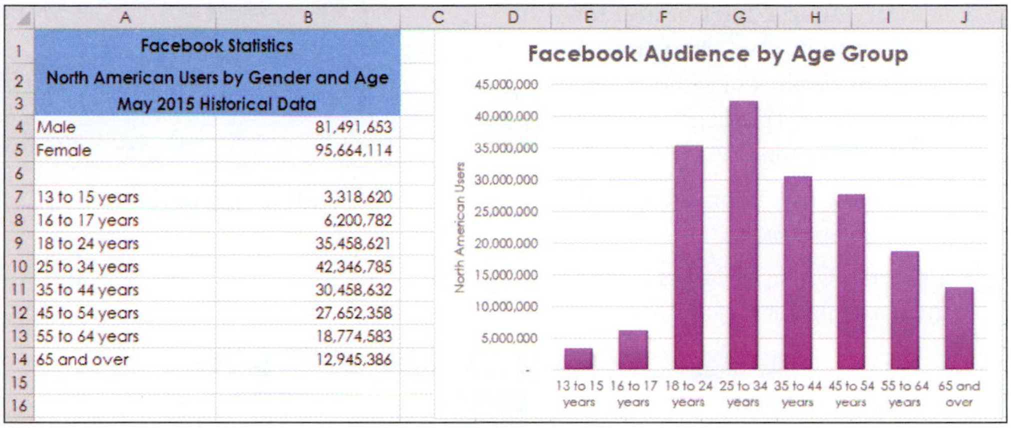

Figure 9.2

Shown above is a column chart for Facebook North American Audience Statistics by Age Group.

Alternative Method Inserting and Modifying a Chart Using the Ribbon

Buttons in the Charts group on the Insert tab can also be used to create a chart. Select the data range, click the Insert tab, and then click the button for the desired chart type in the Charts group. Once a chart has been inserted, the Chart Tools Design and Format tabs contain the same options to modify the chart as those found in the *Chart Elements* and *Chart Styles* galleries.

App Tip

Microsoft added six new chart types to Excel 2016: Treemap, Sunburst, Histogram, Box & Whisker, Funnel, and Waterfall.

Beyond Basics Recommended Charts

Not sure which chart type best represents your data? Select the data you want to graph and Excel shows a series of customized charts that best suit the selection when you click the Charts tab from the Quick Analysis button. Use the *More Charts* option to view other chart types. Alternatively, click the Insert tab and then click the Recommended Charts button in the Charts group to view recommended charts in the Insert Chart dialog box.

9.8 Creating and Modifying a Line Chart

Skills

Create a line chart

Move a chart to a new sheet

Format an axis

Format data labels

Line charts are best suited for data where you want to illustrate trends and changes in values over a period of time. With a **line chart**, a reader can easily spot a trend, or identify growth spurts, dips, or unusual points in the series. Line charts are also often used to help predict future values based on the direction of the line.

1. With the **SocialMediaStats-YourName** workbook open, click the FacebookUserTimeline sheet tab.
2. Select A4:B15.
3. Click the Quick Analysis button, click Charts, and then click *Line*.
4. With the chart selected, click the Move Chart button in the Location group on the Chart Tools Design tab.

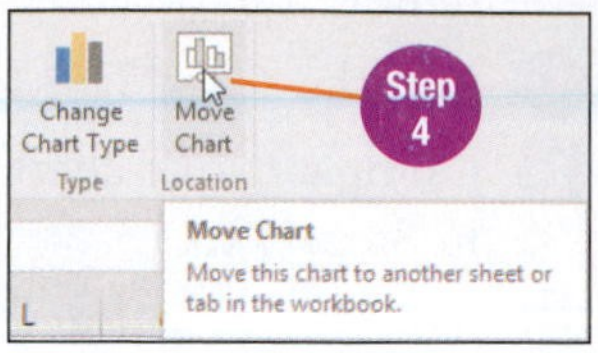

5. Click *New sheet*, type FBTimelineChart, and then press Enter or click OK.

Click the **Move Chart** button to move a chart to its own chart sheet, which automatically scales the chart to fit a letter-size page in landscape orientation.

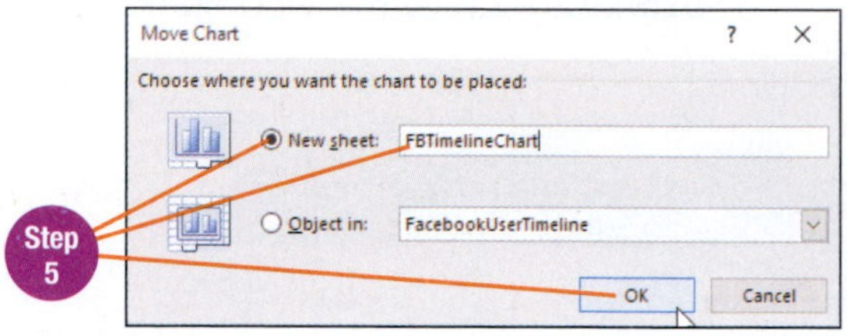

6. With the Chart Tools Design tab active, click the second option in the *Chart Styles* gallery (*Style 2*).
7. Click the Change Colors button in the Chart Styles group and then click the third row in the *Colorful* section of the color gallery (*Color 3*).

Oops!

No border around dates? Click the axis labels a second time. Sometimes the chart is selected the first time you click.

8. Edit the Chart Title to Facebook Active Users Historical Timeline.

In the next step you will correct the axis labels. The dates in column A were incorrectly converted, changing *Dec* to *Jan*.

9. Click to select the dates in the category axis along the bottom of the chart. Make sure you see a border and selection handles around the axis labels.
10. Double-click inside the selected axis labels to open the Format Axis task pane at the right side of the window.
11. Click *Text axis* in the *Axis Options* section of the task pane.

Notice the axis labels change to show the December dates as they appeared in the worksheet.

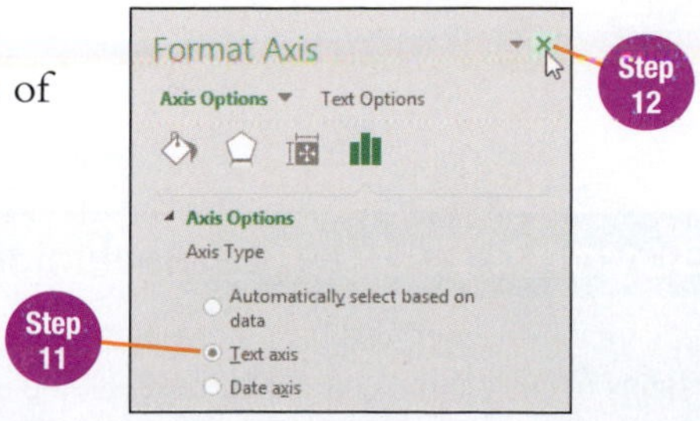

12. Close the Format Axis task pane.

13 Click any data value on a data point in the line chart to select the entire series of data labels.

14 Right-click any of the selected data values and then click *Format Data Labels* at the shortcut menu.

This opens the Format Data Labels task pane.

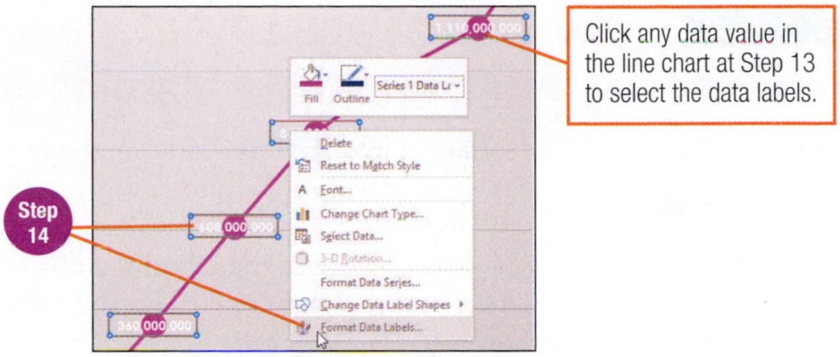

15 Click *Above* in the *Label Position* section of the Format Data Labels task pane with the Label Options tab active.

16 Click Text Options and then click *Text Fill* to expand the options list.

17 Click the Color button and then click *Black, Text 1* (second color in first row).

18 Close the Format Data Labels task pane and then click in the window outside the chart to deselect the data labels.

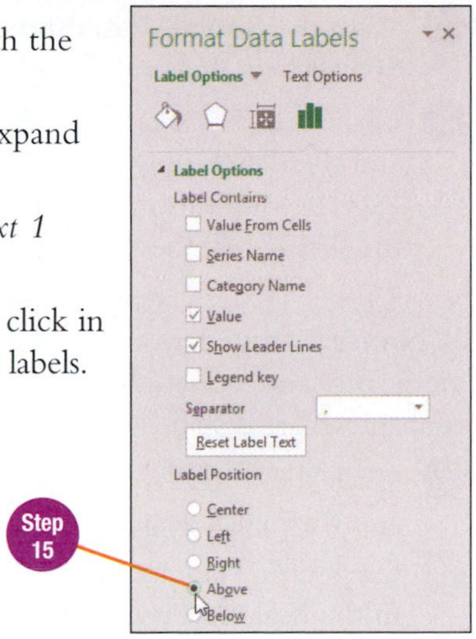

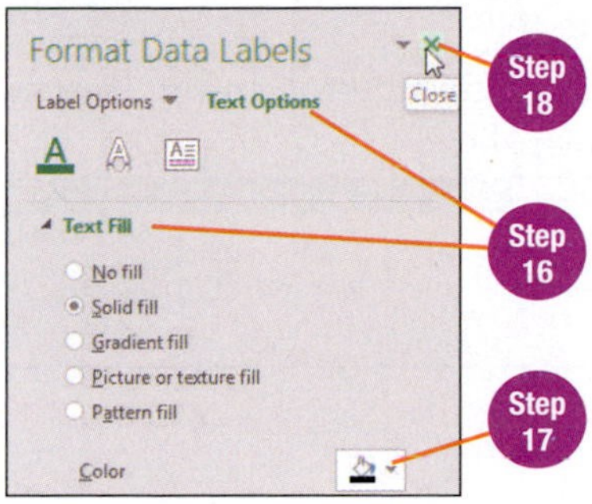

19 Compare your chart with the chart shown in Figure 9.3 and make corrections if necessary.

20 Save the revised workbook using the same name (**SocialMediaStats-YourName**). Leave the workbook open for the next topic.

Quick Steps

Create a Line Chart

1. Select range.
2. Click Quick Analysis button.
3. Click Charts.
4. Click *Line*.
5. Move and/or modify chart elements as required.

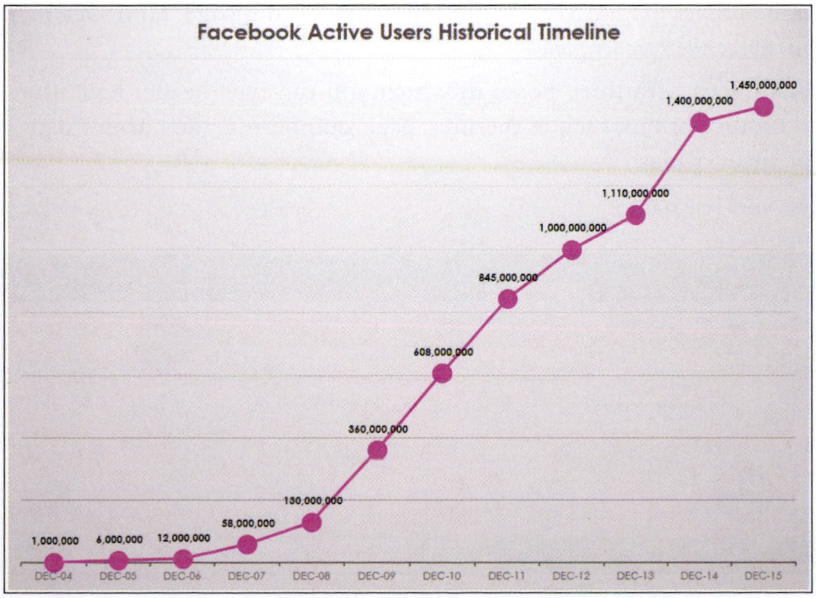

Figure 9.3

Line chart for Facebook Active Users Historical Timeline created in new chart sheet

9.9 Using Page Layout View, Adding a Header, and Changing Margins

Skills

Work in Page Layout view

Add a header

Change margins

Center worksheet horizontally and vertically

Tutorials

Changing Page Layout Options

Inserting Headers and Footers

Inserting an Image

In **Page Layout view**, you can preview page layout options similarly to Print Preview; however, you also have the advantage of being able to edit the worksheet. The worksheet is divided into pages with white space around the edges of each page showing the size of the margins and a ruler along the top and left of the column letters and row numbers. Pages and cells outside the active worksheet are grayed out; however, you can click any page or cell to add new data.

1. With the **SocialMediaStats-YourName** workbook open, click the SocialMediaWebsites sheet tab and then click E1.

2. Click the View tab and then click the Page Layout button in the Workbook Views group.

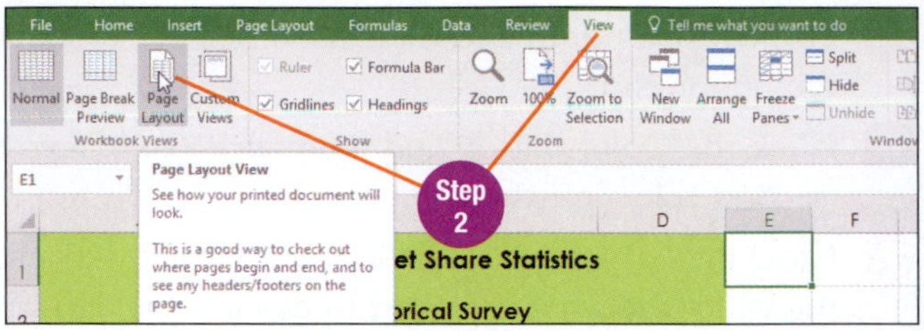

Notice in Page Layout view you can see that the right pie chart is split over two pages.

3. Click the Page Layout tab, click the Orientation button in the Page Setup group, and then click *Landscape* at the drop-down list.

4. Click the *Width* list arrow in the Scale to Fit group (displays *Automatic*) and then click *1 page* at the drop-down list.

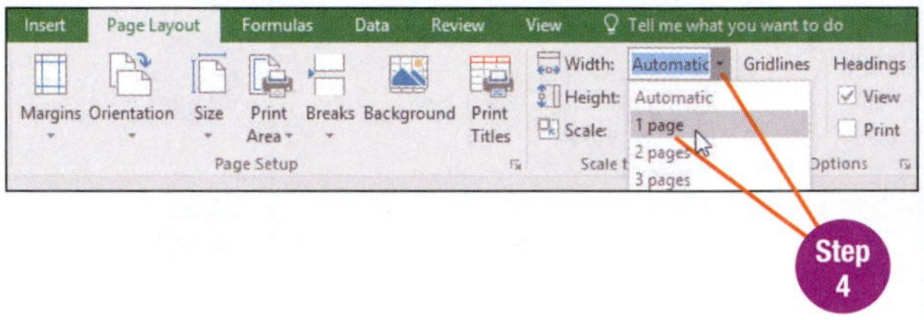

Inserting a Header or Footer

A header prints at the top of each page and a footer prints at the bottom of each page. Headers and footers are divided into three sections, with the left section left-aligned, the center section centered, and the right section right-aligned by default.

5. Click the dimmed text *Add header* near the top center of the page. ***Hint:*** *You may need to scroll up to see the Header pane.*

The Header pane opens with three boxes in which you can type header text and/or add header and footer options, such as pictures, page numbering, the current date or time, and file or sheet names.

6. Type your first and last names.

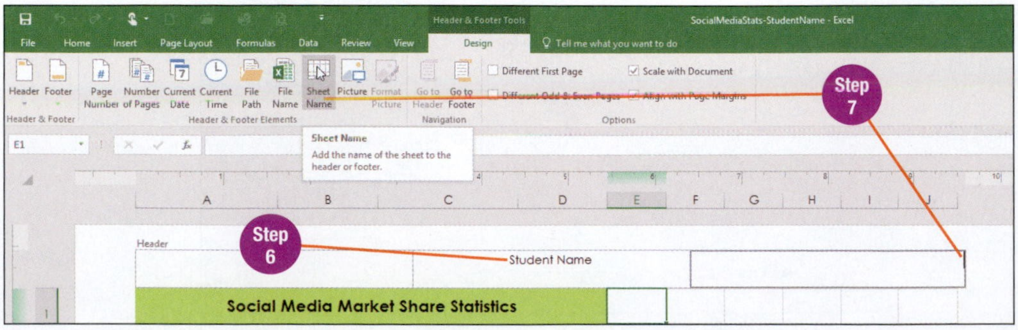

App Tip

View buttons are also at the right end of the Status bar next to the Zoom buttons. Page Layout view is the middle of the three view buttons.

App Tip

Click the Go to Footer button in the Navigation group on the Header & Footer Tools Design tab to move to the *Footer* sections.

Oops!

Can't see the full width of the page? If you're using a tablet or device with a small screen, decrease the Zoom to less than 100 percent until you can view the page width.

7 Click at the right of the center section text box in the Header pane to open the right section text box and then click the Sheet Name button in the Header & Footer Elements group on the Header & Footer Tools Design tab.

Excel inserts the code *&[Tab]*, which is replaced with the sheet tab name when you click outside the *Header* section.

8 Click at the left of the Header pane to open the left section text box and then click the File Name button in the Header & Footer Elements group.

Excel inserts the code *&[File]*, which is replaced with the file name when you click in the worksheet area.

9 Click any cell in the worksheet area.

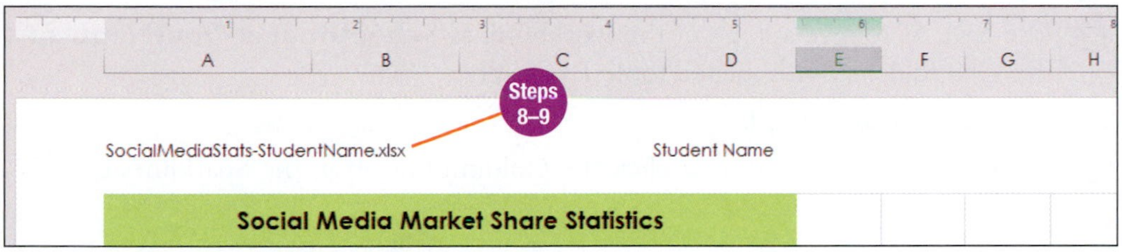

Changing Margins

Worksheet margins are 0.75 inch top and bottom and 0.7 inch left and right with the header or footer printing 0.3 inch from the top or bottom of the page. Adjust margins to add more space around the edges of a page, or between the header and footer text and the worksheet. Center a smaller worksheet horizontally and/or vertically to improve the page appearance.

10 Click the Page Layout tab, click the Margins button in the Page Setup group, and then click *Wide*.

The *Wide* preset margin option changes the top, bottom, left, and right margins to 1 inch and the header and footer margins to 0.5 inch.

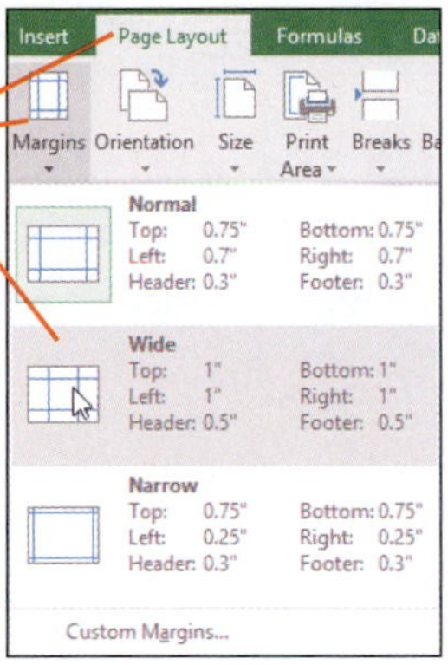

11 Click the Margins button and click *Custom Margins*.

12 Click the *Horizontally* and the *Vertically* check boxes in the *Center on page* section to insert a check mark in each box and then click OK.

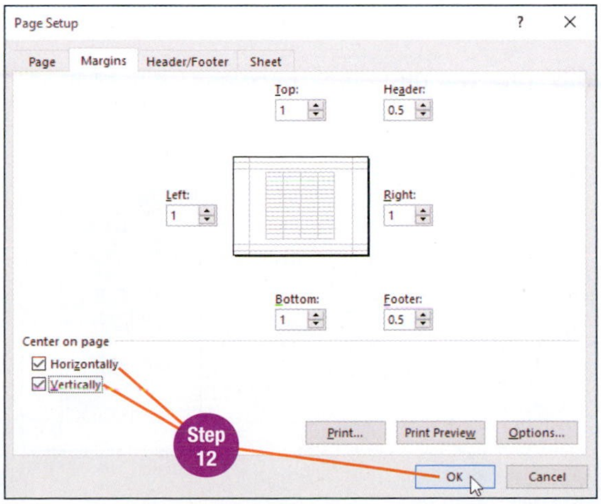

13 Click the Facebook sheet tab, click A6, change to Page Layout view, and modify print options by completing steps similar to those in Steps 3 to 12 to improve the appearance of the printed worksheet.

14 Save the revised workbook using the same name (**SocialMediaStats-YourName**) and then close the workbook.

Quick Steps

Add a Header
1. Switch to Page Layout view.
2. Click *Add header.*
3. Type header text in center section or click in left or right section and type header text.
4. Add header elements as required.
5. Click in worksheet area.

Change Margins
1. Click Page Layout tab.
2. Click Margins button.
3. Click preset option or click *Custom Margins* and change margins at Page Setup dialog box.

Center the Worksheet
1. Click Page Layout tab.
2. Click Margins button.
3. Click *Custom Margins.*
4. Click *Horizontally* and/or *Vertically* check boxes.
5. Click OK.

App Tip

Page Layout view is not available for chart sheets; however, you can add a header or change margins in Print Preview by using the Margins button or Page Setup hyperlink.

View

Model Answer

Compare your completed file with the model answer.

9.10 Creating and Modifying Sparklines and Inserting Comments

Skills

Insert sparkline charts

Insert a comment

Edit a comment

Tutorials

Summarizing Data with Sparklines

Inserting, Editing, and Printing Comments

A **sparkline chart** is a miniature chart inserted into an individual cell within a worksheet. Sparkline charts are used to draw attention to trends or variations in data on a smaller scale than a column or line chart. Excel offers three types of sparkline charts: Line, Column, or Win/Loss.

A comment attached to a cell pops up when the reader points or clicks the cell. Comments are used to add explanatory information, pose questions, or provide other feedback to readers when a workbook is shared.

1. Open the workbook named ***SchoolBudget***.
2. Use Save As to save a copy of the workbook as **SchoolBudget-YourName** in the Ch9 folder in CompletedTopicsByChapter.
3. Make K3 the active cell.
4. Click the Insert tab and then click the Column button in the Sparklines group.

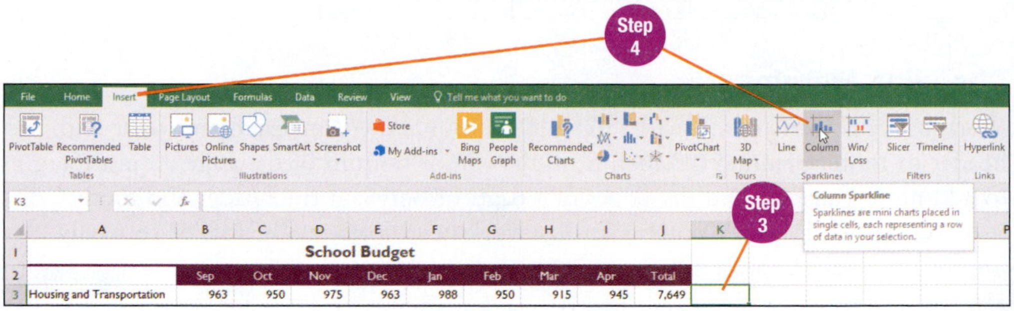

5. Type b3:i3 in the *Data Range* text box at the Create Sparklines dialog box and then press Enter or click OK.

Excel embeds a column chart within the cell.

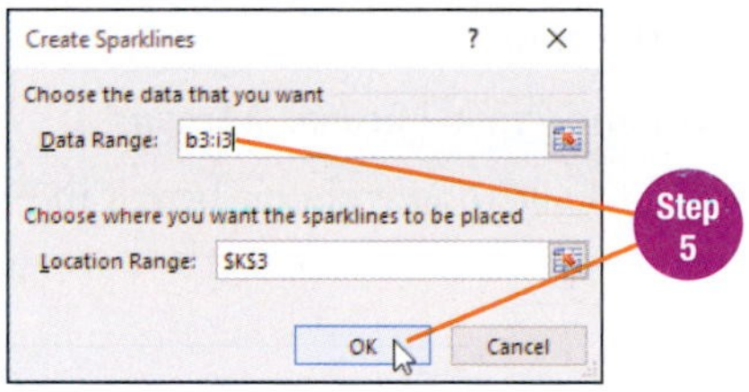

App Tip

Increase the row height and/or column width to enlarge sparkline charts.

6. Use the fill handle to copy the sparklines column chart from K3 to K4:K11.

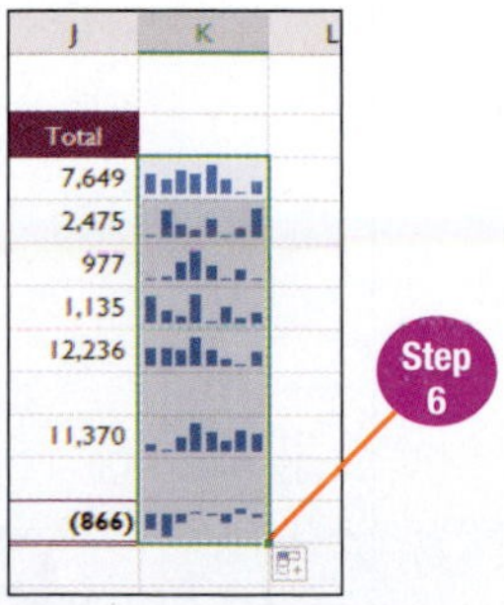

7 Click the *High Point* check box in the Show group on the Sparkline Tools Design tab to insert a check mark.

Excel highlights the bar in the column chart with the highest value by coloring it red. Other options in the tab are used to change the type or style, emphasize other points, show markers, or edit the data source.

Step 7

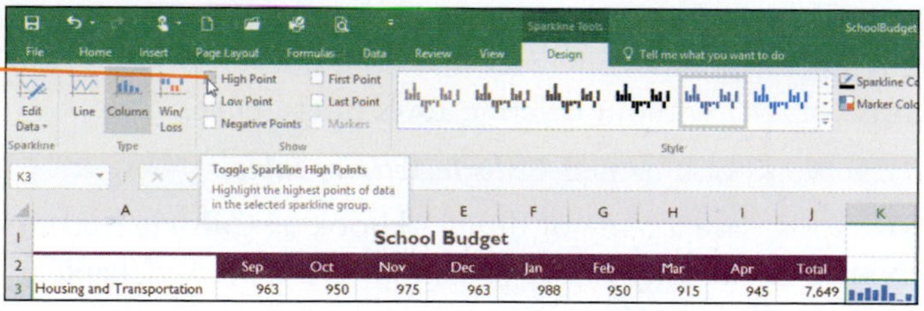

8 Make K2 the active cell, type Trend, and then click E9.

9 Click the Review tab and then click the New Comment button in the Comments group.

10 Type Assuming extra hours during Christmas break. and then click I3.

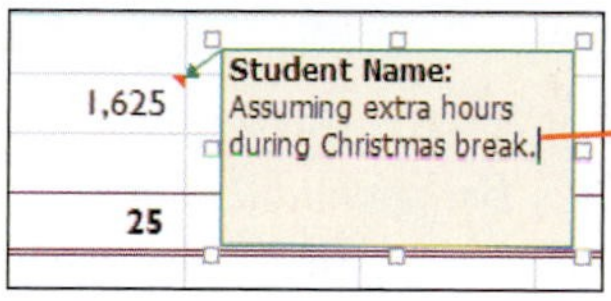

Step 10

Excel inserts a red triangle in the upper right corner of a cell to indicate a comment exists for the cell.

11 Click the New Comment button, type May be able to use last month's rent., and then click any cell.

12 Point to I3 with the mouse to display the comment in a pop-up box.

Step 12

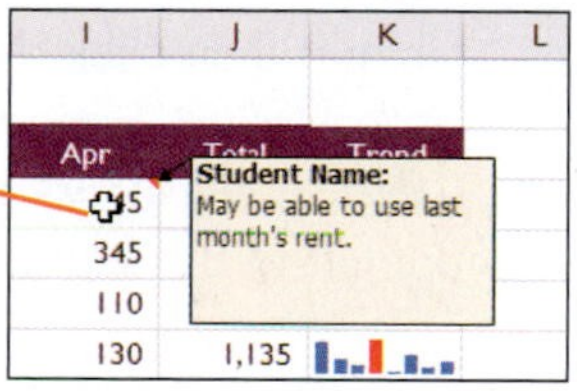

13 Click I3 to activate the cell.

14 Click the Edit Comment button in the Comments group and edit the comment text to *May be able to use last month's rent, which lowers this value to 55.*

Step 14

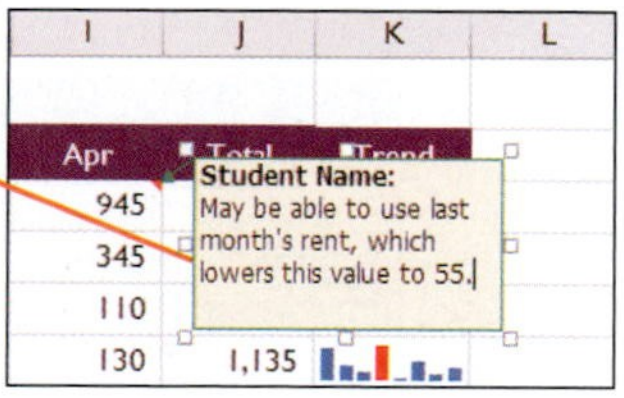

15 Click any cell to finish editing the Comment box.

16 Click the Show All Comments button in the Comments group to display both comment boxes in the worksheet.

17 Click the Show All Comments button to turn off the display of comment boxes.

18 Save the revised workbook using the same name (**SchoolBudget-YourName**) and then close the workbook.

Quick Steps

Insert Sparklines

1. Activate cell.
2. Click Insert tab.
3. Click required sparklines chart button.
4. Type source data range.
5. Click OK.

Insert a Comment

1. Activate cell.
2. Click Review tab.
3. Click New Comment button.
4. Type comment text.
5. Click any cell.

View

Model Answer

Compare your completed file with the model answer.

Beyond Basics Printing Comments

By default, comments do not print with a worksheet. You can choose to print a list of comments on a separate page after the worksheet prints or you can turn on the display of the comment boxes and print the worksheet with the comments as shown in the worksheet. Use the *Comments* option in the *Print* section of the Page Setup dialog box with the Sheet tab active to specify the print option.

9.11 Working with Tables

Skills

Format a range as a table

Sort a table

Filter a table

Tutorials

Formatting Data as a Table

Adding Rows to a Table

Sorting a Table

Filtering a Table

Filtering Data Using Conditional Formatting or Cell Attributes

Applying Conditional Formatting Using Quick Analysis

Format a range of cells as a table to analyze, sort, and filter data as an independent unit. A worksheet can have more than one table, which means you can isolate and analyze data in groups. A table also allows you to choose from a variety of preformatted table styles, which is faster than manually formatting a range. Use tables for any block of data organized in a list format.

A **filter** temporarily hides any data that does not meet a criterion. Use filters to look at subsets of data without deleting rows in the table.

1. Open the workbook named ***CalorieActivityTable***.
2. Use Save As to save a copy of the workbook as **CalorieActivityTable-YourName** in the Ch9 folder in CompletedTopicsByChapter.
3. Select A3:D23.
4. Click the Quick Analysis button, click the Tables tab, and then click the *Table* option.
5. Select A1:A2 and apply *White, Background 1, Darker 5%* fill color (first color in second row).
6. Make A4 the active cell.
7. Click the Table Tools Design tab and then click the *Table Style Medium 1* option in the *Table Styles* gallery (option to the left of the active style).

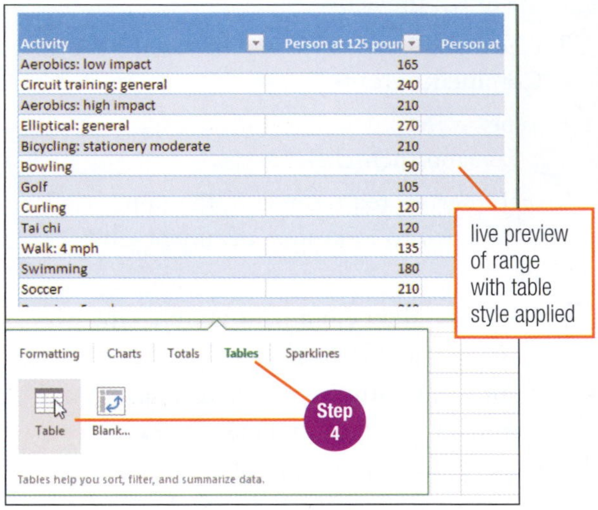

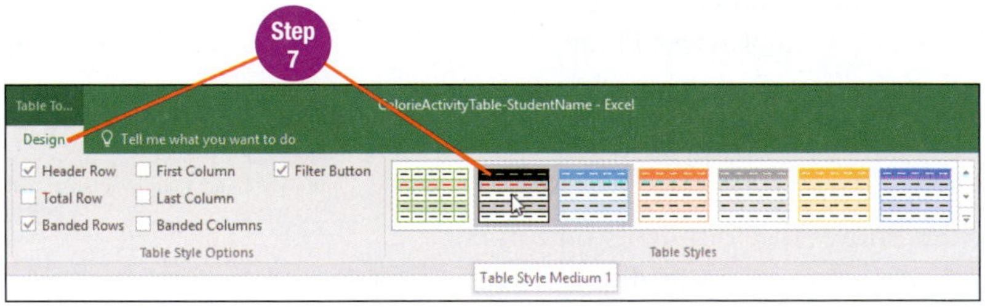

8. Click the filter arrow button at the top of the *Activity* column in the table (displays as down-pointing arrow).
9. Click *Sort A to Z* at the drop-down list.

The table rows are sorted in ascending order by the activity descriptions.

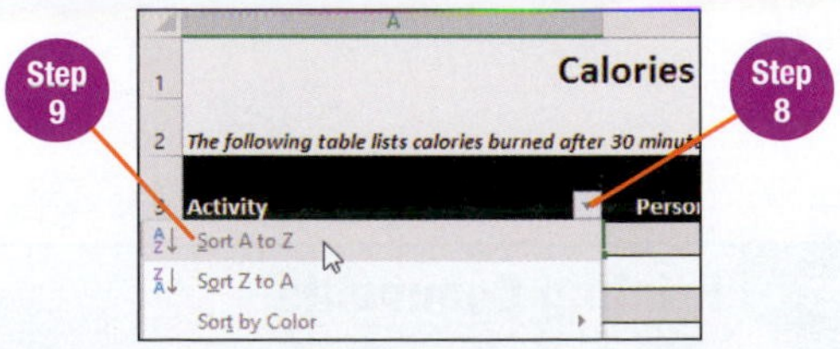

10. Click the filter arrow button at the top of the *Person at 155 pounds* column.

App Tip

Recall from Chapter 7 that different formatting applied to every other row is referred to as *banded rows* and is used to improve readability. The fill color, border style, and other options vary by table style.

A check box is included for each unique value within the column. Filter a table by clearing check boxes for values or items you do not want to see in the filtered list or use the *Filter by Color* and *Number Filters* options to specify a filter condition.

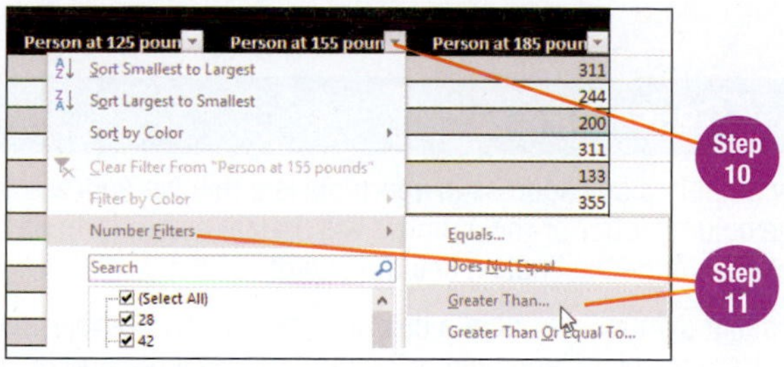

11. Point to *Number Filters* and then click *Greater Than*.
12. Type 200 at the Custom AutoFilter dialog box with the insertion point positioned in the text box at the right of *is greater than* and then click OK.

Excel filters the table and displays only those activities in which the calories burned are more than 200 for a person at 155 pounds.

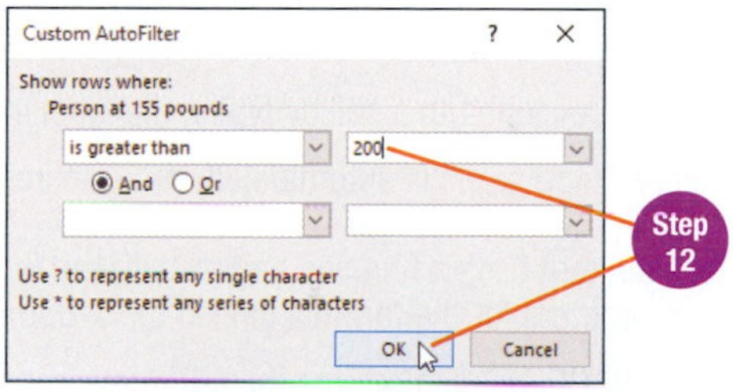

13. Click the filter arrow button at the top of the *Person at 155 pounds* column and click *Clear Filter From "Person at 155 pounds"*.

Clearing a filter redisplays the entire table.

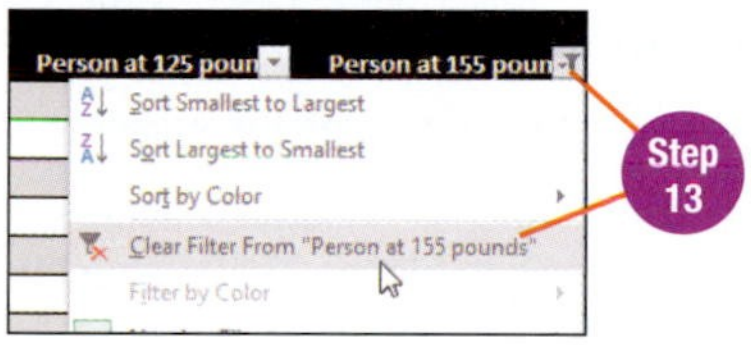

14. Change the orientation to landscape and center the worksheet horizontally.
15. Save the revised workbook using the same name (**CalorieActivityTable-YourName**) and then close the workbook.

Quick Steps

Format a Table
1. Select range.
2. Click Quick Analysis button.
3. Click Tables tab.
4. Click the *Table* option.

Sort a Table
1. Click the filter arrow button at the top of the column you want to sort.
2. Click *Sort A to Z* or *Sort Z to A*.

Filter a Table
1. Click filter arrow button at the top of the column you want to filter.
2. Clear check boxes for items you want to hide or point to *Text Filters* or *Number Filters* and specify criterion.

App Tip

A funnel icon appears in the filter arrow button in the column being used to filter a table, and the row numbers display in blue.

View

Model Answer

Compare your completed file with the model answer.

Alternative Method: Filtering a Table Using the Filter Slicer Pane

A Slicer pane contains all the unique values for a column within the table. Click a value within the pane to filter the table. Use the Insert Slicer button in the Tools group on the Table Tools Design tab and insert a check mark for each column heading for which a Slicer pane is needed.

App Tip

You can filter a table by one column and then filter again by another column to further drill down to the data you want to analyze.

Beyond Basics: Conditional Formatting

Another tool that is used to highlight or review cells is conditional formatting. Conditional formatting applies formatting options only to cells that meet a specified criterion. Select a range, click the Quick Analysis button, and then click the desired conditional formatting button on the Formatting tab. More conditional formatting options are available from the Conditional Formatting button in the Styles group on the Home tab.

Topics Review

Topic	Key Concepts	Key Terms
9.1 Using Absolute Addresses and Range Names in Formulas	By default, a cell address in a formula is a relative address, which means the column letter or row number will update as the formula is copied relative to the destination column and row. A dollar symbol in front of a column letter or row number makes an address absolute, and means the reference will not update when the formula is copied. A formula that has both relative and absolute addresses is referred to as a *mixed address*. A descriptive label can be assigned to a cell or range and used in a formula. A name is assigned to a cell by typing the label in the Name box. A cell or range name is automatically an absolute address.	relative address absolute address mixed address
9.2 Entering Formulas Using Statistical Functions	A formula that uses a function begins with the function name followed by the parameters for the formula (called the *argument*) within parentheses. The AVERAGE function returns the arithmetic mean from the range used in the formula. The MAX function returns the largest value from the range. The MIN function returns the smallest value from the range. The Insert Function dialog box accessed from the Insert Function button provides tools to find and enter a function and argument. The *Count Numbers* option from the AutoSum drop-down list returns the number of cells with values in the range, while COUNTA returns a count of cells with values or text.	argument
9.3 Entering, Formatting, and Calculating Dates	A valid date or time entered into a cell is stored as a numerical value and can be used in formulas. The TODAY function enters the current date into the cell and updates the date whenever the worksheet is opened or printed. Date and time cells can be formatted to a variety of month, day, and year combinations at the Format Cells dialog box with the *Date* category selected. The format in which Excel expects a date to be entered is dependent on the Region setting in the Control Panel. In the United States, the date is expected to be in the format m/d/y.	
9.4 Using the IF Function	The IF function performs a comparison of a cell with a value of another cell and performs one of two calculations depending on whether the comparison proves true or false. Use the Insert Function dialog box to assist with entering an IF statement's arguments. The *logical_test* argument is the statement you want Excel to evaluate to determine which calculation to perform. The *value_if_true* argument is the value or formula if the logical test proves true. The *value_if_false* argument is the value or formula if the logical test proves false.	

continued...

Topic	Key Concepts	Key Terms
9.5 Using the PMT Function	Financial functions can be used for a variety of calculations that involve saving or borrowing money. The PMT function calculates a regular loan payment from a specified interest rate, term, and amount borrowed. Make sure the interest rate and terms are in the same units as the payment you want calculated. For example, divide the interest rate by 12 and/or multiply the term times 12 to calculate a monthly payment from an annual rate or terms. In the PMT argument, *Rate* means the interest rate, *Nper* means the term, and *Pv* means the amount borrowed. The FV function calculates the future value of a regular series of payments that earn a constant interest rate.	
9.6 Creating and Modifying a Pie Chart	Charts are often used to portray a visual snapshot of data. A pie chart shows each data point as a pie slice. The size of each slice in the pie chart represents the value of the data point in proportion to the total of all the values. Use the Charts tab in the *Quick Analysis* gallery to create a pie chart from a selected range. The Chart Elements button is used to add or modify a chart title, data labels, or legend.	pie chart
9.7 Creating and Modifying a Column Chart	A column chart shows one bar for each data point extending upward from a horizontal axis with the height of the bar representing its value. The horizontal axis in a column chart is the category axis, also called the *x-axis*, and shows the labels for each bar. The vertical axis in a column chart is called the *value axis*, also known as the *y-* or *z-axis*, and is scaled to the values of the bars graphed. A column chart is often used to illustrate trends or comparisons over time or by category. The Chart Styles button is used to choose a preformatted style for a column chart, or to change the color scheme. The *Axis Titles* option from the Chart Elements button is used to add titles to each axis in a column chart. The Recommended Charts feature provides a set of customized charts recommended for the data you have selected.	column chart category axis value axis
9.8 Creating and Modifying a Line Chart	A line chart helps a reader identify trends, growth spurts, dips, or unusual points in a data series. Use the Move Chart button in the Location group on the Chart Tools Design tab to move a chart from the worksheet into a chart sheet. A chart in a chart sheet is automatically scaled to fill a letter-sized page in landscape orientation. Change axis options in the Format Axis task pane, or data label options in the Format Data Labels task pane.	line chart Move Chart button

continued…

Topic	Key Concepts	Key Terms
9.9 Using Page Layout View, Adding a Header, and Changing Margins	In Page Layout view the worksheet is divided into pages with white space depicting the size of the margins, and a ruler along the top and left edges. You can see page layout and print options in Page Layout view while viewing and editing the worksheet. Add a header in Page Layout view by clicking the dimmed text *Add header*. Use buttons in the Header & Footer Tools Design tab to add options to a header or footer such as a picture, page numbering, date or time, or file or sheet names. Change to a preset set of margins from the Margins button in the Page Layout tab, or choose *Custom Margins* to enter your own margin settings. Open the Page Setup dialog box with the Margins tab active to center a worksheet horizontally and/or vertically.	Page Layout view
9.10 Creating and Modifying Sparklines and Inserting Comments	A miniature chart embedded into a cell is called a *sparkline chart*. Sparkline charts emphasize trends or variations in data on a smaller scale. Activate a cell and choose a Line, Column, or Win/Loss Sparkline chart from the Sparklines group on the Insert tab. Once created, add or modify sparkline options using buttons on the Sparkline Tools Design tab. A comment appears in a pop-up box when you point or click a cell with an attached comment. Excel displays a red triangle in a cell containing a comment. Use the New Comment button on the Review tab to add a comment in the active cell. To change the text in an existing comment, activate the cell containing the comment and use the Edit Comment button.	sparkline chart
9.11 Working with Tables	A block of data set up in list format can be formatted as a table for formatting, analyzing, sorting, or filtering purposes. A filter temporarily hides data that does not meet a criterion. Use a filter to review subsets of data without deleting rows. Click the filter arrow button at the top of a column to sort or filter a table. Click the filter arrow button at the top of a filtered column and then use the *Clear Filter From (column title)* option to redisplay the hidden rows in the table. Conditional formatting applies formatting options to cells within a range that meet a criterion.	filter

Recheck

Recheck your understanding of the topics covered in this chapter.

Workbook

Chapter review and assessment resources are available in the *Workbook* ebook.

Chapter 10

Creating, Editing, and Formatting a PowerPoint Presentation

Precheck
Check your understanding of the topics covered in this chapter.

Learning Objectives

10.1 Create a new presentation based on a theme, insert slides, and add content to slides

10.2 Change the design theme and theme variant, and insert a table

10.3 Format text using font and paragraph options

10.4 Create a slide with the comparison layout and select, resize, align, and move slide placeholders

10.5 Use Slide Sorter view and duplicate, move, and delete slides

10.6 Modify the slide master

10.7 Add notes and comments to slides

10.8 Run a presentation in Slide Show view and Presenter view

10.9 Prepare slides for audience handouts or speaker notes

Presentations occur in meetings, seminars, and classrooms for a variety of purposes. Some presentations are informational, while others are designed to persuade you to buy a product or service. Some people use presentations at weddings, anniversaries, or family reunions to entertain an audience. In some organizations, presentations are used to provide information at a kiosk where a slide show is set up to run continuously for individuals to view as they walk by or enter a booth. For example, at a trade show, a company might provide a slide show with information about a product. At school you may have used a presentation as a study guide to prepare for an exam.

A presentation is made up of a collection of slides (referred to as a **slide deck**) containing text and multimedia. PowerPoint is the **presentation application** in the Microsoft Office suite. The program is widely used to create a slide deck for presentations. In this chapter, you will learn how to create, edit, and format a presentation. You will create a presentation with a variety of text-based slide layouts; edit content and placeholders; move, duplicate, and delete slides; format slides using a variety of techniques; add notes and comments; and preview the presentation as a slide show. Finally, you will preview options for audience and speaker handouts.

Note: *If you are using a tablet, consider connecting it to a USB or wireless keyboard because you will be typing text in several slides for new presentations in this chapter.*

SNAP If you are a SNAP user, go to your SNAP Assignments page to complete the Precheck, Tutorials, and Recheck.

Data Files
Before beginning this chapter, be sure you have copied the student data files for this course to your storage medium. Steps on downloading and extracting the data files are provided in Chapter 1, Topic 1.8, on pages 22–23.

10.1 Creating a New Presentation and Inserting Slides

Skills

Create a new presentation

Choose a theme and theme variant

Insert a slide

Edit text on a slide

Tutorials

Opening a Presentation Based on a Template

Exploring the PowerPoint Screen

Navigating to Slides

Choosing a Slide Layout

Changing Views

Changing Slide Layout

Inserting and Deleting Text in Slides

Changing the Display of a Slide in the Slide Pane

Inserting a New Slide

Selecting Text

Checking Spelling

App Tip

Double-click a theme to start a new presentation using the theme default style and color scheme.

Begin creating a new presentation at the PowerPoint Start screen by choosing a template, a theme and variant on a theme, or by starting with a blank presentation. The first slide in a presentation is a **title slide** with a text **placeholder** for a title and a subtitle. A placeholder is a rectangular container on a slide that can hold text or other content. Each placeholder on a slide can be manipulated independently.

PowerPoint starts a new presentation with a title slide displayed in Normal view. In Normal view, the current slide displays in widescreen format in the **slide pane**. Numbered slide thumbnails display in the **slide thumbnail pane** at the left of the current slide. A notes pane at the bottom of the slide pane and a Comments pane at the right of the slide pane can be opened as needed.

1. Start PowerPoint 2016.
2. At the PowerPoint Start screen, click the *Ion* theme.

PowerPoint 2016 starts with a gallery of design themes. Click to preview a theme along with the theme variants. A **variant** is a different style and color scheme included in the theme family.

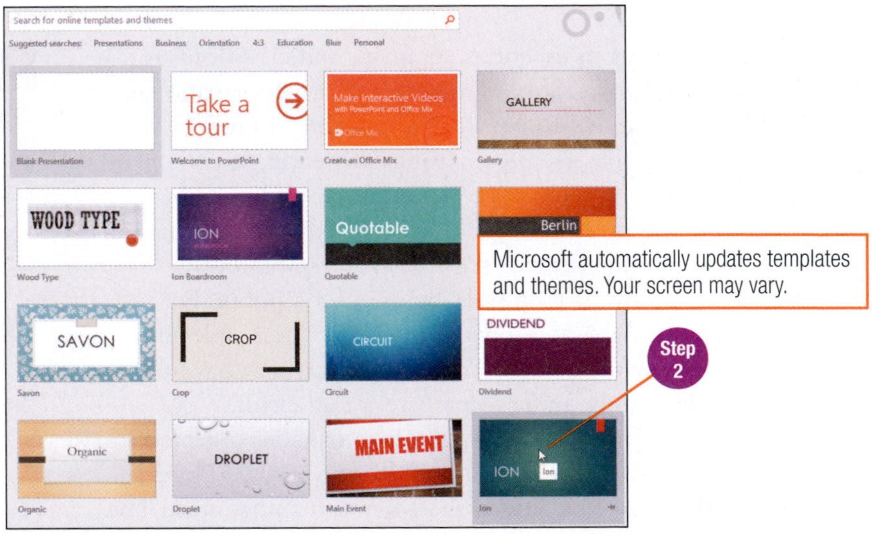

3. Click the last variant (orange color scheme), and then click the right-pointing arrow below the preview slide next to *More Images*.

When previewing a variant, browse through the *More Images* slides to view the color scheme with a variety of content. This allows you to get a better perspective of the theme or variant style and colors before making your selection.

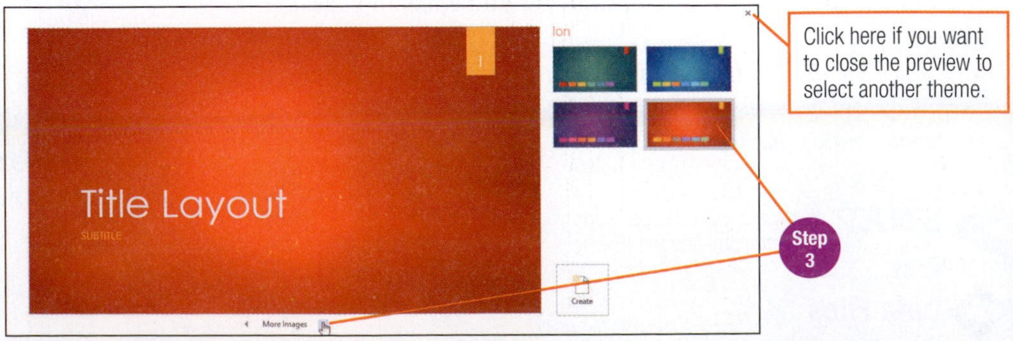

4. Click the second variant (blue color scheme), and then click the right-pointing arrow below the preview slide to view the blue color scheme with a Title and Content layout depicting a chart.

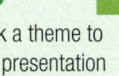

5. Click the right-pointing arrow below the preview slide two more times to view other types of content with the blue color scheme.
6. With the Photo Layout preview displayed, click the Create button.

7. Compare your screen with the one shown in Figure 10.1.

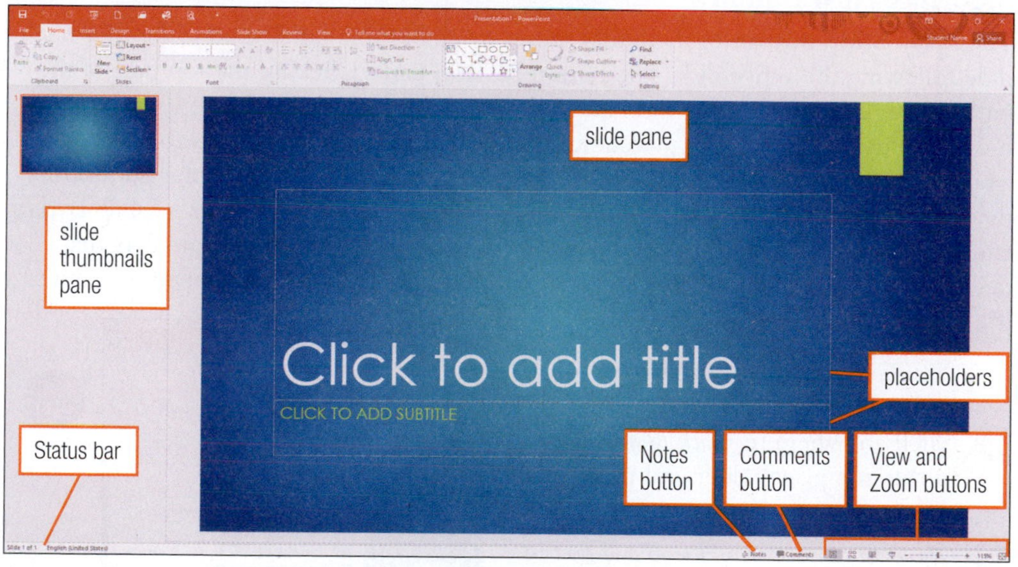

Figure 10.1

A new PowerPoint presentation with Ion theme and blue color variant in the default Normal view is shown above. See Table 10.1 for a description of screen elements.

> **Quick Steps**
>
> **Start a New Presentation**
> 1. Start PowerPoint 2016.
> 2. Click theme.
> 3. Click variant.
> 4. Click Create button.
>
> **Insert a Slide**
> Click New Slide button in Slides group.
> OR
> 1. Click down-pointing arrow on New Slide button.
> 2. Click required slide layout.
>
> **Edit Text**
> 1. Activate slide.
> 2. Select text or click in placeholder and move insertion point as needed.
> 3. Type new text or change text as required.

Table 10.1

PowerPoint Features

Feature	Description
Comments button	Button to turn on or turn off Comments pane at the right side of the slide pane.
Notes button	Button to turn on or turn off the notes pane at the bottom of the slide pane.
placeholders	Containers in which you type or edit text, or insert other content such as an image or audio clip.
slide pane	Pane that displays the active slide. Add or edit content on a slide in this area.
slide thumbnails pane	Pane that displays numbered thumbnails of the slides in the presentation. Navigate to, insert, delete, or duplicate a slide in this pane.
Status bar	Bar that displays active slide number with total number of slides in the presentation and displays a message about an action in progress.
View and Zoom buttons	Buttons to change the display of the PowerPoint window. View buttons in order are: Normal, Slide Sorter, Reading View, and Slide Show. Zoom buttons enlarge or shrink the display of the active slide.

> **App Tip**
> In PowerPoint 2016, slide size is *Widescreen (16:9)* by default. If necessary, change to *Standard (4:3)* using the Slide Size button in the Customize group on the Design tab.

8. Click anywhere in *Click to add title* in the title slide on the slide pane and then type Car Maintenance.
9. Click anywhere in *CLICK TO ADD SUBTITLE* in the title slide on the slide pane and then type Tips for all seasons.

The subtitle text displays in all capital letters regardless of the case used when you type the text because the Ion theme uses the All Caps font effect for the subtitle text.

10. Click in an unused area of the slide to deactivate the subtitle placeholder.

Inserting New Slides

> **App Tip**
> Change the layout for a slide after a slide has been inserted using the Layout button in the Slides group on the Home tab.

The **New Slide button** in the Slides group on the Home tab is used to insert a new slide following the active slide. The button has two parts. Clicking the top part of the button adds a new slide with the Title and Content layout, which is the layout used most frequently. The content placeholder in this layout provides options to add text or a table, chart, SmartArt graphic, picture, or video to the slide. Clicking the bottom of the New Slide button (down-pointing arrow) provides a drop-down list of slide layouts and other new slide options. A **slide layout** is an arrangement of placeholders that determine the number, position, and type of content placeholders included in a slide.

11. Click the top part of the New Slide button in the Slides group on the Home tab.
12. Click anywhere in *Click to add title* in the title placeholder and then type Why maintain a car?.
13. Click anywhere in *Click to add text* in the content placeholder, type Preserve vehicle value, and then press Enter.

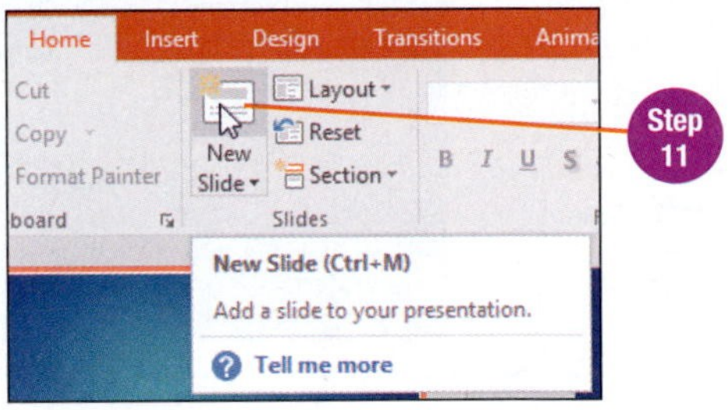

Typing text in the content placeholder automatically creates a bulleted list. In the Ion theme, the bullet character is a green, right-pointing arrow.

14. Type the remaining bulleted list items, pressing Enter after each item except the last one.
    Prolong vehicle life
    Improve driver safety
    Spend less for repairs
    Lower operating costs
    Improve vehicle appearance
    Reduce likelihood of breakdowns

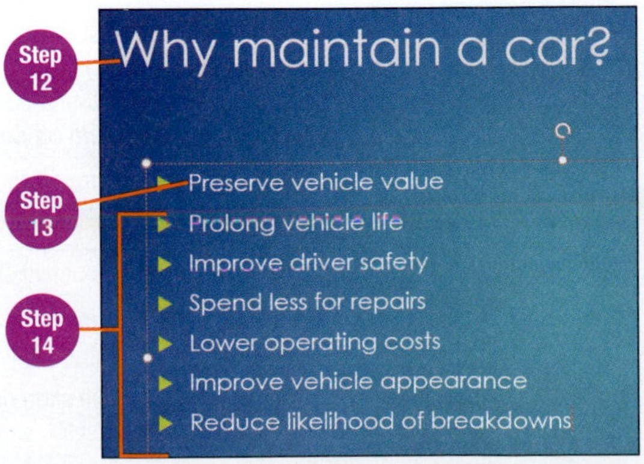

15. Click the top part of the New Slide button in the Slides group.
16. Type the text in the third slide as shown in the image below.

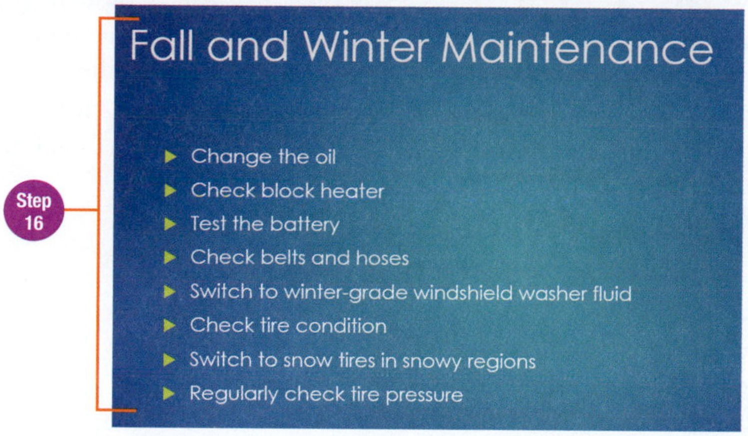

App Tip

Press Ctrl + Enter to move to the next placeholder on a slide or to create a new slide when pressed in the last placeholder.

Editing Text on Slides

Activate the slide you want to edit by clicking the slide in the slide thumbnails pane. Select the text you want to change or delete or click in the placeholder to place an insertion point at the location where you want to edit text and then type new text, change text, or delete text as needed.

17. Click to select Slide 1 in the slide thumbnails pane.
18. Select ALL SEASONS in the subtitle text placeholder and then type car owners so that the subtitle text now reads TIPS FOR CAR OWNERS.

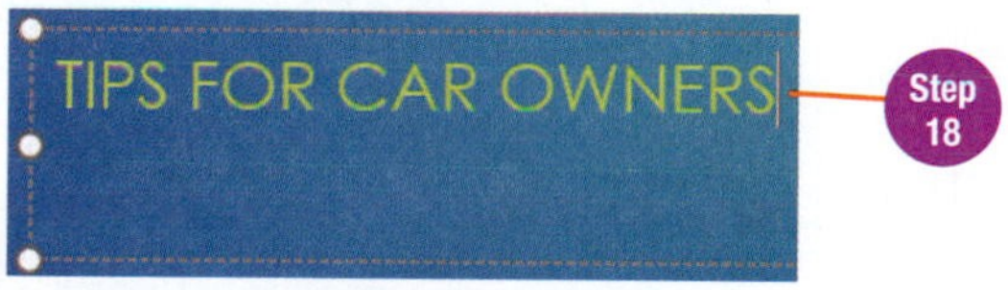

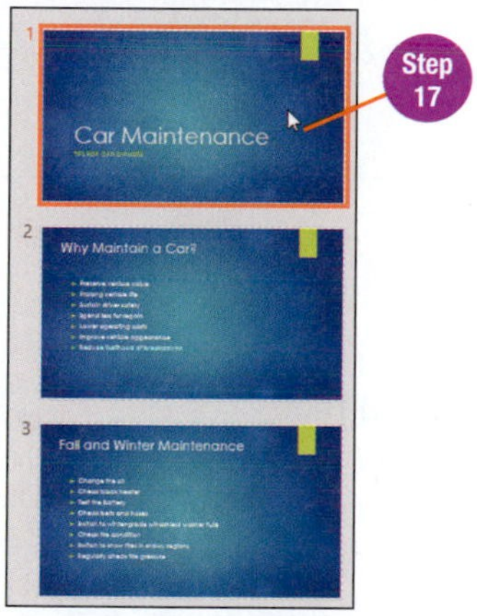

App Tip

Always carefully spell check and proofread each slide in your presentation. Use the Spelling button in the Proofing group on the Review tab as a starting point.

19. Click to select Slide 2 in the slide thumbnails pane.
20. Click at the beginning of the text in the third bulleted list item, delete *Improve*, and then type Sustain.

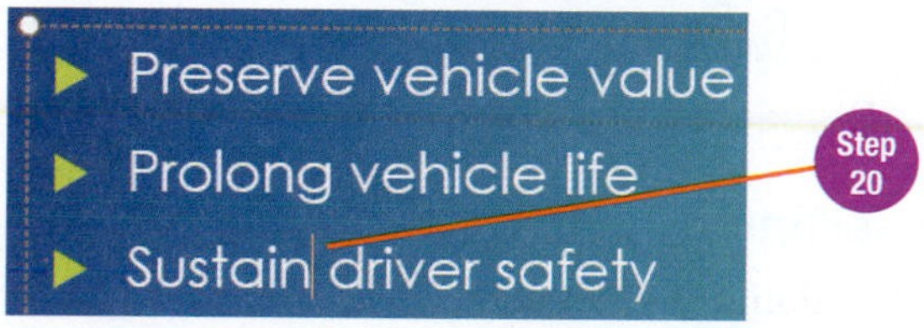

21. Click to place an insertion point within the title placeholder and edit the title text so that *m* in *maintain* and *c* in *car* are capital letters. The title should now read Why Maintain a Car?
22. Click in an unused area of the slide to deactivate the title placeholder.
23. Save the presentation as **CarMaintenance-YourName** in a new folder named *Ch10* in the CompletedTopicsByChapter folder on your storage medium. Leave the presentation open for the next topic.

10.2 Changing the Theme and Inserting and Modifying a Table

Skills

Change theme

Change variant

Insert a table on a slide

Modify table layout

Tutorial
Changing and Modifying Design Themes

The presentation theme and/or variant can be changed after a presentation has been created. To do this, click the Design tab and browse the themes and theme variants in the Themes and Variants galleries.

1. With the **CarMaintenance-YourName** presentation open, click Slide 1 in the slide thumbnails pane.
2. Click the Design tab.
3. Click the *Facet* theme in the Themes gallery (third option).

When deciding upon a theme, roll the mouse over the various theme options to view the active slide with a live preview of the theme. Changing the theme after slides have been created may cause some changes in capitalization in placeholders. For example, a theme that uses the All Caps font in a title or subtitle may mean that you have to do some corrections after the theme is changed if the new theme does not use the All Caps font.

4. Click the More button located at the bottom right of the Variants gallery.

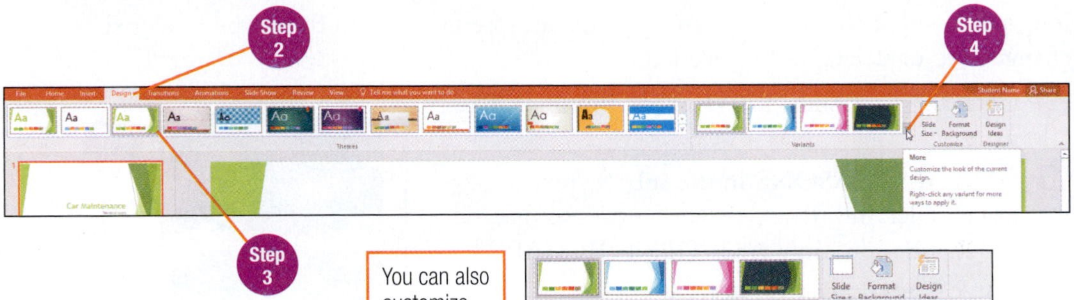

5. Point to *Colors* and then click *Red Orange* in the Colors gallery.
6. Click Slide 3 in the slide thumbnails pane.

You can also customize the theme variant by changing the Fonts, Effects, or Background Styles.

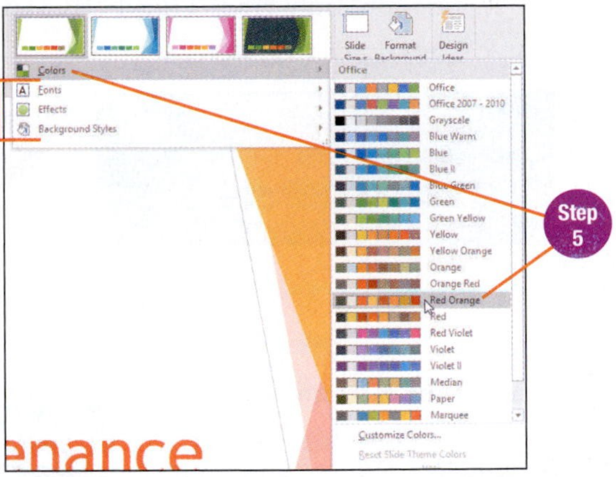

Inserting a Table on a Slide

PowerPoint includes a Table feature for organizing text on a slide in columns and rows similar to the Table feature in Word. To insert a table on a slide, click the Insert Table button in the content placeholder.

7. Click the Home tab and then click the top part of the New Slide button to insert a new slide with the Title and Content layout.
8. Click anywhere in *Click to add title* in the title placeholder and then type Typical Annual Maintenance Costs.
9. Click the Insert Table button in the content placeholder.
10. Select *5* in the *Number of columns* text box at the Insert Table dialog box and then type 2.

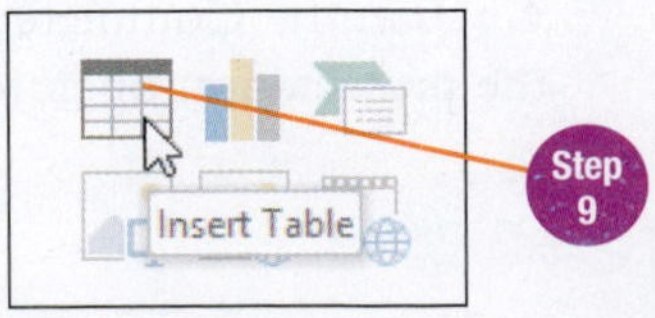

11 Select *2* in the *Number of rows* text box, type 6 and then click OK.

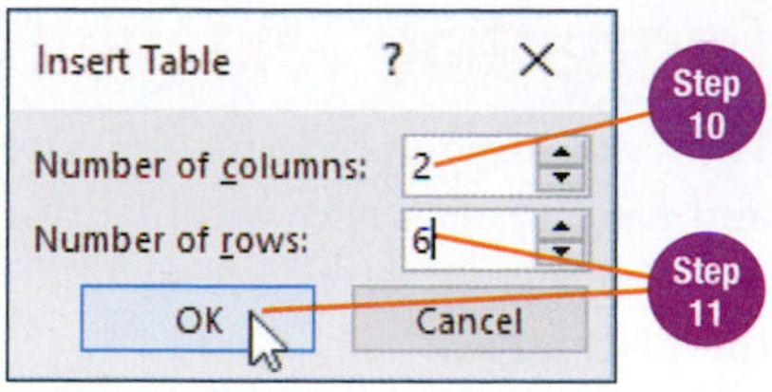

PowerPoint inserts a table in the slide with the colors in the theme variant.

12 With the insertion point positioned in the first cell in the table, type Type of Car and then press Tab or click in the second cell.

13 Type Cost.

14 Type the remaining entries in the table by pressing Tab to move to the next cell or by clicking in the next cell and then typing the text as follows:

Small size	$600
Medium size	$675
Large family sedan	$750
Minivan	$775
SUV	$825

Quick Steps

Change Theme
1. Click Design tab.
2. Click desired option in Themes gallery.
3. If desired, click variant option.

Insert a Table on a Slide
1. Insert new slide.
2. Click Insert Table button in content placeholder.
3. Enter number of columns.
4. Enter number of rows.
5. Click OK.

Oops!

Pressed Tab after last entry and added a new row by mistake? Click the Undo button to remove the extra blank row.

Modifying a Table

The Table Tools Design and Layout tabs provide options for modifying and customizing a table with the same tools you learned about in Word. Use the sizing handles to enlarge or shrink the table size. Drag the border of a table to move the table to a new position on the slide.

15 Drag the right middle sizing handle to the left until the right border of the table ends approximately below the first *e* in *Maintenance* in the title text as shown in the image below.

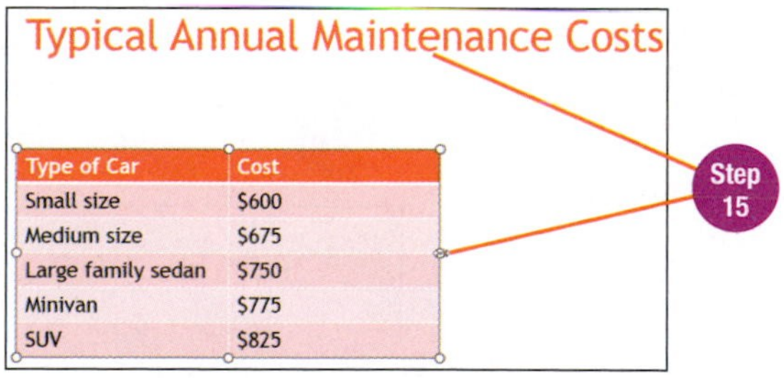

16 Click in any cell in the second column of the table.

17 Click the Table Tools Layout tab, click the Select button in the Table group, and then click *Select Column* at the drop-down list.

18 Click the Center button in the Alignment group.

19 Click in any cell in the first column of the table, select the current entry in the *Width* text box in the Cell Size group, type 3.5, and then press Enter.

20 Drag the top border of the table to move the table until it is positioned at the approximate location shown in the image at right.

21 Save the revised presentation using the same name (**CarMaintenance-YourName**). Leave the presentation open for the next topic.

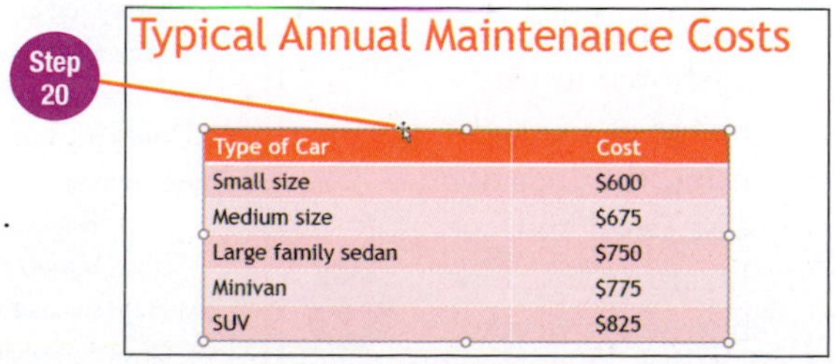

Oops!

Table appears too small with first column wrapping text? You probably changed the width using the *Width* text box in the Table Size group instead of the Cell Size group. Use Undo and then try Step 19 again.

10.3 Formatting Text with Font and Paragraph Options

Skills

Create a multilevel bulleted list

Change the font color

Center text in a placeholder

Tutorial
Increasing and Decreasing Indent

Font and paragraph formatting options in PowerPoint are the same as those in Word and Excel. Select text within a placeholder and apply a formatting option to only the selected text or select a placeholder and apply a formatting option to all the text in the placeholder.

A multilevel bulleted list is created using the **Increase List Level button** and the **Decrease List Level button** in the Paragraph group on the Home tab. Each time you click the Increase List Level button, the insertion point or text is indented to the next tab and the bullet character changes to indicate the text is being demoted to the next list level. Use the Decrease List Level button to move the insertion point or text back to the previous tab and promote the text to the previous list level.

1. With the **CarMaintenance-YourName** presentation open, click Slide 3 in the slide thumbnails pane.
2. Insert a new slide with the Title and Content layout.

New slides are inserted after the active slide. The new slide should be positioned between the Fall and Winter Maintenance slide and the Typical Annual Maintenance Costs slide.

3. With the new Slide 4 the active slide, type Spring and Summer Maintenance as the slide title.
4. Type Thoroughly clean vehicle as the first bulleted list item in the content placeholder and then press Enter.
5. With the insertion point positioned at the beginning of the second bulleted list item, click the Increase List Level button in the Paragraph group on the Home tab.
6. Type Prevent rust by removing sand and salt accumulated from winter driving and then press Enter.
7. With the insertion point positioned at the beginning of the third bulleted list item, click the Decrease List Level button in the Paragraph group to move the bullet back to the previous level, type Check cooling system, and then press Enter.
8. Type the remaining text on the slide as shown in the image at the right using the Increase List Level and Decrease List Level buttons as needed.

Step 5

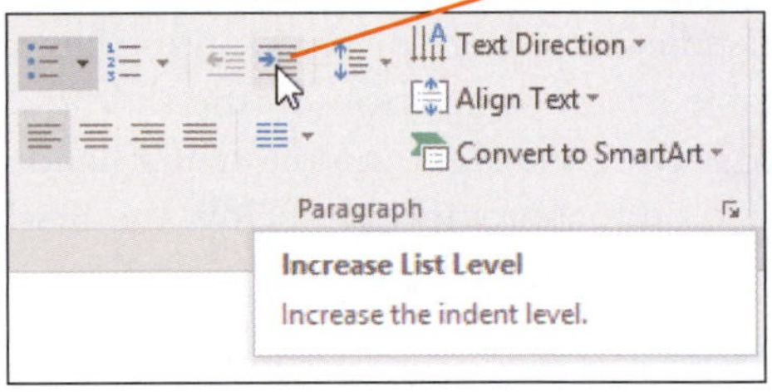

Step 7

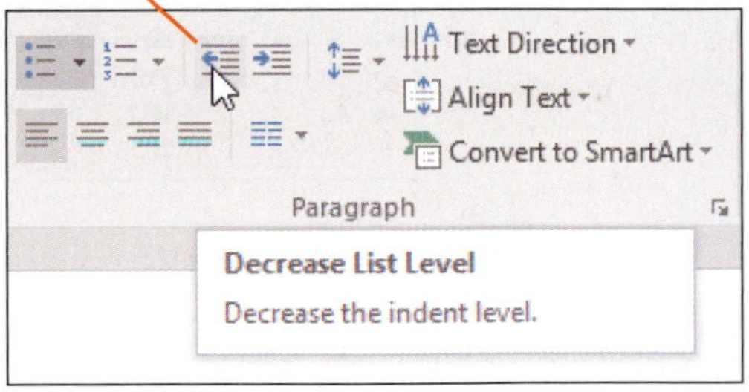

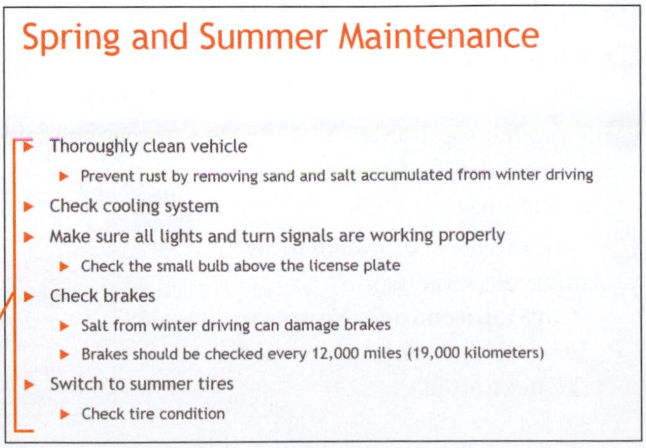
Spring and Summer Maintenance
Thoroughly clean vehicle
Prevent rust by removing sand and salt accumulated from winter driving
Check cooling system
Make sure all lights and turn signals are working properly
Check the small bulb above the license plate
Check brakes
Salt from winter driving can damage brakes
Brakes should be checked every 12,000 miles (19,000 kilometers)
Switch to summer tires
Check tire condition

Steps 4–8

App Tip
A bulleted list can have up to eight levels.

App Tip
You can also press Tab to increase the list level and Shift + Tab to decrease the list level.

Good to Know
When preparing a bulleted list, consider the size of room and number of people attending the presentation to make sure the slide will be readable by everyone in the room. If necessary, divide the content over two slides rather than cramming too much text on one slide.

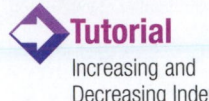

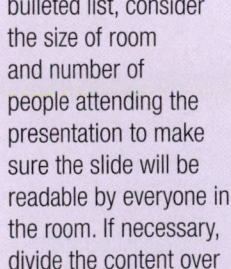

9. Select *12,000* in the content placeholder, click the Font Color button arrow in the Mini toolbar or in the Font group on the Home tab and then click *Red, Accent 1* (fifth option in first row of *Theme Colors* section).

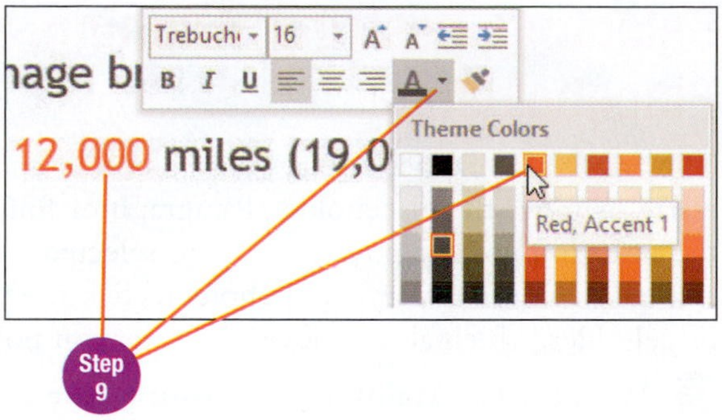

10. Click the Bold button in the Font group.
11. Click in the title text to activate the title placeholder.
12. Click the Center button in the Paragraph group.

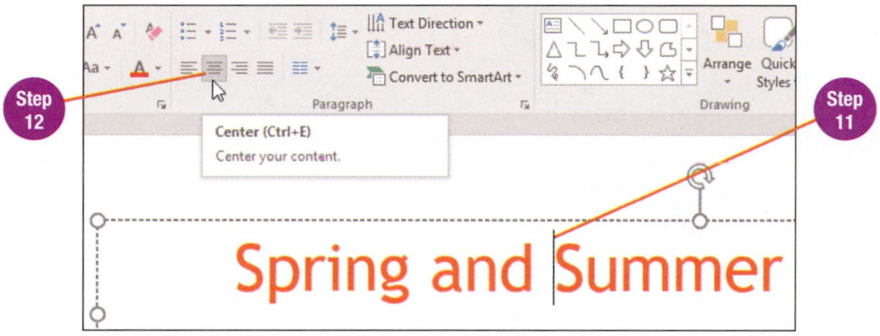

13. Click the Align Left button in the Paragraph group to return the title placeholder to the default paragraph alignment.

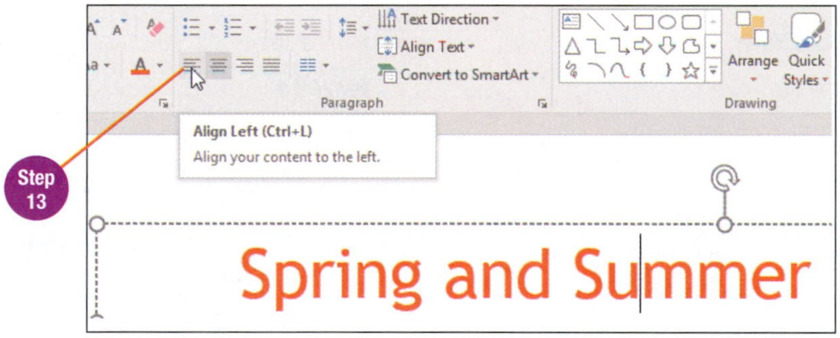

14. Save the revised presentation using the same name (**CarMaintenance-YourName**). Leave the presentation open for the next topic.

Quick Steps

Change Font Options

1. Select text.
2. Click font option in Mini toolbar or Font group on Home tab.

Change Paragraph Options

1. Activate placeholder or select text.
2. Click paragraph option in Mini toolbar or Paragraph group on Home tab.

App Tip

The default paragraph spacing is single line spacing with 10 points of space before and 0 points of space after each paragraph. Use the Line Spacing button or open the Paragraph dialog box to make changes to these settings.

Beyond Basics Changing the Bullet Symbol

The bullet symbols vary with each theme; however, you can change the bullet character to another symbol from the Bullets button arrow in the Paragraph group on the Home tab for an individual list item or for an entire list. To access more bullet symbol options, click *Bullets and Numbering* at the Bullets drop-down list to open the Bullets and Numbering dialog box. Choose the Picture button in the dialog box to select a bullet image or the Customize button to open a Symbol dialog box from which you can select a bullet character. You can also change the size and color of the bullet character in the Bullets and Numbering dialog box.

10.4 Selecting, Resizing, Aligning, and Moving Placeholders

Skills

Insert a slide with the comparison layout

Change a bulleted list to a numbered list

Resize a placeholder

Align a placeholder

Move a placeholder

Tutorial
Modifying Placeholders

The active placeholder displays with a border and selection handles, which are used to resize or move the placeholder. Paragraph or font options apply to the text in which the insertion point is positioned or to selected text. To apply a font or paragraph change to all the text in a placeholder, click the placeholder border to select the placeholder, which also removes the insertion point or deselects text.

1. With the **CarMaintenance-YourName** presentation open, click Slide 5 in the slide thumbnails pane.
2. Click the down-pointing arrow on the New Slide button and then click *Comparison* at the drop-down list.
3. With the new Slide 6 the active slide, type Top 5 Cars Rated by Maintenance Costs as the slide title.
4. Type the title and bulleted list text in the left and right content placeholders as shown in the image below.

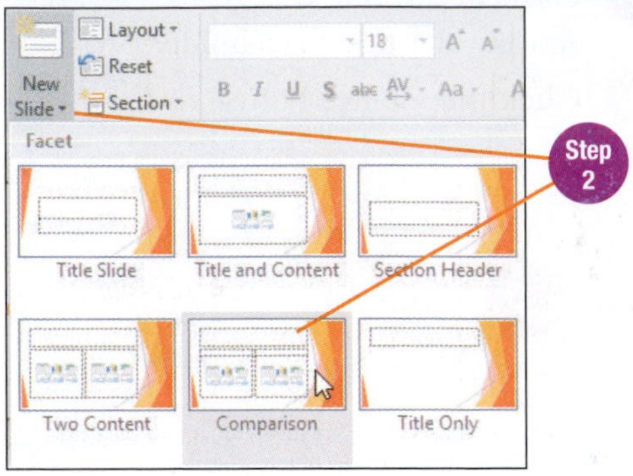

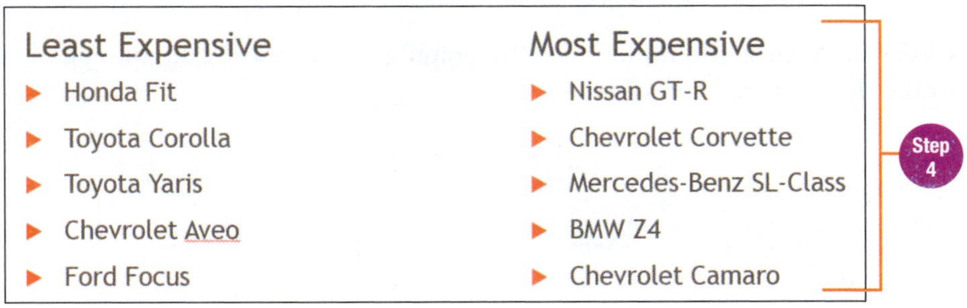
Least Expensive
Honda Fit
Toyota Corolla
Toyota Yaris
Chevrolet Aveo
Ford Focus
Most Expensive
Nissan GT-R
Chevrolet Corvette
Mercedes-Benz SL-Class
BMW Z4
Chevrolet Camaro
Step 4

5. Click anywhere in the bulleted list below the heading *Least Expensive* to activate the placeholder.
6. Click anywhere along the border of the active placeholder to remove the insertion point, selecting the entire placeholder.

The placeholder border changes to a solid line from a dashed line when the entire placeholder is selected. The next action will affect all the text within the placeholder.

7. Click the Numbering button in the Paragraph group to change the bulleted list to a numbered list. (Do *not* click the down-pointing arrow on the button.)

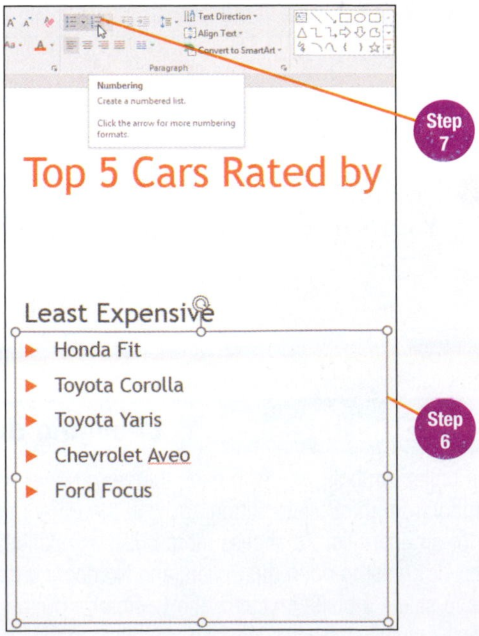

Oops!

Only one bullet changed to a number? This occurs if you have an insertion point within the placeholder; only the item in the list at which the insertion point was positioned is changed. Go back to Step 6 and try again.

8 Click anywhere in the bulleted list below *Most Expensive*, click along the border of the active placeholder to select the entire placeholder, and then click the Numbering button.

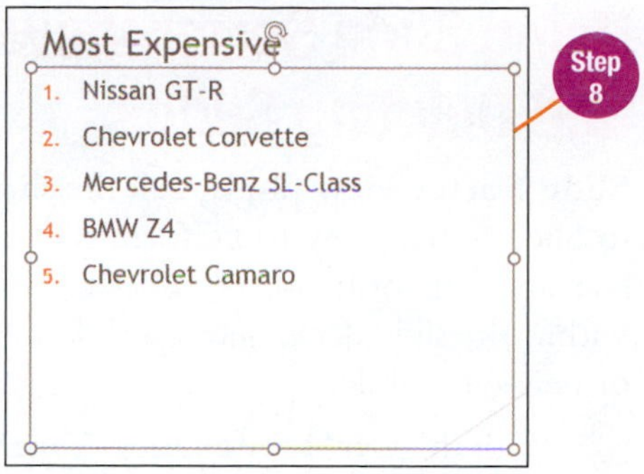

9 Select the numbered list placeholder below the title *Least Expensive*.

10 Drag the right middle sizing handle to the left until the right border of the placeholder is at the approximate location shown in the image below.

11 Select the *Least Expensive* title placeholder and then drag the right middle sizing handle to the left to resize the placeholder until the smart guide appears, indicating the title placeholder is the same width as the content placeholder below it.

Smart guides, also called *alignment guides*, appear automatically when moving or resizing objects. A **smart guide** is a colored horizontal and/or vertical guideline that helps you align, space, or size placeholders or objects evenly.

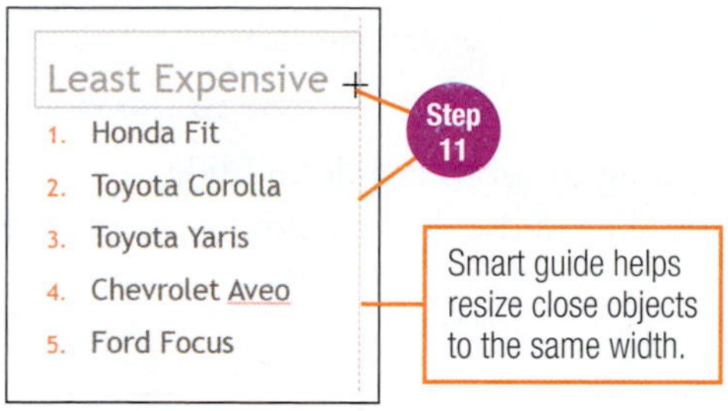

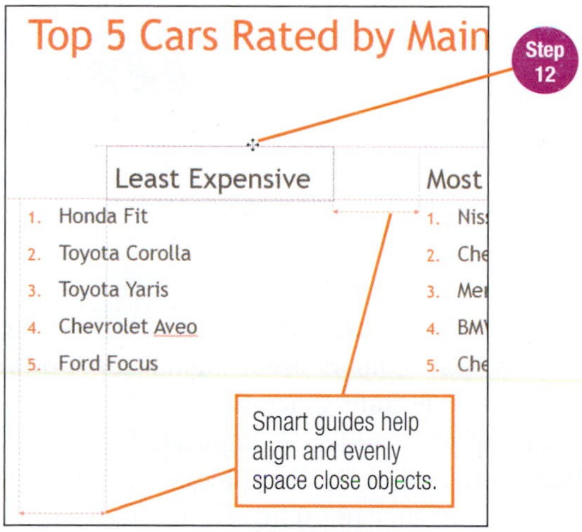

12 With the *Least Expensive* placeholder still selected, drag the border of the placeholder right when the pointer displays with the move icon attached to move the placeholder until the smart guides appear as shown in the image at right.

13 Select the numbered list placeholder below *Least Expensive* and drag right until left, right, top, and bottom smart guides appear, indicating the placeholder is aligned evenly with the placeholders above and right.

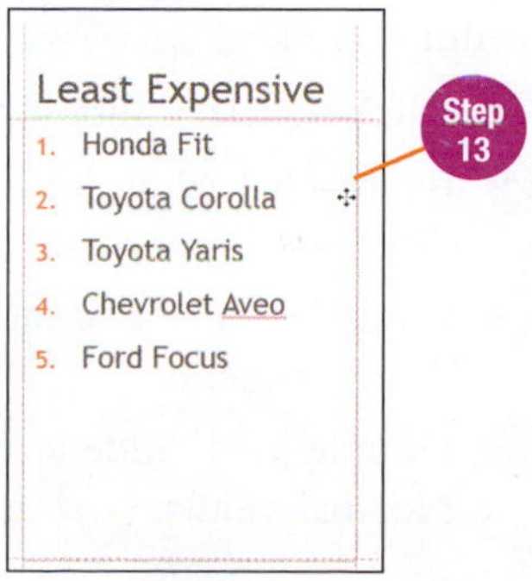

14 Save the revised presentation using the same name (**CarMaintenance-YourName**). Leave the presentation open for the next topic.

Quick Steps

Resize a Placeholder
1. Select placeholder.
2. Drag sizing handle as needed.

Move a Placeholder
1. Select placeholder.
2. Drag placeholder border as needed.

App Tip

The AutoFit feature, which is on by default, automatically scales the font size and adjusts spacing between points to fit text within a placeholder.

Oops!

No right middle sizing handle? On a smaller-screened tablet, the right middle sizing handle may not appear. Use the top right or bottom right sizing handle instead. Remove your finger when you see two smart guides—one at the bottom and one at the right.

10.5 Using Slide Sorter View and Moving, Duplicating, and Deleting Slides

Skills

Use Slide Sorter view

Move a slide

Duplicate a slide

Delete a slide

Tutorials

Rearranging Slides

Deleting Slides

Hiding and Unhiding Slides

Slide Sorter view displays all the slides in a presentation as slide thumbnails. Change to Slide Sorter view to perform slide management tasks. For example, you can easily rearrange the order of the slides by dragging a slide thumbnail to a new position within the slide deck. Select a slide in Slide Sorter view or Normal view to duplicate or delete the slide.

1. With the **CarMaintenance-YourName** presentation open, click the View tab and then click the Slide Sorter button in the Presentation Views group.

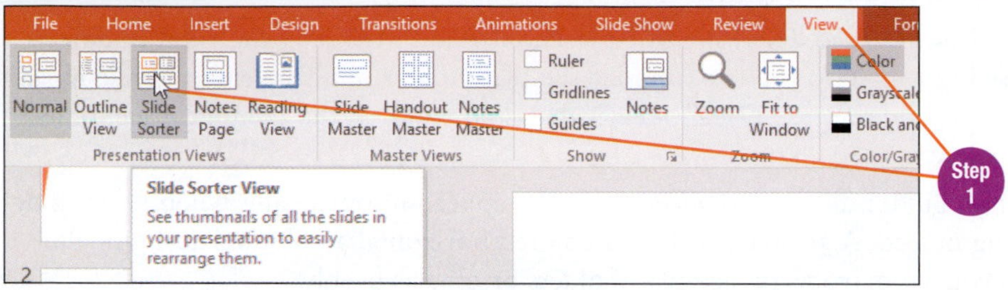

Oops!

Using Touch? Slide right first and then upward to move the slide to the first row.

2. Click Slide 5 to select the slide.
3. Drag Slide 5 to place the slide to the right of Slide 2, and then release the mouse.

As you drag to move a slide in Slide Sorter view, the existing slides rearrange around the slide and are automatically renumbered.

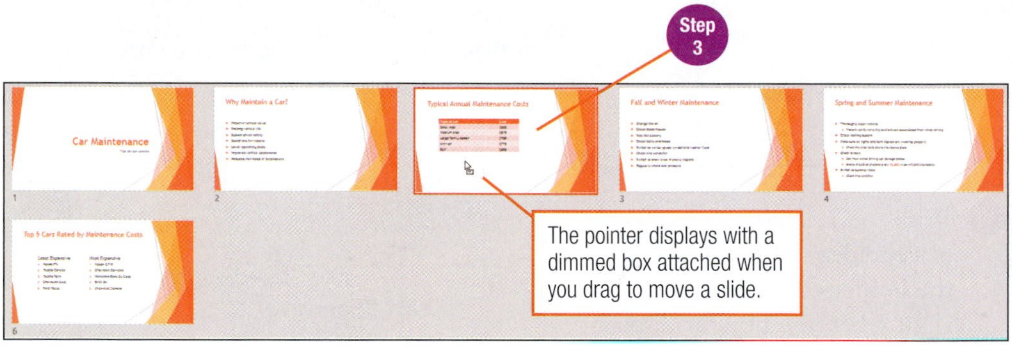

Duplicating a Slide

When you need to create a new slide with the same layout as an existing slide and with the placeholders sized, aligned, and positioned the same, make a duplicate copy of the existing slide. Once the slide is duplicated, all you have to do is change the text inside the placeholders. A duplicated slide is inserted in the presentation immediately after the slide selected to be duplicated.

4. Click to select Slide 6.
5. Right-click Slide 6 to display the shortcut menu.
6. Click *Duplicate Slide* at the shortcut menu.
7. Double-click Slide 7 to return to Normal view.

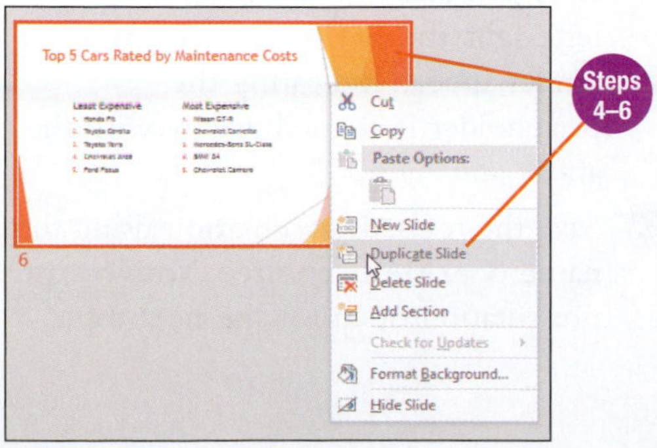

Deleting a Slide

Slides can be deleted in Slide Sorter view or Normal view by selecting the slide, displaying the shortcut menu, and then choosing *Delete Slide* or by pressing the Delete key on the keyboard. Multiple slides can be deleted all at once. To do this, begin by holding down the Ctrl key while clicking each slide you want to remove. When all slides to be deleted have been selected, right-click any selected slide and then choose *Delete Slide* at the shortcut menu.

8. Right-click Slide 7 in the slide thumbnails pane to display the shortcut menu.
9. Click *Delete Slide* at the shortcut menu.
10. Save the revised presentation using the same name (**CarMaintenance-YourName**). Leave the presentation open for the next topic.

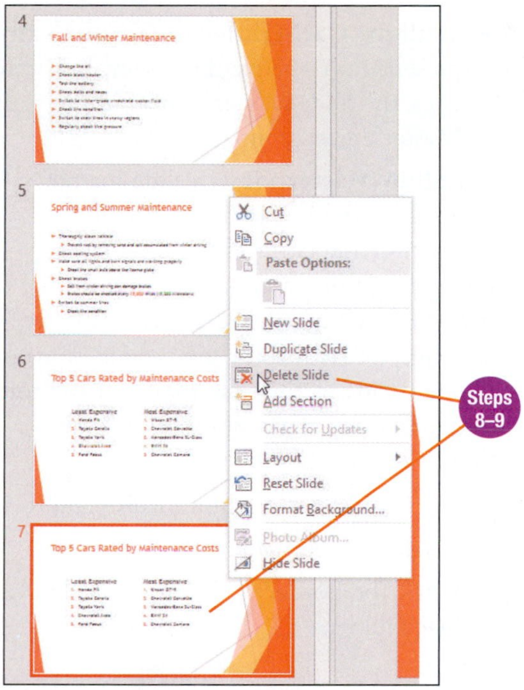

Quick Steps

Slide Sorter View
Click Slide Sorter button in Status bar. OR
1. Click View tab.
2. Click Slide Sorter button.

Move a Slide
Drag slide in Slide Sorter view to required location.

Duplicate a Slide
1. Select slide.
2. Display shortcut menu.
3. Click *Duplicate Slide*.

Delete a Slide
1. Select slide.
2. Display shortcut menu.
3. Click *Delete Slide*.

Alternative Method: Moving or Duplicating Slides

Move slide	In Normal view, drag slide up or down slide thumbnails pane.
Duplicate slide	Select slide, click down-pointing arrow on New Slide button in Slides group on Home tab, and then click *Duplicate Selected Slides*.

Beyond Basics: Hiding a Slide

You may have a slide in a presentation that you want to hide during a particular slide show because the slide does not apply to the current audience or provides more detail than you have time to explain. In Slide Sorter view or Normal view, right-click the slide to be hidden and choose *Hide Slide* from the shortcut menu. A hidden slide is dimmed and has a diagonal line drawn through the slide number in the slide thumbnails pane or in Slide Sorter view. Hide Slide is an on or off feature—redisplay a hidden slide by choosing the Hide Slide option again.

10.6 Modifying the Slide Master

Skills

Display slide master

Format a placeholder on a slide master

Tutorials

Formatting with a Slide Master

Formatting the Slide Background

Inserting Headers and Footers

Each presentation that you create includes a slide master. A **slide master** determines the default formatting and paragraph options for placeholders when you insert new slides. If you want to make a change to a font or paragraph option for the entire presentation, making the change in the slide master will apply the change automatically to all slides in the presentation. For example, if you want a different font color for all the slide titles, change the color on the slide master.

1. With the **CarMaintenance-YourName** presentation open and the View tab active, click the Slide Master button in the Master Views group.

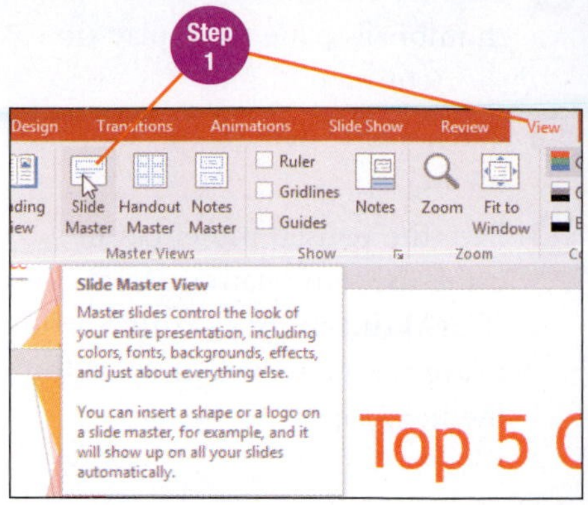

In **Slide Master view**, a slide master at the top of the hierarchy in the slide thumbnails pane controls the font, colors, paragraph options, and background for the entire presentation. Below the slide master is a variety of layouts for the presentation. Changes made to the slide master at the top of the hierarchy affect all the slide layouts below it except the title slide.

App Tip

A slide master is also available for formatting handouts and notes.

App Tip

Formatting changes made on individual slides override the slide master. Presentations should have a consistent look; therefore, limit individual slide formatting changes to only when necessary, such as to indicate a change in topic or speaker.

2. Scroll up the slide thumbnails pane to the first slide at the top of the hierarchy.
3. Click to select Slide 1.
4. Click the border of the Master title placeholder on the slide master to select the placeholder.

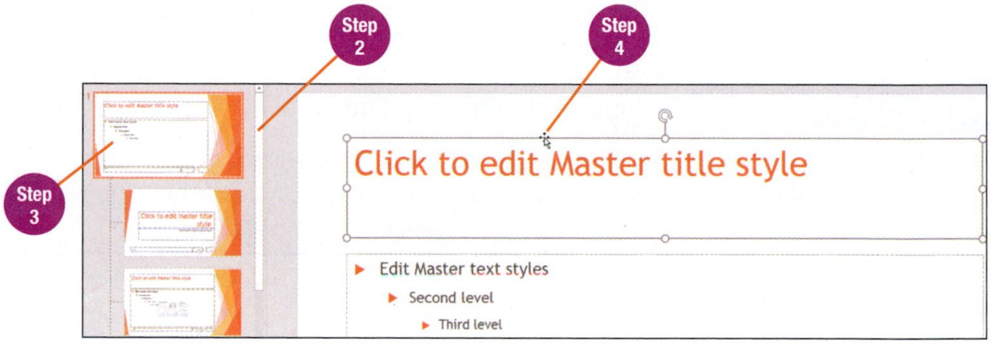

5. Click the Home tab, click the Font Color button arrow, and then click *Dark Red, Accent 6* (last color in first row of *Theme Colors* section).

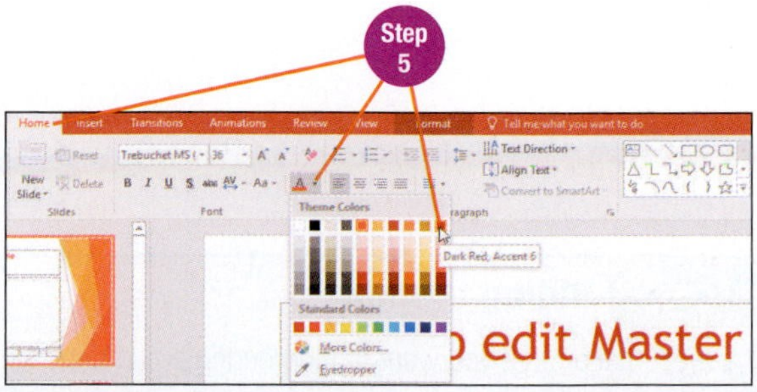

6. Click the border of the content placeholder to select the placeholder and then click the Bullets button arrow in the Paragraph group.

7 Click *Bullets and Numbering* at the drop-down list.

8 Click the Color button in the Bullets and Numbering dialog box and then click *Dark Red, Accent 6*.

9 Click the *Hollow Square Bullets* option (first option in second row).

10 Click OK.

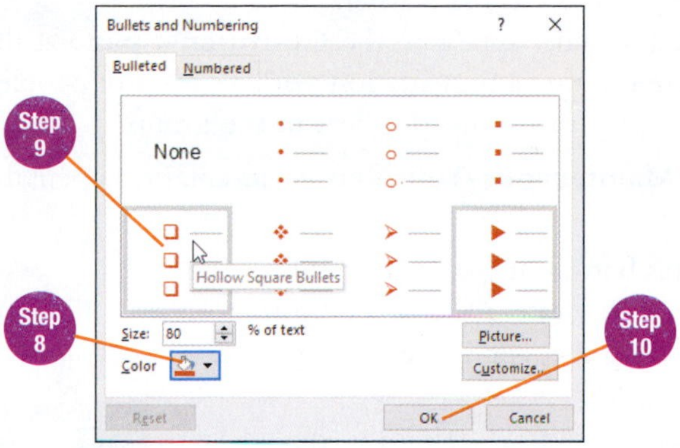

11 Click the Slide Master tab.

12 Click the Close Master View button in the Close group.

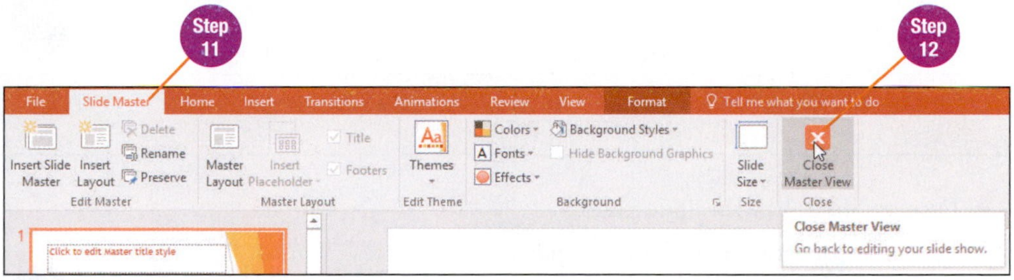

13 Click the Previous Slide or Next Slide buttons at the bottom of the vertical scroll bar or click each slide in the slide thumbnails pane to scroll through and view each slide in the presentation.

Notice that the font color for the title text and the bullet character are changed on each slide *after* the title slide. A title slide has its own slide master and is the first layout below slide 1 in the slide master hierarchy.

14 Save the revised presentation using the same name (**CarMaintenance-YourName**). Leave the presentation open for the next topic.

Quick Steps

Slide Master View

1. Click View tab.
2. Click Slide Master button.

App Tip

Page Up and Page Down also display the previous or next slide in the presentation.

Beyond Basics — Adding Text to the Bottom of Each Slide

Add text to the bottom of each slide in a footer placeholder by selecting the *Footer* check box and typing footer text at the Header and Footer dialog box with the Slides tab active (click Insert tab, then click Header & Footer button in the Text group). Use the slide master to format the footer text to a different font, font size, or color as required. For example, many speakers use the Footer placeholder to add a company name or presentation title at the bottom of each slide.

10.7 Adding Notes and Comments

Skills

Display the notes and Comments panes

Add speaker notes

Add comments

Tutorials

Customizing the Handout Master

Customizing the Notes Master

Notes, generally referred to as *speaker notes*, are text typed in the **notes pane** below the slide pane in Normal view. Use notes to type reminders for the presenter or use this pane to add more details about the slide content for the person giving the presentation. In a presentation designed to be used as a self-study aid, notes are used to provide more explanation to the learner.

Comments added to slides appear in the **Comments pane** at the right side of the slide pane. If you are creating a presentation with a group of people, use comments to provide feedback or pose questions to others in the group.

1. With the **CarMaintenance-YourName** presentation open, display Slide 1 in the slide pane.
2. Click the Notes button in the Status bar to turn on the display of the notes pane at the bottom of the slide pane. Skip this step if the notes pane is already visible.

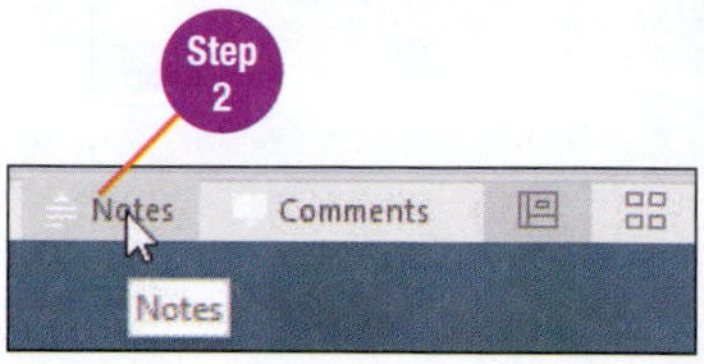
Step 2
Notes
Comments
Notes

3. Click anywhere in *Click to add notes* in the notes pane and then type Begin this slide with the statistic that approximately 5.2% of motor vehicle accidents are caused by vehicle neglect..

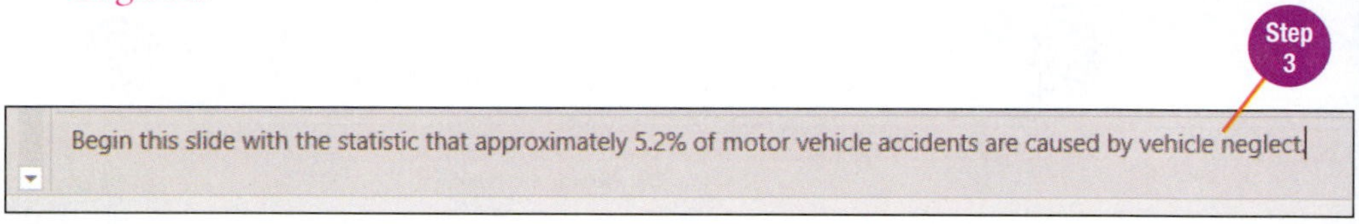
Step 3
Begin this slide with the statistic that approximately 5.2% of motor vehicle accidents are caused by vehicle neglect.

App Tip

Text in the notes pane is visible to the presenter but not the audience during a slide show.

4. Display Slide 3 in the slide pane.
5. Drag the top border of the notes pane upward to increase the height of the pane by approximately one-half inch.

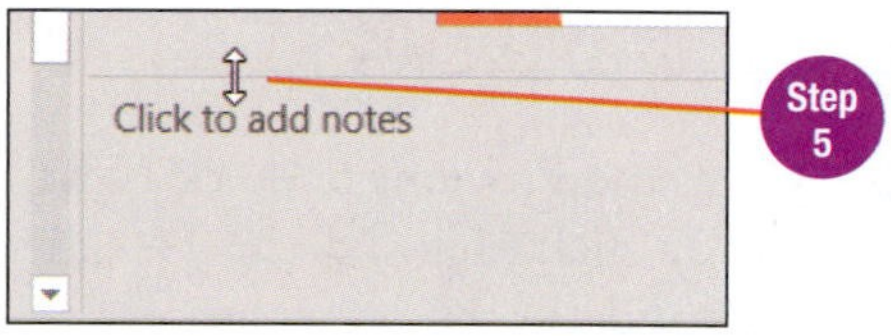
Click to add notes
Step 5

6. Click anywhere in *Click to add notes* in the notes pane and then type Mention that these costs are estimated for a driving distance of 12,000 miles (19,000 kilometers) per year..
7. Press Enter twice and then type Ask the audience if anyone wants to share the total amount paid each year to maintain his or her vehicle..

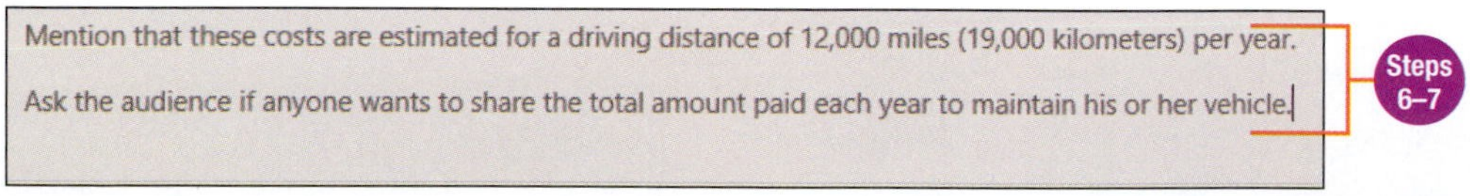
Mention that these costs are estimated for a driving distance of 12,000 miles (19,000 kilometers) per year.
Ask the audience if anyone wants to share the total amount paid each year to maintain his or her vehicle.
Steps 6–7

8. Click the Notes button to turn off the notes pane.
9. Click the Review tab and then click the top part of the Show Comments button in the Comments group to turn on the Comments pane at the right side of the slide pane.
10. Click the New button near the top of the Comments pane.

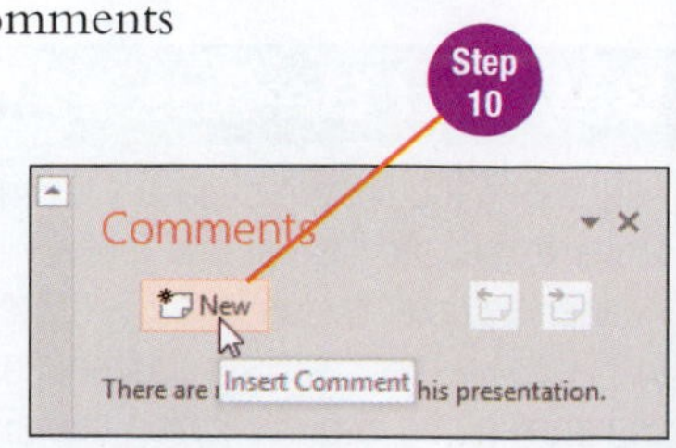
Step 10
Comments
New
Insert Comment
his presentation.

PowerPoint opens a comment box in the Comments pane with your account name associated with the comment.

11. Type Consider adding the source of these statistics to the slide..
12. Click Slide 4 in the slide thumbnails pane, click the New button in the Comments pane, and then type Add more information for any of these points?.
13. Click in the Comments pane outside the Comment box to close the comment.
14. Close the Comments pane.

A comment balloon appears in the top left corner of a slide for which a comment has been added.

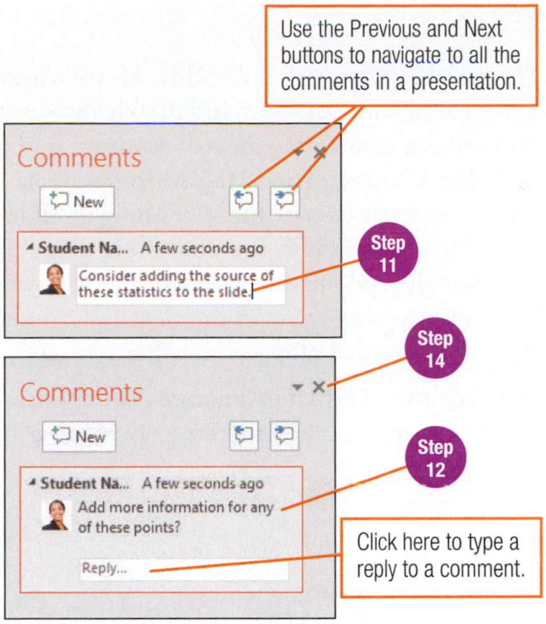

15. Save the revised presentation using the same name (**CarMaintenance-YourName**). Leave the presentation open for the next topic.

Alternative Method: Adding a Comment to Selected Text on a Slide

A comment can also be added to selected text on a slide. The comment balloon displays at the end of the selected text. To do this, select the text and reveal the Comments pane or click the New Comment button in the Comments group on the Review tab.

Quick Steps

Add Notes

1. Activate required slide.
2. Click Notes button.
3. Type note text in notes pane.

Add Comments

1. Activate required slide.
2. Click the Review tab and then click the top part of the Show Comments button.
3. Click New button.
4. Type comment text.

App Tip

A prompt appears in the Status bar when you open a presentation that has comments, informing you of their existence in the file.

Beyond Basics: Deleting or Hiding Comments

Pointing to a comment in the Comments pane displays a Delete icon (black [X]) at the top right of the comment. Click the Delete icon when it appears to remove a comment. To hide comment balloons, click the Show Comments button in the Comments group on the Review tab and then click *Show Markup* at the drop-down list to remove the check mark.

10.8 Displaying a Slide Show

Skills

Display a presentation in Slide Show view

Display a presentation in Presenter view

Tutorials

Running a Slide Show

Changing the Display when Running a Slide Show

Using the Pen Tool during a Slide Show

Display the presentation in **Slide Show view** to preview the slides as they will appear to an audience. Each slide fills the screen with the ribbon and other PowerPoint elements removed; however, tools to navigate and annotate slides are available. Use the **From Beginning button** in the Start Slide Show group on the Slide Show tab to start the slide show at Slide 1.

In **Presenter view**, the slide show displays full screen on one monitor (the monitor the audience will see) and in Presenter view on a second monitor. Presenter view displays a preview of the next slide, notes from the notes pane, a timer, and a slide show toolbar along with other options.

1 With the **CarMaintenance-YourName** presentation open, click the Slide Show tab, and then click the From Beginning button in the Start Slide Show group.

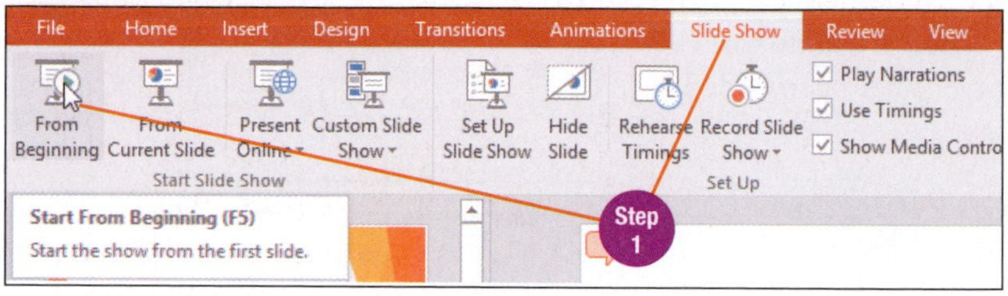

2 Click the right-pointing arrow that appears in the Slide Show toolbar near the bottom left corner of the screen to move to Slide 2. Move the mouse to display the toolbar if the Slide Show toolbar is not visible.

You can also click anywhere on a slide or press the Page Down key to move to the next slide. The buttons on the Slide Show toolbar are shown in Figure 10.2 and described in Table 10.2 below.

App Tip

Press F5 to start a slide show from Slide 1.

Oops!

Using Touch? Tap the slide to display the Slide Show toolbar.

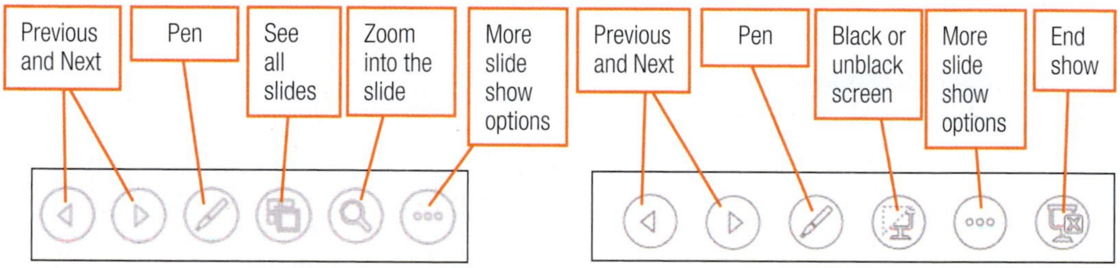

Figure 10.2

The Slide Show toolbar for a mouse-enabled device (left), and for a touch-enabled device (right) is shown above. See Table 10.2 for a description of each button.

Table 10.2

Slide Show Toolbar Buttons

Button	Description
Previous and Next	Displays the previous or next slide in the presentation.
Pen	Displays a pop-up list of options for using the laser pointer, pen, or highlighter when running the presentation.
See all slides	View all slides in the presentation similarly to Slide Sorter view. Use this option to jump to a slide out of sequence during a presentation.
Zoom into the slide	Use this button to click on a portion of a slide that you want to enlarge to temporarily fill the screen for a closer look. Right-click or press the Esc key to restore the slide.
More slide show options	Displays a pop-up list of options for customizing the presentation. On mouse-enabled devices, use this button to end the show or black/unblack the screen during a presentation.
Black or unblack screen	On a touch-enabled device, this button blacks the screen or unblacks the screen.
End show	On a touch-enabled device, use this button to end the show.

3 Continue clicking the Next Slide arrow to navigate through the remaining slides in the presentation until the black screen appears.

After the last slide is viewed, a black screen is shown with the message *End of slide show, click to exit*. Many presenters leave the screen black when their presentation is ended until the audience has left because clicking to exit displays the presentation in Normal view on the screen.

4 At the black screen that appears, click anywhere on the screen to return to Normal view.

5 Display Slide 1 in the slide pane and then click the Slide Show button in the Status bar.

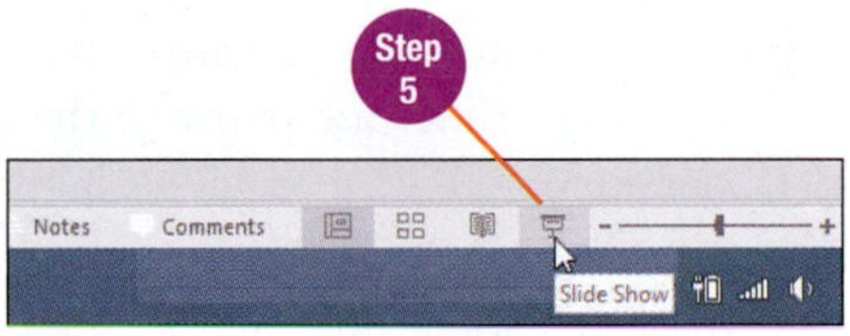

The **Slide Show button** in the Status bar starts the slide show at the active slide.

6 Click the More slide show options button (button with three dots) in the Slide Show toolbar and then click *Show Presenter View* at the pop-up list.

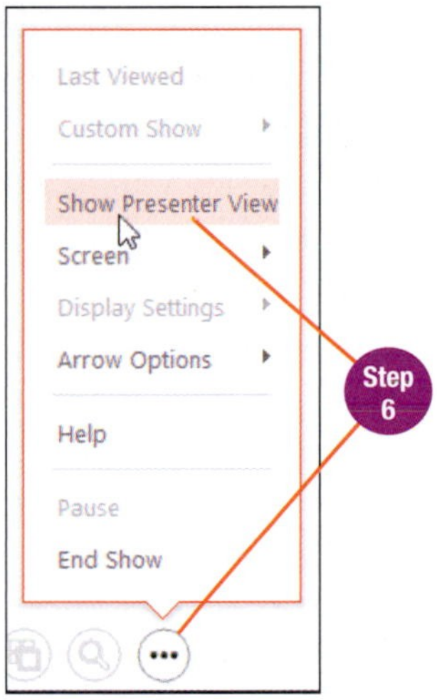

You can use Presenter view on a system with only one monitor to preview or rehearse a presentation. At a presentation venue, PowerPoint automatically detects the computer setup and chooses the correct monitor on which to show Presenter view.

7 Click the Next Slide button in the slide navigator near the bottom of Presenter view until you have navigated to Slide 3 (see Figure 10.3).

8 Compare your screen with the one shown in Figure 10.3.

9 Continue clicking the Next Slide button until you reach Slide 6 and then at the top of the screen click END SLIDE SHOW at the top of Presenter view.

10 Leave the presentation open for the next topic.

Quick Steps

Display a Slide Show

1. Click Slide Show tab.
2. Click From Beginning button.

OR

1. Display Slide 1.
2. Click Slide Show button in Status bar.

Display Presenter View

1. Display presentation as Slide Show.
2. Click More slide show options button.
3. Click *Show Presenter View.*

Good to Know

Many speakers include a closing slide as the last slide in a presentation that is left on the screen until the audience has left. The closing slide contains the speaker's contact information, a favorite or memorable quote related to the topic, or a thank-you message.

App Tip

You can also preview a slide show in Reading view where each slide fills the screen. A Title bar, Status bar, and Taskbar remain visible with buttons to navigate slides in the Status bar.

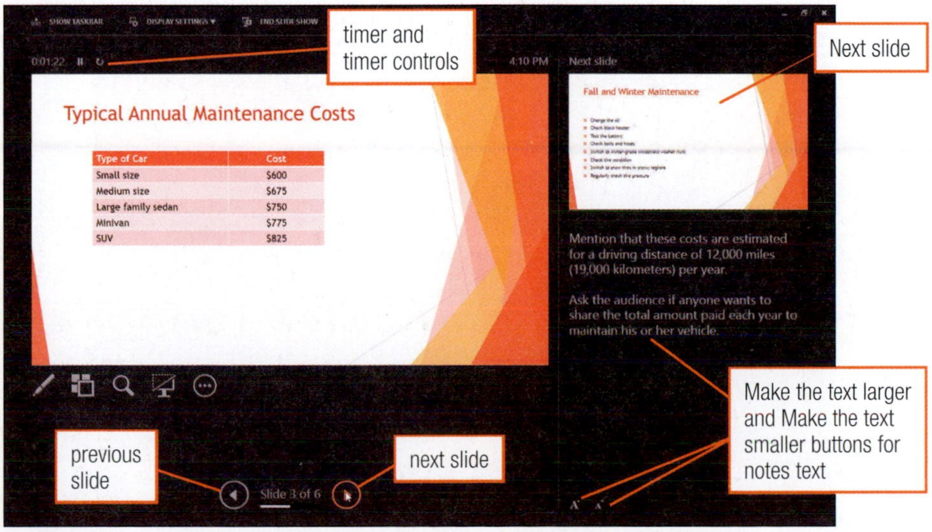

Figure 10.3

Shown above is Slide 3 of the Car Maintenance-YourName presentation in Presenter View

10.9 Preparing Audience Handouts and Speaker Notes

Skills

Preview slides as handouts

Hide comments on printouts

Preview notes pages

Add header and footer text

Tutorial
Previewing Slides and Printing

Some speakers provide audience members with a printout of their slides in a format that allows an individual to add his or her own handwritten notes during the presentation. PowerPoint provides several options for printing slides as handouts. Speakers who do not use Presenter view during a presentation may also print a copy of the slides with the notes included for reference during the presentation.

1. With the **CarMaintenance-YourName** presentation open, click the File tab and then click *Print*.
2. At the Print backstage area, click the Full Page Slides list arrow in the *Settings* category.
3. Click *3 Slides* in the *Handouts* section of the drop-down list.

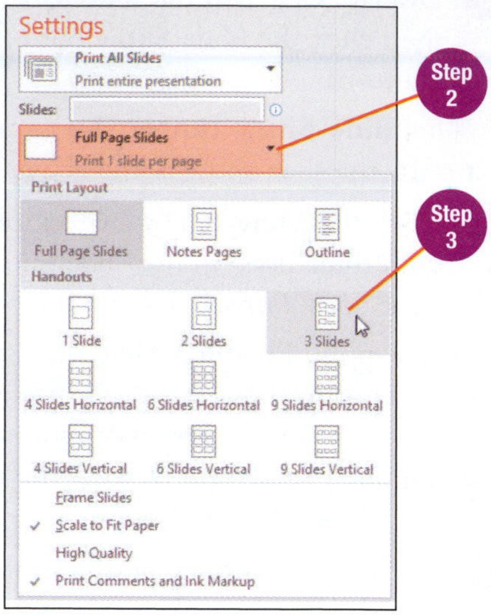

The option to print three slides per page provides horizontal lines next to each slide for writing notes.

4. Click the 3 Slides list arrow and then click *6 Slides Horizontal* at the drop-down list.

Notice that the printout requires two pages even though only six slides are in the presentation. By default, comments print with the presentation; the second page is for printing the comments.

5. Click the 6 Slides Horizontal list arrow and then click *Print Comments and Ink Markup* at the drop-down list to remove the check mark. The printout is now only one page.
6. Click the 6 Slides Horizontal list arrow, and click *Notes Pages* in the *Print Layout* section of the drop-down or pop-up list.

App Tip
Preview various handout options before making a selection to make sure printouts will be legible for most people when slides have a lot of detailed content.

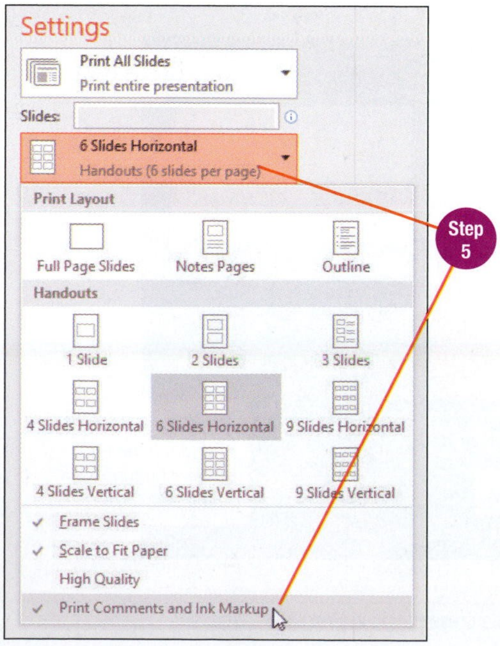

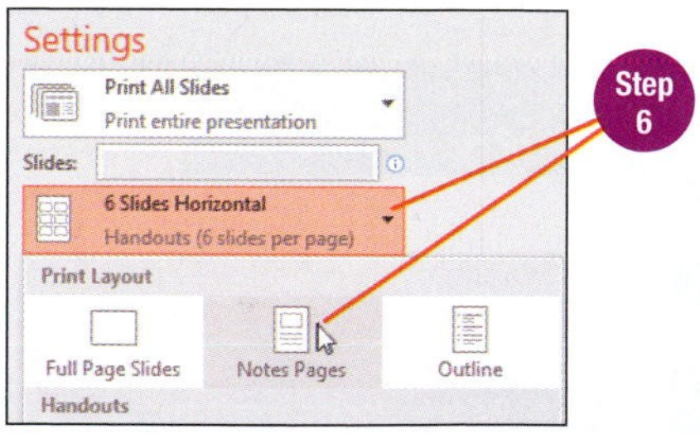

Notes Pages prints one slide per page with the slide at the top half of the page and notes or blank space in the bottom half.

7 Click the Next Page button to display Slide 2 in the *Preview* section.

8 Click the Next Page button to display Slide 3.

Notice the notes text is displayed below the slide.

9 Click the Edit Header & Footer hyperlink at the bottom of the *Settings* section.

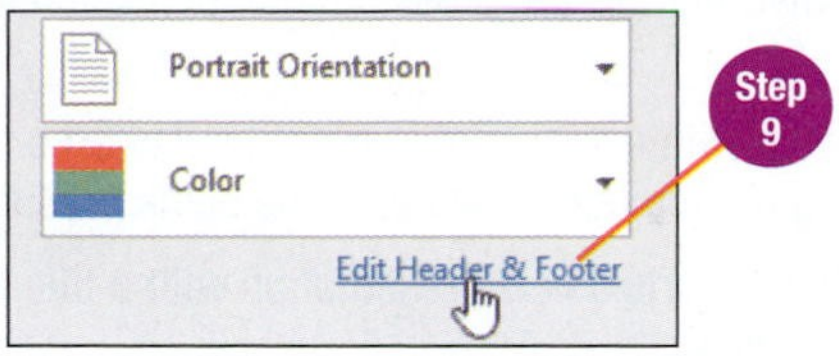

10 At the Header and Footer dialog box with the Notes and Handouts tab active, click the *Header* check box to insert a check mark, click in the *Header* text box, and then type your first and last names.

11 Click the *Footer* check box to insert a check mark, click in the *Footer* text box, and then type your school name.

12 Click the Apply to All button.

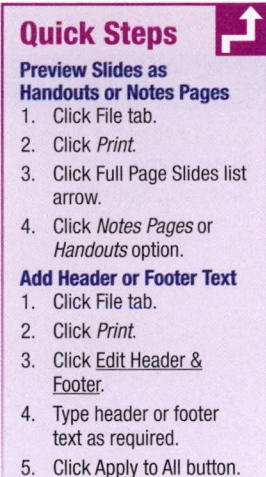

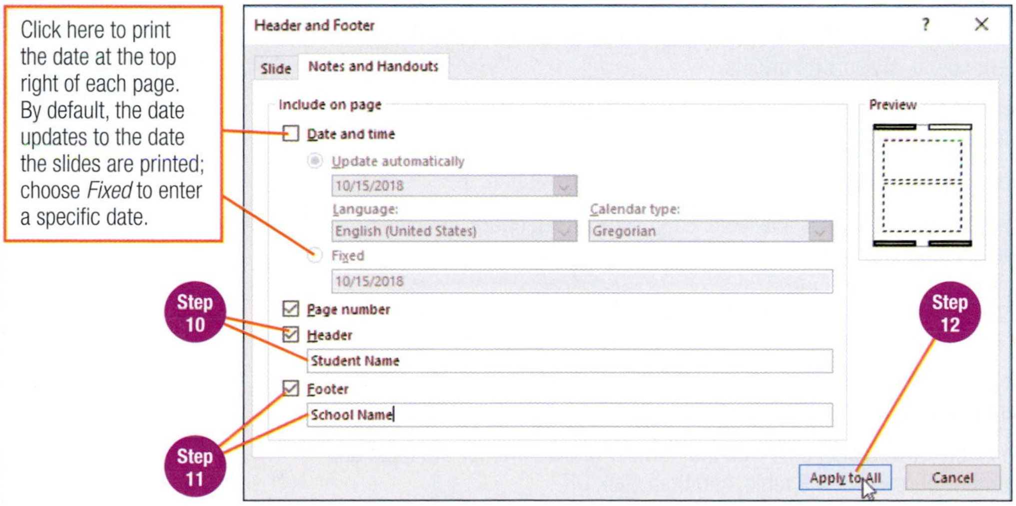

13 Preview the header and footer text by scrolling through the remaining slides.

14 Click the Back button to exit the Print backstage area.

15 Save the revised presentation using the same name (**CarMaintenance-YourName**) and then close the presentation.

Quick Steps

Preview Slides as Handouts or Notes Pages

1. Click File tab.
2. Click *Print*.
3. Click Full Page Slides list arrow.
4. Click *Notes Pages* or *Handouts* option.

Add Header or Footer Text

1. Click File tab.
2. Click *Print*.
3. Click Edit Header & Footer.
4. Type header or footer text as required.
5. Click Apply to All button.

Good to Know

To conserve paper and ink, some presenters publish their presentations to a web service such as SlideShare instead of printing handouts.

Beyond Basics Slide Size and Orientation for Printing

By default, slides print in landscape orientation when printed as slides or in portrait orientation when printed as notes or handouts. Change the orientation with the orientation list arrow in the *Settings* category of the Print backstage area or at the *Custom Slide Size* option from the Slide Size button in the Customize group on the Design tab.

Topics Review

Topic	Key Concepts	Key Terms
10.1 Creating a New Presentation and Inserting Slides	A slide deck is a collection of slides in a presentation. A presentation application is a software program used to create a slide deck. PowerPoint is the presentation application in the Microsoft Office suite. A new presentation is created from the PowerPoint Start screen by choosing a template, a theme, or the blank presentation option. PowerPoint starts a new presentation with a title slide in widescreen format in Normal view. A title slide is the first slide in a presentation. A placeholder is a rectangular container in which you type text or insert other content. Normal view includes the slide pane, which displays the active slide on the right side of the screen, and the slide thumbnails pane, which displays numbered thumbnails of all the slides in a single column along the left side of the screen. A variant of a theme family is based upon the same theme, but with different colors, styles, and effects. Add or edit text on a slide by clicking inside the placeholder and then typing or editing text. Use the New Slide button to add a slide to the presentation. A variety of slide layouts is available. Each slide layout option sets the number, placement, and type of placeholders on a slide.	slide deck presentation application title slide placeholder slide pane slide thumbnail pane variant New Slide button slide layout
10.2 Changing the Theme and Inserting and Modifying a Table	Change the theme and/or variant for a presentation after the presentation has been started using options on the Design tab. Insert a table on a slide using the Insert Table button located within the content placeholder of a new slide. At the Insert Table dialog box, type the number of columns for the table and the number of rows for the table, and then click OK. Use the same methods and tools for entering text and modifying the table layout as the methods and tools that you learned in Word.	
10.3 Formatting Text with Font and Paragraph Options	Select text within a placeholder or select the entire placeholder to apply formatting changes using the options in the Font and Paragraph groups on the Home tab. Create a multilevel bulleted list using the Increase List Level button and the Decrease List Level button in the Paragraph group. Each time you click the Increase List Level button, the insertion point or text is indented to the next tab, and the level changes to the next level. Click the Decrease List Level button to move the insertion point or text back to the previous tab and level. The bullet symbols vary for each theme. You can change the bullet symbol character using the Bullets button arrow.	Increase List Level button Decrease List Level button

continued…

Topic	Key Concepts	Key Terms
10.4 Selecting, Resizing, Aligning, and Moving Placeholders	The active placeholder displays with sizing handles and a border with which you can resize or move the placeholder. Click the border of a placeholder to remove the insertion point and select the entire placeholder to apply a formatting change. A smart guide is a colored line that appears on the slide as you resize or move a placeholder to assist in aligning the placeholder or evenly spacing the placeholder with other close objects.	smart guide
10.5 Using Slide Sorter View and Moving, Duplicating, and Deleting Slides	Slide Sorter view displays all slides as slide thumbnails and is used to rearrange the order of slides or otherwise manage slides in the presentation. Slide or drag a slide in Slide Sorter view to move the slide to a new position within the presentation. Duplicating a slide makes a copy of an existing slide with the placeholders sized, aligned, and positioned the same as the original slide. Delete a slide you no longer need in a presentation by selecting the slide or slides and using the Delete Slide option from the shortcut menu or by pressing the Delete key. A slide can be hidden in the presentation if you do not want the slide to display in a slide show.	Slide Sorter view
10.6 Modifying the Slide Master	Each presentation has a slide master that determines the formatting and paragraph options for placeholders in slides. Display the slide master to make formatting changes that you want to apply to all slides in the presentation automatically. Change to Slide Master view from the View tab to modify the slide master. In Slide Master view, the slide thumbnails pane displays the slide master at the top of the hierarchy. Below the slide master, individual slide layouts are included for formatting separately from the slide master. Add text to the bottom of each slide in a footer placeholder by typing footer text in the Header and Footer dialog box (click Insert tab, then click Header & Footer button in Text group). Use the footer placeholder on the slide master to apply formatting options to the footer text.	slide master Slide Master view
10.7 Adding Notes and Comments	The notes pane appears along the bottom of the slide pane and is used to type speaker notes, reminders for the presenter, or more detailed information about the slide content for a reader. Reveal or hide the notes pane with the Notes button in the Status bar. A comment is added to the active slide by displaying the Comments pane, clicking the New button, and then typing the comment text. Reveal or hide the Comments pane with the Comments button in the Status bar. Delete a comment using the Delete icon that appears when you point to the comment text in the Comments pane. Hide comments by removing the check mark next to *Show Markup* at the Show Comments button drop-down list on the Review tab.	notes pane Comments pane

continued...

Topic	Key Concepts	Key Terms
10.8 Displaying a Slide Show	Slide Show view previews each slide as the audience will see the slide with a full screen. Display a slide show starting at Slide 1 by clicking the From Beginning button in the Start Slide Show group on the Slide Show tab. The Slide Show toolbar provides buttons to navigate slides, annotate slides, zoom into a slide, or black/unblack the screen during the presentation. After the last slide is shown, a black screen displays indicating the end of the slide show. The Slide Show button in the Status bar starts the slide show from the active slide in the slide pane. Display a slide show and click the More slide show options button to switch the view to Presenter view. Presenter view works with two monitors, where one monitor displays the slide show as the audience will see it, and the second monitor displays the slide show in Presenter view. Presenter view can also be seen on a computer with only one monitor so that you can rehearse a presentation. In Presenter view, the speaker's monitor displays a timer and timer controls, a preview of the next slide, notes, and a slide show toolbar along with other options.	Slide Show view From Beginning button Presenter view Slide Show button
10.9 Preparing Audience Handouts and Speaker Notes	Preview slides formatted as handouts at the Print backstage area. The *3 Slides* Handouts option in the *Settings* category at the Print backstage area provides lines next to each slide for writing notes. Various other horizontal or vertical options are available in the *Settings* category of the Print backstage area for printing slide thumbnails as a handout. By default, comments print on a separate page after the slides; to prevent comments from printing, remove the check mark next to *Print Comments and Ink Markup* from the slides option list at the Print backstage area. Choose the *Notes Pages* option at the Print backstage area to print one slide per page with the notes from the notes pane. Add header and/or footer text to a printout using the Edit Header & Footer hyperlink at the bottom of the *Settings* category at the Print backstage area. By default, slides printed as slides print in landscape orientation, while slides printed as handouts or notes pages print in portrait orientation.	Notes Pages

Recheck
Recheck your understanding of the topics covered in this chapter.

Workbook
Chapter review and assessment resources are available in the *Workbook* ebook.

Chapter 11

Enhancing a Presentation with Multimedia and Animation Effects

Precheck

Check your understanding of the topics covered in this chapter.

Presentations are more engaging for audiences when multimedia is used to help speakers communicate their points. Incorporating graphics, sound, and video into PowerPoint slides in a slide deck can help an audience understand the content and remain focused on the presentation.

In this chapter, you will learn how to add graphics to slides using clip art, pictures, SmartArt, WordArt, charts, and drawn shapes. You will also learn to add text in a text box; add sound and video; and complete a slide show presentation by adding transitions and animation effects. Lastly, you will learn how to set up a slide show that advances through the slide deck automatically.

Learning Objectives

11.1 Insert and resize pictures and clip art on a slide

11.2 Insert and modify a SmartArt graphic on a slide

11.3 Convert existing text to a SmartArt graphic and insert and modify a WordArt object on a slide

11.4 Create and modify a chart on a slide

11.5 Draw and modify shapes and text boxes on a slide

11.6 Insert a video clip into a presentation

11.7 Insert a sound clip into a presentation

11.8 Add transition and animation effects into a slide show

11.9 Set up a self-running presentation

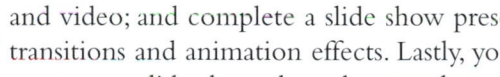

SNAP If you are a SNAP user, go to your SNAP Assignments page to complete the Precheck, Tutorials, and Recheck.

Data Files

Before beginning this chapter, be sure you have copied the student data files for this course to your storage medium. Steps on downloading and extracting the data files are provided in Chapter 1, Topic 1.8, on pages 22–23.

11.1 Inserting Graphic Images from Picture Collections

Skills

Add an image from a file on your storage medium

Add an image from an online resource

Tutorial
Inserting, Sizing, and Moving an Image

Adding a picture, illustration, diagram, or chart on a slide emphasizes content, adds visual interest to a slide, and helps an audience understand and make connections with the information more easily than with text alone. As you did in Chapter 7, you can insert pictures from a file on your PC or from an online resource.

Inserting Pictures from a File on Your Computer

To add a picture to an existing slide, use the Pictures button in the Images group on the Insert tab to add an image stored as a file in a folder on your computer, or a computer to which you are connected. Once inserted, move, resize, and/or modify the picture using buttons in the Picture Tools Format tab. On a new slide, use the Pictures icon in the content placeholder to add a picture to a slide.

1. Start PowerPoint 2016 and open the presentation **PaintedBunting** from the Ch11 folder in Student_Data_Files.
2. Use Save As to save a copy of the presentation as **PaintedBunting-YourName** in a new folder *Ch11* in the CompletedTopicsByChapter folder.
3. Browse through the presentation and read the slides.
4. Make Slide 2 the active slide in the slide pane.
5. Click the Insert tab and then click the Pictures button in the Images group.

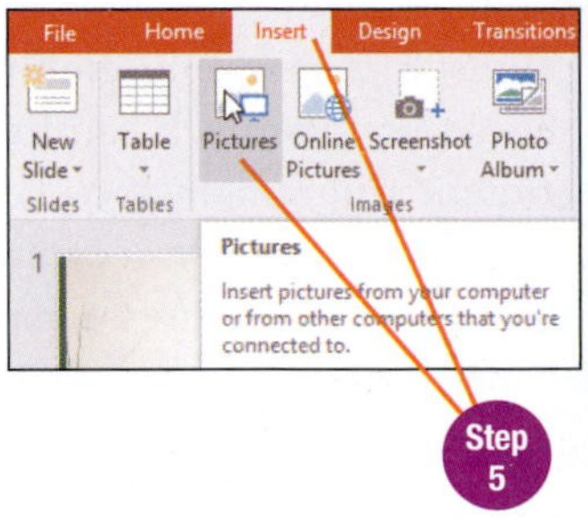

6. At the Insert Picture dialog box, navigate to the Ch11 folder within Student_Data_Files and then double-click the file ***PaintedBunting_NPS***.
7. Using one of the four corner selection handles, resize the image smaller to the approximate size shown in the image below.
8. Drag the image to move the picture to the right side of the slide and then align it with the horizontal and vertical smart guides that appear when the picture is even with the top of the text and the right margin on the slide.

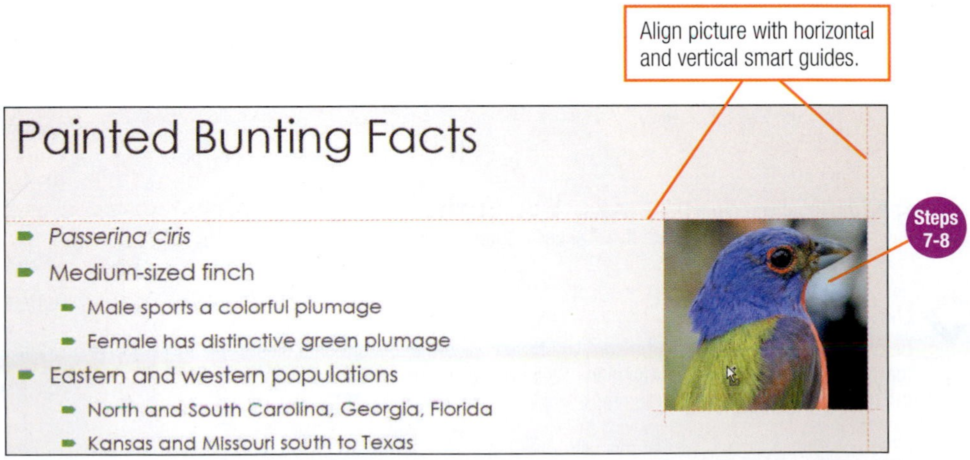

9. Insert the picture ***PaintedBunting_Female*** near the bottom right of the slide as shown on the next page by completing steps similar to Steps 5 to 8.

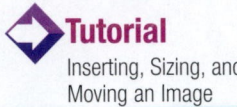

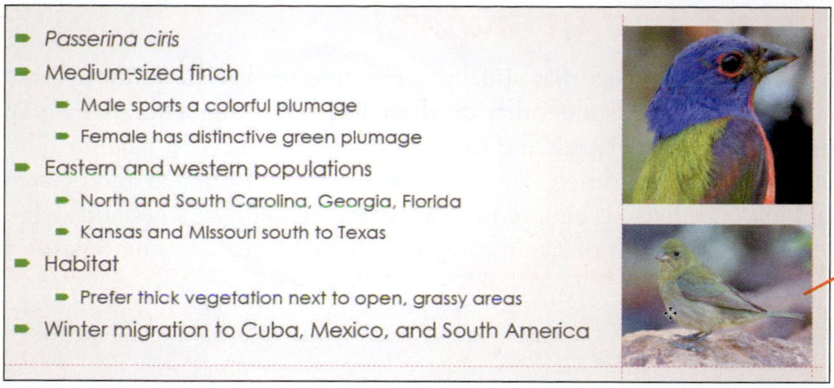
Passerina ciris
Medium-sized finch
Male sports a colorful plumage
Female has distinctive green plumage
Eastern and western populations
North and South Carolina, Georgia, Florida
Kansas and Missouri south to Texas
Habitat
Prefer thick vegetation next to open, grassy areas
Winter migration to Cuba, Mexico, and South America
Step 9

Quick Steps

Insert an Image from the Computer

1. Activate slide.
2. Click Insert tab.
3. Click Pictures button.
4. Navigate to drive and/or folder.
5. Double-click desired image.
6. Resize and/or move as required.

Insert Clip Art or Online Photo

1. Activate slide.
2. Click Insert tab.
3. Click Online Pictures button.
4. Type search keyword.
5. Press Enter.
6. Double-click desired image.
7. Resize and/or move as required.

Inserting a Picture from a Web Resource

The Online Pictures button is in the Images group on the Insert tab or in a content placeholder. Use the Online Pictures button to find a suitable image from a website.

10. Make Slide 6 the active slide in the slide pane.
11. Click the Insert tab and then click the Online Pictures button in the Images group.
12. With the insertion point positioned in the search text box to the right of the *Bing Image Search* option, type team and then press Enter or click the Search button (displays as a magnifying glass).
13. Double-click the picture shown in the image below. If you cannot locate the image shown in the search results list, close the Insert Pictures dialog box and insert the picture from a file in the Ch11 folder in Student_Data_Files using the file ***Team***.
14. Resize and move the picture to the left side of the bullet list and align it with the horizontal smart guide that appears when the center of the image is evenly positioned with the bullet list.

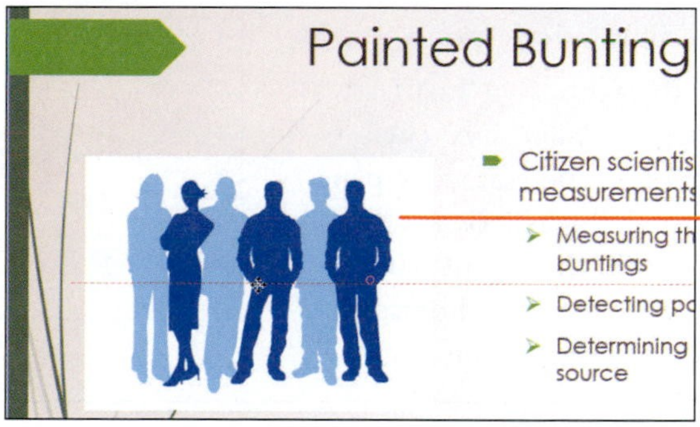
Painted Bunting
Citizen scientis
measurements
Measuring th
buntings
Detecting p
Determining
source
Steps 11-14

15. Save the revised presentation using the same name (**PaintedBunting-YourName**). Leave the presentation open for the next topic.

Beyond Basics Editing Images

Edit an image with buttons on the Picture Tools Format tab using techniques similar to those you learned in Chapter 7. For example, you can apply a picture style or artistic effect; adjust the brightness, contrast, or sharpness; or change the color properties. Use buttons in the Arrange and Size groups to layer the image with other objects, specify the position of the image on the slide, crop unwanted portions of the picture, or specify measurements for height and width.

11.2 Inserting a SmartArt Graphic

Skills

Add a SmartArt graphic

Modify a SmartArt graphic

Tutorials

Inserting, Sizing, and Moving SmartArt

Formatting SmartArt

SmartArt is a graphic object that visually communicates a relationship in a list, process, cycle, hierarchy, or some other diagram. Begin creating a SmartArt graphic by choosing a predesigned layout and then adding text in the Text pane or by typing text directly in the text placeholders within the shapes. You can add and delete shapes to the graphic as needed and choose from a variety of color schemes and styles. See Table 11.1 for a description of layout category diagrams created using SmartArt.

Table 11.1

SmartArt Graphic Layout Categories

Layout Category	Description
List	Nonsequential tasks, processes, or other list items
Process	Illustrate a sequential series of steps to complete a process or task
Cycle	Show a sequence of steps or tasks in a circular or looped process
Hierarchy	Show an organizational chart or decision tree
Relationship	Show how parts or elements are related to one another
Matrix	Depict how individual parts or ideas relate to a whole or central idea
Pyramid	Show proportional or hierarchical relationships that build upward
Picture	Add pictures inside shapes with small amounts of text to show ideas, a process, or a relationship

App Tip

On a new slide with no other content, use the Insert a SmartArt Graphic icon in the content placeholder to create a SmartArt object on a slide.

App Tip

If you are unsure which SmartArt graphic to use, click a layout in the center pane so you can read a description of it in the right pane including suggested usage.

1. With the **PaintedBunting-YourName** presentation open and Slide 6 the active slide in the slide pane, click the Insert tab if the Insert tab is not the active tab.
2. Click the SmartArt button in the Illustrations group.
3. At the Choose a SmartArt Graphic dialog box, click *Process* in the Category pane at the left, click *Basic Chevron Process* in the layout pane in the center (second option in fifth row), and then click OK.

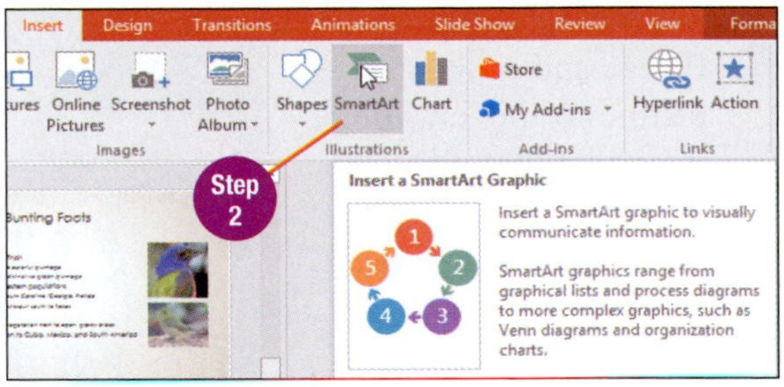

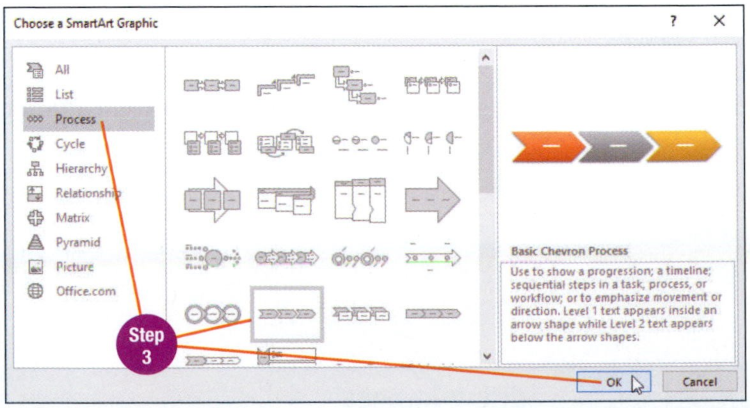

PowerPoint places the SmartArt graphic in the center of the slide. Three shapes are automatically included in the *Basic Chevron Process* layout.

4. Click the left-pointing arrow along the left border of the graphic if the Text pane is not visible and then click in the pane next to the first bullet; if the Text pane is already visible, proceed to Step 5.

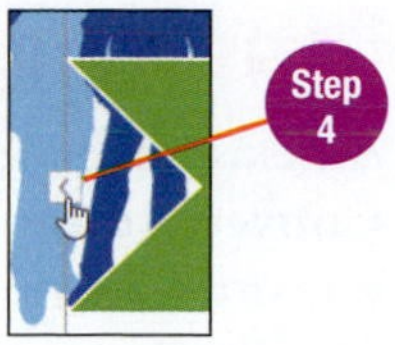

5. With the insertion point in the Text pane next to the first bullet, type Band; click next to the second bullet and type Observe; and click next to the third bullet and then type Analyze.

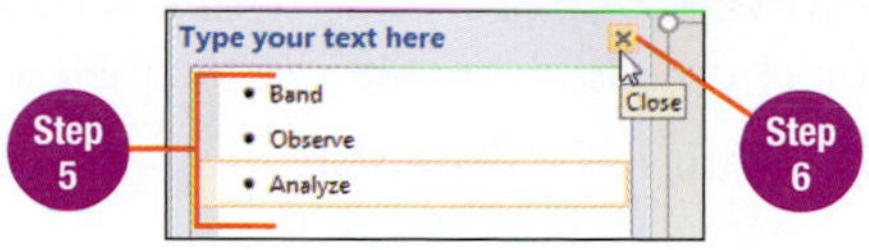

The SmartArt graphic updates as each word is typed in the Text pane to show the text in the shape. You can also add text to the shapes by typing text directly within the text placeholders inside each shape.

6. Click the Close button to close the Text pane.
7. If necessary, click the SmartArt Tools Design tab.
8. Click the More button at the bottom right of the SmartArt Styles gallery.
9. Click *Polished* at the drop-down gallery (first option in *3-D* section).
10. Click the Change Colors button in the SmartArt Styles group and then click *Colorful – Accent Colors* at the drop-down gallery (first option in the *Colorful* section).
11. Drag the border of the SmartArt graphic until the diagram is positioned near the bottom center of the slide, as shown in Figure 11.1.
12. Click in an unused area of the slide to deselect the graphic.
13. Save the revised presentation using the same name (**PaintedBunting-YourName**). Leave the presentation open for the next topic.

App Tip

Press the Down Arrow key to move to the next bullet in the Text pane.

Quick Steps

Insert a SmartArt Graphic

1. Activate slide.
2. Click Insert tab.
3. Click SmartArt button.
4. Select category in left pane.
5. Select layout in center pane.
6. Click OK.
7. Add text in Text pane or in shapes.
8. Format and/or move graphic object as required.

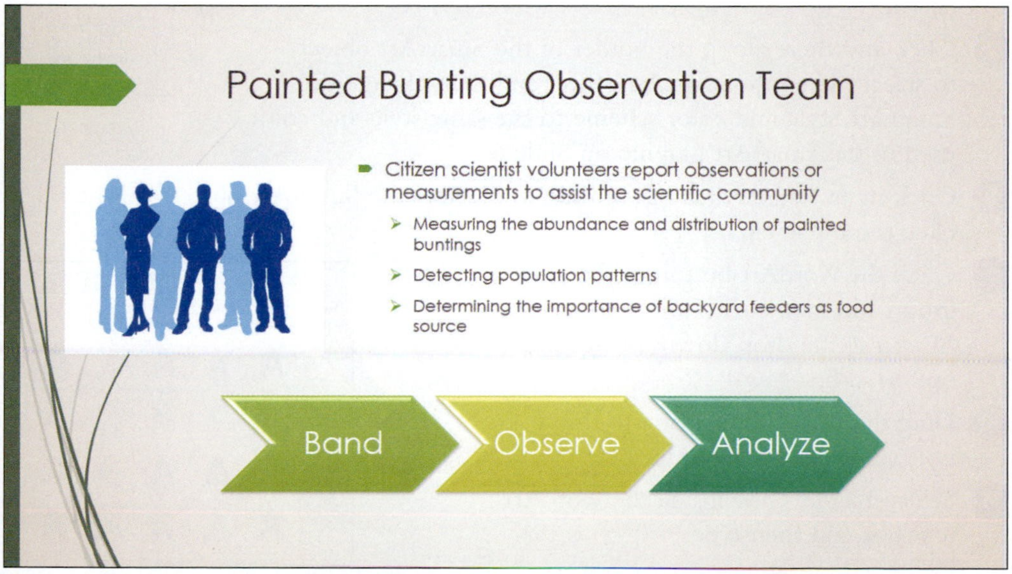

Figure 11.1

The completed Slide 6 with SmartArt graphic is shown here.

Beyond Basics **Modifying a SmartArt Graphic**

Use buttons in the Create Graphic group on the SmartArt Tools Design tab to add shapes, change the direction of the layout (switch between *Right to Left* and *Left to Right*), and move shapes up or down the layout. Each shape in the layout can also be selected and moved or resized individually.

11.3 Converting Text to SmartArt and Inserting WordArt

Skills

Convert text to a SmartArt graphic

Insert and modify a WordArt object

Tutorials

Converting Text and WordArt to a SmartArt Graphic

Inserting and Formatting WordArt

An existing bullet list on a slide can be converted to a SmartArt graphic using the **Convert to SmartArt button** in the Paragraph group on the Home tab. **WordArt** is text that is created and formatted as a graphic object. With WordArt you can create decorative text on a slide with a variety of WordArt Styles and text effects. A WordArt object can also have the text formed around a variety of shapes.

1. With the **PaintedBunting-YourName** presentation open, make Slide 5 the active slide in the slide pane.
2. Click in the bullet list to activate the placeholder.
3. Click the Convert to SmartArt button in the Paragraph group on the Home tab.
4. Click *Hierarchy List* at the drop-down gallery (second option in second row).

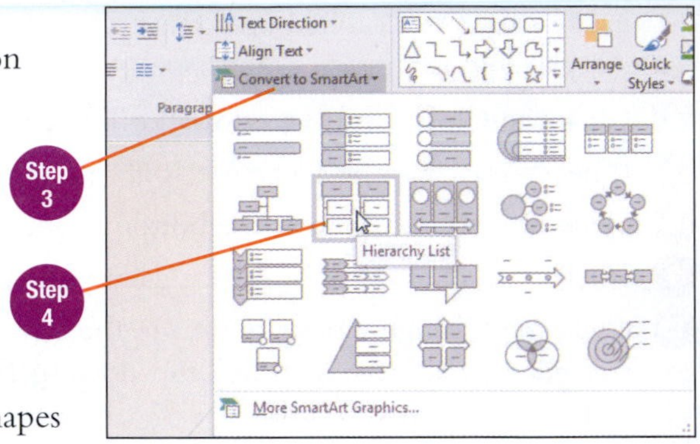

PowerPoint converts the text in the bullet list into the selected SmartArt layout. Level 1 text from the bullet list is placed inside shapes at the top level in the hierarchy diagram, with level 2 text in shapes below the corresponding level 1 box.

5. Close the Text pane if the Text pane is open.
6. Select and delete *Need to* in the second shape in the top level of the hierarchy, and capitalize *m* so that the text inside the shape reads *Manage and preserve natural habitat*.

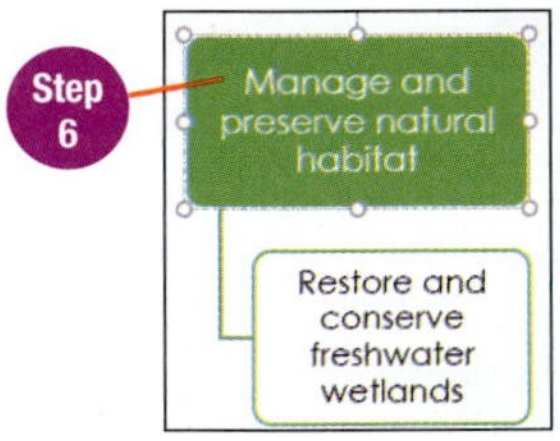

7. Click anywhere along the border of the SmartArt object to select the entire SmartArt object and then change the SmartArt Style and color scheme to the same style and color used in the SmartArt graphic on Slide 6.
8. Click in an unused area of the slide to deselect the SmartArt object and then click the Insert tab.
9. Click the WordArt button in the Text group and then click *Fill – Green, Accent 1, Shadow* at the drop-down list (second option in first row).

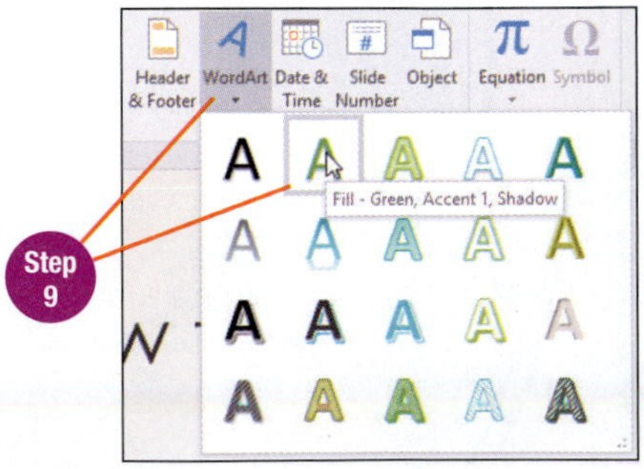

10. Drag the WordArt text box to the bottom center of the slide.
11. Select *Your text here* inside the WordArt text box and then type Help Save the Painted Bunting!.

Oops!

Other text is displayed inside the WordArt text box? This occurs if an insertion point is active inside another object with text when WordArt is created. Proceed to select whatever text is inside the box.

12 Click the border of the WordArt text box to remove the insertion point and select the entire placeholder.

13 Click the Text Effects button in the WordArt Styles group on the Drawing Tools Format tab, point to *Glow*, and then click *Lime, 5 pt glow, Accent color 3* (third option in first row of *Glow Variations* section).

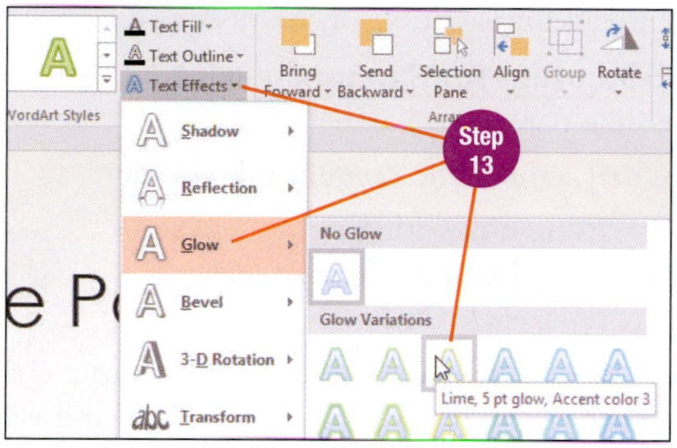

14 Drag the border of the WordArt text box until the smart guide appears, indicating the object is aligned with the center of the object above, as shown in Figure 11.2.

15 Save the revised presentation using the same name (**PaintedBunting-YourName**). Leave the presentation open for the next topic.

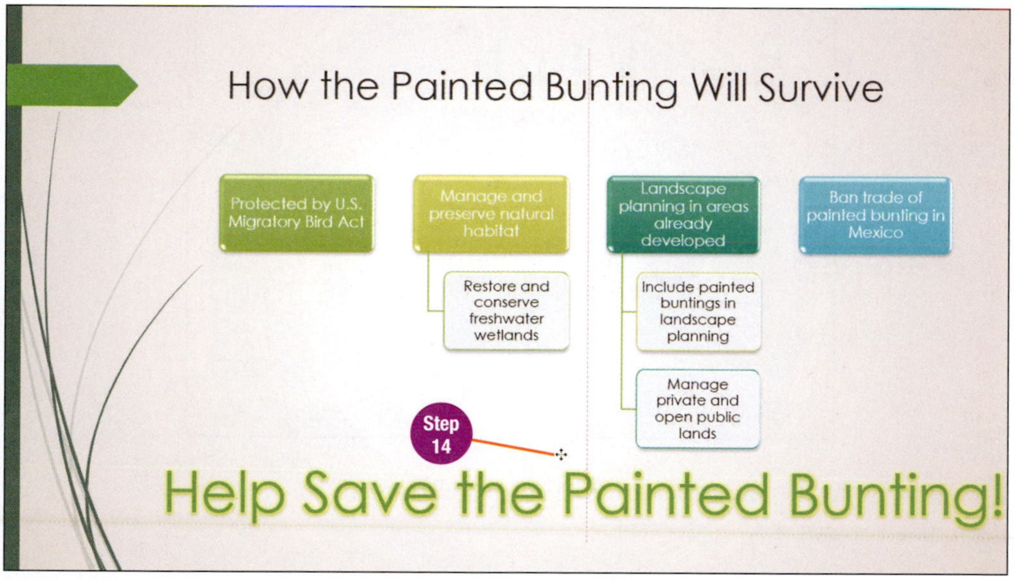

Figure 11.2

Smart guides aid in the alignment of the WordArt object with the center of the SmartArt object.

Quick Steps

Insert WordArt

1. Activate slide.
2. Click Insert tab.
3. Click WordArt button.
4. Select WordArt Style.
5. Move text box as required.
6. Select *Your text here.*
7. Type text.
8. Format WordArt object as required.

App Tip

You can apply more than one text effect to the same object.

App Tip

Select text in a WordArt object and change the font size as you would any other text. Resize the text box using the selection handles if you make the text larger or smaller in size.

Beyond Basics Transforming WordArt Text and Shape Styles

Use the *Transform* option from the Text Effects drop-down list to choose a shape around which WordArt text is formed. Text can be shaped to follow a circular or semicircular path, be slanted, or otherwise be altered to create a distinctive effect. Experiment with options in the Shape Styles gallery to add a rectangular box around the WordArt.

11.4 Creating a Chart on a Slide

Skills

Create a chart on a slide

Modify the chart style and color

Tutorials

Creating a Chart

Formatting with Chart Buttons

Changing Chart Design

Changing Chart Format

Copying and Pasting between Programs

Charts similar to the ones you created with Excel in Chapter 9 can be added to a PowerPoint slide. Add a chart using the Insert Chart icon in a content placeholder or with the Chart button in the Illustrations group on the Insert tab. Charts are commonly used in presentations to show an audience dollar figures, targets, budgets, comparisons, patterns, trends, or variations in numerical data.

1. With the **PaintedBunting-YourName** presentation open, make Slide 3 the active slide in the slide pane.
2. Click the Insert Chart icon in the content placeholder.
3. At the Insert Chart dialog box with *Column* selected in the All Charts category list and *Clustered Column* selected as the chart type, click OK.

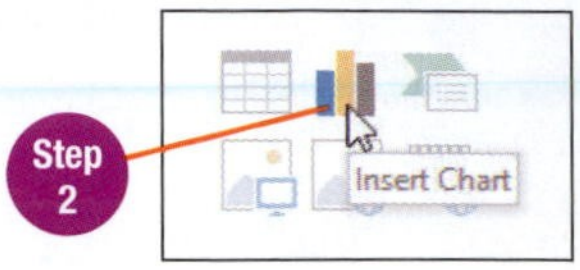

PowerPoint creates a sample chart on the slide and opens a chart data grid into which the data to be graphed is typed. As you enter labels and values into the chart data grid, the chart on the slide updates.

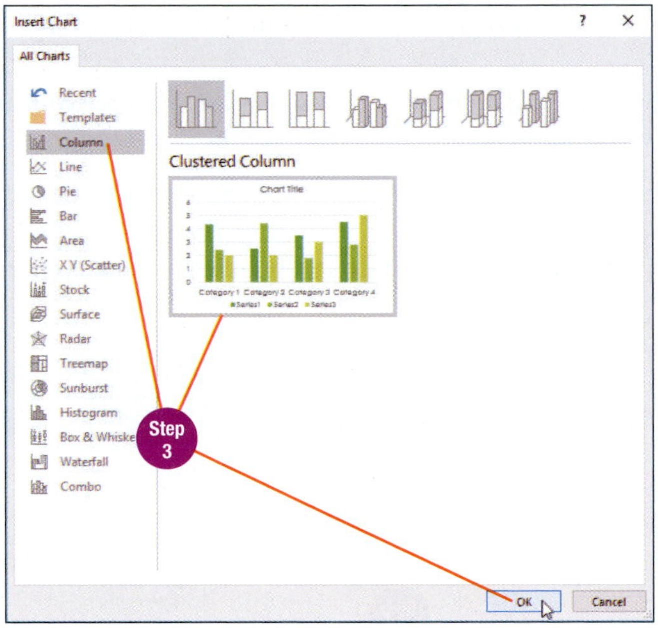

4. With B1 in the chart data grid the active cell, type 2016.
5. Click C1 and then type 2017.
6. Type the remaining data in the cells in the chart data grid as shown in the image below.
7. Close the chart data grid.

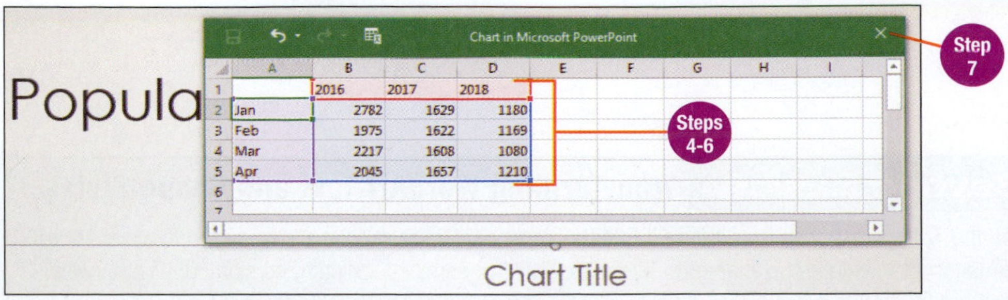

8 Select the text *Chart Title* inside the chart object and then type Monthly Sightings January to April.

9 Click the border of the chart to select the entire chart.

10 Click *Style 4* (fourth option) in the Chart Styles gallery on the Chart Tools Design tab.

11 Click *Color 2* (second row in *Colorful* section) in the Change Colors drop-down list.

12 Click outside the chart to deselect the chart object and then compare your slide with the one shown in Figure 11.3.

13 Save the revised presentation using the same name (**PaintedBunting-YourName**). Leave the presentation open for the next topic.

Quick Steps

Insert a Chart

1. Activate slide.
2. Click Insert Chart icon in content placeholder.
3. Choose category and chart type.
4. Click OK.
5. Add data in chart data grid.
6. Close data grid.
7. Format chart as required.

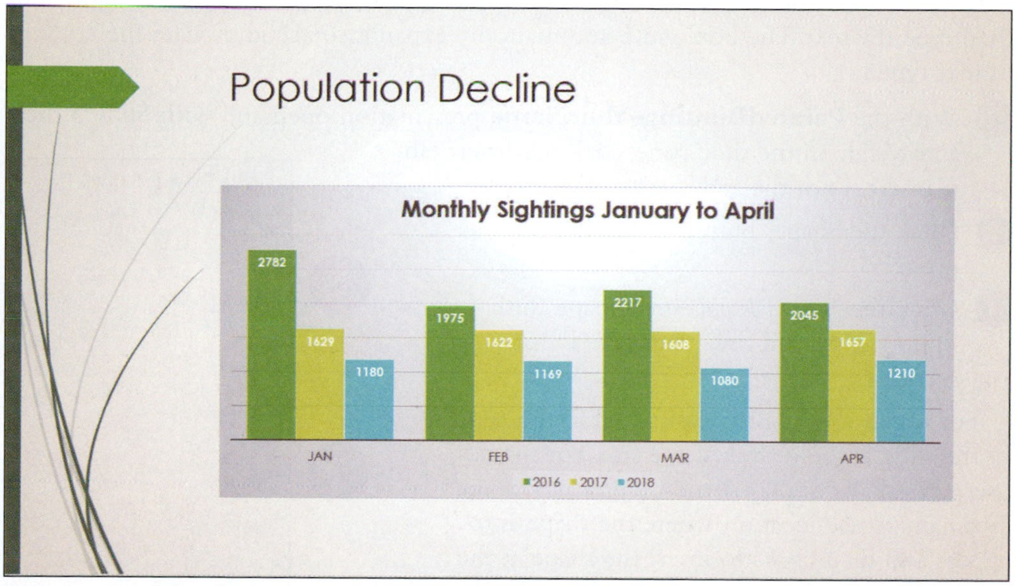

Figure 11.3

Your slide should match the completed Slide 3 with Clustered Column Chart.

Alternative Method **Copying and Pasting a Chart from Excel to PowerPoint**

Sometimes the data needed to create a chart resides in an Excel worksheet. In that case, create the chart in Excel and paste a copy of the chart onto the PowerPoint slide. You will practice this method in Chapter 14.

Beyond Basics **Formatting Charts and Editing Data**

Use the same tools you learned in Excel to modify and format charts in PowerPoint, such as the Chart Elements and Chart Styles buttons at the top right of the chart or with buttons on the Chart Tools Design and Chart Tools Format tabs.

To make a change to the source data for the chart, redisplay the chart data grid by activating the chart and then clicking the top part of the Edit Data button in the Data group on the Chart Tools Design tab.

11.5 Drawing a Shape and Adding a Text Box

Skills

Draw and modify a shape on a slide

Add text inside a shape

Format a shape

Create a text box on a slide

Tutorials

Formatting Shapes

Displaying Rulers, Gridlines, and Guides; Copying and Rotating Shapes

Inserting and Formatting Text Boxes

Inserting Action Buttons

A graphic can be added to a slide by drawing a line, rectangle, circle, arrow, star, banner, or other shape. Once the shape is drawn, text can be added inside the shape, and the shape can be formatted by changing the outline color or fill color or by adding a visual effect. Draw a shape by clicking the **Shapes button** in the Illustrations group on the Insert tab and then selecting the type of shape from the drop-down list. Click the slide where you want the shape to appear to insert a default sized shape or drag the crosshairs to create the desired shape.

A text box is text inside a rectangular object that can be manipulated independently from other objects on a slide. Add a text box using the Text Box button in the Text group on the Insert tab or from the Insert Shapes group on the Drawing Tools Format tab. Drag the downward pointing arrow the approximate length and width desired or click the slide where you want the text box to begin and then type the text. The box width automatically expands to accommodate the amount of text typed.

1. With the **PaintedBunting-YourName** presentation open and with Slide 3 the active slide in the slide pane, click the Insert tab if Insert is not the active tab.

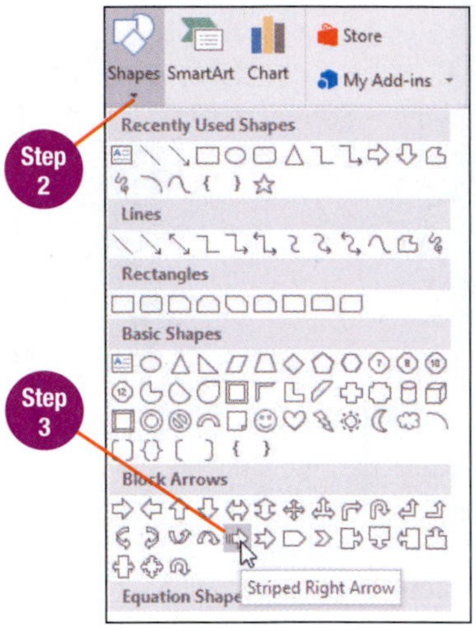

2. Click the Shapes button in the Illustrations group.
3. Click the *Striped Right Arrow* shape (fifth option in second row of the *Block Arrows* section).

For touch users, a shape is placed in the center of the slide at the default shape size. For mouse users, crosshairs display. A mouse user moves the crosshairs to the location where the shape is to appear and then clicks to insert the shape at the default shape size, or drags the crosshairs the desired height and width.

App Tip

When drawing other shapes, hold down the Shift key while dragging the mouse to create a perfect square, circle, or straight line.

4. Click inside the chart near the JAN bar for 2017 (with the value *1629*); if you are using touch, proceed to Step 5.

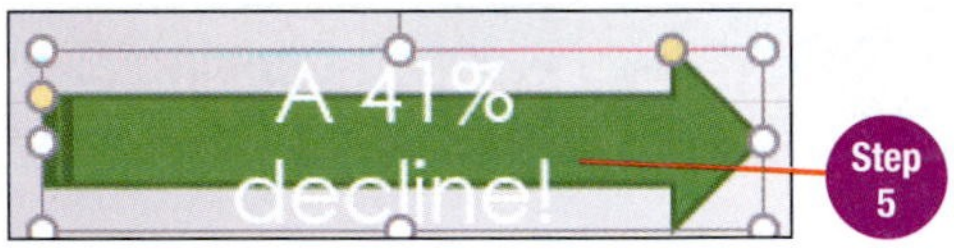

5. With the shape selected, type A 41% decline!
6. Drag the middle right sizing handle to the right until the text fits on one line inside the arrow shape.

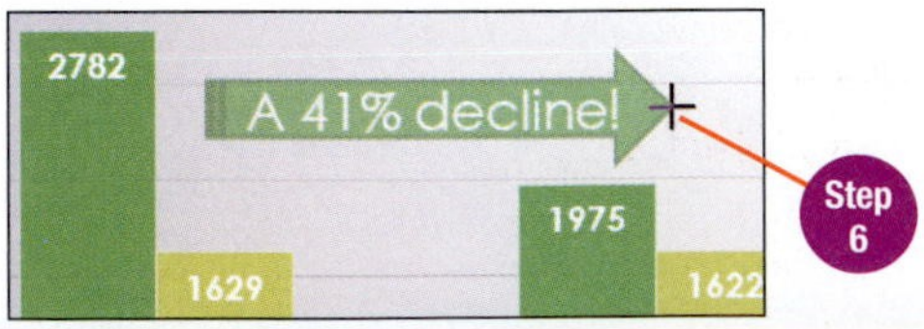

7. Drag the rotation handle (circled arrow above top center sizing handle) in an upward diagonal direction toward the left until the shape is at the approximate angle shown in the image at the right.

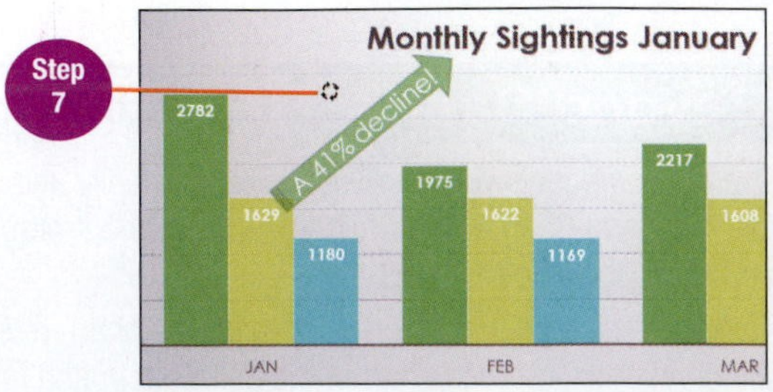

App Tip

Use the yellow handles that appear for a selected shape to change the appearance of the shape. For example, the yellow handle at the top of the arrow can be used to change the length of the arrowhead.

8. Drag the border of the arrow shape down to the bottom left of the chart so that it points to the 2017 January bar, as shown in the image at right.

9. With the arrow shape still selected and the Drawing Tools Format tab active, click the More button at the bottom right of the Shape Styles gallery, and then click *Intense Effect – Turquoise, Accent 6* (last option in last row of *Theme Styles* section in the drop-down gallery).

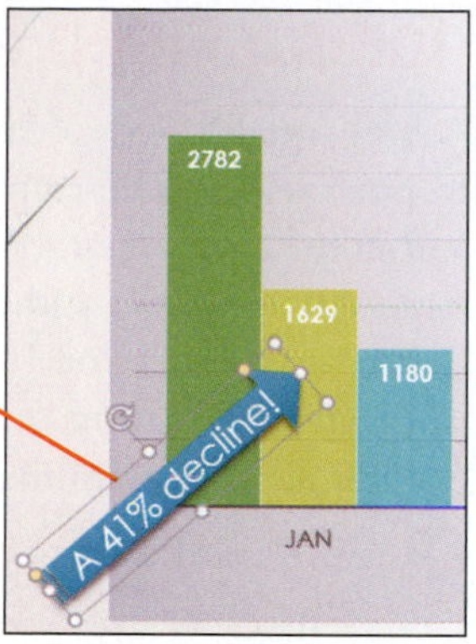

10. Click the Insert tab and then click the Text Box button in the Text group.

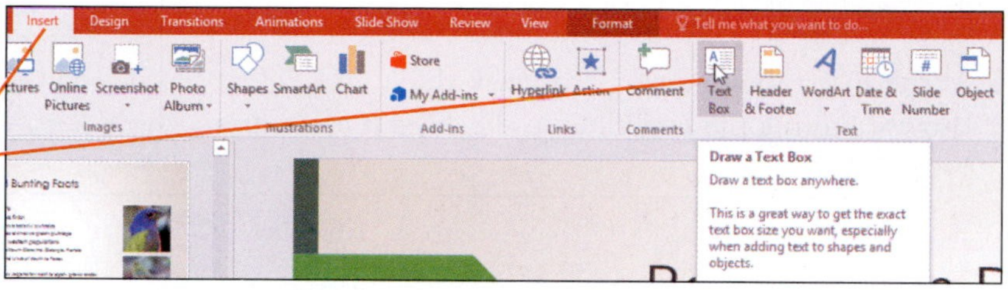

11. Click anywhere at the left side of the slide below the chart to insert a text box with an insertion point; if you are using touch, proceed to Step 12.

12. Type Source: Painted Bunting Observer Team, University of North Carolina, Wilmington.

13. Click the border of the text box to remove the insertion point and select the entire placeholder, click the Home tab if the Home tab is not active, and then click the Italic button in the Font group.

14. Move and/or resize the text box, aligning the text box with the bottom of the chart as shown in the image below.

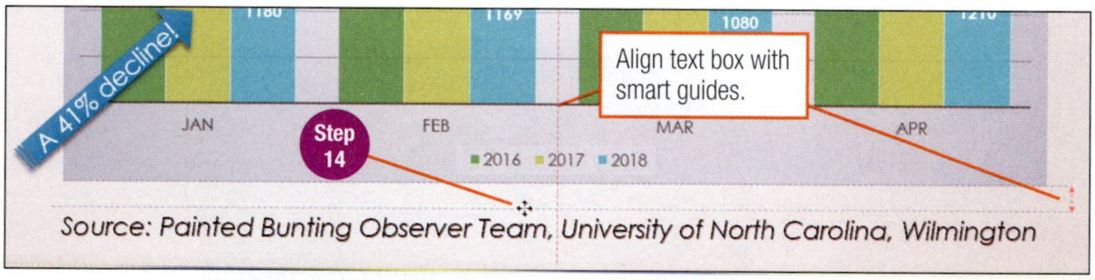

15. Save the revised presentation using the same name (**PaintedBunting-YourName**). Leave the presentation open for the next topic.

Quick Steps

Draw a Shape

1. Click Insert tab.
2. Click Shapes button.
3. Click required shape.
4. Click on slide to insert default shape.
5. Type text if required.
6. Resize, format, and move shape as required.

Create a Text Box

1. Click Insert tab.
2. Click Text Box button.
3. Click on slide.
4. Type text.
5. Resize, format, and move text box as required.

App Tip

Click the View tab and then click the *Gridlines* check box in the Show group to insert a check mark and display evenly spaced horizontal and vertical dotted lines on the slide to assist with placing objects at precise locations.

Beyond Basics Adding an Action Button to a Slide

A category of shapes called *Action Buttons* contains a series of buttons with actions assigned that are used to create a navigation interface or launch other items during a slide show. For example, draw the *Action Button: Home* button (shown at the right) on a slide to move to the first slide in the slide deck when the button is clicked during a slide show.

Home Action Button

11.6 Adding Video to a Presentation

Skills

Insert a video from a file

Trim the video

Set video playback options

Tutorial
Inserting and Modifying Video Files

A high-quality video can demonstrate a process or task that is otherwise difficult to portray using descriptions or pictures. Video is widely used for instructional and entertainment purposes. Appropriately used, video provides a more enjoyable experience for the audience. You can play a video from a file stored on your PC or link to a video at YouTube or another online source. Use the **Trim Video button** in the Editing group on the Video Tools Playback tab to crop a portion of the video playing at the beginning or end of the video clip.

1. With the **PaintedBunting-YourName** presentation open, make Slide 6 the active slide in the slide pane.
2. Insert a new slide with the Title and Content layout and then type A Beautiful Bird as the slide title.
3. Click the Insert Video icon in the content placeholder.
4. At the Insert Video dialog box, click the Browse From a file hyperlink in the *From a file* section.

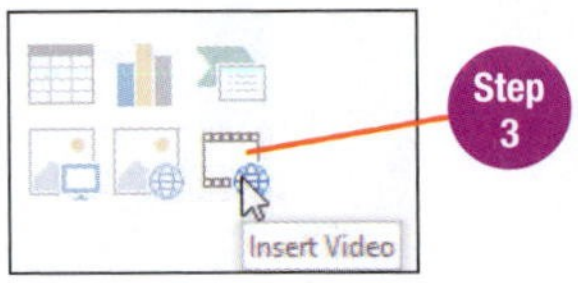

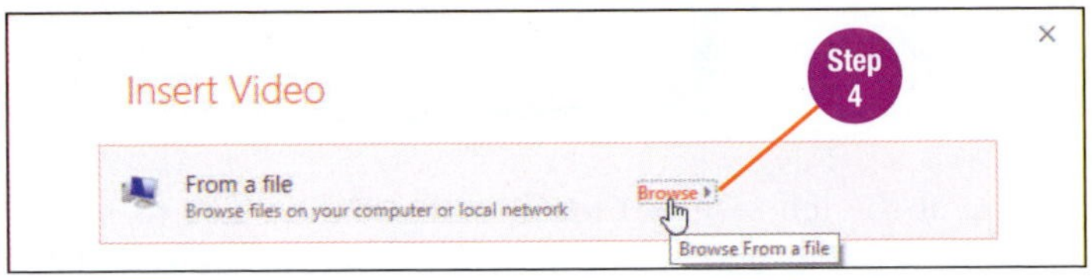

5. Navigate to the Ch11 folder in Student_Data_Files and then double-click the file ***PaintedBuntingVideo***.
6. Click the Play/Pause button below the video to preview the video clip.

The video plays for approximately 52 seconds.

App Tip

PowerPoint recognizes most video file formats, such as QuickTime movies, MP4 videos, MPEG movie files, Windows Media Video (wmv) files, and Adobe Flash Media.

7. Click the Video Tools Playback tab.
8. Click the Trim Video button in the Editing group.

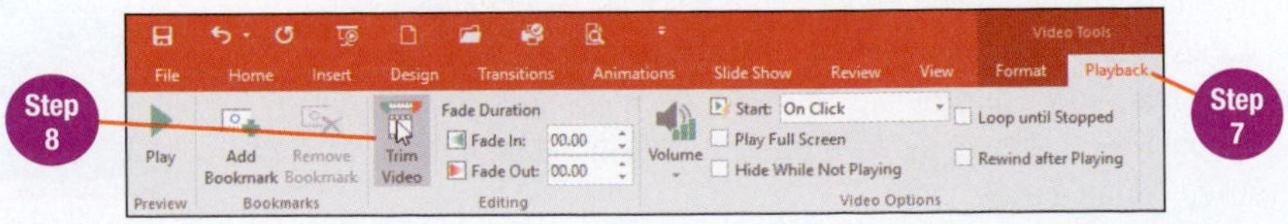

Trimming a video allows you to show only a portion of a video file if the video is too long or if you do not wish to show parts at the beginning or end. Drag the green or red slider to start playing at a later starting point and/or end before the video is finished, or enter the start and end times at the Trim Video dialog box.

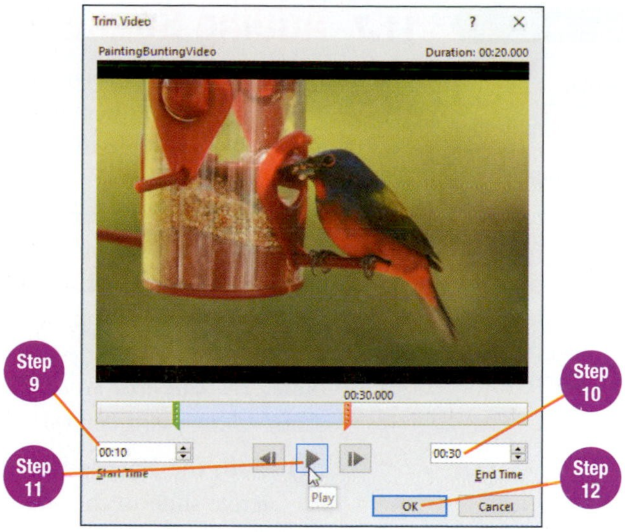

9. At the Trim Video dialog box, select the current entry in the *Start Time* text box and then type 00:10.
10. Select the current entry in the *End Time* text box and then type 00:30.
11. Click the Play button to preview the shorter video clip.
12. Click OK.
13. Click the *Start* list box arrow (displays *On Click*) in the Video Options group and then click *Automatically* at the drop-down list.

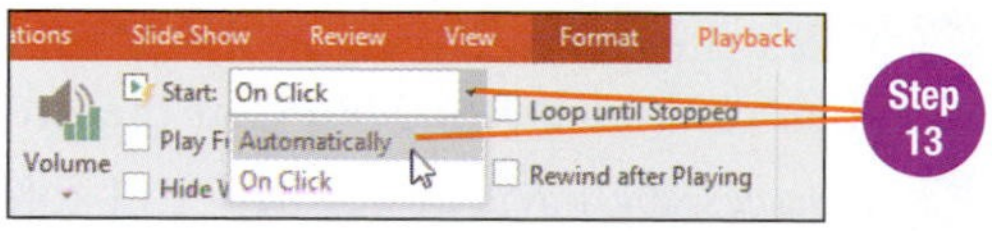

The *Automatically* option means the video will begin playing as soon as the slide is displayed in the slide show.

14. Drag the video object left until the smart guide appears at the left, indicating the object is aligned with the slide title.
15. Click the Video Tools Format tab and then click the *Soft Edge Rectangle* option in the Video Styles group (third option).

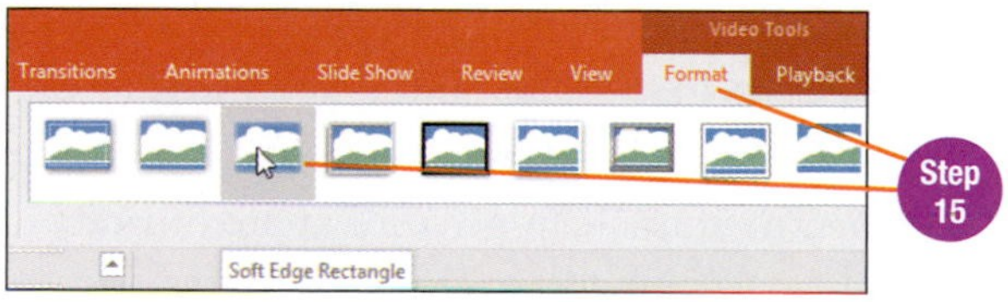

16. Save the revised image using the same name (**PaintedBunting-YourName**). Leave the presentation open for the next topic.

Alternative Method — Adding Video to an Existing Slide and Playing a Video from YouTube

Add video to the active slide by clicking the Insert tab, clicking the Video button in the Media group, and then choosing *Online Video* or *Video on my PC* at the drop-down list.

Link to a video at YouTube by displaying the Insert Video dialog box, typing the name of the video and pressing Enter in the *YouTube* text box, and then double-clicking the desired video in the search results list.

Quick Steps

Add Video from a File on a PC

1. Click Insert Video icon in content placeholder.
2. Click Browse From a file.
3. Navigate to drive and/or folder.
4. Double-click video file.
5. Edit and/or format video clip object as required.

Beyond Basics — Other Video Playback Options

The video can be set to display full screen, to loop continuously so that the video repeats until the slide show has ended, and to fade in or out. Configure these settings in the Editing and Video Options groups on the Video Tools Playback tab.

11.7 Adding Sound to a Presentation

Skills

Insert sound from a file

Set audio playback options

Tutorials

Inserting and Modifying Audio Files

Adding Sound to Slide Transitions

Adding music or other sound during a slide show is another way to interest and entertain your audience. For example, you might time introductory music to play while the title slide displays and your audience gathers, with the end of the music cueing the audience that the presentation is about to begin. Music can also be timed to play during a segment of a presentation to accompany a series of images. To add a sound clip or music to a presentation, activate the slide at which the sound should begin, click the **Audio button** in the Media group on the Insert tab, choose *Audio on My PC* at the drop-down list, and then select the sound or music file at the Insert Audio dialog box.

Note: *You will need headphones or earbuds if you are completing this topic in a computer lab at school where sound through the speakers is disabled.*

1. With the **PaintedBunting-YourName** presentation open, make Slide 1 the active slide in the slide pane and then click the Insert tab if the Insert tab is not the active tab.
2. Click the Audio button in the Media group and then click *Audio on My PC* at the drop-down list.

3. If necessary, navigate to the Ch11 folder in Student_Data_Files at the Insert Audio dialog box, and then double-click the file ***Allemande***.
4. Drag the sound icon to position the icon and playback tools near the bottom right of the slide.
5. Click the Play/Pause button and listen to the recording for a few seconds.

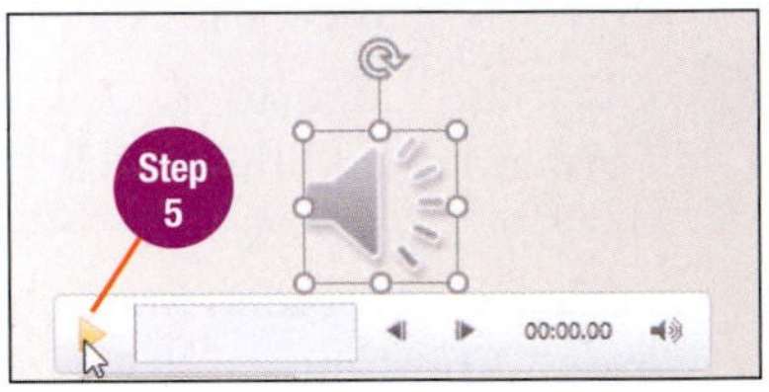

The entire music clip plays for approximately two and a half minutes.

App Tip

Choose *Record Audio* to record a new sound clip using the Record Sound dialog box. Type a name for the sound clip and then use the record, stop, and play buttons.

6. With the Audio Tools Playback tab active, click the *Hide During Show* check box in the Audio Options group to insert a check mark.
7. Click the *Start* list box arrow (displays *On Click*) and then click *Automatically* at the drop-down list.

This option will start the music as soon as the slide is displayed in the slide show.

8. Click the *Loop until Stopped* check box to insert a check mark.

This option will cause the music to replay continuously until the slide is advanced during the slide show.

App Tip

PowerPoint recognizes most audio file formats including MIDI files, MP3 and MP4 audio files, Windows audio files (.wav), and Windows Media Audio files (.wma).

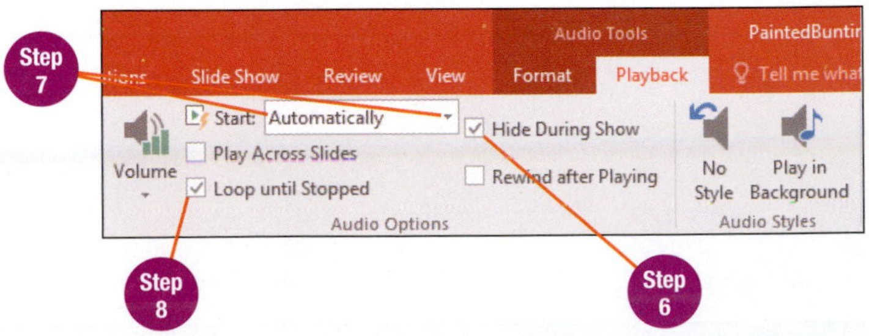

9. Make Slide 7 the active slide in the slide pane.

10 Insert the audio file ***PaintedBunting_Song*** in the slide by completing steps similar to those in Steps 2 to 8.

The audio recording of the Painted Bunting bird song is slightly less than two seconds in length.

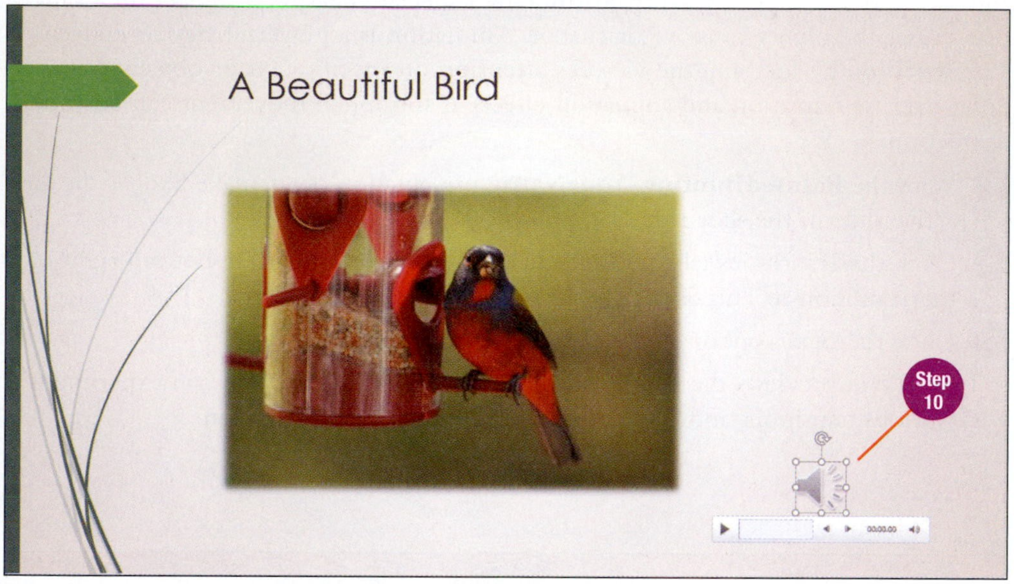

11 Insert a new slide after Slide 7 with the Title and Content layout and then type Photo, Video, and Audio Credits as the slide title.

12 Insert a table, type the information shown in Figure 11.4, and then adjust the layout using your best judgment for column widths and position on the slide.

Always credit the source of images, audio, and video used in a presentation if you did not create the multimedia yourself. In this instance, the music from Slide 1 is not credited because the recording is in the public domain.

13 Save the revised presentation using the same name (**PaintedBunting-YourName**). Leave the presentation open for the next topic.

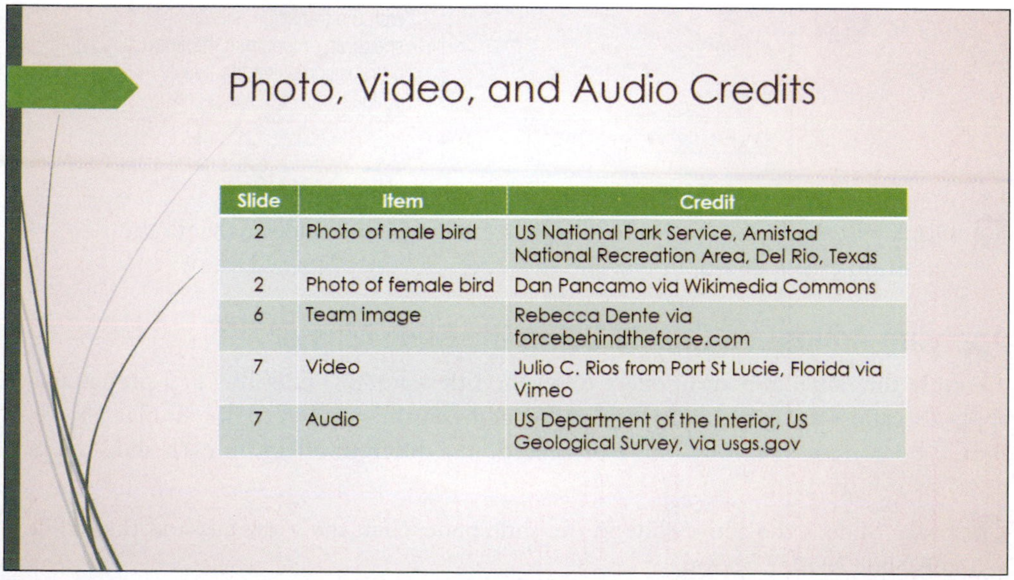

Slide	Item	Credit
2	Photo of male bird	US National Park Service, Amistad National Recreation Area, Del Rio, Texas
2	Photo of female bird	Dan Pancamo via Wikimedia Commons
6	Team image	Rebecca Dente via forcebehindtheforce.com
7	Video	Julio C. Rios from Port St Lucie, Florida via Vimeo
7	Audio	US Department of the Interior, US Geological Survey, via usgs.gov

Figure 11.4

This table for Slide 8 shows multimedia credits.

Quick Steps

Add Audio from a File

1. Click Insert tab.
2. Click Audio button.
3. Click *Audio on My PC.*
4. Navigate to drive and/or folder.
5. Double-click audio file.
6. Edit playback options as required.

Good to Know

Many websites offer copyright-free or public domain multimedia. Include the keywords *copyright free* or *public domain* in a search for a picture, audio, or video file. Check the terms of use at each site to be sure you credit sources appropriately because copyright-free allows free usage but usually requires attribution to the creator.

11.8 Adding Transitions and Animation Effects to Slides for a Slide Show

Skills

Add a transition to all slides

Add an animation effect to an object on the slide master

Add an animation effect to an individual object

Tutorials

Adding Transitions

Applying and Removing Animations

Modifying Animations

Applying an Action to an Object

A **transition** is a special effect that appears as one slide is removed from the screen and the next slide appears. **Animation** adds a special effect to an object on a slide that causes the object to move or change. Animation is a powerful way to enliven a presentation by focusing the viewer's attention on specific text or objects, but don't overuse transition and animation effects as too much movement can become a distraction.

1. With the **PaintedBunting-YourName** presentation open, make Slide 1 the active slide in the slide pane.
2. Click the Transitions tab and then click the More button at the bottom right of the Transition to This Slide gallery.
3. Click the *Blinds* option in the *Exciting* section of the gallery.

PowerPoint previews the effect with the current slide so that you can experiment with various transitions and effects before making your final selection.

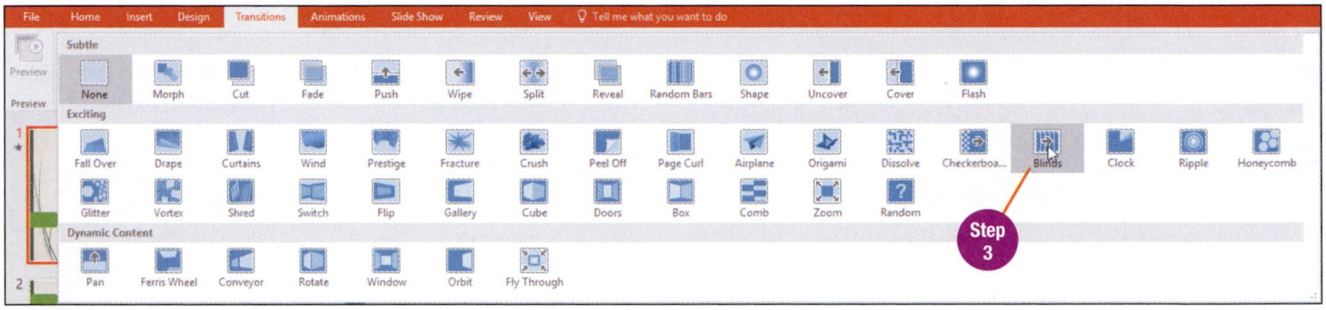

Oops!

Trouble finding *Blinds*? On small-screen devices such as tablets, the Transitions gallery displays fewer buttons per row. Look for *Blinds* further down.

4. Click the Apply To All button in the Timing group.

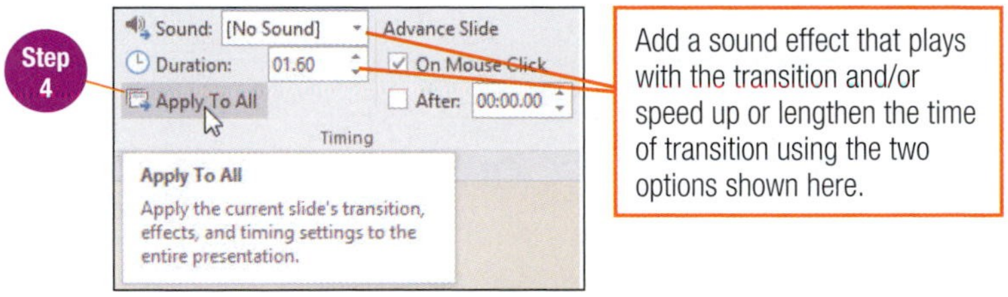

App Tip

Use the Effect Options button in the Transition to This Slide group to choose a variation for the selected transition (such as the direction the blinds move).

5. Display the slide show, advance through the first three slides to view the transition effect, and then end the show to return to Normal view.

Applying Animation Effects Using the Slide Master

To apply the same animation effect to all the titles and/or bullet lists in a presentation, apply the effect using the slide master. Generally, animation effects for similar objects should be consistent throughout a presentation; a different effect on each slide might become a distraction.

6. Make Slide 2 the active slide in the slide pane, click the View tab, and then click the Slide Master button.
7. Click to select the border of the title placeholder on the slide master.

8. Click the Animations tab.
9. Click the *Split* option in the Animation gallery.

See Table 11.2 for a description of Animation categories.

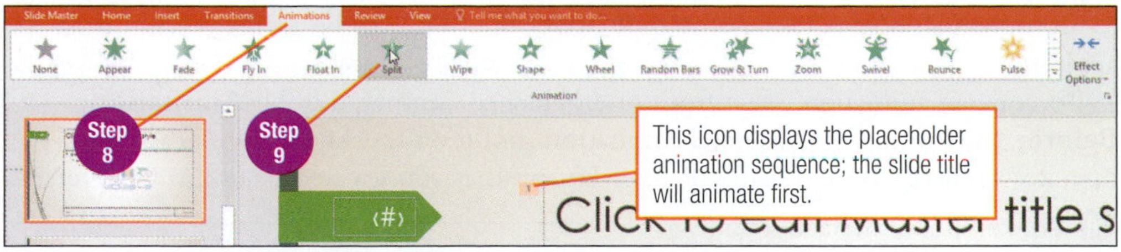

10. Click to select the border of the content placeholder and then click the More button in the Animation gallery.
11. Click the *Zoom* option in the *Entrance* section.

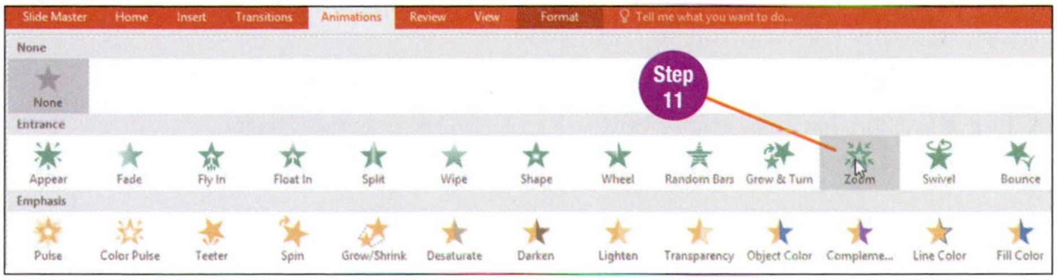

12. Click the *Start* list box arrow (displays *On Click*) in the Timing group and then click *After Previous*.
13. Select the current entry in the *Duration* text box, type 1.5 and then press Enter.

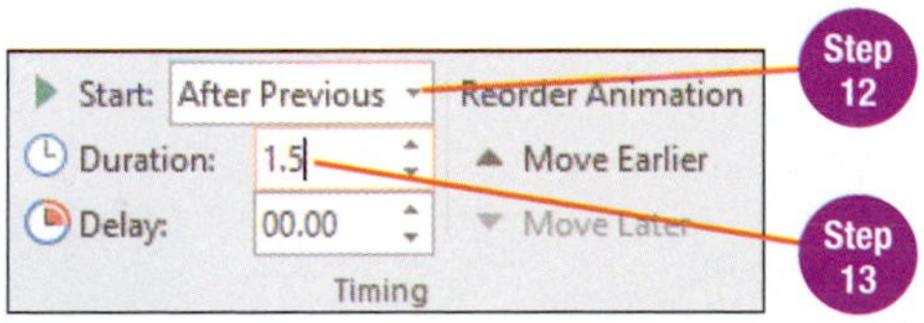

14. Click the Slide Master tab and then click the Close Master View button.
15. Make Slide 1 the active slide in the slide pane, run through the presentation in a slide show to view the transition and animation effects, and then return to Normal view.

App Tip

The Animation gallery provides the most popular effects. View more effects by category using the options at the bottom of the gallery. For example, *More Entrance Effects* shows all 40 options.

Table 11.2

Animation Categories

Category	Description
Entrance	Most common animation effect in which the object animates as it appears on the slide.
Emphasis	Animates text or object already in place by causing the object to move or to change in appearance; includes effects such as darkening, changing color, bolding, or underlining, to name a few.
Exit	Animates the text or object after it has been revealed, such as by fading or flying off the slide.
Motion Paths	An object moves along a linear path, an arc, or some other shape.

Applying Animation Effects to Individual Objects

As you previewed the slide show, you probably noticed that images and other objects, such as shapes or text boxes, appeared on the slide before the title. You may want these items to remain hidden until the title and text have been revealed. To apply animation to an individual object, display the slide, select the object to be animated, and then apply the desired animation option.

To copy an animation effect from one object to another, use the **Animation Painter button** in the Advanced Animation group on the Animations tab, which operates similarly to the Format Painter button that you learned to use in Chapter 3.

16. Make Slide 2 the active slide in the slide pane.
17. Click to select the male bird picture at the top right of the slide.
18. Click the Animations tab and then click the *Wipe* option in the Animation gallery.
19. Click the *Start* list box arrow and then click *After Previous*.
20. Click to select the male bird picture and then click the Animation Painter button in the Advanced Animation group.
21. Click to select the female bird picture at the bottom right of the slide.
22. Make Slide 3 the active slide in the slide pane.
23. Click to select the arrow shape, apply the *Fly In* animation option, and then change the *Start* option to *After Previous*.
24. Copy the arrow shape animation options to the text box object below the chart by completing steps similar to those in Steps 20 and 21.
25. Make Slide 5 the active slide in the slide pane.
26. Click to select the WordArt object at the bottom of the slide, apply the *Float In* animation option, and then change the *Start* option to *After Previous*.
27. Make Slide 6 the active slide in the slide pane.

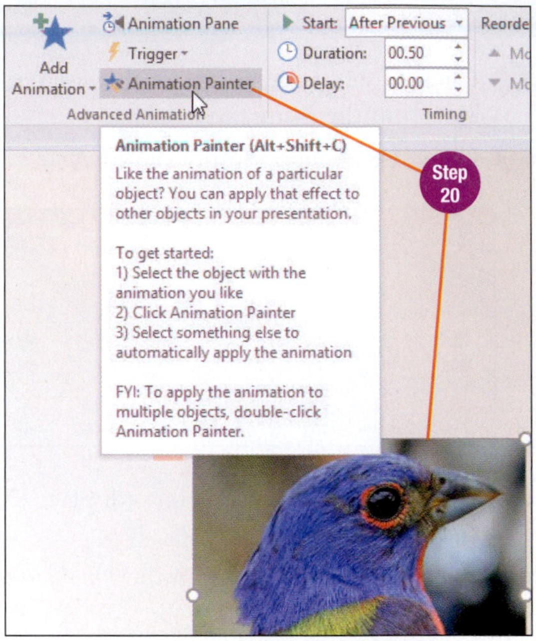

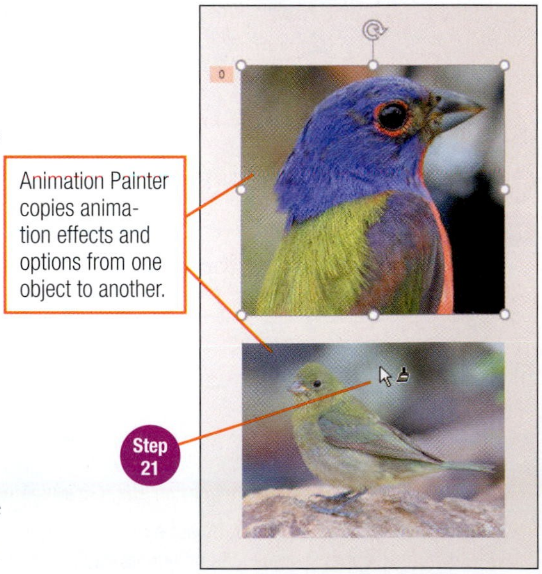

28 Click to select the picture at the left side of the slide, apply the *Shape* animation option, and then change the *Start* option to *After Previous*.

29 Click to select the SmartArt graphic at the bottom of the slide. Make sure the entire graphic is selected and not an individual shape within the graphic.

30 Apply the *Fly-in* animation option and then change the *Start* option to *After Previous*.

31 Click the Effect Options button and then click the *One by One* option in the *Sequence* section of the drop-down list.

This option will cause each chevron in the graphic to animate on the slide one at a time, starting with the leftmost shape first.

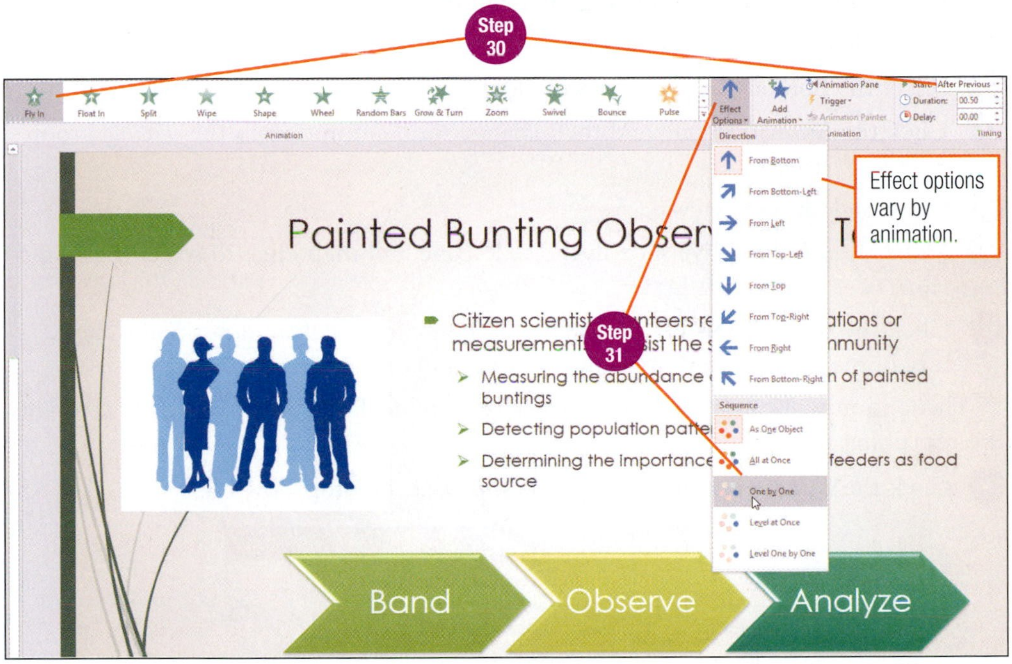

32 Run through the presentation in a slide show from the beginning to view the revised animation effects and then return to Normal view when the slide show ends.

33 Save the revised presentation using the same name (**PaintedBunting-YourName**). Leave the presentation open for the next topic.

Quick Steps

Add a Transition
1. Click Transitions tab.
2. Add transition effect.
3. Change effect options or timing options as required.
4. Click Apply To All button.

Apply Animation to All Slides
1. Display slide master.
2. Click Animations tab.
3. Select placeholder.
4. Add animation effect.
5. Change effect options or timing options as required.
6. Close Slide Master view.

Apply Animation to an Individual Object
1. Activate slide.
2. Click Animations tab.
3. Select object.
4. Add animation effect.
5. Change effect options or timing options as required.

Good to Know

You can deliver a presentation online using the free Office Presentation Service if you are signed in with a Microsoft account. Participants are able to view slides in a web browser. Access the service at the Share backstage area with the Present Online panel.

Beyond Basics Changing the Animation Sequence

To adjust the order in which objects are animated, display the required slide and open the Animation pane at the right side of the window. To do this, click the Animation Pane button in the Advanced Animation group on the Animations tab. Select the object that you want to move in the Animation pane and then use the Move Earlier or Move Later buttons in the Reorder Animation group.

11.9 Setting Up a Self-Running Presentation

Skills

Add timings to slides

Change the show type to kiosk

Tutorials

Advancing Slides Automatically

Setting Timings for a Slide Show

Looping a Slide Show Continuously

Some presentations are designed to be self-running, meaning that the slides are intended to be shown continuously at a kiosk or viewed at a PC by an individual. To create a presentation that advances through slides automatically, you need to set up a time for each slide to display and ensure that each slide animation is set to start automatically for each object. When the animation options and timing settings are complete, open the Set Up Show dialog box to change the show type to *Browsed at a kiosk* by clicking the **Set Up Slide Show button** in the Set Up group on the Slide Show tab.

1. With the **PaintedBunting-YourName** presentation open, use Save As to save a copy of the presentation in the current folder naming it **PaintingBuntingSelfRunning-YourName**.
2. Make Slide 2 the active slide in the slide pane and then display the slide master.
3. Select the border of the title placeholder.
4. Click the Animations tab and then change the *Start* option in the *Timing* group to *After Previous*.
5. Close Slide Master view.
6. Make Slide 1 the active slide in the slide pane and then click to select the sound icon.
7. Click the Audio Tools Playback tab and then click the *Play Across Slides* check box in the Audio Options group to insert a check mark.

This option will cause the music that starts at Slide 1 to continue playing through the remaining slides.

8. Click the Volume button and then click *Low* at the drop-down list.

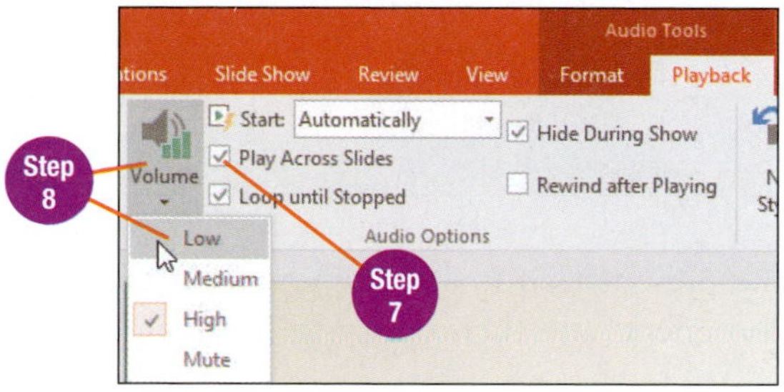

9. Make Slide 7 the active slide in the slide pane and then select and delete the sound icon to remove the audio.
10. Make Slide 8 the active slide in the slide pane and then select and delete the last row in the table.
11. Click the Transitions tab.
12. Click the *After* check box in the *Timing* section to insert a check mark, select the current entry in the *After* text box, type 0:25 and then press Enter.
13. Click the Apply To All button.

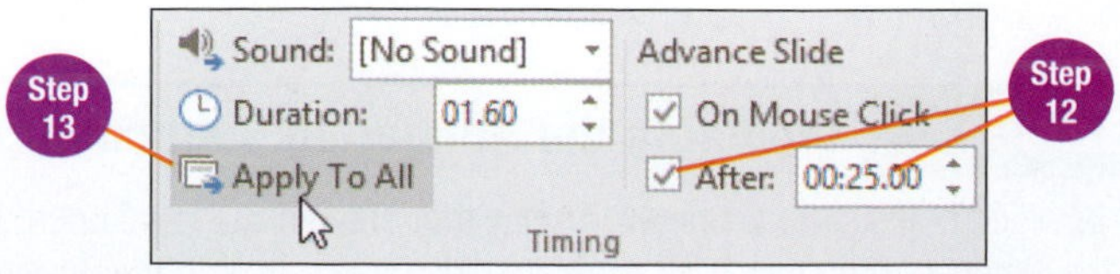

All the slides will advance automatically after the same 25-second duration. To set individual times for slides, activate a slide and enter a different time in the *After* text box.

14 Make Slide 3 the active slide in the slide pane, select the entry in the *After* text box, type 0:10 and then press Enter.

15 Change the *After* time for Slide 5 and Slide 6 to 0:15 and for Slide 8 to 0:10.

16 Click the Slide Show tab and then click the Set Up Slide Show button in the Set Up group.

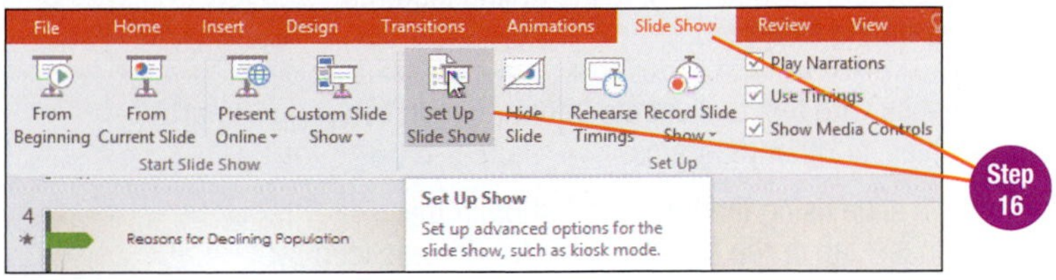

17 At the Set Up Show dialog box, click the *Browsed at a kiosk (full screen)* option in the *Show type* section.

18 Click OK.

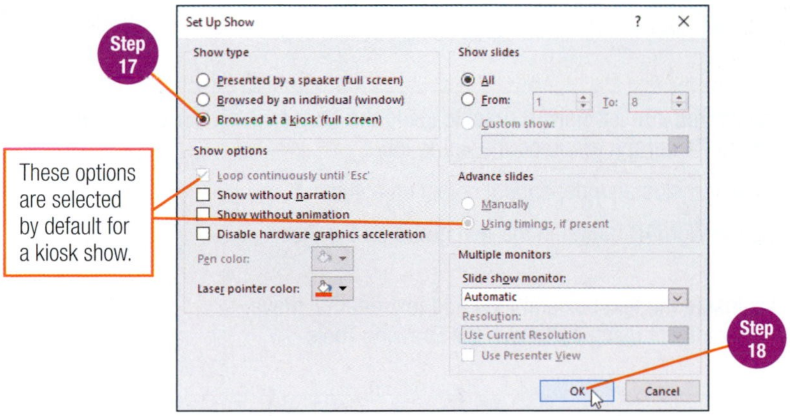

19 Start the slide show from the beginning and watch the presentation as it advances through all the slides automatically. End the show when the presentation starts at Slide 1 again by pressing the Esc key.

20 Save the revised presentation using the same name (**PaintedBuntingSelf Running-YourName**) and then close the presentation.

Quick Steps

Add Timing for a Slide
1. Click Transitions tab.
2. Click *After* check box.
3. Enter time in *After* text box.

Set Up a Kiosk Show
1. Click Slide Show tab.
2. Click Set Up Slide Show button.
3. Click *Browsed at a kiosk (full screen)*.
4. Click OK.

App Tip

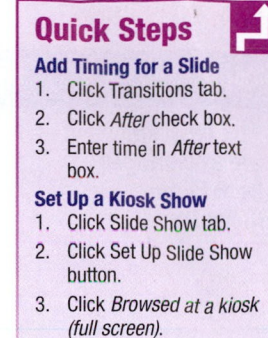

You can create an MPEG 4 (MP4) movie file that you can burn to a disc or upload to a website using the *Create a Video* panel at the Export backstage area.

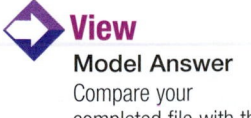

View

Model Answer

Compare your completed file with the model answer.

Beyond Basics Using Rehearse Timings

The Rehearse Timings feature on the Slide Show tab lets you assign a time to each slide as you run through a slide show with a timer active and a Recording toolbar. Use the Next button on the Recording toolbar to advance each slide, and PowerPoint will enter the times for each slide transition. This method lets you time each slide for a typical audience member after a suitable time has elapsed in the slide show.

Topics Review

Topic	Key Concepts	Key Terms
11.1 Inserting Graphic Images from Picture Collections	A picture from your PC can be added to a slide using the Pictures button in the Images group on the Insert tab or with the Pictures icon in the content placeholder on a new slide. Resize, move, or edit a picture by selecting the image and using the selection handles and/or buttons in the Picture Tools Format tab. Find a picture or other image from a website using the Online Pictures button in the Images group on the Insert tab.	
11.2 Inserting a SmartArt Graphic	SmartArt graphics use shapes with text to illustrate information in lists, processes, cycles, hierarchies, or other diagrams. Add a SmartArt graphic to a slide using the SmartArt button in the Illustrations group on the Insert tab or the Insert a SmartArt Graphic icon in a content placeholder. Choose a SmartArt category and layout at the Choose a SmartArt Graphic dialog box and then click OK to enter the desired text. Text can be added to shapes in the Text pane or by typing directly inside a shape. Modify SmartArt styles or colors or edit the graphic using buttons in the SmartArt Tools Design tab.	SmartArt
11.3 Converting Text to SmartArt and Inserting WordArt	A bullet list can be converted into a SmartArt graphic using the Convert to SmartArt button in the Paragraph group on the Home tab. WordArt is decorative text inside an independent object on a slide. Create WordArt using the WordArt button in the Text group on the Insert tab. Type the WordArt text inside the text box and then add text effects, move, and or otherwise edit the object using buttons in the Drawing Tools Format tab.	Convert to SmartArt button WordArt
11.4 Creating a Chart on a Slide	Insert a chart using the Insert Chart icon in the content placeholder or the Chart button in the Illustrations group on the Insert tab. Choose the chart category and chart type at the Insert Chart dialog box and then click OK. Type the data to be graphed in the chart data grid, which is a small Excel worksheet object on top of the slide placeholders. Modify the chart using the buttons in the Chart Tools Design and Chart Tools Format tabs.	
11.5 Drawing a Shape and Adding a Text Box	Draw your own graphics on a slide using the Shapes button on the Insert tab. Type text inside a selected shape and then resize, move, or otherwise modify the shape using buttons in the Drawing Tools Format tab. A text box is a rectangular object in which you can type text and that can be moved, resized, or formatted independently. Create a text box using the Text Box button on the Insert tab or the Drawing Tools Format tab.	Shapes button

continued...

Topic	Key Concepts	Key Terms
11.6 Adding Video to a Presentation	Add a video clip to a slide using the Insert Video icon in a content placeholder or with the Video button in the Media group on the Insert tab. You can select a video clip from a file on your PC or by finding a video clip at YouTube or another website. Use buttons in the Video Tools Playback tab to edit a video or change the video options. Use the Trim Video button to change the starting and/or ending position of the video if you do not want to play the entire clip. Change the *Start* option if you want the video to start automatically when the slide is displayed in a slide show. Options in the Video Tools Format tab are used to format the video object.	Trim Video button
11.7 Adding Sound to a Presentation	Add audio to a slide using the Audio button in the Media group on the Insert tab. Use buttons in the Audio Options group on the Audio Tools Playback tab to hide the sound icon during a slide show, start the audio automatically, play the sound in the background across all slides, or loop the audio continuously until the slide is advanced. Always credit the sources of all multimedia used in a presentation that you did not create yourself.	Audio button
11.8 Adding Transitions and Animation Effects to Slides for a Slide Show	A transition is a special effect that appears as one slide is removed from the screen and another is revealed during a slide show. Animation causes an object to move or transform in some way. Select a transition at the Transition to This Slide gallery on the Transitions tab. The Apply To All button in the Timing group on the Transitions tab sets the same transition effect to all slides. Add an animation effect to a placeholder on the slide master to apply the effect to all slides in the presentation. Animation effects are selected in the Animation gallery on the Animations tab. Specify how the animation will start and the animation duration using options in the Timing group. The Animation Painter button copies the animation effect and effect options from one object to another. Animate an individual object on a slide by selecting the object and then adding an animation effect from the Animation gallery. Animation effects are grouped into four categories: *Entrance*, *Emphasis*, *Exit*, and *Motion Paths*. To change the sequence in which objects are animated, display the Animation pane, select the object to be reordered, and then use the Move Earlier or Move Later buttons in the Reorder Animation group.	transition animation Animation Painter button

continued...

Topic	Key Concepts	Key Terms
11.9 Setting Up a Self-Running Presentation	A self-running presentation is set up to run a slide show continuously. To create a self-running presentation, each slide needs to have a time entered in the *After* text box in the Timing group on the Transitions tab, and each animated object needs to be set to start automatically. Open the Set Up Show dialog box from the Set Up Slide Show button on the Slide Show tab, and then choose *Browsed at a kiosk (full screen)* to instruct PowerPoint to play the slide show continuously until stopped. As an alternative to manually entering each slide time, you can use the Rehearse Timings feature from the Slide Show tab to set a time for each slide to display while watching a slide show with a timer and Recording toolbar active.	Set Up Slide Show button

Recheck

Recheck your understanding of the topics covered in this chapter.

Workbook

Chapter review and assessment resources are available in the *Workbook* ebook.

Chapter 12

Using and Querying an Access Database

Precheck

Check your understanding of the topics covered in this chapter.

Organizations and individuals rely on data to complete transactions, make decisions, and otherwise store and track information. Data that is stored in an organized manner to provide information to meet a variety of needs is called a **database**. Microsoft Access is a software program designed to organize, store, and maintain data in an application referred to as a **database management system (DBMS)**. You interact with a DBMS several times a day as you complete your daily activities. Examples of the types of transactions that involve a DBMS include withdrawing cash from your bank account, completing a purchase, looking up a telephone number, or programming your GPS to find a route to an address.

In this chapter you will learn database terminology and how to navigate a DBMS, including how to open and close objects; add and maintain records using a datasheet and form; find and replace data; sort and filter data; and use queries to look up information and perform a calculation on a numeric field.

Learning Objectives

12.1 Identify a database table, query, report, and form; and define *field*, *field value*, and *record*

12.2 Add a record using a datasheet

12.3 Edit and delete records using a datasheet

12.4 Add, edit, and delete records using a form

12.5 Find and replace data, and adjust column widths in a datasheet

12.6 Sort and filter records in a datasheet and form

12.7 Create a query using a wizard

12.8 Create a query using Design view

12.9 Select records in a query using criteria

12.10 Select records in a query using AND and OR criteria, and sort query results

12.11 Modify a query to insert and remove a field, add a calculated field to a query, and preview a database object

SNAP If you are a SNAP user, go to your SNAP Assignments page to complete the Precheck, Tutorials, and Recheck.

Data Files

Before beginning this chapter, be sure you have copied the student data files for this course to your storage medium. Steps on downloading and extracting the data files are provided in Chapter 1, Topic 8, on pages 22–23.

12.1 Understanding Database Objects and Terminology

Skills

Open and close a database

Identify objects in a database

Open and close objects

Tutorials

Opening an Existing Database

Closing a Database and Closing Access

Opening and Closing an Object

An Access database is structured and organized specifically to keep track of a large amount of similar data. For example, a library database is organized so that information such as the title, author, and publisher is maintained for each book in the library. Making sure that the data is entered and updated in the same manner for each item is important so that information is complete and accurate. For this reason, a database is created with a structure that defines the data that will be collected for each item. Working with objects and data in an existing database will help you understand the terms that are used and how data is organized before you create your own database.

Identifying Database Objects

An Access database is a collection of related objects in which data is recorded, edited, and viewed. Access opens with a Navigation pane along the left side of the window that is used to open an object. Objects are grouped in the Navigation pane by type. The four most common types are tables, queries, forms, and reports. See Table 12.1 for a description of each type.

Table 12.1

Access Objects

Object	Description
Table	Data is organized into tables, each of which opens in a datasheet that displays data in columns and rows. A table stores data about one topic or subject only. For example, in the LibraryFines database, one table contains data about each student and another table contains data about each fine.
Query	A query is used to extract information from one or more tables in a single datasheet that shows all the data or a subset of data that meets a specific condition. For example, a query could show all library fines that have been assessed or only those fines that remain unpaid.
Form	A form provides a user-friendly interface to enter or update data where one record is viewed at a time. The layout of a form can be customized to match closely an existing paper form used in a business.
Report	Reports are used for viewing or printing data from a table or query. Reports can include summary totals and a customized layout.

1 Start Access and open the database named ***LibraryFines*** from the Ch12 folder in Student_Data_Files.

2 Click the Enable Content button in the SECURITY WARNING message bar that appears below the ribbon. If a SAVE CHANGES message bar appears with a Save to SharePoint Site button, click the Close this message button at the right end of the bar.

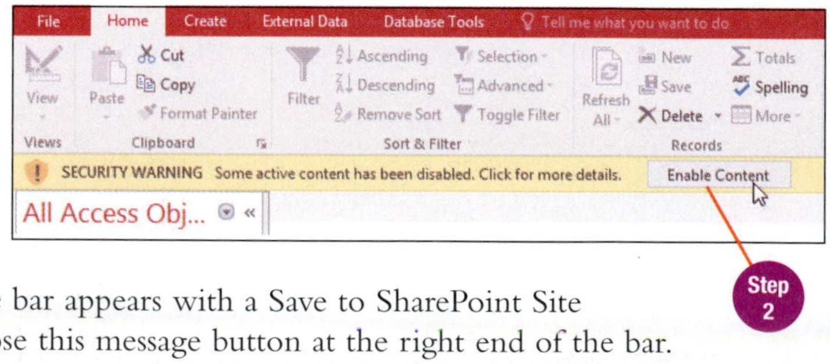

The Security Warning message bar appears each time you open a database unless the settings for Access on your PC have been changed. Microsoft disables some content as a way to protect your PC from potentially harmful files that may be embedded in the database without your knowledge (such as a virus). The data files provided with this textbook are safe, so you can click the Enable Content button.

3 Compare your screen with the one shown in Figure 12.1 on page 289.

Oops!

A Connect to dialog box appears asking for your user name and password and then a Save a Local Copy dialog box appears? If you open data files from your OneDrive account, you may be prompted to enter your OneDrive account name and password and then save a copy of the database to your PC. It will be easier for you to copy the student data files for Chapter 12 and 13 to a folder on a USB flash drive or other hard drive. Close the dialog box, exit Access, and then copy the files to another folder. Start Step 1 again, opening the database from the new folder.

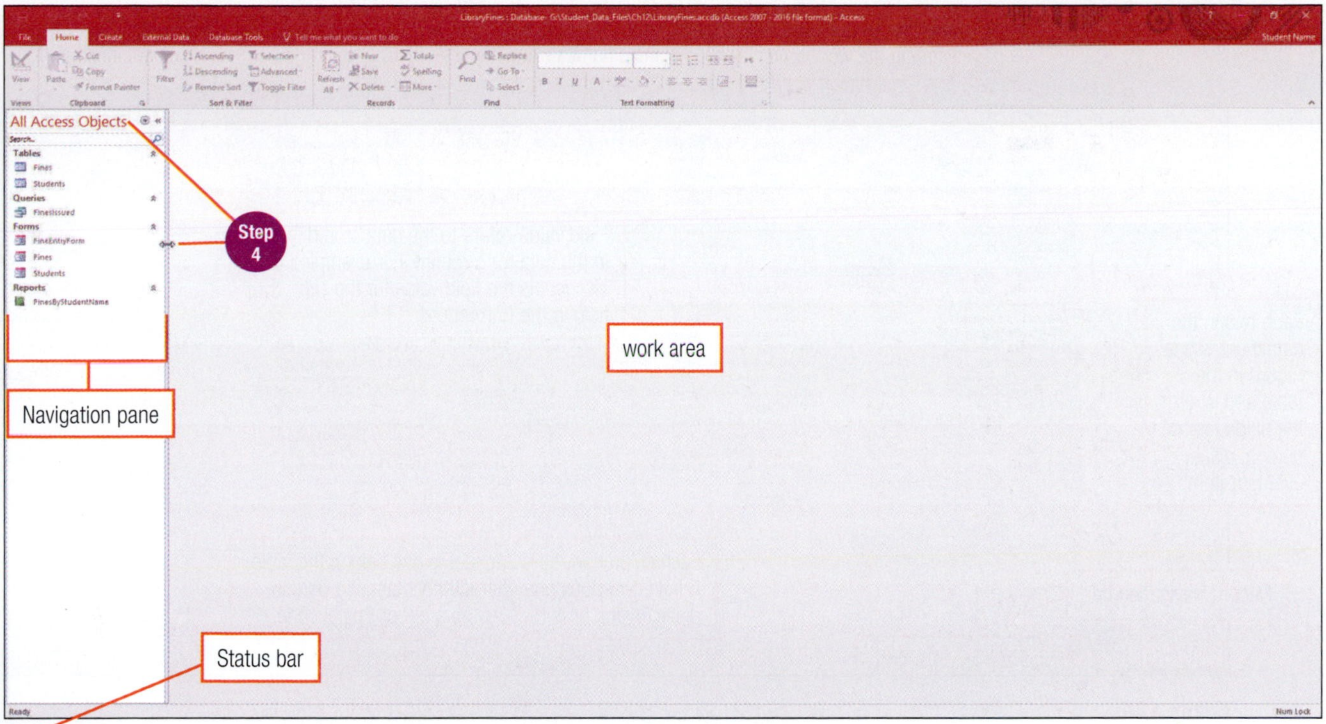

Figure 12.1

The LibraryFines database is shown opened in the Access window.

4 If necessary, drag the gray border along the right side of the Navigation pane to the right to expand the width of the pane until the title *All Access Objects* is entirely visible.

Opening and Closing Objects

Data in a database is organized by topic or subject about a person, place, event, item, or other category grouping in an object called a **table**. A database table is the first object that is created. The number of tables varies for each database depending on the information that needs to be stored. Tables are the building blocks for creating other objects, such as a query, form, or report. In other words, you cannot create a query, form, or report without first creating a table.

5 Double-click *Fines* in the Tables group in the Navigation pane.

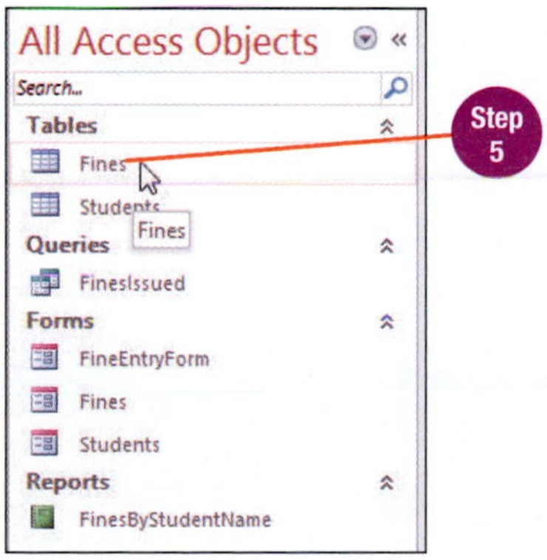

The table opens in Datasheet view within a tab in the work area as shown in Figure 12.2 on page 290. A datasheet resembles a spreadsheet with the data organized in columns and rows. The information about the subject or topic of a table (such as library fines) is divided into columns, each of which is called a **field**. A field should store only one unit of information about a person, place, event, or item. For example, a mailing address is split into at least four fields so the street address, city, state or province, and zip or postal code are separated. This allows the database to be sorted, filtered, or searched by any piece of information.

Oops!

Trouble opening a table? Another way to open the table is to right-click the object name and then choose *Open* at the Shortcut menu.

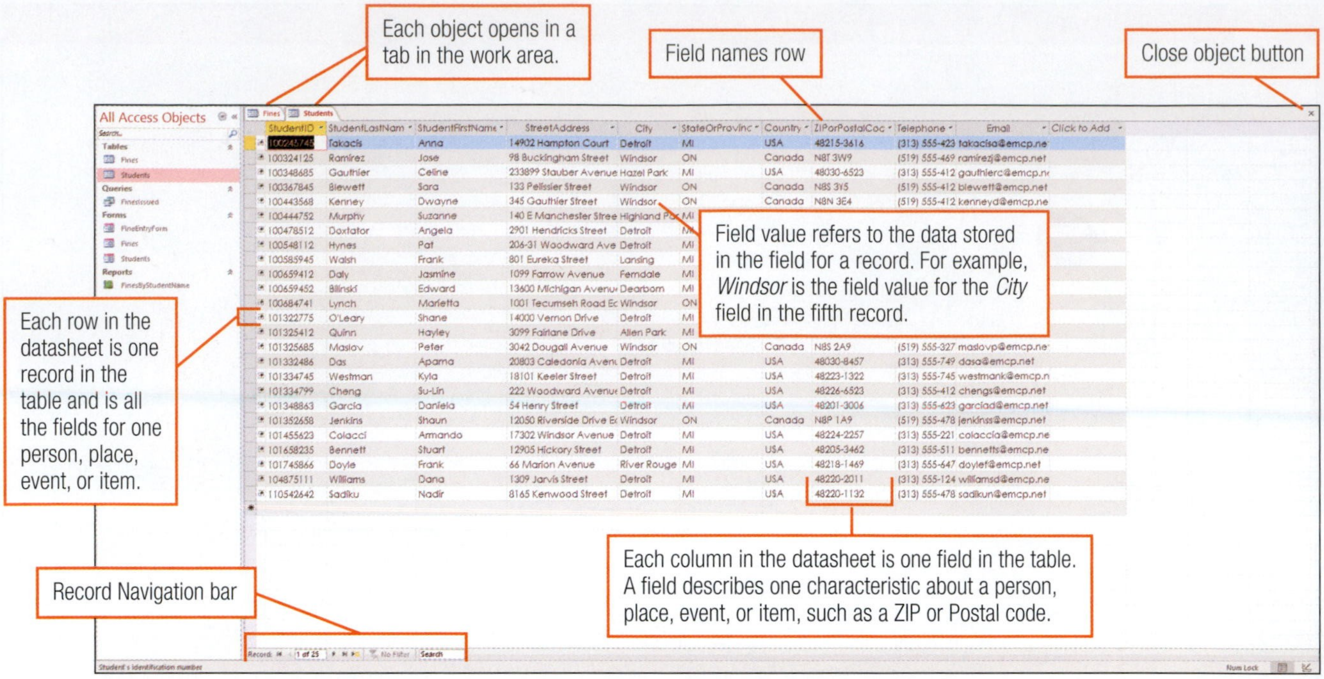

Figure 12.2

Shown is the Datasheet view for the Students table in the LibraryFines database.

Each row in the datasheet shows all the fields for one person, place, event, or item and is called a **record**. The data that is stored in one field within a record is called a **field value**.

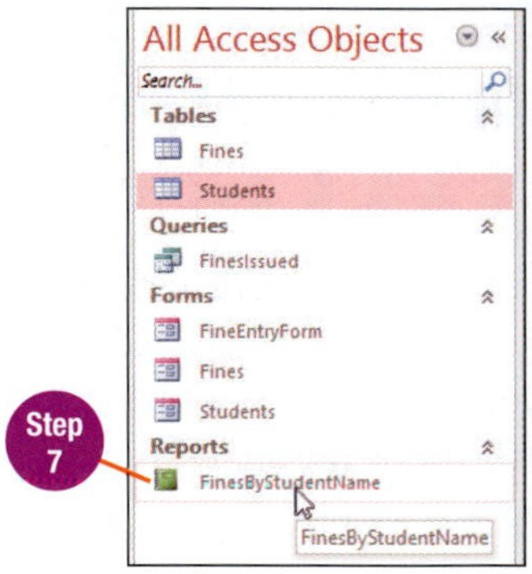

6 Double-click *Students* in the Tables group in the Navigation pane and then compare your screen with the one shown in Figure 12.2.

7 Double-click *FinesByStudentName* in the Reports group in the Navigation pane and review the report content and layout in the work area.

A **report** is designed to view or print data from one or more tables or queries in a customized layout and with summary totals. In this report, library fines are arranged and grouped by student name.

8 Click the Close button at the top right of the work area to close the report.

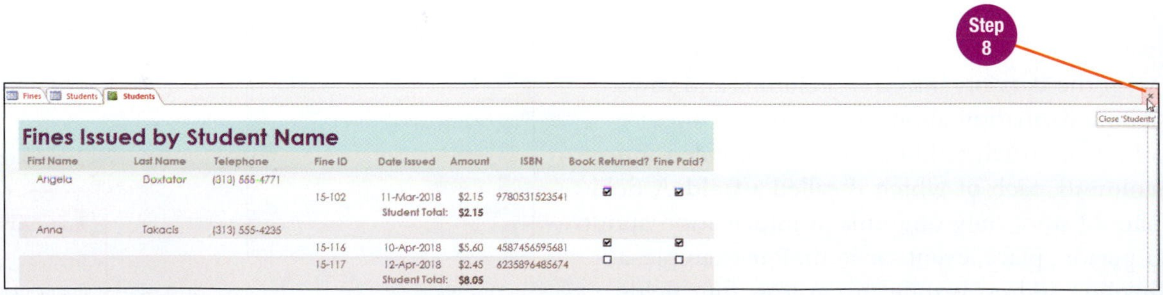

9 Double-click *FineEntryForm* in the Forms group in the Navigation pane.

A **form** is used to enter, update, or view one record at a time.

10 Click the Next record button (right-pointing arrow) in the Record Navigation bar located at the bottom of the form.

Buttons in the Record Navigation bar are used to move to the first record, previous record, next record, or last record. Use the search text box to navigate to a record by typing a field value.

11 Click the Previous record button (left-pointing arrow).

12 Click the Last record button (right-pointing arrow with vertical bar) to move to the last record in the form.

13 Click the First record button (vertical bar with left-pointing arrow) to move to the first record in the form.

14 Click the Close button at the top right of the work area to close the form.

15 Double-click *FinesIssued* in the Queries group in the Navigation pane.

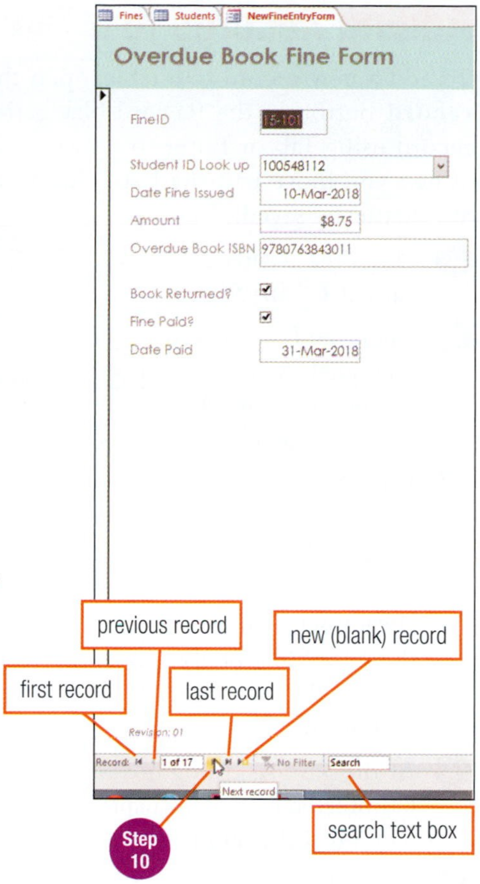

A **query** opens in a datasheet similar to a table. A query displays information from one or more tables and may show all the records or only a subset of records that meet a specific condition.

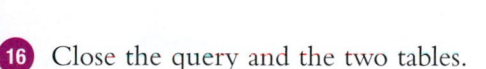

FineID	DateIssued	StudentFirstName	StudentLastName	Telephone	Amount	OverdueBookISBN	BookReturned	FinePaid
15-101	10-Mar-2018	Pat	Hynes	(313) 555-6569	$8.75	9780763843011	☑	☑
15-102	11-Mar-2018	Angela	Doxtator	(313) 555-4771	$2.15	9780531523541	☑	☑
15-103	12-Mar-2018	Pat	Hynes	(313) 555-6569	$1.25	9780412533145	☑	☐
15-104	12-Mar-2018	Marietta	Lynch	(519) 555-3214	$1.40	9784123524158	☑	☐
15-105	13-Mar-2018	Edward	Bilinski	(313) 555-9200	$4.25	9784125312517	☑	☑
15-106	13-Mar-2018	Stuart	Bennett	(313) 555-5112	$3.25	8745125412352	☑	☐

A query can show data from more than one table and display the fields in any order as seen in the first six rows in the FinesIssued query shown here.

16 Close the query and the two tables.

17 Click the File tab and then click *Close* at the backstage area.

Always close a database file using the backstage area before exiting Access so that all temporary files used by Access while you are viewing and updating records are properly closed.

Quick Steps

Open a Database Object

1. Open database file.
2. Double-click object name in Navigation pane.

App Tip

Forms can be created to resemble paper-based forms used within an organization.

App Tip

Close objects as soon as you are finished viewing or updating data. Some Access commands will not run if an object is open in the background.

Beyond Basics — One Database at a Time

Unlike Word, Excel, or PowerPoint, Access allows only one file to be open at a time in the current window. If you open a second database in the current window, Access automatically closes the existing database before opening the new one.

12.2 Adding Records to a Table Using a Datasheet

Skills

Add a new record using a datasheet

Tutorial

Adding and Deleting Records in a Table

To add a new record to a table, open the table and click the **New (blank) record** button in the Record Navigation bar. Type the field values for the new record using Tab or Enter to move to the next column (field) in the datasheet. When you move past the last column in a new row in the datasheet, the record is automatically saved.

1. Open the database named ***LibraryFines***.
2. Click the File tab and then click *Save As* to open the Save As backstage area.
3. With *Save Database As* already selected as the *File Types* option and *Access Database* already selected as the *Save Database As* option, click the Save As button.

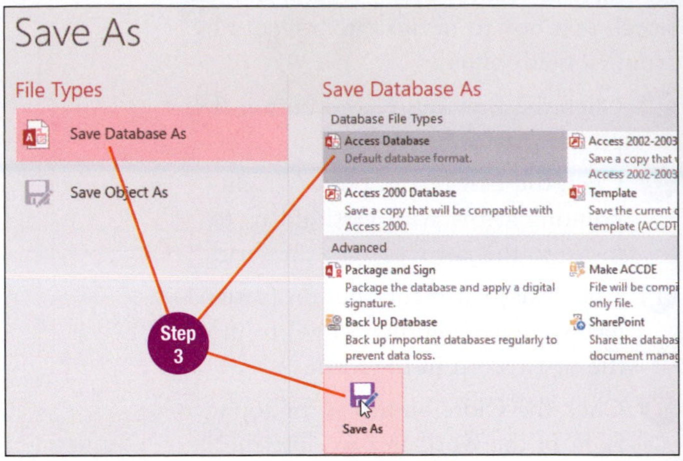

4. At the Save As dialog box, create a new folder named *Ch12* in the CompletedTopicsByChapter folder on your storage medium, change the file name to **LibraryFines-YourName**, and then click the Save button.
5. Click the Enable Content button in the SECURITY WARNING message bar. Close the SAVE CHANGES message bar if the bar appears.
6. Open the Fines table.
7. Click the New (blank) record button in the Record Navigation bar.

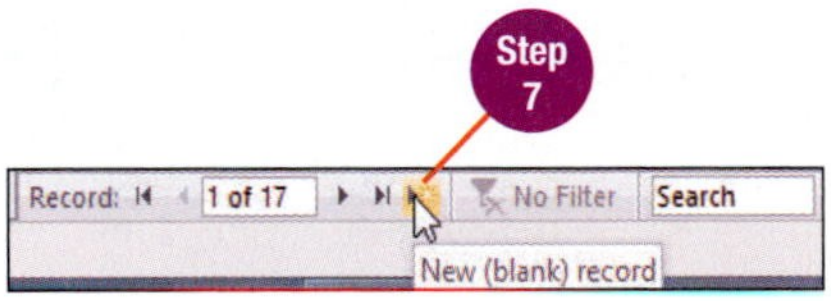

8. Type 15-118 in the *FineID* field and then press Tab to move to the next field.

   The field *StudentID* looks up names and ID numbers in the Students table using a drop-down list.

9. Click the down-pointing arrow in the *StudentID* field, click *100478512 Angela Doxtator* in the drop-down list, and then press Tab.

   The student ID number becomes the field value, which is connected to Angela Doxtator's record in the Students table.

The Pencil icon indicates the record is being edited. The pencil disappears when Access saves the changes.

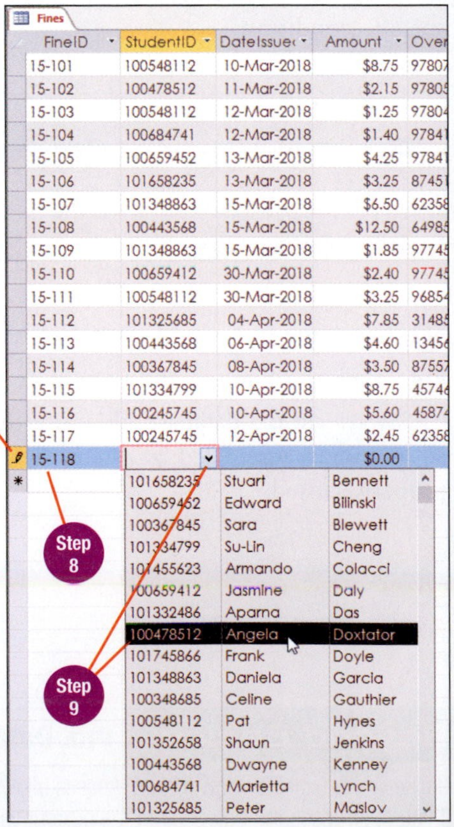

App Tip

You can also move to the next field by pressing the Enter key or by clicking in the next column.

10 Type 12apr2018 in the *DateIssued* field and then press Tab.

The date field has been set up to display underscores and dashes as soon as you begin typing to help you enter the date in the correct format *dd-mm-yyyy*. This configuration also ensures that all dates are entered consistently in the database.

11 Type 8.75 in the *Amount* field and then press Tab.

12 Type 4348973098226 in the *OverdueBookISBN* field and then press Tab.

13 Press the spacebar to insert a check mark in the *BookReturned* field and then press Tab.

BookReturned is a field that has been set up to store only one of two possible field values: *Yes* or *No*. Inserting a check mark stores *Yes*, while an empty check box stores *No*.

14 Click the check box to insert a check mark in the *FinePaid* field and then press Tab.

15 Type 15apr2018 in the *DatePaid* field and then press Tab.

Moving to the next row in the datasheet automatically saves the record just typed and starts a new record.

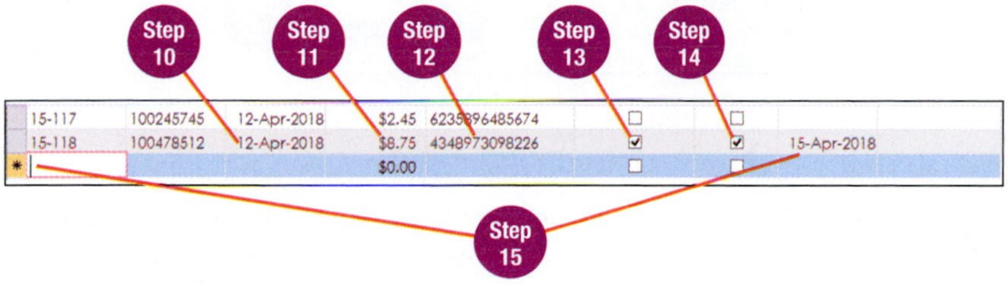

16 Add the following field values in the new row in the fields indicated pressing Tab after typing the data to move to the next field:

FineID	15-119	*OverdueBookISBN*	7349872345760
StudentID	*101348863 Daniela Garcia*	*BookReturned*	Yes
DateIssued	15apr2018	*FinePaid*	No (leave blank)
Amount	5.25	*DatePaid*	(leave blank)

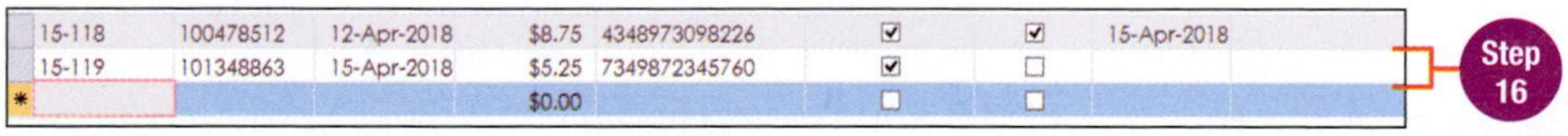

17 With the insertion point positioned in the *FineID* field in a new row, close the Fines table. Leave the database open for the next topic.

Alternative Method

Adding New Records Using the Ribbon or Keyboard Commands

New records can be added to a table using any of these methods:

- Click the New button in the Records group on the Home tab
- Keyboard shortcut Ctrl + + (hold down Ctrl key and press plus symbol)
- Click in the last cell in the table and then press Tab

Quick Steps

Add New Record

1. Open table.
2. Click New (blank) record button.
3. Type field values in new row in datasheet.
4. Close table.

App Tip

Saving in a database is not left to chance! As soon as you complete a new record, Access saves the data to disk.

12.3 Editing and Deleting Records Using a Datasheet

Skills

Edit a record using a datasheet

Delete a record using a datasheet

Edit a field value in a table using a datasheet by opening the table, selecting the text to be changed and then typing the new text, or by clicking in the table cell to place an insertion point and then inserting or deleting text as required. Select a record for deletion by clicking in the gray record selector bar along the left edge of the datasheet next to the record and then clicking the Delete button in the Records group on the Home tab. Access requires confirmation before deleting a record.

See Beyond Basics at the end of this topic for information about precautions to take to back up data in a database before deleting a record.

1. With the **LibraryFines-YourName** database open, open the Students table.
2. Select the text *Murphy* in the *StudentLastName* column in the sixth row in the datasheet and then type Hall as the new last name for Suzanne.

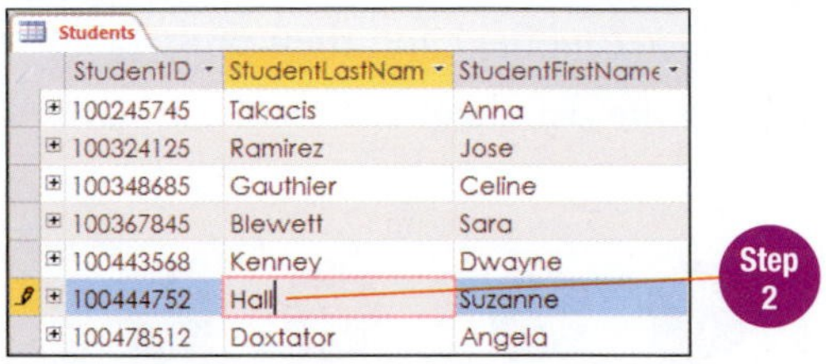

App Tip

As soon as you move to another record in the datasheet, the changes are automatically saved.

3. Press Tab eight times to move to the *Email* field.
4. Press F2 to open the field for editing, move the insertion point as needed, delete *murphy* at the beginning of the email address, and then type hall so that the email address becomes *halls@emcp.net*.

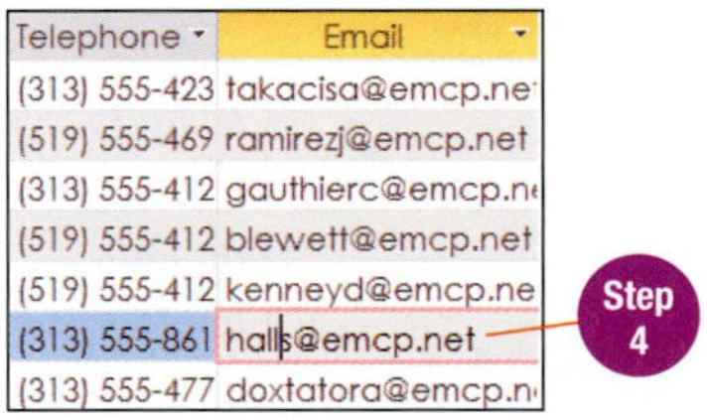

Quick Steps

Edit a Record
1. Open table.
2. Click in table cell to place insertion point.
3. Insert or delete text as required.

Delete a Record
1. Open table.
2. Select record.
3. Click Delete button.
4. Click Yes.

5. Click at the end of *N8T 3W9* in the *ZIPorPostalCode* field in the second row in the datasheet to position the insertion point, press Backspace to remove *3W9*, and then type 2E6.

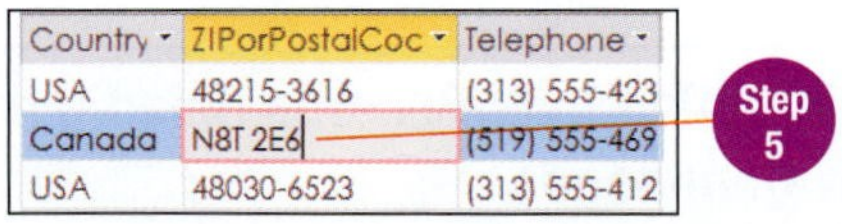

6. If necessary, scroll left until you can see the student names.

7 Click in the record selector bar next to the record for the student *Das Aparna* when you see the mouse pointer change to a right-pointing black arrow.

The gray bar at the left edge of the datasheet is used to select a record. When using a mouse, the pointer displays as a black right-pointing arrow when positioned next to a record in the gray record selector bar.

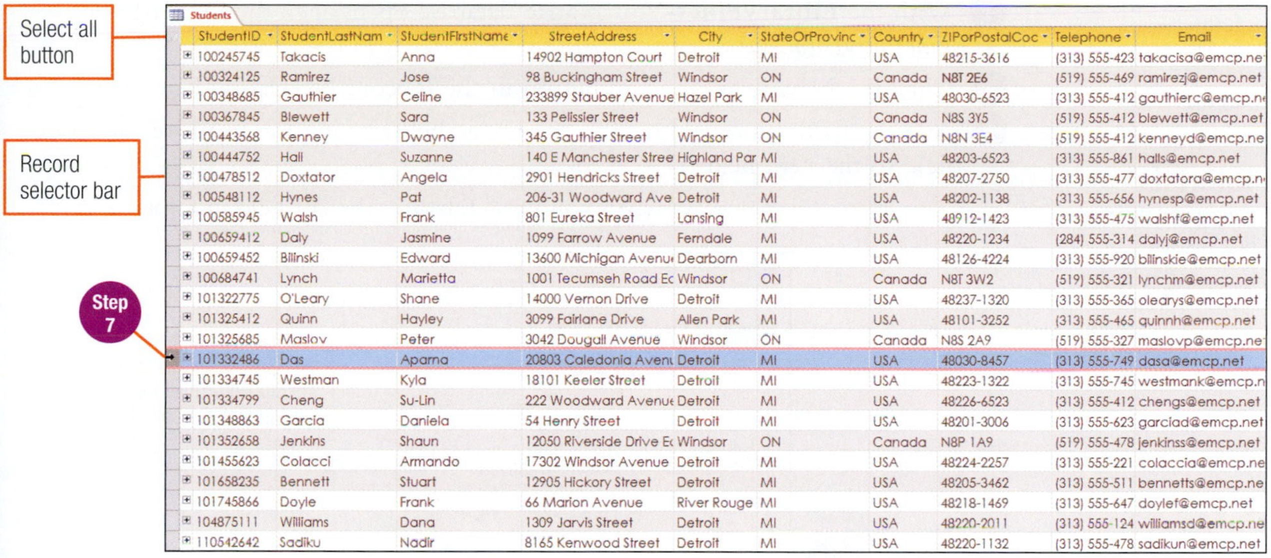

StudentID	StudentLastNam	StudentFirstName	StreetAddress	City	StateOrProvinc	Country	ZIPorPostalCoc	Telephone	Email
100245745	Takacis	Anna	14902 Hampton Court	Detroit	MI	USA	48215-3616	(313) 555-423	takacisa@emcp.ne
100324125	Ramirez	Jose	98 Buckingham Street	Windsor	ON	Canada	N8T 2E6	(519) 555-469	ramirezj@emcp.net
100348685	Gauthier	Celine	233899 Stauber Avenue	Hazel Park	MI	USA	48030-6523	(313) 555-412	gauthierc@emcp.n
100367845	Blewett	Sara	133 Pelissier Street	Windsor	ON	Canada	N8S 3Y5	(519) 555-412	blewett@emcp.net
100443568	Kenney	Dwayne	345 Gauthier Street	Windsor	ON	Canada	N8N 3E4	(519) 555-412	kenneyd@emcp.ne
100444752	Hall	Suzanne	140 E Manchester Stree	Highland Par	MI	USA	48203-6523	(313) 555-861	halls@emcp.net
100478512	Doxtator	Angela	2901 Hendricks Street	Detroit	MI	USA	48207-2750	(313) 555-477	doxtatora@emcp.n
100548112	Hynes	Pat	206-31 Woodward Ave	Detroit	MI	USA	48202-1138	(313) 555-656	hynesp@emcp.net
100585945	Walsh	Frank	801 Eureka Street	Lansing	MI	USA	48912-1423	(313) 555-475	walshf@emcp.net
100659412	Daly	Jasmine	1099 Farrow Avenue	Ferndale	MI	USA	48220-1234	(284) 555-314	dalyj@emcp.net
100659452	Bilinski	Edward	13600 Michigan Avenu	Dearborn	MI	USA	48126-4224	(313) 555-920	bilinskie@emcp.net
100684741	Lynch	Marietta	1001 Tecumseh Road Ec	Windsor	ON	Canada	N8T 3W2	(519) 555-321	lynchm@emcp.net
101322775	O'Leary	Shane	14000 Vernon Drive	Detroit	MI	USA	48237-1320	(313) 555-365	olearys@emcp.net
101325412	Quinn	Hayley	3099 Fairlane Drive	Allen Park	MI	USA	48101-3252	(313) 555-465	quinnh@emcp.net
101325685	Maslov	Peter	3042 Dougall Avenue	Windsor	ON	Canada	N8S 2A9	(519) 555-327	maslovp@emcp.ne
101332486	Das	Aparna	20803 Caledonia Aven	Detroit	MI	USA	48030-8457	(313) 555-749	dasa@emcp.net
101334745	Westman	Kyla	18101 Keeler Street	Detroit	MI	USA	48223-1322	(313) 555-745	westmank@emcp.n
101334799	Cheng	Su-Lin	222 Woodward Avenu	Detroit	MI	USA	48226-6523	(313) 555-412	chengs@emcp.net
101348863	Garcia	Daniela	54 Henry Street	Detroit	MI	USA	48201-3006	(313) 555-623	garciad@emcp.net
101352658	Jenkins	Shaun	12050 Riverside Drive E	Windsor	ON	Canada	N8P 1A9	(519) 555-478	jenkinss@emcp.net
101455623	Colacci	Armando	17302 Windsor Avenue	Detroit	MI	USA	48224-2257	(313) 555-221	colaccia@emcp.ne
101658235	Bennett	Stuart	12905 Hickory Street	Detroit	MI	USA	48205-3462	(313) 555-511	bennetts@emcp.ne
101745866	Doyle	Frank	66 Marion Avenue	River Rouge	MI	USA	48218-1469	(313) 555-647	doylef@emcp.net
104875111	Williams	Dana	1309 Jarvis Street	Detroit	MI	USA	48220-2011	(313) 555-124	williamsd@emcp.ne
110542642	Sadiku	Nadir	8165 Kenwood Street	Detroit	MI	USA	48220-1132	(313) 555-478	sadikun@emcp.net

8 Click the Delete button in the Records group on the Home tab. Do *not* click the down-pointing arrow on the button.

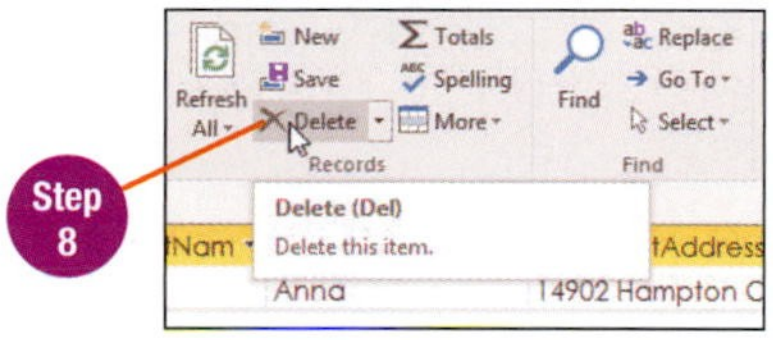

9 Click Yes at the message box that appears asking if you are sure you want to delete the record.

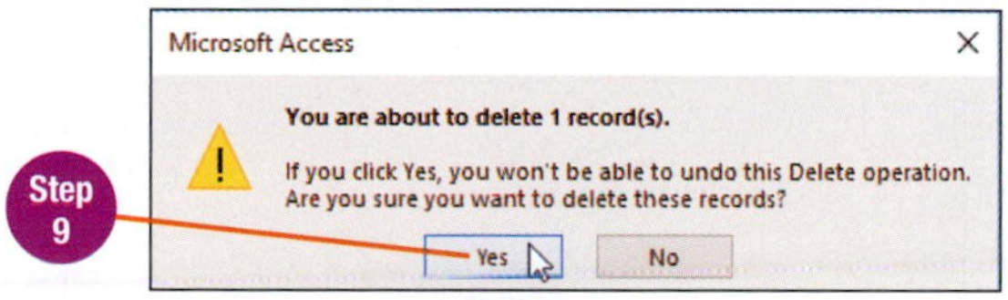

10 Close the Students table. Leave the database open for the next topic.

App Tip

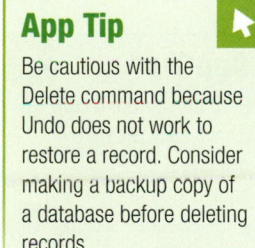

Be cautious with the Delete command because Undo does not work to restore a record. Consider making a backup copy of a database before deleting records.

Beyond Basics Best Practices for Deleting Records

Depending on the purpose of the database, deleting records is generally not done until the records to be deleted are first copied to an archive database and/or a backup copy of the database has been made. In many cases, records need to be retained for historical purposes. Always check before deleting a record to make sure you are following proper procedure.

12.4 Adding, Editing, and Deleting Records Using a Form

Skills

Add a record using a form

Edit a record using a form

Delete a record using a form

Tutorials

Adding and Deleting Records in a Form

Navigating in Objects

A form is an Access object that provides a different view for the data stored in a table. Generally only one record at a time is displayed in a columnar layout instead of the spreadsheet style datasheet. Forms are usually preferred over a datasheet for adding, editing, and deleting records because the user can focus on one record at a time.

1. With the **LibraryFines-YourName** database open, open the form named *FineEntryForm*.
2. Click the New (blank) record button in the Record Navigation bar.
3. Add the field values as shown in the image below, using Tab to move from one field to the next field.

A new blank form displays when you press Tab after the last field in a form.

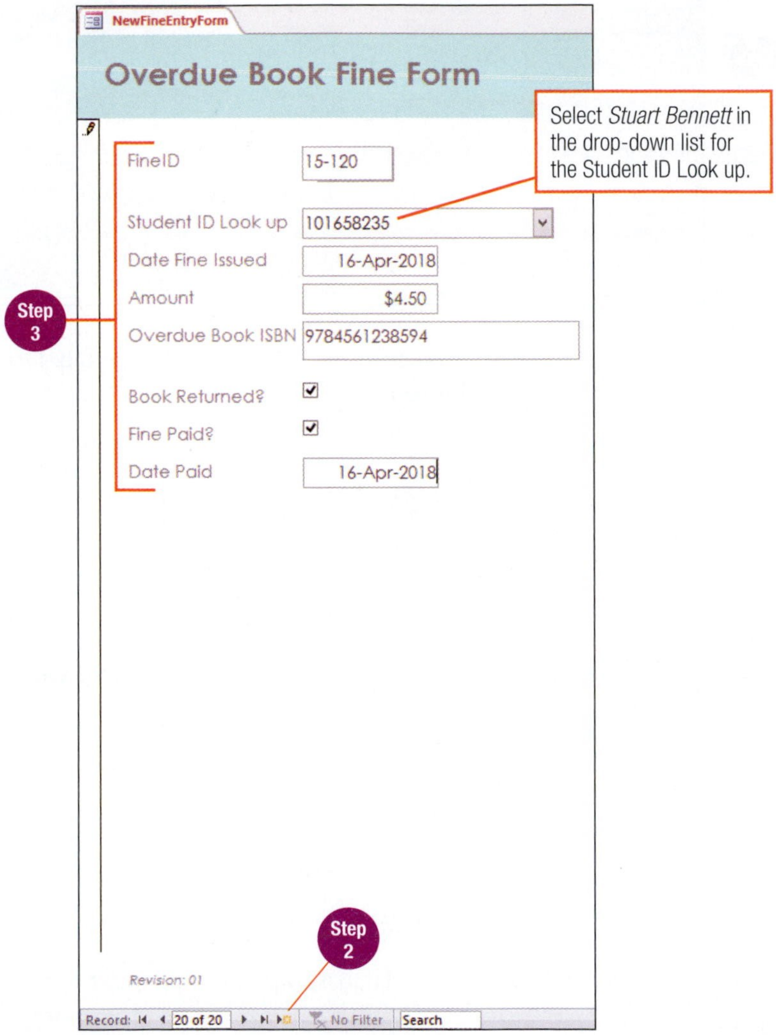

App Tip

Print the current record displayed in a form by displaying the Print backstage area, clicking *Print*, and then clicking *Selected Record(s)* in the *Print Range* section of the Print dialog box.

4. Click the First record button in the Record Navigation bar to display the first record in the form.
5. Select $8.75 in the *Amount* field and then type 7.25.

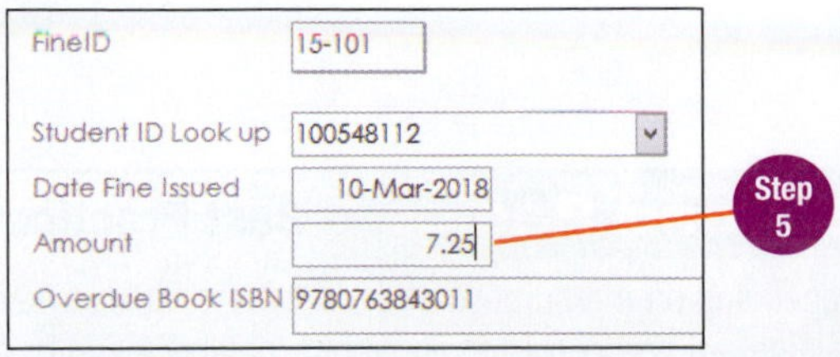

6 Click the Next record button two times to display record 3 in the form.

7 Click the Delete button arrow in the Records group on the Home tab and then click *Delete Record* at the drop-down list.

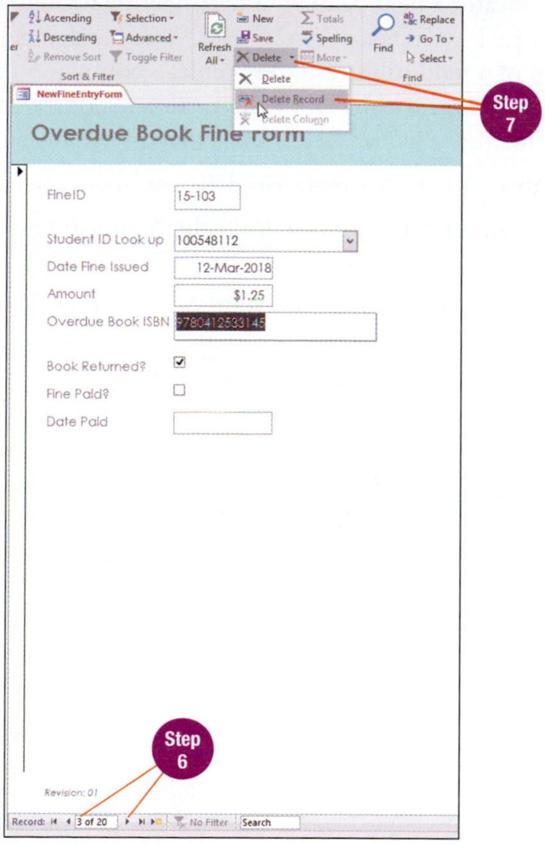

8 Click Yes at the message box that appears asking if you are sure you want to delete the record.

9 Close the form. Leave the database open for the next topic.

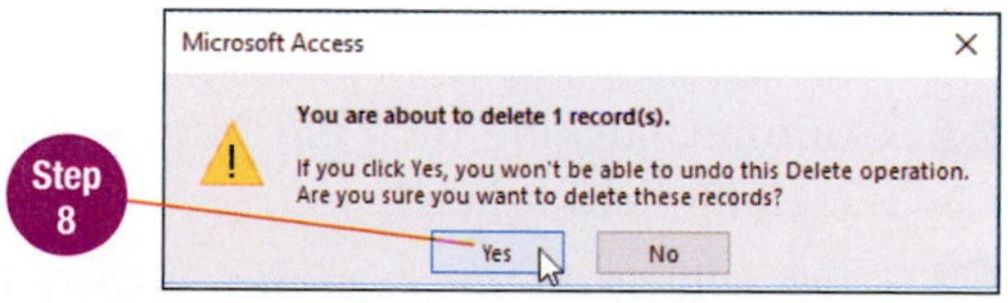

Quick Steps

Delete a Record Using a Form

1. Open form.
2. Navigate to desired record.
3. Click Delete button arrow.
4. Click *Delete Record*.
5. Click Yes.

Oops!

Only the current field value is deleted? This occurs when you do not use the arrow on the button to select the option to delete the entire record. Try Step 7 again, making sure to choose *Delete Record*.

Alternative Method: Navigating Records in a Form Using Keyboard Shortcuts

These keyboard shortcuts can be used in a form to move to another record:

Page Down	Next record	Page Up	Previous record
Ctrl + Home	First record	Ctrl + End	Last record (last field)

Beyond Basics: Using Find to Move to a Record

As databases expand to store hundreds or thousands of records, using the navigation buttons at the bottom of the form to locate a record that needs to be changed or deleted is not feasible. The Find feature locates a record instantly when you search by a name or ID number. You will use Find in the next topic.

12.5 Finding and Replacing Data and Adjusting Column Widths in a Datasheet

Skills

Find and replace data using a datasheet

Adjust column widths in a datasheet

Tutorials

Finding Data

Finding and Replacing Data

Adjusting Field Column Width

The Find feature locates a field value in a datasheet or form and moves the insertion point to each occurrence of the data. When a change needs to be made to all occurrences of a field value, use the Replace command to make the change automatically. The column width for a column in a datasheet can be made wider to fully display data for those fields that do not currently show all the field values.

1. With the **LibraryFines-YourName** database open, open the Fines table.
2. Click to place an insertion point within the *StudentID* field value in the first record.
3. Click the Find button in the Find group on the Home tab.

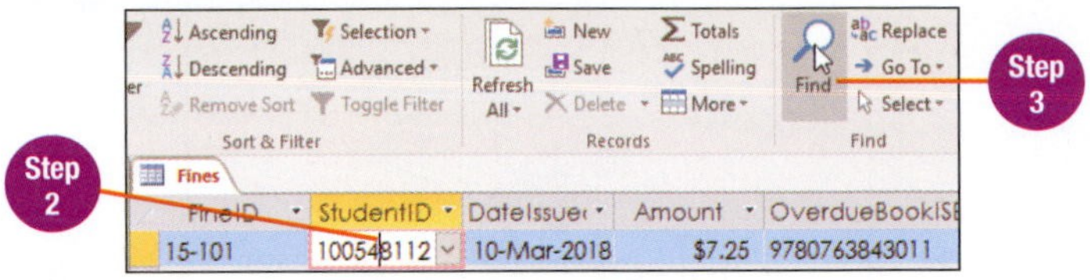

4. Type 101348863 in the *Find What* text box and then click the Find Next button.

   The first record (record 6) that matches the field value is made active.

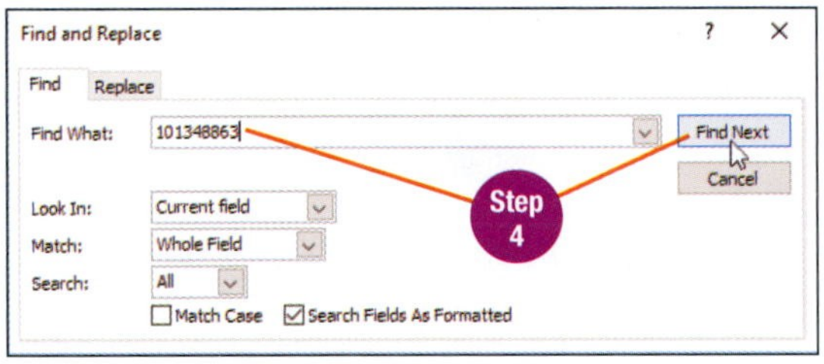

5. Continue clicking the Find Next button to review all occurrences of the matching field value.
6. Click OK at the message that Microsoft Access has finished searching records.

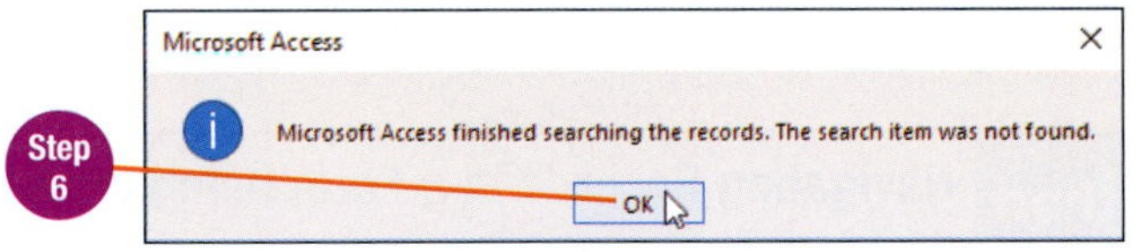

7. Click the Cancel button or the Close button to close the Find and Replace dialog box.
8. Click to place an insertion point within the *FineID* field in the first record.
9. Click the Replace button in the Find group.

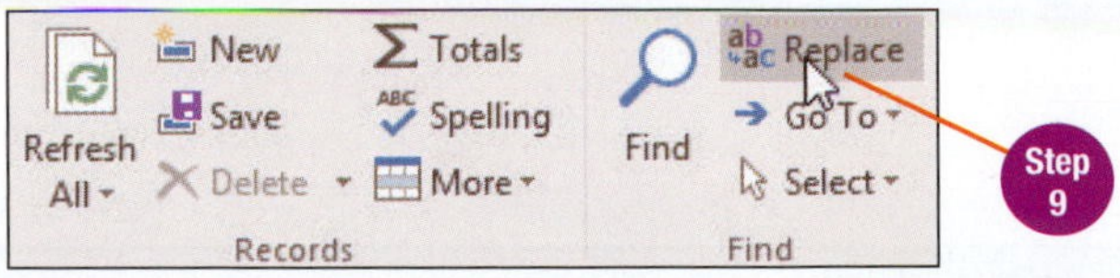

Oops!

No records found? Tap or click OK and then check that you typed the ID number without errors.

10 Type 15- in the *Find What* text box and then press Tab.

11 Type MCL- in the *Replace With* text box.

12 Click the *Match* option box arrow and then click *Any Part of Field* at the drop-down list.

13 Click the Replace All button.

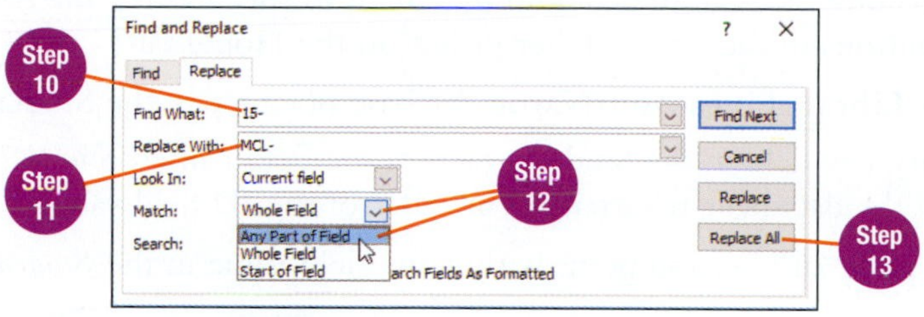

14 Click Yes at the message asking if you want to continue and informing you that the Replace operation cannot be undone.

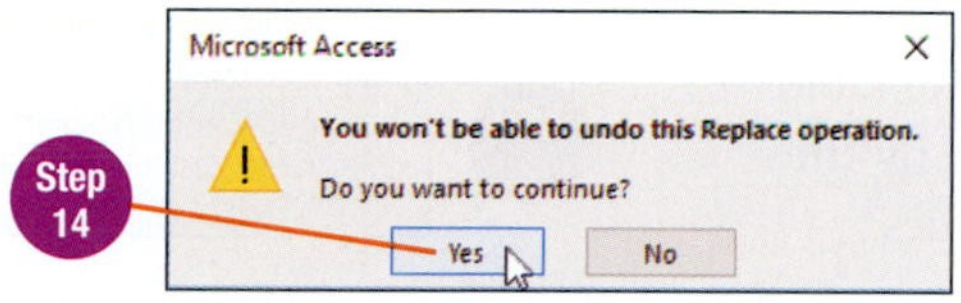

15 Close the Find and Replace dialog box.

16 Click to place an insertion point in any record within the *DateIssued* field.

17 Click the More button in the Records group on the Home tab and then click *Field Width* at the drop-down list.

18 Click Best Fit at the Column Width dialog box.

Best Fit adjusts the width of the column to accommodate the length needed to display the longest field value.

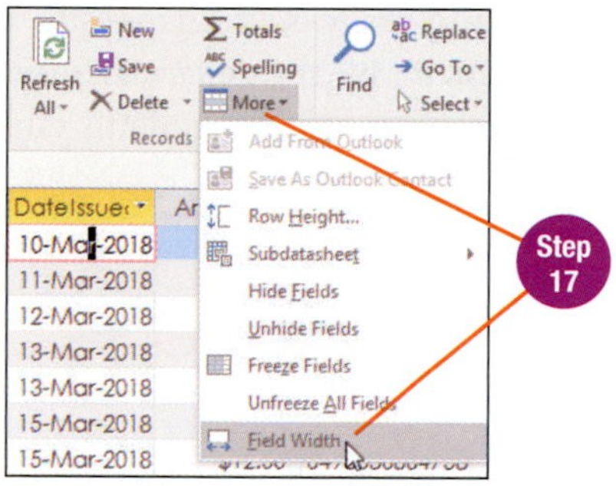

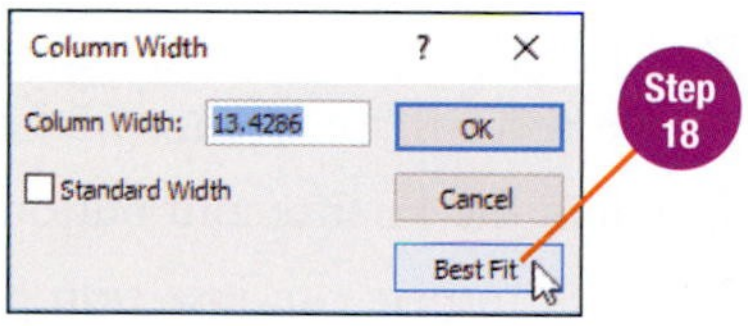

19 Close the Fines table. Click Yes when prompted to save the changes to the layout of the table. Leave the database open for the next topic.

Saving changes to the layout of the table means that Access will retain the new column width for the *DateIssued* field when the table is reopened.

Quick Steps

Find a Record

1. Open table or form.
2. Click in field to be searched.
3. Click Find button.
4. Type field value to find in *Find What* text box.
5. Click Find Next until done.
6. Click OK.
7. Close dialog box.

Replace a Field Value

1. Open table or form.
2. Click in field to be searched.
3. Click Replace button.
4. Type field value to find in *Find What* text box.
5. Type new field value in *Replace With* text box.
6. Click Replace or Replace All as needed.
7. Click Yes.
8. Close dialog box.

Adjust Column Width

1. Open table.
2. Click in any record in column.
3. Click More button.
4. Click *Field Width*.
5. Type value or click Best Fit.

Alternative Method Adjusting the Column Width in a Datasheet

You can also adjust column widths using the following methods:

- Drag the right column boundary in the field names row right to lengthen, or left to shorten the column width.
- Double-click the right column boundary to best fit the column width.
- Type a value in the *Column Width* text box at the Column Width dialog box.

12.6 Sorting and Filtering Records

Skills

Sort records

Filter records

Tutorials

Sorting Records in a Table

Filtering Records

Records are initially arranged in the datasheet alphanumerically by the field in the table that has been defined as the primary key. A **primary key** is a field that contains the data that uniquely identifies each record in the table. Generally, the primary key is an identification number, such as *StudentID* in the Students table. To change the order of the records, click in the column by which to sort and use the Ascending or Descending buttons in the Sort & Filter group on the Home tab.

1. With the **LibraryFines-YourName** database open, open the Students table.

   The primary key field in the Students table is the field named *StudentID*. Notice the records in the datasheet are arranged in order of the ID field values.

2. Click to place an insertion point within any field value in the *StudentLastName* column.

3. Click the Ascending button in the Sort & Filter group on the Home tab.

   Notice the records in the table are now arranged in order by the student last name field values.

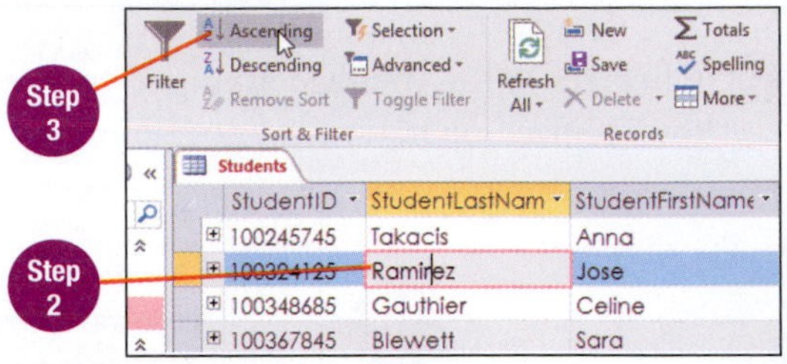

4. Close the Students table. Click Yes when prompted to save the changes to the design of the table.

   Selecting Yes to save changes to the design of the table means that the table will remain sorted by the *StudentLastName* field when you reopen the datasheet. Each object based upon the Students table can have its own sort option saved.

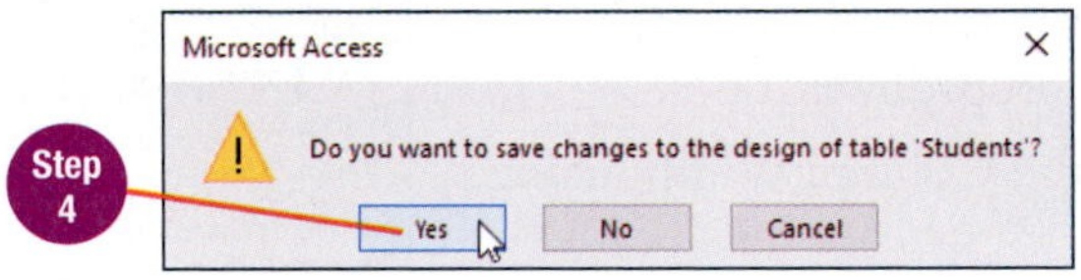

5. Open the Students form.
6. Click the Next record button a few times to view the first few records. Notice the records are arranged by *StudentID*.
7. Click the First record button to return the display to the first record.
8. Click to place an insertion point in the *Student Last Name* field.
9. Click the Ascending button in the Sort & Filter group.

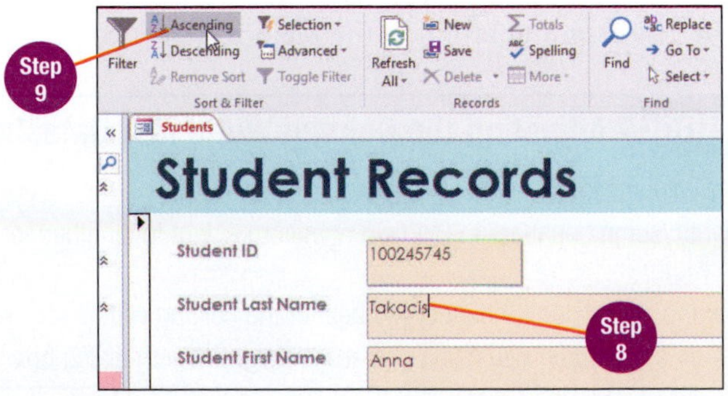

10. Scroll through the first 10 records in the form to view the sorted order and then close the form.

App Tip

When a datasheet is sorted by a field other than the primary key, an up-pointing arrow (ascending order indicator) or down-pointing arrow (descending order indicator) displays next to the field name used to sort.

11 Open the Students table. Notice the up-pointing arrow next to *StudentLastName* in the field names row indicating the records are arranged alphabetically by the student last names.

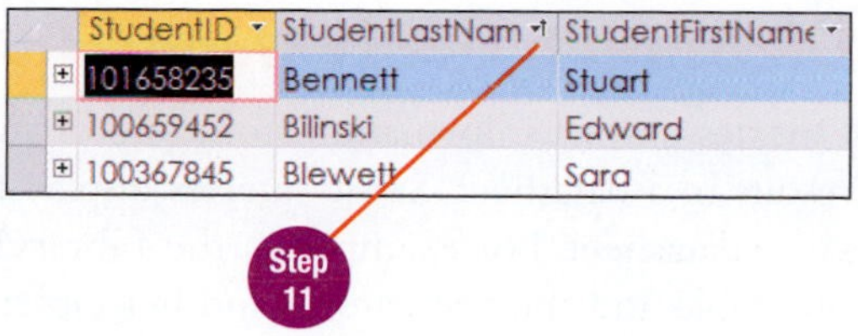

You can filter a datasheet in Access using the same techniques you learned for filtering a table in Excel in Chapter 9. Recall that a filter temporarily hides the rows that you do not want to view.

12 Click the filter arrow (down-pointing arrow) next to *Country*.

13 Click the check box next to *USA* to clear the check mark from the box at the Sort & Filter list box and then click OK.

The datasheet is filtered to show records for students who reside in Canada only.

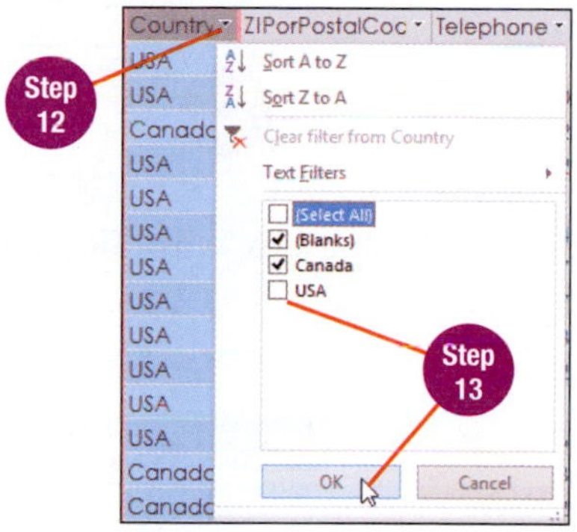

14 Click the Toggle Filter button in the Sort & Filter group to clear the filter.

All records are now redisplayed.

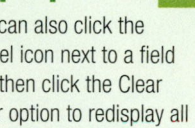

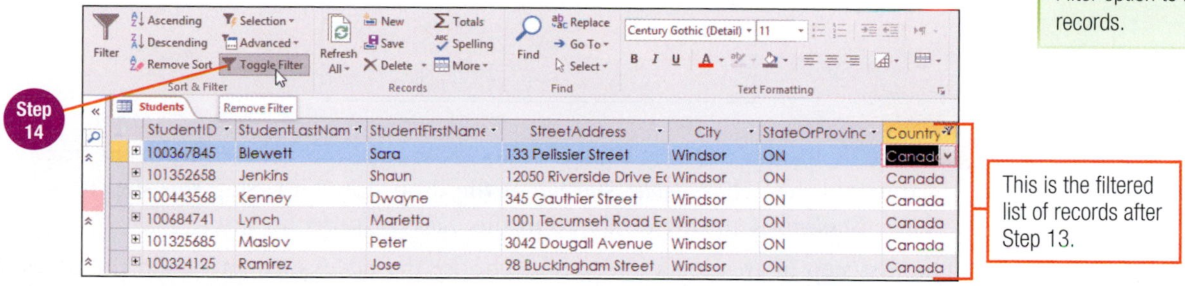

15 Close the Students table. Click No when prompted to save changes to the design of the table. Leave the database open for the next topic.

Quick Steps

Sort a Datasheet or Form

1. Open table or form.
2. Click in field by which to sort.
3. Click Ascending or Descending button.

Filter a Datasheet

1. Open table.
2. Click filter arrow next to field.
3. Clear check boxes as needed.
4. Click OK.

App Tip

Access displays a funnel icon next to a field used to filter a datasheet and displays *Filtered* highlighted in orange in the Record Navigation bar as indicators that all records are not currently displayed.

App Tip

You can also click the funnel icon next to a field and then click the Clear Filter option to redisplay all records.

Beyond Basics — Sorting by More Than One Field

Sort by more than one field in a datasheet by dragging across the field names to select the columns by which to sort and then clicking the Ascending or Descending button. Access sorts fields left to right. For example, if *StudentLastName* and *StudentFirstName* columns are selected, Access sorts first by last names and then by first names when two or more records have the same last name. To sort first by a field other than the leftmost column, move the column before sorting to change the sort order by clicking the field name to select the column, and then dragging the field name left to the desired location.

12.7 Creating a Query Using the Simple Query Wizard

Skills

Create a query using a wizard

Tutorial

Creating a Query Using the Simple Query Wizard

Queries extract information from one or more tables in the database and display the results in a datasheet. Some queries display fields from more than one table in the same datasheet. For example, in the LibraryFines database, the student names are in one table and the fines are in another table; a query can combine the names and fines in one datasheet. Other queries are designed to answer a question about the data; for example, *Which library fines are unpaid?* The **Simple Query Wizard** assists a user with creating a query by prompting the user to make selections in a series of dialog boxes.

1. With the **LibraryFines-YourName** database open, click the Create tab.
2. Click the Query Wizard button in the Queries group.

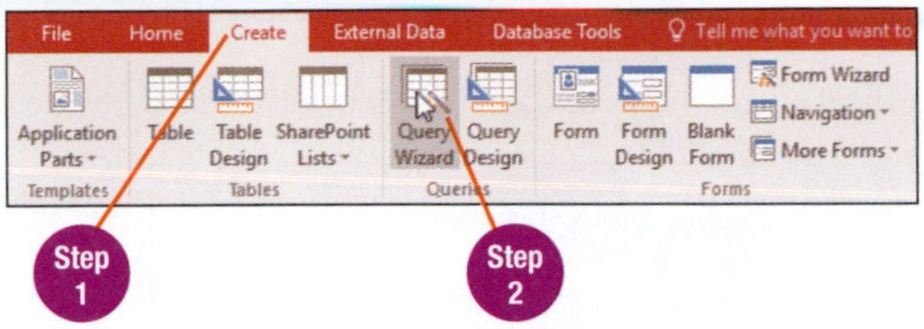

3. Click OK at the New Query dialog box with *Simple Query Wizard* already selected.

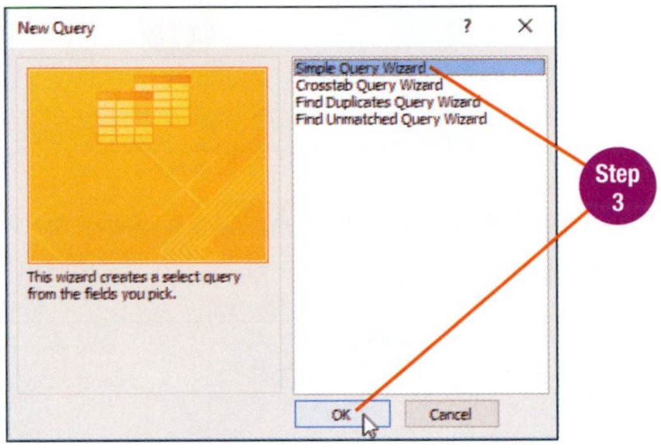

4. At the first Simple Query Wizard dialog box, click the *Tables/Queries* list box arrow and then click *Table: Students* at the drop-down list. Skip this step if *Table: Students* is already displayed in the *Tables/Queries* list box.

The first step in creating a query is to choose the tables or queries and the fields from each table or query that you want to display in a datasheet.

5. With *StudentID* already selected in the *Available Fields* list box, click the Add Field button (displays as a right-pointing arrow) to move *StudentID* to the *Selected Fields* list box.

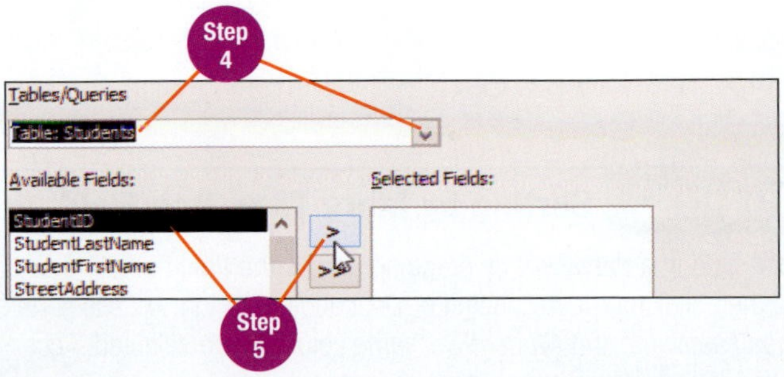

6 Double-click *StudentFirstName* in the *Available Fields* list box to move the field to the *Selected Fields* list box.

You add fields to the *Selected Fields* list box in the order that you want the fields displayed in the query results datasheet.

7 Double-click the following fields in the *Available Fields* list box to move each field to the *Selected Fields* list box.

StudentLastName
Telephone
Email

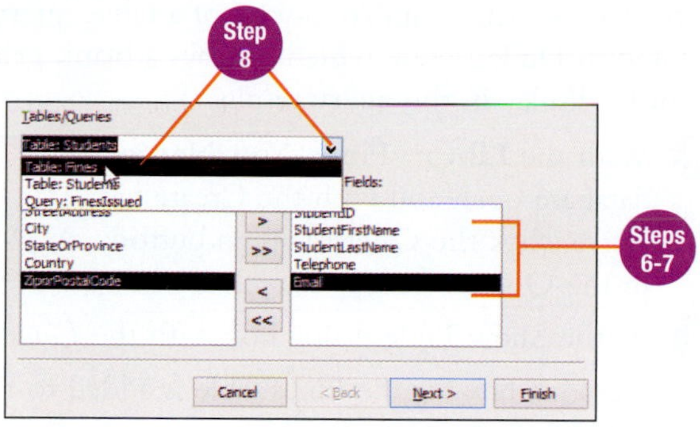

8 Click the *Tables/Queries* list box arrow and then click *Table: Fines*.

9 Double-click the following fields in the *Available Fields* list box to move each field to the *Selected Fields* list box.

DateIssued
Amount
FinePaid

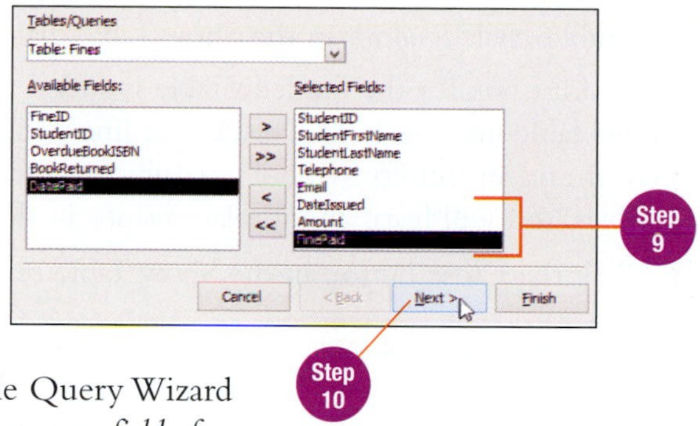

10 Click Next.

11 Click Next at the second Simple Query Wizard dialog box to accept *Detail (shows every field of every record)* for the query results.

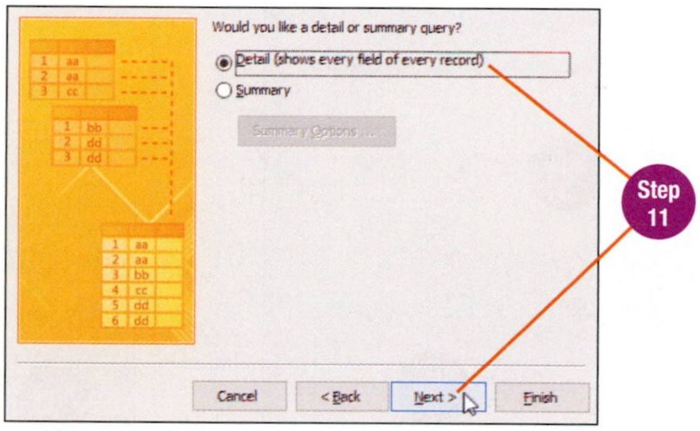

12 At the third Simple Query Wizard dialog box, select the current text in the *What title do you want for your query?* text box, type StudentsWithFines, and then click Finish.

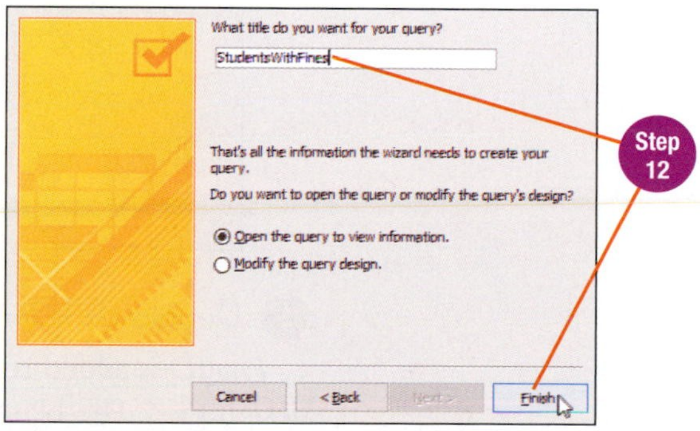

13 Review the query results datasheet. Notice the fields are displayed in the order selected at the first Simple Query Wizard dialog box.

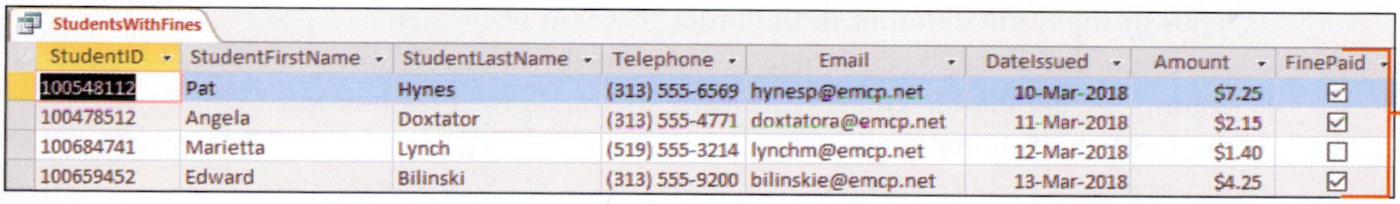

StudentsWithFines

StudentID	StudentFirstName	StudentLastName	Telephone	Email	DateIssued	Amount	FinePaid
100548112	Pat	Hynes	(313) 555-6569	hynesp@emcp.net	10-Mar-2018	$7.25	☑
100478512	Angela	Doxtator	(313) 555-4771	doxtatora@emcp.net	11-Mar-2018	$2.15	☑
100684741	Marietta	Lynch	(519) 555-3214	lynchm@emcp.net	12-Mar-2018	$1.40	☐
100659452	Edward	Bilinski	(313) 555-9200	bilinskie@emcp.net	13-Mar-2018	$4.25	☑

first four rows of query results datasheet

14 Close the StudentsWithFines query. Leave the database open for the next topic.

Oops!

Added the wrong field or the order is wrong? Move a field back to the *Available Fields* list box by selecting the field and using the Remove Field button (left-pointing arrow).

Quick Steps

Create a Query Using Simple Query Wizard

1. Click Create tab.
2. Click Query Wizard button.
3. Click OK.
4. Choose each table and/ or query and fields in required order.
5. Click Next.
6. Click Next.
7. Type title for query.
8. Click Finish.

12.8 Creating a Query Using Design View

Skills

Create a query using Design view

Tutorials

Creating a Query in Design View

Creating a Query in Design View Using Multiple Tables

Every Access object has at least two views. In one view, you browse the data in the table, query, form, or report. This is the view that is active when you open the object from the Navigation pane. Another view, called **Design view**, is used to set up or define the structure and/or layout of a table, query, form, or report. A query can be created in Design view, which displays a blank grid into which you add the fields you want to display in the query results.

1. With the **LibraryFines-YourName** database open and with the Create tab active, click the Query Design button in the Queries group.

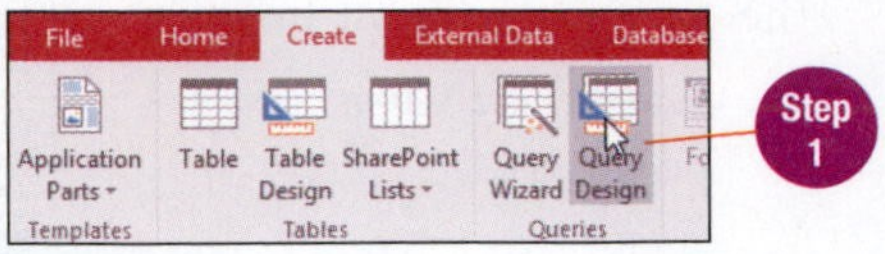

2. At the Show Table dialog box with the *Fines* table selected, click the Add button.

A field list box for the Fines table is added to the top of the *Query1* design grid in the work area.

3. Double-click *Students* in the Show Table dialog box.

A field list box for the Students table is added to the top of the design grid beside the *Fines* table field list box. A black join line connects the two tables. The black line displays 1 and an infinity symbol (∞), which indicates the type of relationship for the two tables. You will learn about relationships in the next chapter.

4. Click the Close button in the Show Table dialog box.

Oops!

Closed the Show Table dialog box by mistake? Reopen the dialog box using the Show Table button in the Query Setup group on the Query Tools Design tab.

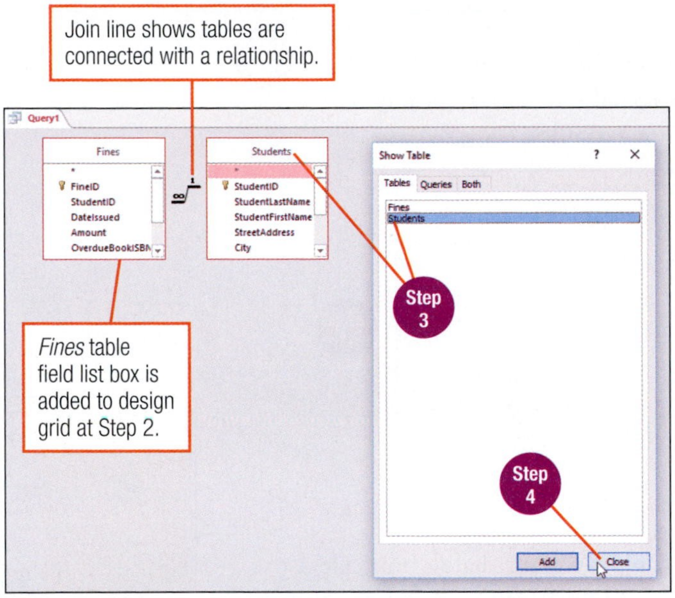

5. Double-click *FineID* in the *Fines* table field list box.

FineID is added to the *Field* text box in the first column of the design grid. The blank columns in the bottom of the window represent the query results datasheet. You build the query by adding fields to the blank columns in the order that you want them to appear in the datasheet. A field is added to the next available column by double-clicking a field name in a table field list box in the top half of the window.

6 Double-click the following fields in the *Fines* table field list box to add each field to the next available column in the query design grid.

DateIssued
Amount
BookReturned (scroll down the table field list box to the field)

7 Double-click the following fields in the *Students* table field list box to add each field to the next available column in the query design grid.

StudentFirstName
StudentLastName

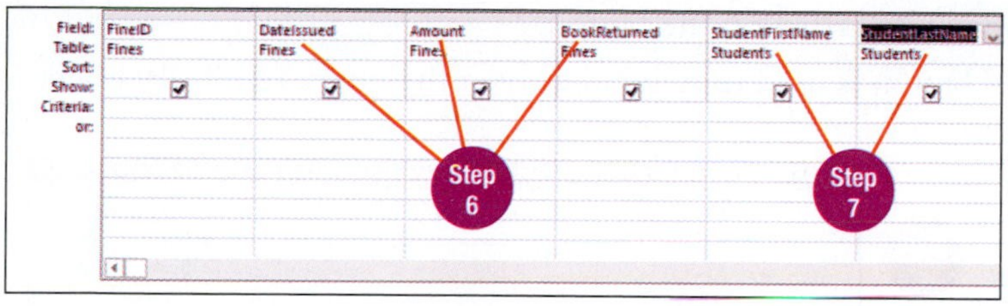

8 Click the Run button in the Results group on the Query Tools Design tab to view the query results datasheet.

The **Run button** instructs Access to produce the query results datasheet by assembling the data from the tables according to the query instructions. A query is a set of instructions with table names and field names to display in a datasheet. The query results datasheet is not a duplicate copy of the data—each time a query is opened or run, the data is generated by extracting the field values from the tables.

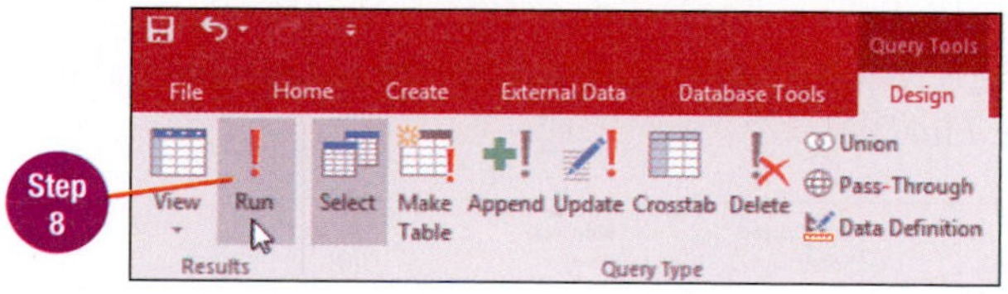

9 Click the Save button on the Quick Access toolbar.

10 Type FinesWithBookReturnsList at the Save As dialog box and then press Enter or click OK.

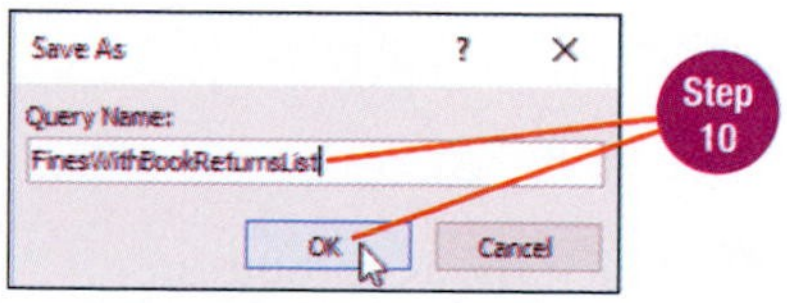

11 Close the FinesWithBookReturnsList query. Leave the database open for the next topic.

Quick Steps

Create a Query Using Design View

1. Click Create tab.
2. Click Query Design button.
3. Add tables to design grid.
4. Close Show Table dialog box.
5. Double-click field names in table field list boxes in desired order for query results datasheet.
6. Click Run button.
7. Click Save button.
8. Type query name.
9. Click OK.

Alternative Method Adding Fields to Columns in the Query Design Grid

Add fields to the design grid from the table field list boxes using these other methods:

- Drag a field name from the table field list box to the Field text box in the desired column; if a field already exists in the column, the field is moved to the column to the right.
- Click in a blank Field text box in the design grid, click the down-pointing arrow that appears, and then click the field name in the drop-down list.

12.9 Entering Criteria to Select Records in a Query

Skills

Select records in a query using criteria

Tutorial

Extracting Records Using Criteria Statements

Both query results datasheets for the queries you created using the Simple Query Wizard and using Design view displayed all records in the tables. Queries are often created to select records from tables that meet one or more conditions. For example, in this topic you will add a criterion to show only those records in which the fines are unpaid.

1. With the **LibraryFines-YourName** database open, open the StudentsWithFines query.
2. Click the View button in the Views group on the Home tab. Do *not* click the down-pointing arrow on the button.

The View button is used to switch between the query results datasheet and Design view.

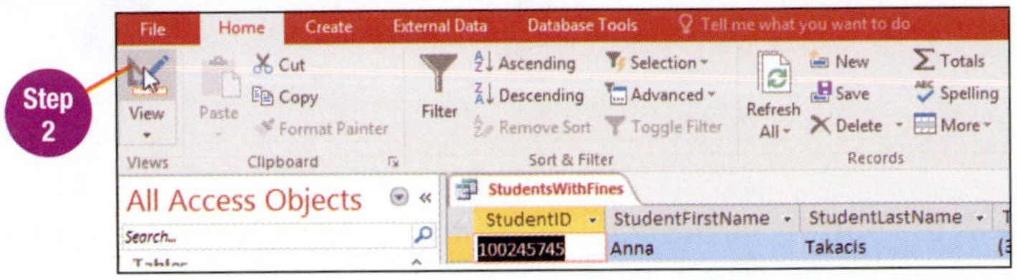

3. Click in the *Criteria* box in the *FinePaid* column in the design grid, type No, press the spacebar, and then press Enter.

Access displays functions in a drop-down list as you type text that matches the letters in a function name. As you type *No*, the function wizard displays *Now* in a drop-down list. Typing a space after *No* causes the *Now* function to disappear. *FinePaid* is a field in which the field value is either *Yes* or *No*. By typing *No* in the *Criteria* box, you are instructing Access to select the records from the *Fines* table in which *No* is the field value for *FinePaid*.

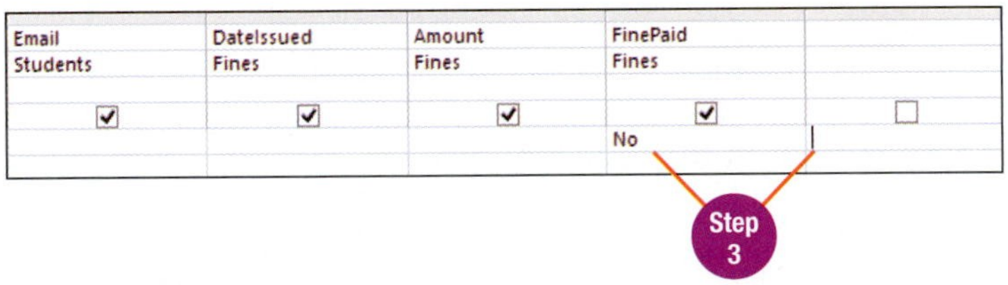

Oops!

Empty datasheet? Use the View button to return to Design view and check that you typed *No* in the *FinePaid* column and/or that *No* is entered in the *Criteria* box of the column.

4. Click the Run button.

Notice that 10 records are selected in the query results datasheet and that the check box in the *FinePaid* column for each record is empty.

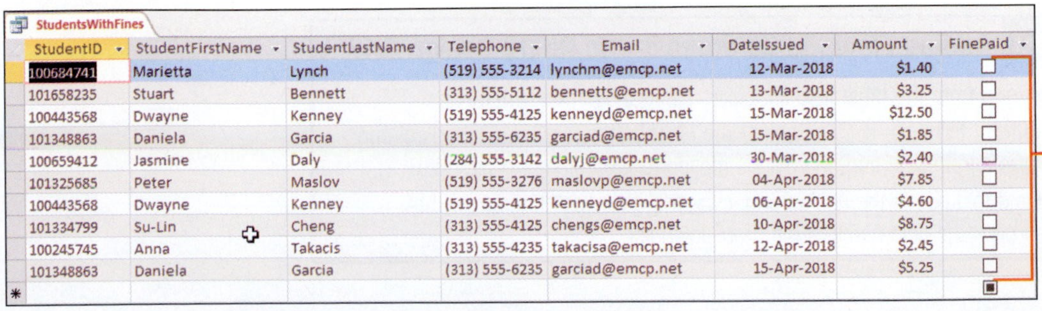

StudentsWithFines

StudentID	StudentFirstName	StudentLastName	Telephone	Email	DateIssued	Amount	FinePaid
100684741	Marietta	Lynch	(519) 555-3214	lynchm@emcp.net	12-Mar-2018	$1.40	☐
101658235	Stuart	Bennett	(313) 555-5112	bennetts@emcp.net	13-Mar-2018	$3.25	☐
100443568	Dwayne	Kenney	(519) 555-4125	kenneyd@emcp.net	15-Mar-2018	$12.50	☐
101348863	Daniela	Garcia	(313) 555-6235	garciad@emcp.net	15-Mar-2018	$1.85	☐
100659412	Jasmine	Daly	(284) 555-3142	dalyj@emcp.net	30-Mar-2018	$2.40	☐
101325685	Peter	Maslov	(519) 555-3276	maslovp@emcp.net	04-Apr-2018	$7.85	☐
100443568	Dwayne	Kenney	(519) 555-4125	kenneyd@emcp.net	06-Apr-2018	$4.60	☐
101334799	Su-Lin	Cheng	(313) 555-4125	chengs@emcp.net	10-Apr-2018	$8.75	☐
100245745	Anna	Takacis	(313) 555-4235	takacisa@emcp.net	12-Apr-2018	$2.45	☐
101348863	Daniela	Garcia	(313) 555-6235	garciad@emcp.net	15-Apr-2018	$5.25	☐

This is the query results datasheet showing unpaid fines only.

5 Click the File tab and then click *Save As* at the backstage area.

6 Click *Save Object As* at the Save As backstage area and then click the Save As button in the *Save the current database object* panel.

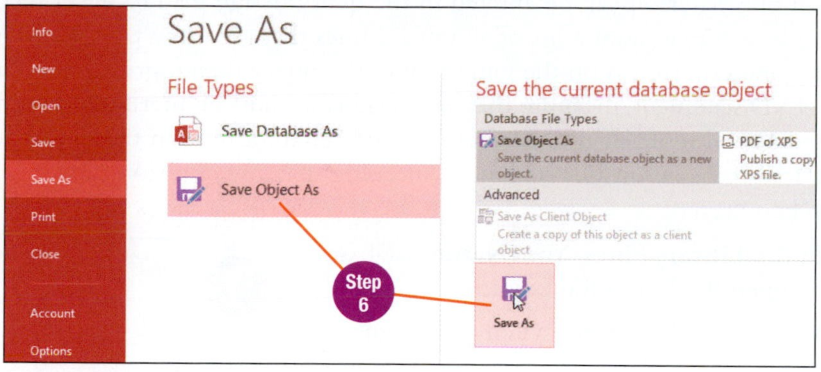

7 Type UnpaidFines in the *Save 'StudentsWithFines' to* text box at the Save As dialog box and then press Enter or click OK.

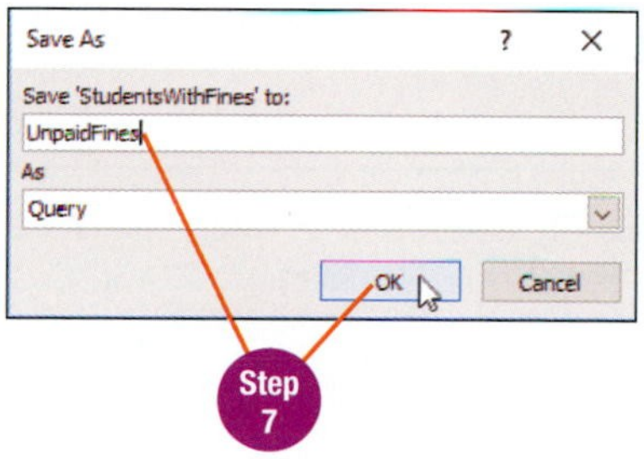

8 Close the UnpaidFines query. Leave the database open for the next topic.

See Table 12.2 for more criteria statement examples.

Table 12.2

Criteria Examples

Field	Entry Typed in *Criteria* Box	Records Selected
Amount	<=5	Fines issued that were $5.00 or less
Amount	>5	Fines issued that were more than $5.00
DateIssued	March 15, 2018 (entry converts automatically to *#3/15/2018#*)	Fines issued on March 15, 2018
StudentLastName	Kenney (entry converts automatically to "Kenney")	Fines issued to student with the last name *Kenney*.

Quick Steps

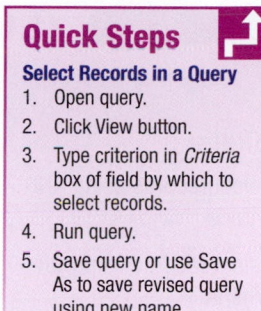

Select Records in a Query

1. Open query.
2. Click View button.
3. Type criterion in *Criteria* box of field by which to select records.
4. Run query.
5. Save query or use Save As to save revised query using new name.

App Tip

A query that extracts records is referred to as a *select query*.

Beyond Basics Selecting Records Using a Range of Dates

Table 12.2 provides the example that typing March 15, 2018 in the *DateIssued* field selects records of fines issued on March 15, 2018. What if one wanted to view a list of all fines issued in the month of March? To do this, type *Between March 1, 2018 and March 31, 2018* in the *Criteria* box of the *DateIssued* column. Access converts the entry to Between #3/1/2018# And #3/31/2018#.

12.10 Entering Multiple Criteria to Select Records and Sorting a Query

Skills

Select records using AND criteria

Select records using OR criteria

Sort query results

Tutorials

Designing a Query with an AND Criteria Statement

Designing a Query with an OR Criteria Statement

Sorting Data and Showing/Hiding Fields in Query Results

More than one criterion can be entered in the query design grid to select records. For example, you may want a list of all unpaid fines that are more than $5.00. When more than one criterion is on the same row in the query design grid, it is referred to as an *AND* statement, meaning that each criterion must be met for a record to be selected. When more than one criterion is on different rows in the query design grid, it is referred to as an *OR* statement, meaning that any criterion can be met for a record to be selected.

1. With the **LibraryFines-YourName** database open, open the UnpaidFines query.
2. Click the View button to switch to Design view.
3. Click in the *Criteria* box in the *Amount* column, type >5, and then press Enter.
4. Click the Run button.

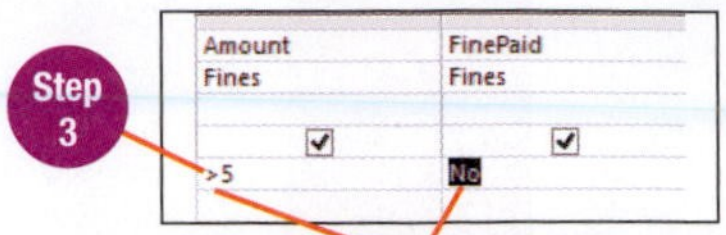

Multiple criteria typed in the same *Criteria* row means each condition must be met for a record to be selected.

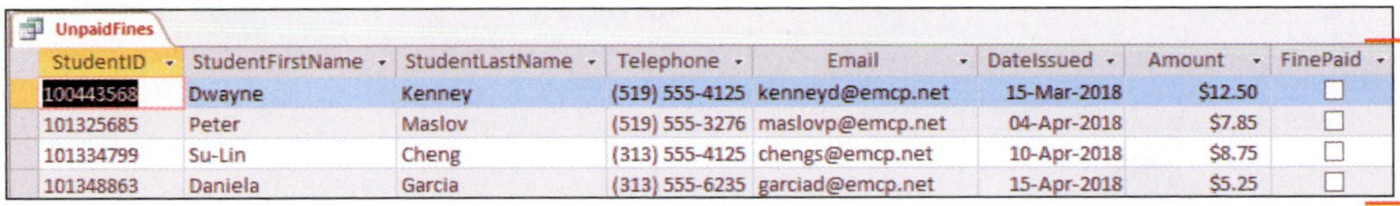

UnpaidFines

StudentID	StudentFirstName	StudentLastName	Telephone	Email	DateIssued	Amount	FinePaid
100443568	Dwayne	Kenney	(519) 555-4125	kenneyd@emcp.net	15-Mar-2018	$12.50	☐
101325685	Peter	Maslov	(519) 555-3276	maslovp@emcp.net	04-Apr-2018	$7.85	☐
101334799	Su-Lin	Cheng	(313) 555-4125	chengs@emcp.net	10-Apr-2018	$8.75	☐
101348863	Daniela	Garcia	(313) 555-6235	garciad@emcp.net	15-Apr-2018	$5.25	☐

This is the query results datasheet showing unpaid fines over $5.00.

5. Use *Save Object As* at the Save As backstage area to save the revised query as *UnpaidFinesOver$5*.
6. Close the UnpaidFinesOver$5 query.
7. Click the Create tab and then click the Query Design button.
8. Double-click *Students* in the Show Table dialog box and then click the Close button.
9. Double-click the following fields in the *Students* table field list box to add each field to the next available column in the query design grid.

   City
   StudentID
   StudentFirstName
   StudentLastName
   Telephone (scroll down the table field list box to the field)

10. Click in the *Criteria* box in the *City* column, type Detroit, click in the row below *Detroit* next to *or*, type Windsor, and then press Enter.

Access inserts double quotation marks at the beginning and end of a criterion for a field that contains text such as a city, name, or other field not used for calculating values.

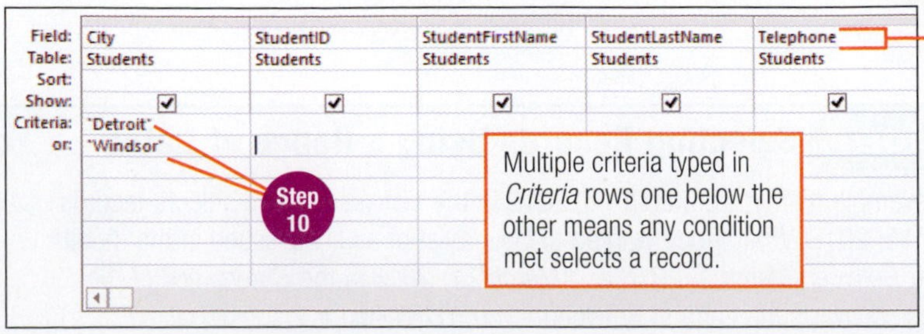

These fields are added to the design grid at Step 9.

Multiple criteria typed in *Criteria* rows one below the other means any condition met selects a record.

11 Click the Run button.

Students who reside in Detroit *or* Windsor are shown in the query results datasheet.

12 Click the View button to return to Design view.

A query is sorted by choosing *Ascending* or *Descending* in the *Sort* list box of the column by which you want to sort. At Step 9, City was placed first in the design grid because Access sorts query results by column left to right. To arrange the records alphabetically by student last name grouped by cities, the *City* field needed to be positioned left of the *StudentLastName* field.

13 Click in the *Sort* list box in the *City* column to place an insertion point and display the list box arrow, click the *Sort* list box arrow, and then click *Ascending*.

14 Click in the *Sort* list box in the *StudentLastName* column, click the list box arrow that appears, and then click *Ascending*.

15 Click the Run button.

The query results datasheet is sorted alphabetically by city and then by the student last name within each city.

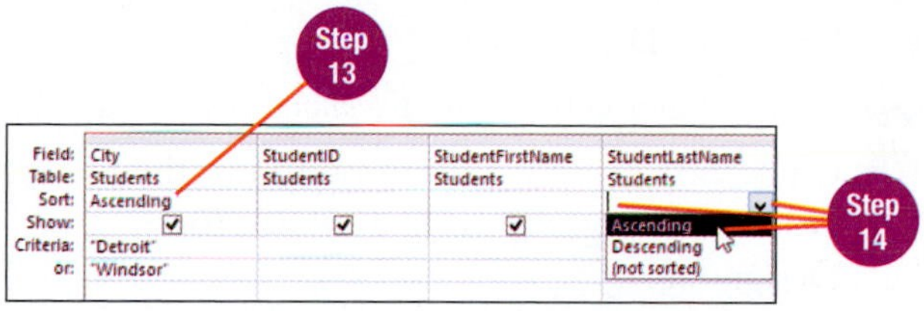

16 Save the query and name it **DetroitAndWindsorStudents**.

17 Close the DetroitAndWindsorStudents query. Leave the database open for the next topic.

DetroitAndWindsorStudents

City	StudentID	StudentFirstName	StudentLastNam	Telephone
Detroit	101658235	Stuart	Bennett	(313) 555-511
Detroit	101334799	Su-Lin	Cheng	(313) 555-412
Detroit	101455623	Armando	Colacci	(313) 555-221
Detroit	100478512	Angela	Doxtator	(313) 555-477
Detroit	101348863	Daniela	Garcia	(313) 555-623
Detroit	100548112	Pat	Hynes	(313) 555-656
Detroit	101322775	Shane	O'Leary	(313) 555-365
Detroit	110542642	Nadir	Sadiku	(313) 555-478
Detroit	100245745	Anna	Takacis	(313) 555-423
Detroit	101334745	Kyla	Westman	(313) 555-745
Detroit	104875111	Dana	Williams	(313) 555-124
Windsor	100367845	Sara	Blewett	(519) 555-412
Windsor	101352658	Shaun	Jenkins	(519) 555-478
Windsor	100443568	Dwayne	Kenney	(519) 555-412
Windsor	100684741	Marietta	Lynch	(519) 555-321
Windsor	101325685	Peter	Maslov	(519) 555-327
Windsor	100324125	Jose	Ramirez	(519) 555-469

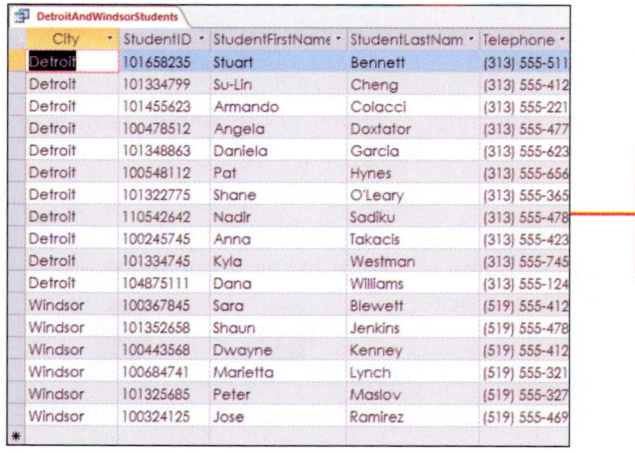

Sorted query results datasheet showing students who reside in either Detroit or Windsor.

Quick Steps

Select Records Using AND
1. Open query in Design view.
2. Type criterion in *Criteria* box of first field by which to select.
3. Type criterion in *Criteria* box of second field by which to select.
4. Run query.

Select Records Using OR
1. Open query in Design view.
2. Type criterion in *Criteria* box of first field by which to select.
3. Type criterion in *or* box of second field by which to select.
4. Run query.

Sort a Query
1. Open query in Design view.
2. Click in *Sort* list box of column by which to sort.
3. Click *Sort* list box arrow.
4. Click *Ascending* or *Descending*.

Beyond Basics — Selecting Using a Wildcard Character

A criterion can be entered that provides Access with a partial entry to match for selecting records. The asterisk is a wildcard character that can be inserted in a criterion in place of characters that you do not want to specify. For example, to select all students with the last name beginning with *C*, type *C** in the *Criteria* box in the *StudentLastName* column.

12.11 Inserting and Deleting Columns, Creating a Calculated Field in a Query, and Previewing a Datasheet

Skills

Delete and insert columns in a query

Create a calculated field

Format a field

Print Preview a datasheet

Tutorials

Modifying Field Properties in Datasheet View

Performing Calculations in a Query

Previewing and Printing a Table

A calculated field can be created in a query that performs a mathematical operation on a numeric field. A database design best practice is to avoid including a field in a table for storing data that can be generated by performing a calculation on another field. For example, assume that in the LibraryFines database, each fine is assessed a $2.50 administrative fee. Because the fee is a constant value, adding a field in the table to store the fee is not necessary. In this topic, you will use a query to calculate the total fine, including the administrative fee.

1. With the **LibraryFines-YourName** database open, open the FinesIssued query.
2. Switch to Design view.
3. Click in any cell in the *Telephone* column in the query design grid.
4. Click the Delete Columns button in the Query Setup group on the Query Tools Design tab.

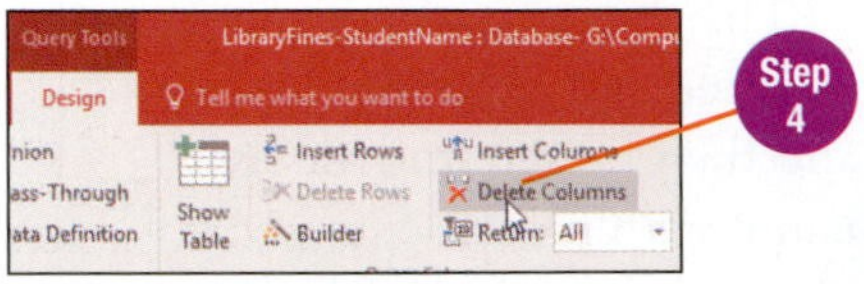

Buttons in the Query Setup group are used to modify a query by deleting columns or inserting new columns between existing fields.

5. Delete the *OverdueBookISBN* and *BookReturned* fields by completing steps similar to Steps 3 and 4.
6. With *FinePaid* the active field, click the Insert Columns button in the Query Setup group.
7. With an insertion point positioned in the *Field* box in the new column between *Amount* and *FinePaid*, type Fine with Admin Fee: [Amount]+2.50 and then press Enter.
8. Drag the right column boundary line in the gray field selector bar at the top of the design grid to widen the column as shown in the image below. Note that Access drops the zero at the end of the formula.

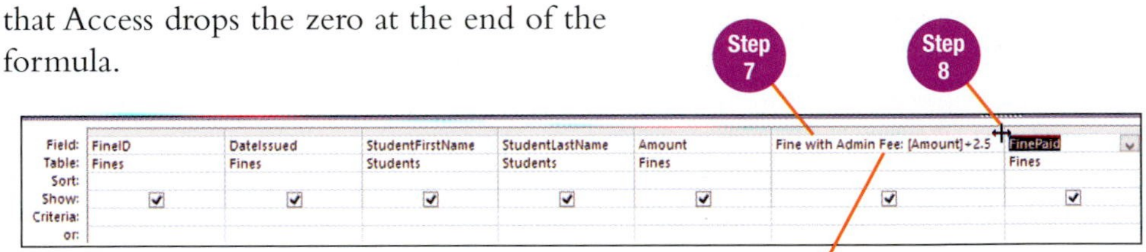

The text before the colon is the column heading for the new field *Fine with Admin Fee*. After the colon the mathematical expression *[Amount]+2.5* is stored. A field name used in a formula is typed within square brackets.

9. Click the Run button.

Notice that the calculated field is not formatted the same as the *Amount* field, and that the column needs to be widened to show the entire column heading.

10. Click in any cell in the *Fine with Admin Fee* column, click the More button in the Records group, click *Field Width*, and then click the Best Fit button in the Column Width dialog box.
11. Switch to Design view.

Oops!

Error message appears? Check your typing to make sure you typed a colon after *Fine with Admin Fee*, used square brackets, and that the entry has no other spelling errors.

App Tip

Use the same mathematical operators in Access that you would use in a formula in Excel: + to add, - to subtract, * to multiply, and / to divide.

12 Click in any cell in the calculated column in the query design grid and then click the Property Sheet button in the Show/Hide group on the Query Tools Design tab.

13 Click in the *Format* box in the Property Sheet task pane, click the list box arrow that appears, and then click *Currency* at the drop-down list.

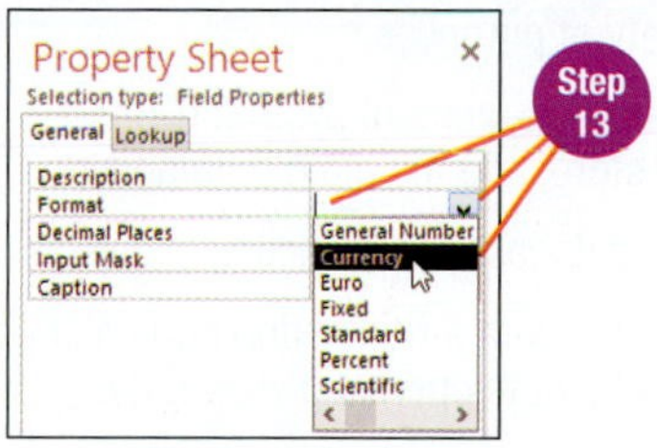

14 Close the Property Sheet task pane.

15 Click the Run button.

16 Use *Save Object As* at the Save As backstage area to save the revised query as *FinesWithAdminFee*.

Quick Steps

Create a Calculated Field in a Query

1. Open query in Design view.
2. Insert column if necessary.
3. Click in *Field* box for calculated column.
4. Type formula.
5. Press Enter.
6. Run query.
7. Save query.

A table datasheet or query results datasheet should be viewed in Print Preview before printing to make adjustments as necessary to the orientation and margins.

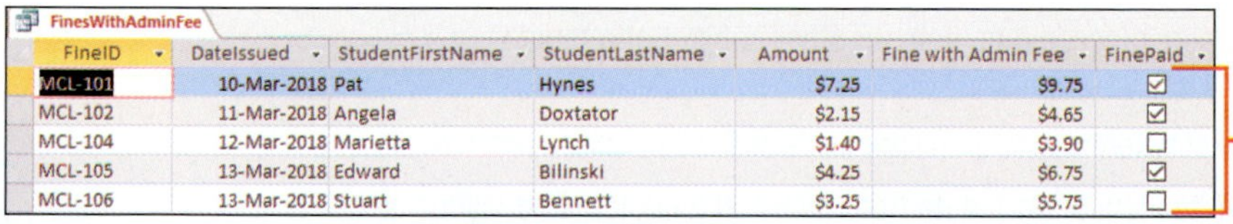
FinesWithAdminFee

FineID	DateIssued	StudentFirstName	StudentLastName	Amount	Fine with Admin Fee	FinePaid
MCL-101	10-Mar-2018	Pat	Hynes	$7.25	$9.75	☑
MCL-102	11-Mar-2018	Angela	Doxtator	$2.15	$4.65	☑
MCL-104	12-Mar-2018	Marietta	Lynch	$1.40	$3.90	☐
MCL-105	13-Mar-2018	Edward	Bilinski	$4.25	$6.75	☑
MCL-106	13-Mar-2018	Stuart	Bennett	$3.25	$5.75	☐

These are the first five records in the FinesWithAdminFee query showing the *Fine with Admin Fee* column.

17 Click the File tab, click *Print*, and then click *Print Preview* at the Print backstage area.

The entire datasheet does not fit on one page in the default Portrait orientation.

18 Click the Landscape button in the Page Layout group on the Print Preview tab.

Notice that Access prints the query name and the current date at the top of the page and the page number at the bottom of the page.

19 Click the Close Print Preview button in the Close Preview group.

App Tip

Access does not save page layout options. If you change the datasheet orientation to landscape for printing purposes and then close the table, the datasheet reverts to the default portrait orientation when the table is reopened.

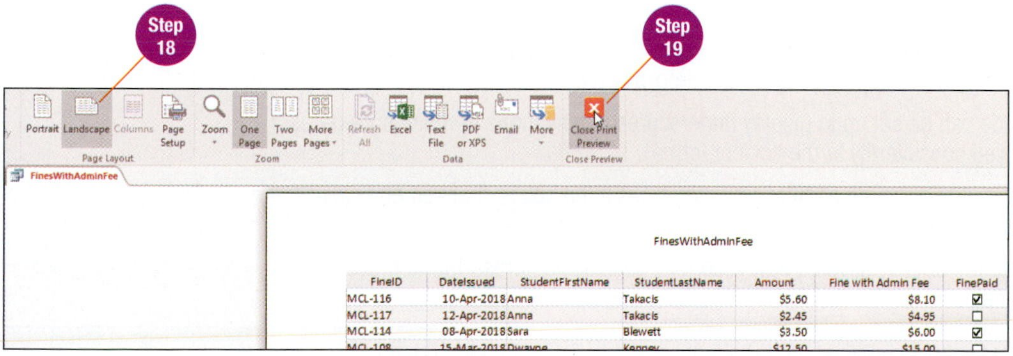

20 Close the FinesWithAdminFee query and then close the LibraryFines database.

View Model Answer
Compare your completed file with the model answer.

Beyond Basics: Exporting Data from Access

Buttons in the Data group on the Print Preview tab are used to export the active table, query, form, or report shown in the work area. For example, click the PDF or XPS button to save a copy of a query results datasheet in a PDF file.

Topics Review

Topic	Key Concepts	Key Terms
12.1 Understanding Database Objects and Terminology	A database includes data stored in an organized manner to provide information for a variety of purposes. A database management system (DBMS) is a software program designed to organize, store, and maintain a database. An Access database is a collection of objects used to enter, maintain, and view data. Access opens with a Navigation pane along the left side of the window used to select an object to open and view data. A table stores data about a single topic or subject such as people, places, events, items, or other category. Each characteristic about the subject or topic of a table is called a *field*. The data stored in a field is called a *field value*. A set of fields for one person, place, event, item, or other subject of a table is called a *record*. A table opens in a datasheet where the columns are fields and the rows are records. A report is an object used to view or print data from tables in a customized layout and with summary totals. A form is another interface to view, enter, or edit data that shows only one record at a time in a customized layout. Use buttons in the Record Navigation bar to scroll records in a form. A query is used to combine fields from one or more tables in a single datasheet and may show all records or only some records that meet a condition.	database database management system (DBMS) table field record field value report form query
12.2 Adding Records to a Table Using a Datasheet	New records are added to a table by opening the table datasheet and then clicking the New (blank) record button in the Record Navigation bar. Type field values in a new row at the bottom of the table datasheet, pressing Tab to move from one field to the next field. A field that displays with a down-pointing arrow means that you can enter the field value by selecting an entry from a drop-down list. Date fields can be set up to display underscores and hyphens to make sure dates are entered consistently in the correct format. A field that displays with a check box stores *Yes* if the box is checked and *No* if the box is left empty. Access automatically saves a new record as soon as you press Tab to move past the last field.	New (blank) record
12.3 Editing and Deleting Records Using a Datasheet	Edit a field value in a datasheet by selecting text to be changed and type new text, or by clicking to place an insertion point within a field (cell) and inserting or deleting text as required. Function key F2 opens a field for editing. The gray record selector bar along the left edge of a datasheet is used to select a record. Click the Delete button in the Records group on the Home tab to delete the selected record from the table. Access requires that you confirm a deletion before the record is removed. Generally, records are not deleted until data has been copied to an archive database and/or a backup copy of the database has been made.	

continued...

Topic	Key Concepts	Key Terms
12.4 Adding, Editing, and Deleting Records Using a Form	A form is the preferred object for adding, editing, and deleting records because one record at a time is displayed in a columnar layout in the work area. Add new records and edit field values in records using the same techniques that you used for adding and editing records using a datasheet. To delete a record using a form, display the record, click the Delete button arrow in the Records group on the Home tab, and then click *Delete Record* at the drop-down list. In a database with many records, navigating to a record using the Find feature is more efficient.	
12.5 Finding and Replacing Data and Adjusting Column Widths in a Datasheet	Click in the column in a datasheet that contains the field value you want to locate and use the Find command to move to all occurrences of the *Find What* text. Use the Replace command to find all occurrences of an entry and replace the field value with new text. Activate any cell in a column for which the width needs to be adjusted, click the More button in the Records group on the Home tab, click *Field Width*, and then enter the desired width or click the Best Fit button. The Best Fit button in the Column Width dialog box adjusts the width of the column to accommodate the longest entry in the field.	Best Fit
12.6 Sorting and Filtering Records	Initially, a table is arranged alphanumerically by the primary key field values. A primary key is a field in the table that uniquely identifies each record such as *StudentID*. To sort by a field other than the primary key, click in the field by which to sort and then click the Ascending or Descending button in the Sort & Filter group on the Home tab. Filter a datasheet by clearing check boxes for items you do not want to view in the Sort & Filter list box accessed from the filter arrow next to the field name. Use the Toggle Filter button in the Sort & Filter group to redisplay all records. Sort by more than one field by selecting the columns before clicking the Ascending or Descending button. Change the sort order by moving a column left if you want to sort first by a field other than the leftmost column.	primary key
12.7 Creating a Query Using the Simple Query Wizard	Queries extract information from one or more tables in a single datasheet. The Simple Query Wizard helps you build a query by making selections in three dialog boxes. At the first Simple Query Wizard dialog box, choose each table or query and the fields in the order that you want them in the query results datasheet. At the second Simple Query Wizard dialog box, choose a detail or summary query. Assign a name to the query at the third Simple Query Wizard dialog box.	Simple Query Wizard

continued…

Topic	Key Concepts	Key Terms
12.8 Creating a Query Using Design View	Every object in Access has at least two views. Opening an object from the Navigation pane opens the table, query, form, or report in Datasheet view. Design view is used to set up or define the structure or layout of an object. Design view for a query presents a blank grid of columns in which you add the fields in the order you want them in the query results datasheet. Add table field list boxes to the query design grid at the Show Table dialog box. Double-click field names in the table field list boxes in the order you want the columns in the query results datasheet. The Run button is used after building a query in Design view to instruct Access to generate the query and show the query results datasheet.	Design view Run button
12.9 Entering Criteria to Select Records in a Query	Queries can be created that show only those records that meet one or more conditions. Use the View button in the Views group on the Home tab to switch between Datasheet view and Design view in a query. Type the criterion by which you want records selected in the *Criteria* box of the column by which records are to be selected. In a field that displays check boxes, the criterion is either *Yes* or *No*.	
12.10 Entering Multiple Criteria to Select Records and Sorting a Query	More than one criterion entered in the same *Criteria* row in the query design grid is an AND statement, which means each criterion must be met for the record to be selected. More than one criterion entered in *Criteria* rows one below the other is an OR statement, which means that any condition can be met for the record to be selected. Choose *Ascending* or *Descending* in the *Sort* list box for the column by which to sort query results in Design view. Access sorts a query by column left to right. If necessary, position the field to be sorted first to the left of another field that is to be sorted.	
12.11 Inserting and Deleting Columns, Creating a Calculated Field in a Query, and Previewing a Datasheet	A calculated field can be created in a query that generates values using a mathematical expression. Use the Delete Columns and Insert Columns buttons in the Query Setup group on the Query Tools Design tab to remove or add new columns in a query. A calculated column is created by typing in the *Field* box a column heading, a colon (:), and then the mathematical expression. Type a field name in a mathematical expression within square brackets. Open the Property Sheet task pane to change the format of a calculated field. A table or query results datasheet should be previewed before printing to make adjustments to page orientation and/or margins.	

Recheck

Recheck your understanding of the topics covered in this chapter.

Workbook

Chapter review and assessment resources are available in the *Workbook* ebook.

Chapter 13

Creating a Table, Form, and Report in Access

Precheck

Check your understanding of the topics covered in this chapter.

Creating a new database involves understanding the purpose of the database and the information the database user will need. The database designer needs to carefully analyze the collected data and decide how best to define and group the elements into logical units. Tables are created first because they are the basis for all other objects. Tables that need to be connected for queries, forms, or reports are joined in a relationship. Objects such as queries, forms, and reports are created after the tables and relationships are defined.

In Chapter 12, you examined an existing database and added and edited data in a table and form. You also created queries to select records for a variety of purposes. Now that you have seen how Access data interacts with objects, you are ready to build a new database on your own. In this chapter you will learn to create a new database, create a new table, assign a primary key, modify field properties, edit relationships, create a form, create a report, compact and repair a database, and create a backup copy of a database.

Learning Objectives

- **13.1** Create a new database and describe guidelines for designing tables
- **13.2** Create a new table using Datasheet view and assign a caption to a field
- **13.3** Create a new table using Design view and assign a primary key
- **13.4** Add a field to a table
- **13.5** Change the field size and add a default value for a field using Design view
- **13.6** Create a lookup list for a field
- **13.7** Identify a one-to-one relationship and a one-to-many relationship, and edit a relationship
- **13.8** Create and edit a form
- **13.9** Create, edit, and view a report
- **13.10** Compact and repair, and back up a database

SNAP If you are a SNAP user, go to your SNAP Assignments page to complete the Precheck, Tutorials, and Recheck.

Data Files

Before beginning this chapter, be sure you have copied the student data files for this course to your storage medium. Steps on downloading and extracting the data files are provided in Chapter 1, Topic 1.8, on pages 22–23.

Skills

Create a new database file

13.1 Creating a New Database File and Understanding Table Design Guidelines

The first step in creating a database is to assign a name and storage location for the new database file. Because Access saves records automatically as data is added to a table, the file name and storage location are required in advance. Once the file is created, Access displays a blank table for you to fill in. Before you create a new table, you must carefully plan the fields and field names and identify a primary key. Although the tables you will create in this chapter have already been planned, the guidelines in Table 13.1 provide you with an overview of the table design process.

Table 13.1

Guidelines for Planning a New Table

Guideline	Description
Divide data into the smallest possible units	A field should be segmented into the smallest units of information to facilitate sorting and filtering. For example, a person's name could be split into three fields: first name, middle name, and last name.
Assign each field a name	Up to 64 characters can be used in a field name with a combination of letters, numbers, spaces, and some symbols. Database programmers prefer short field names with no spaces. A field to store a person's last name could be assigned the name *LName*, *Last*, *LastName*, or *Last_Name*. Short names are preferred because Access provides the ability to enter a longer descriptive title for column headings in datasheets, forms, and reports that is separate from the field name.
Assign each field a data type	Data type refers to the type of information that will be entered as field values. Look at examples of data to help you determine the data type. By assigning the most appropriate data type, Access can verify data as it is being entered for the correct format or type of characters. For example, a field defined as a Number field will cause Access to reject alphabetic letters typed into the field. The most common data types are Short Text, Number, Currency, Date/Time, and Yes/No. Data types are described in Table 13.2 in the next topic.
Decide the field to be used as a primary key	Each table should have one field that uniquely identifies a record, such as a student number, receipt number, or email address. Access creates an ID field automatically in a blank datasheet that can be used if the table data does not have a unique identifier. In some cases, a combination of two or more fields is used as a primary key.
Include a common identifier field in a table that will be joined to another table	Data should not be duplicated in a database. For example, a book title would not be stored in both the Books table and the Sales table. Instead, the book title is stored in the Books table only and a book ID field in the Sales table is used to join the two tables in a relationship. You will learn more about relationships in a later topic.

1. Start Access 2016.
2. Click *Blank desktop database* at the Access Start screen.

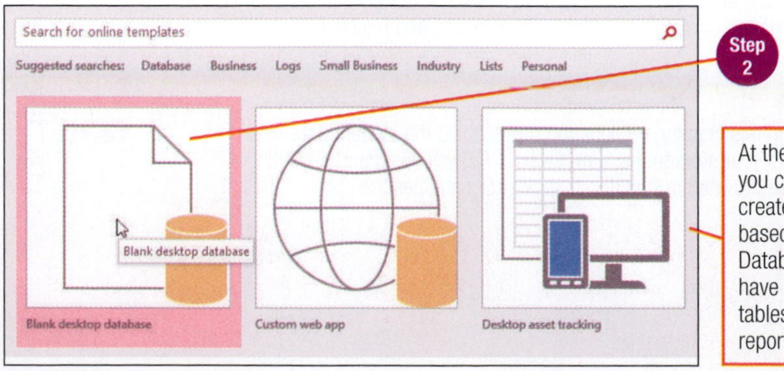

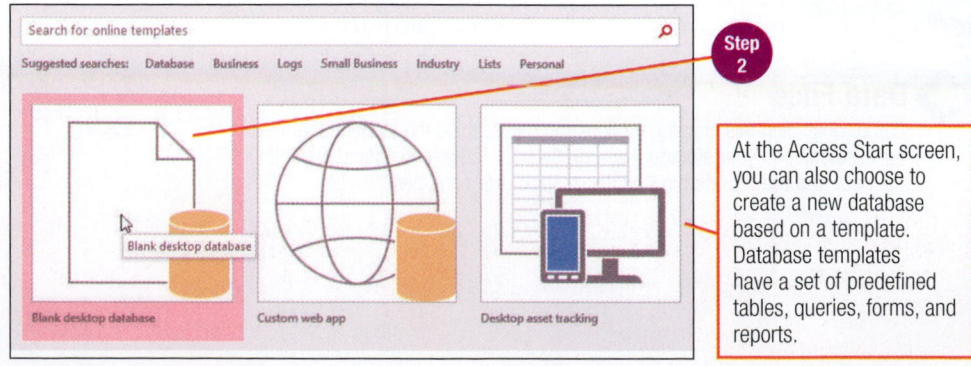

At the Access Start screen, you can also choose to create a new database based on a template. Database templates have a set of predefined tables, queries, forms, and reports.

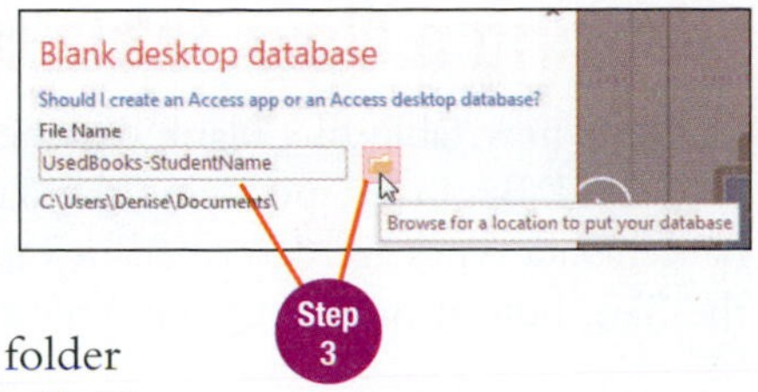

3. Select the current text in the *File Name* text box, type UsedBooks-YourName, and then click the Browse button (file folder icon).
4. At the File New Database dialog box, navigate to the CompletedTopicsByChapter folder on your storage medium, create a new folder *Ch13*, double-click to open the Ch13 folder, and then click OK.
5. Click the Create button.

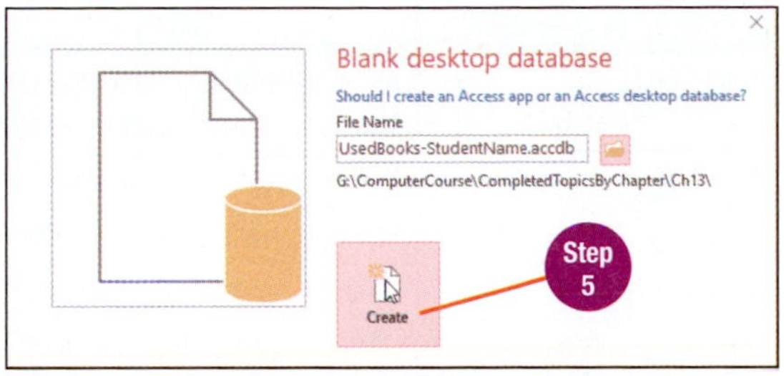

Access creates the database file and opens a new table datasheet named *Table1* in the work area, as shown in Figure 13.1. You can create a new table using the blank datasheet.

> **Quick Steps**
>
> **Create a New Database**
> 1. Start Access 2016.
> 2. Click *Blank desktop database*.
> 3. Type file name.
> 4. Click Browse button.
> 5. Navigate to drive and/or folder location.
> 6. Click OK.
> 7. Click Create.

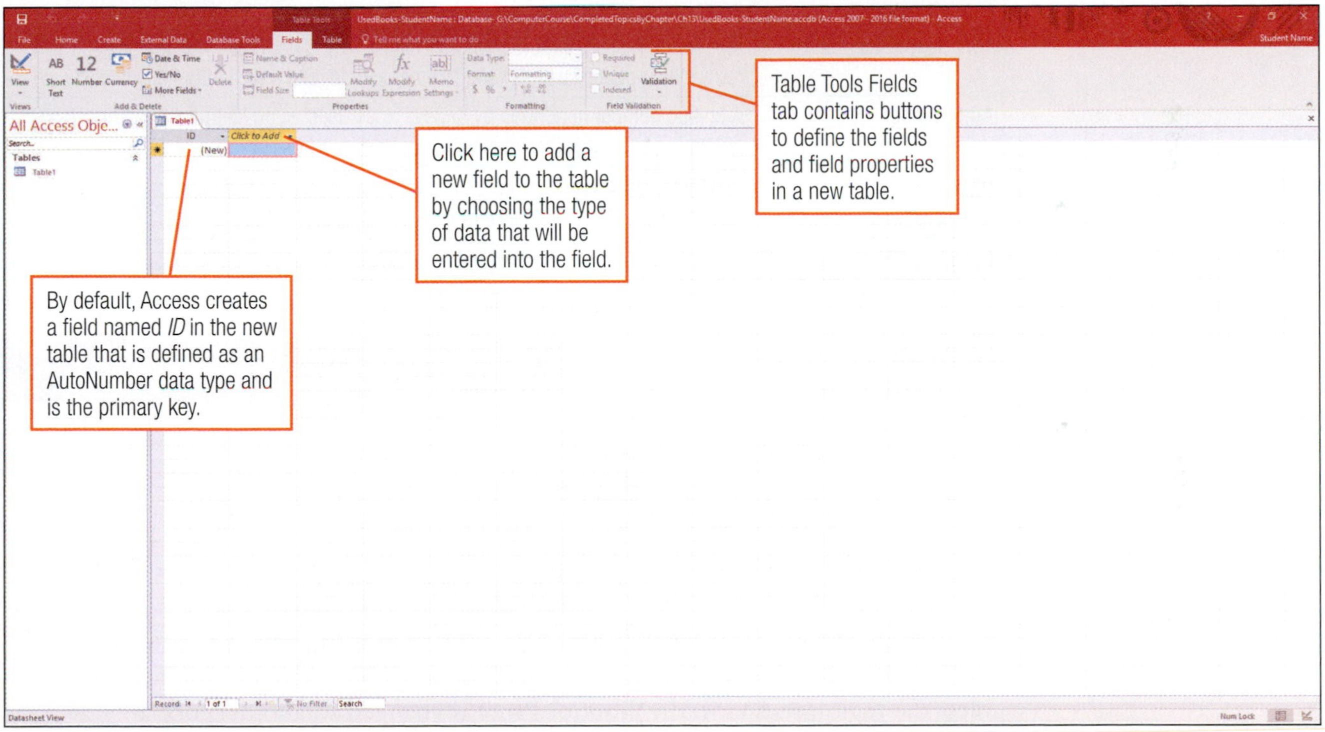

Figure 13.1

Access creates a blank table datasheet in a new database file.

6. Leave the blank table datasheet open for the next topic.

Each table in a database should contain information about one subject only. In this chapter, you will create tables for a used-textbook database that a student organization may use to keep track of students, textbooks, and sales. The three tables you will create in this chapter are described as follows:

Books: shows the title, author, condition, and asking price for each book
Sales: tracks each sale with the date, amount, and payment method
Students: shows information about each student with textbooks for sale

> **App Tip**
>
> A database designer may use data models by creating sample forms and reports before creating tables to make sure all data elements are included in the table design.

13.2 Creating a New Table Using a Datasheet

Skills

Create a new table using a Datasheet

Add a caption for a field

Tutorial

Creating a Table in Datasheet View

Create a new table in a blank datasheet in Datasheet view by adding a column for each field. Begin by specifying the data type for a field and then typing the field name. Data types are described in Table 13.2. Once the fields have been defined, use the Save button on the Quick Access Toolbar to assign the table a name.

Table 13.2

Field Data Types

Data Type	Use for This Type of Field Value
Short Text	Alphanumeric text up to 255 characters for names, identification numbers, telephone numbers, or other similar data.
Number	Numeric data other than monetary values.
Currency	Monetary values such as sales, costs, or wages.
Date & Time or Date/Time	Dates or times that you want to verify, sort, select, or calculate.
Yes/No	Data that can only be Yes or No, or True or False.
Lookup & Relationship or Lookup Wizard	A drop-down list with field values from another table, or from a predefined list of items.
Long Text or Rich Text	Alphanumeric text of more than 255 characters. Select Rich Text to enable formatting options such as font, font color, bold, and italic in the field values.
AutoNumber	A unique number generated by Access to be used as an identifier field. Access generates sequential numbers starting from 1.
Hyperlink	Stores web addresses.
Attachment	Attach a file such as a picture to a field in a record.
Calculated Field	A formula calculates the field value using data in other fields.

1. With the **UsedBooks-YourName** database open and with the blank datasheet for Table1 open, click the Date & Time button in the Add & Delete group on the Table Tools Fields tab.

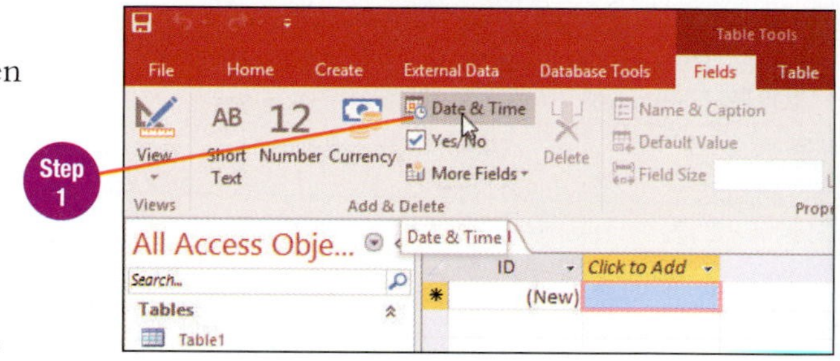

Choosing the most appropriate data type for a field is important for sorting, calculating, and verifying data. Access expects dates to be entered in the format m/d/y unless the region setting in the Control Panel is changed to another format.

2. With *Field1* selected in the field name box for the new column, type SaleDate and then press Enter.

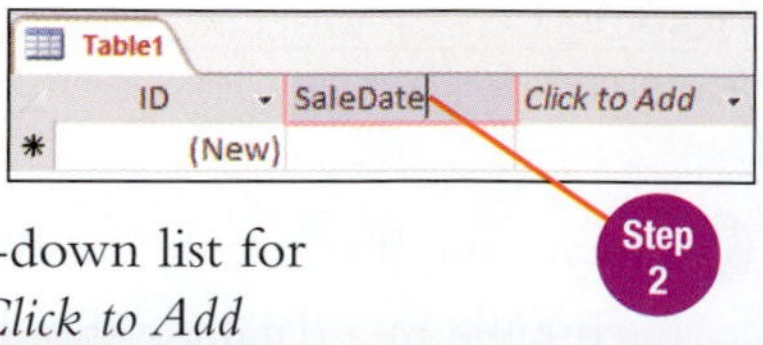

The *Click to Add* column opens the data type drop-down list for the next new field. Add a new field using either the *Click to Add* drop-down list or the buttons in the Add & Delete group on the Table Tools Fields tab.

3. Click *Short Text* in the *Click to Add* drop-down list.

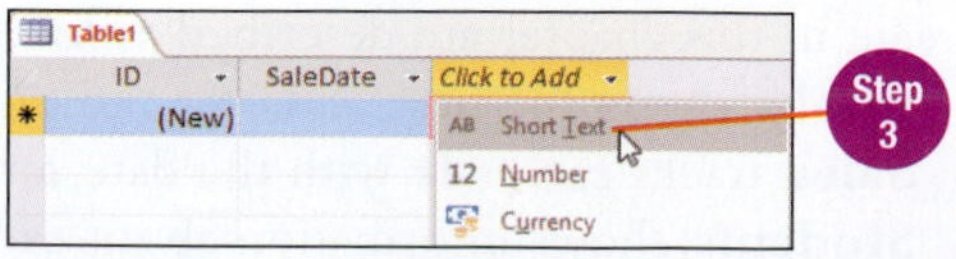

App Tip

Access displays the field name as the column title in a datasheet unless an entry exists in the Caption property, in which case the caption text becomes the column title. (See Step 8.)

4. Type BookID as the field name and then press Enter.
5. Click *Currency* in the *Click to Add* drop-down list, type Amount, and then press Enter.
6. Click *Short Text*, type PayMethod, and then press Enter.
7. Click the *SaleDate* field name to select the field.
8. Click the Name & Caption button in the Properties group on the Table Tools Fields tab.

The **Caption property** is used to type a descriptive title for a field that includes spaces between words or the full text of an abbreviated field name.

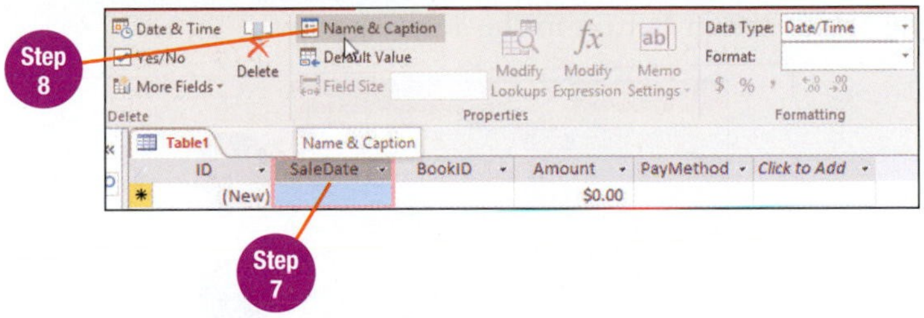

9. Click in the *Caption* text box, type Sale Date, and then press Enter or click OK at the Enter Field Properties dialog box.

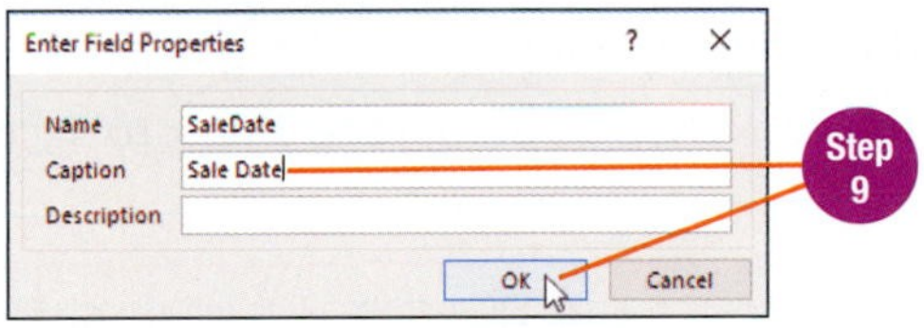

10. Click to select the *Amount* field, click the Name & Caption button, click in the *Caption* text box, type Sale Amount, and then press Enter or click OK.
11. Drag the right column boundary of the *Sale Amount* column until the entire column heading is visible.

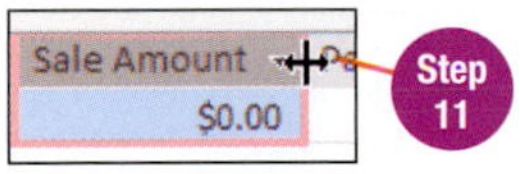

12. Click to select the *PayMethod* field, click the Name & Caption button, click in the *Caption* text box, type Payment Method, and then press Enter or click OK.
13. Drag the right column boundary of the *Payment Method* column until the entire column heading is visible.
14. Click the Save button on the Quick Access Toolbar.
15. Type Sales in the *Table Name* text box in the Save As dialog box and then press Enter or click OK.

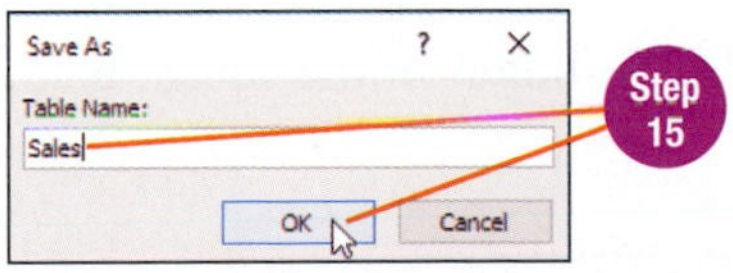

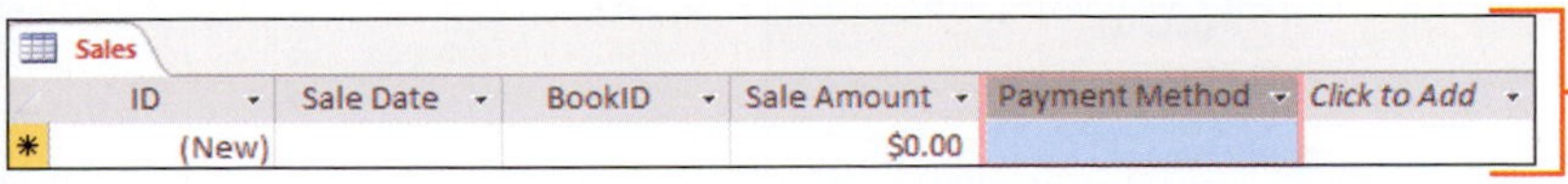

completed Sales table datasheet

16. Close the Sales table. Leave the database open for the next topic.

Quick Steps

Create a Field in a New Table

1. With blank table datasheet open, click required data type button in Add & Delete group on Table Tools Fields tab.
2. Type field name.
3. Press Enter.

OR

1. With blank datasheet open, click *Click to Add*.
2. Click required data type.
3. Type field name.
4. Press Enter.

Add a Caption to a Field

1. Select field.
2. Click Name & Caption button.
3. Click in *Caption* text box.
4. Type caption text.
5. Click OK.

Save a Table

1. Click Save button.
2. Type table name.
3. Click OK.

App Tip

Double-click the right column boundary to best fit the column width.

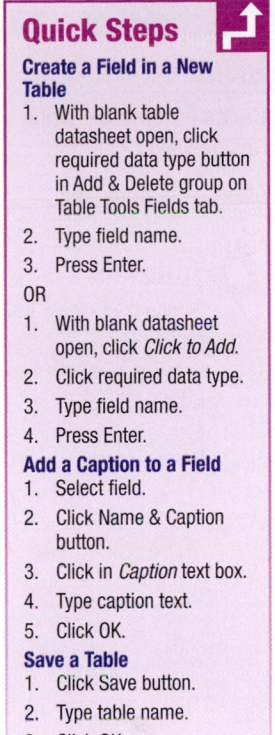

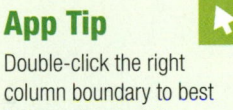

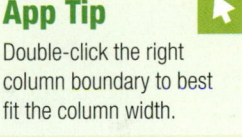

13.3 Creating a New Table Using Design View and Assigning a Primary Key

Skills

Create a new table using Design view

Assign a primary key

Tutorials

Setting the Primary Key Field

Creating a Table in Design View

Managing Fields in Design View

A new table can be created in Design view in which fields are defined in rows in the top half of the work area. In the previous topic, the Sales table, created in a blank datasheet, had an ID field automatically created and designated as the primary key. In Design view, an ID field is not created for you. After creating the fields in the Design view window, assign the primary key to the field that will uniquely identify each record and then save the table.

1. With the **UsedBooks-YourName** database open, click the Create tab.
2. Click the Table Design button in the Tables group.

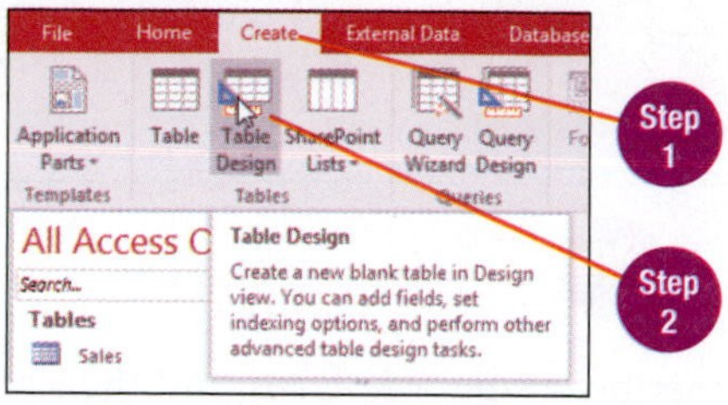

3. With the insertion point positioned in the first row of the *Field Name* column, type StudentID and then press Enter.
4. With *Short Text* in the *Data Type* column, press Enter to accept the default data type.

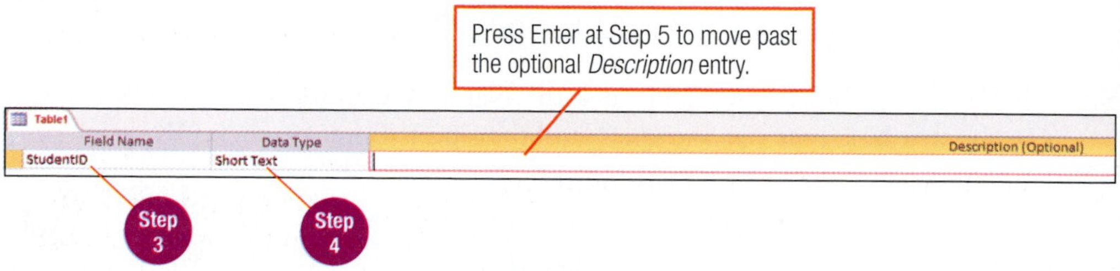

5. Press Enter to move past the *Description* column and move down to the next row to start a new field.

Descriptions are optional entries. A description can be used to type additional information about a field or to enter instructions to end users who will see the description in the Status bar of a datasheet when the field is active.

6. Type LName in the *Field Name* column and then press Enter three times to move to the next row.
7. Enter the remaining fields as shown in the image below by completing a step similar to Step 6.

App Tip

You can also use the Tab key to move to the next column in Design view.

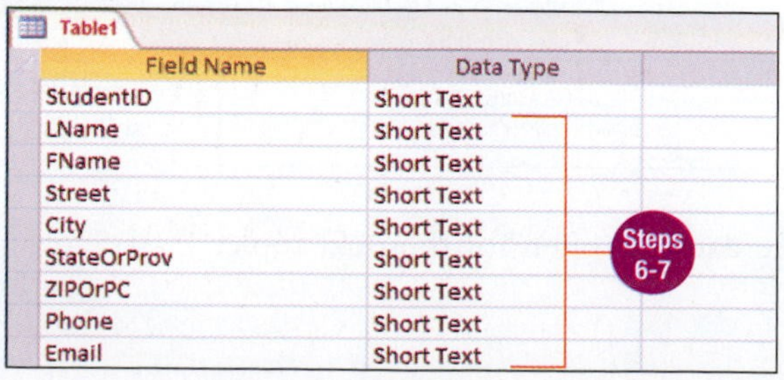

Table1
Field Name
Data Type
StudentID Short Text
LName Short Text
FName Short Text
Street Short Text
City Short Text
StateOrProv Short Text
ZIPOrPC Short Text
Phone Short Text
Email Short Text
Steps 6-7

8 Click to place an insertion point within the *StudentID* field name.

9 Click the Primary Key button in the Tools group on the Table Tools Design tab.

A key icon in the field selector bar (gray bar along left edge of *Field Name* column) indicates the field is designated as the primary key for the table.

Key icon indicates field is the primary key.

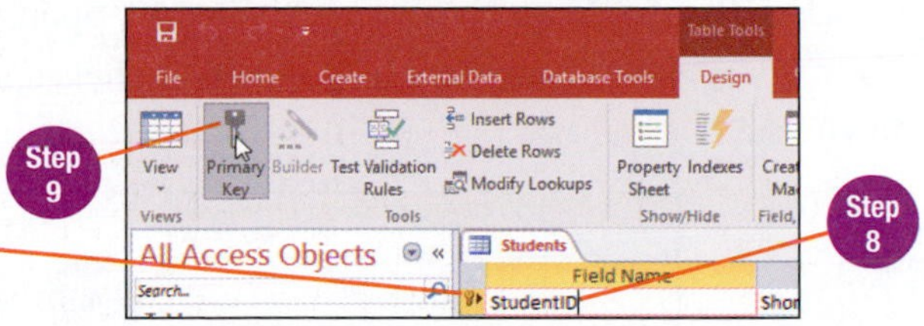

10 Click the Save button on the Quick Access Toolbar, type Students, and then press Enter or click OK.

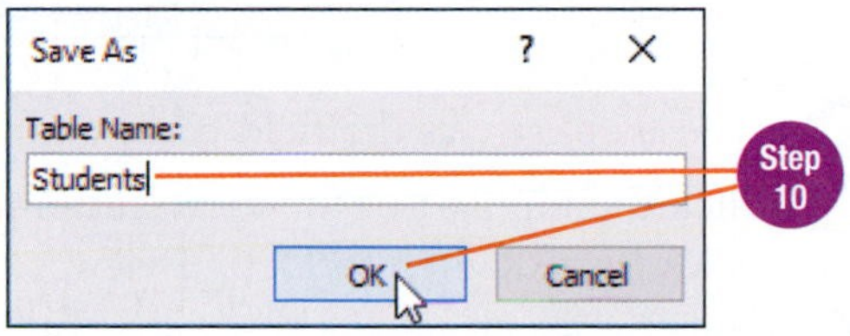

11 Close the Students table.

12 Click the Create tab and then click the Table Design button.

13 Create the first five fields in the new table using the default Short Text data type and without descriptions as follows:

BookID
StudentID
Title
Author
Condition

14 Type AskPrice as the field name in the sixth row and then press Enter.

15 Click the *Data Type* list box arrow and then click *Currency* at the drop-down list.

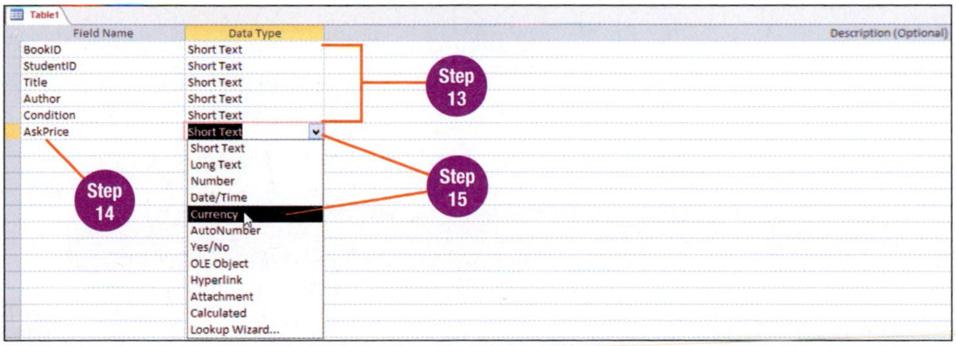

16 Click to place an insertion point within the *BookID* field name and then click the Primary Key button.

BookID is shown as the primary key field after Step 16 is completed.

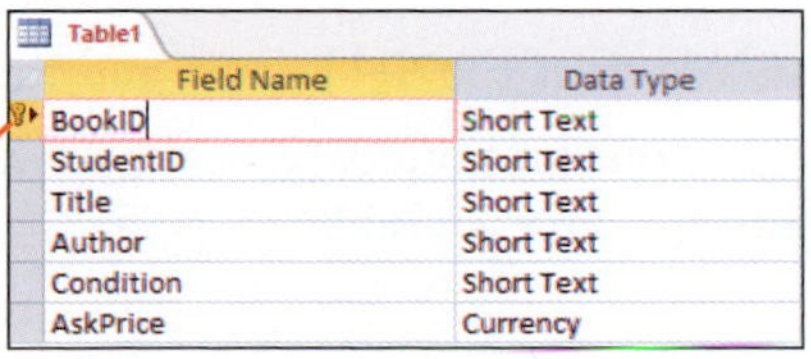

17 Click the Save button on the Quick Access Toolbar, type Books, and then press Enter or click OK.

18 Close the Books table. Leave the database open for the next topic.

App Tip

Access will not allow field values to be duplicated in a primary key—always choose a primary key field that you are sure will never have field values that repeat.

Quick Steps

Create a Table in Design View

1. Click Create tab.
2. Click Table Design button.
3. Type field name.
4. Press Enter.
5. If necessary, change data type.
6. Press Enter until new row is active.
7. Repeat Steps 3–6 until finished.
8. Assign primary key.
9. Save table.

Assign a Primary Key

1. If necessary, open table in Design view.
2. Click to place an insertion point in primary key field name.
3. Click Primary Key button.
4. Save table.

13.4 Adding Fields to an Existing Table

Skills

Add a field to a table

Open a table in Datasheet view and use the *Click to Add* column to add a new field, or make active a field in the datasheet and use the buttons in the Table Tools Fields tab to add a new field after the active field.

1. With the **UsedBooks-YourName** database open, open the Books table.
2. Click the *Click to Add* column heading and then click *Currency* at the drop-down list.

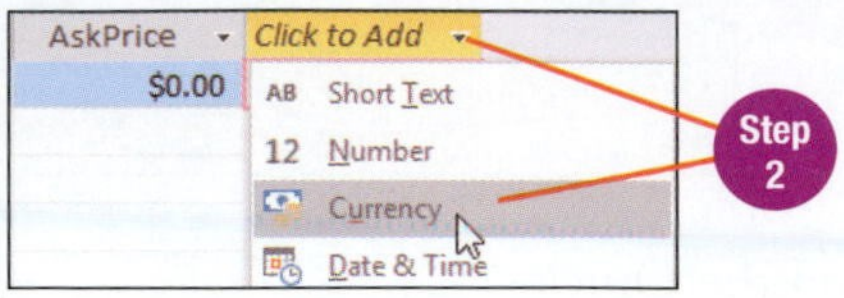

3. Type StopPrice as the field name and then press Enter.
4. Click the top part of the View button in the Views group on the Table Tools Fields tab to switch to Design view.
5. Click in the *Description* column in the *StopPrice* field row and then type Do not sell for lower than the student's stop price value.

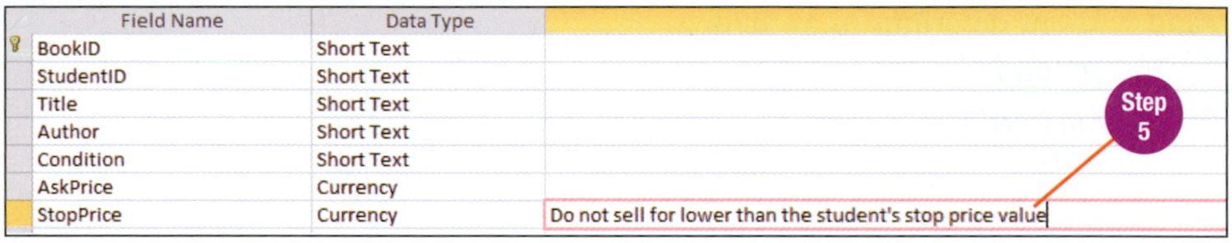

Field Name
Data Type
BookID
Short Text
StudentID
Short Text
Title
Short Text
Author
Short Text
Condition
Short Text
AskPrice
Currency
StopPrice
Currency
Do not sell for lower than the student's stop price value
Step 5

6. Save and then close the Books table.
7. Open the Students table.
8. Click the *Phone* field name to select the column.
9. Click the Table Tools Fields tab and then click the Yes/No button in the Add & Delete group to add the new field in the column to the right of the *Phone* field.

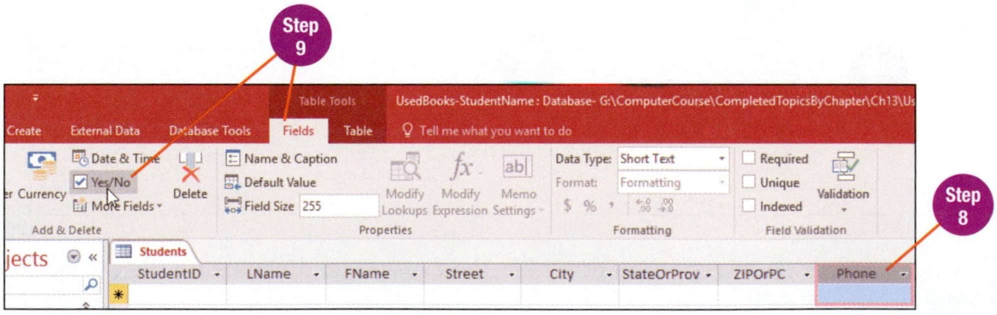

10. Type DirectDeposit as the field name and then press Enter.
11. Drag the right column boundary of the *DirectDeposit* field to the right until the entire column heading is visible.

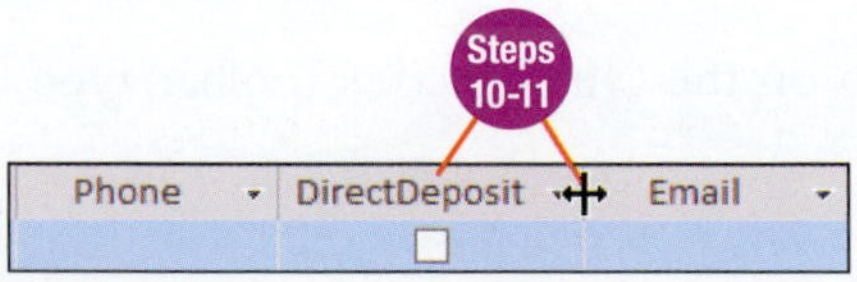

12 Save and then close the Students table.

13 Open the Books table.

14 Click the *StopPrice* field name to select the column.

15 Look at the message that displays in the Status bar.

Notice that the text typed in the *Description* column for the field in Design view at Step 5 displays here. Description entries also display in the Status bar when a form is open that is based upon the same table.

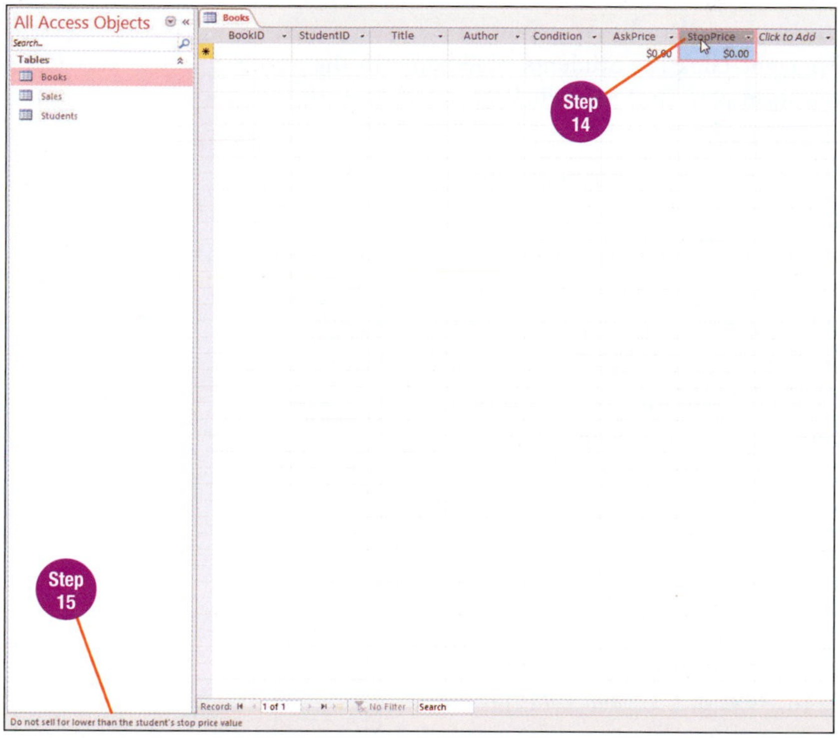

16 Close the Books table. Leave the database open for the next topic.

Quick Steps

Add a Field

1. Open table.
2. Click *Click to Add* column.
3. Click required data type.
4. Type field name.
5. Press Enter.
6. Save table.

OR

1. Open table.
2. Click field name to select column left of where you want the new field located.
3. Click the required data type button.
4. Type field name.
5. Press Enter.
6. Save table.

Alternative Method Adding a New Field to a Table Using Design View

Open a table in Design view and type a new field name in the next available row or make a field active and use the Insert Rows button in the Tools group on the Table Tools Design tab to add a new field above the active field.

Beyond Basics Deleting Fields

Generally, a field that contains data should not be deleted, because deleting a field causes all field values to be removed from the database. However, if a field added to a table is considered unnecessary, remove the field by opening the table in either Datasheet view or Design view. In Datasheet view, make the field active and use the Delete button in the Add & Delete group on the Table Tools Fields tab. In Design view, make the field active and use the Delete Rows button on the Table Tools Design tab.

13.5 Modifying Field Properties Using Design View

Skills

Change the field size

Add a default value

Add a caption in Design view

Tutorials

Modifying Field Properties in Design View

Applying a Validation Rule in Design View

Applying a Validation Rule in Datasheet View

Each field in a table has a set of field properties associated with the field. A **field property** is a single characteristic or attribute of a field. For example, the field name is a field property, and the data type is another field property. The properties in each field can be modified to customize, format, or otherwise change the behavior of a field. The lower half of the work area of a table in Design view contains the **Field Properties pane** that is used to modify properties other than the field name, data type, and description.

1. With the **UsedBooks-YourName** database open, right-click the Students table name in the Navigation pane and then click *Design View* at the shortcut menu.

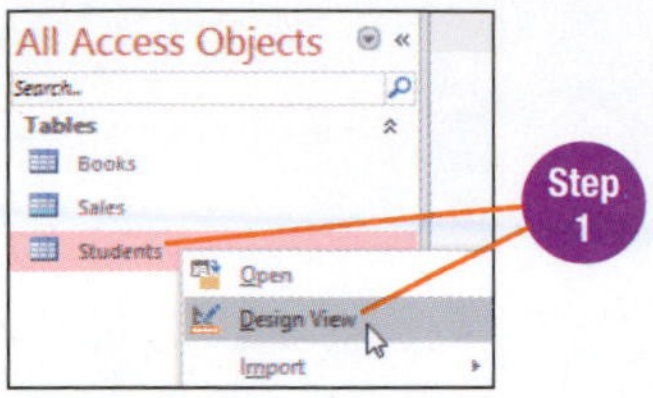

2. Click in the *StateOrProv* field name to select the field.
3. Double-click or drag to select *255* in the *Field Size* property box in the Field Properties pane, type 2, and then press Enter.

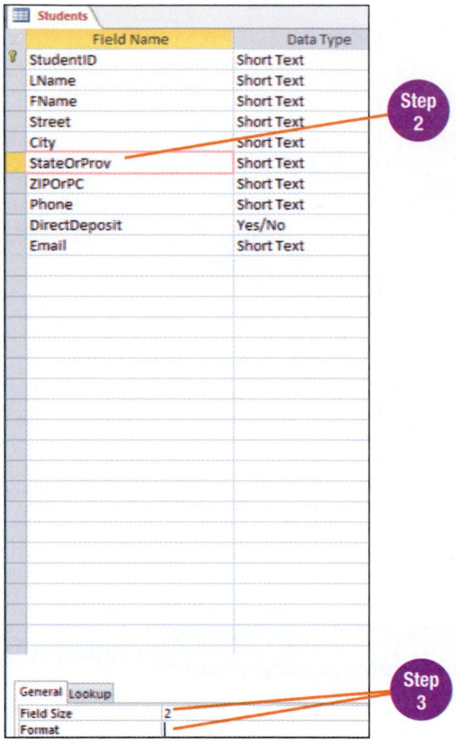

Setting a field size for a state or province field ensures that all new field values use the two-character abbreviation for addressing letters or creating labels from the database.

4. Click in the *Default Value* property box, type MI, and then press Enter.

Access automatically adds quotation marks to the text in a *Default Value* property box for a Short Text data type. The text entered into a *Default Value* property box is automatically entered as the field value in new records; the end user presses Enter to accept the value, or types an alternative entry.

5. Click in the *Caption* property box and then type State or Province.

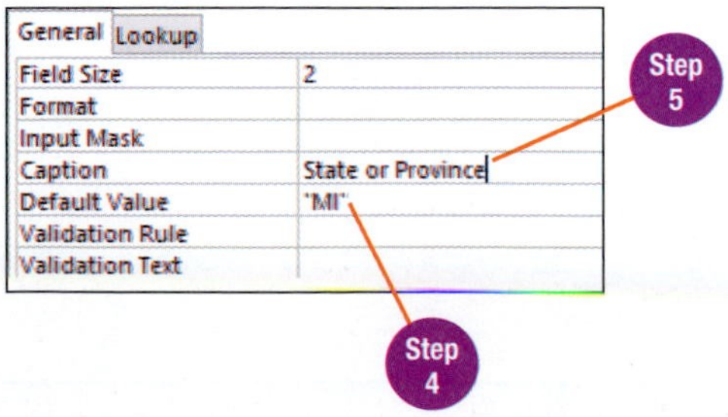

6. Click in the *StudentID* field name to select the field, click in the *Caption* property box, type Student ID, and then press Enter.

App Tip

Options in the Field Properties pane vary by the field data type. For example, a Date & Time field does not have the Field Size property.

App Tip

Adding an entry to the Default Value property not only saves time when a new record is added to the table, it also makes sure a field value is entered consistently and with correct spelling.

7 Add the following caption properties by completing a step similar to Step 6.

Field Name	Caption
LName	Last Name
FName	First Name
Street	Street Address
ZIPOrPC	ZIP or Postal Code
Phone	Telephone
DirectDeposit	Direct Deposit
Email	Email Address

8 Save the table.

9 Click the top part of the View button in the Views group to switch to Datasheet view.

10 Double-click the right column boundary of column headings that are not entirely visible to best fit the column widths.

Notice that *MI* appears in the *State or Province* column by default.

11 Type your name and a fictitious student ID and address into a new record in the datasheet. If necessary, adjust column widths to show all data in all columns.

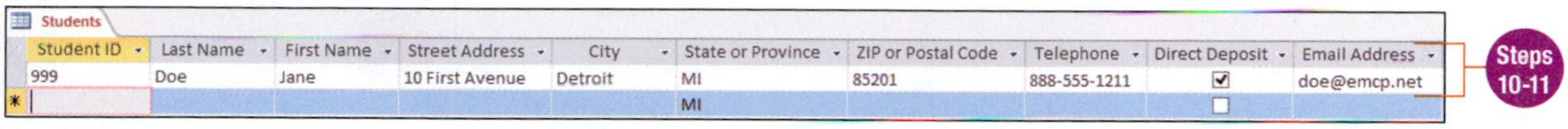

12 Close the table, saving the changes to the table layout. Leave the database open for the next topic.

Quick Steps

Modify a Field Property

1. Open table in Design view.
2. Click in field name in top half of work area.
3. Click or select current value in field property box.
4. Type or select option from drop-down list.
5. Save table.

Alternative Method — Modifying Field Properties Using a Datasheet

Field properties can also be changed for a table open in Datasheet view. Buttons in the Properties group on the Table Tools Fields tab can be used to enter a caption, default value, or field size. Modify or apply format, data validation, or required properties (see Beyond Basics) with buttons in the Formatting and Field Validation groups on the Table Tools Fields tab.

Beyond Basics — Formatting and Data Validation Field Properties

There are other properties that are often changed for a field:

- *Format.* Modifies the display of the field value. For example, a date can be formatted to display as a long date or a medium date.
- *Validation.* Use a validation rule to enter an expression that is tested as each new field value is typed into a record. For example, the expression *>=5* in the *SaleAmount* field would ensure no amounts less than $5.00 are entered.
- *Required.* Select *Yes* to ensure that the field is not left blank in a new record. For example, a ZIP or Postal Code field should not be left blank.

13.6 Creating a Lookup List

Skills

Create a lookup list for a field

Tutorial

Creating a Lookup Field

A **lookup list** is a drop-down list of field values that appears when a field is made active while new records are added in a datasheet or form. The list entries can be a fixed list or field values from another table can be shown in the list. A lookup list has many advantages, including consistency, accuracy, and efficiency when adding data in new records. Access provides the **Lookup Wizard** to assist with creating a lookup list's field properties by choosing options and typing values using dialog boxes.

1. With the **UsedBooks-YourName** database open, right-click the Books table name in the Navigation pane and then click *Design View* at the shortcut menu.
2. Click in the *Condition* field name to select the field.
3. Click the *Data Type* list box arrow and then click *Lookup Wizard* at the drop-down list.

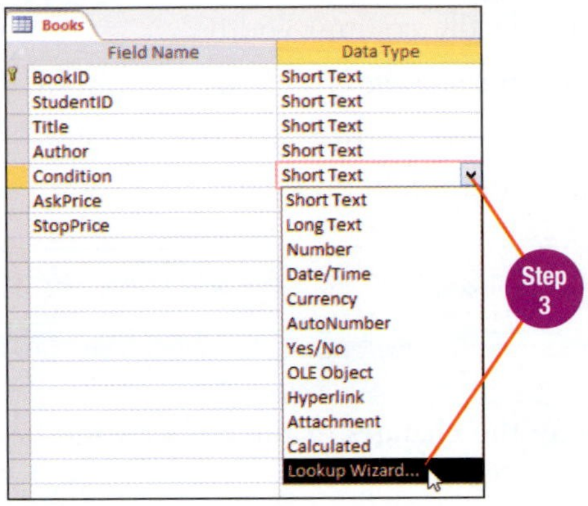

4. Click *I will type in the values that I want.* at the first Lookup Wizard dialog box and then click Next.
5. Click in the first blank row below *Col1* at the second Lookup Wizard dialog box and then type Excellent - No wear or markings.
6. Drag the right column boundary approximately two inches to the right to increase the column width.
7. Click in the second row and then type Very Good - Minor wear to cover.
8. Type the remaining entries in the list as shown in the image at right.
9. Click Next.

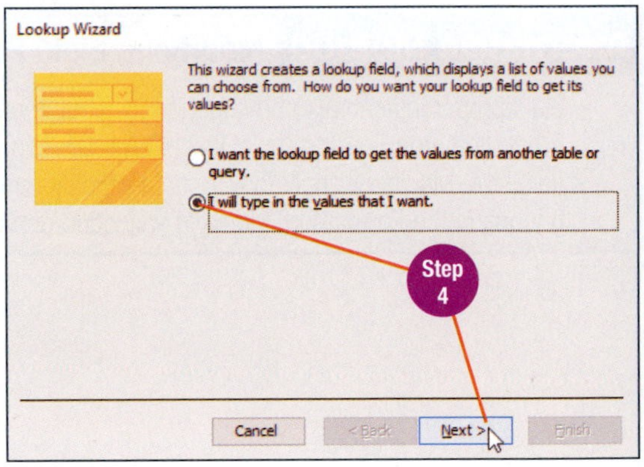

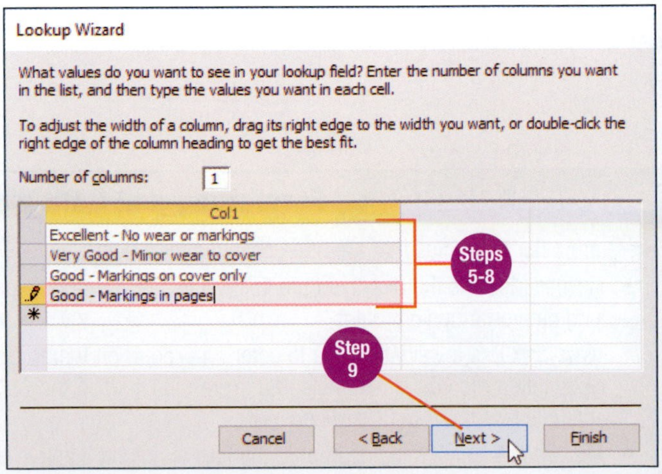

App Tip

You can also use the Tab or Down Arrow key to move to the next row in the column.

Oops!

Pressed Enter by mistake? Click the Back button to return to the list entries.

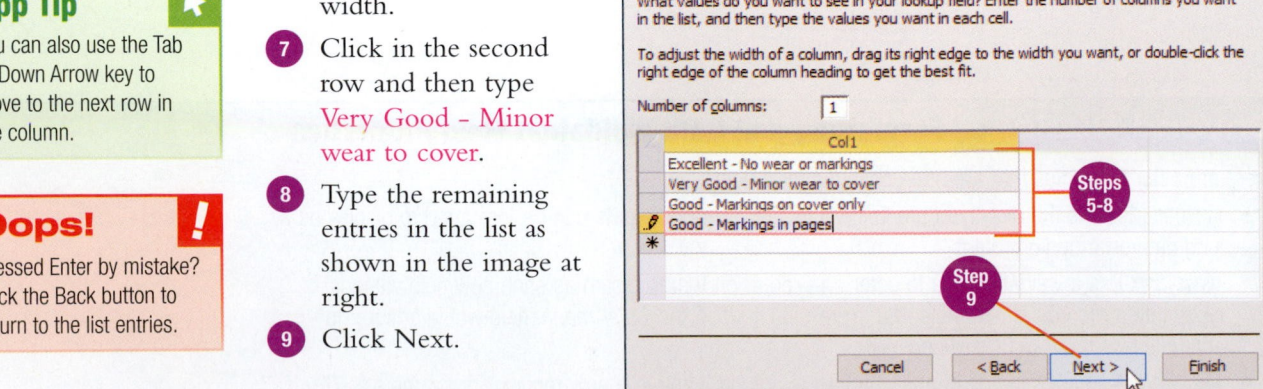

10 Click Finish at the last Lookup Wizard dialog box.

11 Click the Lookup tab in the Field Properties pane.

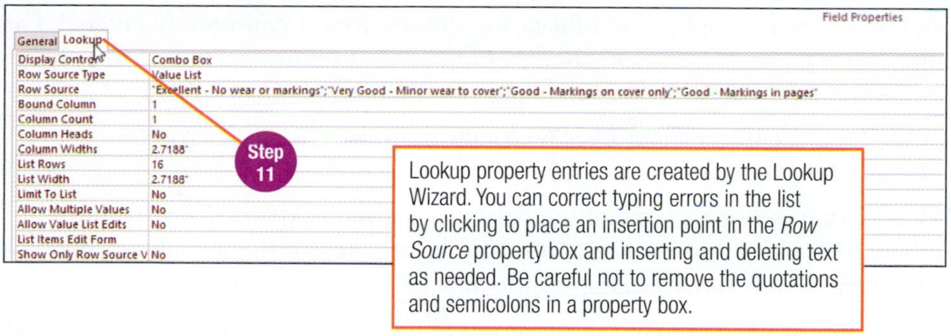

12 Save the table and then switch to Datasheet view.

13 Enter the following record as shown in the image below with the fictitious ID you created for yourself in the *StudentID* column. At the *Condition* field, click the down-pointing arrow that appears and then click *Good - Markings on cover only* at the drop-down list.

14 Adjust column widths as needed to show all data in each column.

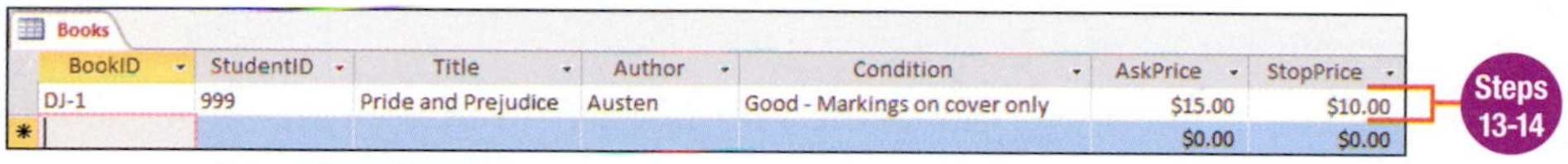
Books
BookID
StudentID
Title
Author
Condition
AskPrice
StopPrice
DJ-1
999
Pride and Prejudice
Austen
Good - Markings on cover only
$15.00
$10.00
$0.00
$0.00
Steps 13-14

15 Close the table, saving the changes to the table layout.

16 Close the database.

App Tip

You can limit field values to only those items in the list by changing the *Limit To List* property to *Yes*.

Quick Steps

Create a Lookup List

1. Open table in Design view.
2. Click *Data Type* list arrow for field.
3. Click *Lookup Wizard.*
4. Click *I will type in the values that I want.*
5. Click Next.
6. Type list entries in *Col1* column.
7. Adjust column width.
8. Click Next.
9. Click Finish.
10. Save table.

View

Model Answer

Compare your completed file with the model answer.

Beyond Basics

Creating a Lookup List with Field Values in Another Table

To create a lookup list in which the entries are field values from a field in another table, proceed through the dialog boxes in the Lookup Wizard as follows:

1. Select *I want the lookup field to get the values from another table or query.*
2. Select the table or query name that contains the field values you want to use in the list.
3. Move the fields you want displayed in the drop-down list from the Available Fields list box to the Selected Fields list box.
4. Select a field to sort the list entries or leave empty for an unsorted list.
5. Adjust column widths as needed and/or uncheck *Hide key column.*
6. Select the field that contains the field value you want to store if more than one field was chosen at Step 3.

13.7 Displaying and Editing a Relationship

Skills

Identify a one-to-one relationship

Enforce referential integrity

Identify a one-to-many relationship

Tutorials

Creating a One-to-One Relationship

Creating a One-to-Many Relationship

Creating a Relationship Report

A relationship allows you to create queries, forms, or reports with fields from two tables by connecting the two tables on a common field. Joining two tables in a relationship prevents duplication of data and ensures data is consistently entered. For example, an ID, name, or title of a book can be looked up in one table rather than repeating the information in another table.

1. Open the database named ***UsedTextbooks*** from the Ch13 folder in Student_Data_Files.
2. Use Save As to save a copy of the database as **UsedTextbooks-YourName** in the Ch13 folder in CompletedTopicsbyChapter. Accept the default options *Save Database As* and *Access Database* at the Save As backstage area.
3. Click the Enable Content button in the SECURITY WARNING message bar and close the SAVE CHANGES message bar if the message bar appears.

This file is similar to the database you have been working on in this chapter but with the Books table modified, additional lookup lists, and with 10 records added to each table.

4. Open the Books table, review the datasheet, and then close the table.
5. Open the Sales table, review the datasheet, and then close the table.
6. Open the Students table and then change *Doe* in the last record of the *Last Name* field to your last name.
7. Change *Jane* in the last record of the *First Name* field to your first name and then close the table.
8. Click the Database Tools tab and then click the Relationships button in the Relationships group.

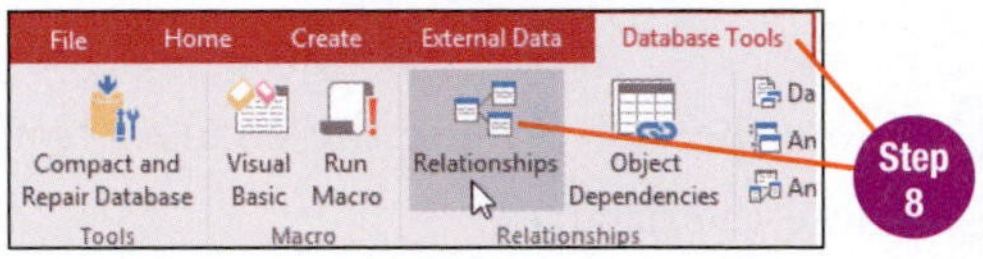

A field list box for each table is located in the Relationships window. A black join line connecting two table field list boxes indicates a relationship. Observe that each join line connects the tables on a common field name.

9. Click to select the black join line that connects the Books table field list box to the Sales table field list box, and then click the Edit Relationships button in the Tools group on the Relationship Tools Design tab.

In the Edit Relationships dialog box that appears, *One-To-One* is shown in the *Relationship Type* section. A **one-to-one relationship** means that the two tables are joined on the primary key in each table. (*BookID* displays a key next to the field name in each table field list box.) In this type of relationship, only one record can exist for the same *BookID* in each table.

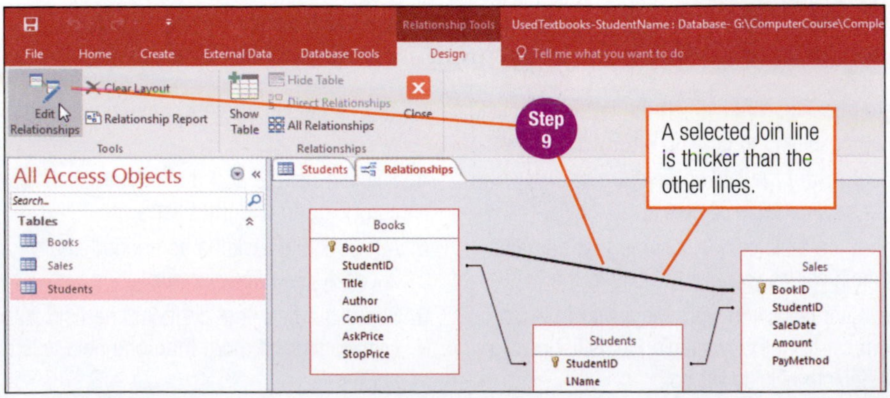

App Tip

When you create a lookup list that looks up field values from a field in another table, Access automatically creates a relationship between the two tables if one does not exist.

App Tip

Delete a relationship at the Relationships window by clicking to select the black join line between the table field list boxes and then pressing the Delete key.

10 Click to insert a check mark in the *Enforce Referential Integrity* check box and then click OK.

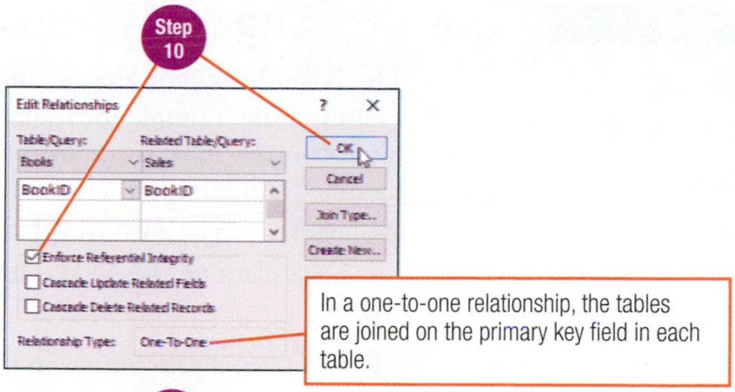

Turning on **Enforce Referential Integrity** means that a record in Books is entered first before a record with a matching *BookID* is entered in Sales. Books is the left table name below *Table /Query*, and Sales is the right table name below *Related Table/Query*. The table below *Table /Query* is the one for which referential integrity is applied—the table in which new records are entered first. The table shown at the left is also referred to as the **primary table** (the table in which the joined field is the primary key and in which new records should be entered first).

11 Click to select the black join line that connects the Books table field list box to the Students table field list box and then click the Edit Relationships button.

12 Click to insert a check mark in the *Enforce Referential Integrity* check box and then click OK.

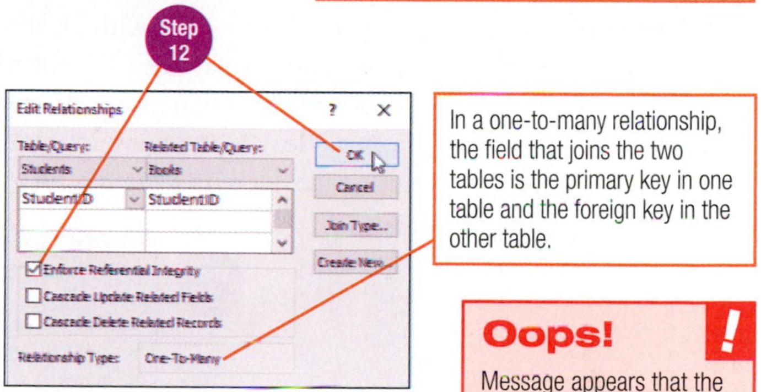

A **one-to-many relationship** occurs when the common field used to join the two tables is the primary key in only one table (the primary table). *One* student can have *many* textbooks for sale. In this instance, a record must first be entered into Students (primary table) before a record with a matching student ID can be entered into Books (related table). A field added to a related table that is not a primary key and is included for the purpose of creating a relationship is called a **foreign key**.

13 Click the Close button in the Relationships group. Click Yes if prompted to save changes to the layout of the relationships and leave the database open for the next topic.

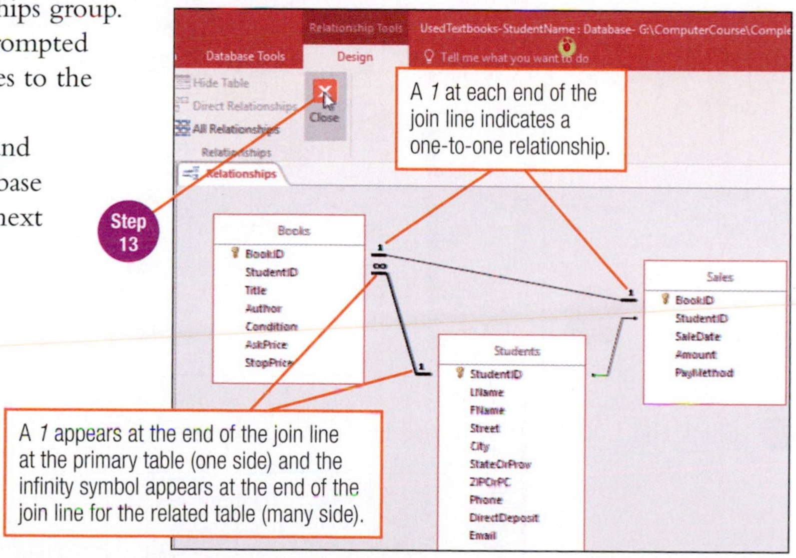

Oops!

Message appears that the database engine could not lock table? This happens when the Students table is currently open. Click Cancel, close the Students table and then try Step 12 again.

Quick Steps

Display Relationships

1. Click Database Tools tab.
2. Click Relationships button.

Enforce Referential Integrity

1. Display Relationships.
2. Click to select black join line.
3. Click Edit Relationships button.
4. Click *Enforce Referential Integrity* check box.
5. Click OK.

App Tip

A one-to-many relationship is the most common type of relationship in databases.

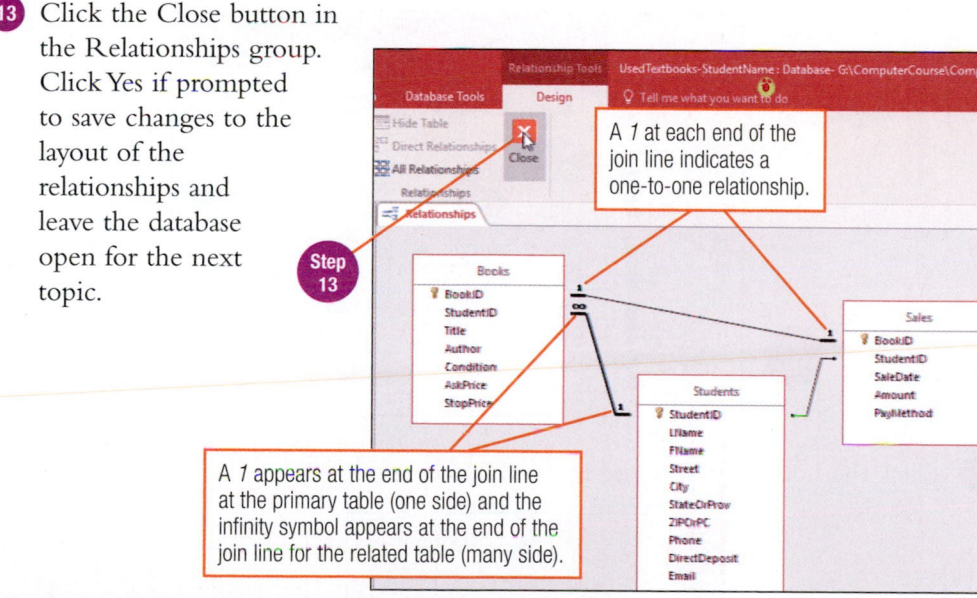

Beyond Basics Creating Relationships

To create a new relationship, open the Relationships window and then drag the common field name from the primary table field list box to the related table field list box. Always drag the field name starting from the primary table. Use the Show Table button in the Relationships group if you need to add a table to the Relationships window in order to create a relationship.

13.8 Creating and Editing a Form

Skills

Create a form

Apply a theme

Add and format a picture on a form

Format the form title

Tutorials

Formatting Table Data

Managing Control Objects in a Form

Applying Conditional Formatting to a Form

Creating a Form Using the Form Button

The Forms group on the Create tab includes buttons to create forms ranging from a tool to create a simple form that adds all the fields in the selected table, to tools for more complex forms that work with multiple tables. Once created, a form can be modified using buttons on the Form Layout Tools Design, Arrange, and Format tabs.

1. With the **UsedTextbooks-YourName** database open, click to select the Books table name in the Navigation pane if Books is not already selected.
2. Click the Create tab.
3. Click the Form button in the Forms group.

A form is created with all the fields in the selected table arranged in a vertical layout and displayed in Layout view. **Layout view** is the view in which you edit a report or form structure and appearance using buttons on the Form Layout Tools tabs. **Form view** is the view in which data is viewed, entered, and updated in the form and is the view in which a form is opened from the Navigation pane.

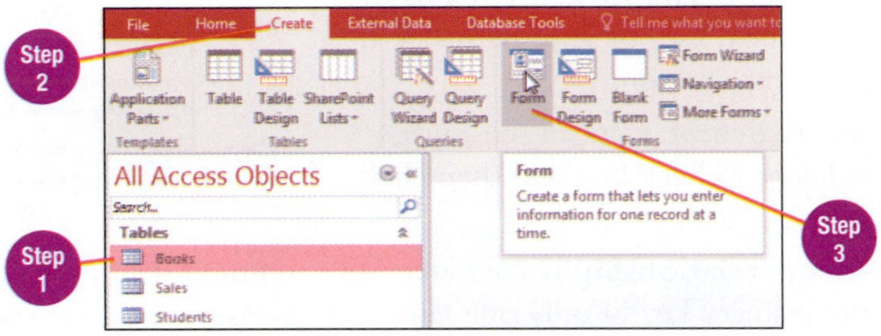

App Tip

Buttons to switch between views are at the right end of the Status bar.

4. Click the Form Layout Tools Design tab if the tab is not already active and then click the Themes button in the Themes group.
5. Click *Slice* in the *Office* section.

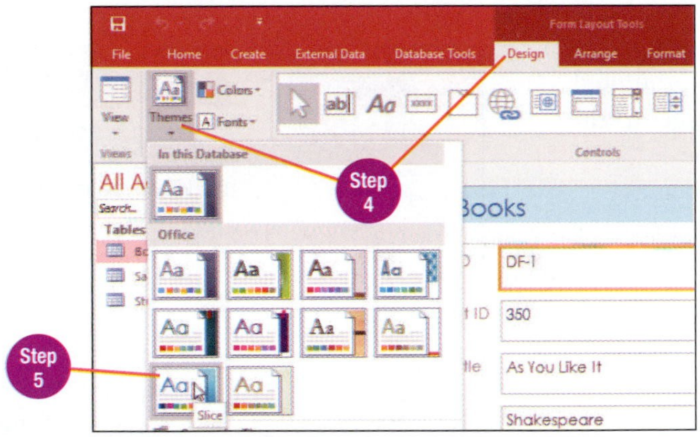

6. Click the Logo button in the Header/Footer group.

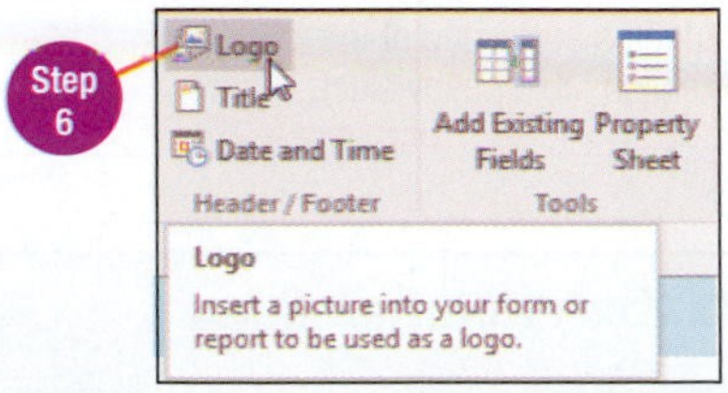

7 At the Insert Picture dialog box, navigate to the Ch13 folder in Student_Data_Files and then double-click the file named ***Textbooks***.

The picture is inserted into the selected logo **control object** near the top left of the form. A control object is a rectangular content placeholder in a form or report. Each control object can be selected and edited to modify the appearance of the content.

8 With the logo control object still selected, click the Property Sheet button in the Tools group.

9 Click the Format tab in the Property Sheet task pane, click in the *Size Mode* property box, click the down-pointing arrow that appears, and then click *Zoom*.

10 Select the current value in the *Width* property box and then type 1.75.

11 Select the current value in the *Height* property box and then type 1.25.

12 Close the Property Sheet task pane.

13 Click the *Books* title to select the control object.

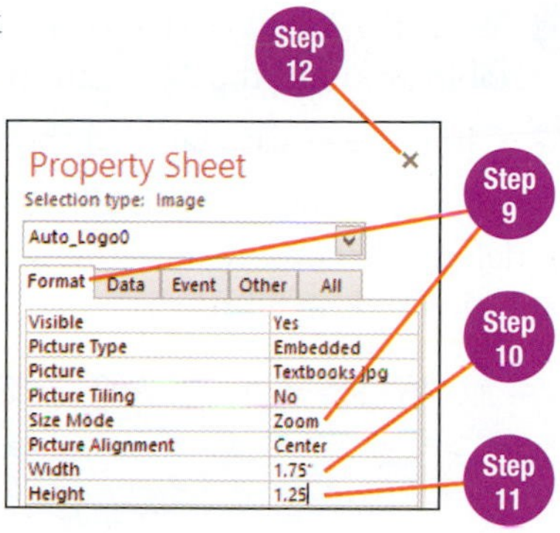

An orange border around the control object indicates the object is selected.

14 Click the Form Layout Tools Format tab.

15 Click the Font Size option box arrow and then click *48* at the drop-down list.

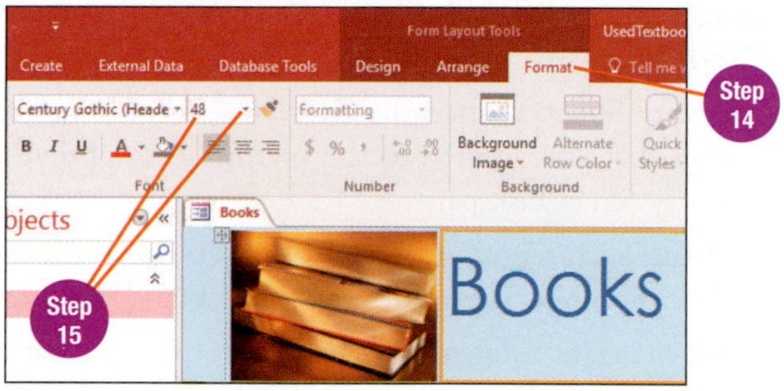

16 Click the Save button on the Quick Access Toolbar and then click OK at the Save As dialog box to accept the default form name *Books*.

17 Close the Books form.

18 Double-click the Books form name in the Navigation pane to reopen the form, scroll through a few records, and then close the form. Leave the database open for the next topic.

App Tip

Control objects are placeholders for pictures, text, field names, and field values.

App Tip

The *Zoom* option for the *Size Mode* property fits the picture to the control object size maintaining proportions.

App Tip

You can also drag the orange border on a selected control object to resize the object.

Quick Steps

Create a Form

1. Click to select table or query name in Navigation pane.
2. Click Create tab.
3. Click Form button.
4. Modify form as required.
5. Click Save button.
6. Type form name.
7. Click OK.

Beyond Basics — Creating a Form Using the Form Wizard

Use the Form Wizard button in the Forms group on the Create tab to create a form that uses fields from one or more tables. With the wizard, you also have control over the fields from each table that are included on the form and the form layout. Fields from related tables can be arranged in a columnar, tabular, datasheet, or justified layout.

13.9 Creating, Editing, and Viewing a Report

Skills

Create a report

Resize control objects

Tutorials

Creating a Report

Creating a Report Using the Report Wizard

Formatting a Report

Managing Control Objects in a Report

Customizing a Report in Print Preview

Create a report using techniques similar to those used to create a form. The Reports group on the Create tab has a Report tool similar to the Form tool. Other buttons in the Reports group include options to design a report from a blank page, create a report using the Report Wizard, or generate mailing labels using the Label Wizard. Modify a report with buttons in the Report Layout Tools tabs. Change the page layout options for printing purposes with buttons in the Report Layout Tools Page Setup tab.

1. With the **UsedTextbooks-YourName** database open, click to select the Sales table name in the Navigation pane.
2. Click the Create tab and then click the Report button in the Reports group.

A report is created with all the fields in the Sales table arranged in a tabular layout. By default, Access includes the current date and time, page numbering, and totals for numeric fields in all reports.

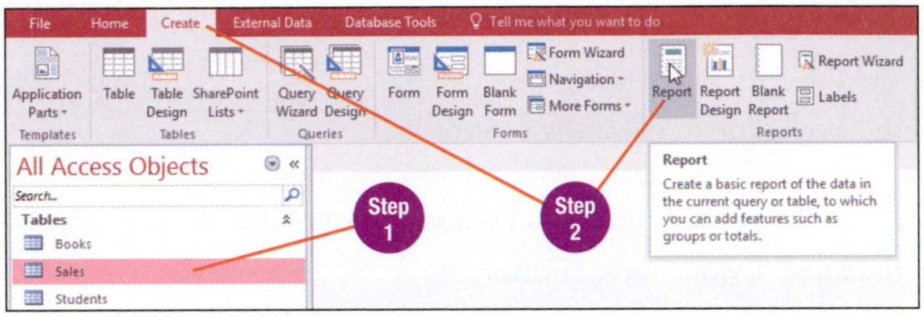

App Tip

Reports use the same theme as forms so that all objects have a consistent look.

Oops!

Textbooks image not shown? Access defaults to the last folder used at the Insert Picture dialog box. If necessary, navigate to the Ch13 folder in Student_Data_Files.

App Tip

A control object is filled with pound symbols (#) if the object is made too narrow for the content to be fully displayed. In that case, increase the width of the control object until the content redisplays.

3. Click the Logo button in the Header/Footer group and then double-click the file named ***Textbooks***.
4. Open the Property Sheet, change the *Size Mode*, *Width*, and *Height* properties to the same settings that you applied to the picture in the previous topic, and then close the Property Sheet task pane.
5. Click to select the *Sales* report title control object, click the Report Layout Tools Format tab, click the Font Size option box arrow, and then click *48*.
6. Click to select the current date control object near the top right of the report.
7. Drag the right border of the control object to the left until the control ends just left of the vertical dashed line that extends the height of the report. If pound symbols display after resizing the control, drag the left border to the left until the date displays again.

The vertical dashed line indicates a page break. Resize control objects so that all objects are to the left of the vertical dashed line to fit on one page.

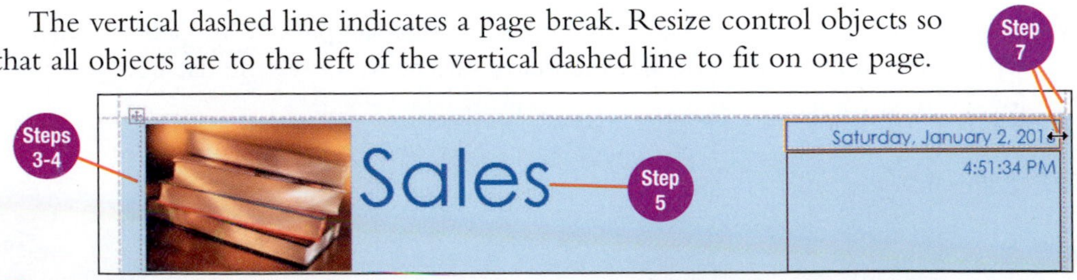

8. Click to select the *Book ID* column heading control object.
9. Drag the right border of the control object left approximately one-half inch to resize the object to the approximate width shown in the image at right.

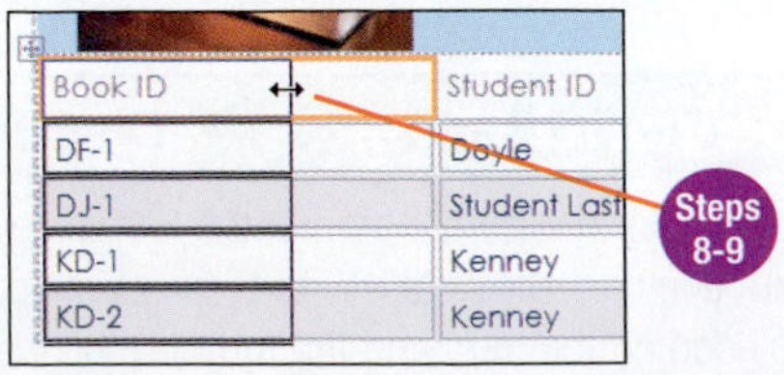

Notice that resizing a column heading control object resizes the entire column.

10 Click to select the *Page 1 of 1* control object and resize the control until the right border is just left of the vertical dashed line.

11 Click to select the control object with the total at the bottom of the *Sale Amount* column and then drag the bottom border of the control down until the value is entirely visible within the object.

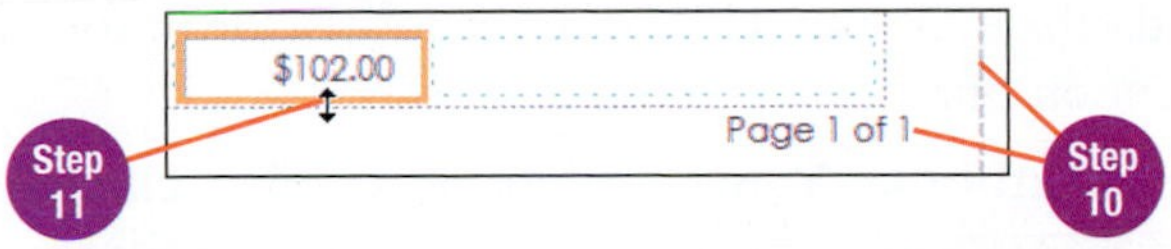

12 Click the Print Preview button near the right end of the Status bar. Compare your report with the one shown in Figure 13.2. If necessary, switch to Layout view, resize control objects, and then switch back to Print Preview.

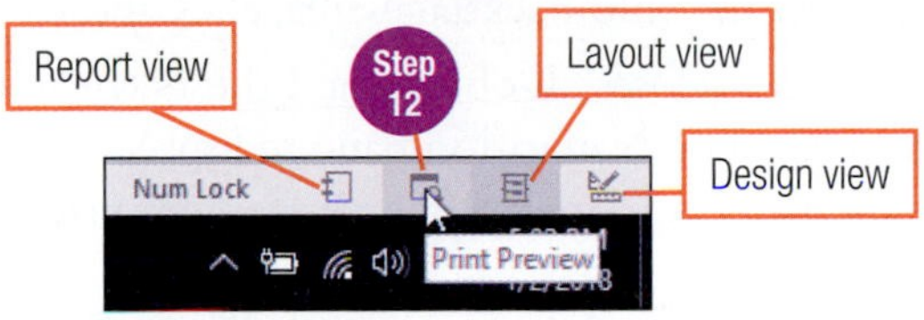

13 Click the Close Print Preview button in the Close Preview group.

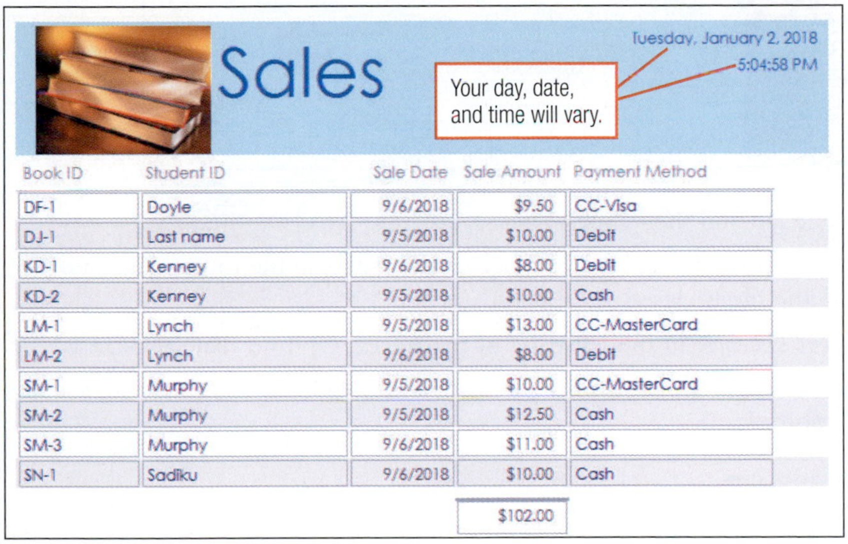

Book ID	Student ID	Sale Date	Sale Amount	Payment Method
DF-1	Doyle	9/6/2018	$9.50	CC-Visa
DJ-1	Last name	9/5/2018	$10.00	Debit
KD-1	Kenney	9/6/2018	$8.00	Debit
KD-2	Kenney	9/5/2018	$10.00	Cash
LM-1	Lynch	9/5/2018	$13.00	CC-MasterCard
LM-2	Lynch	9/6/2018	$8.00	Debit
SM-1	Murphy	9/5/2018	$10.00	CC-MasterCard
SM-2	Murphy	9/5/2018	$12.50	Cash
SM-3	Murphy	9/6/2018	$11.00	Cash
SN-1	Sadiku	9/6/2018	$10.00	Cash
			$102.00	

Figure 13.2

Shown is the Sales report for Topic 13.9.

14 Click the Report View button near the right end of the Status bar.

Report view is the view in which a report opens from the Navigation pane. Report view is used to view data on the screen instead of printing a hard copy. A report cannot be edited in Report view.

15 Close the Sales report, saving changes to the report design and accepting the default report name of *Sales*. Leave the database open for the next topic.

Oops! !

Having difficulty resizing controls using touch? Open the Property Sheet for a selected control and change the *Width* and *Height* values. Use *.25* for the *Height* of the column total control.

Quick Steps

Create a Report

1. Click to select table or query name in Navigation pane.
2. Click Create tab.
3. Click Report button.
4. Modify report as required.
5. Click Save button.
6. Type report name.
7. Click OK.

App Tip

Select the control object for a column heading to change color or alignment options on the Report Layout Tools Format tab to make column headings stand out from the report. You can also select the control objects for the data below the column heading and change format options so that the data is formatted differently than the headings. For example, column data can be centered below a long column heading.

Beyond Basics Grouping and Sorting a Report

The Group & Sort button in the Grouping & Totals group on the Report Layout Tools Design tab toggles on and off the Group, Sort, and Total pane at the bottom of the work area. Turn on the pane and use the Add a group and Add a sort buttons to change the arrangement of records in the report.

13.10 Compacting, Repairing, and Backing Up a Database

Skills

Compact and repair a database

Create a backup copy of a database

A database file becomes larger and fragmented over time as new records are added, edited, and deleted. The file size for the database may become larger than is necessary if the space previously used by records that have since been deleted is not compacted. Access provides a **Compact & Repair Database button** that compresses unused space reducing the file size. The compacting process eliminates unused space in the file. Backing up a database file should be done regularly for historical record keeping and data loss prevention purposes.

1 With the **UsedTextbooks-YourName** database open, click the File tab.

2 At the Info backstage area, click the Compact & Repair Database button.

Access closes all objects and the Navigation pane during a compact and repair routine. The Navigation pane redisplays when the compacting and repairing is complete. For larger database files, compacting and repairing may take a few moments to process.

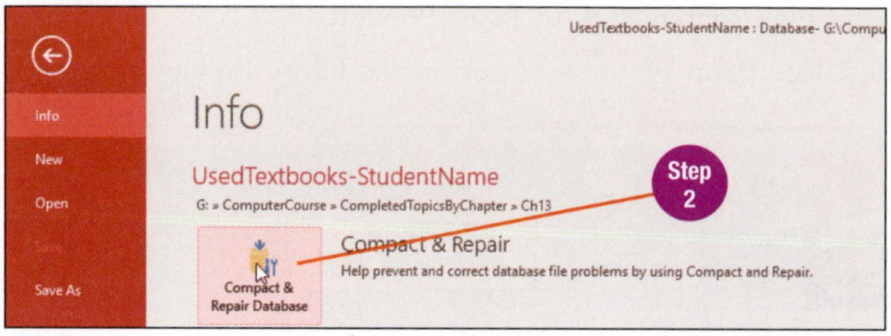

App Tip

If a database is shared, make sure no one else is using the database before starting a compact and repair operation.

3 Click the File tab and then click *Options*.

At the Access Options dialog box, you can set the database file to compact and repair each time the file is closed.

4 Click *Current Database* in the left pane of the Access Options dialog box.

5 Click to insert a check mark in the *Compact on Close* check box in the *Application Options* section.

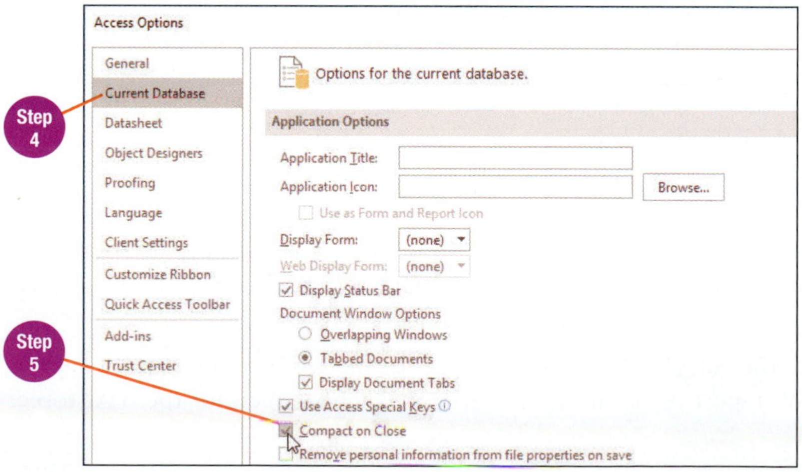

6 Click OK to close the Access Options dialog box.

7 Click OK at the message box that says the database must be closed and reopened for the option to take effect.

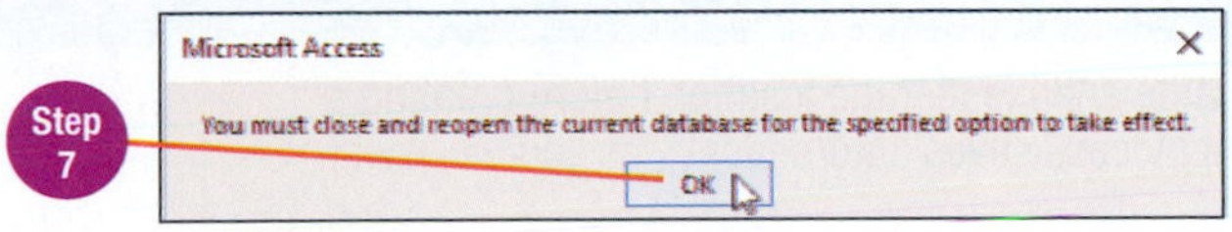

8 Click the File tab and then click *Save As*.

9 At the Save As backstage area, click *Back Up Database* in the *Advanced* section of the Save Database As panel.

10 Click the Save As button.

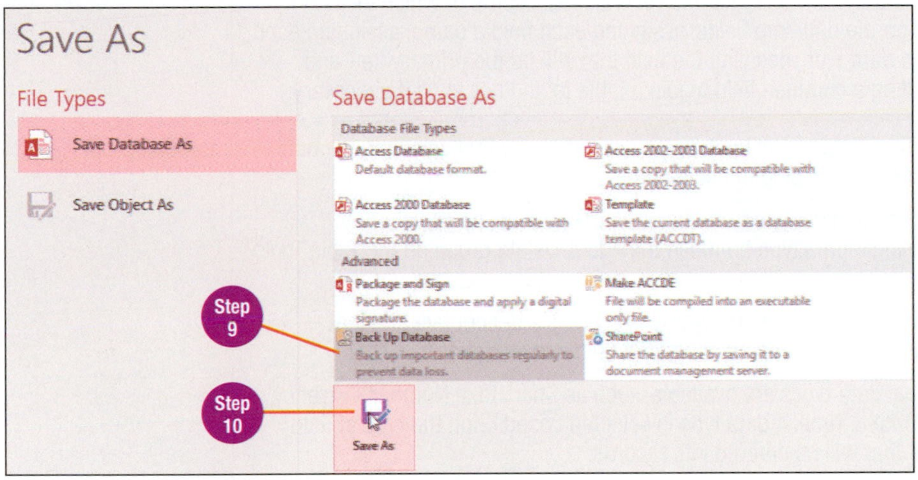

11 Click the Save button at the Save As dialog box.

By default, the backup copy of the database is saved in the same folder as the current database and the file name is the same database file name with the current date added after an underscore at the end of the name, for example, UsedTextbooks-YourName_*currentdate*.

12 Close the database.

Quick Steps

Compact and Repair a Database
1. Click File tab.
2. Click Compact & Repair Database button.

Turn on Compact on Close
1. Click File tab.
2. Click *Options*.
3. Click *Current Database*.
4. Click *Compact on Close*.
5. Click OK twice.

Back Up a Database
1. Click File tab.
2. Click *Save As*.
3. Click *Back Up Database*.
4. Click Save As button.
5. Click Save.

App Tip

A backup should normally be saved on another storage medium. At the Save As dialog box, consider navigating to another drive or copy the backup file to another storage medium afterward.

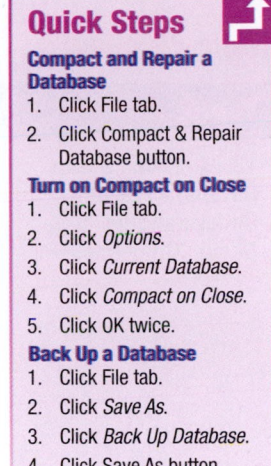

Beyond Basics — Encrypting a Database with a Password

Assign a password to a database to prevent unauthorized access to confidential data stored in a database. A database has to be opened in exclusive mode to assign a password. To do this, close the current database and then display the Open dialog box. Navigate to the location of the database, select the database file, and then use the down-pointing arrow on the Open button to choose *Open Exclusive*. Enable content and then display the Info backstage area. Click the Encrypt with Password button and then type the password twice in the Set Database Password dialog box.

Topics Review

Topic	Key Concepts	Key Terms
13.1 Creating a New Database File and Understanding Table Design Guidelines	Access requires the name and file storage location before creating a new database because Access saves automatically as you work with data. To create a new database file, choose *Blank desktop database* at the Access Start screen, type the file name, and browse to the desired drive and/or folder. When a new database is created, Access displays a blank table datasheet. Planning a new table involves several steps, some of which include dividing the data into fields, assigning each field a name, assigning each field a data type, deciding the field that will be the primary key, and including a common field to join a table to another table if necessary.	
13.2 Creating a New Table Using a Datasheet	In a blank table datasheet, begin a new field by first selecting the data type and then typing the field name. Choose the data type from the *Click to Add* drop-down list or by choosing a data type button in the Add & Delete group on the Table Tools Fields tab. An entry in the Caption property is used as a descriptive title that becomes the column heading for a field in a datasheet. Several data types are available, such as Short Text, Number, Currency, and Date & Time. A data type is selected based upon the type of field value that will be entered into records. Save a table by clicking the Save button on the Quick Access Toolbar and then entering a name for the table.	Caption property
13.3 Creating a New Table Using Design View and Assigning a Primary Key	In Design view, a new table is created by defining fields in rows in the top half of the work area. Type a field name in the first row in the *Field Name* column and then specify the data type using the data type drop-down list. An optional description can be added for a field with additional information about the purpose of the field or with instructions on what to type into the field. Once the fields are defined, assign the primary key by placing an insertion point anywhere within the field name and then clicking the Primary Key button in the Tools group on the Table Tools Design tab.	
13.4 Adding Fields to an Existing Table	Open a table and use the *Click to Add* column to add a new field to the end of an existing table datasheet. Select a column in a datasheet and use the buttons in the Add & Delete group on the Table Tools Fields tab to add a new field to the right of the selected field.	

continued…

Topic	Key Concepts	Key Terms
13.5 Modifying Field Properties Using Design View	Each field in a table has a set of associated field properties. A field property is a single characteristic or attribute of a field that customizes, formats, or changes the behavior of the field. The lower half of the Design view window is the Field Properties pane in which properties for a selected field are modified. The Field Size property is used to limit the number of characters that can be entered into a field. The Default Value property is used to specify a field value that is automatically entered in the field in new records. Other field properties that are often modified are the *Format*, *Validation*, and *Required* field properties.	field property Field Properties pane
13.6 Creating a Lookup List	A lookup list is a drop-down list of items that displays when a field is made active in a datasheet or form. Items in the lookup list can be predefined or extracted from one or more fields in another table. The Lookup Wizard presents a series of dialog boxes to help create the field properties for a lookup list field. Create a custom list of predefined entries by choosing *I will type in the values that I want.* at the first Lookup Wizard dialog box. Type the list entries in the *Col1* column and adjust the column width at the second Lookup Wizard dialog box. Click Finish at the third dialog box.	lookup list Lookup Wizard
13.7 Displaying and Editing a Relationship	A relationship is when two tables are joined together on a common field. Black join lines connecting a common field between two table field list boxes indicates a relationship has been created. A one-to-one relationship means that the two tables are joined on the primary key in each table. *Enforce Referential Integrity* causes Access to check that new records are entered into the primary table first before records with a matching field value can be entered into the related table. A primary table is the table in which the common field is the primary key and into which new records are entered first. The primary table name is the table name at the left below *Table/Query* in the Edit Relationships dialog box. In a one-to-many relationship, the common field used to join the tables is the primary key in only one table (the primary table). A field added to a table that is not a primary key and is added for the purpose of creating a relationship is called a *foreign key*.	one-to-one relationship Enforce Referential Integrity primary table one-to-many relationship foreign key

continued…

Topic	Key Concepts	Key Terms
13.8 Creating and Editing a Form	The Form button in the Forms group on the Create tab creates a new form with all fields in the selected table or query arranged in a columnar layout. Layout view is the view in which you modify a report or form structure and appearance using buttons in the three Form Layout Tools tabs. Form view is the view in which a form is displayed when opened from the Navigation pane and is used to add, edit, and delete data. The Themes button is used to change the color scheme and fonts for a form. Use the Logo button to choose a picture to display in the Logo control object near the top left of the form. A control object is a rectangular placeholder for content. Each control object can be selected and modified to change the appearance of the control content. Open the Property Sheet task pane to make changes to the appearance of a selected picture. Change the *Size Mode* property of a picture to *Zoom* to fit the content to the object size with the height and width proportions maintained. A control object can be resized by changing the values for the *Width* and *Height* in the Property Sheet task pane.	Layout view Form view control object
13.9 Creating, Editing, and Viewing a Report	The Report tool in the Reports group on the Create tab creates a report with all the fields in the selected table or query in a tabular arrangement. Buttons in the Report Layout Tools Page Setup tab are used to change page layout options for printing purposes. Access creates a current date and time control, a page number control, and a total control for each numeric column in a new report. The vertical dashed line in a report indicates a page break. Resizing a column heading control object resizes the entire column. Report view is the view in which a report is displayed when opened from the Navigation pane and is the view that displays the data in the report.	Report view
13.10 Compacting, Repairing, and Backing Up a Database	The compact and repair process eliminates unused space in the database file. Use the Compact & Repair Database button at the Info backstage area to perform a compact and repair operation. During the compact and repair routine, Access closes all objects and the Navigation pane. Turn on the *Compact on Close* option at the Access Options dialog box with *Current Database* selected to instruct Access to perform a compact and repair operation each time the database is closed. Display the Save As backstage area and choose *Back Up Database* in the *Advanced* section to create a backup copy of the current database. Access adds the current date after an underscore character to the end of the current database file name when a backup is created.	Compact & Repair Database button

Recheck

Recheck your understanding of the topics covered in this chapter.

Workbook

Chapter review and assessment resources are available in the *Workbook* ebook.

Chapter 14

Integrating Word, Excel, PowerPoint, and Access Content

Precheck

Check your understanding of the topics covered in this chapter.

Learning Objectives

14.1 Import Excel worksheet data into a table in Access

14.2 Export an Access query to Excel

14.3 Embed an Excel chart into a Word document

14.4 Embed Excel data into a PowerPoint presentation and edit the embedded data

14.5 Link an Excel chart with a PowerPoint presentation, edit the chart, and update the link

The Microsoft Office suite is designed to easily share and integrate data or objects among the programs. For some tasks, you may have portions of a project distributed across more than one application. For example, you may have a chart in Excel and a list in Access that you want to add into a report in Word. The ability to integrate data from one application to another means that you can use the program that best fits each task and/or the expertise of each person and assemble the portions into a complete product without duplicating individual efforts.

In Chapter 3, you used the Copy and Paste buttons in the Clipboard group to copy text, a picture, and a chart between Word, Excel, and PowerPoint. Copy and paste is the best method for situations when the data to be shared is not large and is not likely to need updating. In this chapter, you will learn other methods for integrating data and objects that include importing, exporting, embedding, and linking.

SNAP If you are a SNAP user, go to your SNAP Assignments page to complete the Precheck, Tutorials, and Recheck.

Data Files

Before beginning this chapter, be sure you have copied the student data files for this course to your storage medium. Steps on downloading and extracting the data files are provided in Chapter 1, Topic 1.8, on pages 22–23.

14.1 Importing Excel Worksheet Data into Access

Skills

Create a table by importing Excel data

Modify imported table design

Tutorials

Importing Data to a New Table

Linking Data to a New Table

A new Access table can be created from data in an Excel worksheet, or Excel data can be appended to the bottom of an existing Access table. Because an Excel worksheet and an Access datasheet use the same column and row structure, the two programs are often used to interchange data. To facilitate the import, the Excel worksheet should be set up like an Access datasheet, with the field names in the first row and with no blank rows or columns within the data. The **Import Spreadsheet Wizard** in Access is used to facilitate the import operation by providing a series of dialog boxes that prompt the user through the steps to create the table or add data to the bottom of an existing datasheet.

1. Start Access 2016 and open the **Parking** database from the Ch14 folder in Student_Data_Files.
2. Use Save As to save a copy of the database as **Parking-YourName** in a new folder *Ch14* within CompletedTopicsByChapter. Accept the default options *Save Database As* and *Access Database* at the Save As backstage area.
3. Click the Enable Content button in the SECURITY WARNING message bar.
4. Click the External Data tab.
5. Click the Excel button in the Import & Link group.

App Tip

In Excel click the Data tab and use buttons in the Get External Data group to import data from other sources into a worksheet. You can import into Excel from an Access table, from a web page, and from a text file.

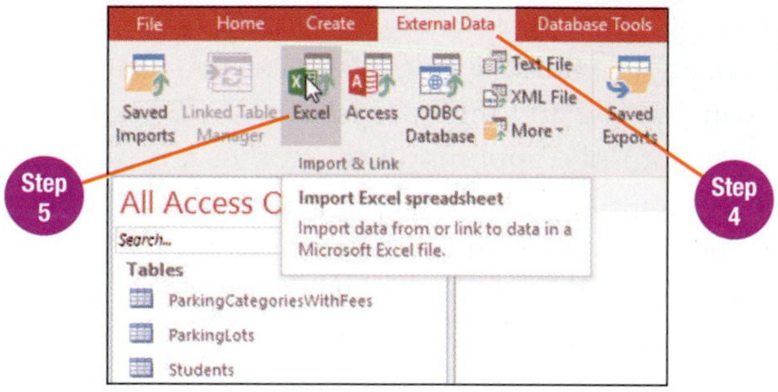

6. Click the Browse button in the Get External Data – Excel Spreadsheet dialog box.
7. Navigate to the Ch14 folder in Student_Data_Files at the File Open dialog box and then double-click ***ParkingRecords***.
8. Click OK to accept the default option *Import the source data into a new table in the current database.*

Use the Append option if the table already exists in the database and you want to add new records from an Excel worksheet to the end of the existing datasheet table.

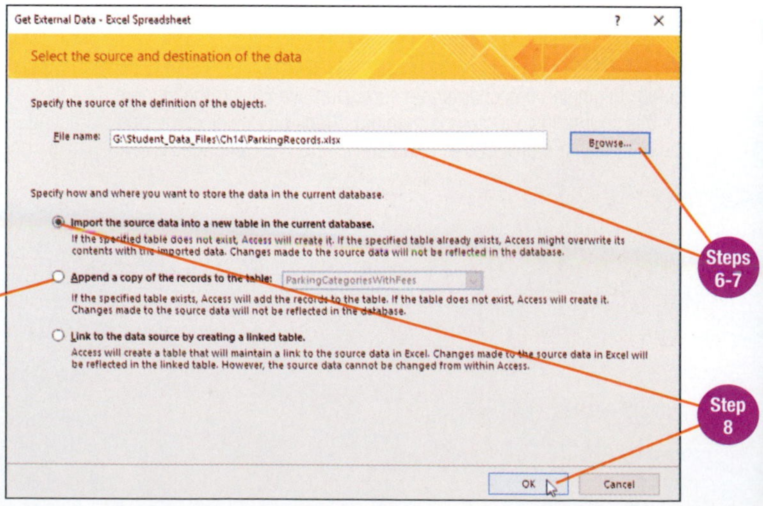

9 At the first Import Spreadsheet Wizard dialog box, Click Next to accept the worksheet labeled *Student Parking Records*.

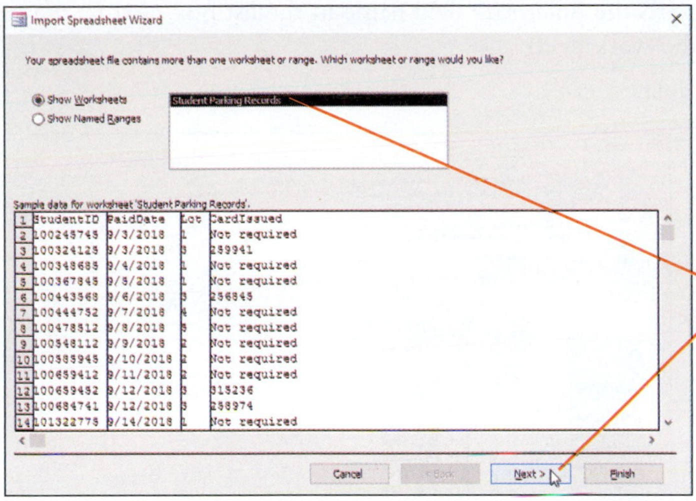

10 At the second Import Spreadsheet Wizard dialog box, click Next with a check mark already inserted in the *First Row Contains Column Headings* check box.

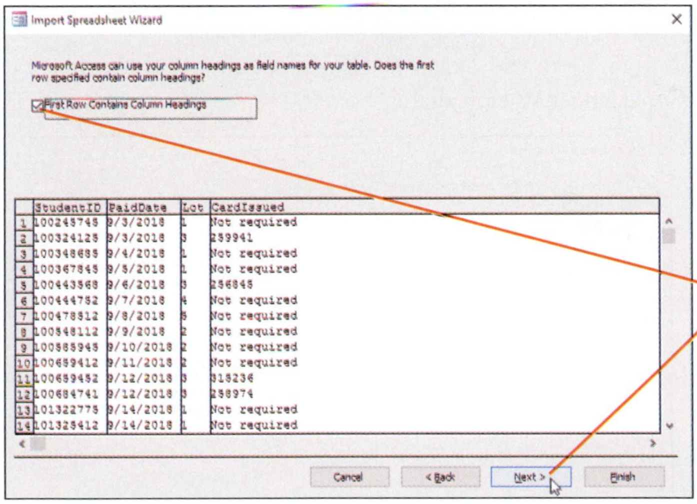

11 At the third Import Spreadsheet Wizard dialog box, click the *PaidDate* column heading and look at the option selected in the *Data Type* list box.

Notice that Access has correctly identified the data as a Date field. At this dialog box, you can review each column and modify the options in the *Field Options* section as needed, or you can elect to make changes in Design view after the import is completed. If a column exists in the Excel worksheet that you do not wish to import into the table, select the column and insert a check mark in the *Do not import field (Skip)* check box.

12 Click Next.

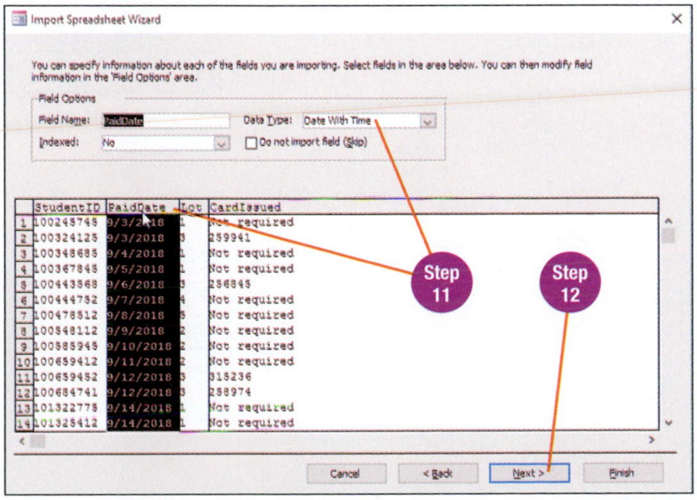

13 At the fourth Import Spreadsheet Wizard dialog box, click *Choose my own primary key*.

Access inserts the *StudentID* field name in the list box next to the option (the first column in the worksheet).

14 Click Next.

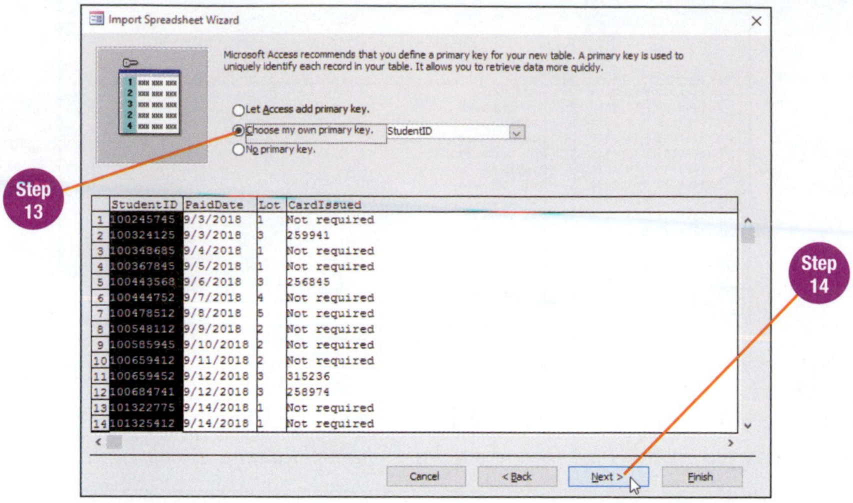

15 Type ParkingSales in the *Import to Table* text box and then click Finish at the last Import Spreadsheet Wizard dialog box.

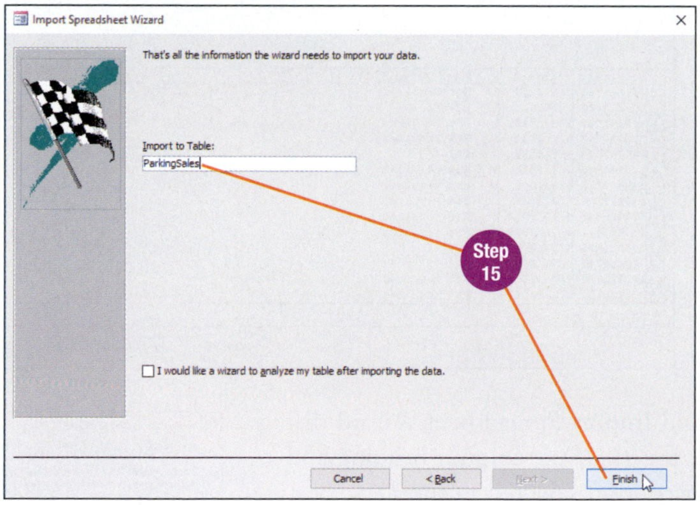

16 Click Close to finish the import without saving the import steps at the Get External Data - Excel Spreadsheet dialog box.

For situations in which you frequently import from Excel to Access, you can save the import specifications so that you can repeat the import later using the same settings.

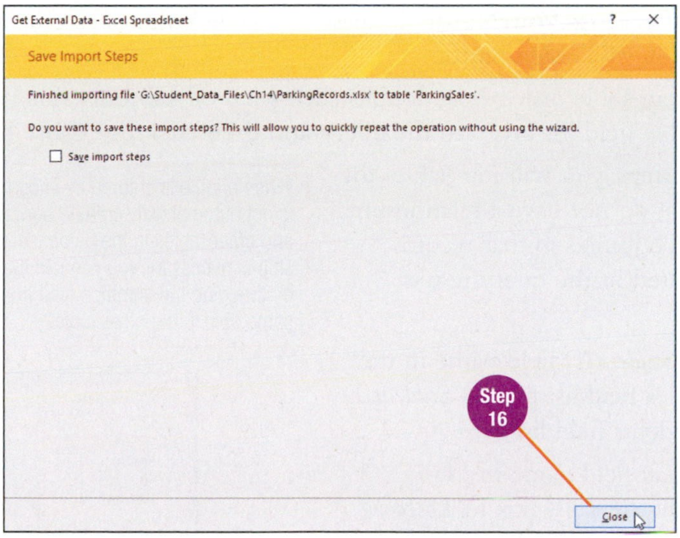

17 Open the ParkingSales table from the Navigation pane and review the datasheet.

18 Switch to Design view and review the field names and data types for the new table.

19 Click the *Data Type* list box arrow for the *Lot* field name and then click *Short Text*.

In the Parking database, the Lot field should be defined as Short Text, because lot numbers are not field values that you would add or subtract.

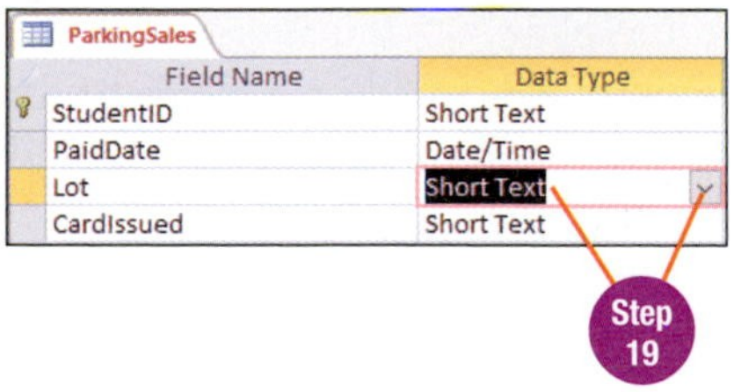

20 Save and then close the table. Leave the database open for the next topic.

Quick Steps

Import Worksheet Data into Access

1. Open destination database.
2. Click External Data tab.
3. Click Excel button in Import & Link group.
4. Click Browse button.
5. Navigate to and double-click Excel file.
6. Click OK.
7. Click Next with worksheet selected.
8. Click Next with *First Row Contains Column Headings* selected.
9. Change *Field Options* for columns if desired and click Next.
10. Choose primary key field and click Next.
11. Type table name and click Finish.
12. Click Close.
13. If necessary, modify table design.

App Tip

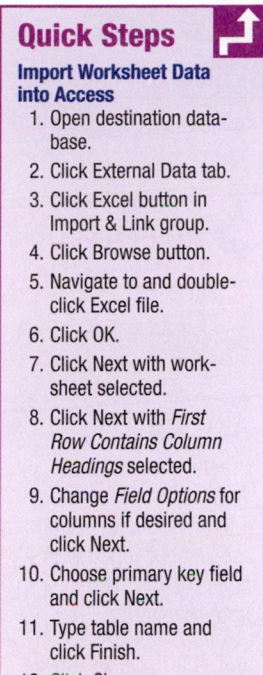

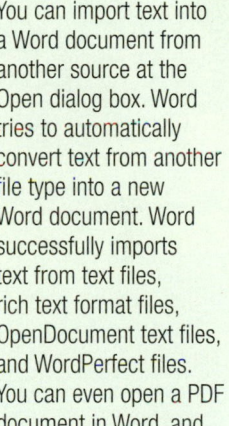

You can import text into a Word document from another source at the Open dialog box. Word tries to automatically convert text from another file type into a new Word document. Word successfully imports text from text files, rich text format files, OpenDocument text files, and WordPerfect files. You can even open a PDF document in Word, and Word converts the PDF file into an editable Word document.

View Model Answer

Compare your completed file with the model answer.

Beyond Basics — Linking an Excel Worksheet to an Access Table

The option *Link to the data source by creating a linked table* at the Get External Data – Excel Spreadsheet dialog box is used when the data that is being imported is likely to be updated within Excel after the import is performed. Access will create a link between the source Excel worksheet and the Access table. Changes made to the Excel data will be automatically reflected in Access. Note that with this option the data cannot be changed from within Access.

14.2 Exporting an Access Query to Excel

Skills

Export an Access query to Excel

Tutorials

Exporting Access Data to Excel

Exporting Access Data to Word

App Tip

Create relationships in the Relationships window if the tables to be joined will be used together in other objects such as a form or report.

Access table data can be exported to use the mathematical analysis tools in Excel. Access creates a copy of the selected table or query data in an Excel worksheet file in the drive and/or folder that you specify. Buttons in the Export group on the External Data tab provide options to send a copy of Access data in a variety of file formats.

1. With the **Parking-YourName** database open, click the Create tab and then click the Query Design button.
2. At the Show Table dialog box, double-click each of the four table names to add all four table field list boxes to the query and then click the Close button.

In the next steps, you will join tables for those tables that do not have a relationship. Tables should be joined so that records are not duplicated in the query results datasheet.

When a table is created by importing, a relationship is not automatically created between the new table and other tables in the database. When a relationship is necessary, you can join the tables in a query by dragging the common field from one table to the same field in the other table.

3. Drag the *StudentID* field name in the ParkingSales field list box to *StudentID* in the Students field list box.
4. Drag the *Lot* field name in the ParkingSales field list box to *LotNo* in the ParkingLots field list box.

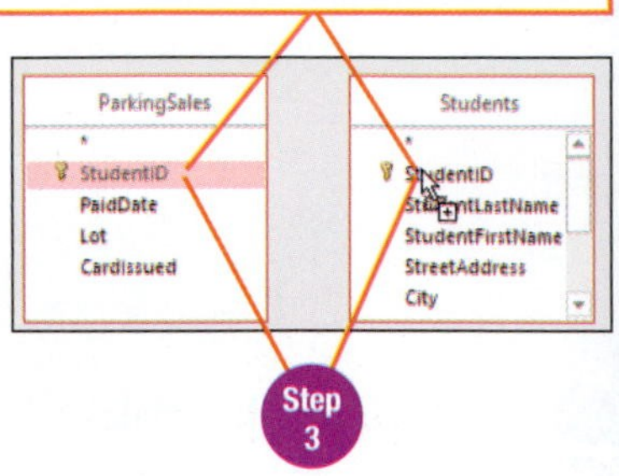

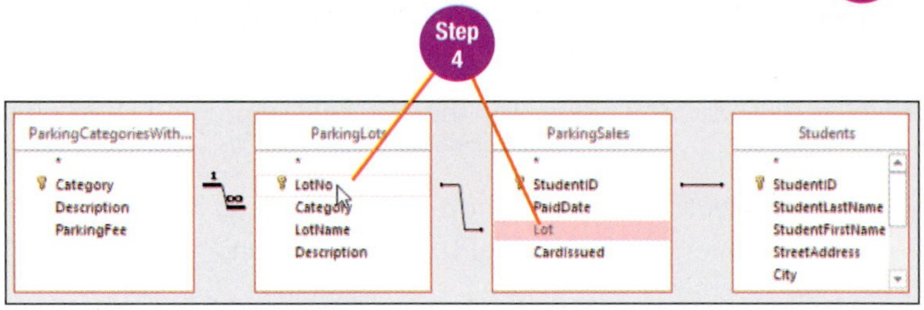

5. Double-click the following fields to add the fields to the query design grid. (Note that you are selecting fields in all four table field list boxes.)

Field Name	**Table Name**
StudentID	ParkingSales
StudentFirstName	Students
StudentLastName	Students
PaidDate	ParkingSales
Lot	Parking Sales
Description	ParkingLots
ParkingFee	ParkingCategoriesWithFees

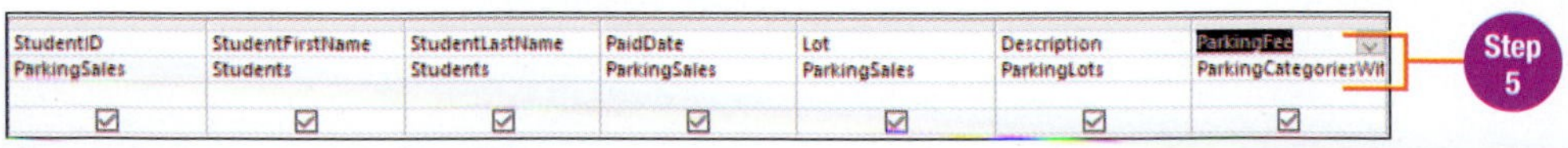

6. Click the Run button in the Results group on the Query Tools Design tab.
7. Save the query as **ParkingSales2018** and then close the query.

8 Click to select the *ParkingSales2018* query name in the Navigation pane.

9 Click the External Data tab and then click the Excel button in the Export group.

Step 9

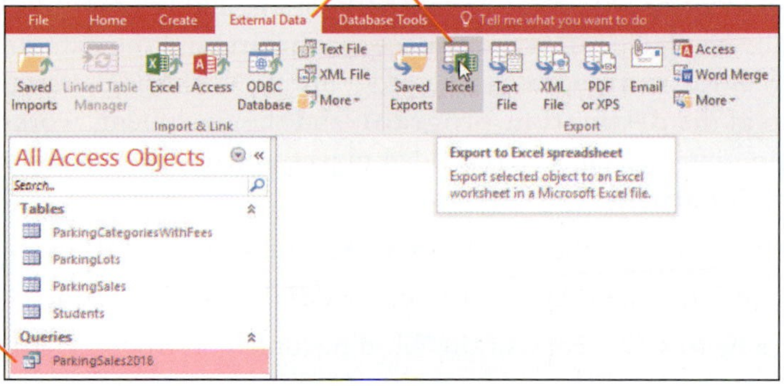

Step 8

Quick Steps

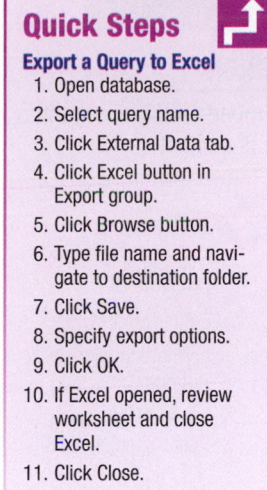

Export a Query to Excel

1. Open database.
2. Select query name.
3. Click External Data tab.
4. Click Excel button in Export group.
5. Click Browse button.
6. Type file name and navigate to destination folder.
7. Click Save.
8. Specify export options.
9. Click OK.
10. If Excel opened, review worksheet and close Excel.
11. Click Close.

10 At the Export – Excel Spreadsheet dialog box, click the Browse button, type ParkingSales-YourName in the *File name* text box, navigate to the Ch14 folder in CompletedTopicsByChapter, and then click Save.

11 Click to insert a check mark in the *Export data with formatting and layout* check box.

12 Click to insert a check mark in the *Open the destination file after the export operation is complete* check box and then click OK.

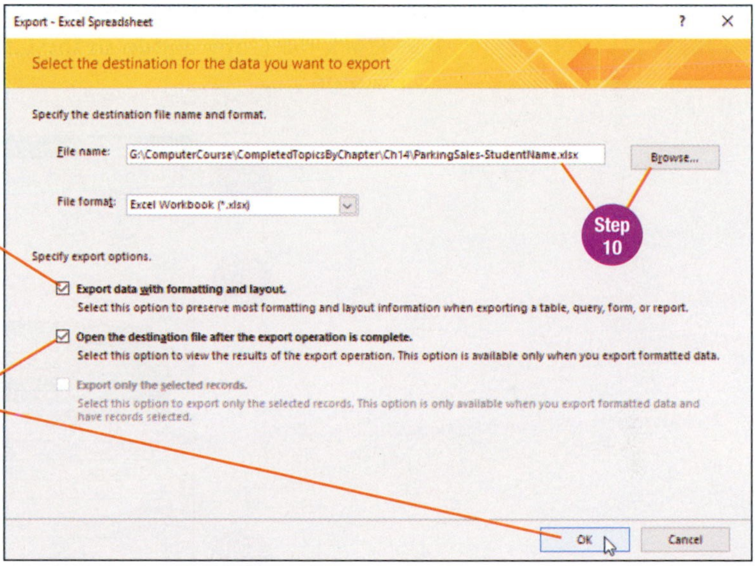

Excel is started automatically with the data from the query results datasheet shown in a worksheet. Notice the first row contains the field names from the query and the worksheet tab is renamed to the query name.

13 Close Excel to return to Access.

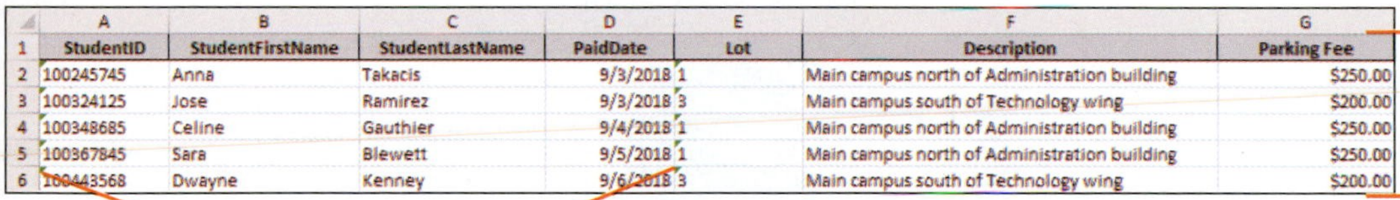

	A	B	C	D	E	F	G
1	StudentID	StudentFirstName	StudentLastName	PaidDate	Lot	Description	Parking Fee
2	100245745	Anna	Takacis	9/3/2018	1	Main campus north of Administration building	$250.00
3	100324125	Jose	Ramirez	9/3/2018	3	Main campus south of Technology wing	$200.00
4	100348685	Celine	Gauthier	9/4/2018	1	Main campus north of Administration building	$250.00
5	100367845	Sara	Blewett	9/5/2018	1	Main campus north of Administration building	$250.00
6	100443568	Dwayne	Kenney	9/6/2018	3	Main campus south of Technology wing	$200.00

First six rows in Excel after query is exported.

Green triangles are shown in the *StudentID* and *Lot* columns because the data is numeric but was exported from Access as text. Green triangles flag data that is a potential error. You can ignore the error flags here.

14 Click Close at the Export - Excel Spreadsheet dialog box to finish the export without saving the export steps.

15 Close the database and then close Access.

App Tip

Go to the Export backstage area in Word, Excel, and PowerPoint to find options for sending data outside the source program.

View Model Answer

Compare your completed file with the model answer.

14.3 Embedding an Excel Chart into a Word Document

Skills

Embed an Excel chart into a document

Tutorials

Copying and Pasting Data into Word

Editing Chart Data

Formatting with Chart Buttons

Pasting Data Using Paste Special Options

In Chapter 3, you used Copy and Paste features to duplicate text and a chart between programs. You can also embed content as an object within a document, worksheet, or presentation. Embedding, like copying and pasting, inserts a duplicate of the selected text or object at the desired location. The program in which the data originally resides is called the **source program**, and the data that is copied is referred to as the **source data**. The program in which the data is embedded is referred to as the **destination program**, and the document, worksheet, or presentation into which the embedded object is placed is referred to as the **destination document**.

1. Start Excel 2016 and then open **SocialMediaStats**.
2. Start Word 2016 and then open **SocialMediaProject**.
3. Use Save As to save a copy of the Word document as **SocialMediaProject-YourName** in the Ch14 folder within CompletedTopicsByChapter.
4. Click the Excel button on the taskbar to switch to Excel and then click to select the pie chart with the title *Global Market Share*.
5. If necessary, click the Home tab.
6. Click the Copy button in the Clipboard group. (Do *not* click the arrow on the button.)

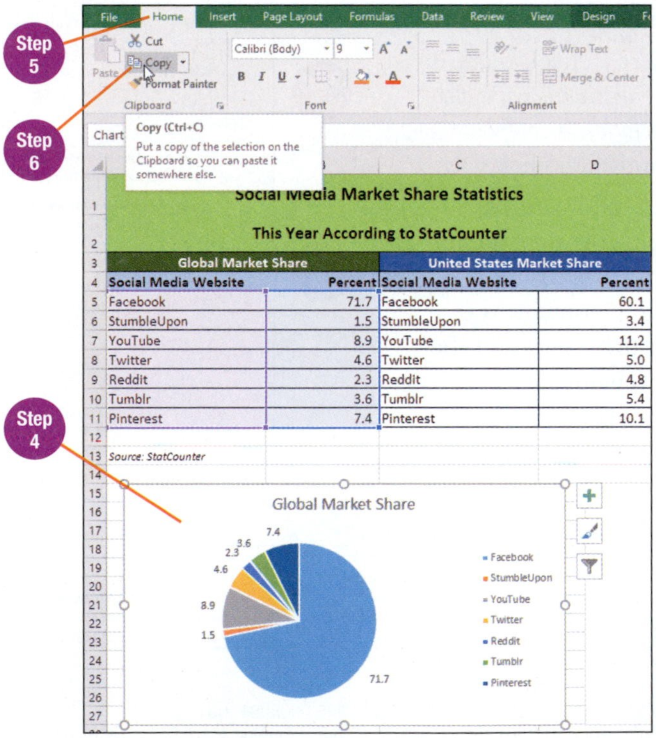

7. Click the Word button on the taskbar to switch to Word and then click to position the insertion point at the left margin on the blank line a double-space below the first table.

8 Click the Paste button arrow and then click *Use Destination Theme & Embed Workbook* (first button in *Paste Options* section) at the drop-down list.

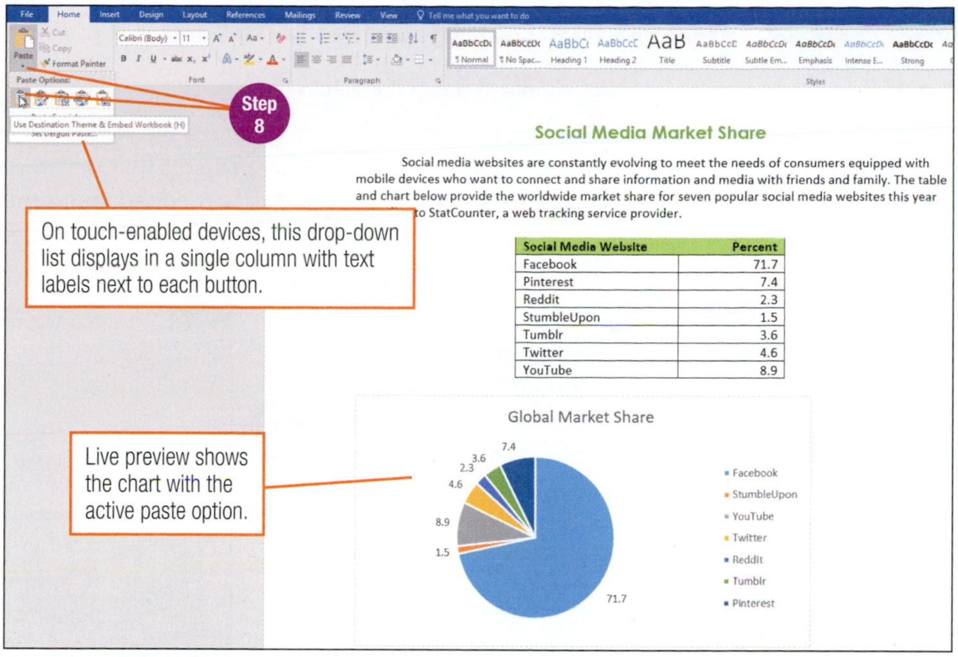

9 Click to select the chart object and then click the Center button in the Paragraph group on the Home tab.

The Chart feature is standardized in Word, Excel, and PowerPoint. A chart embedded within any of the three programs offers the Chart Tools tabs and three chart editing buttons with which the chart can be modified after being embedded.

10 Click the Chart Elements button (plus symbol), point at *Legend* (right-pointing arrow appears), click the right-pointing arrow, click *Bottom*, and then click in the document outside the chart to deselect the chart object.

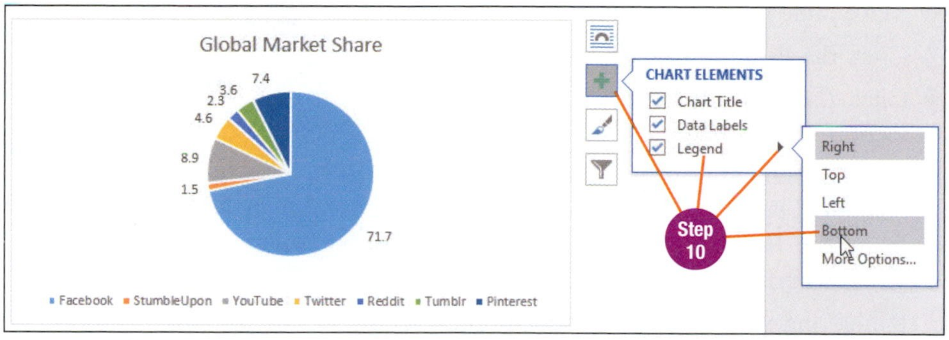

Quick Steps

Embed an Excel Chart into Word

1. Open worksheet in Excel.
2. Open document in Word.
3. Make Excel active, select and copy chart.
4. Switch to Word.
5. Position insertion point.
6. Click Paste button arrow.
7. Click *Use Destination Theme & Embed Workbook.*

11 Switch to Excel and select and copy the pie chart with the title *United States Market Share.*

12 Switch to Word, position the insertion point at the bottom of the document, and then embed, center, and format the pie chart by completing steps similar to Steps 8 through 10.

13 Save the revised document using the same name (**SocialMediaProject-YourName**) and then close Word. Leave Excel and the **SocialMediaStats** workbook open for the next topic.

View

Model Answer

Compare your completed file with the model answer.

Alternative Method **Embedding Copied Data Using Paste Special Dialog Box**

Another way to embed copied data is to select *Paste Special* at the Paste button arrow drop-down list in the destination document. This opens the Paste Special dialog box in which you select the source object in the *As* list box and then click OK.

14.4 Embedding Excel Data into PowerPoint and Editing the Embedded Data

Skills

Embed Excel data into a presentation

Edit an embedded table

Tutorials

Embedding Objects

Using Paste Options

Embedding text or worksheet data uses the same process as embedding a chart. Double-click an embedded object to edit text or worksheet data in the destination location. Embedded text or cell data is edited using the tools on the ribbon from the source program. Click outside the embedded object to end editing and to restore the ribbon of the destination program.

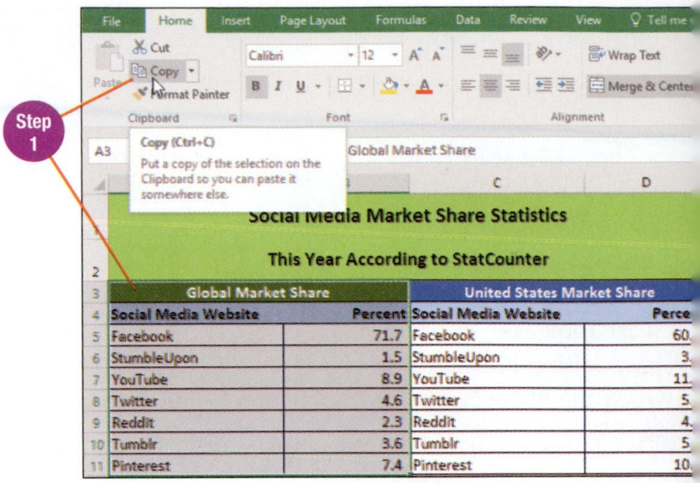

1. With Excel active and the **SocialMediaStats** workbook open, select and copy A3:B11.
2. Start PowerPoint 2016 and open **SocialMediaPres**.
3. Use Save As to save a copy of the presentation as **SocialMediaPres-YourName** in the Ch14 folder within CompletedTopicsByChapter.
4. Make Slide 3 the active slide.
5. Click the Paste button arrow.
6. Click *Embed* (third button in *Paste Options* section).
7. Click the Drawing Tools Format tab, click the Shape Fill button in the Shape Styles group, and then click *White, Text 1* (second option in *Theme Colors* section).
8. Resize and position the embedded object to the approximate size and position shown in the image below.

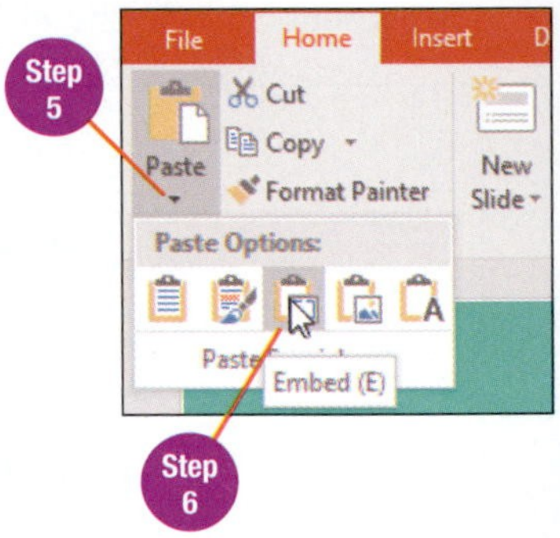

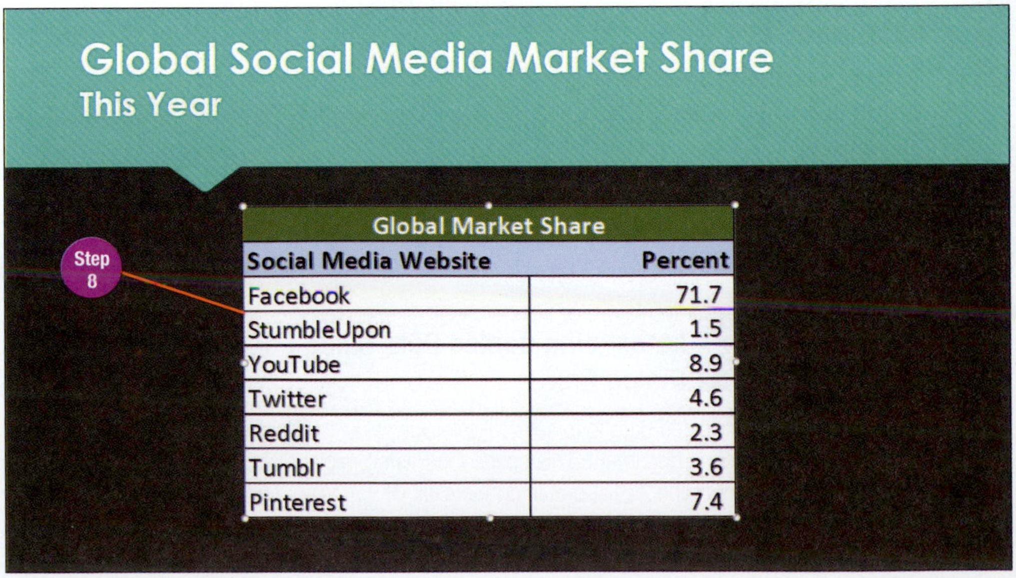
Global Social Media Market Share
This Year
Step 8
Global Market Share
Social Media Website
Percent
Facebook 71.7
StumbleUpon 1.5
YouTube 8.9
Twitter 4.6
Reddit 2.3
Tumblr 3.6
Pinterest 7.4

9. Double-click the inserted cells to open the embedded object for editing.

   Notice the embedded cells open in an Excel worksheet and the ribbon changes to Excel's ribbon.

10. Select B5:B11 and then click the Decrease Decimal button in the Number group on the Home tab.

11. Click on the slide outside the embedded object to end editing and restore PowerPoint's ribbon.

12. Switch to Excel and select and copy C3:D11.

13. Switch to PowerPoint, make Slide 4 the active slide, and embed, format, resize, and position the copied cells by completing steps similar to those in Steps 5 through 11.

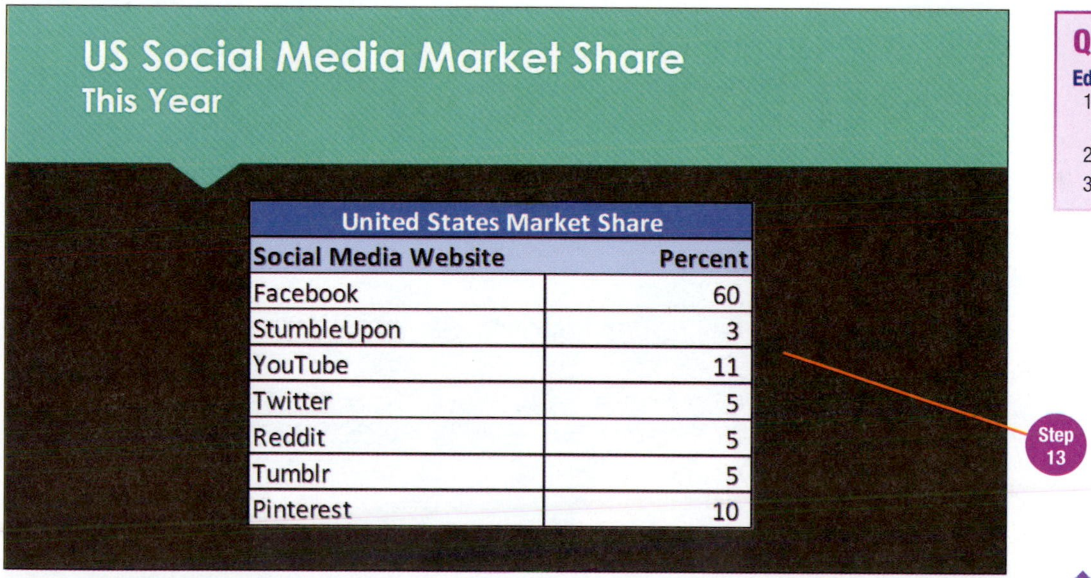

Quick Steps

Edit an Embedded Object

1. Double-click embedded object.
2. Make desired changes.
3. Click outside object.

14. Save the revised presentation using the same name (**SocialMediaPres-YourName**) and then close PowerPoint. Leave Excel and the **SocialMediaStats** workbook open for the next topic.

View Model Answer

Compare your completed file with the model answer.

Beyond Basics **Embedding an Entire File**

Embed an entire document or worksheet using the Object button on the Insert tab. At the Object dialog box, click the Create from File tab and then use the Browse button to navigate to the desired file name. Note that this method embeds the entire file contents at the insertion point, active cell, or active slide.

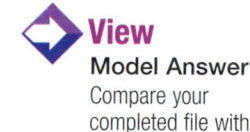

14.5 Linking an Excel Chart with a Presentation and Updating the Link

Skills

Link an Excel chart with a presentation

Turn on automatic link updates

Edit a linked chart

Update links

Tutorials

Linking Data

Linking Objects

Good to Know

Linking is not just for integrating data between two different programs; you can link two documents in Word, two worksheets in Excel, or two tables in Access.

If the data that you want to integrate between two programs is continuously updated, copy and link the data instead of copying and pasting or copying and embedding. When copied data is linked, changes made to the source data can be automatically updated in any other document, worksheet, or presentation to which the data is linked. Linking avoids duplicating work and ensures that errors are not made when the same data is changed in more than one location. Linked objects are managed using the **Links dialog box**, where a link can be set to update automatically, a link can be broken, or the source location for a linked object can be changed.

1. With Excel active and the **SocialMediaStats** workbook open, use Save As to save a copy of the workbook as **LinkedSocialMediaStats-YourName** in the Ch14 folder within CompletedTopicsByChapter.
2. Start PowerPoint 2016 and then open **SocialMediaPres**.
3. Use Save As to save a copy of the presentation as **LinkedSocialMediaPres-YourName** in the Ch14 folder within CompletedTopicsByChapter.
4. Switch to Excel, select and then copy the *Global Market Share* pie chart.
5. Switch to PowerPoint and then make Slide 3 the active slide.
6. Click the Paste button arrow.
7. Click *Use Destination Theme & Link Data* (third button in *Paste Options* section).
8. Resize and move the chart to the approximate size and position shown in the image below.

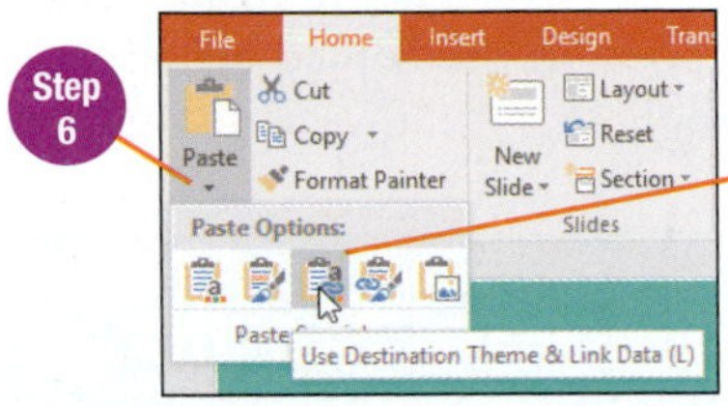

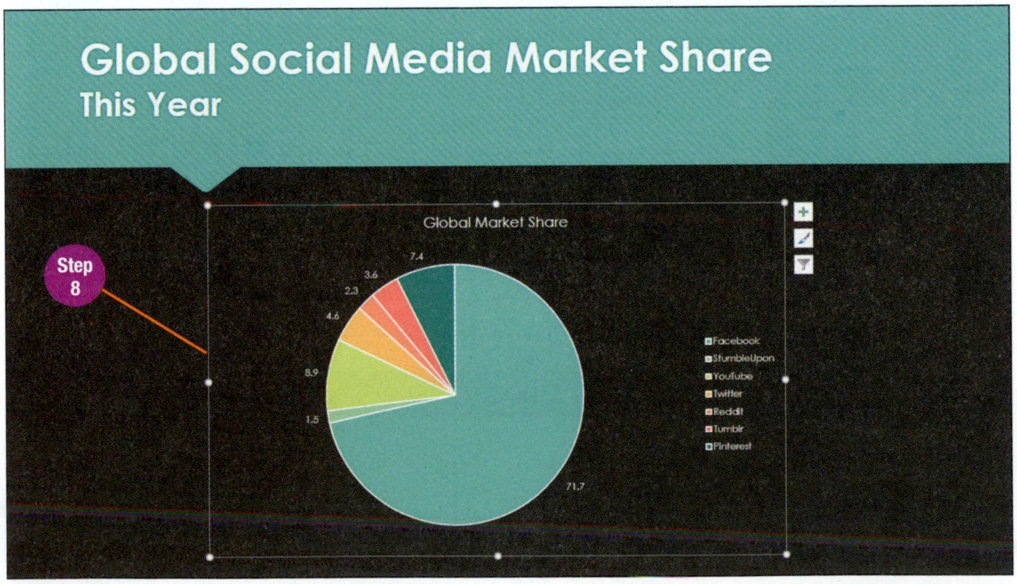

9. Switch to Excel, select and then copy the *United States Market Share* pie chart.

10 Switch to PowerPoint, make Slide 4 the active slide, and link, resize, and move the chart by completing steps similar to those in Steps 6 through 8.

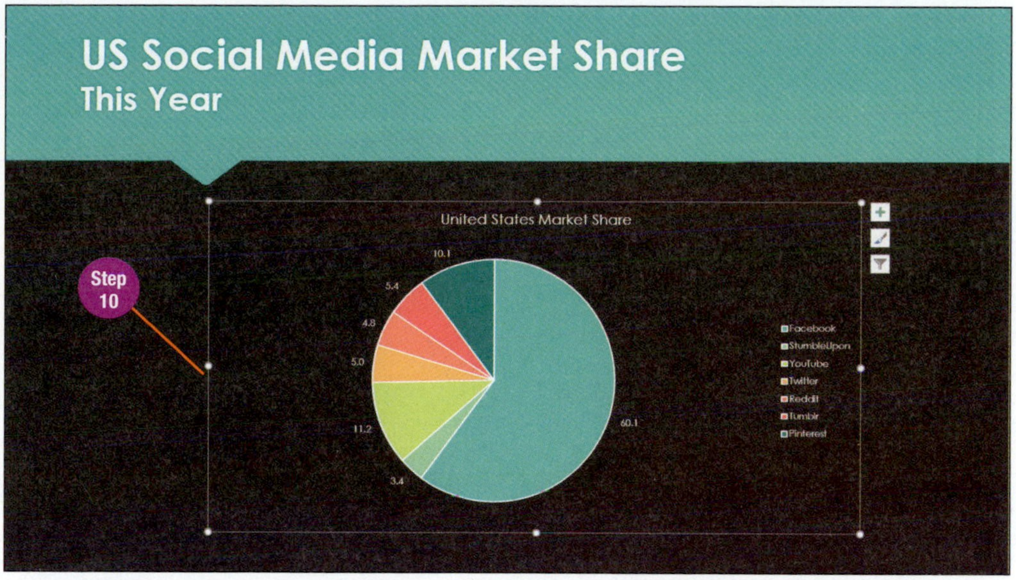

11 Click the File tab and then click *Edit Links to Files* in the *Related Documents* section at the bottom of the Properties panel (bottom right) at the Info backstage area.

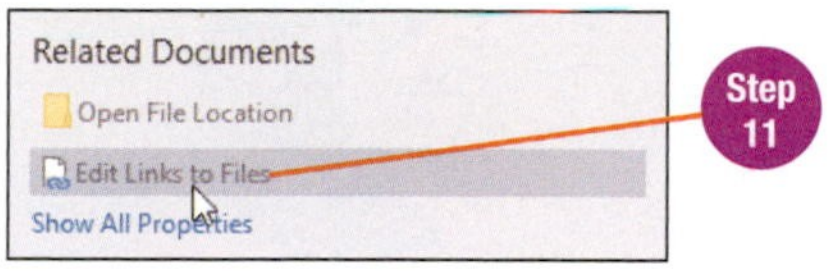

12 At the Links dialog box, click to select the first link in the *Links* list box and then click to insert a check mark in the *Automatic Update* check box.

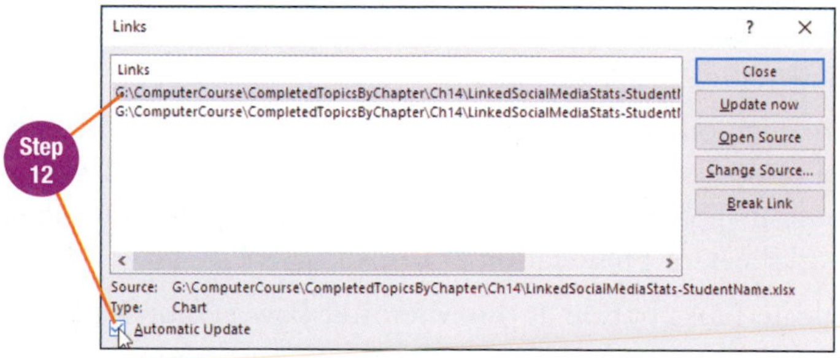

13 Click to select the second link and then click to insert a check mark in the *Automatic Update* check box.

14 Click Close.

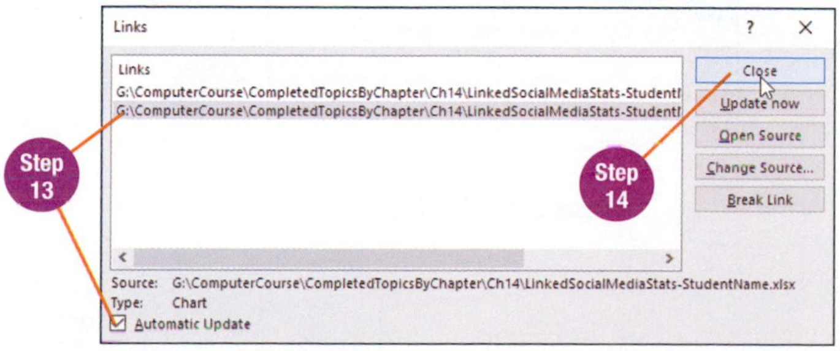

15. Click the Back button at the Info backstage area to return to the presentation.
16. Save the revised presentation using the same name (**LinkedSocialMediaPres-YourName**) and then close the presentation.
17. Switch to Excel.
18. Change the value in D6 from *3.4* to *2.9*.
19. Change the value in D7 from *11.2* to *19.3*.
20. Change the value in D11 from *10.1* to *2.5*.

Notice the pie chart updated after each change in value. The revised chart is noticeably different from the original pie chart.

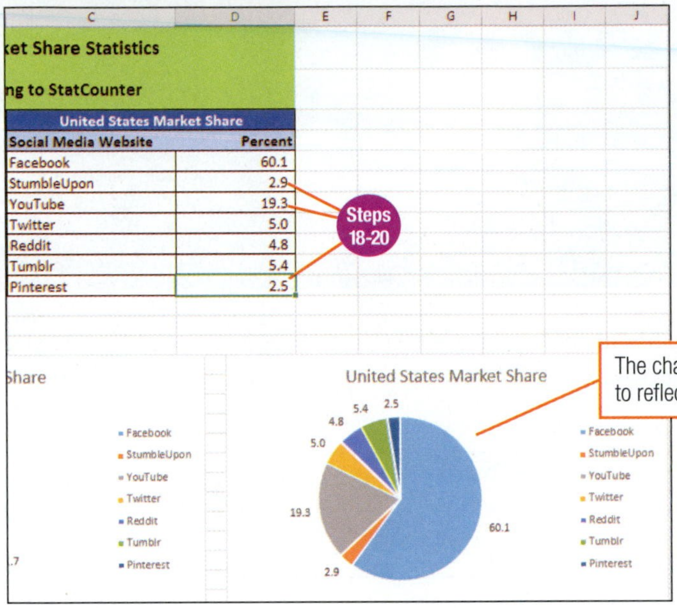

21. Save the revised worksheet using the same name (**LinkedSocialMediaStats-YourName**) and then close Excel.
22. Switch to PowerPoint if PowerPoint is not already active and then open **LinkedSocialMediaPres-YourName**.

App Tip

If the source and destination files are both open at the same time, changes made to the source reflect in the destination file immediately.

Because the presentation contains linked data that is set to automatically update, you are prompted to update links. A dialog box with a security notice and the **Update Links** button appears when you open a file that has links to objects outside the document, worksheet, or presentation.

23. Click the Update Links button at the Microsoft PowerPoint Security Notice dialog box.

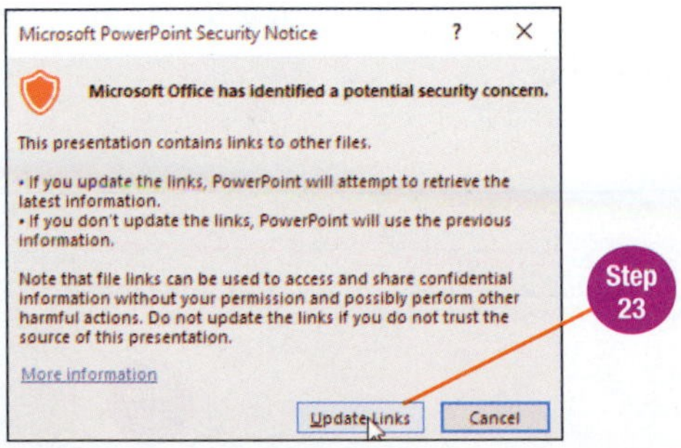

24 Make Slide 4 the active slide. Notice that the chart is updated to reflect the same data as the revised Excel chart.

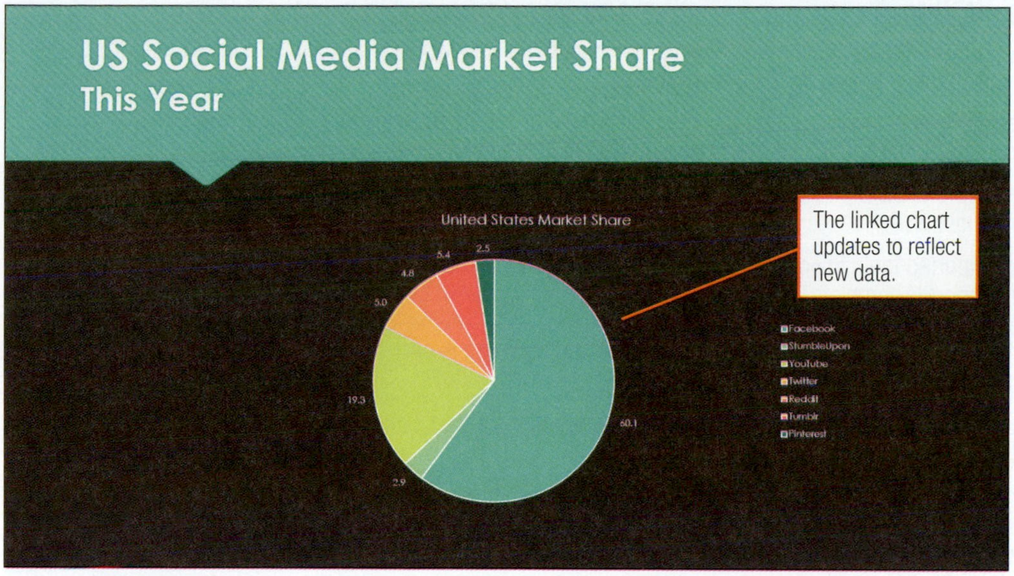

25 Make Slide 3 the active slide and then delete the title inside the chart above the pie.

26 Make Slide 4 the active slide and then delete the title inside the chart above the pie.

27 Save the revised presentation using the same name (**LinkedSocialMediaPres-YourName**) and then close PowerPoint.

Alternative Method — Linking Copied Data Using Paste Special Dialog Box

Another way to link copied data is to select *Paste Special* at the Paste button arrow drop-down list in the destination document. At the Paste Special dialog box, click *Paste link*, make sure the correct source object is selected in the *As* list box, and then click OK.

Security Alert — Update Links with Caution

At Step 23, you clicked the Update Links button because you knew the linked file was from a trusted source. Be aware before you click Update Links when opening a document, workbook, presentation, or database that you know where the linked object originates and that it is from a trusted source. In 2015, Sophos (an IT security company) reported a resurgence of malware circulated in Microsoft Office documents. Sophos reported the malware is targeted more towards Word and Excel files and the files are usually attached to email messages.

Quick Steps

Link Data
1. Open source program and file.
2. Open destination program and file.
3. With source program active, select and copy data.
4. Switch to destination program.
5. Activate destination location.
6. Click Paste button arrow.
7. Click *Use Destination Theme & Link Data*.

Turn on Automatic Link Updates
1. Make destination file active.
2. Click File tab.
3. Click *Edit Links to Files*.
4. Select link.
5. Click *Automatic Update* check box.
6. Click Close.

View Model Answer
Compare your completed file with the model answer.

Beyond Basics — Managing Links

Open the Links dialog box (see Steps 11 and 12) if the drive and/or folder for the source data in a linked file changes to update the location for the source data file, or if you want to break a link to stop updating the destination data.

Topics Review

Topic	Key Concepts	Key Terms
14.1 Importing Excel Worksheet Data into Access	The Import Spreadsheet Wizard starts when you click the Excel button in the Import & Link group on the External Data tab. Five dialog boxes in the Import Spreadsheet Wizard guide you through the steps to create a new table using data in an Excel worksheet. You can save the Excel import settings to repeat the import later using the same settings. Open an imported table in Access in Design view to modify the table design after the import is complete.	Import Spreadsheet Wizard
14.2 Exporting an Access Query to Excel	Export table or query data to Excel using the Excel button in the Export group on the External Data tab. Specify the file name, drive and/or folder, and export options at the Export – Excel Spreadsheet dialog box. You can elect to export the data with formatting and layout options in the datasheet, and automatically open Excel with the worksheet displayed when the export is complete. Export specifications can be saved to repeat the export later.	
14.3 Embedding an Excel Chart into a Word Document	Embedding inserts a copy of selected data as an object in a document, worksheet, or presentation. The program from which data is copied is called the *source program*. The data that is copied is referred to as the *source data*. The destination program is the program that receives the copied data. The destination document refers to the document, worksheet, or presentation into which copied data is pasted as an object. Click the Paste button arrow and then choose the desired embed option to embed copied data as an object in the destination document.	source program source data destination program destination document
14.4 Embedding Excel Data into PowerPoint and Editing the Embedded Data	Double-click an embedded object to open the object data for editing using the source program's ribbon and tools. Click outside the embedded object to end editing and restore the source program's ribbon. An entire document can be embedded using the Object button on the Insert tab.	
14.5 Linking an Excel Chart with a Presentation and Updating the Link	Source data that is continuously updated should be linked instead of copied and pasted or copied and embedded, to avoid duplication of work and reduce errors made when data is entered more than once. Click the Paste button arrow in the destination document and then choose the desired link option to link copied data. Click *Edit Links to Files* in the Properties panel at the Info backstage area to open the Links dialog box in which you manage links to source data. Select a link in the Links dialog box and insert a check mark in the *Automatic Update* check box to turn on automatic updates for the link. Click the Update Links button in the Security Warning dialog box that appears when you open a file with a linked object to update data from the source.	Links dialog box Update Links

Recheck

Recheck your understanding of the topics covered in this chapter.

Workbook

Chapter review and assessment resources are available in the *Workbook* ebook.

Chapter 15

Using OneDrive and Other Cloud Computing Technologies

Precheck

Check your understanding of the topics covered in this chapter.

Learning Objectives

15.1 Create a document in Word Online

15.2 Create a worksheet in Excel Online

15.3 Create a presentation in PowerPoint Online

15.4 Edit a presentation in PowerPoint Online

15.5 Upload and download files to and from OneDrive

15.6 Share a document in OneDrive

15.7 Create a document using Google Docs

Office Online is the web-based version of Word, Excel, PowerPoint, and OneNote, which can be accessed from OneDrive. Computing, software, and storage services accessed entirely from the Web is called **cloud computing**. With cloud computing, all you need is a computer with a web browser to create and edit a document, worksheet, or presentation. With cloud computing technology, you do not need to install software on your PC or mobile device, because all software and storage of documents is online. Google also offers a web-based productivity suite that is popular with many people. Both Microsoft and Google offer their web-based productivity apps free to account holders.

In Chapter 3, you learned how to save a presentation to OneDrive within PowerPoint. In this chapter, you will learn to create and edit files using Office Online from OneDrive; upload, download, and share files in OneDrive; and create a document using Google Docs from Google Drive.

***Note:** If you are using a tablet, consider connecting it to a USB or wireless keyboard because parts of this chapter involve a fair amount of typing. In this chapter, you will need to sign in with a Microsoft account and a Google account. If necessary, create a new account at each website. You may wish to check with your instructor before completing this chapter to confirm the required topics.*

SNAP If you are a SNAP user, go to your SNAP Assignments page to complete the Precheck and Recheck.

Data Files

Before beginning this chapter, be sure you have copied the student data files for this course to your storage medium. Steps on downloading and extracting the data files are provided in Chapter 1, Topic 1.8, on pages 22–23.

15.1 Creating a Document Using Word Online

Skills

Create a document in Word Online

With Word Online, you create and edit documents within a web browser. **Word Online** is similar to the desktop version of Word that you used in Chapters 6 and 7; however, Word Online has fewer features than the desktop version. The program looks similar to the full-featured Word, but you will notice that for some features, functionality within a browser environment is slightly different than the desktop version.

Note: *Microsoft may update Office Online after publication of this textbook, in which case the information, steps, and/or screens shown here may vary.*

1. Open a browser window.
2. If necessary, click in the Address bar or select the current web address. Skip this step if you are using a browser where the insertion point is already positioned in a blank address bar.
3. Type https://onedrive.live.com and then press Enter.
4. If necessary, click Sign in, type the email address or phone number for your Microsoft account and click Next, then type your password and click the Sign in button at the second sign-in screen. Skip this step if you are already signed in to OneDrive, which occurs with the Microsoft Edge browser when you are already signed in to your Microsoft Account for Windows.

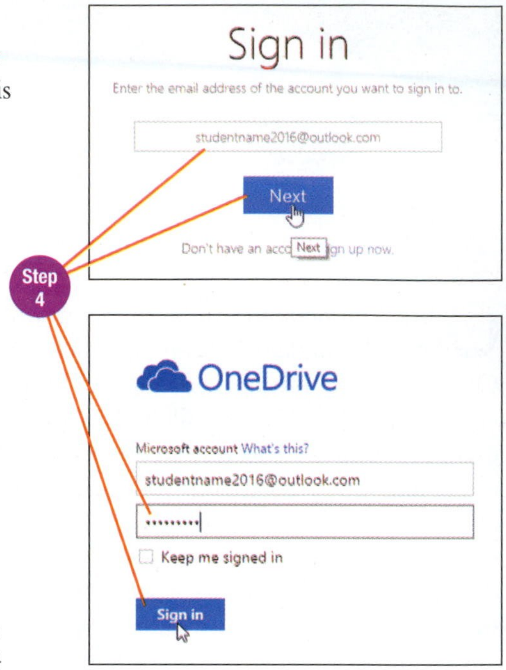

> **Oops!**
>
> Don't know your Microsoft account? If you have a hotmail.com, live.com, or outlook.com email address, your email login is your Microsoft account; otherwise, click the Sign up button or link and create a new account.

Once signed in, the OneDrive window appears similar to the one shown in Figure 15.1.

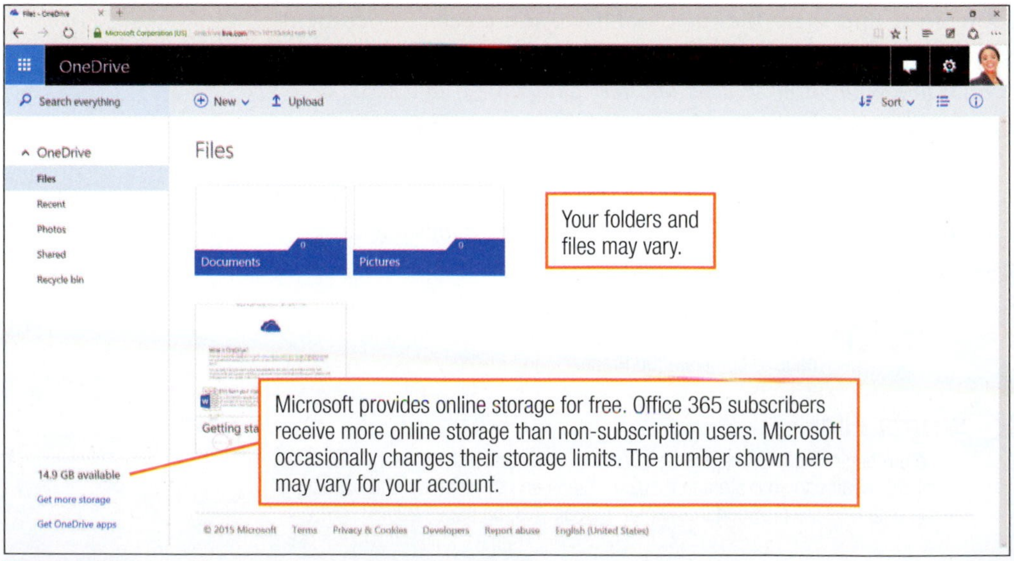

Figure 15.1

This is how the OneDrive window appears for a signed-in user.

5 Click the Microsoft Apps button in the upper left of the screen next to OneDrive (it displays as a waffle icon and is sometimes called the waffle button) and then click the Word tile.

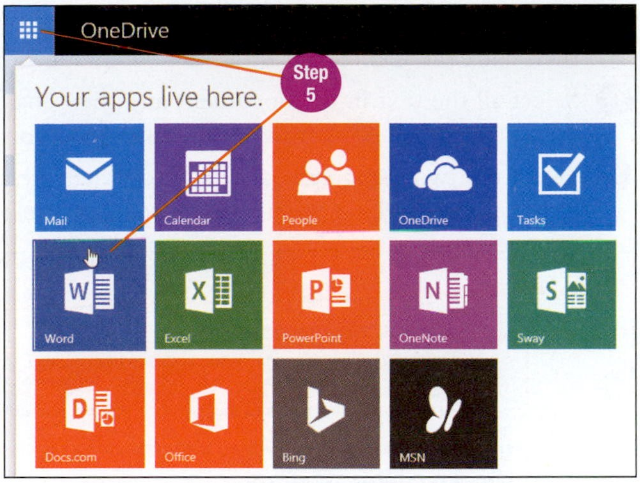

6 Click Got it! if a screen displays with information about new features in Office Online; this message appears the first time you use Office Online, or when changes have been made to the software.

7 Click New blank document at the Word Online Start screen.

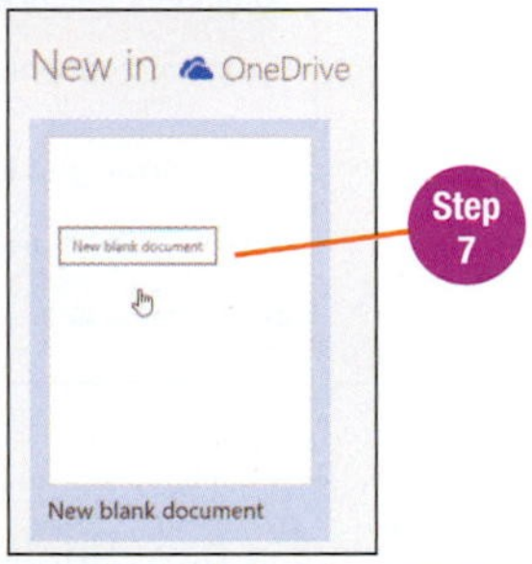

Word Online launches, as shown in Figure 15.2.

> **Check This Out**
>
> **http://CA2.ParadigmCollege.net/Office**
>
> Go here to start Word Online without first starting OneDrive. You can access all the same web-based apps from office.com. Click the desired tile and then sign in with a Microsoft account or a school account.

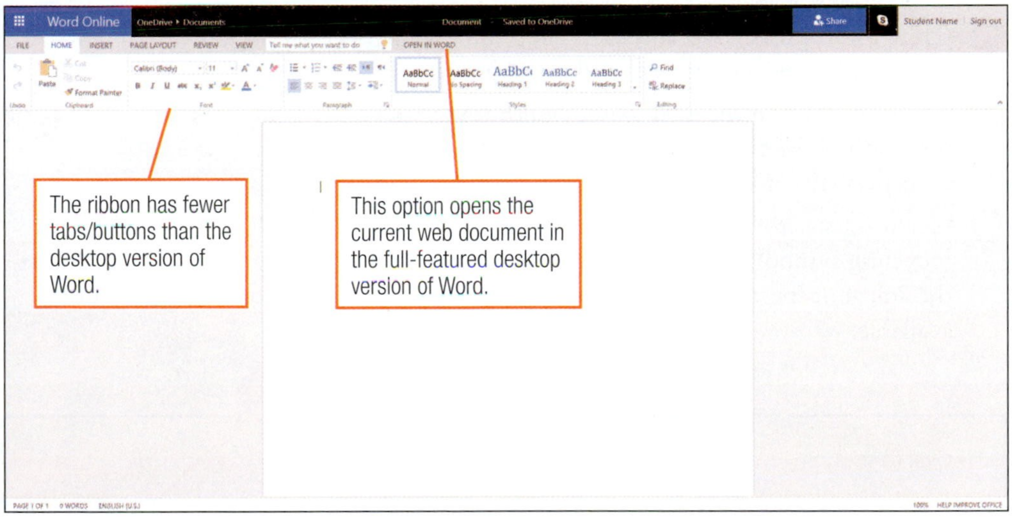

Figure 15.2

The Word Online new document window is shown.

8 Type the following text in the document window using all the default settings:

What Is Green Computing?

Green computing refers to the use of computers and other electronic devices in an environmentally responsible manner. Green computing can encompass new or modified computing practices, policies, and procedures. This trend is growing with more individuals and businesses adopting green computing strategies every year.

Strategies include the reduction of energy consumption by computers and other devices; reduction in use of paper, ink, and toner; and reuse, recycling, or proper disposal of electronic waste.

9 Proofread carefully and correct any typing errors that you find. If necessary, use the Spelling button in the Spelling group on the REVIEW tab to spell check the document.

> **App Tip**
>
> Use the same editing and formatting techniques in Word Online as you learned in the desktop edition of Word.

App Tip

Word Online documents are saved automatically as you work. They are saved using the same file format as the desktop version of Word, which means documents are transferable between editions.

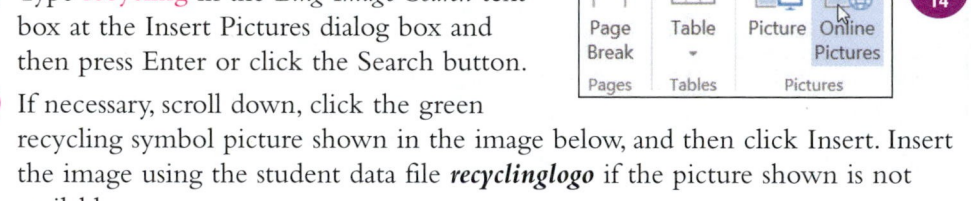

10. Click to place the insertion point within the title *What Is Green Computing?* and then click the Center button in the Paragraph group on the HOME tab.
11. Select all the text in the document and then change the font size to 12 using the *Font Size* option box arrow in the Font group on the HOME tab.
12. Select the two paragraphs of text below the title and then change the line spacing to 1.5 using the Line Spacing button in the Paragraph group on the HOME tab.

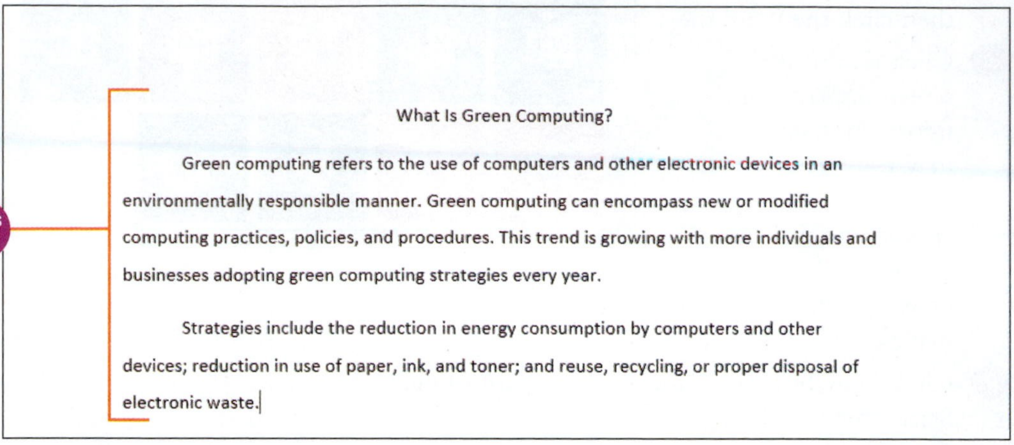
Steps 8-12
What Is Green Computing?
Green computing refers to the use of computers and other electronic devices in an environmentally responsible manner. Green computing can encompass new or modified computing practices, policies, and procedures. This trend is growing with more individuals and businesses adopting green computing strategies every year.
Strategies include the reduction in energy consumption by computers and other devices; reduction in use of paper, ink, and toner; and reuse, recycling, or proper disposal of electronic waste.

13. Position the insertion point at the end of the last paragraph and press Enter to create a new line.
14. Click the INSERT tab and then click the Online Pictures button in the Pictures group.
15. Type recycling in the *Bing Image Search* text box at the Insert Pictures dialog box and then press Enter or click the Search button.
16. If necessary, scroll down, click the green recycling symbol picture shown in the image below, and then click Insert. Insert the image using the student data file ***recyclinglogo*** if the picture shown is not available.

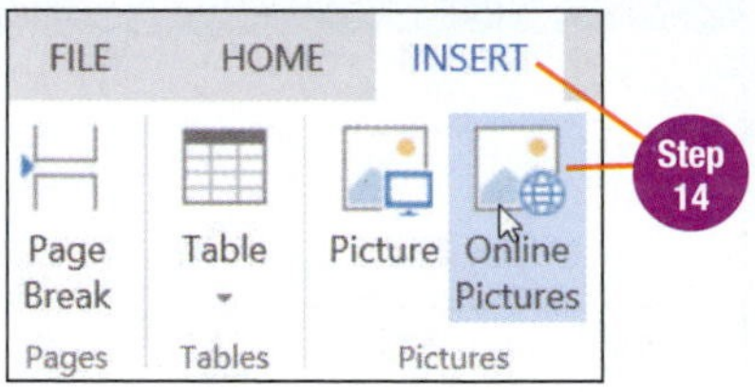
FILE
HOME
INSERT
Page Break
Table
Picture
Online Pictures
Pages
Tables
Pictures
Step 14

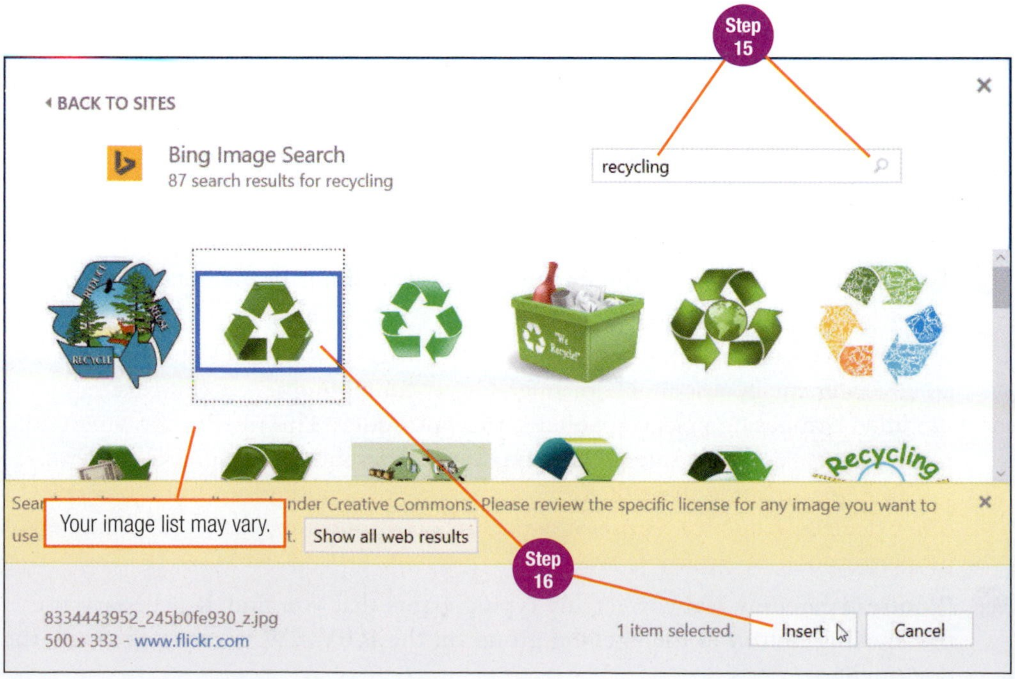
Step 15
BACK TO SITES
Bing Image Search
87 search results for recycling
recycling
Your image list may vary.
Show all web results
Step 16
8334443952_245b0fe930_z.jpg
500 x 333 - www.flickr.com
1 item selected.
Insert
Cancel

Quick Steps

Create a Document in Word Online

1. Open a browser window.
2. Navigate to https://onedrive.live.com.
3. If necessary, sign in with Microsoft account.
4. Click Microsoft Apps button (waffle icon) next to OneDrive.
5. Click Word tile and then New blank document.
6. Type, edit, and format document.
7. Use Save As to rename document.
8. Close document tab.

17 If necessary, click to select the green recycling symbol image and then click the PICTURE TOOLS FORMAT tab.

18 Select the current value in the *Scale* text box in the Image Size group, type 35, and then press Enter.

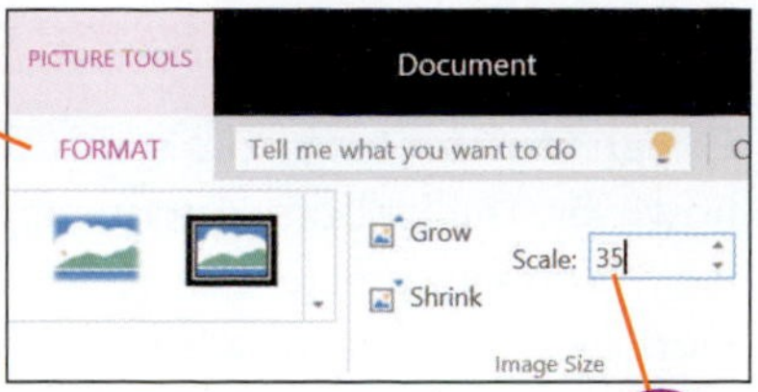

19 With the image still selected, click the HOME tab and then click the Center button in the Paragraph group.

20 Click within the document text to deselect the image.

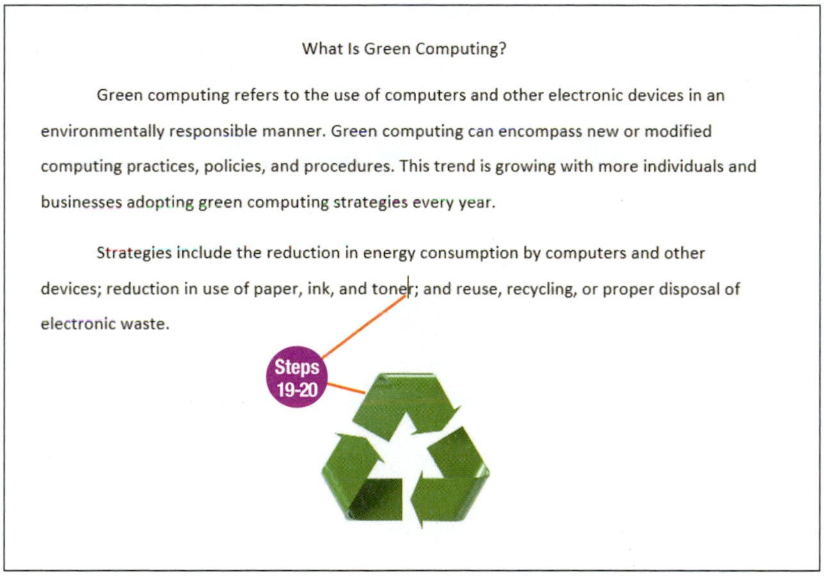
What Is Green Computing?
Green computing refers to the use of computers and other electronic devices in an environmentally responsible manner. Green computing can encompass new or modified computing practices, policies, and procedures. This trend is growing with more individuals and businesses adopting green computing strategies every year.
Strategies include the reduction in energy consumption by computers and other devices; reduction in use of paper, ink, and toner; and reuse, recycling, or proper disposal of electronic waste.
Steps 19-20

21 Click the FILE tab and then click *Save As*.

22 At the Save As backstage area, click Rename.

23 Type GreenComputing-YourName in the *Enter a name for this file* text box at the Rename dialog box and then press Enter or click OK.

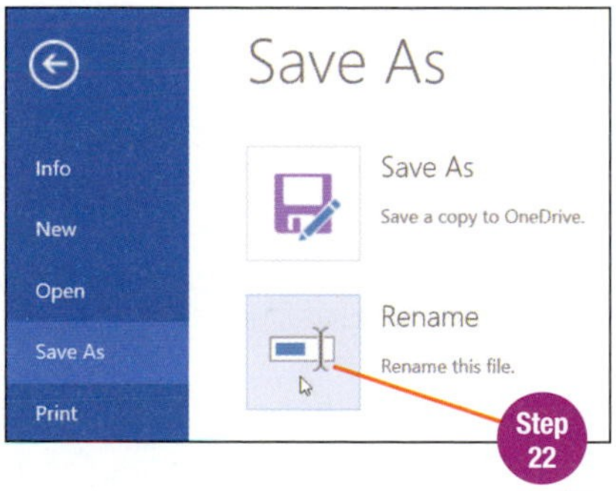

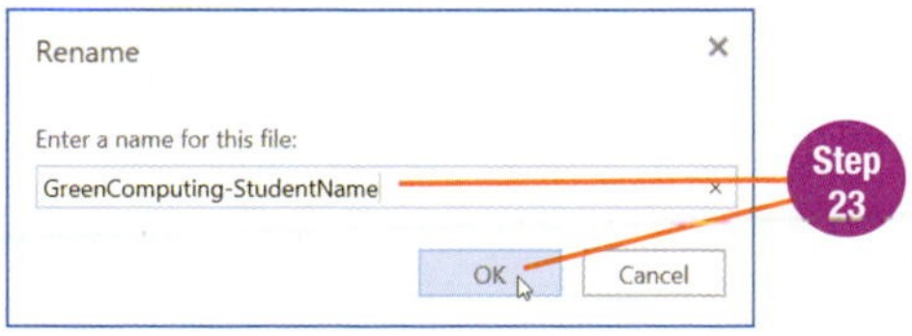

24 Close the document browser tab. Leave OneDrive open for the next topic.

A Word document thumbnail is added to the *Files > Documents* list in OneDrive. Additional options appear in the bar along the top of the OneDrive window when a document is selected. You will use some of these options in later topics.

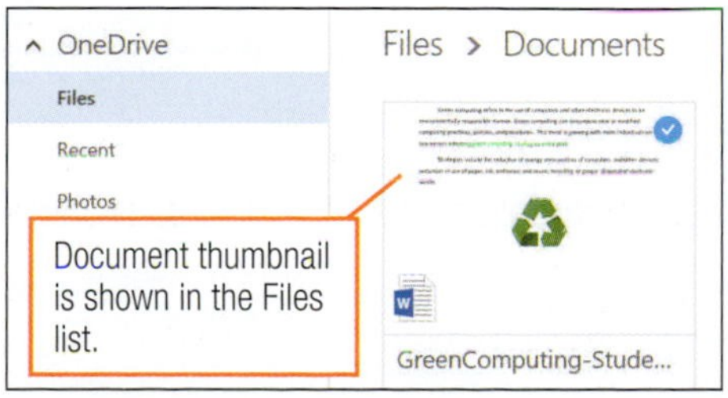

App Tip

Switch to the desktop version of Word if you need access to the full set of picture formatting and editing tools.

App Tip

Create a printable PDF of the document at the Save As backstage area using the Download as PDF option.

Oops!

OneDrive closed when you closed the Word Online document tab? Sometimes, OneDrive operates within a single browser tab, and closing the document tab also exits OneDrive. Restart OneDrive and sign back in to your OneDrive account. Next time, click the Microsoft Apps button and then click the OneDrive tile instead of closing the browser tab when you finish a topic.

15.2 Creating a Worksheet Using Excel Online

Skills

Create a worksheet in Excel Online

Excel Online looks the same as the full-featured desktop edition of Excel; however, the ribbon contains fewer options, and functionality for some features will vary. You can create a basic worksheet in the web-based version of Excel, but for worksheets that need advanced formulas or editing, the desktop version of Excel is preferred.

1. With OneDrive open, click the Microsoft Apps button (displays as a waffle icon), click the Excel tile, and then click New blank workbook at the Excel Online Start screen.

Excel Online launches and opens a window similar to the window shown in Figure 15.3. Like Word Online, Excel Online workbooks are saved in the same file format as the desktop version of Excel and are transferable between software editions.

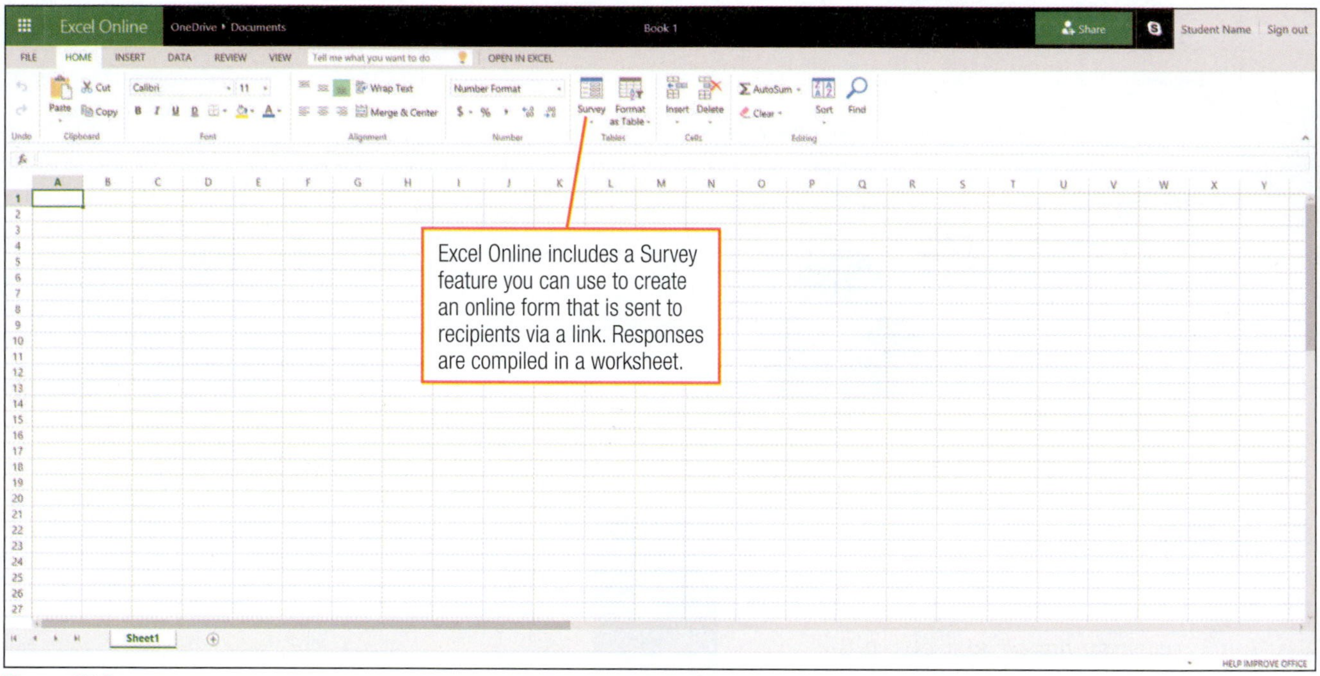

Figure 15.3

As you can see from the Excel Online window, the ribbon has fewer tabs and buttons than the full-featured desktop version of Excel.

2. Type the labels and values in the cells as shown in the image below, substituting your first and last names for *Your Name* in A1.

	A	B	C	D	E	F	G	H	I	J	K
1	Your Name Energy Savings Calculator										
2											
3	Annual electricity cost to run computer continuously:										
4			Watts used		Kilowatts used		Cost per kilowatt hour (cents)			Total Cost	
5	Dell PC		200				10.9				
6											
7	Annual electricity cost to run computer only two hours per day (turned off or put in sleep mode when not in use):										
8											
9	Dell PC		200				10.9				
10											
11	Energy savings by turning off PC when not in use or using sleep mode:										

Step 2

3. Click E5 to make it the active cell and then type the formula =(c5*24*365)/1000.

The formula multiplies the watts used by a PC running continuously 24 hours per day, 365 days per year and then divides the result by 1000 to convert watts to kilowatts.

4. Click J5 to make it the active cell and then type the formula: =e5*(g5/100).

The cost per kilowatt hour in G5 is divided by 100 to convert 10.9 to a decimal value representing cents.

5. Type the remaining formulas in the cells indicated:

   E9 =(c9*2*365)/1000
   J9 =e9*(g9/100)
   J11 =j5-j9

E	F	G	H	I	J
nuously:					
Kilowatts used		Cost per kilowatt hour (cents)			Total Cost
1752		10.9			190.968
two hours per day (turned off or put in sleep mode when not in use)					
146		10.9			15.914
use or using sleep mode:					175.054

Steps 3–5

6. Select A1:J1 and then click the Merge & Center button in the Alignment group on the HOME tab.
7. With A1:J1 still selected, apply bold formatting and change the font size to 12.
8. Click J5 to make it the active cell, click the *Number Format* option box in the Number group on the HOME tab, and then click *Accounting* at the drop-down list.
9. Apply the Accounting Number Format to J9 and J11.
10. With J11 the active cell, click the Borders button in the Font group on the HOME tab and then click *Outside Borders* at the drop-down list.

Notice that fewer border options exist in Excel Online.

11. With J11 still the active cell, apply bold formatting and the *Dark Green* font color (sixth color in *Standard Colors* section).
12. Click in a blank cell to view the border in J11 and then proofread carefully and correct any typing errors that you find.

	A	B	C	D	E	F	G	H	I	J
1	**Your Name Energy Savings Calculator**									
2										
3	Annual electricity cost to run computer continuously:									
4			Watts used		Kilowatts used		Cost per kilowatt hour (cents)			Total Cost
5	Dell PC		200		1752		10.9			$ 190.97
6										
7	Annual electricity cost to run computer only two hours per day (turned off or put in sleep mode when not in use):									
8										
9	Dell PC		200		146		10.9			$ 15.91
10										
11	Energy savings by turning off PC when not in use or using sleep mode:									**$ 175.05**

This is how the worksheet should be formatted after Steps 6 to 11 are completed.

13. Rename the workbook EnergySavings-YourName and then close the workbook tab by completing steps similar to Steps 21 to 24 in the previous topic. Leave OneDrive open for the next topic.

An Excel workbook thumbnail is added to the *Files > Documents* list in OneDrive.

Quick Steps

Create a Workbook in Excel Online

1. Open a browser window.
2. Navigate to https://onedrive.live.com.
3. If necessary, sign in with Microsoft account.
4. Click Microsoft Apps button.
5. Click Excel tile and then New blank workbook.
6. Type cell entries and format worksheet.
7. Use Save As to rename workbook
8. Close workbook tab.

App Tip

Changes to the worksheet are saved automatically to the workbook in OneDrive.

App Tip

Display the worksheet in a printer-friendly format in a separate browser window and then click the Print button at the Print backstage area.

15.3 Creating a Presentation Using PowerPoint Online

Skills

Create a presentation in PowerPoint Online

A basic presentation that does not need to incorporate a chart or audio can be created using **PowerPoint Online**. Other PowerPoint Online features that vary from the full-featured desktop version include fewer animation and transition options, the inability to customize a slide show with timings, set up slide show options, and fewer views.

Quick Steps

Create a Presentation in PowerPoint Online

1. Open a browser window.
2. Navigate to https://onedrive.live.com.
3. If necessary, sign in with Microsoft account.
4. Click Microsoft Apps button.
5. Click PowerPoint tile and then click New blank presentation.
6. Enter and format slides.
7. Rename presentation.
8. Close presentation tab.

1. With OneDrive open and with the Documents folder displayed, click the Microsoft Apps button (displays as a waffle icon), click the PowerPoint tile, and then click New blank presentation at the PowerPoint Online Start screen.
2. Click the DESIGN tab, click the More Themes button ( ) located at the right end of the Themes gallery, and then click *Banded*.

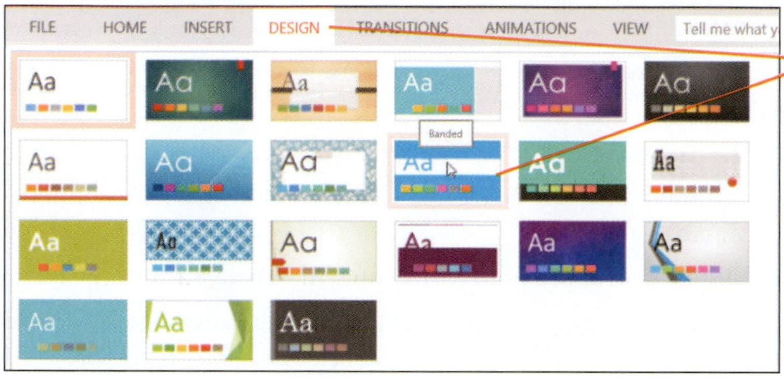

3. Click *Variant 4* in the Variants gallery.

A new presentation with the selected theme is started in the PowerPoint Online window, as shown in Figure 15.4. Similar to Word and Excel, presentations are saved in the same file format and are transferable between PowerPoint Online and the desktop version of PowerPoint.

App Tip

Create a printable PDF of full slides from the Print backstage area.

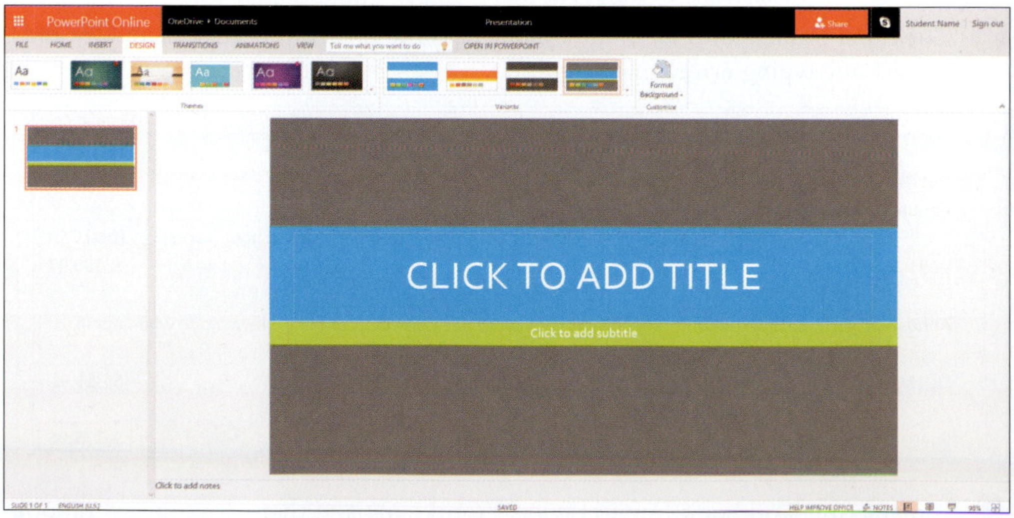

Figure 15.4

The PowerPoint Online window is shown. PowerPoint Online does not have the Slide Show or Review tab found in the desktop version of PowerPoint.

4. Click anywhere in *CLICK TO ADD TITLE* in the title slide and type Green Computing. Click anywhere in *Click to add subtitle* and then type your name.

Note that the font for this theme converts titles to all uppercase text.

5. Click the HOME tab and then click the New Slide button in the Slides group.
6. At the New Slide dialog box with the *Title and Content* layout selected, click Add Slide.

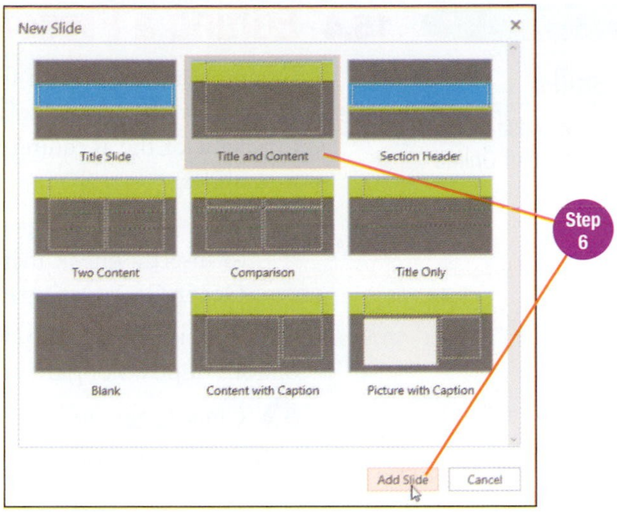
New Slide
Title Slide
Title and Content
Section Header
Two Content
Comparison
Title Only
Blank
Content with Caption
Picture with Caption
Add Slide
Cancel
Step 6

7. Type the text on Slide 2 as follows:

   Slide title What Is Green Computing?
   Bulleted list Use of computers and other electronic devices in an environmentally responsible manner including new or modified:
   computing practices
   computing policies
   computing procedures

8. Add another new slide with the *Title and Content* layout and then type the text on Slide 3 as follows:

   Slide title Green Computing Strategies
   Bulleted list Reduction in energy consumption
   Reduction in use of paper, ink, and toner
   Reuse or recycling of devices
   Proper disposal of e-waste

App Tip

A slight delay may occur after typing or clicking outside a placeholder as the screen refreshes.

9. Make Slide 2 the active slide, click the INSERT tab, and then click the Online Pictures button in the Images group.
10. Type computer in the *Bing Image Search* text box at the Insert Pictures dialog box and then press Enter or click the Search button.
11. Scroll down to the image shown at the right and then double-click to insert it on the slide. Insert the image using the student data file ***computer*** if the image shown is not available.
12. Move the image to the approximate position as shown in the slide at the right.

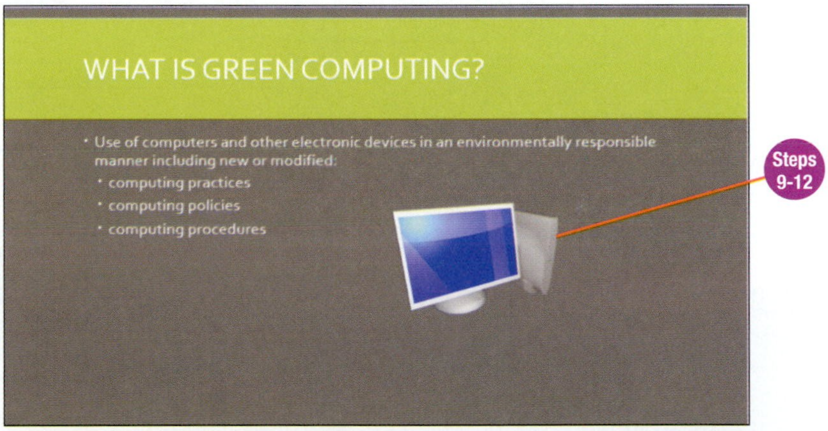
WHAT IS GREEN COMPUTING?
Use of computers and other electronic devices in an environmentally responsible manner including new or modified:
computing practices
computing policies
computing procedures
Steps 9-12

13. Make Slide 3 the active slide. Insert and position the image as shown in the slide at the right. Search for the image by typing recycling in the *Bing Image Search* text box. If necessary, insert the image using the student data file ***worldrecycling***.
14. Rename the presentation GreenComputingPres-YourName and then close the presentation tab. Leave OneDrive open for the next topic.

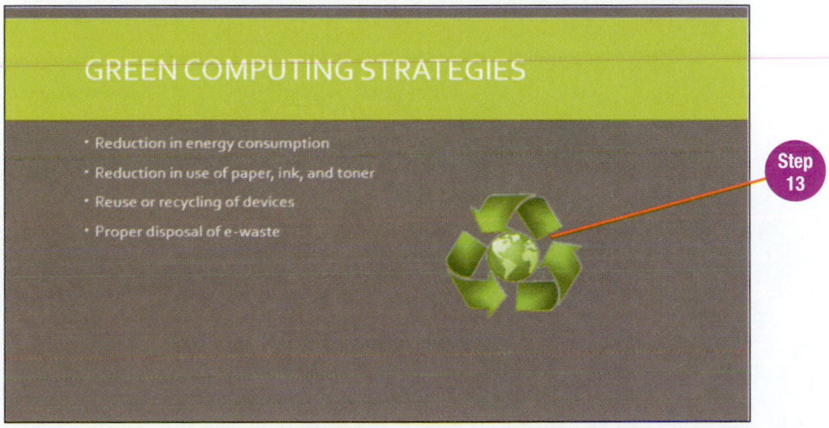
GREEN COMPUTING STRATEGIES
Reduction in energy consumption
Reduction in use of paper, ink, and toner
Reuse or recycling of devices
Proper disposal of e-waste
Step 13

15.4 Editing a Presentation in PowerPoint Online

Skills

Edit a presentation in PowerPoint Online

Opening a presentation from OneDrive in PowerPoint Online displays the slides in Reading view. Switch to editing mode using the Edit Presentation button near the top right of the Reading view window to make changes to slide content or to add new slides.

1. With OneDrive open and with the Documents folder displayed, click to insert a check mark in the check circle at the top right corner of the **GreenComputingPres-YourName** thumbnail if the check circle is empty.

   A check mark in the check circle indicates the presentation is selected. Additional options display along the top of the OneDrive window when a presentation is selected.

2. Click Open and then click Open in PowerPoint Online.

   The presentation opens in Reading view, as shown in Figure 15.5.

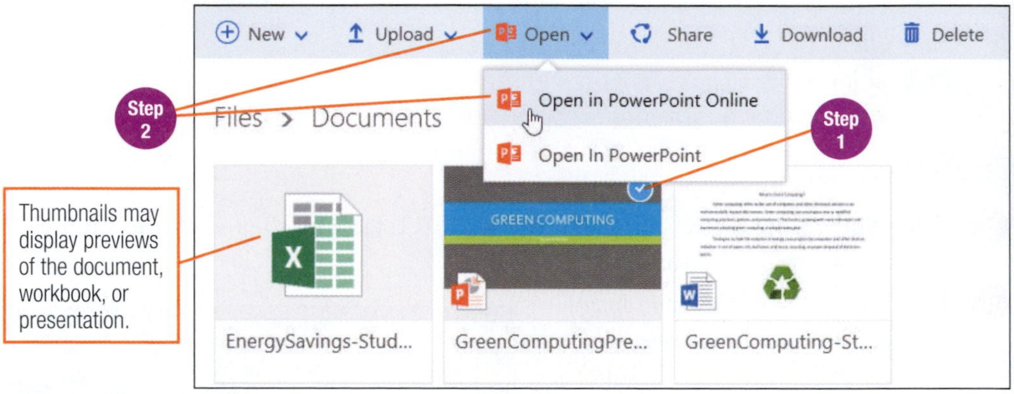

3. Click the Next Slide button (displays as a right-pointing arrow) in the Status bar to view Slide 2 in the window.

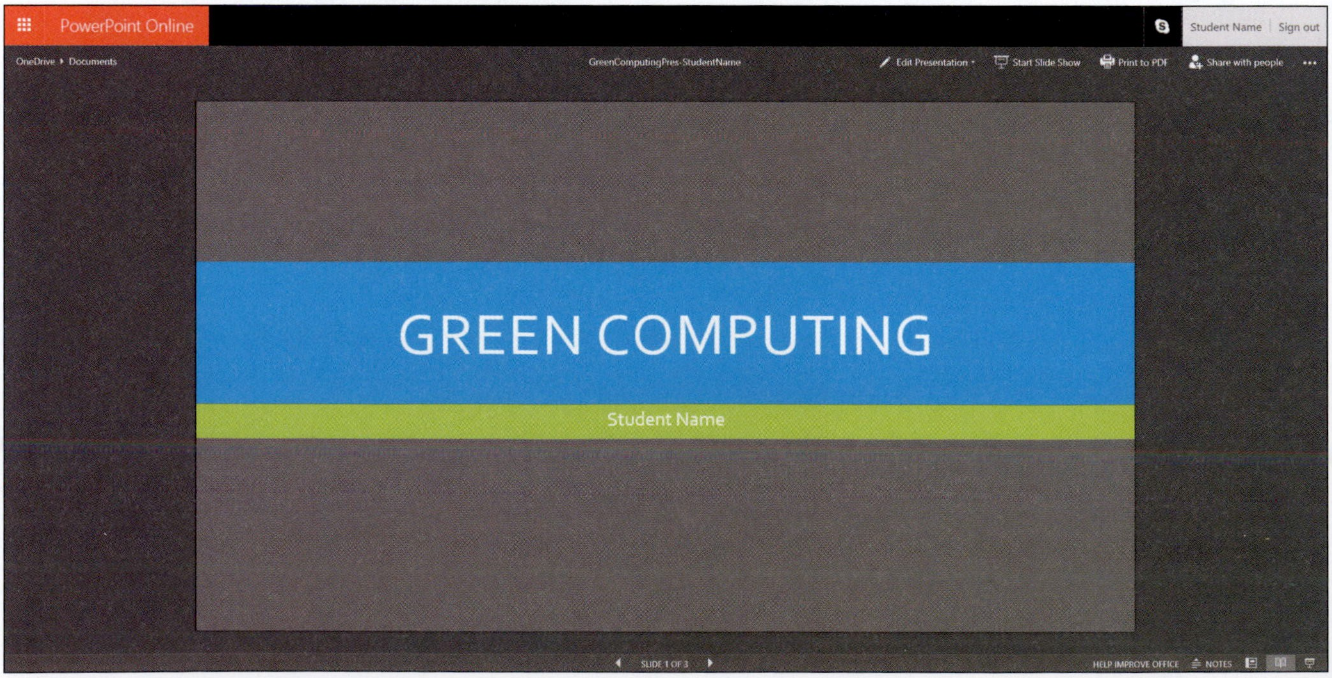

Figure 15.5

A presentation displays in Reading view in PowerPoint Online when opened from OneDrive.

4 Click the Next Slide button again to view Slide 3.

5 Click the Edit Presentation button and then click *Edit in PowerPoint Online*.

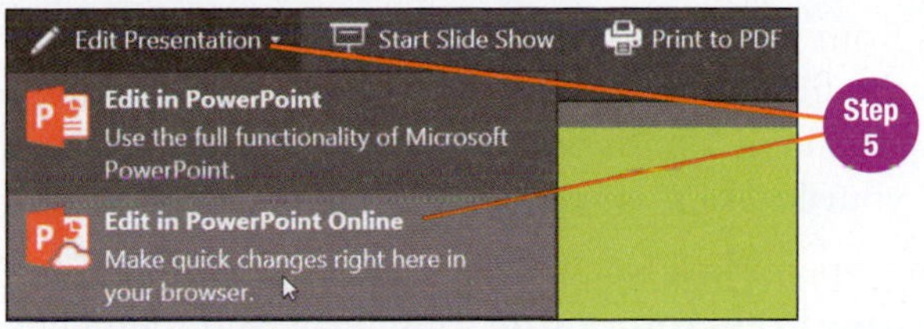
Edit Presentation
Start Slide Show
Print to PDF
Edit in PowerPoint
Use the full functionality of Microsoft PowerPoint.
Edit in PowerPoint Online
Make quick changes right here in your browser.
Step 5

6 If necessary, make Slide 3 the active slide.

7 Add a new slide with the *Title and Content* layout and then type the following text on Slide 4:

Slide title Green Computing Example

Bulleted list A desktop PC can use up to 1700 kilowatt hours per year if left on continuously

Turning off or putting the PC in sleep mode when not in use can save over 1600 kilowatt hours per year for average use of 2 hours per day

This strategy can save $175 per year for electricity cost at 10.9 cents per kilowatt hour

8 Search for the image shown below using the key phrase *power on*. Insert and move the image to the approximate position as shown. Insert the image using the student data file ***poweron*** if the image shown is not available.

9 Close the presentation tab. Leave OneDrive open for the next topic.

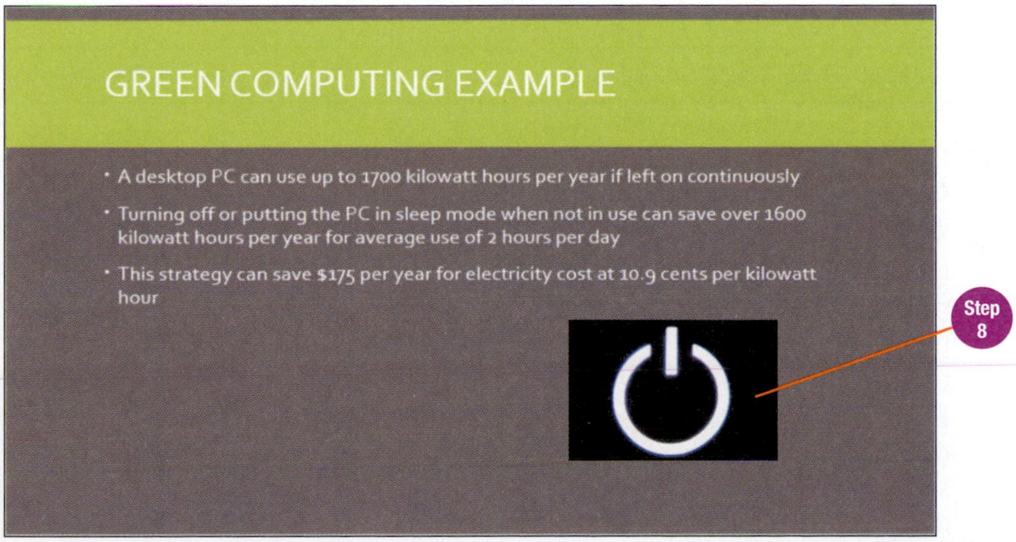
GREEN COMPUTING EXAMPLE
A desktop PC can use up to 1700 kilowatt hours per year if left on continuously
Turning off or putting the PC in sleep mode when not in use can save over 1600 kilowatt hours per year for average use of 2 hours per day
This strategy can save $175 per year for electricity cost at 10.9 cents per kilowatt hour
Step 8

Alternative Method **Editing a Document, Workbook, or Presentation in Desktop Version of Word, Excel, or PowerPoint**

Select the document, workbook, or presentation thumbnail for the file to be edited, click Open, and then click the option to open the file in the full-featured desktop version of Word, Excel, or PowerPoint.

Quick Steps

Edit a Presentation in PowerPoint Online

1. Open a browser window.
2. Navigate to https://onedrive.live.com.
3. If necessary, sign in with Microsoft account.
4. Select presentation thumbnail.
5. Click Open.
6. Click Open in PowerPoint Online.
7. Click Edit Presentation button.
8. Click *Edit in PowerPoint Online.*
9. Edit as required.
10. Close presentation tab.

15.5 Downloading Files from and Uploading Files to OneDrive

Skills

Download files from OneDrive

Upload files to OneDrive

Move files to a folder on OneDrive

You can copy files from your PC or mobile device to OneDrive for backup storage purposes; to access the files from another device instead of copying the files to a USB flash drive; or to share the files with other people. Conversely, you can download a file from OneDrive to your local PC or mobile device to view or edit the file offline.

1. With OneDrive open, click to clear the check mark in the check circle for the **GreenComputingPres-YourName** thumbnail, and then click to insert a check mark in the check circle for the **GreenComputing-YourName** Word document.

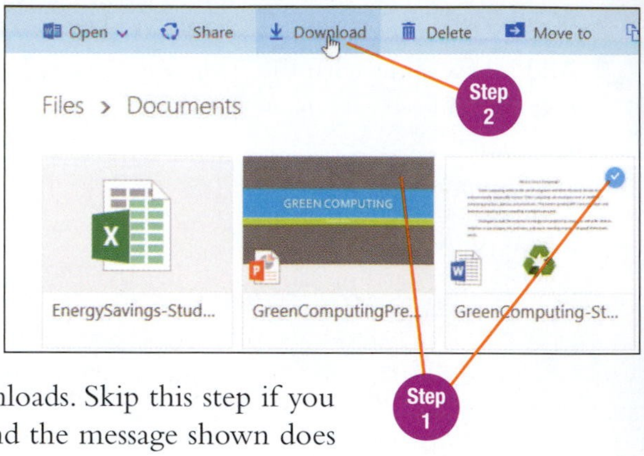

2. Click Download at the top of the OneDrive window.
3. Click the Close button at the right end of the pop-up message at the bottom of Microsoft Edge with the options to Open or View downloads. Skip this step if you are using a different browser and the message shown does not display.

> **Oops!**
> No check circle visible on thumbnail? Move the mouse over the thumbnail and a selection circle will appear.

> **App Tip**
> You can copy and paste files to and from OneDrive from a File Explorer window. OneDrive is shown in the File Explorer Navigation pane above This PC.

By default, files downloaded from OneDrive are saved in the Downloads folder for the signed in user when you are using OneDrive in the Microsoft Edge browser. Another browser may display a Save As dialog box when you click the Download option. In that case you can select to save the file in the Downloads folder on your computer.

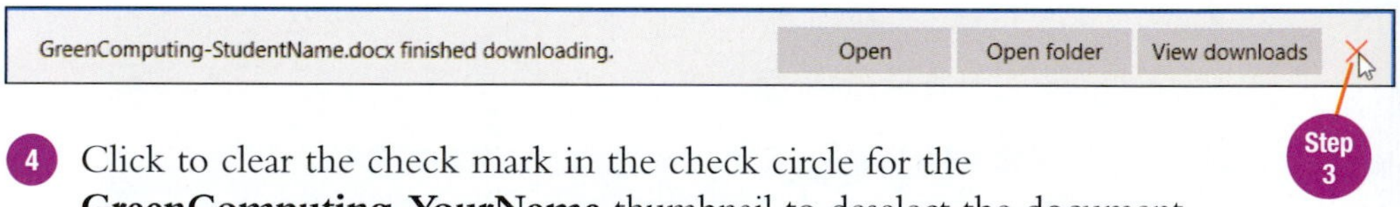

4. Click to clear the check mark in the check circle for the **GreenComputing-YourName** thumbnail to deselect the document.
5. Select and download the **EnergySavings-YourName** workbook to the Downloads folder by completing steps similar to those in Steps 1 through 3.
6. Clear the check mark for the **EnergySavings-YourName** thumbnail to deselect the workbook and then select and download the **GreenComputingPres-YourName** presentation to the Downloads folder by completing steps similar to those in Steps 1 through 3.
7. Click the File Explorer button on the taskbar to open File Explorer.
8. Click *Downloads* in the Navigation pane.

> **App Tip**
> You can select and download multiple files in one operation. OneDrive creates a zipped folder when more than one file is downloaded.

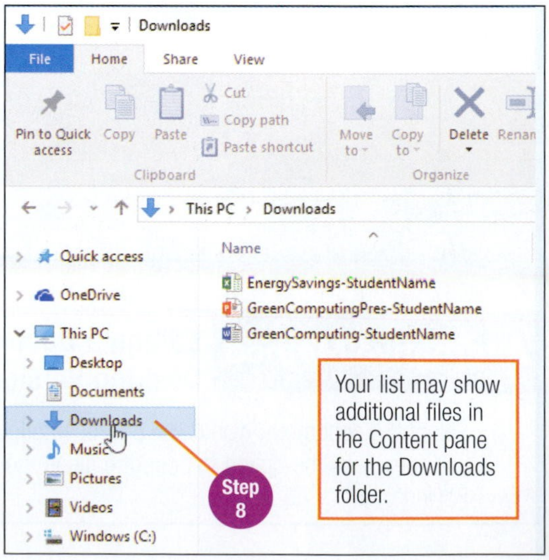

The three files downloaded from OneDrive are shown in the Content pane.

9 Select and copy the three downloaded files to a new folder *Ch15* in the CompletedTopicsByChapter folder on your storage medium. Refer to Chapter 1, Topic 1.9 if you need assistance with this step.

10 Close the File Explorer window and return to the browser window with OneDrive active. Clear the check mark in the check circle for the GreenComputingPres-YourName thumbnail if the file is still selected.

In the next steps you will copy three pictures from your storage medium to your account storage at OneDrive.

11 Click Upload in the bar at the top of the OneDrive window, and then click Files at the drop-down list.

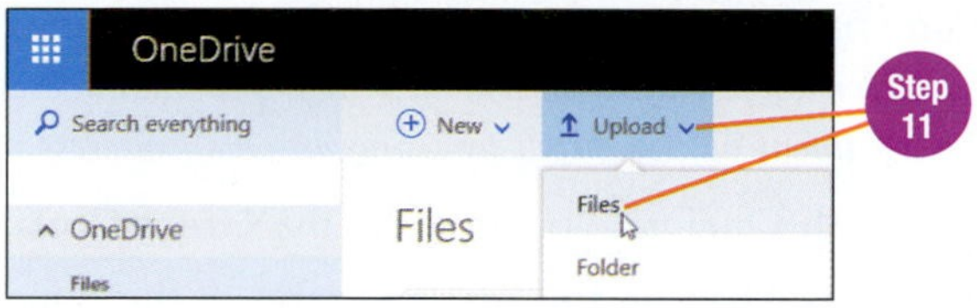

12 At the Open dialog box, navigate to the Ch15 folder in Student_Data_Files on your storage medium, select the three files in the folder whose names begin with ***PaintedBunting***, and then click Open.

The three files are uploaded to the current folder in your account storage in OneDrive. A progress message appears near the right end of the bar at the top of the window as the files are uploaded.

13 Select the three painted bunting picture thumbnails and deselect the thumbnail from Step 6 if the presentation is still selected.

14 Click Move to in the bar at the top of the window.

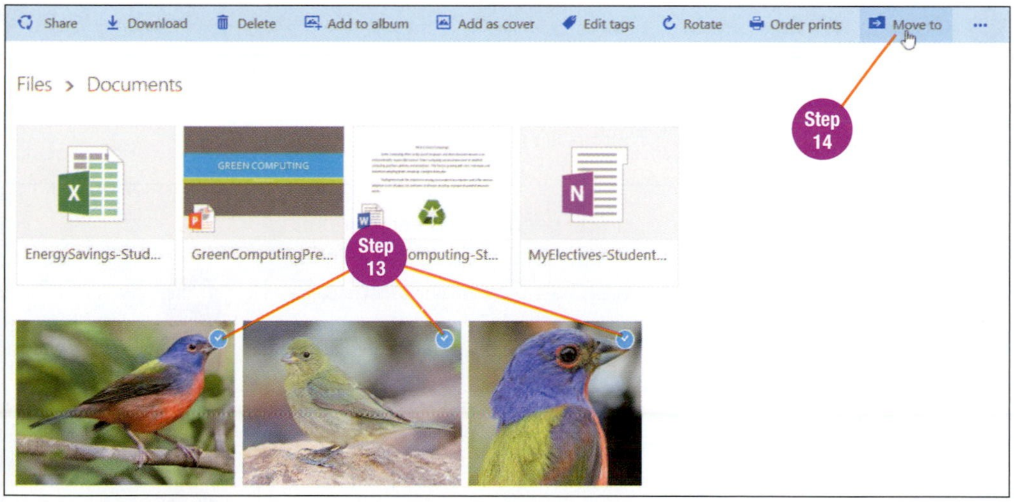

15 Click *Pictures* in the Move items to panel at the right side of the window and then click Move at the top of the panel. Leave OneDrive open for the next topic.

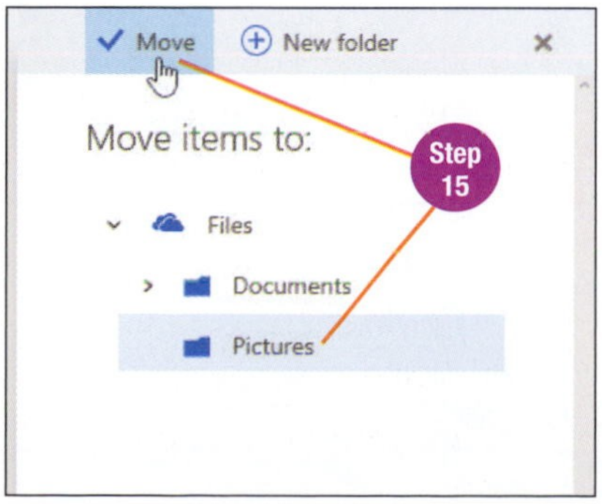

Quick Steps

Download a File from OneDrive

1. Sign in to OneDrive.
2. Select file.
3. Click Download.
4. Close message bar at bottom of browser window if message bar displays.
5. Open File Explorer.
6. Display Downloads folder in Content pane.
7. Select, copy, and paste downloaded file to desired location.

Upload a File to OneDrive

1. Sign in to OneDrive.
2. Click Upload, then Files.
3. Navigate to drive and/or folder.
4. Select file(s) to upload.
5. Click Open.
6. If necessary, move files to desired destination folder.

App Tip

Files are uploaded to the active folder; consider displaying the Pictures folder and then uploading files instead of uploading first and then moving files.

15.6 Sharing a File on OneDrive

Skills

Share a file on OneDrive

OneDrive is an excellent tool for collaborating on documents when working with a team. A team leader can create or upload documents to OneDrive and then share the files with the team members who need them. An individual with shared access to a document receives an email with a link to the file. Changes to the file are made to the copy in OneDrive so that only one document, worksheet, or presentation has to be managed. Collaborating by sharing a file on OneDrive is less cumbersome than sending a file as an email attachment and then trying to manage multiple versions of the same document.

Note: *In this topic, you will share a Word Online document with a classmate. Check with your instructor for instructions on with whom you should share the Word document. If necessary, share the document with yourself by using an email address other than your Microsoft account.*

1. With OneDrive open, select the **GreenComputing-YourName** document.
2. Click Share in the bar at the top of the window.
3. Type the email address for a classmate in the *To* text box in the Share dialog box with the Invite people panel active.

   More than one email address can be entered at the *To* text box. As with email messages, use a semicolon to separate email addresses.

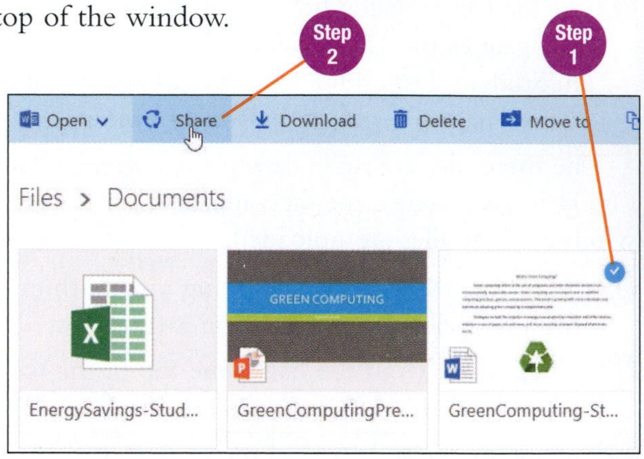

4. Click in the message box and then type Please make your changes to the file accessed from this link..
5. Click Share.

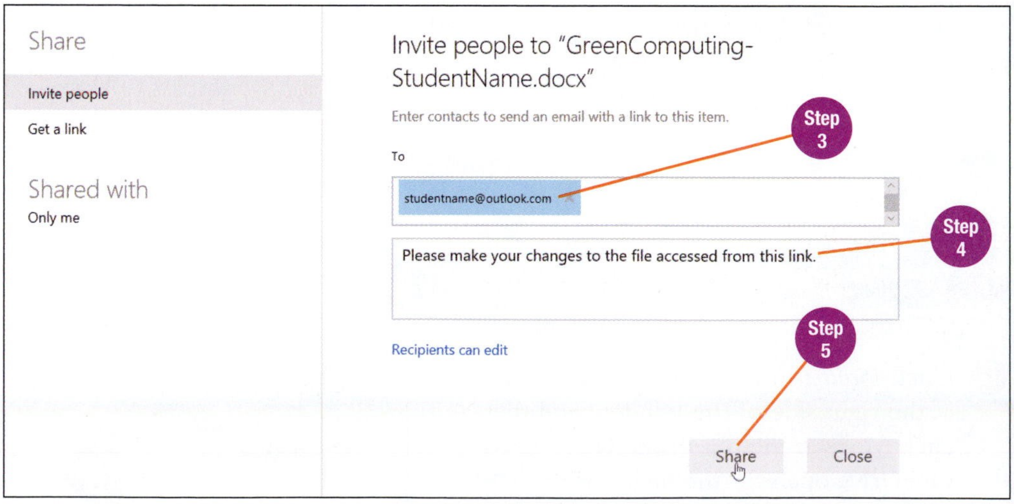

App Tip

You can share files with anyone with a valid email address—the recipient does not have to have a Microsoft account.

Oops!

Sharing from your account is blocked? Sometimes, for new accounts, sharing is blocked until the account is verified. Click the link to verify your account below the message. You may need to give a mobile number that can receive a text message. Enter the code received on your phone, click Next, and then click Done. If necessary, use the Microsoft Apps button to switch from the Outlook tab back to OneDrive when verification is complete and repeat Steps 1 through 5 a second time.

6 Click Close when the classmate's name appears in the *Shared with* section.

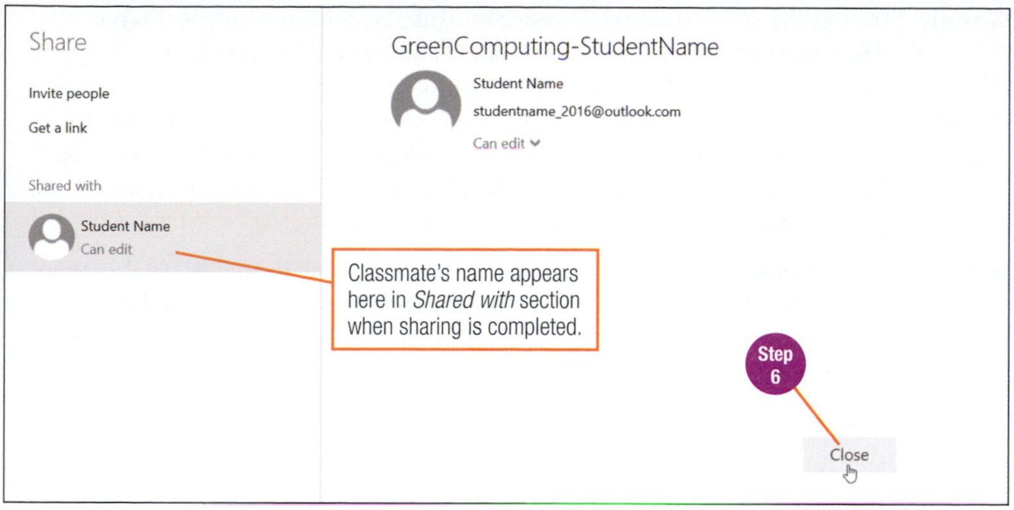

7 Click the Microsoft Apps button next to OneDrive.

8 Click the Mail tile.

9 With *Inbox* the active mail folder, open the message received from a classmate with the subject line informing you the **GreenComputing-StudentName.docx** file has been shared with you in OneDrive.

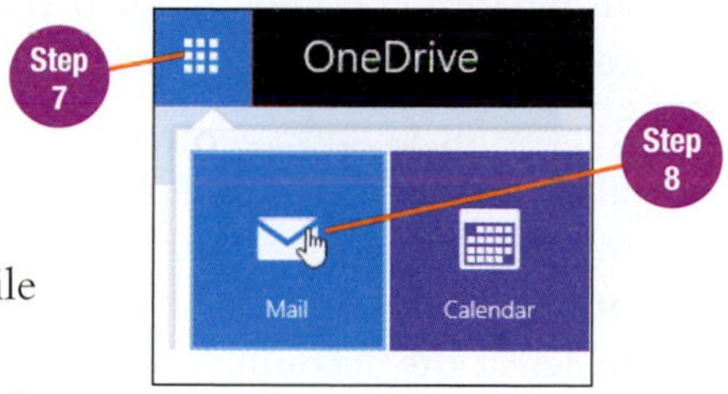

10 Click the link to the file in the message window.

The file opens in Word Online in Reading view. Notice the Edit Document button in the bar at the top of the window.

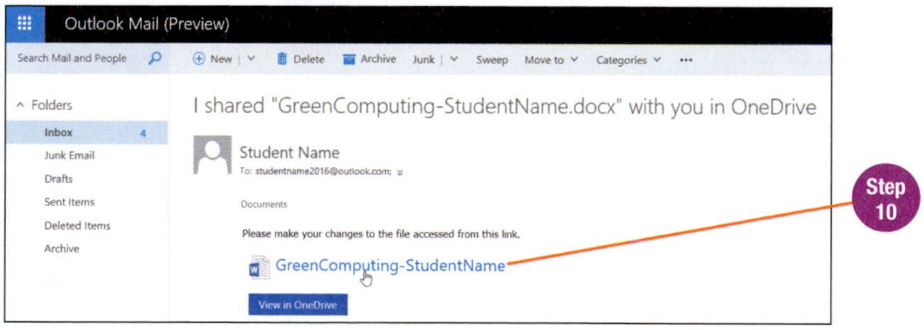

11 Close the document tab.

12 Use the Microsoft Apps button to switch back to OneDrive.

13 Click Shared in the Navigation pane (left pane) of OneDrive to view the file details of files shared by you and with you in the Content pane.

You will have two entries in the Shared panel because you shared the document with a classmate and a classmate shared his or her document with you.

14 Click the Account button that displays your account picture or the generic user silhouette at the right end of the OneDrive bar and then click Sign out.

15 Close the browser window.

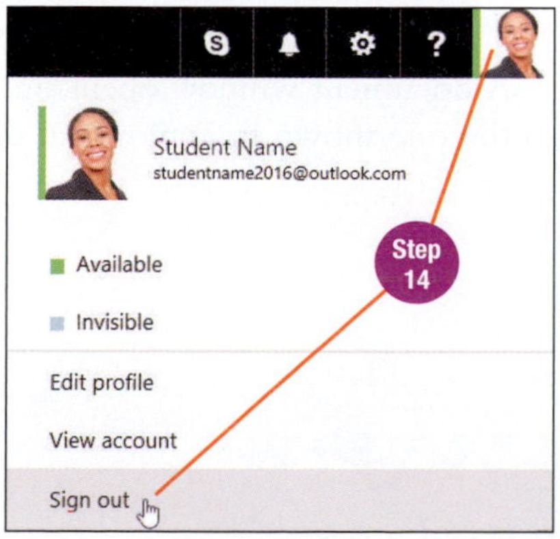

Quick Steps

Share a File on OneDrive

1. Sign in to OneDrive.
2. Select file.
3. Click Share.
4. Type recipient's email address in *To* box.
5. Type message in message box.
6. Click Share.
7. Click Close.

Oops!

No message? Check the email address that the classmate used to ensure the correct address was typed. If an address other than Outlook, Hotmail, or Live was used, you need to go to another mail program to find the message with the link. In that case, sign out of OneDrive, launch your other mail program, and complete Steps 9 and 10. Note also that some mail programs may flag the message as Junk Mail. Check your Junk Mail folder if the message is not in your Inbox.

15.7 Creating a Document Using Google Docs

Skills

Create a document in Google Docs

Google Docs is the web-based word processor offered within **Google Drive** (Google's cloud storage service). With a Gmail account, you can sign in to Google Drive and create a document, presentation, spreadsheet, form, or drawing. Gmail accounts and the Google web productivity apps are free to use. Having an introduction to using one of the Google cloud applications is a good idea, because you may encounter someone at your workplace or volunteer organization who prefers to use the cloud technologies offered by Google.

Note: *This is an optional topic. Check with your instructor or check the course syllabus to see if you are required to complete this topic. Also note that Google may update Google Drive and/or Google Docs after publication of this textbook, in which case the information, steps, and/or screens shown here may vary.*

Oops!

Don't know your Google account? If you have a gmail.com email address, your email login is your Google account; otherwise, click the Sign in with a different account hyperlink near the bottom of the sign-in page to add a new account using the Add account button.

1. Open a browser window.
2. Navigate to google.com.
3. Click the Sign in button near the top right of the window. If you are automatically signed in when you go to the Google page, skip to Step 5.
4. Type your Google account information and click Sign in. If multiple Gmail accounts are set up on the computer you are using, click to select the account you want to use, type your password, and click Sign in.
5. Click the Google Apps button located near the top right of the page (displays as a waffle icon).
6. Click Drive at the drop-down list.
7. Click Got it or a Close button to close a message if a message appears about new features in Google Drive. A message generally displays the first time you access Drive after creating a new account.
8. Click the NEW button below *Drive* at the left side of the page and then click Google Docs at the drop-down list.
9. Click NO THANKS if a message box appears next to the Docs home button with a message about using templates.

A document window opens similar to the one shown in Figure 15.6 on page 371.

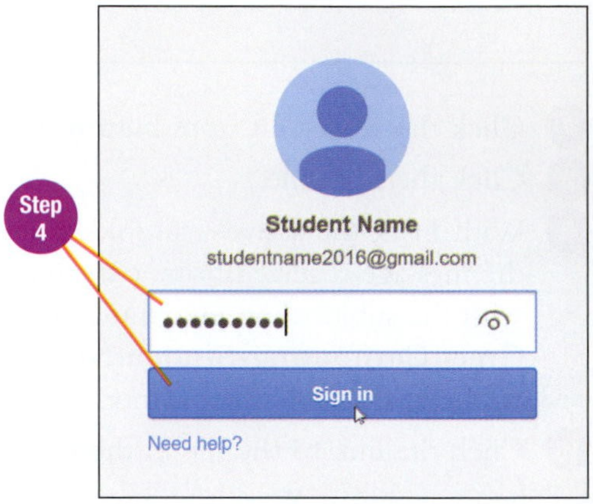

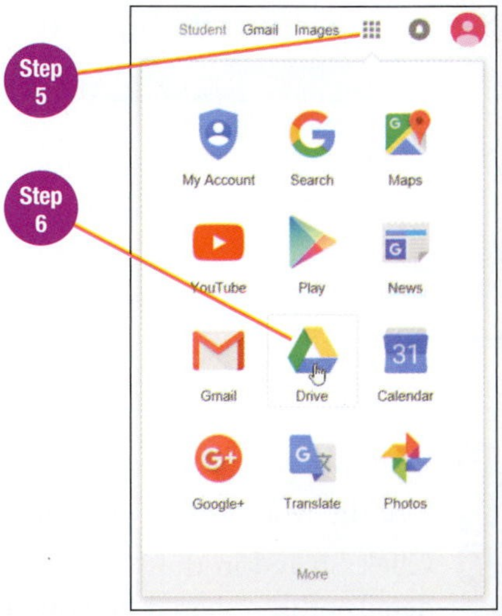

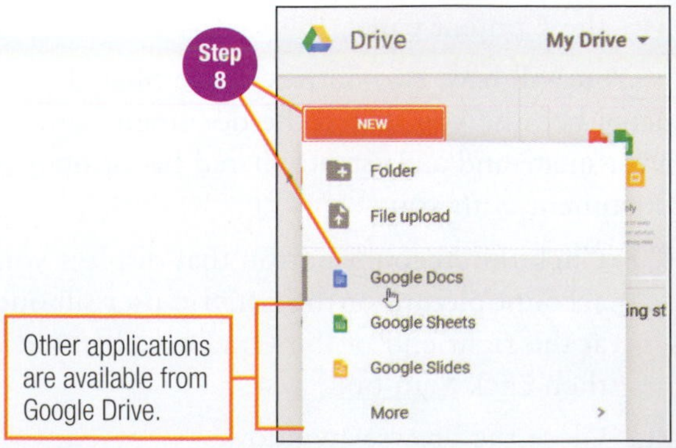

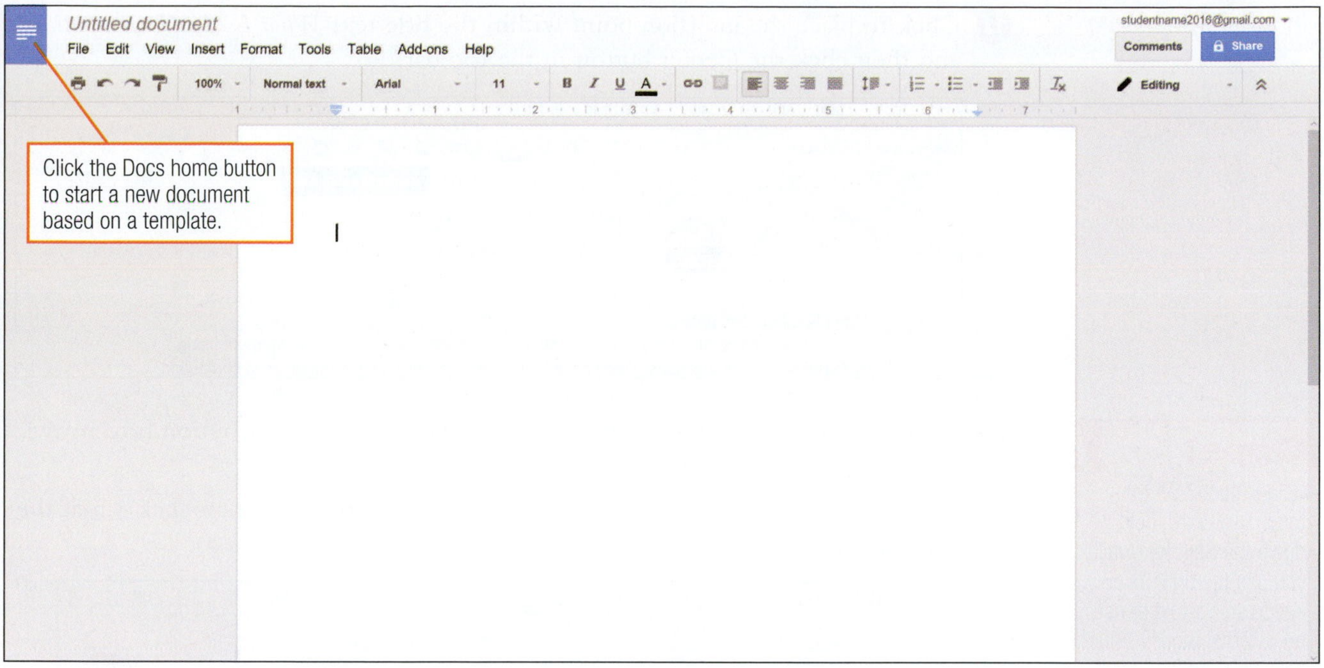

Figure 15.6

A Google Docs document window is shown. Google Docs automatically saves changes every few seconds to a document named *Untitled document*.

App Tip

You can upload and view a Word document in Google Docs.

10 Type the following text in the document window using all the default settings:

What Is Cloud Computing?

Cloud computing refers to a delivery model of software and file management using web-based service providers where all resources are online. Consumers of cloud computing services access software and files via a web browser. Some cloud-based services are free, with fees charged to access more storage or software features. [Press Enter twice after the period.]

11 Click the File menu and then click Rename at the drop-down list.

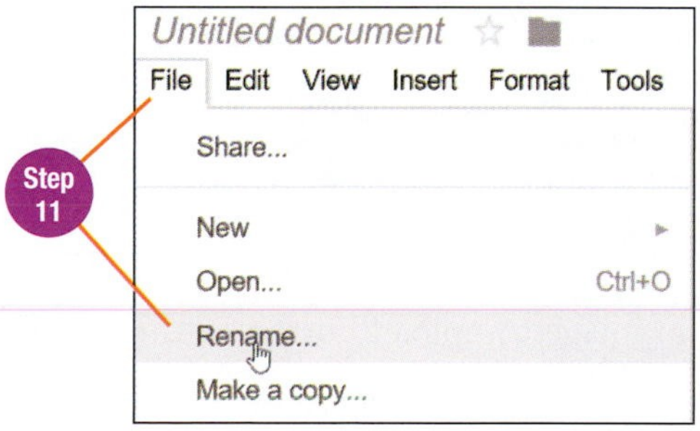

12 Type CloudComputing-YourName in the file name text box above the menu bar and then press Enter.

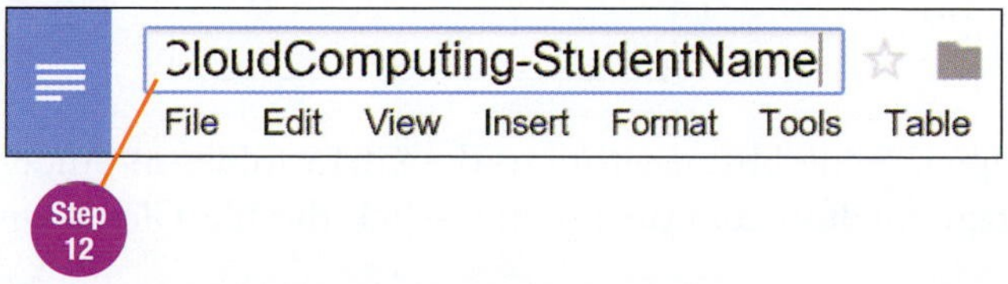

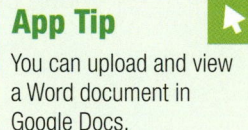

13 Click to place the insertion point within the title text *What Is Cloud Computing?* and then click the Center button in the toolbar.

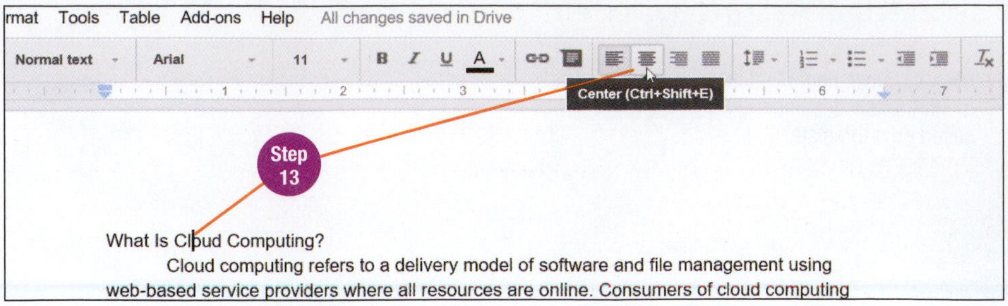

Oops!

Using Touch? On the touch keyboard, hold down the Shift key while you use the right arrow key to select text or use an external mouse. Touch selection gestures for Microsoft apps do not apply in Google Docs.

14 Select the title text, click the Bold button, click the *Font Size* option box arrow, and then click 14 at the drop-down list.

15 Select the paragraph text, click the Line spacing button, and then click 1.5 at the drop-down list.

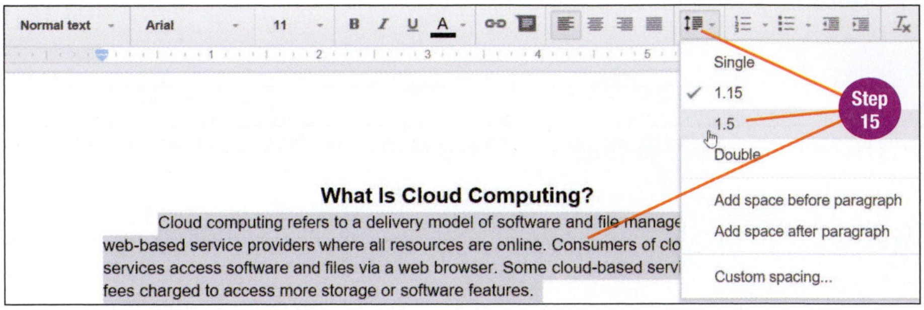

16 Deselect the text and then position the insertion point on the blank line at the bottom of the document.

17 Click the Insert menu and then click Image at the drop-down list.

18 Click the Choose an image to upload button in the middle of the Insert image dialog box.

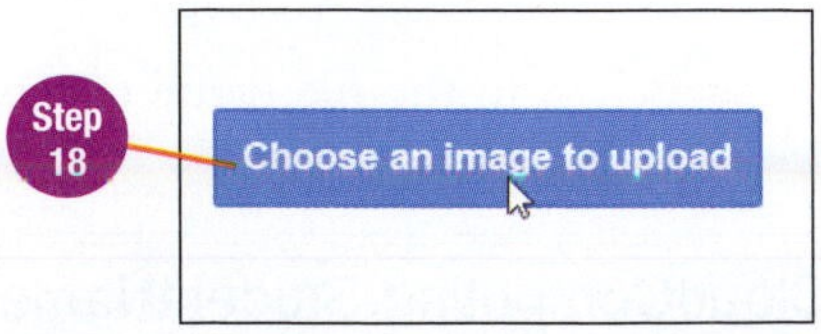

19 At the Open dialog box, navigate to the Ch15 folder in Student_Data_Files on your storage medium and then double-click the file ***Cloud-computing***.

20 Click to select the image, resize the image using the resizing handles to approximately 2 inches wide by 1.5 inches tall, and then click the Center button.

21 With the image still selected, click the Insert menu and then click Footnote at the drop-down list.

22 Type Cloud computing image courtesy of Wikimedia Commons. in the Footnote pane.

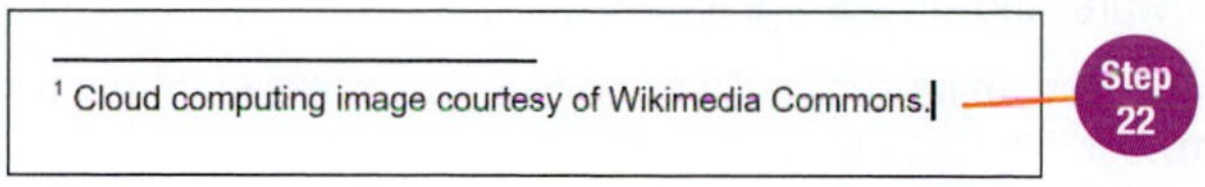

[1] Cloud computing image courtesy of Wikimedia Commons.
Step 22

23 Scroll up to the top of the page.

24 If necessary, click at the end of the paragraph text to deselect the image.

25 Close the tabbed window for the document to return to Google Drive.

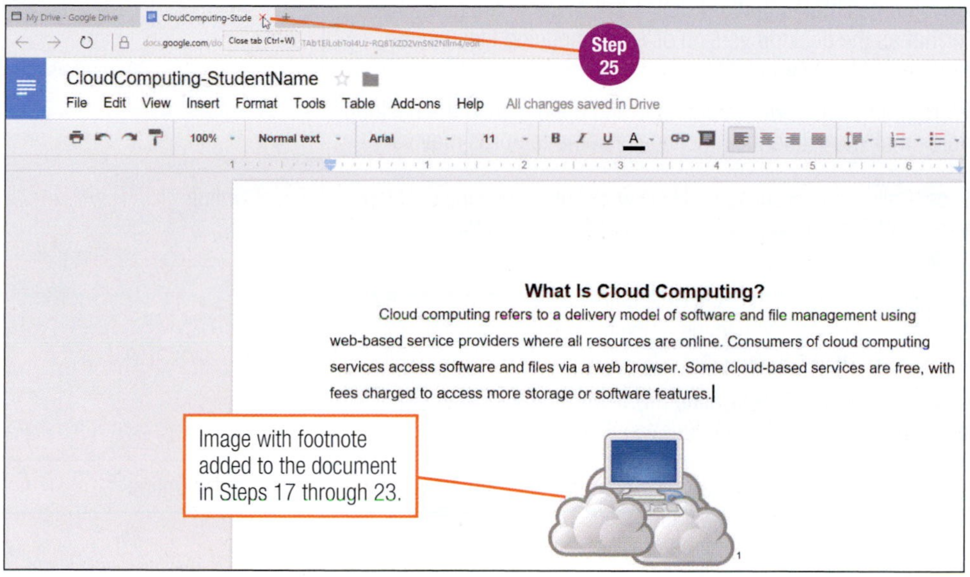

My Drive - Google Drive
CloudComputing-Stude
Close tab (Ctrl+W)
Step 25
CloudComputing-StudentName
File Edit View Insert Format Tools Table Add-ons Help All changes saved in Drive
100% Normal text Arial 11
What Is Cloud Computing?
Cloud computing refers to a delivery model of software and file management using web-based service providers where all resources are online. Consumers of cloud computing services access software and files via a web browser. Some cloud-based services are free, with fees charged to access more storage or software features.
Image with footnote added to the document in Steps 17 through 23.

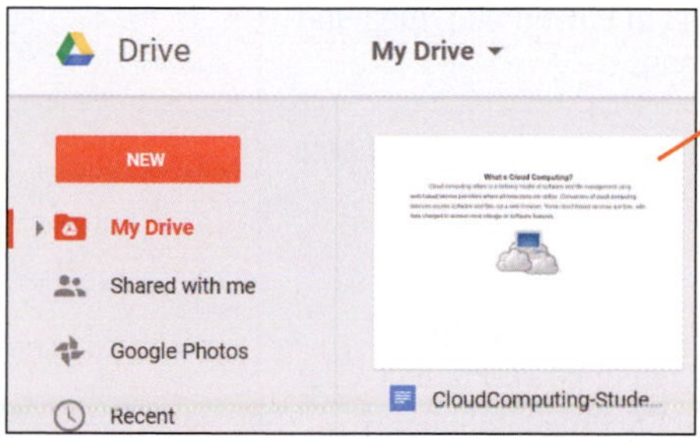

A document in *My Drive* list is shown with a thumbnail.

26 Click your account icon near the top right of the window and then click Sign out.

27 Close the browser window.

Alternative Method **Navigating directly to Google Drive or Google Docs**

Type the URL drive.google.com to navigate directly to Google Drive or docs.google.com to navigate directly to Google Docs.

Quick Steps

Create a Document Using Google Docs

1. Open a browser window.
2. Navigate to google.com.
3. Sign in with Google account.
4. Click Google Apps button, then Drive.
5. Click NEW button, then Google Docs.
6. Type, edit, and format document.
7. Click File.
8. Click Rename.
9. Type document name.
10. Press Enter.
11. Close window tab.

App Tip

Google Docs can be shared with others by selecting the file in the Google Drive list and using the Share button in the bar above the file list.

Check This Out

http://CA2.ParadigmCollege.net/Zoho

Go here to check out another popular web-based productivity suite. Register for a free account at Zoho to access several web-based applications including Writer (word processor), Show (presentation), and Sheet (spreadsheet).

View

Model Answer

Compare your completed file with the model answer.

Topics Review

Topic	Key Concepts	Key Terms
15.1 Creating a Document Using Word Online	Cloud computing is a service in which computer resources, software, and storage are provided online. Cloud computing applications and files are accessed from a web browser. Word Online is the web-based version of Word accessed from OneDrive. Sign in to OneDrive with a Microsoft account, click the Apps button, click the Word tile, and then click New blank document to start a new document. Documents created in Word Online are saved in the same file format as the desktop version of Word, meaning files can be transferred between editions. Word Online has fewer ribbon tabs and options than the desktop version of Word, and the functions of some features may vary.	cloud computing Word Online
15.2 Creating a Worksheet Using Excel Online	Excel Online is best suited for basic worksheets; use the desktop version of Excel for worksheets that need advanced formulas or editing. Worksheets created in Excel Online are saved in the same file format as the desktop version of Excel, meaning files can be transferred between editions. Like Word Online, Excel Online has fewer features than the desktop version, and some functionality may vary.	Excel Online
15.3 Creating a Presentation Using PowerPoint Online	Use PowerPoint Online to create a presentation that does not need charts, audio, advanced animation or transition effects, or advanced slide show set up options. Presentations created in PowerPoint Online are saved in the same file format as the desktop version of PowerPoint, meaning files can be transferred between editions.	PowerPoint Online
15.4 Editing a Presentation in PowerPoint Online	To open a presentation, select a presentation file thumbnail and use Open from OneDrive. A presentation opens in Reading view from OneDrive. Use the Edit Presentation button and choose to open the presentation in either the desktop version of PowerPoint or PowerPoint Online to make changes to the presentation.	
15.5 Downloading Files from and Uploading Files to OneDrive	Select a file by clicking in the check circle at the top right of a tile to insert a check mark. Click Download to copy a selected file from OneDrive to the Downloads folder on your computer. Open a File Explorer window to copy and paste the file to the desired location. Click Upload to select and copy a file from your computer to your OneDrive storage.	

continued...

Topic	Key Concepts	Key Terms
15.6 Sharing a File on OneDrive	OneDrive can be used to collaborate with team members by sharing one copy of a file among several users. Select a file and choose Share to type the email address of any individual you want to share a file with. Individuals receive an email message with a link to the shared file on OneDrive.	
15.7 Creating a Document Using Google Docs	The web-based word processor offered by Google is called *Google Docs*. Sign in to Google with a Gmail account, click the Google Apps button, click Drive in the drop-down list, and then click the NEW button to start a document, presentation, spreadsheet, form, or drawing. Google Drive is the online file-storage service from Google. Google Docs saves changes automatically every few seconds to an untitled document. Use the Rename option from the File menu to assign a name to the untitled document. Use options from the Menu bar drop-down lists and toolbar to add elements, edit, and format a document.	Google Docs Google Drive

Recheck

Recheck your understanding of the topics covered in this chapter.

Workbook

Chapter review and assessment resources are available in the *Workbook* ebook.

Glossary/Index

A

absolute address Excel address with a dollar symbol before the column letter and/or row number so that the address will not change when the formula is copied to another column or row, 214

Accept button used to send a message to a meeting organizer indicating acceptance of a meeting request, 125

Access 2016 database management application in Microsoft Office suite used to organize, store, and manage related data such as customers, vendors, employees, or products, 64, 66, 288–311, 315–335

Accounting Number Format button in the Number group on the Home tab in Excel adds a dollar symbol, a comma in the thousands place, and displays two digits after the decimal point, 191–192

Action Center panel in Windows 10 opened from the Notification icon on the taskbar that displays notifications from settings, apps, applications, and connected accounts and shows quick action tiles to perform system changes, 15

active cell the cell with the green border around its edges and in which the next entry will be stored or that will be affected by a command, 186

Add Page control in OneNote that displays as a plus symbol inside a circle used to add a new page in a section; pages organize note content within a section, 96

Address bar the area in a web browser in which the web address (also called a URL) for a web page is viewed or typed, 41, 43

Align Left paragraph alignment in which lines of text are aligned at the left margin; left edge of page appears even, 147

alignment guide colored vertical and/or horizontal line that appears while dragging an object to help you align and place the object; also called smart guides, 77, 249

Align Right paragraph alignment in which text is aligned at the right margin; right edge of page appears even, 147

Angle Counterclockwise option from Orientation button in Alignment group of Home tab in Excel that rotates text within the cell boundaries by 45 degrees, 209

animation involves adding a special effect to an object on a slide that causes the object to move or change in some way during a PowerPoint slide show, 278

Animation Painter button used in PowerPoint to copy animation effects from one object to another object, 280

app a small program used on a smartphone, tablet, or PC designed usually for one purpose, to work on a touchscreen, use less power than an application, and fewer network resources, 4

B

C

D

S

Y

Z

Photo Credits: Microsoft images used with permission from Microsoft.

Chapter 1 *Page 3*: ©Shutterstock/svetikd. *4*: ©istockphoto.com/Mihai Simonia. *6*: ©istockphoto.com/AlexGul; ©istockphoto.com/Peng Wu; ©istockphoto.com/Malgorzata Beldowska; ©istockphoto.com/Kamil Krawczyk.

Chapter 2 *39*: ©Shutterstock/Rawpixel.com. *40*: ©Shutterstock/Tetiana Yurchenko.

Chapter 3 *63*: ©Shutterstock/Andrey Popov.

Chapter 4 *93*: ©Shutterstock/Goodluz.

Chapter 5 *111*: ©Shutterstock/Rawpixel.

Chapter 6 *135*: ©Shutterstock/bikeriderlondon.

Chapter 7 *157*: ©Shutterstock/Monkey Business Images.

Chapter 8 *185*: ©Shutterstock/Rido.

Chapter 9 *213*: ©Shutterstock/Monkey Business Images.

Chapter 10 *239*: ©Shutterstock/Tyler Olson.

Chapter 11 *263*: ©istockphoto/simonkr.

Chapter 12 *287*: ©Shutterstock/Gragon Images.

Chapter 13 *315*: ©iStock/bo1982.

Chapter 14 *339*: ©Shutterstock/iofoto.

Chapter 15 *355*: ©Shutterstock/arek_malang.